crime victims

AN INTRODUCTION TO VICTIMOLOGY

NINTH EDITION

ANDREW KARMEN

John Jay College of Criminal Justice
City University of New York

CENGAGE
Learning®

Australia • Brazil • Mexico • Singapore • United Kingdom • United States

P9-CRM-170

CENGAGE
Learning·

Crime Victims: An Introduction to Victimology,
Ninth Edition
Andrew Karmen

Product Director: Marta Lee-Perriard

Sr. Product Manager: Carolyn Henderson Meier

Content Developer: Michael B. Kopf,
S4Carlisle Publishing Services, Inc.

Product Assistant: Julia Catalano

Media Developer: Andy Yap

Marketing Manager: Kara Kindstrom

Art and Cover Direction, Production
Management, and Composition:
Lumina Datamatics, Inc.

Manufacturing Planner: Judy Inouye

Cover Image Credit: © Dmitrydesign/
Shutterstock

© 2016, 2013 Cengage Learning

WCN: 01-100-101

ALL RIGHTS RESERVED. No part of this work covered by the copyright
herein may be reproduced, transmitted, stored, or used in any form or by
any means graphic, electronic, or mechanical, including but not limited to
photocopying, recording, scanning, digitizing, taping, Web distribution,
information networks, or information storage and retrieval systems,
except as permitted under Section 107 or 108 of the 1976 United States
Copyright Act, without the prior written permission of the publisher.

For product information and technology assistance, contact us at
Cengage Learning Customer & Sales Support, 1-800-354-9706.

For permission to use material from this text or product,
submit all requests online at **www.cengage.com/permissions.**
Further permissions questions can be e-mailed to
permissionrequest@cengage.com.

Library of Congress Control Number: 2015932824

ISBN: 978-1-305-26103-7

Cengage Learning
20 Channel Center Street
Boston, MA 02210
USA

Cengage Learning is a leading provider of customized learning solutions
with employees residing in nearly 40 different countries and sales in more
than 125 countries around the world. Find your local representative at
www.cengage.com.

Cengage Learning products are represented in Canada by
Nelson Education, Ltd.

To learn more about Cengage Learning Solutions, visit
www.cengage.com.

Purchase any of our products at your local college store or at our
preferred online store **www.cengagebrain.com**.

Printed in the United States of America
Print Number: 02   Print Year: 2016

Brief Contents

Contents

Boxes, Tables, and Figures

BOXES

TABLES

PREFACE

In the early 1980s, I became interested in the victims' rights movement that was campaigning to reform criminal justice policies. I decided to develop an experimental course about crime victims, but I found that no comprehensive and up-to-date textbook existed. After discovering this absence of scholarly books appropriate for classroom use, I accepted the challenge and decided to write one.

When I began working on the first edition during 1983, it was difficult to locate reliable social science data or even well-informed speculation about a number of crucial aspects about people who experienced interpersonal violence and theft. When I prepared the second edition in the late 1980s, I encountered the opposite problem. Instead of a scarcity of material, there was too much. Large amounts of data and lengthy analyses were becoming available, especially about rape, spouse abuse, child abuse, and elder abuse. By the mid-1990s, when I prepared the third edition, this "knowledge explosion" had become even more difficult to manage. Entire issues of scholarly journals had been devoted to, and whole books had been written about, the plight of these victims. When I wrote the fourth edition, the most striking change that I encountered was how the recently developed Internet could provide readily available and continuously updated information about a wide variety of victims. As a result, I added an appendix of websites that faculty and students could check out periodically to view the latest statistics and the most recent developments concerning new laws, programs, and services. (Now there are too many to list.) The fifth edition introduced readers to the problems faced by victims of identity theft, cyberstalking, sexual abuse by clergy, drug-facilitated date rape, bias-driven hate crimes, and unfortunately, terrorist attacks. It also contained many more research findings as a growing number of studies about violence and theft found their way onto the information highway via government agencies, advocacy groups, and scholarly journals focused on specific types of victims. By the time the sixth edition was published, so many new topics and controversial issues had accumulated over the years that I had to break up 7 long chapters into 13 more manageable ones; this repackaging of themes and issues has worked out very well for courses that run 14 or 15 weeks. The seventh edition featured a closer look at several groups of victims who faced special problems, such as college students, casualties of road rage, and feloniously assaulted police officers. In the eighth edition, this list expanded to include increased coverage of assaulted high school students, persons trafficked into the United States, and prisoners.

Ever since the seventh edition, a table right at the outset in Chapter 1 has assembled victimology-bashing quotes that show how the scientific study of victimization is often confused with the controversial political ideology of victimism. This misunderstanding of what victimology actually is all about has led some influential commentators to condemn the entire discipline and brand it with an undeserved bad reputation. Unfortunately this problem continues, and some students might enter the class with a negative impression of victimology.

WHAT'S NEW?

In revising this textbook once again, I have maintained a focus on all the groups of victims that appeared in the previous eight editions. Although nothing important has been cut out, I have changed the order of presentation of a few subjects, and I have paid greater attention to a number of timely issues. In response to feedback from reviewers, this edition has more extensive and more concentrated discussions about the competing theories that explain who gets victimized and why. But it also has an additional number of concise real-life cases culled from high-profile news stories that put a human face on the many empirical generalizations and statistics that are cited in each chapter. These emotionally charged items help to promote students' engagement with the scholarly material that is the backbone of this textbook. These gripping excerpts spark discussions and debates about what happened to real individuals in actual cases, and in the process concretize abstract principles, hypotheticals, and procedures. (As in all the past editions, I continue to respect the privacy of persons who have been harmed by criminals by withholding their names and locations. However, the references provide that information for those students who might want to delve into these cases in greater detail.)

The most useful change in each of the 13 chapters is that I have reformulated clear and measurable learning objectives that will be useful for professors undertaking outcomes assessment. The questions at the end of each chapter, which encourage discussion and debate as well as critical thinking, can serve as the corresponding performance measures. I also provide ideas at the end of each chapter for hands-on research projects. These could form the basis for term papers that can serve as additional indicators of what students gained from taking your class.

In preparing this ninth edition, as always, I have thoroughly updated all the statistical evidence that is needed to back up my analyses and conclusions. For those instructors who relish evidence-based claims and sound policy recommendations, plenty of reliable empirical material from official sources of data appears in the many graphs, tables, and boxes.

As in the previous eight editions, I have sought out and highlighted the many controversies that involve victims as they interact with offenders, criminal justice officials and agencies, policy makers, the news media, social movements, and businesses selling security products and services. These contested issues are emotionally unsettling, hotly debated, and divisive, but they make a college course more meaningful and relevant to the real world of competing interests and polarized politics. I strive to be fair and balanced by presenting the strongest arguments of both sides in each controversy. I do not endorse some of the points of view that I present or their implications for social policy, of course. But I firmly believe that a textbook ought to call attention, whenever possible, to sharp clashes between well-meaning people with differing evidence-based views and divergent interpretations of the same data. Two examples of controversies featured in this ninth edition include whether individuals who sense that they are at risk would fare better if they were armed with concealed handguns for self-protection, as well as the best ways to address alcohol-fueled sexual assaults on campus.

Some highlights of the specific revisions, additions, and improvements I have made in each chapter are described below:

- Chapter 1, "What Is Victimology?" has been sharpened to make sure that students find the upcoming course and its reading assignments to be engaging, relevant to their career plans, and meaningful to their personal concerns. This lead-off chapter contains new real-life cases that dramatize the suffering of college students as the targets of ruthless offenders. That is followed by a streamlined discussion stressing the need for objectivity, and then a new section on the necessity of engaging in research. Bystander intervention, which is an insufficiently studied aspect of society's reaction to victimization, is now covered in greater depth in a box that provides a typology, an example, and an up-to-date review of research findings. Another set of actual cases illustrates how the reactions of victims under attack and their resiliency in its aftermath often can be inspirational and uplifting. That leads to the observation that victimology's unavoidable preoccupation with suffering can and should be balanced out by another more positive and upbeat line of inquiry, termed "survivorology." A section asking "Why Study Victimology?" was expanded to further motivate students to consider the practical value of the course and the importance of the entire enterprise.

- Chapter 2, "The Rediscovery of Crime Victims," provides a great many new references that will prove useful to students who want to investigate the plights of particular groups that have not yet received sufficient attention and assistance. The coverage of victims of human trafficking, a problem of great concern and outrage to many students, now more clearly illustrates how the rediscovery process goes through four distinct stages.

- Chapter 3, "Victimization in the United States: An Overview," has been reorganized to better explain and illustrate how official statistics can provide preliminary answers to important questions. The graph showing historical

trends in homicides has been moved to the end of this chapter to round out
the idea of the big picture. The extensive FBI Uniform Crime Report data
as well as the findings from the Bureau of Justice Statistics' (BJS) National
Crime Victimization Survey in the tables and graphs have been updated
and simplified. The discussion of comparative risks (mortality due to illnesses and accidents) has been expanded and updated.

- Chapter 4, "A Closer Look at the Victims of Interpersonal Violence and
  Theft," replaces the more narrowly focused chapter formerly entitled
  "Violent Crimes: Murders and Robberies." It starts out with an examination of the latest United Nations statistics comparing murder rates for a
  great many countries and their leading cities in order to demonstrate the
  importance of location as a major determinant of risk levels. The chapter
  now also includes discussions about people who suffered near death
  experiences and other aggravated assaults, robberies, burglaries, vehicle
  thefts, and even identity theft. Engaging questions are posed, such as which
  individuals face the gravest chances of being murdered and which motorists
  should be most concerned when parking their cars. Throughout the chapter, differential risks are the focus of attention: how various demographic
  groupings experience much higher or much lower rates of victimization.

- Chapter 5, "The Ongoing Controversy over Shared Responsibility," is a
  sharpened reformulation of the previous edition's "Victims' Contribution
  to the Crime Problem." But as always, it presents all sides of this controversial topic. The debate over individual responsibility (in the form of
  facilitation, precipitation, and provocation) is characterized as victim blaming versus victim defending. The chapter now features enhanced coverage
  of the theories that account for the differential risks experienced by entire
  demographic groups. New material highlighted in boxes provides pragmatic advice from experts about how to avoid being burglarized, getting
  robbed, and being impersonated by an identity thief, and what to do if
  these unwanted events happen.

- Chapter 6, "Victims and the Police," replaces "Victims and the Criminal
  Justice System: Cooperation and Conflict; Part 1: The Police." This
  streamlined chapter contains updated tables, including the clearance rates
  for index crimes for the entire nation, and the homicide clearance rates for
  many big-city police forces (data that still does not appear in other victimology, criminology, or criminal justice textbooks, to my knowledge). The
  controversy surrounding charges that some police departments try to
  manipulate crime statistics downward by discouraging victims from reporting incidents is explored in greater depth. Other issues examined in more
  detail include efforts by victims to recover their stolen property and the
  filing of dishonest and false complaints.

- Chapter 7, retitled as "Victims' Rights and the Criminal Justice System,"
  now provides a systematic review of the many recently enacted procedural
  rights (material that formerly appeared in the final chapter of the book).
  The enumeration and assessment of these rights is integrated into the

discussions about interactions with prosecutors, defense attorneys, judges, juries, and corrections officials This expanded chapter includes some new Supreme Court decisions impacting victims and a strengthened examination of the need for protection against intimidation and reprisals.

- Chapter 8, "Victimized Children," contains expanded discussions and updated statistics in tables and graphs that reveal the latest trends in child maltreatment cases and fatalities. Differential risks of being abused are explored in greater detail. The latest revelations about sexual abuse as well as cover-ups of systematic molestations are summarized. A summary of a study about the sudden rise and rapid fall of prosecutions and lawsuits based on repressed memories of childhood abuse helps to understand what happened to this formerly burning issue.

- Chapter 9, "Victims of Violence by Lovers and Family Members," benefits from new real-life cases and updated research findings. The many ways that victims suffer now is explored in greater detail. The clash between maximalist and minimalist perspectives has been updated and sharpened. Theories that address "why does she stay with an abusive partner?" are presented more effectively. Orders of protection and gun surrender laws are described more clearly.

- Chapter 10, "Victims of Rapes and Other Sexual Assaults," contains new real-life cases and updated statistics in the graph and the table. The discussion about sexual assaults on campus now appears here, rather than in Chapter 11, and a great deal of material has been added, including best practices for handling these cases. Coverage about sexual assaults in the military was added. Updated estimates about differential risks and unanalyzed rape kits enhance the analysis of these issues.

- Chapter 11, "Additional Groups of Victims with Special Problems," has been reorganized and streamlined and benefits from many fresh real-life examples. New material has been added about cyberstalking, line-of-duty deaths of police officers, and murders and woundings attributed to terrorism. The analysis of offenses against high school and college students, of inmate vs. inmate violence, and of hate crimes has been updated and strengthened.

- Chapter 12, "Repaying Victims," contains some new material about civil lawsuits and state compensation funds, as well as practical advice addressing the challenges of collecting insurance reimbursements in the wake of burglaries.

- Chapter 13, "Victims in the Twenty-First Century: Alternative Directions," now features a greatly expanded and yet carefully balanced presentation of the controversy surrounding arming for self-protection, with a wealth of new material about victims using guns to defend themselves. Approaches to conflict resolution that seek to achieve restorative justice now stand out in sharp contrast to arming for self-protection because the discussion about legal rights and remedies has been moved to Chapter 7.

Once again, this edition accentuates the positive by repeatedly focusing on the unanticipated but much-welcomed trend that became evident by the late 1990s: an impressive nationwide drop in victimization rates. Across the country, fewer people are being murdered, robbed, raped, assaulted, or suffering losses from burglaries and car thefts than at any time in the past several decades. This improvement in public safety is well documented in the many tables and graphs throughout the text. Of course, no one knows how much longer the ebbing of the crime wave that began in the 1960s and peaked in the early 1990s will last because no consensus exists among criminologists and victimologists about why crime rates rise and fall.

USING THIS TEXTBOOK

This ninth edition is intended to meet several distinct needs. The optimal situation is to use this textbook as the foundation for an undergraduate elective course on victimology that runs for an entire term. In fact, more than enough material is provided to sustain even a graduate-level course. A number of chapters can be used to address victim-centered problems, such as violence in American society, that arise in either an advanced criminology class or as selected issues in criminal justice course.

Similarly, other chapters might fit neatly into courses that focus on policy analysis or research methods.

For classes that require a term paper or group project, this edition provides loads of up-to-date references, suggestions for short research projects at the end of each chapter, plenty of graphs and statistics, and numerous observations about problems of measurement and interpretation. For example, the extensive compilation of the types of victimization that recently have been recognized or are just waiting to be rediscovered (see the list at the end of Chapter 2) can serve as a launching pad for exploratory research and term projects. For courses that incorporate writing requirements via essay exams, each chapter has several questions for discussion and debate plus a few that stimulate critical thinking. An instructor's manual with short answer questions is also available, as are Microsoft PowerPoint® visual aids.

I maintain a personal Web site (www.crimevictimsupdates.com) geared to this textbook's chapters that provides links to the very latest newspaper and magazine articles, radio and television interviews, and reports issued by government agencies and think tanks. The website can be useful for extra credit and make-up assignments and serves as a constant reminder that the subjects examined in the course are closely connected to the real world outside the classroom.

MY GROWING "CREDENTIALS" AS A CRIME VICTIM

Each time I revise this textbook, my credentials (unfortunately) broaden and deepen. Direct experience often is the best teacher and a source of sensitivity and insight about life's problems and the challenges imposed by misfortunes.

In the preface of each previous edition, I listed these credentials: I am not only a criminologist and victimologist, I am also a crime victim.

I know from personal encounters what it is like to be a victim of a range of street and white-collar crimes (thankfully, none of them were really serious). In fact, my very first experience was something to laugh at, in retrospect, although it was very aggravating at the time. After I graduated from college, I got my first car: a brand-new 1966 Mustang. I drove it around upstate New York, where I was attending graduate school, for about a week before a thief stole its gleaming wire wheel covers—all four of them in a single night! Amazingly enough, crime was not yet a widespread problem, so my minor misfortune actually appeared in the police blotter of the local newspaper. This incident contributed to my life-long interest in law-breaking, victimization, and the search for justice.

Before the first edition was written:

- I was held up twice (in one month!) by pairs of knife-wielding robbers.
- I lost a car to thieves. The police discovered it completely stripped, burned, and abandoned.
- I experienced a series of thefts of car radios and batteries.
- I suffered a break-in that left my apartment in shambles.

By the time the second edition of this textbook came out, my already impressive résumé as a street crime victim had grown considerably:

- A thief stole the bicycle that I used to ride to the train station by cutting the fence to which it was chained.
- Someone ran off with a fishing rod I had left unattended for a few minutes on a pier while I was buying more bait. (It surely was not pulled over the railing by a big fish).
- A teenager singled out my car in a crowded parking lot for some reason and smashed the rear window with a rock. An eyewitness pointed out the young man to the police, and his foster parents volunteered to pay my bills for the damage. (I minimized their expenses by going to a salvage yard to find a low-cost replacement window.)
- A thief broke into the trunk of my car and stole my wallet and my wife's pocketbook while we spent an afternoon at the beach. Our wallets were later recovered from a nearby mailbox, emptied of our cash and credit cards.
- One hot summer night, an intruder entered our kitchen through an unlocked screen door. He ran off with a purse while we talked to guests in the living room.
- A car I was riding in was sideswiped by a vehicle driven by a fugitive who was being hotly pursued by a patrol car. No one was hurt, and the offender escaped.
- A thief smashed the side window of my car, which was parked at a meter a block away from the college where I teach. Sitting in the passenger seat, he

began to pry out the radio. When the alarm went off, he fled, leaving his screwdriver behind (it is now my favorite tool).

By the third edition, I had a few more misfortunes to add to the list:

- My car was broken into two more times, on busy streets, during the day. One time, the alarm sounded and apparently scared off the thief, cutting short his depredations and minimizing my losses to a handful of quarters kept for tolls in an ashtray and some items in the glove compartment.

Shortly before the fourth edition was completed, my family was the victim of a con game that turned out to be a rather common scam:

- We picked a moving company out of the Yellow Pages because it advertised low rates and accepted credit cards. I should have been suspicious when they arrived in a rented truck, but I foolishly signed some papers authorizing them to charge me for packing materials. While we loaded computer components, valuables, and pets into our cars and shuttled them to our new house, they quickly used an enormous amount of shrink-wrap and cardboard boxes on our old furniture, cheap picture frames, and clothing. When their rented van arrived at our new home 10 miles away, they presented me with a bill that was inflated by about $1,000 worth of unnecessary packaging. They demanded immediate payment in cash before they would unload our stuff that Saturday night, or else they would drive away with all our possessions and charge us for unloading and storage. I called the police, but they insisted it was a business dispute and said that they could not intervene. I had no choice but to visit several ATMs, to take out loans from all our credit cards, and hand over the cash. On Monday, I contacted some colleagues at John Jay College of Criminal Justice who have close connections with law enforcement agencies. They made inquiries and warned me that this company was known to have mob ties. Because these gangsters literally knew where we lived, I regret to admit that a fear of reprisals intimidated me from pursuing my claims about fraud in civil court or through state regulatory agencies or consumer affairs bureaus. Years later, I read in the newspaper that some victims received protection as witnesses for the prosecution and that this moving scam crew eventually was put out of business and incarcerated.

By the time I completed the fifth edition, my credentials had "improved":

- Like many other New Yorkers, I knew some victims of terrorism who barely escaped death by evacuating the World Trade Center before the Twin Towers collapsed.
- My daughter's backpack was stolen by a thief who pried open the trunk of our automobile after watching her park the car and walk away.
- More importantly, I received just a taste of what it is like to be a victim of identity theft. The fraud detection unit of a credit card company called one morning and asked if anyone in my family had recently charged exactly $400 at a department store and $200 at a computer software store about

40 miles away. When I answered no, and wondered aloud how such round number amounts could be charged for merchandise that is taxed, they simply said, "Don't worry, just fill out an affidavit." When the paperwork finally arrived weeks later, I did what they asked and never heard anything about these peculiar financial transactions again.

By the time the sixth edition came out, I had received plenty of fraudulent e-mails (called "phishing"—see the discussion of identity theft in Chapters 4 and 5) warning me to immediately update my account at some bank or credit card company or eBay before it was frozen. Besides these pathetic attempts to con me, very little else happened, which probably reflected the nationwide drop in crime that has lowered virtually everyone's risks of being victimized (see Chapter 3).

However, while preparing the seventh edition, my family was victimized twice—in other countries! My daughter's car was broken into near a museum in Montreal, Canada, and her husband's digital camera was stolen (and we paid a hefty bill for a new door lock and rear window for the damaged vehicle). In London's theater district, a pickpocket deftly removed my wife's wallet from her backpack (see Chapter 1). Fortunately, although she lost some cash and her driver's license, whoever ended up with her credit cards was not able to purchase anything or steal her identity. Meanwhile, back home, I suspected that someone entered our car one night while it was parked unlocked in our driveway because the glove compartment was open the next morning. As far as I could tell, nothing was taken. Sure enough, the next night the thief returned and stole the remote for our garage door opener from the car's sun visor while we were eating dinner. Fortunately, just an hour later I discovered that the remote was missing due to my habitual carelessness about not locking my car's doors (see Chapter 5), so I disconnected the garage door opener. I did not report these two minor matters to the police. The incidents in Montreal and London were reported to the authorities, but they never contacted us, so presumably the car thief and the pickpocket were never caught and our stolen property was not recovered (see Chapter 6).

One other incident is worth recounting because it is humorous: I keep my canoe chained to a rack at the town beach during warm weather. I came down one hot summer day to do some paddling and fishing and discovered that someone had stolen the chain and the padlock—but left the canoe behind, undamaged. Go figure!

After finishing the eighth edition, I had only one additional trivial incident to report. Someone stole a small anchor from my motorboat while it was moored in a nearby bay. I reported this petty larceny to the harbor patrol.

Now that this ninth edition is complete, I have just one more minor incident to share. Someone used my credit card to purchase stuff I would never buy and enroll in various costly Web-based services of no interest to me. The credit card security department flagged these peculiar transactions and notified me. I did not have to pay for the expensive goods and services this identity thief charged in my name.

Obviously, victimization is rarely a laughing matter and nothing to scoff at. Others have suffered far more severely than I have. People endure devastating losses and try to cope with traumatic ordeals. But these many brushes with an odd assortment of offenders over the last four decades have sensitized me to the kinds of expenses, emotional stresses, and physical injuries that taken together constitute the "victim's plight." I suspect that many victimologists and victim advocates have been drawn to this humanistic discipline because their own painful experiences inspired them to try to alleviate the suffering of others.

ANCILLARIES

To further enhance the teaching of victimology courses, the following supplements are available to qualified adopters. Please consult your local sales representative for details.

Online Instructor's Manual

The instructor's manual contains a variety of resources to aid instructors in preparing and presenting text material in a manner that meets their personal preferences and course needs. It presents chapter-by-chapter suggestions and resources to enhance and facilitate learning.

Online Test Bank

The Test Bank contains multiple choice and essay questions to challenge your students and assess their learning.

Online PowerPoints®

These vibrant, Microsoft PowerPoint® lecture slides for each chapter assist you with your lecture, by providing concept coverage using images, figures, and tables directly from the textbook!

ACKNOWLEDGMENTS

I would like to thank the following people who helped me prepare this ninth edition of my textbook:

At Cengage Learning: Carolyn Henderson Meier, Senior Product Manager for Criminal Justice; Julia Catalano, Product Assistant for Criminal Justice; Kara Kindstrom, Marketing Manager for Criminal Justice; at S4Carlisle Publishing Services: Michael B. Kopf, Development Production Editor; and at Lumina Datamatics: Kailash Rawat.

I would like to express my appreciation to these reviewers of all the previous editions:

Kelly Asmussen, *Peru State College*

Frankie Bailey, *State University of New York, Albany*

Kevin M. Beaver, *Florida State University*

Susan Beecher, *Aims Community College*

Bonnie Black, *Mesa Community College*

Ashley Blackburn, *University of North Texas*

Pam Nielson Boline, *Dakota Wesleyan University*

John Bolinger, *MacMurray College*

Willie D. Cain, *Campbell University*

Faith Coburn, *University of Wisconsin–Milwaukee*

Ellen G. Cohn, *Florida International University*

Andria L. Cooper, *Fort Hays State University*

Susan Craig, *University of Central Florida*

Greg Dawson, *College of Central Florida*

Elizabeth DeValve, *Fayetteville State University*

Rhonda Dobbs, *The University of Texas at Arlington*

William Doerner, *Florida State University, Tallahassee*

John Dussich, *California State University, Fresno*

Deborah Eckberg, *Metropolitan State University*

Martha Earwood, *University of Alabama at Birmingham*

Gerald P. Fisher, *Georgia College and State University*

Linda Fleischer, *The Community College of Baltimore County*

Gilbert Geis, *University of California at Irvine*

Alan Harland, *Temple University*

Sidney Harring, *John Jay College of Criminal Justice*

Matasha Harris, *John Jay College of Criminal Justice*

Carrie Harter, *Sam Houston State University*

Debra Heath-Thornton, *Messiah College*

Scott Hedlund, *Pierce College*

Elizabeth Hegeman, *John Jay College of Criminal Justice*

Michael Herbert, *Bemidji State University*

Stacey Hervey, *Metro State College*

Eric W. Hickey, *California State University, Fresno*

Lin Huff-Corzine, *Kansas State University*

Amanda M. Humphrey, *Mount Mercy University*

David Johnson, *University of Baltimore*

Dan Jones, *Governors State University*

Lynn Jones, *Northern Arizona University*

Janice Joseph, *Richard Stockton College of New Jersey*

Betsy Kreisel, *University of Central Missouri*

Fred Kramer, *John Jay College of Criminal Justice*

Janet Lauritsen, *University of Missouri–St. Louis*

Daniel P. LeClair, *Boston University*

Joseph Linskey, *Centenary College*

Cheng-Hsien Lin, *Lamar University*

Karol Lucken, *University of Central Florida*

Donal MacNamara, *John Jay College of Criminal Justice*
Liz Marciniak, *University of Pittsburgh at Greensburg*
Michael G. Maxfield, *Rutgers University*
Thomas McDonald, *North Dakota State University*
Jackye McClure, *San Jose State University*
Markita McCrimmon, *Central Carolina Community College*
Melissa Owens McKenna, *Hiwassee College*
Stephen J. Morewitz, *San Jose State University*
Christine Mouton, *University of Central Florida*
George Muedeking, *California State University, Stanislaus*
Ann Weaver Nichols, *Arizona State University*
Sharon Ostrow, *Temple University*
Leanne Owen, *Holy Family University*
Elicka S. L. Peterson, *Florida State University*
Amy Pinero, *Baton Rouge Community College*
Elizabeth Quinn, *Fayetteville State University*

Roy Roberg, *San Jose State University*
Kevin Roberts, *Grace College*
Lorie Rubenser, *Sul Ross State University*
Edward Sagarin, *John Jay College of Criminal Justice*
Ken Salmon, *Arizona State University*
Stanley Saxton, *University of Dayton*
Brent Smith, *University of Alabama, Birmingham*
David Sternberg, *John Jay College of Criminal Justice*
Mark Stevens, *North Carolina Wesleyan College*
James Stewart, *Northeastern Junior College*
Thomas Underwood, *Washburn University*
Joseph Victor, *Mercy College*
Karen Weiss, *West Virginia University*
Tamara Tucker Wilkins, *Minnesota State University, Mankato*
Janet K. Wilson, *University of Central Arkansas*
Thomas G. Ziesemer, *College of Central Florida*

Finally, I want to thank all those professors who provided valuable feedback through a survey about the eighth edition which helped me to prepare this ninth edition:

Andrew Karmen, February 2015

1

What Is Victimology?

LEARNING OBJECTIVES

To practice looking at victims and victimization
through a scientific lens.

To appreciate why objectivity is worth striving for
when examining the victims' plight.

To discover why some people have a negative
impression about what they brand as victimology.

To be able to recognize how victimology is similar to
as well as different from criminology.

To become familiar with the steps to follow when
conducting a victim-centered analysis.

FOCUSING ON THE PLIGHT OF CRIME VICTIMS

The concept of a **victim** can be traced back to ancient societies. It was connected to the notion of sacrifice. In the original connotation of the term, a victim was a person or an animal put to death during a religious ceremony in order to appease some supernatural power or deity. Over the centuries, the word has picked up additional meanings. Now it commonly refers to individuals who suffer injuries, losses, or hardships for any reason. People can become victims of accidents, natural disasters, diseases, or social problems such as warfare, discrimination, political witch hunts, and other injustices. Crime victims are harmed by illegal acts.

Victimization is an asymmetrical interpersonal relationship that is abusive, painful, destructive, parasitical, and unfair. While a crime is in progress, offenders temporarily force their victims to play roles (almost as if following a script) that mimic the dynamics between predator and prey, winner and loser, victor and vanquished, and even master and slave. Many types of victimization have been outlawed over the centuries—specific oppressive and exploitative acts, like raping, robbing, and swindling. But not all types of hurtful relationships and deceitful practices are forbidden by law. It is permissible to overcharge a customer for an item that can be purchased for less elsewhere, or to underpay a worker who could receive higher wages for the same tasks at another place of employment, or impose exorbitant interest rates and hidden fees on borrowers who use credit cards and take out mortgages, or to deny food and shelter to the hungry and the homeless who cannot pay the required amount.

Victimology is the scientific study of the physical, emotional, and financial harm people endure because of illegal activities. Victimologists first and foremost investigate the victims' plight: the impact of the injuries and losses inflicted by offenders on the people they target. In addition, they carry out research into the public's political, social, and economic reactions to the suffering of victims. They also study how victims are handled by officials and agencies within the criminal justice system, especially interactions with police officers, detectives, prosecutors, defense attorneys, judges, probation officers, and members of parole boards.

Victimologists want to know whether and to what degree crime victims experience physical wounds, economic hardships, or emotional turmoil. One aim, of course, is to devise ways to help them recover. In the aftermath of the incident, are they saddened, depressed, frightened, terrorized, traumatized, infuriated, or embittered? Also, victimologists want to find out how effectively the injured parties are being assisted, supported, served, accommodated, rehabilitated, and educated to avoid further trouble. Victimologists are equally curious to determine the extent to which their suffering is being totally ignored, largely neglected, belittled, manipulated, and commercially or politically exploited. Some individuals who sustain terrible injuries and devastating losses might be memorialized, honored, and even idolized, while others might be mocked, discredited, defamed, demeaned, socially stigmatized, and even condemned for bringing about their own misfortunes. Why is this so?

Victimologists also want to examine why some injured parties find their ordeals life transforming. Some become deeply alienated and withdraw from social relationships. They may become burdened by bouts of depression, sleep disorders, panic attacks, and stress-related illnesses. Their healing process may require overcoming feelings of helplessness, frustration, and self-blame. Others might react to their fear and fury by seeking out fellow sufferers, building alliances, and discovering ways to exercise their "agency"—to assess their options and make wise decisions, take advantage of opportunities, regain control of their lives, rebuild their self-confidence, and restore a sense of trust and security. Why do people experience such a wide range of responses, and do personality or social factors primarily determine how a person initially reacts and then recovers?

Direct or **primary victims** experience the criminal act and its consequences firsthand. **Indirect** or **secondary victims** (such as family members and loved ones) are not immediately involved or physically injured in confrontations. But they might be burdened, even devastated, as the following examples illustrate.

> *A teenager who shot and killed a high school athlete is about to be sentenced to prison. The distraught father of the murdered boy tells the judge, "We always hope our little guy will come through the door, and it will never be. We don't have lives. We stay in every day. We can't function."* (MacGowan, 2007)

···

> *As an argument with a stranger escalates and he pulls out a gun, a wife is wounded when she puts out her hand to try to shield her husband from the bullet that causes his death. She tells an interviewer, "I was just so excited and looking forward to spending the day with the love of my life…. And just to think that in the blink of an eye, my whole world just got shattered into a million pieces. And now I'm left trying to pick them all up and putting them back together."* (Gutman, 2014)

First responders and rescue workers who race to crime scenes (such as police officers, forensic evidence technicians, paramedics, and firefighters) are exposed to emergencies and trauma on such a routine basis that they also can be considered secondary or indirect victims who periodically might need emotional support themselves to prevent burnout (see Regehr and Bober, 2005; and Abel, 2013).

Note that victimologists are social scientists and researchers, as opposed to practitioners who directly assist injured parties to recover from their ordeals or who advocate on their behalf. Doctors, nurses, psychiatrists, psychologists, therapists, counselors, social workers, caseworkers, lawyers, clergy, and dedicated volunteers provide hands-on services, emotional support, and practical advice to their clients (see Williams, 2002). Victimologists step back and evaluate the effectiveness of these well-intentioned efforts by members of the healing and helping professions. Conversely, people who minister to those in distress can gain valuable insights and useful suggestions from the findings of studies carried out by victimologists.

The term *victimology* can mean different things to different people, and detectives can consider themselves "victimologists" too. In police work, the term *victimology* is applied to a type of background investigation. To homicide detectives, victimology is the process of reconstructing events and learning as much as possible about a person who was murdered in order to help figure out who the killer is (see Box 1.1).

STUDYING VICTIMIZATION SCIENTIFICALLY

The suffering of victims and of the people who are very close to them always has been a popular theme for artists and writers to interpret and for political and religious leaders to address. But this long and rich tradition embodies what might be categorized as the **subjective approach** to the plight of victims, since issues are approached from the standpoint of morality, ethics, philosophy, personalized reactions, and intense emotions. Victimologists examine these same topics and incidents from a fresh, new angle: through a social science lens. **Objectivity** is the hallmark of any social scientific endeavor. Scientific objectivity requires that the observer try to be fair, open-minded, evenhanded, dispassionate, neutral, and unbiased. Objectivity means not taking sides, not showing favoritism, not allowing personal prejudices to sidetrack analyses, not permitting emotion to cloud reasoning, and not letting the dominant views of the times dictate conclusions and recommendations.

Prescriptions to remain disinterested and uninvolved are easier to abide by when the incidents under scrutiny happened long ago and far away. It is much harder to maintain social distance when investigating the plight of real people right here and right now. These scientific tenets are extremely difficult to live up to when the subject matter—the depredations inflicted by lawbreakers—connects to widely held beliefs about good and evil, right and wrong, and justice and unfairness. Most offenders show such callous disregard and depraved

BOX 1.1 What the Police Mean by the Term *Victimology*

When homicide squad detectives say they are engaged in victimology, they mean piecing together clues and leads from the dead person's life in order to help discover the killer's identity. Police investigators want to find out as much as possible about the deceased from interviews with the next of kin and eyewitnesses, e-mail messages, diaries, banking deposits and withdrawals, computer files, and records of telephone calls. Detectives look into the victim's associates (by compiling lists of contacts, including friends, family members, acquaintances, rivals, and enemies), social background (lifestyle, occupation, education, marital status, secret lovers), criminal history (any prior record of arrests, convictions, and incarcerations plus any cases in which the departed served as a complainant, plaintiff, or witness against others), financial situation (sources of income, debts owed, investments, and who is next in line to inherit any property), and health issues (drinking habits, substance abuse, and other problems). Autopsy findings shed light on the final meal, the presence of any traces of recent drinking and drug taking, the cause of death, and the approximate time interval when the fatal confrontation took place.

For example, if a drug dealer is found shot to death in an alley, detectives would construct a timeline of his last known whereabouts and activities. What were his known hangouts (bars, clubs, parks, etc.)? Investigators would seek clues to determine whether he was killed by someone above him in the hierarchy of drug trafficking or someone below who worked for him or bought controlled substances from him. Was he recently embroiled in any disputes or court cases, and did he secretly serve as a confidential informant? Who had a motive and an opportunity to slay him? (NYPD homicide detectives, 2008). When police discovered the scattered remains of a number of young women in a stretch of deserted sand dunes near a popular beach, their victimological inquiries soon established a common thread: that they all had been prostitutes apparently slain by a serial killer (Swartz, 2013).

Clearly, whereas victimologists want to uncover trends, patterns, and regularities that hold true for many injured parties in general, police investigators seek to establish in great detail everything that can be unearthed about the life and death of a particular person. "Forensic victimology" in this very pragmatic and immediate sense is undertaken to increase the odds of solving a case, apprehending a suspect, and testifying in court on behalf of a person who is no longer able to pursue justice on his or her own (see Petherick and Turvey, 2008).

indifference toward the human beings they have cold-bloodedly targeted as depersonalized objects that it is difficult to avoid being caught up and swept away by strong emotional currents. Consider how natural it is to identify with those on the receiving end of violent attacks, to feel empathy and sympathy toward them, and to bristle with hostility toward the aggressors, as in the following real-life cases (all involving college students):

A 22-year-old student government president is carjacked and kidnapped by two armed young men, 21 and 17 years old, and forced to withdraw money from an ATM. Next, they drive their hostage to a remote location in the woods, molest her, and then decide to kill her since she could identify them. She pleads for her life and urges them to pray with her. Instead, one shoots her four times. But she still can move and talk, so he blasts her with a shotgun to finish her off. The two assailants are caught and convicted of murder. (Velliquette, 2011)

■■■

A 22-year-old college student who aspires to become a police officer works in a bakery. But he is gunned down in his home by a gang of young men who barge in and mistake him for his look-alike younger brother, who had gotten them in trouble with the authorities. "He was one of the best boys you will ever find," his mother laments. (Bultman and Jaccarino, 2010)

■■■

A sophomore attends a campus party and leaves alone around midnight. About 2 am, footage from a surveillance camera shows her walking in a downtown pedestrian mall followed by a man. After that she disappears, and her family, friends and volunteers undertake the largest hunt for a missing person in the state's history. Over a month later, her remains are discovered on an abandoned property about 8 miles away from the mall, and the police arrest the man in the video, who is linked by forensic evidence to other attacks. Students at her university organize a memorial during homecoming weekend, and her parents thank the police and the volunteers who searched for her, but add, "We are devastated by the loss of our beautiful daughter." (Martinez, 2014)

•••

A classroom door swings open, and a mentally deranged undergraduate barges in and shoots the professor who is lecturing by the blackboard. Then, starting with those in the front rows, the silent and expressionless gunman methodically starts firing away at the horrified students, who hit the floor and turn over desks to shield themselves. "There were a couple of screams, but for the most part it was eerily silent, other than the gunfire," a student reports. As the mass murderer wanders off, another student recalls, "I told people that were still up and conscious, 'Just be quiet because we don't want him to think there are people in here because he'll come back in.'" Indeed, he tries to return to resume the slaughter, but a wounded classmate keeps the door wedged shut. Still determined to reenter into the classroom, the deeply disturbed young man fires repeatedly at the door. When he eventually stalks off, frantic students call 911 on their cell phones and holler for help out the windows. The attacker is later found dead from a self-inflicted gunshot wound to the head, in another classroom, alongside the bodies of some other undergrads he murdered. (Hernandez, 2007)

Doesn't basic human decency demand that observers identify with the wounded, fallen, downtrodden, and underdogs and condemn vicious predatory behavior? Why would anyone even consider striving for objectivity to be an indispensable prerequisite of each and every scientific analysis?

WHY OBJECTIVITY IS DESIRABLE

At first glance, the importance of reserving judgments, refraining from jumping to conclusions, and resisting the urge to side with those who are in pain might not be self-evident. An angry, gut reaction might be to ask, "What kind of person would try to remain detached and dispassionate in the midst of such intense suffering? What is wrong with championing the interests of people whose

lives have been upended by unjust and illegal actions? Why is neutrality a worthwhile starting point in any analysis?"

The simple and direct answer to the question "Why shouldn't victimologists be openly, unabashedly, and consistently pro-victim?" is that, unlike the situations described in the examples above, on many occasions this formula offers no real guidance. So when is a person worthy of sympathy and support? Most people would consider an individual to be an innocent victim only when the following conditions apply (what sociologists would call the **ideal type** or positive stereotype): The person who suffered harm was weaker in comparison to the apparent aggressor and was acting virtuously (or at least was engaged in conventional activities and was not looking for trouble or breaking any laws), the wrongdoer was a complete stranger whose predatory behavior obviously was illegal and unprovoked, and the one who resorted to force was not a member of a governmental agency authorized to use coercion (such as police officers or prison guards). Using the language of sociology, the status of being a legitimate or bona fide victim worthy of support is socially constructed and conferred (see Christie, 1986; and Dignan, 2005).

Sometimes It Is Difficult to Distinguish Victims from Villains

But real-life confrontations do not consistently generate simple clear-cut cases that neatly fall into the dichotomies of good and evil, innocence and guilt. Not all victims were weak, defenseless, unsuspecting "lambs" who, through tragic or ironic circumstances or just plain bad luck, were pounced upon by cunning, vicious "wolves." In some instances, observers may have reasonable doubts and honest disagreements over which party in a conflict should be labeled the victim and which should be stigmatized as the villain. These complicated situations dramatize the need for impartiality when untangling convoluted relationships in order to make a rational argument and a sound legal determination that one person should be arrested, prosecuted, and punished, and the other defended, supported, and assisted. Unlike the black-and-white examples presented above, many messy incidents reported in the news and processed by the courts embody shades of gray. Clashes frequently take place between two people who, to varying degrees, are simultaneously both victims, or both wrongdoers. Consider the following two accounts of iconic, highly publicized incidents from past decades that illustrate just how difficult it can be to try to establish exactly who seriously misbehaved and who acted appropriately:

> *A wealthy couple are at home in their mansion watching television and eating ice cream when someone shoots the man point-blank in the back of the head and then blasts his wife with a shotgun a number of times in the face. The police search for the killers for six months before the couple's two sons, 21 and 18, concede that they did it. In a nationally televised trial for first-degree murder and facing possible execution, the sons give emotionally compelling (but uncorroborated) testimony describing how their father sexually molested and mentally abused them when they were little boys. The brothers contend they acted in self-defense, believing that their parents were about to murder them to keep the alleged incestuous acts a family secret. The prosecution argues that these boys killed their parents in order to get their hands on their $14 million inheritance (they had quickly spent $700,000 on luxury cars, condos, and fashionable clothing before they were arrested). The jurors become deadlocked over whether to find them guilty of murder or only of the lesser charge of voluntary manslaughter, and the judge declares a mistrial. In the second trial, the prosecution ridicules their "abuse excuse" defense. The jury convicts them of premeditated murder and sentences them to life in prison without parole. Soon afterwards, each brother gets married (the older one divorces and has a second wedding behind bars) even though the prison system does not permit conjugal visits for lifers. (Berns, 1994; Mydans, 1994; Associated Press, 1996a; and Hubbard, 2012)*

∎∎∎

> *An ex-Marine who works as a bouncer in a bar wakes up in his bed and discovers to his horror that his wife has sliced off his penis with a kitchen knife.*

> *Arrested for "malicious wounding," she tells the police that she mutilated him because earlier that evening in a drunken stupor he forced himself upon her. He is put on trial for marital sexual abuse but is acquitted by a jury that does not believe her testimony about a history of beatings, involuntary rough sex, and other humiliations. When she is indicted on felony charges (ironically, by the same prosecutor) for the bloody bedroom assault, many people rally to her side. To her supporters, she has undercut the debilitating stereotype of female passivity; she literally disarmed him with a single stroke and threw the symbol of male sexual dominance out the window. To her detractors, she is a master of manipulation, publicly playing the role of a sobbing battered wife deserving of sympathy to divert attention from her act of rage against a sleeping husband who had lost his sexual interest in her. Facing up to 20 years in prison, she declines to plead guilty to a lesser charge and demands her day in court. The jury accepts her defense—that she was traumatized, deeply depressed, beset by flashbacks, and susceptible to "irresistible impulses" because of years of cruelty and abuse—and finds her not guilty by reason of temporary insanity. After 45 days under observation in a mental hospital, she is released. Soon afterwards, the couple divorces, and then they each take financial advantage of all the international media coverage, sensationalism, titillation, voyeurism, and sexual politics surrounding their deeply troubled relationship. Over the years, he is arrested seven times, gets married three more times, stars in porn movies, and brags that about 70 women have been sexually attracted to him because of his ordeal and re-attachment surgery. She is arrested for punching her mother but then sets up a charitable organization that attempts to prevent domestic violence. (Margolick, 1994; Sachs, 1994; and Moye, 2013)*

In both of the classic cases that were resolved by the criminal justice system years ago in ways that caused quite an uproar and still provoke many heated discussions, the persons officially designated as the victims by the police and prosecutors—the dead parents, the slashed husband—arguably could be considered by certain standards as wrongdoers who "got what was coming to them." Indeed, they were viewed just that way by substantial segments of the public and by some jurors. The defendants who got in trouble with the law—the shotgun-toting brothers, the knife-wielding wife—insisted that they should not be portrayed as criminals. On the contrary, they contended that they actually were the genuine victims who should not be punished: sons sexually molested by their father, a battered woman who was subjected to marital rape.

Now consider three confusing and controversial cases that made headlines and provoked heated public debates in recent years:

A 17-year-old boy wearing a hooded sweatshirt on a rainy night is on the phone with his girlfriend as he walks home from a store after buying a can of soda and some candy. A member of a neighborhood watch group on patrol in a gated community of townhouses that has recently suffered a rash of break-ins drives by, spots him, and calls the police, voicing his suspicions that, "He is up to no good…". The 911 dispatcher tells the 28-year-old man, who had taken some criminal justice courses at a community college, not to follow and confront the youth. But he does, and after he gets out of his SUV, they exchange words and become embroiled in a fistfight. Neighbors hear someone screaming and pleading for help, and call 911. When officers arrive, they find the man bloodied and the teenager dead from a bullet to his heart. The man claims that he was the actual victim and that he had a right to fire his licensed handgun in self-defense. When the news spreads that the local police department has decided not to arrest the armed crime watch volunteer, demonstrations erupt across the country, demanding his arrest as an overzealous police wannabe who acted as a vigilante. Protesters also condemn provisions of the state's "stand your ground" law for causing needless bloodshed and denounce the shooter for engaging in racial profiling because he trailed after what he deemed to be a "suspicious outsider." The local police chief steps down, the county prosecutor and the Justice Department re-open the investigation, and President Obama identifies with the unarmed youth who was tragically and needlessly killed, telling journalists that, "If I had a son, he'd look like {the victim}." A jury of six women acquits the defendant of charges of second

degree murder, and even of the lesser charge of manslaughter. The jurors reject the prosecution's version of the events: that the man had deliberately pursued the hoodie-clad black teenager and instigated the fight that led to the fatal shooting. The jury accepts the injured man's contention that the teenager knocked him to the ground, punched him and repeatedly slammed his head against the sidewalk; and that he was justified in firing to protect himself because he feared grave bodily harm or death. The testimony and evidence at the trial does not clearly resolve key questions about what really happened that rainy night: who initiated the confrontation and started the fight by throwing the first punch, who screamed for help, and at what point was the handgun drawn? Angry protesters insisting that the dead teen was the genuine victim chant, "No justice, no peace." After the controversial "not guilty" verdict, the man is featured in the news several times for brushes with the law involving violent outbursts. (Alvarez and Buckley, 2013; and Jauregui, 2014)

■ ■ ■

At around 4:30 am, a 55-year-old white man hears loud pounding and shouting at his front door and then at his side door. He grabs a shotgun and fires a blast through his locked screen door into the face of a teenage black girl standing on his front porch, killing her instantly. He is arrested and put on trial. Although he initially told the police that his weapon discharged accidentally, he tells the jury that he thought his home was about to be invaded by several intruders and, fearing for his life, vowed that "I wasn't going to cower in my house, I didn't want to be a victim." The prosecution contends that he went to the door armed because he wanted to confront and frighten vandals who had defaced his vehicle with paintballs a few weeks earlier. The jury rejects his claim of firing in self-defense, and finds the man guilty of second degree murder and manslaughter. The young woman he killed turned out to be 19, unarmed, and intoxicated. Apparently she was making a commotion because she was seeking help after being involved in a car crash nearby several hours earlier. (Anderson, 2014; and Abby-Lambertz, 2014)

■ ■ ■

A 29-year-old mother of 3 enters her home to gather her belongings so she can escape from her abusive estranged husband, whose periodic beatings have inflicted injuries that have sent her to a hospital. But he returns home unexpectedly, accompanied by two of her stepsons. The 10-year-old and 13-year-old watch in horror as he beats and strangles her. She runs into the garage to get into her car but finds herself trapped, so she grabs her licensed handgun and returns to their house. When he curses and charges towards her, she fires what she contends are three warning shots into the kitchen ceiling to ward him off. But he calls the police, and her shots are viewed as angry attempts to hurt or kill him and his sons. She rejects a plea offer and is put on trial, and after the jury deliberates for a mere 12 minutes, she is convicted of three counts of aggravated assault with a deadly weapon, which could keep her in prison for 20 years. A grassroots movement of supporters fights for her release and for the charges to be dropped, viewing her as a battered woman who used a weapon to defend herself from imminent bodily injury. When her conviction is overturned because of faulty jury instructions, the prosecution vows to retry her and to seek consecutive sentences that would keep her behind bars for 60 years. (Shepeard, 2014)

In all three of these recent high-profile cases presented above, one other question arose: whether the race of the participants, and especially whether negative racial stereotypes, colors the thinking of various groups about which person should be designated as the genuine victim (see Ghandnoosh, 2014). Also, in all three of these cases, individuals perceiving themselves to be facing a threat of imminent bodily harm reached for their gun, triggering a debate between advocates of armed self-defense and supporters of gun control legislation (the arguments of both sides of this controversy appear in Chapter 13). Sharply different points of view were aired in dinner table discussions, news media columnists' interpretations, courtroom proceedings, and even political rallies about the role of race in decision making and about the use of deadly weapons for self-protection These are the kind of issues that victimologists need to study scientifically.

Whenever different interpretations of the facts lead to sharply divergent conclusions about who is actually the guilty party and who really is the injured party, knee-jerk pro-victim impulses provide no useful guidance for action. The confusion inherent in the unrealistically simplistic labels of 100 percent culpable criminal and 100 percent innocent victim underscores the need for objectivity when trying to figure out who is primarily responsible for whatever lawbreaking took place. Clearly, the dynamics between victims and victimizers need to be sorted out in an evenhanded and open-minded manner, not only by victimologists but also by journalists, police officers, prosecutors, judges, and juries.

In rare instances, even the authorities can't make up their minds, as this unresolved incident demonstrates:

A pizza parlor chef and a mob henchman become embroiled in a knife fight that spills out on to a city street. They stab and slash each other and wind up in different hospitals. The police arrest both of the injured parties on charges of attempted murder as well as other offenses. However, each of the combatants refuses to testify in front of a grand jury against his adversary, fearing self-incrimination if he has to explain his motives and actions. The district attorney's office declines to grant immunity from prosecution to either of the two parties because detectives cannot figure out who was the attacker and who fought back in self-defense. As a result, neither is indicted, and a judge dismisses all the charges pending from the melee. Both wounded men, and the lawyers representing them, walk out of court pleased with the outcome—that no one will get in trouble for an assault with a deadly weapon. (Robbins, 2011)

Criminals Can Be Victims Too

To further complicate matters, impartiality is called for when the injured party clearly turns out to be an undeniable lawbreaker. To put it bluntly, predators prey upon each other as well as upon innocent members of the general public. Some assaults and slayings surely can be characterized as "criminal-on-criminal." Researchers (see Singer, 1981; and Fattah, 1990) noted long ago that people who routinely engage in illegal activities are more likely to get hurt than their law-abiding counterparts. When an organized crime syndicate "puts out a contract" on a rival faction's chieftain, the gangster who gets "whacked" in a "mob rub-out" is not an upstanding citizen struck down by an act of randomly directed violence. Similarly, when a turf battle erupts between drug dealers and one vanquishes the other, it must be remembered that the loser aspired to be the victor. When youth gangs feud with each other by carrying out "drive-by" shootings, the young members who get gunned down are casualties of their own brand of retaliatory "street justice." Hustlers, con men, high-stakes gamblers, pimps, prostitutes, fences, swindlers, smugglers, traffickers, and others living life in the fast lane of the underworld often get hurt because they enter into showdowns with volatile persons known to be armed and dangerous. What could it possibly mean to be pro-victim in these rather common cases in which lawbreakers harm other wrong-doers? The designations "victim" and "offender" are not always at opposite poles but sometimes can be pictured as overlapping categories somewhere near the middle of a continuum bounded by complete innocence and full legal responsibility.

Of course, it is possible for people engaged in illicit activities to be genuine victims qualifying for protection and redress through the courts. For example, prostitutes who trade sexual favors for money are frequently beaten by sadistic johns, robbed of their earnings by exploitative pimps (see Boyer and James, 1983; and Brents and Hausbeck, 2005), and occasionally targeted by serial killers. The harms they suffer are more serious than the "offenses" they commit (see Coston, 2004). Similarly, drug addicts who get beaten and robbed merit assistance. Next, consider the possibility of the intergenerational transmission of misusing force—a cycle of violence over time that transforms a victim into a victimizer (see Fagan, Piper, and Cheng, 1987). For example, a child subjected to periodic beatings might grow up to parent his sons in the same excessively punitive way he was

raised. A study that tracked the fortunes of boys and girls known to have been physically and sexually abused over a follow-up period of several decades concluded that being harmed at an early age substantially increased the odds of future delinquency and violent criminality (Widom and Maxfield, 2001). Another longitudinal study of molested males estimated that although most did not become pedophiles, more than 10 percent grew up to become sexual aggressors and exploiters (Skuse et al., 2003). Similarly, the results of a survey of convicts revealed that they were much more likely to have been abused physically or sexually as children than their law-abiding counterparts (Harlow, 1999).

Even more confusing are the situations of certain groups of people who continuously switch roles as they lead their messy and deeply troubled daily lives. For instance, desperate heroin addicts are repeatedly subjected to consumer fraud (dealers constantly cheat them by selling heavily adulterated packets of this forbidden powder). Nevertheless, after being swindled over and over again by their suppliers, they routinely go out and steal other people's property to raise the cash that pays for their habits (see Kelly, 1983). Similarly, teenage girls who engage in prostitution are arrested by the police and sent to juvenile court as delinquents, in accordance with the law. But reformers picture them as sexually abused by their pimps and by johns who actually commit statutory rape upon these underage sex workers. Are they victims who need help rather than offenders who deserve punishment (see Kristof, 2011)? To further complicate matters, offenders can morph into victims right under the noses of the authorities. For example, when delinquents are thrown in with older and tougher inmates in adult jails, these teenagers face grave risks of being physically and sexually assaulted ("New study," 2008). In penal institutions, convicts become victims entitled to press charges and to protection when they are assaulted, gang raped, or robbed by other more vicious inmates (who seek to stifle any complaining and reporting as "snitching"). About half of all inmates in state prisons told interviewers that they had been shot at in their past lives on the street, and more than a fifth had been wounded by gunfire (Harlow, 2001).

Violence begets violence, to the extent that those who suffer today may be inclined to inflict pain on others tomorrow, For example, a group of picked-upon students might band together to ambush their bullying tormentors; or a battered wife might launch a vengeful surprise attack against her brutal husband.

Victims Can Find Themselves at Odds with the "Good Guys"

Striving for objectivity is important for yet another reason. Crime victims can and do become embroiled in conflicts with persons and groups besides the perpetrators who have directly inflicted physical wounds and economic losses. Injured parties might nurse grievances against journalists reporting about their cases; police officers and detectives investigating their complaints; prosecutors ostensibly representing them in court; defense attorneys working on behalf of the accused; juries and judges deciding how to resolve their cases; probation, parole, and corrections officers supervising convicts who harmed them; lawyers handling their lawsuits in civil court; governmental agencies and legislative bodies shaping their legal rights; social movements either speaking on their behalf or opposing their wishes; and businesses viewing them as eager customers for security products and services. Impartiality helps social scientists to understand why friction can develop in these situations and how to find solutions if these relationships become antagonistic.

First consider the situation in which some victims are pitted against others. This can arise in the aftermath of a Ponzi scheme collapse, when it comes to parceling out whatever funds remain to the many investors who were defrauded. Those investors who bought in and cashed out earlier made money at the expense of those who jumped in right before the pyramid scheme was uncovered (see Henriques, 2010). Which victims are truly the "good guys," and which are more deserving of inaccurate depictions than others? Objectivity

is needed to resolve this victim versus victim infighting.

Next, consider how victims of highly publicized crimes could be outraged by the way the news media portrays them. Rather than side with the injured parties or with the journalists covering their cases, shouldn't a victimologist adopt the stance of a detached and disinterested observer who investigates these charges of insensitivity and inaccuracy perhaps by carrying out a fine-grained content analysis of press coverage in those high-profile cases?

Third, consider those situations where well-intentioned officials and groups put forward competing criminal justice policies, both of which claim to be pro-victim. For instance, prosecutors' offices have adopted one or the other of two alternative ways of responding to violence between intimate partners. One policy enables a battered woman to remain in control of "her" case and ultimately decide if she wants to press charges against her husband or lover whom she had arrested for assaulting her. Advocates of letting her choose whether to prosecute or not emphasize that this approach empowers her to weigh her alternatives and take her personal safety into account. The other policy mandates that the prosecution of the arrestee should go forward on the basis of the available evidence (police officer testimony, photos of bruises, eyewitness accounts, hospital records, and 911 recordings), even if the injured party wants to drop the charges (either because she fears reprisals or seeks rapprochement). Supporters of this policy believe that when batterers know they will be held responsible and punished, domestic violence will subside as a societal problem. In other words, her ability to determine what she wants to do about her individual situation must be sacrificed for the "greater good," which is to use cases like hers to generally deter would-be batterers from assaulting their partners. Only an impartial analysis of scientifically gathered evidence can determine which of these two ostensibly pro-victim approaches best serves the long-term interests of most domestic violence victims (see O'Sullivan, Davis, Farole, and Rempel, 2007; and Nichols, 2014).

The Pentagon has tried for several decades to reduce the number of sexual assaults inflicted by members of the marines, army, navy, air force, and even the coast guard upon their comrades in arms in service academies, barracks, military bases, and even foreign battlefields. After the U.S. Senate debated alternative ways to bring the problem under control, two competing bills, both claiming to be pro-victim, came up for a vote. Supporters of one proposal argued that soldiers, sailors, and marines who are sexually assaulted fear that if they dare to file a complaint, their superiors may not act in their behalf. So they urged legislation that would have stripped commanding officers of their ability to decide which cases reported to them should lead to a court martial and would have empowered military prosecutors to make that decision about pressing charges or not. But the majority voted against this proposal, and instead the Senate passed the Victims Protection Act of 2014 that provides complainants with special counsels to advise them about the pros and cons of pursuing their cases in the military as opposed to the civilian criminal justice system (Jordan, 2014). Which of these two competing approaches would have been better for victims of sexual assaults? Will the new reform bring about substantial improvements? Objectivity, not partisanship, is needed to answer these questions.

The above examples underscore how important it is for researchers to remain neutral at the outset of a study. Now consider the dilemmas many everyday people face because of their competing loyalties: their desire to back crime victims in their struggle for justice versus remaining true to their other commitments. The following examples illustrate how objectivity and impartiality are sorely needed whenever pro-victim impulses must be balanced against other priorities and allegiances—for instance, enthusiastic support for the police or for the pro-life movement.

The mission of police departments is to protect and serve the public, and most people respect and admire the courage of officers who risk their lives to rescue hostages taken by kidnappers. But who would a person who is pro-victim as well as pro-police side with when these well-intentioned officers accidentally kill by "friendly fire" a captive they are seeking to free from the clutches of a captor? Would they agree

with the distraught relatives who launch civil lawsuits for damages that criticize the department for inadequate training and an overreliance on military-style SWAT tactics rather than hostage negotiation techniques, or would they stand shoulder-to-shoulder with the police fraternal organizations that predictably insist that the courageous officer did nothing wrong? Clearly, objectivity is called for when examining the effectiveness of existing law enforcement strategies and departmental policies in these tragedies that periodically seize the attention of the news media and the public (for example, see Dewan, 2005; Rubin, 2008; Murphy, 2014; and Haake, 2014).

People who are pro-choice would agree that a girl or woman who has been compelled to submit to incestuous relations or a forced penetration that results in a pregnancy should not have to bear the rapist's child. But those who want to minimize the suffering of these females and yet are also passionately pro-life might find themselves torn between their conflicting loyalties. This dilemma is fought out in public whenever candidates running for office declare their support for strict antiabortion bills that would permit no exceptions, not even for terminating pregnancies resulting from incest or rape (see Redden, 2013). Evaluating the impact of these controversial policies and proposals about terminating desperately unwanted pregnancies requires an open-minded and even-handed approach to the arguments advanced by both sides about how many pregnancies each year arise from incest or rape, and what are the consequences for the mother who is compelled to bear the rapist's child and for that baby as it grows up. In many states, the man, unless he is convicted of rape, can sue for visitation and custody rights, like any other estranged father (see Chapter 10).

SOURCES OF BIAS THAT THWART OBJECTIVITY

To sum up the arguments presented in earlier sections, when choosing projects to research and when gathering and interpreting data, victimologists must put aside their personal political orientations toward criminal justice policies (such as conservatism or liberalism); their allegiances to causes (such as preserving civil liberties or advancing women's rights or outlawing abortion); and any positive or negative feelings toward entire groups (such as being pro-police or hostile to gun owners). Advocacy, whether for or against some policy or practice, should be kept separate from assessing the facts or drawing conclusions based on the available data. Scientific skepticism in the face of claims ("Prove it! Where is the evidence?")—not self-interest or preconceived notions—must prevail when evaluating whether victims' rights legislation, prevention strategies, antitheft hardware, and recovery programs genuinely work or are ineffective or even counterproductive in reaching their stated goals. Expert opinion, in reports, in court testimony, or in the classroom, must be based on facts, not faith. Research, policy analyses, and program evaluations must tell the whole truth, no matter who is disappointed or insulted.

Three types of biases undermine the ability of any social scientists (not just victimologists) to achieve objectivity and draw conclusions based on solid evidence (see Myrdal, 1944). The first may arise from personal experiences, taking the form of individual preferences and prejudices. For example, victimologists who have been personally harmed in some way (beaten by a lover, robbed, or raped, for example) might become so sensitized to the plight of their fellow victims that they can see issues only from that point of view. Conversely, those who have never been through such an ordeal might be unable to truly grasp what the injured parties must endure. In either case, the victimologist may develop a bias, whether it be oversensitivity and overidentification or insensitivity and lack of identification.

A second type of bias derives from the legacy of the discipline itself. The language, concepts, theories, and research priorities can reflect the collective preferences and priorities of its founders and their followers. For instance, it is widely acknowledged that the pioneers in this field of study introduced a victim-blaming orientation into the new discipline, but over the decades the tide has decisively turned. Today, the vast majority

of victimologists make no secret of their opposite commitments: not to find fault with those who are suffering but rather to devise more effective means of aid, support, and recovery.

Although subtle, a third type of bias can be traced back to the mood of the times. Victimologists, like all other members of a society, are influenced by their social environment. The events that shape public opinion during different periods of time can also affect scientific thought. During the 1960s and early 1970s, for example, many people demanded that the government devise ways to help victims get back on their feet financially, medically, and emotionally. This insistence about expanding the social safety net to cushion the blows inflicted not only by corporations laying off workers and hospitals and doctors charging exorbitant fees for medical treatments but also by criminals reflected the spirit of egalitarianism and mutual aid of this stage in American history. The belief that society—through the instrument of the government—could and should do more to help out inspired a great deal of research and policy advocacy. But these ambitious goals have been voiced less often ever since the 1980s, when the themes of "strive for self-reliance," "reduce social spending by government," and "cut taxes" gained popularity. This emphasis on individuals taking responsibility for their own well-being as opposed to holding the socioeconomic system accountable for its shortcomings and failings (especially chronically high rates of unemployment and a growing gap between the super rich and the desperately poor) has become the dominant ideology since the financial meltdown of 2008 and the onset of the "Great Recession." Consequently, research projects and proposals about government-funded victim assistance programs have shifted their focus to matters such as only providing seed money for demonstration projects, imposing "sunset provisions" (to phase out efforts that don't rapidly produce results), stressing cost effectiveness, and exploring the feasibility of self-help, privately financed, or faith-based charitable alternatives.

Clearly, inquiries into how victims suffer at the hands of criminals as well as other groups such as journalists and criminal justice officials is unavoidably a value-laden pursuit that arouses intense passions and sharply dissenting views. As a result, some have argued that objectivity is an impossible and unrealistic goal that should be abandoned in favor of a forthright affirmation of values and allegiances. They say that victimologists (and other social scientists) should acknowledge their biases at the outset to alert their audiences to the slant that their analyses and policy recommendations will take. Others argue that objectivity is worth striving for because subjectivity thwarts attempts to accurately describe, understand, and explain what is happening, why it came about, and how conditions can be improved.

For the purposes of a textbook, the best course of action is to present all sides of controversial issues. Nevertheless, space limitations impose hard choices. This book focuses almost entirely on victims of interpersonal violence and theft (street crimes such as murder, rape, robbery, assault, kidnapping, burglary, larceny, and motor vehicle theft). There are many other categories of lawbreaking: crimes in the suites involving a betrayal of trust and an abuse of power by high government officials against their rivals or to the detriment of the general public, and by corporate executives who can illegally inflict massive losses and injuries upon their company's workers, customers, stock owners, or competitors. White-collar crimes such as embezzlement by employees against their employers or fraud by citizens against government programs also impose much greater financial costs than street crimes. Organized rackets run by mobsters (drug smuggling, gun trafficking, counterfeiting of documents and currency, gambling, extortion) generate millions of dollars, undermine everyday life, and stimulate official corruption (bribes to look the other way). Crimes without complainants—victimless activities to some, vice to others—are controversial because the social reaction and criminal justice response might be worse than the original deviant behavior involving transactions between consenting adults (such as prostitution, illegal wagering, and street-level drug selling and buying). Clearly these other categories of crimes are as serious and merit attention from scholars, law enforcement agencies, and concerned citizens.

But they are not the types of lawless deeds that come to mind when people talk about "the crime problem" or express fears about being harmed. Street crime scares the public, preoccupies the media, keeps police departments busy, and captures the notice of politicians. These conventional, ordinary, depressingly familiar, and all-too-common predatory acts have tangible, visible, and readily identifiable victims who are directly affected and immediately aware of their injuries and losses.

In contrast, in the other categories of crime, especially white-collar crime and crime in the suites, the deleterious consequences are experienced by abstractions (such as "a competitive economy" or "national security"), impersonal entities (such as the U.S. Treasury or multinational corporations), or vaguely defined collectivities (such as voters, taxpayers, investors, shareholders, or consumers). It is difficult to grasp precisely who has suffered in these cases, and it is nearly impossible to describe or measure the background characteristics or reactions of the injured parties. It is extremely tough to establish in court specifically who the flesh-and-blood victims are in cases of drug smuggling, money laundering, insurance scams, false advertising, bribe taking, software piracy, counterfeiting of trademarked goods, dumping of toxic wastes, insider trading, electoral fraud, illegal campaign contributions, and income tax evasion. But individuals hurt by assailants, robbers, and rapists can be easily identified, observed, contacted, interviewed, studied, counseled, assisted legally, and treated medically. As a result, a wealth of statistical data has accumulated about their wounds, losses, and emotional reactions. For these reasons, victims of interpersonal violence and theft will be the primary focus of attention and concern throughout this text, even though many of the illegal activities cited above inflict much more severe social and economic damage (see Naim, 2005). But note that this decision immediately introduces a bias into this introduction to the field of victimology, one that reflects the experiences of authors of articles and textbooks, the collective priorities of the discipline's founders and most prolific researchers, and the mood of the times!

Victimology's Undeserved "Bad Reputation"

Not very long after the term entered mainstream culture, *victimology* (undeservedly!) became a "dirty word." Some prominent and insightful people who ought to know better misuse "victimology" as an epithet spit out through clenched teeth. This disturbing trend emerged during the 1990s and unfortunately is becoming even more entrenched and pronounced during the twenty-first century. For example, in an article condemning a speech delivered by President Obama, an editor of a political journal used the term *victimology* in a negative way four times (such as "Obama has now put the presidential imprimatur on the crudest kind of racial victimology….") (MacDonald, 2013). Similarly, a former speechwriter for President Bush wrote an editorial headlined, "The Victimology of Hillary Clinton" (Frum, 2014). And a nationally syndicated radio talk show host, responding to a caller who characterized "victimology" as a mindset about feeling guilty for being privileged, responded, "But this whole notion of victimology, I totally get it" (Limbaugh, 2014)—but does he really? Some dramatic illustrations of how victimology has been bad-mouthed in the media as muddled thinking or even denounced as a contemptible point of view over the years appear in Box 1.2.

What were these commentators thinking when they issued these sweeping denunciations of what they branded as "victimology"? Why is this relatively new academic discipline being singled out for such harsh criticisms?

Evidently, those who condemn what they label "victimology" are railing at something other than scientific research focused on people harmed by criminals. The mistake these commentators are making is parallel to the improper usage of the phrase "sociological forces" rather than "social forces," and "psychological problems" instead of "mental problems." Victimology is just one of many "-ologies" (including such narrowly focused fields of study as volcanology, penology, or suicidology, or such broad disciplines as sociology and psychology). The suffix *-ology* merely means "the study of." If the phrase "the objective study of crime victims" is substituted for "victimology" in the excerpts quoted above, the sentences make no sense. Victimology, sociology, and psychology are disciplines that adopt a certain approach to their subject matter or a method of analysis that maintains a particular focus, but they do not impose a partisan point of view or yield a set of predictably biased conclusions.

It appears that what these strident denunciations are deriding is a victimization-centered orientation that can be categorized as the ideology of **victimism** (see Sykes, 1992). An **ideology** (such as conservatism or liberalism) is a coherent, integrated set of beliefs that shapes interpretations and leads to political action. Victimism is the outlook of people who share a sense of common victimhood. Individuals who accept this outlook believe that they gain insight from an understanding of history: of how their fellow group members (such as women, homosexuals, or racial and religious minorities) have been seriously "wronged" by some rival group (to put it mildly; viciously slaughtered would be a better way to phrase it in many historical cases!) or held back and kept down by unfair social, economic, or political institutions built upon oppressive and exploitative roles and relationships.

For example, in a well-known speech in 1964 (right before Congress passed civil rights legislation officially dismantling segregation), Malcolm X, the fiery spokesman for the black nationalist movement, adopted a victimist outlook when he proclaimed (see Breitman, 1966) "I'm one of the 22 million black people who are the victims of Americanism … victims of democracy, nothing but disguised hypocrisy … I'm speaking as a victim of this American dream system. And I see America through the eyes of the victim. I don't see any American dream; I see an American nightmare." A victimist review of the history of African Americans up to the present would stress how the evils of slavery were "perfectly legal"; how Jim Crow segregation and institutionalized racism in housing, employment, education, and public accommodations until the 1950s were permitted by a Supreme Court decision; how lynch mobs rarely got into trouble for their extrajudicial

BOX 1.2   Some Striking Examples of "Victimology Bashing"

The context and then the statement denouncing "victimology"

Concerning male/female relations:

- During a nationally televised interview, a critic of contemporary feminism (Paglia, 1993) declared, *"I hate victimology. I despise a victim-centered view of the universe. Do not teach young women that their heritage is nothing but victimization."*

- A collection of letters written to the editors of the *New York Times* (1996, p. E8) was published under the headline *"What women want is a lot less victimology."*

- A reviewer (Harrop, 2003) of a book about the difficulties facing boys wrote, *"The art of victimology requires three easy steps: (1) Identify a group suffering real or perceived injustices. (2) Exaggerate the problem. (3) Blame the problem on a group you don't like. Conservatives have long condemned the "victimology industry" as a racket, especially when practiced by women and minorities. As it happens, conservatives also play the game, and very well indeed.... The latest victimized group seems to be American boys."*

- A political analyst subtitled her provocative article about an alleged "Campus Rape Myth" as *"The reality: bogus statistics, feminist victimology, and university approved sex toys"* (MacDonald, 2008a).

Concerning heterosexual/homosexual relations:

- In a newspaper opinion piece about the controversy surrounding homosexuals serving in the military, the author (Sullivan, 1993, p. A21) observed, *"The effect that ending the ban could have on the gay community is to embolden the forces of responsibility and integration and weaken the impulses of victimology and despair.... A defeat would send a signal to a gay community at a crossroads between hopeful integration and a new relapse into the victimology of the ghetto."*

Concerning race and ethnic relations:

- An author of a book about race relations called a well-known reverend and civil rights activist a *"professional victimologist"* (see Dreher, 2001).

- A former governor of Colorado (Lamm, 2004) warned that a plot to "destroy America" through immigration and multiculturalism would include the following strategy: *"establish the cult of victimology ... start a grievance industry blaming all minority failure on the majority population."*

- A newspaper columnist and political activist (Kuhner, 2011) lamented: *"Victimology and racial set-asides dominate large swathes of American life, from university admissions and government bureaucracies to big business and construction."*

Concerning international relations:

- A former Soviet intelligence officer (Pacepa, 2005) denounced the United Nations as a breeding ground for *"a virulent strain of hatred for America, grown from the bacteria of Communism, anti-Semitism, nationalism, jingoism, and victimology."*

- A prominent commentator (Brooks, 2006a) wrote about the public's perception of the Middle East: *"What these Americans see is fanatical violence, a rampant culture of victimology and grievance, a tendency by many Arabs to blame anyone but themselves for the problems they create."*

- A reviewer (Anderson, 2008) of a book about the war on terrorism wrote: *"The Left's victimology now sickens [the author]."*

- The secretary of defense in both the Bush and Obama administrations (Gates, 2009) told members of the armed forces: *"I think most of our families don't regard themselves as victims and don't appreciate sometimes the victimology piece. They are very proud of the service of their soldiers overseas...."*

Concerning "culture wars":

- In his syndicated column, a leading conservative partisan (Buckley, 1994, p. 30a) condemned the thinking of the 1960s Woodstock generation: *"The countercultural music is the perfect accompaniment for the culture of sexual self-indulgence, of exhibitionism, of crime and illegitimacy, and ethnic rancor and victimology."*

Concerning courtroom strategies:

- A news magazine columnist (Leo, 2002) took a swipe at certain lawsuits: *"Yes, everybody is a victim now, but some breakthroughs in victimology are more noteworthy than others. The year's best example was the trio of supersize teens who sued McDonald's, claiming the burger chain made them fat by enticing them to eat its meals nearly every day for five years."*

- In a critique of several jury verdicts that found defendants "not guilty," a news magazine commentator (Leo, 1994) complained, *"We are deep into the era of the abuse excuse. The doctrine of victimology—claiming*

(Continued)

BOX 1.2 (Continued)

victim status means you are not responsible for your actions—is beginning to warp the legal system..... *The irony of this seems to escape victimologists. A movement that began with the slogan, 'Don't blame the victim' now strives to blame murder victims for their own deaths."*

Concerning academia and life on college campuses:

- A columnist (Seebach, 1999, p. 2B) berated liberal professors for producing college grads whom employers would reject because the students were *"experts only in victimology or oppression studies."*

- A political analyst (MacDonald, 2007) interpreted the selection of a new university president as evidence that *"Harvard will now be the leader in politically correct victimology."*

- Arguing that resentment against highly educated candidates might be going too far during the 2008 presidential campaign, a political analyst (MacDonald, 2008c) agreed with her allies: *"I am as depressed as anyone by the university's descent into ignorant narcissism and victimology over the last 30 years."*

Concerning everyday life:

- A Pulitzer Prize–winning conservative commentator (Will, 1998, p. 42) titled his syndicated column opposing the Clinton administration's antismoking campaign as *"President feeds the culture of victimology."*

- One journalist (Parker, 1999, p. B10) even insisted that *"Americans are fed up with twentieth-century victimology."*

---

murders; how Klan terror often went unpunished; and how injustices within the criminal justice process such as police brutality and racial profiling continue right up to the present.

Similarly, a leading figure in the women's liberation movement of the late 1960s analyzed "sexual politics" in a victimist way (Millet, 1970): "Oppressed groups have been denied education, economic independence, the power of office, representation, an image of dignity and self-respect, equality of status, and recognition as human beings. Throughout history women have been consistently denied all of these, and their denial today, while attenuated and partial, is nevertheless consistent." A victimist perspective about the history of female oppression would point out how in the past girls and young women who testified that they had been raped felt as if they were put on trial; how battered women's pleas for help were ignored by the men at the helm of the criminal justice system; and how females were barred from serving on juries and were strongly discouraged from pursuing various careers, such as becoming a police officer, lawyer, or judge.

Staunch critics of current conditions often connect the dots by tracing the roots of today's

social problems back through centuries of systematic subjugation. Activists believe that the unfair practices of the past persist right up to the present. But the commentators cited in Box 1.2 claim that adopting this kind of victimist orientation leads to an unhealthy preoccupation of dwelling on past wrongs that impedes efforts to make progress today.

This debate over who or what is to blame for persisting injustices surrounding sex, class, and race is part of an ongoing political battle for the hearts and minds of the American people—a continuing ideological struggle that is often categorized as "identity politics," which is part of the "culture wars." Unfortunately, victimology has become confused with victimism and as a result has been caught up in the cross fire between partisans of the Right and Left. But victimology, as an "-ology" and not an "-ism," is an objective, neutral, open-minded, and evenhanded scientific endeavor that does not take sides, play favorites, or speak with just one voice in these political debates. So there is no reason to condemn the whole scholarly enterprise of victimology and dismiss it as flawed, distorted, or slanted, as the commentators quoted in Box 1.2 did. To put it bluntly, victimology has received a bum rap by those who mockingly equate it with victimism. Read on and this confusion will be dispelled. Victimology will take shape as a challenging, meaningful, balanced, enlightening, socially constructive, and relevant field of study that focuses on a very old problem from a fresh, new angle.

WHY EMPHASIZE RESEARCH?

As a branch of social science that closely focuses on how people behave and react, victimology must be research oriented. Yet, a criticism that often is voiced is, "Why spend all that time and money trying to establish what everyone already knows? The answer is that research is always necessary because "common sense" or "conventional wisdom" is sometimes mistaken, and what people think they already know is incorrect.

For example, consider what happened in this real-life incident:

A 43-year-old grad student enters a classroom in which about 20 students had assembled a few minutes before class. Armed with a military semiautomatic rifle loaded with a 30-round clip, he points the weapon at his classmates and pulls the trigger, but the rifle jams. He tries again, but again the gun does not fire. The students realize they are under attack and drop to the floor, overturn their desks, and try to hide behind them. One courageous student shoves his desk at the gunman, enabling the others to bolt out into the hallway and then out of the building. The gunman flees too but is captured within an hour back at his home. (Asmussen and Creswell, 1995)

Everyone knows what happened in the immediate aftermath, since—unfortunately—violence on college campuses has erupted many times in recent decades. Students in nearby classrooms heard a commotion and set up makeshift barricades while the 20 distraught students raced away in a panic from the scene of the potential slaughter and immediately sought out counselors provided by the administration, right? Wrong! Only a few were openly emotional and cried. Most were in a state of denial and milled around the entrance to the building kidding each other about their near-death experience, dismissing it as though it was trivial. No one called the campus mental health center right away. Most sought out the company of friends or hung out in nearby bars, according to two researchers who interviewed some of the students who thought they were about to die that fateful day (Asmussen and Creswell, 1995).

Next consider what is "known" about robbers: They single out targets that they consider weak and vulnerable, who are easy prey and are unlikely to put up much of a struggle to escape or to try to overpower and capture them. Therefore, it seems predictable that elderly ladies would be robbed much more often than young men, right? Wrong. Data derived from a national survey of the public carried out by a government agency, the Bureau of Justice Statistics, each year reveals that robbers go after teenage boys and young men much more often than older women.

As a final example, most people are familiar with the military's problem of sexual assaults within the ranks (mentioned above). Few would be surprised that servicemen, especially those of higher ranks, exploit their power over the women in uniform to coerce them to submit to sexual acts against their will. But it may be quite a shock to most observers to discover that a little more than half of all reports gathered by researchers of "unwanted sexual contacts" imposed by men were directed at other men. Men therefore made up the majority of the targets of sexual assaults, although women suffered disproportionately high rates (females make up only 15 percent of all members of the armed forces but almost 50 percent of all victims). Clearly, the findings of the Pentagon's survey indicate that the problem of sexual violence goes far beyond the confines of male–female relations among enlistees serving in the army, navy, air force, and marines (see Dao, 2013).

Research is always needed because unexpected findings often are uncovered. Victimologists rely upon the same methods used by all social scientists: case studies, surveys and polls based on questionnaires and interviews, carefully designed social experiments, content analyses of various forms of communication (like movies and song lyrics), secondary analyses of documents and files, records of focus group interactions, and up close and personal ethnographic inquiries based upon systematic field observations.

COMPARING VICTIMOLOGY TO CRIMINOLOGY

Victimology is an interdisciplinary field that benefits from the contributions of sociologists, psychologists, social workers, political scientists, doctors, nurses, criminal justice officials, lawyers, spiritual leaders, and other professionals, volunteers, advocates, and activists. But academically and organizationally, victimology is best conceived of as an area of specialization within criminology, on par with other fields of intensive study, such as delinquency, drug abuse, and penology. All these subdisciplines merit elective courses and textbooks of their own in colleges and graduate programs. In other words, criminology is the older parent discipline and victimology is the recent offshoot.

Criminology can be defined as encompassing the scientific study of illegal activities, offenders, their victims, criminal law and the justice system, and societal reactions to the crime problem.

The Many Parallels between Criminology and Victimology

Even though it is a rapidly evolving subdiscipline, victimology parallels its parent, criminology, in many ways. Criminologists ask why certain individuals become involved in lawbreaking while others do not. Their studies concentrate on the offenders'-backgrounds and motives in order to uncover the root causes of their misbehavior. Victimologists ask why some individuals, households, and entities (such as banks) are targeted while others are not. Research projects aim to discover the sources of vulnerability to criminal attack and the reasons why some victims might act carelessly, behave recklessly, or even instigate others to attack them.

Criminologists recognize that most people occasionally break certain laws (especially during adolescence) but are otherwise law-abiding; only some who engage in delinquent acts graduate to become hardcore offenders and career criminals. Victimologists realize that anyone can suffer the misfortune of being at the wrong place at the wrong time but wonder why certain individuals are preyed upon over and over again.

Although the law holds offenders personally accountable for their illegal conduct, criminologists explore how social, economic, and political conditions "breed" or foster or generate criminal activity. Similarly, although certain victims might be accused of sharing some degree of responsibility with their offenders for the outbreak of specific incidents, victimologists examine personality traits, agents of socialization, and cultural imperatives that compel some people to take chances and put their lives in danger (like teenagers), while others seem to accept their fate. Just as aggressive criminal behavior can be learned, victims may have been taught to lead high-risk lifestyles or alternatively, even to play and accept their subordinate roles.

Both criminologists and victimologists place a great emphasis on following the proper ways of gathering and interpreting data as evidence. Criminologists and victimologists calculate statistics, compute rates, compile profiles, draw graphs, and search for patterns and trends. Criminologists collect and analyze information about individuals engaging in illegal behaviors, especially their typical ages and social backgrounds (such as educational attainments and income levels). Victimologists look over statistics about the sex, ages, and social backgrounds of the people who are harmed by unlawful activities.

Criminologists apply their findings to devise local, regional, and national crime-prevention strategies. Victimologists scrutinize the patterns and trends they detect to learn from other people's misfortunes and mistakes. They then develop personalized victimization-prevention strategies and risk reduction tactics.

Both criminologists and victimologists study how the criminal justice system actually works, in contrast to the way the system is supposed to operate according to agency regulations, official roles, federal and state legislation, court decisions, and politicians' promises. Criminological research reveals how suspects, defendants, and convicts are really handled, while victim-centered studies examine the way injured parties are actually treated by police officers, prosecutors, defense attorneys, and judges. Criminologists assess the needs of offenders for counseling, psychotherapy, additional education, job training, and drug treatment. In addition, criminologists evaluate the effectiveness of various rehabilitation programs offered behind bars or available to probationers or parolees that are intended to reduce recidivism rates. Similarly, victimologists want to diagnose the emotional problems that beset people after they have been harmed by offenders, and to test out the usefulness of programs designed to facilitate their recovery (see Lurigio, 1990; and Roberts, 1990). Criminologists try to calculate the social and economic costs that criminal activity imposes on a community or on society as a whole. Victimologists estimate the losses and expenses that individuals and businesses incur due to acts of violence, theft, or fraud.

Some Differences and Issues about Boundaries

Criminology and victimology differ in several important ways. For starters, criminology is several hundred years old, whereas victimology did not emerge until the second half of the twentieth century.

Criminologists agree among themselves that they should limit their studies to illegal activities and should exclude forms of social deviance that do not violate any criminal law. For instance, the unwanted attention and advances that constitute sexual harassment at a workplace are no longer considered to be a private matter or a personal problem but are a type of discrimination that can lead to a lawsuit—but not an arrest. Similarly, certain aspects of bullying are clearly against the law (physical attacks), while other expressions (mocking, teasing, taunting) are upsetting and ought to be discouraged but are not illegal acts. Both criminologists and victimologists would study bullying in those instances where the intentional acts of aggression rise to the level of criminal behavior and result in vandalism or theft, or, worse yet, erupt into violence (such as the object of scorn suffering a severe beating; or conversely, when the pushed-around individual switches roles by bringing a deadly weapon to school to fight back against his tormentors) (see DeGette, Jenson, and Colomy, 2000; Unnever and Cornell, 2003; and Lipkins, 2008).

However, victimologists, unlike criminologists, cannot reach a consensus about the appropriate outer limits of their field. Some victimologists argue that their scientific studies should not be restricted to criminal victimization. They believe that additional sources of harm, anguish, and loss are worthy of systematic analysis: vicious political repression (brutality, torture, execution) carried out by despotic regimes that violate basic human rights; manmade slaughters (such as wars and genocide); natural disasters (such as floods and earthquakes); and maybe even sheer accidents (like meltdowns of nuclear power plants). There are victims of cancer, famines, ethnic cleansing, and torture who suffer in similar ways to people injured in crimes. The common thread would be to understand the nature of tribulations and travails, and the consistent goal would be to develop effective strategies for short-run relief as well as long-term solutions to alleviate emotional and physical pain stemming from all kinds of calamities.

However, the majority of victimologists believe that their studies should remain focused on criminal victimization so that there are precise, readily identifiable limits and clear directions for further research and theorizing. Actually, criminal victimization may not be more serious (financially), more injurious (medically), or more traumatic and longer lasting (emotionally) than other types of harm. But it is necessary to rein in the boundaries of the field in order to make it manageable for the practical purposes of holding conferences, publishing journals, writing textbooks, and teaching college courses. (For the pros and cons of these alternative visions of what the scope of victimology ought to be, see

Schafer, 1968; Viano, 1976, 1983, and 1990a; Galaway and Hudson, 1981; Flynn, 1982; Scherer, 1982; Schneider, 1982; Friedrichs, 1983; Elias, 1986; Fattah, 1991; and Dussich, 2009b.)

The dividing line between victimology and mainstream criminology is not always clear-cut. Invariably, the two fields overlap. Historically, much of criminology can be characterized as **offenderology** because of its preoccupation with the reasons why criminals behave as they do, a focus on the wrongdoers' personal motives and the underlying root causes of their antisocial behavior, and whether punishment or treatment will make them stop. Lawbreakers always have been under a spotlight while the people they harmed remained shadowy figures on the fringes. But now victimology enriches criminology by yielding a more balanced and comprehensive approach that sheds light on both parties and their interactions.

Another way to differentiate the priorities of criminology versus victimology is to examine the social reaction to crime as opposed to the social reaction to victimization.

Once again, it is difficult to try to draw a sharp line between what issues criminologists should explore in contrast to what parallel or comparable topics victimologists should scrutinize. Yet such an exercise might be worthwhile because it helps clarify how the two fields have different focuses and also points to areas where research about victims and victimization remains sparse.

Since the offender is of primary interest to criminologists, analyzing the social reaction to lawbreaking might include issues like the public's willingness to pay for increased criminal justice expenses (hiring more police officers, supplying them with more powerful weaponry, and building more prisons in contrast to investing in job training, drug treatment, and inmate reentry programs) and the degree of voter support for tough new laws or for stiffening existing penalties (such as "three strikes" legislation or expanded use of electronic monitoring) or for police crackdowns (zero tolerance campaigns). The focus remains on the wrongdoers and how to best handle them, whether through punishment or rehabilitation. Long-term crime prevention strategies that criminologists propose and debate include efforts to eradicate the social roots of street crime, such as poverty, unemployment, failing schools, and dysfunctional families.

For victimology, the emphasis shifts to the public's reaction to the plight of injured parties. Consequently, researching the social reaction to victimization translates to examining the degree of voter support for victims' rights initiatives and the willingness of taxpayers to earmark revenue for government-run assistance programs and compensation funds. Also of great interest are the many self-help and direct aid projects set up by former victims, such as child search organizations, shelters for battered women, crisis centers for rape victims, and similar advocacy organizations. Another dimension of the social reaction is the many steps fearful individuals might undertake to reduce their own risks of becoming targets. These victimization prevention efforts on a personal level (in contrast to crime prevention efforts on a community or societal level) include taking self-defense classes and buying guns for self-protection, purchasing antitheft devices (such as burglar and car alarms), and buying insurance policies for reimbursement of crime-inflicted losses (life, health, home, and car insurance as well as for identity theft and fraud protection).

One of the most intriguing aspects of the social reaction to lawbreaking behavior is how often and in what manner eyewitnesses respond while a crime is in progress. Criminology and victimology overlap whenever researchers focus upon the interaction between offenders, their intended victims, and onlookers, an emerging area of study that could be referred to as **bystanderology**, to coin a term (see Box 1.3).

Interfacing with Other Disciplines

A number of academic orientations enrich victimology. Researchers who pursue a mental health/ forensic psychology orientation might explore how victims react to their misfortunes. They ask why some injured parties experience

B O X 1.3 The Social Reaction to Victimization: A Look at the Interplay between Victims, Offenders, and Bystanders

Bystanderology

If a third party is present when an offender confronts his intended victim, this presence of an audience introduces a situational variable or contextual factor that can become the focus of what can be called "bystanderology."

One or more onlookers were watching in about 70 percent of all fights, around 50 percent of all robberies, and almost 30 percent of all rapes and other sexual assaults, according to an analysis of government surveys of victims' experiences during the 1990s (Planty, 2002).

Individuals who witness a crime in progress as it unfolds right before their eyes may react in essentially two ways. First of all, there is nonintervention: Bystanders may avert their gaze, steer clear of trouble, mind their own business, and not get involved in the dispute. Or they may simply watch, become confused and immobilized, and consequently not do anything to help out. In extreme cases, they may run away, as when shots are fired. Alternatively, onlookers could become engaged and intervene to some degree while a crime is in progress or in its immediate aftermath (see Shotland and Goodstein, 1984; and Takooshian, 2014).

The following example, which took place on a busy big city street, illustrates this spectrum of possibilities, as an onlooker who intervened in behalf of a victim becomes mortally wounded himself and then fails to receive any aid from other spectators:

> A man angrily confronts a woman and threatens violence. A homeless immigrant who sometimes works as a day laborer comes to her aid and is stabbed. A nearby surveillance camera records how he collapses and lies face down in the gutter for over an hour. Passersby show some curiosity but hurry along. One man lifts the wounded Good Samaritan's body, sees a pool of blood, and then walks away. Another snaps a photo and then departs. By the time the police are summoned and help arrives, he is dead. (Sulzberger and Meenan, 2010)

Police officers are third parties who have a duty to intervene and can be counted upon to enter the fray in behalf of an innocent person under attack. Bystanders and onlookers have no such duty and may or may not take action as a robber, rapist, or assailant confronts a victim. A typology of possible responses by bystanders could include the following categories, ranked in terms of the desirability/undesirability of the outcome (making the situation better or worse for the person under attack):

a) Effectively intervene to rescue the victim from harm and also apprehend the apparent offender by making a citizen's arrest until the police arrive.

b) Minister to the victim after the attack is over by providing physical and emotional first aid until first responders like police officers, emergency medical technicians, and ambulance crews arrive.

c) Scream for help and summon the authorities by calling 911; or at least take pictures that can later be used as evidence.

d) In the aftermath of an attack, come forward and serve as a witness for the prosecution.

e) Do nothing, take no action, look the other way, or melt away due to apathy or indifference; but also some noninterveners may be immobilized by fear.

f) Become a victim; the **Good Samaritan** who steps in can get injured or killed by the offender.

g) Accidentally injure or kill the victim while carrying out a rescue mission (this disaster can happen when a SWAT team tries to overpower a hostage-taker but the captive is killed during the raid).

h) Intervene in behalf of the wrong party by erroneously sizing up the situation, resulting in the injury or death of the genuine victim. This can happen when uniformed officers mistake an undercover officer for an "armed perpetrator" who is training a gun on a suspect, and they shoot the officer in disguise thinking they are rescuing a victim (a tragic mistake referred to by the military term "friendly fire")

i) Intentionally join in on the side of the wrongdoer, undermining the victim's ability to effectively resist and inflicting additional losses and injuries, which may even be fatal (these bystanders who knowingly make things worse have been called "Bad Samaritans"). Bystanders who rally to the side of lawbreakers while a crime is in progress can get swept up into a type of crowd psychology that leads to the looting of stores, mob attacks, lynchings, race riots, and gang rapes.

The social reaction of the bystander(s) may decisively shape the outcome of an attempted crime. The presence of onlookers might cause the would-be offender to back down or cut short his attempt to inflict harm. On the other hand, the existence of an audience might cause both parties to escalate their conflict in order to save face and protect their reputations on the street. This might encourage the aggressor to deliver additional wounds in order to demonstrate his prowess, as in clashes between gang members.

When surveyed about whether the presence of a third party helped or worsened the situation, half of all victims reported "neither helped not hurt." But when bystanders actively interceded, victims judged the impact of their

(Continued)

BOX 1.3 (Continued)

actions as "helpful" more often than as "harmful." Passersby play a constructive role if they prevent further injuries and recover stolen property, and their intervention is counterproductive if they further enrage the attacker (Hart and Miethe, 2008).

A phenomenon known as the "bystander effect" has been studied extensively by social psychologists, often by simulating emergencies in an experimental setting. Their findings reveal that as the number of bystanders increases, the likelihood that any particular individual will intervene decreases. Also, as the number of onlookers increases, the time that elapses until someone takes action increases. Bystanders are more inclined to get involved if they are directly beseeched for assistance. When bystanders are slow or reluctant to make a move, it may be due to audience inhibition (each person is afraid of being publicly embarrassed if the effort fails) or because of the diffusion of responsibility (each onlooker assumes someone else will take charge of the situation and take the first step) (see Scroggins, 2009).

Passersby might have a moral duty to be "their brother's keepers." But in most states (except in Vermont since 1967, and later Minnesota and Wisconsin), they bear no legal obligation to undertake any risks (unless they are police officers, firefighters, and doctors, even when they are off-duty). Civil statutes shielding Good Samaritans from out-of-pocket expenses and lawsuit liability are meant to encourage

individuals to get involved. Criminal laws prevent people from harming one another, but they do not compel individuals to help one another, even if one knows that another person is in imminent danger or has sustained a serious physical injury (Silver, 2012).

Police departments and community organizations sometimes help set up civilian anticrime patrols and neighborhood watch committees. On college campuses, rape prevention campaigns include efforts to train potential bystanders (especially male athletes and sorority sisters) to step in to creatively outmaneuver aggressive classmates from crossing the line separating drunken partying from carrying out sexual assaults. Ever since the late 1980s, role playing exercises and poster campaigns have urged students, especially incoming freshmen, to "Do something" with slogans like "Don't be a passive bystander," "Don't just stand there," and "If she can't stop him, you can" (Winerip, 2014). Intervention by onlookers (playing the role of "capable guardians") is counted upon by some victimization prevention strategies (such as alerting the authorities if an alarm goes off). Honoring those who didn't stand idly by and placed themselves at risk as "heroes" demonstrates the public's appreciation for coming to the assistance of victims when a crime is in progress (also see Hart and Miethe, 2008; Lateano, Ituarte, and Davies, 2008; Reynald, 2010; Gidcyz et al., 2011; Moynihan, 2011; and Banyard, Arnold, Eckstein, and Stapleton, 2011).

post-traumatic stress disorder (PTSD) (occasionally feeling very frightened long after a dangerous "fight or flight" situation has passed) while others who suffer through comparable calamities do not. Professionals engaged in therapeutic relationships with patients who endured vicious violence need to discover which crisis intervention techniques work best (see Roberts and Roberts, 2005). Researchers who take an historical perspective trace developments from the past to better understand the present, while those who adopt an economic perspective try to measure individual and collective costs, losses, and expenses that result from criminal activities. The anthropological orientation compares victimization in other societies far away and long ago in order to transcend the limitations of analyses rooted in the here and now. Victimologists

who adopt a sociological perspective develop profiles (statistical portraits) of the characteristics of people who are harmed, analyze the interactions within the victim–offender relationship, examine the way other people and social institutions (such as the public welfare and health care systems) deal with injured parties, and seek to evaluate the effectiveness of new policies and programs. Scholars who apply a legalistic/criminal justice orientation (that focuses on department regulations, Supreme Court decisions, and legislation) explore how victims are supposed to be handled by the police, prosecutors, defense attorneys, judges, probation officers, and parole boards, and they scrutinize the provisions of recently enacted laws designed to empower victims as the adversary system resolves their cases.

Divisions within the Discipline

Victimology does not have the distinct schools of thought that divide criminologists into opposing camps, probably because this new subdiscipline lacks its own well-developed theories of human behavior. However, in both criminology and victimology, political ideologies—conservative, liberal, and radical left/critical/conflict—can play a significant role in influencing the choice of research topics and in shaping policy recommendations.

The conservative tendency within victimology focuses primarily upon street crimes. A basic tenet of conservative thought is that everyone—both victims and offenders—must be held strictly accountable for their decisions and actions. This translates into an emphasis on self-reliance rather than governmental assistance. Individuals should strive to take personal responsibility for preventing, avoiding, resisting, and recovering from criminal acts and for defending themselves, their families, and their homes from outside attack. In accordance with the crime control model of criminal justice, the primary purpose of the legal system is to protect the innocent from those who want to harm them. As a result, lawbreakers must be punished in proportion to the suffering they inflicted on their victims (the philosophy of retribution, or **just deserts**). Making criminals pay also is supposed to accomplish the goals of general deterrence (to make a negative example of them, to serve as a warning to other would-be offenders that they should think twice and decide not to break the law), as well as specific deterrence (to teach them a lesson so they won't repeat this forbidden conduct in the future). Incapacitating predators behind bars keeps them away from the targets they would like to prey upon.

The liberal tendency sees the scope of the field as stretching beyond street crime to include criminal harm inflicted on persons by reckless corporate executives and corrupt officials. A basic theme within liberal thought is to endorse societal intervention through the instrument of government to try to ensure fair treatment and to alleviate needless suffering. This position leads to efforts to extend the "safety net" mechanisms of the welfare state to cushion shocks and losses due to all kinds of misfortunes, including crime. To "make the victim whole again," aid must be available from such programs as state compensation funds, subsidized crime insurance plans, rape crisis centers, and shelters for battered women. Some liberals are enthusiastic about restorative justice experiments that, instead of punishing offenders by imprisoning them, attempt to make wrongdoers pay restitution to their victims so that reconciliation between the two estranged parties might become possible.

The radical left/critical/conflict tendency seeks to demonstrate that the problem of victimization arises from the exploitative and oppressive relations that are pervasive throughout the social system. Therefore, the scope of the field should not be limited simply to the casualties of criminal activity in the streets. Inquiries must be extended to cover the harm inflicted by industrial polluters, owners and managers of hazardous workplaces, fraudulent advertisers, predatory lenders (for example, of mortgages with deceptive provisions for repayment of the loan), brutally violent law enforcement agencies, and discriminatory institutions. Victims might not be particular individuals but whole groups of people, such as factory workers, minority groups, customers, or neighborhood residents. From the radical/critical/conflict perspective, victimology can be faulted for preferring to study the more obvious, less controversial kinds of harmful behaviors, mostly acts of personal violence and crude theft by desperate individuals, instead of the more fundamental injustices that mar everyday life: the inequitable distribution of wealth and power that results in poverty, malnutrition, homelessness, family dysfunction, chronic structural unemployment, substance abuse, and misplaced aggression toward potential allies who are in similar circumstances. The legal system and the criminal justice apparatus are considered part of the problem by criminologists as well as victimologists working within this tradition because these institutions that supposedly promote fairness actually primarily safeguard the interests of influential groups and privileged classes (see Birkbeck, 1983; Friedrichs, 1983; Viano, 1983;

Elias, 1986, 1993; Fattah, 1986, 1990, 1992a, 1992b; Miers, 1989; Reiman, 1990; Walklate, 1991; and Mawby and Walklate, 1993).

WHAT VICTIMOLOGISTS DO

The current parameters of the field are evident in the kinds of questions victimologists try to answer. In general, these questions transcend the basics about "who, how, where, and when," and tackle the questions of "why?" and "what can be done?"- Victimologists explore not only the interactions between victims and offenders, but also victims and the criminal justice system as well as victims and the larger society.

A selection of some intriguing and imaginative studies that illustrate the kinds of issues concerning offender–victim relationships addressed by researchers over the decades appears in Box 1.4.

Victimologists, like all researchers, must adopt a critical spirit and a skeptical stance to see where the trail of evidence leads. In the search for truth, myths must be exposed, unfounded charges dismissed, and commonsense notions put to the test. The following guidelines outline the step-by-step reasoning process that can be followed when carrying out research (see Parsonage, 1979; Birkbeck, 1983; and Burt, 1983).

Step 1: Identify, Define, and Describe the Problem

The most basic task for victimologists is to determine all the different ways that a violation of the law can inflict immediate and long-term harm: the extent of any physical injuries, emotional damage, and economic costs, plus any social consequences (such as loss of status). For example, as they grow up, severely abused children might suffer from post-traumatic stress disorder, dysfunctional interpersonal relationships, personality problems, and self-destructive impulses (see Briere, 1992).

Sometimes a group is difficult to study because there isn't an adequate expression that describes its common misfortune or captures the nature of its plight. Now that terms like date rape, stalking, cyberstalking, carjacking, battering, elder abuse, identity theft, and bias crime have entered everyday speech, government agencies and researchers are exploring in what manner and how frequently people are harmed by these offenses. On occasion, victimologists help break the silence about situations that long have been considered taboo topics by studying activities such as sibling abuse, incestuous sexual impositions in stepfamilies, and marital rape (see Hines and Malley-Morrison, 2005).

Victimologists analyze how the status of being a "legitimate victim" is socially defined. They explore why only some people who suffer physical, emotional, or economic harm are designated and treated as full-fledged, bona fide, and officially recognized victims and as such, are eligible for aid and encouraged to exercise rights within the criminal justice process. But why are other injured parties left to fend for themselves? One key question is, "Is the social standing of each of the two parties taken into account when government officials and members of the general public evaluate whether one person should get into legal trouble for what happened and the other should be granted assistance?"

Clearly, the status of being an officially recognized victim of a crime is **socially constructed**. The determination of who is included and who is excluded from this privileged category is carried out by actors within the criminal justice process (police officers and detectives, prosecutors, judges, even juries) and is heavily influenced by legislators (who formulate criminal laws) and the media that shapes public opinion about specific incidents.

Step 2: Measure the True Dimensions of the Problem

Because policy makers and the general public want to know how serious various kinds of illegal activities are, victimologists must devise ways to keep track of the frequency and consequences of prohibited acts. The accuracy of statistics kept by government bureaus and private agencies must be critically examined to ferret out any biases that might inflate or deflate these estimates to the advantage of those who, for

BOX 1.4   A Sampling of the Wide Range of Studies about the Interaction between Offenders and Victims

Identifying the Cues that Trigger a Mugger into Action

Pedestrians, through their body language, may signal to prowling robbers that they are "easy marks." Men and women walking down a city street were secretly videotaped for several seconds, about the time it takes a criminally inclined person to size up a potential victim. The tapes were then shown to a panel of "experts"—prisoners convicted of assaulting strangers—who sorted out those who looked as if they would be easy to corner from those who might give them a hard time. Individuals who received high **muggability ratings** tended to move along awkwardly, unaware that their nonverbal communication might cause them trouble (Grayson and Stein, 1981).

Explaining Public Indifference toward Victims of Fraud and Con Games

People who have lost money to swindlers often are pictured as undeserving of sympathy in the media, and they may encounter callousness, suspicion, or contempt when they turn to the police or consumer affairs bureaus for help. This second-class treatment seems to be due to negative stereotypes and ambivalent attitudes that are widely held by the public as well as criminal justice officials. A number of aphorisms place blame on the "suckers" themselves—"fraud only befalls those of questionable character," "an honest man can't be cheated," and "people must have larceny in their hearts to fall for a con game."

For example, white-collar crime investigators picture even sophisticated investors who lose their money to scammers in Ponzi schemes as being so blinded by their greed for suspiciously high returns that they ignore the red flags that should have alerted them to the likelihood that they were being drawn into a too-good-to-be-true business arrangement (Goldstein, 2011).

Con artists count on exploiting the anticipated behavior of their "marks." Their targets may get so preoccupied with some "convincer" (such as a large sum of money awaiting them) that they are too distracted to realize what is really going on. Marks could be socially compliant to someone impersonating an authority figure (for example, they reveal their password in response to an e-mail allegedly from a bank's security officer and subsequently are taken in by a "phishing" scheme). They may let their guard down and assume there is safety in numbers if it seems that lots of other people are willing to take a chance on some risky venture. They may be willing to do something illegal (such as to buy stolen goods) and end up too compromised to go to the police. They could be so trusting and naïve that they fall for tear-jerking emotional appeals for financial help. And under pressure to "act now or it will be too late," they could make impulsive decisions they later regret. In well-planned con games pulled off by professionals, nothing is what it seems to be (Stajano and Wilson, 2011).

The stereotype of defrauded parties is that they disregarded the basic rules of sensible conduct regarding financial matters. They don't read contracts before signing and don't demand that guarantees be put in writing before making purchases. Their apparent foolishness, carelessness, or complicity undermines their appeals for redress and makes others reluctant to activate the machinery of the criminal justice system and regulatory agencies on their behalf. Their claims to be treated as authentic victims worthy of support may be rejected if they are scorned as money-hungry "dupes" who were merely outsmarted (Walsh and Schram, 1980; Moore and Mills, 1990; and Shichor, Sechrest, and Doocy, 2000).

Using a broad definition of fraudulent schemes (including various rip-offs such as dishonest home, auto, and appliance repairs and inspections; useless warranties; fake subscription, insurance, credit, and investment scams; phony charities, contests, and prizes; and expensive 900-number telephone ploys), a nationwide survey found victimization to be widespread. More than half the respondents had been caught up in some scam or an attempt at deception at least once in their lives, costing an average loss of more than $200. Contrary to the prevailing negative stereotype, the elderly were not any more trusting and compliant; in fact, they were deceived less often than younger people (Titus, Heinzelmann, and Boyle, 1995).

Examining How Pickpockets View their Targets

According to a sample of 20 "class cannons" (professional pickpockets) working the streets of Miami, Florida, their preferred marks (victims) are tourists who are relaxed, off guard, loaded with money, and lacking in clout with criminal justice officials. Some pickpockets choose "paps" (elderly men) because their reaction time is slower, but others favor "bates" (middle-aged men) because they tend to carry fatter wallets. A "moll buzzer" or "hanger binger" (sneak thief who preys on women) is looked down on in the underworld fraternity as a bottom feeder who acts without skill or courage. Interaction with victims is kept to a minimum. Although pickpockets may "trace a mark" (follow a potential target) for some time, they need just a few seconds to "beat him of his poke" (steal his wallet). This is done quietly and deftly, without a commotion or any jostling. They rarely "make a score" (steal a lot in a single incident). The class cannon

(Continued)

BOX 1.4 (Continued)

"passes" (hands over) "the loot" (wallet, wad of bills) to a member of his "mob" (an accomplice) and swiftly leaves the scene of the crime. Only about one time in a hundred do they get caught by the mark. And on those rare occasions when the theft is detected, they can usually persuade their victims not to call the police. They give back what they took (maybe more than they stole) and point out that pressing charges can ruin a vacation because of the need to surrender the wallet as evidence, plus waste precious time in court appearances. Cannons show no hatred or contempt for their marks. In general, they rationalize their crimes as impersonal acts directed at targets who can easily afford the losses or who would otherwise be fleeced by businesses or allow their money to be taken from them in other legally permissible ways (Inciardi, 1976).

Exploring the Bonds between Captives and their Captors

Hostages (of terrorists, skyjackers, kidnappers, bank robbers, rebelling prisoners, and gunmen) are used by their captors to exert leverage on a third party—perhaps a family, the police, or a government agency. These captives could react in an unanticipated way to being trapped and held against their will. Instead of showing anger and seeking revenge, these pawns in a larger drama may emerge from a siege with positive feelings for, and attachments to, their keepers. Their outrage is likely to be directed at the authorities who rescued them for acting with apparent indifference to their well-being during the protracted negotiations. This surprising emotional realignment has been termed the **Stockholm syndrome** because it was first noted after a 1973 bank holdup in Sweden. Several psychological explanations for this "pathological transference" are plausible. The hostages could be identifying with the aggressor, and they might have

become sympathetic to acts of defiance aimed at the power structure. As survivors, they might harbor intense feelings of gratitude toward their keepers for sparing their lives. As helpless dependents, they might cling to the powerful figures who controlled their every action because of a primitive emotional response called "traumatical infantilism." After the ordeal, terrorized hostages need to be welcomed back and reassured that they did nothing wrong during—and right after—their captivity. People in occupations that place them at high risk of being taken prisoner—ranging from convenience store clerks and bank tellers to airline personnel and diplomats—need to be trained about how to act, what to say, and what not to do if they are held and used as a bargaining chip during a stand-off. Law enforcement agencies need to set up and train hostage negotiation units as an alternative to solely relying on heavily armed SWAT teams whose military-style assaults endanger the lives of the captives they are trying to save. Crisis negotiators no longer consider the bonding that may occur between captives and captors to be detrimental. The development of the Stockholm syndrome actually can increase the hostages' chances of surviving the ordeal. However, it could also mean that law enforcement cannot count on the victims' cooperation in working for their own release and for later prosecuting their violent and dangerous kidnappers in court. In terms of frequency of occurrence, it is likely that this type of coping mechanism by captives has been overemphasized and inaccurately assumed in cases that were diagnosed by commentators in the media. Identifying with the aggressor and seeing rescuers as adversaries rarely takes place, according to an analysis of the narratives contained in the FBI's Hostage/Barricade Database System (see Ochberg, 1978; Fattah, 1979; Symonds, 1980a; Turner, 1990; Louden, 1998; Fuselier, 1999; and De Fabrique, Romano, Vecchi, and Van Hasselt, 2007).

some self-serving reason, wish to either exaggerate or downplay the real extent of the problem.

In order to make measurements, victimologists have to **operationalize** their concepts by developing working definitions that specify essential characteristics and also mark boundaries, clarifying which cases should be included and which should be excluded. For example, when trying to determine how many students have experienced school violence, should youngsters who were threatened

with a beating be counted, even if they were not actually physically attacked?

Once victimologists measure the frequency of some unwanted event per year, they can begin to search for changes over time to see if a particular type of criminal activity is marring the lives of a greater number or fewer people as time passes. To grasp the importance of making accurate measurements, consider the problem of child abuse. Suppose that statistics gathered by child protection agencies indicate a huge increase in the number of reported instances of suspected abuse. How can this upsurge be explained? One possibility is to interpret this spike as evidence that parents are neglecting, beating, and molesting their children these days like never before. But another explanation could be that new compulsory reporting requirements recently imposed on physicians, school nurses, and teachers are bringing many more cases to the attention of the authorities. Thus, a sharp rise in reports might not reflect a genuine crime wave directed at children by their caretakers but merely a surge in official reports because of improvements in detecting and keeping records of maltreatment. Victimologists can make a real contribution toward resolving this controversy by devising ways to estimate the actual dimensions of the child abuse problem with greater precision. Other pressing questions that can be answered by careful measurements and accurate statistics include the following: Are huge numbers of children being snatched up by kidnappers demanding ransoms? Or are abductions by strangers rare? Are husbands assaulted by their wives about as often as wives are battered by their husbands? Or is female aggression of minor concern when compared to male violence? Is forced sex a common outcome at the end of an evening, or is date rape less of a danger than some people believe (see Loseke, Gelles, and Cavanaugh, 2005)?

Once injured parties have been identified, and their ranks measured, researchers can carry out a **needs assessment** through interviews or via a survey to discover what kinds of suffering they are experiencing and what sorts of assistance and support they require to resolve their problems and return to the lives they were leading before the crime occurred. Such studies might reveal their unmet material and emotional needs, and weaknesses in existing programs and policies.

Step 3: Investigate How Victims Are Handled

Researchers scrutinize how victims actually are treated by the criminal justice and social service systems that are ostensibly designed to help them. Their studies can pinpoint the sources of tension, conflict, mistreatment, and dissatisfaction that alienate victims from the agencies that are supposed to serve them. Program evaluations determine whether stated goals are being met. For instance, many victimologists have studied how well or how poorly the police, prosecutors, judges, and family therapists are responding to the plight of abused children, sexually assaulted persons, and also battered women (see Hilton, 1993; Roberts, 2002; Hines and Malley-Morrison, 2005; Roberts and Roberts, 2005; and Barnett, Miller-Perrin, and Perrin, 2005).

Step 4: Gather Evidence to Test Hypotheses

Victimologists investigate all kinds of hypotheses: suspicions, hunches, impressions, accusations, assertions, and predictions. Like all social scientists, when presented with claims about what is true and what is false, their proper response is not to accept or reject the assertion but to declare: "Prove it! Show me! Where is the evidence?"

Testing hypotheses yields interesting findings, especially discoveries that cast doubt on common-sense notions (challenging what everyone "knows" to be true) and widely held beliefs. A major goal is try to sort out myths from realities.

For example, will the "dos and don'ts" tips offered on websites for women who are being stalked by ex-lovers actually work to reduce the risks of violent outbursts; or are these bits of advice largely ineffective; or could following these instructions actually be counterproductive, escalating tensions and heightening dangers?

In order to illustrate each of the four steps that victimologists might follow when researching a particular type of suffering, a systematic analysis of the problem of "road rage" is presented in Box 1.5.

B O X 1.5   An Illustration of How to Analyze a Specific Type of Victimization: Road Rage

Step 1: Identify, Define, and Describe the Problem:

The analysis begins with a brief history that recounts when the problem was recognized and the way in which the victims' plight was originally portrayed.

For decades, concern about the risks surrounding automobile travel centered on accidents caused by hazardous road conditions, speeding, and drunk driving. Although flare-ups between motorists with short fuses must have been taking place since the onset of the automobile age well over 100 years ago, they remained under the radar until the news media began to report on a spate of "freeway shootings" (in California in 1977, in Houston in 1982, in Los Angeles in 1987, and in Detroit in 1989). Newspaper headlines originally dubbed the frightening situations as "road assaults," "freeway free-for-alls," "highway violence," "highway hostility," "motorist mayhem," and even merely "unfriendly driving." Yet concerns about becoming a casualty of one of these confrontations on wheels did not mount until a media account coined the phrase "road rage" in 1988; the catchy alliteration was meant to capture the essence of an armed attack in which a Florida driver shot a passenger in a car that had cut him off (see Best, 1991; and Roberts and Indermaur, 2005). During the 1990s, the sudden emergence and rapid diffusion (across the country and around the globe) of substantial media attention to this "new crime" demonstrated how large audiences of frazzled commuters and anxious travelers considered this amorphous yet omnipresent threat to be of great relevance. Colorful accounts—about 10,000 stories between 1990 and 1996, and nearly 4,000 in 1997 alone—described a "spreading epidemic" of "ugly acts of freeway fury" in which cursing, seething, and stressed-out motorists were "driven to destruction," because it was "high noon on the country's streets and highways." Roads were pictured as "resembling something out of the Wild West," "highways to homicide," "shooting galleries," "war zones," and even "terror zones." Journalists, reflecting the popular movies of their day, originally branded offenders as "road warriors" and "Rambos," who rejected the prevailing outlook of "have a nice day" in favor of a "make my day" chip-on-the-shoulder approach to dealing with strangers. Drivers lost their tempers and took their frustrations out on each other in numerous ways, ranging from fistfights to intentional collisions to gunfire (see Best, 1991; Mizell, 1997; Fumento, 1998; and Roberts and Indermaur, 2005).

Today, cases like this one are widely recognized to be examples of "road rage:"

A man in a SUV with his wife and two-year-old daughter is driving down a big city highway known for its traffic jams when he suddenly finds himself surrounded by a swarm of men on motorcycles. He panics and bumps one of the motorcyclists; another dismounts and he accidently runs over him. Fearing for his safety and the well-being of his family, he races down an exit ramp with the motorcycle riders in hot pursuit. They catch up with him on a busy street, smash his vehicle's windows, and drag him from his SUV. A video of the beatdown goes viral, drawing a great deal of international attention, as viewers ask, "Where were the police—what took them so long to break up this attack on this besieged motorist?" (It turns out that one of the "bikers" actually was an undercover officer infiltrating the gang, but he is indicted for assault, along with 10 others.) (Long and Peltz, 2013)

Step 2: Measure the True Dimensions of the Problem

The analysis proceeds by estimating the frequency of occurrence of this sort of incident and examining the victim–offender interaction in order to draw evidence-based portraits of the typical aggressors and their usual targets, and of the amount of harm done.

Unfortunately, chilling accounts often were laced with hyperbole and sensationalism. Consequently, heated discussions erupted about whether fears were out of proportion to actual threats. Investigations that attempted to estimate the actual toll that road rage imposed on motorists adopted definitions that were way too broad: media coverage, and even some of the earliest research undertakings, characterized road rage as synonymous with extremely aggressive driving habits that embodied hostility toward other motorists. Part of the continuum included noncriminal acts, such as screaming curses out the window, making threatening or obscene gestures, flashing headlights on and off, honking horns repeatedly, weaving in and out of traffic, cutting others off, tailgating in a way that resembles stalking, and getting out of the vehicle to argue face-to-face. From the targeted motorist's point of view, as well as from a police and traffic safety perspective, this inclusive definition that ranged from trivial to life-threatening actions seemed to make sense, in terms of recognizing all the different dimensions of an infuriating and ominous encounter. But from the standpoint of both criminology and victimology, the definition should be much more restrictive and exclude insults and implied threats as well as bad driving maneuvers that at most result in summonses for moving violations in traffic court. A more limited and precise definition of road rage would count only those interpersonal conflicts that are matters for the criminal justice system to resolve: outbreaks of violence in which either one of the drivers—or one of the passengers—intentionally or recklessly injures or kills another driver, passenger, cyclist, or even a pedestrian, or damages a vehicle on purpose; or uses the vehicle to make a serious attempt to do harm to another party embroiled in the fracas (see Smart and Mann, 2002). A driver who is threatened can be considered a victim of harassment, and if a gun is pointed, the crime becomes "menacing." If a shot is fired, an assault with a deadly weapon has taken place. One difficult methodological decision confronting researchers is whether to include or exclude incidents in which the two warring parties were not complete strangers. For example, some car chases are really extensions of ongoing quarrels that fall under the category of "domestic violence" (Mizell, 1997). Upon investigation, other clashes could turn out to be drive-by shootings involving members of warring street gangs or competing drug-dealing crews. But putting these exceptional cases aside, road rage generally constitutes a type of physical attack perpetrated by a stranger in a vehicle who approaches a victim just by chance in an anonymous public space—a street or highway (Roberts and Indermaur, 2005).

Criminologists zero in on the perpetrators' possible mental problems, anger and aggression, drug and alcohol use, and risk-taking propensities while victimologists focus on the characteristics of the injured parties and how they respond to the incidents. Both sets of researchers seek to discover how often punishable acts of road rage break out. Not all cases are considered newsworthy by editors and journalists, so scholarly studies must be based on access to "official sources of data": the arrest records of police departments and the transcripts of court proceedings, perhaps supplemented by the files of insurance companies. However, descriptions of the events leading up to the confrontation may be fragmentary or incomplete, or the versions of who did what to whom could be completely one-sided. Furthermore, just as with media coverage, official statistics present an underestimate. Some criminal acts that could lead to arrest and prosecution go unreported because the authorities were not notified by either party or by eyewitnesses. On the other hand, accounts from unofficial sources could yield overestimates because the working definition of road rage used by the general public and the media has expanded far beyond the original narrower

notion of violence on wheels. Other unofficial sources of data, including the findings of surveys, that ask motorists if they were ever subjected to or eyewitnesses to road rage may be cluttered with huge numbers of judgmental interpretations about incidents that would not wind up in the criminal justice system. For example, using a broad definition, an annual survey estimated that the most afflicted cities in 2009 were New York, Dallas/Fort Worth, Detroit, Minneapolis/St. Paul, and Atlanta; far fewer incidents reportedly took place in Portland, Cleveland, Sacramento, Baltimore, and Pittsburgh (AP, 2009).

Several websites that welcome postings by motorists infuriated by encounters with inconsiderate, rude, careless, or just plain inept drivers also use a definition that is too vague and inclusive. Overly broad definitions tend to generate exaggerated estimates. The **prevalence rate** of ever experiencing, perpetrating, or witnessing road rage can approach 100 percent if the database includes motorists' complaints about drivers who suddenly cut in front of them, honked incessantly, braked hard without warning, swerved dangerously, hurled insults, or even forced them on to the shoulder. These experiences might be unnerving and insulting, and some might be violations of traffic ordinances, but as merely subjective and undocumented accusations, they don't rise to the level of criminal matters, so the aggrieved parties are not genuine "victims" of physical violence or deliberate property destruction.

The task for scholarly researchers is to sort through this collection of media and police reports about aggressive and reckless driving and focus on the incidents of intentional collisions, assaults, shootings, and even murders. For example, a comprehensive review of over 10,000 records of events that took place from 1990 through 1996 yielded an estimate of over 200 deaths and about 12,600 injuries directly attributable to road rage, or about 1,500 casualties a year resulting from collisions arising from dangerously aggressive driving (see Mizell, 1997; and Garase, 2006). On the other hand, as real as the threat may be, criminal acts of road rage seems to be a relatively infrequent event, statistically speaking, at least according to self-report surveys of drivers (Roberts and Indermaur, 2005). Pedestrians and cyclists felt the most vulnerable; believed that they were specifically targeted; suffered more physically and mentally; and were more likely to alter their behavior after the incidents, according to a survey of a small sample of self-identified victims (Cavacuiti et al., 2013).

(Continued)

B O X 1.5   (Continued)

Road rage needs to be **operationalized** (precisely defined so that it can be measured) in a restrictive manner to include only incidents in which one driver knowingly injures or kills another motorist, passenger, or pedestrian or uses a vehicle as a weapon to attack someone or something. Then criminologists could focus their attention on the defendants who get arrested and prosecuted for their angry outbursts, by asking questions like: Do people who pick fights when driving also start altercations in everyday life? Do they drive as they live? Do these hyperaggressive drivers differ demographically and socially from average motorists? Psychologically oriented criminologists could ask whether these belligerent drivers are burdened with pent up anger, poor impulse control, short fuses, and hair triggers that reflect deep-seated personality problems (and maybe even mental disorders) that make them a danger to themselves and anyone who strays into their path. These emotional disturbances might include an obsession with minimizing travel time to the point of always being in a great rush; a need to try to come in first in a highly competitive environment; a tendency to perceive the driving mistakes of others as personal attacks on themselves or their vehicles; and even a sense that they need to punish others to teach others a lesson to improve their driving skills (see Ayar, 2006).

But these issues about the presumed shortcomings of offenders are not the immediate focus of victim-centered investigations, which seek to expand and balance out the inquiry into the hostile encounter by paying close attention to the injured party and to the behaviors of both individuals during their confrontation. The victim–offender interaction must be carefully reconstructed. Two strikingly different possibilities arise. The first scenario is that road rage casualties were innocent travelers who were cruising along and just minding their own business when they were randomly targeted by belligerent drivers. This image of a routine activity being interrupted "out of the blue" by senseless violence is especially chilling because automobile travel unavoidably brings strangers from very different social backgrounds into close proximity as they attempt to share the road with one another. Road rage is a serious problem that must be addressed immediately if ordinary motorists can become embroiled in a feud without warning; if some hothead's wrath can be vented on anyone who is unlucky enough to gets in his way; and if any motorist—just like getting into a collision—can find himself under attack at anytime.

But the alternative scenario paints an entirely different picture: that the injured party was a violence-prone individual himself. He was spoiling for a fight and was easily inflamed and incited into action. These mutual combatants overreacted to each other's overtures. The initial event was misperceived as embodying a hostile intent, and this presumed threat was countered with an inappropriately bellicose response, thereby escalating the incident to the point of bloodshed or a crash. The misbehavior of the victim can be as important a catalyst in this interaction as the aggressive actions of the assailant. In essence, offenders and victims "find each other" as they interact within a vast pool of fellow drivers. The question arises, in what proportion of cases are the injured parties not totally innocent victims? How often do those who get wounded or killed share some degree of responsibility with the complete strangers who attacked them? Presumably, the violations of traffic laws would not have spiraled into a criminal matter were it not for the victim's inadvertent triggering of the aggressive driver's violent response; or worse yet, the victim's furious overreaction to the offender's bad driving led to the next round of escalating hostilities. Researchers who examine the victim–offender interaction can provide estimates of the percent of cases in which victims are totally innocent of any incitement to violence, and the remaining percent in which those who wind up hurt are partially at fault for triggering the aggressive driver's illegal response.

Media accounts portray road rage victims as tending to be young males in their twenties and thirties (Asbridge, Smart, and Mann, 2003). Some researchers who have studied both parties suggest that they have uncovered situations that illustrate the **principle of homogamy**: that both offenders and victims share a great deal in common, socially and demographically (according to surveys about aggressive driving that asked about lesser skirmishes in addition to violent episodes). The picture they have painted from their data is that the two persons caught up in the confrontation tend to closely resemble each other. Both usually are males; often in their twenties and thirties; generally of lower socioeconomic status; frequently with drug and drinking problems; perhaps exhibiting a "macho" personality; sometimes driving around in a high-performance vehicle or sports car with tinted windows; and most disturbingly, all too often going around armed with guns (see Asbridge et al., 2003, 2006; Roberts and Indermaur, 2008; Hemenway, Vriniotis, and Miller, 2006; and Fierro, Morales, and Alvarez, 2011).

These angry young men, who have poor impulse control and a propensity to get into fights while trying to share the road, seem to be one and the same as those who spend a lot of time away from home and get into brawls on street corners and in bars. Additional studies that derive profiles of both parties from police files and court proceedings could settle this question about the possibility of homogamy. The research hypotheses would be that both the offenders and their victims would tend to be low-income, young, urban males, rather than females, older persons, suburbanites or rural residents, and more affluent people (Asbridge et al., 2003). Furthermore, those whose routine activities involve a great deal of driving may have more opportunities to become embroiled in confrontations (Asbridge and Butters, 2013).

Step 3: Investigate How Victims Are Faring

Zero in on the criminal justice system's response.

Motor vehicle collisions are a major cause of injury, disability, and death, especially of young people. On a societal level, vehicle crashes are a major source of shattered lives, emotional damage (including phobias, and in extreme cases, post-traumatic stress disorder), truncated opportunities, missed work, and other losses and expenses. Since some unknown proportion of highway carnage is attributable to road rage, this societal problem may impose serious unrecognized consequences for public safety and social well-being. How are the police, courts, and insurance companies addressing these issues of?

Criminologists and criminal justice officials debate whether offenders might need to be punished (through stiff fines and time behind bars) to teach them a lesson not to drive recklessly again (specific deterrence), and to hold them up as negative role models to serve as a warning to other would-be road warriors (general deterrence). Incapacitation (through license suspensions and incarceration) will serve to protect other motorists by removing them from the driver's seat. Treatment (such as anger management, time management, and stress management) might be called for if that is the source of their dangerously aggressive behavior behind the wheel. But what could and should be done for the objects of their wrath? If the homogamy thesis is correct, then victims might be negatively stereotyped as potential perpetrators themselves. The authorities might automatically handle the "ostensible targets" of road rage differently than other innocent victims of physical violence because these

individuals might bear some responsibility for the breaking of laws this time—and the next time, they could be the offenders.

Victim-centered questions that researchers need to address include these: What happens in police stations, courtrooms, and in insurance offices when the authorities believe that both parties are partially to blame? Are charges against the defendant reduced or dismissed if it appears that the injured party contributed in some way to the escalation of the confrontation? Do insurance companies reduce the amounts of reimbursement for damages or medical treatment, or deny the applications entirely, in cases of mutual combat? In contrast, in cases where the injured parties are blameless, are the sentences harsher on those convicted of highway mayhem than of comparable street brawls? Do innocent targets of road rage get the same assistance and exercise the same rights as innocent victims of violent street crimes? How these victims' cases actually are handled ought to be a prime concern of victimologists.

Step 4: Gather Evidence to Test Hypotheses

See if this criminal activity is linked to other social problems and whether effective responses have been devised and implemented.

Now that the term road rage is firmly entrenched in the vocabulary of law, criminal justice, and journalism, discussions of the problem generate many interesting hypotheses. For example, a number of possible societal causes have been suggested. Can increases or decreases in road rage be correlated with other indicators of changes in the pace of life and the level of tension, frustration, alienation, and cutthroat competition in an area at a given time and place? Does the problem have deeper societal roots than just the chance encounter of two foul-tempered/short-fused individuals? To what extent is road rage the outgrowth of underlying social problems, such as alcohol consumption and drug abuse; overall levels of aggression, rage, and untreated mental illness; as well as increases in commuting time, road traffic, construction delays, and rush-hour congestion (see Smart and Mann, 2002; and Asbridge et al., 2003).

Another interesting hypothesis that needs investigation is: Does the yearly incidence of highway violence closely track the level of violence on the streets—in other words, if public safety improves and the streets become more peaceful, does the occurrence of road rage also decline?

(Continued)

BOX 1.5 (Continued)

The next set of hypotheses to be tested is whether the measures to curb road rage are working effectively. Legislatures in a number of states passed tough new laws against recklessly aggressive driving, hoping to deter or weed out the problem drivers who are at high risk of causing road rage incidents. Police departments and state highway patrol agencies devised new ways of monitoring and videotaping traffic flow and accidents, and launched crackdowns to vigorously enforce traffic laws. Criminologists need to evaluate whether these crime control strategies are bringing roadway violence under control.

At the same time, the National Safety Council, the AAA Foundation for Traffic Safety, insurance companies, and government agencies such as the National Highway Traffic Safety Administration developed awareness and education campaigns, warning the public about how quickly minor traffic confrontations could escalate into dangerous showdowns. Is there much that fearful motorists can do to minimize their chances of becoming the target of another driver's wrath, or at least to halt the up-and-back interplay before it spirals out of control? As soon as the problem was recognized, articles in the popular press and road safety educational materials alerted motorists about "How to avoid getting shot at" and "How to handle on-the-road hostility" plus other practical suggestions for those on the receiving end of aggressive driving (see Best, 1991; and Mizell, 1997). In 2007, the governor of Michigan, and in 2009, the governor of Alabama, responding to an educational campaign against "emotional driving" sponsored by a self-help group founded by a parent of a woman killed in an incident, proclaimed the

middle of July as "Road Rage Awareness Week" (Targeted News Services, 2009). Are the pragmatic tips disseminated in driver education campaigns really effective as a way of preventing victimization? If road rage incidents decline after practical advice is widely disseminated, then these victim-oriented countermeasures might deserve some credit for helping concerned motorists stay out of trouble. Comparisons of changes in the levels of reported road rage crimes in similar jurisdictions that did and did not implement these strategies should shed light on this matter.

Finally, what have been the long-term trends over the decades? Is road rage (as distinct from changes in media coverage) genuinely increasing or decreasing as the years roll by? In 1997, the House Subcommittee on Surface Transportation held hearings about a reported epidemic of "auto anarchy" that was "transforming the nation's roadways into crime scenes." In the midst of all this publicity, however, skeptics pointed out that statistics showed that the numbers of accidents, highway deaths, and crash-related injuries actually were trending downward, especially when the increases in the number of drivers, registered vehicles, and the total miles traveled were taken into account. Perhaps the entire road rage problem had been blown way out of proportion right at the outset by journalists trying to attract large audiences, politicians seeking campaign donations and votes, therapists looking to profit from heightened fears of a newly recognized emotional "disorder," and lobbyists representing publicity-hungry agencies and organizations (see Drivers.com staff, 1997; Fumento, 1998; Rathbone and Huckabee, 1999; Hennessy and Wiesenthal, 2002; and "Rising Rage," 2005).

WHY STUDY VICTIMOLOGY?

One last parallel between criminology and victimology merits highlighting. Criminology and victimology are not well-paying fields ripe with lucrative opportunities for employment and advancement. Studying the modus operandi of criminals and the mistakes made by the individuals they injured certainly doesn't make a person invincible to physical attacks, thefts, or swindles, although this heightened awareness might reduce the risks a student of human behavior and criminal conduct faces. Yet for several good reasons a growing number of people are investing time, energy, and money to study victimology in training academies and college courses.

First of all, those who study the plight of victims benefit intellectually, as do all social scientists, by gaining insights into everyday life, solving puzzling and troubling issues, better appreciating life's subtleties, seeing phenomena more clearly, and understanding complex situations more profoundly. Second, intellectually curious individuals can profit from pursuits that expand their horizons, transcend the limits of their own experiences in the familiar routines of everyday life, free them from irrational fears and unfounded concerns, and enable them to overcome gut reactions of fatalism, cynicism, emotionalism, and deep-seated prejudices. Third, the findings generated from theorizing and applied research have practical applications that simultaneously ease the distress of others and foster a sense of purpose, self-worth, accomplishment, and satisfaction that comes from combating social injustices.

Those who study how individuals shape and in return are influenced by the realities around them are developing their "sociological imagination" (Mills, 1959)—a recognition of how their particular personal troubles usually are outgrowths of and can be traced back to larger social problems (like poverty, unemployment, dysfunctional families, and failing schools). Specifically, by exercising their "criminological imagination" (see Young, 2011), those who focus on lawbreaking can raise their consciousness about the connections between individual difficulties, historic injustices, prevailing social institutions and ideologies, contemporary culture, and the shortcomings of academic research and theorizing in order to recognize the sharp contrast between what is and what could be.

Besides paying these dividends, it's possible to profit in other ways by studying various aspects of victimization.

Scrutinizing victim–offender interactions can shed light on how miscommunication, misunderstandings, desires, obsessions, demands, stereotypes, reckless behavior, and provocative acts can trigger harsh reactions that can lead to needless conflict and avoidable tragedies.

Analyzing the way that certain victims are criticized and blamed for their own downfall raises vital questions about the degree to which individuals are able to determine their own fate as opposed to the extent to which larger social forces and pressures shape a person's behavior and social circumstances.

Exploring how some victims are assisted by social programs while others are left to fend for themselves raises profound issues about the proper role of government and its collectively funded and organized safety net meant to cushion the fall of individuals reeling from the impact of serious losses and major expenses.

Examining how some individuals and groups stress self-reliance and taking responsibility for one's well-being, especially in terms of arming in self-defense against troublemakers, while others

emphasize relying on police protection and collective undertakings meant to eradicate the social roots of crime, helps to clarify the differing assumptions and values that underlie political conflicts between those believing in right wing as opposed to left wing ideologies.

Delving into the dark side of family life—child abuse, spouse abuse, and elder abuse—sheds light on the all-too-common dysfunctional relationships that undermine the notion of being "safe at home" as a sanctuary from the cruelties of the outside world, and suggests ways to prevent or correct these difficult situations.

Investigating how the police and courts handle the casualties of interpersonal violence uncovers the criminal justice system's priorities, and the extent to which agencies that are supposed to deliver "blind justice" and treat persons equally actually take into account the victim's social class, race, sex, and age. It also reveals how injured parties define the elusive ideal of "justice" in terms of varying beliefs about vengeance, penitence, forgiveness, and reconciliation.

Examining the way victims were treated in the past and how they are responded to in other societies reveals what has been, what might be, what should be avoided, and what ought to be emulated and adopted.

RECOGNIZING EXEMPLARY BEHAVIOR UNDER VERY DIFFICULT CIRCUMSTANCES

Criminologists generally study people who are labeled as "predators" and "convicts" because of the most antisocial and harmful acts they are known to have committed. Those who are sympathetic to offenders as troubled souls argue that people should not be judged solely by the worst things they have done. Victimologists generally study individuals at the most vulnerable and miserable points in their lives. But examining the range in reactions of persons under attack sometimes provides an opportunity to see people at their very best, not just at their low points. Consider how these individuals who were targeted by offenders responded in ways that are worthy of respect, even admiration:

> A mother visiting a friend's house logs in to her sophisticated home-surveillance system to see if a snowstorm has started yet, and using her infrared camera trained on her backyard is startled to spot an intruder climbing into her house. As he begins to ransack her home, she watches in real time video, and then hurriedly calls 911. When the burglar spies the flashlight beams of the responding officers, he panics and bolts outside. She directs the police to his hiding spot, and after a brief chase, he is captured. (Yan, 2014)

■■■

> A 15-year-old girl opens the door to what appears to be a deliveryman in uniform. She recognizes him as her former uncle who is furiously looking for his ex-wife, and tries to slam the door shut, but he kicks it in. He pulls out a gun and ties her up, along with her four sisters and brothers. When her parents return home, the man ties them up too and orders all seven members of the family to lie face-down on the floor and to tell him where he can find his ex-wife. When his former in-laws and their children insist they don't know where she is, he methodically shoots each one in the head. The girl is wounded but plays dead until he runs out. Then she quickly calls 911, tells the police that her parents and siblings have been murdered, and warns them that the killer is on his way to his ex-wife's parents' home. He is intercepted and apprehended before he can shoot anyone else. (Fredericks, 2014)

■■■

> A 27-year-old woman who stands four feet, five inches and weighs 90 pounds is behind the counter of her family's suburban convenience store when a six-foot-tall man wearing a mask pulls a gun and brandishes it in her face. The angry gunman screams, "Hurry up! Give me the money!," but she stalls and makes believe she can't open the cash register. When the robber turns to see if anyone is looking, she grabs a three-foot ax hidden behind the counter and starts

swinging it wildly, yelling, "Get out of here!" He flees empty-handed. She confides to detectives and a reporter that "I was scared, I was shaking. I didn't want to hit him, I just wanted him to get out." (Crowley, 2007)

■■■

> A 31-year-old social worker is about to go to dinner after a long day on a cold night when he is suddenly confronted by a teenager wielding a knife. He hands over his wallet to the young robber and then offers him his coat too, surmising, "If you are willing to risk your freedom for a few dollars, then I guess you must really need the money." Then he takes the emotionally confused adolescent to a restaurant. When it is time to pay for the meal, the teenager gives back his wallet, and even hands over his knife. The social worker sums up their encounter to an interviewer: "If you treat people right, you can only hope that they treat you right. That's as simple as it gets in this complicated world." (NPR, 2008)

■■■

> A "gentleman" holds a lobby door open for a 101-year-old woman who is on her way to church. But then he hits her so hard that blood spurts out her mouth and nose. A surveillance camera in the hallway shows the robber striking her over and over until she finally relinquishes her grip on her handbag containing $23. Her face bleeds for two weeks and her right arm never heals properly. But nearly a year later, she hobbles into a courtroom to identify the 45-year-old defendant as the man who mugged her. Her testimony at this special evidentiary hearing is preserved on videotape just in case she is unable to appear as a witness for the prosecution at the trial. (Farmer, 2008)

■■■

> A 35-year-old woman is beaten, robbed, and repeatedly raped for two hours in a dingy garage. In court, the courageous single mother testifies that while the gunman kept sexually assaulting her, "I had to keep myself from going crazy. I just hummed to myself." Realizing that the humming also calmed the rapist, she begins to give him a massage and to talk

soothingly to him. As they converse, the 45-year-old assailant apologizes, and then discloses his name and even his date of birth, which later enables detectives to track him down. (Shifrel, 2007a)

■■■

A 45-year-old teacher is kidnapped in a shopping mall parking lot by a gun-toting teenage carjacker. She secretly turns on a micro-cassette recorder to gather evidence just in case she can't convince the youth to let her go. During her final 46 minutes, she persuades the carjacker to discuss his childhood and his experiences in the military, descriptions which later provide detectives with valuable clues. She also reads passages to him from a psychology textbook; urges him to live a meaningful life and to find God; promises to help him land a job; and sobs as she describes how she treasures being a mother to her young son. But it is all to no avail. He doesn't shoot her, but smothers her with her own coat, which contains the tape recorder in a pocket that leads to his capture. (Jones, 2007)

Victimology is not the cold or dismal discipline it might appear to be at first glance. Victimologists are not morbidly curious about or preoccupied with misfortune, loss, tragedy, pain, grief, death, and mourning. Of course, because of its inherently negative subject matter, the discipline is problem-oriented by nature. However, victimologists also take part in furthering positive developments and constructive activities when they seek to discover effective ways of coping with hardships, transcending adversity, reimbursing financial losses, speeding up the healing process, promoting reconciliation between parties enmeshed in conflicts, and restoring harmony to a strife-torn community.

What insights that could advance an understanding of resilience in the struggle to fully recover from a shattering, life-threatening experience might be gleaned from these cases?

A mentally deranged 60-year-old woman shoots a member of a sheriff's department SWAT team in the neck. Formerly known as "the most in shape" deputy by his fellow officers, he wakes up as a quadriplegic, confined to a wheel chair. But with great determination he remains focused on his goal of returning to work at a desk job in the narcotics squad, observing "Your future is kind of bleak when you've got tubes coming out of you and everyone is saying you'll never walk again.... But if you stay mad about it all the time, you're not doing anything good for yourself." Supported by his family and colleagues, he optimistically reports signs of progress. "There have been a lot of little instances, like being able to pick up a ... potato chip and eat it with my hands." (Young, 2008)

■■■

As part of a gang initiation ritual, a thirteen-year-old boy is given a gun and told to use it. He confronts a young mother, yells, "Give it up!" and shoots her in a panic when she screams. The bullet rips through her jaw and teeth, requiring her to undergo ten years of agonizing reconstruction surgery. When he is caught, he is prosecuted as an adult and sentenced to life imprisonment without the possibility of parole. And yet, when he telephones her from prison after several years, she accepts the collect charges, even though she still is in terrible pain and can't eat. He apologizes for his "mistake" and for decades afterwards, they write letters to each other. She becomes friends with her assailant's mother and brother, and despite concerns by her husband and friends, urges the judge (unsuccessfully) to release him from prison (Kristof, 2014).

■■■

A member of congress is shaking hands with constituents at a supermarket, when a deranged college student emerges from the crowd and opens fire. Six people are killed, and thirteen are wounded, including the congresswoman, who is shot in the forehead. Doctors estimate she has a one in ten chance to live, but she pulls through. At her lowest ebb, she is not even able to smile, and experts doubt that she will ever speak or walk again. But with the help of her astronaut husband, her family, and dedicated members of the hospital staff, she summons up astonishing tenacity and one breath and one hard fought word at a time, recovers from her catastrophic head wound better than expected. When asked in a television interview if she was ever angry about what happened to her, she replies haltingly, "No. No. No. Life. Life." A few years later, she tells a crowd "I am working hard, lots of therapy: speech therapy, physical therapy, and yoga too." She insists, "My spirit is strong as ever"… and "I am still fighting to make the world a better place and you can too." (Curry, 2011; Freking, 2011; and Walshe, 2014)

Evidently, studying how injured parties respond to their plight can yield some unanticipated benefits. Victimologists can gain a more complete understanding and appreciation of the full range of possible reactions to attacks. Some individuals cope with their misfortunes in ways that are clever, bold, even courageous, and demonstrate a determination to behave with dignity and to pursue an unwavering commitment to justice. These persons can serve as positive role models for other wounded people who are seeking to recover from setbacks and overcome hardships.

"SURVIVOROLOGY:" TOWARD A MORE INSPIRING AND UPBEAT TRAJECTORY WITHIN VICTIMOLOGY

Some people who have been seriously harmed by criminals prefer to be called **survivors** rather than victims because of the term's positive connotations—that they are rebounding are exercising "agency" to take charge of their lives and demonstrating their resiliency to adversity. They see the term "victim" as carrying a lot of unwanted baggage, such as being "bested," "vanquished," and a "loser." Already, the expressions "survivors of incest, rape, intimate partner violence, and child abuse" are widely used (but not of robberies or shootings—at least not yet).

Similarly, some people initially attracted to the discipline of victimology may begin to fear that it is mired in negativity and preoccupied with pain, loss, sorrow, hostility, and recriminations. Learning bitter lessons from mistakes and feeling empathy toward those who are suffering may not be sufficient incentives to study victimology. What advocates, members of the helping professions, and injured parties

themselves need to find out more about is how certain seriously wounded persons are able to go beyond "just coping." As it is put glibly in everyday language, some seem able to "get over it," "get past it," "put it behind them," and "get on with their lives." How do they do it? What is the secret of their success? What personality traits, coping skills, inner resources, and belief systems enable individuals who have endured shattering experiences to emerge from a period of bereavement, depression, and anger, reconsider their priorities, and return to their previous lives or perhaps reorient themselves to new lifestyles (see Ai and Park, 2005; and Underwood, 2009).

This potentially upbeat tendency within victimology could be termed **survivorology**. Just as gravely ill persons, refugees from war-torn countries, captives who were cruelly tortured, or severely wounded soldiers can demonstrate great resolve to make the most out of their remaining time on earth and make impressive strides to piece back together their disrupted lives, so too might individuals who sustained vicious attacks want to make the transition from victim to survivor. Researchers—and the general public—can find the outlooks and actions of certain exemplary individuals who have suffered through shocking ordeals to be admirable, uplifting, and even inspiring. Within victimology, survivorology could focus on these success stories, in which individuals whose lives looked so bleak in the immediate aftermath of a terrible crime made great progress, surmounted obstacles, overcame severe limitations, and transformed a crisis into an opportunity.

The overarching theme of survivorology could be to "discover the common threads that underlie the secrets of their success" and determine how they did it: Was their recovery and new trajectory built upon faith and spirituality, inner strengths and outstanding character traits, the crucial support provided by others (family members, close friends, volunteers and mentors, or perhaps fellow sufferers in self-help groups), government-funded social programs, immersion in activism, or some other source of courage and perseverance? And what special opportunities would other individuals in similar dire straits need to make a successful reentry back into society? To spur the

---

BOX 1.6 Questions to Spur the Development of Survivorology

- How can the concept of "survivor" be operationalized so that it is not too restrictive and yet not too inclusive?
- What is resilience, and how can it be measured as a matter of degree?
- What is recovery, and how can it be measured as a matter of degree?
- Which groups of victims (such as those who have endured repeated beatings, childhood sexual abuse, rapes, shootings, or the loss of a loved one who died violently) have the most success—and the most difficulty—recovering from their ordeals?
- Which groups of victims show the most resilience in terms of characteristics such as age, sex, race and ethnicity, education, income, and occupation?

- What forms of social support (such as strong family ties, close bonds with friends, financial reimbursement, government programs, individual and group counseling, and camaraderie from a self-help group) improve the prospects for as well as the rate of recovery?
- What aspects of an individual's character and which personality traits foster resiliency and recovery?
- What can crime victims learn about resiliency and recovery from the travails of individuals who endured devastating losses due to political oppression, natural disasters, life-threatening illnesses, and other near-death experiences—and vice-versa.

---

development of survivorology as an area of concentration within victimology that accentuates the positive, two key concepts need to be operationalized: resiliency (roughly speaking, the ability to rebound after a serious setback) and recovery (basically, regaining control over one's life, recuperating, restoring, returning to the condition the person was in before the crime took place). Once these two concepts of resiliency and recovery are operationalized as variables whose magnitude can be estimated numerically and not designated simply as a dichotomous all or nothing situation, then different degrees of resilience and rates of recovery need to be investigated for various groups of victims.

The more survivorology is developed, the less victimology will be preoccupied solely with suffering, loss, and negativity (see Box 1.6).

SUMMARY

Victimization is an asymmetrical relationship that is abusive, parasitical, destructive, unfair, and illegal. Offenders harm their victims physically, financially, and emotionally. Until recently, the plight of crime victims was largely overlooked, even by most criminologists. When some researchers began to study victims, their initial interest betrayed an antivictim bias: They sought evidence that the victims' behavior before and during the incidents contributed to their own downfall. Since the 1960s, the majority of the social scientists attracted to this new discipline have labored to find ways to ease the suffering of victims and to prevent future incidents. But a commitment to strive for objectivity rather than to be reflexively pro-victim is the best stance to adopt when carrying out research or evaluating the effectiveness of policies.

Victimology is best viewed as an area of specialization within criminology. Both criminologists and victimologists seek to be impartial in their roles as social scientists when investigating lawbreaking, its social consequences, and the official responses by the justice system. But much of criminology in the past can be characterized as "offenderology," so the new focus on those who are on the receiving end of interpersonal violence and theft provides some balance and rounds out any analysis of problems arising from lawbreaking behavior.

Victimologists carry out studies that seek to identify, define, and describe all the ways that illegal activities harm targeted individuals; to measure the seriousness of the problem; to discover how victims' cases are actually handled by the legal system; and to test research hypotheses (for example, about bystanders or survivors) to see if they are supported by the available evidence.

KEY TERMS DEFINED IN THE GLOSSARY

bystanderology, 20	just deserts, 23	post-traumatic stress disorder (PTSD), 22	subjective approach, 3
criminology, 18	muggability ratings, 25	prevalence rate, 29	survivorology, 36
direct or primary victims, 2	needs assessment, 27	principle of homogamy, 30	survivors, 36
ideal type, 5	objectivity, 3	socially constructed, 24	victim, 2
ideology, 14	offenderology, 20	Stockholm syndrome, 26	victimism, 14
indirect or secondary victims, 2	operationalize, 26		victimization, 2
	operationalized, 30		victimology, 2

QUESTIONS FOR DISCUSSION AND DEBATE

1. Why should victimologists strive for objectivity rather than automatically adopt a pro-victim bias?

2. Give several examples of the kinds of research questions that victimologists find interesting and the kinds of studies they carry out.

3. In what ways are victimology and criminology similar, and in what ways do they differ?

4. Should bystanders be required to notify the police about serious crimes that they directly witness?

CRITICAL THINKING QUESTIONS

1. How should the police and the public react when hardcore criminals, such as mobsters, drug dealers, and street gang members fight among themselves and become casualties of violence?

2. Generate a list of questions about stabbings that would be of great interest to a victimologist working within (a) an anthropological framework, (b) a historical approach, and (c) an economic perspective.

SUGGESTED RESEARCH PROJECTS

1. Perform a keyword search of a comprehensive database of magazines and newspaper articles and blog postings to discover whether the term *victimology* is still being misused and confused with the ideology of victimism.

2. Use a comprehensive database of magazines and newspaper articles to determine whether any cases currently in the news illustrate the difficulty of identifying which party clearly is the criminal and which is the victim.

2

The Rediscovery
of Crime Victims

LEARNING OBJECTIVES

To trace how changes in the criminal justice system over the centuries have impacted the role of victims in the legal process.

To find out how and why the plight of victims has been rediscovered in recent decades by various social movements and groups.

To become familiar with the stages of the rediscovery process.

To apply the concept of rediscovery to specific groups of victims mentioned in the news.

THE DISCOVERY, DECLINE, AND REDISCOVERY OF CRIME VICTIMS

Each law that prohibits a certain act as being harmful defines the wrongdoer as a criminal subject to punishment and at the same time specifies that the injured party is a victim deserving some sort of redress. The laws forbidding what are now called **street crimes**—murder, rape, robbery, assault, burglary, and theft—can be traced back several thousand years. Hence, victims of interpersonal violence and theft were "discovered" ages ago, in the sense that they were formally identified and officially recognized.

Scholars of the history of the legal system report that in past centuries victims played a leading role in the resolution of criminal matters. To discourage retaliation by victims and their families—acts that could lead to endless feuding if offenders and their kin counterattacked—societies in simpler times established direct repayment schemes. Legal codes around the world enabled injured parties to receive money or valuables from wrongdoers to compensate for the pain, suffering, and losses they endured.

This process of victim-oriented justice prevailed mostly in small villages engaged in farming, where social relations were based on personal obligations, clear-cut family ties, strong religious beliefs, and sacred traditions. But the injured party's role diminished as industrialization and urbanization brought about business relations that were voluntary, secular, impersonal, rationalized, and contractual. Over the centuries, victims lost control over the process of determining the fate of the offenders who hurt them. Instead, the local governmental structure dominated judicial proceedings and extracted fines from convicts, physically punished them, or even executed them. The seriousness of the wounds and losses inflicted upon victims were of importance only for determining the charges and penalties wrongdoers faced upon conviction. Restoring injured parties to the condition they were in before the crimes occurred was no longer the main concern. In fact, the recovery of damages

became a separate matter that was handled in another arena (**civil court**) according to a different set of rules (**tort law**) after criminal proceedings were concluded (Schafer, 1968).

Historically, in the United States and in other parts of the world, the situations of victims followed the same evolutionary path from being at the center of the legal process to being relegated to the sidelines. When the 13 American colonies were settled initially by immigrants from Great Britain in the 1600s, the earliest penal codes were based on religious values as well as **English common law**. During the colonial era, police forces and public prosecutors had not yet been established. Victims were the key decision makers within the rudimentary criminal justice system and were its direct beneficiaries. They conducted their own investigations, paid for warrants to have sheriffs make arrests, and hired private attorneys to indict and prosecute their alleged attackers. Convicts were forced to repay those they harmed up to three times the value of the goods they had damaged or stolen (Schafer, 1968).

But after the American Revolution and the adoption of the Constitution and the Bill of Rights, crimes were reconceptualized as hostile acts directed against the authority of the government, which was defined as the representative of the people. Addressing the suffering imposed upon individuals was deemed to be less important than dealing with the symbolic threat to the social order posed by lawbreakers. **Public prosecutors**, acting on behalf of the state and in the name of the entire society, took over the powers and responsibilities formerly exercised by victims. Federal, state, and county (district) attorneys were granted the discretion to decide whether to press charges against defendants and what sanctions to ask judges to impose upon convicts.

The goals of deterring crime through punishment, protecting society by incapacitating dangerous people in prisons or through executions, and rehabilitating transgressors through treatment came to overshadow victims' demands to be restored to financial, emotional, and physical health.

Over the last two centuries, the government increasingly has assumed the obligation of providing jail detainees and prison inmates with food, clothing, housing, supervision, medical care, recreational opportunities, schooling, job training, psychological counseling, and legal representation—while leaving victims to fend for themselves. As they lost control over "their" cases, their role dwindled to just two contributions: filing a complaint with the police that initiated an investigation and, if necessary, testifying for the prosecution as another piece of evidence in the state's presentation of damning facts against the accused.

When **plea negotiation** (a settlement worked out by the prosecutor and the defense attorney) replaced a trial as the most common means of resolving criminal cases, victims lost their last opportunity to actively participate in the process by presenting their firsthand experiences on the witness stand to a jury. Victims rarely were included and consulted when the police and prosecution team decided upon their strategies and goals. To add insult to injury, often they were not even informed of the outcomes of "their" cases. Thoroughly marginalized, victims frequently sensed that they had been taken advantage of twice: first by the offender and then by a system that ostensibly was set up to help them but in reality seemed more intent on satisfying the needs of its core agencies and key officials (see Schafer, 1968; McDonald, 1977; and Davis, Kunreuther, and Connick, 1984).

After centuries of neglect, those on the receiving end of violence and theft were given renewed attention and, in effect, were rediscovered during the late 1950s and early 1960s. A small number of self-help advocates, social scientists, crusading journalists, enlightened criminal justice officials, and responsive lawmakers helped channel the public's attention to a festering problem: the total disregard of the needs and wants of victims. Through publications, meetings, rallies, and petition drives, these activists promoted their message: that victims were forgotten figures in the criminal justice process whose best interests were systematically overlooked but merited attention. Discussion and debate emerged during the late

1960s and has intensified throughout the following decades over why this injustice existed and what could be done about it. Various groups with their own distinct agendas formed coalitions and mobilized to campaign for reforms. As a result, new laws favorable to victims are being passed, and criminal justice policies are being overhauled.

A number of distinct groups and constituencies are responsible for this ongoing process of rediscovery. They include a wide variety of social movements; elected officials; commercial interests; the news media; and scholars, researchers, and advocates.

Social Movements: Taking Up the Victims' Cause

Aside from suffering harm at the hands of criminals, victims as a group may have very little else in common. They differ in terms of age, sex, race/ethnicity, religion, social class, political orientation, and many other important characteristics. Therefore, it has been difficult to organize them into self-help groups and to harness their energies into a political force for change. Despite these obstacles, a crime victims' movement emerged during the 1970s. It has developed into a broad alliance of activists, support groups, and advocacy organizations that lobbies for increased rights and expanded services, demonstrates at trials, maintains a variety of websites, educates the public, trains criminal justice professionals and caregivers, sets up research institutes and information clearinghouses, designs and evaluates experimental policies, and holds conferences to share experiences and develop innovative programs.

The guiding principle holding this diverse coalition together is the belief that victims who otherwise would feel powerless and enraged can attain a sense of empowerment and regain control over their lives through practical assistance, mutual support, and involvement in the criminal justice process (see Friedman, 1985; Smith, 1985; Smith, Sloan, and Ward, 1990; and Weed, 1995).

The victims' movement has greatly benefited from the work of advocates, who, by definition, speak in behalf of someone else, especially in legal matters. Originally, advocates were referred to as "ombudsmen." Rape crisis centers and shelters for battered women were the first to empower their clients in the early 1970s by furnishing them with the services of dedicated and knowledgeable people to consult with who understood how the criminal justice process worked and how to make the system more responsive to their clients' needs. These pioneers in advocacy usually were former victims who knew firsthand what the injured parties were going through. A Florida police department and a Chicago legal services organization were the first components of the justice system to routinely provide advocates in the mid-1970s. Shortly afterward, prosecutors' victim–witness assistance programs (VWAPs) and family courts (responsible for assigning *guardians ad litem* to represent the best interests of abused children) followed suit. In addition to survivors and volunteers, professionals in the helping fields (such as social workers, nurses, psychologists, psychiatrists, counselors, and lawyers) began to offer their specialized skills. Agencies provided short-term training in crisis intervention techniques and practical assistance with financial claims, court proceedings, and referrals to medical, mental health, and legal services. Courses and career preparation became available on college campuses. Two forms of advocacy developed: Case advocacy involves a one-on-one relationship with a client who needs specific assistance and focused guidance for a short period of time. System advocacy involves representing an entire group as part of an organized lobbying campaign to bring about procedural reforms that will ease their plight (Dussich, 2009a).

Major Sources of Inspiration, Guidance, and Support Several older and broader social movements have greatly influenced the growth and orientation of the victims' movement. The most important contributions have been made by the **law-and-order movement**, the **women's movement**, and the **civil rights movement**.

The law-and-order movement of the 1960s raised concerns about the plight of victims of street crimes of violence and theft. Alarmed by surging crime rates, conservatives adopted the "crime control" perspective and campaigned for hard-line, get-tough policies. They insisted that the criminal justice system was society's first line of defense against internal enemies who threatened chaos and destruction. The "thin blue line" of law enforcement needed to be strengthened. A willingness to tolerate too much misbehavior was viewed as the problem, and a crackdown on social and political deviants who disobeyed society's rules and disrupted the lives of conventional people was offered as the solution. To win over people who might have been reluctant to grant more power to government agencies—police, prosecutors, and prison authorities—they argued that the average American should be more worried about becoming a victim than about being falsely accused, mistakenly convicted, and unjustly punished (Hook, 1972). Conservative crime control advocates pictured the scales of justice as being unfairly tilted in favor of the "bad guys" at the expense of the "good guys"—the innocent, law-abiding citizens and their allies on the police force and in the prosecutor's office. In a smooth-running justice system that they envisioned, punishment would be swift and sure. Attorneys for defendants would no longer be able to take advantage of practices that were dismissed as "loopholes" and "technicalities" that undermined the government's efforts to arrest, detain, convict, imprison, deter, incapacitate, and impose retribution on wrongdoers.

"Permissiveness" (unwarranted leniency) and any "coddling of criminals" would end: More offenders would be locked up for longer periods of time, and fewer would be granted bail, probation, or parole. Liberals and civil libertarians who opposed these policies as being too repressive and overly punitive were branded as "pro-criminal" and "antivictim" (see Miller, 1973; and Carrington, 1975).

In contrast, liberal activists in the women's movement have focused their energies since the late 1960s on aiding one group of victims in particular: females who were harmed by males and then failed to receive the support they deserved from the male-dominated criminal justice system. Feminists launched both an antirape and an antibattering movement. The antirape movement set up the first rape crisis centers in Berkeley, California, and Washington, D.C., in 1972. These centers were not just places of aid and comfort in a time of pain and confusion. They also were rallying sites for outreach efforts to those who were suffering in isolation, meeting places for consciousness-raising groups exploring the patriarchal cultural traditions that encouraged males to subjugate females, and hubs for political organizing to change laws and policies (see Rose, 1977; Largen, 1981; and Schechter, 1982). Some antirape activists went on to protest the widespread problem of sexual harassment on the street, uniting behind the slogan "Take back the night" (see Lederer, 1980).

Other feminists helped organize battered women's shelters. They established the first "safe house" in St. Paul, Minnesota, in 1974. Campaigns to end battering paralleled activities to combat rape in a number of ways. Both projects were initiated for the most part by former victims who viewed their plight as an outgrowth of larger societal problems and institutional arrangements, rather than as personal troubles stemming from their own individual shortcomings. Both sought to empower women by confronting established male authority, challenging existing procedures, providing peer support and advocacy, and devising alternative places to turn to in a time of need. The overall analysis that originally guided these pro-victim efforts was that male versus female offenses (such as rape, wife beating, sexual harassment in the streets and at work, and incest at home) pose a threat to all women and slows progress toward equality between the sexes. The gravest dangers are faced by women who are socially disadvantaged because of racial discrimination and economic insecurity. According to this philosophy, girls and women victimized by boys and men cannot count on the privileged males at the helm of criminal justice agencies to lead the struggle to effectively protect or assist them—instead, women must empower each other (see Brownmiller, 1975).

Similarly, liberal activists in the civil rights movement focused their energies on opposing entrenched racist beliefs and discriminatory practices that encouraged members of the white majority to intimidate, harass, and attack people of color. Over the decades since the 1950s, this movement has brought together organizations representing the interests of a wide range of minority groups, in order to direct attention to the special threats posed by racist violence, from lynch mobs to Ku Klux Klan terrorism in the form of bombings and assassinations.

In recent years, one of the movement's major concerns has been convincing the government to provide enhanced protection to individuals who are the targets of **bias crimes**, which are motivated by the perpetrators' hatred of the "kind of person" the victim represents. Bias crimes can range from harassment and vandalism to arson, beatings, and slayings. Civil rights groups have been instrumental in lobbying state legislatures to impose stiffer penalties on attackers whose behavior is fueled by bigotry and in establishing specialized police squads to more effectively deter or solve these inflammatory violations of the law. Otherwise, these divisive crimes could polarize communities along racial and ethnic lines and thereby undermine the ongoing American experiment of fostering multicultural tolerance and the celebration of diversity (see Levin and McDevitt, 2003).

Civil rights organizations also try to mobilize public support to demand evenhandedness in the administration of justice. A double standard, although more subtle today than in the past, may still infect the operations of the criminal justice system. Crimes by black perpetrators against white victims always have been taken very seriously—thoroughly investigated, quickly solved, vigorously prosecuted, and severely punished. However, crimes by white offenders against black victims, as well as by blacks against other blacks (see Ebony, 1979) have rarely evoked the same governmental response and public outrage. The more frequent imposition of the death penalty on murderers who kill whites, especially blacks who slay whites, is the clearest example of a discriminatory double standard (see Baldus, 2003). Civil rights activists also point out that members of minority groups continue to face graver risks of becoming victims of official misconduct in the form of racial profiling and police brutality—or even worse, the unjustified use of deadly force—as well as false accusations, frame-ups, wrongful convictions, and other miscarriages of justice.

Additional Contributions by Other Social Movements Social movements that champion the causes of civil liberties, children's rights, senior citizens' rights, homosexual rights, and self-help also have made significant contributions to bettering the situation of victims.

The **civil liberties movement**'s primary focus is to preserve constitutional safeguards and due process guarantees that protect suspects, arrestees, defendants, and prisoners from abuses of governmental power by overzealous criminal justice officials. However, civil liberties organizations have won court victories that have benefited victims of street crime in two ways: by furthering police professionalism and by extending the doctrine of "equal protection under the law."

In professionalized police departments, officers must meet higher educational and training requirements and must abide by more demanding standards. As a result, victims are more likely to receive prompt responses, effective service, and sensitive treatment. If they don't, channels exist through which they can redress their grievances. Guarantees of equal protection enable minority communities to gain access to the police and prosecutorial assistance to which they are entitled and to insist upon their right to improved, more professionally trained law enforcement in contrast to the under-policing they endured until recently. This improves the prospects for careful and responsive handling for complainants whose calls for help were given short shrift in the past when officials discriminated against them due to their race, ethnicity, sex, age, social class, disability, or some other disadvantage (Walker, 1982; and Stark and Goldstein, 1985).

Children's rights groups campaign against sexual abuse, physical abuse, severe corporal punishment, gross neglect, and other forms of maltreatment of youngsters. Their successes include stricter reporting requirements of cases of suspected abuse; improved procedures for arrest, prosecution, and conviction of offenders; greater sensitivity to the needs of victimized children as complaining witnesses; enhanced protection and prevention services; and more effective parenting instruction programs.

At the other end of the age spectrum, activists in senior citizens' groups have pressured some police departments to establish special squads to protect older people from younger robbers and swindlers and have brought about greater awareness of the problem of **elder abuse**—financial, emotional, and physical mistreatment by family members or caretakers (see Smith and Freinkel, 1988).

The gay rights movement originally called attention to the vulnerability of male homosexuals and lesbians to blackmail, exploitation by organized crime syndicates that ran bars and clubs, and police harassment of those who deserved protection (see Maghan and Sagarin, 1983). The movement now focuses on preventing street assaults ("gay-bashing") against suspected homosexuals and lesbians—hate crimes that are motivated by the offenders' disdain for the victims' presumed sexual orientation.

Groups that are part of the **self-help movement** have set up dependable support systems for injured parties by combining the participatory spirit of the grassroots protest movements of the 1960s with the self-improvement ideals of the human potential movement of the 1970s. The ideology of self-help is based upon a fundamental organizing principle: that people who have directly experienced the pain and suffering of being harmed and are still struggling to overcome these hardships themselves can foster a sense of solidarity and mutual support that is more comforting and effective than the services offered by impersonal bureaucracies and emotionally detached professional caregivers (Gartner and Riessman, 1980).

Even the prisoners' rights movement of the late 1960s and early 1970s may have inspired victim activism. Inmates rebelled at a number of correctional institutions, often in vicious and counterproductive ways. They protested overcrowded conditions; demanded decent living standards; insisted on greater ways of communicating with the outside world (via uncensored mail, access to the mass media, more family visits, and meetings with lawyers); asked for freedom of religion; called for more opportunities for rehabilitation, education, and job training; and complained about mistreatment and brutality by guards (see ACLU, 2008). Many people harmed by these incarcerated offenders surely wondered, "if convicts deserve better treatment from the authorities, don't we, too?"

The task for victimologists is to assess the impact that all these other social movements have had on shaping the course of the victims' movement over the decades, as well as on alleviating the suffering of persons harmed by criminals these days. How effective and influential have the victories of these campaigns really been?

Elected Officials: Enacting Laws Named after Victims

Legislators engaged in the political process of enacting new laws have helped to rediscover specific groups and address their plight. Starting in the 1980s, federal, state, and local representatives realized that if they proposed a new law and named it after someone who had suffered terribly in a highly publicized crime, their campaign would gain a great deal of favorable media coverage that would help build support for the law's passage as well as for their own reelection. All suggestions for revisions and additions to the existing body of laws can be controversial and might provoke opposition, but officeholders who dare to argue against proposed legislation that enshrines the name of an innocent person harmed by a vicious predator run the risk of being branded "antivictim."

Probably the best-known example of a law bearing the name of a crime victim is the **Brady Bill**, or more formally, the *Handgun Violence Prevention Act*. The title honors James Brady, President Reagan's press secretary, who was shot in the head in 1981 by an assassin trying to kill the president (the gunfire killed two persons guarding the president). Passed in 1993, it imposed a computer-based FBI

criminal background check on anyone who seeks to buy a firearm from a federally licensed dealer, in a stepped-up attempt to protect the public from individuals deemed to be dangerous (who had been forbidden by federal law from purchasing firearms since 1968, as a reaction to the assassination of President Kennedy in 1963).

Another bill bearing a victim's name is the *Jeanne Clery Disclosure of Campus Security Policy and Campus Crime Statistics Act* (originally referred to as the Crime Awareness and Campus Security Act). Named to memorialize a 19-year-old freshman who was raped and murdered in her dorm by another student, it was enacted in 1990. This federal law requires all colleges that receive federal aid to maintain and disclose annual reports about a long list of crimes that take place on or near their campuses so that prospective students and their parents can assess the relative risks of attending various institutions of higher learning.

The *Emmett Till Unsolved Civil Rights Crime Act* went into effect in 2008. It set up a cold case unit within the U.S. Department of Justice to reopen and investigate bias-motivated murders committed before 1970. Emmett Till, a 14-year-old black teenager, was kidnapped, tortured, shot, and dumped into a river in 1955 by two white racists for flirting with the wife of one of the two men at a grocery store in rural Mississippi (see Anderson, 2011).

The *Matthew Shepard and James Byrd Jr. Hate Crimes Prevention Act* was passed by Congress in 2009. Named to commemorate a gay college student who was beaten to death by bigots, and an African-American man who was dragged to his death behind a pickup truck by white supremacists, the legislation expanded the coverage of the federal government's hate-crime law, which was originally passed in 1969.

The *Adam Walsh Child Protection and Safety Act*, also known as the Sex Offender Registration and Notification Act (SORNA), was enacted by Congress in 2006. Named in the memory of a six-year-old who was abducted from a department store and then viciously murdered, the act strengthened sex offender registration requirements, stiffened the penalties of existing laws forbidding sexually abusing and exploiting children, and extended federal authority over kidnappings.

Over the decades, many state legislatures have passed statutes named after victims, such as New Jersey's *Megan's Law*. Commemorating a seven-year-old girl slain in 1994 by her next-door neighbor, a habitual child molester, each state's version of *Megan's Law* mandates that convicted sex offenders register with their local police department and that community residents be notified of their whereabouts, so that parents—in theory, at least—can take steps to better shield their children from these potentially dangerous strangers.

Since the 1980s, state and county legislatures nationwide have enacted thousands of new laws named after victims (see Editors, *New York Post*, 2006; and Lovett, 2006). Two very different conclusions about the rediscovery of the victim's plight by lawmakers can be drawn. The first is to view certain headline-making tragedies as a "final straw" that focused much-needed attention on a festering problem, mobilized public opinion, and triggered long overdue legislative action by well-meaning elected officials. The other response is to suspect that vote-seeking politicians are exploiting the media attention surrounding highly emotional but very complicated situations for their own personal advantage (to advance their careers). They grab headlines by proposing a change in the existing body of law that will allegedly prevent such an incident from happening again. The strong feelings evoked by a recent tragedy make it difficult for opponents to question the wisdom of implementing the "reforms" these ambitious, headline-seeking politicians propose in the name of the victim.

The task for victimologists is to start out as impartial observers and to gather data to see whether the legislation bearing the name of a victim actually offers any tangible assistance to ease the plight of individuals harmed in this particular manner. Also, are these measures really effective in preventing innocent people from being hurt by these kinds of offenses in the future, or do they just punish offenders more severely on behalf of those they already injured? Some of these recent legal reforms

enacted to ostensibly reduce the occurrence of a certain kind of victimization might turn out to be ill-conceived, seriously flawed, ineffective, or even counterproductive (for example, see Cooper, 2005).

The News Media: Portraying the Victims' Plight

The news media deserve a great deal of credit for rediscovering victims. In the past, offenders received the lion's share of coverage in newspapers and magazines and on radio and television stations. Stories delved into their backgrounds, their motives, and what should be done with them—usually how severely they should be punished. Scant attention was paid to the flesh-and-blood individuals who suffered because of the offender's illegal activities.

But now those who are on the receiving end of criminal behavior are no longer invisible or forgotten people. Details about the injured parties are routinely included to inject some human interest into crime stories. Balanced accounts can vividly describe the victims' plight: how they were harmed, what losses they incurred, what intense emotions distressed them, what helped or even hindered their recovery, how they were treated by caregivers, and how their cases were handled by the legal system. By remaining faithful to the facts, journalists can enable their audiences to transcend their own limited direct experiences with lawbreakers and to see emergencies, tragedies, and triumphs through the eyes of the injured parties. Skillful reporting and insightful observations allow the public to better understand and empathize with the actions and reactions of those who suffered harm. In certain highly publicized cases, interviews by journalists have given victims a voice in how their cases ought to be resolved in court, and even how the problem (such as child snatchings by an angry ex-spouse, easy access to firearms, or collisions caused by drunk drivers) should be handled by the criminal justice system. Media coverage also has given these individuals with firsthand experiences a public platform to campaign for wider societal reforms (Dignan, 2005).

However, victims—and if they perish violently, their next of kin—often complain about **sensationalism**, a kind of coverage that has been branded as "scandal-mongering," "pandering," "yellow journalism," and "tabloidism." Newspapers, magazines, radio stations, and television networks are prone to engage in sensationalism because they are profit-oriented businesses. Shocking stories attract readers, listeners, and viewers. Blaring headlines, gripping accounts, colorful phrases, memorable quotes, and other forms of media hype build the huge audiences that enable media enterprises to charge advertisers high rates. Producers, editors, and reporters who seek to play up the human-interest angle may exploit the plight of persons who have suffered devastating losses and debilitating wounds. Not surprisingly, the "infotainment" shows have found that crime stories attract a lot more notice if they are spiced up with a heavy dose of sex, gore, and raw emotions. In the quest for higher ratings, market-driven coverage can sink to an "If it bleeds, it leads" rule of thumb. If reporters turn a personal tragedy into a media circus and a public spectacle, their intrusive behavior might be considered an invasion of privacy. Overzealous journalists frequently are criticized for showing corpses lying in a pool of blood, maintaining vigils outside a grieving family's home, or shoving microphones into the faces of bereaved, dazed, or hysterical relatives at funerals. The injured party receives unwanted publicity and experiences a loss of control as others comment upon, draw lessons from, and impose judgments on what he or she allegedly did, or did not do, or should have done.

Incidents receive intensive and sustained coverage only when some aspect of the victim–offender relationship stands out as an attention-grabber: The act, the perpetrator, or the target must be unusual, unexpected, strange, or perverse. Suffering harm in ways that are typical, commonplace, or predictable is just not newsworthy. Editors and journalists sift through an overwhelming number of real-life tragedies that come to their attention (largely through contacts within the local police department) and select the cases that are most likely to seize center stage, go viral, shock people out of their complacency, and either stir up deep-seated fears or arouse the public's empathy and social conscience.

The stories that are featured strike a responsive chord in audiences because the incidents symbolize some significant theme—for example, that anyone can be chosen at random, simply for being at the wrong place at the wrong time; that complete strangers cannot be trusted; and that bystanders might not come to a person's aid, especially in anonymous, big-city settings (Roberts, 1989). Historically, heinous crimes that have received the most press coverage have had one or more of these elements in common: Either the injured party or the defendant is a child, woman, or a prominent or wealthy person; intimations of "promiscuous" behavior by the victim or defendant help explain the event; some doubts linger about the guilt of the convict; and the circumstances surrounding a slaying seemed unusual (Stephens, 1988; and Buckler and Travis, 2005).

Furthermore, media attention may reflect the unconscious biases of talk show hosts, correspondents, and editors who work in the newsroom. For example, members of minority communities have charged that national news outlets, especially those on cable TV, focus relentless attention on the disappearance of attractive white people, particularly young women and children, but overlook equally compelling cases involving individuals who do not share these characteristics (see Lyman, 2005; Memmott, 2005; and Barton, 2011).

Hence, it is predictable that the unsolved Christmas Eve murder of a six-year-old beauty contest winner in her own upscale home, with her parents and brother upstairs, would be the subject of incessant tabloid sensationalism (Johnson, 2008). Similarly, the disappearance of a 24-year-old intern after jogging in a park set off an avalanche of lurid speculation when it was revealed that she was having an affair with a married congressman (the case was solved years later when her killer turned out to be a complete stranger who had attacked other women in that same park at about the same time) (Tavernise, 2011). If these charges are true, the problem may go deeper and may reflect the shortcomings of market-driven journalism. The gatekeepers, under organizational pressures to sell their product, sift through a huge pool of items and select stories they perceive will resonate with the general public, at the expense of presenting an accurate sampling of the full range of tragedies taking place locally, nationally, and around the world (see Buckler and Travis, 2005).

And yet, it can be argued that media coverage of crime stories is an absolute necessity in an open society. Reporters and news editors have a constitutional right, derived from the First Amendment's guarantee of a free press, to present information about lawbreaking without interference from the government. Illegal activities not only harm particular individuals but also pose a threat to those who may be next. People have a right as well as a need to know about the emergence of dangerous conditions and ominous developments, and the media has an obligation to communicate this information accurately.

The problem is that the public's right to know about crime and the media's right to report these incidents clash with the victim's right to privacy. Journalists, editors, and victims' advocates are addressing questions of fairness and ethics in a wide variety of forums, ranging from blogs and posted comments on the Web and letters to the editor in newspapers, to professional conferences and lawsuits in civil court.

Several remedies have been proposed to curb abusive coverage of a victim's plight. One approach would be to enact new laws to shield those who suffer from needless public exposure, such as an unnecessary disclosure of names and addresses in dispatches or on websites. An alternative approach would be to rely on the self-restraint of reporters and their editors. The fact that most news accounts of sexual molestations of children and of rapes no longer reveal the names of those who were harmed is an example of this self-policing approach in action. A third remedy would be for the media to adopt a code of professional ethics. Journalists who

abide by the code would "read victims their rights" at the outset of interviews, just as police officers read suspects their Miranda rights when taking them into custody (see Thomason and Babbilli, 1987; and Karmen, 1989).

Victimologists could play an important role in monitoring progress by studying how accurate widely broadcast initial accounts are; how frequently and how seriously reporters insult and defame the subjects of their stories; and how successfully the different reform strategies prevent this kind of exploitation, or at least minimize any abusive invasions of privacy (see Duwe, 2000).

Commercial Interests: Selling Security Products and Services to Victims

Just as the rediscovery of victims by elected officials and the news media has benefits as well as drawbacks, so too does the new attention paid to injured parties by businesses. An emerging market of people seeking out protective services and anti-theft devices simultaneously raises the possibility of meeting consumer needs but also of commercially exploiting these eager customers. Profiteers can engage in fear mongering and false advertising in order to cash in on the legitimate concerns and desires of individuals who feel particularly vulnerable and even panicky. In situations where entrepreneurs issue bold claims about some gadget's effectiveness, objectivity takes the form of scientific skepticism. Victimologists must represent the public interest and demand, "Prove those assertions about this product or service! Where is the evidence?"

Consider the question of whether expensive automobile security systems actually work as well as their manufacturers' advertisements say they do. For instance, do car alarms really deliver the layer of protection against break-ins that their purchasers seek and that sales pitches promise? In New York, the City Council passed regulations restricting the installation of new car alarms because the devices were deemed to be largely ineffective as well as a serious source of noise pollution. Rather than agreeing with frustrated motorists that the wailing sirens do no good, or trying to defend the alarm industry's reputation and profits, nonpartisan victimologists can independently evaluate the effectiveness of these antitheft devices. Are car alarms really useful in deterring break-ins; in minimizing losses of accessories such as car stereos, navigation systems, or air bags; in preventing vehicles from being driven away; and in aiding the police to catch thieves red-handed?

Similarly, research projects could attempt to determine whether burglar alarms actually deter or cut short intruders' invasions and are therefore worth the price of installation and monthly monitoring fees, and whether identity theft insurance protection is a wise investment.

VICTIMOLOGY CONTRIBUTES TO THE REDISCOVERY PROCESS

The emergence and acceptance of victimology as a scholarly endeavor has propelled the rediscovery process onward.

The beginnings of the academic discipline of victimology can be traced back to several articles, books, and research projects initiated by criminologists during the 1940s and 1950s. Until that time, criminology's attention was focused entirely on those who violated the law: who they were, why they engaged in illegal activities, how they were handled by the criminal justice system, whether they should be incarcerated, and how they might be rehabilitated. Eventually, perhaps through the process of elimination, several criminologists searching for solutions to the crime problem were drawn to—or stumbled upon—the important role played by victims.

These criminologists considered victims to be worthy of serious study primarily because they were the completely overlooked half of the dyad (pair). The first use in English of the term *victimology* to refer to the scientific study of people harmed by criminals appeared in a book about murderers written by a psychiatrist (Wertham, 1949). The first scholars to consider themselves victimologists examined the presumed vulnerabilities of certain

kinds of people, such as the very young, the very old, recent immigrants, and the mentally incompetent (Von Hentig, 1948); the "kinds of people," (in terms of factors such as age and sex), whose actions contributed to their own violent deaths (Wolfgang, 1958); and the degree of resistance put up by rape victims (Mendelsohn, 1940).

Beniamin Mendelsohn, a defense attorney in Romania, wrote and spoke during the 1940s and 1950s about how victims were ignored, disrespected, and abused within the criminal justice process. He proposed ways to help and protect them by creating victim assistance clinics and special research institutes, and he campaigned for victims' rights. For his foresight, he might be deemed "the father of victimology" (Dussich, 2009b).

During the 1960s, as the problem of street crime intensified, the President's Commission on Law Enforcement and the Administration of Justice argued that criminologists ought to pay more attention to victims (thereby inspiring some to become victimologists). The Commission's Task Force on Assessment (1967, p. 80) concluded:

> One of the most neglected subjects in the study of crime is its victims: the persons, households, and businesses that bear the brunt of crime in the United States. Both the part the victim can play in the criminal act and the part he could have played in preventing it are often overlooked. If it could be determined with sufficient specificity that people or businesses with certain characteristics are more likely than others to be crime victims, and that crime is more likely to occur in some places rather than in others, efforts to control and prevent crime would be more productive. Then the public could be told where and when the risks of crime are greatest. Measures such as preventive police patrol and installation of burglar alarms and special locks could then be pursued more efficiently and effectively. Individuals could then substitute objective estimation of risk for the general apprehensiveness that today restricts—perhaps unnecessarily and at best haphazardly—their enjoyment of parks and their freedom of movement on the streets after dark.

In this call for a shift in focus, the Commission's Task Force stressed the potential practical benefits: More crimes could be prevented and more criminals caught, unrealistic fears could be calmed and unwarranted complacency dispelled, and needless expenditures could be eliminated or reduced. These ambitious goals have not yet been attained. Other goals not cited by the commission that have been added over the years include reducing suffering, making the criminal justice system more responsive, and restoring victims to the financial condition they were in before the crime occurred.

During the 1960s and 1970s, criminologists, reformers, and political activists argued persuasively that offenders themselves were in some sense "victims" too—of the desperation caused by poverty in the midst of plenty, dysfunctional families, failing school systems, rundown housing, job shortages, discrimination, police brutality, and other social problems (for example, see Ryan, 1971). In reaction to this sympathetic characterization of lawbreakers, many people asked, "But what about the real flesh-and-blood individuals that they preyed upon who were innocent, law-abiding, and vulnerable? What can be done to ease their suffering?" While grappling with that question, reformers came to recognize that persons targeted by criminals were being systematically abandoned to their fates and that institutionalized neglect had prevailed for too long. A consensus began to emerge that people harmed by illegal acts deserved better treatment. Plans for financial assistance were the focus of early discussions; campaigns for enhanced rights within the legal system soon followed.

By the 1970s, victimology had become a recognized field of study with its own national and international professional organizations, conferences, and journals. Courses in victimology sprang up on many campuses, in part because students wanted to discuss their own personal experiences—which must be explored with great sensitivity (see Cares, 2012). By the end of the 1990s, students were taking victimology classes at more than 240 colleges and universities.

The milestones that mark victimology's relatively brief history, plus the major pioneering efforts to provide tangible help to crime victims are presented in Box 2.1.

REDISCOVERING ADDITIONAL GROUPS OF VICTIMS

This process—in which people whose plight was recognized long ago but is neglected for many years until it finally attracts the attention it deserves—goes on and on with no end in sight. Some rediscovered groups that have received a great deal of study and support include abused children, battered women; females who have suffered date rapes; kidnapped youngsters; people targeted by bigots; individuals attacked by enraged motorists; pedestrians, passengers, and drivers killed in collisions caused by drunk drivers; and prisoners sexually assaulted by fellow inmates or members of the custodial staff. The suffering of other groups unfortunately is also becoming quite well known and increasingly attended to: students shot in high schools and colleges, employees subjected to workplace violence, and police officers assaulted and fired at by felons.

And yet, there are still other groups under the radar or waiting in the wings to be rediscovered by those academics and scholars, practitioners, social movements, elected officials, the news media, and commercial interests who continue to drive the process forward. A steady stream of fresh revelations serves as a reminder that these neglected groups still are "out there" and that they have compelling stories to tell, unmet needs, and legitimate demands for assistance and support. Usually, they continue to escape public notice until some highly unusual or horrific incident reveals how they are being harmed. The types of victims whose plight is now being rediscovered—but who require much more scrutiny and analysis, and creative remedies—are listed in Box 2.2.

BOX 2.1 Highlights in the Brief History of Victimology and Victim Assistance

Year	Event
1924	Edwin Sutherland writes the first criminology textbook that includes a short discussion about victims.
1941	Hans Von Hentig publishes an article focusing on the interaction between victims and criminals.
1947	Beniamin Mendelsohn coins the term victimology in an article written in French.
1957	In Great Britain, Margery Fry proposes legislation that would authorize the government to reimburse victims for their losses.
1958	Marvin Wolfgang studies the circumstances surrounding the deaths of murder victims and discovers that some contributed to their own demise.
1964	The U.S. Congress holds hearings on the plight of crime victims but rejects legislative proposals to cover their losses.
1965	California becomes the first U.S. state to set up a special fund to repay victims for crime-inflicted expenses.
1966	The first nationwide victimization survey to find out about crimes that were not reported to the police is carried out, and its findings are considered so enlightening that it becomes an annual undertaking.
1967	A presidential commission recommends that criminologists study victims.
1968	Stephen Schafer writes the first textbook about victims.
Early 1970s	The first sex crime squads and rape crisis centers are established.
1972	The federal government initiates a yearly National Crime Victimization Survey of the general public to uncover firsthand information about street crimes.
1973	The first international conference of victimologists is convened in Jerusalem.
1974	The first shelter for battered women is set up in Minnesota. The first victim advocates in law enforcement are assigned by the police department in Fort Lauderdale, Florida. The first lawyers serving as advocates for victims in legal proceedings are made available on the South East Side of Chicago.
Mid-1970s	Prosecutors initiate victim–witness assistance programs.
1976	The first scholarly journal devoted to victimology begins publication. A National Organization for Victim Assistance (NOVA) is established to bring together service providers working for government agencies and nonprofits. The probation department in Fresno, California, is the first to instruct its officers to interview victims to find out how the crime impacted them physically, emotionally, socially, and financially.
1977	New York State enacts the first "Son of Sam" law to prevent offenders from profiting from telling about their exploits.
1979	The World Society of Victimology is founded.
1981	President Reagan proclaims Victims' Rights Week every April.
1982	Congress passes a Victim and Witness Protection Act that suggests standards for fair treatment of victims within the federal court system.
1983	The President's Task Force on Victims of Crime recommends changes in the Constitution and in federal and state laws to guarantee victims' rights.
1984	Congress passes the Victims of Crime Act, which provides federal subsidies to state victim compensation and assistance programs.
1985	The United Nations General Assembly unanimously adopts a resolution that urges all members to respect and extend the rights of victims of crimes and of abuses of power.
1986	Victims' rights activists seek the passage of constitutional amendments on the federal and state levels guaranteeing victims' rights.
1987	The U.S. Department of Justice opens a National Victims Resource Center in Rockville, Maryland, to serve as a clearinghouse for information.
1990	Congress passes the Victims' Rights and Restitution Act.
1994	Congress passes the Violence Against Women Act.
2003	The American Society of Victimology is set up to encourage collaboration between academicians, researchers, and practitioners.
2004	Congress enacts the Crime Victims' Rights Act, which pledges fair treatment and opportunities for input in federal court proceedings.
2005	A bipartisan group of 18 members of Congress forms a Victim's Rights Caucus.
2007	VictimLaw, a user-friendly website set up by the National Center for Victims of Crime, provides a searchable database about state legislation concerning restitution and compensation for financial losses.
2008	The National Museum of Crime & Punishment opens in Washington, D.C., with exhibits that dramatize the plights of victims.
2011	The Office of Justice Programs (OJP) of the federal government's Department of Justice (DOJ) launches a website, www.crimesolutions.org, that evaluates the effectiveness of programs on behalf of crime victims.
2014	The Bureau of Justice Statistics develops a webpage that presents tables of data about victims in a user-friendly format.
2014	California becomes the first state to pass a "Yes Means Yes" law that requires explicit mutual consent before engaging in sex in college campus settings.

SOURCE: Galaway and Hudson, 1981; Schneider, 1982; Lamborn, 1985; National Organization for Victim Assistance (NOVA), 1989, 1995; Dussich, 2003; Walker, 2003; Garlock, 2007; Rothstein, 2008; Dussich, 2009a, 2009b; and Chappell, 2014.

B O X 2.2 The Process of Rediscovery Goes On and On

These recently recognized groups of victims face special problems that require imaginative solutions. They eventually will receive the assistance and support they need as the rediscovery process continues to focus attention and resources on their plight:

- Individuals who are deaf, blind, mentally retarded, mentally ill, or afflicted by other disabilities that attracted molesters, assailants, robbers, or other criminals who preyed upon them more often than other potential targets (Office for Victims of Crime, 2003; Barrow, 2008; and Harrell, 2014), particularly when they were young (Smith and Harrell, 2013; and Tabachnick, 2013).

- People whose attackers cannot be arrested and prosecuted because as members of foreign delegations they have been granted "diplomatic immunity" and are able to escape justice by returning home (Ashman and Trescott, 1987; Sieh, 1990; Lynch, 2003; and Grow, 2011)

- Pedestrians and passengers killed by drivers who speed, run red lights, or ignore stop signs and may be guilty of criminally negligent homicide (Goodman, 2013; and Lerner, 2014).

- Motorists and pedestrians slammed into during high-speed chases by fugitives seeking to avoid arrest or by squad cars in hot pursuit (Gray, 1993; Crew, Fridell, and Pursell, 1995; and Schultz, Budak, and Alpert, 2010)

- Motorists, cyclists, and pedestrians injured or killed by hit-and-run drivers (Bisnar and Chase, 2011).

- Native Americans living on the nation's 310 Indian reservations who suffer much higher victimization rates for murder, rape, and other interpersonal crimes but receive less protection and redress from the criminal justice system than other U.S. citizens (Williams, 2012a, 2012b; and Erdrich, 2013).

- Immigrants who feel they cannot come forward and ask the police for help without revealing that they are "illegal aliens" who lack the proper documents and are subject to deportation (Davis and Murray, 1995; Davis, Erez, and Avitabile, 2001; Chan, 2007; and Hoffmaster, Murphy, McFadden, and Griswold, 2010)

- Homeless adults robbed, assaulted, and murdered on the streets and in shelters (Fitzpatrick, LaGory, and Ritchey, 1993; and Green, 2008)

- Homeless runaway teens who are vulnerable to sexual exploitation and rape (Tyler, Whitbeck, Hoyt, and Cauce, 2005)

- Hotel guests who suffer thefts and assaults because of lax security measures (Prestia, 1993; Owsley, 2005; and Ho, Zhao, and Brown, 2009)

- Cruise ship passengers who suffer attacks and thefts from fellow voyagers and members of the crew (Anderle, 2013).

- Tourists who blunder into dangerous situations avoided by streetwise locals and are easy prey because they let their guard down (Rohter, 1993; Glensor and Peak, 2004; Lee, 2005; and Murphy, 2006)

- Delivery truck drivers who are targeted by robbers, hijackers, and highway snipers (Sexton, 1994; and Duret and Patrick, 2004)

- Prostitutes soliciting complete strangers on the streets or over the Internet who face risks of being beaten, raped, and murdered that are many times higher than for other women in their age bracket (Boyer and James, 1983; Salfati, James, and Ferguson, 2008; and Mueller, 2014)

- Unwanted newborns abandoned or killed by their distraught mothers (Yardley, 1999; and Buckley, 2007)

- Suspects brutally beaten by police officers who used more force than the law allows (Amnesty International USA, 1999; and Davey and Einhorn, 2007)

- Teachers attacked, injured, and even killed by their students (Fine, 2001; Parker, 2014; and Freie Universitaet Berlin, 2014)

- Underage students who experience statutory rape when they are seduced by their high school teachers (Zernike, 2014).

- Youngsters sexually molested or physically abused through prohibited forms of corporal punishment by parents and teachers (Goodnough, 2003; and Larzelere and Baumrind, 2010)

- High school and college students subjected to abusive hazing and bullying by older students that results in injury or death (Salmivalli and Nieminen, 2002; Montague, Zohra, Love, McGee, and Tsamis, 2008; and Zernike and Schweber, 2014)

- Terrified residents whose homes were invaded by armed robbers (Hurley, 1995; Copeland and Martin, 2006; and Thompson, 2011)

- "Mail-order brides," lured to the United States by unregulated international matchmaking services on the Internet, who fear deportation if they complain to the authorities about their husbands' violence (Briscoe, 2005; Morash, Hoan, Yan, and Holtfreter, 2007; and Greenwood, 2008)

- Teenage girls and young women kidnapped and held captive as "sex slaves" by vicious rapists (Hoffman, 2003; Jacobs, 2003; Maslin, 2011; Kaufman, 2012; and Williams, 2013)

- Unsuspecting people, usually women, who feel symbolically violated sexually after being secretly videotaped during private moments by voyeurs using hidden spy cameras (Lovett, 2003; and Williams, 2005)

- Female motorists sexually abused by highway patrol officers (Tyre, 2001)

- People deceived by robbers and rapists impersonating uniformed officers as well as plainclothes detectives (Long, 2008; and Van Netta, 2011)

- Persons arrested for drug law violations who are pressured by detectives to become confidential informants and end up wounded or murdered by dealers (Goodman, 2013)

- Good Samaritans who try to break up crimes in progress and rescue the intended victims but wind up injured or killed themselves (Mawby, 1985; Time, Payne, and Gainey, 2010; and Cunningham et al., 2012)

- Innocent bystanders wounded or killed by bullets intended for others, often when caught in crossfire between rival street gangs or drug dealers fighting over turf (Sherman, Steele, Laufersweiler, Hoffer, and Julian, 1989; and Williams, 2009)

- People being blackmailed who are reluctant to turn to the authorities for help because that would lead to exposure of their embarrassing secrets (see Katz, Fletcher and Altman, 1993; and Robinson, Cahill, and Bartels, 2010)

- Recipients, some of them children, of crank phone calls laced with threats or obscenities, made by individuals who range from "heavy breathers" and bored teenagers to dangerous assailants (Savitz, 1986; Warner, 1988; Leander, Granhag, and Christianson, 2005; and Renshaw, 2008)

- Residents injured by fires or burned out of their homes, unaware that they were harmed by acts of arson until fire marshals determine that the suspicious blazes were intentionally set (Sclafani, 2005)

- Homeowners who wind up evicted because of swindles like mortgage fraud and foreclosure-rescue fraud (FBI, 2008b)

- Consumers who lose money in Internet cyber swindles and "dotcons," such as online pyramid investment (Ponzi) schemes, bogus auctions, fake escrow accounts, and other computer-based frauds (Lee, 2003b; and Stajano and Wilson, 2011)

- "Missing persons" who have vanished and are presumed dead by their frantic relatives, but, since they were adults with a right to privacy, cannot be the objects of intense police manhunts unless there is evidence of foul play (McPhee, 1999; Gardiner, 2008; and NCMA, 2008). Sometimes their remains lie unidentified until "cybersleuths" and other amateur detectives poring over online coroners' files and missing-persons databases are able to match a body to a disappearance and notify the local police department about solving one of their cold cases, thereby helping these deceased individuals get a proper burial, and maybe even securing "justice" for them if their killer is convicted (Halber, 2014; and Latson, 2014)

- Unrelated individuals whose lives are snuffed out by vicious and demented serial killers (Holmes and DeBurger, 1988; Hickey, 1991; Egger and Egger, 2002; Pakhomou, 2004; Flegenheimer and Rosenberg, 2011; and AP, 2011c); and especially prostitutes, hitchhikers, and stranded motorists, whose bodies are dumped near highways by violence-prone long-haul truckers (Glover, 2009; and Dalesio, 2011)

THE REDISCOVERY PROCESS IN ACTION, STEP BY STEP

The rediscovery process is more than just a well-intentioned humanitarian undertaking, media campaign, or example of special pleading. It has far-reaching consequences for everyday life, and the stakes are high. Injured people who gain legitimacy as innocent victims and win public backing are in a position to make compelling claims on government resources (asking for compensation payments to cover the expenses they incurred from their physical wounds, for example). People who know from first-hand experience about the suffering caused by illegal acts also can advance persuasive arguments about reforming criminal justice policies concerning arrest, prosecution, trial procedures, appropriate sentences, and custodial control over prisoners. Finally, redis-covered victims can assert that preventing others from suffering the same fate requires a change in prevailing cultural values about tolerating social conditions that generate criminal behavior. Victims even can make recommendations that are taken seriously about the ways people should and should not behave (for instance, how husbands should treat their wives, and how closely parents should supervise their children) and even the proper role of government (such as how readily the state should intervene in "private" matters such as violence between intimates).

The process of rediscovery usually unfolds through a series of steps and stages. The sequential model that is proposed below incorporates observations drawn from several sources. The notion of developmental stages arises from the self-definition of the victimization process (Viano, 1989). The natural history, career, or life-cycle perspective comes from examining models of ongoing social problems (see Fuller and Myers, 1941; Ross and Staines, 1972; and Spector and Kitsuse, 1987). The focus on how concerns about being harmed are first raised, framed, and then publicized arises from the constructionist approach (see Best, 1989b). The idea of inevitable clashes of opposing interest groups battling over governmental resources and influence over legislation comes from sociology's conflict approach. The realization that there is an ongoing struggle by victimized groups for respect and support in the court of public opinion is an application of the concept of stigma contests (Schur, 1984).

Stage 1: Calling Attention to an Overlooked Problem

The rediscovery process is set in motion whenever activists begin to raise the public's consciousness about some type of illegal situation that "everybody knows" happens but few have cared enough to investigate or try to correct. These moral entrepreneurs, who lead campaigns to change laws and win people over to their point of view, usually have first-hand experience with a specific problem as well as direct, personal knowledge of the pain and suffering that accompany it. Particularly effective self-help and advocacy groups have been set up by parents who endured the ordeal of searching for their missing children, mothers whose children were killed in collisions caused by drunk drivers, and the families of officers slain in the line of duty, among others. Additional individuals who deserve credit for arousing an indifferent public include the targets of hate-driven bias crimes, adults haunted by the way they were molested when they were young, women brutally raped by acquaintances they trusted, and wives viciously beaten by their husbands. They called attention to a state of affairs that people took for granted as harmful but shrugged off as "What can anyone do about it?" These activists responded, "Things don't have to be this way!" Exploitative and hurtful relationships don't have to be tolerated—they can be prevented, avoided, and outlawed; governmental policies can be altered; and the criminal justice system can be made more accountable and responsive to its "clients."

As Stage 1 moves along, activists function as the inspiration and nucleus for the formation of self-help groups that provide mutual aid and solace and also undertake campaigns for reform. Members of support networks believe that only people who have suffered through the same ordeal can really understand and appreciate what others just like them are going through (a basic tenet borrowed from therapeutic communities that assist substance abusers to recover from drug addiction).

Activists also state that victims' troubles stem from larger social problems that are beyond any individual's ability to control; consequently, those who suffer should not be blamed for causing their own misfortunes. Finally, activists argue that recovery requires empowerment within the criminal justice process so that victims can pursue what they define as their own best interests, whether to see to it that the offender receives the maximum punishment permitted by law, is compelled to undergo treatment, and/or is ordered to pay their bills for crime-related expenses.

To build wider support for their causes, moral entrepreneurs and self-help groups organize themselves into loosely structured coalitions such as the antirape and antibattering movements. Usually, one or two well-publicized cases are pointed to as symbolic of the problem. Soon many other victims come forward to tell about similar personal experiences. Then experts such as social workers, detectives, and lawyers testify about the suffering that these kinds of victims routinely endure and plead that legal remedies are urgently needed. Extensive media coverage is a prerequisite for success. The group's plight becomes known because of investigative reports on television, talk radio discussions, magazine cover stories, newspaper editorials, and the circulation of these accounts on blogs. Meanwhile, press conferences, demonstrations, marches, candlelight vigils, petition drives, ballot initiatives, lawsuits, and lobbying campaigns keep the issue alive and the pressure on.

Sociologically, what happens during the first stage can be termed the social construction of a social problem, along with **claims-making** and typification (see Spector and Kitsuse, 1987; and Best, 1989b). A consensus emerges that a pattern of behavior is harmful and should be subjected to criminal penalties. This crystallization of public opinion is a product of the activities of moral entrepreneurs, support groups, and their allies. Spokespersons engage in a claims-making process by airing grievances, estimating how many people are hurt in this manner, suggesting appropriate remedies to facilitate recovery, and recommending measures that could prevent this kind of physical, emotional, and financial suffering from burdening others. Through the process of typification, advocates point out classic cases and textbook examples that illustrate the menace to society against which they are campaigning.

Stage 2: Winning Victories, Implementing Reforms

The rediscovery process enters its second stage whenever activists and advocacy groups begin to make headway toward their goals.

At first, it might be necessary to set up independent demonstration projects or pilot programs to prove the need for special services. Then government grants or funding from private foundations can be secured. Next, federal, state, and local agencies or nonprofit organizations can copy successful models or take over some responsibility for providing information, assistance, and protection. For instance, the battered women's movement set up shelters, and the antirape movement established crisis centers. Eventually, local governments funded safe houses where women and their young children could seek refuge, and hospitals and universities organized their own 24-hour rape hotlines and crisis-intervention services.

Individuals subjected to bias crimes were rediscovered during the 1990s. During the 1980s, only private organizations monitored incidents of hate-motivated violence and vandalism directed against racial and religious minorities, as well as homosexuals. But in 1990, the government got involved when Congress passed the Hate Crime Statistics Act, which authorized the FBI to undertake the task of collecting reports about bias crimes from local police departments. Achievements that mark this second stage in the rediscovery process include the imposition of harsher penalties and the establishment of specially trained law enforcement units in many jurisdictions to more effectively recognize, investigate, solve, and prosecute bias crimes. Self-help groups offer injured parties tangible forms of support. The best example of a rediscovery campaign that has raised consciousness, won victories, and secured reforms is the struggle waged since the early 1980s by Mothers Against Drunk Driving (MADD). These anguished parents argued that for too long the "killer drunk" was able to get away with a socially acceptable and judicially excusable form of homicide because more people identified with the intoxicated driver than with the innocent person who died from injuries sustained in the collision. Viewing themselves as the relatives of bona fide crime victims, not merely persons who perished from accidents, these crusaders were able to move the issue from the obituary page to the front page by using a wide range of tactics to mobilize public support, including candlelight vigils, pledges of responsible behavior by children and family cooperation by their parents, and demonstrations outside courthouses. Local chapters of their national self-help organizations offered concrete services: Pamphlets were distributed through hospital emergency rooms and funeral parlors, bereavement support groups assisted grieving relatives, and volunteers accompanied grieving families to police stations, prosecutors' offices, trials, and sentencing hearings.

Buoyed by very favorable media coverage, their lobbying campaigns brought about a crackdown on DUI (driving under the influence) and DWI (driving while intoxicated) offenders. Enforcement measures include roadblocks, license suspensions and revocations, more severe criminal charges, and on-the-spot confiscations of vehicles. Their efforts also led to reforms of drinking laws, such as raising the legal drinking age to 21 and lowering the blood alcohol concentration levels that officially define impairment and intoxication (Thompson, 1984). Along with the 55 mph speed limit, mandatory seat belt laws, improved vehicle safety engineering, better roads, and breakthroughs in emergency medical services, the achievements of MADD and its allies have saved countless lives (Ayres, 1994).

Stage 3: Emergence of an Opposition and Development of Resistance to Further Changes

The third stage in the rediscovery process is marked by the emergence of groups that oppose the goals sought by victims of rediscovered crimes. The victims had to overcome public apathy during Stage 1 and bureaucratic inertia during Stage 2. During Stage 3, they encounter resistance from other quarters. A backlash arises against perceived excesses in their demands. The general argument of opponents is that the pendulum is swinging too far in the other direction; that people are uncritically embracing a point of view that is too extreme, unbalanced, and one-sided; and that special

interests are trying to advance an agenda that does not really benefit the law-abiding majority.

Spokespersons for a group of recently rediscovered victims might come under fire for a number of reasons. They might be criticized for overestimating the number of people harmed when the actual threat to the public, according to the opposition, is much smaller. Advocates might be condemned for portraying all those who were hurt as totally innocent of blame—and therefore deserving of unqualified support—when in reality some are partly at fault and shouldn't get all the assistance that they demand. Activists might be castigated for making unreasonable demands that will cost the government (and taxpayers) too much money. They also might be denounced for insisting upon new policies that would undermine cherished constitutional rights, such as the presumption of innocence of persons accused of breaking the law. For example, allegations about child abuse or elder abuse can lead to investigations that permanently stigmatize the alleged wrongdoers even if the charges later turn out to be unfounded (see Crystal, 1988).

When the antirape movement claimed to have discovered an outbreak of date rapes against college students, skeptics asked why federally mandated statistics about incidents reported to campus security forces showed no such upsurge. They contended that hard-to-classify liaisons were being redefined as full-fledged sexual assaults, thereby maligning some admittedly sexually aggressive and exploitative college men as hard-core criminals (see Gilbert, 1991; Hellman, 1993; and MacDonald, 2008a). When the battered women's movement organized a clemency drive to free certain imprisoned wives who had slain their abusive husbands (in self-defense, they contended, but prosecutors and jurors disagreed), critics charged that these abused women would be getting away with revenge killings. When adults who believed that they had endured incest insisted that new memory retrieval techniques were helping them recall repressed recollections of sexual molestations by parents, stepparents, and other guardians, some accused family members banded together and insisted they were being unfairly slandered because of a therapist-induced **false memory syndrome** (see Chapters 8, 9, and 10 for an in-depth analysis of these three controversies).

Even the many accomplishments of the entire victims' movement can be questioned (see Weed, 1995). Under the banner of advancing victims' rights, pressure groups might advocate policies that undermine whatever progress has been made toward securing humane treatment for offenders and reentry opportunities for ex-prisoners. Victim activism can unnecessarily heighten fear and anxiety levels about the dangers of violence and theft and divert funds toward repressive measures and away from social programs designed to tackle the root causes of street crime.

Groups that focus their energies on the plight of individuals injured by interpersonal violence also can distract attention from other socially harmful activities such as polluting the environment or marketing unsafe products, and their reforms can raise expectations about full recovery that just cannot be reasonably met (Fattah, 1986). It is even possible that what was formerly a grassroots movement run by volunteers who solicited donations has metamorphosed into a virtual "victim industry." It engages in a type of mass production, churning out newly identified groups of victims by dwelling on kinds of suffering that can arise from noncriminal sources such as bullying, emotional abuse, sexual harassment, sexual addiction, eating disorders, and credit card dependency (see Best, 1997).

Stage 4: Research and Temporary Resolution of Disputes

It is during the fourth and last stage of the rediscovery process that victimologists can make their most valuable contributions. By getting to the bottom of unsolved mysteries and by intervening in bitter conflicts, researchers can become a source of accurate assessments, by helping to evaluate competing claims about whether the problem has or has not been brought under control, and by determining whether treatment and prevention measures are genuinely effective. By maintaining objectivity,

victimologists can serve as arbiters in these heated disputes.

For example, during the 1980s, a series of shocking shootings by disgruntled gun-toting employees led to the rediscovery of victims of workplace violence. In the aftermath of these slaughters, worried employees insisted that employers call in occupational safety specialists to devise protection and prevention programs. Anxious managers usually acceded, fearing expensive lawsuits and lowered morale and productivity. But researchers have determined that these highly publicized multiple murders accounted for just a tiny fraction of a multifaceted but far less newsworthy set of dangers. Most of the cases of workplace violence across the country involve robberies, unarmed assaults, and complaints about stalkers acting in a menacing way. Many incidents that disrupt the smooth functioning of factories and offices are not even criminal matters, such as instances of verbal abuse, bullying, and sexual harassment (Rugala, 2004).

During Stage 4, a standoff, deadlock, or truce might develop between victims' advocates who want more changes, and their opponents who resist any further reforms. But the fourth phase is not necessarily the final phase. The findings and policy recommendations of neutral parties such as victimologists and criminologists do not settle questions once and for all. Concerns about some type of victimization can recede from public consciousness for years, only to reappear when social conditions are ripe for a new four-stage cycle of rediscovery of (1) claims making, (2) reform, (3) opposition, and (4) temporary resolution.

A number of types of formerly overlooked victims have reached Stage 4 in the rediscovery process. Recently collected data can be analyzed to try to put the public's fears into perspective, to attempt to resolve ongoing controversies, and to assess the impact of countermeasures designed to assist those who are suffering and to prevent others from sharing their same fate (an example that stirs up strong emotions in a great many people, trafficking in human beings, appears in Box 2.3).

BOX 2.3   An Illustration of the Four Stages in the Rediscovery Process: The Plight of Victims of Human Trafficking

Stage One: Reviving Public Outrage About a Longstanding Problem:

Trafficking in human beings is widely recognized as a lucrative racket and a major aspect of the crime problem in a great many source, transit, and destination countries across the globe. But it is not a new development: Its victims were first discovered over 100 years ago. (The slave trade that brought Africans in chains to the Americas during the age of European colonialism is a different problem that goes back further in history, and its horrors transcend the confines of crime and victimization.)

During the early years of the twentieth century, a worldwide movement against "white slavery" arose. Its stated goal was to stop prostitutes from Europe from being sent to brothels throughout the colonial empires of the Western powers. The sexual enslavement of white females eventually proved to be what social scientists call a moral panic because the problem turned out to be far smaller and less significant than was popularly depicted. And yet, the campaign to stop it led to a series of treaties, including the International Agreement for the Suppression of the White Slave Traffic (1904), the League of Nation's International Convention for the Suppression of Traffic in Women and Children (1921) and its Convention for the Suppression of Traffic in Women of Full Age (1933), and the United Nation's Convention for the Suppression of the Traffic in Persons and the Exploitation of the Prostitution of Others (1949) (Lobasz, 2009).

Compelling girls and women to take part in the sex trade is only part of this problem. The other part is the economic exploitation of migrant workers who are smuggled across borders to toil in homes, factories, and fields. Starting in the late 1980s, reformers began to call attention to their plight. A number of factors came together to heighten concern and provoke outrage: a new focus by human rights groups on the many ways females are exploited around the world; the growing desperation in many societies of single mothers to find ways to support their children (what sociologists call the feminization of poverty); the collapse of the Soviet Union and its Eastern European satellites, which caused many young women to search for a means of survival abroad; environmental degradation due to the mismanagement of natural resources that triggered large-scale migrations across national borders of workers seeking opportunities in a rapidly globalizing economy; and the consolidation of organized crime's hold over the smuggling of weapons, drugs, and people (Jahic and Finckenauer, 2005; Lobasz, 2009; Chuang, 2010; and Smilowitz, 2014).

When prominent people began to characterize human trafficking as "a form of modern-day slavery" and warn that profiting from the "controlled service" of others was one of the fastest growing criminal industries in the world, a social movement developed to oppose it. It brought together international organizations, human rights groups, religious leaders, charitable organizations, political figures, criminal justice officials, social workers, victim advocates, and thousands of well-intentioned grassroots "abolitionists" motivated by stirring phrases like "free the slaves" and "break the chains of bondage." Two rather unlikely allies joined together to campaign for stronger laws against sex trafficking. The first were certain American feminists who viewed prostitution as an entrenched institution of male dominance and its female providers as subordinates compelled to sell their bodies because of a lack of meaningful economic alternatives. The second political force was a coalition of conservative evangelical Christians, whose concerns about men who take advantage of "fallen women" stemmed from matters of conscience and strongly held beliefs about purity, innocence, virtue, sin, evil, and immorality. Their religiously motivated crusade centered on preserving traditional marriages and families rather than on liberating women from subordination to patriarchal control by opening up better opportunities that would enable them to become financially independent (see Chuang, 2010; and Bernstein, 2010).

The rediscovery process moved forward quickly after prominent figures spoke out.

President Clinton (2000) announced "...anti-trafficking provisions represent a major step forward in my Administration's ongoing effort to eradicate modern-day slavery. In 1998, I issued an Executive Memorandum directing my Administration to combat this insidious human rights abuse through a three-part strategy of prosecuting traffickers, protecting and assisting trafficking victims, and preventing trafficking.... Over the past several years, we have taken every opportunity to shine a bright light on this dark corner of the criminal underworld, in part by continually raising with leaders around the world the need to work together to combat this intolerable and reprehensible practice...."

President Bush (2003) intoned, "It takes a special kind of depravity to exploit and hurt the most vulnerable members of society. Human traffickers rob children of their innocence, they expose them to the worst of life before they have seen much of life. Traffickers tear families apart. They treat their victims as nothing more than goods and commodities for sale to the highest bidder.... Many victims are beaten. Some are killed. Others die spiritual and emotional deaths, convinced after years of abuse that their lives have no worth. This trade in human beings brings suffering to the innocent and shame to our country, and we will lead the fight against it."

President Obama advanced similar arguments. He echoed the views of previous chief executives that human trafficking should be called by its real name, "modern slavery" and that the focus of strategies to combat this crime should continue at home, not just abroad. He declared, "The bitter truth is that trafficking also goes on right here. It's the migrant worker unable to pay off the debt to his trafficker.... The teenage girl—beaten, forced to walk the streets. This should not be happening in the United States of America" (Flock, 2012).

The discovery that sex trafficking wasn't only a problem in distant lands but that it was cropping up here too added a sense of urgency that spurred people to action. As President Bush (2004) put it, "It is estimated that between 14,500 and 17,500 victims of trafficking cross our borders every year. U.S. law enforcement has documented cases of Latvian girls trafficked into sexual slavery in Chicago, or Ukrainian girls trafficked in Los Angeles, and Maryland, or Thai, Korean, Malaysian and Vietnamese girls trafficked in Georgia, or Mexican girls trafficked in California, New Jersey and here in Florida. Many of the victims are teenagers, some as young as 12 years old."

In order to gain the greatest amount of support for the campaign, advocates socially constructed a "perfect victim" who did not voluntarily choose to leave her family and to sell her body. They promoted the image of an innocent young girl who was kidnapped from her remote village and then drugged, beaten, and broken in spirit until she was obedient and submissive; passed around and then sold into slavery; and later transported from her poverty-stricken source country through some transit country until she wound up as a virtual prisoner in a cruelly run brothel in some strange, far-off destination country. This socially constructed perfect victim—young, female, helpless, yearning to be rescued, protected, assisted, and given sanctuary—captured the public's imagination. But what about those who did not fit this sympathy-evoking stereotype of the perfect victim? Women who were willing to be smuggled across borders and agreed to be "sex workers" in foreign settings, but did not foresee that they would be intimidated, stripped of their false identity papers, and strictly controlled, do not evoke the same degree of compassion from the public, police officers, prosecutors, judges, and immigration officials. Indifference can easily turn to outright hostility toward these "illegal aliens" who chose and consented to "prostitute themselves." Somewhere in between are those naïve young women who were procured by

organized crime recruiters via employment scams: false promises of decent-paying legitimate jobs in domestic settings as maids or nannies, or in modeling, or even as dancers in strip clubs. Instead, after overstaying their visa limits or entering the country with counterfeit documents that were later confiscated by the trafficker, they wound up as exploited undocumented workers, forced to submit to the demands of pimps, brothel managers, and customers in the commercial sex trade in order to pay off their border-crossing debts and to protect their families abroad from retaliation by the trafficker's syndicate (Rieger, 2007; Lobasz, 2009; and Uy, 2011).

The United Nations declared its first "World Day against Trafficking in Persons" on July 30, 2014. Its Protocol to Prevent, Suppress and Punish Trafficking in Persons defined human trafficking as "the recruitment, transportation, transfer, harboring, or receipt of persons, by means of the threat or use of force or other forms of coercion, of abduction, of fraud, of deception, of the abuse of power or of a position of vulnerability or of the giving or receiving of payments or benefits to achieve the consent of a person having control over another person, for the purpose of exploitation." Banned activities included "the exploitation of the prostitution of others or other forms of sexual exploitation, forced labor or services, slavery or practices similar to slavery, servitude, or the removal of organs" (Smilowitz, 2014).

In the United States, the definition of sex trafficking has broadened substantially over the years. Physical transport across international borders no longer was an essential part of the definition; crossing state boundaries within the United States became a sufficient trigger for federal prosecution (U.S. Department of State, 2007). Later expansions of the definition even dropped the requirement of movement across state lines and simply focused on the use of force, coercion, or fraud to keep someone trapped in a condition of servitude (Farrell, McDevitt, and Fahey, 2010). The working definition of sex trafficking used by local law enforcement agencies often boils down to a simple formulation: adult prostitution that involves coercion and any sexual exploitation of children (Gonzalez, 2013).

Because the definition has evolved so dramatically, activists currently work to raise awareness by dispelling the following myths and misconceptions: Trafficking does not necessarily involve smuggling or forced movement, transportation, or border-crossing; physical force, physical abuse, or physical restraint does not have to take place; victims are not only foreign nationals or immigrants but can be males as well as females, adults as well as minors, and even well educated

(Continued)

B O X 2.3 (Continued)

and affluent persons, not just poorly educated, poverty-stricken people; and the offense of trafficking can occur even if the victim consents and receives payment. However, certain populations remain especially vulnerable: undocumented immigrants; refugees and asylum seekers; runaways and homeless youth; members of groups that have been oppressed, marginalized, and impoverished; and individuals who have been severely abused and traumatized. Trafficked persons were mostly mired in the sex trade (brothels, escort services, massage parlors, street prostitution, and even strip clubs), or they were stuck performing backbreaking labor, like planting and picking crops or landscaping and construction, or menial jobs, especially in the hotel and hospitality industry; janitorial services; home, health, and elder care; and factories and sweatshops (Polaris Project, 2012). For example, a woman from another country who is hired as a nanny to tend to a child around the clock without any time off, is provided with sparse meals and cramped quarters, and then is threatened with exposure and deportation (because she has overstayed her visa) if she complains about her predicament can be considered trafficked. Similarly, an undocumented day laborer who picks up occasional construction jobs but then is cheated out of his wages and intimidated from protesting because the employer warns him about a call to the immigration authorities is also being coercively exploited (Grant, 2013). As the original definition broadened to encompass so many more people and such a wide variety of situations, the number of persons designated as victims and the number of programs designed to assist them grew dramatically.

A search of journalism databases revealed that media coverage of the problem grew exponentially from a mere handful of articles at the start of the 1990s to about 3,750 in 2008 alone (Farrell et al., 2010).

Stage Two: Passing Legislation and Setting Up Assistance Programs

Raids against transnational trafficking rings, statements by world leaders, international conferences, and articles as well as popular movies depicting sexual slavery heightened pressures to "do something." In response, the Clinton administration drafted a comprehensive approach that embodied the prosecution of profiteers, protections for trafficked persons, and prevention measures. In 1994, the U.S. Department of State declared trafficking across borders to be a severe violation of human rights and began to issue an annual "Trafficking in Persons Report" that monitored what other countries were doing to try to bring the problem under control. The State Department's Office to Monitor and Combat Trafficking in Persons originally focused on the sexual exploitation of women and girls smuggled by international rings feeding the demand for prostitutes but broadened its scope to include forced labor. Foreign nationals who assist investigations and prosecutions are eligible for the designation

"qualified victims," and they might be granted "continued presence" and immigration relief (from deportation), which can lead to permission to work in legitimate jobs, legal residency, and eventual citizenship. Federally funded services (provided through contracts with NGOs) include medical, dental, and mental health care; sustenance and shelter; help with translation and interpretation; legal assistance; and transportation (Jahic and Finckenauer, 2005; Lobasz, 2009; Chuang, 2010; and U.S. Department of State, 2011). However, to be eligible for these forms of support, plus possibly restitution and a visa, the U.S. Department of Health and Human Services must certify that the person meets the hard to prove standards of a "severe trafficking victim" (George, 2012).

In 2000, an international agreement went into effect: the United Nations Protocol to Prevent, Suppress and Punish Trafficking in Persons, Especially Women and Children. That same year, Congress passed the Trafficking Victims Protection Act (TVPA). Both laws defined trafficking as the recruitment and movement of children, women, and men for the purpose of subjecting these victims to involuntary servitude in labor-intensive activities. The TVPA was reauthorized and strengthened in 2003, 2005, 2008, and 2013. The 2013 reauthorization strengthened efforts to ban child marriage and to prevent the purchase of products made by labor trafficking victims. The National Defense Authorization Act of 2013 enables government agencies to terminate any contracts with organizations and individuals that engage in or support trafficking (Polaris Project, 2014a; 2014b).

An Anti-Trafficking in Persons Division was set up in the Office of Refugee Resettlement that is part of the U.S. Department of Health and Human Services. It funds the National Human Trafficking Resource Center (NHTRC), which staffs a hotline and tipline.

The U.S. Department of Justice runs a Bureau of Justice Assistance (BJA) and an Office for Victims of Crime (OVC). The BJA in cooperation with the OVC has funded 42 Anti-Human Trafficking Task Forces across the country, which pair law enforcement agencies with service providers in order to offer effective first responses to exploited persons. The Immigration and Customs Enforcement Division of the Department of Homeland Security runs a Human Smuggling and Trafficking Unit that seeks to locate individuals brought in from other countries. A Human Smuggling and Trafficking Center is a collaborative effort that involves the Department of State, Department of Justice, Department of Homeland Security, and the Office of the Director of National Intelligence that functions as a repository of information about these illegal activities (Polaris Project, 2014a).

Besides the Department of Health and Human Services, the State Department, the Department of Homeland Security, and the Department of Justice, at least 15 international organizations participate in the global struggle to suppress human trafficking, including the United Nations, the International Labor Organization, the Organization of American States, the Association of Southeast Nations, and the World Bank (Lobasz, 2009).

On the home front, all 50 states and the District of Columbia have passed legislation to combat sex and labor trafficking. However, most states still lack adequate laws to support and assist persons who have escaped, and 12 states had failed by 2014 to make even minimal efforts to pass such legislation, according to a rigorous rating system. The FBI's efforts to disrupt human trafficking draw upon its Civil Rights Unit (CRU) and the Violent Crimes Against Children Section (VCACS). The CRU investigates forced labor; sex trafficking of adults by force, fraud, or coercion; and the sexual exploitation of foreign minors, while the VCACS focuses on the commercial exploitation of Americans under the age of 18 who have been drawn into the sex trade. The FBI has established close to 70 Child Exploitation Task Forces that operate around the country, in which its agents work in tandem with victim specialists from its Office for Victim Assistance, as well as state and local law enforcement agencies. The Bureau announced in 2014 that a nationwide crackdown on the sex trafficking of underage persons, part of its Innocence Lost initiative, swept up about 280 pimps and similar exploiters and led to the rescuing of nearly 170 minors from their control. Since its creation in 2003, the Innocence Lost sting operations have resulted in the identification and recovery of approximately 3,600 sexually exploited minors (FBI, 2014a).

Activists have identified the immediate needs of persons extracted from the clutches of traffickers that ought to be provided by local law enforcement and social welfare agencies: temporary housing, assistance to relocate to another area, transportation on a daily basis, legal advice, and of course physical protection. Ideally, a trained counselor should be assigned to the rescued person's case within a few hours (Gonzalez, 2013). Advocacy groups are developing and then recommending various "best practices" that fit within a victim-centered approach to prevent the smuggling and sale of human beings across national boundaries, to safeguard these rescued individuals from further harm, and to repatriate them to their country of origin or else reintegrate them into the destination society, at first with legal immigrant status and eventually with citizenship rights.

Stage Three: Challenges Arise and Opposition Emerges

No one approves of or defends involuntary servitude and sexual violence, but the crusade against human trafficking has provoked some opposition among thoughtful people and concerned groups for a number of reasons.

First of all, some activists share the moral outrage of the crusaders but feel that the widespread use of the

shocking phrase *modern-day slavery* is overly dramatic and an historically inaccurate equation of contemporary forms of servitude with the horrific institutionalized barbarism of the transatlantic slave trade that for several centuries relentlessly brought fresh supplies of captive Africans to the new world as chattel to be bought, sold, and worked to near death (similarly, the very serious terms *lynching*, *genocide*, and *holocaust* can be inappropriately applied to lesser crimes).

Other critics are dismayed that this reform movement has become drawn into a divisive and intractable debate over the "oldest profession": whether the sale of sexual favors is inherently coercive, invariably embodies female subordination, and must be driven out of business by punishing profiteers, pimps, the women themselves, and their customers. Some argued that becoming a sex worker as an adult can be a voluntary and rational choice, and that these employees or independent contractors deserve economic rights, medical care, and basic legal protections rather than further stigmatization and permanent criminal records that just drive their forbidden exchanges of erotic acts for money deeper underground where they become even more dangerous (see Grant, 2013). In 2003, the Bush administration reaffirmed its opposition to pimping, pandering, and maintaining brothels as inherently harmful and dehumanizing and as furnishing an incentive for the international sex trade in females. This stance prohibited any nongovernmental service organizations that receive federal funding to help victims from supporting any toleration of prostitution as a solution to the trafficking problem. As a result, advocacy groups have become embroiled in a debate over prostitution, instead of focusing their energies on devising improved services for individuals who feel trapped (see DeStefano, 2007; Chuang, 2010; Cavalieri, 2011; and Uy, 2011). Some defense attorneys representing indigents estimate that many, but not all, of their clients arrested on prostitution charges are, in fact, trafficked according to the current broadened definition, and many more have survived an extensive amount of brutality and trauma. But they ask why hyperbolic rhetoric that conflates prostitution with slavery usually leads to crackdowns in which the ostensible victims who are supposed to be rescued by raids instead are prosecuted, resulting in their facing jail time, possible deportation, warrants for failure to appear in court, and rap sheets that undermine their efforts to find jobs and housing in order to leave "the life" (Mugulescu, 2014).

Many concerned activists and advocacy groups feel that the media's preoccupation with lurid stories about sex trafficking causes lawmakers and law enforcement agencies to lose sight of the more pervasive forms of people smuggling for the purposes of taking terrible advantage of them as migrant

(Continued)

B O X 2.3   (Continued)

laborers as they toil in the fields, factories, and private homes of their exploitive employers (see Chuang, 2010; and Uy, 2011).

Similarly, an emphasis on the criminal justice approach to trafficking as a threat to border security (especially in a post-9/11 world) and as a way of smashing transnational organized syndicates draws substantial amounts of very limited resources toward "crime-fighting" and away from efforts to protect and address the needs of victims (see Lobasz, 2009; Chuang, 2010; and Uy, 2011).

Finally, some skeptics suspect that the true magnitude of the problem has been exaggerated by campaigners who disseminate shocking overestimates in order to arouse an otherwise jaded public (see Grant, 2013). They point out that the actual number of cases, successful prosecutions, and verified victims are tiny fractions of these large, widely circulated figures. For example, between 2000 and early 2007, federal agencies had certified only 1,175 people from 77 countries as victims of human trafficking (U.S. Department of State, 2007). During 2009, the State Department issued only about 600 T visas and Continuing Presence orders to cooperating victims (U.S. Department of State, 2011). Yet a CIA report in 2000 estimated that up to 50,000 women and children are trafficked into the United States each year for the sex trade (see Rieger, 2007). Other estimates came in lower; the yearly figure cited above by President Bush was about one-third the size of the CIA estimate but still way beyond the tiny number of rescued persons. On New York's Long Island, an area reputed to be a hotbed of trafficking, not one arrest was made during 2005, and only one woman was rescued from prostitution (Mead, 2006). As for the importation of teenage girls from abroad and from other parts of the United States to the streets of New York City for the purposes of prostitution, a federally funded ethnographic study of underage sex workers found very few that could be considered "trafficked." The estimates derived from the field interviews were surprising: Nearly half were boys; almost half were recruited into the sex trade by friends; only 1 in 10 were involved with pimps; over 9 in 10 were born in the United States; and more than half were native New Yorkers (see Curtis et al., 2008; and Hinman, 2011).

Several explanations attempt to account for this discrepancy between rough estimates and actual statistics. One is that the low numbers indicate that the U.S. government has not allocated sufficient resources to thoroughly train law enforcement officers and to fund extensive investigations into this problem and extract people from the clutches of traffickers and exploiters. A variation on this theme is that there is insufficient cooperation and coordination between the agencies tasked by the TVPA enforcement provisions with bringing this problem under control. But others suspect that the low numbers of substantiated cases reveal that political figures and advocacy groups may have greatly overestimated the prevalence of trafficking into (as well as within) the United States (see Farrell et al., 2010).

Stage Four: Research Findings Temporarily Resolve Disputes

The true intensity of the problem remains unknown since trafficking often goes undetected and unreported due to its covert nature, the reluctance of victims who feel vulnerable and fear reprisals to turn to the authorities for help, misconceptions about its definition, and a lack of awareness about it in some localities (Polaris Project, 2014b).

The first set of reasonably accurate statistics about the profiles of victims in human trafficking cases was derived from those federal task forces that collected "high-quality" data about their investigations during the period of 2008–2010. A little over 525 confirmed victims were located in about 390 cases. Most of the investigations concerned sex trafficking rather than labor trafficking. In the sex trafficking cases, the overwhelming proportion of victims were female (94 percent). Also, the vast majority were younger than 25 years old (87 percent) and U.S. citizens (83 percent). As for the victims' race and ethnicity, more were black (40 percent) and white (26 percent) than Hispanic or Asian. In the labor trafficking cases, most of the victims were over 24 years of age (62 percent), and more were males (32 percent), Hispanics (63 percent), and Asians (17 percent). None were U.S. citizens (Banks and Kyckkelhahn, 2011).

A portrait of the problem was drawn from nearly 1,500 individuals who considered themselves to be caught up in sex and labor trafficking and who directly contacted a hotline for victims during the five-year period from 2007 to 2012. The most common complaints about sex trafficking involved prostitutes controlled by pimps. The majority of these pimps recruited these young women in social settings by feigning romantic interest, by promising them that they would earn enough to enjoy the material comforts they longed for, and by discouraging them from having casual sex "for free." Then they pressured them to perform sex acts at hotels, motels, truck stops, brothels, and streets for customers solicited through online advertisements. Most of the complaints about labor trafficking came from women from foreign nations stuck doing domestic work in the Northeast as well as in southern Florida and southern California, and from migrant farm workers. Minors were more likely to be exploited sexually than through unpaid labor. Callers reported that they most often became trapped because of lies, false promises, and debts (Polaris Project, 2013).

Victimologists want to discover why many individuals caught up in these oppressive situations do not run to the authorities for help. In other words, what can be done to increase the reporting rate? Exactly how do the traffickers lure or deceive their targets (presumably through false promises of a better life and ploys about legitimate jobs); how do they recruit children (perhaps by capitalizing on their innocence and naïveté, sometimes with parental complicity); and how do they dominate and intimidate those who find themselves trapped into involuntary servitude, even when chances to escape their predicament repeatedly arise? Are victims immobilized because their exploiters confiscate all their documents, take advantage of language barriers, threaten reprisals against loved ones at home in the source country, and scare them about deportation if they dare seek help? Perhaps some individuals who enter the country improperly and toil mightily don't perceive themselves to be trafficking victims—they don't realize that exploitive relationships that might be acceptable back home may fall under the heading of trafficking here. Whether these explanations are sufficient, relevant, and comprehensive needs to be further researched by directly interviewing victims who have been extracted, perhaps unwillingly, from their perilous lifestyles (see George, 2003; Landesman, 2004; Bureau of Public Affairs, 2005; Glaberson, 2005; Saunders, 2005; Rieger, 2007; Uy, 2011; and Dank, 2014).

The murder of several border crossers in Arizona by smugglers (called "coyotes") holding them hostage in frustrated attempts to extort more money from their families back home indicated the depth of the perils victims face (Fulginiti, 2008). A surge of unaccompanied minors from Central America across the nation's southern border during 2014 raised the specter of homeless youth ripe for sexual exploitation (Hulse, 2014). Furthermore, studies based on surveys completed by municipal and county police departments have concluded that most of these law enforcement agencies lacked sufficient policies and adequate training to accurately identify trafficking victims and successfully investigate their cases (Wilson, Walsh, and Kleuber, 2006; Farrell et al., 2010; and George, 2012).

The FBI and the U.S. Department of Homeland Security have compiled lists of behaviors and situations to help investigators from the U.S. Department of Labor, the U.S. Equal Employment Opportunity Commission, the Immigration and Naturalization Service, and state and local law enforcement and child protection agencies, to better recognize trafficking victims if they encounter them in their daily duties. Officers and concerned members of the general public should be on the lookout for the potential signs of being trafficked for the purpose of exploitation in the sex trade or for debt peonage. These clues appear in Table 2.1.

Whether the problem is growing or subsiding and whether specific government assistance and rescue efforts are effective remain subjects of controversy that require additional research. This is why the plight of trafficking victims within the United States can be considered to have arrived at Stage 4 of the rediscovery process.

TABLE 2.1   Possible Indicators That a Person Is a Trafficking Victim

Does the individual ...?

- Live on or very close to the work premises
- Bunk in a sparse place with many other occupants
- Lack personal space and possessions
- Frequently move from one work site to another
- Appear unfamiliar with how to get around the neighborhood
- Seem unable to travel around freely
- Admit that he/she cannot socialize with outsiders and attend religious services
- Disclose that he/she was recruited for one line of work but then was compelled to perform other tasks
- Confide that earnings are garnished and held by someone else
- Indicate that identification and travel documents are held by someone else
- Appear to have been coached about what to say to immigration and police officers
- Seem unable to talk openly and to communicate freely with family and friends
- Look injured from beatings or show signs of malnourishment or lack of medical treatment
- Defer to someone else who insists on speaking or interpreting for him/her
- Claim to be represented by the same attorney that handles the cases of many other undocumented workers (illegal aliens)

SOURCES: Blue Campaign, 2010; Walker-Rodriguez and Hill, 2011.

SUMMARY

Laws that recognized that individuals harmed by offenders deserved governmental support and economic aid were passed centuries ago, but until the middle of the twentieth century, the plight of crime victims was largely overlooked, even by most criminologists.

Today, the plight of victims is being brought to the public's attention by journalists covering the crime beat, social movements mobilizing in behalf of certain individuals and groups who embody their causes and agendas, elected officials seeking voters' support, and commercial interests advertising products and services to guard against victimization.

The rediscovery process goes through four stages. After a group's plight becomes known and reforms are implemented, an opposition frequently arises that resists further changes that might be to the group's advantage. When conflicts arise, victimologists can help resolve them by studying how seriously these newly rediscovered groups actually suffer, if their numbers are really growing or declining, and whether reform measures and efforts designed to assist them are genuinely working as intended.

KEY TERMS DEFINED IN THE GLOSSARY

bias crimes, 43

Brady Bill, 45

children's rights groups, 44

civil court, 40

civil liberties movement, 44

civil rights movement, 42

claims-making, 55

elder abuse, 44

English common law, 40

false memory syndrome, 57

law-and-order movement, 42

Megan's Law, 46

plea negotiation, 41

public prosecutors, 40

self-help movement, 44

sensationalism, 47

street crimes, 40

tort law, 40

trafficking in human beings, 58

women's movement, 42

QUESTIONS FOR DISCUSSION AND DEBATE

1. Identify some of the most important milestones in the history of academic victimology.

2. Highlight some of the first breakthroughs in victim assistance.

3. Summarize what happens at each stage of the rediscovery process.

4. Explain how the campaign to rescue victims of human trafficking has sparked some controversies.

CRITICAL THINKING QUESTIONS

1. Identify a group of victims of some specific illegal activity who still has not been rediscovered and was not mentioned in this chapter. Describe the kinds of harm this group might be experiencing.

2. Argue that the rediscovery of victims by the news media, elected officials, and commercial enterprises is a "mixed blessing" by stressing the downside: the potential for exploiting their plight for some ulterior purpose such as personal gain or profiting from their suffering.

SUGGESTED RESEARCH PROJECTS

1. Find out about some recently proposed or passed laws in your state that have been named in honor of crime victims. In each case, ask whether this legislation offers anything specific—other than ratcheted-up punishment of the offender—to ease the victim's plight.

2. Choose a group from the list in Box 2.2 whose plight is currently being rediscovered. Pose questions that researchers ought to examine. Find out about the composition of this group, the nature of its losses, and the efforts now underway to ease its suffering.

3. Choose several groups whose plight is now well known, such as physically abused children, kidnapped children, battered women, abused elders, or carjacked motorists. Find out about how their plight was first rediscovered by looking up the oldest or earliest articles that appear in a comprehensive database of newspaper, magazine, and journal articles.

3

Victimization in the United States: An Overview

LEARNING OBJECTIVES

To appreciate how statistics can be used to answer important questions.

To become aware of the ways statistics can be used to persuade and mislead.

To find out what information about crime victims is collected routinely by the federal government's Department of Justice.

To become familiar with the ways that victimologists use this data to estimate how many people were harmed by criminal activities and what injuries and losses they suffered.

continued

LEARNING OBJECTIVES

continued

To explore the kinds of information about victims that can be found in the Federal Bureau of Investigation's annual *Uniform Crime Report.*

To learn how the FBI's *National Incident-Based Reporting System* is extracting more information drawn from police files about victims.

To appreciate the strengths and weaknesses of this source of official statistics.

To discover what data about victims and their plight can be found in the federal government's alternative source of information, the Bureau of Justice Statistics' *National Crime Victimization Survey.*

To recognize the strengths and weaknesses of this alternative source of government statistics.

To assemble official statistics to spot trends, and especially whether the problem of criminal victimization has been intensifying or diminishing over recent decades.

To develop a feel for historical trends in the level of violence in the United States.

To be able to weigh the threat of crime against other perils by understanding comparative risks.

VICTIMIZATION ACROSS THE NATION: THE BIG PICTURE

Victimologists gather and interpret data to answer crucial questions such as: How many people are harmed by criminals each year? Is victimization becoming more of a problem or is it subsiding as time goes by? And which groups are targeted the most and the least often? Researchers want to find out where and when the majority of incidents occur, whether predators on the prowl intimidate and subjugate their prey with their bare hands or use weapons, and if so, what kinds? It is also important to determine whether individuals are attacked by complete strangers or people they know, and how these intended targets act when confronted by assailants. What proportion try to escape or fight back, how many are injured, what percentage

need to be hospitalized, and how much money do they typically lose in an incident?

The answers to specific questions like these yield statistical portraits of crime victims, the patterns that persist over the years, and the trends that unfold as time passes; when taken together, they constitute what can be termed the **big picture** —an overview of what is really happening across the entire United States during the twenty-first century. The big picture serves as an antidote to impressions based on direct but limited personal experiences, as well as self-serving reports circulated by organizations with vested interests, misleading media images, crude stereotypes, and widely held myths. But putting together the big picture is not easy. Compiling an accurate portrayal requires careful planning, formulation of the right questions, proper data collection techniques, and insightful analyses.

The big picture is constructed by making systematic observations and accurate measurements on the local level. Then, these village, city, and county reports must be aggregated so victimologists and criminologists are able to characterize the situation in an entire state, region of the country, and ultimately the nation as a whole. (Sociologists would call this process as going from an up-close and personal micro level up to a more institutional and systemwide macro level of analysis.) An alternative path to follow is to assemble a randomly selected nationwide sample and then ask those people to share their experiences about what offenders did to them during the past year. If the sample is representative and large enough, then the findings from this survey can be generalized to project estimates about what is happening in the country as a whole. Once the big picture is assembled, it becomes possible to make comparisons between the situation in the United States and other postindustrial societies around the world. The similarities are increasing and cultural differences are diminishing as globalization is fostering a modern way of life, which involves seeking higher education, commuting over congested highways to work, shopping in malls, watching cable TV programming, using the Internet, and calling the police on smartphones for help, that has spread to even the most remote regions of the planet.

Until the 1970s, few efforts were made to routinely monitor and systematically measure various indicators of the plight of the nation's victims. By the 1980s, a great many social scientists and agencies were conducting the research needed to bring the big picture into focus. Also, all sorts of special-interest groups began keeping count and disseminating their own estimates about the suffering of a wide variety of victims, including youngsters wounded at school, college students hurt or killed on campus, children reported missing by their parents, and people singled out by assailants who hate their "kind."

The statistics presented in this chapter come from official sources and shed light on the big picture concerning "street crimes" involving interpersonal violence and theft.

Making Sense of Statistics

Statistics are meaningful numbers that reveal important information. Statistics are of crucial importance to social scientists, policy analysts, and decision makers because they replace vague adjectives such as "many," "most," and "few" with precise numbers.

Both victimologists and criminologists gather their own data to make their own calculations, or they scrutinize **official statistics**, which are compiled and published by government agencies. Why do they pore over these numbers? By collecting, computing, and analyzing statistics, researchers can answer intriguing questions. Accurate and credible statistics about crimes and victims are vital because they can shed light on these important matters:

- Statistics can be calculated to estimate **victimization rates**, which are realistic assessments of threat levels that criminal activities pose to particular individuals and groups. What are the odds various categories of people face of getting robbed or even murdered during a certain time period? Counts (such as death tolls) answer the question "How many?" Better yet, rates (number of persons who get robbed out of every 100,000 people in a year)

can provide relative estimates about these disturbing questions.

- Statistics can expose **patterns** of criminal activity. Patterns reflect predictable relationships or regular occurrences that show up during an analysis of the data year after year. For instance, a search for patterns could answer these questions: Is it true that murders generally occur at a higher rate in urban neighborhoods than in suburban and rural areas? Are robberies committed more often against men than women, or vice versa?

- Statistical **trends** can demonstrate how situations have changed over the years. Is the burden of victimization intensifying or subsiding as time goes by? Are the dangers of getting killed by robbers increasing or decreasing?

- Statistics can provide estimates of the costs and losses imposed by illegal behavior. Estimates based on accurate records can be important for commercial purposes. For example, insurance companies can determine what premiums to charge their customers this year based on actuarial calculations of the typical financial expenses suffered by policyholders who were hospitalized last year after being wounded by robbers.

- Statistics can be used for planning purposes to project a rough or "ballpark figure" of next year's workload. Law enforcement agencies, service providers, and insurance companies can anticipate the approximate size of their caseloads for the following year if they know how many people were harmed the previous year.

- Statistics also can be computed to evaluate the effectiveness of criminal justice policies and to assess the impact of prevention strategies. Are battered women likely to lead safer lives after their violent mates are arrested, or will they be in greater danger? Do gun buyback programs actually save lives or is their impact on the local murder rate negligible?

- Finally, statistical **profiles** can be assembled to yield an impression of what is usual or typical about victims in terms of their characteristics such as sex, age, and race/ethnicity. For example, is the widely held belief accurate that most of the people who die violently are young men from troubled families living in poverty-stricken, big-city neighborhoods? Portraits based on data can also provide a reality check to help ground theories that purport to explain why some groups experience higher rates of predation than others. For example, if it turns out that the frail elderly are robbed far less often than teenagers, then any theory that emphasizes only the physical vulnerability of robbers' targets will be totally off-base or at best incomplete as an explanation of which groups suffer the most, and why.

However, statistics might not only be used, they can also be abused. Statistics never speak for themselves. Sometimes, statistics can be circulated to mislead or deceive. The same numbers can be interpreted quite differently, depending on what **spin** commentators give them—what is stressed and what is downplayed. Cynics joke that statistics can be used by a special-interest group just like a lamppost is used by a drunkard—for support rather than for illumination.

Officials, agencies, and organizations with their own particular agendas may selectively release statistics to influence decision makers or shape public opinion. For example, law enforcement agencies might circulate alarming figures showing a rise in murders and robberies at budget hearings to support their arguments that they need more money for personnel and equipment to better protect and serve the community. Or these same agencies might cite data showing a declining number of victimizations in order to take credit for improving public safety. Their argument could be that those in charge are doing their jobs so well, such as hunting down murderers or preventing robberies, that they should be given even more funding next year to further drive down the rate of violent crime. Statistics also might serve as evidence to argue that existing laws and policies are having the intended desirable effects or,

conversely, to persuade people that the old methods are not working and new approaches are necessary.

Interpretations of mathematical findings can be given a **spin** that may be questionable or debatable—for example, emphasizing that a shelter for battered women is "half empty" rather than "half full," or stressing how much public safety has improved, as opposed to how much more progress is needed before street crime can be considered under control. As useful and necessary as statistics are, they should always be viewed with a healthy dose of scientific skepticism.

Although some mistakes are honest and unavoidable, it is easy to "lie" with statistics by using impressive and scientific-sounding numbers to manipulate or mislead. Whenever statistics are presented to underscore or clinch some point in an argument, their origin and interpretation must be questioned, and certain methodological issues must be raised. What was the origin of the data, and does this source have a vested interest in shaping public opinion? Are different estimates available from other sources? What kinds of biases and inaccuracies could have crept into the collection and analysis of the data? How valid and precise were the measurements? How were key variables operationalized—defined and measured? What was counted and what was excluded, and why?

Victimologists committed to objectivity must point out the shortcomings and limitations of data collection systems run by the government. They try to interpret statistics without injecting any particular spin into their conclusions because (it is hoped) they have no "axe to grind" other than enlightening people about the myths and realities surrounding the crime problem.

THE TWO OFFICIAL SOURCES OF DATA

As early as the 1800s, public officials began keeping records about lawbreaking to gauge the "moral health" of society. Then, as now, high rates of interpersonal violence and theft were taken as signs of social pathology—indications that something was profoundly wrong with the way people generally interacted in everyday life. Annual data sets were compiled to determine whether illegal activities were being brought under control as time passed. Monitoring trends is even more important today because many innovative but intrusive and expensive criminal justice policies intended to curb crime have been implemented.

Two government reports published each year contain statistical data that enable victimologists to keep track of what is happening out on the streets. Both of these official sources of facts and figures are disseminated each year by the U.S. Department of Justice in Washington, D.C. Each of these government data collection systems has its own strengths and weaknesses in terms of providing the information victimologists and criminologists are seeking to answer their research questions. The Federal Bureau of Investigation's *Uniform Crime Report (UCR): Crime in the United States* is a massive compilation of all incidents "known" to local, county, and state police departments across the country. The FBI's *UCR* is a virtual "bible" of crime statistics based on victims' complaints and direct observations made by officers. It is older and better known than the other official source, the Bureau of Justice Statistics' *National Crime Victimization Survey (NCVS): Criminal Victimization in the United States*. The BJS's *NCVS* provides projections for various regions and for the entire country based on incidents voluntarily disclosed to interviewers by a huge national sample drawn from the general public.

Facts and Figures in the Federal Bureau of Investigation's *Uniform Crime Report* (*UCR*)

The *UCR* was established in 1927 by a committee set up by the International Association of Chiefs of Police. The goal was to develop a uniform set of definitions and reporting formats for gathering crime statistics. Since 1930, the FBI has published crime data in the *UCR* that was forwarded voluntarily to Washington by police departments across the United States. In recent years, more than 18,000 village, town, tribal, college, municipal,

county, and state police departments and sheriff's departments in all 50 states, the District of Columbia, and several territories that serve about 97 percent of the more than 300 million inhabitants of the United States participate in the data collection process, usually by sending periodic reports to state criminal justice clearinghouses. Several federal law enforcement agencies now contribute data as well (FBI, 2014).

The FBI divides up the crimes it tracks into two listings. Unfortunately, both Part I and Part II of the *UCR* have been of limited value to those interested in studying the actual flesh-and-blood victims rather than the incidents known to police departments or the characteristics of the persons arrested for allegedly committing them.

Part I of the *UCR* focuses on eight index crimes, the illegal acts most people readily think about when they hear the term "street crime." Four index crimes count violent attacks directed "against persons": murder, forcible rape, robbery, and aggravated assault. The other four monitor crimes "against property": burglary, larceny (thefts of all kinds), motor vehicle theft, and arson. (The category of arson was added in 1979 at the request of Congress when poor neighborhoods in big cities experienced many blazes of suspicious origin. However, incidents of arson are still unreliably measured because intentionally set fires might remain classified by fire marshals as being "of unknown origin.") These eight crimes (in actual practice, seven) are termed **index** crimes because the FBI adds all the known incidents of each one of these categories together to compute a "crime index" that can be used for year-to-year and place-to-place comparisons to gauge the seriousness of the problem. (But note that this grand total is unweighted; that means a murder is counted as just one index crime event, the same as an attempted car theft. So the grand total [like "comparing apples and oranges"] is a huge composite that is difficult to interpret.)

The *UCR* presents the number of acts of violence and theft known to the authorities for cities, counties, states, regions of the country, and even many college campuses (since the mid-1990s; see

Chapter 11). For each crime, the FBI compiles information about the number of incidents reported to the police, the total estimated losses in billions of dollars due to property crimes, the proportion of cases that were solved, and some characteristics of the suspects arrested (age, sex, race)—but, unfortunately for victimologists, nothing about the people who suffered harm and filed the complaints.

In **Part II**, the *UCR* only provides counts of the number of people arrested for 21 assorted offenses (but no estimates of the total number of these illegal acts committed nationwide). Some Part II crimes that lead to arrests do cause injuries to individuals, such as "offenses against women and children," as well as "sex offenses" other than forcible rape and prostitution. Others do not have clearly identifiable victims, such as counterfeiting, prostitution, gambling, drunkenness, disorderly conduct, weapons possession, and drug offenses. Still other Part II arrests could have arisen from incidents that directly harm identifiable individuals, including embezzlement, fraud, vandalism, and buying/receiving/possessing stolen property.

The Uniform Crime Reporting Division furnishes data in separate annual publications about how many hate crimes were reported to police departments (see Chapter 11). It also issues a yearly analysis of how many law enforcement officers were feloniously assaulted and slain in the line of duty, the weapons used against them, and the assignments they were carrying out when they were injured or killed (also analyzed in Chapter 11).

From a victimologist's point of view, the *UCR*'s method of data collection suffers from several shortcomings that undermine its accuracy and usefulness (see Savitz, 1982; and O'Brien, 1985). First of all, underreporting remains an intractable problem. Because many victims do not inform their local law enforcement agencies about illegal acts committed against them and their possessions (see Chapter 6), the FBI's compilation of "crimes known to the police" is unavoidably incomplete. The annual figures about the number of reported crimes recorded as committed inevitably are lower than the actual (but unknown) number of crimes that really were carried out. Second, the *UCR*

focuses on accused offenders (keeping track of the age, sex, and race) but does not provide any information about the complainants who reported the incidents. Only information about murder victims (their age, sex, and race) is collected routinely (see Chapter 4). Third, the *UCR* lumps together reports of attempted crimes (usually not as serious for victims) with completed crimes (in which offenders achieved their goals). Fourth, when computing crime rates for cities, counties, and states, the FBI counts incidents directed against all kinds of targets, adding together crimes against impersonal entities (such as businesses and government agencies) on the one hand, and individuals and households on the other. For example, the totals for robberies include bank holdups as well as muggings; statistics about burglaries combine attempted break-ins of offices with the ransacking of homes; figures for larcenies include goods shoplifted from department stores in addition to thefts of items swiped from parked cars.

Another shortcoming is that the FBI instructs local police departments to observe the **hierarchy rule** when reporting incidents: List the event under the heading of the most serious crime that took place. The ranking in the hierarchy from most terrible to less serious runs from murder to forcible rape, robbery, aggravated assault, burglary, vehicle theft, and finally larceny. For instance, if an armed intruder breaks into a home and finds a woman alone, rapes her, steals her jewelry, and drives off in her car, the entire incident will be counted for record-keeping purposes only as a forcible rape (the worst crime she endured). The fact that this person suffered other offenses at the hands of the criminal isn't reflected in the yearly totals of known incidents. If the rapist is caught, he could also be charged with armed robbery, burglary, motor vehicle theft, possession of a deadly weapon, and possession of stolen property, even though these lesser offenses are not added to the *UCR*'s compilations.

Phasing in a *National Incident-Based Reporting System*   Fortunately, the *UCR* is being overhauled and is becoming a much more useful source of information about individuals who are harmed by lawbreakers. The FBI is converting its data collection format to *a National Incident-Based Reporting System (NIBRS)*.

Law enforcement officials began to call for a more extensive record-keeping system during the late 1970s. The police force in Austin, Texas, was the first to switch to this comprehensive data collection and reporting system. However, other big-city police departments that deal with a huge volume of crime reports have had trouble meeting *NIBRS* goals and timetables, so complete implementation has been postponed repeatedly. North Dakota and South Carolina were the first two states to adopt *NIBRS* formatting in 1991. As of 2008, *NIBRS* data collection was taking place in 32 states and the District of Columbia, covering 25 percent of the nation's population, 26 percent of its reported crimes, and 37 percent of its law enforcement agencies (IBR Resource Center, 2011). But the switchover seems to be proceeding very slowly. A 2012 *NIBRS* national report compiled figures submitted by 6,115 law enforcement agencies (only 33 percent of the over 18,000 participating departments) in 32 states that covered about 30 percent of the nation's population and 28 percent of all crimes known to police departments across the country (FBI, 2014b).

One major change is the abandonment of the hierarchy rule of reporting only the worst offense that happened during a sequence of closely related events. Preserving a great many details makes it possible to determine how often one crime evolves into another, such as a carjacking escalating into a kidnapping, or a robbery intensifying into a life-threatening shooting. For the incident cited above that was categorized as a forcible rape under the hierarchy rule, this new record-keeping system also would retain information about the initial burglary; the resulting robbery; the vehicle theft; other property stolen from the victim and its value; other injuries sustained; the woman's age, sex, and race; whether there was a previous relationship between her and the intruder; and the date, time, and location of the incident. Until the advent of the *NIBRS* computer database, only in cases of homicide were some of these facts extracted from police files and retained.

Another significant aspect of the overhaul is that the *NIBRS* provides expanded coverage of additional illegal activities. Instead of just eight closely watched *UCR* index offenses, FBI computers are now prepared to keep track of 46 Group A offenses derived from 22 categories of crimes. In addition to the four "crimes against persons" and the four "against property" of the *UCR*'s Part I, the new Group A monitors offenses that formerly had been listed in Part II or just not collected at all. Victim-oriented data are becoming available for simple assault (including intimidation), vandalism (property damage and destruction), blackmail (extortion), fraud (swindles and con games), forcible sex crimes (sodomy, sexual assault with an object, and fondling), nonforcible sex offenses (statutory rape and incest), kidnapping (including parental abductions), and the nonpunishable act of justifiable homicide. The data collected about a victim of a Group A offense include these variables: sex, age, race and ethnicity, area of residence, type of injury, any prior relationship to the offender, and the circumstances surrounding the attack in cases of aggravated assault and murder. If items were stolen, the details preserved about them include the types of possession taken and their value, and in cases of motor vehicle theft, whether the car was recovered. Also, the *NIBRS* makes a distinction between attempted and successfully completed acts (from the criminal's point of view) (IBR Resource Center, 2011).

Already, some data mining studies based exclusively on the *NIBRS* archives from selected states and cities address some intriguing issues. For example, an analysis of roughly 1,200 cases of abductions in the 12 states that had switched over to *NIBRS* by 1997 shed light on a previously overlooked subcategory of "holding of a person against his or her will," called acquaintance kidnapping. This newly recognized offense includes situations such as when a teenage boy isolates his former girlfriend to punish her for spurning him, to pressure her to return to him, to compel her to submit sexually, or to evade her parents' efforts to break them up. Also included are incidents in which street gang members spirit off rivals to intimidate them, retaliate against them, or even recruit them. In these types of hostage takings, the perpetrators tend to be juveniles just like their teenage targets, the abductions often take place in homes as opposed to public places, and the captives are more likely to be assaulted (Finkelhor and Ormrod, 2000).

Several studies using *NIBRS* data from certain jurisdictions have revealed important findings about various types of murders. In general, elderly men are murdered at twice the rate as elderly women (Chu and Kraus, 2004). Specifically, older white males are the most frequent victims of "eldercide"; they are killed predominantly by offenders who are below the age of 45 and tend to be complete strangers. Female senior citizens are more likely to be slain by assailants who are older than 45 and are often either a spouse or grown child (Krienert and Walsh, 2010). Murders of intimate partners tend to be committed late at night, during weekends, and in the midst of certain holidays more often than at other times (Vazquez, Stohr, and Purkiss, 2005). Also, the higher homicide rate in Southern cities actually may not be due to a presumed subculture of violence or "code of honor" that supposedly compels individuals likely to lose fights and suffer beatings to nevertheless stand up to the aggressors to save face (Chilton, 2004).

Facts and Figures in the Bureau of Justice Statistics' *National Crime Victimization Survey* (*NCVS*)

Victimologists and criminologists have reservations about the accuracy of the official records kept by police departments that form the basis of the FBI's *UCR* as well as its *NIBRS*. Tallies maintained by local law enforcement agencies surely are incomplete due to victim nonreporting. Also, on occasion, these closely watched statistics may be distorted by police officials as a result of political pressures to either downplay or inflate the total number of incidents in their jurisdiction in order to manipulate public opinion about the seriousness of the local crime problem or the effectiveness of their crime-fighting strategies (for example, see Eterno and Silverman, 2012).

Dissatisfaction with official record-keeping practices has led criminologists to collect their own data. The first method used was the **self-report survey**. Small samples of people were promised anonymity and confidentiality if they would "confess" on questionnaires about the crimes they had committed. This line of inquiry consistently revealed greater volumes of illegal acts than were indicated by official statistics in government reports. Self-report surveys confirmed the hypothesis that large numbers of people broke the law (especially during their teens and twenties), but most were never investigated, arrested, or convicted, especially if they were members of middle- or upper-class families. But self-reports about offending did not shed any light on those who were on the receiving end of these illegal acts.

After establishing the usefulness of self-report surveys about offenses, the next logical step for researchers was to query people from all walks of life about any street crimes that may have been committed against them rather than by them. These self-report studies originally were called "victim surveys." But that label was somewhat misleading because most respondents answered that they were not victims—they had not been harmed by street crimes during the time period in question.

The first national survey about victimization (based on a random sample of 10,000 households) was carried out in 1966 for the President's Commission on Law Enforcement and the Administration of Justice. It immediately confirmed one suspicion: A sizable percentage of individuals in the sample who told interviewers that they had suffered losses and/or sustained injuries acknowledged that they had not reported the incident to the police. This proof of the existence of what was termed the "dark figure" (meaning a murky, mysterious, imprecise number) of unreported crimes further undercut confidence in the accuracy of the FBI's *UCR* statistics for all offenses except murder. Confirming the existence of unreported crime also underscored the importance of continuing this alternative way of measuring victimization rates and trends by directly asking members of the general public about their recent experiences.

In 1972, the federal government initiated a yearly survey of businesses as well as residents in 26 large cities, but the project was discontinued in 1976. In 1973, the Census Bureau began interviewing members of a huge, randomly selected, nationwide, stratified, multistage sample of households (clustered by geographic counties). Until 1992, the undertaking was known as the *National Crime Survey (NCS)*. After some revisions, it was retitled the *National Crime Victimization Survey (NCVS)*.

The Aspects of Victimization That It Measures *NCVS* respondents answer questions from a survey that runs more than 20 pages. They are interviewed every six months for three years. The questioning begins with a series of screening items, such as, "During the last six months did anyone break into your home?" If the respondent answers yes, follow-up questions are asked to collect details about the incident.

When completed, the survey provides a great deal of data about the number of violent and property crimes committed against the respondents, the extent of any physical injuries or financial losses they sustained, and the location and time of the incidents. It also keeps track of the age, sex, race/ethnicity, marital status, income level, and place of residence of the people disclosing their misfortunes to survey interviewers. The survey records the victims' perceptions about the perpetrators (in terms of whether they seemed to have been drinking and if they appeared to be members of a gang), whether they used weapons, and what self-protective measures—if any—the respondents took before, during, and after the attack. Additional questions probe into any prior relationships between them, as well as the reasons why they did or did not report the crime to the police.

The survey is person-centered. It is geared toward uncovering the suffering of individuals 12 years of age or older and the losses experienced by entire households (but not of workplaces, such as burglaries of offices or robberies of banks). The questionnaire focuses on crimes of violence (forcible rape, robbery, and aggravated assault) just like the *UCR*, plus simple assault, but not murder.

It also inquires about two kinds of thefts from individuals (personal larceny with contact like purse snatching and pickpocketing, and without any direct contact), and three types of stealing directed at the common property of households—burglary, larceny, and motor vehicle theft—again, just like the *UCR* (except that crimes against collectivities like organizations and commercial enterprises are not included in the *NCVS* but are counted in the *UCR*). Identity theft is now examined, but the list of possible offenses is far from exhaustive. For example, respondents are not quizzed about instances of kidnapping, swindling, blackmail, extortion, and property damage due to vandalism or arson.

The benefit of survey research is that it eliminates the futility of attempting the impossible: interviewing every person (of the nearly 265 million people 12 years old or older residing in the entire United States in 2013) to find out how he or she fared in the past year. The combined experiences of just about 160,000 individuals over the age of 11 living in roughly 90,000 households randomly selected to be in the national sample in 2013 can be projected to derive estimates of the total number of people throughout the country who were robbed, raped, or beaten, and of households that suffered burglaries, larcenies, or car thefts (Truman and Langton, 2014).

Shortcomings of the Data At the survey's inception, the idea of asking people about their recent misfortunes was hailed as a major breakthrough that would provide more accurate statistics than those found in the *UCR*. But, for a number of reasons, the technique has not turned out to be the foolproof method for measuring the "actual" amount of interpersonal violence and theft that some victimologists had hoped it would be. (For more extensive critiques of the methodology, see Levine, 1976; Garofalo, 1981; Skogan, 1981b, 1986; Lehnen and Skogan, 1981; Reiss, 1981, 1986; Schneider, 1981; O'Brien, 1985; Mayhew and Hough, 1988; Fattah, 1991; and Lynch and Addington, 2007).

First, the findings of this survey, like any other, are reliable only to the extent that the national sample is truly representative of the population of the whole country. If the sample is biased (in terms of factors connected to victimization, such as age, gender, race, class, and geographical location), then the projections made about the experiences of the roughly 250 million people who actually were not questioned in 2013 will be either too high or too low. Because the *NCVS* is household based, it might fail to fully capture the experiences of transients (such as homeless persons and inmates) or people who wish to keep a low profile (such as "illegal" immigrants or fugitives).

Second, the credibility of what people tell pollsters is a constant subject of debate and a matter of continuing concern in this survey. Underreporting remains a problem because communication barriers can inhibit respondents from disclosing details about certain crimes committed against them (incidents that they also probably refused to bring to the attention of the police). Any systematic suppression of the facts, such as the unwillingness of wives to reveal that their husbands beat them, of teenage girls to divulge that they suffered date rapes, or of young men to admit that they were robbed while trying to buy illicit drugs or a prostitute's sexual services, will throw off the survey's projection of the true state of affairs. Furthermore, crimes committed against children under 12 are not probed (so no information is forthcoming about physical and sexual abuse by caretakers, or molestations or kidnappings by acquaintances or strangers). **Memory decay** (forgetting about incidents) also results in information losses, especially about minor offenses that did not involve serious injuries or expenses.

But overreporting can occur as well. Some respondents may exaggerate or deliberately lie for a host of personal motives. Experienced detectives filter out any accounts by complainants that do not sound believable. They deem the charges to be "unfounded" and decide that no further investigation is warranted (see Chapter 6). But there is no such quality control over what people tell *NCVS* interviewers. The police don't accept all reports of crimes at face value, but pollsters must. "Stolen" objects actually may have been misplaced, and an accidentally shattered window may be mistaken as

evidence of an attempted break-in. Also, no verification of assertions takes place. If a person in the sample discusses a crime that was supposedly reported to the local police, there is no attempt to double-check to see if the respondent's recollections coincide with the information in the department's case files. **Forward telescoping** is the tendency to vividly remember traumatic events and therefore believe that a serious crime occurred more recently than it actually did (within the survey's reference period of "the previous six months"). It contributes to overreporting because respondents think a crime should be counted, when actually it was committed long before and ought to be excluded.

Because being targeted within the previous six months is a relatively rare event, tens of thousands of people must be polled to find a sufficient number of individuals with incidents worthy of discussion to meet the requirements for statistical soundness. For example, about 1,000 people must be interviewed in order to locate just a handful who were recently robbed. Estimates derived from small subsamples (such as robbery victims who are elderly and female) have large margins of error. The *NCVS* therefore requires a huge sample and becomes very expensive to carry out.

Even with a relatively large number of participants, the findings of the survey can only describe the situation in the nation as a whole. The seriousness of the crime problem in a particular city, county, or state cannot be accurately determined because the national sample is not large enough to break down into local subgroups of sufficient size for statistical analysis (with a few exceptions). Furthermore, the projected absolute number of incidents (offenses committed and victims harmed) and the relative rates (victims per 1,000 people per year) are really estimates at the midpoint of a range (what statisticians call a **confidence interval**). Therefore, *NCVS* rates always must be regarded as approximate, plus or minus a certain correction factor (margin of error) that depends mostly on the size of the entire sample (all respondents) and becomes statistically questionable for a very small specific subsample, such as low-income young men, living in cities, who were robbed within the last six months.

The *NCVS* has improved over the years as better ways have been devised to draw representative samples, to determine which incidents coincide with or don't fit the FBI's uniform crime definition, and to jog respondents' memories (Taylor, 1989). In particular, more explicit questions were added about sexual assaults (involving unwanted or coerced sexual contact) that fell short of the legal definition of forcible rape and about instances of domestic violence (simple assaults) (Hoover, 1994; and Kindermann, Lynch, and Cantor, 1997).

Over its four decades, the survey's questions have been refocused, clarified, and improved. But the accuracy of the *NCVS* has suffered because of waves of budget cuts. To save money, the sample size has been trimmed repeatedly. Over the decades, expensive "paper and pencil interviews" (PAPI) carried out at people's homes have been replaced by follow-up phone calls (computer-assisted telephone interviews [CATI]) and mail-in questionnaires. The response rate for individuals who were invited to participate has held steady at about 88 percent; in other words, 12 percent of the people chosen for the study declined to answer questions in 2010 as well as in 2013 (Truman, 2011; and Truman and Langton, 2014).

Comparing the *UCR* and the *NCVS*

For victimologists, the greater variety of statistics published in the *NCVS* offer many more possibilities for analysis and interpretation than the much more limited data in the *UCR*. But both official sources have their advantages, and the two can be considered to complement each other.

The *UCR*, not the *NCVS*, is the source to turn to for information about murder victims because questions about homicide don't appear on the BJS's survey. (However, two other valuable, detailed, and accurate databases for studying homicide victims are death certificates as well as public health records maintained by local coroners' and medical examiners' offices. These files may contain information about the slain person's sex, age, race/ethnicity, ancestry, birthplace, occupation, educational attainment, and zip code of last known address [for examples of how this non-*UCR* data can be analyzed, see Karmen, 2006]).

The *UCR* is also the publication that presents information about officers slain in the line of duty, college students harmed on campuses, and hate crimes directed against various groups. The *UCR* is the place to go for geographically based statistics; it provides data about the crimes reported to law enforcement agencies in different towns and cities, entire metropolitan areas, and counties, states, and regions of the country. *NCVS* figures are calculated for the whole country, four geographic regions, and urban/suburban/rural areas, but are not available for specific cities, counties, or states (because the subsamples would be too small to analyze). The *UCR*, but not the *NCVS*, calculates the overall proportion of reported crimes that are solved by police departments. Incidents counted in the *UCR* can be considered as having passed through two sets of authenticity filters: Victims felt what happened was serious enough to notify the authorities shortly afterward, and officers who filled out the reports believed that the complainants were telling the truth as supported by some evidence. Although limited information about arrestees is provided in the *UCR*, this annual report doesn't provide any descriptions of the persons harmed by those accused rapists, robbers, assailants, burglars, and other thieves (until the *NIBRS* replaces current record-keeping formats).

NCVS interviewers collect a great deal of information about the respondents who claim they were harmed by street crimes. The *NCVS* is the source to turn to for a more inclusive accounting of what happened during a given year because it contains information about incidents that were but also were not reported to the police. The yearly surveys are not affected by any changes in the degree of cooperation—or level of tension—between community residents and their local police, by improvements in record-keeping by law enforcement agencies, or by temporary crackdowns in which all incidents are taken more seriously. But the *NCVS* interviewers must accept at face value the accounts respondents describe. Also, the *NCVS* annual report has nothing to offer about murders, line-of-duty assaults and deaths of police officers, offenses committed against children under 12, robberies and burglaries directed at commercial establishments, and injuries and losses from intentionally set fires.

Even when both of these official sources collect data about the same crimes, the findings might not be strictly comparable. First of all, the definitions of certain offenses (such as rape) can vary, so the numerators may not count the same incidents. The *UCR* kept track only of rapes of women and girls (sexual assaults against boys and men were considered as "forcible sodomy") until a gender-neutral definition that explicitly described all forms of intrusive bodily invasions was adopted in 2011. The *NCVS* counts sexual assaults against males as well as females. Similarly, the definitions of robbery and burglary are not the same in the two official record-keeping sources. For example, the *UCR* includes robberies of commercial establishments and burglaries of offices, but the *NCVS* does not.

In addition, the denominators differ. While the FBI computes incidents of violence "per 100,000 people," the BJS calculates incidents "per 1,000 people age 12 or older." For property crimes, the *NCVS* denominator is "per 1,000 households," not individuals (the average household has between two and three people living in it).

Therefore, it is difficult to make direct comparisons between the findings of the *UCR* and the *NCVS*. The best way to take full advantage of these two official sources of data from the federal government is to focus on the unique information provided by each data collection system.

Even when the new and improved *NIBRS* data storage system is taken into account, several important variables are not tracked by any of these government monitoring systems. For example, information about the victims' education, occupation, ancestry, birthplace, and rap sheet is not collected by the *UCR*, the *NIBRS*, or the *NCVS*. Yet these background variables could be crucial to investigate certain issues (like robbers preying on

recent immigrants or murders of persons known to be involved in the drug scene).

A First Glance at the Big Picture: Estimates of the Number of New Crime Victims Each Year

To start to bring the big picture in focus, a first step would be to look up how many Americans reveal that they were victims of street crimes each year.

The absolute numbers are staggering: Police forces across the nation learned about nearly 1.25 million acts of "violence against persons" during 2013, according to the FBI's (2014) annual *Uniform Crime Reports*. In addition, over 9 million thefts were reported to the police (however, some were carried out against stores or offices, not individuals or families). The situation was even worse, according to the BJS' *National Crime Victimization Survey*. It projected that people 12 years old and over suffered an estimated 6.1 million acts of violence, and households experienced close to 16.8 million thefts during 2013 (Truman and Langton, 2014).

Some individuals and households are victimized more than once in a year, so the number of incidents might be greater than the number of people. Then again, in some incidents, more than one person might be harmed, so the number of people could be larger than the number of criminal events. Either way, it is obvious that each year, millions of Americans are initiated into a group that they did not want to be part of: They join the ranks of those who know what it is like from firsthand experience to endure crime-inflicted injuries and losses.

A Second Look at the Big Picture: Watching the FBI's Crime Clock

Consider another set of statistics intended to summarize the big picture that are issued yearly by the FBI in its authoritative *UCR*. This set is called the **Crime Clock**, and it dramatizes the fact that as time passes—each and every second, minute, hour, and day—the toll keeps mounting, as more and more people join the ranks of crime victims (see Figure 3.1).

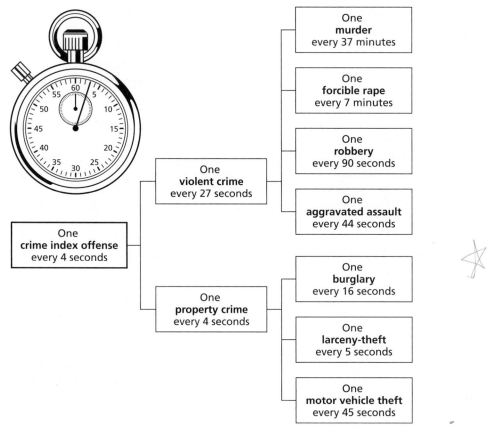

F I G U R E 3.1   The FBI's Crime Clock, 2013
SOURCE: FBI, 2014.

The Crime Clock's statistics are calculated in a straightforward manner. The total number of incidents of each kind of crime that were reported to all the nation's 18,000 plus police departments is divided into the number of seconds (60 × 60 × 24 × 365 = 31,536,000) or minutes (60 × 24 × 365 = 525,600) in a year. For instance, about 14,200 people were slain in the United States in 2013. The calculation (525,600/14,200 = 37) indicates that every 37 minutes another American was murdered that year (FBI, 2014).

Just a glance at this chart alerts even the casual reader to its chilling message. The big picture it portrays is that crimes of violence (one every 27 seconds) and theft (one every 4 seconds) are all too common. As the Crime Clock ticks away, a steady stream of casualties flows into morgues, hospital emergency rooms, and police stations throughout the nation. At practically every moment, someone somewhere in the United States is experiencing what it feels like to be harmed by a criminal. These grim reminders give the impression that becoming a victim someday is virtually inevitable. It seems to be just a matter of time before one's "number is called" and disaster strikes. Sooner or later, it will be every American's "turn"—or so it appears.

Furthermore, it can be argued that these alarming figures revealed by the Crime Clock are actually underestimates of how dangerous the streets of the United States really are, due to a shortcoming in the report's methodology. The big picture is really much worse. The FBI's calculations are based solely upon crimes known to police forces across the country. But, of course, not all illegal acts are brought to the attention of the authorities. The police find out about only a fraction of all the incidents of violence and an even smaller proportion of the thefts that occur because many victims do not share their personal troubles with the uniformed officers or detectives of their local police departments. The reporting rate varies from crime to crime, place to place, year to year, and group to group (see Chapter 6 for more details about victim reporting rates). Hence, one way to look at these Crime Clock statistics is to assume that they represent the tip of the iceberg: The actual number of people harmed by offenders in these various ways must be considerably higher.

However, the only disclaimer the FBI offers is this: "The Crime Clock should be viewed with care. The most aggregate representation of *UCR* data, it conveys the annual reported crime experience by showing a relative frequency of occurrence of the Part I index offenses. It should not be taken to imply a regularity in the commission of crime. The Crime Clock represents the annual ratio of crime to fixed time intervals" (FBI, 2014, p. 44). In other words, the reader is being reminded that in reality, the number of offenses carried out by lawbreakers ebbs and flows, varying with the time of day, day of the week, and season. These Crime Clock numbers represent projections over the course of an entire year and not the actual timing of the attacks. These street crimes do not take place with such rigid regularity or predictability.

The Crime Clock mode of presentation—which has appeared in the *UCR* for decades—has inherent shock value because as it ticks away, the future seems so ominous. Members of the public can be frightened into thinking they may be next and that their time is nearly up—if they haven't already suffered in some manner at least once.

This countdown approach lends itself to media sensationalism, fear-mongering political campaigns, and marketing ploys. Heightened anxieties can be exploited to garner votes and to boost the sales of burglar alarms, automobile antitheft devices, or crime insurance. For example, according to the Better Business Bureau (2014), a common phone scam begins with a warning based on this type of Crime Clock "data": "The FBI reports that there is a home break-in in the United States every 15 seconds…." The robocall then invites the frightened recipient to sign up for a "free" security system that, of course, has many hidden costs.

Delving Deeper into the Big Picture: Examining Victimization Rates

Statistics always must be scrutinized carefully, double-checked, and then put into perspective with some context. Victimologists and criminologists look at both raw numbers and rates. **Raw numbers** reveal the actual numbers of victims. For example, the body count or the death toll is a raw number indicating how many people were dispatched by murderers. **Rates** are the appropriate measurements to use when comparing the incidence of crime in populations of unequal size, such as the seriousness of the violence problem in different cities or countries, or at different periods of time.

The *UCR* could offer another disclaimer—but doesn't—that the Crime Clock's figures are unnecessarily alarming because they lack an important measurement of risk—the recognition that there are millions of potential targets throughout the nation. The ticking away of the Crime Clock is an unduly frightening way of depicting the big picture because it uses seconds, minutes, hours, or days as the denominator of the fraction. An alternative formulation could be used in the calculation: one that places the reported number of victimizations in the numerator of the fraction and the (huge) number of people or possessions who are in danger of being singled out by criminals into the denominator. Because there are so many hundreds of millions of residents, homes, and automobiles that could be selected by predators on the prowl, the actual chances of any given individual experiencing an incident during the course of a year may not be so high or so worrisome at all. This denominator provides some context.

This alternative calculation—using a large denominator, "per 100,000 persons per year"—puts the problem in perspective and can yield a very different impression. In fact, the *UCR* does present these "crime rates"—which also could be called "victimization rates"—right after the Crime Clock in every yearly report. It seems to make a world of difference in terms of context. The implicit message when rates are calculated is almost the opposite: Don't worry so much about being targeted. These misfortunes will probably burden someone else.

Indeed, the *UCR*'s yearly findings seem relatively reassuring, suggesting that the odds of being harmed are not at all as ominous as the Crime Clock implies. For example, the Crime Clock warned that a violent crime took place about every 27 seconds during 2013. That understandably sounds frightening because violence is the part of the street crime problem that the public worries about the most. However, when the *UCR* findings are presented with a huge denominator as a rate (per 100,000 persons per year), the figure seems less worrisome. For every 100,000 Americans, only 368 were subjected to a violent attack during 2013. Another way of expressing that same rate is that 99,632 out of every 100,000 persons made it through the year unscathed. Put still another way, only about 0.4 percent (far less than 1 percent) of the public complained to the police that they had been raped, robbed, or assaulted that year (or they were murdered). (Remember, however, that not all acts of violence are reported; some robberies were of stores or banks, or other commercial enterprises or offices; and also, some individuals face much higher or much lower risks of being targeted, as will be explained in Chapter 4.)

As described above, victimization rates also are computed and disseminated by another branch of the U.S. Department of Justice, the BJS. Its estimates about the chances of being harmed come from a different source—not police files, but a nationwide survey of the population: the *NCVS*. The survey's findings are presented as rates per 1,000 persons per year for violent crimes, and per 1,000 households per year for property crimes (in contrast to the *UCR*'s per 100,000 per year; to compare the two sets of statistics, just move the *NCVS* figure's decimal point two places to the right to indicate the rate per 100,000). The *NCVS*'s findings indicated that 23.2 out of every 1,000 residents age 12 and over in the United States (or 2,320 per 100,000, or 2.3 percent) were on the receiving end of an act of violence during 2013. (This estimate is substantially greater than the *UCR* figure because it includes those incidents that were not reported to the police but were disclosed to the interviewers; and it counts a huge number of less serious simple assaults while the UCR only counts more serious aggravated assaults—for definitions, see Box 3.1 below.) Furthermore, the *NCVS* supplies some reassuring details that are not available from the *UCR*: The rate of injury was about 6 per 1,000 (Truman and Langton, 2014). In other words, the victim was not physically wounded in about three quarters of the confrontations. Accentuating the positive (interpreting these statistics with an "upbeat" spin), despite widespread public concern, for every 1,000 residents of the United States (over the age of 11), 977 were never confronted and 994 were not wounded during 2013.

In sum, the two sources of data—the *UCR* and the *NCVS*—published by separate agencies in the federal government strive to be reasonably accurate and trustworthy. What differs is the way the statistics are collected and presented. Each format lends itself to a particular interpretation or spin. The *UCR*'s Crime Clock calculations focus on the number of persons harmed per hour, minute, or even second. But stripped of context, these figures are unduly alarming because they give the impression that being targeted is commonplace. They ignore the fact that the overwhelming majority of

Americans went about their daily lives throughout the year without interference from criminals. The rates per 100,000 published in the *UCR* and per 1,000 in the *NCVS* juxtapose the small numbers who were preyed upon against the huge numbers who got away unscathed in any given year. This mode of presenting the same facts yields a very different impression: a rather reassuring message that being targeted is a relatively unusual event.

Tapping into the *UCR* and the *NCVS* to Fill in the Details of the Big Picture

The two official sources of government statistics can yield useful information that answers important questions about everyday life, such as, "How often does interpersonal violence break out?" (Note that when working with statistics and rounding off numbers such as body counts and murder rates, it is easy to forget that each death represents a terrible tragedy for the real people whose lives were prematurely terminated, and a devastating loss for their families.)

The BJS's definitions that are used by *NCVS* interviewers appear side by side in Table 3.1 with the FBI's definitions that are followed by police departments transmitting their figures to the *UCR*. Also shown are the estimated numbers of incidents and victimization rates for 2013 derived from both data collecting programs.

Glancing at the data from the *UCR* and the *NCVS* presented in Table 3.1, the big picture takes shape. Note that the numbers of incidents and the victimization rates from the *NCVS* are often higher than the *UCR* figures for each type of offense. The main reason is that the *NCVS* numbers include crimes not reported to the police, and therefore not forwarded to FBI headquarters for inclusion in the *UCR*.

Both sources of data expose a widely believed myth. Contrary to any false impressions gained from news media coverage and television or movie plots, people suffer from violent crimes much less frequently than from property crimes. Every year, larceny (thefts of all kinds, a broad catch-all category) is the most common crime of all. Burglary is the second most widespread form of victimization, and motor vehicle theft ranks third. According to *NCVS* findings, thefts of possessions—the stealing of items left unattended outdoors plus property or cash taken by someone invited into the home, such as a cleaning person or guest—touched an estimated 10,050 out of every 100,000 households, or roughly 10 percent, in 2013. Fortunately, this kind of victimization turns out to be the least serious; most of these thefts would be classified as petty larcenies because the dollar amount stolen was less than some threshold specified by state laws, such as $1,000). The *NCVS* finding about how common thefts are each year is confirmed by the *UCR*. Larcenies of all kinds (including shoplifting from stores in the *UCR* definition) vastly outnumber all other types of crimes reported to police departments.

As for violent crimes, fortunately a similar pattern emerges: The most common is the least serious type. Simple assaults (punching, kicking, shoving, and slapping) are far more likely to be inflicted than aggravated assaults, robberies, rapes, or murders. Aggravated assaults, which are intended to seriously wound or kill, ranked second in frequency on the *NCVS*. According to the *UCR*, aggravated or "felonious assaults" were the most common type of violent offense reported to the police, but that is because the *UCR* doesn't monitor the number of simple assaults committed. Only the number of arrests for simple assaults, not the number of incidents, appears in Part II of the *UCR*; the *NIBRS* keeps track of statistics for both simple and aggravated assaults but a nationwide tally is not yet possible.

Because so many complicated situations can arise, interviewers for the *NCVS* receive instructions about how to categorize the incidents victims disclose to them. Similarly, the FBI publishes a manual for police departments to follow when

T A B L E   3.1   Estimated Nationwide Victimization Rates from the UCR and the NCVS, 2013

Crime	Definition	Incidents	Rate (per 100,000)
FBI's UCR Definitions			
Murder	The willful (nonnegligent) killing of one human being by another; includes manslaughter and deaths due to recklessness; excludes deaths due to accidents, suicides, and justifiable homicides.	14,200	4.5
Forcible Rape	The carnal knowledge of a female forcibly and against her will; includes attempts; excludes other sexual assaults and statutory rape.	80,000	25
Robbery	The taking of or attempting to take anything of value from the care, custody, or control of a person or persons by force or threat of force; includes commercial establishments and carjackings, armed and unarmed.	345,000	109
Aggravated Assault	The unlawful attacking of one person by another for the purpose of inflicting severe bodily injury, often by using a deadly weapon; includes attempted murder and severe beatings of family members; excludes simple, unarmed, minor assaults.	724,000	229
Simple Assault	No weapon used, minor wounds inflicted	Not measured	Not computed
Burglary	The unlawful entry of a structure to commit a felony or theft; includes unlawful entry without applying force to residences and commercial and government premises.	1,928,000	610
Larceny-Theft	The unlawful taking, carrying, leading, or riding away of property from the possession of another; includes purse snatching, pocket picking, thefts from vehicles, thefts of vehicles, and shoplifting; excludes the use of force or fraud to obtain possessions.	6,004,000	1,900
Motor Vehicle Theft	The theft or attempted driving away of vehicle; includes automobiles, trucks, buses, motorcycles, snowmobiles, and commercially owned vehicles; excludes farm machinery and boats and planes.	700,000	221
BJS's NCVS Definitions			
Murder	Not included in the survey	Not measured	Not computed
Rape/Sexual Assault	Rape is the unlawful penetration of a male or female through the use of force or threats of violence; includes all bodily orifices, the use of objects, and attempts as well as verbal threats. Sexual assaults are unwanted sexual contacts, such as grabbing or fondling; includes attempts and may not involve force; excludes molestations of children under 12.	174,000	110
Robbery	The taking directly from a person of property or cash by force or threat of force, with or without a weapon; includes attempts; excludes hold-ups of commercial establishments.	369,000	240
Aggravated Assault	The attacking of person with a weapon, regardless of whether an injury is sustained; includes attempts as well as physical assaults without a weapon that result in serious injuries; excludes severe physical abuse of children under 12.	633,000	380
Simple Assault	The attacking of person without a weapon resulting in minor wounds or no physical injury; includes attempts and intrafamily violence.	2,047,000	1,580
Household Burglary	The unlawful entry of residence, garage, or shed, usually but not always, for the purpose of theft; includes attempts; excludes commercial or governmental premises.	2,458,000	2,570 (per 100,000 households)
Theft	The theft of property or cash without contact; includes attempts to take possessions and stealing by persons invited inside.	9,071,000	10,050 (per 100,000 households)
Motor Vehicle Theft	The driving away or taking without authorization of any household's motorized vehicle; includes attempts.	556,000	520 (per 100,000 households)

NOTES: All *UCR* and *NCVS* figures for incidents were rounded off to the nearest 1,000, except for murder, which is rounded off to the nearest 100.
All *NCVS* rates were multiplied by 100 to make them comparable to *UCR* rates.
The FBI definition of rape is the old narrow one, referred to as the "legacy" definition, not the new expanded one.
SOURCES: FBI's *UCR*, 2013; BJS's *NCVS*, 2013 (Truman and Langton, 2014).

they submit records to the *UCR* about the crimes they are aware of that were committed in their jurisdiction. These guidelines are intended to insure that the annual crime reports are genuinely "uniform"—in the sense that the same definitions and standards are used by each of the roughly 18,000 participating law enforcement agencies. For example, all police and sheriffs' departments are supposed to exclude from their body count of murders all cases of vehicular homicides caused by drunk and impaired drivers; accidental deaths; justifiable homicides carried out by officers of the law or by civilians acting in self-defense; and suicides. But some very complex situations may arise on rare occasions and need to be clarified, so guidelines for scoring them on the *UCR* are disseminated by the FBI. Some of these instructions appear in Box 3.1 below. (Note that local prosecutors might view these crimes differently.)

Poring over "details" like the precise wording of definitions and arguing over what should and should not be included and counted, or excluded and not monitored, may seem like a rather dry technical exercise and even a "boring" waste of time. However, definitions and the statistics derived from them can really matter. For example, consider the implications of this issue:

> Police officials and women's groups …
> applauded a recommendation by the Federal Bureau of Investigation subcommittee that the definition of rape used by the agency be revised. The definition, written more than 80 years ago, has been criticized as too narrow, resulting in thousands of rapes being excluded from the FBI's Uniform Crime Report. The subcommittee recommends a broader definition, to include anal and oral rape as well as rapes involving male victims. (Goode, 2011).

What would be the consequence of adopting the more inclusive definition? Initially, forcible rape rates as monitored by this government source would rise, reflecting a more comprehensive and accurate count of the actual amount of sexual violence in the United States. That larger statistic could result in the allocation of additional federal, state, and local resources to fund efforts to catch and prosecute more rapists, and to provide support and assistance to a greater number of victims (Goode, 2011).

Searching for Changes in the Big Picture: Detecting Trends in Interpersonal Violence and Theft

The data in the annual *UCR* as well as the *NCVS* represent the situation in the streets and homes of America after a particular year has drawn to a close. These yearly reports can be likened to a snapshot at a certain point in time. But what about a movie or video that reveals changes over time? To make the big picture more useful, a crucial question that must be answered is whether street crime is becoming more or less of a problem as the years roll by.

Sharp increases in rates over several consecutive years are commonly known as **crime waves**. Downward trends indicating reduced levels of criminal activity can take place as well. Ironically, there isn't a good term to describe a sudden yet sustained improvement in public safety. Perhaps the term **crime crash** (see Karmen, 2006) captures the essence of such a largely unexpected, year-after-year downturn (just as a quick plunge in the price of shares on the stock market is called a crash, except that a "crime crash" goes on for years before it is noticeable, and then is welcomed).

During the late 1960s, a major crime wave engulfed the country, according to the FBI's *UCR*, which was the only annual source of nationwide data during that decade. Since 1973, the findings of the Bureau of Justice Statistics' (BJS) *NCVS* have provided an additional set of figures to monitor the upward and downward drifts in victimization rates. The establishment of a second, independent reporting system to measure the amount of street crime in contemporary American society initially appeared to be a major breakthrough in terms of bringing the big picture into sharper focus. In theory, the federal government's two monitoring systems should support and confirm each other's findings, lending greater credence to all official statistics shared with the

---

BOX 3.1   The FBI's Instructions About How to Classify Certain Complicated
Crimes: Guidelines from the *Uniform Crime Reporting Handbook*

Part A. Does the death of the victim fall into the category of a murder?
  What if the victim...:

SITUATION 1) ...is confronted by a robber or other assailant and suffers a heart attack and dies?

  ANSWER: Do not count this as a murder, but simply as a robbery or as an assault (because it is not a "willful killing").

SITUATION 2) ...is a woman in the ninth month of pregnancy who is stabbed in the stomach; she survives, but the fetus dies?

  ANSWER: Do not categorize this as a murder. Score this as an aggravated assault against the woman (because the definition of murder excludes deaths of unborn fetuses).

SITUATION 3) ...is a firefighter or a police officer who enters a burning building and dies; later it is determined that the blaze was intentionally set by an arsonist?

  ANSWER: Do not count this as a murder because it is understood that firefighting and police work is hazardous and requires taking grave risks.

SITUATION 4) ...is a motorist embroiled in a road rage incident who dies because his adversary intentionally crashes his vehicle into the motorist's car?

  ANSWER: Score this as a murder. If the victim survives, then consider the incident to be an aggravated assault (the vehicle is the deadly weapon), no matter how minor the injury to the person or the damage to the car.

Part B. Is it a rape?
  What if the victim...

SITUATION 1) ...is slipped a date-rape drug in her drink by a man who is after her, but he is unable to lure her away from her friends?

  ANSWER: Count this as an attempted forcible rape, since he intended to have intercourse with her against her will (she would be incapable of giving consent because of her temporary mental or physical incapacity) but was thwarted by his inability to get her alone.

SITUATION 2) ...is married to a man who beats her until she submits to intercourse?

  ANSWER: Count this as a forcible rape. Ever since marital rape was recognized as a crime, the law no longer permits a husband to be exempt from arrest for forcing himself on his wife.

Part C. Is the incident an armed robbery?
  What if the victim...

SITUATION 1) ...is a cashier in a store who is ordered to hand over money by a man who claims to have a weapon in his pocket but does not brandish it, so the cashier does not actually see it?

  ANSWER: Score this as an armed robbery, since the robber claimed to have a weapon (or perhaps had a fake knife or gun).

SITUATION 2) ...returns home and surprises a burglar, who then assaults him with a crowbar, steals valuables, and escapes out the door?

  ANSWER: Score this as an armed robbery, since the resident was confronted and attacked by the intruder.

SOURCE: Adapted and reworded from *Uniform Crime Reporting System Guidelines* (FBI, 2009).

---

public. But in practice, estimates from the *UCR* and the *NCVS* have diverged for particular categories of offenses during certain brief stretches of time, clouding the big picture about national trends (Rand & Rennison, 2002).

The *UCR* measures the violent crime rate by adding together all the known cases of murder, forcible rape, aggravated assault, and robbery. The *NCVS* doesn't ask about murder (a relatively small number) but it does inquire about simple assaults (a huge number). The BJS then combines all disclosed cases of simple and aggravated assault, all sexual assaults (of males as well as females), and some robberies (only of people, not banks or stores) into its violent crime rate. Other differences in data collection methodology plus divergent definitions that were discussed above may help explain some of the inconsistent results in the years between 1973 and the start of the 1990s, when the two trend lines were not in synch. But one finding clearly emerges: According to both of these monitoring systems, violent crime rates "crashed" during the 1990s and have continued to drift downward, as the graph in Figure 3.2 demonstrates.

A parallel set of problems and findings arise when the changes over time in property crime rates are graphed. The *UCR* defines property crime to include burglary, motor vehicle theft, and larcenies against persons and households but also against commercial enterprises, government offices, and nonprofit entities. The *NCVS* counts burglaries, vehicle thefts, and larcenies but only if they are directed against individuals and their households. Once again, despite differing signals during the first 20 years, the takeaway message of

the graph in Figure 3.3 echoes that of Figure 3.2: Property crime rates "crashed" during the 1990s and have fallen farther during the twenty-first century.

In sum, both the FBI's *UCR* and the BJS's *NCVS* confirm that diminishing numbers of residents of the 50 states are being affected by the social problems of violence and theft. In other words, even though each year millions of new individuals join the ranks of crime victims, the rate of growth has been slowing down for about two decades. This substantial decline in victimization rates since the early 1990s is certainly good news. But how much longer will this crime crash continue? Few social scientists, politicians, or journalists would dare declare that the "war on crime" has been won. And since the experts can't agree about the reasons why this substantial improvement in public safety took place, if someday there is a return to the

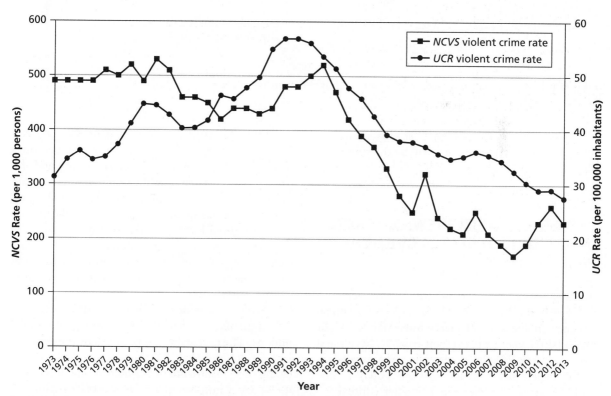

FIGURE 3.2 Trends in Violent Victimization Rates, United States, 1973–2013
SOURCES: FBI's *UCRs* 1973–2013; BJS's *NCVSs* 1973–2013.

FIGURE 3.3   Trends in Property Crime Rates, United States, 1973–2013
SOURCES: FBI's *UCR*s 1973–2013; BJS's *NCVS*s 1973–2013.

"bad old days" of much higher rates of victimization, the causes of this reversal will be the subject of bitter debate (see Karmen, 2006).

TAKING A LONGER VIEW: MURDERS IN THE UNITED STATES OVER THE PAST CENTURY

Another aspect of the big picture involves getting a feel for historical trends. Is the level of criminal violence in the United States today far worse or much better than in the distant past? Is the United States becoming a safer place to live or a more dangerous society as the decades pass by? Today's crime problem needs to be seen in a broader context.

Historians write about the carnage of the past, especially when the first European settlers arrived,

and then during the time period of the Thirteen Colonies, the American Revolution, the centuries of slavery, the Civil War, Reconstruction, and the frontier days of the "Wild West." But accurate records are hard to find before industrialization took place, cities sprang up, and urban police forces began to guard local residents on a daily basis.

Graphs are particularly useful for spotting historical trends at a glance. Trends in homicide rates can be traced further back than changes over time for the other interpersonal crimes.

Murder is the most terrible crime of all because it inflicts the ultimate harm, and the damage cannot be undone. The irreparable loss is also felt by the departed person's loved ones. But the social reaction to the taking of a person's life varies dramatically. It is determined by a number of factors: the state's laws, the offender's state of mind, the deceased's possible contribution to the escalation of hostilities, the social standing of each party, where the crime was committed, how the person was dispatched, and whether the slaying attracted media coverage and public outcry. Some murders make headlines, while others slip by virtually unnoticed except by the next of kin. Some killings lead to the execution of the perpetrator; others ruled to be justifiable homicides result in no penalty and possibly even widespread approval.

Homicide is broadly defined as the killing of one human being by another. Not all homicides are punishable murders. All murders are socially defined: How to handle a specific killing is determined by legislators, police officers, and detectives; prosecutors and defense attorneys; judges and juries; and even the media and the public's reaction to someone's demise. Deaths caused by carelessness and accidents are not classified as murders (although if the damage was foreseeable, they might be prosecuted as manslaughters). Acts involving the legitimate use of deadly force in self-defense whether carried out against felons by police officers or by private citizens under attack (see Chapter 13) are also excluded from the body counts, as are court-sanctioned executions.

The law takes into account whether a killing was carried out intentionally (with "express malice"), in a rational state of mind ("deliberate"), and with advance planning ("premeditation"). These defining characteristics of first-degree murders carry the most severe punishments, including (depending on the state) execution or life imprisonment without parole. Killing certain people—police officers, corrections officers, judges, witnesses, and victims during rapes, kidnappings, or robberies—may also be capital offenses.

A homicide committed with intent to inflict grievous bodily injury (but no intent to kill) or with extreme recklessness ("depraved heart") is prosecuted as a second-degree murder. A murder in the second degree is not a capital crime and cannot lead to the death penalty.

A homicide committed in the "sudden heat of passion" as a result of the victim's provocations is considered a "voluntary" (or first-degree) manslaughter. The classic example is the "husband who comes home to find his wife in bed with another man and kills him." Offenders convicted of manslaughter are punished less severely than those convicted of murder.

A loss of life due to gross negligence usually is handled as an "involuntary" (second-degree) manslaughter, or it may not be subjected to criminal prosecution at all. Involuntary manslaughter in most states occurs when a person acts recklessly, or appreciates the risk but does not use reasonable care to perform a legal act, or commits an unlawful act that is not a felony and yet a death results.

Some types of slayings have special names (see Holmes, 1994): infanticide (of a newborn by a parent), filicide (of a child by a parent or stepparent), parricide (of a parent by a child), eldercide (of an older person), intimate partner homicide (of a spouse or lover), serial killing (several or more victims dispatched one at a time over an extended period), mass murder (several people slaughtered at the same time and place), felony murder (committed during another serious crime, like robbery, kidnapping, or rape), and contract killing (a professional "hit" for an agreed-upon fee).

The *UCR* has been monitoring murder (combined with manslaughter) rates since the beginning of the 1930s, but in the beginning only big-city police departments forwarded their records to FBI headquarters. Fortunately, another source of data is available that is drawn from death certificates (maintained by **coroner's offices**, which are called **medical examiners** offices in some jurisdictions) that list the cause of death. This database, compiled by the National Center for Health Statistics, can be tapped to reconstruct what happened during the earliest years of the twentieth century up to the present. Graphing this data facilitates the identification of crime waves and spikes but also sharp drops and deep "crashes" in the homicide rate over the decades. Long-term trends can then be considered in context (against a backdrop of major historical events affecting the nation as a whole).

The Rise and Fall of Murder Rates Since 1900

It is possible to look back over more than a century to note how the homicide rate has surged and ebbed in America during various historical periods.

As the trend line in Figure 3.4 indicates, homicide rates appeared to rise at the outset of the 1900s as states' coroners' offices joined the statistical reporting system. From 1903 through the period of World War I, which was followed by the prosperous "Roaring Twenties" until the stock market "crash" of 1929, the murder rate soared. It rose even further for a few more years until it peaked in 1933. So during the first 33 years of the twentieth century, the homicide rate skyrocketed from less than 1 American killed out of every 100,000 each year to nearly 10 per 100,000 annually.

The number of violent deaths plummeted after Prohibition—the war on alcohol—ended in 1933, even though the economic hardships of the Great Depression persisted throughout the 1930s. During the years of World War II, when many young men were drafted to fight overseas against formidable enemies trying to conquer the world, only 5 slayings took place for every 100,000 inhabitants. A brief surge in killings broke out as most of the soldiers returned home from World War II, but then interpersonal violence continued to decline during the 1950s, reaching a low of about 4.5 slayings for every 100,000 people by 1958.

During the turbulent years from the early 1960s to the middle 1970s, the number of deadly confrontations shot up, doubling the homicide rate. This crime wave reflected the demographic impact of the unusually large baby-boom generation passing through its most crime-prone teenage and young-adult years, as well as the bitter conflicts surrounding the sweeping changes in everyday life brought about by social protest movements that arose during the 1960s and lasted well into the 1970s. The level of lethal violence during the twentieth century reached its all-time high in 1980, when the homicide rate hit 10.2 deaths per 100,000 inhabitants. After that peak, murder rates dropped for several years until the second half of the 1980s, when the crack epidemic

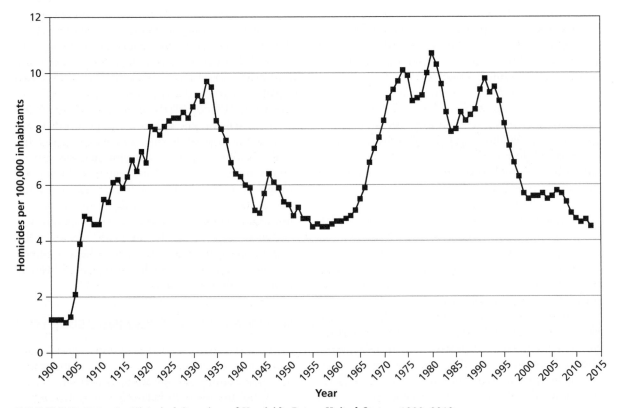

FIGURE 3.4 An Historical Overview of Homicide Rates, United States, 1900–2013

touched off another escalation of bloodshed. By the start of the 1990s, murder rates once again were close to their highest levels for the century. But as that decade progressed, the fad of smoking crack, selling drugs, and toting guns waned; the economy improved; the proportion of the male population between 18 and 24 years old dwindled; and consequently, the murder rate tumbled (see Fox and Zawitz, 2002; and Karmen, 2006). The death toll has continued to drift downward throughout the twenty-first century, even during the hard times of the Great Recession that set in after the subprime mortgage meltdown, stock market crash, and corporate bailouts of 2008, as Figure 3.4 shows.

Returning to the *UCR* database, the impressive improvement in public safety became strikingly evident in 2013, when the body count declined to about 14,200, about 10,500 fewer victims than in 1991, when the death toll had reached an all-time record of close to 24,700. Taking population growth into account, the U.S. murder rate in 2013 stood at 4.5 killings per 100,000 inhabitants, an overall "crash" of about 50 percent since 1991 (Cooper and Smith, 2011). The U.S. murder rate hadn't been as low as 4.5 since 1958.

PUTTING CRIME INTO PERSPECTIVE: THE CHANCES OF DYING VIOLENTLY—OR FROM OTHER CAUSES

One final way to grasp the big picture involves weighing the relative threats posed by different types of misfortunes. The chance of being harmed by a criminal needs to be compared to the odds of being hurt in an accident or of contracting a serious illness. The study of **comparative risks** rests on estimates of the likelihood of experiencing various negative life events. One purpose of studying comparative risks is to determine what kinds of threats (crimes, accidents, or diseases) merit greater precautionary measures by both individuals and government-sponsored campaigns. (A list of calamities could be expanded to include plagues, fires, and natural

disasters such as floods, tornadoes, earthquakes, and hurricanes.) Once the chances of being stricken by dreaded events are expressed in a standardized way, such as rates per 100,000 people, the dangers can be compared or ranked, as they are in Table 3.2. The data is derived from death certificates filed in all 50 states and the District of Columbia. It is collated by the National Center for Health Statistics into a National Vital Statistics System (Xu et al., 2014).

The nationwide data assembled in the first column of Table 3.2 pertains to people of all ages, both sexes, and varying backgrounds. The statistics in column 2 indicate that overall, about 800 out of every 100,000 Americans died in 2010. That year, the number of deaths from natural causes (diseases) greatly exceeded losses of life from external causes (accidents, suicides, and homicides). In particular, heart disease, cancer, and stroke were by far the leading causes of death in the United States at the end of the first decade of the twenty-first century. As for other untimely demises, more people died from accidents (including car crashes) than from homicide (murders plus deaths by "legal intervention"—justifiable homicides by police officers as well as executions of death row prisoners). In fact, more people took their own lives through suicides than lost them due to violence unleashed by others (homicide was added to the bottom of the list and did not rank in the top 10 leading causes of death). Tentatively, it can be concluded that most people worry too much about being murdered and ought to focus more of their energies toward their health, eating habits, and lifestyles instead.

However, this inspection of comparative risks surely doesn't seem right to some readers. For example, dying from Alzheimer's disease might be a very real and scary prospect to aging baby boomers, but it is off the radar screen for most millennials. The usefulness of comparing the mortality rates assembled in the second column of Table 3.2 to each other is limited. The reason is simple: The data in the second column of the table ignores the key factor of age. Column 2's figures about the causes of death describe the dangers faced by the "average" American, a social construct that each person resembles to some extent. But the actual odds a specific individual faces may differ tremendously from this fictitious composite norm.

TABLE 3.2   Comparing the Risks of Death Posed by Crime, Accidents, and Certain Diseases, 2010 and 2012

Cause of Death	Death Rate per 100,000, All Americans, 2010	Death Rate per 100,000, 20–24 years olds, 2010	Death Rate per 100,000, All Americans, 2012
All causes	800	87	733
1) Heart problems (cardiovascular disease)	194	3	171
2) Cancers (malignant neoplasms)	186	5	167
3) Lung problems (pulmonary and respiratory diseases)	45	Fewer than 1	42
4) Strokes (cerebrovascular disease)	42	Fewer than 1	37
5) Accidents (unintentional injuries)	39	36	39
6) Alzheimer's disease	27	Fewer than 1	24
7) Diabetes	22	Fewer than 1	21
8) Kidney problems (nephritis)	16	Fewer than 1	13
9) Influenza and pneumonia	16	1	14
10) Suicides (intentional self-harm)	12	14	13
Homicides (including legal intervention) (assault)	6	13	5*
All other causes	194	12	

NOTE: Homicide rate for 2012 is estimated from the FBI's *UCR* for 2012.

SOURCE: Centers for Disease Control and Prevention's (CDC) National Center for Health Statistics, *National Vital Statistics Report*, 2013; Yu et al., 2014 (column 5)

Besides age, the most important determinants of mortality rates are sex, race/ethnicity, social class, and place of residence. To make more meaningful comparisons, some of these key variables, especially age, must be controlled, or held constant (see Fingerhut, Ingram, and Feldman, 1992). Death rates for young adults appear in the third column of Table 3.2.

Comparing the rates in column 3 to those in column 2 reveals some sharp differences. For example, of all Americans between the ages of 20 and 24 (of both sexes and all races), only 87, not 800, out of every 100,000 died in 2010. For people in their early twenties, homicide was a real threat—the third leading cause of death—after accidents (especially involving motor vehicles) and suicides. Few young adults died from heart attacks, cancer, strokes, influenza, or other diseases like HIV/AIDS (NCHS, 2013). Also, although this is not shown in the table, within every age group, being murdered loomed as a greater danger to boys and men than to girls and women, and to racial minorities as compared to members of the white majority. These observations raise an important issue. Besides comparative risks, victimologists have to also study

differential risks. The perils facing different groups (in terms of age, sex, race/ethnicity, social class, and other factors) can vary dramatically. Differential risks will be scrutinized in the next chapter.

Another problem with risk comparisons is that the ranking represents a snapshot image of a fluid situation. Thus, Table 3.2 captures a moment frozen in time—the relative standing of dangers of accidents, diseases, and lethal violence in 2010. But it cannot indicate underlying trends. The chances of something terrible ending a life can change for everyone substantially over the years. That is why yearly data must be assembled into tables and graphs in order to spot trends.

For example, an encouraging downward trend in fatal accidents took place during the 1980s. Deaths due to plane crashes, falls, drownings, fires, and poisonings all dropped during that decade, probably as a result of greater safety consciousness, new devices such as smoke detectors and car seats for children, and new policies such as mandatory seat belt laws and tougher penalties for drunk driving. By 1990, the risk of dying in a car crash had fallen to its lowest level since the 1920s, according to a study by the National Safety Council (Hall, 1990). During the

1990s, the chances of being murdered diminished impressively, as did the odds of perishing shortly after contracting full-blown HIV/AIDS. As the chances of dying from a particular disease, a terrible accident, or a fatal assault rise or fall over time, listings of comparative risks must undergo periodic revision (CDC, 1999).

Column 4 in Table 3.2 shows that mortality rates did change somewhat over a time span of just two years. In general, the trends were in the desirable direction. The death rate for the diseases listed in Table 3.2 all declined, which means the life expectancy of the average American increased. The only disappointing trend was a small rise in the suicide rate. Accidental deaths remained at the same level in 2012 as in 2010.

To further complicate the picture, occupation must be taken into account when comparing the risks of becoming a homicide victim to the risk of suffering a fatal injury at work. Risks are closely tied to tasks; some jobs are far more dangerous than others. Focusing on deaths in the workplace, studies conducted by the National Institute for Safety and Health and by the federal government's Bureau of Labor Statistics established that fatal accidents take place most often in jobs related to construction, farming and forestry, and transportation. Putting accidents aside, researchers discovered that certain lines of work, such as law enforcement and cab driving, carry much greater risks of being murdered on the job. (See Chapters 4 and 11 for a discussion of homicides at workplaces.)

In sum, individuals face widely varying risks of being murdered, depending on which groups they fall into (who they are, where they live, and what they do on a daily basis).

Now that the big picture has been studied from a number of angles—nationally, historically, and comparatively—it is time to zoom in on specific crimes. The analysis of the big picture has revealed that the most terrible of all violent crimes—homicide—is also the least likely to take place. Data from official sources will help reveal what suffering it inflicts on the population of the United States. In addition to murders, aggravated assaults as well as robberies (two crimes that potentially could escalate into slayings) will be the focus of the next chapter.

SUMMARY

Statistics can convey important information about crimes and their victims, but consumers of numerical data must ascertain exactly what was counted, how accurate the measurements are, and whether vested interests are promoting particular interpretations. The two leading sources of data about crime victims published annually by the U.S. Department of Justice are the FBI's *Uniform Crime Report* and the BJS's *National Crime Victimization Survey*. The *UCR* draws on police files and is useful to victimologists who want to study murders, but it is of limited value for research into other kinds of victimizations until the *National Incident-Based Reporting System* is completely phased in and replaces it. The *NCVS* contains information about interpersonal violence as well as property crimes and gathers data directly from members of a large national sample who answer questions about their misfortunes over the past six months.

Victimization rates are expressed per 1,000 in the *NCVS* or per 100,000 in the *UCR* in order to facilitate fair comparisons between groups, cities, or countries of different sizes.

According to both the *NCVS* and the *UCR*, the twin problems of interpersonal violence and theft have subsided so substantially since the early 1990s up to the present that these crime rates can be said to have "crashed." The homicide rate in 2013 was just about the same as in the late 1950s, before "crime in the streets" became a matter of great public concern.

Comparative risks reveal which kinds of misfortunes are more or less likely than others: Homicide is not the leading cause of death for any group. Comparative risks show how crime is often not as great a threat to well-being as injuries and deaths from accidents and diseases.

KEY TERMS DEFINED IN THE GLOSSARY

big picture, 67

comparative risks, 89

coroner's offices, 87

Crime Clock, 77

crime crash, 83

crime waves, 83

differential risks, 90

forward telescoping, 75

hierarchy rule, 71

index, 70

medical examiners, 87

memory decay, 75

National Crime Victimization Survey (NCVS), 70

official statistics, 68

Part I crimes, 70

Part II crimes, 71

patterns, 68

profiles, 68

range (confidence interval), 75

rates, 79

raw numbers, 79

self-report survey, 73

spin, 69

statistics, 68

trends, 68

Uniform Crime Report (UCR), 70

victimization rates, 68

QUESTIONS FOR DISCUSSION AND DEBATE

1. Choose some statistics presented in this chapter and interpret them in two ways: First, make them seem as alarming as possible; and second, portray them as reassuringly as possible.

2. What kinds of information about victims of interpersonal violence and theft can be found in the FBI's annual *Uniform Crime Reports*?

What are the sources of inaccuracies in these statistics?

3. What kinds of information about victims of interpersonal violence and theft can be found in the BJS's annual *National Crime Victimization Survey*? What are the sources of inaccuracies in these statistics?

CRITICAL THINKING QUESTIONS

1. What information about the people who get injured or killed by offenders is *not* systematically collected by the *UCR* and the *NCVS*, or even the *NIBRS*? Why would this additional information be important? How could it be used and what issues could it shed light on?

2. Make up some hypothetical scenarios in which people with a vested interest in convincing the public that victimization rates are either going up or going down could "shop around" for *UCR* or *NCVS* statistics about robberies or burglaries to support their claim.

SUGGESTED RESEARCH PROJECTS

1. Find out the latest rates per 100,000 people for the seven index crimes for your home state by searching the FBI website where the *UCR* statistics are posted. What crime rates are substantially higher or lower in your state than for the entire United States (as shown in Table 3.1)?

2. Find out the definitions and the precise wording of the questions that are asked in the *NCVS* by downloading the survey instrument from the BJS website. Discuss how the inquiries about aggravated assault, rape, and other sexual assaults are phrased, and why respondents might be confused or unclear about how to answer these questions.

4

A Closer Look at the Victims of Interpersonal Crimes of Violence and Theft

LEARNING OBJECTIVES

To understand the meaning of differential risks.

To appreciate the complications of making international comparisons.

To discover which countries and which cities across the globe have the highest and lowest homicide rates.

To use official statistics to spot national trends in murders, aggravated assaults, and robberies in recent decades.

To discover the profile of the typical victim in order to determine which demographic groups face the highest and lowest chances of getting murdered and also of being robbed.

To appreciate the strengths and weaknesses of statistical projections about the risk any given individual faces of being on the receiving end of violence.

To grasp the meaning of cumulative risks.

To become acquainted with the suffering of people whose homes are burglarized.

To become knowledgeable about the situation of people whose cars are stolen.

To become familiar with the aggravation arising from identity theft.

ADDRESSING SOME TROUBLING QUESTIONS

The previous chapter painted the "big picture" about all forms of victimization in the entire country in recent years. This chapter focuses on certain interpersonal crimes of violence and theft in greater depth. People attacked by murderers, other dangerous assailants, and robbers are examined first. Individuals and households whose homes are burglarized, whose cars are driven off by thieves, and whose identities are stolen by impostors are investigated later in the chapter. (The plight of abused children is examined in Chapter 8; the dilemma faced by intimate partners who are beaten by batterers is explored in Chapter 9; and the suffering imposed by rapists is examined in Chapter 10.)

Victimologists gather and interpret data to answer disturbing questions such as: How many people are robbed, wounded, and even murdered by criminals each year? How rapidly are the ranks of people who have suffered these misfortunes growing? Researchers want to find out where and when the majority of crimes occur, and, in the age of globalization, where in the world are the streets much more dangerous and where are they dramatically safer?

A matter of particular concern is which groups are targeted the most and the least often.

Specifically, which groups are at a higher risk of getting slain, shot, stabbed, or robbed? Data from the *UCR* and the *NCVS* will be used to answer a set of unsettling questions:

- What are the odds of being attacked during any given year? **Incidence rates** measure the number of new victims per 1,000 or per 100,000 persons annually and thereby reveal the risks people face.

- How many people know what it is like to be confronted by a robber who growls, "Your money or your life!" **Prevalence rates** estimate the proportion of people per 1,000 or per 100,000 who have ever experienced some misfortune.

- What are the chances that a person will be harmed by a violence-prone opponent at least once during his or her entire life (not just in a single year) [incidence rate], or during previous years [prevalence rate]? **Cumulative risks** estimate these lifetime likelihoods by projecting current situations into the future.

- Is violence a growing problem in American society, or is it subsiding? **Trend analysis** provides the answer by focusing on changes over time.

- Does violent crime burden all communities and groups equally, or are some categories of people more likely than others to be held up, physically injured, and killed? **Differential risks** indicate the odds of an unwanted event taking place for members of one social demographic group as compared to another.

Identifying Differential Risks: Which Groups Suffer More Often Than Others?

The first step in a victim-centered analysis addresses the issue, "Which groups sustain the greatest casualties? Which groups face lesser threats of harm?

Victimization rates for the entire population indicate how frequently murders, rapes, robberies, and assaults are committed against "average" Americans and how often "typical" households suffer burglaries, motor vehicle thefts, and identity theft. It is reasonable to suspect that the chance of becoming a victim is not uniform for everyone but is more likely for some types and less likely for others.

The discussion about comparative risks at the conclusion of Chapter 3 revealed that different age groupings of people do not all face the same odds of getting killed accidentally—say, from a skiing mishap—or of dying from a particular disease, such as cancer. People with attributes in common such as age or sex may be affected by crime much more or much less often than others. If these suspicions can be documented, then any overall rate that projects a risk for all Americans might mask important variations within subgroups. In other words, it is necessary to "disaggregate" or "deconstruct" or break down victimization rates into their component pieces in order to reveal the differential risks faced by particular categories of people.

A pattern within a victimization rate is recognizable when one category suffers significantly more than another. The most obvious example is the incidence of rape: Females are much more likely to be sexually violated than are males. Searching for patterns means looking for regularities within a seemingly chaotic mass of information and finding predictability in what at first appear to be random events.

The differential risks derived from patterns identified in the data will be investigated in this chapter for the violent crimes of murder and robbery and for the property crimes of burglary, motor vehicle theft, and identity theft.

FOCUSING ON MURDERS

Where It Is Safer or More Dangerous: Making International Comparisons

In order to bring the big picture into sharper focus during the era of globalization, it is important to remember that victimization rates vary dramatically not only from time to time but also from one place to another. The greatest variations can be found by comparing one society to another. Cross-national comparisons reveal the magnitude of the crime problem in different countries at one point in time.

The main source of data about victimization rates in other countries is a branch of the United Nations—its Office on Drugs and Crime Control—which periodically surveys its members' law enforcement agencies. Also, the European Union (EU) collects data from the criminal justice systems of its member states and publishes an annual European Sourcebook of Crime and Criminal Justice Statistics. In the past, the International Police Organization (Interpol) also publicly posted data.

Since 1989, most European countries have participated in an International Crime Victim Survey that generates statistics that are considered more reliable than data from police departments. Police in the various countries use different definitions for common crimes like rape, burglary, and robbery. Also, some police forces are more scrupulous about recording incidents and forwarding their data to headquarters than others. Differences in record-keeping practices can make comparisons difficult too (for example, some countries do not follow the "hierarchy rule"), and, of course, the willingness of victims to reveal their troubles to the authorities varies dramatically from place to place (Van Dijk et al. 2007; and Loftus, 2011).

Making international comparisons of victimization rates continues to be difficult, and hasty conclusions can be misleading. Some governments do not routinely disclose reliable and up-to-date data about their crime rates, or they publish figures that seem unrealistically low, probably because their regimes fear that high rates will damage their nations' public images and scare off potential tourists and investors.

Researchers who studied cross-national crime data decades ago came to these conclusions: Compared to other nations providing trustworthy statistics, U.S. victimization rates for violent crimes were very high, for auto theft were fairly high, and for burglary were near the middle of the range (Kalish, 1988). Violence is more of a problem in the United States than in many other highly developed societies, but theft is not (Zimring and Hawkins, 1997).

Narrowing the focus strictly to the number of murders in various societies still requires careful attention to methodological issues. Each country's definitions of intentional, wrongful, punishable killings reflect laws and local customs that govern the way deaths are classified. For international comparisons to be valid, definitions of killings that constitute murder must be consistent. For example, not all countries consider infanticides as murders. Also, certain countries may count attempted murders as intentional homicides, but in the United States (and most other societies) cases in which wounded people survive are classified as aggravated assaults. Other inconsistencies result if a nation's body count includes deaths from legal interventions (such as the use of deadly force by police officers and court-ordered executions), totally unintentional deaths (like negligent manslaughter and vehicular homicides), and assisted suicides.

The United Nations asks its member states about their crime problems and promotes the use of definitions that are as consistent as possible. These official statistics have been assembled in Table 4.1 in order to present a picture of the variations in murder rates across the globe.

What very important factor do Austria, China, Denmark, the Czech Republic, France, Germany, Hungary, Ireland, Indonesia, Japan, the Netherlands, Poland, Saudi Arabia, Spain, South Korea, and Switzerland have in common? They are among the most peaceful societies on the planet, with a murder rate close to just one slaying per 100,000 inhabitants. As for the English-speaking advanced industrial countries, citizens of the United States have a lot more to worry about in terms of

succumbing to lethal interpersonal violence than people who reside in the United Kingdom, Australia, New Zealand, and Canada. Most of the countries in the EU have very low murder rates. Some of the developing nations of Asia, Africa, and Latin America report that they experience levels of lethal violence that are lower than those in the United States: Morocco, Turkey, Liberia, Egypt, Vietnam, Chile, and Cuba.

Table 4.1 reveals that the people who suffer the greatest casualties tend to live in Central and South America and the offshore island nations in the Caribbean Sea, especially Honduras and Venezuela, but also Belize, Guatemala, El Salvador, Jamaica, the Dominican Republic, Colombia, Trinidad and Tobago, the Bahamas, the U.S. Commonwealth of Puerto Rico, Brazil, Mexico, and Panama. South Africa, despite the dismantling of apartheid several decades ago, also is still burdened by disturbingly high levels of bloodshed.

Note that some of the killings that boost the body count in strife-torn societies across the globe are not the outgrowth of ordinary street crime but are the result of intense political polarization, expressed as vigilantism (including slayings by death squads), terrorism, and low-intensity guerrilla warfare waged against governments by insurgent groups and drug trafficking cartels. War-torn countries like Iraq, Syria, and Afghanistan were excluded from Table 4.1.

Some countries are strikingly different from others in terms of their economies, criminal justice systems, cultural traditions, and age distributions (for example, many developing societies have huge populations of young people and relatively few old people). Therefore, it might make more sense to limit comparisons of murder rates to fairly similar, highly industrialized nations. Because a key determinant of the murder rate in any country is simply the proportion of the population that falls into the highest risk group (young males), one way to deal with variations would be to calculate the homicide rate for every 100,000 teenage boys and young men in each society. Following this procedure and then restricting the comparison only to other highly industrialized societies, the United

TABLE 4.1   Murder Rates Across the Globe: Selected Countries, 2012

Country	Murder Rate per 100,000 Inhabitants	Country	Murder Rate per 100,000 Inhabitants
Australia	1	Italy	1
Austria	1	Jamaica	39
Bahamas	30	Japan	0.3
Belgium	2	Liberia	3
Belize	45	Mexico	22
Bolivia	12	Morocco	2
Brazil	25	Netherlands	1
Canada	2	New Zealand	1
Chile	3	Nicaragua	11
China	1	Nigeria	20
Colombia	31	Pakistan	8
Costa Rica	9	Panama	17
Cuba	4	Peru	10
Czech Republic	1	Philippines	9
Denmark	1	Puerto Rico (U.S.)	27
Dominican Republic	22	Poland	1
Egypt	3	Russian Federation	9
El Salvador	41	Saudi Arabia	1
Estonia	5	South Africa	31
Finland	2	South Korea	1
France	1	Spain	1
Germany	1	Switzerland	1
Greece	2	Thailand	5
Guatemala	40	Trinidad/Tobago	28
Honduras	90	Turkey	3
Hungary	1	United Kingdom (England and Wales)	1
Ireland	1	Ukraine	4
Israel	2	United States	5
India	4	Venezuela	54
Indonesia	1	Vietnam	3
Iran	4		

NOTES: All rates are rounded off to the nearest whole number, except for those less than 1 per 100,000.

The latest figures available for a few of the countries are from 2011, not 2013.

The Commonwealth of Puerto Rico is a U.S. territory.

SOURCE: United Nations Office on Drugs and Crime Control, 2014.

States stood out as having the worst murder rate during the late 1980s (Deane, 1987; Rosenthal, 1990). Another way to take the substantial demographic differences from country to country into account is to calculate the murder rate of a population and then adjust that number to reflect a standardized age distribution in order to improve comparability over time and between countries.

When 1980s murder rates in different nations were analyzed, higher rates tended to be associated with great economic inequality (huge gaps between the wealthy and the poor), limited government funding of social programs for the disadvantaged, cultural supports for legitimate violence by government officials and agencies (frequent executions and few restraints on the use of force by the police), family breakdown (high divorce rates), high rates of female participation in the labor force, and ethnic heterogeneity (see Gartner, 1990).

Clearly, geographic location—in which society a person resides—is a major factor that determines murder risks around the globe. Substantial variations also can be anticipated between different cities in foreign countries. The wide range in murder

TABLE 4.2   Murder Rates in Selected Cities Around the World

Country—City	Murder Rate per 100,000 Residents, 2012
Australia—Sydney	1
Austria—Vienna	1
Bahamas—Nassau	44
Belgium—Brussels	3
Belize—Belize City	105
Brazil—Sao Paulo	14
Canada—Toronto	1
China—Hong Kong	0.4
Colombia—Bogota	17
Costa Rica—San Jose	18
Czech Republic—Prague	1
Denmark—Copenhagen	1
Dominican Republic—Santo Domingo	29
El Salvador—San Salvador	53
Estonia—Tallinn	6
Egypt—Cairo	2
Finland—Helsinki	2
France—Paris	2
Germany—Berlin	1
Greece—Athens	2
Guatemala—Guatemala City	117
Honduras—Tegucigalpa	102
Hungary—Budapest	2
Indonesia—Jakarta	0.7
Italy—Rome	1
Jamaica—Kingston	50
Japan—Tokyo	0.2
Kenya—Nairobi	6
Mexico—Mexico City	9
Netherlands—Amsterdam	2
New Zealand—Auckland	0.7
Panama—Panama City	53
Poland—Warsaw	2
Portugal—Lisbon	0.6
Russia—Moscow	4
Spain—Madrid	1
South Korea—Seoul	0.8
Trinidad—Port of Spain	17
United Kingdom—London	1
United States—Detroit	45*
United States—New Orleans	41*
United States—St. Louis	38*
United States—New York	4*
Venezuela—Caracas	100**

NOTES: All rates are rounded off to the nearest whole number, except for those less than 1 per 100,000.

For some cities, 2011 is the latest year available.

*U.S. city rates are for 2013, the latest figures available.

**Estimated for 2013 (Cawthorne and Rawlins, 2014).

SOURCE: United Nations Office on Drugs and Crime Control, 2014.

rates in the world's leading cities is evident in Table 4.2. Note that cities, which have much smaller populations than entire countries, have the potential to show more volatility in homicide rates per 100,000 inhabitants from one year to the next. The rampages of a relatively small number of offenders can have a noticeable statistical impact. Ciudad Júarez, Mexico, may be the most dramatic case to illustrate this point. Its body count stood at about 300 homicides in 2007. Then a wave of drug-related violence engulfed the city, and during 2010 about 3,000 murders took place, a shocking tenfold increase (Valencia, 2010).

The cities with the most violent deaths per capita (taking the size of the population into account) are mostly in Central and South America and on certain Caribbean islands: Nassau (Bahamas), Belize City (Belize), Santo Domingo (Dominican Republic), San Salvador (El Salvador), Guatemala City (Guatemala), Tegucigalpa (Honduras), Kingston (Jamaica), Panama City (Panama), and Caracas (Venezuela). When these big city rates assembled in Table 4.2 are compared to the entire country's rates that were presented in Table 4.1, a pattern can be discerned: The leading city often has a higher murder rate than the rest of that country. However, there are some exceptions to this pattern, in which the leading city is safer than the country as a whole, such as Mexico City (Mexico) and Moscow (Russia). Reliable statistics are not available for certain cities known to be burdened by terribly high levels of violence, such as Cape Town as well as Johannesburg, South Africa (Rueda, 2013).

As for the United States, four cities in 2013 had murder rates that were in the same league as some of the roughest cities in the world: Detroit (with 45 per 100,000), New Orleans (with 41), St. Louis (with 38), and Baltimore (with 37). New Yorkers (at 4) were murdered at a rate that was slightly lower than "average Americans" (4.5 per 100,000). But New Yorkers have much more to fear than the inhabitants of large European cities of over several million inhabitants on the list, such as London, Paris, or Rome. Tokyo, the largest city on the list, was the most peaceful place of all. Other huge urban areas with extremely low murder rates of less than 1 per 100,000 were Hong Kong, China; Seoul, South Korea; Jakarta, Indonesia; and Auckland, New Zealand.

The above examination of international comparisons has revealed a crucial risk factor: where a person lives (and by extension, the people one interacts with on a daily basis) has a major impact on the chance of being murdered. People who reside in certain foreign countries and certain cities face much graver dangers of dying violently than inhabitants of other places. So "location" is a substantial determinant of differential risks of becoming a victim of homicide.

Those who lose their lives tend to be permanent residents of a city. Tourists, business travelers, conventioneers, and other visitors rarely get caught up in deadly showdowns far from home, according to a detailed analysis of murders in New York City (see Karmen, 2006).

The Geographic Distribution of Violent Deaths in the United States

Now that the murder rates in different countries and their biggest cities have been analyzed, the next logical step is to zoom in on the United States. The international comparisons in Tables 4.1 and 4.2 highlight the well-known fact that some parts of the world are much more violent—or much more peaceful—than others. But what about the spatial distribution of lethal violence within the United States? Are there striking differences in the murder rate for different parts of the country, for different cities, and even for various neighborhoods within cities?

The answer, as everyone knows, is of course "yes!" A number of geographic factors strongly influence differential risks. As for the four sections of the country, historically the highest homicide rates have been recorded in the South (with 5.3 per 100,000 in 2013); the lowest have been in the Northeast (at 3.5 per 100,000) and the West (at 4.0). The rates in the Midwest generally have fallen in-between (at 4.5). Residents of metropolitan areas (urban centers rather than suburbs) face higher risks of violent death than do inhabitants of rural counties or of small cities beyond the fringe of metropolitan areas.

Geography-based risks can even be further fine-tuned by calculating murder rates for U.S. cities. A closer look at the FBI's data from municipal police departments confirms that some urban centers were much more dangerous places to dwell in than others. The map in Figure 4.1 shows vertical bars that depict the number of residents who were murdered out of every 100,000 inhabitants of that city (taking size into account is the only sound way to make such comparisons).

The map indicates that among the largest cities, Detroit had the dubious distinction of being the homicide capital of the country in 2013. (When Detroit had to declare fiscal bankruptcy in 2013, it was a more dangerous place, with a murder rate of 45 per 100,000 residents, than it was in 2010, when its murder rate was 34 per 100,000.) The most well-known medium-size city with some of country's roughest neighborhoods is New Orleans (which became even more dangerous after the floods caused by Hurricane Katrina but then improved substantially, as its murder rate tumbled from a sky-high level of 95 per 100,000 residents in 2007 down to still intolerable level of 41 in 2013). In fact, as far as trends go, outbursts of lethal violence diminished in nearly all big U.S. cities from the 1990s up to 2013. Despite the nationwide decline in murder rates, the risks facing residents remain much higher in Detroit, Philadelphia, Washington D.C., Atlanta, and Miami than in Denver, San Francisco, San Jose, San Antonio, Los Angeles, and New York. The nation's safest big cities were Seattle and San Diego (see Figure 4.1).

According to researchers, the disparities are not simply a function of size but seem to be determined by conditions such as population density, the local economy (poverty and unemployment rates, wage scales, and the gap between rich and poor), special problems (the easy availability of illegal handguns, the extent of drug trafficking, and the ineffectiveness of police strategies), traditions and customs (including the persistence of a subculture that condones violence), and demographic factors (especially divorce rates and the proportion of the population that is poor, male,

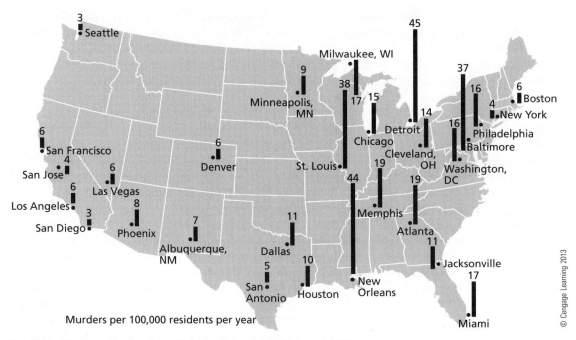

FIGURE 4.1   Murder Rates In Major Cities, United States, 2013

young, and of a marginalized minority group) (see Tardiff, Gross, and Messner, 1986; Chilton, 1987; Land, McCall, and Cohen, 1990; Messner and Golden, 1992; and Karmen, 2006).

To complicate matters further, murder rates vary dramatically within the confines of a city's limits. Upscale urban neighborhoods are rarely crime scenes while the mean streets on the "wrong side of the tracks" are virtual battlefields between rival street gangs, drug dealing crews, or hostile factions of organized crime. Also, neighborhood homicide rates can flare up or die down substantially over a span of just a few years as local conditions deteriorate or improve (see Karmen, 2006).

Who Gets Killed by Whom? How, Where, and Why?

Now that some patterns in the level of lethal violence have been spotted, it is time to focus more closely on some common threads that run through thousands of slayings, and what has been pieced together about the relationships between victims and their killers in recent years. Did the victims know their offenders? How did they perish? What caused the confrontations that led to their untimely deaths? To answer these questions, it is necessary to derive a **profile** or **statistical portrait** of the "typical" murder, victim, and killer.

NCVS interviewers ask no questions about murders of household members, and coroners' records only maintain information about the deceased but not about the killer or the crime, so the *UCR* is the only source of detailed data that links the individual who perished to the murderer. *UCR* guidelines urge police officials to fill out a **Supplementary Homicide Report** (SHR) about each killing in their jurisdiction. The resulting SHR database provides information about the age, sex, and race of the victim and—if detectives solved the case and made an arrest—the accused person's age, sex, race, weapon, possible motive, and his or her prior relationship—if any—with the slain person.

The first question that can be answered with the help of data from the SHRs is, "How many murders involved just a single killer and a lone victim." Nearly one half of all the homicides in which the police were able to figure out what happened were simply confrontations between two people. The remainder were either unknown or involved more than one attacker and/or more than one person who perished, according to the 2013 *UCR*.

Another issue that can be readily addressed is "How were the victims killed?" For decades, the majority of killers have dispatched their adversaries with firearms. Sometimes murderers use rifles and shotguns, but usually they prefer handguns (revolvers and pistols account for about two-thirds of all gun deaths). The proportion of victims who expired from bullet wounds rose from 64 percent in 1990 to just about 70 percent in 1993, before subsiding to 65 percent in 1998, lurching back up to 70 percent in 2004, and staying just about at that level (69 percent) in 2013. Knives and other sharp instruments ran a distant second as the weapons of choice, accounting for 12 percent of all deaths. The rest were slain by blunt instruments; fists and feet; hands (largely via strangulation and smothering); and by various other ways (explosions, arson, poisons, by being pushed, and other less frequent means).

Another issue that can be addressed with data from the SHRs is, "By whom? Did the victim know the killer?" Recall that this is the kind of issue that intrigued the founders of victimology. They were criminologists who wanted to study the interaction between victims and offenders. They were especially interested in uncovering any prior relationships between the two parties in cases of lethal interpersonal violence. For example, they wondered whether the killer and the mortally wounded person previously had known each other (as intimates, adversaries, or casual acquaintances). To shed light on this pattern within slayings, victim–offender relationships need to be broadly categorized. Perhaps the two were complete strangers brought together by fate. Maybe both were members of the same family (nuclear or extended). The third possibility is that the killer and his target were acquaintances, neighbors, or friends (including girlfriend or boyfriend). According to data in the SHRs derived from police investigations from the 1990s up to 2013, in the most

common situation (ranging from 29 percent to 38 percent) the offender was a friend or acquaintance. Killings of one family member by another added up to an additional 12 percent to 14 percent each year. Slayings by strangers accounted for about 12 percent to 16 percent of cases for which the relationship could be surmised by detectives. Unfortunately for researchers, unsolved homicides of "unknown relationship" (at the time the SHRs were submitted) made up the largest category, hovering between 35 and 45 percent in recent decades (36 percent in 2013) (FBI, 2014).

If detectives could determine the victim–offender relationship in this residual grouping (which presumably contains many difficult-to-solve slayings by complete strangers), the percentages due to family quarrels and conflicts with friends and acquaintances probably would be much smaller. Nevertheless, looking only at solved cases, the old adage remains true: A person is more likely to be killed by someone he or she knows than by a complete stranger. In 45 percent of all solved murders in 2013, the killer was an acquaintance or even a former friend. Family members killed each other in 25 percent of all solved cases. Strangers were deemed to be the killers in nearly 20 percent of all solved cases. Because so many slayings remain unsolved, it is difficult to determine if the proportion of murders committed by strangers is rising. It remains an important issue for further research because it is more difficult to anticipate and guard against attacks by unknown assailants (see Riedel, 1987). (SHRs are filled out shortly after killings take place. Police departments usually do not send updated reports to the *UCR* for "cold cases" that they solve months or years later. Some departments do not submit SHRs to the *UCR* for each killing, as they are supposed to do in this voluntary reporting system.)

A third question that can be answered is, "Why? What were these sudden violent outbursts all about?" The reasons for the confrontations that claimed lives are called the "circumstances" by police departments and the FBI. The SHRs expose some widely held myths arising from TV shows and movies. Of the 6,681 murders committed during 2013 whose circumstances were known, in only

13 were the deceased categorized as engaged in prostitution. Gangland killings of mobsters claimed 138 lives (up from 78 in 2007) but amounted to just 2 percent of all murders across the country that year. Drug dealers' turf battles (386) and drug-fueled brawls (59) added up to another 7 percent. Killings arising from clashes between rival juvenile street gangs (584) accounted for nearly 9 percent of all murders in which the motive was known. Although this nationwide gang death toll dropped from about 670 in 2010 to nearly 585 in 2013, gang membership remained a risky activity in many urban neighborhoods. Robbers stole around 685 lives, about 10 percent of the 2013 body count (FBI, 2014b).

However, the largest category was "other arguments—not specified" (more than 25 percent of all cases solved during 2013). This miscellaneous grouping of heated disputes includes some that were trivial or based on misunderstandings and others that must have seemed to be matters worth killing for and dying over to the participants at the time. If this vague grouping is added to "unknown reasons" surrounding cases the police couldn't solve then the motives for around half of all the 2013 killings remain a mystery and can't be meaningfully analyzed. In sum, the available data does not provide definitive answers to the key concern, "what brought about their deadly showdown?"

Who Faces the Gravest Threats of Being Murdered?

The 2013 U.S. murder rate of 4.5 means that out of every collection of 100,000 people, nearly 5 people were killed and 99,995 survived. Who were these unfortunate few that were marked for death? This statistic captures the odds of being slain for fictitious "average" Americans of all backgrounds, which is a useful social construct for certain purposes (for example, as shown above, to compare the perils faced by U.S. residents to the dangers confronting the average Canadian or Mexican). But this composite statistic conceals as much as it reveals. When the SHRs are used to deconstruct the body count, differential risks

of getting killed become evident. These findings should be especially alarming for those who fall into some or all of the high-risk categories and should be somewhat reassuring for members of other groups. The odds of suddenly expiring vary greatly from place to place: by region of the country, area of residence (urban, suburban, or rural), and specific location (which city) as was shown above. Hence, differential risks already have been uncovered in terms of geography: where people reside. It should come as no surprise that three other important factors are sex, age, and race or ethnicity.

SHR statistics indicate that a person's sex is a crucial determinant of risks. Men die violently much more frequently than women. Year after year, at least three-quarters of the corpses are of boys and men (almost 78 percent in 2013). This proportion has remained roughly the same since the early 1960s. Expressed as rates, boys and men are killed at least three and during some years four times as often as girls and women. Also, over recent decades, about 9 out of 10 of the known offenders were teenage boys or men (roughly 90 percent of the arrestees were males in 2013). Therefore, most murders can be categorized as male-on-male. When females get killed, the murderers usually turn out to be males (91 percent of all girls and women were slain by boys and men in 2013). On infrequent occasions when females kill, they tend to slay their own small children or the men in their lives rather than other women.

As for the race of those whose lives were snuffed out prematurely, the *UCR* recognizes only these categories: white, black, and other (Asians) plus undetermined or unknown. (Note that most Hispanics were counted as whites on the SHRs.) During 2013, roughly half (51 percent) of all those who perished were black, a little less than half were white (45 percent), and the small remainder (3 percent) were of other races (mostly Asians) or of unknown origin (1 percent). Because half of all those who were killed were black, but only about 13 percent of the population identified themselves as people of African descent according to the U.S. Census Bureau, these *UCR* calculations confirm that black communities across the country suffer from disproportionately high rates of lethal violence. Whites, who comprise 78 percent of the population but only 45 percent of the departed, experience disproportionately low risks. Put another way, the dangers of getting murdered are disproportionately higher for blacks than for whites or others. As for ethnicity, the SHRs indicated that 18 percent of all those who were murdered were Hispanic, which is in line with the proportion of the population that was classified as Latino or Hispanic (17 percent) by the Census Bureau (see Harrell, 2007).

As for victim–offender relationships, most slayings turn out to be intraracial, not interracial, a longstanding pattern according to decades of record-keeping (see Wood, 1990). Focusing solely upon lone-offender/single-victim killings carried out during 2013, the *UCR*'s SHRs documented that 90 percent of black victims were slain by black offenders, and 83 percent of white victims were killed by white perpetrators.

Besides sharp differences in risks by sex and race, murder rates also have varied dramatically by age, a pattern that was discerned decades ago (see Akiyama, 1981). Children between 9 and 12 years old are the least likely age group to be slain. The risks of being murdered rise during the teenage years and peak during the early twenties, between ages 20 and 24. After age 25, the body count drops substantially with each passing year, indicating an inverse relationship: As a person grows older, risks decline smoothly. The typical victims were in their late teens, twenties, and thirties when they were killed. Almost two-thirds (62 percent in 2014) of those who died way before their time were between the ages of 17 and 39. An even higher proportion of perpetrators fall into this age range. As a result, most murders can be characterized as young adults slaying other relatively young persons.

So far, this listing of differential risks has been based on the 2013 *UCR*. But what about the recent past? A statistical portrait of all the people who were slain and all the persons arrested for murder and manslaughter between the years 1980 and 2008 appears in Box 4.1. The picture that emerged from this comprehensive analysis of the FBI's SHRs shows that the differential risks detected in

2013 are consistent with the patterns that prevailed over almost three decades.

From this review of the demographic factors that are correlated with murder rates, a profile can be drawn indicating which groups of people run the greatest risks of suddenly dying from an act of violence. They are Southerners, urban residents, males, teenagers, and young adults between 18 and 24, and African-Americans. Those who fall into the opposite groups face the lowest risks of all: Northeasterners, residents of small towns in rural areas, females, children and the elderly, whites, and Asians.

One additional factor profoundly influences the dangers of becoming embroiled in lethal showdowns: financial status. Lower income people fall into the high-risk group while affluent persons enjoy life in the low-risk group. But this pattern cannot be unearthed from the SHRs because police files and FBI compilations do not collect information about the social class of the deceased. However, an analysis of New York City murders determined from death certificates that the overwhelming majority of the victims had never been to college and that the zip code of their last known address often indicated they had resided in a low-income neighborhood. Furthermore, of the persons arrested for these homicides, about 85 percent qualified as "indigent" in court and were provided with an attorney at no cost by the government. Furthermore, the majority of crime scenes were located in precincts in poverty-stricken neighbors. These findings underscore the connection between violence and economic standing: Being poor is a major risk factor for getting killed as well as for committing murder. Many murders can be characterized as "poor on poor" (Karmen, 2006).

It seems that the attitudes and behaviors of entire groups—such as males, young adults, low-income earners, and city dwellers—determine, to some degree, their fate.

Changes over Time in Near Death Experiences: Trends in Aggravated Assault Rates

Murder and robbery are the two violent crimes that are the main focus of this chapter, but at this point a look at trends in aggravated assaults also would be

BOX 4.1   A Statistical Picture of Murders in the United States, 1980–2008

An analysis of a massive database of hundreds of thousands of SHRs containing details about homicides committed over a span of 28 years established that the perpetrators and their victims were not a representative cross-section of all Americans. On the contrary, murderers and the people they killed were more likely to be male, young, and black, in terms of their demographic characteristics.

By Sex:

Males were disproportionately involved as the accused perpetrators (nearly 90 percent of all arrestees) and as their targets (over 75 percent of the deceased), although males comprise only about 50 percent of the population. Their rate of offending was about 15 for every 100,000 American boys and men, but for females it was less than 2 arrests per 100,000 girls and women per year. The victimization rate for males was close to 12 per 100,000, but for females it was much lower, close to 3 per 100,000 per year. Clearly, the typical murder was male-on-male.

   Males mostly killed other males, but also killed females. Females rarely killed, and when they did, they usually killed males.

By Age:

Americans 18–24 years old made up nearly 11 percent of the population but accounted for more than one-third (38 percent) of all the accused killers and about one-quarter (24 percent) of the deceased. Eighteen- to 24-year olds had the highest rates of offending (29 per 100,000 per year) and of dying violently (17 per 100,000) of any age group. Twenty-five- to 34-year-olds suffered the second highest rate of involvement as offenders as well as victims. Nearly two-thirds of all victims and more than three-quarters of all arrestees were under 35 years of age. Therefore, the typical murder involved young adults killing other young adults.

By Race:

Americans of African descent were overrepresented as both victims and offenders. The victimization rate for blacks was 28 per 100,000 per year while for whites it was less than 5 per 100,000. The offending rate for blacks was over 34 per 100,000 while for whites it was less than 5. People identifying themselves as black comprised about 13 percent of the population but made up nearly half (47 percent) of all those who died violently and a little more than half (53 percent) who were arrested for manslaughter and murder. The typical murder was intraracial. Eighty-four percent of whites were slain by whites, and 93 percent of blacks were killed by blacks.

Victim–offender relationships:

Strangers were responsible for about one-fifth (22 percent) of all homicides in which the police could determine the victim–offender relationship.

   Of the remaining 78 percent of killings carried out by nonstrangers, the victim was a spouse in 10 percent of the cases, another family member in 12 percent, and a boyfriend or girlfriend in 6 percent. The remaining half (49 percent) involved other types of acquaintances.

Circumstances:

Arguments over all kinds of miscellaneous matters (other than issues surrounding street gangs and drugs, which are separate categories) made up the largest heading each year.

   Homicides involving members of juvenile or adult gangs increased from 220 deaths (about 1 percent of all killings) in 1980 to 960 (about 6 percent) in 2008.

   The majority of drug-related and gang-related killings took place in large cities.

SOURCE: Cooper and Smith, 2011.

appropriate. Aggravated or felonious assaults are the most frequent category, outnumbering the other serious interpersonal crimes of violence (murder, rape, robbery) monitored by the *UCR* every year.

   By definition, aggravated assaults result in serious wounds or involve attacks (or threats of harm) with a deadly weapon. Therefore, some aggravated assaults are attempted murders in which the injured parties barely survived (a bullet missed its mark, a stabbing was not fatal, and a severe beating almost claimed a life). To put it differently, homicides are aggravated assaults in which victims do not recover from the wounds inflicted by their adversaries. With some bad luck or poor timing or ineffective medical care, an aggravated assault easily could wind up as a murder. Conversely, with good fortune, a tragedy might be averted by ambulance crews, paramedics, and hospital emergency room personnel, and a vicious act of violence that would have added to the body count remains a near death experience and is officially recorded as an aggravated assault.

Whether a victim of an aggravated assault lives or dies depends on several factors, including the weapon used, the severity of the wound, the injured party's preexisting health condition, and the quality of medical care received. According to a nationwide study that analyzed the caliber of various trauma care systems in selected counties across the country, a continuous drop in the lethality of assaults since 1960 can be primarily attributed to advances in emergency medicine (Harris, Thomas, Fischer, and Hirsch, 2002). The policy implication is that the most important way to drive the murder rate down is to help critically wounded people stay alive by having competent ER doctors, nurses, and EMTs on call, ready to spring into action.

Both the *UCR* and the *NCVS* keep records of the annual number of aggravated assaults. Because two sources of official data can be tapped, a graph depicting changes over time in the rates of assaults with a deadly weapon or serious attacks can have two trend lines: one according to the *UCR* and the other according to the *NCVS*. The graph shown in Figure 4.2 displays the estimated rates for aggravated assaults committed across the United States from 1973 to 2013.

The *NCVS* trend line shows that close calls and near death experiences of people shot or stabbed declined slightly in frequency from the early 1970s until the early 1990s. Then the *NCVS* was redesigned; the rate of aggravated assaults jumped in part because of the new measurement methods. However, by the end of the 1990s and for several years into the new century, a dramatic improvement in the level of serious interpersonal violence became

evident from *NCVS* estimates. Between 1993 (when the survey was redesigned and the rate hit a peak) and 2009, aggravated assaults disclosed to *NCVS* interviewers plummeted about 60 percent. By 2013, the rate had leveled off a bit above its lowest point in 40 years, at a little less than 4 persons per 1,000, way down from its peak in the early 1990s at 12 per 1,000.

UCR data shows a somewhat different pattern up to the early 1990s. After years of rising numbers of reports about serious attacks, complaints to the police about felonious assaults peaked in 1993 at about 430 per 100,000 people. From that high point, the level of violence subsided substantially during the second half of the 1990s and continued to diminish gradually through the twenty-first century, which is the same downward drift indicated by the *NCVS* line on the graph. The *UCR* rates combining shootings, stabbings, and other felonious assaults in 2013 were way down at about 230 per 100,000. But unlike the *NCVS* data points, they still had not quite fallen to their lowest levels in 40 years.

But the good news about this very positive trend must be tempered by a recognition that a growing number of totally innocent persons are sustaining aggravated assaults from gun violence that comes out of the blue.

During 2013, President Obama signed into law the Investigative Assistance for Violent Crimes Act. It authorized the U.S. Department of Justice to look into attempted mass killings in places of public use in order to provide federal, state, and local law enforcement agencies with data that will help them to better understand how to prepare for, prevent, respond to, and recover from these violent outbursts. The FBI began in 2014 to report about the casualties of "active shooter" incidents, in which an offender attempts to kill people in a confined and populated area such as a school, workplace, shopping center, house of worship, transportation hub, or some other gathering place like a movie theater. The monitoring system does not count all mass killings (of three or more persons) or all mass shootings (for example, gang fights and turf battles between rival drug dealing crews are excluded). It focused on 160 active shooter incidents that broke out between

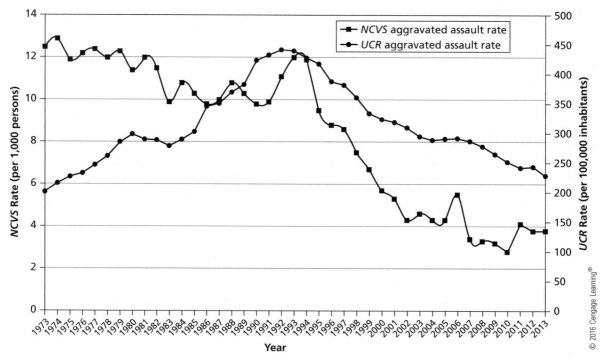

FIGURE 4.2   Trends in Aggravated Assaults, United States, 1973–2013

2000 and 2013. The gunmen collectively inflicted 1,043 casualties on the general public, murdering 486 people and wounding 557. The median number of people slain per incident was 2, with another 2 injured. During the first seven years from 2000 to 2006, an average of around six incidents broke out each year. During the next seven-year interval up to 2013, more than 16 outbreaks took place annually; so the trend, unfortunately, is upward. The gunfire erupted in 40 of the 50 states, and 60 percent of the attacks were over before the local police could arrive to save lives. Most of the shootings lasted five minutes or less. Even when the police arrived at the scene in time to intervene, the victims still had to make desperate life-and-death decisions. The worst bloodshed took place at an elementary school, a college campus, an army base, and a movie theater. The year with the highest number of casualties (a total of 90 murdered and 118 victims of aggravated assaults) was 2012; during 2000, only seven people were killed or injured in these kinds of armed attacks.

Ten percent of the shooters went after women with whom they had or formerly had a romantic relationship. In 12 of these 16 incidents, these women were killed; an additional 42 innocent onlookers were murdered, and another 28 were wounded. In 13 percent of all the incidents (21 of 160), the gunfire stopped after unarmed bystanders and victims courageously, safely, and successfully restrained the shooter. The FBI concluded that the study supports the importance of training ordinary citizens (including members of the college campus community) as well as law enforcement officers by holding what-to-do-if exercises (FBI, 2014c).

FOCUSING ON ROBBERIES

Robbers are usually complete strangers on the prowl for suitable prey. Therefore, they are among the most feared and hated of all street criminals. The offense combines stealing with extortion or outright violence (often including the use of weapons), so it carries some of the stiffest prison sentences permissible under law. And yet, throughout history, bandits were considered much more interesting than their victims, and their exploits were often romanticized. The highwaymen of Robin Hood's band, pirates who plundered ships laden with treasure, frontier outlaws who ambushed stagecoaches and trains, and gangsters who held up banks during the Great Depression—all were the subjects of stories and songs sympathetic to, or at least understanding of, the impulses that drove their dramatic deeds. But the glitter has largely faded and in its place is the image of the mugger or gunman as a vicious thug, a cruel predator, and an exploiter of weakness—one whose random violence casts a shadow over everyday life. This reversal in the imagery of robbers has sparked renewed concern for their victims.

Robbers and the People They Prey Upon

Completed robberies are face-to-face confrontations in which perpetrators take something of value directly from victims against their will, either by force or by threats of violence. Whether the holdup is completed or just attempted, the law considers armed robberies more serious than unarmed ones (**strong-arm robberies, muggings**, or **yokings**).

Robberies: Who, How Often, How, Where, When

Because nearly all robbery victims live to tell about their experiences, more details can be gathered about them than about people who were murdered. Some limited information about robberies that were reported to and solved by local police departments appears annually in the FBI's *UCR*. The data indicates the number of incidents and describe the people who were arrested—but not the people who were accosted. The *NCVS*—not the *UCR*—is the source to tap to find out "how often, who, how, where, when," plus information concerning losses, injuries, stolen property recovery rates, and reactions during the confrontations (Harlow, 1987).

Respondents in the sample who confided that they had been robbed within the past six months provided *NCVS* interviewers with a wealth of data. They described the assailants who robbed them and the weapons used against them, and they disclosed whether the robbers got what they were after, where and when the crimes took place, if they resisted, whether they got hurt, and if so, how seriously. The answers from these unfortunate individuals in the sample were used to derive projections about the experiences of all Americans over the age of 11 who were robbed. To simplify matters, only single-victim/single-offender incidents will be analyzed (Harrell, 2005; 2007).

Nearly 370,000 people were robbed during 2013, according to projections derived from the *NCVS* sample. That translated to a rate of a little more than 2 per 1,000 persons over the age of 11. In a little more than half of the face-to-face confrontations, the robbers were unarmed, but in 17 percent they brandished a firearm (almost always a handgun) and in 14 percent they pulled out a knife. Almost 45 percent of the victims (but especially the males) said the offenders were complete strangers, but a surprising proportion, 17 percent (almost exclusively the female victims), characterized the robber as an "intimate" and another 11 percent recognized the offender as a relative. Most of the rest (22 percent) were described as acquaintances, either casual or even well-known. Over 67 percent of the individuals who were robbed that year informed the police about their harrowing experiences, according to the BJS analysis tool customized report (BJS, 2014).

The primary motive behind robbery is theft. But offenders did not always get what they wanted. About one-quarter (27 percent) of robberies ended up as unsuccessful attempts to steal cash and valuables. The typical victim lost about $150. Most often, they were relieved of personal effects such as portable electronic or photographic gear, and jewelry, followed by purses and wallets containing credit cards and cash. Most robbery victims never recovered any of these valuables on their own or after an investigation by the police in 2008, the last year that such detailed analyses were available (*NCVS*, 2011).

Robbers, armed or not, hurt their victims for a number of reasons. They may do so initially to intimidate the target into submission. They may become violent during the holdup in reaction to resistance, lack of cooperation, or stalling. Offenders may relish taking advantage of a helpless person or may seize the opportunity to show off to accomplices. Injuring their targets may be a sign of panic, disappointment in the haul, anger, scorn, contempt, sadism, or loss of self-control. Unleashing violence may also be instrumental: Wounding individuals can render them incapable of later identifying the robbers, pursuing them, or even calling for help. Explosive outbursts at the end of the transaction may be intended to shock, stun, or preoccupy victims, their associates, and any bystanders so that they will hesitate to summon the police.

Despite all these possible motives for inflicting injuries, most robbers didn't wound their victims. Only a little more than one-third (37 percent) of those who suffered either completed or attempted robberies were wounded. However, some who escaped injuries were grabbed, shoved, and otherwise roughed up. Among the wounded, most victims experienced minor injuries, such as cuts, scratches, bruises, and swellings. A small proportion suffered serious injuries, such as broken bones, lost teeth, loss of consciousness, or gunshot wounds that required medical care in a hospital emergency room. About 8 percent of robbery victims in 2008 incurred medical expenses, usually from visiting a hospital emergency room (BJS, 2011). Similarly, in 2013 about 40 percent of the people who were accosted told interviewers they were injured in the incident, but most of them (62 percent) did not need any medical treatment for their wounds, according to the customized table generated by the BJS analysis tool.

Changes over Time in Robbery Rates

Robbery is often cited as the offense most people worry about when they express their fears about street crime. Robbery is a confrontational crime in which force is used, or violence is threatened (…"or else"). Figure 4.3 displays the trends in robbery rates according to *UCR* and *NCVS* data. The *UCR* trend line shows that robberies soared after 1977, peaked in 1981, plunged until 1985, and then shot up again to record levels in the early 1990s. After that, reports of muggings and holdups plummeted impressively until 2001. Known cases of robberies largely continued to drift downward during the first decade of the twenty-first century (bottoming out in 2010), and then ending up in 2013 a little above their lowest level in 40 years (FBI, 2014b).

The *NCVS* trend line tells a very similar, but not identical, story. It indicates that the robbery rate fell between 1974 and 1978, rebounded until 1981 when it hit an all-time high, dropped sharply during the early 1980s, but then climbed back up from 1985 until 1994. The robbery rate then tumbled an impressive 65 percent between 1993 and 2002 before creeping back up a little. By 2013, disclosures to interviewers about robberies had reached their lowest levels since the *NCVS* surveys began 40 years earlier.

Checking Out Whether More Robberies Are Turning into Murders

One bit of good news about robbery is often overlooked: Most victims are not injured, and of those who are, most don't need medical attention in an emergency room. And yet, because robbery is such a potentially devastating crime, a troubling question ought to arise: How often do robberies escalate into murders? In other words, what are the chances of being killed by a robber? Robbers may wound their victims (and perhaps inadvertently kill them) to quell resistance or to prevent them from calling for help and reporting the crime or to intimidate them from pressing charges and testifying in court.

On occasion, claims are made that robbers these days are more viciously violent than ever before. The impression that robbers kill more readily "these days" than in the past is part of a

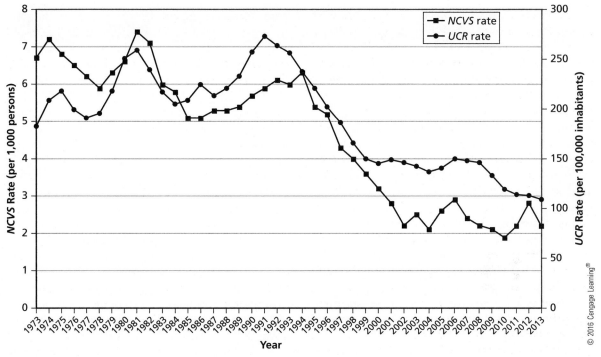

F I G U R E 4.3   Trends in Robberies, United States, 1973–2013

gloomy larger perception that American society is falling apart, that civilization is collapsing, and that predators today are more depraved than ever before. In the aftermath of a particularly gruesome slaying, journalists sometimes play up this theme. But this is nothing new.

For example, during the "good old days" of the 1940s and 1950s, when street crime was not a major issue in electoral campaigns because it wasn't perceived to be a pressing problem, some people feared robbers would kill them even if they surrendered without a fight and cooperated. A reporter at the time (Whitman, 1951, p. 5) wrote: "The hoodlum will bash in your head with a brick for a dollar and ninety-eight cents. The police records of our cities are spotted with cases of 'murder for peanuts' in which the victims, both men and women, have been slugged, stabbed, hit with iron pipes, hammers, or axes, and in a few cases kicked to death—the loot being no more than the carfare a woman carried in her purse or the small change in a man's pocket."

Several decades later, a newsmagazine's cover story (Press et al., 1981, p. 48) titled "The Plague of Violent Crime" observed: "Another frightening difference in the crime picture is that life is now pitifully cheap. Law enforcement officials think they have witnessed a shift toward gratuitous slaughter. 'It used to be *Your money or your life,*'says a Bronx assistant district attorney.... 'Now it's *Your money and your life.*'"

So a journalist had the impression at the start of the 1950s that robbers were becoming more vicious. The same assertion was made by a journalist at the start of the 1980s. Were these frightening media images based on facts? Is it true, as some people fear, that more and more robberies are escalating into murders (see Cook, 1985, 1987)? Researchers must undertake a fine grained analysis. Victimologists can combine *UCR* statistics on murders and *NCVS* findings about robberies to shed some light on this grisly question (see the data assembled in Table 4.3 inside Box 4.2).

BOX 4.2 "Your Money or Your Life!"

Using both the *UCR* and the *NCVS*, it is possible to derive rough estimates of how many robbery victims get killed each year, and whether that percentage is growing or shrinking.

The number of robberies committed annually can be estimated from *NCVS* figures. However, the *NCVS* excludes robberies of establishments like convenience stores and banks and thereby unavoidably undercounts commercial robberies where some employee or bystander might get slain. *UCR* figures are always smaller because they represent only the robberies known to the police. The SHRs' annual number of slayings that were felony murders starting out as robberies is surely an undercount because homicide detectives are unable to determine the motive and solve the crime in around one-third of all cases. Also, in certain murders, the killer might have robbed the deceased person's corpse as an afterthought, according to a study of robbery-related homicides in Baltimore during 1983 (see Loftin, 1986).

Acknowledging these methodological caveats, rough calculations can be performed to derive ballpark estimates of how often targeted individuals—whether they are cooperating or resisting—are murdered by robbers. (See the data assembled in Table 4.3.)

Several tentative conclusions can be reached from this statistical evidence drawn from official sources: The nationwide annual death toll is disturbing but at least it is diminishing. Nearly 2,500 people died at the hands of robbers in 1980, and about 685 perished in 2013. But, thankfully, slayings committed during the course of holdups are rare, considering the huge numbers of confrontations (well over a million in 1980, nearly 370,000 in 2013) in which a life could have been taken along with money or possessions. In 2013, the proportion of robbery victims who were slain—less than two-tenths of 1 percent, was within the same range as during the past 33 years. So predators these days are not more inclined to snuff out the lives of their prey while trying to relieve them of their valuables before making their escape.

And yet, this advice remains sound: When accosted by an armed offender who growls, "Your money or your life!" statistics confirm that the correct response is to hand over the money and hang on to your life, according to a detailed study of more than 100 solved homicides that occurred in Chicago during 1983 (Zimring and Zuehl, 1986).

TABLE 4.3   Yearly Estimates of Murders Committed During Robberies

	1980	1990	2000	2010	2013
Number of persons murdered (from the *UCR*)	23,040	23,438	15,586	14,748	12,253
Number of persons murdered during a robbery (from the *UCR*)	2,488	2,156	1,077	780	686
Total number of robbery victims (from the *NCVS*)	1,179,000	1,150,000	732,000	480,750	369,000
Murdered victims as a percentage of all robbery victims	0.21%	0.19%	0.14%	0.16%	0.19%

SOURCE: FBI's *UCR*, 1980, 1990, 2000, 2010, 2013; BJS's *NCVS*, 1980, 1990, 2000, 2010, 2013.

Differential Risks: Which Groups Get Robbed the Most and the Least Often?

To discover patterns in robberies, researchers must sort through data collected each year about various groupings of people and households that participated in the *NCVS* survey. According to the *NCVS* for 2013, the robbery rate was 2.4 per 1,000. That means just about 2 individuals out of every 1,000 residents over the age of 11 got robbed that year. But, just as with murder rates, sharp differences in robbery risks become evident when the odds facing the average American are disaggregated or deconstructed. Breaking down the *NCVS* sample into subcategories, certain demographic groupings were robbed much more often than others. Patterns that prevailed when robbery was a huge problem in 1993 and patterns that still persisted when the robbery rate was dramatically lower in 2013 can be discerned from the data assembled in Table 4.4.

To put the issue bluntly, although everyone might be apprehensive about being robbed at a certain time and place, particular groups of people have a lot more to fear on a regular basis than

TABLE 4.4   Robbery Rates for Various Groups, 1993 and 2013

Victim Characteristics	1993 Rate	2013 Rate
Overall rate	8 per 1,000	2 per 1,000
Sex		
Male	11	3
Female	6	2
Race and Ethnicity		
White	7	2
Black	21	3
Other	9	4*
Hispanic	14	3
Age		
15–17	13	3*
18–20	16	3*
21–24	11	4
25–34	11	4
35–49	6	2
50–64	2	2
65 and older	2	0.4*
Family income**		
Less than $7,500	15	10
$7,500–$14,999	12	8
$15,000–$24,999	10	5
$25,000–$34,999	6	2
$35,000–$49,999	6	3
$50,000–$74,999	7	1
$75,000 or more	5	0.6
Location of the Incident		
Urban	15	3
Cities with more than 1 million residents	34**	4
Suburban	7	2
Rural	4	2*
Marital status**		
Married	3	0.8
Widowed	2	3*
Divorced	12	4
Separated	19	9*
Never married	17	4

NOTES: Rates are per 1,000 people with these characteristics per year. All rates are rounded off to the nearest whole number, except for those smaller than 1.0.

*Estimate is based on very few cases and could be unreliable.

**Figure is for 1995, not 1993.

SOURCE: BJS's *Victimization Analysis Tool, 2014*.

others. The differential risks vary dramatically by demographic characteristics.

Starting with sex, the first pattern that stands out is that males are singled out more often than females. The rate for males was 11 per 1,000 in

1993, compared to 6 for females. By 2013, boys and men were getting robbed a lot less frequently than in 1993 (down sharply to just 3 per 1,000) but they still tangled more often with robbers than girls and women (down substantially to just 2 per 1,000).

With regard to race and ethnicity, in 1993 blacks and Hispanics were accosted several times as often as whites and others (mostly Americans of Asian ancestry). By 2013, the rates for all four racial and ethnic groups had tumbled and the differences had nearly disappeared, although whites still enjoyed lower risks than blacks, Hispanics, and others.

As for age, the analysis of the survey's findings for 1993 revealed that younger people (between the ages of 15 and 34) were confronted much more often than older people. Individuals in their late teens faced the gravest risks of all. After those peak years, risks decline steadily with advancing age. In other words, an inverse relationship prevails: As age increases, the dangers of being robbed decrease. In 2013, the differences in victimization rates had narrowed dramatically but the overall pattern persisted: People younger than 35 were targeted more often than those who were older. Contrary to the impression that robbers prefer to prey upon the elderly and frail, the statistics demonstrate that senior citizens are singled out the least often of any age group.

Family income also appeared to be negatively correlated with robbery rates. As income increased, the chances of being robbed generally decreased, with just one exception. In 1993, the differences between the lowest and highest income groups were dramatic. Twenty years later, the gap had narrowed considerably, but the pattern persisted: The desperately poor were robbed of their meager possessions much more often than others with higher household incomes. Clearly, robbers are no Robin Hoods.

Robbery is thought to be a big-city problem, and that perception is supported by the data.

In 1993, residents of urban areas were targeted much more often than suburbanites, while inhabitants of small towns and rural areas led safer lives. Inhabitants of the largest cities with populations of over 1,000,000 suffered a shockingly high victimization rate of 33 per 100,000. Two decades later, city people still faced higher risks and country people still enjoyed lower odds, but the dangers of getting robbed in all areas had tumbled, especially in the nation's largest cities.

In addition to sex, age, race and ethnicity, income, and area of residence, marital status made a big difference: In 1993, individuals who had never been married or who were separated or divorced endured much higher robbery rates than either married or widowed people (who generally were older and tended to be female). By 2013, risks were lower for all groups (except for the widowed, but that statistic was based on very few cases), but the pattern persisted: Those who were not married were more likely to find themselves in trouble. Chances are that most robbers don't check for wedding rings before striking; lifestyle choices may explain the disparate rates. This pattern provides an important clue that will be cited later to explain differential risks.

To sum up the patterns gleaned from Table 4.5, in both the early 1990s and on the safer streets during 2013, higher robbery risks were faced by men rather than women; minorities than whites; younger people than middle-aged or elderly people; single individuals than married couples; poor people than those who are better off financially; and city residents than those living in suburbs or small towns. Combining these factors, the profile of the person facing the gravest dangers of all is an impoverished, young, black or Hispanic man living in an inner-city neighborhood. Affluent, elderly white ladies living in rural areas lead the safest lives.

Unfortunately, the *NCVS* does not calculate a victimization rate for comparison purposes for an individual who falls into all of the high-risk or all of the low-risk subcategories. However, the survey findings cited in Table 4.4 indicated that black teenage boys living in low-income families and residing in the biggest cities (thereby falling into all five of the high-risk categories) must have suffered a robbery victimization rate in the "bad old days" of the early 1990s that was off the charts compared with persons from other backgrounds.

However, two decades later, people falling into this highest risk grouping faced dramatically improved odds of avoiding a sharply reduced number of robbers on the prowl.

One additional variable is worthy of consideration—occupation. Robbery rates differ substantially depending on the nature of a person's work. Statistics from the *NCVS* indicated that people holding the following (generally less desirable) jobs were much more likely to be robbed: taxi drivers, gardeners, busboys, dishwashers, carnival and amusement park workers, car wash attendants, messengers, newspaper carriers, peddlers, and certain construction workers. However, musicians and composers, painters and sculptors, and photographers also were victimized at above-average rates. Least likely to be accosted were inspectors, line workers, bank tellers, opticians, farmers, professional athletes, elementary school teachers, engineers, and psychologists (Block, Felson, and Block, 1985). Another study determined that retail sales workers, especially clerks at convenience stores and liquor stores, were robbed the most, along with cab drivers. College professors faced the lowest risks of being accosted (Warchol, 1998).

Differential risks also show up clearly when a particular kind of robbery—carjacking—is the focus of attention. Some people are more likely than others to have their vehicles taken from them by robbers, as the information assembled from official sources in Box 4.3 indicates.

In general, it appears that the daily activities of individuals as well as the behavior patterns of entire groups—such as poor young men living in cities—determine, to some degree, whether or not robbers will single them out as possible prey.

The takeaway message in the graphs depicted in Figures 4.2 and 4.3 confirm that the rates of these three violent crimes have fallen dramatically, even crashed, from their historically high levels that were socially as well as politically intolerable. In general, Americans have been getting along much better with each other since the early 1990s, even during the hard times of the Great Recession that developed during 2008 and persisted for several years. The dramatic downward trends in murders,

BOX 4.3 Carjacked Drivers

In the movies, as well as in real life, motorists are yanked out of their cars and trucks by highwaymen who hop in behind the wheel and make a quick getaway. In the early 1990s, the catchy term **carjacking** was coined to describe the robbery of a motor vehicle directly from a driver, as distinct from the theft of a parked car. Once the crime had a name, the news media started to report the most outrageous cases (such as the death of a woman who, while trying to rescue her toddler from the back seat of her commandeered BMW, became entangled in her seat belt and was dragged more than a mile).

Police departments began to keep track of carjacking incidents separately from the general category of "robberies of all types," and state legislatures began to impose stiffer penalties for the crime. In 1993, Congress passed the Anti-Car Theft Act, which made robberies of motorists carried out with a firearm a federal offense, under the legal rationale that vehicles and guns are involved in interstate commerce (see Gibbs, 1993a). The 1994 Violent Crime Control and Law Enforcement Act made killings arising from carjackings punishable by death.

Although the probability of being robbed of an automobile, SUV, or truck is low, the potential for disastrous consequences is high. With luck, occupants are forced out of their vehicles and left standing at the roadside, shaken but uninjured. However, this frightening type of confrontational crime can easily escalate from a robbery into an aggravated assault, abduction, rape, and even murder.

Because this combination of circumstances is relatively uncommon, researchers had to merge the findings from a number of years of *NCVS* surveys to assemble a sufficient number of cases to analyze. During each of the 10 years from 1993 to 2002, the *NCVS* projected that roughly 38,000 carjackings took place nationwide. That worked out to about 0.17 incidents (some involved more than one person)

per 1,000 people, or 17 per 100,000—making this kind of robbery about three times more common than murder. Almost 25 percent of these motorists were hurt; of these casualties, about 9 percent suffered gunshot or knife wounds, broken bones, or internal injuries.

Each year, up to 15 motorists were killed during carjackings, according to the FBI's SHRs. As for trends, this kind of holdup, like other varieties of robberies, tapered off after the mid-1990s (Klaus, 2004).

Many of the differential risks surrounding carjackings paralleled the patterns for other robberies. Male motorists faced greater risks of being accosted than females. Cars driven by people from households with incomes less than $50,000 were seized more frequently than vehicles owned by more affluent families (which probably also means that robbers took less expensive cars more often than high-end vehicles). Higher risks were faced by black and Hispanic motorists, drivers between the ages of 25 and 49, people who were not married, and city residents (Klaus, 1999a, 2004).

In the vast majority of the incidents, the driver was alone; in almost half of all confrontations, the robber acted alone. Males committed more than 90 percent of these crimes and were armed in about 75 percent of the incidents (45 percent wielded a gun).

Two-thirds of the drivers put up resistance. About one-quarter used confrontational tactics, such as fighting back against the assailant, trying to capture him, chasing him, or threatening him. About one-third tried nonconfrontational tactics like bolting out of the car and/or screaming for help. Nearly all motorists (98 percent) reported their losses to the police if the robber drove away with their vehicle, but only 58 percent of attempts were brought to the attention of law enforcement agencies. About one-quarter of the owners never recovered their vehicles, but about half suffered some financial losses (Klaus, 1999a, 2004).

aggravated assaults, and robberies (see above) through 2013 indicate that even the nation's meanest streets have become substantially safer. But to conclude from these very positive developments that began during the early 1990s that the "worst is over" might be overly optimistic. No criminologist or victimologist knows for sure why crime rates rise and fall, or what the future holds. Predictions about upcoming crime waves or crashes must be based on projected changes in a number of

underlying variables. Developments in some of these root causes are very hard to anticipate. Another crime wave could break out, or the unanticipated but much welcomed improvement in America's crime problem might continue for an additional number of years. But it is safe to conclude that the ranks of victims were not growing during the twenty-first century as rapidly as they were during the 1960s, 1970s, 1980s, and 1990s, when pessimists made dire predictions that violence by superpredators soon would be getting out of hand and spiraling out of control.

FOCUSING ON BURGLARIES

Burglaries are the most common of all serious crimes tracked by the FBI. Larcenies, which are thefts of all kinds, are more numerous, but more than half were just petty larcenies resulting in minor losses. Burglaries of residences resulted in substantial losses, averaging over $2,100 in 2013, according to the *UCR* (FBI, 2014a). Residential burglaries are particularly upsetting because the intruder violates one's private and personal space, and fears about the threat of a surprise return visit can linger for a long time.

Single-family homes are more attractive to burglars than apartments, condominiums, and other multifamily residences because private houses have more access points and are more difficult to secure, and often contain greater rewards. However, private homeowners can take their own initiatives to protect their possessions and usually have both the incentive and the resources to do so. Intrusions are much more likely to occur during the day and on weekdays when the premises are unoccupied than on weekends and at night. Besides preferring to strike when no one is at home, it appears that burglars select targets that are familiar to them and convenient (often close to their own homes), accessible, easy to watch, and vulnerable (lacking security devices). Specifically, the most likely targets are located near potential offenders (in high-crime urban neighborhoods or in the vicinity of transit hubs, shopping centers, sports arenas, and places where young men and drug abusers congregate), either near busy thoroughfares or on the quiet outskirts of neighborhoods. Houses vacant for extended periods, homes without barking dogs, and those on corners or bordering on alleys or in secluded locations shrouded by shrubbery, walls, or fences attract prowlers. Ironically, mansions with expensive cars parked outside actually dampen interest because they are more likely to remain occupied or to be protected by sophisticated security systems. Houses that were struck once are more likely to be struck again because the features that determine their attractiveness are difficult to change, because the burglar returns to remove additional goods left behind during the first invasion, or because the burglar has told others about the vulnerability of this target. Simple tools like screwdrivers and crowbars typically are used to pry open locks, windows, and doors (Weisel, 2002).

Trends and Patterns in Burglaries

The changes in the burglary rate over a 30-year span appear in Figure 4.4.

Residents of nearly 2.5 million households told *NCVS* interviewers in 2013 that someone had tried or had succeeded in entering their home to steal things. This translates to a rate of 26 for every 1,000 households, or more than 2 percent. That same year, over 1.9 million burglaries were reported to police departments across the nation, according to the *UCR*. (Roughly 25 percent of those break-ins were of commercial establishments and government agencies, not residences; on the other hand, many completed as well as attempted residential burglaries were not brought to the attention of the police.) Burglars carted off an estimated $4.6 billion in stolen goods, yielding an average loss of over $2,000 per incident in 2013 (FBI, 2014b).

NCVS findings can be used to reveal differential risks. Burglars, just like robbers, are the opposite of Robin Hoods. They steal from the poor much more than the rich. The dwellings of the most poverty-stricken families in the *NCVS*, those with an income of under $7,500, suffered at a much higher rate (55 per 1,000 households, which is over 5 percent) than any other financial bracket on the survey in 2013. As for race and ethnicity, white households experienced nearly 23 intrusions or attempted break-ins per 1,000 while black families suffered about 35, and Hispanic families endured just about the same rate, at 34 per 1,000. Family size seems to count. Households of six or more people were burglarized at a rate of 53 per 1,000, while individuals

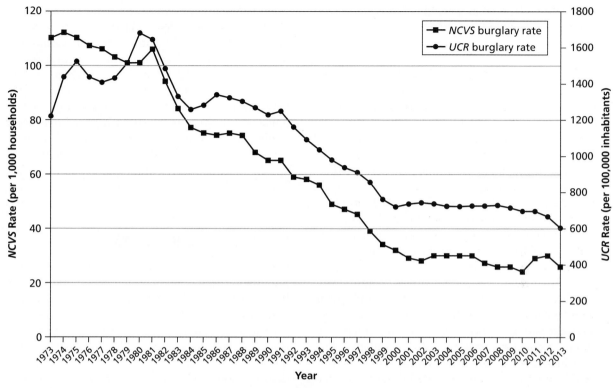

FIGURE 4.4 Trends in Burglaries, United States, 1973–2013

NOTE: *UCR* figures include commercial and office burglaries.

SOURCES: FBI's *UCRs* 1973–2013; BJS's *NCVSs* 1973–2013.

living alone came home to ransacked dwellings much less often, at 30 per 1,000. As for where the targeted home was located, a surprising change has taken place over the years. Burglary used to be a much bigger problem in large cities. In 1996, the burglary rate for urban dwellers in cities with a population of 1 million or more was a shocking 62 per 1,000 households. By 2013, that figure had drifted downward to just 22 per 1,000. The 2013 burglary rate for suburban families also was 22, while it was substantially higher in rural areas, at 30 per 1,000, according to the BJS's *Victimization Analysis Tool.* Hence, burglary had shifted from a big city problem to a headache of country living.

It appears that a family's financial status, decisions about where to live, and everyday behaviors determine, to some degree, whether a burglar invades their personal space.

FOCUSING ON MOTOR VEHICLE THEFT
Stealing Cars for Fun and Profit

About 556,000 households suffered a vehicle theft (or an attempted vehicle theft) during 2013, a slight bump up from previous years, according to the *NCVS.* That volume of incidents translated to a rate of a little more than five vehicle thefts for every 1,000 households. The *UCR* for 2013 indicated that police departments across the country received almost 700,000 complaints about completed or attempted thefts of cars, vans, trucks, buses, motorcycles, and ATVs from households (and also from businesses and agencies, which explains why this figure is larger than the number of vehicle thefts estimated by the *NCVS*), yielding a rate of a bit over 220 thefts for every 100,000 inhabitants. Therefore, both official sources confirm that vehicle theft takes place much less often than larceny or burglary but is much more common than any of the serious violent crimes in the FBI's crime index.

Surprisingly, some commentators mistakenly portrayed auto theft as the "happy crime" in which no one loses and everyone gains (see Plate, 1975). Their argument proposes that the thief makes money and that the owner is reimbursed by the insurance company and then enjoys the pleasure of shopping for a new car. Meanwhile, the manufacturer gains a customer who wasn't due back in the showroom for another couple of years, and the insurance company gets a chance to raise comprehensive fire and theft loss premiums and invest that money in profitable ventures.

But in actuality, most victims of auto theft are quite upset for a number of reasons. Many motorists devote a great deal of time, effort, and loving care to keeping their vehicles in good shape. Second, the shock of discovering that the vehicle vanished touches off a sense of violation and insecurity that lingers for a long time. Third, not all owners purchase theft coverage, usually because they cannot afford it. Even those who are insured almost always must suffer a hefty deductible out of their own pockets, and they might owe more on the car loan than the vehicle is worth, so the insurance payoff does not cover the outstanding balance they must repay. Personal items left in the vehicle are gone, as are any expensive add-ons. The loss is always unanticipated, necessitating time-wasting emergency measures such as filing a complaint at a police station, taking cabs, renting a car, and canceling important appointments. Many end up buying a more expensive replacement. Finally, motorists who collect insurance reimbursement might find that either their premiums are raised or their policies cannot be renewed.

Collectively, vehicle thefts cost owners nearly $4.1 billion, with losses averaging nearly $6,000 per stolen vehicle in 2013, the *UCR* reported (FBI, 2014). Insurance coverage for comprehensive fire and theft damages and losses cost the average policyholder about $140 per year (III, 2011).

Victims of grand theft auto (also termed grand larceny auto, or GLA) ought to notify the police immediately, since the authorities will assume that the owner was behind the wheel if that stolen vehicle is involved in a crime, such as a hit-and-run, or is used as a getaway car in a bank robbery. Also, there is a chance of recovering it if the police locate the vehicle after it is pulled over for a traffic violation, parked, or abandoned. If it is insured for comprehensive fire and theft damage and loss, a case number from a law enforcement agency will be necessary in order to receive reimbursement.

Trends in Motor Vehicle Theft

Changes in motor vehicle theft rates over the past few decades are shown in Figure 4.5. One trend line, based on *NCVS* findings, portrays yearly rates of thefts of noncommercial vehicles disclosed to survey interviewers, whether successful completions or failed attempts, for every 1,000 households. The other trend line, from the *UCR*, depicts yearly rates of completed or attempted thefts of all motorized vehicles, per 100,000 people, reported to police departments across the country. Both of these sets of statistics indicate that rates of auto theft rose during the late 1980s, reached an all-time high at the start of the 1990s, subsided as the twentieth century drew to a close, and then dropped further during the first 13 years of the twenty-first century (tumbling an impressive 40 percent just from 2001 to 2010, according to the *UCR*).

By contrast, however, thefts were climbing after the late 1990s for one type of vehicle: motorcycles. In 1998, about 27,000 were stolen. That number doubled to more than 55,000 by 2003, then soared to around 71,000 in 2004 before dropping back down to 56,000 in 2009 and 46,000 in 2012. As more motorcycles filled the roads and as they became more expensive, their attractiveness to thieves rose. Motorcyclists lavish great attention on their cherished possessions by installing high-performance engines and exhaust systems, chromed parts, and specialized frames. The most often stolen

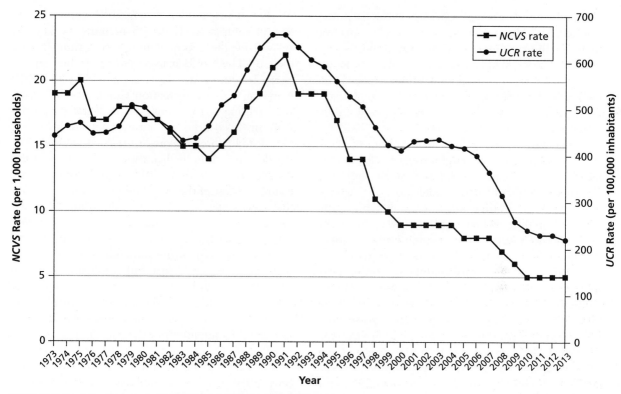

FIGURE 4.5 Trends in Motor Vehicle Thefts, United States, 1973–2013

NOTE: *UCR* figures include thefts of taxis, buses, trucks, and other commercial vehicles.
SOURCES: FBI's *UCRs* 1973–2013; BJS's *NCVSs* 1973–2013.

brands were Honda, Yamaha, Suzuki, and Kawasaki. Harley-Davidson, despite being the most popular bike, ranked in fifth place, comprising just 8 percent of all missing motorcycles. The highest theft rates burdened owners in California, Florida, Texas, North Carolina, and Indiana. The cities where a lot of the stealing took place were New York, Las Vegas, San Diego, Indianapolis, and Miami. Just like riding, stealing shows seasonal variations: More thefts are carried out in the summer than in the winter (Scafidi, 2013).

Which Motorists Should Be Most Concerned When Parking?

A truck is stolen from the parking lot of a hotel. Inside it are three presidential seals, three lecterns, and $200,000 worth of electronic equipment,
including a teleprompter. The truck is recovered a few hours later—it was abandoned in the parking lot of another hotel and looted of a high-end audio system. The Department of Defense investigates the theft of the unguarded truck from the lot, which was monitored by closed circuit TV, but is unable to determine if this was just a crime of opportunity or whether the equipment used by President Obama to deliver speeches was specifically targeted. (Geller, 2011).

The theft of a truck from the president's entourage is surely a rare occurrence, but it underscores the fact that determined thieves can steal almost any vehicle.

To begin an investigation into differential risks, it is necessary to ask, "Which cars do thieves find most attractive?" The chances of losing a vehicle depend upon its make, model, and year. A prime consideration centers on the appeal or black market value of the various cars, SUVs, vans, and pickup trucks to those who make a living by repeatedly fencing stolen parts. Professional thieves prowl the streets looking for specific makes and models on their shopping lists. Which parked cars do they enter and drive away most often?

The answer, in the form of a ranking of vehicles, should be fairly straightforward. Consumers need to know this information when shopping for used cars (brand new models do not yet have track records) if they are concerned about the chances of their vehicles spirited away or about the costs of insuring them—premiums to cover comprehensive theft and fire damage (coverage for collisions and personal injuries is more important and more expensive). In other words, crime-conscious motorists ought to be aware of how desirable or undesirable their prized possessions are to thieves cruising around. But each year, the answer to the question, "Which cars are stolen the most" depends upon which organization is asked and which criteria were used to compile the ranking (see Gibson, 2004). Three distinct listings that bear little resemblance to each other appear in Table 4.5.

For vehicles stolen during 2013, the list in the second column in Table 4.5 presents the ranking derived by the National Insurance Crime Bureau (NICB). The NICB analyzes police car theft reports assembled in the database maintained by the FBI's National Crime Information Center (NCIC) each year. During 2013, about half of all stolen vehicles were made by domestic automakers and half were produced by foreign manufacturers. What the ranking does not show is that a high proportion of the vehicles stolen during 2013 were very old. For example, most of the nearly 54,000 Honda Accords that were stolen across the nation during 2013 first hit the road during the 1990s; relatively few Accords manufactured after 1997 were taken from their rightful owners (not shown in Table 4.5). This pattern is surprising at first until it is realized that the older cars are stolen to be stripped of their sheet metal parts, which are then used to repair crash-damaged newer cars—unless the manufacturer changes the dimensions of the later models (Scafidi, 2014b).

But what about the theft of brand new cars? If only 2013 makes and models that were stolen somewhere within the United States during 2013 are the focus of attention, then an entirely different list emerges. This ranking appears in the third

T A B L E   4.5   Which Vehicle Owners Suffered the Most Thefts?

Rank	All Vehicles Stolen During 2013 Make/Model NICB	Only New 2013 Models Stolen During 2013 NICB	Theft Rate of 2011 Models Stolen During 2011 NHTSA	Rate per 1,000
1	Honda/Accord	Nissan/Altima	Dodge/Charger	5
2	Honda/Civic	Ford/Fusion	Mitsubishi/Galant	4
3	Chevrolet/Pickup Trucks	Ford/Full Size Pickup	Cadillac/STS	4
4	Ford/Pickup Trucks	Toyota/Corolla	Lamborghini/Gallardo	4
5	Toyota/Camry	Chevrolet/Impala	Hyundai/Accent	4
6	Dodge/Pickup Trucks	Hyundai/Elantra	Chevrolet/HHR	3
7	Dodge/Caravan	Dodge/Charger	Chevrolet/Aveo	3
8	Jeep/Cherokee	Chevrolet/Malibu	Chevrolet/Impala	3
9	Toyota/Corolla	Chevrolet/Cruze	Nissan/Infinity FX35	3
10	Nissan/Altima	Ford/Focus	Nissan/GT-R 1	3

NOTES: Column 1: NICB rankings are based on a grand total of the number of thefts of a particular make and model manufactured in previous years that were stolen during 2013, according to the FBI's NCIC database.

Column 2: NICB rankings are based on the number of thefts of a particular make and model manufactured in 2012–2013 that were stolen during 2013, according to the FBI's NCIC database.

Column 3: NHTSA rankings also are drawn from the FBI's NCIC as well as manufacturers' production totals. Theft rate is per 1,000 vehicles manufactured and sold to the U.S. public during 2011 and is rounded off to the nearest integer.

SOURCE: First list from NICB (Scafidi, 2014b), second list from NICB (Stewart, 2014), third list from NHTSA (2014).

column. It also was compiled by the NICB and is derived from the FBI's NCIC database.

A completely different ranking appears in the fourth column. This list is based on a theft rate for each vehicle that is calculated by taking into account not only the number of cars of a given make and model that are reported stolen to the police (in 2011, the latest year available) but also the number of these cars (not SUVs or trucks) that were produced and sold during 2011. In other words, this third and final ranking uses "number owned by motorists" as its denominator. The resulting rate is the number reported stolen (during 2011) for every 1,000 cars of this type on the road (during 2011). This list from the National Highway Transportation and Safety Administration (NHTSA) also is calculated from stolen car reports in the FBI's NCIC database. (No ranking system uses insurance company files about vehicles reported by their owners as stolen.) This ranking appears in the fourth column of Table 4.5.

Obviously, Table 4.5 demonstrates that there are no simple and direct answers to the crucial questions, "Which cars are most attractive to thieves?" and "Which drivers should be most cautious about where they park their cherished possession?" The key risk factors appear to be the make, model, and year of the car; its resale value; the demand for it by chop shops that fence stolen parts; and how easy or difficult it is to break into, start up, and drive away. Insurance records confirm a counterintuitive pattern: For several reasons, as cars age, they are more likely to be targeted. If the model lines are not substantially redesigned, then stolen sheet metal crash parts from the older cars can be used by illicit collision body shops to repair damaged newer ones. Also, older cars are less likely to be equipped with the latest state-of-the-art antitheft devices that thieves have not yet learned how to defeat. Another reason is that as cars wear out and depreciate, their owners have less incentive to maintain security devices in good working order and to vigilantly observe precautions about where they park their less valuable vehicles. Because most cars have a life expectancy of 7–10 years, security experts warn owners never to let their guard down (see

Clark and Harris, 1992; NICB Study, 1993; and Krauss, 1994).

Finally, to make matters more complex, the desirability of particular vehicles on the black market varies around the country. For example, thieves concentrated on Japanese models in Los Angeles, pickup trucks in Dallas, and American sedans in Chicago, reflecting the preferences of consumers in those metropolitan areas (Sparkman, 2003). The insurance industry generates detailed lists annually of the most frequently targeted cars that are tailored for every state and even each large city so that companies can maximize their profits by fine-tuning premiums to reflect payouts to their local customers for theft losses.

Differential risks are determined by a number of factors besides the attractiveness of the target in the stolen car market. Another set of determinants of risk must be the number of professional thieves and chop shops operating in a given area, as well as the effectiveness of the efforts by local police departments to put them out of business.

As for geography, where a vehicle is parked is a key variable. Owners in the South and West suffered substantially higher theft rates than in the North and Midwest. Residents of urban areas reported their cars stolen more often than suburbanites and people living in rural areas. The significance of the geographic factor is illustrated in Table 4.6, which demonstrates how important the location where the car is parked is when it comes to vehicle theft. This listing of vehicle theft rates for many of the nation's metropolitan areas is based on data from police reports collected by the FBI and analyzed by the NICB (Toups, 2014; and Scafidi, 2014a).

From a motorist's point of view, this ranking indicates that the meanest streets to park a car are in California's metropolitan areas. In general, drivers in Western states have the most to worry about in terms of their vehicles vanishing. Those who find parking spaces in downtown areas of a metropolitan area usually have even more to fear than those who park in that city's nearby suburbs. Some cities that have a reputation for being safe in terms of violence, such as San Jose and San Diego, are not so safe for parked cars; conversely, some places like New Orleans and

T A B L E 4.6   Vehicle Theft Rates in U.S. Metropolitan Areas, 2013

Metropolitan Area	Rank	Vehicle Theft Rates per 100,000 Residents	Metropolitan Area	Rank	Vehicle Theft Rates per 100,000 Residents
Bakersfield, CA	1	725	Las Vegas, NV	27	395
Fresno, CA	2	710	Omaha, NE	28	390
Modesto, CA	3	680	Los Angeles/Long Beach, CA	29	385
San Francisco/Oakland, CA	4	650	Little Rock, AK	30	385
Stockton, CA	5	635	Houston, TX	35	365
Redding, CA	6	625	Atlanta, GA	48	315
Spokane, WA	7	600	Denver–Mesa, CO	50	310
Vallejo/Fairfield, CA	8	600	New Orleans, LA	51	305
San Jose/Santa Clara, CA	9	570	Cleveland, OH	52	300
Yuba City, CA	10	550	Portland, OR	54	300
Riverside/San Bernardino, CA	11	525	Milwaukee, WI	59	295
Odessa, TX	12	510	Miami-Fort Lauderdale, FL	65	280
Seattle/Tacoma, WA	13	500	Tucson, AZ	68	275
Merced, CA	14	495	Honolulu, HI	69	275
Visalia/Porterville, CA	15	490	Dallas-Fort Worth, TX	70	270
Salinas, CA	16	490	Chicago, IL,	82	255
Salt Lake City, UT	17	470	St. Louis, MO	93	235
Chico, CA	18	470	Minneapolis, MN–St. Paul, WI	131	185
Yakima, WA	19	465	Philadelphia, PA	138	180
Albuquerque, NM	20	445	Boston–Cambridge, MA	235	125
Grants Pass, OR	21	440	New York City, NY–Newark, NJ	242	120
Oklahoma City, OK	22	440	Pittsburgh, PA	310	80
Detroit/Dearborn, MI	23	430	Madison, WI	320	75
Sacramento, CA	24	410	Binghamton, NY	365	45
Wichita, KS	25	405	State College, PA	379	25
San Diego, CA	26	400			

NOTES: The boundaries of metropolitan statistical areas are defined by the U.S. Census and often include nearby counties and suburban towns. Rankings were calculated by the NICB based on *UCR* rates.

Rates are rounded to the nearest 5.

SOURCE: NICB, 2014b.

St. Louis that are known to be dangerous in terms of being murdered are not so risky when it comes to leaving vehicles unattended (refer back to Figure 4.1). Drivers who walk away from their cars in the university towns of Madison, Wisconsin; Binghamton, New York; and State College, Pennsylvania, can rest assured (statistically speaking) that their vehicles will still be there when they return.

Combining the findings displayed in Tables 4.7 and 4.8, it can be concluded that motorists who drive vehicles that are on thieves' hottest cars list and who park them on the meanest streets of certain hot spot metropolitan areas face unusually high odds of discovering that their prized possession has disappeared.

Besides vehicle attractiveness and geographic location, two other factors surely influence the vulnerability of a parked car: the effectiveness of factory-installed and after-market add-on antitheft devices, and the immediate microenvironment—such as traffic patterns, the presence or absence of pedestrians, and the intensity of lighting at night in the vicinity of the street, driveway, or lot where the vehicle sits unguarded. These two factors are under the control of individuals to some degree, except that many motorists cannot afford secure but expensive parking arrangements and costly antitheft hardware.

Once again, various categories of people face either higher or lower levels of danger from criminals. In terms of differential risks, those who faced the greatest odds of losing their cars were apartment dwellers, residents of inner-city neighborhoods, African-Americans and Hispanic-Americans, low-income families, and households headed by people under the age of 25. Those whose cars were least likely to be stolen were residents of rural areas, homeowners, and people over age 55, according to an analysis of a database of more than 12 million attempted and completed vehicle thefts disclosed to *NCVS* interviewers between 1973 and 1985 (Harlow, 1988).

Decades later, the pattern was similar. Motorists in big cities with a population of a million or more lost their cars to thieves at a rate of 10 per 1,000 households per year. In rural areas, the theft rate was only 3 per 1,000. White families living in the suburbs experienced a vehicle theft rate of 2, while black families living in cities suffered much more, nearly 9 thefts per 1,000 households. Cars owned by people between 20 and 34 years old disappeared at a rate of 9 per 1,000 households, compared to just 2 for motorists over 65, according to the BJS's *Victimization Analysis Tool* of *NCVS* 2013 data.

It seems that drivers' decisions about where to reside, spending priorities, and parking habits—in other words, their attitudes and behaviors—determine, to some degree, the fate of their vehicles.

FOCUSING ON INDIVIDUALS WHOSE IDENTITIES WERE STOLEN

> *The crime of identity theft undermines the basic trust on which our economy depends. When a person takes out an insurance policy, or makes an online purchase or opens a savings account, he or she must have confidence that personal financial information will be protected and treated with care. Identity theft harms not only its direct victims, but also many businesses and customers whose confidence is shaken. Like other forms of stealing, identity theft leaves the victim poor and feeling terribly violated.*
>
> PRESIDENT GEORGE BUSH, 2004 (REMARKS WHEN SIGNING THE IDENTITY THEFT PENALTY ENHANCEMENT ACT)

The Nature of the Problem and How Many People Experience Its Aggravations

Throughout history, people seeking to evade capture have used disguises, false papers, and aliases to pass themselves off as someone else. Spies, saboteurs, infiltrators, terrorists, and fugitives from justice used fictitious histories, documents, and résumés to fool authorities. But now computer databases and high-tech devices provide incentives for impersonators for a different reason: monetary gain.

The relatively new, increasingly sophisticated, and surprisingly common white-collar crime of **identity theft** arises from the illegal appropriation of someone's personal information—such as the individual's name, address, date of birth, Social Security number, and mother's maiden name. Identity fraud is defined as the unauthorized use of another individual's personal information to try to achieve illicit financial gain. Identity thefts are measured as attempted as well as successful misuses of these personal identifiers to loot an existing account (for example, a bank savings or checking account) or to open a new account (for instance, with a telephone or credit card company), plus impersonations for other fraudulent purposes (such as to collect undeserved government benefits like someone else's income tax refund) (Javelin Strategy and Research, 2011; and Langton and Planty, 2011).

Even though identity theft is a relatively new type of offense, it draws upon traditional interpersonal crimes such as pickpocketing, thievery, robbery, and burglary of wallets as well as established white-collar crimes like forgery, counterfeiting, fraud, and impersonation. For example, those who steal cars might be able to parlay a vehicle theft into an identity theft if the driver left a copy of the license or registration in the glove compartment and a laptop, smartphone, briefcase, or wallet in the trunk (ITRC, 2014a). Cutting-edge criminals increasingly commit their offenses online by compromising other people's existing Internet accounts (such as Amazon, eBay, and PayPal). These high-tech fraudsters also engage in account takeovers in which they add new properties to somebody else's existing utility account (such as for a smartphone) and run up huge unauthorized charges for premium services (Javelin, 2014).

No one is immune from being preyed upon, not even the most wealthy and privileged, as the following example shows.

> *A purse, containing a checkbook and a Social Security card, is swiped from the wife of the chairman of the Federal Reserve Bank while she is sitting in a coffee shop. Months later, a woman is arrested who uses wigs to impersonate her victims when cashing bad checks and draining their accounts. It turns out that she is part of a sophisticated ring that defrauded more than $2 million from hundreds of people who banked at 10 financial institutions.* (Lucas and Melago, 2009)

Victims of identity theft were discovered during the 1990s when nearly all state legislatures criminalized the unlawful possession of personal identification information for the purposes of committing fraud. Hearings held by congressional committees during the 1990s revealed that police departments usually did not view individuals whose identities were appropriated by fraudsters as actual victims, since the immediate monetary losses usually were incurred by credit card companies, not account holders. In 1998, Congress passed the Identity Theft and Assumption Deterrence Act. The legislation made it a federal crime to knowingly transfer and use any name or number without lawful authority in order to commit or aid and abet any illegal activity. The law not only imposed stiff sentences and fines on those who committed this new federal offense but also stipulated that the impersonated individual was a crime victim deserving of financial protection and entitled to reimbursement via court-ordered restitution obligations imposed on convicted thieves. However, a persistent problem is that this crime often goes unreported, uninvestigated, and/or unsolved. In 2000, the International Association of Chiefs of Police (IACP) urged police departments that were reluctant to accept complaints to

revise their policies and provide incident reports and other forms of assistance to impersonated individuals (Newman, 2004). A provision of the Fair and Accurate Credit Transactions Act of 2003 enabled customers to get one free credit report each year (from www.annualcreditreport .com) so they can check for any suspicious activity in their accounts at the three major companies. Congress authorized the Department of Homeland Security to get involved when it passed the REAL ID act in 2005 (NCJRS, 2005; Kelleher, 2006; and President's Task Force, 2007). State laws require companies and agencies to notify their customers and clients so that they can be vigilant whenever the personal information in their records is stolen by hackers.

Reports of ID thefts do not wind up in the tallies of incidents known to the police in any category of Part 1 of the FBI's *UCR*. Although the huge grouping entitled "larceny-theft" includes all kinds of acts of stealing, whether petty or grand larcenies, it specifically excludes aspects of identity thefts that appear in Part 2 (but only if there is an arrest), such as embezzlements, forgeries, check frauds, and confidence games and other scams (Velasquez, 2013). In other words, because of outdated definitions, acts of stealing carried out by breaking a window or snatching an unguarded purse are counted, while incidents of stealing perpetrated by using a skimmer, a keyboard, or a spyware program are not counted as larceny-thefts.

Several problems continue to undermine the effectiveness of efforts by law enforcement agencies to come to the aid of identity theft victims. First, many officers lack necessary training, and their departments lack the needed resources to provide an adequate response. Second, multijurisdictional complications undercut an agency's commitment to follow through on a complaint. When a victim in one city reports to a local police department that a thief has stolen personal information and is carrying out fraudulent financial transactions in another city, state, or country, which law enforcement agency bears primary responsibility for seeing the investigation through to completion?

If the authorities seem unsympathetic, betray skepticism, and appear reluctant to officially file their complaints and take action, victims understandably get upset. They sense that they are being suspected of wrongdoing as they fill out forms that must be notarized, telephone merchants who are demanding payment, fend off collection agencies, and write lengthy explanations to credit rating bureaus. They bear the burden of proof and are held financially responsible unless and until they can establish their innocence and clear their names.

Because law enforcement countermeasures are not yet effective, identity snatchers know that the risks of apprehension, conviction, and punishment are relatively low, while the returns are potentially high. These crimes are difficult, time-consuming, and expensive to investigate, especially when multiple jurisdictions are involved. In fact, offenders exploit these problems by misusing the stolen information far from the original crime scene, preferably in another county, state, or country (Collins and Hoffman, 2004).

Losses and Suffering

This potentially serious type of larceny can damage a person's finances, reputation, and credit history, as well as cause great emotional distress that can trigger relationship problems. A targeted individual must undertake tasks that are confusing and infuriating because the burden of proving innocence falls to the victim.

Identity theft can be viewed as going through a series of stages. People discover they have been preyed upon when they get a call from a credit card fraud division or when a purchase is declined at the point of sale because a card's limit has been exceeded. Others find out when they are harassed by a bill collector demanding payment on a delinquent account or when a monthly statement marked "overdue" arrives in the mail. Others notice unauthorized charges on credit card statements, peculiar and costly long-distance calls on phone bills, cashed or bounced checks they never wrote, or suspicious withdrawals from their bank accounts. In extreme cases, they discover they have been targeted when the police take them into custody as a fugitive on an outstanding warrant, and then it becomes clear that a lawbreaker was released after showing false documents and posting bail. It can take weeks, months, maybe even years before individuals become aware that they have been targeted because the crooks want to get away with the charade for as long as possible. Some don't discover the extent of the damage until they are denied new credit cards, turned down for student loans, disconnected from utilities, or charged extra high interest rates for mortgages and car loans. Out-of-pocket expenses and time spent on paperwork depend on how long it takes to discover the fraud (Collins and Hoffman, 2004). It takes lower income and less educated people longer to discover the impersonation and consequently they suffer more, in terms of problems with their accounts, harassment by debt collectors, and utility cutoffs (Newman, 2004).

ID theft poses a special problem for military personnel, civilians working for defense contractors, and employees of the criminal justice system who need security clearances. A person who was defrauded might be considered a security risk and could be denied a clearance or might have the privilege of access to classified information revoked if a background check turns up evidence of a maxed out credit card, bounced checks, or an arrest that really was the fault of an impersonator (Velasquez, 2014).

ID scams and swindles exact a serious toll on society as a whole, adding up to billions of dollars in losses annually. New account fraud is more costly but less frequent. Depletion of existing accounts is less common but more expensive to recover from. Businesses sustain most of the financial losses because individuals usually are not held responsible for charges that turn out to be fraudulent. But individuals collectively spend billions in their efforts to repair their credit worthiness. Individuals also suffer indirect costs in the form of businesses' expenses for fraud prevention and lost revenue that are passed on to them as higher fees; for legal bills to pay for civil litigation initiated by creditors over disputed purchases; and for time lost and aggravation they endure while undoing the damage inflicted by the impostor (President's Task Force, 2007, p. 11). Adding business losses to consumer expenses, each incident might cost from $2,800 to $5,100 (Piquero, Cohen, and Piquero, 2011).

Just as the different databases yield inconsistent projections about general prevalence, yearly incidence, and twenty-first-century trends, so too are there varying estimates of the actual collective costs of this white-collar crime, and whether overall losses are increasing or decreasing.

Over $13 billion was lost due to identity thefts that took place during 2010, and that figure nearly doubled to $25 billion during 2012, according to the *NCVS* self-report survey (Harrell and Langton, 2013). However, the impression that losses are being brought under control emerges from the findings of a financial services company's annual self-report survey that uses a broader definition but a smaller sample. Identity frauds of all kinds cost Americans $48 billion in 2008, rose to $56 billion in 2009, and then plunged to $37 billion in 2010, further tumbled to $21 billion in 2012, and added up to a mere $18 billion in 2013 (Javelin, 2011, 2014).

The next question to be answered is, "In what ways can impersonators hurt their victims?" Unscrupulous impostors can use identifiers to max out existing charge accounts and obtain new credit cards in their target's name and then run up huge bills that are ignored. ID thieves empty people's savings accounts and pass bad checks (another type of account takeovers). They secure car loans that will never be repaid based on another person's credit history and enjoy using gas heat, electricity, cell phones, and landlines while disregarding the costs and consequences of overdue bills. They drive around and get tickets with a license that has their picture but someone else's name, apply for government benefits and tax refunds they didn't earn, get hired for jobs by pretending to be an applicant with better credentials, and may even get arrested under an assumed name before jumping bail and disappearing.

One peculiar aspect of identity theft is its parasitical nature: the offender, unless detected and put out of action, often repeatedly feeds off the same person in a variety of ways over a prolonged period of time, by maxing out credit cards, emptying bank accounts, and taking out loans that will never be repaid.

Now that the range of possible swindles and scams has been outlined, the question arises, "How did impersonators actually harm their victims?" Table 4.7 shows the relative frequency of each of these forms of fiscal exploitation as the percentage of all complainants to the FTC's clearinghouse. Credit card fraud was the most common category, afflicting about one-quarter of all victims; loan fraud was the least likely swindle exposed during 2006. As Table 4.7 reveals, by 2010, credit card fraud, bank account fraud, loan fraud, employment fraud, and cell phone/telephone fraud had diminished, while government benefits fraud (filing a false tax return for a refund) plus assorted other scams had intensified. By 2013, fraud related to government documents and benefits, especially where thieves collected their victims' income tax refunds, had grown substantially to become the biggest category. Other scams, especially credit card fraud, loan fraud, and utilities fraud had declined over the years since 2006, as a comparison of the percentage of complaints to the FTC in columns 2, 3, and 4 in Table 4.7 reveals.

Findings from the *NCVS* show a slightly different ranking. The 2012 *NCVS* projected that unauthorized use of an existing credit card was the most widespread problem, more common than draining an existing savings or checking account or using personal information to open a new credit card account or to secure a loan (Baum, 2007). In 2010, the most prevalent type of scam continued to be the unauthorized use or attempted use of a credit card, experienced by 3.8 percent of all respondents, which projected to 4.6 million persons across the country. The second most common type of theft was from a bank's debit, checking, or savings account. Perhaps as many as 1.8 percent of all households, adding up to as many as 2.2 million people experienced this intrusion in 2010. Between 2005 and 2010, there was a decline in the number of households that suffered because some impostor used fraudulent

TABLE 4.7   How Victims of Identity Theft Were Harmed, Nationwide, 2006, 2010, 2013

Nature of the Crime	Total Number of Complaints 2006 246,000 Percentage of All Complaints	Total Number of Complaints 2010 251,000 Percentage of All Complaints	Total Number of Complaints 2013 290,000 Percentage of All Complaints
Credit Card Fraud			
Charging items to existing accounts	11	7	6
Opening new accounts in their names	15	9	11
Bank Frauds			
Draining existing accounts	6	3	2
Receiving electronic fund transfers	8	5	4
Opening new accounts in their names	3	3	2
Utilities Fraud			
Getting a new cell phone in their names	7	4	4
Getting a new telephone in their names	4	2	1
Getting gas or electric service in their names	6	9	9
Loan Fraud			
Taking out business/personal/student loans in their names	3	2	2
Taking out auto loans/leases in their names	2	1	1
Taking out mortgages in their names	1	1	1
Employment-Related Fraud			
Working under their victims' names	14	11	6
Government Document Frauds			
Filing false tax returns for refunds in their names and wage fraud	6	16	30
Obtaining driver's licenses in their names	1	1	1
All Other Purposes and Ways, including attempts	24	29	31

NOTES: Complaints received by the Federal Trade Commission (FTC) from individuals and participating agencies were rounded off to the nearest 1,000 for the calendar year. Percentages exceed 100 percent due to rounding and because some victims were harmed in more than one way.
SOURCE: Federal Federal Trade Commission Sentinel Network (FTC, 2011, 2014).

documents, such as to obtain undeserved medical treatment charged to someone else's health insurance policy, or to pretend to be the victim when stopped by the police for a traffic violation or a more serious offense (Langton, 2011).

However, estimates and projections about the actual amount of suffering varied dramatically according to different sources. For example, only 1 percent told *NCVS* interviewers in 2012 that the impersonation caused significant problems at work or school. And merely 4 percent said they experienced significant relationship problems with their families and friends because of the theft. Only 14 percent of those who discovered that their identity had been appropriated by an impostor experienced any out-of-pocket expenses. Of these unfortunate persons, about half lost less than $100. As for aggravation, over half of all victims were able

to resolve any problems in just one hour up to one day. However, nearly 30 percent spent a month or more straightening out the mess in which their good names were used for fraudulent purposes. As for their personal reactions, 10 percent told interviewers that the theft caused severe emotional distress, and about 25 percent reported moderate levels of distress. When crooks opened brand new accounts and ran up big bills, their victims experienced greater financial, credit, and relationship problems and more intense emotional distress. (Harrell and Langton, 2013).

However, according to a different survey, the average fraud loss per incident cost victims about $630 in out-of-pocket expenses in 2010, a substantial increase from the 2009 estimate of about $390 per incident. The amount of time it took consumers to undo the damage from an identity theft jumped to 33 hours from 21 hours in 2009 (Javelin, 2011).

In sum, reactions can range from a minor annoyance and maybe even mild amusement (in terms of what the thieves purchased using credit cards) to fury about a complicated and costly mess. As a result, a cottage industry has sprung up over the past decade to address the public's fears and genuine concerns about preventing identity theft and recovering from it. Companies sell protection policies that pledge they will monitor their customers' financial records for suspicious activities and intercede to repair the damage if successful impersonations take place. Whether the fees these companies charge and the actual services they deliver are really a wise investment and worth the expenses have not yet been evaluated by victimologists.

The emotional toll of trying to restore their financial reputation can cause some victims to become highly suspicious of other people's motives and profoundly distrustful of officials and agencies they had counted upon to help them. A wide range of responses are possible, from denial to humiliation to outrage. The level of distress is compounded if the crime is never solved and the real name of the thief never becomes known. Some feel overwhelmed and powerless, as well as ashamed and embarrassed for appearing to be spendthrifts and deadbeats. Others join self-help groups that have websites to share advice and facilitate mutual support with those who know firsthand what it is like to repair a lifetime record of credit worthiness (Busch-White, 2002; and Savage, 2003).

Is the Problem Growing or Subsiding?

How many people know what it is like to be impersonated? How rapidly are their ranks increasing? To address these concerns, it is necessary to ask "What are the yearly incidence and longer term prevalence rates?" A wide range of estimates can be found because of variations in the definitions used (what is included and excluded) and the methods of collecting data (complaints filed vs. survey findings and subsequent projections to the entire population). Inconsistencies about definitions of

the crime and its victims persist. Three databases estimate the size of the problem and indicate how its dimensions are changing over time. But the findings of these three monitoring efforts do not always match or coincide. The oft-repeated warning that identity theft is America's fastest growing crime implies a steady upward trend that is difficult to verify. Different impressions can be derived from the data assembled in Table 4.8.

The *NCVS* is a valuable source of estimates about the prevalence and incidence of identity theft. Questions about identity theft were added to the *NCVS* in 2004. The percentage of victimized households rose between 2005 and 2009 from 5.5 to 7.3 percent but then declined a bit in 2010 to 7 percent. Figures for 2011 are not available, but in 2012 the proportion remained constant at 7 percent of that year's sample. Therefore, the proportion of the sample that has experienced identity theft had leveled out. In terms of sheer numbers, an estimated 16.6 million persons experienced one or more successful deceptions or attempts at impersonation in 2012. Over 34 million people over the age of 16 had experienced one or more incidents of attempted or completed identity theft at some point in their lives as of 2012, according to the *NCVS* (Harrell and Langton, 2013) (see the third column in Table 4.8).

The FTC operates an identity theft data clearinghouse called the **Consumer Sentinel Network**. It receives information from about 150 law enforcement agencies and collects details from online complaint forms and calls to its hotline (877-IDTHEFT). The FTC bases its estimates about how many people have had their identities stolen on unverified incident reports that have been pouring in to this monitoring system since it was set up in 1997 (FTC, 2011). From these complaints, the FTC projected that as many as 8 million Americans suffered from a brush with identify theft during 2008. That figure rose to an estimated 9 million during 2010. As for the actual number of complaints, they peaked in 2008 and then declined, but bounced back to an all-time high in 2012 before slipping a bit in 2013 (FTC, 2014) (see the second column in Table 4.8).

T A B L E 4.8   Estimates About the Number of Identity Theft Victims per Year, 2001–2013

Source of Estimate and Year	Federal Trade Commission (FTC) Complaints and Projections	National Crime Victimization Survey (NCVS) Households	Javelin Strategy and Research Survey
2001	86,000	not available	not available
2002	162,000	not available	not available
2003	215,000 15 Million = 5%	not available	not available
2004	247,000	3.6 M = 3.1%	not available
2005	256,000 8.3 M = 3.7%	6.4 M = 5.5%	not available
2006	246,000	7.9 M = 6.7 %	10.6 M
2007	259,000	7.9 M = 6.6%	10.2 M
2008	315,000	not available	12.5 M
2009	278,000	8.9 M = 7.3%	13.9 M
2010	251,000 = 9 M	8.6 M = 7.0%	10.2 M
2011	279,000	not available	11.6 M
2012	369,000	17 M = 7.0%	12.6 M
2013	290,000	not available	13.1 M = 6.5%

NOTES: Figures for certain years are not available.

For the FTC, figures are for the number of complaints filed with the ID Theft Clearinghouse, rounded to the nearest 1,000.

For the *NCVS*, the number refers to households with victimized persons over the age of 16. The percentage refers to a projection of all U.S. households.

For the Javelin survey, the numbers and percentages refer to all adult U.S. residents.

SOURCES: FTC = Sentinel annual reports, 2002–2013; BJS *NCVS* = Baum, 2006, 2007; Baum and Langton, 2010; Langton, 2011 Langton and Planty, 2011; Javelin, 2011; 2014).

But the number of identity theft victims reached new heights in 2009 before dropping back in 2010. The number of victims then rose substantially for the next three years and in 2013 was not far below its all-time high, according to an annual self-report survey sponsored by a financial services company (Javelin, 2014) (see the last column in Table 4.8).

In sum, as of 2013, the problem of identity theft had stabilized at an intolerably high level that was bothersome to millions of people each year, according to the Justice department's self-report survey, a private company's annual survey, and the federal government's repository for consumer complaints. Regardless of which of these three sources of data is cited, two conclusions must be drawn from Table 4.8. First, in terms of trends, the problem of identity theft is no longer steadily getting worse with each passing year. Second, in terms of relative frequencies, the projected estimates of many millions of individuals and households afflicted by identity theft are much greater each year than the total number suffering from serious property crimes, as recorded by the

UCR as well as the *NCVS*. The ranks of those who were impersonated by an impostor far outnumber the sum total of people whose homes were burglarized and whose motor vehicles were stolen.

As with other categories of interpersonal crime, underreporting undercuts the accuracy of these official and unofficial statistics. Some persons who detect telltale signs of identity theft do not bring their monetary troubles to the attention of law enforcement agencies, and some who do seek assistance are rebuffed. In both 2010 and 2013, most persons (a little over 60 percent) who contacted the FTC to file a complaint that their identities were stolen also notified a law enforcement agency about their situation. However, 7 percent said that the police would not take their report (FTC, 2011; 2014). Reporting rates to the police actually might be much lower and declining when measured by a different method. Of all those who told interviewers that their identities had been stolen, only about 17 percent filed complaints with their local law enforcement agency in 2007, according to the *NCVS* (Langton and Planty, 2010). By 2012, the reporting rate to the police had slipped to a mere 9 percent (although nearly 90 percent reported the misuse to a credit card company or bank, 9 percent contacted a credit bureau, and 6 percent contacted one of the credit monitoring services [Harrell and Langton, 2013]).

Who Faces the Greatest Risks?

Several obstacles hamper attempts to derive accurate estimates of the frequency of these thefts and the profile of those who are targeted most often. First, some people do not yet know that impostors have assumed their identities. Second, some victims are not aware that the FTC has been designated as the national clearinghouse for complaints. Third, certain individuals and businesses are unwilling to report their personal financial problems to law enforcement agencies and government hotlines for an assortment of reasons. For example, businesses might fear that disclosures will harm their reputations, while individuals might decide that the time it will take will not be worth their trouble.

One of the earlier attempts to derive a profile of the average victim determined that the typical

age was 42, the place of residence was a large metropolitan area, and the amount of time it took the person to detect the fraud was 14 months. Seniors were targeted less frequently, and African-Americans tended to suffer more than other groups from check fraud and from theft of utility and telephone services (see Newman, 2004).

But more recent studies cast doubt on the continuing accuracy of this preliminary statistical portrait. The *NCVS* provides more details about differential risks. As for age, the two intervals that experienced lower rates were those between 18 and 24, and also those over 65. People between the ages of 35 and 49 suffered the most (8 percent per year in 2012). As for race and ethnicity, whites experienced higher rates and blacks and Hispanics lower rates. As for sex, males and females were victimized at roughly the same rate. When it comes to social class, the survey found that families earning $75,000 or more were targeted more often than those in lower income brackets (Harrell and Langton, 2013).

As with other types of crimes, where people live plays a major role in shaping differential risks. Table 4.9 presents a ranking of the five worst states and the five safest states in 2013. Many more reports

T A B L E   4.9   States Where Residents Faced the Highest and Lowest Risks of Identity Theft, 2013

Rank 2013	State	Victimization Rate per 100,000 Inhabitants 2010	Victimization Rate per 100,000 Inhabitants 2013
1	Florida	115	193
2	Georgia	97	134
3	California	102	105
4	Michigan	70	97
5	Nevada	96	97
6	Maryland	83	96
7	Arizona	103	91
8	Texas	96	88
9	New York	85	87
10	Illinois **Lowest risks**	81	86
46	Iowa	38	40
47	Maine	32	39
48	Hawaii	43	38
49	South Dakota	25	33
50	North Dakota	30	32

NOTES: Based on complaints received by the FTC from individuals and participating law enforcement agencies during 2010 and 2013. Many incidents were not reported; complaints were not checked for credibility.

SOURCE: Federal Trade Commission Sentinel Network (FTC, 2011, 2014).

of being impersonated came from Florida, Georgia, and California (over 100 per 100,000 residents) than from other states. Risks were much lower, about about 40 per 100,00 or even less than that, in Iowa, Maine, Hawaii, and South and North Dakota, according to the Sentinel Network administered by the FTC (2014).

The geographic factor can be fine-tuned further by focusing on specific cities. The 10 metropolitan areas where residents filed the most complaints and therefore presumably faced the greatest dangers of being impersonated were Miami–Fort Lauderdale–West Palm Beach, Florida (with a sky-high rate of more than 340 victims per 100,000 inhabitants); Columbus, Georgia; Naples–Marcos Island, Florida; Jonesboro, Arkansas; Tallahassee, Florida; Cape Coral–Fort Myers, Florida; Atlanta, Georgia; Port Saint Lucie, Florida; Beckley, West Virginia; and Tampa–St. Petersburg, Florida. As for entire regions, people living in the South and West needed to be more vigilant than those residing in the Northeast and Midwest, according to the FTC's (2014) state and city rankings, which are volatile and can vary substantially from year to year.

It appears that spending habits, lifestyle choices, and decisions about where to reside—in other words, attitudes and behaviors—determine, to some degree, whether an individual's identity will be misappropriated by some thief or hacker.

PREDICTING THE CHANCES OF BECOMING A VICTIM SOMEDAY: PROJECTING CUMULATIVE RISKS

Yearly victimization rates might lull some people into a false sense of security. Annual rates give the impression that crime is a rare event. Only a handful of people out of every thousand fall prey to offenders; most people get through a year unscathed. But fears about victimization do not conform to a January-to-December cycle. People worry that they might be robbed, raped, or murdered at some point during their lives. As the years

go by, the small annual rates can add up to a formidable level for individuals who fall into several high-risk categories.

Lifetime likelihoods are estimates of the cumulative risks of victimization, viewed over a span of 60 or more years (from age 12 into the 70s, the average life expectancy in the United States today). These projections yield a very different picture of the seriousness of the contemporary crime problem. What appears to be a rare event in any given year looms as a real possibility over the course of an entire lifetime (Koppel, 1987), according to the gloomy projections in Table 4.10.

(Note the difference between lifetime likelihoods and prevalence rates. A prevalence rate refers to the proportion of the population that has already experienced victimization. It adds together the current year's casualties to those who suffered during previous years. Expressed as a fraction, the numerator would be this year's new cases plus a larger number of old or preexisting cases from previous years; the denominator would be the size of the population. Lifetime likelihoods are estimates about what the grand total might be in the years ahead, calculated by projecting current rates into the future.)

Over a span of about 60 years, nearly everybody will experience at least one theft, and most people may eventually suffer three or more thefts, according to the projections made on the basis of the relatively high rates of reported crimes that prevailed during the late 1970s and early 1980s. Although the chance that a girl or woman will be forcibly raped in a given year is minuscule, it rises to a lifetime threat of 80 per 1,000, or 8 percent (about 1 female in every 12). For black females, the risk is somewhat greater (at 11 percent, or nearly one in nine) over a lifetime. (Note that these projections don't differentiate between date rape, acquaintance rape, and attacks by strangers—see Chapter 10.) Robbery is a more common crime, so the projection is that about 30 percent of the population will be robbed at least once over a 60-year period. Of this group, 5 percent will be robbed twice, and 1 percent will be robbed three or more times.

T A B L E   4.10   Chances of Becoming a Victim over a Lifetime

Type of Victimization and Person's Race, Sex, and Age	Percentage of Persons Who Will Be Victimized Someday over the Next 60 years			
	Once or more	Once	Twice	Three times or more
Rape				
All females, over a lifetime beginning at age 12	8	8	—	—
Whites	8*	7	—	—
Blacks	11	10	1	—
Robbery				
All persons, over a lifetime beginning at age 12	30*	25	5	1
Males	37	29	7	—
Females	22*	19	2	—
Whites	27	23	4	4
Blacks	51	35	12	—
Assaults				
All persons, over a lifetime beginning at age 12	74	35	24	15
Males	82	31	26	25
Females	62	37	18	7
Whites	74*	35	24	16
Blacks	73*	35	25	12
Burglary				
All households, over a span of 20 years	72	36	23	14
Motor Vehicle Theft				
All households, over a span of 20 years	19	17	2	—

NOTES: *Figures do not add up to total shown in "once or more column" because of rounding.
Estimates include attempts.
Projections are based on average victimization rates calculated by the National Crime Survey (earlier name for the *NCVS*) for the years 1975–1984; for rape, 1973–1982.
___ indicates that the lifetime likelihood is miniscule, less than 0.5 percent.
For burglary and motor vehicle theft, the unit of analysis is households, not individuals; and the time span is only 20 years, not 60 years or more.
SOURCE: Adapted from Koppel, 1987.

Taking differential risks by sex and race into account, males are more likely to be robbed at least once in their lives (37 percent) than females (22 percent), and blacks are more likely to be robbed one or more times than whites (51 percent compared to 27 percent). When it comes to assault, the terms *likelihood* and *probability* take on their everyday meanings as well as their special statistical connotations. Being assaulted at least once in a lifetime is probable for most people—roughly three out of every four persons. (However, this alarming prediction includes failed attempts to inflict physical injury, threats of bodily harm that were not carried out, minor scuffles, and intrafamily violence.) Males face a greater likelihood of becoming embroiled in a fight someday than females (82 percent compared to 62 percent).

Similarly, the projected cumulative risks are unnerving for property crimes committed against households (not individuals) over a time span of 20 years (not a lifetime of over 60 years starting at age 12). Based on the relatively high rates of burglary that prevailed in the late 1970s and early 1980s, the prediction was that over 70 percent of all families would experience a burglary or an attempted break-in over the next 20 years, and nearly one quarter would suffer twice, and about one in seven would be targeted three times or more. On the other hand, only a little less than 20 percent would lose a car to thieves over a 20-year span (see the rows in Table 4.10).

However, the mathematical and sociological assumptions underlying these unnerving projections are very complex and subject to challenge. The calculations were based on estimates derived by averaging victimization rates for the years 1975 to 1984, and then extrapolating these numbers into the future (Koppel, 1987). If crime rates drop substantially over the next 40 years or so, as they already have during the 1990s and 2000s, these projections will turn out to be overly pessimistic. Conversely, if the crime problem intensifies during the next few decades of the twenty-first century, the real odds will be much greater than the percentages in Table 4.10.

Lifetime likelihoods of being murdered also have been computed. Unlike the projections above, which are based on *NCVS* findings, murder risk estimates are derived from *UCR* data. Differential cumulative risks can be presented as ratios, such as "1 out of every x people will be murdered." All the remaining individuals ($x - 1$) within this category are expected to die from diseases and other natural causes, accidents, or suicides. A small x indicates a grave danger. Overall, roughly 1 American out of every 200 will die a violent death (based on the homicide levels of the late 1990s). But the risks vary tremendously, depending on personal attributes, especially sex and race. In general, males are more likely to be slain than females, and blacks are more likely than whites. But when data for both sex and race is included, black females turn out to be in greater danger of being murdered (1 out of every 171) than white males (1 out of every 241). White females have the least to fear, relatively speaking, of the four groupings (1 will be killed out of every 684). But the prospects facing black males are frightening. If the rates of the late 1990s continue over the decades, 1 out of every 35 black males (about 3 percent) eventually will become a victim of homicide (FBI, 1999). In the early 1980s, the crime problem was more severe so the projected threat was even greater: the prediction was that 1 out of every 21 black males (nearly 5 percent) would die violently (Langan, 1985).

The recognition of differential risks touches off another round of questions for victimologists to grapple with as they analyze *UCR* and *NCVS* data. Why does the burden of victimization fall so heavily on some groups of people and not others? Did crime victims do something "wrong" to jeopardize their well-being, or were their misfortunes basically due to bad luck or fate? What can each person—who by definition is a potential target—do to minimize risks? Are there policies the government or society can implement to help all of its members lead safer lives? To what degree is an individual responsible for his or her own future, and to what extent do forces beyond any individual's ability to control determine the risks of becoming a crime victim? These controversial issues are carefully investigated in the next chapter.

SUMMARY

This chapter focused on the people harmed by interpersonal crimes, especially acts of violence by murderers, assailants, and robbers; but also by stealing, like burglary, motor vehicle theft, and identity theft.

Various groupings of people face different risks of being harmed by criminals. International comparisons demonstrate that societal conditions and traditions greatly affect a country's murder rates: The United States stands out as suffering higher rates of violence than similar advanced industrialized societies. Where a person lives and interacts with others is a major determinant of differential risks.

Trends capture changes in victimization rates over time, while patterns indicate connections between the attributes of victims and the frequency with which they are targeted. Data from the *UCR* and the *NCVS* indicates that many types of victimizations are taking place far less frequently in recent years than during their peak period of the late 1980s and early 1990s.

Murders and serious assaults are down sharply since the early 1990s. The gravest risks still are faced by poor young men in urban settings. Robberies take place much less frequently as well, but the same categories of people—poor young men in big cities—still are the most likely targets.

The differential risks of experiencing a property crime—burglary, motor vehicle theft, and a stolen identity—vary substantially by location more so than by the characteristics of the persons who are directly affected. Whereas burglaries and vehicle thefts have dropped sharply over the decades, identity theft has mushroomed into a common aggravation—and for some, a huge source of distress—during the twenty-first century.

Cumulative risks indicate the odds of being victimized over the course of a lifetime: suffering an assault someday is a danger most people will endure; and experiencing a burglary over a 20-year span is likely for most households Studying the reasons for differential risks yields theories that explain why certain groups are more vulnerable to attack than others. This will be the focus of the next chapter.

KEY TERMS DEFINED IN THE GLOSSARY

carjacking, 113

Consumer Sentinel Network, 126

cumulative risks, 94

differential risks, 94

identity theft, 121

incidence rates, 94

muggings, 107

prevalence rates, 94

profile, 100

statistical portrait, 100

strong-arm robberies, 107

Supplementary Homicide Report, 100

trend analysis, 94

yokings, 107

QUESTIONS FOR DISCUSSION AND DEBATE

1. Describe some trends in interpersonal crimes of violence and theft that became evident during the 1990s. Which of these trends has continued right up to the present?

2. Discuss the contention that property crime really hasn't subsided so much—it has just shifted toward identity theft.

CRITICAL THINKING QUESTIONS

1. Try to explain why violent and property crime rates are surprisingly stable and predictable from one year to the next. Speculate as to why last year's rate for the entire United States was so close to this year's rate.

2. All the graphs presented in this chapter show that victimization rates have dropped since the early 1990s. Identify the factors that might explain this much welcomed but largely unexpected improvement in public safety for the following crimes: murder, robbery, burglary, and vehicle theft.

SUGGESTED RESEARCH PROJECTS

1. Make a list of some of the most dangerous countries and cities in the world, based on their murder rates. Ask some people you know if they have ever visited these places and whether they were aware of the statistically high rates of violence while they were there.

2. Monitor this year's murders in your hometown by carefully searching through local newspapers for articles that provide the necessary details. Assemble a database that includes profiles of the victims and the offenders, breakdowns of the victim–offender relationship, weapons used, and circumstances categorizing of the killings. How do these slayings compare statistically to the national averages presented in this chapter?

3. Develop a table that lists the same cities from the map in Figure 4.1. But instead of murder rates, assemble robbery rates from the FBI's *UCR*. Does the ranking of these large U.S. cities by robbery rates come out the same as for murder rates?

4. Find out from insurance companies' websites the makes, models, and years of vehicles stolen most often in your state and, if possible, in your nearest metropolitan area. See if your vehicle is on the list of those most wanted by thieves.

5. Find out from the FTC website the seriousness of identity theft in your state and in the metropolitan area nearest to where you live.

5

The Ongoing Controversy over Shared Responsibility

LEARNING OBJECTIVES

To realize why the concept of shared responsibility is so controversial.

To recognize victim-blaming, victim-defending, and system-blaming arguments.

continued

LEARNING OBJECTIVES

continued

To understand the distinctions between victim facilitation, precipitation, and provocation.

To be able to apply the concepts of victim facilitation, victim blaming, and victim defending to burglary, automobile theft, and identity theft.

To be able to apply the concepts of victim precipitation, victim provocation, victim blaming, victim defending, and system blaming to murder and robbery.

To realize what is at stake in the debate between victim blamers and victim defenders.

To be able to recognize the institutional roots of crime, which overshadow the victim's role.

To become familiar with the competing theories that attempt to explain why some groups suffer higher victimization rates than others.

To recognize how the issue of shared responsibility impacts the operations of the criminal justice system.

To debate the appropriate role of risk management and risk reduction strategies in everyday life.

To appreciate the difference between crime prevention and victimization prevention.

HOW SOME VICTIMS CONTRIBUTE TO THE CRIME PROBLEM

The first few criminologists drawn to the study of victims were enthusiastic about the concept of **shared responsibility** as a possible explanation for why a particular person was harmed by a certain offender. By raising questions previous researchers had overlooked about victim proneness, individual vulnerability, and personal accountability for one's misfortunes, they believed they were developing a more complete explanation about why laws are broken and people get hurt. But they also touched off a controversy within victimology as well as in the arena of public opinion that still rages today.

Consider these situations:

- A motorist shows no concern about where he parks his car, even though he knows that it ranks high on the list of most frequently stolen vehicles. Sure enough, after he leaves it unlocked on a dark quiet street, it is gone when he comes back the next morning.

- A college student tosses out bank statements and credit card bills without worrying whether personal information in them will end up in the wrong hands. Her carelessly discarded paperwork enables an identity thief to open up a credit card account and run up a large balance in her name.

- A man gets drunk at a bar, even though he is among complete strangers, and recklessly begins to stare at a woman who is sitting next to her formidable-looking boyfriend. They exchange insults, and the jealous boyfriend beats him up.

Until victimology emerged, mainstream criminology had consistently ignored the role that injured parties might play in setting the stage for lawless behavior. Victimologists have pledged to correct this imbalance by objectively examining all kinds of situations to determine whether people who were harmed might have played a part in their own downfall.

Thus, victimologists have gone beyond offender-oriented explanations that attribute lawbreaking solely to the exercise of free will by the wrongdoer. Victimologists suggest that certain criminal incidents be viewed as the outgrowths of a process of interaction between two parties. What has emerged is a dynamic model that takes into account initiatives and responses, actions and reactions, and each participant's motives and intentions.

Several expressions coined by the pioneers of victimology capture their enthusiasm for examining interactions: the "duet frame of reference" (Von Hentig, 1941), the "penal couple" (Mendelsohn, 1956), and the "doer–sufferer relationship" (Ellenberger, 1955). Reconstructing the situation preceding the incident can provide a more balanced and complete picture of what happened, who did what to whom and why, and thereby represents an improvement over earlier one-sided, static, perpetrator-centered accounts (Fattah, 1979).

A well-known line of inquiry (albeit a controversial one) within criminology centers on the differences, if any, between lawbreakers and law-abiding people. Criminologists ask, "What is 'wrong' with them? Are there physical, mental, or cultural differences that distinguish offenders from the rest of us?" In a similar vein, victimologists ask, "What distinguishes victims from nonvictims? Do individuals who get targeted think or act differently from those who don't?"

Just posing these questions immediately raises the possibility of shared responsibility. Victimologists have borrowed the terminology of the legal system, traditionally used to describe criminal behavior, to describe the motives and actions of the injured parties as well. The words *responsibility, culpability, guilt,* and *blame* crop up routinely in discussions based on dynamic, situational accounts of the interactions between two people. In the broadest sense, the concept of shared responsibility implies that certain persons—not just their offenders—did something "wrong." Adopting this framework leads to the proposition that some—but certainly not all—of the individuals who were hurt or experienced losses did not do all they could have done to limit their exposure to dangerous people or threatening circumstances, or to abort confrontations that were escalating.

REPEAT AND CHRONIC VICTIMS: LEARNING FROM PAST MISTAKES?

One day in October, a woman hears someone banging on her front door. She opens it and sees her neighbor, a 21-year-old man, lying on his back. He pleads, "Call 911, I'm dying." The ambulance rushes the man to a nearby hospital, but he is dead on arrival. Detectives discover that he had been shot at on two different occasions a few days apart back in July, and briefly hospitalized from the second attack. However, the alleged assassin in those two prior armed assaults was still in jail awaiting trial at the time of the third shooting. (Koehler, 2011)

Researchers looking for clear-cut cases of shared responsibility often focus on individuals who have suffered a series of thefts or attacks.

Offenders seem to set their sights on certain individuals and households more than once during a given period of time. "Repeat victims" are burdened twice. Suffering three or more times during a relatively short time span qualifies a person for the dubious distinction of being a "chronic victim." Having been hurt in the past turns out to be the single best predictor of becoming harmed again in that very same way—or by some other perpetrator or from some other type of offense. Furthermore, the greater the number of prior victimizations, the higher the likelihood will be of trouble in the near future. Revictimization often takes place soon after the initial incident, and then the risks begin to decline as time passes. All these incidents are most likely to break out in very localized high-crime areas, dubbed **hot spots**. Just as a great many crimes can be traced back to just a few perpetrators, a relatively small number of individuals—termed "**hot dots**"—often sustain a large proportion of these attacks. If the police can recognize these recurring patterns by applying their knowledge about the suspected offenders, the likely scenes of the crimes, and the probable targets, then they can become effective guardians to head off further trouble (Pease and Laycock, 1996).

Such "series incidents" accounted for about 1 percent of all victimizations and 4 percent of all episodes of violence disclosed to *NCVS* interviewers in 2013 (Truman and Langton, 2014).

Just as criminals have careers in which they offend in various ways over the years, those on the receiving end might also be said to endure "victim careers" over the course of their lifetimes. The career consists of the frequency, duration, and seriousness of the hurtful experiences suffered by a person from childhood until death. The total number of incidents, the date of their onset, their timing (bunching up or spreading out), and the nature of the injuries and losses sustained as they grow older might be gained by interviewing people and asking them to try to recall all their misfortunes retrospectively. Another approach would involve periodically reinterviewing them or an entire birth cohort every few years as part of an ongoing longitudinal study. The goal would be to empower these individuals to reduce their risks of future turmoil, to improve social support programs and police interventions intended to help them, and to further the development of victim-centered theories that explain the disproportionate burdens certain persons endure (Farrell et al., 2001).

One implication of this focus on revictimization and victim careers is that particular individuals might be making the same mistakes over and over again. Maybe they periodically permit their judgment to become clouded by drinking too much, by failing to safeguard their personal property, by allowing themselves to become isolated from bystanders who could intervene in their behalf, or by hanging out with persons known to be armed and dangerous. The most well-documented examples include bank branches suffering holdups frequently, residences being burglarized a number of times, cars getting broken into on a regular basis, battered wives getting struck repeatedly, and bullied children being picked on by a series of tormentors. Yet their unfortunate track records may not be entirely their fault, according to crime analysts working on behalf of police departments who look for patterns that may indicate where offenders will strike next and precisely whom they might target. These analysts have come up with two primary reasons to account for repeat victimizations: a **boost explanation** that focuses on the offender's abilities, and a **flag explanation** that emphasizes target vulnerability (see Weisel, 2005).

Boost explanations of repeat victimizations point out that career criminals gain important information about the people and places they repeatedly attack based on firsthand knowledge from the successful perpetration of their initial illegal act. They use this inside information to plan their next attack against the same target. Examples of boost explanations would be that burglars learn when a particular home is unoccupied or how to circumvent a certain warehouse's alarm system. Car thieves figure out how to open the door of a specific make and model of car without a key. Robbers discover where a storekeeper

hides his cash right before closing time. In contrast, flag explanations of repeat victimizations are victim-centered. They point out that unusually vulnerable or attractive targets might suffer the depredations of a number of different offenders as opposed to the same criminal over and over. For example, apartments with sliding glass doors are easily broken into, convenience stores that are open around the clock are always accessible to desperate shoplifters and robbers, and taxi drivers and pizza deliverers are particularly easy to rob of the cash they are carrying (Weisel, 2005).

THE ENTIRE SPECTRUM OF POSSIBILITIES: RECOGNIZING COMPLETE INNOCENCE AND FULL RESPONSIBILITY

A **typology** is a classification system that aids in the understanding of what a group has in common and how it differs from others. Over the decades, victimologists have devised many typologies to try to illustrate the degree of shared responsibility, if any, that injured parties might bear in particular incidents. Some of the categories of people identified in typologies include those who are "ideal" (above criticism), "culturally legitimate and appropriate" (seen as fair game, outcasts), "deserving" (asking for trouble), "consenting" (willing), and "recidivist" (chronic) (see Fattah, 1991; also Mendelsohn, 1956; Fattah, 1967; Lamborn, 1968; Schafer, 1977; Sheley, 1979).

Up to this point, the degree of responsibility a victim might share with an offender has ranged from "some" to a "great deal." But the spectrum of possibilities extends further in each direction. A typology of shared responsibility must include at least two more categories in order to be exhaustive. At one extreme is "no shared responsibility at all" or complete innocence. The other endpoint can be labeled as full responsibility.

Several teenagers have a beef with some boys across the street. They go up to the roof of a nearby building and start shooting at the rival group using an automatic pistol. A 34-year-old mother, who is waiting to pick up her children from school, hears the sounds of gunfire and tries to shield several nearby youngsters by throwing herself on top of them. She is fatally struck in the chest, and two other bystanders are wounded by the stray bullets. (Baker and Maag, 2011)

Completely innocent individuals, such as the mother killed in the tragedy described above, cannot be faulted for what happened to them. In some cases, they were targeted at random and suffered simply because they were at the wrong place at the wrong time. Others were crime-conscious people who tried to avoid trouble. They did what they reasonably could to reduce the risks they faced. To avoid violence, they did nothing to attract the attention of predators and nothing to incite otherwise law-abiding people to attack them. Blameless targets of property crimes took proactive steps to safeguard their possessions in anticipation of the possibility of arson, vandalism, burglary, larceny, or vehicle theft. They did all they could to hinder rather than help any would-be thieves hungry for their possessions.

If taking precautions, keeping a low profile, and minding one's own business qualify as the basis for blamelessness and complete innocence, then at the other extreme, total complicity becomes the defining characteristic for full responsibility. Logically, a victim can bear sole responsibility only when there is no offender at all. Individuals who are totally responsible for what happened are, by definition, really not victims at all. They suffered no harm from lawbreakers and actually are offenders posing as victims for some ulterior motive. Phony complainants usually seek either reimbursement from private insurance policies or government aid for imaginary losses. They file false claims and thereby commit fraud. For instance, someone who falls down a flight of steps might insist he was pushed by a robber. Fake victims may have motives other than financial gain. Some people may pretend to have been harmed in order to cover up what really occurred. For example, a husband who gambled away his paycheck might tell his wife and detectives that he was held up on the way home.

WHO OR WHAT IS TO BLAME FOR SPECIFIC INCIDENTS?

Since the 1970s, the notion of shared responsibility has become a subject of intense and sometimes bitter debate. Some criminologists and victimologists have expressed concern over the implications of studies into mutual interactions and reciprocal influences between the two parties. Those who raised doubts and voiced dissent might be seen as loosely constituting a different school of thought. Just as criminology (with a much longer, richer, and stormier history than victimology) has recognizable orientations and ideological camps within it (for example, adherents of conflict models vs. sociobiological explanations for violent behavior), so too does victimology have its rifts and factions. To put it bluntly, a victim-blaming tendency clashes repeatedly with a victim-defending tendency over many specific issues.

Arguments that specific victims bear some responsibility along with their offenders for what happened have been characterized as **victim blaming**. Countering this approach by challenging whether it is accurate and fair to hold the targeted individual accountable for injuries and losses that a wrongdoer inflicted can be termed **victim defending**.

Two opposing ideologies might imply that there are two distinct camps, victim blamers and victim defenders. However, victimologists cannot simply be classified as victim blamers and victim defenders. The situation is complex, and people may change sides, depending on the crime or the persons involved. In fact, most individuals are inconsistent when they respond to criminal cases. They criticize specific individuals but defend others, or they find fault with certain groups (for example, viciously abusive husbands who eventually are killed by their battered wives) but not other groups (such as inebriated women who are sexually assaulted by their predatory dates).

What Is Victim Blaming?

Victim blaming assumes that the offender and the victim are somehow partners in crime, and that a degree of mutuality, symbiosis, or reciprocity may exist between them (see Von Hentig, 1948). To identify such cases, both parties' possible motives, reputations, actions, and records of past arrests and convictions must be investigated (Schultz, 1968).

The quest for evidence of shared responsibility captivated the first criminologists who became interested in the behavior of victims before, during, and after the incident. Leading figures encouraged their colleagues to focus upon the possibility of shared responsibility in their research and theorizing. Some of their statements, excerpted from studies that appeared decades ago, are assembled in Box 5.1.

Victimology, despite its aspirations toward objectivity, may harbor an unavoidable tendency toward victim blaming. It is inevitable that a careful reconstruction of the behavior of a victim before, during, and after a crime will unearth rash decisions, foolish mistakes, errors in judgment, and acts of carelessness that, with 20–20 hindsight, can be pointed to as having brought about the unfortunate outcome. Step-by-step analyses of actions and reactions are sure to reveal evidence of what injured parties did or failed to do that contributed to their suffering.

Victim blaming follows a three-stage thought process (see Ryan, 1971). First, the assumption is made that there is something wrong with these individuals. They are said to differ significantly from the unaffected majority in their attitudes, their behaviors, or both. Second, these presumed differences are thought to be the source of their plight. If they were like everyone else, the reasoning goes, they would not have been targeted for attack. And third, victims are warned that if they want to avoid trouble in the future, they must change how they think and act. They must abandon the careless, rash, or provocative patterns of behaviors that brought about their downfall.

Victim blaming is a widely held view for several reasons. It provides specific and straightforward answers to troubling questions such as, "Why did it happen?" and "Why him and not me?" Victim blaming also has psychological appeal because it draws upon deep philosophical and even theological beliefs. Fervent believers in a **just world outlook**—people get what they deserve before their lives end—find victim blaming a comforting notion. Bad things happen only to evil characters; good souls are rewarded for following the rules. The alternative—imagining a world governed by random events where senseless and brutal acts might afflict anyone at any time, and where wrongdoers get away unpunished—is unnerving. The belief that victims must have done something neglectful, foolish, or provocative that led to their misfortunes dispels feelings of vulnerability and powerlessness, and gives the blamer peace of mind about the existence of an orderly and just world (Lerner, 1965; Symonds, 1975; Lambert and Raichle, 2000 and Stromwall, Alfredsson, and Landstrom, 2013).

The doctrine of personal accountability that underlies the legal system also encourages victim-blaming explanations. Just as criminals are condemned and punished for their wrongdoing, so, too, must victims answer for their behavior before, during, and after an incident. They can and should be faulted for errors in judgment that only made things worse. Such assessments of blame are grounded in the belief that individuals exercise a substantial degree of control over events in their everyday lives. They may not be totally in command, but they are not powerless or helpless pawns and should not be resigned to their fate, waiting passively to become a statistic. Just as cautious motorists should implement defensive driving techniques to minimize car accidents, crime-conscious individuals are obliged to review their ways of relating to people and how they behave in stressful situations in order to enhance their personal safety. By following the advice of security experts about how to keep out of trouble, cautious and concerned individuals can find personal solutions to the social problem of street crime.

Victim blaming also sounds familiar because it is the view of offenders. According to the criminological theory known as "**techniques of neutralization**," delinquents frequently disparage their intended targets as having negative traits ("He was asking for it," or "They are a bunch of crooks themselves"). In extreme cases, youthful

BOX 5.1 Early Expressions of Support for Inquiries into the Victim's Role

- A real mutuality frequently can be observed in the connection between the perpetrator and the victim, the killer and the killed, the duper and the duped. The victim in many instances leads the evildoer into temptation. The predator is, by varying means, prevailed upon to advance against the prey. (Von Hentig, 1941, p. 303)

- In a sense, the victim shapes and molds the criminal. Although the final outcome may appear to be one-sided, the victim and criminal profoundly work upon each other, right up until the last moment in the drama. Ultimately, the victim can assume the role of determinant in the event. (Von Hentig, 1948, p. 384)

- Criminologists should give as much attention to "victimogenesis" as to "criminogenesis." Every person should know exactly to what dangers he is exposed because of his occupation, social class, and psychological constitution. (Ellenberger, 1955, p. 258)

- The distinction between criminal and victim, which used to be considered as clear-cut as black and white, can become vague and blurred in individual cases. The longer and the more deeply the actions of the persons involved are scrutinized, the more difficult it occasionally will be to decide who is to blame for the tragic outcome. (Mannheim, 1965, p. 672)

- In some cases, the victim initiates the interaction, and sends out signals that the receiver (doer) decodes, triggering or generating criminal behavior in the doer. (Reckless, 1967, p. 142)

- Probation and parole officers must understand victim-offender relationships. The personality of the victim, as a cause of the offense, is oftentimes more pertinent than that of the offender. (Schultz, 1968, p. 135)

- Responsibility for one's conduct is a changing concept, and its interpretation is a true mirror of the social, cultural, and political conditions of a given era ... Notions of criminal responsibility most often indicate the nature of societal interrelationships and the ideology of the ruling group in the power structure. Many crimes don't just happen to be committed—the victim's negligence, precipitative actions, or provocations can contribute to the genesis of crime.... The victim's functional responsibility is to do nothing that will provoke others to injure him, and to actively seek to prevent criminals from harming him. (Schafer, 1968, pp. 4, 144, 152)

- Scholars have begun to see the victim not just as a passive object, as the innocent point of impact of crime on society, but as sometimes playing an active role and possibly contributing to some degree to his own victimization. During the last 30 years, there has been considerable debate, speculation, and research into the victim's role, the criminal–victim relationship, the concept of responsibility, and behaviors that could be considered provocative. Thus, the study of crime has taken on a more realistic and more complete outlook. (Viano, 1976, p. 1)

- There is much to be learned about victimization patterns and the factors that influence them. Associated with the question of relative risk is the more specific question (of considerable importance) of victim participation, since crime is an interactional process. (Parsonage, 1979, p. 10)

- Victimology also postulates that the roles of *victim* and *victimizer* are neither fixed nor assigned, but are

---

offenders believe the suffering they inflict is retaliatory justice that merits praise ("We deserve a medal for doing that"). Their consciences would burden them with pangs of guilt if they saw these same incidents in a more conventional way (see Sykes and Matza, 1957; and also Schwendinger and Schwendinger, 1967). Those offenders who are devoid of empathy and pity are so desensitized that they do not feel the guilt, shame, remorse, or moral inhibitions that otherwise would constrain their behavior. By derogating and denigrating the victim, juvenile delinquents or adult criminals can

validate their hurtful acts as justifiable. Outbursts of stark cruelty and savagery become possible when the injured party is viewed as worthless, less than human, an appropriate object for venting hostility and aggression, or an outcast deserving mistreatment (Fattah, 1976, 1979).

Defense attorneys may persuasively articulate the victim-blaming views of their clients, especially in high-profile murder cases. A "trash-the-reputation" (demonization of the deceased) approach, coupled with a "sympathy" (for the accused) defense, might succeed in swaying a mutable and interchangeable, with continuous movement between the two roles.... This position, understandably, will not be welcomed by those who, for a variety of practical or utilitarian reasons, continue to promote the popular stereotypes of victims and victimizers, according to which the two populations are as different as black and white, night and day, wolves and lambs. (Fattah, 1991, p. xiv)

Calls for Research into the Victim's Role in Specific Crimes

- *Murder:* In many crimes, especially criminal homicide, which usually involves intense personal interaction, the victim is often a major contributor to the lawless act.... Except in cases in which the victim is an innocent bystander and is killed in lieu of an intended victim, or in cases in which a pure accident is involved, the victim may be one of the major precipitating causes of his own demise. (Wolfgang, 1958, pp. 245, 264)

- *Rape:* The offender should not be viewed as the sole "cause" and reason for the offense, and the "virtuous" rape victim is not always the innocent and passive party. The role played by the victim and its contribution to the perpetration of the offense becomes one of the main interests of the emerging discipline of victimology. Furthermore, if penal justice is to be fair it must be attentive to these problems of degrees of victim responsibility for her own victimization. (Amir, 1971, pp. 275–76)

- *Theft:* Careless people set up temptation–opportunity situations when they carry their money or leave their valuables in a manner which virtually invites theft by pickpocketing, burglary, or robbery. Carelessness in handling cash is so persistently a part of everyday living that it must be deemed almost a national habit.... Because victim behavior today is conducive to criminality, it will be necessary to develop mass educational programs aimed at changing that behavior. (Fooner, 1971, pp. 313, 315)
  Victims cause crime in the sense that they set up the opportunity for the crime to be committed. By changing the behavior of the victim and potential victim, the crime rate can be reduced. Holders of fire insurance policies must meet fire safety standards, so why not require holders of theft insurance to meet security standards? (Jeffrey, 1971, pp. 208–209)

- *Burglary:* In the same way that criminologists compare offenders with nonoffenders to understand why a person commits a crime, we examined how the burglary victim and nonvictim differ in an attempt to understand the extent to which a victim vicariously contributes to or precipitates a break-in. (Waller and Okihiro, 1978, p. 5)

- *Auto theft:* Unlike most personal property, which is preserved behind fences and walls, cars are constantly moved from one exposed location to another; and since autos contain their own means of locomotion, potential victims are particularly responsible for varying the degree of theft risk by where they park and by the occasions they provide for starting the engine. The role of the victim is especially consequential for this crime; many cases of auto theft appear to be essentially a matter of opportunity. They are victim-facilitated. (McCaghy, Giordano, and Henson, 1977, p. 369)

jury and securing an acquittal or in convincing a judge to hand down a lesser sentence. For example, in cases where children slay their parents, the dead fathers and mothers may be pictured as callous abusers and perverse molesters, while their offspring are portrayed as defenseless objects of adult cruelty (see Estrich, 1993b; Hoffman, 1994).

What Is Victim Defending?

Victim defending rejects the premise that those who suffer are partly at fault and challenges the recommendation that people who were targeted must change their ways to avoid future incidents. First of all, victim blaming is criticized for overstating the extent to which careless habits, foolhardy actions, attention-grabbing behavior, and verbal instigation explains the genesis of an illegal act. Motivated offenders would have struck their chosen targets even if the victims had not made their tasks easier, called attention to themselves, or aroused angry reactions. Second, victim blaming is condemned for confusing the exception with the rule and overestimating the actual proportion of

> **BOX 5.2** Early Criticisms of the Notion of Shared Responsibility
>
> - The concept of victim precipitation has become confused because it has been operationalized in too many different, often incompatible ways. As a result, it has lost much of its usefulness as an empirical and explanatory tool. (Silverman, 1974, p. 99)
>
> - The study of victim precipitation is the least exact of the sociological approaches; it is part *a priori* guesswork and part "armchair detective fun and games" because the interpretation rests, in the final analysis, on a set of arbitrary standards. (Brownmiller, 1975, p. 353)
>
> - A tendency of investigators to assign responsibility for criminal acts to the victims' behavior reinforces similar beliefs and rationalizations held by most criminals themselves.... Scientific skepticism should be maintained regarding the concept of victim participation, especially for crimes of sudden, unexpected violence where the offender is a stranger to the victim. (Symonds, 1975, p. 22)
>
> - Victims of crime, long ignored but now the object of special scholarly attention, had better temper their enthusiasm because they may be more maligned than lauded, and their plight may not receive sympathetic understanding. Some victimologists have departed from the humanitarian, helping orientation of the founders of the field and have turned victimology into the art of blaming the victim. If the impression of a "legitimate victim" is created, then part of the burden of guilt is relieved from the perpetrator, and some crimes, like rape for example, can emerge as without either victims or offenders. (Weis and Borges, 1973, p. 85)
>
> - Victim precipitation explanations are plagued by the fallacy of circular reasoning about the cause of the crime, suffer from oversimplified stimulus–response models of human interaction, ignore incongruent facts that don't fit the theory, and inadequately

cases in which blameworthy conduct took place. Shared responsibility is said to be unusual, not common. A few people's mistakes don't justify placing most victims' attitudes and behaviors under a microscope, or under a cloud of suspicion. Third, exhorting people to be more cautious and vigilant is not an adequate solution. This advice is unrealistic because it overlooks the cultural imperatives and social conditions that largely shape the attitudes and behaviors of both parties in a conflict.

Over the past several decades, many victimologists have embraced the tenets of victim defending, and have sharply denounced crude expressions of victim blaming as examples of muddled thinking and confused reasoning about the issue of shared responsibility. Excerpts of the earliest victim defending arguments condemning victim blaming views appear in Box 5.2.

Victim defending is clear about what it opposes, but it is vague about what it supports. Two tendencies within victim defending can be distinguished concerning who or what is to be faulted. The first can be called **offender blaming**. Offender blaming removes the burden of responsibility from the backs of victims and restores it entirely onto the shoulders of lawbreakers,

"where it belongs." Victim defending coupled with offender blaming leads to traditional criminological thinking, characterized earlier as "offenderology." The question once again becomes, "What is 'wrong' with the offender? How does he differ from the law-abiding majority?" If the answer is that the offender has physical defects or even genetic predispositions to act violently, then the sociobiological theories of criminology become the focus of attention. If the offender is believed to suffer from mental illness, personality disorders, or other emotional problems, then the theories of forensic psychology are relevant. If the offender is said to have knowingly and intentionally chosen to prey upon others, then the explanations center on the classical/rational choice/free-will and deterrence theories about pleasure and pain, benefits and costs, and conclude with the necessity of punishing those who decide to steal and rob.

What Is System Blaming?

The second tendency is to link victim defending with **system blaming**, wherein neither the offender nor the victim is the real culprit. If the lawbreaker is viewed as largely a product of his or her environment, explore the victim's intentions. (Franklin and Franklin, 1976, p. 134)

- An analytical framework must be found that salvages the positive contributions of the concept of victim precipitation, while avoiding its flaws—its tendency to consider a victim's provocations as both a necessary and sufficient condition for an offense to occur; its portrayal of some offenders as unrealistically passive; and its questionable moral and legal implications about who is the guilty party. (Sheley, 1979, pp. 126–127)

- Crime victimization is a neglected social problem in part because victim precipitation studies typically fail to articulate the distress of the victims and instead suggest that some may be to blame for their own plight. The inferences often drawn from these studies—that some individuals can steer clear of trouble by avoiding certain situations—suffer from the *post hoc ergo propter hoc* fallacy of treating the victims' behavior as both

necessary and sufficient to cause the crime. (Teevan, 1979, p. 7)

- To accept precipitation and provocation as legitimate excuses for attenuating responsibility for violent crime is false, illogical, psychologically harmful to victims, and socially irresponsible.... Victim-blaming has been injected into the literature on crime by well-meaning but offender-oriented professionals. It becomes the basis and excuse for the indifference shown to supposedly "undeserving" victims. (Reiff, 1979, pp. 12, 14)

- The eager acceptance of arguments about victim responsibility by scholars and the public alike is undeserved; these accounts of why the crime occurred often lack empirical verification, can lead to cruel insensitivity to the suffering of the victim, and tend to exonerate or even justify the acts of the offenders, especially rapists. (Anderson and Renzetti, 1980, p. 325)

and the victim is too, then the actions of both parties have been influenced by the agents of socialization—parental input, peer group pressures, subcultural prescriptions about what's cool and respectable and what's not, school experiences, media images, religious doctrines—along with criminal justice practices, economic imperatives, and many other social forces. Victim defending coupled with system blaming is a more complex and sophisticated outlook than victim defending/offender blaming. According to this more nuanced sociological type of analysis, the roots of the crime problem are to be found in the basic institutions upon which the social system is built. Then the focus of attention moves to the social-economic-political theories in criminology that assert that the causes of criminality are closely connected to other unsolved social problems (debilitating poverty, chronic unemployment, dysfunctional families, failing schools, injustices arising from growing levels of inequality, unreasonable cultural pressures to succeed, and subsequent strains between means and goals) (among many others, see Franklin, 1978; and Balkan, Berger, and Schmidt, 1980). To many observers, the explanations flowing from the system blaming approach

end up "excusing" the offender from being held accountable in the criminal justice process.

To illustrate the differences between victim blaming and victim defending coupled with system blaming, several types of interpersonal violence and theft will be explored. First, explicit charges of victim facilitation in burglary, automobile theft, and identity theft will be examined. Then the focus will shift to what the injured persons might have done "wrong" in cases of murder and robbery.

MISTAKES INDIVIDUALS MAKE: FACILITATION

Arguments stressing personal accountability focus on the notions of victim facilitation, precipitation, and provocation. All three of these blameworthy behaviors are derived from the broader theme of shared responsibility. Each concept describes the specific, identifiable, and undesirable actions taken by certain individuals immediately before they were harmed. Provocation is the most serious charge that can be leveled at an injured party, while facilitation is the least serious. Unfortunately, these three terms have been used somewhat loosely and inconsistently by criminologists and victimologists to the point that important distinctions have been blurred or buried.

The term **facilitation** ought to be reserved for situations in which victims carelessly and inadvertently make it easier for a thief to steal. Those who negligently and unwittingly assist their offenders share a minor amount of blame. They increase the risks of losing their own property by their thoughtless actions. Facilitation is more like a catalyst in a chemical reaction that, given the right ingredients and conditions, speeds up the interaction. Facilitating victims attract criminally inclined people to their poorly guarded possessions and thereby influence the spatial distribution of crime, but not the number of incidents.

Auto theft, burglary, and identity theft are three property crimes where the problem of facilitation can arise. A motorist who thoughtlessly exits his vehicle but leaves the engine running can be considered blameworthy if a juvenile joyrider seizes the opportunity and impulsively hops behind the wheel and drives off. Similarly, a ransacked home is the price a person might pay for neglecting to observe standard security measures. Those who are careless about protecting their personal information are highly susceptible to identity theft.

How Many Burglaries Were Victim-Facilitated?

Elderly folks often talk fondly about the "good old days" when they left their doors unlocked. That practice wouldn't be prudent these days.

A residential burglary can be considered to be facilitated if the offender did not need to break into the premises because a homeowner or apartment dweller had left a front door, back door, garage door, or window wide open or unlocked. By definition, these burglaries are not "forcible entries"; they are "unlawful entries"—acts of trespass by intruders seeking to steal valuables. A reasonable implication is that the number of successful burglaries could be cut in half if

residents would take greater care to lock up their homes, garages, and other entrances. If they did, burglars would have to work harder and in some cases would be deterred, thwarted, scared off, or caught red-handed.

Details about victim-facilitated burglaries appear in the *National Crime Victimization Survey (NCVS)* as well as the *Uniform Crime Report (UCR)*.

The *NCVS* keeps track of three categories of household (not commercial) burglaries: forcible entries (break-ins), attempted forcible entries, and unlawful entries without force. (Attempted, unsuccessful no-force invasions are not counted because survey respondents usually would be unaware of these close calls.) Throughout the 1990s and into the early years of the twenty-first century, about 50 percent or more of all completed burglaries reported to *NCVS* interviewers were unlawful entries without force. But over the decades these facilitated burglaries have dropped sharply, from more than 40 per 1,000 households in the early 1970s down to only 12 per 1,000 in 2008 (the last time the *NCVS* published such detailed findings). More and more people have become crime-conscious about residential security. Apparently, burglars must work harder because fewer people are making it easy for intruders to invade homes and spirit off their possessions.

In recent years, about one-third of all residential and commercial burglaries were unlawful entries in which it was not necessary to use physical force to break down doors or smash locks or windows, according to the *UCR* for 2010 as well as for 2013 (Hardison et al., 2013; and FBI, 2014).

Some kinds of people are more likely to be "guilty" of facilitating a burglary than others, according to the breakdowns about no-force entries presented in recent *NCVS* annual reports. The age of the head of the household turned out to be an important determinant of whether or not someone would be so thoughtless as to facilitate a burglary. Younger people were much less careful than senior citizens.

The number of people in the household mattered a great deal: the more people living under the same roof, the more likely carelessness would take its toll. Individuals living alone experienced fewer facilitated burglaries; households with six or more people suffered rates that were much greater. As for the race and ethnicity of the head of the household, black and Hispanic families suffered higher rates of no-force entries. Another key factor was financial: the lower-income families in the survey suffered much higher rates of no-force entries (Hardison et al., 2013). Victims reported 44 percent of all no-force entries to the police, according to the *NCVS* for 2008 (BJS, 2011). But even the affluent sometimes act thoughtlessly:

> *Residents of an upscale urban community are jarred when they receive an e-mail from the neighborhood association alerting them that four homes in just five days experienced unlawful entries through open windows or unlocked doors. "This neighborhood is so safe, but not everybody puts on their city smarts and remembers to do the common sense thing and lock their doors," the e-mail states. Police officers post hundreds of warning fliers and even lock several doors themselves after diamond earrings, bracelets, expensive watches, and electronic goods are pilfered during a crime spree by intruders who did not need to use force to enter those premises. (Robbins, 2011)*

Leaving a front door, side door, back door, sliding glass door, garage door, or window open makes a trespasser's tasks easier. Defending against intrusion by installing an alarm system ought to make a would-be burglar's tasks more difficult. Crime-conscious persons who have already been burglarized once, plus concerned individuals who fear that they might be targeted, have been buying security systems for their residences at a rate of about 1.8 million new systems per year. Security systems cost between $100 and $1200 to install (depending upon their features), and monitoring services charge fees of over $400 a year. About one-fifth of all residences were guarded by alarms early in the twenty-first century (Sampson, 2007).

The problem that arises from the widespread sale and installation of security systems is that a huge number of false alarms occur, which use up limited police resources and therefore waste taxpayers' money. Police departments across the country responded to roughly 36 million alarm activations, about 95 percent of which were false alarms, at an annual cost of $1.8 billion in 2002. Nationwide, false burglar alarm calls accounted for 10 to 25 percent of all calls for assistance to police departments in the early 2000s. Each alarm activation that turns out to be false wastes about 20 minutes of police time, usually for two officers. The three main causes of false alarms are user errors, faulty equipment, and improper installation. Bad weather and monitoring-center mistakes by alarm company personnel also contribute to the drain on police time. In most jurisdictions, the financial costs of responding to false alarms that repeatedly emanate from the same residential or commercial premises are not recouped by imposing fines on the crime-conscious but negligent owners. Ironically, although residential burglaries tend to be concentrated in or around poverty-stricken urban neighborhoods, the false alarms tend to come from well-protected, affluent homes in low crime communities (Sampson, 2007).

It might be assumed that one reason why the threat of residential burglary has diminished is that more renters and owners have installed security systems—but this explanation would not explain the simultaneous drop in murders, robberies, and vehicle thefts since the start of the 1990s (refer back to the discussion of the big picture in Chapter 3). Some more profound changes in American society must account for the "crime crash."

Burglary prevention strategies go far beyond installing an alarm or getting a dog and leaving a light on at night. The list of do's and don'ts has grown much more extensive than that, as the advice from the experts assembled in Box 5.3 shows.

How Many Vehicle Thefts Were Victim-Facilitated?

> *No intelligent person would put from $1,000 to $5,000 in good money in the street and expect to find it there an hour later, yet that is exactly what a large number of people do when they leave an automobile in the street without locking it. Even more, not only are they leaving money at the curb but they*

BOX 5.3   Advice from Experts About Burglary

What to Do to Safeguard a Residence:

Following these tips can greatly reduce the chances of being burglarized, police officials insist:

1. Never go out and leave a door or window open or unlocked.
2. Check the door and door frame to see if they are sturdy enough or need to be repaired or replaced. Have a licensed locksmith install a heavy duty dead bolt lock with a highly pick resistant cylinder.
3. Secure all windows properly by replacing the inadequate crescent locks that come as standard equipment. Air conditioners should be secured to the window sash so they can't be pulled out or pushed in.
4. Illuminate the perimeter of the house, especially the door areas with enough light to see a silhouette. Install the floodlight fixture out of reach, in a tamperproof and weather resistant housing. Use timers throughout the house that turn lights in various rooms on and off on a varied schedule. Shrubbery should be trimmed or designed to provide maximum visibility and no opportunities for concealment.

5. It pays to comparison shop for alarm systems. Get estimates from at least three established companies.
6. Make an inventory of all valuable items like jewelry and electronics, and take photos for insurance purposes. Make a list of their serial numbers and ask the local precinct for a tool to engrave each item with a unique number that can be traceable if it gets stolen and then recovered by a police department. Ask the precinct to send out a burglary prevention officer to conduct a confidential home security survey that will identify existing vulnerable points of entry.

What to Do If the Alarm Has Been Set Off or the Home Is Ransacked:

1. Call the police immediately to report the crime but do not enter the premises because the intruder might still be lurking inside. Secure the crime scene until detectives arrive to look for clues.
2. Notify the insurance company to begin the paperwork to file a claim for reimbursement.

SOURCE: NYPD, 2014.

---

are also putting four wheels under it to make it easier for the thief to take it.

AUGUST VOLLMER, POLICE CHIEF, BERKELEY, CALIFORNIA
(VOLLMER AND PARKER, 1936: 65)

Yet through all this practical, emotional, and monetary attachment to the automobile, there emerges convincing evidence that it is one of the motorist's most carelessly neglected possessions.

J. EDGAR HOOVER, FBI DIRECTOR (HOOVER, 1966)

Use common sense: Lock your car and take your keys. It's simple enough, but many thefts occur because owners make it easy for thieves to steal their cars.

FRANK SCAFIDI, NATIONAL INSURANCE CRIME BUREAU (2014a)

Who or what is to blame for the theft and attempted theft of roughly 556,000 cars in 2013 (according to the *NCVS* [BJS, Truman and Langton, 2014]) or the approximately 700,000 vehicles reported as stolen that year (according to the *UCR* [FBI, 2014])?

As the statements above demonstrate, victim-blamers over the decades have been quick to scold negligent drivers for facilitating thefts by leaving their vehicles unlocked, or, even worse, for leaving keys dangling in the ignition lock. Car stealing seems to be the only crime for which there is an organized victim-blaming lobby, a peculiar situation that developed long ago. Composed of representatives of automakers, insurance companies, and law enforcement agencies, this lobby has castigated motorist carelessness since the dawn of the automobile age.

The problem of car-stealing is certainly not new—it emerged more than 100 years ago, at the dawn of the automobile age. As long ago as 1919, Congress passed the Dyer Act, which authorized the FBI to investigate organized theft rings that drove stolen vehicles across state borders to evade local police forces with limited jurisdictions. Then, as now, cars were taken for a number of reasons.

Professional thieves steal cars for profit. These career criminals don't rely on driver negligence;

they know how to start a car without a key. It takes them just a few minutes with the right tools to disarm alarm systems and defeat standard security hardware such as door, ignition, and steering wheel locks. If necessary, they can tow away a vehicle on a flatbed truck and defeat its security system at their leisure (Hazelbaker, 2011). Working in league with commercial theft rings, these pros steal cars either to sell or to strip for parts. Steal-to-sell (retagging) operations alter the registration and title documents and vehicle identification number, and then pass off the car as used. Steal-to-strip operations (chop shops) dismantle vehicles and sell the sheet metal crash replacement parts (such as the hood, trunk lid, fenders, and doors) as if they came from legitimate salvage and recycling pipelines to auto body repair shops.

Another motive for stealing a vehicle is to use it for temporary or short-term travel, often as a getaway car after committing some other crime, such as a bank robbery.

Joyriders take cars for a spin just for fun. Juvenile joyriding (which the law calls "unauthorized use of a motor vehicle" and treats as a delinquent act) has been a craze among teenage boys ever since cars were marketed with the message that owning one is a sign of manhood and a basis for independence. These amateurs—who seek the status, thrills, and challenge of "borrowing" cars to impress their friends—often prey upon careless motorists who leave their keys handy.

Evidence of poor habits is not hard to find, according to a survey of drivers sponsored by the insurance industry in 2007. About 20 percent of all respondents admitted that they did not always lock their vehicles. Seven percent sometimes left spare keys in their vehicle. One-third conceded that they have left their car unattended while it was running (RMIIA, 2011). To counter this mindset of being lax about taking security seriously, educational campaigns advise motorists to follow a number of tips to safeguard their vehicles (see Box 5.4).

The actual contribution of victim facilitation to auto theft usually has been measured as the percentage of recovered stolen cars in which

there was evidence that the thieves had used the owners' keys. Although this methodology has its limitations, surveys based on it reveal a trend that casts doubt on the continued relevance of negligence as an important factor. Data from insurance company records from the 1940s through the 1960s indicate that between 40 percent and 90 percent of all thefts were facilitated by motorists' carelessness. During the 1970s, police, FBI, and insurance industry records showed that facilitation was a factor in 13 percent to 20 percent of all thefts (Karmen, 1979; National Institute of Justice, 1984). In the early 1990s, an insurance industry publication reported that only 13 percent of all vehicle thefts were still victim facilitated (National Insurance Crime Bureau, 1993). But law enforcement agencies as well as insurance and security companies still emphasize that outbreaks of negligence leading to crimes of opportunity remain a significant problem. The Austin, Texas, police department (2011) estimated that nearly 20 percent of all stolen vehicles were taken using the keys left in them. A 2008 study of vehicle stealing in Texas determined that keys were used in about 50 percent of all thefts. A 2009 study of thefts in Arizona concluded that 20 percent of the vehicles had been taken using keys. A Baltimore study determined that a stunning 85 percent had been driven off using keys left inside the cars in 2010 (Egan, 2011).

However, it is likely that most of the recovered vehicles in these studies were taken impulsively by juvenile joyriders who later abandoned them. Vehicles stolen by professionals who dismantled them or else resold them intact are rarely recovered and therefore cannot be examined for evidence of victim facilitation. Furthermore, some of the cars stolen by using keys might not have been victim-facilitated thefts—the keys were bought, not left behind by negligent owners. "Jigglers"—thin pieces of metal shaped like keys—are sold over the Internet in sets as "master keys" that can open most locks, for legitimate purposes—such as by locksmiths and auto repossessors (Gardiner, 2010).

The available statistics support the following conclusion: At one time, when the public was less

---

BOX 5.4 Advice to Motorists About Vehicle Theft

What the Insurance Industry Recommends in Order to Safeguard the Vehicle:

The insurance industry advises it customers to take a "layered approach" that involves four sets of precautions

1. Use Common Sense:
2. Park in well-lit areas. Be aware of surroundings and avoid parking near suspicious looking people. Always lock the car's doors and close all windows completely. Remove the keys from the car. Never leave the engine running unattended—not even for a minute. Take all valuable items from the car or hide them from view.
3. Install Visible or Audible Anti-Theft Devices:
4. Activate a car alarm system; steering wheel locks; steering column collars; and wheel locks. Get the vehicle identification number (VIN) etched on all windows and attach a theft deterrent decal to them.
5. Add a vehicle immobilizer:

6. Purchase smart keys which have computer chips that must be present to start the car; fuse cut-offs; hidden kill-switches; and starter, ignition, and fuel disablers.
7. Buy a transmitter for a tracking system so a stolen vehicle can be quickly located and recovered (Scafidi, 2014b).

What to Do If the Vehicle Is Stolen:

1. Call the police immediately to report the crime so that they won't assume the owner is behind the wheel if the vehicle is used as a getaway car or is involved in a hit-and-run accident. The police might be able to recover the vehicle if it is abandoned.
2. Call the tracking system company to alert them so they can seek to locate the vehicle.
3. Notify the insurance company to begin the paperwork to file a claim for a temporary replacement and eventual reimbursement.

---

conscious about crime, facilitation may have contributed substantially to joyriding escapades. But teenage amateurs are no longer responsible for most car thefts. Professionals—often working for commercial rings that may be affiliated with organized crime syndicates—now represent the greater threat. As the years roll by, key facilitation is declining in significance as a reason for losing a car to thieves.

Facilitating a car theft by leaving keys behind in the ignition could in rare instances lead to a civil judgment against a victim if the thief injures someone else. Some states now require that a car be locked whenever a motorist leaves it (see Sweet, 2011). Some insurance companies have exclusion clauses in their policies that threaten loss of coverage and a denial of reimbursement if the owner acts recklessly or even negligently and leaves keys dangling in unattended vehicles.

The clash in outlooks between victim blaming and victim defending is an example of a half-empty/half-full debate. Victim blaming focuses on the proportion of motorists who have bad habits. Victim defending emphasizes that the

overwhelming majority of people whose cars were stolen did nothing wrong. These drivers don't have self-defeating attitudes and didn't act carelessly. According to victim defenders, the image of the absentminded owner that is frequently conjured up by victim-blaming arguments is an outmoded stereotype that no longer fits (Karmen, 1980).

Owners of motorcycles that are stolen also can be subjected to victim-blaming. For example, the insurance industry warned them to follow theft-prevention tips with this slogan: "Be an easy rider—not an easy target!" (Scafidi 2006).

A similar debate surrounds the issue of who or what is to blame for the surge of identity thefts in the twenty-first century.

How Many Identity Thefts Were Victim-Facilitated?

Protect your Social Security number and other personal information.
Don't let identity thieves rob you of your educational future!

INSPECTOR GENERAL JOHN HIGGINS, U.S. DEPARTMENT OF EDUCATION *[ADDRESSING COLLEGE STUDENTS]* , (2005)

■■■

We're all vulnerable to identity theft—that's the bad news. The good news is that you can protect yourself.

FBI AGENT JEFF LANZA, 2006 (FBI, 2008)

■■■

The first line of defense against identity theft often is an aware and motivated consumer who takes reasonable precautions to protect his information. Every day unwitting consumers create risks to the security of their personal information. From failing to install firewall protection on a computer hard drive to leaving paid bills in a mail slot, consumers leave the door open to identity thieves. Consumer education is a critical component of any plan to reduce the incidence of identity theft.

PRESIDENT'S TASK FORCE ON IDENTITY THEFT (2007, P. 39)

■■■

Awareness is an effective weapon against many forms of identity theft. Be aware of how information is stolen and what you can do to protect yours, monitor your personal information to detect any problems quickly, and know what to do when you suspect your identity has been stolen. Armed with the knowledge of how to protect yourself and take action, you can make identity thieves' jobs much more difficult.

FEDERAL TRADE COMMISSION (2008)

■■■

Consumers should remain vigilant and be careful not to expose personally identifiable information over social networks and to acquaintances.

STEVE COX, CEO, COUNCIL OF BETTER BUSINESS BUREAUS (QUOTED IN JAVELIN, 2011)

As the threat of identity theft mushroomed, a victim-blaming versus victim-defending debate emerged. Victim blaming accentuates the many ways careless people can make the thieves' tasks easier. Victims of identity theft sometimes are blamed—explicitly or implicitly—for failing to take this threat seriously. They ignored the long and growing lists of dos and don'ts, did something careless, and singled themselves out for trouble (see Kelleher, 2006). Because of thoughtlessness or foolishness, they facilitated the ruination of their credit worthiness. This point of view proceeds from the assumption that carelessness is the most frequent cause of the problem, and that conscientiously taking measures to protect personal data is the solution. Victim defending points out the many opportunities that thieves can seize to purloin information that are beyond the ability of individuals to control or counter.

College students might be especially vulnerable to identity theft for several reasons. They store personal data in shared, largely unguarded dormitory rooms. Many undergraduates might not take precautions because they do not have much money or assets. They do not realize that they could be targeted for their unblemished "good names and reputations," and not the limited amounts of cash in their bank accounts. Surveys document that lax attitudes toward handling personal identifiers persist on some campuses (Office of the Inspector General, 2005). Many universities hold workshops on identity theft awareness (President's Task Force, 2007, p. 40). One theme is that users of social networking sites are warned not to post bits of information that identity thieves and burglars could exploit. Examples of what should not be revealed online include addresses, dates of vacations, and information about daily routines. Telling the world about one's place of birth, mother's maiden name, favorite song, and even pets' names could be providing thieves with answers to questions that are commonly asked for security purposes to sign in to Internet accounts (Schultz, 2010).

Thieves can resort to a range of methods to get the information they need to become effective impostors. They can employ old-fashioned methods such as grabbing wallets and purses during burglaries and robberies or breaking into parked cars to find personal papers and laptops. Identity crooks can commit a federal offense by sorting through a person's mail for bank and credit card statements, preapproved credit card offers, new checkbooks, telephone bills, or tax receipts. Patient criminals can even file a "change of address" form at a post office to physically divert a target's mail to a location of their choosing. Gutsy thieves can pry loose secrets by "pretexting": posing as representatives of a government agency or business with a legitimate need to know personal information. They can pilfer records kept by an employer or bribe an employee who has access to confidential files. When desperate, they can stoop to "**dumpster diving**" by rummaging through an individual's garbage or the trash thrown away by businesses or hospitals, searching for discarded receipts and bank statements.

Besides these low-tech means, some thieves have mastered sophisticated high-tech methods to take advantage of their intended prey. "**Shoulder surfers**" find out passwords by watching their marks at ATMs. Corrupt employees can use "**skimmers**" to scan and capture crucial information during credit card transactions at restaurants and other stores. Others obtain what they need to know via the Internet by searching agency records (especially about births, marriages, and deaths). Cyberthieves, perhaps operating on some other continent, can engage in "**phishing**" and "**pharming**." "Phishermen" try to fool, entice, or frighten unsophisticated email recipients into disclosing account numbers, user names, and passwords on authentic-looking yet bogus websites; they pretend that they need to update an existing account or repair a security breach with a bank or other financial institution. Sophisticated cybercrooks engage in **caller ID phone spoofing**: the recipient's phone displays a phone number that seems to originate from a trusted party; consequently the naïve person is deceived into divulging confidential information. Pharmers attack legitimate websites with malicious codes that steer traffic to look-alike fake sites that "harvest" (intercept and decode) encrypted online transactions. "Keystroke logging" spyware, planted inside a computer with a malicious code or virus, betrays everything an unsuspecting user types. "Screenscrapers" can snatch and transmit whatever is on

a monitor of an infected PC. All of these techniques are intended to exploit the weaknesses, vulnerabilities, and impulsiveness of unsuspecting targets who fail to remain vigilant at all times, and thereby facilitate the scammers' tasks (FTC, 2002; Slosarik, 2002; Collins and Hoffman, 2004; NCJRS, 2005; Shanahan, 2006 and Acohido, 2014).

As for the victim–offender relationship, the thief is usually but not always a complete stranger. "Friendly fraud" carried out by persons known to their target—such as roommates or relatives—appears to be on the rise, especially against consumers between the ages of 25 and 34 (Javelin, 2011). Clearly, the victim–offender relationship can range from trusted employees, former intimate partners, roommates, and estranged relatives to casual acquaintances (like dishonest bank tellers or postal workers), to total strangers like car thieves and electronic intruders who hack into files maintained by supposedly secure websites. It is extremely difficult to guard against all these different lines of attack (Acohido, 2014; and ITRC, 2014a).

Indeed, the implicit victim blaming message underlying theft-prevention educational campaigns is that those who don't conscientiously take precautions will be sorry someday when impostors hijack their identities. If they ignore the long and growing lists of dos and don'ts, they are singling themselves out for trouble (see Kelleher, 2006). Victims who accept blame often obsess over how they inadvertently must have given their secrets away. What they might have done "wrong" appears in Box 5.5.

Victim defenders argue that facilitation is not the heart of the impersonation problem. Consistently following theft prevention recommendations would reduce a person's risks by making a thief's tasks more difficult to carry out. But even the most scrupulous observance of all these suggestions at all times still might prove ineffective. More and more people have sharpened their "cyber-streetwise" skills. And yet even as they foil attempted scams, ID crooks devise clever new ways to rip them off (Shanahan, 2006). Therefore, it seems unfair to blame most victims because sophisticated identity pirates can overcome any obstacles cautious individuals place in their paths. Victim defenders cite observations by experts such as these:

> *It has been said that the theft of one's identity and personal information is not a matter of "if" but a matter of "when."*

ELIOT SPITZER, NEW YORK STATE ATTORNEY GENERAL, 2005 (QUOTED IN KATEL, 2005, P. 534)

■ ■ ■

> *Firewalls and virus protection programs are routinely penetrated by sophisticated hackers seeking ID information.*

BRUCE HELLMAN, SUPERVISOR OF THE FBI'S NEW YORK COMPUTER HACKING SQUAD (QUOTED IN SHERMAN, 2005, P. 24)

■ ■ ■

> *Even if you take all of these steps, however, it's still possible that you can become a victim of identity theft.*

U.S. DEPARTMENT OF JUSTICE, FRAUD DIVISION, 2008

Furthermore, many people would consider abiding by the long lists of dos and don'ts recommended in Box 5.4 to be unreasonable (such as workers grilling their employers about how well their personnel files are safeguarded); impractical (customers refusing to provide Social Security numbers to creditors); burdensome (like devising new passwords containing many letters and numbers every few months); or unworkable (emptying home mailboxes at midday). Living this way—always being vigilant and suspicious—is emotionally exhausting.

A nagging question is "Why me?" or "How did it happen?" Unfortunately, most victims never figure that out. Several sets of answers from various sources shed light on this issue.

A study commissioned in 2005 focused on the relatively small proportion that did discover how the thieves got their personal identifiers. Lost or stolen wallets, credit cards, and checkbooks were the source of the problem in less than 30 percent of all identity theft cases in which victims thought they knew why it happened to them (Katel, 2005).

Only about 40 percent of all self-identified victims told *NCVS* interviewers that they thought they knew what caused their problems. The leading reasons were that personal identifiers were compromised during a purchase or other transaction; fell into the wrong hands because of a lost or stolen wallet or checkbook; and were lifted from personnel files maintained in offices. But the majority had no clue as to why they were targeted and how the fraud took place (Langton and Planty, 2010). Similarly, "How did it happen?" remained a mystery to the majority of respondents in the 2012 *NCVS*. Nearly 67 percent could not determine how the thief obtained their personal information, and over ninety percent did not know anything about the person who impersonated them (Harrell and Langton, 2013). Tapping into another source of data, only about 30 percent of "verified victims" who used the free services offered by the Identity Theft Assistance Center (ITAC) had figured out how it happened to them. The leading causes were computer hacking/viruses/phishing schemes, followed by lost or stolen wallets, checkbooks, or credit cards. Other less frequent explanations were data breaches beyond their ability to control; betrayals by relatives, friends, and in-home employees; stolen or diverted mail; disclosures by corrupt employees; and, lastly, burglaries of their residences—this according to a 2011 study of about 760 persons commissioned by an organization that is funded by the financial services industry and reportedly engages in victim advocacy (ITAC, 2011).

But there are many other ways that thieves can steal information from their unsuspecting prey during a range of everyday activities. Personal identifiers can be intercepted in technologically sophisticated ways while customers are engaged in banking transactions online or when they are buying merchandise or tickets over the Internet. Cell phone transmissions can also be intercepted to hijack information. Birth certificates can be obtained under false pretenses from records maintained by county governments. Crooks posing as landlords or employers conducting background checks can get other people's credit reports (Office of the Inspector General, 2005).

BOX 5.5 The Perils of Identity Theft: What to Do and What Not to Do, According to the Experts

Many identity-theft prevention and self-help guidebooks suggest ways of avoiding trouble (for example, see May, 2001; Vacca, 2002; Frank, 2010; and Kelly, 2011). The recommendations are much more extensive and demanding than the advice given to individuals who want to protect their homes from burglars and their vehicles from car thieves.

Preventive Measures

Government agencies do their part in the campaign against victim facilitation by warning the public to manage personal information "wisely and cautiously." The Fraud Division of the U.S. Department of Justice (2008) summarizes its advice about four ways to minimize risks by using the acronym SCAM.

- Be "stingy" about giving out personal information.
- "Check" your financial records regularly.
- "Ask" to see a free credit report from one of the three credit bureaus every four months.
- "Maintain" careful records of financial accounts.

The Federal Trade Commission (2008; 2011) spells out in greater detail the many precautions it recommends:

- Keep important documents such as bank books and tax returns under lock and key, as well as computers and laptops full of personal information.
- Stash away personal records so they aren't readily available to roommates, party guests, domestic employees, or repairmen.
- Use a paper shredder to destroy unsolicited preapproved credit card invitations, as well as unneeded receipts, bills, applications, forms, and account statements, to thwart thieves who pick through trash and recycling bins for items revealing personal information.
- While away from home, destroy receipts from financial transactions at banks, ATMs, restaurants, and gasoline stations.

- Promptly remove incoming letters from a mailbox, and take outgoing bills and checks directly to post office collection boxes.
- Devise clever (rather than easily remembered but also easily guessed) passwords using a combination of letters, numbers, and special characters. Substitute creative alternatives for a birth date or a mother's maiden name for electronic accounts. Change these unique hard-to-crack passwords on a regular basis for each account.
- Scrutinize bills and account statements for unauthorized transactions.
- Request information about security procedures at doctors' offices, businesses, educational institutions, and workplaces, such as who has access to databases, whether records are kept in a safe location, and how old files are disposed of.
- Don't carry a Social Security card in a wallet or write that number on a check. If it is requested in a business transaction, ask: "Why is it needed? How will it be used? What law requires that it be divulged? What measures are taken to protect this number? What will happen if it isn't provided?" See if a substitute number can be used on a state driver's license or for a health insurance policy.
- Go to the trouble of opting out of telephone solicitations, direct mail lists, and preapproved credit card offers.
- If scrupulously abiding by this lengthy list of "dos" and "don'ts" is not sufficiently reassuring, cautious persons intent on avoiding trouble can purchase identity theft insurance package plans.

If state law permits it, a cautious person can place a "freeze" on his or her credit files with each of the three major agencies, so that third parties cannot access the account or open a new one without permission to temporarily lift it.

VICTIM PRECIPITATION AND PROVOCATION

Victim facilitation is a possibility in burglaries, motor vehicle thefts, and identity thefts. Charges of precipitation and provocation are hurled at victims of murder, robbery, assault, and rape (see Chapter 10 for an extensive analysis).

A husband-and-wife team, each with a history of robbery arrests and drug abuse, embark on a dangerous course of action to solve their financial problems. Armed with a submachine gun, they barge into storefront social clubs operated by organized crime families and seize the mobsters' ill-gotten gains. After hitting four Mafia social clubs in different neighborhoods over three months, their highly provocative and predictably short-lived crime spree comes

Concerned customers must pay a fee for this transaction, but the expense is waived for victims of identity theft. Those who have their ID stolen can also impose a "fraud alert" that compels potential creditors to notify victims about any applications for new credit cards or loans in their name.

Red Flags That Indicate a Theft May Have Taken Place

The Federal Trade Commission (2011) emphasizes the importance of early detection as a way to minimize harm. It suggests that consumers monitor their accounts regularly and be on the alert for any suspicious activities, such as the following signs that impostors may have recently stolen their identities:

- Unfamiliar or suspicious debits, purchases, and cash withdrawals appear on accounts.
- Inaccurate information appears on credit reports.
- Bills that were anticipated do not arrive in the mail, signaling that the billing address may have been changed.
- Credit cards arrive in the mail that were not applied for.
- Credit is denied, or high rates are imposed on mortgages or car loans, indicating elevated risks and delinquent accounts.
- Bill collectors call about overdue debts.
- Notices arrive referring to mysterious houses that were bought, apartments rented, or jobs held in the victim's name.

Recovery and Restoration After an Impersonation

Individuals who have evidence that their personal accounts have been penetrated and their identities appropriated by impostors should follow these four steps in order to recover from the theft, according to advice provided by the Federal Trade Commission (2011):

- Place a fraud alert on credit inquiries, applications, and reports with the three major companies. Monitor these accounts carefully for at least one year.

- Close any accounts that appear to have been fraudulently opened or tampered with, and notify the company's security or fraud department, in writing, about the intrusion. Obtain forms to dispute any fraudulent transactions and debts, and keep records and copies of all correspondence.
- Notify the local police and file a detailed complaint called an "Identity Theft Report" either in person, over the phone, or online, and get the report's number. If the local police are reluctant to accept the complaint, ask to file a "Miscellaneous Incident Report" or try another jurisdiction, such as the state police, or ask the state attorney general's office for assistance. Provide reluctant officers with a copy of the FTC's "Law Enforcement Cover Letter" that explains the impact of this type of crime on victims and the finance industry, as well as the FTC's "Remedying the Effects of Identity Theft" that underscores the necessity of police reports as a way to ensure victim's rights.
- Contact the Federal Trade Commission, file a complaint using its online form or the hotline, and obtain an "ID Theft Affidavit," which can be circulated to law enforcement agencies (such as the FBI, the Secret Service, and the U.S. Postal Inspection Service).
- Also, notify the IRS, U.S. Passport Office, and the state department of motor vehicles. Speak to counselors at an FTC hotline who offer advice about the steps to be followed and how to use their standard ID Theft Affidavit to simplify the process of settling disputed charges with defrauded creditors. Persons who continue to suffer lingering consequences and repeated intrusions may appeal to the Social Security Administration for a new identification number, but this step still may not resolve all their problems (FTC, 2011; U.S. General Accounting Office, 2002; Slosarik, 2002; and Lee, 2003a and Albrecht, Albrecht, and Tzafrir, 2011).

to a sudden end on Christmas Eve. As the couple sits in their car at a traffic light on a congested street, a man walks up and shoots each robber in the head several times. Rival mob factions both claim credit for arranging the rubout until the police finally arrest one of their gangsters a dozen years later. (Rashbaum, 2005)

■■■

Two young women who seem to be intoxicated give a $50 bill to a cashier at a fast food joint. When the cashier questions its authenticity, one of the women leaps over the counter and the other goes around it. The two women curse and cuff the cashier. He grabs a metal rod and savagely beats them. Later, it is discovered that he is out on parole for killing a classmate 10 years earlier, and that one of the women may *suffer permanent brain damage from being bludgeoned on the head. The cashier is fired and held on charges of felonious assault, and the two unruly customers are arrested for menacing, criminal trespass, and disorderly conduct.* (Sandoval, 2011)

The accusation embedded in the term **precipitation** is that the individual who gets hurt contributed significantly to the outbreak of violence.

A charge of **provocation** embodies a stronger condemnation than precipitation; it accuses the loser of being more responsible than the victor for the fight that ensued. The injured party instigated an attack that would not have taken place otherwise. The person condemned for provocation goaded, challenged, or incited a generally law-abiding person into taking defensive measures in reaction to forceful initiatives. When the battle ended, the aggressor was the one who was wounded or killed.

(Unfortunately, over the years, victimologists and criminologists have used the terms *precipitation* and *provocation* loosely, and even interchangeably, obscuring the distinction between lesser responsibility for precipitation and greater responsibility for provocation.)

The first in-depth investigation of what was termed victim precipitation centered on homicides committed in Philadelphia from 1948 to 1952 (Wolfgang, 1958). Precipitation was the label applied to those cases in which the person who was killed had been the first to use force by drawing a weapon, striking the first physical blow during an argument, or in some way initiating violence to settle a dispute. Often, the victim and the offender knew each other; some had quarreled previously. Situations that incited them to violence included charges of infidelity, arguments over money, drunken brawls, and confrontations over insults or "fighting words."

Victim-precipitated cases differed in a number of statistically significant ways from homicides in which those who were slain did not bring about their own demise. Nearly all the precipitative victims were men; a sizable minority of the innocent victims were women. Conversely, relatively few women committed homicide, but a substantial proportion of those who did so were provoked by violent initiatives by the men they killed. Alcohol was consumed before most killings, especially prior to precipitated slayings—usually, the victim had been drinking, not the offender.

In cases of precipitation, the one who died was more likely to have had a previous run-in with the law than in other murders. More than a third of the precipitative victims had a history of committing at least one violent offense, as opposed to one-fifth of the blameless ones.

Overall, about one murder of every four in Philadelphia from 1948 to 1952 was labeled by the researcher as victim-precipitated. Hence, in a quarter of the cases, widely held images of victims (as weak and passive individuals shrinking from confrontations) and of offenders (as strong, brutal aggressors relentlessly pursuing their prey) didn't fit the facts as reconstructed from the police department files. In many of the victim-precipitated homicides, the characteristics of the victims closely resembled those of the offenders. In some cases, two criminally inclined people clashed, and chance alone determined which one would emerge as the winner or the loser in their final showdowns (Wolfgang, 1958).

Petty quarrels escalate into life-and-death struggles through a sequence of stages, or a series of transactions. The initial incident might be a personal affront, perhaps something as minor as a slur or gesture. Both parties then contribute to the unfolding of a "character contest." As the confrontation escalates, each person attempts to "save face" at the other's expense by hurling taunts, insults, and threats, especially if onlookers are pressuring them to fight it out (Luckenbill, 1977).

The term **subintentional death** has been applied to situations in which those who got killed played contributory roles in their deaths by exercising poor judgment, taking excessive risks, or pursuing a self-destructive lifestyle (Allen, 1980). This charge—that some people want to end their emotional suffering and consciously or unconsciously enter risky situations or engineer tragic events—is leveled most commonly at repeat victims. In homicide cases, the argument rests on a record of several "near misses" preceding the final violent outburst. If the deceased person's outright dares and subliminal invitations are interpreted within this framework, victim-provoked homicide is tantamount to suicide (Mueller, in Edelhertz and Geis, 1974); it is as if a mentally disturbed individual had a death wish but could not quite carry it through without help (Wolfgang, 1959; Reckless, 1967). This assumption of hidden motives is unsympathetic to the deceased who allegedly manipulated others to kill them, and it fosters a tendency to view them in a harsh light—as troublemakers whose demise is really not a tragedy.

Perhaps those who lost their final showdowns didn't welcome their fate. What might be misinterpreted as a death wish was really an adherence to the norms of street culture that extols the use of force to settle disputes (Singer, 1986). This readiness to resort to combat to resolve arguments is not a sign of psychopathology but is instead learned behavior. Cultural norms that require people to fight it out and not back down are reported to be most prevalent among Southerners (Butterfield, 1999) as well as among young men in poor, urban neighborhoods who conform to a "code of the streets" to prove their manhood and gain their peers' respect (Anderson, 1999). In many serious assaults, detectives often discover that both the injured party and the victorious assailant were mutual combatants (Lundsgaarde, 1977).

Note that according to the law, not all people wounded or killed by shootings or stabbings are classified as crime victims. For example, an armed robber slain in a gun battle with a bank guard would be categorized as a dead offender, not a provocative victim. His demise would not be a murder but an act of **justifiable homicide** if the security officer resorted to deadly force in self-defense. Some casualties of justifiable homicides apparently committed "suicide by cop" (see Klinger, 2001) by provoking police officers to shoot them—for example, advancing in a menacing manner while brandishing an unloaded gun, and ignoring urgent warnings of "Stop or I'll shoot!"

Victims of police brutality often are condemned for having provoked the officers into using excessive force (beyond the necessary amount allowed by law) to subdue and arrest them. This image of instigating an officer to unleash retaliatory violence is reinforced if the person who was beaten was openly defiant and resisted arrest or even assaulted the officer. The brutality victim's allegations are difficult to prove in criminal court (and in civil lawsuits) if any officers who witnessed key events abide by a "code of silence" and take part in a "blue wall" cover-up of misconduct—unless the incident was videotaped. Also, intense pressures to drop the brutality complaint are brought to bear on the injured person during plea negotiations if he is charged with crimes.

Consequently, it is difficult to assess the extent of the problem of police brutality as well as the problem of victim provocation of officers. Reliable nationwide data and monitoring systems don't exist. Yet charges of police brutality and countercharges of arrestee provocation must be taken seriously and investigated carefully because these divisive incidents can polarize the public, strain police–community relations, and even touch off riots.

How Many Violent Crimes Were Precipitated or Provoked?

The issue of the victims' roles in street crimes was systematically explored in the late 1960s by the National Commission on the Causes and Prevention of Violence (NCCPV). As its name suggests, the blue-ribbon panel was searching for the roots of the problem and for practical remedies. If large numbers of people were found to be partly at fault for what happened to them, then changing the behavior of the general public might be a promising crime-prevention strategy. Social scientists working for the commission took a definition of victim precipitation derived from previous studies by criminologists and victimologists, and they applied it to four types of crimes: murders, aggravated assaults, forcible rapes, and robberies. Then they drew a sample of reports from police files from 17 cities and made a judgment in each case about whether the person who was attacked shared any responsibility with the assailant.

Victim-precipitated homicides (defined as situations in which the person who died was the first to resort to force) accounted for 22 percent of all murder cases in the 17 cities: as much as 26 percent in Philadelphia (Wolfgang, 1958; see above), and as high as 38 percent in Chicago (Voss and Hepburn, 1968). About 14 percent of aggravated assaults were deemed to be precipitated (in which the seriously injured person was the first to use physical force or even merely offensive language and gestures, sometimes referred to as "fighting words"). Armed robberies were committed against precipitative individuals "who clearly had not acted with reasonable self-protective behavior in handling money, jewelry, or other valuables." Eleven percent of the holdups in the 17 cities were deemed to be precipitated, about the same as in a study conducted in Philadelphia (Normandeau, 1968). Forcible rapes that led to arrests were designated as precipitated if the woman "at first agreed to sexual relations, or clearly invited them verbally and through gestures, but then retracted before the act." Only 4 percent of all rapes were classified as precipitated in the study of 17 cities. However, as many as 19 percent of all sexual assaults in Philadelphia were deemed to be precipitated by females (Amir, 1967). (This controversial notion of victim-precipitated rape will be explored and critiqued in Chapter 10.)

The commission concluded that instances of victim complicity were not uncommon in cases of homicide and aggravated assault; precipitation was less frequent but still empirically noteworthy in robbery; and the issue of shared responsibility was least relevant as a contributing factor in rapes (National Commission on the Causes and Prevention of Violence, 1969b; Curtis, 1974).

Research projects that look into victim complicity have shed some light on the role that alcohol plays in terms of precipitation and provocation. Alcohol is a drug (a depressant) and its consumption has been implicated even more consistently than the use of illicit drugs in fueling interpersonal

conflicts leading to fatal outcomes or serious injuries (see Spunt et al., 1994; Parker, 1995). For example, the *UCR*'s Supplementary Homicide Reports (SHRs) for 2013 reveal that "brawls due to the influence of alcohol" claimed many more lives than "brawls due to the influence of narcotics" (121 compared to 58 in 2010; 93 compared to 59 in 2013) (FBI, 2014).

The first comprehensive analysis of urban murders (in Philadelphia around 1950) determined that the victim, the offender, or both were drinking before the killing took place in 64 percent of the cases (Wolfgang, 1958). Reports from medical examiners in eight cities in 1978 revealed that the percentage of corpses testing positive for alcohol ranged from a low of 38 percent to a high of 62 percent (Riedel and Mock, 1985). In New York City between 1973 and 1997, the proportion of victims who had been drinking before they were murdered was as low as 29 percent and as high as 42 percent, according to autopsies performed by the Office of the Chief Medical Examiner (Karmen, 2006). In a study of nearly 5,000 homicides committed in Los Angeles between 1970 and 1979, researchers reported that they detected alcohol in the blood of nearly half the bodies autopsied. The blood-alcohol content in about 30 percent of these 5,000 murder victims was high enough to classify the person as intoxicated by legal standards at the time of death. The typical alcohol-related slaying involved a young man who was stabbed to death in a bar on a weekend as the result of a fight with an acquaintance or even a friend (Goodman et al., 1986).

Binge drinking is a dangerous practice that some people—including college students—have slipped into. Two mechanisms explain the link between consuming large quantities of alcohol and violence due to precipitative or provocative conduct. The **selective-disinhibition perspective** suggests that if one person binges—or worse yet, if both parties do—judgment will become clouded, and these individuals are likely to misinterpret each other's intentions, cues, and actions, and then behave in a less restrained manner. The **outlet–attractor perspective** proposes that at certain drinking locations (such as liquor stores, bars, and clubs) people gather with the expectation that they will seek "time out" from normal constraints and act "out of character" in an "anything goes" environment (Parker and Rebhun, 1995).

Some outbreaks of mortal combat that arise from intense conflicts—often fueled by alcohol—can be viewed as the outcome of a sequence of events in a transaction. The initial incident might be a personal affront, perhaps something as minor as a slur or gesture. Both the offender and the victim contribute to the escalation of a **character contest**. As the confrontation unfolds, at least one party, but usually both, attempts to "save face" at the other's expense by not backing down. The battle turns into a fatal showdown if both participants are steeped in a tradition that favors the use of force as the way to settle bitter disputes (Luckenbill, 1977). Recall that the largest category in the listing of "circumstances" comprised people who were slain as a result of a dispute of some kind. Most of the deaths that resulted from these fights were unplanned and led to manslaughter indictments and convictions.

TRANSCENDING VICTIM BLAMING AND VICTIM DEFENDING: SYSTEM BLAMING

The analysis above of murders, robberies, burglaries, auto thefts, and identity thefts uncovered some strengths and weaknesses of both victim blaming and victim defending. Contrary to sweeping characterizations made by some victimologists, victim blaming is not inherently an exercise in scapegoating, an example of twisted logic, or a sign of callousness. It depends on which crime is the focus of attention, who the victims are, and why some people condemn their behavior. Similarly, victim defending is not always a noble enterprise engaged in by those who champion the cause of the downtrodden. Certain victims deserve to be criticized.

Victim blamers are not necessarily liberal or conservative, rich or poor, young or old, or male or female. Sometimes they switch sides and

become victim defenders—depending on the facts of the case, the nature of the crime, and the parties involved. Individuals are not consistent; nearly everyone blames certain victims and defends others.

The strengths of victim blaming and victim defending lie in their advocates' willingness to scrutinize specific criminal acts and reconstruct real-life incidents. The two clashing perspectives dissect in great detail who said and did what to whom and under what circumstances. Victim-blaming and victim-defending arguments bridge the gap between theoretical propositions and abstractions on the one hand, and how people genuinely think and act on the other.

The most serious drawback of both perspectives is a tendency to be microscopic rather than macroscopic. Victim-blaming and victim-defending arguments get so caught up (or bogged down) in the particular details of each case that they tend to ignore the larger social forces and environmental conditions that shape the attitudes and behaviors of both criminals and victims. Thus, whenever partisans of the two perspectives clash, they inadvertently let the system—with its fundamental institutions (established ways of organizing people to accomplish tasks) and culture (way of life, traditions)—off the hook. Yet these outside influences compel the actors in the drama to play the well-rehearsed roles of offender and victim and to follow a well-known script in an all-too-familiar tragedy. Policymaking often swings back and forth between attempts to control the behavior of either would-be predators or their potential prey—but not their larger social environment, which is what a system-blaming analysis of social institutions would recommend.

Clearly, transcending the analytical confines of both victim blaming and victim defending requires that the researcher go beyond criminology and victimology and into the broader realm of social science: sociology, anthropology, psychology, economics, and political science. Only then can the effects of the social system on shaping the thoughts and actions of specific offenders and their victims, and on creating the vested interests that have grown up around the problems of burglary, vehicle theft and identity theft, be appreciated and understood. Doling out the proper mix of exoneration and blame to just two people is of limited value because the influences of outside forces are eliminated from consideration.

As for murders, system-blaming would center on the glorification of violence in the media as a source of entertainment, from murder-mysteries to movies to video games. Resorting to physical force is also widely accepted as a means of conflict resolution, not only on the meanest streets of poverty stricken neighborhoods where young men immersed in a subculture of violence congregate, but also in policy-making circles at the highest levels of government where plans to go to war are developed. The reliance on deadly force is also encouraged by the firearms industry through the manufacture of increasingly powerful weapons, with easy access to them due to lax laws regulating gun purchases.

As for robberies, system-blaming would start out by pointing out the longstanding and now growing gulf between the well-off and the desperately poor, and the over-importance of material possessions in a consumer-oriented society.

In the case of burglary, system-blaming would emphasize the organized nature of fencing as an incentive to thievery. Imagine if burglars had to peddle their stolen stuff on the street themselves, rather than cashing it in at some fencing operation that accepts "second-hand goods," no questions asked.

In the case of identity theft, system blaming would stress how the numerous data breaches (estimated at almost 650 per week in October 2014) expose personal data to thieves regardless of the efforts by conscientious customers to protect their secrets by regularly changing their passwords. From January 2005 up to October 2014, nearly 570 million records containing sensitive personal information were exposed because of over 4,850 security breaches. These breaches compromised the names, social security numbers, financial account information, medical records, and email addresses and passwords kept in the files of banking, finance, credit,

educational, government, military, and medical organizations (ITRC, 2014c). These data breaches, not individual acts of carelessness, are often the basis for identity thefts. In 2011, one in every five persons who received data breach notification letters later became a victim of at least one subsequent fraud. In 2012, that victimization rate rose to one in every four. By 2013, one out of every three customers who got a warning later got into financial trouble in some way. Almost half (46 percent) of all consumers with breached debit cards from banks discovered that their accounts were drained. About 15 percent of all persons whose Social Security numbers were taken eventually were defrauded, according to an annual survey (Javelin, 2014).

Also, surprising amounts of personal information are readily available in databases accessible through the Internet. The lax security measures of some businesses put their consumers at risk. Online stores, car dealerships, retail chains, and regional banks are rarely held accountable for unauthorized disclosures of confidential information about their customers, and are reluctant to publicly acknowledge intrusions into their files. Organizations often are not vigilant guardians of the records of their students, employees, or patients (Newman, 2004). Data brokers who sell personal information for commercial purposes need to take additional measures to protect the public from raids on their files by cybercrooks and fraudsters who seek credit, debit, and ATM card account information (like PIN codes), Social Security numbers, and birthdates. Stolen identifiers are for sale through global black market channels.

Most federal and state legislation passed to date focuses on deterring and punishing offenders. It offers little protection or relief in the form of government compensation or restitution by offenders for those who lose money, and fails to hold accountable the commercial ventures whose careless practices enable thieves to periodically swipe databases full of confidential data. Most state governments have passed laws to compel organizations that maintain databanks to notify people put at risk when a breach of security takes place. But Congress could pass stricter regulations that would impose higher internal security standards on the operations of agencies and companies that suffer breaches with infuriating regularity but only reluctantly admit that intruders broke into their record-keeping systems, office files, and computer databases. Thefts of personal data from supposedly secure repositories can endanger hundreds of thousands of people at a time (Editors, *New York Times*, 2005a; Sherman, 2005; President's Task Force, 2007; and Consumer's Union, 2008; and Acohido, 2014).

The system-blaming approach also questions the sincerity of the efforts made by the giant corporations (especially banks and credit card companies) that ostensibly suffer losses when their customers fall prey to identity thieves. Even though this kind of fraud initially costs them billions of dollars annually, ultimately they pass along most of these expenses to their customers by raising rates and fees, just as large stores charge higher prices to cover "inventory shrinkage" due to shoplifting and employee theft. Any remaining losses can be written off at tax time. It appears that top executives have calculated that it is better for their businesses' bottom line to recoup money from honest customers than it is to spend more on fraud prevention or to pay more to pursue and help bring to justice impostors masquerading as someone else.

Sensing that this problem has become a deeply entrenched feature of the financial landscape, companies have discovered that every "crisis" presents an opportunity to make money by marketing credit monitoring services to detect suspicious activity and by selling a new form of insurance that repays policyholders for expenses arising from misappropriations of their good names (May, 2002; Edwards and Riley, 2011; and Albanesius, 2011).

Many law enforcement agencies still lack experts in forensic computing and remain far behind the curve when it comes to detecting intrusions, figuring out who did it, and gathering evidence that will stand up in court. The odds are in the thieves' favor. Convictions take place in only 1 out of every 700 to 1,000 reported instances of identity theft (Katel, 2005).

In the case of car theft, victim-blaming and victim-defending arguments nearsightedly dwell on the actions of motorists and thieves. What is excluded from the analysis is as important as what is included. A comprehensive battle plan must take into account how sophisticated and organized commercial thievery has become, and how profitable the black market for "hot" cars and stolen parts continues to be. It must also grasp how the practices of insurance companies provide incentives for thieves to steal cars for parts, and how salvage yards make it easy to infiltrate stolen items into the flow of recycled parts to auto body repair shops (see Goodman, 2014) An effective anticrime strategy must also come to grips with the inadequacies in record-keeping and in the stamping of serial numbers on crash parts. These shortcomings, which have been known for years but are not yet been adequately resolved (see Karmen, 1980; NIJ, 1984), make it difficult for law enforcement officers to detect and prove thievery.

Even more important, it is necessary to go beyond victim blaming and victim defending to realize that the manufacturers bear responsibility for the ease with which their products are taken from their customers. Pros brag that they need just a minute or two (and an ordinary screwdriver or some shaved-down keys) to defeat standard antitheft locks on the doors and ignitions of many makes and models (see Kesler, 1992; Behar, 1993; "Auto Theft Alert," 1994; S. Smith, 1994; and McKinley, 2006).

Perhaps blaming victims for auto theft serves to distract attention from engineering issues. The most virulent victim blaming has emanated from automobile industry spokespersons, insurance company representatives, and top law-enforcement officials. Who or what are they protecting? Certainly, they are not apologists for the lawbreakers, either the joyriding juveniles or the professional crooks. Apparently, condemning the motorists who left their cars vulnerable to thieves is intended to divert attention away from the automobile manufacturers who design and sell cars that are so easily stolen. Considerable evidence exists to substantiate the charge that until recently vehicle security (like passenger safety) was assigned a low priority by automakers, probably because thefts stimulate new car sales (see Karmen, 1981a). Vehicle security is likely to remain a problem until manufacturers are compelled by law to post theft-resistance ratings from an independent testing bureau or government laboratory on new-car showroom stickers.

THE IMPORTANCE OF DETERMINING RESPONSIBILITY IN THE CRIMINAL JUSTICE PROCESS

A wife returns home late at night after having a tryst with her landscaper at a motel. Her husband, an executive and former professor, becomes enraged and slams her face into the floor of the garage, splitting her head open. The police find her blood-soaked body behind the wheel of her SUV in a creek, but when they determine that the apparent driving accident was staged, the husband is arrested. He is prosecuted for her murder, but the jury finds him guilty of the lesser charge of passion/provocation manslaughter. The judge sentences him to eight years in prison. He will be eligible for parole after five and a half years. (Miller, 2005)

The process of fixing responsibility for crime unavoidably rests on judgments that are subject to challenges and criticisms. These judgments are based on values, ethics, allegiances, and prejudices concerning the crucial question of whether (and to what degree) the victim shares responsibility with the offender for a violation of the law. A number of important decisions that affect the fate of the offender, the plight of the victim, and the public's perception of the crime hinge on this issue of victim responsibility.

Whether or not the victim facilitated, precipitated, or provoked the offender is taken into account by police officers, prosecutors, juries, judges, compensation boards, insurance examiners, politicians, and crime control strategists. Victim responsibility is an issue at many stages in the criminal justice process: in applications for compensation; in demands for restitution and compensatory damages; in complaints about how crime victims are treated by family, friends, and strangers at home, in hospital emergency rooms, in court, and in the newspapers; and in the development of crime prevention programs and criminological theories.

At every juncture in the criminal justice process, judgments must be made about the degree of responsibility, if any, the complainant bears for what happened. The police confront this issue first. For example, when called to the scene of a barroom brawl, officers must decide whether to arrest one or both or none of the participants and what charges to lodge if they do make arrests. Often the loser is declared the victim, and the combatant still on his feet is taken into custody for assault.

When prosecutors review the charges brought by the police against defendants, they must decide if the complainants were indeed totally innocent victims. If some degree of blame can be placed on them, their credibility as witnesses for the prosecution becomes impaired. A district attorney may decide that the accused person would probably be viewed by a jury or a judge as less culpable and less deserving of punishment and therefore has less of a chance of being convicted. Because relatively few cases are brought to trial, the prosecution will engage in plea bargaining (accepting a guilty plea to a lesser charge) if a blameworthy victim would be an unconvincing witness. Such cases might even be screened out and charges dropped. For instance, a study of files in the District of Columbia during the early 1970s revealed that evidence of victim blameworthiness halved the chances that a case would be prosecuted (Williams, 1976).

Killings that resulted from extreme provocations by the deceased are likely to be considered justifiable homicides and won't be prosecuted. Jurisdictions use different standards to determine what constitutes provocation and justification. For example, a study of slayings in Houston, Texas, determined that 12 percent were justifiable, but in Chicago only 3 percent of all killings were considered justifiable by local authorities. It appears that the legal definition of justification was broader in Texas than in Illinois (Block, 1981).

If the provocation by the person who died is considered insufficient to render a homicide justifiable, it might be treated as an extenuating circumstance. Evidence of victim provocation can persuade the district attorney to charge the defendant with manslaughter instead of murder. In a homicide or assault case, the victim's provocation must have been "adequate" in order for the charges to be reduced or for the defendant to be acquitted on the grounds of justifiable self-defense. In most states, that means that the defendant's violent responses to the victim's provocations must have occurred during the heat of passion, before a reasonable opportunity for intense emotions to cool (Wolfgang, 1958; Williams, 1978).

If the defendant is convicted, the judge may view the injured party's provocation as a mitigating factor that makes a lesser sentence appropriate. In jurisdictions where restitution by offenders is permitted or even mandated, the culpability of victims can be a cause for reducing the amount of repayment that convicts must undertake. Similarly, the judge or the jury in civil court is likely to consider a plaintiff's blameworthy actions as a reason for reducing the monetary damages a defendant must pay for causing loss, pain, and suffering. Parallel considerations arise when persons wounded in violent crimes apply to a criminal injury compensation board for reimbursement. If the board members determine in a hearing that the victim bears some responsibility for the incident, they will reduce the amount of the award or may, in extreme cases of shared guilt and provocation, entirely reject the application for financial assistance (see Chapter 12).

In some conflicts that erupt after extensive interaction between two mutually hostile parties, the designations "offender" and "victim" simply do not apply. When both people behaved illegally, adjudication under the adversary system may not be appropriate. Neighborhood justice centers have been set up to settle these shared responsibility cases through mediation and arbitration. Compromises are appropriate when both disputants are to some degree "right" as well as "wrong" (see Chapter 13).

In sum, widely held beliefs and stereotypes about shared responsibility can profoundly shape the way a case is handled within the criminal justice process. The frustrations of trying and failing to deter or rehabilitate criminals periodically propels public safety campaigns in the opposite, presumably easier, direction toward crackdowns on victim facilitation, precipitation, and provocation. What follows is a satire that was written decades ago but remains quite relevant, in which a fictitious professor of victimology puts forward preposterous proposals to reduce street crime (see Box 5.6).

Applying Deterrence Theory to Victims

For more than two centuries, since the time of Cesare Beccaria and Jeremy Bentham, the originators of the **classical school** of **free will** or **rational choice** theory, a fierce debate has raged over whether would-be offenders are deterred by the prospects of apprehension, conviction, and punishment. Rarely, if ever, is the debate about deterrence applied to past and potential victims.

Simply put, **deterrence theory** holds that swift and sure punishment is the solution to the crime problem. According to the tenets of specific deterrence, punishing offenders teaches them a lesson they won't forget, so they will not repeat the forbidden act. According to the doctrine of general deterrence, publicly punishing offenders makes them into negative role models that serve as a warning to others to avoid committing similar misdeeds.

Proponents and opponents argue whether offenders really learn the intended lesson (especially in jails and prisons, which can serve as "graduate schools" that churn out individuals with advanced degrees in criminality). Do would-be lawbreakers really mull over their decisions rationally, think twice, and decide not to commit illegal acts? Or do they often act impulsively, disregarding the possible consequences in the heat of passion? Do others who hear about the crime and the punishment that followed truly make the connection, think, "That could be me!" and become "scared straight" and dissuaded from violating the law?

BOX 5.6 Prof Calls for Crackdown on Crime Victims

There is so much talk about crime in the streets and the rights of the criminal that little attention is being paid to the victims of crime. But there is a current of opinion that our courts are being too soft on the victims, and many of them are going unpunished for allowing a crime to be committed against them. One man who feels strongly about this is Professor Heinrich Applebaum, a criminologist who feels that unless the police start cracking down on the victims of criminal acts, the crime rate in this country will continue to rise.

"The people who are responsible for crime in this country are the victims. If they didn't allow themselves to be robbed, the problem of crime in this country would be solved," Applebaum said.

"That makes sense, Professor. Why do you think the courts are soft on victims of crimes?"

"We're living in a permissive society and anything goes," Applebaum replied. "Victims of crimes don't seem to be concerned about the consequences of their acts. They walk down a street after dark, or they display jewelry in their store window, or they have their cash registers right out where everyone can see them. They seem to think that they can do this in the United States and get away with it."

"You speak as if all the legal machinery in this country was weighted in favor of the victim, instead of the person who committed the crime."

"It is," Applebaum said. "While everyone is worried about the victim, the poor criminal is dragged down to the police station, booked and arraigned, and if he's lucky he'll be let out on bail. He may lose his job if his boss hears about it and there is even a chance that if he has a police record, it may prejudice the judge when he's sentenced."

Applying the principles of general deterrence to law-abiding people, many parallel questions arise: Do victims learn a lesson from their mistakes? Do they realize how they may have facilitated, precipitated, or even provoked criminal activities? Do they vow to not repeat these errors, to take "dos and don'ts" tips more seriously, and to change their careless or even reckless ways? Or do they disregard the persistent threats, continue to take their chances, plow ahead stubbornly, and become repeat victims, suffering serial victimizations (two or more incidents during a relatively short time)?

And does their suffering serve as a warning to the general public about "how not to behave"? Does news media coverage of specific incidents strike fear in the hearts and minds of large numbers of would-be victims, making them think twice and conclude that the potential costs outweigh the benefits? Do members of this audience exercise their free will and rationally decide the particular risky behavior engaged in by a victim isn't worth pursuing, and do they then choose a more prudent course of action? Does the frightening prospect of becoming a casualty lead to constructive responses, such as incorporating risk avoidance and risk management precautions into lifestyles?

The answers to these queries require careful research by victimologists.

Facilitation, precipitation, and provocation are recognized as the blameworthy actions of specific individuals in particular incidents. However, the data presented in Chapter 4 from the *UCR* and the *NCVS* confirmed a widely held belief that certain entire groups of people are more likely than others to be murdered, robbed, assaulted, or to lose their valuables to burglars, car thieves, and other crooks. Why is that? What, if anything, did they do—or fail to do—that caught the attention of criminals? What, if anything, marks them as different from the rest of the potential targets in the general population? Which risk factors heighten dangers and make these high-risk demographic groups and their possessions more vulnerable to attack (Dussich, 2011).

Although victimologists cannot agree among themselves about precisely which behaviors and practices increase susceptibility, being singled out definitely does not appear to be a random process, striking people just by chance. When individuals ask, "Why me?" victimologists suggest that the reason in most cases goes beyond simply "being in the wrong place at the wrong time." However, "being at the wrong place at the wrong time" indeed can

"I guess in this country people always feel sorrier for the victim than they do for the person who committed the crime."

"You can say that again. Do you know that in some states they are even compensating victims of crimes?"

"It's hard to believe," I said.

"Well, it's true. The do-gooders and the bleeding hearts all feel that victims of crimes are misunderstood, and if they were treated better, they would stop being victims. But the statistics don't bear this out. The easier you are on the victim, the higher the crime rate becomes."

"What is the solution, Professor?"

"I say throw the book at anybody who's been robbed. They knew what they were getting into when they decided to be robbed, and they should pay the penalty for it. Once a person has been a victim of crime and realizes he can't get away with it, the chances of his becoming a victim again will be slim."

"Why do people want to become victims of crime, Professor?"

"Who knows? They're probably looking for thrills. Boredom plays a part, but I would think the biggest factor is that victims think they can still walk around the streets of their cities and get away with it. Once they learn they can't, you'll see a big drop in crime statistics."

"You make a lot of sense, Professor. Do you believe the American people are ready to listen to you?"

"They'd better be, because the criminal element is getting pretty fed up with all the permissive coddling of victims that is going on in this country."

SOURCE: From "Victim Precipitation," by Art Buchwald, copyright © *The Washington Post*, February 4, 1969.

---

be a sufficient explanation, as this tragic carjacking case demonstrates:

A father gets a call from his daughter about some good news. So he pulls over to the shoulder of the highway to safely talk on his cell phone. A parolee who had served time for attempted murder suddenly appears. "Who are you running from?" the father asks. The parolee doesn't answer but yanks him out of the car, shoots him in the head, and speeds off in the stolen vehicle. The fugitive had just murdered a police officer and wounded another before fleeing and chancing upon the driver on his cell phone. The cop-killer is captured but the father dies. (Ruderman and Goodman, 2012)

Consider robberies as an example of the interplay of different responses that can lead to strikingly different outcomes. Potential victims can learn a great deal from other people's experiences, especially their mistakes. Successful robbers, armed or unarmed, are skilled at "target manipulation" or "victim management" (Letkemann, 1973). From a close-up, symbolic interactionist perspective within sociology, victim–offender initiatives and responses can be analyzed as a set of complementary roles. Robbers are the initiators and aggressors; the people they are preparing to pounce upon are usually passive, at least at the start. But the individuals who discover that they are under attack can refuse to play their assigned role, reject the script, and struggle against the scenario imposed on them. The intended prey might even gain the upper hand, switch roles, and disrupt the final act, or end it in a way dreaded by the aggressors. In other words, the incident may or may not proceed according to the offender's game plan. When analyzed as a transaction based on **instrumental coercion** (applying force to accomplish a goal), a typical robbery proceeds through five stages or phases: planning, establishing co-presence, developing co-orientation, transferring valuables, and leaving (Best and Luckenbill, 1982).

1. During the planning stage the offenders prepare to strike by choosing accomplices, weapons, sites, getaway routes—and intended targets. They look for certain favorable characteristics, such as valuable possessions, vulnerability to attack, relative powerlessness to resist, and isolation from potential protectors. Strangers are preferred because they will have greater difficulty in providing descriptions to the police and in identifying suspects from pictures or lineups.

2. During the second phase of the interaction, the offenders establish **co-presence** by moving within striking distance. The robbers try not to arouse their intended prey's suspicion or to provoke either unmanageable opposition or fright and flight. Some offenders rely on speed and stealth to approach unsuspecting individuals. Others employ deceit to trick people into letting down their guard.

3. The third stage is developing **co-orientation**. At this stage the robbers announce their intentions to dominate the situation and exploit their advantages. They order their targets to surrender valuables and they demand compliance. Their prey can either acquiesce or may contest the robbers' bid to take charge, depending on an assessment of the aggressors' "punitive resources" (ability to inflict injury). Robbers who fail to develop co-orientation (to secure cooperation and submission) through threats may resort to violence to intimidate or incapacitate their opponents.

4. If the robbers successfully gain and maintain the upper hand, the interaction moves into its fourth phase. Victims are searched and their valuables are seized. But the interaction is terminated prematurely (from the offenders' point of view) if the targets uncooperatively resist, have no valuables, are unexpectedly rescued, or escape.

5. The fifth stage is the exit. It is marked by the robbers' attempts to break off the relationship at a time and under conditions of their choosing. As they prepare to leave the scene, they may inflict injuries to prevent interference with the getaway, or they may issue threats about the dangers of pursuing them or reporting the crime to the authorities (Best and Luckenbill, 1982).

This breakdown of robbery transactions into distinct stages and discrete steps helps to anticipate possible outcomes. Targeted individuals may or may not suffer financial losses from stolen (or damaged) property. Robbers may or may not injure their victims at the outset or at the end. Their prey may or may not be able to resist the aggressors' advances and may or may not be able to prevent successful completions of the unwanted transfer of valuables. Officers on patrol may or may not become involved. And a very small proportion who resist may be killed in tragic incidents that escalate from robbery to homicide. When an attempted forced transfer of valuables from one person to another is deconstructed in this manner, many opportunities can arise to change the script and the sequence of events to the victim's advantage. A lot can be learned from other people's mistakes. Suggestions from experts about how to prevent or at least survive robberies appear in Box 5.7.

Carjacking is a type of robbery that is very difficult to anticipate and defend against. There are no foolproof precautions, and drivers always must be on the alert for many different scenarios when starting or stopping and while parking. Victims of this crime of opportunity sometimes are criticized for not being vigilant enough when loading or unloading packages; driving while preoccupied with music or cell phone conversations; traveling with their car doors unlocked and windows open; blundering through dangerous neighborhoods rather than taking safer routes; or falling into a trap by stopping after being bumped into, as part of a staged accident by a vehicle full of robbers.

Theorizing About Risk Factors: Figuring Out Why Certain Groups Suffer More Often Than Others

Theoretical explanations start as hypotheses that answer questions that begin with "Why?" After making an empirical generalization (an observation based on patterns or trends that emerged when the data were analyzed) theorists are inclined to ask, "What accounts for this?" For example, during the warmer months, there are more unlawful entries (burglaries accomplished without using force to get in) and stranger rapes. This empirical generalization about the seasonality of certain illegal activities requires an explanation. Why should

B O X 5.7 Robbery: What the Experts Recommend

Police experts recommend these ways of minimizing the chances of being robbed:

1. Walk alertly and confidently, while scanning the vicinity forwards and backwards. Try not to walk alone. At night, consider taking a taxi cab even for short trips.
2. Trust your instincts and avoid uncomfortable situations, especially groups congregating and hanging out. Do not take shortcuts through unlit, sparsely traveled paths such as trails, stairwells or alleys.
3. Carry only as much cash as needed. Avoid outdoor ATMs, particularly at night and those in secluded interior areas. Be alert at banks or check cashing businesses since carrying large wads of bills can attract robbers.

What to Do During a Robbery

1. Try to remain calm. Do not resist. Try not to be a hero. Take no action that would jeopardize safety. Follow the robber's directions, but do not volunteer more than asked for. Assure the robber of full cooperation.
2. Meanwhile, make mental notes of the robber's race, age, height, sex, clothing, complexion, hair, and eye color. Note anything unusual about the robber such as scars or tattoos. Also note the number of accomplices and how they left the scene, their direction of travel, and the type and color of their vehicle. Get the license number if it is safe to do so. Try to remember any conversations the suspects may have with one another, what the suspect's weapon looked like, and what the suspect touched that may have left fingerprints.
3. After the robbery, go to a safe location close to the crime scene and call 9-1-1 immediately. Ask all witnesses to remain until the officers arrive. If a witness must leave, obtain his/her name, address, and telephone number. Witnesses should write down or remember their account of the suspects and their actions. Do not discuss the robbery or compare notes about the robber's appearance with anyone. Protect the crime scene. Try not to touch anything.

SOURCE: Houston, Texas Police Department, 2014.

burglary and rape exhibit a predictable cycle of increases and decreases during the course of a year? An offender-centered explanation might propose that burglars and rapists are more active during warmer weather. Another line of thought could be that something about their intended targets changes with the seasons. Perhaps behavior patterns during warm weather create greater opportunities for predators to stalk their quarry. During the summer, people spend more time outside and are more likely to leave windows open while they are away from home. As a result, strangers find more occasions to assault girls and women sexually, and prowlers find more unprotected homes to invade (Dodge, 1988).

One of the founders of victimology (see Von Hentig, 1941, 1948) zeroed in on presumed weaknesses and special vulnerabilities of entire groups— what today would be called risk factors. He was convinced that certain personal attributes played a part in determining susceptibility to attack. The mentally retarded (because they were less aware of dangers), newly arrived immigrants (unfamiliar with the language and customs), minorities (not given the same degree of protection by law enforcement authorities), less-educated individuals, and very inexperienced people were pictured as attractive targets for exploitation by offenders employing deception and fraud. Con artists swindled those who were greedy, heartbroken, depressed, or lonesome with legendary ease. Physically handicapped people, the elderly and frail, the very young, and persons with impaired judgment and dulled senses due to intoxication were assumed to be easy prey for robbers and assailants. According to this typological approach, a varied collection of psychological, biological, social, and demographic factors set whole categories of people apart as particularly vulnerable (McShane and Emeka, 2011).

Why Various Groups Experience Differential Risks: Routine Activities and Specific Lifestyles

Most victimologists are not satisfied with explanations that emphasize a single vulnerability factor that is biological (gender, age, or race), psychological (loneliness or greed), social (income or occupation), or situational (just arrived as an immigrant; or just got paid in cash). A number of more elaborate theories attempt to figure out why certain groups suffer more than others. These theories draw upon a number of factors as building blocks.

From an offender's standpoint, potential targets (individuals, homes, and cars) can be rated along several dimensions. One dimension is **attractiveness**. Teenage muggers assault classmates to rob them of stylish shoes or coats or the latest electronic devices. Some people and things appear "ripe for the taking," while others present more of a challenge to the robber or burglar and raise the specter of being thwarted or even captured. Certain prizes can easily be snatched, spirited off, and cashed in (such as car airbags or smartphones), while others would take a long time and a lot of trouble to fence, and the net return might be minimal (such as used automobile tires of a specific size).

Situational factors highlight how people and their possessions are temporarily more susceptible at certain times, periods, or stages than at others. For example, muggers might lie in wait as payday approaches or when Social Security checks or public assistance allotments arrive in the mail (direct deposit eliminates this danger). Armed robbers might approach storekeepers at closing time.

Proximity describes whether the offender can get within range of the intended target, geographically (by direct contact) and socially (through interaction). Offenders might have great difficulty getting within striking distance of certain attractive targets, such as millionaires or their mansions. Proximity is a disadvantageous working condition for certain occupations such as mental health attendants and corrections officers who deal with dangerous people on a regular basis (see Garofalo, 1986; Siegel, 1998). Mental patients in hospitals for the criminally insane also endure high rates of assault and theft because of the proximity factor (see Seager, 2014). Certain individuals might be singled out simply because they are conveniently accessible, such as nonviolent inmates locked in with hardened convicts in prisons, jails, and holding cells. Similarly, elderly people trapped in high-crime housing

projects or meek students stuck in troubled high schools also suffer grave dangers because they are readily available targets.

Vulnerability is a dimension that refers to a target's ability to resist and repel an attack, and ranges from well protected to largely undefended. For instance, at one extreme, rare coins in a museum are attractive to thieves and can be viewed up close but usually are displayed in tightly guarded settings. At the other extreme, it can be a costly mistake to leave valuables in plain sight in autos. The same vulnerability factors apply to people: Bodyguards may accompany corporate chieftains, but storekeepers walk home alone late at night.

The combination of the two factors of proximity and vulnerability can turn deadly, as this tragic case shows:

> A young woman moves from a small farming community to a tough neighborhood in a sprawling big city. Her motivation is to help drug abusers kick their habits by becoming devoutly religious. Soon after making contacts and inviting addicts over to discuss religious teachings, she is found slain in her apartment. (McShane and Emerka, 2011)

Taking these factors into account leads to an explanation of how entire groups might face heightened risks. Tourists often are preyed upon because of the confluence of a number of factors: exposure, attractiveness, proximity, situational vulnerability, and hot spots. Robbers, pickpockets, sneak-thieves, hustlers, and other swindlers gravitate to sites where tourists congregate as hot spots for crime because they figure that they can take advantage of the high population turnover and the anonymity of crowds to move into striking distance, while their prey will be readily identifiable (sporting backpacks, cameras, and maps and driving rental cars). Their attractive targets also will be carrying large sums of money and valuables, while being unusually vulnerable: relaxed and off-guard, distracted, careless, adventuresome, even reckless, unfamiliar with signs of danger, naïve about notorious scams avoided by knowledgeable locals, perhaps disinhibited from drinking too much, and often cut off from potential guardians by language barriers. The offenders also know from experience that tourists are not inclined to waste precious time filling out forms in police stations, looking at mug shots of potential suspects, and staying around to take part in drawn-out court proceedings. To discourage offenders from damaging the lucrative tourist trade that is so vital to the local economy, some prime travel destinations have organized special police units to protect and serve visitors as well as special prosecutorial units (to fly in crucial eyewitnesses to testify in behalf of the state, or at least to use videoconferencing to facilitate their pressing charges and securing convictions) (Glensor and Peak, 2004).

Routine activities theory stresses the interactions of three key variables: the existence of motivated criminals (for example, drug addicts desperate for cash), the availability of suitable targets (people or their possessions), and the presence or absence of capable guardians. These guardians can be gadgets (motion detectors, burglar alarms, gates and fences, bright lights, safes) or people (such as alert parents, watchful neighbors, or police officers on patrol) or even animals (barking dogs). Would-be offenders seize opportunities to strike whenever attractive targets are not well protected. If one of the three elements is absent, a successful completion of a direct contact predatory crime won't take place. Consequently, concerned individuals should take preventive steps to make themselves and their possessions less vulnerable to attack by anticipating how, where, and when offenders might probe and test their defenses. Everyday living arrangements that can affect victimization risks include patterns of commuting, shopping, attending school, going to work, and pursing hobbies.

Daily activities govern the **social ecology of victimization**: the kinds of people who will be harmed and the manner, time, and location of the incidents. For example, in recent decades, the vulnerability of women to robbery and murder increased, according to routine activities theory, because they go far away from home to work and experience more interactions with nonfamily members. Those who spend most of their time at home (like the elderly) are not in much danger of being murdered by strangers; if they do meet a violent

end, it is likely to be at the hands of family members or close friends (Cohen and Felson, 1979; Messner and Tardiff, 1985; Maxfield, 1987; Burke, 2009; and Felson and Boba, 2010).

The routine activities explanation for differential risks links several major themes within criminology and victimology. One is that social conditions continuously generate criminally inclined individuals. Another is that opportunities for committing thefts and robberies multiply as possessions proliferate. A third theme is that preventive measures can be more effective if they rest on "collective efficacy" derived from unofficial guardianship and informal mechanisms of social control (such as when nosy neighbors assume some responsibility for the well-being of others). The fourth theme is that certain activities and circumstances expose people and their possessions to heightened dangers (see Cohen and Felson, 1979; Cohen, Kluegal, and Land, 1981; Felson, 1994; Finkelhor and Asdigian, 1996; and Siegel, 1998).

Given the interplay of these factors (offender motivation, guardianship, and target suitability), how people actually behave can account to some degree for their observed differences in susceptibility to violence and theft. The sociological term **lifestyle** refers to attitudes and behaviors that govern how people spend their time and money at work and at leisure, and the social roles they play (such as traveler, parent, student, or homemaker). Lifestyle theory stresses the importance of three aspects of **exposure**: to high-risk persons; at high-risk locations; and during time periods of high-risk. Associating with high-risk persons in high-risk locations during dangerous times doesn't guarantee that tragedy will strike, but it sure raises the mathematical probability of a person suffering a misfortune (Hindelang et al., 1978). Lifestyles that place people in jeopardy may appear to be freely chosen (such as pursuing thrill-seeking forms of entertainment) but also are strongly influenced by culturally shaped role expectations (such as how teenagers "ought" to spend Saturday evenings) as well as structural constraints (like the financial necessity of depending upon public transportation late at night).

To further illustrate the significance of life-styles, consider the *NCVS* findings presented in Table 4.4 earlier, which indicated that single young men and women were robbed at much higher rates than their married counterparts. Surely muggers don't feel guilty about preying upon people sporting wedding bands. It could be the willingness of young singles to venture out alone at night to seek the company of acquaintances and even strangers that accounts for much of the difference in the dangers they face. The relatively low rates of robbery, rape, and assault by strangers for young married men and women with small children can also be understood as a function of lifestyle. In their interactions with relatives and friends, leisure activities, and family-centered obligations, young mothers and fathers are less exposed to dangerous people and hotspots for criminal activity than their counterparts without spouses or sons or daughters (Skogan, 1981a; Felson, 1994; Finkelhor and Asdigian, 1996; and Siegel, 1998). In contrast, the pursuit by single people of certain forms of late-night amusements such as cruising around, congregating in parks, drinking and partying with complete strangers, and frequenting bars and clubs near closing time inject elements of uncertainty and volatility. Seeking excitement from daring and edgy activities boosts risk levels too.

Engaging in unconventional **deviant lifestyles** greatly heighten risks. For example, prostitutes working the streets seem particularly prone to hold-ups, rapes, beatings, and on rare occasion violent deaths (especially by serial killers). These young women are easy targets because they operate in the shadows, are willing to accompany complete strangers to isolated or desolate locations, and often abuse alcohol or other drugs that loosen their inhibitions, increase their desperation for money, and impair their judgment. Crimes committed against them often are not taken very seriously by the public or the authorities, and witnesses on their behalf (usually other prostitutes, pimps, drivers from escort services, or johns) are often disreputable, unreliable, or uncooperative with the authorities and therefore ineffective protectors (see Boyer and James, 1983). This case, although

unusual according to the SHRs, dramatizes the possible perils of pursuing a deviant lifestyle:

A prostitute who advertises her services on an Internet website is dropped off by her driver, but soon runs out of the customer's house, terrified, and disappears into some nearby woods at night. A police dog sent out to track her down instead unearths the remains of several people along a deserted stretch of a highway near a popular beach. Further searching and digging with heavy machinery over the course of a year eventually turns up her corpse, plus the remains of 9 victims. Some of them had been reported missing, several were dismembered, and others could not be positively identified. The police theorize that they were all linked to the sex trade, and were dispatched by one or more serial killers over a number of years. (AP, 2011b; Mueller, 2014)

A related concept, the **deviant place factor**, calls attention to exact locations rather than the general lifestyle of particular individuals. Certain settings attract predators on the prowl and troublemakers looking for some action. Hot spots for crime tend to be concentrated in urban settings (Sherman, Gartin, and Buerger, 1989) and include crowded public spaces that serve as crossroads for a wide range of people (like downtown bus or train terminals), desolate areas where the police rarely patrol, or hangouts where heavy drinking and drug consumption regularly take place (perhaps seedy clubs or empty parking lots). Those who frequent these locations by necessity or choice expose themselves to greater risks.

In sum, lifestyles (including congregating at hot spots and spending time at deviant places) largely determine the quantity and quality of the contacts between potential targets and criminally inclined individuals. Differences in lifestyles lead to variations in exposure to risks. In the long run, exposure is the primary determinant of a group's victimization rate (for example, compare teenagers to senior citizens) (see Hindelang, Gottfredson, and Garofalo, 1978; Garofalo, 1986; Jensen and Brownfield, 1986; Mustaine and Tewksbury, 1998b).

Some Victims Were Criminals: The Equivalent Group Explanation

The **equivalent group** explanation portrays victims who engage in certain high-risk deviant lifestyles in a less-than-sympathetic light. It emphasizes the possibility that certain pairs of victims and victimizers share the same interests, participate in the same activities, and are drawn from homogenous or overlapping lifestyle groups. According to this theory, offenders select their victims from their own circles of adversaries, acquaintances, and even former friends. Adherence to and participation in the norms of certain deviant subcultures can sharply raise the chances of becoming a casualty. Fellow lawbreakers may be viewed as "fair game" or "easy prey" because their own involvement in criminal behavior discourages them from turning to the authorities they despise for help (see Fattah, 1991; Siegel, 1998).

Many murders can be pointed to as illustrations of the explanation that both parties were drawn from overlapping social groupings. Most perpetrators and many of their victims had been in trouble with the law before their final showdowns, according to a survey of more than 8,000 prosecutions carried out in the nation's 75 largest counties during 1988. About 45 percent of the deceased turned out to have criminal records (arrests or convictions for misdemeanors or felonies) as did 75 percent of all defendants (see Dawson and Langan, 1994).

Entire categories of killings and armed assaults are reminders that not all murder victims were totally innocent, law-abiding people minding their own business. A considerable proportion across the country could be characterized as "criminal-on-criminal." The most obvious examples of overlapping illegal lifestyles leading to violence include mob wars between organized crime families engaged in racketeering who try to get rid of the competition; drive-by shootings of street gang members embroiled in turf battles; fights to control the trade among rival drug-dealing crews; and inmates consumed by pent-up rage attacking each other over minor matters.

Conflicts among participants in the drug scene spark many casualties: cutthroat competition between dealers, disputes between buyers and sellers (quarrels over high prices, money owed, misrepresentation of the contents, and scams surrounding inferior quality); robberies of dealers or customers; and what the FBI calls "brawls due to the influence of narcotics" by people acting out of character because they were high from crack smoking, cocaine snorting, and methamphetamine injecting. Adding these categories together, drug-related murders can soar to staggering body counts in metropolitan areas at certain times (see Tardiff, Gross, and Messner, 1986; Spunt et al., 1993). Nationwide, a number of slayings that were deemed narcotics-related claimed many lives during the height of the crack epidemic in the late 1980s, and peaked in 1989 at about 1,400 (Timrots and Snyder, 1994). In Washington, D.C., drug-related murders boosted the homicide rate more strikingly than anywhere else during the late 1980s. About 20 percent of murders (in which the motive was known to the police) in 1985 were drug-related; either the coroner determined the victim was under the influence of drugs, traces of controlled substances or paraphernalia were discovered at the crime scene, or the killing occurred in a drug hangout such as a "shooting gallery" or "crack house," according to the Office of Criminal Justice in the District of Columbia. This proportion rose to 34 percent the following year, jumped to 51 percent in 1987, soared to 80 percent in 1988, and crested at 85 percent of all homicides in D.C. during the first part of 1989 (Berke, 1989; Martz et al., 1989). In New York City, drug-related killings also peaked by the close of the 1980s at over one-third of all slayings but dropped by half to 17 percent by the end of the 1990s as the crack epidemic waned (see Karmen, 2006).

Criminals attacking other criminals behind bars in the nation's jails and prisons was long considered to be a part of daily life in institutions. Perhaps the problem was even tolerated to some degree because the casualties were considered by many to be expendable persons who deserved to suffer. In addition, the constant threat of violence was presumed to enhance the deterrent effects of being "sent away." Between the years 2001 and 2012, about 255 inmates were murdered by other inmates in the nation's county jails and 670 were slain in state prisons (Noonan and Ginder, 2014).

The equivalent group explanation also helps account for the carnage among teenage boys that intensified from the mid-1980s into the early 1990s. The overwhelming majority (about 85 percent) of these premature deaths were from gunfire. A cycle of aggression and retaliation developed as growing numbers of young men from poverty-stricken families in drug-ravaged communities armed themselves, both for self-protection and for prestige—whether or not they were directly involved in the crack, cocaine, or heroin trade that was thriving in their neighborhoods. When they fought each other with weapons, often over minor beefs that seemed matters of life and death at the time, the body count soared. These young gunslingers did not "freely choose" their lifestyles, however. The root causes of this teenage arms race were economic hardships, failing schools, dwindling legitimate job opportunities, limited supervised recreational activities, family instability, and a pervasive subculture of violence (see Fingerhut, Ingram, and Feldman, 1992; and Blumstein and Rosenfeld, 1998).

The **subculture of violence** theory explains why fighting may be the first resort, rather than a last resort, for certain offenders and their victims. Drawn from the study of murders in Philadelphia cited earlier, the theorist (Wolfgang, 1958) contended that young, inner-city males had been raised in an environment that stressed using physical force to settle disputes. The ready resort to fighting as a means of conflict resolution was viewed as positive, necessary, and even respectable by fellow members immersed in this subculture, although using such violent means to settle arguments would be condemned as inappropriate and downright illegal in mainstream culture. The roots of this subculture (to the extent that it really exists as a distinct way of life within a larger militarized society) might be traced back to the old South and the old West, as well as to "lower class culture" in general. The focus of the values, beliefs, and traditions in this subculture is on achieving respect and on the recognition of manhood, which is socially constructed to emphasize the ideal of "machismo."

To be viewed as "manly," a teenage boy or young adult must react forcefully to even perceived slights. In the process, members of the subculture of violence engage in constant spontaneous fights that blur the distinction between aggressor and victim (Wolfgang and Ferracuti, 1967; and Pearson-Nelson, 2009).

Controversies surround all of the explanations that center on deviant lifestyles and the membership of victims and offenders in equivalent groups. A blame-the-victim bias slips into the interpretations. Research findings about the number and percent of murder victims who got high on alcohol or controlled substances before they died raise the possibility that some casualties of deadly showdowns may have been partly at fault for the escalation of tensions and the outbreak of violence because their behavior "under the influence" was similar to the disinhibited actions of their attackers. Similarly, teenagers and young adults in gangs who end up injured or mortally wounded are written off as troublemakers who "got themselves killed" while taking part in illegal activities. Branded as young "gangbangers," "thugs," or drug abusers, they are demeaned as full-time lawbreakers who become part-time casualties ("today's victim was yesterday's offender"). Their entire lives are judged and stigmatized solely on the basis of the worst incidents that are known, assumed, or alleged about them: their criminal records. The unmistakable implication is that their suffering is less deserving of compassion, support, and respectful treatment by the authorities who handle their cases.

What's the Difference Between Crime Prevention and Victimization Prevention?

The concept of **crime prevention** has been defined in a number of ways. A rather inclusive definition would be the sum total of all proactive state policies and private initiatives (by individuals, community groups, businesses, and other organizations) intended to reduce the damage inflicted by lawbreaking activities. Another formulation would include any interventions in mechanisms believed to cause criminal incidents that would reduce the probability of these occurrences. A third definition does not emphasize intentions but focuses on results: any strategy or program that reduces the number of offenses or offenders or victims, or the amount of damage (see Schneider, 2014). In a practical sense, crime prevention means "the anticipation, recognition, and appraisal of a risk, and the initiation of some action to remove or reduce it" (National Crime Prevention Institute, 1978).

Prevention relies on proactive strategies that discourage the development of illegal activities, as opposed to reactive **crime control** measures taken by the justice system in response to acts that have already been committed. Formerly, crime prevention strategies centered on government programs designed to eradicate the social roots of lawbreaking behavior, such as desperation for money, job shortages, failing school systems, and racial discrimination. Community-based crime prevention campaigns focused on lowering the dropout rate in school systems, providing decent jobs for all those who want to work, and developing meaningful recreational outlets and summer jobs for otherwise idle youth. But since the 1970s, this approach, which relies upon social investments by government to ameliorate conditions that generate street crime, has fallen out of favor because the considerable expenses of these approaches require substantial revenue from taxation.

Over the decades, a subtle shift has taken place in so-called crime prevention measures. A better term than crime prevention for some of these preemptive moves, like installing surveillance cameras, is **victimization prevention** (see Cohn, Kidder, and Harvey, 1978).

Victimization prevention is much more modest in intent than crime prevention. Its goal is to discourage criminals from attacking particular targets, such as certain homes, warehouses, stores, cars, or people. Like defensive driving, victimization prevention hinges on the dictum, "Watch the other guy, and anticipate his possible moves." The shift from crime prevention on a societal and governmental level to victimization prevention on a neighborhood, group (business, campus, office building), and personal level demands that potential victims become **crime conscious** (or "street smart"). The responsibility for keeping out of trouble increasingly falls on the possible targets themselves, who must outmaneuver would-be offenders and keep one step ahead of them. Crime-conscious individuals are compelled to follow victimization prevention tips, which are long lists of dos and don'ts compiled from observations of other people's misfortunes. The recommendation derived from studies of other people's mistakes is that cautious persons should take measures that make them appear to be well protected and their property well guarded, so that criminally inclined prowlers will look elsewhere for easier pickings (Moore, 1985).

Intense interest in the part played by lifestyles and routine activities has led to many new strategies to diminish the odds of being singled out for trouble. The ways people try to diminish their odds are called **risk-reduction activities**.

Avoidance strategies (Furstenberg, 1972) are actions people take to limit personal exposure to dangerous people and frightening situations, such as not allowing strangers into their homes or ignoring passersby who attempt to strike up conversations on deserted streets.

Risk-management tactics (Skogan and Maxfield, 1981) minimize the chances of being harmed when exposure is unavoidable. Examples include walking home with other people rather than alone, or carrying a concealed weapon.

Situational crime prevention rests upon interventions that are designed to block criminal opportunities from developing in a particular time and place through the management, design, or manipulation of the human and physical environment (Schneider, 2014).

Crime prevention through environmental design (referred to by the acronym CPTED) stresses the importance of creating well-protected, defensible space (Newman, 1972) by **target hardening** (adding locks, erecting fences) and maintaining effective surveillance (limiting the number of entrances, improving visibility by trimming bushes and adding bright lights). In public housing projects, certain architectural designs can enhance defensible space by erecting barriers to channel traffic and consequently limit the escape routes used by intruders. Extending defensible space requires that neighbors take some responsibility and ownership for semipublic and semiprivate areas by nurturing a sense of community spirit (collective efficacy) and encouraging self-help initiatives like block associations and neighborhood watch patrols (Golden, 2009).

Crime resistance means making an offender's task more difficult through threat assessment and advanced planning. Risk-reduction actions can be categorized as individual or collective (when arranged in cooperation with others) (Conklin, 1975), and as either private-minded or public-minded (Schneider and Schneider, 1978).

However, the **valve theory of crime shifts** predicts that the number of offenses committed actually will not drop when targets are hardened because criminal activity simply will be displaced. If one area of illegal opportunity is shut off (for example, if robbing bus drivers is made unprofitable by the imposition of exact fare requirements or prepaid cards), those who are desperate for cash will shift their attention to comparable but more vulnerable targets (such as cabdrivers or storekeepers) (National Commission on the Causes and Prevention of Violence, 1969a). When crime is displaced and criminals are deflected, the risk of victimization goes down for some but rises for others, assuming that offenders are intent on committing crimes and are flexible in terms of time, place, target, and tactics (Allen et al., 1981).

Victimization prevention strategies adopted by very crime conscious individuals actually might endanger other people who may be less cautious or less able to implement countermeasures. Victimization will be redistributed spatially, geographically, and socially—a far cry from genuine crime prevention, which would lower the risks everyone faces. For example, a pamphlet distributed by the country's largest police department frankly acknowledged that self-protective measures might merely redirect offenders elsewhere: "No vehicle is theft-proof. You must approach this problem with the attitude that it will not be my car that becomes part of the statistics. As selfish as it may sound, if

the thief wants a car of your year, make, and model, let it be someone else's. If you follow these guidelines and take all the necessary precautions to protect your car, the chances are it will not be stolen" (New York Police Department, 1992).

The contention that victimization prevention methods simply shift the burden on to others, while alleviating the dangers faced by cautious people and their well-guarded possessions, is a plausible hypothesis that researchers must examine. One thing is clear: target-hardening strategies certainly lend themselves to commercial exploitation. Advertisements constantly proclaim that new, virtually foolproof, security-enhancing products are for sale. As these goods and services are purchased by a growing market share of people who desperately don't want to become statistics, victimologists can test the claims to see which devices work best, or if they have any appreciable impact at all.

Should each prudent person worry only about his or her own safety and take protective measures to ward away prowlers and fend off thieves? How many anticrime devices and precautions are sufficient? Is there a limit, a point of diminishing returns?

Reducing Risks: How Safe Is Safe Enough?

When social scientists estimate risks, they are predicting how many people will experience unwanted incidents. Statistical concepts underlying risk estimates can be difficult to grasp. Only three distinct probabilities can be readily understood: "0," which signifies that an event is impossible; "1," which means that an event is inevitable; and "0.5," which indicates a toss-up, or a 50–50 chance (as in seeking "heads" when flipping a coin). But risks that are 0.1 (1 in 10) or 0.01 (1 in 100) or 0.001 (1 in 1,000) are harder to fathom or evaluate. If the odds of something happening were one in a million, statisticians would advise people not to worry about it (or count on it if the event is desirable, such as winning a lottery). But when two or three people in every thousand are robbed each year, what importance should be placed on the risk of robbery when planning one's daily schedule? How much preparation and anxiety would be rational in the face of these odds? What sacrifices would be appropriate in terms of forgoing necessary or welcomed activities (such as taking evening classes or watching the sun set on a deserted beach)? At what point does disregarding risks and ignoring precautions become foolhardy?

In general, it is safer to stay at home, especially at night; to travel in pairs or groups and use cars or taxis; to avoid public spaces, unfamiliar places, and complete strangers; to steer clear of known hot spots and dangerous characters; and to not let down one's guard by becoming intoxicated or distracted. Those precautions are a price that many older people are willing to pay to avoid putting themselves in harm's way. But many teenagers and young adults reject such restrictions in their quest for entertainment and nightlife (see Felson, 1997; Mustaine and Tewksbury, 1998a).

To illustrate the nature of the dilemma, consider the much lower robbery rate of the elderly compared to people in their early twenties, even though senior citizens are presumed to be especially vulnerable to the young men who use force to steal. This apparent paradox can be explained by noting that older people usually incorporate many risk-reduction strategies into their lifestyles and routine activities to the point that these self-imposed restrictions become second nature. For instance, to find young adults out after midnight drinking in bars, nightclubs, and gambling casinos seems normal; to encounter elderly people in such settings at those hours is surprising. Teenagers and young adults ride home alone on public transportation late at night; old people rarely do.

Since entire demographic groups experience very different rates of victimization for robbery and murder, as documented in Chapter 4, risk-reduction strategies seem to work. But it is difficult to demonstrate the effectiveness of specific precautions, such as keeping away from known hot spots and volatile people who engage in deviant lifestyles. It is hard to pinpoint particular instances in which these strategies clearly have prevented a crime from taking place. Therefore, whether to sacrifice certain freedoms and pleasures for enhanced safety is a trade-off that each person must confront and weigh. The proper balance between safety and risk is ultimately a personal decision. But it is also a matter of public debate. In general, more protection can be secured by greater expenditure. Dangers can be reduced if individuals and groups are willing to pay the price for more police patrols, improved lighting, surveillance cameras, and other security measures. However, a demand for absolute safety (zero risk) is irrational in statistical terms. Probabilities of unwanted events can be reduced but never entirely eliminated. At some point, it is reasonable for a person to declare that the odds pose an acceptable risk (Lynn, 1981). Furthermore, many people lack the opportunities and resources to reduce the risks they face. They are unable to alter their means of travel, their hours of work, the schools their children attend, or the neighborhoods in which they live. Many of the suggestions and stern admonitions about dos and don'ts directed at the general public turn out to be impractical, unrealistic, and out of reach for such people.

In economics, a **cost–benefit analysis** can determine the point of diminishing returns, when additional outlays to attempt to achieve a goal exceed the value or return on that investment. Obviously, the price of a second lock on a door is outweighed by its benefit if the door comes with a standard lock that is flimsy. Just as obviously, adding a third lock to a door that already has two imposes more costs than benefits, especially if the hinges are weak.

But what about comparisons that are less clearcut? What about installing floodlights and a burglar alarm? How about stepped up police patrols in a neighborhood plagued by break-ins? At what point are there too many police officers to justify their salaries? Can the pain and suffering of victims or the public's fear of street crime (or terrorism) be converted by some formula to determine how much taxpayers or consumers should spend on security expenses? How much is peace of mind worth, in terms of money? "How safe is safe enough?" turns out to be a value judgment that each person must grapple with.

Ambivalence About Risk Taking

Contradictory messages permeate American culture on the subject of risk taking. On the one hand, the prevailing entrepreneurial ideology extols the financial risk taking of investors, especially daring "venture capitalists." Similarly, popular heroes go beyond their comfort zones and boldly take on daunting challenges: pioneers, explorers, inventors, private detectives, secret agents, soldiers of fortune, high-stakes gamblers, and other adventurers. Adolescence by definition is a period of experimentation, and risk taking is part of growing up.

On the other hand, middle-age and middle-class values emphasize order, stability, predictability, and control over one's destiny. This leads to prudence in the face of danger. Conscientious, responsible,

"mature" adults plan, build, save, and invest so that they are prepared for adversity, illness, retirement due to old age, accidents, or devastating losses inflicted by criminals. They prize safety, peace of mind, insurance, and protective devices.

The ambivalent attitudes toward risk taking in American culture are mirrored by contradictory responses to victimization. Some readily rush to the defense of victims while others impulsively criticize them as reckless people who have failed in their gambits. Their suffering evokes sympathy, but it also invites second-guessing about what might be altered in their attitudes, daily routines, and lifestyles to avoid future troubles.

SUMMARY

When victims ask, "Why me?" victimologists suggest explanations that range far beyond the notions of being in the wrong place at the wrong time, fate, or just plain bad luck. Explanations that raise the possibility that the victim, along with the offender, shares some degree of responsibility for what happened are the subjects of bitter debate.

Victim-blaming arguments focus on facilitation through negligence, precipitation due to recklessness, and provocation because of instigation. Victim blaming insists that injured parties must change their ways if they want to live safer lives. Victim defending either places the entire blame for what happened on lawbreakers (offender blaming) or finds fault with social institutions and cultural values that shape the lives of both offenders and victims (system blaming).

Differential risks are largely determined by routine activities and lifestyles that result in more or less exposure to dangerous individuals in the vicinity of hot spots for illicit behavior. Involvement in illegal activities with criminally inclined persons surely heightens risks, according to the equivalent group hypothesis. Some people do not learn lessons from the misfortunes of others or from their own brushes with trouble and are not deterred from high-risk behaviors, so they face higher risks of becoming repeat victims.

Each person must perform a cost–benefit analysis about precautions in everyday life and expenditures for risk-reduction measures, and determine on an individual basis just how safe is safe enough.

One final note needs to be emphasized. All the precautions listed in the boxes above to avoid robbery, burglary, motor vehicle theft, and identity theft are recommendations from police detectives and other justice professionals based on past experiences. These experts and professionals look at the way criminals operate and they scrutinize the apparent mistakes victims have made. That is how these victimization prevention tips were derived. But what seems to be plausible, reasonable, sound advice needs to be carefully researched. Victimologists have to conduct studies to determine whether or not each of these tips and recommendations really work as touted and as intended. For example, do alarms actually scare off car thieves or at least cut short their attacks? Does it pay to install a burglar alarm and then incur the unending expense of monthly monitoring fees? If timers turn lights on and off at night to make a home look like it is occupied, does that actually deter burglars from attempting to break in? If a person rejects simple passwords that are easy to remember and conscientiously devises and changes strong passwords routinely, does that really help to stave off attempts at identity theft? Crime conscious people need to know if these tactics do any good and if these expenses are worthwhile investments. Only careful research can answer these tough questions. Until then, "how safe is safe enough" is a very difficult question to answer because evidence-based support for various common sense tips and recommendations is not yet available.

KEY TERMS DEFINED IN THE GLOSSARY

attractiveness, 166

avoidance strategies, 171

boost explanation, 137

caller ID phone spoofing, 150

character contest, 157

classical school, 161

co-orientation, 164

co-presence, 164

cost–benefit analysis, 173

crime conscious, 171

crime control, 171

crime prevention, 170

crime prevention through environmental design, 171

crime resistance, 172

deterrence theory, 161

deviant lifestyles, 168

deviant place factor, 168

dumpster diving, 150

equivalent group, 169

exposure, 167

facilitation, 144

flag explanation, 137

free will, 161

hot dots, 136

hot spots, 136

instrumental coercion, 163

just world outlook, 139

justifiable homicide, 155

lifestyle, 167

offender blaming, 142

outlet–attractor perspective, 156

pharming, 150

phishing, 150

precipitation, 154

provocation, 154

proximity, 166

rational choice, 161

risk-management tactics, 171

risk-reduction activities, 171

routine activities, 167

selective-disinhibition perspective, 156

shared responsibility, 135

shoulder surfers, 150

situational crime prevention, 171

situational factors, 166

skimmers, 150

social ecology of victimization, 167

subculture of violence, 170

subintentional death, 154

system blaming, 142

target hardening, 171

techniques of neutralization, 139

theoretical explanations, 164

typology, 137

valve theory of crime shifts, 172

victim blaming, 138

victim defending, 138

victimization prevention, 171

vulnerability, 166

QUESTIONS FOR DISCUSSION AND DEBATE

1. Which high-risk groups—if any—do you fall into, when it comes to the following four crimes: robbery, burglary, vehicle theft, and identity theft?

2. Compare and contrast victim facilitation, victim precipitation, and victim provocation. Make up scenarios to illustrate the differences.

3. Describe the process of victim blaming step by step, and then argue that people whose identities were stolen may have made the thieves' tasks easier. How can they avoid revictimization?

4. Describe the victim-defending point of view, and then apply it to motor vehicle theft.

5. Explain system blaming in general, and then apply this perspective to identity theft.

CRITICAL THINKING QUESTIONS

1. Is it possible to be too crime conscious—too concerned about being victimized? Defend your point of view by providing examples of risk reduction strategies that demand sacrifices that might be considered by some to be prudent but by others to be unreasonable.

2. Review the statements for and against scrutinizing the victim's role that appear in Boxes 5.1 and 5.2. Select quotes from victimologists with whom you strongly agree and several with whom you strongly disagree, and explain your views.

3. Although it is impossible to prevent victimization, it is possible to reduce risks—but it will cost individuals, companies, and governments much more money. Explain this observation and give some examples of expensive measures that could be undertaken.

4. Review your own lifestyle and routine activities. What are the most dangerous things you do, in terms of exposure to criminally inclined persons and entering hot-spot zones? What could you do to reduce your risks? What changes would be unreasonable, impractical, or unworkable?

5. Argue that undertaking crime prevention on a governmental level is a more socially responsible approach than simply encouraging individuals to incorporate victimization prevention strategies into their everyday lives.

SUGGESTED RESEARCH PROJECTS

1. Find more examples of victim-blaming accusations for various crimes by searching through databases of newspaper and magazine articles, and in lists of victimization prevention tips.

2. Develop a brief questionnaire about high-risk activities and survey some people you know. Ask whether they feel these activities are too dangerous in their opinion, in terms of being robbed. See if the willingness to take precautions (adopt victimization prevention strategies) is connected to age, sex, or past misfortunes.

6

Victims and the Police

LEARNING OBJECTIVES

To establish the ways in which victims suffer.

To find out what the criminal justice system can accomplish in behalf of victims.

To become familiar with the ways that the police can serve the best interests of crime victims.

To uncover issues and relationships where victims and law enforcement agencies can find themselves in conflict rather than in an alliance.

To become acquainted with the kind of evidence that is useful to evaluate whether a police department is effectively meeting the needs of victims in its jurisdiction.

To recognize the features of a victim-oriented police department.

Though our homes and neighborhoods are safer than they have been in decades, millions of Americans still become victims of crime each year. For many citizens, a sense of security remains painfully elusive, and we must continue to fight crime wherever it exists. (President Barack Obama, 2011)

The primary mission of the criminal justice system is to "fight crime." But in terms of delivering justice, the system has an additional obligation: to serve those who are harmed by offenders. Criminology and criminal justice courses focus on the actions and operations of law enforcement agencies, prosecutors' offices, defense attorneys, judges, juries, probation departments, corrections departments, and parole authorities. Criminologists investigate how this system handles perpetrators—specifically, suspects, arrestees, defendants, convicts, inmates, probationers, parolees, and other formerly incarcerated persons. Victimologists explore how this same system handles the individuals who suffer injuries and losses due to illegal activities: how the police respond to complainants; how prosecutors, defense attorneys, and judges treat these witnesses for the state; and how corrections, probation, and parole officials react to the special requests that individuals previously harmed by the convicts under their custody and control ask of them, such as for information, protection, and restitution.

Sociologists who analyze social institutions from a functionalist perspective point out that the criminal justice system is supposed to serve as the first line of defense for innocent, law-abiding people against the depredations of the "criminal element." In other words, the legal system's mission is to protect the general public, and then, failing that, to help specific individuals recover from the losses inflicted by offenders. But those who adopt a conflict perspective see this same system in a different light. Agencies and officials act to some extent on their own behalf and follow policies that are in their own self-interest, as well as to the advantage of even more powerful interest groups that dominate society (see Reiman, 2005). Therefore, from the conflict perspective, it is not surprising to discover that some victims enjoy cooperation from justice professionals while others find themselves at odds concerning certain practices or policies pursued by the officials and agencies whose ostensible mission is to protect and assist them.

VICTIMS INTERACTING WITH THE CRIMINAL JUSTICE SYSTEM: COOPERATION OR CONFLICT?

The criminal justice system is the one branch of government that comes under scathing attack from all political quarters. Conservative crime control proponents, treatment-oriented liberals, civil libertarians, civil rights activists, feminists, and victim advocates—all find fault with its priorities and procedures. Over the past few decades, even some officials who run its agencies and shape its daily operations have joined the chorus of critics calling for change. However, they sharply disagree over how to reform the system.

The consensus among the experts who focus on victim issues is that the criminal justice system does not measure up to expectations. It fails to deliver what it promises. It does not meet the needs and wants of victims as its clients or consumers of its services. Serious problems persist, and the indictments of the system voiced over the years appear in Box 6.1. Even though the crime problem has subsided, and the shortcomings of other social institutions attract more attention, occasional criticisms of the way the system treats victims persist (see Box 6.1).

What Would Be Ideal?

Suppose a person is robbed and injured. What could and should the system do to dispense justice in this case?

Law enforcement agencies are at the intake end of the legal system and are the criminal justice professionals that victims initially encounter. Ideally, police officers could rush to help the person in distress and provide whatever physical and psychological first aid might be needed. Then they should help the victim to file a complaint. Hopefully, they would catch the culprit and properly collect evidence of guilt that will stand up in court.

They could recover any stolen goods taken by the robber and speedily return these items to the rightful owner.

The prosecutor could make sure the defendant is indicted and then press for a swift trial. In the meantime, the injured party, who is serving as a key witness for the government, should be protected from intimidation and reprisals. After conviction, the victim's views about a fair resolution of this case could be fully aired. The judge could hand down a sentence that would balance the victim's wishes with the community's desires and the robber's needs. Correctional authorities could see to it that the probationer, prisoner, or parolee doesn't harass or attack the person whose complaint set the machinery of criminal justice into motion. If the convict was ordered by the judge to reimburse the individual he harmed for losses and expenses, then correctional authorities could ensure that these restitution payments or services are delivered in a timely fashion, as promised.

But this "best-case scenario" frequently does not materialize. Instead of enjoying the cooperation of officials and supportive services from agencies as the system handles "their" cases, victims might find themselves sorely disappointed or even locked into conflicts with the police, prosecutors, judges, wardens, and parole boards.

WHAT DO VICTIMS WANT: PUNISHMENT? TREATMENT? RESTITUTION?

Why should victims bring their problems to the attention of a law enforcement agency that functions as the intake valve or first component of the legal system? What motivates them when they ask the police to set the crime justice process into motion? What kinds of results are they seeking from the authorities? What would be in their best interests? What does "justice" mean to them?

Rather than answer these questions that others must decide for themselves, the victims' rights movement has sought empowerment. That means

the ability to have some input into important decisions at every step in the criminal justice process, from initially filing a complaint with the police up to the release of the perpetrator from custody, or probation, or parole. Empowerment would enable the injured parties to exercise their "agency"— taking actions in pursuit of outcomes that embody their sense of fair play, self-interest, and desire for closure.

But why demand inclusion? Why insist on having a chance to participate at key junctures in the criminal justice process?

Victims can pursue one or even a combination of three distinct goals. The first is to see to it that hard-core offenders who act as predators are punished and removed from the streets so that they can't harm their victims again, or prey upon others. The second is to use the justice process as leverage to compel lawbreakers to undergo rehabilitative treatment to counteract their criminal inclinations. The third possible aim is to get the court to order convicts to make restitution for any expenses arising from injuries and losses.

Make "Them" Suffer

A serial killer terrorizes a small city by binding, torturing, and killing his victims. He taunts the local police for three decades by sending them clues, but they fail to figure out his identity until finally they trace a disk he sent them to his church's computer. After a court hearing, the son of his tenth and final victim denounces him to reporters as "a rotting corpse of a wretch of a human hiding under a human veneer. I'm spiteful, I'm vengeful, and I relish the thought that he knows that he'll walk into that prison but he'll be carried out." (Wilgoren, 2005).

■■■

A man is convicted of murdering three younger men with whom he was arranging a drug deal by shooting them point-blank in the back of the head as they sat in a car parked near a university. When the judge hands down the maximum sentence, life without parole, family members of the victims shout "Yes! Yes!" and weep. One mother declares "Justice was

BOX 6.1 Notable Criticisms of How the Criminal Justice System Handles Victims

If there is one word that describes how the criminal justice system treats victims of crimes and witnesses to crimes, it is "badly."

JAMES REILLY, DIRECTOR OF THE VICTIM/WITNESS ASSISTANCE PROJECT OF THE NATIONAL DISTRICT ATTORNEYS' ASSOCIATION (1981, P. 8)

Crimes that terrorize take many forms, from aggravated assault to petty thievery. But one crime goes largely unnoticed. It is a crime against which there is no protection. It is committed daily across our nation. It is the painful, wrongful insensitivity of the criminal justice system toward those who are the victims of crime.... The callousness with which the system again victimizes those who have already suffered at the hands of an assailant is tragic.

SENATOR JOHN HEINZ, SPONSOR OF THE OMNIBUS VICTIMS PROTECTION ACT PASSED BY CONGRESS (1982, P. A19)

Without the cooperation of victims and witnesses in reporting and testifying about crime, it is impossible in a free society to hold criminals accountable. When victims come forward to provide this vital service, however, they find little protection. They discover instead that they will be treated as appendages of a system appallingly out of balance. They learn that somewhere along the way the system has lost track of the simple truth that it is supposed to be fair and to protect those who obey the law while punishing those who break it. Somewhere along the way, the system began to serve lawyers and judges and defendants, treating the victim with institutionalized disinterest.... The neglect of crime victims is a national disgrace.

LOIS HERRINGTON, CHAIR OF THE PRESIDENT'S TASK FORCE ON VICTIMS OF CRIME (1982, PP. VI–VII)

---

done. He's going to suffer more than I have suffered." (McKinley, 2013)

■ ■ ■

A 23-year-old is four months pregnant when a young man enters her mobile home under the pretext of seeking directions, and then forces her into the bedroom and rapes her. Three decades later, he is finally convicted and sentenced for first degree criminal sexual conduct. Exercising an opportunity to voice her opinion, she tells the judge, "it's been a rough 31 years.... My sex life has been screwed up ... I hope he goes away for the rest of his life. (Deiters, 2013)

Penalizing offenders for the pain and losses they imposed on their victims is what comes to most people's minds first when discussing the meaning of "justice."

Besides physical injuries, victims can suffer socially and emotionally in the aftermath of a serious violent crime such as rape, sexual assault, aggravated assault, and robbery. Just about two-thirds of the persons subjected to serious violent crimes told *NCVS* interviewers that they were burdened by socio-emotional problems, including moderate to severe levels of distress (manifested as anxiety,

depression, anger, and sleep disturbances), strained relationships with family members and friends, and/or disruptions of their usual activities at school or work. But only a little more than half of those who experienced these upsetting consequences informed the police about their plight, and only slightly more than one in every ten received help from some service agency during the years 2009 to 2012 (Langton and Truman, 2014).

Many people hurt by acts of interpersonal violence and theft want the justice system to punish convicts in their behalf so that they will suffer too. Throughout history, people have always punished one another. However, they may disagree about their reasons for subjecting a wrongdoer to deprivations and hardships. Most deliberations in court concern questions of punishment: who, why, when, where, and how much?

Punishment—imposing unpleasant and unwanted consequences—is usually justified on utilitarian grounds as a necessary evil. It is argued that making transgressors suffer curbs future criminality in a number of ways. According to the doctrine of specific deterrence, the perpetrator who experiences negative sanctions learns a lesson and is discouraged from breaking the law again. Making an example of

For too long, the rights and needs of crime victims and witnesses have been overlooked in the criminal justice system.... we have begun to address this problem [through federal legislation passed in 1994 and 1996]. But those important measures are not enough.

PRESIDENT BILL CLINTON (1996, P. 1)

[According to a recent survey] victims often feel that they are treated as a piece of evidence, helpful only when they help prove the prosecution's case and when they help a police officer find the bad guy. But they often feel disrespected and ignored and that their interests and concerns are irrelevant.

SUSAN HERMAN, DIRECTOR OF THE NATIONAL CENTER FOR VICTIMS OF CRIME (1999)

In the year 2000, Americans were victims of millions of crimes. Behind each of these numbers is a terrible trauma, a story of suffering and a story of lost security. Yet the needs of victims are often an afterthought in our criminal justice system. It's not just, it's not fair, and it must change. As we protect the rights of criminals, we must take equal care to protect the rights of the victims....

But too often our system fails to inform victims about proceedings involving bail and pleas and sentencing and even about the trials themselves. Too often, the process fails to take the safety of victims into account when deciding whether to release dangerous offenders. Too often, the financial losses of victims are ignored.... When our criminal justice system treats victims as irrelevant bystanders, they are victimized for a second time.

PRESIDENT GEORGE W. BUSH (2002)

a convict also serves as a warning to would-be offenders contemplating the same act, according to the doctrine of general deterrence. (Whether convicts actually learn lessons and whether would-be offenders really think twice and decide not to carry out a crime are subjects of heated debate among criminologists.) Punishment in the form of imprisonment has been promoted as a method of enhancing public safety by incapacitating dangerous predators so that they can no longer roam the streets preying upon innocents. Another rationale for punishment by the government is that it satisfies the thirst for revenge of angry victims and their supporters, who otherwise may harbor an urge to engage in vigilantism and get even on their own. Finally, imposing severely negative sanctions also has been justified on the grounds of "just deserts" as a morally sound practice, regardless of any value it has in deterring or incapacitating criminals. According to this theory of punishment as retribution, it is fair to make offenders suffer in proportion to the misery they inflicted on others. Since biblical times, people have believed in the formula of retaliation in kind: *lex talionis,* or "an eye for an eye." According to this point of view, retribution rights a wrong, evens the score, and restores balance to the moral order, as

long as the severity of the punitive sanction is in proportion to the gravity of the offense. Punishment in behalf of the victim by criminal justice professionals is touted as the equitable and practical solution to the thirst for payback. In other words, the legal system serves as the official avenger for injured parties by imposing adequate and proportional retribution so that wrongdoers get their just deserts.

Despite the current popularity of punishment as the antidote to victimization and the cure for crime, the punitive approach remains controversial. Utilitarian opponents have documented how impractical, expensive, ineffective, and even counterproductive high rates of mass imprisonment can be. Civil libertarians have condemned such harsh punishments as a tool of domination and oppression used by tyrants and totalitarian regimes to terrorize their subjects into submission (see for example Menninger, 1968; Wright, 1973; Prison Research, 1976; Pepinsky, 1991; Elias, 1993; Mauer, 1999; Dubber, 2002; and Alexander, 2012).

The quest for vengeance has shaped history. Incorporated into the customs and consciousness of entire groups, classes, and nations, it is expressed in simmering hatreds, longstanding feuds, ongoing vendettas, and even repeated outbreaks of retaliatory military strikes leading to full-scale war. To feel a sense of fury and rage toward a vicious predator or cruel enemy is entirely human. Revenge fantasies can sustain individuals and even give purpose and direction to their lives. For example, people who sustained terrible losses were at the forefront of a campaign to deprive inmates of whatever comforts and privileges they "enjoyed" behind bars so they would be even more miserable in bleak, "no-frills" prisons (see Hanley, 1994).

Openly calling for revenge is usually frowned upon, and most people don't want to appear vindictive. They are told to forget what the offender did, to put vivid memories of the harrowing event behind them, and to move on with their lives. But vengeance has its supporters, who reject charges that the urge to extract a pound of flesh is barbaric, shortsighted, and pointless, a moral failing or a sign of mental pathology, or even a willingness to go overboard and commit a new crime. They contend that wanting to strike back is connected to a biologically rooted sense of justice and, when successful and savored, can bring about a feeling of relief, catharsis, fulfillment, and completeness. If the urge to get even is stifled, then individuals who are dismayed and ashamed about their own vulnerability might take out the desire for revenge on themselves and engage in self-defeating or—worse yet—self-destructive behavior (Carey, 2004; and Nesbo, 2014). A similar motivation driving victim behavior is spite (defined as the desire to punish, hurt, humiliate, or harass someone, even when the injured party gains no apparent benefit and may well pay a cost). Studies using surveys and experiments suggest that men are generally more spiteful than women and that young adults are more spiteful than older folks (Angier, 2014).

However, the thirst for vengeance can undercut recovery if it becomes an obsession. Even when fulfilled, acts of revenge are rarely as satisfying as had been imagined. In the hours and days following a crime, it is psychologically useful and even cathartic for persons nursing wounds to dream of inflicting pain on those who wronged them. But a chronic preoccupation with striking back needlessly prolongs angry memories and painful flashbacks about the incident. Individuals consumed by a desire to get even never break free of the pernicious influence of their victimizers. Former victims learn that the best revenge of all is to transcend their offender's grip, put the experience behind them, rise above what happened, regain the moral high ground, and strive to lead a fulfilling life (Halleck, 1980; also see Carey, 2004). The next of kin whose loved ones were murdered sometimes arrive at this conclusion, as the following cases indicate:

> *A man whose wife was killed when a right-wing extremist blew up a federal building undergoes a long and painful journey through anger, hate, and ultimately forgiveness. When the killer is first captured and brought to court, he confides to a reporter, "I wanted to grab my rifle, go sit by the highway and give him a proper greeting." But now he acknowledges that he has reached a surprising conclusion: that the execution of the bomber is wrong. "It is not about justice—it is about revenge. It's blood lust. And if I don't stand up now and say this, well, it's just cowardice," he declares.* (Goodell, 2001)

■■■

> *Three white supremacists, hoping to trigger racial conflict, chain a black man to their truck and drag him along a country road until he is dead. Thirteen years later, one of the murderers is about to be executed. The dead man's sister tells reporters, "I had to forgive because if I didn't, hate would eat me up just like it ate him up…. And I refuse to live life like that. Life is too precious to just be consumed with hate."* (Miller, 2011)

Make "Them" Get Treatment

Some persons do not look to the criminal justice system to exact revenge by tormenting their victimizer in their behalf. Instead, they want professionals and experts to help wrongdoers become decent, productive, law-abiding citizens. Victims are most likely to endorse treatment and rehabilitation services if their perpetrators are not complete strangers.

They realize that it is in their enlightened self-interest to try to salvage, save, rescue, and cure troubled family members, other loved ones, friends, neighbors, classmates, or close colleagues at work. Rehabilitation might take the form of counseling, behavior modification, intense psychotherapy, detoxification from addictive drugs, medical care, additional schooling, and job training. "Helping" offenders remains as much a part of the justice system's mission as making them sorry for what they did. Rehabilitation was the original motivation of critics of corporal punishment and the widespread imposition of the death penalty (like the Quakers) who invented "penitentiaries" and "reformatories" and "houses of correction" in the early 1800s. Unfortunately, the ascendancy of a pessimistic, "nothing works" point of view (popularized because of a mistaken interpretation of a major study [see Martinson, 1974]) has led to disenchantment with the longstanding practice of investing in rehabilitation programs within prison walls.

Rehabilitation followed by reintegration into the community (currently termed "reentry") is a long-term strategy that benefits both victims and society. Incapacitating antisocial predators is a short-term strategy that merely buys time and promotes a false sense of security that doesn't last long. Angry and frustrated inmates may pose even greater threats to public safety when they are released from custody. Victims who overcome their initial emotional outrage over what offenders did to them might become equally infuriated about ineffective, heavy-handed, punitive policies as well as inept efforts to change the personalities and conduct of inmates in jails or prisons, or of convicts on probation or parole.

Make "Them" Pay for Losses and Expenses

As a third alternative, some victims seek restitution rather than retribution or rehabilitation. They want the legal system's help to recoup their losses and pay their bills—a necessary prerequisite for full recovery. Restitution collected from offenders can help restore victims to the financial condition they were in before the crimes occurred. Once perpetrators

make amends monetarily, reconciliation becomes a realistic possibility (see Chapter 12).

Whether they desire that something be done to the offender (punishment), for the offender (treatment), or for themselves (restitution), victims want the professionals who run the criminal justice system—police, prosecutors, judges, wardens, probation officers, parole officers, members of parole boards—to take effective actions in response to violations of law. What they don't want is inaction, lack of interest, neglect, abuse, empty promises, or attempts at manipulation.

VICTIMS AND THE POLICE

Law enforcement agencies are the first representatives of the criminal justice system that victims encounter in the immediate aftermath of crimes. If their cases are not solved with an arrest, then police officers in metropolitan areas and sheriff's deputies in rural areas will be the only criminal justice professionals with whom victims will have contact. Therefore, how the police handle the individuals who summon them for help during emergencies or who walk in to precinct station houses to fill out paperwork requires careful examination.

These first responders can help out in many ways. The police can arrive quickly when summoned and can provide on-the-spot first aid. Detectives can launch thorough investigations and solve crimes by taking suspects into custody, recovering stolen property, and gathering evidence that will lead to convictions in court.

Victims are direct consumers of police services. Their opinions, based on their direct experiences, can greatly influence police–community relations. Unfortunately, these "clients" or "customers" can become bitterly disappointed with the performance of law enforcement agencies ostensibly committed to "serve and protect" them if officers are slow or reluctant to respond, don't believe their accusations, conduct superficial investigations, don't solve their cases by making arrests, and fail to recover their stolen property.

Reporting Incidents

Criminal justice authorities want people to "report, identify, and testify." Officials fear that if would-be predators believe that their intended prey won't complain to the authorities about their depredations, then the deterrent effect of the risk of getting caught and punished will be undermined. Furthermore, if the public provided more complete information about where and when crimes were committed, then crime analysts working for the police could more effectively anticipate where career criminals will strike next. In other words, victims who fail to report incidents actually are endangering others. Also, they forfeit important rights and opportunities, such as eligibility for services and reimbursement of losses through compensation plans, tax deductions, and insurance policies. Despite these appeals to self-interest and civic responsibility, most individuals still do not tell the authorities about incidents in which their property was stolen, and just half call on the police when they are harmed by violent perpetrators. Within each of these two broad categories, certain types of incidents are more likely to be reported than others.

Of all the crimes inquired about on the *NCVS*, completed auto theft emerges each year as the category with the highest reporting rate (close to 90 percent of cars driven off, about 50 percent of all attempts). Most vehicle owners notify law enforcement agencies about their loss for several sound reasons: There is a good chance their missing cars, SUVs, and trucks will be recovered if officers are aware of the disappearance; filing a formal complaint is required for insurance reimbursement; and motorists do not want to be held responsible for any accidents or crimes involving their vehicles. (For example, detectives will assume that the owner was behind the wheel of a getaway car used in a bank robbery.) The lowest reporting rates were registered for thefts of household property worth less than $50. As for the category of violent crimes, robberies and aggravated assaults were reported most frequently and simple assaults least often. The only reporting rate that rises and falls substantially from year to

year is for rapes and other sexual assaults. Sometimes it approaches one-half of all incidents disclosed to *NCVS* interviewers, but during other years the reporting rate tumbles to less than one-third of all rapes disclosed to interviewers (Harlow, 1985; Rennison, 1999; Catalano, 2005; and Truman, 2011).

Differential reporting rates have been uncovered by the *NCVS*. Certain groups of victims are more or less likely to bring their problems to the attention of the authorities. During the 1990s, females were more inclined to report violent incidents than were males, and older people were more willing than younger ones (especially teenagers). Those who had never been married were less inclined to file complaints than their married or divorced counterparts. Urban residents notified their local police a little more often than suburbanites. In general, reporting rates were higher by persons who faced violence than by those who lost property; were confronted by an armed assailant; attacked by a stranger; physically injured (especially shot); or were harmed by someone who seemed high on drugs or alcohol. Reporting rates were relatively lower for incidents involving offenders thought to be gang members. Despite public misimpressions, lower-income people were somewhat more willing to call the police than higher-income individuals, and black victims reported attacks more readily than white or Asian victims (Hart and Rennison, 2003).

The *NCVS* asks victims to explain why they did or did not report to the police the very same incidents that they are willing to disclose to survey interviewers. Different reporting rates reflect rational calculations about advantages and disadvantages that can vary from group to group (see Biblarz, Barnowe, and Biblarz, 1984; Greenberg and Ruback, 1984; Gottfredson and Gottfredson, 1988). When victims reported violent crimes, their leading reasons were "to prevent future violence," "to stop the offender," and "to protect others." Smaller percentages of respondents told interviewers their motivations were "to catch and punish the offender" and "to fulfill their civic duty." When people did not file complaints, their most common explanations were that the incidents were "a private/personal matter," "not important enough to involve the police," or "some other officials were notified," and that the perpetrators were unsuccessful in achieving their intentions. Insurance coverage was not a significant factor in deciding whether or not to report incidents (Hart and Rennison, 2003; BJS, 2011).

Victimologists have long suspected that reporting rates vary from department to department, depending on the closeness of the working relationships between local law enforcement agencies and the residents they are supposed to protect and serve. Those suspicions were confirmed when the *NCVS* carried out a comparative study of reporting rates in 12 cities during 1998. Fewer victims of violence called the cops in Spokane, Washington (31 percent), and New York City (32 percent) than in Washington, D.C. (50 percent) or Springfield, Missouri (58 percent). A smaller percentage of the people who suffered property crimes filed complaints in San Diego, California (28 percent), and New York City (29 percent) than in Kansas City, Missouri (45 percent), and Savannah, Georgia (47 percent) (see Smith et al., 1999).

Note that these differential reporting rates from department to department undercut the accuracy of making city-to-city comparisons of crime rates based on the FBI's *UCR* compilation of crimes known to the police. City-by-city rankings of murder rates can be accurate because they don't depend on voluntary reports by victims, of course

Police departments face contradictory pressures. On the one hand, they want victims to come forward and share their misfortunes with the authorities, so that officers and detectives can effectively do their jobs. On the other hand, if that effort at outreach is too successful, the entire department might look inept, and individual precinct commanders and squad leaders might look incompetent.

Police forces that successfully cultivate closer ties to their communities learn about a greater proportion of the crimes committed within their jurisdiction. "User-friendly" departments that have won the trust of local residents can wind up

penalized in terms of their reputations. A department that suddenly becomes victim-oriented might appear to be engulfed by a crime wave. The apparently rising crime rates could merely be the result of improving reporting rates. Ironically, departments that alienate the people whom they are supposed to protect and serve look better by comparison—they may seem to be effectively suppressing illegal activities, when the actual reason for the low numbers of reported incidents is that a smaller proportion of the inhabitants turn to them for help.

Commanding officers and supervisors of the robbery, burglary, and sex crimes squads also face contradictory pressures. They need a steady stream of cases to work on, but they do not want to appear to be overwhelmed or seen as ineffective. Evaluating performance by using up-to-date computer-generated statistics is a foundation of the **Compstat** approach pioneered by the New York Police Department (NYPD) in the middle 1990s (and adopted since then by law enforcement agencies worldwide). As a result, victimization and arrest statistics have been monitored as closely as companies keep track of sales and profits. Precinct commanders are largely evaluated on their ability to continuously reduce the number of crimes known to have been committed in their jurisdictions. This is a positive development because Compstat-oriented departments now are constantly striving to devise more effective ways to improve public safety. However, the pressures to come to a meeting with the latest numbers of reported crimes being even lower than the last time has tempted some commanders and their subordinates to try to artificially suppress statistics about criminal activities. Some ways to reduce the apparent crime rate is to discourage victims from reporting about their misfortunes, to refuse to accept their complaints into the record-keeping system, or to downgrade serious charges into minor offenses whose numbers are not so closely monitored (see Levitt, 2004; Baker, 2011; Rayman, 2012; Eterno and Silverman, 2012; and Matson and Turk, 2013). For example, the NYPD was pressured to set up a watchdog panel in 2011 to look into the numbers of reported offenses in its Compstat database after a city councilman declared, "I believe that the statistics were in fact being manipulated. I have spoken to many current and former police officers who unfortunately refused to go on the record but have corroborated that fact. And I've spoken to many civilians whose valid complaints were not accepted by the Police Department" (see Baker and Rashbaum, 2011). In an apparent response, the police commissioner sent a memo to officers telling them to make it easier for New Yorkers to report crimes and to count each complaint. Officers were instructed to fill out reports even if the complainant wouldn't agree to be interviewed by detectives, couldn't identify the suspect or refused to view photographs in mug books, didn't want to press charges, and couldn't provide receipts for items that were stolen (Parascandola, 2012).

Similar problems of brushing off would-be complainants or downplaying the seriousness of their accounts have cropped up in many other jurisdictions. For example, in Milwaukee, the department misreported hundreds of beatings, stabbings, and child abuse cases to artificially deflate the *UCR*'s calculation of the violent crime rate for that city from 2009 to 2011 (Poston, 2012). In Los Angeles, 1,200 serious violent crimes were allegedly misclassified as minor offenses by Los Angeles Police Department (LAPD) record-keepers, according to a newspaper's investigation (Rubin and Poston, 2014). Manipulation in the form of downgrading could have consequences for the complainants: They might not be eligible for the services and financial compensation available to certified victims of violence. Similarly, in Houston, "a pattern of deceit" to keep publicly published numbers down during 2010 was uncovered by investigative reporters. They unearthed several "hidden homicides"—deaths due to arson which were not counted as murders, and deaths ruled as suicides in which the deceased was shot several times. When the police department reluctantly reopened certain recent cases of suspicious deaths and ended up reclassifying some as murders, the next of kin of 20 deceased persons became eligible for victim compensation payments from a state fund (Greenblatt and Razio, 2010).

Police departments generally want recent immigrants—both those who arrived in the United States legally as well as those who did not—to report attacks upon them and to serve as witnesses for the prosecution because criminals often prefer to target them (Altman and Aguayo, 2006). For that reason, many departments do not want to be compelled to engage in the enforcement of federal immigration laws because that activity would undermine trust and cooperation with recent arrivals to their community (Preston, 2011). Another potential problem is that language barriers can cause confusion and conflict during stressful interactions such as emergency calls and filing complaints (as well as in stop-and-frisks, car stops, investigations, arrests, bookings, and interrogations). Since 2002, the U.S. Department of Justice has carried out about 50 routine audits of police departments that serve substantial populations of inhabitants with limited proficiency in English to determine if the police are complying with civil rights laws mandating fair and equal treatment of all persons. Officers might find themselves unable to make sense of accusations and unable to communicate their own requests or orders to disputants, complainants, and suspects. Solutions to this communication problem include having linguists on standby to translate what is said during 911 calls or at crime scenes, finding third-party bystanders to speak to victims in their native language, and hiring more multilingual officers. One particularly difficult situation involves intervening in domestic disputes. Officers unable to find an interpreter might refuse to accept a complaint and will fill out "uncooperative" or "refused" in the space on the form that is labeled "victim's statement" (Rivera, 2010b). A review of the NYPD by the Justice Department's Office for Civil Rights in 2010 concluded that the department often failed to ensure that New Yorkers seeking assistance had critical access to certified interpreters if their first language was not English (most commonly, it was Spanish, Chinese, Russian, and Italian). For instance, despite having many Spanish-speaking officers, the NYPD had only 12 certified Spanish interpreters on call in its multilingual database, one for every 75,000 Spanish-speaking residents in its jurisdiction (Baker and Rivera, 2010).

As for trends, reporting rates are supposed to go up as the years go by. Criminal justice officials launched a campaign to promote calling the police for help decades ago (see "Crime Victims Digest," 1985). At the start of the twenty-first century, a government publication accentuated the positive by emphasizing how reporting rates, particularly for acts of violence, had risen modestly over the years (see Hart and Rennison, 2003; also Catalano, 2005). But in 2010, the BJS concluded that any progress had stalled, and no statistically significant improvements in reporting rates for violent offenses had been achieved since 2001 (Truman, 2011).

Table 6.1 shows the reporting rates for various types of crimes since the *NCVS* began its surveys in 1973. It shows that in 2013, the reporting rate for rapes and other sexual assaults was less frequent than when the survey began

40 years earlier (and had actually tumbled to an all time low of 23 percent in 1995 and again in 2009). However, the reporting rate for robberies was higher in 2013 than in previous years (except 2007). Aggravated assaults, motor vehicle thefts, and burglaries also were reported a little more often in 2013 than during most years in recent decades (see Table 6.1).

A victim advocacy group has argued that the public should be shocked—rather than reassured— by the stubborn persistence of relatively low reporting rates and the spotty progress in improving them despite years of campaigns to boost them. Their interpretation accentuated the negative, pointing out that the millions of incidents that victims decide not to bring to the attention of the authorities each year reflect a continuing and widespread lack of confidence in the criminal justice system. The persistence of this underreporting problem can be taken as evidence that police forces across the country have had only limited success over the decades in enlisting the public to cooperate more closely

T A B L E   6.1   Trends in Reporting Crimes to the Police, Selected Years, 1973–2013

	1973	1983	1988
All crimes	32 percent	35	36
Rapes and sexual assaults	49	47	45
Robberies	52	53	57
Aggravated assaults	52	56	54
Simple assaults	38	41	41
Burglaries	47	49	51
Household larcenies	25	25	26
Motor vehicle thefts	68	69	73

	1998	2006	2010	2013
All crimes	38	41	NA	NA
Rapes and sexual assaults	32	41	50	35
Robberies	62	57	58	68
Aggravated assaults	58	59	60	64
Simple assaults	40	44	47	39
Burglaries	49	50	59	57
Household larcenies	29	32	32	29
Motor vehicle thefts	80	81	83	76

NOTES: Figures are percentages and include reports of both attempted and completed acts.

Survey redesign influenced rape reporting rates after 1992.

NA = not available any longer.

Reporting includes information provided by third parties, such as eyewitnesses, family members, school authorities, or officers at the crime scene.

SOURCES: Bastian, 1993; Truman, 2011; Truman and Langton, 2014; BJS's *NCVS, Criminal Victimization in the United States*, selected years.

with law enforcement (National Center for Victims of Crime, 2003).

In most jurisdictions, victims are not legally obliged to inform authorities about violations of law committed against them or their property. But if they go beyond silence and inaction, and conspire or collaborate in a cover-up to conceal a serious crime (like a shooting), they can be arrested themselves and charged with **misprision of a felony**. The failure of witnesses to report certain kinds of offenses, especially the abuse of a child or an elderly person, is a misdemeanor in many jurisdictions (Stark and Goldstein, 1985).

Responding Quickly

When victims call for help, they expect officers to spring into action immediately. To meet this challenge, police departments have 911 emergency systems. But incoming calls have to be prioritized by dispatchers who determine each one's degree of urgency. Obviously, reports about immediate danger—such as screams in the night for help or calls about prowlers or shots fired—merit a higher priority than calls about cars that have disappeared from parking spots. If officers reach crime scenes quickly, they have a better chance of rescuing someone who is in grave danger, catching the culprit, recovering stolen property, gathering crucial evidence, and locating eyewitnesses. Police departments have been experimenting for decades with ways to reduce response times to calls about emergencies. But *NCVS* findings fuel suspicions that a substantial proportion of victims still might be dissatisfied with the amount of time it took officers to arrive at crime scenes.

Less than one third of all persons who were under attack told survey interviewers that the rescuers arrived within five minutes, according to *NCVS* findings. No improvement in response times materialized from 1990 to 2008, even though crime rates and consequently workloads have fallen sharply across the nation, and many police forces have grown in patrol strength. In 1990, the police arrived within 10 minutes at the scene of a 911 emergency nearly 60 percent of the time; by 2008

(the latest figures available), their track record was no better. An officer came within 60 minutes in roughly 90 percent of all calls for help in the midst or aftermath of a violent incident, but in certain explosive confrontations that response certainly would not be fast enough.

In New York City, the City Council ordered the NYPD to issue an annual report of its response times. The department was able to improve how long it took to get to crime scenes after receiving an emergency 911 "critical" call for help from a little over 6 minutes in 1999 to just under 5 minutes in 2014, which was faster than the arrival time for ambulances but slower than for fire engines (Mayor's Management Report, 2014).

To be fair to the officers responding to 911 calls, travel time is only one reason for delays. More importantly, precious moments are lost most often when people at the scene hesitate before reporting a crime in progress. There are several reasons for such delays on the part of bystanders and participants. They might be confused about whether an illegal act really occurred. Injured parties and eyewitnesses might want to first cope with emotional conflicts, personal trauma, and physical wounds, and then regain their composure before informing the authorities of what happened. (Before the advent of cell phones, delays arose if a landline or telephone booth wasn't nearby.) (Spelman and Brown, 1984). As for policy implications, reducing the time elapsed on the police department's end remains a matter of life and death and ought to be a priority for victim advocates to tackle.

A study of how long it took officers in Houston, Texas, to reach the scene of a burglary in progress discovered that response times were shorter in disadvantaged neighborhoods, improving the likelihood of nabbing the intruder (Cihan et al., 2012).

Handling Victims with Care

People who bring their problems to a police station expect procedural justice. They want officers and detectives to listen to them without bias as they explain their situation. They anticipate that the police will be sensitive and polite, treat them with dignity, respect their rights, and make decisions in an open and transparent manner (see Murphy and Barkworth, 2014).

In the aftermath of a street crime, victims are likely to feel powerless, disoriented, and infuriated. Fear, guilt, depression, and revenge fantasies engulf them. They expect authority figures to calm and console them, to help them restore their sense of equilibrium, and dispel lingering feelings of helplessness. After the first injury inflicted by the criminal, victims are particularly susceptible to a **second wound**. If officers unwittingly make them feel worse by being dismissive or callous, they will feel rejected and betrayed by those they counted on for support (Symonds, 1980b; and Ogawa, 1999).

Studies of police work suggest that what victims are encountering is the protective coating of emotional detachment that officers develop to shield themselves from becoming overwhelmed by the misery they routinely see around them. If officers appear unmoved, distant, and disinterested, it might be that they fear "contamination" (Symonds, 1975). Such "distancing" is a defense mechanism and is part of a "working personality" officers must develop because of the constant potential for danger in a hostile environment and the need to maintain objectivity in the face of complicated situations and conflicting witness accounts. A frighteningly unusual event for the victim can be a rather unexceptional incident for a seasoned officer (Ready, Weisburd, and Farrell, 2002). To avoid **burnout**, law enforcement officers (like others in helping professions) sense that they must inhibit their impulses to get emotionally involved in their cases. The paramilitary nature of police organizations and the bureaucratic imperatives of specialization and standardization reinforce their inclinations to deal with tragedies as impersonally as possible. In addition, the "macho" norms of police subculture—with its emphasis on toughness, camaraderie, suspicion of outsiders, insider jokes, graveyard humor, and profound cynicism—put pressure on members of law enforcement agencies to act businesslike when dealing with profoundly upsetting situations (Ahrens, Stein, and Young, 1980).

Many departments have initiated training programs to prepare at least a portion of their force to act sensitively when they deal with victims with acute needs. Officers and detectives are taught how to administer "psychological first aid" to people in distress. They are instructed to respond swiftly, listen attentively, show concern, and refrain from challenging the victims' versions of events or judging the wisdom of their reactions while the crime was in progress. Officers are told to not show any skepticism when a rape victim is not badly bruised or bleeding, a child did not report molestation immediately, an elderly person has trouble communicating, or a blind person offers to assist with the identification of a suspect. At the conclusion of training sessions, officers should be informed that responsiveness to victims carries a high priority within the department and has become a criterion for evaluating performance and a consideration in granting promotions (Symonds, 1980b; President's Task Force, 1982; National Sheriffs' Association, 1999). By 2000, more than 70 percent of all big-city police departments (serving more than 250,000 residents) had set up special victim assistance units, and more than 90 percent had officers on call who were trained to handle cases of child abuse, missing children, and domestic violence (Reaves and Hickman, 2002).

One of the most emotionally draining tasks in police work is notifying the next of kin of people who have been murdered. Anecdotal evidence indicates that many officers are inept at delivering bad news in plain language and with compassion. To rectify this problem, some departments have developed guidelines and manuals so that survivors are not further traumatized by disturbing memories of clumsy and uncaring behavior by officers carrying out these most unpleasant death notification obligations (Associated Press, 1994d).

Challenging the Victim's Version of Events

When people fill out a complaint form in a police station, they want their versions of what transpired to be accepted. From a detective's point of view, however, it is a necessary part of the job to maintain some healthy skepticism and handle complainants as "presumptive" victims until they pass a credibility test to weed out those whose stories are bogus. Obviously, the police should not automatically treat all complainants as if they are up to no good because of the misdeeds of a few fakers. The following examples demonstrate that on rare occasions individuals who tell what appear to be compelling stories may be attempting to manipulate and mislead investigators in order to conceal their role in a serious offense or just for a self-serving reason.

A man and his estranged girlfriend are sitting in a car arguing over visitation arrangements concerning their 14-month-old son, who is in the back seat. A robber comes up to them, shoots her fatally and then shoots him in the leg. After he tells slightly different versions of events to detectives, they become suspicious. When he is visited in the hospital by a cousin who closely fits the description of the gunman, they are both arrested and charged with murder. (Baker, 2008)

■■■

A 20-year-old Army private tells detectives at a hospital that he was shot in the knee during a robbery. But the police investigators determine that he arranged to be wounded to avoid having to return to combat duty in Iraq. He pleads guilty to the misdemeanor of falsely reporting an incident, and receives a sentence of one year in jail. He also is ordered to return to his military base, where he may be subjected to a court martial. His wife and the accomplice who shot him for a fee of $500 also face conspiracy, assault, false reporting, and illegal gun possession charges. (Chan, 2007)

■■■

The founder and leader of a nationwide civilian anticrime patrol garners favorable media coverage when he tells reporters that he was injured when he tried to capture three rapists at a subway station. He also shows off bruises that he claims he sustained when he came to the rescue of a person being mugged but actually were the result of an accident. Years later, after nearly dying from a shooting, the anticrime crusader and talk-show host admits that he conspired with other members of the newly formed group to

stage a series of six publicity stunts to further the organization's reputation for courage and effectiveness. About a dozen years after that, this acknowledged fabrication is used by a defense attorney to undermine his credibility with a jury when he testifies against a mob boss who, the prosecution alleges, ordered his assassination for mocking and taunting the Mafia on his talk-radio show. (Gonzalez, 1992; Preston, 2005; and Cornell, 2006).

■■■

A television network weather forecaster tells detectives that she was attacked twice by the same man, once while jogging in the park and again near her home. When the police can't find any eyewitnesses, she confesses that "I made it up for attention. I have so much stress at work, with my personal life, and with my family." Facing a jail sentence for filing a false complaint, the judge sentences her to probation and 350 hours of community service, the same amount of time the police spent investigating her phony claims. (Cornell, 2011).

It is always possible that the person alleging to be a bona fide victim is making a fraudulent claim for some ulterior purpose. People might falsely swear under penalty of perjury that they were harmed by criminals for a number of reasons. An angry person may exact revenge against an enemy by getting him in trouble with the law. An individual who did something improper may want to cover up the true circumstances surrounding an event (for example, when a husband claims he was robbed to account for the loss of his pay, which he actually spent on a prostitute or gambled away).

Hoaxes can be very socially divisive and damaging to race relations, especially when whites falsely claim they were viciously attacked by black suspects, setting off manhunts. Highly publicized examples include a husband who killed his wife but insisted she was shot during a hold-up (until his lie was exposed and he jumped off a bridge), and a young mother who drowned her unwanted little children by driving her vehicle down a boat ramp but swore that they were kidnapped and driven off by a carjacker (see Russell-Brown, 2008).

A more mundane motive for lying is to commit insurance fraud. For example, tourists may dishonestly claim that they were robbed of their cash-filled wallets or expensive cameras as part of a scam to get reimbursement for nonexistent losses from insurance policies sold to travelers (Associated Press, 1999b). One area in which false claims of victimization routinely constitute a major problem concerns allegations of vehicle theft. Detectives on the auto squad and insurance company investigators suspect that as many as 10 percent of all persons who enter police stations with tales of woe about vehicles that have vanished are faking in order to collect reimbursements they are not entitled to (Jay, 2011). "Owner give-ups" refer to illegal transactions where the vehicle is driven off a pier or ramp into a body of water ("splashed"), set on fire ("torched"), or simply abandoned so that it can be reported as stolen in order to avoid debts. As a result of schemes like this, a list of signs of suspicious behavior has been compiled to weed out the fraudsters from the genuine victims of grand larceny auto (see Box 6.2).

It is appropriate for detectives to take all plausible complaints seriously and to search for evidence that will substantiate a person's account of what happened. Deceptions are exposed by thorough investigations that look into vague descriptions and turn up inconsistencies each time the account is repeated, pieces of the puzzle that don't add up, an absence of witnesses, and events in the complainant's background that raise suspicions and undermine credibility. Unfortunately, major hoaxes as well as petty false claims can waste taxpayer money and precious police resources that could be put to better use investigating real crimes and helping genuine victims (Radford, 2013).

Two categories of errors are possible when handling complaints from people insisting they are innocent victims. The first type, illustrated by the above examples, occurs when detectives initially believe a person who later is exposed as a liar. The other type of mistake, illustrated below, is to disbelieve the account of someone who really is telling the truth.

A 26-year-old mother of two accepts a ride from a stranger who kidnaps her. For the next two months, this retired handyman with an ailing wife holds her captive in a concrete bunker in his backyard and repeatedly rapes her. When he finally releases her, she runs to the police and tells of her ordeal as a sex slave. They don't take this kidnap and rape victim's story seriously, finding it hard to believe. Eventually, four additional young runaways and drug abusers recount horrific tales that are similar. Finally, the police launch an investigation, locate the bunker, and arrest the man who quickly pleads guilty to these vicious crimes. (Jacobs, 2003; Smalley and Mnookin, 2003)

Unfounding, illustrated by the above case, is a process in which the police reject a person's claim about being harmed by a criminal as unbelievable or at least unprovable in court. **Defounding** means that detectives believe an offense really did take place, but it was not as serious as the complainant described (Lundman, 1980). For example, what was initially reported as a burglary might upon further investigation be classified as merely an instance of criminal trespass—which is a misdemeanor rather than a felony—if nothing of value was stolen.

Just as individuals might have a motive to lodge a false charge, police investigators might have an incentive to declare a report of a crime completely unfounded or to defound it down to a lesser offense. By defounding and unfounding complaints, detectives can reduce the number of serious crimes recorded in their precincts, perhaps because their supervisors want to convince the public that the crime rate is decreasing impressively. Detectives might cut down the number of difficult cases they must try to solve by abusing their discretion and writing off legitimate pleas for help. For example, for more than 20 years, Chicago detectives dismissed about 21 percent of their complaints about serious crimes as unfounded; the average rate for other big-city departments was less than 2 percent, according to the FBI. Detectives were inclined to dismiss victims' accounts as unfounded because they would receive higher ratings and faster promotions if they

---

BOX 6.2 Which Individuals Who Claim to Be "Victims" of Auto Theft Might Be Suspected of Engaging in Fraud by Law Enforcement and Insurance Investigators?

The following warning signs could arouse the suspicion of auto squad detectives and insurance company adjusters that the person who reports that his car was stolen might not be a genuine crime victim and that the alleged theft might be a "QC" (questionable claim) that merits closer scrutiny as a possible attempt at fraud:

Red Flags: The Auto Theft "Victim"...

- Filed a false claim in the past
- Received insurance reimbursement for a vehicle theft in the past
- Is very knowledgeable about the process for filing a claim and insurance terminology
- Owns a car that has a history of expensive mechanical repairs (a "lemon") or gets very poor mileage (a "gas guzzler")
- Asserts that very expensive items were in the vehicle when it was taken
- Has fallen behind in loan payments on the vehicle and faces repossession, has many outstanding tickets, or is beset by serious financial problems
- Has very recently taken out the policy with this insurance company, the coverage is about to expire, or a cancellation notice has been sent out
- Has recently moved into the current address or uses a post office box, does not have a telephone or only has a

cell phone, is difficult to contact, or has just been hired or just lost a job
- Has purchased the policy by walking off the street into an insurance agency and putting down cash for a binder
- Has paid only for minimum liability coverage but for maximum comprehensive fire/theft coverage on an expensive late model vehicle
- Has waited several days before notifying the police of the alleged disappearance
- Is notified that the vehicle has been recovered but was stripped, burned, severely damaged, or found with a seized engine or blown transmission but without a compromised steering column or ignition lock shortly after it was reported missing
- Has documents (title, registration, license plate, vehicle identification number) that contain mistakes or irregularities
- Presses for a quick settlement but avoids making statements under oath and requests that the check be picked up by a friend or relative
- Has contacted a salvage yard or repair shop that takes an unusual interest in the claim

SOURCES: Jay, 2011; Ohio Insurance Board, 2011; Louisiana State Police's Insurance Fraud Unit, 2011.

"closed" more cases. Auditors reviewing these police files concluded that as many as 40 percent of the rape, robbery, burglary, and theft reports disregarded as unfounded probably did take place as the victims claimed. The kinds of cases that were prime candidates for official disbelief involved victims who were difficult to contact, knew their assailants, or did not lose much money ("Chicago Police," 1983; "Burying Crime in Chicago," 1983).

In Oakland, California, overworked detectives in the late 1980s dismissed 24 percent of the rape complaints they received as unfounded. At that time, the FBI reported that other departments across the country disbelieved about 9 percent of all rape charges. After a newspaper article questioned why there was such a disparity in the unfounding rate,

the police chief conceded that perhaps 200 cases were tossed aside too quickly and merited reexamination. But detectives in this California city advanced several arguments in their own defense. First, they asserted that the nationwide figure of 9 percent was a misleading standard for comparison, since many departments keep the unfounding rate artificially low by classifying cases as "filed pending further investigation" (not officially closed) rather than "closed due to baseless or false charges." Second, they pointed out that because of budget constraints, the sexual assault unit's six investigators were so swamped with cases that they had to prioritize their workload. They felt pressured to disregard complaints from women who would appear uncooperative, untruthful, or unsympathetic in court, such as prostitutes and drug abusers who would be inclined to lie about the circumstances surrounding the sexual assaults for fear of getting in trouble for solicitation or possession of controlled substances. Finally, the detectives insisted that many of the complainants refused to agree to medical examinations and failed to appear for follow-up interviews, making the investigation of their charges difficult, time consuming, and unlikely to lead to convictions (Gross, 1990).

Similarly, in New Orleans five detectives in the special victims squad were transferred for failing to thoroughly investigate hundreds of sexual assault complaints from 2011 to 2013. Many of the complaints were simply filed under the heading "miscellaneous," and no further action was taken. In hundreds of other cases, an initial report was filled out but no effort was made to gather evidence. Detectives also routinely discouraged complainants in sexual assault cases from pursuing prosecution of the alleged rapists (Robertson, 2014).

Investigators do not want to be manipulated or deceived, of course. Even though lie detector tests are not admissible in court because their findings are not considered reliable, NYPD detectives received authorization in 2005 to use polygraphs during the early stages of an investigation to test their suspicions that a suspect, a witness, or a complainant was lying to them (Celona, 2005).

People who knowingly fill out false complaints are breaking the law in most states if they gratuitously volunteer unsolicited, incorrect information to the police. The laws that make it a misdemeanor to file a false instrument (statement) are intended to deter perjury and thereby protect innocent individuals from the embarrassment and hardships caused by untrue accusations. A lying complainant who instigates a wrongful arrest for an improper motive such as revenge also can be sued in civil court for malicious prosecution.

However, to encourage citizen cooperation with law enforcement, most jurisdictions have adopted a doctrine of witness immunity that shields complainants who furnish information to the police "in good faith" from any subsequent lawsuits by innocent individuals they mistakenly identified as

suspects (Stark and Goldstein, 1985). But those who waste the time and money of law enforcement agencies by filing patently false accusations can get into legal trouble, as the following example demonstrates.

> A young woman mysteriously disappears while jogging just four days before her elaborate wedding. Hundreds of neighbors, wedding guests, and police officers search the area and pass out missing person flyers, while bloodhounds scour the banks of a nearby river and media outlets across the country broadcast her description. Her fiancé, the last person to see her, comes under suspicion but resists pressures by the police to take a lie detector test. Several days later and hundreds of miles away she reappears; she calls 911 and tells the authorities that she just was released by a Hispanic man and a white woman who had kidnapped her. A few hours later, the "runaway bride" admits she had gotten "cold feet" and had taken a long bus ride. Her friends, family, and neighbors are both relieved and furious that she was not a victim of foul play. Their views and her problems become the fodder for talk shows and tabloid headlines. In court, she pleads no contest to one felony count of making a false statement to the police, and the judge imposes a sentence of two years on probation, 120 hours of community service, plus a fine. (Johnston, 2005)

Investigating Complaints and Solving Crimes

Victims who report crimes expect their local police and sheriff's departments to launch investigations that successfully culminate with the apprehension of suspects and the seizure of solid evidence pointing to their guilt (Brandl and Horvath, 1991).

The FBI's annual *UCR* calculates and publishes average **clearance rates** for each of the seven index crimes for police departments across the country. In general, clearing crimes means making arrests. FBI guidelines instruct police departments to consider cases to be solved when they are closed by taking suspects into custody, lodging charges against them, and turning them over to courts for prosecution. Exceptional clearances take place when situations beyond the control of law enforcement agencies prevent them from arresting and formally charging someone, even though sufficient evidence has been gathered and the exact whereabouts of the suspect are known. For example, the suspect cannot be arrested because he has died or is otherwise beyond reach (such as, he can't be extradited) or the victim refuses to further cooperate with the prosecution. Old cases that are closed by an arrest count toward the current year's clearance rate. In calculating clearance rates, the *UCR* program counts the number of reported offenses that have been closed and not the number of persons charged with these crimes. The arrest of just one person may clear several crimes, and yet the arrest of several accomplices may close only one reported incident (FBI, 2011). Note that the police consider the crime solved even if the sole arrestee is not ultimately convicted of the original charge or even any lesser charge. If the accused is found not guilty after a trial, the case usually is not reopened. In other words, there is no "case tracking" or follow-up, and once clearance rates are calculated and published in the *UCR*, they are not later corrected or updated to reflect what ultimately happened in court. Therefore, clearance rates tend to be overestimates of the proportion of criminals who are brought to justice and made to pay for their crimes because the FBI and local departments do not monitor what eventually happens to these cases at later stages of the criminal justice process. Some charges are dropped by prosecutors or dismissed by judges, freeing those arrestees. Of those who are prosecuted, many engage in negotiations via their defense attorneys and plead guilty to lesser charges in order to get milder punishments, or are not convicted by a jury after a trial (see the leaky net diagram in Chapter 12).

Police departments routinely compile the percentages of cases that are closed by arrests because this indicator of effectiveness ought to be calculated and submitted to the FBI's *UCR* division. These clearance rates are used to evaluate the performance of individual detectives, specialized squads (such as those concentrating on homicide, burglary, and sex crimes), and the department as a whole.

But these same statistics can be interpreted from a different angle and for a different purpose. From a victim's point of view, the police have successfully completed their mission when, acting on sufficient evidence, all the wrongdoers in a particular incident have been charged with what they really did. The proportion of cases that are solved can indicate the percentage of complainants who have a solid basis for being satisfied or dissatisfied with the investigatory services provided by local police forces. Victims want suspects to be taken into custody because it symbolizes that justice has been served. An arrest means that their misfortunes have been considered significant enough to warrant official action, and their request for assistance has been taken seriously by those in authority. Victims who report crimes and cooperate with investigations want someone to be held directly accountable for the injuries and losses they have suffered. That person might be ordered by the judge to make restitution to repay losses and expenses. Besides restitution, injured parties might demand retribution in order to gain solace from the knowledge that the government is punishing the wrongdoer in their behalf. Also, those with a sense of civic responsibility might want to see the offender removed from society and incapacitated behind bars in order to make the streets safer for others. For all these reasons, solving cases by making arrests can be considered a high-priority issue and a crucial performance measure from the standpoint of victims who report crimes and cooperate with law enforcement authorities.

By the conclusion of most movies and television shows, the wrongdoer has been captured, reinforcing the message that crime doesn't pay. But victimologists need to ask, "In real life, how often do law enforcement agencies figure out (and also, fail to figure out) who did it?" Data from selected years over the past five decades appear in Table 6.2. These statistics summarize the overall accomplishments of roughly 17,000 law enforcement agencies during the second half of the twentieth century and the first 13 years of the twenty-first. The most recent solution rates appear in the last column.

T A B L E   6.2   Trends in Clearance Rates, United States, Selected Years, 1953–2013

Type of Crime	1953	1963	1973	1983	1993	1998	2003	2006	2010	2013
Murder	93%	91	79	76	66	69	62	61	64	64
Rape	78	69	51	52	53	50	44	41	40	40
Aggravated assault	75	76	63	61	56	59	56	54	56	58
Robbery	36	39	27	26	24	28	26	25	28	29
Burglary	27	27	18	15	13	14	13	13	12	13
Larceny	20	20	19	20	20	19	18	17	21	23
Vehicle theft*	26	26	16	15	14	14	13	13	12	14

NOTES: *Since the 1970s, this category of the *UCR* has included the theft of all motorized vehicles, including trucks, vans, motorcycles, and buses.
SOURCES: FBI *UCRs*, selected years, 1953–2013.

Accentuating the positive, the figures for 2013 reveal that police forces nationwide had greater success at solving violent crimes, which are more serious and threatening to public safety than property crimes. Accentuating the negative and looking at these numbers from the victims' point of view, it is obvious that the vast majority of people who go to the trouble to report thefts to the police will not be pleased with the outcome of their cases: The investigations will be discontinued before any arrests are made. Put another way, 87 percent of burglary complainants, 86 percent of persons reporting that their vehicle was stolen, and 78 percent of theft victims had good reasons to be frustrated in 2013—their offenders had escaped detection and arrest.

Similarly, many victims of interpersonal violence did not gain the satisfaction of knowing that someone got in trouble for harming them. Of those who reported robberies, 71 percent endured the aggravation of learning that no one was apprehended for accosting them. Of all those who had the courage to tell the authorities in 2013 that they had been raped or otherwise sexually assaulted, 60 percent did not experience the relief of knowing that their attackers had been arrested. Presumably, these assailants who remained at large were mostly strangers and not the perpetrators of acquaintance rapes. Of all those who were subjected to an aggravated assault like a shooting or stabbing, 42 percent were disturbed to find out that no arrests were made in their cases (FBI, 2014).

The highest clearance rates of all are achieved by homicide squads. But even these seasoned detectives who devoted considerable time and effort to these important cases were not able to figure out who did it in a little more than 35 percent of the slayings that took place in 2013. To put it dramatically, that means that more than one out of every three killers got away with murder that year. Thousands of dangerous assailants annually join the ranks of murderers who are still roaming the streets unpunished for their heinous crimes.

As for changes over time, the *UCR* clearance rates compiled in Table 6.2 reveal a disturbing national trend. For six of the seven index crimes (except for larcenies, the least damaging but the only bright spot) a general downward drift is evident from the early 1950s through the first 13 years of the twenty-first century. During the 1950s, police departments were able to solve practically all murders and most rapes and aggravated assaults. Clearance rates for these three violent crimes as well as for robberies dropped sharply during the crime wave of the late 1960s and never bounced back up. During the 1970s and 1980s, the solution rates for rapes and serious assaults remained stable, while the ability of the police to solve murders continued to decline. Burglaries and auto thefts led to arrests roughly twice as often in the 1950s as in the 1990s. Grand and petit larcenies (major and minor thefts of all kinds) have always been difficult to solve (except for shoplifting arrests). During the early 1990s, clearance rates hit new lows across the board, but then improved slightly by 1998 (for murders, serious assaults, and robberies), as crime rates and consequently detectives' caseloads fell throughout the nation. Disappointingly, solution rates (especially for murder and rape) dipped again at the beginning of the twenty-first century. By 2006, the overall ability of police departments across the country to solve a reduced volume of cases of interpersonal violence and theft had sunk to an all-time low. These dismal national figures had recovered just a bit in a few categories by 2013.

These statistics from the FBI's *UCR* reveal a shocking conclusion: during the twenty-first century, police departments are having more trouble than ever in solving cases despite breakthroughs in forensic science (like DNA matching), the proliferation of surveillance cameras, and the establishment of massive databases of known offenders and their identifying features like scars, tattoos, and fingerprints. Taken collectively, the nation's 17,000 federal, state, county, and municipal law enforcement agencies had never before had such a disappointing track record as they did during the twenty-first century.

Translating these statistical trends into human terms, most victims have good reasons to be dissatisfied with the performance of their local police and sheriffs' departments. Because property crimes vastly outnumber violent offenses, and relatively few thieves are caught, most victims will be disappointed if they count on law enforcement agencies to arrest somebody for harming them. Ironically, decades ago, long before the victims' rights movement began to demand improved services, local law enforcement agencies were much more effective at accomplishing their basic mission of catching culprits.

As might be suspected, some police forces are better than others when it comes to solving crimes. *UCR* statistics confirm the existence of differential rates for solving crimes from department to department. As Table 6.3 indicates, some urban police forces were able to solve a much greater percentage of murder cases than their counterparts in other large cities. Some departments caught killers at rates substantially above the national average for cities of a quarter of a million inhabitants or more, which was 60 percent in 2003 but sunk to 54 percent in 2006 before bouncing back to 61 percent in 2010 and 63 percent in 2013. On the other hand,

the kin of murder victims in cities with subpar performance records were likely to remain tormented by the lack of closure due to the inability of their local police departments to arrest any suspects.

According to the data assembled in Table 6.3, in most cities the proportion of solved cases rose and fell quite dramatically from year to year. In Phoenix, Washington, D.C., Boston, Oklahoma City, and Las Vegas, the police forces were able to achieve clearance rates that were way above the national big city average of 57 percent in 2012. The families and close friends of people murdered in these cities were more likely to experience the closure of learning that someone was charged with the slayings of their loved ones than in other urban centers. The cities where the next of kin were likely to be very upset due to particularly disappointing solution rates included Memphis, Seattle, Portland, Detroit, and especially Columbus. Police departments in Cincinnati, Cleveland, Newark, and Atlanta also reported disturbingly low homicide clearance rates to the *UCR* for 2012 (not displayed in Table 6.3).

Note that the two largest police forces in the nation, in New York and Chicago, did not participate in the *UCR's* voluntary reporting program during the period 2003 to 2012 (the NYPD's clearance rate of 73 percent was achieved in 2013), and that the third largest department, the LAPD, disclosed a peculiar drop in 2011 to 39 percent and then a surge in solved murder cases from previous years that artificially boosted the 2012 rate to over 100 percent).

A number of factors might account for the wide range in clearance rates and their volatility over the years. The ability to solve homicide cases depends in part on practices and policies that a department can control, such as ensuring that the first officer who arrives at the crime scene is trained to follow proper procedures, assigning a sufficient number of detectives to a case, having them respond quickly, and devoting a substantial amount of resources to homicide investigations. Clearance rates also are shaped by factors beyond a department's control, such as the particular mix of difficult versus easy-to-solve cases in its jurisdiction (Wellford and Cronin, 2000).

TABLE 6.3 Clearance Rates for Homicide Cases (Murder and Manslaughter) in Major U.S. Cities, Selected Years, 2003–2012

City and State	2003	2004	2005	2006	2009	2012
All cities of 250,000 or more inhabitants	60	58	57	54	61	57
Phoenix, AZ	41	34	41	40	63	93
Los Angeles, CA	57	56	57	57	58	70**
San Diego, CA	58	92	88	56	48	56
San Jose, CA	79	83	96	62	71	63
Denver, CO*	49	51	—	—	71	60
Washington, D.C.	60	61	61	64	75	81
Jacksonville, FL	61	54	62	65	79	55
Chicago, IL *	—	—	—	—	—	—
Indianapolis, IN	82	87	80	74	65	65
Baltimore, MD	76	59	54	53	55	50
Boston, MA	64	28	29	47	56	79
Detroit, MI	50	37	30	28	23	34
Las Vegas, NV	38	54	74	68	79	78
New York, NY*	—	—	—	—	—	73****
Columbus, OH*	—	37	56	—	52	22
Oklahoma City, OK	63	97	63	64	75	78
Portland, OR	44	45	45	60	37	36
Philadelphia, PA	65	65	63	56	75	70
Memphis, TN	80	79	72	66	70	56
Dallas, TX	64	59	74	81	66	60
Houston, TX	57	60	59	70	70	76
San Antonio, TX	67	78	70	—	87	75
Seattle, WA	78	71	72	70	100***	37
Milwaukee, WI	80	82	63	59	78	62

NOTES: *The FBI's *UCR* Division did not receive statistics from the police departments in Chicago, New York City, Denver, and Columbus for certain recent years.

**The clearance rate for Los Angeles was estimated to be around 70 percent because only 39 percent of all homicides were solved in 2011 and over 100 percent were solved in 2012; apparently many previously unsolved cases were cleared in 2012.

***The clearance rate in Seattle exceeded 100 percent because unsolved murders from previous years were cleared by arrests in 2009.

****The NYPD figure is for 2013, since the 2012 rate was not disclosed.

SOURCE: "Return A Record Cards," 2002–2012, FBI's Uniform Crime Reporting Division, released to the author by special request.

For example, murder/suicide cases virtually solve themselves, such as when a husband kills his wife and then himself and leaves a note behind. "Smoking gun" cases are also cleared on the spot. On the other hand, slayings among mobsters, rival street gangs, or drug dealers are much more difficult to successfully close because of the lack of cooperation of witnesses and other knowledgeable people. Even the best departments find murders of robbery victims by complete strangers to be tough to solve.

Furthermore, victims and witnesses who are immersed in the "code of the streets" that prevails in poverty-stricken neighborhoods generally view helping the authorities solve crimes as "snitching." Consequently, one strategy to boost clearance rates would be to improve police–citizen interactions in a way that restores the legitimacy of the police (see Stewart et al., 2008). However, several factors widely assumed to be crucial—who the victim was, where the slaying took place, and the detective's workload and degree of experience—actually may not significantly affect homicide clearance rates, according to a study of more than 800 killings between 1984 and 1992 (Puckett and Lundman, 2003).

Of all the homicide cases that are eventually solved, half are closed within a week, and 93 percent are solved within a year, according to a study of nearly 800 cases in four large cities during 1994–1995 (Wellford and Cronin, 2000). Even though the prognosis is not promising if no one has been identified as a suspect after one year, departments seeking to improve their clearance rates establish **cold case squads** to take a fresh look at old, unsolved serious crimes. Crimes that are finally closed with an arrest are credited to that year's clearance rate, which can be boosted to over 100 percent whenever the cold case squad is unusually effective. With the passage of time, some positive developments might take place: Investigators who were overly focused on the wrong suspects might be reassigned or retire; eyewitnesses who originally were afraid to talk might become more cooperative; former partners in crime might experience a falling out; old evidence, as long as it is not contaminated, might be retested in police labs using powerful new techniques; and formerly overburdened detective squads now might have more time to do thorough investigations. Media coverage of an unsolved case can stimulate renewed public interest, and persistent relatives who keep checking in and inquiring about any new clues can pressure homicide detectives to take a second look (Dahl, 2011).

As for missing adults who could be victims of foul play, the National Institute of Justice has set up a National Missing and Unidentified Persons System (NamUs) database to assist detectives, private eyes, and concerned relatives search for clues. It listed between 80,000 and 90,000 names and descriptions filed by police departments across the country during 2013, but it is deemed to be underutilized (Sottile, 2014).

Because there is no statute of limitations for murder, on rare occasions a deceased person's relatives might be relieved to learn that a killer who thought he had escaped the long arm of the law has been brought to justice, as these two examples demonstrate:

The mother of an 18-year-old woman is sexually assaulted and then strangled in her apartment. Twenty-five years later, an ex-convict is arrested

when his DNA matches evidence found at the crime scene. The woman's 43-year-old daughter tells reporters, "I've called these guys so many times to try and keep this case alive. If there are any other families out there, they need to do whatever it takes." After a sleepless night, she declares, "This was the happiest and saddest day of my life." (Charkes, 2008)

∎∎∎

A young woman serving as a federal intern leaves her apartment building to go off jogging and then disappears. Under unrelenting pressure from the media and her parents, the police search for her fruitlessly for a year, until a man stumbles upon her remains in a nearby park. Accusations are hurled at her hometown congressman, with whom she was secretly having an affair. He vehemently denies any involvement, but the revelations ruin his political career. Ten years after her slaying, a jury, basing its verdict largely on the testimony of another inmate who says he heard a confession, convicts a man—who had served time for attacking other women—of first degree murder. Before the judge sentences him to 60 years, the young woman's mother calls him a "hideous creature" who is "lower than a cockroach." She asks, "Did you really take her?" and then insists, "Look into my eyes right now and tell me!" He asserts "I am very sorry… but I had nothing to do with it. I am innocent." (Tavernise, 2011)

On the other hand, family members and close friends can suffer endless frustration and anguish if a killer gets away with murder:

The parents of a little girl who wins beauty contests wake up early one morning to prepare for a family vacation—and discover a ransom note on the staircase inside their home. The kidnapper demands $118,000: exactly the amount that the father had just received as a bonus from his company. Shortly after they summon the police, the father discovers the child's body in the basement. She had been sexually abused and then strangled. Because inexperienced officers do not conduct an effective investigation and no one is ever arrested for the murder, a cloud of suspicion hangs over the grieving parents and her brother. Years later, a new, highly sensitive test is *performed on traces of DNA on the murdered child's clothing and her father, younger brother, and mother (now deceased) are officially eliminated as suspects in her slaying. These secondary victims, who suffered additional emotional turmoil as the subjects of conspiracy theories for over a decade, receive a note from the district attorney's office, stating, "No innocent person should have to endure such an extensive trial in the court of public opinion." (Ramsey and Ramsey, 2000; Bellamy, 2005; and Johnson, 2008)*

To sum up, after fruitless searches for clues and leads, most victims of property crimes and many who suffered interpersonal violence will wind up feeling defeated by the lack of closure in their cases. If more criminals were brought to court, then a higher proportion of residents would be satisfied with the performance of their local police or sheriff's department on this most fundamental aspect of a law enforcement agency's mission.

Arresting Suspects

When victims formally lodge complaints, they expect action in the form of thorough investigations and the collection of evidence culminating in an arrest—in a proper lawful manner that will hold up in court.

When police officers carry out custodial interrogations or make arrests, they have a legal obligation to inform suspects of their Miranda rights to remain silent and to be represented by a lawyer. When victims file complaints, they immediately discover that the police are under no comparable constitutional pressure to read them their "rights" about their obligations and opportunities. To start with, victims need to know the names and badge numbers of the officers and the detectives handling their cases, where and when they can be reached, case identification numbers, whether suspects have been apprehended, and if so, whether they are being detained in jail or are being released on bail.

But findings from the *NCVS* indicated that a large percentage of victims during the 1980s never were informed whether their cases were solved and

arrests were made. Even when police were successful in closing a case with an arrest, they might not have shared this good news with these most interested parties (FBI, 2007; Whitaker, 1989). To guarantee that these basic rights (endorsed by a presidential task force in 1982) are respected, a number of states have passed statutes that specify that police departments must keep victims posted on the status of their cases. But in the remaining states, victims must depend on departmental policies and the good will of individual detectives.

Dissatisfaction also can arise when detectives deem a complainant's misfortunes to be too minor to merit official action. It is difficult to justify the expenditure of the department's limited human resources, time, and money to solve minor cases. Some departments issue directives that specify cutoff points below which no action will be taken beyond simply making a formal note of the complaint. For example, in Dade County, which includes Miami, Florida, reports about stolen cars were taken solely over the telephone and only during certain hours (Combined News Services, 1993). In New York City during the 1980s, a detective from the burglary squad was assigned to a case only if the reported loss exceeded a figure of several thousand dollars (Gutis, 1988). Sometimes the police might be reluctant to expend much effort if victims are likely to receive insurance reimbursement.

Many complainants discover that with the passage of time, their cases have been closed even though they remain unsolved. How long an investigation remains open depends on the workload in the jurisdiction and the seriousness of the offense. If the police are unable to establish the identity of a suspect or cannot obtain sufficient evidence to justify an arrest, then they can exercise their discretion to discontinue any active effort to solve the crime. Victims have no formal means of compelling law enforcement agencies to continue to work on unsolved mysteries. Dissatisfied complainants have been unable to convince judges to intervene in matters of police discretion unless a pattern of noninvestigation reflects racial or religious discrimination on the part of government officials sworn to serve and protect the public (Austern, 1987).

Even when a trail of evidence leads to a suspect, an arrest is never automatic. Police officers exercise a great deal of personal and departmental discretion in deciding whom to take into custody and book, and whom to let go, especially for misdemeanors. The factors that influence these decisions include pressures from colleagues and superiors, the individual predilections of officers, the nature of the offense, and the relationship of the victim to the suspect. Victims can become angry when officers don't arrest these suspects.

One solution for victims is to convince judges to issue arrest warrants based on their sworn complaints which officers must then carry out. A second solution is to exercise the dangerous do-it-yourself option known as a **citizen's arrest**. Private citizens are empowered to use whatever force necessary to prevent a suspect from escaping until the police arrive to take charge of the situation. Civilians must directly witness the offenses, apprehend and detain their suspects immediately after the crimes are committed, and turn their captives over to the authorities without delay. Police officers are generally obligated to accept custody of suspects taken prisoner by victims or bystanders. In some states, citizens can make arrests only for felonies, but in other jurisdictions they may act even if the offense they directly witnessed is only a misdemeanor (Cicchini and Kushner, 2010).

But citizen's arrests are risky undertakings. Suspects are likely to resist capture and endanger victims or onlookers who intervene. In cases of mistaken identity, even victims who acted with probable cause and in good faith can be sued in civil court for false arrest and false imprisonment in some states. The use of excessive force can also be grounds for a lawsuit, even if the wrongdoer is later found guilty. Police officials generally discourage civilians from thinking of themselves as deputized to make arrests. They point to the lengthy training sworn officers receive in self-defense tactics, the use of firearms, the application of laws governing arrests, the seizure of evidence, and suspects' rights. Because attempts to make citizen's arrests can easily devolve into acts of vigilantism, law enforcement officials encourage activist-oriented civilians to become involved in police auxiliary units or neighborhood anticrime patrols instead (Hall, 1975; Stark and Goldstein, 1985; and Cicchini and Kushner, 2010).

Recovering Stolen Property

Besides catching culprits, the police can satisfy victims' needs by recovering their stolen items. Just as clearance rates indicate the approximate percentage of victims who receive optimum service in terms of arrests, recovery rates show how often the police succeed in retrieving stolen goods. Unfortunately, unlike clearance rates, user-friendly recovery rates are not routinely tabulated and published by police departments or the FBI.

The *UCR* notes the overall dollar value of recovered stolen goods for all kinds of reported incidents. For example, police departments were able to recover 55 percent of the value of "locally stolen" motor vehicles but only about 1 percent of all cash taken by thieves, burglars, and robbers during 2013 (FBI, 2014).

Recovery rates for various crimes used to be available from the *NCVS* until 2008. Interviewers asked respondents whether all or part of the money and property taken from them was returned to them (not counting insurance reimbursement). Police recovery rates can then be estimated. But the figures will be biased upward because some victims are able to get back their stolen property through their own efforts. Unfortunately, this statistic cannot be refined further to determine the percentage of victims who recovered items by themselves and what percentage was retrieved by the police. Furthermore, these estimates combine partial and full recoveries, again biasing the statistics upward and presenting the abilities of police departments across the nation as more effective than they really are. Partial recoveries might not satisfy victims; a discarded wallet emptied of any cash or credit cards, for example, or a badly stripped automobile with a traceable vehicle identification number would count as partial recoveries. With these reservations in mind, the following observations can be made: This aspect of police work will leave most people who suffered robberies, burglaries, and household larcenies dissatisfied with the outcomes of their cases. The recovery rates are very low. Even though crime rates have fallen substantially across the nation since the 1990s, enabling detectives to have more time to investigate the remaining cases, the ability of police departments to retrieve stolen goods apparently has not improved. In fact, these disappointing percentages dropped to new lows over the decades for burglaries, larcenies, and vehicle thefts. A mere 7 or 8 percent of all victims of burglaries and household larcenies recovered some or all of what was taken from them in 2008. For valuables stolen during robberies, the recovery rate did not change; victims got back some or all of their items in 24 percent of the cases in 2008, the same figure as in 1980. Only owners of stolen vehicles are likely to get back their cars. But these statistics don't indicate the condition the vehicles were in when they were found—the recovered cars may have been severely damaged or stripped. A vehicle was recovered in 65 percent of all cases in 1980 but that figure slipped to 58 percent in 2008, according to *NCVS* annual reports. That disappointing overall rate (which varies dramatically by state and by make/model/year) slid further to just 55 percent in 2013, according to the *UCR* (FBI, 2014). However, vehicles equipped with a tracking device that can be detected by specially programmed computers provided to police departments were recovered better than 90 percent of the time in 2013, according to the manufacturer (Lojack, 2014).

Even if the police recover stolen property, some victims might not get it back for a while. Law enforcement agencies have the authority to hold seized items if they are of value in continuing investigations. Prosecutors are allowed to maintain custody of pieces of evidence until after the trial or even until those convicted have exhausted all appeals. Victims frustrated by that delay are now assisted in some states by statutes that compel the police to return stolen property "expeditiously"—as soon as it is no longer needed for law enforcement purposes (Stark and Goldstein, 1985).

As noted above, sometimes victims themselves deserve credit for retrieving stolen items, as these cases illustrate:

A young man advertises on a popular website that his car is for sale. A prospective buyer takes it for a spin, but doesn't return. The trusting soul reports the theft to the police but soon becomes impatient when he sees a new posting about a car for sale that suspiciously resembles his on the same website. He arranges with the "owner" to meet at a gas station to take it for a test drive. The do-it-yourself sting operation succeeds when the thief drives up in the stolen car, the victim calls the police, and they arrest the crook red-handed as he bolts from the vehicle. (Doyle and Fredericks, 2011)

■■■

A young man's laptop is stolen by a burglar. The owner activates a built-in spyware program that snaps pictures of the thief and captures screenshots of his email, including a business address of a company. The owner searches for the company's address and then plots its exact location on a mapping website. Then he notifies the local police department in that jurisdiction; however, the police deem the theft of his laptop to be a very low-priority matter. So he posts pictures and details about the apparent thief on a website, and then mobilizes his friends via social networking until the story goes viral. He is invited to appear on a national television network's morning news program, and vents his frustration about law enforcement's inaction. Shortly after his appearance in the mainstream media, he receives a call from the local police department that the thief has been arrested and that his laptop has been recovered. (Lindzon, 2011)

Measuring Progress Toward a Victim-Oriented Police Department

The adoption of a **community policing** approach by many departments symbolizes a commitment to granting residents a larger say in guiding the operations and policies of a branch of local government that is supposed to protect and serve them. Community policing also has opened the door to a more victim-oriented approach within law enforcement. What would a "consumer-centered" or "user-friendly" model entail? What **performance measures** indicate that a department is effectively carrying out its mission to protect and serve the residents of its jurisdiction?

First of all, a victim-oriented department would extend outreach efforts to neighborhood residents to build their confidence that they get an appropriate reception if they bring their problems to a police station. A user-friendly department would facilitate the process for lodging complaints, making it as stress free and as streamlined as possible. Complaints about very minor matters might even be taken over the phone or by filling out a form online. If a greater proportion of victims become encouraged to come forward, an indicator of success would be a temporary rise in the crime rate because a higher percentage of incidents would be reported and recorded. (A localized version of the *NCVS* could be used to discover what percentage of victims still are not reporting various types of crimes, and why.)

When victims come forward, they expect to be handled with care. To achieve this goal, a department would have to train its officers to deliver death notifications with compassion, to better comfort traumatized persons, to provide physical and psychological first aid, and to avoid inflicting second wounds in the form of victim-blaming accusations. The particular needs of children, battered women, rape victims, and disabled persons also would be addressed effectively by specialized squads of highly trained detectives (see Chapters 9 and 10). Officers could also be better trained to spot a complainant who is making a false charge, so that all complainants would not be greeted with skepticism as possible fakers and liars, and detectives would not subject them to needless accusatory questioning. Customer-satisfaction surveys could be an appropriate way to measure whether complainants felt departments were handling their cases with care.

A victim-oriented department would dispatch officers quickly to 911 calls for help. Statistics showing downward trends in response times to emergencies would indicate progress along this front. Presumably, police forces constantly work to solve as many crimes

as possible. But victim-oriented forces would not only seek to make arrests in high-profile cases that merit intense media coverage, but also in the much more common minor cases that revolve around stolen property. Clearance rates should rise in departments that are becoming more user-friendly, indicating that victims and witnesses are cooperating with investigations to a greater degree, sharing all they know, looking at mug shots, and picking suspects out of lineups. Similarly, local law enforcement agencies would make greater efforts to recover stolen property and return it to its rightful owner after it is no longer needed for court proceedings. Officers and detectives would gather evidence properly so that it can be entered as a prosecution exhibit against the accused. Court records about the percent of charges at the time of arrest that are later dropped by the prosecutor, or dismissed by the judge, or that are dramatically reduced because of improperly obtained evidence can be examined to monitor progress along this front. All these performance measures reporting rates, average response times to emergencies, clearance rates, and stolen property recovery rates— would be published and posted on the department's website each year, reflecting its commitment to transparency and accountability.

A victim-oriented department would also set up a victim advocacy unit. The advocates would provide guidance and support for complainants as their cases are processed through the system, refer them to counseling, walk them step by step through the proper channels to obtain orders of protection or emergency shelter or compensation from a state fund, and make sure that they are safe and reasonably satisfied with the way they were treated (Duncan, 2014). Besides potentially achieving higher reporting rates, more tips from the public, greater levels of cooperation from witnesses, and better clearance rates, a victim-friendly department might benefit in an additional way. Its officers might enjoy higher morale and enhanced job satisfaction (IACP, 2009).

A key criterion for evaluation could be this: Does a department that claims to be victim-oriented do all that it can to provide the same high-quality services to the public as it delivers to fellow officers and to members of their families whenever they are directly harmed by criminals? If the department falls far short on this bottom-line performance indicator, then it needs to re-examine its priorities and revamp its operations.

SUMMARY

In their pursuit of justice—whether the goal is punishment of or treatment for the offender or restitution for their losses—victims might find themselves in conflicting rather than cooperative relationships with police officers and detectives.

When they report crimes, victims want the police to respond quickly, administer psychological and physical first aid effectively, believe their accounts, apprehend suspects, gather evidence that is admissible in court, and get back any property that was taken from them. However, uniformed officers and detectives might be slow to arrive, handle victims insensitively, consider their versions of events unbelievable or exaggerated, fail to solve their cases, and be unable to recover their stolen goods. Various statistical measures collected by the *NCVS* and the *UCR* (such as reporting rates, response times, clearance rates, and property recovery rates) can be used as performance indicators to provide some rough estimates about how often victims receive the services and assistance they seek from their local police and sheriff's departments that pledge to serve and protect them.

KEY TERMS DEFINED IN THE GLOSSARY

burnout, 189

citizen's arrest, 200

clearance rates, 193

cold case squads, 198

community policing, 201

Compstat, 185

defounding, 191

differential reporting rates, 184

misprision of a felony, 188

performance measures, 202

second wound, 189

unfounding, 191

QUESTIONS FOR DISCUSSION AND DEBATE

1. Make up some details about three very different robberies. Then, explain why, in your opinion, it is in their best interest for these victims to seek either punishment, offender rehabilitation, or restitution in each of these cases.

2. Make up some details about a shooting, and then discuss what a police department ideally could do for the injured person in this case. Then reverse the outcomes, and highlight every problem with the local police that could further compound the suffering of this victim.

CRITICAL THINKING QUESTIONS

1. From the viewpoint of police chiefs, argue that victims have unrealistically high expectations and make unreasonable demands in terms of the department's priorities, resources, and personnel.

2. Speculate about the causes of the falling clearance rates for solving crimes of violence in recent decades.

3. Speculate about the reasons why stolen property recovery rates are so low.

SUGGESTED RESEARCH PROJECTS

1. Interview local residents who have suffered crimes such as robberies, vehicle break-ins, petty thefts, and burglaries, and find out whether they reported the incidents to the police. Question them about why they did or did not. Ask those who reported crimes whether they know if their cases were solved by an arrest.

2. Meet with local police officials and discover what the department's clearance rate is for the seven index crimes, its response time to 911 calls, the percentage of auto theft or robbery complaints that were determined to be unfounded, and the recovery rate for stolen motor vehicles. See if this information is contained in a publicly available annual report or on a departmental website. If these statistics are not made public, should they be?

3. Draw up a comprehensive checklist of all the victim-oriented services that could and should be offered by a user-friendly police department. Rate your local department on how well it provides each form of assistance and support to crime victims.

4. Evaluate the websites of a number of police departments of interest to you. Are performance measures disclosed? Does the information that is posted on the Internet appear in a victim-friendly format (for example, what to do if…, how to…) and is some of it translated into different languages?

7

Victims' Rights and the Criminal Justice System

LEARNING OBJECTIVES

To realize that some cases of interpersonal violence and theft will be handled in the juvenile justice system.

To become familiar with the legal rights victims have gained in recent decades.

continued

THE ADULT CRIMINAL JUSTICE SYSTEM VERSUS THE JUVENILE JUSTICE SYSTEM

This chapter examines what might happen in cases that the police have solved by arresting an adult. As the fate of the accused person is determined by the criminal justice system, victims will interact with prosecutors, defense attorneys, judges, juries, and—if the defendant is convicted—corrections officials. Cooperation is the desired outcome, but conflict might erupt over certain divisive issues with these criminal justice professionals and the agencies that employ them.

Note that this chapter focuses on how cases are processed by the legal system when adults are arrested by the police. Each state has the authority under the constitution to determine at what age adulthood begins and for which crimes this distinction applies. For example, in New York, state legislators decided that persons as young as 16 might be considered as adults, and their cases could be processed in the adult system. When the police arrest a suspect as young as 13 for murder, he could be considered as sufficiently mature to face adult penalties, such as a life sentence, if the prosecutor chooses to pursue this get-tough option. In nearly all the other states, the age when individuals can be held fully responsible for their criminal behavior is 18.

In each state, arrestees who are not old enough to be considered adults are handled by its juvenile justice system. The nation's first juvenile court was set up in Cook County Illinois (covering Chicago) in 1899. Most states quickly followed suit. Consequently, ever since the early 1900s, a "double standard of justice" has prevailed. Almost everyone feels that a double standard based on the defendant's—or the victim's—race or social class is not fair, but most people will agree that handling a case differently because the suspect is young and immature is justifiable. For example, if a youngster steals a car, drives off, and later wrecks it and then abandons it, this vehicle theft ought to handled differently than a case in which a grown-up steals a car and drives it off to a chop shop where it is dismantled so that its sheet metal parts can be sold on the black market to repair crash damaged vehicles. Yet, in both cases, a motorist has lost a car to a thief. Similarly, if a 14-year-old breaks into a house to steal things, the authorities will view the crime in a different light than if an adult burglarized the dwelling, even though the losses experienced by the home-owner might be identical.

This separate system is supposed to operate according to a different set of principles (which in many states emphasize treatment over punishment, and sometimes, "restorative justice," which is analyzed in Chapter 13). Consequently, not only arrestees but also their victims are handled differently. The individuals injured by juvenile delinquents are not permitted to play an active role and can exercise fewer options and rights in family courts or juvenile courts, where judges have much more discretion to shape outcomes. For example, in about one quarter of the states, all the proceedings will be held behind closed doors and victims will be barred from attending. The names of the accused teenagers might not be disclosed in news reports, even if the identities of the persons they robbed, shot, or stabbed are revealed. Young arrestees won't be released on bail but they are likely to be sent home to their parents or legal guardians, and those who feel directly threatened by their return to the community (often, teenagers themselves) won't have input into this decision. Injured parties won't testify in front of jurors and television cameras because jury trials aren't held. Youthful offenders "adjudicated" as delinquents probably will be placed on probation, but their victims won't have much of a say in that outcome either. However, more research needs to be carried out to determine how these procedural differences actually affect the persons these juveniles harm (for example, see Carr, Lord, and Maier, 2003).

What is known is that juveniles account for a considerable proportion of all persons accused of crimes involving interpersonal violence and theft. In 11 percent of the violent crime cases that police cleared, the arrestees were under the age of 18. In 16 percent of the solved property crimes, juveniles were taken into custody, according to the FBI's *Uniform Crime Report* for 2013. Therefore, a considerable number of victims will discover that their solved cases will be diverted into the juvenile justice system or family courts.

TOWARD GREATER FORMAL LEGAL RIGHTS WITHIN THE CRIMINAL JUSTICE SYSTEM

The struggle to gain guarantees and protections from the government has motivated reformers and dissidents throughout history. Legal rights serve as a remedy for injustice and abuse as well as a basis for independent and autonomous action. A number of movements seeking liberation, empowerment, equality, and social justice have sought greater rights for their constituencies. The most well-known and influential include the civil rights, women's rights, workers' rights, consumers' rights, students' rights, children's rights, gay rights, mental patients' rights, and prisoners' rights movements. The victims' rights movement that arose during the 1960s falls within this reformist tradition.

The legal rights of journalists, political activists, criminal defendants, and convicts have been derived from the safeguards and guarantees specified in the first 10 amendments to the Constitution, which taken together are referred to as the Bill of Rights. But the framers of the Constitution did not enumerate any specific rights for crime victims. The pledges, entitlements, privileges, benefits, options, practices, and opportunities for redress commonly referred to as **victims' rights** spring from several different sources. A few rights originated as idiosyncratic policies adopted by certain caring and innovative officials, such as police chiefs, district attorneys, trial judges, and probation officers. Other rights were derived from case law based on court decisions. The remainder was established by laws passed by city and county governments, statutes enacted by state legislatures, acts approved by Congress, and referenda placed on the ballot by advocacy groups and endorsed by voters. As a result, an inconsistent assortment of rights has developed that varies markedly from state to state, jurisdiction (county or municipality) to jurisdiction, and even courthouse to courthouse.

One trend is certain: Since the 1960s, victims' rights have been proliferating in the legislative arena and expanding geographically because of the successful campaigns of a social movement. Composed of activists, support groups, concerned professionals (like lawyers and doctors), nonprofit organizations, and coalitions forging broad alliances, this movement has won many victories and has changed the way the public, the media, businesses, and elected officials view the crime problem and the individuals who suffer because of it. The driving force behind the movement is the personal commitment of its leading grassroots activists. Most are survivors in the best sense of the word—they are individuals who have endured terrible ordeals or are close family members of people who perished; they have summoned up the strength to demonstrate exemplary resiliency to overcome adversity, and effectively channeled their grief and anger into constructive outlets. They have struggled for social change and justice so that fewer people in the future will have to suffer what they went through. Some examples of people on the frontlines of reform who were chosen by fate to become organizers and leaders with a new sense of purpose appear in Box 7.1.

A self-reinforcing cycle is operating: As more victims become aware of their rights and begin to exercise them, these rights become accepted and honored within the criminal justice system. These victories encourage victims and their allies to raise new demands for further rights (Stark and Goldstein, 1985; and Viano, 1987).

Recent improvements in cruise ship passenger safety illustrate this self-reinforcing cycle in action. After a rash of incidents in which passengers were murdered, assaulted, raped, or mysteriously disappeared at sea, Congress responded to recommendations made by a group of victimized passengers and passed the Cruise Vessel Security and Safety Act in 2010. The law required these huge floating five-star hotels to better address the needs of their customers who were harmed far from home. Ships must have

---

B O X   7.1   Inspiring Examples of Victim Activism

Mobilizing against drunk drivers

A mother whose teenage daughter was run over by an intoxicated driver starts a group that successfully changes public attitudes about mixing drinking with driving and persuades criminal justice officials that people injured in drunk driving collisions are victims of crimes—not accidents.

Assisting law enforcement agencies to track down fugitives

A father whose son is kidnapped and decapitated by a killer who is never caught hosts a television program that broadcasts cases from police departments' "most wanted" lists so viewers can phone in tips to capture these suspects.

Covering trials of the rich and famous from a pro-victim angle

A novelist and journalist whose actress daughter is murdered by her ex-lover writes a book about attending her killer's trial and then hosts a television program that focuses on powerful and privileged people who get in trouble with the law and the people they harm.

Assisting the search for missing children

A father whose 12-year-old daughter was abducted and murdered establishes a foundation that helps locate missing children.

Setting up a foundation to protect children from kidnappers

A young woman who was abducted by a husband and wife team and repeatedly raped during her nine months of captivity finally is rescued, goes to college, gets married, writes an autobiography, and establishes a nonprofit organization that teaches children how to take defensive measures to resist a stranger's aggression.

Establishing one of the first victims' rights organizations

A wealthy woman may have been poisoned by her husband (his original conviction for attempted murder was overturned and he was acquitted after a second trial; she remained in a coma for 28 years before dying in 2008). Her son and daughter, convinced that their mother's coma resulted from a crime, use a portion of her fortune to found one of the first organizations that helps all kinds of victims.

Compelling college administrations to publicize information about crimes on campus

The parents of a daughter whose murder in a dormitory was initially downplayed by college authorities set up a watchdog group that convinces Congress to impose crime reporting requirements on image-conscious university administrations.

Campaigning for restrictions on gun availability

A White House press secretary, who was shot in the head by an assassin aiming to kill the president, becomes a leading

medical personnel on board to treat those who suffer sexual assaults and to stockpile rape kits to collect and preserve evidence. The industry had to install stronger room locks and peepholes on cabin doors, and surveillance cameras in corridors and lounges, to reduce the risks of crew-on-passenger and passenger-on-passenger interpersonal offenses, and to help solve the crimes that did take place during the journey. Cruise ships also must establish and publicize crime reporting procedures to notify the coast guard and the FBI about incidents at sea when they return to American ports. After the law was passed, the House of Representatives held hearings on whether the act was being effectively implemented, as well as about additional ways to

safeguard the millions of vacationers that the ships carry from port to port each year (Anglen, 2014). Apparently, the crime statistics released voluntarily by the giant corporations operating various cruise lines under differing names understate the true scope of the problems at sea and in ports. Only homicides, suspicious deaths, attacks resulting in bodily injury, sexual assaults, and thefts in excess of $10,000 have to be reported to the authorities, and the coast guard only discloses information about incidents that are no longer being investigated by the FBI. Congress discovered in 2013 that only accounts of about 30 crimes were made public out of 950 received, a highly unsatisfactory situation according to the U.S. Government

figure along with his wife in legislative efforts to make it more difficult for emotionally volatile and mentally disturbed people to buy handguns.

A nurse whose husband is shot dead and whose son is severely injured by a man who goes berserk on a commuter train and shoots passengers at random testifies so dramatically for stricter controls over handguns and assault weapons before Congress that she is later elected to the House of Representatives.

A college student who survived a campus massacre produces a film about it and campaigns for an improved National Instant Criminal Background Check System to prevent guns on sale in stores from getting into the wrong hands.

Working to help poverty-stricken teenagers

A social worker whose son was riddled with bullets in a senseless street killing becomes an advocate for at-risk teens from abusive and neglectful families similar to those of the two men who murdered her child.

Mobilizing for community notification laws

The parents of a seven-year-old girl who was raped and murdered by a recently released pedophile living across the street help gather support for state and federal legislation that authorizes criminal justice officials to alert the public whenever a convicted sex offender moves into their neighborhood.

Lobbying for additional DNA testing

A woman whose rapist was finally caught after six years because of a DNA cold hit (match) sets up a group that lobbies for more federal funding to pay for the testing of forensic evidence collected from rape victims. Her advocacy efforts are so successful that Congress places her name on legislation intended to eliminate DNA testing backlogs.

Establishing a support group for parents of murdered children

A mother and father whose daughter was slain by her boyfriend set up a self-help group for grieving families that not only serves their emotional needs during their bereavement but also promotes violence prevention activities and lobbies for greater rights for the next of kin within the legal process.

Organizing a national coalition of victim activists

A murdered young woman's parents establish a network of survivors and activists that pledges to be "of the victims, by the victims, and for the victims" in its support and crime prevention actions.

SOURCES: Weed, 2005; Rondeau and Rondeau, 2006; National Coalition of Victims in Action, 2008; Nemy, 2009; Tobias, 2009; Goodman, 2012; Gross, 2013; and Maloney, 2014.

Accountability Office as well as a victim's group (Hill, 2014). Over the years, the scope of this organization has broadened from seeking improvements in the safety, security and protection of not only passengers but also of members of the crew, and not only from crime but also from medical emergencies (Business Wire, 2014).

The victims' rights movement has institutionalized this self-reinforcing cycle of calling attention to a festering problem and then mobilizing a coalition to bring about reforms by setting aside special days, weeks, and even months each year to attract media attention. Events are held to raise public awareness about the plight of particular groups of victims and the rights that have been recently granted to them to ease their suffering and assist their recovery. Besides a high-profile National Crime Victims Week each April, the calendar is now filled with special events that commemorate a wide variety of persons who have been harmed by all sorts of criminals, from drunk drivers and identity thieves to rapists and murderers (see Box 7.2).

The Quest for a Constitutional Amendment Guaranteeing Victims' Rights

One goal for those seeking to empower victims that has not yet been achieved is to insert pro-victim language into the Bill of Rights. The Sixth Amendment contains provisions that specify how defendants are to be handled in court. Activists and advocacy groups first raised the possibility of updating the Sixth Amendment after a presidential task force recommended rewording it in 1982. But in 1986, reformers decided to postpone this plan to inject additional phrases into the Sixth Amendment in favor of concentrating on a "states first" strategy of securing amendments to state constitutions. By 2011, this approach had succeeded in 33 states (NVCAP, 2011). Also, since 1980, almost every

---

B O X 7.2 Events That Call Attention Not Only to the Plight but also to the Rights of Various Kinds of Victims

Type of Victimization	Awareness Time
National Slavery and Human Trafficking Month	January
National Stalking Awareness Month	January
National Teen Dating Violence Awareness Week	early February
National Youth Violence Prevention Week	late March
National Child Abuse Prevention Month	April
National Sexual Assault Awareness Month	April
National Crime Victims Week	late April
National Peace Officer's Memorial Day	mid-May
National Missing Children's Day	late May
World Elder Abuse Awareness Day	mid-June
National Night Out Against Crime	early August
National Campus Safety Awareness Month	September
National Day of Remembrance for Murder Victims	late September
National Crime Prevention Month	October
National Domestic Violence Awareness Month	October
National Bullying Prevention Awareness Week	early October
Days of Activism Against Gender Violence	late November
Identity Theft Prevention and Awareness Month	December
National Drunk and Drugged Driving Prevention Month	December

SOURCES: Office for Victims of Crime, 2014; and Congressional Victims' Rights Caucus, 2012.

state legislature has passed packages of statutes called a "Victim's Bill of Rights." The common threads running through these amendments and Bill of Rights packages were these promises to victims: to be handled with fairness, respect, and dignity; to be notified in a timely manner about, to be present and to be heard at important judicial proceedings; to promptly get back stolen property that was recovered and held as evidence; to be protected from intimidation and harassment; and to receive restitution or compensation (NCVC, 2011c).

A large but insufficient number of Republicans and Democrats in both the House and the Senate over the years have voiced support for adding to the wording of the Sixth Amendment, as have Presidents Bill Clinton and George Bush.

Proponents of this movement to update the Bill of Rights argued that these federally backed promises would rectify a constitutional imbalance—its enumeration of many rights for suspects, defendants, convicts, and inmates versus its silence on victims' issues. A reworded Sixth Amendment could serve as an equalizer that could end institutionalized second-class treatment. However, the degree of opposition is substantial, even from pro-victim quarters. Civil liberties groups voice a different set of concerns. Adding pro-victim measures to the Sixth Amendment could undermine the presumption of innocence before the defendant's guilt has been established. Empowering victims actually strengthens the coercive powers of the government (police, prosecution, corrections) to detain, punish, imprison, and even execute its citizens. (Senate Committee, 2003).

In 2004, advocates in Congress of a constitutional amendment adopted a compromise strategy and passed the Crime Victim's Rights Act (CVRA) by a vote of 96 to 1. Also known as the Justice for All Act, the CVRA was anticipated to be a formula for success and a model for the states. It resembled the proposed amendment but applied only to the federal criminal code. The act stated that victims of federal offenses have the right to be treated with fairness and with respect for their dignity, privacy, and safety. It pledged that victims would have the right to confer with prosecutors, to be notified about proceedings, and to be heard on issues involving release, negotiated pleas, and sentences. Victims also would have the right to full and timely restitution. Employees of the Department of Justice and other federal agencies as well as federal judges must undertake their best efforts to ensure that these enumerated rights are made known and implemented. The CVRA has the potential to bring about fundamental changes in the Federal Rules of Criminal Procedure that would thoroughly integrate victims into all stages of the justice system's decision-making process, if it is vigorously enforced. If the CVRA proves to be ineffective in the years ahead, then the campaign to amend the Sixth Amendment to the Constitution would resume, its backers vowed (Senate Committee, 2003; Morgenstern and Fisher, 2005; Wood, 2008; and Cassell, 2010).

The Achievements of the Victims' Rights Movement

The rights that crime victims have fought for and secured are so numerous and varied that they must be grouped for comparison and analysis. One way to categorize these newly achieved rights is to note which groups of victims directly need, want, and benefit from a specific right. For example, in 1984, Wisconsin was the first state to adopt a Child Victims' Bill of Rights. Among other provisions, it stipulated that all legal proceedings must be carefully explained to the young complainant in language he or she can understand.

Another way to keep track of rights is to note at which stage of the criminal justice process these options can be exercised. For example, the right to be present at all court proceedings (with the presiding judge's approval) begins at arraignment when bail is considered. At the other end of the spectrum, the right to address the parole board arises years after the convict has been imprisoned. Still another way to classify victims' rights is to note at whose expense they were gained. Conflicts among individuals, groups, and classes permeate society. Rights gained by one group or class enhance its position with respect to its competitors or adversaries. In this **zero-sum game model**, three categories of victims' rights can be discerned: those gained at the direct expense of criminals (more precisely: arrestees, defendants, convicts, inmates, probationers, and parolees); those gained at the expense of the criminal justice system (agency budgets and the privileges and convenience of law enforcement, judicial, and corrections officials); and those gained at the expense of either offenders or officials, depending on how victims exercise their newly authorized influence.

Rights Gained at the Expense of Offenders

Some advocates argue that victims' rights ought to be gained at the expense of offenders' rights. Too much concern has been shown for the rights of criminals, they say, and not enough for the plights of the innocent people they harm. In the unending battle between lawbreakers and law-abiding citizens, the "bad guys" have gained certain advantages within the legal system over the "good guys." To restore some semblance of evenhandedness to the scales of justice that have been tipped or tilted in favor of the wrong side, victims need rights that can match, counter, or even trump the rights of offenders. In this context, reform means reversing certain court decisions and legal trends and shifting the balance of power away from wrongdoers and toward the parties they injured (see Hook, 1972; Carrington, 1975; and President's Task Force, 1982).

Collisions between the rights of victims versus those of suspects, defendants, convicts, probationers, parolees, and prisoners can arise over many issues.

Those who emphasize punishing offenders on behalf of the individuals they harmed assume that the interests of victims and government officials largely coincide: apprehension, prosecution, conviction, and imprisonment. Victims' rights gained at the expense of offenders' rights would include provisions that facilitate conviction of the accused without unreasonable delays, close legal loopholes that enable the defendants to escape their just deserts, increase the likelihood of incarceration, and eliminate unwarranted acts of leniency toward these prisoners, such as early release from confinement. The President's Task Force on Victims of Crime (1982) proposed many

recommendations of this nature, and some were enacted in California in 1982. Other gains that victims might secure at the expense of convicts would be the right to preview and perhaps object to the terms of a proposed plea agreement, and to the recommendations in a presentence report (Cassell and Joffee, 2011).

Some provisions that have been characterized as pro-victim reforms and fit within this punitive and retribution framework are listed in Table 7.1.

Critics of this approach of enhancing victims' rights at the expense of suspects, defendants, convicts, inmates, probationers, and parolees raise a number of objections. First, making convicts suffer more does not mean that the people they hurt suffer less. Second, many of these measures do not really empower victims but simply strengthen the government's ability to control its citizens. Civil libertarians who fear the development of a repressive police state warn that the implementation of antidefendant, pro-police, and pro-prosecutor measures undermines cherished principles: the presumption of innocence and the state's burden of proof. These due process safeguards are subverted when defendants are denied pretrial release, when improperly obtained evidence is used against them, and when the victims' desires for revenge are manipulated by the government to enhance its punitive powers (see Henderson, 1985; Fattah, 1986; Hellerstein, 1989; Hall, 1991; Abramovsky, 1992; Simonson, 1994; and Dubber, 2002).

Rights Gained at the Expense of the System

Some rights that victims gain should come at the expense of justice system officials and agencies that have neglected the needs and wants of their ostensible clients for far too long, advocates say. Society, or more precisely the social system, is partly at fault for the crime problems that plague communities. The state, therefore, is obligated to minimize suffering and to help injured parties recover and become whole again through government intervention, even if offenders cannot be caught or convicted. A preoccupation with punishing lawbreakers must not overshadow the need to assist and support the people they harmed. New laws must guarantee that

TABLE 7.1   Victims' Rights Gained at the Expense of Suspects, Defendants, and Convicts

Subject	Right of Victims
Denial of bail	To be protected from suspects whose pretrial release on bail might endanger them
Protection from further harm	To be reasonably protected during the pretrial release period from the accused through orders of protection and by increased penalties for acts of harassment and intimidation
Defenses	To be assured that defendants cannot avoid imprisonment by pleading not guilty by reason of insanity, through the substitution of guilty and mentally ill, which requires treatment in a mental institution followed by incarceration in prison
Privacy	To be assured that medical records and statements divulged to counselors remain confidential even if requested by the defense during the discovery phase of court proceedings
Evidence	To be assured that defendants cannot benefit from the exclusion of illegally gathered evidence by having all evidence obtained by the police in good faith declared admissible in trials
Offender's age	To be assured that juvenile offenders do not escape full responsibility for serious crimes by having such cases transferred from juvenile court to adult criminal court
Restitution	To receive mandatory repayments from convicts who are put on probation or parole unless a judge explains in writing the reasons for not imposing this obligation
Appeals	To appeal sentences that seem too lenient
Notoriety for profit	To have any royalties and fees paid to notorious criminals confiscated and used to repay victims or to fund victim services
Abuser's tax	To have penalty assessments collected from felons, misdemeanants, and traffic law violators to pay for victim services, compensation, and assistance programs

SOURCES: BJS, 1988; MADD, 1988; NOVA, 1988; NVCAP, 2008.

standards of fair treatment be met that respect the dignity and privacy of injured people. Because extra effort, time, and money must be expended to provide services that were not formerly available on a routine basis, these rights can be considered to have been gained by victims at the expense of the prerogatives of officials (including detectives, assistant district attorneys, and probation officers) and the budgets of agencies (such as court systems and parole boards).

Rights gained at the expense of officials and agencies first were enacted in 1980, when Wisconsin's state legislature passed a comprehensive Bill of Rights for victims and witnesses. The President's Task Force (1982) endorsed similar proposals that were incorporated into federal statutes when Congress approved the Victim/Witness Protection Act. Many states have proclaimed similar assurances, either through specific laws or via more comprehensive legislative packages (see Table 7.2).

In addition to gaining rights at the expense of the criminal justice system, victims have also achieved some protection from the whims of employers in the private as well as the public sectors. Since the start of the new century, a number of states have passed statutes prohibiting employers from threatening, penalizing, or firing victims of sexual assault, domestic violence, and stalking who must take time off from their jobs (work leave) to attend to legal or therapeutic matters (Brown, 2003; and Bulletin Board, 2004).

Rights Gained at the Expense of Offenders, the System, or Both

The boldest demands raised by advocacy groups within the victims' rights movement concern power. Some victims want to influence the outcome of the criminal justice process at key stages from bail hearings to jury selection to sentencing. Instead of being relegated to the role of passive observers,

T A B L E   7.2   Victims' Rights Gained at the Expense of Criminal Justice Agencies and Officials

Subject	Rights of Victims
General rights	To be read their rights as soon as a crime is reported, or to be provided with written information about all obligations, services, and opportunities for protection and reimbursement
Case status	To be kept posted on progress in their cases; to be advised when arrest warrants are issued or suspects are taken into custody
Court appearances	To be notified in advance of all court proceedings and of changes in required court appearances
Secure waiting areas	To be provided with courthouse waiting rooms separate from those used by defendants, defense witnesses, and spectators
Employer intercession	To have the prosecutor explain to the complaining witness's employer that the victim should not be penalized for missing work because of court appearances
Creditor intercession	To have the prosecutor explain to creditors such as banks and landlords that crime-inflicted financial losses require delays in paying bills
Suspect out on bail	To be notified that a suspect arrested for the crime has been released on bail
Negotiated plea	To be notified that both sides have agreed to a plea of guilty in return for some consideration
Sentence and final disposition	To be notified of the verdict and sentence after a trial and of the final disposition after appeals
Work release	To be notified if the convict will be permitted to leave the prison to perform a job during specified hours
Parole hearings	To be notified when a prisoner will be appearing before a parole board to seek early release
Pardon	To be notified if the governor is considering pardoning the convict
Release of a felon	To be notified when a prisoner is to be released on parole or because the sentence has expired
Prison escape	To be notified if the convict has escaped from confinement
Return of stolen property	To have stolen property that has been recovered and held as evidence returned expeditiously by the police or prosecution
Restitution	To repay victims first from any funds collected by the court from the convict before any other legal obligations or fines are paid off
Compensation	To be reimbursed for out-of-pocket expenses for medical bills and lost wages arising from injuries inflicted during a violent crime

SOURCES: BJS, 1988; MADD, 1988; NOVA, 1988; and NVCAP, 2008.

they want to be active participants in the events that shape the outcomes of their cases. This point of view leads to the provision that the injured parties should be present and heard whenever suspects, defendants, and convicts are present and heard.

Participatory rights that victims gain may come at the expense of offenders, agency officials, or both, depending on how this leverage actually is applied. Victims can be seen as allies of the government and as junior partners on the same side as the police and the prosecution in the adversarial system.

Therefore, empowering them means strengthening the coalition of forces seeking to arrest, detain, convict, and punish persons accused of wrongdoing. Enhancing the powers of a potentially repressive state apparatus alarms civil libertarians concerned about safeguarding constitutional rights and maintaining checks and balances. But if victims are visualized as independent actors, then they may not agree with the courses of action taken by their ostensible governmental allies. Calls to empower them might provoke resistance from criminal justice professionals who fear that their agency's mission will be compromised and its budget strained, and that their personal privileges and discretionary authority will be jeopardized (see Karmen, 1992; and Marquis, 2005).

The critical junctures for victim input are arraignments where bail is set, plea negotiations, sentencing hearings, and parole board appearances.

It is often asserted or assumed that victims' highest priority is retribution and that they are likely to seize every opportunity to press for harsher handling of offenders. Vengeful victims might insist that defendants not be offered low bail or generous concessions in return for guilty pleas, that sentences imposed on convicts be as severe as the law allows, and that parole boards reject prisoners' petitions for early release.

In contrast, victims might have different priorities and find themselves at odds with the authorities over how to handle particular cases. For instance, a battered woman's greatest concern might be securing treatment for a violence-prone lover. If so, she might favor diversion of the case from the criminal justice system to allow the wrongdoer to enter a rehabilitation program. Burglary victims focused on receiving full and prompt reimbursement of their financial losses might favor an alternative to incarceration, such as restitution as a condition of probation.

Thus, involving the victim in the decision-making process constrains the free exercise of discretion formerly enjoyed by prosecutors' offices, judges, probation departments, and parole boards. What victims seek when they exercise participatory rights—whether mild or severe punishment, treatment for the offender, or restitution - their wishes might not align with the inclinations of the prosecutor or the judge or members of the parole board.

Pledges about the chance to participate in crucial decisions raise several contentious philosophical and policy questions. Should such formal rights also be extended to someone who does not fit the profile of an innocent, law-abiding, mature victim of a serious crime? For example, should assault victims from unsavory backgrounds—who have arrest records as street gang members, drug dealers, mobsters, and prostitutes, or are currently serving time behind bars—be permitted a say in plea negotiations and

sentencing? If so, should their requests carry less weight? Should victimized children have input? Should people who represent the victim (in their capacity as next of kin, executor of the estate of the deceased, the legal guardian of a minor, lawyer for the family, or volunteer advocate) be granted participatory rights? Should participatory rights be restricted to victims of serious crimes such as felonies or, even more narrowly, only to persons physically injured by violence? And what happens when these participatory rights are violated? What remedies should victims have when criminal justice agencies fail to involve them in the decision-making process or don't live up to the standards for fair treatment?

The lack of enforcement mechanisms highlights another related problem: the absence of clear lines of responsibility for implementation. Which officials or agencies can be held accountable for keeping victims informed of their rights? For example, does the duty of notifying the victim about the right to allocution before sentencing fall to the police officer or civilian employee who records the initial complaint; to the assistant district attorney who prosecutes the case; to the probation officer who prepares the presentence investigation report; or to the clerk in the office of court administration who schedules the postconviction hearing? And how many times must the responsible official attempt to contact a victim before giving up and declaring that a good-faith effort was made?

Providing all complainants with advocates from the outset would be one way to make sure that injured parties find out about all their rights and options and exercise them as best they can. But as yet, no jurisdiction has institutionalized and universalized the practice by assigning an advisor to every complainant who wants one, in the same way that lawyers are routinely provided to all suspects, defendants, and convicts.

Furthermore, if victims were read their rights the same way officers read suspects their Miranda warning prior to interrogation, complainants would learn that they have a right to remain vocal about how they are treated and about what they believe should happen at bail hearings, plea negotiations, sentencing hearings, and parole board meetings (see Karmen,

1995). Complainants would also learn, from advocates, that they have a right to consult with a lawyer and to refuse to answer questions or disclose any personal information that was not directly relevant to the investigation (and usually protected by privacy privileges) about subjects such as sexual history, sexual orientation, medical or mental health records; or disclose information in conversations with doctors, therapists, spouses, attorneys, or religious counselors. At the outset, victims would be warned that any disclosures about personal matters would come to the attention of not only the prosecutor but also the defense counsel, the defendant, expert witnesses, and the judge, in addition to the media and the public, during court proceedings (see Murphy, 1999; Cassell, 2010; and Wood, 2008).

There is no shortage of new ideas about what benefits, services, and rights ought to be developed to address unmet needs. In city councils, state legislatures, and the halls of Congress, new bills are constantly being introduced. Most do not get much support the first or second time around, but as time passes additional sponsors are found and constituencies are organized to lobby for their approval. A listing of bills that were introduced in Congress by Republicans and Democrats who have formed a "victims' rights caucus" during sessions 2009 to 2014 appear in Box 7.3.

VICTIMS AND PROSECUTORS

Prosecutors are the chief law enforcement officials within their jurisdictions. They represent the interests of the county, state, or federal government. But their agencies also supply the lawyers that deal directly with victims. Therefore, prosecutors' offices can be viewed as public law firms offering free legal services to complainants who are willing to cooperate and testify as witnesses. County prosecutors, referred to as **district attorneys** (or state attorneys), usually are elected

---

BOX 7.3 Legislation Introduced in Congress Sponsored by the Crime Victims Caucus

Bills were introduced in the House and Senate from 2009 to 2014 to:

Set up a national database about missing persons and unidentified human remains

Protect youngsters from people with criminal backgrounds who seek to provide child care services

Authorize the use of tax records to help locate a missing or abducted child

Assist child welfare agencies to train employees in identifying and counseling children at risk of becoming victims of human trafficking

Compel parents, legal guardians, or caregivers to quickly notify authorities if a child dies or is considered missing and in grave danger

Make affinity scams as well as fraudulent Internet, television, mail, and telemarketing schemes aimed at senior citizens a federal crime

Set up a national Silver Alert communication network to help locate missing senior citizens

Set up a national Blue Alert system to quickly disseminate information to the public that an on-duty law enforcement officer has been murdered or seriously wounded or is missing after responding to an emergency call, and to provide a description of the suspect

Make the U.S. Department of Defense improve its preventive measures and responses to sexual assault and domestic violence, including the establishment of a sexual assault victim advocate in military units who can receive confidential information

Prevent backlogs of DNA evidence collected from sexual assaults from accumulating at state and local law enforcement agencies and to avoid charging victims for the expenses arising from forensic examinations and rape kits

Expand provisions about family and medical leaves to enable workers to address the plight of relatives who suffer consequences from domestic violence, sexual assault, and stalking

Require institutions of higher learning to include in their campus crime reports incidents involving dating violence, stalking, and domestic violence

Make stalking (with intent to kill, injure, harass, or intimidate) across state lines a federal crime

Be informed in a timely manner about any negotiated plea

Protect money earmarked for the federal Crime Victims Fund derived entirely from fines, forfeitures, and other penalties from being used for other purposes or from being cut

SOURCE: Adapted from the Congressional Victims' Rights Caucus Legislation Compendium for 2011 and 2014 (VRC.org, 2014).

officials (but may be appointed by a governor). The lawyers who actually handle criminal cases and personally work with victims are called **assistant district attorneys** (ADAs) but are also referred to as assistant prosecutors or assistant state attorneys in some jurisdictions. Around the nation, approximately 2,340 prosecutors' offices pursue felony cases in state courts of general jurisdiction. These government lawyers representing victims can become injured parties themselves. About 3 percent of the chief prosecutors and 6 percent of their ADAs reported that they personally had been assaulted in 2005, according to a nationwide survey (Perry, 2006).

To a great extent, victims are on the same side as the government in the criminal justice process. Prosecutors and victims therefore are natural allies who ought to cooperate with each other. Prosecutors might want to do what is best for victims, but they also are concerned about their careers and political futures, the well-being of their agencies, and the general good of the entire community and society. Attending to these concerns and juggling these competing interests can cause conflicts to erupt between prosecutors and the injured parties they purport to represent.

Prosecutors' offices can and should serve victims in a number of different ways. First of all, they can keep their clients informed of the status of their cases, from the initial charges lodged against defendants to the release of convicts on parole. Second, ADAs can help the individuals they represent achieve justice by conveying to the attention of judges their clients' views on questions of bail, continuances, dismissed cases and dropped charges, negotiated pleas, sentences, and restitution arrangements. Third, they can take steps to protect their clients from harassment, threats, injuries, and other forms of intimidation and reprisals. Fourth, ADAs can try to resolve cases as quickly as possible without unnecessary delays and help their clients minimize losses of time and money by notifying them of upcoming court appearances and scheduling changes. Fifth, ADAs can assist victims in retrieving stolen property recovered by police and seized as evidence (President's Task Force, 1982).

Sometimes prosecutors are able to balance the interests of the government, their own bureaucracies,

and their clients without much conflict. But in certain cases, prosecutors cannot do what is best for all of their constituencies simultaneously. Conflicts can arise between the aims of the government and the outcome desired by those who were harmed. Conflicts also can emerge between the bureaucracy that employs prosecutors and injured parties who are the clients, customers, or consumers of their services. Finally, prosecutors advancing their careers may not follow unpopular courses of action favored by their clients.

In all of these potential conflicts, if prosecutors must sacrifice the interests of any party, it is most likely to be those of the victim, and not of the government, their bureaucracy, or their own careers. Victims can feel betrayed if their lawyers do not look after their needs and wants. Or to put it another way, a lawyer—assigned without choice by the government and charging no fee—might not do a satisfactory job from a client's standpoint.

Assisting Victims and Other Witnesses for the State

The difficulties, inconveniences, and frustrations faced by people serving as witnesses for the prosecution have been well-known for decades. As far back as 1931, the National Commission on Law Observance and Enforcement commented that the administration of justice was suffering because of the economic burdens imposed on citizens who participated in trials. In 1938, the American Bar Association noted that witness fees were deplorably low, courthouse accommodations were inadequate, intimidation went unchecked, and witnesses' time was often wasted. In 1967, the President's Commission on Law Enforcement and Administration of Justice reached similar conclusions. In 1973, the Courts Task Force of the National Advisory Commission on Criminal Justice Standards and Goals noted that the failure of victims and witnesses to appear at judicial proceedings when summoned was a major reason for cases being dismissed. Noncooperation was attributed to the high personal costs of involvement incurred by citizens who initially were willing to meet their civic obligations (see McDonald, 1976).

In the past, victims serving as prosecution witnesses often were mistreated in a number of ways. They would be subpoenaed to appear at a courtroom, grand jury room, or prosecutor's office. They would wait for hours in dingy corridors or in other grim surroundings. Busy officials would ignore them as they stood around bewildered and anxious. Often, they wouldn't be called to testify or make statements because of last-minute adjournments. Accomplishing nothing, they would miss work and lose wages, be absent from classes at school, or fail to meet their responsibilities at home. In most jurisdictions, they would receive insultingly low witness fees for their time and trouble. In certain metropolitan areas, they would receive no compensation at all because no official informed them of their eligibility and of the proper application procedures. Their experiences often could be characterized as dreary, time-consuming, depressing, exhausting, confusing, frustrating, and frightening (Ash, 1972).

In 1974, the National District Attorneys Association (NDAA) commissioned a survey to determine the extent to which victims and other witnesses for the prosecution encountered these types of problems. The survey documented that about 10 percent never were notified that an arrest had been made in their case. Nearly 30 percent never got their stolen property back, even though it had been used as evidence. About 60 percent of injured persons were not informed of their right to file a claim for financial reimbursement. Roughly 45 percent reported that no one had explained to them what their court appearance would entail. About 25 percent of witnesses, including victims, summoned to court ultimately were not asked to testify. Even though nearly 80 percent lost pay to appear, about 95 percent received no witness fees. As a final insult, around 40 percent were never notified of the outcome of the case (Lynch, 1976).

To address these problems, the Law Enforcement Assistance Administration funded the first **Victim/ Witness Assistance Projects (VWAPs)** through the NDAA. Pilot programs were set up in prosecutors' offices in California, Illinois, Utah, Colorado, Kentucky, Louisiana, Pennsylvania, and New York during the mid-1970s (Schneider and Schneider,

1981; and Geis, 1983). Since then, most prosecutors' offices have established VWAPS. A nationwide survey determined that victim advocates made up 6 percent of all the persons working for prosecutors' offices. Large offices in big cities employed 13 advocates on average, although the median in all offices, large and small, was just one person (Perry, 2006).

Several assumptions underlie the growth and development of these programs. One is that providing services will elicit greater cooperation from victims and witnesses. Presumably, well-briefed, self-confident witnesses who have benefited from such programs will be more willing to put up with the hardships of testifying in court, leading to lower dismissal rates and higher conviction rates, the standards by which prosecutors' offices are judged. Also, offering services to a group perceived to be highly deserving of governmental assistance will be good for community relations. Public confidence and faith in the criminal justice system will thus be restored, resulting in higher levels of cooperation within jurisdictions that have these programs (Rootsaert, 1987).

Most VWAPs are charged with the laudable but vaguely defined mission of helping victims, aiding witnesses, and furthering the goals of law enforcement. In the best programs, agency personnel intervene as soon as possible after an offense is committed, providing immediate relief to the injured parties through services that include hotlines; crisis counseling; and emergency shelter, food, transportation, and immediate lock repairs. Some projects provide translators, guidance about replacing lost documents, and assistance in getting back stolen property recovered by the police. Most make referrals to social service and mental health agencies for those needing long-term care and counseling. All programs furnish information about opportunities for reimbursement of losses and eligibility for compensation benefits (see Chapter 12). A few offer mediation services for victims who seek to reconcile their differences with their offenders (see Chapter 13). To encourage witness cooperation, pamphlets are distributed about the adjudication process (with titles like "What Happens in Court?" and "Your Rights as a Crime Victim"). Through a case-monitoring and notification system, the staff keeps victims and other witnesses advised of indictments, postponements and continuances, negotiated pleas, convictions, acquittals, and other developments. Linked to the notification system is a telephone alert or on-call system to prevent unnecessary trips to court if dates are changed on short notice, which also avoids wasting the time of police officers who serve as witnesses.

Some programs also have set up reception centers exclusively for prosecution witnesses in courthouses to provide a secure waiting room so that offenders and their families and friends won't get any last-minute opportunities for intimidation. Transportation to and from court, escorts, and child care frequently are available. Help in obtaining witness fees also is provided. The staff in some programs may go as far as to intercede with employers and landlords and other creditors who might not appreciate the stresses and financial difficulties witnesses face (Schneider and Schneider, 1981; Geis, 1983; Weigend, 1983; and Rootsaert, 1987).

Requirements about notification, protection (such as separate waiting areas in courthouses), and intercession (with employers and creditors) increase the justice system's workloads and costs. A nationwide survey of prosecutors' offices at the end of the century discovered that most district attorneys reported that new victims' rights laws had imposed significant unfunded burdens on their limited budgets in the form of additional staff and more mailings and phone contacts (Davis, Henderson, and Rabbitt, 2002).

Some signs that VWAPs are reducing the mistreatment of victims are evident. In 1974, only 35 percent of the offices of district attorneys routinely notified victims of felonies of the outcomes in their cases; 97 percent of these offices did so by 1992, according to the National Prosecutor Survey Program (Dawson, Smith, and DeFrances, 1993).

The establishment of VWAPs has raised some constitutional and ethical concerns. To deny services to a victim whose cooperation is not needed (or who desires to pursue a case that the prosecutor's office wants to drop) would be unfair but not illegal, since the aid is granted as a privilege rather than as a right. To deny similar services (free parking, child care, last-minute phone calls canceling a scheduled appearance) to witnesses for the defense would violate notions of fairness within the adversary system. As long as the defendant is presumed

innocent unless proven guilty, evenhanded treatment of all witnesses should prevail. Rapport between victims and VWAP personnel that becomes too close can cause another problem: The testimony given in court can be considered coached or rehearsed if it departs from the original statements the complainants and witnesses made and covers up contradictions in order to make the most convincing case against the defendant.

Protecting Victims Who Serve as Witnesses for the Prosecution

A 19-year-old alleges he was shot in the face in a playground by a 21-year-old (a repeat offender who has a history of intimidating witnesses). The accused is jailed. A month before the trial, someone fires close to 20 bullets into the 19-year-old's mother's home while he is away and three children and a grandchild are inside. The 19-year-old, who has been living with out-of-town relatives, decides not to testify as a witness for the prosecution. "I'm scared for my family. I'm sorry for the danger I put them in. They don't deserve this. If I testify and put him away for good, what does that even do? He's in jail now, and somebody still shot at my family." (Newall, 2011)

People who are unsure about whether to report crimes, press charges, and testify in court certainly could be dissuaded by chilling tales like this one. Victims who agree to serve as prosecution witnesses need to be protected from intimidation and reprisals. The gravest dangers are faced by individuals harmed by drug-dealing crews, defectors from street gangs and mob syndicates, and battered women trying to break free from abusive mates. Intimidation can range from nuisance phone calls, stalking, and explicit threats of physical attacks to property damage (vandalism) and even deadly assaults. Offenders or the defendants' friends or relatives can attempt to scare victims during face-to-face confrontations that can take place in police stations and courthouses, as well as in neighborhoods and homes. The fear of reprisals can cause a victim to ask that charges be dropped, or simply to not show up to testify, or to recant earlier testimony when cross-examined. When intimidation succeeds, prosecutors are forced to drop charges, judges dismiss cases, juries fail to convict, and guilty parties go free (Gately, 2005).

Because complainants' perceptions of the risks of cooperation determine whether they will testify in court, the primary responsibility for safeguarding the well-being of witnesses for the state falls to the lawyer handling the case for the government. When prosecutors don't react to acts of intimidation by providing police protection, one of the victim's worst fears is confirmed—namely, that the criminal justice system can't provide security from further harm and that the only way to avoid reprisals is to stop cooperating. If left unaddressed, these incidents convey the message that complainants are on their own, and they signify to offenders that witness tampering is worth a try. It may have the desired effect, and usually it carries little risk of additional penalties (see Docksai, 1979; President's Task Force, 1982; Davis, 1983; and Healy, 1995).

Just how serious is the problem of intimidation? How many complainants suffer acts of intimidation after seeking help from the authorities? How many crimes go unreported because the victim fears retaliation? The annual rates of nonreporting due to fear of reprisal are measured by the NCVS. Each year only a small percentage of respondents admit to interviewers that worries about retaliation stopped them from informing the police about violent crimes. Fear inhibits around 10 percent of all rape victims each year from trying to get their attackers in trouble with the law. Worries about what the offender might do are less of a deterrent to reporting in cases of simple assaults, aggravated assaults (like shootings and stabbings), and robberies (BJS, 2008c). (The percentages can fluctuate considerably from year to year because the number of survey respondents who were harmed in these specific ways is extremely small, statistically speaking.) As for changes over time, intimidation levels apparently have not changed substantially over the past few decades; if anything, the percentages might be rising when it comes to robbery and minor assaults. The situation certainly is not improving. However, based on this evidence from NCVS findings from

the 1980s up to 2008, overall, it appears that this problem actually is not of major importance.

But these statistics might yield false impressions. Measuring intimidation is very difficult, in part because would-be complainants (and witnesses) who are successfully intimidated might be too afraid to disclose their plight not only to detectives and prosecutors but also to NCVS interviewers. Also, intimidation can be based on "what if…" fears even if offenders don't actually threaten reprisals. The actual number of nonreporting and noncooperating individuals really cannot be accurately determined. Various studies have yielded contradictory findings about how often injured parties are effectively intimidated by the persons that they accuse of harming them (see Fried, 1982; and Glaberson, 2003).When investigative journalists contended that witness fear was a factor in virtually every violent crime prosecution in Philadelphia, a senator proposed to make witness intimidation into a federal offense (Phillips and McCoy, 2010).

Several aspects of the intimidation problem still need further study. Which groups are more vulnerable to fears of reprisals than others (in terms of age, sex, race/ethnicity, immigration status, and prior involvement with the justice system either as a complainant or as a defendant)? What behaviors or consequences are considered to be most threatening? What form of retribution do victims fear more, acts directed against themselves or their loved ones? Why do some persons brave the risks despite efforts to silence them? What services do some injured parties insist must be provided in order for them to be willing to cooperate and testify? Where do the complainants live and work vis-à-vis the intimidators who threaten them? At what times of day or at what stages in the legal process (before or after lineups or court proceedings), and places (schools, job sites, recreational areas) do they feel most vulnerable? Are issues of shared responsibility, prior victim–offender relationships, family ties, and neighborhood subcultures significant factors in the intimidation equation (see Dedel, 2006)?

The problem of intimidation goes beyond direct threats. Would-be complainants may experience strong pressures from families and friends not to come forward and tell police what happened. As one journalist dramatically put it, in many urban neighborhoods, "talking to the law has become a mortal sin, a dishonorable act punishable by social banishment—or worse" (Kahn, 2007). Subjected to this "cultural intimidation" by their community to not "snitch," to the authorities, the casualties of beatings, stabbings, and shootings may be forced to either settle the score privately or to let the matter rest. But that only perpetuates a cycle of attacks and retaliatory strikes as part of a neighborhood subculture of violence that adds to the level of danger and misery in high-crime areas, especially in poverty-stricken inner-city areas. Government officials and community activists need to counteract this drift toward "do-it-yourself" acts of revenge that are deemed to be "street justice" (see Chapter 13) by developing creative ways to protect those who are urged by officials to cooperate with law enforcement agencies and the prosecution (Kahn, 2007).

This often-cited example shows how a person who did her civic duty by cooperating with the authorities ended up murdered, along with her family, sparking a public outcry for more effective witness protection strategies:

> *A woman repeatedly files complaints with the police against the dealers who sell drugs in front of her row house in a tough urban area. One night, an angry 21-year-old dealer kicks open her front door and throws a firebomb inside. The woman, her husband, and her five children are burned to death in the resulting inferno. The dealer is sentenced to life behind bars without parole, and local residents hold a vigil each year to commemorate her courage and sacrifice. After remaining boarded-up for years, the row house is renovated and turned into a "safe haven community center" named after her. It offers a computer lab, an arts and crafts program, and other activities to children who live nearby. A bright blue light flashes 24 hours a day, reminding passers-by—as well as street-level dealers—that a surveillance camera is trained on that corner. (Simmons, 2007)*

Much of the intimidation problem can be traced to officials who have shirked their responsibilities to victims. Police officers might con victims into cooperating by making empty promises of added protection, knowing full well that their precincts don't have the resources to provide such special attention. Because attrition lightens their workload, ADAs might allow cases to collapse when key witnesses and complainants fail to appear after being subpoenaed—perhaps due to intimidation. Judges may not be vigilant for the same reason: Intimidation leads to nonappearances and ultimately dismissals, which reduces caseloads. To reduce fears about reprisals, the American Bar Association's Committee on Victims (1979) put forward five recommendations decades ago, but these measures still have not been implemented in many jurisdictions. The ABA urged that legislatures should make attempts at intimidation a misdemeanor. Police forces ought to set up victim/witness protection squads. Judges should issue orders of protection and consider violations as grounds for contempt-of-court citations and revocations of bail. Also, judges should grant continuances rather than drop all charges against defendants if complaining witnesses mysteriously fail to appear when subpoenaed. Prosecutors must avoid carelessly revealing information concerning the whereabouts of victims, even after cases are resolved.

Prosecutors always have had to coax victims and other witnesses to cooperate by offering them protective services until the trial is over, or even longer. However, inadequate funding limits the ability of prosecutors' offices to offer these protective measures to all who need them (New York State Law Enforcement Council, 1994). Also, some victims understandably are reluctant to accept offers of protection if it means uprooting their families and virtually starting their lives over, as this case illustrates.

> *A mother's house is riddled with bullets because her son is willing to testify against a young man who allegedly shot him. The district attorney's office offers to move her and her family to another town with the help of the state's witness relocation program. The program would pay for 120 days of temporary housing, moving expenses, storage costs, and two months' rent. But the family would have to agree never to return to the neighborhood where they*

have other family members and friends. The mother turns down the government's offer. Her fiancé explains, "That house is everything she's earned in life. It's hard for her to turn her back on it." Noting that she has nearly finished paying off the mortgage after living in her home for 16 years and raising seven children in it, she despairs, "It just doesn't work for us. We will do our best to hang in there, I guess." When she tells her son to keep away from the neighborhood, he decides he won't testify.
(Newall, 2011)

The establishment of witness-protection programs on the state and federal levels represents the government's greatest possible commitment to address the threat of reprisals. These secretive programs provide tight security to victims, witnesses, and their immediate families. Their services are intended primarily to safeguard witnesses willing to testify against criminal organizations like mob families, street gangs, and drug trafficking networks. Often the beneficiaries are not really victims but lawbreakers like mob turncoats, former drug dealers, and defectors from street gangs. The federal Witness Security Program promises relocation, new identities, new jobs, and payment of moving expenses (U.S. Marshals Service, 2011). Successful relocation, even if at a temporary shelter or safe house and on an emergency basis, requires a multi-agency response that usually involves police, prosecutors, public housing agencies, and social service providers. Lesser measures require sturdier locks, alarm systems, stepped-up police patrols, and escorts; efforts to avoid publicly identifying cooperating witnesses so they won't be labeled as "rats" or "snitches"; measures to limit contacts with potential intimidators (through unlisted numbers, caller ID, and call blocking); and supportive services through existing VWAPS. Also, the authorities must admonish potential intimidators, assist victims to obtain restraining orders and no-contact conditions of bail, and enforce speedy trial provisions and witness tampering statutes. Compelling victims to testify by holding them as material witnesses or threatening them with contempt of court usually is ineffective (Dedel, 2006).

In sum, jurisdictions that fail to adequately confront the problem of victim and witness intimidation will suffer from high levels of retaliatory violence, low levels of public confidence in the ability of the criminal justice system to protect them, low reporting rates, subpar clearance rates, and reduced conviction rates.

To be fair and balanced, one additional type of intimidation must be addressed. One-sided formulations of the intimidation problem imply that it is improper for anyone other than law enforcement agents to contact witnesses and victims. But an important principle of the adversary system is that a person accused of a crime has a constitutional right to confront his accusers. Therefore, defense attorneys must be allowed to interview witnesses and compel them to testify truthfully. But reluctant witnesses who have information that will help the case of the accused also can be intimidated—not by the threat of violence but by worries about unfavorable media coverage and by fear of harassment by the authorities, especially in highly publicized "must-win" cases (see American Bar Association Committee on Victims, 1979).

Dismissing Charges and Rejecting Cases

Crime victims, police officers, and prosecutors are all supposed to be on the same side within the adversary system. Yet their alliance—based in theory on a common commitment to convict people guilty of crimes—often unravels. Victims may feel rebuffed and abandoned when prosecutors dismiss or reduce charges and counts against suspects. A decision not to go forward means no further official action will be taken, and injured parties will not achieve the goals they sought when they reported the crime, whether they were looking for maximum punishment as revenge, compulsory treatment of the offender, or court-ordered restitution.

To prosecutors, these decisions, even if they infuriate victims, are unavoidable. It is impossible for prosecutors to fulfill their legal mandate to enforce every law and to seek the conviction of all lawbreakers. When evaluating the cases brought before them by police and deciding whether to go forward, ADAs must take into account many other considerations besides the victims' wishes: How are cases of this kind usually handled in this jurisdiction? What are the odds of a conviction rather than an acquittal? Are there serious doubts about the guilt of the accused? How credible and how cooperative are the victim and other witnesses? Does the complainant have any improper motives for pressing charges? Was the evidence obtained according to constitutional guidelines, or will it be tossed out of court under the exclusionary rule? Is the whole undertaking worth the state's limited resources? How much will it cost in time and money to resolve the matter? Would indictment, prosecution, and conviction of the defendant serve as a general deterrent to others who are contemplating committing the same type of offense (an application of the theory of general deterrence)? Would punishment discourage the offender from repeating this illegal act (an application of the theory of specific deterrence)? Would pressing charges and seeking conviction enhance the community's sense of security and boost confidence in the criminal justice system? Could the accused cooperate with the authorities as a police informant or as a key witness for the prosecution in other cases in return for leniency? Would pressing or dropping charges set off protests from powerful interest groups in the community? If this office declines to prosecute, would the case be pursued by another branch of government or in a different jurisdiction? Are appropriate pretrial diversion programs available that provide treatment to wrongdoers as an alternative to adjudication? And last but certainly not least, would a victory in this case substantially advance the careers of the ADA handling the case and of the prosecutor heading up the office? (see the National Advisory Commission, 1973; Sheley, 1979; and Boland and Sones, 1986).

When all these factors are taken into account, it is clear that the victim is only one of several key players who influence the decisions of prosecutors. Police officials, other colleagues in the prosecutor's office, defense attorneys, judges, community leaders, journalists covering the story, and vocal interest groups all affect prosecutorial decision making.

Cases that have been solved by arrests might not be pursued for a number of reasons. Prosecutors might screen them out because of perceived weaknesses that undercut the chances of conviction. Judges might dismiss charges on their own initiative if they feel that the evidence is weak. In general, jurisdictions in which prosecutors weed out many cases before going to court have low case-dismissal rates at later stages of judicial proceedings. Where prosecutors toss out few cases, judges throw out many more. Periodic nationwide surveys of overall felony case processing revealed that nearly half of all cases that were solved by arrest were not carried forward (either rejected at screening by prosecutors, dismissed in court by judges, or diverted out of the system) (Boland and Sones, 1986; and Boland, Mahanna, and Sones, 1992). Clearly, the outcomes of these decisions could cause a great many victims to become dissatisfied with the adjudication process.

One measure that would substantially empower injured parties would be to permit **private prosecution**—allowing them to hire their own lawyers to act as prosecutors—to initiate charges, handle plea negotiations, and present cases at trials. This option is allowed in other countries and was a standard procedure in colonial America. By the end of the 1990s, only a few jurisdictions still authorized a victim's attorney to directly ask a judge or grand jury to initiate proceedings against a defendant (see Beloof, 1999). However, if this reform were implemented, only the prosperous would be able to afford such personalized justice.

Negotiating Pleas

The vast majority of cases that are carried forward (not diverted to treatment programs, screened out by prosecutors, or dismissed by judges) are resolved by out-of-court settlements known as negotiated pleas. **Plea negotiation** is the process in which the ADA and the defense counsel meet in private to hammer out a compromise and thereby avoid holding a public trial. The typical outcome of the "bargaining" (as most observers and participants derisively refer to the offers and counteroffers) is that the defendant agrees to waive his or her constitutional rights to a trial in front of a jury of his or her peers and instead confesses in return for some **consideration** from the government. Many types of concessions from the prosecution are possible, such as dropping certain charges (often the more serious ones carrying the most severe penalties) or the dismissal of particular counts (accusations of harm against specific victims). Often, the consideration is a promise or a recommendation for a lesser punishment: a suspended sentence, probation, a fine, or incarceration for an agreed-upon period of time that is less than the maximum permitted by the law.

Over 95 percent of all felony as well as just about all misdemeanor convictions were secured by the accused admitting guilt rather than by a jury rendering a guilty verdict or by a judge's decision (bench trial), according to a database of cases adjudicated in the 75 busiest urban U.S. counties in 2009 (Reaves, 2013).

Plea negotiation, even though it has been widely condemned for decades, appears to be the only practical way of handling a huge volume of cases. If all the defendants detained in a jail demanded their constitutional right to be judged by a jury of their peers after a trial, the local courts would be paralyzed by gridlock.

Because doing away with deals and inducements is unrealistic, some victims want to play active roles in the plea negotiations that resolve their cases. They justify their quest for empowerment by emphasizing that they were the ones directly involved and personally harmed, and thus it is their case. Unless they are allowed to play a role in this process, they will be effectively shut out of any meaningful participation in the resolution of their cases.

But this demand and formulation of the issue has evoked considerable resistance from prosecutors. They feel threatened by the inclusion of victims (whom they supposedly represent, in addition to the state) at such meetings. They object because victims might try to use the administrative machinery as an instrument of revenge and might put forward unreasonable demands for the imposition of maximum penalties. Deals would fall through, and

risky and costly trials would result (McDonald, 1976; and Rothfeld, 2008).

In general, victims still do not have a right to participate in or even be consulted during the process of plea negotiation. Few jurisdictions grant victims a clearly defined role, and most state laws still do not provide them with any formal mechanisms to challenge the decisions of the prosecuting attorneys who act in their names as well as on behalf of the people. No state legislation empowers complainants to dictate the terms or to nullify a proposed deal. The terms *to confer* or *to consult* are interpreted as merely to notify, inform, or advise. Victims have a right only to make their opinions known and to offer comments, and prosecutors merely have an obligation to consider their views and bring them to the attention of the judge. The terms of the settlement and the sentencing recommendations ultimately are still matters of prosecutorial professional discretion. Most state laws flatly declare that there are no consequences for noncompliance with these rights, and that failure to observe the pledges about opportunities for input shall not be grounds for changing the sentence. Hence, victims only have a voice, not a veto, and even then still are frequently completely excluded from the negotiation process (NCVC, 2002d).

Many victims are convinced that criminals gain an advantage when they accept plea bargains offered by the prosecution. Actually, the expression **plea bargain** gives the erroneous impression that defendants who **cop a plea** invariably get a break or good deal that permits them to escape the more severe punishment they deserve. Actually, police officials and prosecutors routinely engage in **bedsheeting** and **overcharging** so that they will have more bargaining chips in anticipation of the negotiations that will follow. Bedsheeting is the practice of charging a defendant with every applicable crime committed during a single incident. For example, an armed intruder captured while burglarizing an occupied home could face charges of criminal trespass, breaking and entering, burglary, attempted grand larceny, and carrying a concealed weapon, in addition to the most serious charge of all, robbery. Overcharging means filing a criminal indictment for an offense that is more serious than the available evidence might support (for example, charging someone with attempted murder after a fistfight). Some of these charges could not be proven in court, but defendants and their lawyers might be too cautious to gamble and call a prosecutor's bluff. For these reasons and others, most accused individuals who plead guilty in return for concessions receive the penalties that they probably would have received if convicted after a trial (Rhodes, 1978; Beall, 1980; and Katz, 1980).

Resolving cases by negotiating pleas rather than by holding full-scale trials certainly saves taxpayers the expenses incurred from building more courthouses, hiring more judges, bailiffs (court officers), and defense attorneys (for indigents). But out-of-court settlements attained through negotiations might be in the best interests of certain victims. Plea negotiation spares victims the ordeal of testifying in court and undergoing hostile questioning during cross-examination by defense attorneys. For some victims, testifying in painful detail means reliving the horror of the crime, as in this trial:

> A tearful victim tells a jury how she had fallen asleep cuddling her toddler while her husband was working late. She awoke when she heard a prowler enter through a kitchen window, but remained still. Unfortunately he spotted her, pulled out a knife, and put the blade to her daughter's throat. Faced with a nightmare choice, she quietly submitted and was raped. "It was disgusting," she testifies. On cross-examination, she admits that she can't identify the accused because the intruder covered her head with a sheet (but his DNA was lifted from the bedding). (Ginsberg, 2005)

Concerns about emotional distress suffered by a victim on the stand are voiced most often in cases of forcible rape and child molestation. Other types of complainants also may be particularly reluctant to undergo cross-examination if the facts of the case portray them in a negative light or reveal aspects of their private lives that they do not want exposed to the world via media coverage (especially in jurisdictions where trials can be televised).

VICTIMS AND DEFENSE ATTORNEYS

Victims and defense attorneys are on opposite sides and therefore are natural enemies within the adversary system. Whether hired privately for a fee or provided free to indigents, these lawyers have a duty to advise suspects, defendants, and convicts about legal proceedings and the options they can exercise. Defense lawyers have an obligation to zealously represent their clients' best interests, which usually translates to getting out of trouble with the law entirely, or at least being sentenced to less than the maximum punishment.

Conflicts often break out between victims and defense lawyers over two matters: how long the process takes and the number of court appearances needed, as well as the line of questioning directed at victims who testify in court when they appear as prosecution witnesses. From a victim's view, defense attorneys might engage in two abusive practices: asking judges for postponements of their clients' cases to wear victims down and using unfair tactics to undermine the credibility of complainants when they appear as prosecution witnesses.

Postponing Hearings

The Sixth Amendment to the Constitution guarantees the accused the right to a speedy trial. Hence, problems of congested court calendars and needless delays usually have been approached from a defendant's standpoint. Many states and the federal courts have set limits on the amount of time that can elapse between arrest and trial (not counting continuances requested by defense attorneys). But complainants serving as government witnesses also suffer from the uncertainty that envelops unresolved cases, and they share a common interest with defendants in having legal matters settled in as short a time as possible.

If accused people have been released on bail, however, defense lawyers may have an incentive to stall proceedings to "buy time on the streets" and to wear down witnesses for the prosecution. As delays mount and complainants appear in court unnecessarily, they and other crucial prosecution witnesses may lose patience with the protracted deliberations of the legal system. Their commitment to see the case through to its conclusion may erode. Stalling succeeds when a complainant or another key witness gives up in disgust and fails to appear in court as required. For example, a victim who lost her handbag to an unarmed bandit might miss so many days from work that the lost wages far exceed what the robber took, so she may eventually drop out. Stalling for time might also pay off if victims or other witnesses for the prosecution forget crucial details, move away, become ill, or die in the interim. At that point, the defense attorney can move for a dismissal of charges (Reiff, 1979). Prosecutors can also manipulate continuances for their own ends. If defendants are in jail rather than out on bail, then government attorneys may stretch out proceedings to keep them behind bars longer and as a way to pressure them to give in and accept unfavorable plea offers. In the process, the defendant's right to a speedy trial could be violated.

Postponements can prolong and intensify the suffering of complainants. In order to be available if called to testify, they might have to arrange repeatedly for child care, miss school or work, cancel vacations, and break appointments, only to discover (often at the last minute) that the hearings have been rescheduled. To defeat this wear-the-victim-down strategy, some defense motions for postponements could be opposed more vigorously by prosecutors. Similarly, requests for a postponement should be rejected by judges if they suspect the defense's call for a continuance is a stalling tactic (President's Task Force, 1982). To prevent complainants and police officers from showing up in court on days when hearings have been postponed, victim/witness assistance programs in prosecutors' offices operate last-minute notification systems.

As a general rule, the more serious the charges against the defendant are, the longer it takes to resolve the case. Cases resolved by negotiated pleas don't take as long as cases resolved by trials (Boland et al., 1992). Researchers determined that murder cases in state courts took an average of more than one year to be resolved, rape cases required

about 245 days, and robbery cases went on for more than 150 days from arrest to sentencing, according to a study of nearly 50,000 felonies processed in the nation's 75 largest counties during 2009 (Reaves, 2013). However, in some high-crime areas, huge backlogs cause even greater delays, prolonging the anxiety of both complainants and defendants waiting for the final outcome of their conflicts.

Cross-Examining Witnesses During Trials

If they can't wear down victims by stalling, defense attorneys might try to discredit them, along with other prosecution witnesses, before or during a trial. Attorneys for the accused are duty-bound to seek evidence that contradicts or undermines what the accusers contend. In addition to a speedy trial, the Sixth Amendment to the Constitution gives defendants the right to confront their accusers. The burden of proof falls on the prosecution, and the defendant is considered innocent unless proven guilty. The accuser must be presumed to be mistaken until his or her credibility is established beyond a reasonable doubt. The strategy of portraying the victim in a negative light (as a person who makes charges that should not be believed) is employed frequently in rape and sexual assault cases where credibility is a crucial issue, as this example shows.

A 20-year-old woman and a 61-year-old man briefly chat as their flight takes off. Then she puts her feet up on an empty seat between them and falls asleep. When she awakens, she finds that her legs are on his lap. Claiming that he had slipped his hand inside her shorts and molested her, she pushes him away, calls the flight attendant over, and has him arrested when the airplane lands. Weeks later, his attorney informs the prosecution that he has obtained a Facebook post which shows that within a few hours after the alleged sexual assault, the supposedly traumatized young woman had contacted her brother about mundane matters, like what she had eaten that day. The young woman realizes that she mistakenly "friended" someone who later turns out to be connected to the defendant's son, and reports that she feels revitimized by this invasion of her privacy. Court proceedings will determine whether the defendant's constitutional right to confront his accuser trumps the victim's right under the rape shield law to be free from inquiries into her past sexual behavior and lifestyle, and whether communications disseminated by social media like Facebook and Twitter are public information or private matters. (McDonald, 2011)

Because defense attorneys are obliged to be vigorous advocates for their clients, they may advance arguments at a trial or during plea negotiations that the defendant is in fact innocent. In casting doubt on the version of events cobbled together by police and the prosecution, defense attorneys draw upon their skills and training to undermine the accusatory testimony of victims. Under the adversary system, each side puts forward its best case and assails the version of events presented by the opposition. Cross-examination is the art of exposing the weaknesses of witnesses. The intent is to impugn credibility by revealing hidden motives, lapses of memory, unsavory character traits, embarrassing indiscretions, prejudices, or dishonest inclinations.

Cross-examinations can be ordeals for witnesses. But if defense attorneys were not allowed to sharply question prosecution witnesses, then the right of defendants to try, through their lawyers, to refute the charges against them would be undermined. The concerns of complainants and other witnesses (including defense witnesses who are cross-examined by prosecutors) of being embarrassed on the stand under oath must be balanced against the public humiliation suffered by defendants who are arrested and put on trial.

The defense attorney goes up against a formidable professional foe when the witness for the government is an expert in forensic science or forensic psychology, or is a seasoned law enforcement officer (although the credibility of police testimony has become the subject of much debate). But when the full brunt of the defense's well-honed counterattack is directed at a novice, the complainant, the potential for adding insult to injury reaches disturbing proportions. At its best, the confrontation in the courtroom puts the victim

as eyewitness to the test. At its worst, the victim is a target to be injured again by being made to look like a liar, a fool, or an instigator who got what he or she deserved.

Because defense attorneys have a duty to vigorously represent the best interests of their clients, their courtroom tactics might seem harsh. To rattle a witness, discredit damning testimony, and sow seeds of doubt and confusion among jurors, they may have to resort to theatrics and hyperbole. The Code of Professional Responsibility that guides legal strategies permits a zealous defense to gain an acquittal or a lenient sentence, but it prohibits any line of questioning that is intended solely to harass or maliciously harm a witness. Experts and the public often disagree over whether a defense attorney or prosecutor crossed the line and acted unethically by badgering a witness during a cross-examination. Cases that provoke the greatest controversy are those in which defense attorneys cast aspersions on the character of victims or blame them for their own misfortunes (Shipp, 1987).

Trials are relatively rare events, so most victims are not called to testify and undergo cross-examination. Because the outcomes of trials are uncertain and involve risks, attorneys for both sides usually prefer to strike a deal out of court. However, statistically speaking, most trials are successful from the point of view of victims and prosecutors: Defendants usually are found guilty.

The percentage of criminal indictments that result in trials before juries or in bench trials before judges varies according to two factors: the jurisdiction and the nature of the charges. Some prosecutors are more willing to put defendants on trial. Cases involving serious felony charges such as murder, rape, aggravated assault, and robbery go to trial more often than cases involving lesser crimes such as burglary or auto theft. Rape complainants are the most likely to be subjected to hostile cross-examination by defense attorneys. But only about 5 percent of rape cases were resolved through trials with the help of the complainants' testimony in the nation's largest prosecutorial jurisdictions in 2000 (Rainville and Reaves, 2003).

In murder trials, families and friends of the deceased find it particularly upsetting if defense attorneys attack the attitudes and actions of the deceased persons to try to justify or exonerate the behavior of the accused killers. Unlike cross-examinations, these attempts to sully the reputation (or trash the memory) of murder victims are peculiarly one-sided affairs. The deceased subjects of nasty insinuations are not around to rebut the inflammatory things that the alleged offenders say about them during trials. The defense attorney pictures the accused as respectable and believable and the departed as a person of ill repute, as the two cases below show. In the first case, which was highly publicized, the preppy's defense was that his partner enjoyed engaging in sex that was dangerously rough.

An 18-year-old dies of strangulation late at night in a public park in the arms of a six-foot-four 19-year-old she was dating. He tells police that she passed away accidentally as he protected himself during "rough sex play." His lawyer subpoenas her diary, in which she allegedly graphically described aggressive sexual exploits with other young men—but later, it turns out that the diary doesn't contain such information. Some members of the jury are swayed by the defense's arguments. The jury remains deadlocked for days. Before it can render a unanimous verdict, a last-minute plea is negotiated that permits the defendant to admit guilt to the lesser charge of manslaughter instead of murder. At a press conference, the father denounces the defense's portrayal of his dead daughter, and calls it a bizarre pack of lies. After serving 15 years, the killer is released. He later develops a heroin habit and gets convicted of selling cocaine. He is sentenced to 19 years behind bars. (Hackett and Cerio, 1988; Lander, 1988; and Eligon, 2008)

Similarly, in another case that was widely covered in the news media, the defense attorney for a famous TV detective portrayed the dead wife in such a highly negative way that jurors might consider her undeserving of any sympathy.

An actor is on trial for shooting his wife. According to the prosecutor, he referred to her as a "pig" whom he wanted to "snuff." The defense attorney raises doubts about each of the prosecution's specific charges, and portrays the murdered woman as a "sleazy grifter" who recruited rich and famous men by sending them form letters attached to nude pictures of herself. The defense claims she told friends that she always wanted to marry a celebrity. Calling her a "scam artist," the defense tells the jury that she used at least a dozen aliases and left behind 10 former husbands. She allegedly pressured the 71-year-old star into a loveless marriage by getting pregnant in order to get at his money. The jury decides he is not guilty of murder and is deadlocked over the charge that he sought to hire a TV stuntman to kill her. (LeDuff, 2005; and AP, 2005)

VICTIMS AND JUDGES

Judges are supposed to act as referees within the adversary system. Defendants often consider them to be partisans representing the state and favoring the prosecution. Angry victims, however, frequently see judges as guardians of the rights of the accused rather than protectors of injured parties. Victims who have been mistreated by the offender, police officers, the prosecutor, and the defense attorney expect that the judge will finally accord them the evenhanded justice they seek. But conflicts between victims and judges can erupt over bail decisions and sentencing.

Granting Bail

Police officers often resent the granting of bail as a repudiation of their hard work and the risks they took to apprehend perpetrators. To them, releasing defendants on bail is tantamount to turning dangerous criminals loose. Victims also can be outraged by judges' decisions to grant bail to defendants whom they consider to be the culprits who harmed them and who may come back to get even with them for informing the police.

The Eighth Amendment to the Constitution prohibits the setting of excessive bail. Whether it establishes a chance to be bailed out as an affirmative right, however, is a subject of scholarly debate and considerable public concern. State and federal courts routinely deny bail to defendants accused of first-degree murder. In noncapital cases, bail can be denied to jailed suspects who have a history of flight to avoid prosecution or who have tried to interfere with the administration of justice by intimidating a witness or a juror. Otherwise, defendants generally are given the chance to raise money or post bond to guarantee that they will show up at their hearings and trials.

The amount of bail is usually determined by the judge and is set according to the nature of the offense and the record of the defendant. The prosecutor usually recommends a high figure while the defense attorney argues for a sum that is within the defendant's reach. Making bail is a major problem for defendants who are poor and have no prosperous friends or relatives. Across the country, houses of detention are crammed with people unable to raise a few hundred dollars to purchase their freedom until their cases are resolved. Nationwide, a little more than half of all victims of violent crimes faced the prospect that the person accused of harming them would be let out on bail in the 75 largest counties in 2009 (Reaves, 2013).

The question of bail versus jail raises a number of troubling issues. When accused people are denied bail and subjected to preventive detention, or are unable to raise the necessary amount, they are sent to jail and thereby immediately undergo punishment before conviction. The living conditions in houses of detention are usually far worse than in prisons, which hold convicted felons. Yet the release of a defendant who is genuinely guilty and may strike again poses an immediate danger to the entire community and a direct threat to the complainant who will serve as a witness for the state. A possible solution to this dilemma is for the judge to impose and strictly enforce as a condition of bail that the defendant must avoid all contact with the complainant and other prosecution witnesses or else forfeit the privilege of pretrial release.

Statutes in California, Oregon, Texas, Missouri, and Mississippi specifically instruct judges to take the victim's safety into account when determining the conditions of an arrestee's pre-trial release. In cases with unusual dangers and high rates of repeat offenses, such as accusations of domestic violence, child abuse, stalking, sex offenses, and violations of orders of protection, defendants might be denied pre-trial release in many states. Victims have a right to attend and speak out at bail hearings in Alaska, Arizona, California, Missouri, Oregon, South Carolina, Tennessee, Utah, and Washington. Electronic monitoring devices that are activated if the defendant approaches can be provided to victims in Arkansas, Connecticut, Illinois, Louisiana, Michigan, Mississippi. Oklahoma, Tennessee, and Texas (NCSL, 2013).

Sentencing Offenders

After a defendant is convicted—by an admission of guilt as part of a negotiated plea or by a jury verdict after a trial—the judge has the responsibility of imposing an appropriate sentence. Judges can exercise a considerable amount of discretion when pronouncing sentences unless there are mandatory minimums or explicit guidelines. Sentences can involve incarceration, fines, enrollment in treatment programs, community service, and obligations to repay victims. The particular objectives that guide sentencing are specific deterrence, general deterrence, incapacitation, retribution, rehabilitation, and restitution.

The substantial variation among judges in the severity of punishment they mete out in comparable cases is termed **sentence disparity**. Civil libertarians find great disparities troubling because judges might be expressing their social prejudices, to the extent that they deal more harshly with certain groups of offenders. Convicts might view sentence disparities as a sign of unjustifiable arbitrariness. Crime control advocates consider wide ranges as evidence that judges on the low end are too soft or lenient toward offenders. Activists in the victims' rights movement find the spectrum of possible punishments as a motivation to press for greater input in sentencing.

Historically, excluding victims from the sentencing process has been justified on several grounds.

If the purpose of punishing offenders is to deter others from committing the same acts, then sanctions must be swift, sure, and predictable, and not subject to uncertainty and modification by injured parties. If the objective is retribution, then lawbreakers must receive the punishments they deserve and not the penalties their victims request. If the goal of sentencing is to rehabilitate offenders, then the punitive urges of the people they harmed cannot be allowed to interfere with the length and type of treatment prescribed by experts (McDonald, 1979).

The potential impact of victims' desires on sentencing is limited because so many other parties already shape those decisions. Victims who want to help determine their offenders' sentences have to compete for influence with other individuals and groups that routinely affect judicial discretion. State legislatures pass laws that set maximum and minimum limits for periods of confinement and for fines. Prosecutors make recommendations based on deals arrived at during plea negotiations and draw upon the courtroom work group's mutual understandings about appropriate penalties for specific crimes in that jurisdiction at that time (the **going rate**). Defense attorneys use whatever leverage they have on behalf of their clients. Defendants determine their own sentences to some degree by their demeanor, degree of remorse, prior record of convictions, and other mitigating or aggravating personal characteristics and circumstances. Probation officers conduct background investigations and make recommendations to guide judges. Parole boards determine the actual time served when they release convicted felons from prison ahead of schedule or keep them confined until their maximum sentences expire. Corrections officers influence whether or not convicts earn "good-time" reductions and parole by filing reports about cooperative or troublesome behavior. The news media can shape case outcomes by their coverage or lack of it. The public's reactions also can affect the handling of cases, prompting harshness or leniency. And ultimately, state governors can shorten terms of imprisonment and even stop executions by issuing pardons or commuting sentences. Therefore, the victim's notion of what would be an appropriate sentence is just one of many.

If victims want to compete against this constellation of forces and play a role in shaping sentences, they can make their wishes known in two ways: by conveying their requests to judges in writing or by expressing their views orally (**allocution**) at sentencing hearings. Written **victim impact statements** enable judges to learn about the actual physical, emotional, and financial effects of the offense on the injured parties and their families. Questionnaires ask (under the threat of penalties for perjury) about wounds, medical bills, counseling costs, other expenses, insurance reimbursements, and lifestyle changes resulting from the crime. Statements of opinion ask victims what they would consider to be fair and just. In most jurisdictions, the victim impact statement is incorporated into the **presentence investigation report** (PSIR) prepared by a probation officer.

Allocution enables injured parties to directly convey to the judge (and the public) the extent of their suffering and their beliefs about what an appropriate sentence might be. Whereas written impact statements are permitted in all 50 states and the District of Columbia, allocution at sentencing hearings is allowed at the judge's discretion. Because of allocution's highly subjective and emotional content, civil libertarians feared that direct appeals to judges could undermine the judiciary's professional objectivity by injecting inflammatory considerations into the proceedings that could jeopardize a convict's Eighth Amendment rights to be spared from cruel and unusual punishments (see Frey, 2009). But victims now have the right to speak at sentencing in most states, and what they say if often highly emotional, as this case reveals:

An 11-year-old girl is kidnapped and held for nearly two decades by a middle-aged married couple with demented religious beliefs. She is repeatedly raped and gives birth to two children, when she is 13 and again at age 16. At the couple's sentencing hearing, her statement is read: "There is no God

in the universe who would condone your actions. You stole my life and that of my family… But, you do not matter any more." The kidnapped girl's mother rises and speaks of her own suffering, "I thought I was going insane, my baby was gone. It was you … that broke my heart. I hate you both." The judge sentences the man to 431 years, and his wife to 36 years to life. The wife tells the judge, "I deserve every moment of it."
(McKinley, 2011)

The invention and adoption of impact statements and the granting of the allocution privilege were important victories for the victims' rights movement. Prior to their acceptance and implementation, injured parties had to rely on prosecutors to present their views and to fully describe their wounds and losses. But advocates argued that the situation was unbalanced. Convicted persons did not have to depend solely on their lawyers to speak for them. They were permitted to directly address the court before their sentences were handed down. Yet two lives—the injured party's as well as the wrongdoer's—were profoundly shaped by the sentence, which represented an official evaluation of the degree of harm inflicted. Judges couldn't make informed decisions if they heard from only one side: the defendants themselves and their lawyers, families, friends, and other character witnesses. Notions of fairness dictated that individuals who were harmed also be allowed to write or speak about their experiences before sentences were determined (President's Task Force, 1982).

Just because activists in the victims' rights movement succeeded in securing the right to submit an impact statement or to speak in person at a sentencing hearing does not mean that these practices have become widespread and effective. On the contrary, studies have concluded that few victims took advantage of these opportunities, that when they did their participation had very little influence, and that they did not necessarily feel better after voicing their views at sentencing hearings (Villmoare and Neto, 1987; and Frey, 2009).

When a sentence is handed down, it is possible that the victim is misled into thinking that it is more severe than it actually is. Therefore, the victims' rights movement has urged states to impose a **truth-in-sentencing rule** that would require judges to calculate and announce the earliest possible date (actual time served) that a convict could be released from confinement, taking into account time off for good behavior behind bars and parole immediately upon eligibility (Associated Press, 1994b). For example, during the 1980s, felons sent to prison by state court judges across the country served an estimated 38 percent of their maximum sentences. A harsh federal truth-in-sentencing law, passed in 1987 and adopted since then in most states, requires felons to serve at least 85 percent of their court-imposed sentences (Langan, Perkins, and Chaiken, 1994). A study of more than 300 victims of felonies in eight jurisdictions across the country established that most of them were dissatisfied with the sentences judges handed down in their cases. Eighty-six percent agreed with the statement that guilty offenders are not punished enough (Forst and Hernon, 1984). In 2012, the actual median time served by murderers was a little less than 13 years; robbers were kept behind bars for almost three years; and rapists were released on average after four years (Carson, 2014).

Studies of victims' attitudes toward sentences and of actual time served raise a crucial question: Just how much punishment is enough? Victims might feel that the offenders convicted of harming them don't stay in prison long enough. But no formula or equation exists to calculate the gravity of an offense and translate this rating into the proper amount of time a perpetrator should be incarcerated. Profound disagreements divide people over the issue of whether certain murders should carry the death penalty or life imprisonment without parole. Usually overlooked, however, are the dramatic differences in maximum penalties from state to state for lesser crimes such as rape, robbery, or burglary. Clearly, legislators who have the authority to set the upper limits for penalties can't agree on the maximum length of prison time that one person who harms another really deserves. It is impossible to conclude with any degree of objectivity that a particular offender "got off too lightly" when the maximum sentences differ so sharply from one jurisdiction to another (see Katz, 1980).

Victims do not always call for the judge to impose the toughest penalties permissible by law, as this unusual case underscores:

> A carload of teenagers gleefully hurl a frozen turkey out the window and speed off unconcerned as it bashes the windshield of the vehicle behind them. The heavy object breaks every bone in the driver's face, shatters her eye socket, and knocks her unconscious. After many operations and months of reconstructive surgery, she submits a victim impact statement. It urges the district attorney and the judge to sentence the apologetic and remorseful 19-year-old ringleader to the minimum punishment, six months in the county jail and five years of probation, and not the maximum possible sentence of 25 years in prison. She concludes, "God gave me a second chance at life, and I passed it on." After she recovers, she spends much of her time speaking to teenagers about how a thoughtless decision can wreck their lives. (Finn, 2005; and Chang, 2006)

A bitter controversy rages over whether members of the immediate family of a murder victim should be permitted to try to influence the jury's sentencing decision in **bifurcated capital trials** during the penalty phase (after the defendant has been convicted and faces the possibility of execution). The following case brought before the Supreme Court was at the core of the debate over the admissibility of highly emotional information from victim impact statements or via allocution.

> In the midst of a drug-induced frenzy, a man stabs to death a mother and her two-year-old daughter. During the penalty phase of the trial, the grandmother describes to the jury how the three-year-old boy who survived the attack still cries mournfully for his mother and little sister. The jury sentences the convict to die in the electric chair. (Clark and Block, 1992)

Victims' rights groups and prosecutors' organizations argued that it was illogical to demand that a jury focus all of its attention on the defendant's difficult circumstances and other mitigating factors and then ignore the turmoil of those who were close to the deceased. But civil rights and civil liberties groups argued that the introduction of impact statements could be highly inflammatory and prejudicial in capital cases, diverting the jury's attention toward the victim's character (how much or how little the dead person would be missed and mourned) and away from its duty of evaluating the defendant's blameworthiness and the circumstances of the crime. The first time the high court considered a case that raised this issue, it voted to exclude impact statements. But when this issue came up for a second time, the majority of justices ruled that close relatives could testify during the penalty phase of a capital case (Clark and Block, 1992).

Appealing to the Supreme Court

On rare occasions, a case involving a crime victim raises significant legal issues that have not yet been addressed and resolved by an earlier judicial ruling. In these instances, victims and their supporters, as well as prosecutors and defense attorneys, have turned to the U.S. Supreme Court to make wise and fair decisions that will serve as a precedent for future cases to follow.

The Supreme Court is the highest appellate body in the judicial system. It hears only those cases on appeal from federal and state courts that appear to raise important principles of constitutional law. Its nine justices are appointed by the president (who must secure the approval of the Senate) for life so that they can make decisions without fearing repercussions from powerful outside pressure groups. When a majority of Supreme Court justices (five or more) agree on a decision, that ruling sets a precedent that must be followed in all lower courts throughout the nation. These landmark decisions also guide the procedures followed by police departments, prosecutors, trial judges, corrections officials, and other agencies within the criminal justice system.

Over the past several decades, a number of decisions handed down by the Supreme Court have affected the rights and interests of crime victims (see O'Neill, 1984). Some of these far-reaching rulings are summarized in Box 7.4. In most of these landmark decisions, the Court rejected arguments raised by victims and their supporters.

Note that many of these decisions were decided by just one vote, indicating that a near majority of the justices holding differing political ideologies and priorities voiced strong dissenting opinions.

VICTIMS AND JURIES

The jury system, pioneered hundreds of years ago in England, has been hailed as an inspiring example of participatory democracy because ordinary citizens— not government officials, scientific experts, or criminal justice professionals—decide whether an individual is guilty as charged.

The Sixth Amendment guarantees defendants that they will be judged by a jury of their peers who live in the jurisdiction where the alleged offense took place. Exactly what that means (especially the interpretation of the term *peers*) is a subject of ongoing controversy and has led to many court decisions over the years. In order to choose the 12 people (plus alternates) who will listen to the testimony and evaluate the evidence before deliberating and then rendering a verdict, a complicated set of procedures and steps that vary from state to state (and the federal government) must be followed in a sometimes protracted and costly process. In general, the adversarial system empowers the prosecutor as well as the defense attorney to exercise a certain number of challenges for cause (they must explain why) plus peremptory challenges (no reason needs to be given), in order to eliminate particular potential jurors. Supposedly both of these opponents are seeking thoughtful, reasonable, open-minded individuals who start out as impartial. In reality, the prosecution would prefer to launch

the trial with jurors leaning toward conviction while the defense would hope to seat individuals already skeptical of the government's version of events who will ultimately thwart the achievement of a unanimous verdict. Therefore, picking those who will sit in judgment is a crucial stage in which each side tries to uncover the biases of prospective jurors in that day's pool of citizens called for jury duty (the venire) by carefully questioning them (the process of voir dire).

From a victim-centered perspective, several issues and questions arise: First of all, do victims influence the outcomes of trials either by displaying emotions (that they are appropriately upset, in proportion to the suffering they endured) or by acting so restrained that they come across as less deserving of sympathy and vindication (see Rose, Nadler, and Clark, 2006)? Second, which kinds of jurors will be most likely to accept and trust the testimony of the victim, who is serving as a witness for the prosecution, that the person on trial is truly the one who allegedly committed a harmful act? Third, are those jurors who have been on the receiving end of serious crimes themselves (or who have suffered because of what happened to loved ones) more likely to vote for conviction during jury deliberations than the others who have heard the same arguments advanced by the prosecution and challenged by the defense? Finally, when jurors not only decide whether the accused is guilty beyond a reasonable doubt but also determine what the sentence should be—as in bifurcated death penalty trials—do they factor in the victim's characteristics and status?

The decision making of the members of a jury that takes place behind closed doors precludes researchers from reconstructing who voted to convict or acquit, and why. So most studies either focus on simulated trials in front of mock juries, or they seek out statistical patterns running through the verdicts of many similar cases.

The decision to accept or reject a particular prospective juror is made on the basis of each counsel's stereotypes, hunches, and accumulated wisdom from past experiences as a trial lawyer. But picking a jury has evolved from an "art" to a "science" with

BOX 7.4 Supreme Court Decisions Directly Affecting Victims

Decisions Advancing Victims' Interests and Rights

Victimized Children Can Testify via Closed-Circuit Television
In 1990, in a 5–4 decision *(Maryland v. Craig)*, the Supreme Court held that it was constitutional for a state to pass a law that shields a child who accuses an adult of sexual abuse from a face-to-face confrontation during a trial. The child's testimony and the defense attorney's cross-examination can take place in another room and can be shown to the jury over closed-circuit television if the prosecutor can convince the judge that the young witness would be traumatized by having to testify in the defendant's presence. The majority felt that the state's interest in the physical and psychological well-being of the abused child may outweigh the defendant's Sixth Amendment right to face his or her accuser in person (Greenhouse, 1990).

Rape Victims' Past Experiences Can Be Kept out of Court
In 1991, the Supreme Court ruled by a 7–2 vote that the rape shield laws passed in all 50 states were constitutional. The laws allow judges to suppress as irrelevant attempts by the defense to introduce allegations about past sexual experiences of rape victims (Rauber, 1991).

Victim Impact Statements Can Be Used in Capital Cases
In 1987 *(Booth v. Maryland)*, the Supreme Court overturned a death sentence because the jury during the penalty phase of the trial heard a particularly heartrending impact statement about how the murder of an elderly couple shattered the lives of three generations of their family. The majority ruled that the use of such inflammatory impact statements created a constitutionally unacceptable risk that juries might impose the death penalty in an arbitrary and capricious manner, swayed by the social standing and reputation of the deceased person. The majority believed that the victim's worth was not an appropriate factor for a jury to consider when weighing the killer's fate—imprisonment or execution—because it would undermine the guarantee of equal protection (Triebwasser, 1987b). But in 1991 *(Payne v. Tennessee)*, the Court reversed itself and ruled that prosecutors could introduce victim impact statements and that the survivors of murder victims could testify. The majority held that courts have always taken into account the harm done by defendants when determining appropriate sentences (Clark and Block, 1992).

Victims' 911 Emergency Calls Can Be Used as Evidence If They Can't Testify at a Trial
In 2006, *(Davis v. Washington)*, all nine justices agreed that a victim's 911 call describing a crime in progress and identifying the assailant can be entered as evidence in court proceedings, without violating the defendant's Sixth

Amendment right to confront his accuser, if the complainant can't or chooses not to testify (Greenhouse, 2006).

People Concerned About Crime Have a Right to Keep Handguns in Their Homes
In 2008 *(District of Columbia et al. v. Heller)*, five justices interpreted the Second Amendment as granting individuals who fear that criminals might invade their residences the right to own loaded handguns to defend themselves, their families, and their property, even in large cities with very strict gun control laws. The dissenters cited the dangers of accidental domestic fatalities and the need to protect children from access to firearms (Greenhouse, 2008; Wasserman, 2008).

A Victim's Dying Words Can Be Reported to a Jury
In 2011 *(Michigan v. Bryant)*, six of the eight justices interpreted the Sixth Amendment's confrontation clause as permitting a dying man's identification of his assailant to police officers to be admissible as evidence against the defendant in a murder trial (Liptak, 2011).

Police Can Collect DNA from Arrestees to Use to Solve Crimes Like Rapes
In 2013 *(Maryland V. King)*, by a vote of 5–4, the Court granted the police authority to take DNA samples derived from cheek swabs from the persons they arrest to see if a match will reveal their participation in a crime, especially in cases of sexual assault where such forensic evidence plays a key role in identifying an assailant (RAINN, 2014).

Decisions Opposing Victims' Interests and Rights

Government Has No Constitutional Duty to Protect Individuals
In 1989 *(De Shaney v. Winnebago County Dept. of Social Services)*, six of the nine justices decided that a government agency could not be sued for failing to intervene (on behalf of a child repeatedly beaten and permanently injured by his father) because the state does not have a special obligation to protect individuals from harm by other private persons (U.S. Supreme Court, 1989).

Victims Can't Sue Police Departments for Failing to Enforce Orders of Protection
In 2005 *(Gonzales v. Castle Rock Police)*, the Supreme Court by a 7–2 margin ruled that a victim of domestic violence did not have the right to sue her local police department for failing to enforce a restraining order against her husband who subsequently murdered their three children. The Court upheld the principle that police departments are not liable to lawsuits challenging the way officers exercise discretion in the

performance of their duties, unless there is evidence of extreme negligence (Bunch, 2005).

Victims Cannot Compel Prosecutors to Take Action Against Suspects

A number of decisions handed down in 1967, 1973, 1977, 1981, and 1983 have established that attorneys general and district attorneys have absolute discretion over whether to charge defendants with crimes and what charges to press or drop. Victims cannot compel prosecutors to take particular actions, and courts cannot intervene in this decision-making process (see Stark and Goldstein, 1985).

Victims of Rape and Domestic Violence Can't Sue Attackers in Federal Court

In 2000 (*United States v. Morrison*), the Supreme Court by a 5–4 margin struck down a provision of the 1984 Violence Against Women Act, which had granted injured parties in domestic violence and rape cases the additional option of suing their assailants for monetary damages in federal court. The majority voted to uphold the doctrine of state sovereignty over gender-based violence rather than extend federal authority via the interstate commerce clause (Biskupic, 2000).

Newspapers Can Publish the Lawfully Obtained Names of Rape Victims

In 1989, a majority of six justices argued that the First Amendment's guarantee of freedom of the press protected a newspaper from liability for printing the name of a woman who already was identified as a rape victim in publicly available police reports. However, the decision did not declare unconstitutional state laws in Florida, Georgia, and South Carolina that prohibit the publishing of a rape victim's name as an invasion of privacy (Greenhouse, 1989).

Offenders Can Escape Paying Restitution to Victims

In 1989 (*Pennsylvania Dept. of Public Welfare v. Davenport*), the Court ruled 7–2 that if convicts declare bankruptcy, they can avoid paying court-ordered restitution because restitution obligations are dischargeable debts. In 1990 (*Hughey v. United States*), the Court ruled that a federal judge cannot order a defendant to pay restitution to a victim if the charge involving that victim was dropped as part of a negotiated plea. The Court based its ruling on a provision of the federal Victim and Witness Protection Act of 1982 (Eddy, 1990).

Victims Can't Easily Claim Income Gained by Notorious Offenders

In 1991 (*Simon & Schuster v. New York Crime Victims Board*), the Supreme Court struck down New York's 1977 "Son-of-Sam" statute, which served as a model for 41 other state laws. The law confiscated fees and royalties offenders gained from selling their inside stories to book publishers or moviemakers and permitted victims to claim that money. The unanimous opinion held that the state's worthwhile goals of ensuring that criminals do not profit from their crimes, and of transferring the proceeds to victims, did not justify infringements on the First Amendment right of free speech (Greenhouse, 1991).

Victims of Identity Theft Can't Have Extra Time to Sue Credit Bureaus

In 2001 (*TRW v. Andrews*), the Supreme Court ruled that people who find out that impostors have ruined their financial reputations have only two years from the time the mistake about their real creditworthiness was made to file damage lawsuits against the major credit bureaus that generate ratings, even if they don't discover these errors in sufficient time (Savage, 2003).

The Statute of Limitations on Child Sexual Abuse Charges Cannot Be Extended

In 2003, the Supreme Court struck down a California law that had lengthened the state's statute of limitations to enable criminal prosecutions of alleged molesters whose accusers came forward many years after the events took place. However, the decision did not block victims from pursuing lawsuits in civil court (Garvey and Winton, 2003).

Victims of Child Pornography Have to Return to State Courts to Seek Restitution

In 2014, (*Paroline v. United States*) by a five to four decision, the Court affirmed that a child whose sexual abuse appeared in pornography was entitled to financial compensation under the federal Crime Victims Restitution Act for direct, foreseeable, significant, and repeated harm from the viewing of these images. But the higher court reversed a state court decision and held that only a trial court, on a case-by-case basis, had the authority, using its discretion and sound judgment, to determine the appropriate amount of restitution from the offender for imposing this mental anguish on the victim (NCVLI, 2014).

Insufficient Proof That the Lives of Murdered Black People Count for Less

In 1987 (*McCleskey v. Kemp*), in upholding a death penalty conviction, the Supreme Court rejected a statistical analysis that seemed to show that the deaths of black victims were not taken as seriously as the deaths of white victims by criminal justice decision makers—prosecutors, juries, and judges. The Court ruled that a pattern—in which offenders convicted of killing white people were 11 times more likely to be sentenced to die than those found guilty of murdering black victims—was not compelling evidence of intentional discrimination in violation of the Eighth and Fourteenth Amendments (Triebwasser, 1987a).

the advent of consultants who use statistical methods, especially findings from surveys of the local residents' attitudes and biases, to predict which kinds of people are more likely to convict or acquit in a case based on similar facts and accusations.

One bit of conventional wisdom taught to lawyers is that prospective jurors who disclose that they have been victims in the past can be expected to consciously or subconsciously identify with the injured party who is serving as a star witness for the prosecution. This tendency is presumed to be especially strong if the crime committed against them resembles the charge that the defendant is facing in the upcoming trial (Gobert and Jordan, 2009). Judges often ask venire members about their own past experiences with criminals and send home victims who admit that they will have trouble being open-minded about the presumption of innocence. Although no jurisdiction has strict laws that address the issue of jury ineligibility because of prior victimization, eliminating victims from the pool often might be justified on an individual basis but impractical as a general procedure since being harmed by criminals is such a common experience. Former victims are indeed more likely to vote to convict than other jurors, according to the findings of a simulation in which 2,400 people were asked to decide guilt or innocence after watching a one-hour mock trial about a burglary of a dwelling (Culhane, Hosch, and Weaver, 2004).

Concealing a hidden bias due to past experiences can get a juror in trouble, as the following case demonstrates:

> A young man is serving as a juror in a capital murder case in which a former Marine is accused of stabbing a woman to death. He confides in a court bailiff that he doesn't think he can be impartial because two of his family members had been killed in robberies. The bailiff informs the judge, who angrily asks the young man why he didn't reveal these troubling relationships on a detailed questionnaire or to the two attorneys who vetted him. The judge lectures him about the disruption his tardy disclosure has caused, and warns, "I'm not going to put you in jail, but you're going to forfeit your jury fee ($90). Now, get

> out of here before I change my mind!" The prosecutor and the defense attorney urge the judge not to declare a mistrial and start over, and both agree to continue with just 11 jurors. (Emily, 2010)

The findings of several other studies shed additional light on the victim–juror relationship.

In death penalty cases, prosecutors, judges, and juries seem to be influenced by the race of the victim as much as by the race of the defendant. Blacks who murder whites and whites who dispatch whites are much more likely to be sentenced to die by juries than whites who slay blacks or blacks who kill blacks, according to a statistical study entered as evidence in a case that led to a landmark decision by the Supreme Court (see Baldus, 2003). Murder victims' families (referred to as "co-victims") find death penalty cases understandably burdensome and emotionally frustrating because the legal process marginalizes them, leaving them with a very limited role to play in resolving their traumatic loss. During bifurcated capital trials, prosecutors often urge murder victims' families to attend all the proceedings, and if a conviction takes place, to testify during the penalty phase to provide victim impact evidence that might influence jurors to choose execution over life imprisonment (Karp and Warshaw, 2009). Just as first responders (like police officers and emergency technicians) and caregivers (such as doctors, social workers, and advocates) can suffer vicarious traumatization, so too can sensitive jurors succumb to the stresses generated by gruesome evidence and harrowing testimony and by emotionally draining arguments during protracted jury deliberations behind closed doors (Robinson, Davies, and Nettleingham, 2009).

VICTIMS AND CORRECTIONS OFFICIALS

Corrections officials include jail and prison wardens and guards, and probation and parole officers. Victims whose cases led to successful prosecutions occasionally seek their cooperation but may find themselves in conflict over issues of safety and money.

Keeping Track of Offenders and Receiving Reimbursement from Them

Victims are more likely to have contacts with county probation departments than with county jail, state prison, or state parole authorities. Of those found guilty in state courts, more felons are sentenced to probation for up to several years than are sent to jail for up to a year or to prison for longer stretches (Brown and Langan, 1998).

Victims want two things from probation and parole officers. When offenders are placed on probation or are released on parole after serving time in prison, victims want to be protected from harassment and further harm. They can feel especially endangered by a vengeful, violent ex-offender if their cooperation and testimony was a crucial factor leading to conviction. And if making restitution is a condition of probation or parole, victims want to receive these payments right on schedule. Probation and parole officers share these goals but often find their caseloads so overwhelming that they cannot enforce these requirements effectively.

Corrections officials must safeguard the well-being and best interests of victims by keeping them notified of the inmates' whereabouts, parole board appearances, and release dates, according to legislation in most states. Correctional agencies can go further and develop victim safety plans that make sure prisoners on temporary leave (on furlough, work release, or educational release) or who escape from an institution do not threaten, track down, stalk, and attack the people they injured who helped to send them away (see National Victim Center, 1990; and Gagliardi, 2005).

When victims discover from other sources that their offenders (especially those guilty of aggravated assault, armed robbery, rape, or sexual molestation) are back on the streets, conflicts can erupt with corrections officials who did not meet their notification obligations. A widely used computer-based notification system enables corrections officials to alert registered victims about their jail or prison inmates' whereabouts, including their release on bail; attendance at classes or work outside the institution; completion of sentence; placement on probation or parole; or their escape from custody (Harry, 2002).

Influencing Parole Board Decisions

Statistically, few victims ever deal with members of parole boards because only small percentages of offenders are caught, convicted, and sent away to prison for years. However, parole hearings have received a great deal of attention from the victims' rights movement because they determine the fates of inmates who have inflicted serious harm.

By definition, parole means an early release for felons before the maximum or upper limits of the judges' sentences have been served. Prisoners become eligible for parole after serving a specified proportion of their sentences, but parole is not automatic. After hearings, parole boards turn down most convicts, keeping them incarcerated for many more years. (However, even without parole, early release is still possible because most correctional institutions subtract time off for good behavior.)

The board grants conditional liberty to convicts who have earned the privilege of parole. They may return to their communities but must abide by restrictions on their conduct. Parolees who violate the rules can be returned to prison to finish up the remainder of their unexpired full sentences at the discretion of administrative judges after revocation hearings.

Victims with a punitive outlook will want parole boards to vote to keep convicts behind bars for their entire sentences. Victims seeking reimbursement will want boards to grant parole to convicts but impose strict restitution obligations on them. Victims concerned about offender rehabilitation will want boards to impose treatment obligations as a condition of parole.

Because many parolees commit additional crimes after serving time, boards granting early release have come under intense scrutiny and even criticism. Although the origins of parole date back to the mid-1800s, convicts are finding it much more difficult to earn early release these days. Traditionally, three rationales justify setting up boards to grant the privilege of a shortened sentence to selected prisoners. The first is that ex-convicts can make smoother transitions from a tightly controlled prison regimen to civilian life with the guidance of parole officers. Second, corrections officers can control the behavior of inmates more effectively if a possibility of early release looms as a reward for continuous good behavior. The third justification is that parole enables correctional authorities to better manage the flow of prisoners into and out of institutions, ensuring that sufficient cell space is available for new arrivals.

Prisoners' rights groups have rejected the notion that parole is a form of benevolence that serves as an incentive for rehabilitation. They have criticized the practice as a way of extending the length of time ex-convicts are under governmental control; as a device to prolong punishment; and as a source of anxiety and uncertainty. These groups have called for the abolition of the practice of parole and have suggested determinate or fixed sentences of shorter duration as a replacement for indefinite sentences with widely varying minimums and maximums (Shelden, 1982).

Crime control organizations also have demanded an end to the parole system but for different reasons. They perceive parole boards as granting undeserved breaks and unwarranted leniency because dangerous criminals are let out prematurely. They want parole ended and replaced with definite sentences of longer duration (President's Task Force, 1982). Victims, too, may bitterly resent the practice of parole if it reduces sentences of incarceration that they originally considered too short. If parolees harass victims or fail to pay them restitution in a timely manner, then parole board decisions will be resented for these additional reasons (see Herdt, 2013).

As a result of the widespread dissatisfaction with parole, the federal prison system and a number of state systems have phased it out. In other jurisdictions, parole is granted less often. The reliance on parole reached its peak in 1977, when as many as 72 percent of prisoners returning to society were granted conditional liberty with community supervision. The proportion of inmates achieving discretionary early release had dropped to 35 percent in

2006 (Glaze and Bonczar, 2007). Over 850,000 formerly incarcerated adults were out on parole in 2013 (Herberman and Bonczar, 2014), although some of them, such as drug dealers, had not been sentenced for interpersonal violence. However, since trends in the data reveal that more than one-third of prisoners still do not serve their maximum terms, and hundreds of thousands of convicts were under the supervision of parole officers, it is clear that victims retain an interest in exercising their rights before parole boards.

Although procedures to standardize and rationalize parole board decision making have been implemented, measures also have been adopted to open up the process by providing notice to and soliciting input from groups that were formerly excluded. In 43 states, legislation expressly grants victims (and often law enforcement officers, prosecutors, and judges) the right to attend parole hearings (usually held inside prisons in remote locations) and to personally inform board members of their views. Alternatively, they can submit written or videotaped impact statements. Board members can serve victims by inviting them to participate in decision-making processes, by warning them in advance that the persons they helped send to prison are being let go, and by ordering the convicts to pay restitution as a condition of release. In some states, restitution is a mandatory requirement for parolees unless the board excuses them from it (National Victim Center, 1990; and Parker, 2009). Understandably, the next of kin of murder victims often argue, "don't release the convict on parole," as this case demonstrates:

> An off-duty police sergeant spots an armed robbery-in-progress at an ATM. The robber, a drug addict who has previously served time for two manslaughters, fires at the policeman and kills him; the officer's bullet is deflected by the robber's zipper, and he escapes. An innocent man confesses to the crime. When the actual killer eventually is captured, prosecutors are compelled to negotiate a plea of 15 years to life. After the 15 years are up, the slain officer's father has to attend parole board meetings every two

years. The father, a retired DEA agent who carried out 3,000 arrests without once firing his service revolver, tells the parole board in a written statement, "Anyone who sets this creature free, from this day on, know that innocent blood is on your hands. This is no longer about vengeance. Nothing I say can bring my son back." When the board turns down the convict's application for parole for the third time, the father declares, "There's no celebration. It is what it is." (McShane, 2011a; 2011b)

As with sentencing, the potential impact of victim input on decision making about parole is limited. The boards receive statements not only from victims, but also from prosecutors, judges, and other concerned parties. They interview the inmates and review their criminal records and the prison files summarizing their behavior behind bars. Most of the time, the decisions arrived at by boards are not determined by the wishes of victims but rather by intense political pressures to keep convicts confined longer or by pragmatic administrative considerations to let some out ahead of schedule to make room for new arrivals.

Victimologists have carried out occasional studies to see how the reforms are actually working. In Texas, only about 20 percent of eligible people filed victim impact statements (Schmidt, 2006). Similarly, most failed to appear and speak out at sentencing hearings (Forer, 1980). Those who did exercise their in-person allocution rights exerted very little influence, especially when convicts faced determinate (fixed) sentences (Villmoare and Neto, 1987; Walsh, 1992). A survey of New Yorkers turned up no clear evidence that those who filed victim impact statements experienced a greater sense of involvement or were more satisfied with the city's justice system and the disposition in their cases (Davis and Smith, 1994).

However, when victims submitted impact statements to Pennsylvania parole boards, inmates were less likely to be granted early release (Parsonage, Bernat, and Helfgott, 1994). And when California prosecutors introduced victim impact statements during the penalty phase in capital murder trials, the additional evidence raised the likelihood that the jury

would impose execution rather than sentence the killer to life in prison without the possibility of parole (Aguirre et al., 1999). According to a federally sponsored survey of departments of corrections in various states, 98 percent reported that they were notifying victims of parole dates and release dates (Gagliardi, 2005).

AND JUSTICE FOR ALL?

The Fourteenth Amendment to the Constitution promises **equal protection under the law** for all citizens: Federal and state criminal justice systems ought to regard social factors such as class, race, nationality, religion, and sex as irrelevant to the administration of the law (blind justice). Traditionally, criminologists and political activists have examined whether this important principle of equal protection really governs the way suspects, defendants, and convicts are treated by officials and agencies. The main focus of concern has been whether poor or minority offenders are subjected to discriminatory treatment. Whether certain kinds of victims are handled in a discriminatory manner is an equally significant concern but it has escaped notice.

It is often said that the United States is a country "ruled by laws, not men." This maxim implies that the principles of due process and equal protection limit the considerable discretionary powers of criminal justice officials. **Due process** means procedural consistency (following all the required steps) and equal protection require that different categories of people be treated similarly. Yet enough discretion remains at each stage in the criminal justice process to generate unequal outcomes. Of course, those who do exercise discretion can and do justify their actions. Explanations range from practical considerations about time and money to philosophical rationales about the true meaning of justice. Nevertheless, the actions they take generate, maintain, and reveal double standards, or more accurately (because sometimes more than two groups are involved) **differential handling**, ranging from exemplary service and support for some to **second-class treatment** for others.

Recognizing "Second-Class" Treatment

The wife of a wealthy doctor disappears while walk-ing her dog. The police launch a massive search, hold a press conference, assign two dozen detectives to work full time to canvass the affluent neighborhood, circulate flyers, and try to pick up her trail with a bloodhound. Her body later is found floating in the river, but it cannot be determined if she fell in, jumped in, or was pushed. Less than two months later, a shy and studious African American college student never returns from running an errand in a working-class immigrant neighborhood. Her mother calls 911 the next morning, and two officers fill out a missing persons report—reluctantly, saying that because she is 21 years old, they really are not sup-posed to. Once 24 hours have elapsed, a detective marks the case closed. The family appeals to local elected officials, and after a few days the police department reopens the case. But it is too late—during that time two kidnappers who torture and rape her in a dingy basement a few blocks away decide to kill her. A federal judge permits the victim's mother to file a lawsuit alleging bias in the police depart-ment's response, based on the race, class, and age of the missing person. (Gardiner, 2008)

Many social institutions have two or more tracks and deliver unequal services to their clients or consumers. For instance, the health care system does not treat all patients the same; some get higher quality medical attention than others. Similarly, the school system does not provide all students with equal educational opportunities. Some are chal-lenged, nurtured, and as a result excel, while others are discouraged, neglected, and consequently fail to reach their academic potential.

A systematic examination of how cases are pro-cessed by the criminal justice system must address a crucial question. Now that victims have rights and are no longer routinely overlooked, do some get better service than others?

Criminologists have documented the discrep-ancy between official doctrines and actual practices. For example, race and class ought to be extraneous factors in a system of "blind justice," but, in reality, they are useful predictors of how officials respond to offenders. When victimologists pieced together scattered research findings about how different cat-egories of victims were treated, a comparable pic-ture emerged. Certain victims were more likely to be given first class or VIP treatment, while others tended to be neglected, abused, and treated as second-class complainants by the same agencies and officials. In other words, how a case was han-dled was determined by the victim's as well as the offender's social standing, in addition to the cir-cumstances surrounding the crime.

The findings of many independent studies car-ried out decades ago are summarized in Box 7.5. They yield a profile of the groups of people who in the past tended to be treated far better or much worse than others. Victims who were innocent and from respectable backgrounds and privileged strata were more likely to receive better service from police officers, prosecutors, juries, and judges. Individuals whose backgrounds were tarnished or who came from disadvantaged groups were less likely to get favorable treatment.

Many social handicaps that have held people back in life also impede their ability to receive fair treatment as crime victims. The same discretionary powers that result in overzealous law enforcement in some communities contribute to lax enforce-ment in others. Apparently, calls for help from members of groups that traditionally have suffered discrimination were not perceived as entirely legiti-mate or as compelling by some at the helm of the criminal justice system. The credibility of complai-nants from disadvantaged backgrounds often was eroded by a belief that these same people were the wrongdoers in other incidents. Such stereotyp-ical responses by the authorities poisoned relations between the two camps.

From bitter experience, individuals from the lower strata, and "out groups" marginalized because of their unconventional lifestyles have anticipated that their requests for intervention would be greeted with suspicion or even hostility. They expected perfunctory treatment at best. As a conse-quence, they have turned to the criminal justice system only under the most desperate circumstances (Ziegenhagen, 1977).

BOX 7.5   Which Victims Get Better Treatment?

Arrests

Suspects are more likely to be taken into custody if the victims:

- Request that officers make an arrest in a deferential, nonantagonistic manner (Black, 1968)
- Convince the police that they themselves were not involved in any illegal activity before the incident (La Fave, 1965)
- Prove to officers that they are not a friend, relative, or neighbor of the suspect (Goldstein, 1960; La Fave, 1965; Black, 1968; Reiss, 1971; and Giacinti, 1973)

Prosecutions

Charges are more likely to be lodged against defendants if the victims:

- Are middle-aged or elderly, white, and employed (Myers and Hagan, 1979)
- Have high status in the community ("Prosecutorial discretion," 1969)
- Are women and the offender is a male stranger (Myers, 1977)
- Are women without a reputation for promiscuity (Newman, 1966)
- Are not known to be homosexual (Newman, 1966)
- Are not alcoholics or drug addicts (Williams, 1976)
- Have no prior arrest record (Williams, 1976)
- Can establish that they weren't engaged in misconduct themselves at the time of the crime (Miller, 1970; Neubauer, 1974; and Williams, 1976)
- Can prove that they didn't provoke the offender (Newman, 1966; Neubauer, 1974; and Williams, 1976)
- And the offender are not both black and are not viewed as conforming to community subcultural norms (Newman, 1966; McIntyre, 1968; Miller, 1970; and Myers and Hagan, 1979)

Convictions

Judges or juries are more likely to find defendants guilty if the victims:

- Are employed in a high-status job (Myers, 1977)
- Are perceived as being young and helpless (Myers, 1977)
- Appear reputable and have no prior arrest record (Kalven and Zeisel, 1966; and Newman, 1966)
- Had no prior illegal relationship with the defendant (Newman, 1966)
- In no way are thought to have provoked the offender (Wolfgang, 1958; Kalven and Zeisel, 1966; and Newman, 1966)
- Are white and the defendants are black (Johnson, 1941; and Allredge, 1942; Garfinkle, 1949; and Bensing and Schroeder, 1960)
- And the offender are not both black and are not viewed as acting in conformity to community subcultural norms (Newman, 1966; McIntyre, 1968; Miller, 1970; and Myers and Hagan, 1979)

Punishments

Judges will hand down stiffer sentences to defendants if the victims:

- Are employed in a high-status occupation (Myers, 1977; and Farrell and Swigert, 1986)
- Did not know the offender (Myers, 1977)
- Were injured and didn't provoke the attack (Dawson, 1969; and Neubauer, 1974)
- Are white and the offenders are black (Green, 1964; Southern Regional Council, 1969; Wolfgang and Riedel, 1973; and Paternoster, 1984)
- Are females killed by either males or females (Farrell and Swigert, 1986)

The manner in which police and prosecutors respond to homicides provides some clear examples of differential handling. When a "very important person" is murdered, the police department comes under tremendous pressure from the media, elected officials, and powerful constituencies within the public to arrest someone quickly. To give an illustration, a highly publicized robbery and murder of a foreign visitor was so threatening to Florida's multibillion-dollar tourist trade that local business interests and the Chamber of Commerce generated tremendous pressure to apprehend whoever was preying upon vacationers (see Rohter, 1993; and Boyle, 1994). But when an "undesirable" is slain, overworked and understaffed homicide detectives may carry out only a superficial, routine investigation. For example, the fatal shooting of a street-level prostitute or drug peddler would attract little public notice or official concern and certainly wouldn't merit the establishment of a task force of detectives to track down the killer who carried out what the police mockingly term a "misdemeanor homicide" (see Simon, 1991; and Maple, 1999).

On the other hand, when a member of the police force is slain, the homicide squad will work day and night to follow up every possible lead in order to catch the killer and reinforce the message that the death of an officer will not go unpunished. To illustrate how law enforcement agencies assign capturing the killer of "one of their own" the highest priority, consider this comparison: In 1992, police departments across the country solved 65 percent of murders and 91 percent of the killings of fellow officers (FBI, 1993). Similarly, during 1998, 93 percent of line-of-duty officer killings were cleared, compared to 69 percent of civilian murders across the nation (FBI, 1999). And in 2007, right after homicide solution rates sank to an all-time low of 61 percent, 50 out of 51 murders of police officers were cleared by the arrest of a suspect or by exceptional means (the perpetrator was justifiably killed by the dying officer or by other officers, or the assailant afterward committed suicide or died under other circumstances) (FBI, 2008a).

Most of the research cited in Box 7.5 uncovering evidence of differential handling was conducted before the victims' rights movement scored sweeping legislative victories. Therefore, victimologists need to carry out a new round of investigations to discover whether the past inequity of differential handling persists to this day, or whether the lofty goals of "equal protection under the law" and "justice for all" are becoming more of a reality in state criminal justice systems across America. As social scientists continue to evaluate the effectiveness of informational and participatory rights that have been granted in recent decades, they are likely to discover evidence of **differential access to justice**: that certain groups of people are more likely than others to be informed of their rights, to exercise

them, and to use them effectively to influence the decision-making process (see Karmen, 1990).

Even though many legislatures have added victims' rights amendments to their state constitutions or have passed a victims' bill of rights, much educational work needs to be done, a study conducted by the National Center for Victims of Crime (NCVC, 1999) concluded. It surveyed victims in two states considered to have strong pro-victim protections and in two states where their rights on paper were limited. Overall, those whose cases were processed by the justice systems of states with strong protection fared better, but even they were not afforded all the opportunities they were supposed to get. In the two states that theoretically guaranteed many rights, more than 60 percent of victims interviewed were not notified when the defendant was released on bail, more than 40 percent were not told the date of the sentencing hearing, and nearly 40 percent were not informed that they were entitled to file an impact statement at the convict's parole hearing. Of those who found out in time, most (72 percent) attended the sentencing hearing and submitted an impact statement, but relatively few went to bail or parole hearings. Only about 40 percent of the local officials surveyed in the two strong protection states knew about the new laws enumerating victims' rights (Brienza, 1999; and NCVC, 1999).

Overall, a survey of cases handled by prosecutors across the country at the end of the twentieth century failed to find evidence of substantial changes in outcomes resulting from the passage of victims' rights legislation (Davis et al., 2002).

As a consequence of constraints and obstacles that undermine the effective implementation of victims' rights, some movement activists remain pessimistic, even cynical about the much-heralded reforms that supposedly grant empowerment. Mere pledges of fair treatment do not go far enough. Being notified about the results of a bail hearing, plea negotiation session, sentencing hearing, or parole board meeting falls far short of actually pursuing one's perceived best interests. Attending and speaking out is no guarantee of being taken seriously and truly having an impact. Victims still have no constitutional standing, which means that they cannot go to civil court and sue for monetary damages if their rights are ignored or violated, and they cannot veto decisions about bail, sentences, and parole that are made in their absence without their knowledge and consent (Gewurz and Mercurio, 1992). Lofty pronouncements that the rights of victims to fair treatment will be carefully respected by officials might prove to be lip service, paper promises, and cosmetic changes without much substance (Gegan and Rodriguez, 1992; and Elias, 1993). However, because recent federal legislation grants victims the right to appeal rulings that appear to violate their rights, advocates have convinced the Department of Justice to sponsor victim law clinics to work to boost the degree of compliance by uninformed criminal justice officials (Schwartz, 2007; and Davis and Mulford, 2008). As of 2011, 12 legal clinics across the country served victims seeking to have their rights respected and enforced in court proceedings (NCVLI, 2011).

What is the ultimate goal of victims' rights advocates? What some seek might be called a system of "parallel justice." In the aftermath of serious crimes, "justice is served" when offenders are punished and isolated behind bars, and then rehabilitated and eventually reintegrated into society by reentry programs. But there is no comparable societal response for victims, which would begin with an acknowledgement that what happened to them was wrong, and would culminate with efforts to assist them to rebuild their lives. The guiding principle of parallel justice is that a society has an obligation to its victims too: to help them to heal, regain a sense of security, protect them from further harm, and reintegrate back into the life they were leading before the crime occurred. The public must be mobilized to support a comprehensive approach to making victims whole again that supplements the efforts of government agencies with

additional forms of support from private and nonprofit groups such as community organizations. Local resources must be marshaled to provide a menu of services that can address both the immediate and the long-term welfare of individuals harmed by interpersonal violence (Herman, 2010).

In order to better provide practical assistance and financial compensation for their losses and expenses, the governmental response should include a nonadversarial conference in which victims explain what happened to them, the unwanted event's impact, and what they need to get their lives back on track. The conference should result in an official validation that they have been wronged. Case managers should determine how best to enable them to rebuild their lives with the help of an array of services such as day care, job training, housing, or counseling. Offenders can play a role in constructing a parallel justice system for victims by making restitution and performing community service as part of their own reentry process (Herman, 2000, 2010; and NCVC, 2008).

One necessary step for an action plan to rebalance one-sided criminal justice procedures that exclude victims would be to set up an independent office or commissioner or ombudsperson. This independent body could monitor actual case outcomes to make sure that individual victims are getting the services and opportunities they are supposed to, according to new laws. It could also identify shortcomings in existing procedures that need to be fixed through legislation. Another step forward would entail setting up permanently funded institutes for victims' rights and services, preferably based at universities that would be centers for research and development. The institutes could assemble data, carry out surveys, and conduct and evaluate social experiments about advocacy and innovative services in order to identify best practices (see Waller, 2011).

SUMMARY

Whether they want to see their attacker punished via incarceration, given effective treatment in some rehabilitation program, or ordered to make restitution, victims might find themselves in conflict

rather than in cooperative relationships with prosecutors, judges, and corrections officials.

Victims want prosecutors' offices to provide them with lawyers who will represent their interests faithfully, but they may be disappointed if the assistant district attorneys assigned to handle their cases don't take steps to protect them from reprisals, don't consult with them during plea negotiations, or fail to gain convictions from juries after trials. Victims are not surprised if defense attorneys try to wear them down by stalling tactics and try to impeach their testimony by asking hostile questions during cross-examinations at trials. Victims hope that judges will be evenhanded but can become upset if judges set bail low enough for defendants to secure release and then threaten them, and if judges impose sentences that do not reflect the gravity of the offenses that harmed them. Victims want corrections officials to keep them posted concerning the whereabouts of convicts, protect them from reprisals after release, and effectively supervise restitution arrangements that might have been imposed as conditions of probation or parole.

Several decades ago, before the rise of the victims' movement, insensitive mistreatment by agencies and officials within the criminal justice process was common. Victims from privileged backgrounds clearly were treated much better than others. Researchers need to document whether the system now delivers equal justice for all or if the problem of differential handling persists.

KEY TERMS DEFINED IN THE GLOSSARY

allocution, 230

assistant district attorneys, 217

bedsheeting, 224

bifurcated capital trials, 232

consideration, 224

cop a plea, 224

differential access to justice, 242

differential handling, 239

district attorneys, 216

due process, 239

equal protection under the law, 239

going rate, 230

overcharging, 224

plea bargain, 224

plea negotiation, 223

presentence investigation report, 230

private prosecution, 223

second-class treatment, 239

sentence disparity, 229

truth-in-sentencing rule, 231

victim impact statements, 230

Victim/Witness Assistance Projects (VWAPs), 218

victims' rights, 207

zero-sum game model, 211

QUESTIONS FOR DISCUSSION AND DEBATE

1. Argue that victims should not be allowed to participate in plea negotiations.

2. Argue that victims should have much more of a voice in determining sentences.

3. Argue that victims should not be allowed any input into parole board decisions.

4. Describe how certain decisions by the Supreme Court have had an effect on the rights and best interests of victims.

CRITICAL THINKING QUESTIONS

1. Explain how certain rights might be considered to be gained at the expense of either criminals or criminal justice officials, depending on the way victims exercise them.

2. Identify a group of victims who do not deserve first-class handling by prosecutors, in the opinion of many people.

3. If victims are unable to participate because of their very serious wounds, or are too young to make such important decisions, who—if anyone—should exercise their rights in their name? Be specific, and give plausible scenarios.

4. Why hasn't a victims' rights amendment been added to the Constitution? Look through speeches given by Presidents Clinton and Bush and delivered by members of Congress, and then find out the objections of opponents who defeated this campaign to recast the Sixth Amendment.

SUGGESTED RESEARCH PROJECTS

1. Draw up a checklist of all the ways a prosecutor's office can provide assistance and support to victims of violent crimes. Find out which of these services are offered by the district attorney's office in your jurisdiction, and compare the two lists.

2. For some of the landmark decisions of the U.S. Supreme Court listed in Box 7.4 that had an impact upon victims, find out the facts of the case, the legal reasoning that was accepted by the majority of justices, and the arguments that were put forward in the dissenting minority position.

3. See if there is any evidence in recent articles in newspapers and magazines that wealthy and powerful figures who were victims of interpersonal violence or theft got first-class VIP treatment.

4. See if you can find out whether victims harmed by delinquent youth can exercise any rights in the juvenile and family courts in your local jurisdiction.

8
Victimized Children

LEARNING OBJECTIVES

To understand how two perspectives, a maximalist alarmist stance and a minimalist skeptical viewpoint, clash over the scope and seriousness of problems whenever solid statistical evidence is lacking.

To appreciate how substantial progress has been made along a number of dimensions in addressing the problem of missing children.

continued

LEARNING OBJECTIVES

continued

To recognize how children can be maltreated in a number of ways.

To grasp how maltreatment can cause great and lasting suffering for children as they grow up and become adults.

To appreciate how complicated it is to try to determine exactly how many children endure abuse at the hands of adults, and whether child maltreatment is growing or diminishing.

To recognize the many controversies that surround the issues of recovering memories of child sexual abuse by caretakers and of exposing molestations by members of the clergy.

To become familiar with the many child-centered reforms that have been implemented in the family court and criminal justice system.

To recognize child abuse in all its guises, including attacks by siblings and the statutory rape of minors.

The previous two chapters looked at the way the criminal justice system handles "ordinary" victims—adults harmed by street crimes such as serious assaults, robberies, burglaries, and car thefts. This chapter will analyze the unique vulnerabilities and needs of a group that is particularly susceptible to victimization: children. The focus of attention will be how the criminal justice system provides—or is supposed to accord them—extra-sensitive handling and special care.

Infants, toddlers, youngsters, and even teenagers are vulnerable to physical and sexual abuse by their caretakers: parents, older siblings, other family members such as stepparents, grandparents, babysitters, daycare workers, teachers, and acquaintances. Children are also highly desirable targets for kidnappers and pedophiles who may be complete strangers but could also be acquaintances or even close relatives.

If their offenders are arrested, children face a unique set of problems when their cases are processed by the legal system. If they are very young

and/or if the accused wrongdoers are parents or guardians, they will need someone to advocate on their behalf. They must be questioned with great care, and they face special difficulties in establishing their credibility when testifying. Courtroom procedures and cross-examinations can be intimidating, if not traumatizing. For these reasons, children face unusual challenges that require imaginative solutions that do not violate the constitutional rights of the adult suspects, arrestees, and defendants accused of harming them by investigators and prosecutors.

THE ONGOING DEBATE BETWEEN MAXIMALISTS AND MINIMALISTS

A basic question that arises whenever the particular problems of entire groups are examined is, "How many people suffer in this way?" Two distinct points of view usually can be recognized: a maximalist alarmist perspective and the minimalist skeptical perspective. The ongoing debate between these two viewpoints over the seriousness of a particular facet of the crime problem can become especially acrimonious if the two governmental sources of data, the FBI's *Uniform Crime Report* (*UCR*) and the Bureau of Justice Statistics' *National Crime Victimization Survey* (*NCVS*), do not closely monitor or focus upon these illegal activities and therefore cannot provide any official counts or rates. Other agencies or organizations must be turned to for data in order to derive rough, "ballpark" estimates.

The issues that have generated the most heated exchanges concern the fates of missing children, the extent of physical child abuse, and the prevalence of incest and child molestation. Victimologists can enter into these controversies as objective "claims investigators" and apply the tools of social science research to determine where the truth lies—which is usually somewhere between the high-end estimates of maximalist alarmists and the much smaller numbers offered by minimalist skeptics.

In general, the **maximalist** position argues that a problem is more widespread and intense than most people realize. Maximalists often warn that a type of victimization that routinely has been overlooked is reaching epidemic proportions. Dire consequences will follow unless drastic steps are taken. This outlook can be characterized as maximalist because it assumes the worst—large numbers of people are experiencing the problem, they are suffering greatly, their plight is not receiving sufficient attention and action by government officials, and the situation is spiraling out of control. Maximalists try to mobilize public support and resources to combat what they believe is an emerging crisis or epidemic that was rapidly spreading undetected and "under the radar" until they pinpointed it.

Frightening claims about dangerous conditions that are intensifying provoke a predictable response that can be termed the **minimalist** position. It is marked by a skeptical stance that tends to downplay the scope and seriousness of the problem. Minimalists consider maximalist estimates to be grossly inflated for either some well-intentioned reason or perhaps for a self-serving purpose. The maximalist assessment that massive expenditures and emergency measures are warranted touches off bitter clashes with minimalists who question what they consider to be overreactions. These sharp differences take the form of acrimonious debates at conferences and hearings, strident denunciations in reports and books, and angry letters and emails to the editors of newspapers, magazines, and websites that publish articles espousing the views of the other side.

Just like victim blaming and victim defending, maximalist and minimalist viewpoints actually are ideologies. A person might accept an alarmist point of view on one issue (for example, what happens to missing children) but might take a skeptical stance regarding another (such as the prevalence of stepfather–daughter incest). Therefore, as with victim blaming and victim defending, it is best not to personalize the matters merely as disputes between individuals. It is more constructive to view the controversies as the results of different sources of information, opposing assumptions, clashing political beliefs, and varying socioeconomic interests.

MISSING CHILDREN

The Rediscovery of the Plight of Kidnapped Children

A six-year-old boy wanders over to the toy counter in a department store in a mall near a police station. A few minutes later, his mother realizes he has disappeared. An intensive search is launched, but two weeks later and 120 miles away, a fisherman discovers the boy's severed head. The local police misplace crucial evidence implicating a serial killer as the prime suspect. Twenty-seven years after the abduction took place, and 12 years after the serial killer dies behind bars while serving consecutive life sentences for committing other terrible murders, the police charge him with decapitating the little boy on the basis of circumstantial evidence. Over the years, the boy's father helps set up an organization that aids and comforts parents searching for missing children and helps galvanize support for legislation that compels the FBI to set up a massive computer database to assist investigations to locate youngsters who have disappeared anywhere in the country and creates a nationwide registry to monitor the whereabouts of previously convicted sex offenders. Upon learning that his son's kidnapping has been officially declared "solved" and "closed," he declares, "… he didn't die in vain. For all the other victims who haven't gotten justice, I say one thing: 'Don't give up hope.'" (Almanzar, 2008)

•••

An eight-year-old boy is walking alone for the very first time from his day-camp bus stop to meet up with his parents a few blocks away in a bustling, urban enclave of devoutly religious people. He becomes lost and asks a man for directions. The man offers to drive him home, but first takes him to pay a dentist's bill and later drives him to a suburban community for a wedding. Meanwhile, busloads of members of the close-knit religious community arrive, and soon thousands of volunteers are combing through the neighborhood, putting up posters about the missing child and reviewing footage from surveillance cameras in stores along the child's route home. The next *morning, the man goes off to work but returns home in a panic when he hears that already $100,000 has been collected for a reward fund, and realizes that the entire community has been mobilized to locate the boy. While the child is watching television, the abductor drugs him with painkillers and then smothers him, and then dismembers his body. The police find some remains in a dumpster and quickly close in on the killer. "We pray that none of you should have to ever live through what we did," his parents write on the website of a charity for needy children and families that they establish to "perpetuate the feeling of collective responsibility and love" expressed during the search for their missing son.* (Baker, Robbins, and Goldstein, 2011)

■ ■ ■

An 11-year-old, his brother, and a friend are riding their bicycles on a gravel road by a farm near their home. A masked man carrying a gun appears and orders the boys to throw their bikes into a nearby ditch and lie face down on the ground. He tells two of them to run off into the woods and not look back, and then grabs the 11-year-old and disappears. The police are called, arrive minutes later, and launch a search that soon mobilizes hundreds of volunteers and generates over 50,000 leads. The nearby farm is periodically scoured by the FBI and rescue dogs. Twenty-one years later, the case is featured on a cable network news program and the sheriff's department receives 11 new leads. The boy's mother becomes an activist in behalf of missing children and never loses hope. Whenever she is asked, "How do you do it?" she answers, "How could I not? Every parent knows, you would do anything for your children...." (Wetenhall, 2010; and Kampshroer, 2011)

Kidnapping a youngster symbolizes the ultimate clash between good and evil: innocent and defenseless little children in the clutches of ruthless adults. No other group of crime victims has so captured the attention and hearts of the public. Rarely has citizen involvement been solicited and supplied on such a grand scale as in campaigns to rescue stolen children. Few victims' rights organizations have been so instrumental and successful in drafting new laws and reforming criminal justice procedures as the child-search movement.

Tragedies like the cases above periodically rivet the nation's attention. But how often do such shocking kidnappings take place? How should parents react to this threat? And what is being done to prevent abductions and locate captives before it is too late?

Hundreds of years ago, kidnapping was outlawed as a vicious crime under English common law. In the United States, news reports of abductions began to appear in the late 1800s. During the 1920s, several cases embodied a parent's worst nightmares about stranger danger (Gado, 2005). In the early 1930s, a kidnapper killed the baby of a celebrity aviator even after he picked up money for the child's safe return. Ever since then, demanding a ransom or transporting a hostage across state lines constitutes a federal crime and the FBI can enter the manhunt. Under current state and federal statutes, force is not a necessary element of the crime of taking and holding a person (of any age) against his or her will; the abducted individual can be detained through trickery or manipulation, termed (**inveiglement**). Besides extorting a ransom, the kidnapper might capture and hold someone for some other nefarious reason, such as robbery (for example, to compel an adult to divulge a password to withdraw money from an ATM), or to steal and raise a very young child, or to cruelly exploit someone as a sex object.

At the start of the 1980s, the agony suffered by kidnapped youth and their families was rediscovered by members of the victims' movement, reporters, and government officials. The problem was subsumed under the broader catchphrase **missing children**, which is applied to youngsters whose whereabouts are unknown to their parents and caretakers. In essence, the designation "missing child" refers to the lack of knowledge of a frightened adult responsible for the child's well-being. The designation does not necessarily establish that a youngster is in danger. But many people immediately assume the worst and fear foul play. It was no coincidence that the rediscovery of this age-old parental nightmare took place at the same time (the late 1970s and early 1980s) that widespread concerns were intensifying that the traditional family structure for raising children was disintegrating in America because of teenage pregnancies, single motherhood, divorce, and daycare.

Some of the major developments that marked the rediscovery of the kidnapping problem and the efforts to locate missing children are listed chronologically in Box 8.1.

Fears and Confusion Reigns in the Absence of Data

Statistics about kidnappings measure one of the most heinous crimes imaginable. And yet at the beginning of the 1980s, when a nationwide panic broke out, no organization or government agency was monitoring the scope of this problem. No systematic and comprehensive records were kept about the number of cases in which a distraught parent told police officers that a child was missing, the number of arrests of hostage takers by local departments, the outcomes of state prosecutions for kidnapping, or the number of kidnapped youngsters who were murdered. Because no one knew how many innocent, helpless children were seized and carried off each year, wild estimates circulated, and public fear levels soared.

The official source of data about crimes known to the police, the *UCR*, was of little use because kidnappings are not a Part One index offense. Furthermore, arrests for kidnappings were (and continue to be) combined with lesser crimes under the headings "offenses against family and children" and "all other offenses" in the *UCR*'s Part Two. (However, the emerging National Incident Based Record System, NIBRS, does keep track of kidnappings.) In the other official source, the *NCVS*, respondents were not asked about kidnappings of members of their households. In fact, the interviewers did not (and still don't) inquire about any crimes committed against youngsters under 12. The only estimates about the number of missing children presumed to be victims of foul play were derived from very limited studies of police files or projections from surveys based on small samples.

Insufficient record keeping and sporadic monitoring of the various dimensions of the problem remain a vexing problem to this day.

As a result, a heated debate has periodically erupted during the past three decades between maximalist alarmists and minimalist skeptics over what has happened to youngsters whose whereabouts are not known to their parents. Starting in the early 1980s, maximalists argued that kidnapping had become frighteningly common and that a complacent public ought to get aroused and mobilized. Assuming the worst about the disappearances, alarmists called for emergency measures to halt the apparent surge in abductions by strangers. They warned that child snatchers could strike anywhere, no youngster was ever completely safe, and parents could never be too careful about taking precautions and restricting their children's activities. Two remarks illustrate the near-hysteria of the times: A Congressman offered "the most conservative estimate you will get anywhere" that 50,000 children were abducted by strangers each year (see Best, 1988, 1989a); and a father of a murdered child told a congressional hearing, "This country is littered with mutilated, decapitated, raped, and strangled children" (see Spitzer, 1986:19).

Minimalists suspected that the true scope of the problem was blown out of proportion by well-meaning maximalists whose overestimates unduly alarmed parents. The public's fears were stoked by businesses that sought to profit from selling products and services to panicky adults; by journalists willing to sensationalize stories to attract larger audiences; by politicians looking for a get-tough issue that no one would dare oppose and therefore would gain them favorable publicity and votes; and by child-search organizations seeking a mission, recognition, private contributions, and government funding. Minimalists charged that maximalists were using the most inclusive definitions in order to generate the largest possible numbers (see Schneider, 1987). A child welfare advocate summed up the minimalist position when he charged that inflated statistics were being circulated by "merchants of fear" and "proponents of hype and hysteria" who "have foisted on a concerned but gullible American

BOX 8.1   Highlights of the Rediscovery of the Missing Children Problem

1932   The baby of a famous aviator is abducted from his crib and is later found dead. A man caught with some of the ransom money is executed. State and federal kidnapping laws are strengthened.

1955   The National Child Safety Council is established as the first private and voluntary organization in the field.

1974   Congress passes the Juvenile Justice and Delinquency Prevention Act, which mandates that runaways be sheltered but not arrested and confined.

1977   California becomes the first state to make violating a child custody agreement a felony.

1980   Congress amends the Juvenile Justice and Delinquency Prevention Act to permit police departments to hold chronic runaways under court order until they return home. Congress passes the Parental Kidnapping Prevention Act, which prohibits state courts from modifying original custody decrees issued after divorces and establishes a locator service that tracks down "fugitive parents" by tracing Social Security numbers.

1981   A Senate subcommittee holds the first hearings on the problem of missing children.

Child safety groups form a Child Tragedies Coalition.

Mysterious disappearances of 28 youngsters in Atlanta over a two-year period are solved when a young man is convicted of murder.

1982   Congress declares May 25 National Missing Children's Day and passes the Missing Children's Act, which grants searching parents new rights in their dealings with law enforcement agencies.

1983   A TV docudrama about the abduction and murder of a boy named Adam is viewed by an estimated 55 million people (about one of every four Americans).

1984   Congress passes the Missing Children's Assistance Act, which sets up a National Center for Missing and Exploited Children as a resource base and establishes an advisory board to guide, plan, and coordinate federal efforts.

1985   After a televised documentary, President Reagan appeals to viewers to help find missing children; 60 photos are broadcast and three youths are quickly reunited with their families.

1986   The first annual National Conference on Missing and Exploited Children is held.

1987   A National Association of Missing Child Organizations is formed to share information and maintain professional standards.

1988   Congress amends the Missing Children's Assistance Act to allocate money for establishing and operating clearinghouses on the state level to coordinate local law enforcement, social services, and educational activities.

1990   Congress passes the National Child Search Assistance Act, which requires officers to immediately enter information about disappearances into police computer networks.

1991   Congress enacts the International Parental Child Kidnapping Act.

1993   In response to the kidnap–murder of a 12-year-old girl by a parolee, federal and state lawmakers pass "three strikes and you're out" provisions to incarcerate repeat offenders for life.

1996   The Department of Justice sets up the Victim Reunification Travel Program to assist parents whose children have been unlawfully abducted to other countries by noncustodial family members.

2003   Congress passes a bill that helps states set up a national "Amber Alert" broadcasting system to enlist the public in the hunt for an abducted child.

2006   Congress passes the Adam Walsh Child Protection and Safety Act, which mandates that the FBI must enter information about missing and abducted children into its National Crime Information Center (NCIC) database within two hours of receiving a police report.

2011   The acquittal by a jury of a mother on trial for allegedly murdering her two-year-old daughter (who was "missing" for over a month before the authorities were notified) inspires lawmakers in several states to propose bills that would make it a felony for a parent or legal guardian to fail to quickly report the disappearance or death of a child.

SOURCE: Davidson, 1986; Howell, 1989; Aunapu et al., 1993; Jones, 2003; OJJDP, 2008; National Center for Missing and Exploited Children (NCMEC), 1987; Kallestad, 2011.

public" what he termed "one of the most outrageous scare campaigns in modern American history" (see Treanor, 1986: 8).

As fears escalated during the 1980s, strikingly different estimates were disseminated from maximalist as compared to minimalist sources (see Best, 1988, 1989a; Forst and Blomquist, 1991; and Kappeler, Blumberg, and Potter, 1993). Several factors having to do with vague definitions, police department practices, and pessimistic versus optimistic assumptions account for the sharp divergence. Some departments were less inclined than others to request outside assistance and federal intervention. Consequently, the FBI did not investigate some kidnapping cases in which a stranger might have been involved. The definitions police forces used in classifying crimes directly determined the number of stranger abduction cases in their files. For example, if an incident occurred in which a child was lured into a car, sexually molested, and then abandoned hours later, it might be classified as a sexual assault for record-keeping purposes (in accord with the *UCR*'s hierarchy rule), inadvertently obscuring the fact that an abduction took place, albeit for a relatively short time.

Assumptions about unsolved cases colored the estimates as well. The disappearance of a teenager might be the tragic result of a stranger abduction. But a more likely explanation is that a missing adolescent is a runaway who will eventually return home voluntarily. (Such youth may be victims in a different sense—of parental sexual or physical abuse. Furthermore, while out on their own, they are very vulnerable to sexual exploitation.) Other missing teens are not runaways but **throwaways** expelled from their homes by angry or neglectful parents. Finally, some children were not snatched by strangers but were whisked away by an angry parent who disregarded a court order after a bitter custody battle following a separation or divorce. (Seizures by noncustodial parents obviously can be ruled out in most disappearances.) In some remaining cases, especially those involving very young children, the missing youth may simply be confused and lost for a while. Minimalists suspect that many missing children are merely temporarily lost, were

spirited off by an angry ex-spouse, are runaways or throwaways, or are in the clutches of molesters who will soon release them. Maximalists assume that many missing children are victims of foul play and will never be reunited with their distraught parents.

This debate demonstrates how important technical details—definitions, ways of gathering data, and of making measurements and deriving estimates—can be in bringing social problems to the attention of the media, the public, and policy makers, and in assessing the seriousness of some aspect of criminal activity.

Many worthy causes compete for media coverage, public concern, and governmental action. The first few crusaders to alert people to the danger of kidnappings by strangers issued press releases with shockingly huge estimates that generated widespread fears. They were the only experts on the subject because no officials or agencies were authorized to analyze mysterious disappearances of children across the country. But some journalists and social scientists became skeptical of these statistical projections. Soon, members of the media adopted misleadingly low official estimates with the same uncritical enthusiasm with which they had earlier accepted the activists' overestimates. This capsule history of the controversy confirms these suspicions: Large estimates call attention to neglected social problems more readily than small numbers; figures from official sources carry greater weight than unofficial estimates; and large official estimates are the best of all to galvanize public support and governmental action (Best, 1988, 1989a).

Estimates of the Incidence and Seriousness of the Disappearance Problem

In an effort to try to resolve the maximalist–minimalist debate, the Department of Justice, as mandated by the 1984 Missing Children's Assistance Act, funded a five-year National Incidence Study of Missing, Abducted, Runaway, and Throwaway Children (NISMART). Researchers collected data in several ways: by conducting a telephone survey of nearly 35,000 randomly selected households, by analyzing FBI homicide records and the case files about nonfamily abductions in 83 law enforcement agencies in 21 randomly selected counties across the nation, and by interviewing runaways and the professionals who dealt with them in social service agencies and juvenile facilities. The social scientists clarified definitions, consulted with experts, and generated numbers that led them to the conclusion that the term *missing children* caused endless confusion by mixing five distinct problems that had very different victims, causes, dynamics, and remedies.

The first was the worst-case scenario that fit the stereotype of a kidnapping by a stranger with evil intentions. Thankfully, it turned out to be a rare occurrence. The second type, family abductions, was found to be a much bigger problem than policy makers had realized. Many missing children turned out to be runaways, which was the third type. But some of these homeless youngsters had actually been "cast out," and therefore throwaways constituted the fourth type of missing child. The fifth and final category were children who were missing because they got lost, were injured and couldn't reach their parents, or innocently failed to tell their caretakers where they were going and when they would return home. The report's findings indicated that adherents of the maximalist position were overestimating the real scope of the stranger danger threat to young people, and that those who took the minimalist approach were underestimating its true dimensions (Finkelhor, Hotaling, and Sedlak, 1990).

A follow-up NISMART study was carried out 10 years later but used different data collection methods. The pool of cases of missing children was assembled by a national telephone survey of adult caretakers in about 16,000 households and a mail survey of law enforcement agencies serving 400 counties throughout the nation. In addition, 74 juvenile facilities were contacted to find out how many of the youngsters in their care had run away during 1997. By combining the statistics gathered from these three sources, the researchers were able to address the question of what happened to missing children during the late 1990s and how many really were crime victims. The findings of

NISMART–1 and NISMART–2 are summarized in Box 8.2.

Although the two comprehensive NISMART studies shed much-needed light on many emotionally charged issues, several other key questions were answered by an intensive study of police department records for 1984 in Houston, Texas, and Jacksonville, Florida: What kinds of children are typically the targets of nonfamily abductions? Are they lured away or captured by force? When and where are they approached, and where are they taken? How long are they held? What additional crimes are committed against them?

According to the researchers who analyzed more than 200 cases reported to the police in those two cities that year, girls are targeted much more often (in 88 percent of the cases) than boys (although many young males may not tell their parents about the abduction and subsequent molestation, and their parents may not report the incidents to the police). The typical captive was between 11 and 14 years old. A little more than half (57 percent) of the youngsters were forced to go with their captors (perhaps intimidated by the sight of a weapon or physically overpowered); the remainder were lured or tricked into accompanying their abductors. Most of the victims were taken to secluded spots, either indoors (empty apartments, garages) or outdoors (woods, fields), but a sizable number were kept in a vehicle. Nearly all (98 percent) were released within 24 hours. In the majority of the cases (72 percent), the abductor molested the child; in most of the remaining cases (22 percent), the child escaped unharmed from an attempted kidnapping. About 4 percent were simply held and let go and, tragically, 2 percent were murdered after being sexually assaulted. The researchers discovered that only 15 percent of the cases involving an abduction were primarily classified by the police as a kidnapping. Most of the cases were filed under the heading of sexual assault and consequently were classified that way in the *UCR* (NCMEC, 1986).

Other research that zeroed in on kidnappings of children under 18 that resulted in homicides yielded an estimate of about 100 stranger killings a year

BOX 8.2   How Often Are Children Kidnapped, and What Happens to Them?

The NISMART–2 study analyzed nearly 800,000 cases across the country that were reported to police departments and child-search organizations in the late 1990s. Statistically, about 11 children out of every 1,000 were reported missing during 1999. The analysis yielded the following estimates of the number of victim–offender relationships and the characteristics of abducted children:

90 to 115 Life-Threatening Kidnappings of Children by Adults per Year

These cases fit the stereotype of a kidnapping: A child is detained overnight or longer and/or is transported 50 miles or more. The abductor intends to permanently keep the child, extort a ransom, or commit some other crime, including murder. In most of these extremely serious offenses, the kidnapper is not a complete stranger to the youngster and could be a disgruntled former boyfriend of the child's mother, a friend of the family, a neighbor, or a babysitter.

Most of these 115 captives grabbed by strangers or acquaintances during 1999 were teenagers. Nearly 70 percent were females, and more than 70 percent were white. Unfortunately, in 40 percent of these 115 cases, the child was murdered before the authorities could find her or him. In an additional 4 percent, the victim's body was never recovered (Finkelhor, Hammer, and Sedlak, 2002).

Between 1976 and 1987, as few as 50 and as many as 150 children were murdered by kidnappers each year. There was no discernible trend over the 12-year period. The victims tended to be older (aged 14–17), female, and from racial minority groups. Overall, a teenager's chances of being kidnapped and murdered during this period were calculated to be 7 out of every 1 million; the chances for younger children were 1 out of 1 million per year.

The NISMART–1 study, with data based on different collection methods, yielded a larger estimate that 200 to 300 of this kind of kidnapping took place in 1988.

12,000 Short-Term Abductions by a Nonfamily Member per Year

These cases meet the legal elements of kidnapping: a crime by an acquaintance or by a stranger who takes the child by force, or by threats, or by deceit into a building, vehicle, or other place and/or detains the child for more than an hour, perhaps to commit a sexual assault.

56,500 Long-Term Abductions by a Family Member per Year

In these cases, a family member, usually a parent, takes the child in violation of a decree from family court and tries to conceal his or her whereabouts and/or moves the youngster to another state with the intention of keeping the child permanently and/or altering custodial arrangements. If custody disputes are counted that were directly resolved by the estranged parents and guardians themselves and were not reported to the authorities, then the number of family abductions swells to over 200,000.

Accounting for the Remaining Cases of Children Reported as Missing

The NISMART–2 study concluded that of the nearly 800,000 children who were reported missing to police or child-search agencies, almost 360,000 (45 percent) turned out to be either runaways or throwaways (driven out of their homes). A roughly equal amount, 340,000 (43 percent), were considered missing by their alarmed parents because of "benign explanations"—misunderstandings and miscommunication about where the children were going and when they would return. The remaining youngsters, almost 62,000 (8 percent), did not return home on time because they were lost or injured.

SOURCES: NISMART–1: Finkelhor, Hotaling, and Sedlak, 1990; and Forst and Blomquist, 1991. NISMART–2: Sedlak, Finkelhor, Hammer, and Schultz, 2002.

(about 0.5 percent of murders nationwide in the mid-1990s). More than 7 of every 10 victims were white girls. Their average age was 11. The typical assailant was a single white man about 27 years old, often with a history of past sexual assaults and abductions. Roughly three-fifths of the abductions were characterized as crimes of opportunity by strangers; the rest were carried out by friends or acquaintances of the youngster's family. About 7 out of 10 had

been sexually assaulted or raped before they were slain. Almost half of the youth had been dispatched within the first hour, and almost three-quarters had been murdered within four hours, according to an analysis of 562 child killings carried out in 44 states between the late 1970s and the mid-1990s ("Study Puts Facts," 1997).

Since the two NISMART studies and the others cited above were carried out during time periods when crime rates were much higher, it is likely that the current numbers of youngsters abducted, molested, and murdered have declined substantially. The FBI's National Crime Information Center (NCIC) maintains a missing persons database. During 2013, it contained information about 335 cases that were designated as "abducted by a stranger," down from 518 in 2007 (FBI, 2014d). Nevertheless, horror stories that send shock waves through the media serve as a reminder that the threat of a worst-case scenario always looms as a possibility whenever a child disappears.

Hunting for Children Who Have Vanished

A 12-year-old girl and her two friends are enjoying a slumber party when they hear a knock on the bedroom door. When it is opened, a tall, bearded man wielding a large knife barges in. As her two friends giggle, thinking it is a practical joke, the intruder ties them up and carries the 12-year-old off into the night. The abduction galvanizes a sleepy community into action. Waves of volunteers flock to a storefront command center. Thousands of people beg to be assigned some task, like answering telephones or circulating posters with a picture of the victim and a police artist's sketch of the suspect. Shopkeepers close their stores, and workers give up their vacations to assist the search. A well-known actress donates a huge reward for information leading to an arrest or the safe return of the abducted child. Ironically, the police question a man for trespassing, but they do not know he is the kidnapper and that the missing girl is in the trunk of his vehicle, so they let him go. Two months later he is arrested. A crowd gathers for a vigil outside the jail, chanting, "Tell the truth and set your conscience free." Shortly afterward the middle-aged man, who was out on parole after spending 15 of his last 20 years behind bars for abductions, assaults, and burglaries, confesses that he strangled the girl and leads police to her body. He is sent to death row. An outraged community demands that a "three strikes and you're out" law be passed to prevent hardened convicts like him from ever being released. ("Kidnapping Summons City to Action," 1993; Gross, 1993; and Noe, 2005)

Even though the platitude "our children are our future" was frequently voiced in the early 1980s, only a few groups were prepared to help locate missing children. They were staffed by a handful of people with very limited budgets.

Before child-search organizations were set up, parents were totally dependent on police departments. Unfortunately, working relationships frequently became strained between frantic parents and the law enforcement agencies that were supposed to be carrying out the manhunt. The issues that divided them were delays in police responses, restricted access to law enforcement information, and a reluctance by local authorities to call for nationwide assistance.

When distraught parents turned to missing persons bureaus for help, they expected officers to spring into action by issuing all-points bulletins describing the child who had disappeared and by launching an intensive search. But many departments followed procedures that dictated that a youngster had to be missing for 24, 48, or even 72 hours before an official investigation could be initiated. These mandatory waiting period regulations were based on past experience that indicated the overwhelming majority of cases were not life threatening and would "solve themselves." The missing youths would turn out to be runaways who would soon return home tired, hungry, and broke. But infuriated parents condemned such arbitrary delays as endangering the lives of their children. They claimed that it enabled abductors to escape from the local area to other jurisdictions, where any call for a manhunt would receive an even lower priority, and interest in the case would be difficult to sustain. The crux of the problem for parents was that the burden of proof fell on them to somehow demonstrate that their children were victims of foul play (see Collins et al., 1983).

In 1990, responding to appeals by grieving parents for reform, Congress passed the National Child Search Assistance Act. The legislation prohibited law enforcement agencies from imposing waiting periods before entering the child's description into computer networks linking the FBI's National Crime Information Center, police departments, and state clearinghouses (Girdner and Hoff, 1994). Parents of formerly missing children who volunteer to undergo training have formed teams that provide emotional support and logistical advice to parents in distress. A family survival guide written by parents who have been through this ordeal suggests that immediate steps include putting out a "Be On the Look Out" (BOLO) bulletin to other police departments; preparing photos for dissemination to schools, hospitals, and media outlets; and searching with bloodhounds. Many states require police officers to take in-service training courses about how to investigate missing children cases, to interact with their families, and to follow the FBI's Child Abduction Response Plan.

A federally sponsored National Center for Missing and Exploited Children (NCMEC) operates a network linking 30 federal agencies, 50 state clearinghouses, and more than 60 private and non-profit organizations. It has a cold case unit, operates a national 24-hour hotline, trains police officers and prosecutors, provides parents with references to mental health professionals, furnishes reimbursement for reunification travel expenses, and helps recover missing youngsters (Aunapu et al., 1993; Office of Juvenile Justice and Delinquency Prevention, 1998; and Parilla and Allen, 2010).

In an effort to locate children who have been missing for a long period of time, the Internal Revenue Service has carried out a "Picture Them Home" program that sends photos in the same envelopes as tax forms to millions of homes each year. Since 2001, the program has helped recover more than 80 children (Kocieniewski, 2010).

The Amber Alert System

During the late 1990s, **Amber Alert** systems were set up in many states and received support from the federal government in 2003 to help searchers enlist the cooperation of the public. Amber stands for America's Missing: Broadcast Emergency Response, but the system is named after a nine-year-old girl who was kidnapped while riding her bicycle in Texas in 1996. A neighbor was able to describe to the police the vehicle into which she was lured, but without an effective system to widely disseminate that information, law enforcement agencies were unable to find the car in time. Community residents were outraged four days later when her body was discovered and demanded the establishment of some way to broadcast emergency bulletins so that more people could be rapidly enlisted to hunt for a missing or abducted child. Using the same arrangements as for severe weather warnings, a rapid-response network of radio and television stations broadcasts descriptions of the suspect, the youngster, and other clues like a vehicle's license plate to a huge audience in the immediate area. This voluntary partnership among police departments, broadcasters, and transportation agencies has branched out to incorporate the trucking industry, social networking websites, the wireless industry, and Internet providers (NCMEC, 2010).

Its goals are to deter kidnappings by scaring would-be offenders with the prospect of being swiftly apprehended and severely punished, and failing that, to rescue children quickly, before they are injured or killed. The system sends out a message whenever a law enforcement agency has a reasonable belief that a child under 18 has been abducted and is in imminent danger of severe bodily harm or death. By 2005, all 50 states and an additional 64 localities had set up Amber Alert systems, including the District of Columbia, Puerto Rico, and the U.S. Virgin Islands.

During the period from 2005 to 2010, almost 1,340 alerts were issued nationwide in an effort to recover endangered children. Most of the cases were either family child snatchings (mostly by non-custodial parents) or nonfamily abductions (but not necessarily by strangers); a small number concerned lost children. Each year between 10 and 25 alerts turned out to be based on hoaxes intentionally called in by parents or the youths themselves, and a roughly equal number of reports of emergencies later were deemed to be unfounded (inadvertent mistakes concerning the whereabouts of the child). Issuing the alert directly led to saving one or more endangered children in nearly 290 recoveries. Most of the rescues credited to an Amber

Alert took place when a member of the public or a law enforcement officer spotted the child or the vehicle, or when the abductor became aware of the manhunt, panicked, and released the captive. Unfortunately, over the six-year period, 57 of the children died before they were located (but not all were murdered by their abductors). Most of the foiled hostage takings turned out to be parental abductions. As for a profile of the typical children being sought, most were either infants and toddlers or in their early teens. The majority were not white, and girls outnumbered boys by a small margin each year. As for trends, the number of Amber Alerts issued annually during the seven-year time period dropped substantially, presumably indicating that the abduction problem is decreasing (NCMEC, 2011). The yearly figures drawn from annual reports appear in Table 8.1.

The police in New York City received about 25,000 calls from people worried about missing persons (of all ages) during 2010. About 90 percent were resolved by the end of the year. During the first half of 2011, NYPD detectives investigated about 5,800 missing person cases, of which 3,500 involved children between the ages of 10 and 17. Detectives suspected that about 265 of these youngsters were "victims of involuntary disappearances" for at least a short period of time (Goldstein and Baker, 2011). The NYPD first used the high-tech Wireless Emergency Alert system that automatically sends text messages to all cell phones operating in the city to quickly locate a 7-month-old boy who had been abducted by his

mentally ill mother in 2013 (Hu and Goodman, 2013).

The importance of an immediate mobilization— "the more eyes, the better"—in order to "beat the clock" was underscored by a study of 600 kidnappings that ended in tragedies. About three-quarters of the children were killed within the first three hours, and nine-tenths within the first 24 hours (Jones, 2003; Zgoba, 2004; and NCMEC, 2010). Long-term abductions that eventually lead to a successful recovery are rare, but a case like this illustrates the optimistic view that there may be a ray of hope when a child's fate remains unknown for months:

> A 14-year-old girl is sleeping beside her 9-year-old sister when an intruder puts a knife to her throat and warns, "Don't make a sound. Get out of bed and come with me, or I will kill you and your family." The kidnapper, a homeless street preacher who once briefly worked for her parents, forces her to hike for hours uphill to a campsite in the woods. With the help of his wife, this self-proclaimed "prophet" performs a "marriage" ceremony in a tent that night, rapes her, and then holds her captive, sometimes by chaining her. As part of this polygamous "marriage," she is forced to consume alcohol and other drugs and raped nearly every day, sometimes several times a day. Occasionally the trio travels around in public, with the captive wearing a religious-looking veil. After nine months, a passing motorist recognizes her walking with the couple around a suburb near her home, and she is rescued. Nearly nine years later, the

TABLE 8.1 Accomplishments of the Amber Alert System, 2005–2011

Year	Number of Alerts	Number of Recoveries	Recoveries Directly Resulting from Alerts	Child Recovered Too Late: Deceased
2005	275	220	49	15
2006	261	214	53	10
2007	227	188	48	6
2008	194	166	40	8
2009	208	166	45	9
2010	173	150	28	9
2011	158	144	28	5
Totals	1,496	1,248	291	62

SOURCE: NCMEC's Amber Alert Annual Reports, 2005–2011.

street preacher is judged mentally fit to stand trial. She testifies about her ordeal, and he is convicted of kidnapping as well as unlawful transportation of a minor across state lines for sexual exploitation and is sentenced to spend the rest of his life in prison. "I hope that not only is this an example that justice can be served in America, but that it is possible to move on after something terrible has happened," the girl tells reporters as she walks arm-in-arm with her mother out of the courthouse. (Dobner, 2010a, 2010b; and AP, 2010, 2011a)

Protecting Children from Kidnappers

As parents and their children have become more conscious about "stranger danger," they have incorporated preventive steps into their daily routines in a myriad of ways. Youngsters are instructed by police officers, teachers, and parents "what to do if …" as well as through comic book characters, board games, songs, and books. Potential targets and their guardians are educated to spot **child lures**—deceitful tricks abductors use to entice them into situations where they can be exploited. Child lures involve ways of meeting the intended prey, of gaining their trust—perhaps by playing games—and of evading parental supervision. The training that children receive in recognizing and rejecting child lures far exceeds the old warning of "Don't accept candy from strangers." They are taught to distinguish between good touches and bad touches and to be wary of certain situations and behaviors as well as specific kinds of people. The aim is to build self-confidence rather than to instill unreasonable fears.

The widespread use of social networking sites and youth-oriented websites provides sexual predators with many additional opportunities to lure and then groom their intended prey. They can chat, exchange increasingly explicit photos, and subsequently make plans to meet in person. Parents find it difficult to effectively monitor the communications of naïve or rebellious youngsters (Walker, 2009).

Some risk reduction strategies involve planning, products, and services. At the height of the social panic that gripped many families during the mid-1980s, the maximalist viewpoint was so widespread that many new products flooded the market and department stores set up child safety displays. High-tech outlets sell homing devices that trigger alarms when children stray or are taken beyond a certain range. Dentists offer to bond microchips containing identifying information to children's teeth. Graphic designers can be hired to create images that project what a missing child might look like at different ages. Shopping centers attract crowds by offering fingerprinting for infants and toddlers. Playgrounds, schoolyards, and large stores are designed to limit access and close down escape routes. Tens of thousands of stores have set up **Code Adam** responses (named after a child who was abducted from a store and murdered; see the first real-life example above) that lock down all doors and notify customers and employees that a child has just been reported missing on the premises. The shadow cast by the ominous stranger has eclipsed the mushroom-shaped cloud that haunted the imaginations of previous generations (Wooden, 1984; "Teaching Children," 1999; and Verhovek, 2001).

Understandably, child safety campaigns have provoked a backlash. Skeptics dismiss as "urban legends" most of the accounts that circulate via the Internet and in emails about children of inattentive parents who are hustled out of stores and malls and other public places by kidnappers who quickly alter the youngsters' appearances by changing their clothes or slipping wigs on them. These cautionary tales that urge parents to be vigilant at all times, to never let their guard down, and to not let youngsters out of their sight, even for a moment, reflect widespread fears about predatory strangers that apparently well up in people who reside in increasingly impersonal and anonymous urban and suburban settings and who regret the loss of close-knit communities ("What a way…," 2008).

Some minimalist skeptics worry about the potential social and psychological costs of certain of these victimization prevention measures. They wonder whether an anxious, suspicious, and dependent generation will be cheated out of a carefree childhood and grow up obsessed by security considerations and burdened prematurely by adult's fears. Other critics are concerned about the questionable performance of expensive products and services. They take a dim view of commercial outfits that charge for information, devices, and forms of assistance that can be obtained for free from non-profit child-find organizations or police departments. Other minimalists are suspicious of the motives of the many corporations that have made tax-deductible contributions to child-search projects; amid the hoopla over staged events, they get free publicity and cultivate good public relations. Victimologists can carry out research to determine whether certain widely touted child safety measures really work as intended, fail to be effective, or, worse yet, have unanticipated negative social and emotional side effects (see Karlen et al., 1985; Andrews, 1986; Adler, 1994; Brody, 2003; Hoffman, 2009; and Rochman, 2011).

PHYSICALLY AND SEXUALLY ABUSED CHILDREN

The Rediscovery of Child Abuse

Beliefs about what constitutes child abuse—physical, sexual, and emotional—remain the subject of much debate. Legal definitions of child maltreatment and neglect clearly are socially constructed: They evolve as time passes, and they differ from country to country and even between subcultures within a society. For centuries, parents were permitted to beat their children as they saw fit in the name of imposing discipline. Legal notions of progeny as the property of their parents as well as religious traditions (such as "honor thy father and mother" and "spare the rod and spoil the child") legitimized corporal punishment of youngsters as a necessary, even essential, technique of child rearing. Only if permanent injury or death resulted were adults in danger of being held responsible for going too far, a problem labeled **cruelty to children**.

The **House of Refuge movement** arose in the early 1800s to intervene on behalf of beaten

and neglected children. Its priority was to prevent abused youth from growing up to be delinquents. The movement removed youngsters from their dysfunctional homes, but unfortunately, these victims often were thrown into environments where they mingled with young vagrants and lawbreakers. During the late 1800s, the Society for the Prevention of Cruelty to Animals expanded its mission and began to take responsibility for rescuing children from uncaring foster parents and heartless employers. Cases like this one were brought to its attention:

> A 10-year-old girl testifies, "Mamma has been in the habit of whipping me and beating me almost every day … I never dared speak to anybody, because if I did I would get whipped." This orphan's plight, recounted in a 1874 newspaper article entitled "Inhuman treatment of a little waif" puts a human face on child abuse and inspires reformers to launch a crusade. (Markel, 2009)

As a result of this case, the first child protective agency in the world, the Society for the Prevention of Cruelty to Children, was organized in New York City in 1874. It used its police powers to place abused youngsters from big-city slums into foster homes in rural settings, but the children sometimes wound up in juvenile institutions in a misguided attempt to head off delinquency. During the early 1900s, the "child savers" movement was motivated by the same fear: that neglect and abuse caused lawbreaking later in life. It designed a special court system and developed reform schools strictly for troubled juveniles (see Platt, 1968; and Pfohl, 1984).

The problem festered until the early 1960s, when pediatric radiologists (doctors who study X-rays of children's injuries) sparked the rediscovery of physical abuse. Apparently, the pledge of confidentiality inhibited physicians such as pediatricians and emergency room doctors from exposing the consequences of severe beatings, as did their reluctance to get embroiled in the criminal justice process. Pediatric radiologists, on the other hand, had little direct contact with parents and desired greater recognition within the medical profession. Therefore, they were willing to set the rediscovery process into motion, exposing brutality, labeling it as deviant behavior, and encouraging legislation against it by alerting colleagues and the public to the **battered child syndrome** in 1962. This syndrome was identified as a clinical condition of nonaccidental injuries repeatedly inflicted by parents or guardians, reflecting a cycle pattern of inflicting excessive punishments. In the typical case, the youngster was less than three years of age and suffered traumatic injuries to the head and limbs, and the caretakers claimed that the wounds were caused by accidents and not beatings (see Pfohl, 1984; and Kethineni, 2009).

Social workers, women's organizations, public health associations, and law enforcement groups joined doctors to help raise public consciousness about the suspected dimensions of the problem. Between 1962 and 1966, legislatures in all 50 states passed laws forbidding parents from abusing their children (Pfohl, 1984). Because the victims usually were too young or too frightened to complain, requirements for reporting cases of apparent abuse to child welfare and protection agencies were imposed on doctors, teachers, and others who routinely came into contact with youngsters.

In 1974, Congress passed the Child Abuse Prevention and Treatment Act, amending it in 1978. The law prohibited maltreatment in all its guises (acts of omission as well as commission), including neglect, physical abuse, sexual abuse, and emotional abuse. Neglect ranged from abandonment to failure to meet a child's basic requirements in three areas: physical needs (including inadequate supervision and medical care), emotional needs (denial of nurturing and affection, tolerance of a child's drug or alcohol abuse, or fierce fighting in the child's presence), and educational needs (tolerance of chronic truancy). Physical abuse involved assaults (punching, kicking, scalding, suffocating, shaking, and extended confinement, even if unintended as the consequence of excessive punishment). Sexual abuse was recognized as incest, fondling, sodomy, intercourse, rape, and commercial exploitation (impairment of morals, involvement in pornography, or prostitution). In addition, maltreatment could take the form of emotional abuse (leading to serious behavioral or mental disorders) (see Irwin, 1980; and National Clearinghouse, 1997). During the 1980s, the focus of researchers, practitioners, and an indignant public shifted from physical maltreatment to sexual abuse (Milner, 1991).

When Congress passed the Keeping Children and Families Safe Act of 2003, it broadened the definition of child maltreatment to encompass any act—or failure to act—on the part of a parent or another caretaker that results in death, serious physical or emotional harm, sexual abuse or exploitation, plus any act or failure to act that poses an imminent risk of serious harm. Child neglect (failure to provide adequate supervision, medical care, food, or clothing) turns out to be the most prevalent form of maltreatment but also the most difficult type to recognize and to respond to by social service and criminal justice agencies.

News media coverage of horror stories that described particularly vicious punishments, severe injuries, and disturbing circumstances evoked strong condemnations and helped galvanize a social movement. Initially, journalists focused on battering, but they soon broadened their inquiries to include cases of sexual exploitation and incest as well as of gross neglect and emotional cruelty. There is never a shortage of highly upsetting tragedies that can keep the public focused on the need to adequately fund effective child protective services (CPS), as this case shows:

> *A baby is born prematurely and must stay in a hospital getting special care. When she is finally able to go home, she is severely neglected by her drug-addicted mother. The local child welfare agency arranges for a private company to monitor the little girl's plight because her mother clearly is unable to attend to her daughter's serious medical problems. But the child is routinely beaten and tied to her bed at night to keep her from taking food from the refrigerator and "making a mess." One day, a caseworker inspects the home and discovers the bruised and emaciated corpse of the four-year-old (who weighed just 18 pounds when she died). The 30-year-old mother is arrested for second-degree assault, and the*

front page story shines a spotlight on the many inadequacies of the city's protective services agency, which concedes that a lapse in supervision and investigation occurred. (Rivera, 2010a)

Coverage of these human interest stories fit the organizational needs not only of the news media to attract readers and viewers but also of professional and occupational groups and private and nonprofit agencies seeking increased funding and more recognition for their missions (Johnson, 1989).

From 2008 through 2013, over 785 children died of abuse or neglect while their cases were being monitored by child protection agencies across the country. The authorities knew they were in danger and kept their cases open while investigating their families or guardians in their troubled homes. And yet, these children, mostly under the age of four, were beaten to death, starved, or left unattended and drowned. Many factors probably contributed to these preventable deaths: huge workloads, tight budgets, and shortages of trained caseworkers to follow-up complaints about abuse and neglect to hotlines that consequently were screened out and never investigated, or misclassified. Also, some deaths can be attributed to abusers avoiding detection by moving from state to state, and to a policy that emphasizes keeping families intact, according to a study carried out by the Associated Press (2014b).

The persistence of child abuse always has been of great concern to victimologists. They ask, "Exactly what behaviors by adults toward children can be considered forms of maltreatment?" Is the true scope of the problem adequately recognized and accurately measured? What are the short-term and long-term consequences of suffering maltreatment? What percentages of cases go unreported and unattended? Are existing mandatory reporting requirements sufficient? How are abused youngsters handled by the authorities in family courts and in the criminal justice system? Are treatment, protection, and support services by government agencies as well as private, nonprofit, and religious organizations effective? To anticipate and thereby prevent future cases of abuse, victimologists want to

discover what the risk factors are that might predict which children will face the gravest dangers (see Finkelhor, 2008).

How Children Suffer

A biography of one of the most famous outfielders in the history of major league baseball reveals that he was molested as a child by his teenage half-sister and an older boy. These sexually exploitive incidents severely impacted his life, especially by poisoning his relationship with women, but also by possibly contributing to his heavy drinking and lewd public behavior, the ballplayer's widow suspects. (Madden, 2010)

∎∎∎

A 29-year-old man accuses an assistant football coach of molesting him over 100 times during a period of four years, starting when he was 10 years old. He claims the middle-aged man lavished gifts on him, took him to see football games, and arranged for him to enjoy special privileges at campus facilities. The abuse took place in the coach's basement and in the university's locker room, among other places. When the boy turned 14, he resisted further advances, saying "I'm going to tell …," but the predator reportedly scoffed, "No one will believe you" and then threatened him and his family. But when eight other young men come forward and testify about molestations and sexual assaults, he is charged with 52 counts of sexual abuse of young boys over a span of 15 years. A jury convicts him, and at the sentencing hearing, one young man tells him to his face that his life was ruined and his childhood stolen: "I am troubled with flashbacks of his naked body, something that will never be erased from my memory." Another victim says, "I want you to know I don't forgive you." and a third observes, "There is no remorse, only evil." The judge sentences him to between 30 and 60 years in prison. His downfall leads to the worst scandal in the history of college athletics. When stories surface about a cover-up years earlier of a credible charge against this assistant coach of raping a boy in a campus shower room, the board of trustees fires the university president, along with the revered head coach; students hold a raucous protest against the firings; and critics question the administration's undue emphasis on big-time college athletics. (Berube, 2011; Pennington, 2011; and Peyser, 2012)

∎∎∎

A famous actress reveals that at one point she "wanted to die" after a childhood marred by sexual abuse. At age six, she was molested by a female babysitter. When she was 12, her first heterosexual experience took place when a 25-year-old male acquaintance raped her. After that, she was gang-raped by a boyfriend from school and six of his buddies. As a result, she confides, she always has had a difficult time trusting people. She sets up a foundation that uses her fame, access to world leaders, and fortune to campaign for animal rights and to protect the environment. (Li, 2014)

The U.S. Centers for Disease Control (CDC) deems child abuse and neglect to be a high-priority health problem. The U.S. Department of Health and Human Services (HHS) considers violence against children to be a public health crisis. One researcher summed up the current situation this way, "If 20 million people were infected by a virus that caused anxiety, impulsivity, aggression, sleep problems, depression, respiratory and heart problems, vulnerability to substance abuse, antisocial and criminal behavior, retardation and school failure, we would consider it an urgent public health crisis. Yet, in the United States alone, there are more than 20 million abused, neglected and traumatized children vulnerable to these problems. Our society has yet to recognize this epidemic, let alone develop an immunization strategy" (Perry, 2011, cited in TexProtects).

Physically and sexually abused youngsters might suffer terribly in a myriad of ways. The fear, stress, and trauma they endure can lead to problems that can plague the rest of their lives. Afflicted pupils can fall behind developmentally and consequently may perform poorly in school. They may behave inappropriately with other youngsters and can become enmeshed in troubled relationships when they grow up. Abused children are much more likely than their peers to regress to infantile behaviors like thumbsucking or bed-wetting, mimic sexual behavior when playing with toys, refuse to get undressed, run away from home, become sexually promiscuous, commit crimes, get arrested as teenagers and adults, become depressed or anxious, turn to drinking and drugs for solace, cut or burn themselves, and ultimately commit suicide to end their torment (TexProtects, 2011; and Fernandez, 2011).

Sexually exploited youngsters can suffer complicated, far-reaching, and long-lasting problems. The aftershocks of childhood incest can be devastating. Youngsters reportedly suffer from clinginess, loss of appetite, nightmares, bed-wetting, sexual preoccupations, inappropriate knowledge of sexual matters, and posttraumatic stress disorder (PTSD). As they grow older, they are more prone than others to experience reckless promiscuity, sexual dysfunctions, eating disorders, depression, guilt, self-hatred, self-mutilation, alcoholism, and substance abuse. A review of the literature written by therapists turned up seven groupings of adverse effects. Affective problems were evidenced by guilt, shame, anxiety, fear, depression, anger, low self-esteem, concerns about secrecy, feelings of helplessness, and an inordinate need to please others. Physical repercussions included genital injuries, unwanted pregnancies, venereal diseases, loss of appetite, sleep disruptions, and bed-wetting. Cognitive effects took the form of shortened attention spans and trouble concentrating. Behavioral symptoms materialized as hostile-aggressive acting out, tantrums, drug taking, delinquency, withdrawal, and repetitions of the abusive relationship. Self-destructive impulses were manifested as suicidal thoughts, high-risk behavior, and self-mutilations. Psychopathological repercussions showed up as neuroses, character disorders, psychotic thought patterns, and multiple personalities. Finally, sexual disorders took the form of age-inappropriate sexual knowledge, talk, and involvements. Because sexual abuse can range from a single molestation to an ongoing incestuous relationship, each youngster might exhibit a different mix of symptoms. Although these symptoms are consistent with abuse, they don't constitute legal proof that incest definitely occurred; other problems can bring about these same disorders. There is no specific problem or repertoire of behaviors that definitively and conclusively indicates that a child has been abused (Yapko and Powell, 1988; Whitcomb, 1992; and Kendall-Tackett, Williams, and Finkelhor, 1993).

The problem of child abuse exacts an enormous toll not only on the youngsters who are preyed upon but on the entire society. The direct and indirect social and economic costs show up as expenses for foster homes, medical care, alcohol and drug treatment, and outlays for police protection, court proceedings, and incarceration. For example, many women who receive public assistance because of multiple problems—addiction to alcohol or drugs, disabling bouts of anxiety and depression, and injuries from violent mates—were sexually abused when they were girls (de Parle, 1999).

An intergenerational transmission of poor parenting skills takes place when abused children grow up and harm their own children in the same ways that they were mistreated. Children socialized into a subculture of violence that is very much on display in their homes are taught to use force to settle disagreements in the same imitative manner that they learn other behaviors. Worse yet, experiencing neglect, physical abuse, and sexual abuse as a youngster becomes a serious risk factor for perpetuating a vicious cycle that leads to delinquency, crime, and violence later in life. Those who were physically abused face the gravest risks of becoming lawbreakers, more so than those who were abused sexually or grossly neglected. Of course, suffering during childhood does not inevitably lead to criminal behavior as a grown-up: Most adults who were abused as children don't have arrest records. But the search for risk versus resiliency factors continues to inspire a great deal of theorizing and research (see for example, Gray, 1986; Wyatt and Powell, 1988; Barringer, 1989; Widom, 1989, 1995; Turman, 1999; and Widom and Maxfield, 2001).

Estimates of the Incidence, Prevalence, and Seriousness of Child Abuse

The U.S. General Accounting Office (GAO, 2011) issued a report that concluded that more accurate

statistics are needed because it is difficult to determine the true depth and breadth of the problem in the absence of reliable information. The two official sources of crime statistics, the FBI's *UCR* and the BJS's *NCVS*, contain no data about child maltreatment's incidence (the number of new cases that come to light each year) and prevalence (the proportion of youth who have ever suffered this form of victimization). The *UCR* monitors the age of murder victims, but not all homicides against youngsters were carried out by abusive parents or caretakers. The *NCVS* does not ask respondents younger than 12 about any illegal acts committed against them. Therefore, researchers must turn to other sources of official statistics.

One source of government data comes from the Administration for Children and Families (ACF) of the U.S. Department of Health and Human Services (DHHS). Its Children's Bureau, in conjunction with the Office of Planning, Research and Evaluation, periodically carries out a congressionally mandated National Incidence Study (NIS) of Child Abuse and Neglect. The NIS gathers statistics about children whose mistreatment was investigated by state CPS but it also obtains information about cases that were screened out by CPS agencies and not looked into, as well as incidents that came to the attention of child welfare professionals but not CPS agencies. Therefore, the NIS database is more inclusive than other data collection systems.

The NIS survey defined maltreatment as encompassing both abuse and neglect. Abuse can harm children in three ways: physically, sexually, and emotionally. Neglect can hurt youngsters in three ways: physically, emotionally, and educationally.

The fourth and most recent NIS study analyzed data from a nationally representative sample of 122 counties during the study year 2005–2006. It found that more than 1.25 million children suffered harmful maltreatment. That number corresponds to a rate of one child out of every 58, which was more than 2 percent of all youngsters growing up in the Untied States at that time. Of those who were abused, 58 percent were hurt physically,

24 percent were harmed sexually, and 27 percent experienced emotional abuse. Of those who were neglected, 47 percent were hurt educationally, 38 percent suffered physically, and 25 percent were harmed emotionally. The percents exceed 100 percent because some children were abused or neglected in more than one way (ACF, 2010).

The other source of official statistics also comes from the ACF. It is the National Child Abuse and Neglect Data System (NCANDS). Since 1990, the ACF has issued annual Child Maltreatment reports based on statistics collected from CPS (but also called child welfare agencies) in the 50 states plus the District of Columbia and Puerto Rico. Well over 3 million reports were filed with the state agencies across the country, but only about one-fifth of them were supported by enough evidence to make a determination that the child was indeed a victim. Therefore, about 685,000 children were deemed to be abused or neglected, yielding a victimization rate of about 9 out of every 1,000 children in the population during 2012 (fiscal year). More than 75 percent experienced neglect; more than 15 percent endured physical abuse; and nearly 10 percent suffered sexual abuse, according to the annual Child Maltreatment report based on the NCANDS database (ACF, 2013).

Note that the NCANDS figure (685,000) is a much smaller number than the NIS estimate (1.25 million) because the two systems use definitions and methods of collecting data that are substantially different (also, but less important, they were for two recent but different years). Maximalists sharply disagree with minimalists over how these two sets of numbers should be interpreted, and what actions need to be taken to more effectively bring the problem under control.

Maximalist Versus Minimalist Approaches to the Seriousness of the Problem

Maximalist Arguments   The maximalist perspective contends that the time has come to reject the reluctance of earlier generations to face the facts and to recognize the enormity of the crisis. Parents are abusing and neglecting their children in record numbers, and pedophiles, sadistic adolescents, and other abusers are preying on youngsters as never before. This alarmist perspective puts forward strong arguments to support its case that child abuse is all too common and must be taken much more seriously (see Gardner, 1990, 1994; Finkelhor, 1990; Whitcomb, 1992; Mash and Wolfe, 1991; Feher, 1992; Ceci and Bruck, 1993; De Koster and Swisher, 1994; Kincaid, 1998; and Fernandez, 2011).

Maximalists are convinced that many instances of abuse go undetected—especially crimes of a sexual nature. Hence, the known incidents are only the tip of the iceberg, as this case implies:

> A newly elected U.S. senator writes in his autobiography that he was groped decades ago by a summer camp counselor whom he does not wish to publicly identify. He declares that "if my book has encouraged people to come forward with their own stories of abuse or if it's given comfort to victims who thought they were all alone and that no one would believe them, then that is a good thing." Thirteen former campers, now grown men, hire a lawyer and lodge allegations of abuse. (Goodnough, 2011)

The maximalist perspective assumes that statistics from official sources are gross underestimates of the true depth of the emergency (see Herman, 1981; Russell, 1984, 1986; Peters, Wyatt, and Finkelhor, 1986; and Wyatt, 1985).

- Presumably, a large (but unknown) number of episodes of physical and sexual abuse are never reported to the authorities—not by the child, the abusive parent's spouse, parent, another relative or by a neighbor, doctor, or teacher. Underreporting is a serious problem because many victimized children are too young to know their rights or to be believed, or are too intimidated or even terrorized to tell anyone. They also may consciously wish to forget the past or are too embarrassed to disclose what actually happened. Furthermore, they may distrust the interviewer, may wish to protect their parents, or may believe they deserved the overly harsh punishments. Most abuse and neglect takes place behind closed doors without witnesses, and tangible evidence is lacking unless obvious physical injuries or sexually transmitted venereal diseases appear. Many professionals who are supposed to err on the side of caution fail to file mandatory official reports when they suspect abuse, preferring instead to pressure adults in troubled families to enter counseling, drug treatment, or other programs. The professionals responsible for intervening in child abuse cases often hold cherished beliefs about family privacy and parental rights, which make them reluctant to become enmeshed in court cases. Finally, preschoolers are not as closely observed for signs of abuse by child welfare professionals as older students are.

- Many reports of abuse are mistakenly screened out and dismissed by child welfare agencies that simply do not have sufficient time, money, and staff to do the thorough investigations necessary to verify the charges. Just because a report is deemed to be unsubstantiated (due to a lack of sufficient evidence to meet stringent legal standards of proof) does not mean it is untrue; classifying a report as "unfounded" certainly does not mean it is completely baseless or intentionally and maliciously false.

- Violence against children seems to be the norm in many families. Youngsters are abused on a regular basis but the authorities are not aware of their plight.

Minimalist Views The minimalist point of view makes the following arguments to back up its contention that child abuse is less widespread than the maximalist alarmist perspective would have the public believe (see Siegel et al., 1987; Pagelow, 1989; Besharov, 1990; Wexler, 1990; Robin, 1991; Ceci and Bruck, 1993; and Jenkins, 1998):

- The definition of child maltreatment has been expanding and diluting over the years. Minor instances of bad parenting that were justifiably overlooked in the past are now being routinely reported. All forms of physical discipline (slaps, spankings) should not automatically qualify as child abuse. Various ethnic and religious subcultures have dramatically different notions of where to draw the line between appropriate parenting and maltreatment, but some protection agencies blindly apply a rigid "one standard fits all" approach. No state prohibits parents from using "reasonable corporal punishment" when disciplining their children; in fact, some states expressly permit it. In many studies it is not clear which definition is being applied to real-life cases—the law's, the reporter's, the researcher's, or the child's (especially once the child has grown up). Yet some studies apply the label of "abuse" to acts that most people consider reasonable corporal punishment, instead of reserving it for clearly inappropriate and excessive force. In a 1977 ruling (*Ingram v. Wright*), the Supreme Court held that corporal punishment in school (within reasonable limits, by designated personnel, and with parental approval) is permissible under the Constitution.

- Similarly, certain aspects of maltreatment—especially emotional and educational neglect and abuse—are vague and subjective terms. The expanding definition of maltreatment also has incorporated medical neglect, another very indefinite and controversial concept.

If it appears that child maltreatment is increasing, it may just be that reports of suspected neglect and abuse are growing, skeptics charge. Heightened public awareness and mandatory reporting regulations can produce an apparent crime wave. Over 90 percent of all states require doctors, educators, and child care providers to report suspected abuse or even neglect. In addition, 25 percent of all states require nonprofessionals like parents and community residents to share their suspicions with child protective service agencies. Nearly 50 percent of the states permit tipsters to remain anonymous (Young-Spillers, 2009).

Professionals face civil and criminal penalties if they cover up or are grossly negligent in overlooking abuse. All these mandatory reporting requirements and anonymous tip hotlines generate many baseless charges. Large numbers of honestly mistaken allegations, as well as maliciously false ones, are mixed in with truthful disclosures, making the problem seem worse than it is, minimalists say.

When a failure to report occurs, children could face grave dangers. On the other hand, when unwarranted allegations are entered into government files, the reputations of innocent parents are called into question and agencies waste their limited resources. Caseloads from official sources yield grossly inflated estimates because many allegations are never validated conclusively. **Unfounded reports** (unsubstantiated or not indicated cases) are dismissed or closed when, after an investigation, there is insufficient legally admissible evidence on which to proceed. Unproven allegations about child abuse should not be counted in official statistics. The increase in unproven complaints is caused by the public's emotionally driven desire to "do something," coupled with sensationalized media coverage about a formerly taboo topic, plus the "take no chances" zeal and defensiveness of professionals subjected to mandatory reporting requirements. The high rate of unsubstantiated claims (more than half of all allegations) recorded by many child protection agencies is due, in part, to a lack of screening of calls to hotlines. The inflated figures also result from a willingness to follow up anonymous tips, some of which may be deliberately false and vengeful acts intended to get an adult in trouble (estimated at 3 percent), and an acceptance of complaints from estranged spouses locked in custody battles. Other unsubstantiated cases arise from a reliance on behavioral indicators as possible symptoms of abuse (in the absence of corroboration in the form of statements by the victim or eyewitnesses, or physical evidence) (Besharov, 1987; and Snyder and Sickmund, 1995). What constitutes a substantiated case of neglect or abuse varies from state to state. Less than half of the states impose high standards of proof, such as material or clear and convincing evidence. The majority of states apply lower standards for defining substantiation, such as probable cause or credible evidence (Young-Spillers, 2009).

In sum, minimalists argue that official estimates are overcounts that are inflated by vague definitions

and unsubstantiated reports, whereas maximalists view these same statistics as undercounts of the true scope of the problem largely because of underreporting as well as underfunding that hampers the ability of child welfare organizations to do thorough investigations.

Trends in the Rate of Child Abuse

As for changes over time, the fourth NIS study found that maltreatment declined by 26 percent since the third NIS survey in 1993. The level of maltreatment in 2005–2006 had dropped to the level observed in the second NIS survey, which was carried out in 1986. In other words, after increasing from 1986 to 1993, maltreatment fell back to its 1986 level. The sexual abuse rate tumbled by 44 percent and the physical abuse rate declined by 23 percent over the 12-year period (ACF, 2010:5).

The NCANDS database of all cases of abuse and neglect of children less than 18 years old known to CPS agencies, whether substantiated with sufficient evidence or just indicated, reveals a similar downward trend. The rate of child maltreatment appears to have peaked in 1993 (at 15.3 victims per 1,000 youngsters) and then declined to its lowest level in decades in 2011 and 2012 (to 9.2 per 1,000). (See the upper trend line in Figure 8.1.) Thus, both monitoring systems seem to concur that the problem of abuse and neglect has subsided.

However, a disturbing rise in recent years in the most accurately measured statistic of all—deaths due to extreme abuse and neglect—is also evident in Figure 8.1. (See the lower trend line in that graph.) A fatality is the most horrendous result of either extreme abuse or neglect. In the mid-1990s, about 1,100 children died because adults neglected or abused them. Deaths of children from maltreatment seem to have reached a new high of 1,770, yielding a rate of 2.3 for every 100,000 children in 2009. Caretaker neglect claimed most of these needlessly lost lives, followed by physical abuse, and then medical neglect (ACF, 2010). By 2012, child fatalities had barely decreased to an estimated body

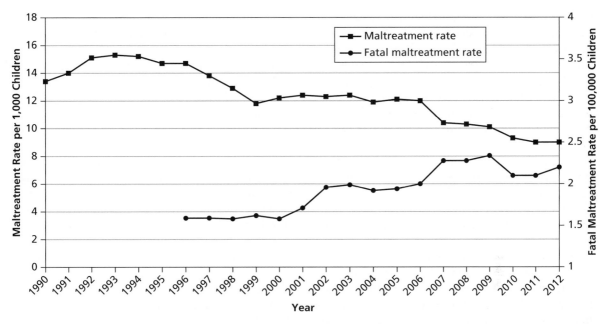

FIGURE 8.1 Trends in Child Maltreatment Rates, United States, 1990–2012
SOURCES: NCANDS, 1990–2012.

count of 1,640 and a mortality rate of 2.2 per 100,000 (ACF, 2013).

This gruesome statistic is being measured more accurately as time passes because more states are closely monitoring and reporting these deaths. In addition, a growing number of jurisdictions have set up a child fatality review team made up of coroners, detectives, prosecutors, and social workers. The first child fatality review teams were set up in California, Oregon, and North Carolina in 1978 to carry out more thorough investigations and to keep better records about these cases. A National Center for Child Death Review and a National Coalition to End Child Abuse Deaths are among the organizations that have been established as information clearinghouses and to advocate for increased support for treatment and prevention programs (Langstaff and Sleeper, 2001).

However, between 2005 and 2009, Congress substantially reduced federal funding to states earmarked to treat and protect abused and neglected children, and 45 states cut vital services for children and families (Every Child Matters, 2011). The

actual annual death toll may have been even higher, according to a report by the General Accounting Office (GAO, 2011), which detected undercounting problems (for example, cases of shaken baby syndrome may have been systematically overlooked). Based on the GAO's findings, a report to a congressional hearing projected an actual body count of about 2,500 (Webster, 2011).

In general, the social factors that contribute to child abuse and neglect are related to poverty and governmental inaction: high levels of violent crime, alcohol and drug problems among adults, teenage motherhood, elevated high school dropout rates, and high rates of imprisonment. The social conditions that decrease maltreatment are upturns in the nation's economy, a trend toward marrying later in life and having fewer children, greater public awareness and condemnation of abuse, investments in treatment and prevention programs, and more shelters for battered women and their offspring. If the seriousness of abuse really did diminish in American society, the improvement may have been due to stepped up prevention efforts, increased prosecutions and incarcerations of offenders, and profound cultural changes in parental attitudes and behaviors toward children. On a societal basis, child maltreatment is less of a problem in nations that offer their citizens universal health insurance, child care, preschool, parental leave, and visiting nurse services (Straus and Gelles, 1986; Finkelhor and Jones, 2004; and Petit, 2011).

Differential Risks Children Face of Being Maltreated

As with all other forms of victimizations, certain groups face greater dangers than others.

For example, geography is an important risk factor: The state (in terms of its social problems and its government services—and possibly its reporting and investigating practices) in which a child grows up appears to be related to levels of abuse, and even more tragically, of premature deaths.

Victimization rates were much higher than the national figure of 9.2 per 1,000 in the District of Columbia, Alaska, Arkansas, Florida, Iowa, Kentucky, Massachusetts, Michigan, and Rhode Island. Maltreatment rates were below the national average in Arizona, Hawaii, New Jersey, Wisconsin, Vermont, and Washington; and these rates were extremely low in Minnesota, Missouri, New Hampshire, Kansas, Virginia, and Pennsylvania during 2012 (ACF, 2013).

Reported child fatality rates (which fluctuate considerably from year to year) were much higher in Arkansas and Florida (over 4 per 100,000) than they were in Hawaii, New Jersey, Iowa, Minnesota, Montana, North Dakota, Connecticut, Vermont, and New Hampshire (all less than 1 per 100,000) in 2012 (ACF, 2013).

As for the chances of being abused or neglected, differential risks can be determined by reviewing the findings of the annual reports derived from the NCANDS database and the periodic NIS studies. The profile of youngsters facing the highest odds of maltreatment can be determined from the statistics in these two official sources. Girls generally

experience slightly higher rates of maltreatment than boys. Sexual abuse is imposed on girls much more often than boys. Another demographic risk factor is race and ethnicity. Disproportionately higher rates of maltreatment (compared to their numbers in the population) were endured by African-American and (to a lesser extent) Hispanic youth, while white and other youngsters experienced disproportionately lower rates. As for social class, youngsters growing up in poverty-stricken homes and in households with an unemployed parent were more likely than others to be maltreated. Children living in families with both biological parents had the lowest rates of abuse and neglect; youngsters whose single parent had a live-in partner suffered the highest rates of abuse and neglect. Larger families (four or more children) were sites of abuse more than average size families (two children). Children growing up in homes beset by domestic violence between the adults were at a greater risk than youth living in more peaceful homes. Families residing in rural areas had more of a problem with neglect and abuse than urban households. Both of these sets of official statistics verify the suspicion that children with physical, emotional, and medical disabilities (such as behavioral disorders, mental retardation, visual and hearing impairment, and learning disabilities) are especially vulnerable and indeed suffer maltreatment at an unusually high rate. However, the NIS concluded that infants and toddlers suffered the lowest rates of maltreatment, while the annual Child Maltreatment report highlighted the greater rates of abuse and neglect faced by babies in their first year of life (ACF, 2010).

Further details about high-risk situations have been discovered from research into the backgrounds of physically abused children. Beatings are more likely to occur in dysfunctional families racked by a combination of symptoms of marital discord: The parents fight viciously (partner abuse); one or both of the parents are currently drug abusers and/or alcoholics; the mother was raised by a substance-abusing parent; and the mother was often beaten while she was growing up (Salzinger, Feldman, and Hammer, 1991).

As for sexual abuse, which is imposed most often on boys and girls between the ages of 7 and 13, poor parent–child communication, parental unavailability, and intense father–mother conflict seem to be risk factors (Finkelhor, 1994). Sexual abuse poses a greater threat for females, according to prevalence studies. As many as 29 percent of women compared to 14 percent of men told interviewers they suffered molestations when they were children, according to a series of telephone surveys conducted from 1992 to 2007 (Stop It Now!, 2011).

More Controversies Surrounding Childhood Sexual Abuse

Intense controversies have broken out over the real extent of sexual abuse during childhood. One area of contention surrounds charges of parent–child incest, especially allegations of father–daughter (and stepfather–daughter) sexual contacts. These accusations usually arise during divorce proceedings or shortly afterward. In addition, molestation charges sometimes are leveled by children against their parents or other trusted adults many years later when repressed memories surface.

Accusations Made During Divorce Proceedings and Custody Battles   When allegations of sexual abuse surface in the midst of a divorce and a tug-of-war over a child, two camps quickly emerge. One side argues that since there are no outsiders who witness violations of the incest taboo within the home, these family secrets usually are not exposed unless the parents break up. This view can be considered a variation of the maximalist perspective because it assumes that many forbidden relationships imposed on youngsters are covered up unless and until the husband and wife separate.

The other side, embodying minimalist skepticism, contends that baseless allegations are being taken too seriously by the authorities and the resulting investigations ruin the lives of innocent parents, usually fathers. In the mid-1980s, an organization was formed to provide support to adults who insisted that they had been falsely accused. They nicknamed their predicament the **SAID syndrome**: sexual

allegations in divorce. Their contention was that in most of these cases, a spiteful mother pressured her daughter to echo a fictitious story about molestations by the father that never occurred. Spreading this vicious lie was a wife's vindictive ploy to discredit her former husband so that the judge in family court (usually an elected official) would issue an order to prevent the girl's father from having further contact with her as she grew up (Fahn, 1991; Sheridan, 1994; and Cantor, 2011).

Data cannot easily resolve this maximalist–minimalist debate. Charges are deemed unsubstantiated in these civil proceedings if the bulk of the evidence is insufficient to confirm that the girl was sexually molested by the defendant. The investigators for the child protection agency who interview the girl and her parents in order to evaluate the family dynamics and home environment often feel a need to resolve the matter quickly and minimize the strain on all three parties. Many jurisdictions are too overburdened by huge caseloads to carry out a thorough investigation. Some caseworkers lack the assessment skills and interviewing techniques necessary to elicit crucial testimony. Faced with a father who vehemently denies everything, an intimidated and confused child torn by divided loyalties, and a lack of corroboration by eyewitnesses, the investigators may have little choice but to conclude that it was unlikely that abuse occurred. However, their verdict might be attributed more to the constraints of time, money, and training than to the merits of the case. An unproven charge is not necessarily untrue (Fahn, 1991).

The Furor over Recalling Repressed Memories of Childhood Sexual Abuse

A therapist who is also a sociologist writes a memoir in which she claims that she can now remember how her father abused her when she was a little girl. She believes she has finally figured out why she suffered pain and bleeding between her thighs when she was five and endured depression, anorexia, despair, and suicidal tendencies while growing up. But her 91-year-old father, a prominent religious leader and retired professor of ancient scripture, denies the charges, and her seven siblings also dispute her recollections. (Wyatt, 2005)

In the early 1900s, Sigmund Freud, the founder of modern psychology, originally believed that many women diagnosed as suffering from "hysteria" were desperately trying to repress memories of childhood sexual abuse. But after several years of psychoanalyzing patients with this diagnosis, he arrived at the conclusion that these women's suspicions about being molested when they were very young actually were just fantasies about incestuous desires, which were strictly taboo. Grownups who claimed they were molested as infants, toddlers, or very young children generally were not believed by adherents of this psychoanalytical approach.

However, during the 1980s, the problem was rediscovered, and allegations made by individuals who suspected they had been sexually abused long ago were no longer quickly dismissed. A memory recovery movement emerged to support these adult "survivors" (as they prefer to be called) of childhood incest and molestations. The movement was composed of a coalition of patients, support groups, authors of self-help handbooks, and therapists who practiced memory retrieval techniques. This movement proclaimed that new treatment methods made it possible for many sufferers of certain common emotional problems and behavioral symptoms to discover that the actual root cause could be traced back to molestation or incest. These patients' efforts to repress memories of traumatic events that were imposed on them years earlier were burdening them with mental disorders. The recovery movement's claims were echoed in confessions issued by well-known figures during interviews in tabloid newspapers and talk show conversations, in the plots of made-for-television movies and magazine cover stories, and in pop psychology best sellers. But these disturbing and emotionally charged allegations also appeared in family therapy journals, on self-help websites, in revelations in incest support groups, and in the testimony of expert witnesses during civil lawsuits.

A maximalist perspective emerged. It contended that the thousands of people recalling childhood sexual abuse (including celebrities and other public figures) represented just the tip of the iceberg. Unfortunately, maximalists predicted, many sexual abuse victims will never become aware of the true source of their misery and anguish and will go through life blaming themselves for their emotional distress (Maltz and Holman, 1986; Bass and Davis, 1992; and Herman, 1992).

Maximalists believe that when adults suspect that unspeakable acts were foisted on them as children, their unsettling hunches are usually well founded. They have been expending great mental energy to unconsciously block, blot out, or deny any recollection of their "terrible secrets." But with the help of new therapeutic techniques involving hypnosis, psychoactive drugs that serve as truth serums, age regression, guided fantasy, and automatic writing, a flood of these submerged memories can be released. Successful patients progress through several stages, proceeding from initial denial to suspicions to realization (after considerable self-examination, probing, dredging up, and digging). Survivors come to recognize that many others have shared their fate. When they speak openly about their past tribulations and join self-help support groups, they further the healing process (Bass and Davis, 1992; and Terr, 1994).

Incest always is difficult to prosecute because the allegation is based on a child's contentions against an adult's denials, and the case usually lacks eyewitnesses or tangible evidence. When children grow older, it is usually too late to bring criminal charges. In most states, the statute of limitations for felonies runs out five to seven years after the crime is committed. Therefore, adults who think they can recall memories of incest seek to punish their tormentors in a different arena—civil court—via lawsuits for monetary damages for pain and suffering. Many state legislatures have recognized the possibility of delayed discovery and the legitimacy of the demands by incest survivors for some avenue of redress. In these jurisdictions, lawmakers have lengthened the statute of limitations for filing civil lawsuits (which previously expired a few years after the youth reached the age of majority, generally at 18) to several years after the adult recalls the alleged abuse (which could be as long as 20 or 30 years or more). This reform can be considered pro-plaintiff (pro-victim, but anti-defendant) because the purpose of a statute of limitation is to protect accused persons from having to fight allegations from the distant past. Defendants might not remember where they were and what they did—and witnesses in their defense may have moved away or died (Mithers, 1990). Thousands of lawsuits have been filed, encouraged by a national center for prosecuting cases of child sexual abuse in civil court.

In reaction to the emergence of the repressed memory movement and its maximalist outlook, a skeptical perspective has emerged that takes a minimalist position. It concedes that the sexual abuse of children, particularly by parents, largely went underreported and unprosecuted until the 1980s. But this perspective questions whether a genuine medical breakthrough has taken place and whether a sound new method of psychological diagnosis really has been developed. The suspicion is that certain intervention techniques do not unearth buried memories but actually invent **pseudomemories** that are delusions arising from the therapist's repetition of persuasive suggestions. As a result, certain practitioners who are so intent on unlocking repressed memories are misguiding some of their highly vulnerable and confused patients.

This minimalist perspective also charges that the maximalist definition of the kinds of behaviors that constitute childhood sexual abuse is much too inclusive (for example, it might condemn unwanted kisses and hugs, or a lack of respect for personal privacy). Similarly, too many vague symptoms on lengthy checklists in self-help manuals are interpreted as likely signs of childhood sexual abuse—everything from ordinary physical ailments (headaches, stomach pains, and dizziness) and common emotional problems (general malaise, alienation, low self-esteem, and phobias) to widespread attitudes and behaviors (like feeling powerless or having difficulties in maintaining long-term relationships). As a result of these overly broad definitions as well as unwarranted assumptions about the

origins of certain symptoms, many therapy patients end up deceiving themselves. They come to believe that they remember awful events that never really happened (Goldstein, 1993; Ofshe and Watters, 1993; Loftus and Ketcham, 1994; Pendergrast, 1994; Yapko, 1994; MacDonald and Michaud, 1995; Beckett, 1996; and Freyd, 2011).

The debate over claims of therapeutic breakthroughs on the one hand versus charges of planted suggestions and intense coaxing on the other became unusually acrimonious during the early 1990s (see Flathman, 1999). Alarmists denounced skeptics who questioned the authenticity of certain claims as "enemies" of incest survivors. Minimalists downplayed the many testimonies about long-forgotten episodes of childhood sexual abuse as part of a modern-day "witch hunt" reflecting a jump-on-the-bandwagon phenomenon and a passing fad. Some psychologists and psychiatrists voiced concerns that the furor over symptom-producing traumatic memories was undermining the reputation of the entire profession of clinical therapy and causing patients who had genuinely suffered to be scoffed at as misguided souls (see Geis and Loftus, 2009). Lengthy bibliographies of books and articles in professional journals about false allegations and recanted charges about abuse were assembled, buttressing the skeptical point of view (see King and Drost, 2005; and Wells, 2011).

Feminists were divided over which side to support in this acrimonious controversy. Some supported the memory recovery movement as a sociopolitical force that could help put an end to the sexual exploitation of children, especially girls, and the subordination of women. They interpreted the resistance as a backlash, just another tactic in the long-standing tradition of silencing, denying, dismissing, belittling, and deriding what women say about their oppression within the family. But other feminists argued that the tendency of the incest survivor movement to blame so many problems that crop up in women's lives on some clearly identifiable villain who might have committed sexual offenses long ago has the counterproductive political consequence of shifting the focus of activism from seeking sweeping social changes to pursuing individual recovery and personal retribution (see Darnton, 1991; Chira, 1993; Horn, 1993; Tavris, 1993; Ofshe and Watters, 1993; and Sivers, Schooler, and Freyd, 2002).

A study of over 600 civil cases and 100 criminal cases during the 1990s centering on repressed memories determined that about 90 percent of the persons alleging childhood sexual victimization were females, most were between the ages of 25 and 45, and almost all insisted the abuse went on for at least two years; half said it started before age 6. The most frequent charge was that the claimant's father sexually abused her beginning at an early age and continuing through much of her childhood, but she could not recall this pattern of repeated traumatic victimization until decades after it ended, and therapy began. Only a handful of these kinds of court cases were filed each year during the 1980s. But during the first half of the 1990s, the total number of civil lawsuits plus some criminal cases surged to over 50 per year, and peaked in 1993 with over 125. After 1996, the number of new filings tapered off dramatically. As for the outcomes, the plaintiffs prevailed in only a handful of the civil suits during the early and mid-1990s. Most were either dropped by the plaintiff or dismissed by the judge because of a lack of credible evidence, or settled out of court. In the 65 criminal cases that were resolved, the defendants were either convicted after a trial or pled guilty rather than go to trial in a total of 24 cases. However, by the end of the 1990s, a different type of lawsuit was being filed: over 150 malpractice claims had been lodged by parents against mental health care providers. In most of these civil suits, the plaintiffs argued that the therapist had mistakenly led their grown child to believe, through suggestive interviewing techniques, that she had been sexually abused at a young age, and that these false allegations based on implanted pseudomemories led to needless suffering, strained relationships, and defamation of the parents' reputations. The researcher concluded that the data showed that a major shift had taken place: the courts which took lawsuits and prosecutions seriously in the first part of the 1990s had become increasingly skeptical of repressed memory claims in

the late 1990s because of significant evidentiary problems inherent in these accusations about events that allegedly happened years ago (Lipton, 1999). These findings supported a minimalist view about repressed memories: that many were not backed up by credible evidence, and that the problem of incest and other forms of severe childhood sexual abuse was not as widespread as maximalists believed.

Parents and others caretakers targeted by lawsuits organized a foundation to defend themselves against what they branded a "false memory syndrome" or a "parent alienation syndrome." Some former patients who recanted their exhumed memories have brought malpractice suits against the therapists who persuaded them to view themselves as incest victims. In criminal courts, some convictions based on recalled memories have been overturned (see Horn, 1993; Sugarman and McCoy, 1997; Achimovic, 2003; and Freyd, 2011).

Sexual Abuse of Children by Religious Figures, Teachers, and Others in Positions of Trust Starting in the 1970s, reports began to circulate about religious figures who took advantage of their positions of authority and trust to sexually exploit members of their flock. The worst offenders appeared to be "gurus" who told the followers of their cults that religious teachings required that they—and sometimes their teenage daughters—should submit to the leader's sexual demands.

During the 1980s, a number of adults identified themselves as survivors of sexual abuse carried out by pedophile priests within the Roman Catholic Church. By the early 1990s, a sufficient number of people had come forward to form self-help groups, which then linked up to become a nationwide support network. Most members were grown men who said they had been molested when they were altar boys during their preteen and teenage years. A small number were women who recounted tales of exploitation during their adolescence.

In the absence of reliable data about the true scope of the problem, a maximalist–minimalist debate erupted. Spokespersons for the two major victims' self-help organizations tended to adopt a maximalist stance. They predicted that the actual number of molested youngsters was far greater than just the hundreds who received monetary settlements from civil lawsuits and the several thousand members who had joined the two major self-help groups. They pointed out that many victims were reluctant to go public because of shame and self-blame. In fact, the degree of denial could be so great that some adults continued to insist that abusive conduct never took place even after a molester confessed in court to sexually exploiting them. They argued that a single pedophile could cause a great deal of suffering if he was not removed from a position of trust and expelled. One defrocked priest seems to have molested between 80 and 130 youngsters during a period of about 30 years. Another sexually abused as many as 200 boys while he worked at a church-run school for the deaf from 1950 to 1974. Despite a steady stream of complaints beginning in the mid-1950s (when the threat of molestation was rarely mentioned), the Vatican declined to defrock him (Goodstein and Callender, 2010).

These maximalists contended that ever since the late 1960s, church officials had covered up the true proportion of the scandal by transferring priests accused of sexual abuse to other parishes as a way of hiding the wrongdoing, and by financially rewarding victims with hush money to remain silent. Reformers urged state legislatures to adopt stringent mandatory reporting requirements that specifically added clergy to the list of occupations (usually including teachers, daycare workers, and doctors), who must bring cases of suspected child abuse to the attention of state protection agencies. Victim advocates also urged lawmakers to extend the statute of limitations for prosecuting sexual offenses, as many survivors don't come forward until they are well into adulthood due to intense guilt as well as impulses to suppress distressing memories of childhood molestations.

Victims and their advocates wanted clerics whom they accused of being pedophiles to be prosecuted on charges of sexual assault, indecent exposure, and endangering the welfare of a child. Self-help groups also encouraged their members to pursue civil lawsuits, even though the testimony,

depositions, and formal inquiries dealt with matters that were intensely personal and painful to relive. Activists also demanded more effective counseling and psychotherapy services, to be paid for by the clerics' employers. They called upon the church's hierarchy to adopt measures fostering greater openness and accountability in its decision making, to cooperate fully with law enforcement investigations, and to acknowledge publicly that the victims' plight had been ignored or dismissed. They felt validated when two reports issued by committees of the United Nations condemned the way the Vatican was handling sexual abuse allegations (see Lobdell, 2002; Pfeiffer, 2002; Serbin, 2002; U.S. Conference of Catholic Bishops, 2002; Ostling, 2003; Stammer, 2003; Wakin, 2003; Jones and Goodnough, 2008; also see Povoledo, 2014; and Yardley, 2014).

Minimalists within the hierarchy of the church and among its most loyal parishioners wondered if some who claimed they were abused years ago simply were seeking money by filing lawsuits in civil court about matters that could no longer be prosecuted and either proven or disproven in criminal court. Minimalists also questioned whether the extent of exploitation and wrongdoing by employees of this very large organization was of a greater proportion, statistically speaking, than for any other similar-sized group that dealt with children, such as teachers or therapists. They expressed concerns that the entire priesthood was being unfairly maligned (see Pfeiffer, 2002; Serbin, 2002; USCCB, 2002; and Wakin, 2003).

In 2003, in an extensive study authorized and paid for by the U.S. Conference of Catholic Bishops, researchers concluded that nearly 4,400 of the roughly 110,000 deacons and priests (4 percent) who served during the period from 1950 to 2002 may have committed sexual offenses against minors. Approximately 10,670 individuals were known to have made allegations of child sexual abuse against priests. About 17 percent of these complainants contended that their siblings also were sexually abused. Nearly 60 percent of the complainants alleged that the abuse lasted for more than one year. Two-thirds of the accusations had been registered after 1993. Most (81 percent) of the complainants were males; the most frequent (40 percent) age range when the abuse took place was between 11 and 14. Almost 90 percent of the allegations concerned molestations that went further than unwanted touching over the youngster's clothing (John Jay College Research Team, 2004; see also Perillo, Mercado, and Terry, 2008). As for trends, a study based on church files plus interviews contended that the frequency of abuse by clergymen had reached its peak during the years of American society's "sexual revolution" in the 1960s and 1970s, and had dropped off significantly by the mid-1980s. Organizations representing victims strongly criticized the study's implications: that the problem had been successfully addressed and contained, and that the crisis was over (see Goodstein, 2011).

The Roman Catholic Church disclosed in 2007 that during the five years since its sexual abuse crisis erupted, it received about 13,000 credible accusations against its clergymen, dating back to 1950. But what about ministers of other religions? Because Protestant denominations are less centralized than the Catholic Church, an indirect way to measure the number of youngsters molested by its clergymen was to monitor the number of claims received by the three companies that insure nearly all Protestant congregations, religious schools, and camps. One insurance company logged about 100 reports of sexual abuse of minors per year over a 10-year period ending in 2007. Another processed an average of 100 reports per year for 20 years. A third handled almost 75 reports per year over a 15-year time span. However, not all the claims were credible, or were adjudicated in civil court, or led to financial settlements (Associated Press, 2007b). Members of an insular Ultra-Orthodox Jewish community in New York City feared they would become stigmatized as "troublemakers" and would end up as outcasts if they filed complaints about child sexual abuse (Vitello, 2008; see also Otterman and Rivera, 2012).

In recent years, accusations of child sexual abuse and cover-ups of the problem have arisen in many other organizations besides religious institutions.

For example, civil lawsuits and other inquiries uncovered evidence at state-run juvenile facilities (Blinder, 2013), scouting (Johnson, 2012), expensive and prestigious private schools (Secret, 2012; and Yee, 2013), and at a devoutly fundamentalist college that discouraged help-seeking efforts by its students who had been sexually abused as children (Perez-Pena, 2014a, 2014b).

Strange Allegations of Child Sexual Abuse During Rituals

A deputy sheriff is arrested and charged with sexually abusing his two daughters, now 18 and 22. Soon the charges emanating from the devoutly religious 22-year-old (who has a history of making unsubstantiated complaints about sexual abuse) grow to alarming proportions: she claims to have attended 850 satanic rituals and to have watched 25 babies being sacrificed and then cannibalized. Eventually, both daughters, the mother, and then even the father, can visualize being present at these ceremonies, where members of a sadistic devil-worshipping cult forced the women to perform sexual acts with goats and dogs. The father is grilled by his police department colleagues and quickly confesses to the abuse, but then hires a new lawyer and tries to withdraw his guilty plea. However, it is too late and he is convicted of six counts of child molestation. His older daughter demands that he receive the most severe punishment possible, and the judge sentences him to 20 years in prison. (Wright, 1994)

One of the most peculiar debates between the maximalist and minimalist viewpoints reached a feverish pitch that resembled what sociologists call a "moral panic" during the late 1980s and early 1990s. It incorporated several elements of great concern at the time: child abuse, sexual exploitation, kidnapping, and repressed memories.

The maximalist position was that tens of thousands of people disappeared each year because they were dispatched by secret cults. Believers in the existence of a satanic conspiracy circulated frightening accounts about bizarre "wedding" ceremonies in which covens of witches and devil worshipers chanted, wore costumes, took drugs, sacrificed animals, and even mutilated, tortured, and murdered newborn infants or kidnapped children. In its most extreme form, the charge was that satanic cults engaged in baby breeding and in kidnapping in order to maintain a fresh supply of victims for human sacrifices and cannibalism. Child care workers, parents, relatives, and other adults in the United States, and soon afterward in Canada, Australia, New Zealand, Great Britain, Belgium, the Netherlands, France, and Germany were accused, arrested, prosecuted, and sometimes convicted of engaging in abusive rituals organized by religious cults (see Neuilly and Zgoba, 2006; and Cole, 2009).

The people who came forward and claimed that they had survived these vicious rituals often were young women undergoing psychotherapy. They told tales of being fondled, raped, sodomized, and exploited as objects in sexual games and pornographic films. Usually, the scenarios they pictured involved groups of adults, sometimes including members of their own families, abusing very young children. Although many of the alleged victims said that they encountered resistance or even outright disbelief when they reported the crimes to officers, some law enforcement agencies took their charges seriously. Newsletters, conferences, and training sessions were organized for detectives, social workers, child welfare investigators, and therapists. Public fears soared after bizarre charges about teachers practicing witchcraft at a California preschool generated one of the longest and costliest trials in American history in 1990 (but no convictions). In response to this outcry, several state legislatures quickly outlawed the "ritual mutilation" of innocents during religious initiation rites (see Bromley, 1991; Richardson, Best, and Bromley, 1991; Lanning, 1992; Sinason, 1994; Kincaid, 1998; and Holmes and Holmes, 2009).

To investigate the deluge of claims about ritual abuse, a study sponsored by the National Center on Child Abuse and Neglect surveyed more than 11,000 psychiatrists, psychologists, clinical social workers, district attorneys, police executives, and social service agency administrators during 1993. The respondents told the survey interviewers that more than 12,000 accusations of ritual abuse had

been brought to their attention, but that not a single case had been proven in which a well-organized, intergenerational ring of satanic followers had sexually molested, tortured, or killed children in their homes or schools. The study only turned up some cases in which lone individuals or isolated couples carried out abusive rituals or perpetrated crimes in the name of some distorted interpretation of religion (Goleman, 1994). Similarly influential studies in other countries also debunked near-hysterical claims that organized groups were routinely sexually abusing children during bizarre rituals. Although some of those accused indeed may have been guilty of certain illegal acts, and some horrific murders surely were committed, many of the convictions that resulted during this "witch hunt" can be viewed as miscarriages of justice (Cole, 2009).

A minimalist position emerged and insisted that the public was overreacting to exaggerated claims and unsubstantiated charges. At first, these minimalists were accused of being secret Satanists engaged in a cover-up of the "truth" and also as "anti-child" by maximalists. Nevertheless, these skeptics kept challenging the widely accepted belief that this was a real problem. The minimalist view attributed these unfounded fears to sensationalism by the tabloid press and irresponsible talk shows that fed a climate of rumors and fears. The time was ripe because of widespread and deep-seated anxieties concerning new brainwashing techniques of mind control and the use of highly manipulative and suggestive questioning methods to unearth memories and get children to accuse adults of unspeakable acts. Social developments and cultural trends also set the stage: youthful experimentation with sex and drugs; the growth of cult-like religious groups; the breakdown of traditionally structured families; the redefinition of male and female roles; increased conflict over abortion, which some opponents condemned as "baby-killing"; and concerns about a growing reliance on daycare services for preschoolers. The resulting moral panic was fueled by an unusual confluence of interests: of religious fundamentalists concerned about inappropriate sexuality undermining the innocence of childhood and of feminists intent on protecting girls from molestation by boys and men. Fears about well-financed, hidden cells of satanic infiltrators seemed to replace the witch-hunt for "communist subversives" as the forces of an "evil underworld" in these updated versions of older conspiracy theories (see Bromley, 1991; Richardson et al., 1991; Lanning, 1992; Sakheim and Devine, 1992; Nathan and Snedeker, 1995; LaFontaine, 1997; Jenkins, 1998; Cole, 2009; Veraa, 2009 and McRobbie, 2014).

Although many people claimed to have witnessed, participated in, and survived these "devilish acts," minimalist skeptics concluded that their credibility was as questionable as that of the hundreds of people who swore they had been abducted by aliens from outer space (see Schemo, 2002; and Clancy, 2005) or who said they remembered events from their past lives as different people.

ABUSED CHILDREN AND LEGAL PROCEEDINGS

Children who survive kidnappings or endure physical and sexual abuse need to bring their problems to the attention of the authorities. Detectives and prosecutors must test the veracity of their accounts in a sensitive manner. If their charges seem credible and adults are arrested on the basis of their complaints, then their cases must be handled with care by the legal system.

Cases revolving around allegations of abuse within a family traditionally are dealt with by child welfare protective services and family courts. Cases involving very serious charges are brought to criminal court. But by trying to protect the child from further harm, the judicial proceedings inadvertently can compound the youngster's suffering. It has become clear that the adult-oriented criminal justice system is not designed to address the emotional and physical needs of traumatized children. As key witnesses for the prosecution, youngsters often find the setting hostile and the proceedings confusing, hard to fathom, and frightening (Munson, 1989).

Taking into Account the Best Interests of the Child

An abused child needs an advocate who will provide support and advice during legal proceedings, especially when the alleged offender is a parent. The law has recognized the inability of the government's prosecutor to play this role and created a special position, the **guardian ad litem** (GAL), to look after the best interests of the child. The Child Abuse Prevention and Treatment Act passed by Congress in 1974 required that youngsters be provided with GALs if CPS lodges charges against their parents in family court. The Victims of Child Abuse Act of 1990 went further and recommended the provision of GALs to young complainants when their serious accusations channeled their cases to criminal court. By 1997, nearly 650 programs operated across the country, providing court-appointed special advocates. In 2007, GALs served as independent voices seeking to protect about 234,000 young clients from further abuse and neglect (Patterson, 2009).

Usually, these court-appointed advocates are attorneys, but in some states they can be especially trained volunteers. Their duties include accompanying the child to legal proceedings and helping arrange for needed social, mental health, and medical services. In criminal proceedings against an abuser, the GAL is supposed to serve as counselor, interpreter, protector against system-induced trauma (insensitive handling), monitor, coordinator, advocate (of rights to privacy and protection from harassment), and spokesperson (about wishes, fears, and needs). Guardians interview caretakers, service providers, therapists, foster parents, and teachers in order to investigate a child's background, home environment, and relationships with family members. In some states, GALs assist the child in preparing a victim impact statement. They also can submit their own recommendations to the court about what would be best for the child's welfare, in terms of maintaining safety and meeting emotional needs. Over 500,000 children wind up in the foster care system. Because youngsters in foster care can suffer from another round of physical and sexual abuse and neglect, some states have set up an independent child advocate's office to serve as a watchdog and intervene on behalf of these especially vulnerable youth (Whitcomb, 1992; Lawry, 1997; Smothers, 2003; and Patterson, 2009).

The creation of the position of guardian ad litem dramatized the importance of a much larger question: What are the injured party's best interests? When children are too young to be able to explain for themselves what would be to their advantage, it is up to GALs to advocate in their behalf. But what are the options, opportunities, perils, and pitfalls of various courses of action?

Two official responses are possible in cases of physical or sexual abuse. One is to view parental wrongdoers as dysfunctional people in need of treatment and rehabilitation. The other is to react to them as criminals who deserve incapacitation and punishment. These two alternatives reflect opposing philosophies. Mental health professionals (psychiatrists, psychologists, counselors, and social workers) tend to see criminal proceedings as unproductive, inhumane, damaging to both victims and perpetrators, and inappropriate in all but the most horrendous cases. Police officials and prosecutors tend to resent therapeutic approaches that, in their view, coddle offenders and excuse their antisocial conduct. But these alternatives have become intertwined, as criminal proceedings have been used to compel abusers to undergo court-mandated and supervised treatment programs as a condition of pretrial diversion or probation (see Berliner, 1987; Harshbarger, 1987; and Newberger, 1987).

The Credibility of Children as Witnesses

A 15-year-old boy testifies that a world-renowned pop singer invited him to his mansion for sleepover parties, got him drunk, and then molested him on several occasions two years earlier while he was undergoing treatment for cancer. The boy's younger brother takes the stand and claims he saw the singer fondle his brother in two additional incidents. But the defense argues that the brothers and their mother are "con artists, actors, and liars" who had taken advantage of the bout with cancer to wheedle money

from celebrities. After a three-month trial, the jury finds the pop star not guilty of molestation and not even guilty of providing alcohol to minors. (Broder and Madigan, 2005)

The testimony of children has been viewed with skepticism ever since the Salem witch trials of 1692, when a number of girls made outrageous claims that they publicly recanted several years later after the "witches" were executed. Historically, when children were drawn into the adult court system as prosecution witnesses, the proceedings were inherently biased against their participation. Their testimony was automatically suspect, and their legitimate needs were routinely overlooked. Now it is widely recognized that young complainants have unique problems that require special handling.

Should youngsters have an automatic credibility problem simply by virtue of their age? Would children lie about important matters? Is there a kernel of truth to most revelations, whether spontaneously volunteered or coaxed out of children, or do hysterical parents and overzealous investigators set off witch hunts and fall for hoaxes?

Social scientists are conducting experiments to determine the accuracy of the memories children acquire, retain, and retrieve. Researchers estimate that about 500 studies have examined the issue of children's "suggestibility" ever since a bitter controversy erupted during the late 1980s (Goldberg, 1998). An estimated 20,000 children were called upon each year to testify in legal proceedings stemming from allegations of sexual abuse, and as many as 80,000 more were questioned by investigators annually about possible molestations at the start of the 1990s (Goleman, 1993). As a result, whether children tend to tell the truth or are prone to concoct stories has become an emotional issue with significant legal repercussions.

Because of their immaturity, very young children suffer from cognitive limitations that can undermine their credibility. They think in very concrete terms and have trouble understanding generalizations. They do not organize their thoughts logically or recount stories sequentially.

They may be unable to properly locate events in space, distance, and time, making it difficult for them to be sure about where and when something happened. They tend to assume that adults know the whole story and think that their partial answers are satisfactory. They also have short attention spans. Finally, they might be uncomfortable confiding in strangers who intimidate them (Whitcomb, 1992).

Two distinct points of view characterize the debate over the issue of credibility (see Ceci and Bruck, 1993; and Lewin, 2002). At one extreme is the pro-prosecution/pro-victim "believe the children" position that says that youngsters are generally competent witnesses about events that happened to them weeks or months earlier, are resistant to suggestions, and do not make up charges about abuse, especially sexual molestations and assaults that didn't happen. In fact, children might even retract accusations that ring true if the social reaction to their disclosure threatens to cause chaos. For example, a girl who reveals an incestuous relationship might recant her original testimony if she fears that she will be rejected and branded as a liar by her father, who faces disgrace and imprisonment; that her mother will become hysterical and enraged; that her siblings will be furious about the disruption of their family life; and that caseworkers and detectives will become more intrusive. The girl could feel she is being blamed for provoking the crisis and might back down in a vain attempt to restore some semblance of normality (Whitcomb, 1992).

At the other extreme is the pro-defendant position that questions the trustworthiness of the testimony of children who serve as witnesses for the prosecution. Children's versions of events should be viewed with skepticism because they are extremely vulnerable to coaching and manipulation by adults. The testimony of very young witnesses loses credibility once they have been subjected to intensive questioning by caseworkers, detectives, prosecutors, and parents who strongly believe that abuse has taken place. If authority figures attempt to validate their preconceived notion of what may have happened, the youngsters might keep repeating the "right answers" to the leading questions

adults ask. Then the youngsters might eventually be swayed and regurgitate the adults' suspicions back to them, as if these events actually occurred. When a high-pressure interviewing technique is imposed upon a hyper-suggestible youngster, the result can be the creation of a false memory. A baseless charge against an innocent adult ultimately could lead to a wrongful conviction.

Whether the version of events offered by a number of preschoolers was believable beyond a reasonable doubt became the subject of many heated discussions in this highly publicized case:

> Nineteen children between the ages of three and five testify at the trial of their nursery school teacher. They tell the jury that over a period of seven months, during naptime, this 22-year-old woman (who had received an excellent evaluation and a promotion) inserted knives, forks, spoons, and Lego blocks into them. Some testify that they played games naked and she made them drink urine, eat feces, and defecate on her. Although no staff members saw, heard, smelled, or suspected anything suspicious, and no parent ever detected any evidence of strange behavior, the jury believes the children. Three years after the alleged incidents, the 10-month trial ends, and the teacher is convicted on 115 counts of sexual abuse and sentenced to 47 years in prison. But five years later, the conviction is overturned on appeal when a three-judge panel rules that prosecution interviewers pressured the children with bribes and threats to confirm the charges. Also, the judge was faulted for violating his impartiality when he coaxed the young witnesses to testify against the teacher over closed-circuit TV in his chambers while sitting on his lap. The prosecution decides not to retry the case, in part because some parents conclude that putting their now teenage children back on the witness stand would be too stressful. (Manshel, 1990; and Nieves, 1994)

Contradictory findings about the reliability of children's claims have filled forensic literature since the mid-1970s. Some studies conclude that youngsters can be swayed only about minor details, but others indicate that repeated interrogations can coerce children to make up tales that they believe are memories.

Professionals who look into and report instances of suspected maltreatment must be scrupulous about carrying out two legal obligations simultaneously: promoting the best interests of their young clients while safeguarding the legal rights of the adults they investigate (Ceci and Bruck, 1993; and Hewitt, 1998).

Ever since the landmark decision of the Supreme Court in 1895 (*Wheeler v. United States*), children have had to pass pretrial competency tests before testifying (unless they were over the age of 14). Nearly 100 years later, the Victims of Child Abuse Act of 1990 reversed that presumption; now children are considered competent witnesses unless there is evidence to the contrary. However, in most state courtrooms across the country, before a trial begins, the judge evaluates whether a youngster understands the difference between truth and falsehood, appreciates the seriousness of the oath to swear to tell the truth, and can remember details of past events. Child welfare advocates welcome these reforms because they believe most children in abuse cases don't lie (Whitcomb, 1992). But civil libertarians are concerned that the presumption of competency might undermine a defendant's right to a fair trial (Austern, 1987; and Dershowitz, 1988).

Devising Child-Friendly Practices

Besides credibility, another special problem requires a special solution: Testifying in legal proceedings can add to the suffering of victimized children. To avoid further traumatizing these youngsters, the idea of developing a child-friendly courtroom setting and protocol quickly caught on (see Libai, 1969).

The right to a public trial always has protected defendants against judicial misconduct and governmental persecution behind closed doors. However, the prospect of testifying in front of a crowd of strangers can deter a youthful complainant from pressing charges. In particular, the spectacle of describing in intimate detail what happened during an episode of sexual abuse is so potentially disturbing to a sensitive youngster that exceptions to the public nature of a trial have been legislated. Some

states grant judges the authority to bar spectators from the courtroom during the testimony of a child who claims to have been sexually abused. In more than half of the states, the release of identifying information by the news media about a complainant in a sexual abuse case is severely limited (Whitcomb, 1992).

The Sixth Amendment guarantees defendants in criminal trials the right to confront their accusers. In theory, looking the defendant in the eye in court as an accusation is repeated has traditionally been considered a test of a complaining witness's truthfulness. But when very young children are the complainants, they often dread seeing the defendant in person. For many years, to avoid last-minute intimidation when the youngster took the stand, prosecutors would position themselves to block the small witness's view of the defendant. Other prosecutors simply instructed the child to look at someone in the spectator section during the testimony, preferably toward a supportive, familiar person. More obvious methods of shielding frightened complainants from the direct gaze of defendants, such as using a screen or one-way glass or having the children turn their backs, were deemed to violate the face-to-face requirement of the confrontation clause.

With the advent of closed-circuit television and videotaping, more options developed. To avoid intimidation and anxiety caused by the presence of jurors and other courtroom personnel, nearly all states allow youngsters to be questioned in another room using two-way, live closed-circuit television. To spare the child the ordeal of reliving unpleasant experiences in front of strangers, most of these states permit testimony and cross-examination previously videotaped at depositions, grand jury proceedings, or preliminary hearings to be used in trials (Kelley, 2009). In 1990, the Supreme Court ruled (in *Maryland v. Craig*) that these alternatives to direct confrontation were constitutionally permissible under certain circumstances (Whitcomb, 1992).

Hearsay is usually not admissible during trials because statements uttered outside the courtroom are not made under oath and are not subject to cross-examination. Yet in child abuse cases, what the youngster said before legal proceedings were initiated may be very compelling evidence. For example, a casual remark by a very young and immature girl might be a surprisingly graphic description of a sexual act that should be unfamiliar to her. Therefore, in the interest of justice in more than half the states, special exceptions to the hearsay rule enable witnesses to tell the court what allegedly sexually abused children have told them (Kelley, 2009). In 1980, the Supreme Court ruled (in *Ohio v. Roberts*) that a statement made by a complainant who does not testify at the trial can be used as evidence if it falls under one of the rules for hearsay exceptions or meets a reliability test (Whitcomb, 1992).

In the late 1970s, investigators began to use anatomically detailed dolls (with prominent genitalia) to facilitate and enhance interviews with children who might have been sexually abused. The rationale was that the presence of a doll would make the interview seem less formal and stressful, enable children with limited vocabularies or overwhelming emotions to demonstrate what happened to them, and permit the information to be disclosed without any reliance on leading questions. The Victims of Child Abuse Act of 1990 endorsed the use of dolls as demonstrative aids during interviews and court proceedings, and some states have followed suit. But critics point out that experiments have shown that even children with no suspected history of abuse play with the anatomically intriguing dolls in a suggestive way that could falsely imply an inordinate interest in sexuality based on personal experiences (see Whitcomb, 1992).

Other reforms that are less controversial and more often implemented include allowing children to use drawings to describe what happened to them, interviewing them in decorated playrooms at police stations rather than in dingy, bare-walled interrogation rooms, and modifying the courtroom's protocol and seating arrangements to make the setting less imposing. Additional child-friendly practices include giving young witnesses an orientation tour of the courthouse, enrolling them in brief "court schools" that explain the role of key figures and the procedures that will be followed,

permitting them to have a supportive person at their side, and using just one trained interviewer to elicit all their testimony. To limit the length of the ordeal of going to trial, some jurisdictions give child abuse cases a high priority in scheduling and try to avoid continuances that cause upsetting delays. To minimize stress, the medical, mental health, treatment, and legal aspects of abuse cases are now coordinated by child protection teams of professionals from different disciplines. Information-sharing procedures eliminate unnecessary interviews. Public funds cover the costs of physical and mental health examinations. Caseworkers from protective services agencies and law enforcement officers are empowered to take children endangered by their situations into emergency custody. Because confused and intimidated youngsters often do not inform anyone of their plight for years, many states have extended their statutes of limitations so they do not begin to run until the complainant reaches a more mature age (see Whitcomb, 1986; "Child Abuse Victims," 1989; Howell, 1989; Myers, 1998; and Kelley, 2009).

A survey revealed that the following percentages of judges have used these approaches to minimize the stress on youngsters who testified in their courtrooms: adjust questions to the child's comprehension level (88 percent); exclude the public during the child's testimony (55 percent); allow the child to testify in the judge's chambers (46 percent); have only the judge ask the questions (45 percent); permit the child to testify while sitting on an adult's lap (41 percent); rearrange courtroom furniture (31 percent); videotape the child's testimony (27 percent); remove the defendant from the child's view (16 percent); have a therapist ask the questions (13 percent); allow the child to testify over closed-circuit television (11 percent); and install a one-way mirror (3 percent) (Hafemeister, 1996).

The **funnel model** of the criminal justice system best describes what typically happens to child abuse cases. Although the legal system starts with a huge workload, cases are removed or lost at each stage in the proceedings (arrest, prosecution, indictment, plea negotiation, trial) until there are very few left at the end of the process—leading to incarceration in jail or prison. Children testifying and being cross-examined, and adults getting convicted and locked up turns out to be a relatively rare event (see Chapman and Smith, 1987; and Whitcomb, 1988, 1992).

PROACTIVE VERSUS REACTIVE STRATEGIES

Strategies to prevent children from being abused take many forms. Proactive approaches attempt to prevent abuse from taking place. They range from screening potential child care workers to weed out known molesters, setting up help lines and crisis nurseries where parents can drop off their children if they feel they are about to lose control of their emotions, organizing Parents Anonymous support groups for abusers, and offering child-rearing courses for new parents (Irwin, 1980).

During the late 1990s, in response to stories in the news about abandoned babies, a social movement developed and successfully persuaded legislators in Texas to pass the country's first "**safe haven law**" in 1999. By 2009, every state had a similar Abandoned Infant Protection Act that allows parents to relinquish unwanted newborns with no questions asked to prevent infanticides (and neonaticides within 24 hours of birth). The parents (who can remain anonymous if they want) will not risk criminal prosecution for neglect or abandonment if the infant (usually defined as less than 21 or 30 days old) is healthy, as determined by a doctor, and handed over to responsible adults at safe environment sites like hospitals, police precincts, or firehouses. (Formally putting the baby up for adoption through an agency is preferred over following this emergency procedure, of course.) The effectiveness of this legislation is difficult to determine because few states keep records of the number of unwanted babies (some resulting from rapes) that are abandoned, dead or alive. Advocates believe the lives of well over 1,000 infants have been saved by these provisions. The governor of Illinois proclaimed April as Save Abandoned Babies Month

to promote awareness after an infant was found dead at a public location in 2014 (Save Abandoned Babies Foundation, 2014; and National Safe Haven Alliance, 2014). In Illinois, 69 unharmed babies were safely relinquished between 2001, when the law was enacted, and 2010. Unfortunately, an almost equal number (63) were illegally abandoned during those 10 years at churches, along roadways, and even in trash cans; 30 perished before they were discovered (McQueary, 2011). The existence of the law and the locations of the places prepared to receive newborns generally are not well publicized. In the New York City area, six discarded babies were found dead during 2006, twice as many as in the preceding year, even though the state's safe haven law went into effect during 2000 (Buckley, 2007).

The problem of child maltreatment touches on many profound issues. Although proactive and preventive strategies are as important as reactive criminal justice responses, sharp differences of opinion surface over the proper role of government in the balance between social nurturance and social control. In reply to the question, "Whose children are they?" one long-standing answer is that children belong to, or are the property of, their parents.

Another way of looking at youngsters is to see them as "junior" citizens: Parents have custody of them, but the larger community has "visiting rights." In extreme cases, the community might even assert joint custody and violate the privacy of the family and the rights of parents. Government agencies step in as the parents of last resort when children face a clear and present danger. Yet in an age when the social conditions experienced by children are generally deteriorating (in the form of reduced parental involvement and support, increased exposure to violence, and persistent poverty during childhood in female-headed households), stepped-up efforts to criminalize the maltreatment of children might not do much to stem the growth of the problem (Garbarino, 1989). On the other hand, the price for inaction or minimal reaction in the name of family preservation on the part of child protection agencies and family courts is heightened risks of serious injury or death.

ADDITIONAL FORMS OF EXPLOITATION AND MISTREATMENT OF YOUNG PEOPLE

Besides the maltreatment of children by their parental caretakers, several other victim–offender relationships fall within the realm of physically abusing and sexually exploiting young people.

Sibling Abuse

Furious fights between siblings over possessions, demands for privacy, pecking orders, and parental attention are the subjects of Bible stories, plays, novels, movies, and family folklore. When brothers and sisters fight each other, their roughhousing is often dismissed as "kids will be kids" or disregarded as a normal expression of sibling rivalry. But this casual, ongoing, everyday violence usually ignored by parents can escalate to such levels of hostility that emotional scars and serious wounds are inflicted. Sons are more violent than daughters, and all-boy families are the most violent of all. The use of force to resolve quarrels breaks out more often between siblings than between parents or between parents and children. Older youths might not only physically assault but also sexually abuse younger male and female siblings. The younger child generally does not tell anyone about the incidents for fear of being blamed, of not being believed, or of suffering reprisals. About one-third of all children are hit or attacked by a sibling each year, according to a survey of 2,000 children and their caretakers (see Straus, Gelles, and Steinmetz, 1980; Wiehe, 1997; Caffaro and Caffaro, 1998; Butler, 2006; Krienert and Walsh, 2011; and Caspi, 2011).

Sibling-on-sibling violence stands out because it is the most frequent yet least studied type of assault, which evidently reflects the difference between the priorities of researchers and the concerns of youngsters. In terms of a typology of victimization during childhood, violence between siblings can be classified as pandemic, or occurring in the lives of a majority of children as they grow up. It is more common than the incidence of robbery, theft, vandalism of a possession, assault

by a peer, and physical punishment by a parent (Finkelhor and Leatherman, 1994; and O'Connor, 2013). Sibling abuse can set the stage for other expressions of violence. For example, victimized boys might grow up to become abusers of their dates during courtship (Simonelli et al., 2002).

Abuse of Adolescents by Parents

The fact that even teenagers can be abused by their parents used to be overlooked entirely or subsumed under the heading "child abuse" and then neglected in favor of a focus on the very young and totally helpless. Attempts to define and measure abuse become confusing because of cultural ambivalence about the thin line between physical abuse and physical discipline (see Jackson et al., 2000). Many adults consider venting parental wrath justifiable when there is "sufficient provocation"—if a teenager is argumentative, defiant, incorrigible, or out of control. Adolescents are not viewed as particularly vulnerable or defenseless, as are infants, toddlers, and children under 12. The same force that could injure a little child might not seriously wound a teenager. The overt consequences of psychological abuse and emotional neglect become less detectable as adolescents mature into independent young adults (see Lourie, 1977; Libbey and Bybee, 1979; and Pagelow, 1989).

As boys grow older, the power differential between parents and their sons decreases and physical abuse declines. As girls become sexually mature and seek greater independence, the power differential between parents and their daughters diminishes more incrementally, leading to conflicts as parents attempt to impose restraints backed up by force. Sons who strike back get into legal trouble for assault. Girls generally do not fight back physically, but they seek to escape a repressive household by running away, acting promiscuously, or taking drugs. The majority of abused teenagers are white and from low-income families where they are either the only child or one of four or more children. The abusive parents tend to be middle-aged, are often stepparents, and are going through their own mid-life crises. Excessive parental force takes the form of hair pulling, slapping, choking, beating, threatening with a knife or gun, and assault with a weapon (see Pagelow, 1989).

Statutory Rape of Minors

Statutory rape generally is defined as sexual intercourse involving a teenager younger than 16 and a partner three or more years older, although the laws of the 50 states show some departures from these standards. A national survey carried out in 2002 discovered that the first sexual experiences of 13 percent of girls and 5 percent of boys technically could be considered as statutory rapes (U.S. Department of Health and Human Services, 2005). The problem has been largely overlooked by criminologists and victimologists because of the absence of reliable data and the presence of a willing victim. But information contained in the FBI's NIBRS database for 21 states during the years 1996–2000 sheds some light on about 7,500 cases that were reported to police departments, either directly by the minor or by the boy or girl's parents or caretakers. The police kept track of these complaints when an older wrongdoer (of any age) engaged in sexual relations with a younger person (between ages 7 and 17) who is not mature enough in the eyes of the law to willingly grant consent. In other words, these cases of nonforcible sexual intercourse would not be illegal if both partners were old enough to make responsible decisions.

A few high-profile cases of female teachers carrying on affairs with underage male students have challenged the prevailing stereotype of exploitative older males taking advantage of teenage girls. But the NIBRS data confirms that this widely held image indeed is based on facts: The overwhelming majority (95 percent) of the complaints centered on allegations by female minors against adult males. Very few adult male homosexuals were involved in exploitive relationships, according to the NIBRS reports. In the relatively rare cases in which boys were considered victimized (5 percent), the overwhelming majority (94 percent) of their sex partners were older females, not older males. The average age difference between the older males and the girls was six years, while the average gap between older females and boys was nine years. About 30 percent of the wrongdoers considered themselves to be boyfriends or girlfriends; 60 percent were classified as acquaintances; 7 percent were members of the victims' families; and the remainder were strangers. The police made an arrest of the older sex partner in a little over 40 percent of the cases (Troup-Leasure and Snyder, 2005). However, many young adults question whether a sexual relationship with a willing partner who is a minor should be treated as a criminal matter, even if it appears to be exploitive, as long as the age gap between them is not more than a few years (Oudekerk, Farr, and Reppucci, 2013).

SUMMARY

The true extent of the victimization of children cannot be accurately measured. As a result, maximalist alarmists assume the worst and call for stepped-up measures to head off a crisis. Minimalist skeptics disagree and believe that the incidence, prevalence, and seriousness of the indisputably real problems of physical child abuse, sexual molestation, and kidnappings are not spiraling out of control.

Although children are highly desirable targets for kidnappers and pedophiles, analyses of reports about missing children yield the somewhat reassuring finding that abductions by strangers that result

in murders are relatively rare. Efforts to recover kidnapped children are much more organized and effective than they used to be when the problem first surfaced at the start of the 1980s.

Infants, toddlers, children, and even teenagers are especially vulnerable to physical and sexual abuse by their caretakers: parents, older siblings, and other family members such as stepparents, as well as babysitters, teachers, and acquaintances. Maximalists and minimalists differ over whether these twin problems of physical and sexual abuse are intensifying or subsiding. It appears maltreatment in its many forms is declining but the worst cases—leading to child fatalities—are not decreasing appreciably.

Bitter controversies surround charges of retrieved memories of molestations during childhood, accusations about parental sexual abuse voiced during divorce proceedings, and claims of abuse by religious figures. Stories about sexual abuse during satanic rituals have faded away.

The legal system's handling of young witnesses for the prosecution has improved dramatically in recent years. Children harmed by their parents are assigned a guardian ad litem to advocate on behalf of their best interests. They are questioned with greater care but still face special difficulties in establishing the credibility of their testimony. Courtroom procedures and cross-examination practices have been reformed so that they are less intimidating and less stressful for youngsters serving as witnesses for the prosecution. However, these new practices must not violate the rights of defendants who may be falsely accused and must be considered innocent unless proven guilty, civil libertarians insist.

KEY TERMS DEFINED IN THE GLOSSARY

Amber Alert, 256

battered child syndrome, 260

child lures, 258

Code Adam, 258

cruelty to children, 259

funnel model, 280

guardian ad litem, 276

House of Refuge movement, 259

inveiglement, 249

maximalist, 247

minimalist, 248

missing children, 249

pseudomemories, 271

safe haven law, 281

SAID syndrome, 269

throwaways, 252

unfounded reports, 266

QUESTIONS FOR DISCUSSION AND DEBATE

1. Why were the views of maximalists and minimalists so far apart on the fate of missing children?

2. Why are the views of maximalists and minimalists so different on the question of whether the problem of neglect and abuse of children is intensifying or subsiding?

CRITICAL THINKING QUESTIONS

1. Suggest a set of procedures concerning the testimony of children serving as witnesses for the prosecution against adults who allegedly molested them that surely would violate the constitutional rights of the defendants.

2. Speculate about why stories of people who claim that they survived satanic rituals have largely disappeared from the news since the 1990s.

SUGGESTED RESEARCH PROJECTS

1. Perform a content analysis of stories about repressed memories of childhood sexual abuse that appeared in the press over the last few decades. Pick a newspaper and magazine database and do keyword searches to see what kinds of accounts made the news and how the

cases were resolved, and whether the number of such articles remains roughly steady or is declining over the decades.

2. Find recent news articles about missing children who have been rescued—but also who have been murdered. See if the number of stories is increasing, decreasing, or staying the same over the past few years.

3. See if you can interview a guardian ad litem or a family court judge about the special court procedures in your jurisdiction that can be implemented to lessen the distress faced by abused children who serve as witnesses for the prosecution.

4. Investigate safe haven provisions in your area: When was the law passed, how well publicized is it, where can distraught mothers hand over unwanted newborns, and how many babies have been rescued from abandonment and possible death in this way?

9

Victims of Violence by Lovers and Family Members

LEARNING OBJECTIVES

To distinguish between all the different forms of domestic violence and intimate partner violence.

To appreciate how wife beating was rediscovered and how attitudes and responses toward wife beating have changed over the centuries.

To recognize victim-blaming, victim-defending, and system-blaming arguments concerning who or what is at fault.

continued

LEARNING OBJECTIVES

continued

To identify maximalist and minimalist perspectives about the seriousness of the problem of intimate partner violence.

To be able to offer a number of convincing answers to the question of why a battered woman stays in an abusive relationship.

To become familiar with the many changes that have taken place in the way that the criminal justice system handles violence between intimate partners as well as the shortcomings that persist.

To become aware of the problem of violence within couples who are dating.

To become alert to the different forms of elder abuse.

To become familiar with the different strategies underlying prevention efforts to reduce family violence.

VIOLENCE WITHIN ROMANTIC RELATIONSHIPS AND FAMILIES

Domestic violence affects every American. It harms our communities, weakens the foundation of our nation, and hurts those we love most. It is an affront to our basic decency and humanity, and it must end…we acknowledge the progress made in reducing these shameful crimes…and recognize that more work remains until every individual is able to live free from fear. (President Barack Obama, 2014)

∎∎∎

A young woman is punched in an elevator by her fiancé, a well-known football player, and crumples to the floor. The league suspends him for two games, but she does not press charges and marries him. When a video taken by the elevator's surveillance camera circulates on the Internet, the disturbing footage provokes public outrage. A debate breaks out over whether cultural changes about domestic violence are needed so that major league sports teams will take greater responsibility for disciplining their professional athletes, or whether to honor the presumption of

innocence and not take action until criminal charges are resolved by the legal system—which has a poor track record of handling this kind of interpersonal conflict between intimates. (Crouse, 2014)

This chapter focuses upon another aspect of family violence—not the abuse of children by parents, but physical attacks by one adult against another. Besides child abuse, the various forms of violence within a family (in the broadest sense of the term) include intimate partner abuse, woman battering and wife beating, husband beating, attacks by teenagers against their parents, elder abuse, and fights among relatives in a household. Family members injured by all these forms of nonstranger interpersonal violence all face special problems because—as in cases of child abuse and neglect—they live in close proximity, if not under the same roof, as their assailants. They usually interact on a routine basis and are dependent upon each other, so they require special solutions that are creative, fine-tuned, and effective. When the police are called upon to quell violence within households, the officers generally refer to these incidents as **domestic disturbances**.

Intimate partner violence (IPV) is the newer and more inclusive name since it refers not only to physical assaults by husbands against wives but also attacks by wives against husbands, fights between persons who are separated or divorced, and assaults within romantic relationships, such as between domestic partners as well as girlfriends and boyfriends IPV is a broader term than spouse abuse because it also embraces the use of force by a person with whom the victim is involved in (or has had) a sexual relationship, and therefore includes any and all assaults by a current live-in lover, a domestic partner, an ex-spouse, or a boyfriend, ex-boyfriend, girlfriend, or former girlfriend, whether heterosexual or homosexual.

THE REDISCOVERY OF "WIFE BEATING"

… we've come a long way…domestic abuse was too often seen as a private matter, best hidden behind

closed doors. Victims too often stayed silent or felt that they had to live in shame, that somehow they had done something wrong. Even when they went to the hospital or the police station, too often they were sent back home without any real intervention or support. (President Barack Obama, 2013)

...

In her autobiography, the daughter of a prominent political figure reveals that she endured many vicious beatings by her first husband, a police officer, shortly after they married. During fits of jealous rage, he punched and kicked her in the head so brutally that she fantasized about killing him. But when she picked up his service revolver, she found she was incapable of pulling the trigger. She told her coworkers, friends, and parents that her cuts and swellings were due to her clumsiness. Her father, a famous actor and former president of the United States, finally discovers the truth about her "bruises from accidents" when he reads her book. (Bruni, 1989)

Wife beating is the old-fashioned name for a problem that has plagued many families since the institution of marriage was first invented thousands of years ago. This kind of violence mars the lives of millions of Americans, and yet it was a taboo topic that was rarely discussed publicly until the start of the 1970s. Now violence between intimates has come out from the shadows and is the most thoroughly studied victim–offender relationship of all— and for several good reasons. The consequences of these beatings can be severe for the injured party (physical wounds, depression, posttraumatic stress, loss of job, homelessness, even death from homicide or suicide), for the offender (arrest, prosecution, probation, incarceration, mandatory therapy), for their children (emotional scars, divorce, custody battles), and for the entire society (costs of medical care and social services, lost productivity, and criminal justice expenses).

The rediscovery of the plight of battered wives by the feminist movement during the 1970s shattered the illusion of **domestic tranquility**—the notion that women were safe from harm as long as they remained at home, protected by their husbands

from the vicious dog-eat-dog world raging outside. Once it was realized that a "silent crisis" burdened so many women and that the perpetrators were not menacing strangers but the men they married, the "look-the-other-way," "mind-your-own-business," and "hands-off" policies toward "lovers' spats" that took place "behind closed doors" could no longer be justified (see Straus, 1978; Pagelow, 1984a, 1984b; Gelles and Cornell, 1990; Straus and Gelles, 1990; and Dobash and Dobash, 1992).

For centuries, legal traditions granted the man—viewed as the "head of the household" whose home was "his castle"—the "right" to "discipline" his wife and children "as he saw fit" because they were regarded as his property or chattels. This outlook served as the basis in English common law (which was adopted into American jurisprudence) for a nonintervention stance that denied women equal protection under the law. Such institutionalized indifference was legally permissible because it was a wife's "duty" to "love, honor, and obey" her husband. Indeed, many battered wives did not even define their beatings as crimes and did not consider themselves to be victims because they accepted the prevailing ideology echoed by authority figures, friends, and parents that they had "stepped out of line" and "had it coming" and therefore "got what they deserved." Such traditional thinking made the marriage license into a hitting license for husbands (Dobash and Dobash, 1979).

As early as the mid-1600s, the pilgrims who settled in New England officially recognized the possibility that wives could be assaulted by their husbands, that husbands could be brutalized by their wives, that children could be harshly mistreated by their parents, and that incestuous sexual relations could be imposed on youngsters. Guided by religious teachings about the virtues of harmonious family life and the sins of disobeying authority, the Puritans in Plymouth Colony and Massachusetts Bay Colony passed the first laws forbidding verbal or physical abuse between family members. Wife beating was punishable by a fine or a whipping; however, the sentence for husband abuse was up to the judge. Child abuse (called

unnatural severity) carried a fine, but if incest was discovered it could result in execution by hanging, according to the interpretation of the Bible at that time.

Even though conformity to all laws was insisted upon and intervening into a neighboring family's affairs was expected, none of these laws were vigorously enforced. Only on rare occasions were wives brought to court for verbally abusing ("nagging") their husbands. Husbands rarely were fined and almost never whipped for beating their wives, and charges were dropped if judges decided wives had provoked their husbands' wrath. Wives who complained that their husbands beat them often recanted their accusations when they got to court. No case of child abuse was ever prosecuted, and no one was ever put to death for incest, according to court records from these New England colonies. Apparently, these laws merely served a symbolic function, outlining rights and responsibilities and setting limits.

Puritan teachings held that God ruled the state, the state supervised the family, and the husband headed the household. The occasional use of force to discipline a wife (what they called **moderate correction** within **domestic chastisement**) was permissible "within reasonable limits"—as long as the beating caused no permanent damage. In those days, the expression **rule of thumb** actually was a guideline that prohibited men from using sticks thicker than their thumbs to beat their wives, whose "provocations" included "passionate language" (scolding) and refusing to engage in sexual relations. The desire to reinforce patriarchal control, uphold parental rights, and shore up the nuclear family necessitated that laws criminalizing abuse within families would be rarely enforced and that "sinners" would receive lenient sentences. The most effective restraints on male violence were informal social controls: community disapproval, pressures from the wife's parents, and in extreme cases, divorce (Rhode, 1989; and Pleck, 1989).

A mistaken impression prevails that the issue of spouse abuse was raised for the first time during the 1970s, primarily by feminists intent on exposing the injustices and cruelties of **patriarchy**, the traditional system of male dominance. Actually, there had been a previous campaign against family violence in American history as part of the war on drinking known as the temperance movement to usher in Prohibition (Pleck, 1989).

As the agricultural way of life gave way to industrialization and urbanization, a wave of concern about family violence developed in the late 1800s. Reformers argued in favor of the principle that the government had a responsibility to enforce morality as codified in law. Fears about immigrants, drifters, and the growing "dangerous classes" of criminals and delinquents in the large cities fueled this movement for change. Temperance advocates hammered away at the evils of drinking by emphasizing how wives and children were abused by drunkards who wasted their time and money in saloons. Offshoots of the Society for the Prevention of Cruelty to Children (SPCC) were set up across the country. Some women's rights activists contended that fines and jail terms were insufficient to deter wife beating and called for the restoration of the whipping post. (Public flogging had been abandoned in most states about 100 years earlier as an uncivilized and barbaric form of corporal punishment.) Other feminists sought ways to help battered wives get orders of protection and divorces (Pleck, 1989).

The wave of reform that directly focused on victim support activities was launched by feminists in the women's liberation movement of the early 1970s. Wife beating symbolized women's oppression within the family, and the lack of responsiveness on the part of the men who ran the criminal justice system demonstrated how women faced institutionalized discrimination in everyday life. Projects such as shelters for battered women exemplified the self-help, tangible aid, and empowerment that women could achieve if they acted collectively.

Before the 1970s, wife beating received very little attention in the journals read by counselors, social workers, and others in the helping professions. This "silent crisis" did not merit much press coverage, either. Now entire conferences, organizations, college courses, websites, journals, books, readers, handbooks, and even an encyclopedia are devoted to reducing the violence that breaks out between intimates (for examples, see Roberts, 2002; Loseke, Gelles, and Cavanaugh, 2005; Payne and Gainey, 2005; Roberts and Roberts, 2005; Sokoloff and Pratt, 2005; Jackson, 2007; Giardino and Giardino, 2010; Meloy and Miller, 2010; and Garcia and McManimon, 2011).

Blaming Her for His Violent Outbursts

The battered women's self-help movement initially encountered resistance and opposition because of the widespread acceptance of victim-blaming arguments that portrayed beaten wives unsympathetically. Many people, including some counselors and family therapists, believed that a high proportion of beatings were unconsciously precipitated or even intentionally provoked. The wives who were said to be responsible for inciting their husbands' wrath were negatively stereotyped as "aggressive," "masculine," and "sexually frigid." Their husbands were characterized as "shy," "sexually ineffectual," "dependent and passive," and even as "mothers' boys." The dynamics of a couple's conflict were set into motion whenever a badgered husband tried to please and pacify his querulous and demanding wife. Eventually, her taunts and challenges would provoke an explosion, and he would lose self-control (see Snell, Rosenwald, and Robey, 1964; and Faulk, 1977).

Victim blaming emphasized the wife's alleged shortcomings: her domineering nature, her coldness, and her secret masochistic cravings for suffering. It placed the entire burden of change on the woman—not the man, the community, or the culture that encouraged male dominance. Activists in the battered women's movement rejected this outlook because it failed to condemn the violence and implied that it was not a criminal matter that should be addressed by police departments and courts. The husband's main problem appeared to be his weakness rather than his resort to force to get his way (see Schechter, 1982; and Beirne and Messerschmidt, 1991).

The battered women's movement succeeded in replacing this victim-blaming outlook with a victim-defending one. This husband-blaming/wife-defending point of view quickly gained adherents, as journalists depicted wife beating in ways surprisingly favorable to a feminist pro-victim perspective during the 1970s and 1980s. Abusers generally were depicted in these media accounts as "super-macho" types who felt that following conventional sex-based roles gave them a right to discipline and control their wives and to beat back any challenges to their manly privileges. The targets of their wrath were pictured as stereotypically feminine women who believed that a wife's place was in the home and that she should be selflessly devoted to her husband, dependent upon him as a breadwinner, and deferential to his rightful authority.

Several progressive themes ran through most of the articles. One was that wife beating was a social problem afflicting millions and not just a personal trouble burdening only a few unfortunate women. Another was that the women did not deserve or provoke the abuse heaped upon them, and that the consequences were serious, even life-threatening. Many articles concluded that this crisis in a fundamental social institution, the family, should be of concern to everyone because domestic violence broke out at all levels of society, even if it was harder to detect in affluent families. Governmental action could bring it under control through social programs coupled with more vigorous criminal justice responses. Most articles identified the root causes as unjust gender relations, buttressed by an ideology that proclaimed that males were superior to females. Male supremacy was perpetuated by socialization practices that exhorted boys to be aggressive, tough, and powerful while teaching girls to be passive, submissive, and supportive, according to a content analysis of stories and reports appearing in widely read magazines during the 1970s and 1980s (Loseke, 1989).

How Victims Suffer

A 39-year-old nurse who is the mother of two boys is attacked by her estranged husband. He breaks into her house, beats her with a baseball bat, and then he squirts industrial strength lye on her from a plastic bottle. She is burned beyond recognition. What remains of her face and much of her body is a patchwork of scar tissue and skin grafts, difficult to look at and even more painful to live with. After six years, doctors locate a recently perished donor's body and she is given a face transplant. She emerges from the operating room with what her mother describes as a puffy surreal mask, but they both are hopeful that she finally is on the road to recovery. (Goodnough, 2013)

The suffering inflicted on victims can range from merely being shaken up to gruesome disfiguring injuries—as the case above dramatizes—to mortal wounds (see Abraham, 2014).

The federal government's Centers for Disease Control (CDC) pictures intimate partner violence as a serious but preventable public health problem that is often intertwined with two additional crimes, stalking (see Chapter 11) plus rape and other sexual assaults (see Chapter 10). The CDC includes four types of behaviors under the heading IPV. The first is emotional abuse, which takes the form of intimidating and controlling behaviors motivated by extreme jealously, and also name-calling, belittling, humiliating insults, and other forms of bullying that undermine a person's sense of self-worth. Denying access to money and isolation from friends and family is also considered a type of emotional abuse, as is threatening to harm a partner's close relatives or possessions (including pets). (Emotional abuse is not a crime.) The second is issuing threats about impending physical or sexual violence, which includes brandishing a weapon but also using gestures and even words that communicate an intent to cause injury, disability, or death. Credible threats of harm could be crimes. Sexual violence, the third aspect of IPV, is a crime whenever one partner is forced to submit to a sex act without granting consent. Physical violence, the fourth and most obvious set of lawbreaking behaviors, includes simple assaults (pushing, shoving, pulling, dragging, shaking, ripping clothing, scratching, biting, burning, tying up, hitting with an open hand, kicking) as well as aggravated assaults evidencing an intent to inflict serious injuries (punching with a closed fist, choking, whipping,

stomping, throwing an object, and wounding with a knife or gun). The full continuum of physical injuries ranges from welts, bruises, swellings, cuts, scratches, sprains, and burns to dizziness, loss of vision or hearing, fractures, broken bones, concussions, and internal bleeding. Using this broad definition, the CDC concludes that intimate partner violence can undermine physical and mental health in a number of ways and observes that the longer the victim endures the violence, the more serious its deleterious effects will be. Emotional harm can appear in the guise of flashbacks, panic attacks, sleep disorders, and other symptoms of trauma. Emotional damage can also manifest itself as lowered self-esteem, distrust of others, anger, stress, depression, eating disorders, and, in extreme cases, suicide. Physical injuries can range from minor wounds to permanent disabilities, and, in worst-case scenarios, even death. The consequences can also lead to digestive disorders, venereal diseases, pregnancy complications, and other acute and chronic health problems that require medical attention in emergency rooms, hospitalization, counseling, and more intensive forms of therapy. Unhealthy responses on the part of the targets to the trauma of IPV include self-destructive habits involving smoking, drinking, drug taking, and unsafe sex (Black et al., 2011; and CDC, 2011b). Battered women who suffered from PTSD but demonstrated some resiliency often benefited from social support and comforting religious beliefs (Astin et. al., 1993).

Two other expressions of intimate partner abuse are worthy of mention: forcibly tattooing a young woman against her will to symbolize that she has been claimed by some guy (see O'Donnell, 2013); and forcing a mate into getting pregnant and bearing a child by removing or sabotaging contraceptive devices ("reproductive coercion") (Castillo, 2013).

Estimates of the Incidence, Prevalence, and Seriousness of Intimate Partner Violence

"I never reported it…. I was intimidated, ashamed. I had nowhere to go. I had five children to raise. I was

told that if I ever left, he would find me and kill me," said the police chief of a small rural department, who suffered broken bones, burns, and stab wounds in a series of beatings that began two weeks after she got married. ("Police Chief ...," 1993)

After "wife beating" was rediscovered in the 1970s, and the broader terms *spouse abuse* and *woman battering* entered everyday language, a number of questions arose. The most basic was, "How widespread is the problem?" The myth that just a very small proportion of married women were beaten by their husbands was hard to dispel because official statistics in those days had no such breakdown under the general heading of assault. When the battered women's movement organized **speakouts**, where wives disclosed their situations to sympathetic audiences, these true confessions indicated that violence between individuals who were supposed to be lovers was all too common. But anecdotal evidence is insufficient to document the genuine dimensions of the problem. A maximalist versus minimalist debate broke out.

The maximalist perspective was that the women whose suffering was known were just the tip of the iceberg. Fierce fighting poisoned many ostensibly romantic relationships, and battering actually was so widespread as to constitute a low-profile epidemic. However, a minimalist reaction arose to challenge maximalist assumptions about just how common and serious the problem actually is. The opposing viewpoints sharply disagreed in part because of some of the complexities surrounding efforts to estimate the true scope and intensity of not only wife beating, or spouse abuse generally, but of intimate partner violence in all its forms.

The first and most basic methodological issue concerns which victim–offender relationships should be included and which should be excluded. Several terms with similar and overlapping but not identical meanings can cause confusion and create inconsistencies from one study to another. Choosing one definition over another can make the scope of the problem seem much larger or much smaller. Restricting attention to wife abuse (strictly beatings of married women) will yield the lowest estimates.

Woman battering focuses on the injured parties regardless of whether they are legally married or not, so the statistical counts will be higher. Measuring the frequency of spouse abuse, which includes male as well as female victims who are legally married, will lead to medium-size estimates. The highest estimates will be generated by counting all aspects of intimate partner violence. This is the broadest term because it refers to all forms of abuse of males and females in romantic relationships, including couples, whether heterosexual or homosexual, who are merely dating, as well as living together, in formally recognized domestic partnerships, or legally separated, as well as after a break-up or divorce.

Besides measurement problems stemming from definitions, other methodological issues can arise from the way the data is collected. Hunting for statistics about domestic disturbances in police files only will turn up cases known to authorities, but these calls for assistance could arise from conflicts between any members of the same household, including grandparents, adolescents, siblings, and relatives, not just intimates. The phrase *domestic violence* refers to the largest grouping of all because it embraces violence in all its forms, which may or may not be reported to the police, between parents, siblings, elders, children, unmarried lovers, and other relatives living under the same roof.

Besides disagreements over which relationships should be included or excluded, additional fuel for the maximalist–minimalist debate arises from disagreements about which specific behaviors constitute abuse, violence, battering, or beatings. There are distinctions among these terms and different shades of meaning and connotations. These ambiguities permit observers to draw very different conclusions. First of all, it must be noted that although verbal and emotional abuse is psychologically harmful, this conduct is not a criminal matter. Similarly, sexual withdrawal (withholding affection, refusing sexual relations) is also destructive to a relationship and can be grounds for a break-up or divorce but cannot be the basis for an arrest. (Of course, physically overpowering a partner to make her submit could constitute forcible rape; if the two are married, it would be marital rape, which is discussed later.) To summarize this set of complications, the question comes down to whether to count words as well as deeds. When researchers try to measure the incidence and prevalence of IPV, should "credible threats" about using force be counted, whether they are reported to the police or not?

Further complications arise from different definitions about the use of force. Not all physical assaults bring about visible injuries. Partners may attack each other by pushing, shoving, arm-twisting, and hair-pulling and yet not inflict tangible injuries sufficient to be labeled as wounds. If physical injury is taken to be the defining criterion, then domestic violence is overwhelmingly a male-on-female crime. But if all kinds of attacks are counted, then females act aggressively against their male partners almost as often as males assault their female lovers. Put succinctly, many men who are attacked by women are not wounded; assaults by males inflict injuries more often than assaults by females (Straus, 1991). Clearly, the precise definition used by the researcher profoundly shapes a study's findings and the interpretation of these numbers.

Social workers, family therapists, feminists, psychologists, criminologists, victimologists, police officers, and prosecutors have tried but failed to reach a consensus about where to draw the line between inclusion and exclusion of actions labeled abusive, violent, or assaultive. It seems that many people approve of, tolerate, or are resigned to some "normal" level of quarreling and fighting among partners in romantic relationships. The lack of public consensus can be called **normative ambiguity** (Straus, 1991), and it reflects the distinction some would make between conflicts that occur within the family and fights between strangers. The cultural support that still exists in some communities for using force to settle family quarrels means that the reporting rate varies from group to group. And that observation brings up a final methodological concern: Which families or couples are queried about domestic violence, and how representative is the sample used in any research endeavor?

In sum, because there is no standard definition that is widely accepted, a researcher's working definition of intimate partner violence must clearly specify how it operationalizes key variables such as the credibility of any threats, the assailant's intentions, the attempts to inflict wounds, the weapons used in the attack, the actual physical injuries sustained, the depth of psychological trauma, and even any injuries suffered by the aggressor (see Loseke, 1989; Rhodes, 1992; and BJS, 2008a).

Maximalist Arguments   Because of these methodological issues, maximalists can cite a number of studies yielding disturbing, even shocking, statistical findings that support their contention that intimate partner violence remains a deeply hidden but extremely widespread and serious problem:

- Intimate partner violence afflicts twice as many women as another much more publicized major concern, breast cancer (Kristof, 2014a).

- A consistent finding running through years of research is that women are much more likely to be harmed by someone they know than by a stranger. For most women, statistically speaking, the most dangerous places they frequent are their homes, and the most dangerous people they interact with are intimates, other family members, and friends (Bernstein and Kaufman, 2004; and Schwartz, 2005). Females were murdered by a male they knew (but not necessarily intimately) 13 times more often than by a male stranger in 2012 (VPC, 2014).

- A substantial proportion of the adult population in the United States will experience some form of intimate partner violence at least once during their lifetimes. Nearly 25 percent of all women will be subjected to serious physical violence perpetrated by an intimate partner (such as being slammed against something or hit with a fist, or worse) within their lifetimes, For men, the corresponding prevalence rate is a surprisingly high (14 percent). Nearly 9 percent of all women will be raped, and another 16 percent will endure other kinds of sexual assaults by an intimate partner over a lifetime, according to the National Intimate Partner and Sexual Violence Survey for 2011 (Breiding et al., 2014).

- Almost half of all incidents of battering were not reported to police departments in recent years, partly because of fears of reprisals but also due to previous negative experiences with officers responding to domestic disturbance calls, according to findings derived from the *NCVS* (Catalano, 2009). In 2013, the reporting rate for IPV had risen slightly, but still was only 57 percent. Even the most serious violent attacks by intimates were reported only 60 percent of the time (Truman and Langton, 2014), despite all the efforts over the years to encourage victims to seek help and protection from the authorities. (Of course, many incidents are not disclosed to survey interviewers either, especially if the assailant is present when the injured party is answering questions.) Other pressures to keep the problem under wraps and behind closed doors inhibit victims from filing complaints, so the actual amount of violence between intimates is worse than the official statistics indicate. For example, hundreds of cities and towns have adopted "nuisance property" or "crime-free housing" ordinances that permit landlords to evict unruly tenants. Battered women might find themselves forced to choose between two dangerous courses of action: either calling attention to their dysfunctional family lives by dialing 911 and thereby risking eviction or enduring the beatings in order to avoid expulsion from their rented homes (Eckholm, 2013).

- The main reasons respondents cited for informing the authorities were to end the attack, to keep it from happening again, and to get the offender in trouble so that he would be punished. The leading reasons for not requesting help were the women's beliefs that the incidents were private and personal matters, that the crime wasn't important enough, that the police wouldn't or couldn't assist them, and that they would be subject to reprisals if they

dared to seek outside protection. *NCVS* data indicates that women who report being assaulted by a mate are likely to report being physically abused again when they are interviewed in later years. Police files confirm fears that the cycle of violence tends to escalate in frequency and severity over time (Langan and Innes, 1986).About one-third of all nonreporting victims suffered more than one violent attack during the six months preceding their *NCVS* interview (Fleury et al., 1998; and Greenfeld et al., 1998).

- Women sustain about 2 million injuries from intimate partner violence each year (CDC, 2008). About 1 million women each year seek medical attention for serious wounds inflicted by a male partner—a husband, ex-husband, boyfriend, or former lover. Somewhere between one-fifth and one-third of all visits by women to hospital emergency rooms are to treat injuries resulting from a partner's assault. Domestic violence poses a greater threat of injury to women between the ages of 15 and 44 than automobile accidents, robberies, and cancer combined (Gibbs, 1993b). IPV may be the source of an even greater proportion of injuries, but women tend to be reluctant to disclose to doctors that they were assaulted, and physicians often shy away from raising the subject ("Screening…," 2006).

- Some violent men continue to beat their mates even when the women are pregnant. Between 6 percent and 8 percent of women queried in various studies conceded to interviewers that they were injured by their husbands or partners during their pregnancy. The prevalence rate of assaults during pregnancy is perhaps as low as 3 percent but may be as high as 25 percent, depending on the sample used in the study (see Goldstein and Martin, 2004; and Futures Without Violence, 2010). Beatings that pregnant women endure cause more birth defects than all diseases for which children are immunized. The greatest risks are faced by young women who are poorly educated, not married, living in crowded households, and unable to get prenatal care (Hilts, 1994). Male violence is the leading cause of deaths stemming from injuries during pregnancy (Frye, 2001). Violence inflicted during pregnancy is a cause of post-partum depression.

- The rate of domestic violence in military families is much higher than it is among civilians. The military concedes it has a "spousal aggression issue," as the Pentagon calls it, but points out that many soldiers are young and come from poverty-stricken families, and these two factors are correlated with high rates of reported domestic violence. However, the armed forces might actually have a more serious domestic violence problem than the figures indicate, because the Department of Defense keeps records only of substantiated attacks against a current legal spouse living on a military base. Incidents that take place off-post might not be entered in the Pentagon's statistics, and assaults against ex-partners, live-in lovers, or dates do not count as "spousal aggression" (Schmitt, 1994; and Houppert, 2005). Civilian spouses of active duty personnel on or near military bases who have children and have been married for two years or less are assaulted the most often. The army consistently has the highest rates of spouse abuse, followed by the marines, navy, and air force. Abused women tend to be afraid to report incidents because of a lack of confidentiality, privacy, and effective services, but also because of a sense of isolation from family and friends (Futures Without Violence, 2014). Similarly, intimate partner violence may be a serious but hidden problem within the ranks of the very same police forces that victims count upon to protect them. Officers may be prone to abuse since they receive special training in hand-to-hand fighting, learn how to control people who challenge their authority, and enjoy the privilege of carrying firearms wherever they go. Their intimate partners may be unusually reluctant to report abuse because they anticipate that their assailants' close colleagues and even prosecutors (who need the daily cooperation of officers) will not take their complaints seriously and may even go to great lengths to cover up what happened and to retaliate against the complainant. The International Association of Chiefs of Police has promoted a model set of "zero tolerance" rules to purge domestic violence offenders from the ranks of law enforcement agencies, but most departments have failed to fully adopt and implement this approach. Reliable statistics still do not exist to measure how often officers abuse their domestic partners, get arrested for it, and subsequently are disciplined by the department for these assaults (Kocieniewski and Flynn, 1998; and Cohen, Ruiz, and Childress, 2013).

- The total social costs of domestic violence—for health care (including mental health), social services (including aid to homeless women fleeing abusive relationships), lost productivity, and criminal justice outlays—add up to between $5 billion and $10 billion a year (Senate Committee on the Judiciary, 1993; and Max et al., 2004). Individuals who are recovering from severe assaults lose nearly 8 million days of paid work each year—the equivalent of more than 32,000 full-time jobs (CDC, 2011b). Battered women are frequently harassed or even attacked when they are at their jobs, resulting in reduced productivity and inflated health care costs for their employers. Violence against women is a leading cause of female homelessness and also is the leading reason for children being homeless, according to a survey sponsored by the U.S. Conference of Mayors (Washington Crime News Service, 2003; and Futures Without Violence, 2009). The overwhelming majority of women incarcerated in jails and prisons have endured severe physical or sexual violence in their lifetimes, during childhood, and/or as adults due to an intimate partner (Williams, 2013).

- Males shooting their female partners to death is a much bigger problem in the United States than in other higher-income countries. The actual death toll might be even greater because some of the females murdered by males were their ex-girlfriends, but the FBI's *UCR* only recognizes current girlfriends, wives, and ex-wives as intimate partners (VPC, 2014).

Minimalist Views   The minimalist position is that violence between intimates, while serious, is not the dire threat to women's physical and mental well-being as maximalist alarmists' calls to action make it seem. Because there are so many unresolved definitional and methodological issues, minimalists can point to studies that yield findings that picture the problem as not so common and not so serious, and actually in decline.

- Intimate partner abuse sometimes is equated with intimate partner violence. But abuse can be defined so broadly that it goes far beyond everyday understandings of what constitutes violence, and subsequent measurements of its frequency of occurrence will be inflated. An example of a definition of intimate partner abuse that is too-inclusive is "any behavior within a current or past intimate relationship that involves actual, attempted, or threatened harm… that may impact or detract from the victim's physical, psychological, sexual, economic, or spiritual well-being" (cited in Demarais et al., 2014).

- In 2013, less than 3 out of every 1,000 persons age 12 or older suffered a simple or aggravated assault from an intimate partner, according to the *NCVS* (Truman, and Langton, 2014).

- Most IPV attacks were only simple assaults, and most of the injuries that resulted were superficial, such as scratches, bruises, and welts (Tjaden and Thoennes, 2000; Rennison, 2003; and Catalano 2009). Many minor assaults that are registered on surveys don't even lead to physical injuries and should not be lumped in with aggravated assaults that inflict severe bodily harm. Some incidents that are counted in studies were just threats or attempted assaults that failed. Also, some of the fighting is initiated by women or can be considered acts of retaliation, so women were not always the

passive recipients of male aggression (see Straus, 1999). Furthermore, an expanded definition of abuse that includes vicious name-calling and controlling behaviors like intimidation and social isolation, which may cause psychological damage but not physical wounds, has been used in some studies, leading to inflated estimates of the numbers of individuals suffering from "violence" unleashed by intimate partners.

- Of all the violence (simple and aggravated assaults, rapes and other sexual assaults; and robberies) disclosed to interviewers by males and females in 2013, strangers were the perpetrators in 38 percent of all incidents; acquaintances, whether casual or well-known, accounted for 32 percent; and intimate partners were the attackers in just 15 percent (the remaining 6 percent were other family members and relatives) (Truman and Morgan, 2014). Therefore, the relative threat of intimate partners as compared to strangers and acquaintances may have been overstated by maximalists.

- Intimate partner violence negatively affects the work victims perform for organizations via absenteeism, tardiness, and distraction, but productivity losses might not be as serious as originally assumed (Reeves and O'Leary-Kelly, 2007).

As for trends, minimalists point out that domestic violence seems to be diminishing in frequency. In fact, the problem may have begun to subside shortly after it was rediscovered at the start of the 1970s.

- Researchers found in a 1975 survey that about 4 out of every 100 couples admitted engaging in at least one serious outbreak of violence within the year. A decade later, however, researchers using the same definitions in interviews (this time with a larger representative sample of married and cohabiting couples) uncovered evidence that the rate had dropped to about 3 couples per 100 per year. Serious incidents were defined as those involving kicking, hitting with a fist, biting, and beating up, or using or threatening to use a gun or knife during a dispute. The overall incidence rate, which included less serious instances of slapping, shoving, pushing, and throwing things, was estimated to be about 16 percent of married and cohabiting couples per year. The prevalence rate was only 33 percent for one or more incidents involving any degree of violence during the entire marriage or cohabitation (Straus and Gelles, 1986).

- *NCVS* data also indicates that intimate partner violence against women and also against men is diminishing (Rennison, 2003; and Catalano, 2009). Between 1993 and 2010, the overall IPV rate tumbled by over 60 percent for both females and males nationally. In 1993, interviewers learned about over 2 million incidents, which translated to a rate of nearly 10 victims for every 1,000 persons over the age of 11 that they interviewed. By 2010, the number of incidents was around 900,000 and the violent victimization rate by a current or former romantic partner was way down to about 3.5 per 1,000. The number of incidents decreased to about 810,000 in 2012, and then dropped further to less than 750,000 in 2013, according to an analysis of *NCVS* files. (However, most of the improvement occurred from the early 1990s up to 2003 [Catalano, 2012b; and Truman and Morgan, 2014]). As for the rate of serious violence between intimates (counting rape, other sexual assaults, aggravated assaults, and robberies but not simple assaults), it fell by more than 70 percent from 3.6 per 1,000 persons in 1994 down to just 1 per 1,000 in 2012 (Truman and Morgan, 2014).

- As for males murdering the females they were formerly intimate with, that rate has declined about 25 percent from 1.6 per 100,000 in 1996 to 1.2 per 100,000 in 2012 (VPC, 2014). Countries and cities across the globe with murder rates of about 1 per 100,000 generally are considered very safe (refer back to Chapter 4).

Recognizing Warning Signs

Besides seeking answers to the question of how many, victimologists also wonder, "What kinds of families are wracked by these problems?" At first there were only media images and personal revelations (true confessions), but this kind of anecdotal evidence might be very unrepresentative and misleading. Atypical cases make the news, but what kinds of women are usually objects of their lovers' wrath?

The statistical profile of a couple in which the woman is at risk for a severe beating is as follows, (the more factors that fit, the higher the risk): The family income is low and the couple is under economic stress. She is young, unemployed, poorly educated, and lives with but is not married to a man of a different religious or ethnic background. He is between the ages of 18 and 30, is unemployed or working in a blue-collar job, did not graduate from high school, beats his children, and abuses alcohol and illicit drugs. His parents were violent toward each other, and he grew up in a rough neighborhood where neighbors were unwilling to intervene in situations where they witnessed violence. She suffers from anxiety and depression, low self-esteem, passivity, dependence, and an inordinate need for attention, affection, and approval. She lives in isolation from family and friends and also may be especially vulnerable due to physical disabilities. He is impulsive, jealous, possessive, verbally domineering, and a firm believer in strictly defined gender roles and male dominance in decision making. He too suffers from a low sense of self-worth and dreads rejection and abandonment. Her threats to move out to escape his clutches provoke fears that he is losing control of her (Ingrassia and Beck, 1994; Healy and Smith, 1998; "Domestic Abusers," 1999; Tjaden and Thoennes, 2000; and CDC, 2011b).

In terms of demography rather than individual situations and traits, the highest risk groups for intimate partner violence, as identified by their disclosures on the *NCVS*, are women who are between the ages of 18 and 34. Women over 50 were assaulted far less frequently. Females heading up households with children were 10 times more likely to be victimized than married women with children. Women who were separated were in much more danger than married women; single women who were never married or were divorced faced moderate levels of risk. African-American women faced higher risks, and Hispanic and Asian women faced lower risks of beatings than white women in 2010 (Catalano, 2012).

Battered women may be in very grave danger of severe or even fatal injuries if a number of these "red flags" are evident: He owns a gun, threatens to kill her, chokes or strangles her during fights, is exceedingly jealous and possessive, compels her to submit to sex, controls most of her daily activities, is a substance abuser and goes on drug-taking or drinking binges, disregards restraining orders and stalks her, and acts violently toward others as well. Social service agencies working with abused women often try to estimate their clients' level of risks by asking about warning signs (like previous episodes of choking) listed on a "lethality assessment tool" (Campbell et al., 2003), but skeptics question whether concerted attempts to murder a partner are really statistically predictable and therefore preventable (see Adame, 2014).

Researchers also have discovered that a substantial age discrepancy raises the risks that one spouse will kill the other. The chances of lethal violence are much higher if the man is at least 16 years older than the woman, or if the woman is at least 10 years older than the man, according to a study of intimate partner homicides that took place in Chicago from the mid-1960s to the mid-1990s (Breitman, Shackelford, and Block, 2004).

Fatal Attractions: Slayings of Intimate Partners

A married couple is walking down a suburban street when a man accosts them, shooting the 27-year-old wife to death and wounding the 26-year-old husband. He tells the police that three men shouting ethnic slurs were the killers. But the wife had recently texted her brother that she can't talk to her husband because he is so abusive, and that "Someday U will

find me dead … he wants to kill me." The police arrest the husband and he confesses that he hired a friend to kill her and then wound him to mislead the authorities. (Stelloh and Barron, 2011)

As with child abuse, the most accurate statistics are kept about the most terrible of all crimes: murder. The FBI's SHRs can be used to focus attention upon those homicides solved by the police that fit the victim–offender relationship of one intimate partner killing another. An analysis of all the homicides committed between 1980 and 2008 unearthed many important findings that shed light on very troubled intimate partner relationships where the degree of violence escalated to lethal levels (Cooper and Smith, 2011):

- In those murders in which the police were able to figure out the victim–offender relationship, about 16 percent arose out of a conflict between intimate partners. One spouse killing another accounted for 10 percent, and a boyfriend or girlfriend slaying one another made up 6 percent of all solved murders during that 28-year span.

- Every year, male violence greatly overshadowed violence by females: The body count from husbands killing wives plus boyfriends killing girlfriends vastly outnumbered the death toll of wives killing husbands added to girlfriends killing boyfriends.

- About 40 percent of female murder victims were slain by an intimate, as opposed to another member of her family, some acquaintance, or a complete stranger. The lowest percent of females killed by an intimate was 38 percent in 1995; the highest percent was 45 percent in 2008, the last year under scrutiny.

- Enraged intimates pose a relatively minor threat to the continued existence of most husbands and boyfriends; but for females, infuriated intimates make up a growing proportion of all killers, approaching the 50 percent mark.

- Over this time period, the proportion of intimate homicides committed by one spouse against another has declined steadily, while the proportion carried out by a boyfriend or girl-friend against one another has risen year after year. In other words, a declining percent of murders involve deadly assaults among husbands and wives, and a growing percent reflect unmarried lovers' embroiled in deadly quarrels. By 2008, about half of all IPV homicides involved people formally married to each other and the other half engulfed unmarried couples.

■ Over the 28 years, the percentage of killings carried out with firearms has declined substantially, from nearly 70 percent to roughly 50 percent. In 2008, 53 percent of all female victims but only 42 percent of deceased males were shot to death (see Cooper and Smith, 2011; also see Zawitz, 1994).

Further insights about the toll intimate partner violence imposes on American society can be gleaned from the bar graph in Figure 9.1, based on data from the FBI's SHRs over more than three and a half decades. The graph reveals that 1988 was the deadliest year for wives and girl-friends: nearly 1,600 perished. The first year tracked by the graph, 1977, was the time period when the most husbands and boyfriends were slain (almost 1,200). The lowest body count for male intimate partners, at about 240, down an astonishing 85 percent from its peak 33 years earlier, was recorded in 2010 and was duplicated in 2013. Clearly, violence by females against their intimate partners has dropped impressively. As for males murdering teenage girls and women they were once romantically involved with, the death toll receded during the 1990s and reached its lowest (best) point in 1999, with fewer than 1,000 female casualties of fatal IPV. But the slaying of girlfriends and wives leveled off during the early years of the twenty-first century, and then ominously reversed course in 2007 and began creeping back up until 2010. By 2013, the

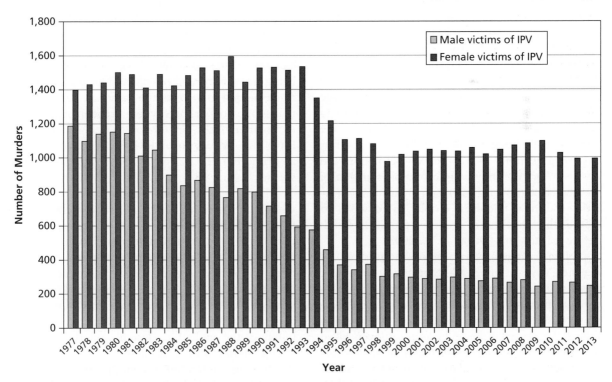

FIGURE 9.1 Trends in Murders Due to Intimate Partner Violence, United States, 1977–2013

SOURCE: FBI's *UCR*s, 1977–2013.

number of murdered wives and girlfriends nation-wide had dropped again to just under 1,000, very close to its lowest level in 36 years. So the problem of fatal intimate partner violence has subsided sub-stantially, especially if population growth over the decades is taken into account. However, female violence directed at males has dropped much more than male violence directed at females. The bar graph dramatizes the observation made above that lethal violence by males against the females they had been romantically involved with remains much more of a threat than deadly assaults by females against the males they once cherished. Between 1977 and 2013, the ratio of female deaths to male deaths widened dramatically from two to one to more than four to one.

A closer inspection of the SHRs for 2012 turned up some additional findings: When males murdered their female partners during arguments, firearms were the weapon of choice; most of the time (70 percent), the murder was carried out with a handgun, with rifles and shotguns a distant second. Alaska, with its relatively small population, had the highest female IPV murder rate, at 3 kill-ings for every 100,000 female residents.

The drop in murders between spouses noted above is probably due in part to a decline in marriage rates over the decades and enhanced selectivity among those who decide to wed, as well as a greater willingness for couples embroiled in bitter conflicts to disengage from each other via separation and divorce. Also, the improving economic situation of women, in terms of greater employment opportu-nities and rising incomes, enables more wives to escape the clutches of violence-prone husbands before it is too late (Dugan et al., 2003).

Note that men may have various motives for slay-ing their wives or girlfriends. Similarly, wives might murder their husbands, and girlfriends might kill their boyfriends, for many reasons; to put an end to physical abuse is one possibility. The bar graph in Figure 9.1 displayed the body count of lovers killed for any and all motives—whether out of fury, re-venge, jealousy, or financial gain. It is not known how many of those IPV homicides of men fall into the pattern of battered women slaying their violent mates.

Just as extensive investigations take place when a child dies from maltreatment, in more than half of all states fatality review boards now conduct postmortems to determine what went wrong and what could have been done differently to prevent romantic relationships from bitter end-ings. The fatality review team delves into the way the criminal justice system and social service agen-cies responded to the first signs of trouble, if any, and how early intervention efforts could have been more effective in protecting the victim (Websdale, 2003).

Explaining Intimate Partner Violence: Why Doesn't She Just Leave Him?

In criminology, an offender-oriented question would be, "Why does he beat her so viciously?" A victim-centered question that is often asked is, "If he is so brutal, then why does she put up with it and stay with him?" Until the 1970s, this compli-cated situation was dismissed with the victim-blaming rejoinder that being regularly beaten must somehow fulfill a pathological need of hers. For example, battered wives have been accused of being masochistic and of enjoying feeling miserable or of looking forward to the passionate lovemaking that supposedly follows when a repentant husband or boyfriend asks her for forgiveness. They could leave the dysfunctional love hate relationship at any time but choose to stay, some victim-blamers say (see Paglia, 1994; and Celock, 2013).

Therapists developed a more nuanced answer when they began to recognize that a cycle of vio-lence often marred the lives of their clients, accom-panied by "learned helplessness," which they termed the **battered-woman syndrome**. Beatings often follow a pattern and escalate in frequency and intensity unless the couple receives help. Three phases make up a cycle that resets and then repeats itself periodically in their relationship: tension building; the violent explosion; and the tranquil, loving aftermath (Walker, 2009).

During the tension-building phase, the aggres-sor hurls insults and even breaks objects while his docile target tries to appease him in a vain attempt to stave off a blow-up and preserve their relationship. She attempts to cope with her mate's bad behavior and conceals it from others, isolating herself from potential rescuers. When her accommodations and sacrifices fail, the second stage of acute violence erupts. He goes on a rampage and savagely assaults her. Feeling trapped, she acts submissively as part of a defense mechanism to avoid his wrath. The injuries that he inflicts shock and confuse her. When he becomes fearful of driving her away, he begins to show shame and remorse, and the third stage—the reconciliation or "honeymoon" phase—commences. He apologizes, pledges it won't happen again, and acts tenderly. Still seeking marital bliss and unwilling to confront the seriousness of her plight, she blames herself for his loss of control and forgives him. Believing she can head off his next round of assaults, she becomes protective of him, covers up what really happened, and decides not to seek outside help or try to leave him. An illusion of normalcy prevails for a while. But nothing has been resolved or corrected, and soon the lull that soothed her into staying with him ends, tensions rise, and the cycle repeats itself. But his next round of attacks may increase in ferocity. He expresses less contrition and she feels less confident about being able to defuse his anger. He ratchets up his efforts to dominate her life, and she finds herself more isolated, trapped, vulnerable, and endangered than before (Walker, 2009).

However, some criticisms of the concept of "syndrome" have arisen, since it implies that virtually every battered woman shares these experiences and their consequences, that the fault lies with her lack of initiative rather than with his coercive conduct, and that she is a passive recipient rather than an active and resilient partner (see Wallace, 2007). Furthermore, findings drawn from files about women undergoing treatment cannot be generalized to the entire population because these battered women in therapy do not constitute a representative sample (this is called the **clinical fallacy**) (Straus, 1991).

Besides the possibility of the battered woman's syndrome, researchers have discovered a number of other plausible reasons why women stay with their violent mates and repeatedly endure the cycle of battering/reconciliation/battering. Some feel dependent, dread being alone, and despair that they have nowhere to go and no one to turn to for aid and comfort. They are intimidated, even terrorized, and fear reprisals if they dare to try to escape their possessive and controlling husbands who are obsessed with a "You belong to me!" and "If I can't have you, no one can!" mentality. They worry about their children's welfare (emotional damage, loss of financial support, and custody and visitation issues). Some still love their tormentors and invoke higher loyalties (a commitment to the institution of marriage and to the vows they took "for better or worse, in good times and in bad, till death do us part"). Some are ashamed of the stigma of "abandoning" or "deserting" a husband and of contributing to a "failed marriage" because of cultural and religious traditions. Many believe they should stand by their men and try to help cure them—attributing the whole mess to external causes such as alcoholism, unemployment, or stress at work. Finally, trying to escape from a batterer is a risky course of action. Some find themselves stalked and beaten more viciously and subject to greater dangers when they try to break up or after they separate from their abusive partners (Frieze and Browne, 1991; Steinman, 1991; Barnett and LaViolette, 1993; Kirkwood, 1993; Hampton, Oliver, and Magarian, 2003; and Malkin, 2013).

Practical considerations also might have deterred her from trying to escape. Abruptly severing an intimate relationship is difficult when a couple has children, property in common, and intertwined families, friends, daily routines, and jobs. A woman who separates from an abusive mate with a good job may lose custody of her children (Catania, 2005).

Before women who are trapped in abusive relationships can be helped, they must begin to recognize that they genuinely are crime victims. They must reject the illusions that they can prevent or maintain control over future outbursts and that the beatings are their fault. They must stop minimizing the extent of the physical and emotional injuries their partner inflicts, and they must resist shifting the blame to his drinking problem or other external triggers. Also they must override their impulses to isolate themselves to hide their troubles and avoid embarrassment (Arriaga and Capezza, 2005).

A number of more elaborate explanations have been put forward to explain why domestic violence remains such a widespread problem and why women endure repeated assaults by the men who profess to love them. Psychological theories emphasize personal pathologies. Most center on the batterers' problems, such as poor impulse control, paranoia, substance abuse, hypersensitivity, an inability to manage anger, or even brain injuries. But some intrapersonal explanations implicate the targets of IPV by contending that they too have personality problems, suffering from low self-esteem and bouts of depression and anxiety. The traumatic bonding theory posits that certain battered women developed unhealthy attachments to their abusive and neglectful parents and recreate these destructive relationships with their violent mates. Investment theory explains repeated attacks in terms of her deep commitment to maintain their love affair. Similarly, a psychological entrapment explanation proposes that the woman stays because she feels she has worked so hard to make the relationship successful that she must endure anything to save it. Wives who become overly dependent, passive, and submissive serve as inviting targets for their husband's displaced aggression and misplaced blame. The women seem resigned, crushed, and defeated and have feel helpless without an exit strategy because attempts to escape seem emotionally destructive to the children, economically disastrous, and likely to trigger even more violence.

But activists in the battered women's movement believe it is a mistake to attempt to "pathologize" intimate partner abuse as a problem that burdens merely a limited number of emotionally unstable couples. But it is also incorrect to try to normalize family violence as a by-product of unavoidable conflicts that occasionally arise in every romantic relationship. The problem of male violence persists because acting aggressively is generally taught and encouraged, as is female passivity and resignation, as part of sex-role socialization,

according to social learning theory. This theory explains how the unleashing of violence as a reaction to internal and external strains is a behavioral response modeled by abusive parents to their children. Intergenerational transmission of IPV takes place when girls who see their mothers beaten by their fathers come to accept periodic outbursts of violence as tolerable; similarly, boys grow up watching their fathers beat their mothers in times of stress or during bouts of heavy drinking.

Social scientists have developed a variety of competing explanations that focus on the dynamics between the two parties to account for the prevalence of partner abuse (see Gelles, 1987; and Hotaling et al., 1988). Those who apply exchange theory start with the explanation that in every couple each partner supplies the other with valued services and benefits. The problem arises when a domineering person employs force to obtain his goals and discovers that the gains outweigh the losses (rough treatment pays off). In nuclear families where couples live in isolation from the scrutiny and support of others, the benefits of violence can exceed the costs because authorities are reluctant to violate the privacy of intimates. Resource theory views power as stemming from economic, social, or psychological benefits and advantages. Decision-making influence within a family flows from the income, property, contacts, and prestige that each partner contributes to the relationship. Because men have advantages in the outside economy, they command much more power in most families, leaving women in a subordinate and therefore vulnerable position. But men lacking these resources can become aggressive as a reaction to a perceived loss of control. Some couples are on a collision course whenever the head of the household feels that his wife's assertions of independence threaten his privileges and social status as protector and provider, and he may hit her in order to once again take charge of a situation. Violence is the outward manifestation of their underlying battle over power and control. Coping theory suggests that when one or both partners in a troubled relationship experience severe stress, resorting to force may be considered a way of regaining normalcy while outside forces work to tear the couple apart. According to the subculture-of-violence theory, resorting to physical force to settle disputes is more acceptable in poor communities than within the middle class, whose members purportedly believe in negotiation and compromise. As a result, more cases of child abuse and intimate partner violence take place in poverty-stricken neighborhoods where this outlook prevails (see Sampson, 2007a; and Winter, 2010).

Feminist theory regards IPV as a consequence of the persistence of patriarchy, a system of male dominance that is promoted and enforced through coercion. Inequities and injustices within relationships are maintained through force, especially if the female shows streaks of independence and challenges his supremacy in decision making. The division of domestic labor in families places the husband in the dominant role and assigns him male prerogatives; the wife is compelled to accept a subordinate position burdened by female duties. These distinctions are legitimized by religion and the state, as symbolized by the wife's marriage vows to "love, honor, and obey" her husband. In a society controlled by giant corporations and large government bureaucracies, some men seize upon domination over their wives and children as a substitute for real autonomy in their personal lives. As long as women with children are financially dependent on men, and both sexes are raised to accept male aggression and tolerate female passivity, woman battering will persist as a serious social problem (see Dobash and Dobash, 1979; Schechter, 1982; Yllo and Bograd, 1988; Rhode, 1989; Viano, 1992; Healy and Smith, 1998; and Walker, 2009).

Enabling Victims Who Feel Trapped to Escape

From its start, the highest priority of the battered women's movement has been to provide tangible aid at a time of great need. To offer immediate support to victims during a crisis, activists established **shelters** as places of refuge. In 1974, following the lead of feminists in England a few years earlier, a self-help group in St. Paul, Minnesota, transformed an old meetinghouse into the first of many women's shelters in the United States (Martin, 1976). These "safe houses" offer a number of services to their temporary residents. First and foremost, they provide short-term room and board in a secure setting for women, and often their children, who are in continuing physical danger. Most also furnish emergency clothing and transportation. By bonding together in self-help groups, the women can give one another emotional support when grappling with transitional issues, particularly about whether to try to sever or to salvage their relationships with abusers. Counselors discuss legal issues (such as pressing charges; obtaining court orders of protection; and navigating the complexities of separation, divorce, child custody, and alimony), educational matters (such as a return to school and retraining for displaced homemakers), and job hunting. Hotline staffers instruct victims where to go, because the addresses of shelters are kept secret to protect the residents from being stalked. Through outreach activities, staff members raise public awareness about the needs for empowering these otherwise dependent women and for reforming the criminal justice and social service systems (Warrior, 1977; Neidig, 1984; Dutton-Douglas and Dionne, 1991; and OJP, 1998). In recent years, service providers at shelters have begun to recognize the importance of being sensitive to racial, ethnic, and cultural differences in order to design effective outreach strategies, therapeutic intervention programs, and criminal justice policies (Bent-Goodley, 2005; and Sokoloff and Pratt, 2005).

Although the first safe houses were set up initially as independent self-help projects staffed by volunteers, many argued that local governments had a responsibility to establish permanent shelters run by social service agencies. As government-sponsored shelters spread during the 1980s, a backlash against them emerged. "Pro-family" organizations sought to limit local, state, and federal funding for shelters, and police referrals of victims to them. These critics contended that shelter workers tended to be home wreckers who contributed to the breakup of marriages by encouraging battered wives to divorce abusive husbands (see Stone,

1984; and Pleck, 1989). Actually, most women who took refuge in a shelter did return to live with their mates again, and many of them suffered additional beatings, according to limited follow-up studies by researchers attempting to assess the effectiveness of this method of intervention (Dutton-Douglas and Dionne, 1991). As might be anticipated, women who flee violent mates and seek refuge in government-sponsored shelters tend to be the poorest and most desperate. Two surveys of women seeking emergency housing estimated that they were suffering between 60 and 70 beatings per year, whereas the average victim endured 6 per year. They also differed from the "norm" in another way: These targets of routine beatings rarely dared to fight back (see Straus, 1991).

By 1987, about 1,200 battered women's shelters were operating across the country. By the end of the 1990s, about 1,900 shelters had been established ("Domestic Abusers," 1999). The first temporary shelter run by a police department opened in Virginia during 2000 (Ellis, 2000). About 1,450 shelters across the country housed nearly 17,000 women and over 19,000 of their children on a typical day in 2013, according to an annual census of service providers (NNEDV, 2014).

Unfortunately, shelters for battered women are not as numerous as needed, and often are filled to capacity, necessitating waiting lists and time limitations. There are also restrictions about the maximum age of children accompanying their mothers. Prohibitions on bringing along dogs and cats deter some women from leaving dangerous living arrangements, so animal welfare organizations have established safe-haven partnerships with shelters to provide short-term boarding for family pets (Humane Society, 2014) but only in a limited number of areas outside of big cities.

Shelter residents still may feel terrified at the thought of having to live in hiding at secret locations like fugitives and of uprooting their children, and might be outraged at the "solution" of abandoning their homes to wrongdoers. Furthermore, they may know of women who are separated or even divorced but still get tracked down and beaten by their former intimates. Refuge seekers who are turned away from overcrowded facilities or whose time runs out face the same limited choices that battered women confronted before there was a movement to shelter them: Return home and face renewed attacks or seek temporary respite with friends, relatives, or parents (Abrams, 1987; Browne, 1987; and Mechanic and Uhlmansiek, 2000).

Battered Women and the Criminal Justice System: Violence Is Violence—or Is It?

A woman is beaten by her husband hundreds of times. She divorces him and then testifies against him in court. He is sent to prison and vows to get even with her some day. A note is placed in his file that she must be warned before he is released from custody. One day he is let out for a brief furlough, but she is not contacted. He catches her by surprise at home and murders her. (Pollitt, 1989)

Decades ago, battered women seeking help from the criminal justice system were regularly mal-treated, discouraged, disappointed, and repeatedly injured as the authorities stood idly by because a double standard prevailed. The assaults were not considered by police departments, prosecutors, and courts as "real crimes" because the violence was not carried out by strangers. The dominant noninterventionist ideology recommended that the long arm of the law shouldn't reach into the sanctuary of the home and intrude into private family squabbles between spouses unless the fighting approached life-threatening levels. Otherwise, battered women were urged to endure their lot and preserve their marriages by forgiving and forgetting.

The consciousness-raising efforts undertaken by activists in the battered women's movement during the 1970s successfully convinced many people that a hands-off policy endangers wives who feel trapped in abusive relationships. Women in distress needed, and were entitled to, the Constitution's pledge of "equal protection under the law." The marriage license did not grant husbands a license to hit their wives. Fights between partners could have grave consequences when left to fester and smolder. Instead of fading away, the conflicts could escalate in intensity and lead to severe injuries—usually for the woman, less often for her tormentor (see Schechter, 1982).

Once the public as well as criminal justice officials became convinced that intervention was the proper course of action, a question arose: "What type of response would lead to the desired results—that the violent men would change their ways?" Three long-standing options were explored: Separate the combatants, arrest the assailant, or refer the couple to marital counseling. Each choice had its possibilities and shortcomings. Battered women, their advocates, and victimologists are still divided over how best to respond to the problem: whether to pursue a legal course of action that depends on criminal justice solutions like arrest and punishment or to follow a social service approach that relies on counseling and reconciliation (see Sherman, 1986; Fagan, 1988; Gondolf, 1988; Ohlin and Tonry, 1989; Pleck, 1989; Buzawa and Buzawa, 1990; Roberts, 1990; Bouza, 1991; Bowman, 1992; Hilton, 1993; Klein et al., 1997; Healy and Smith, 1998; Jasinski and Williams, 1998; Malefyt et al., 1998; Maxwell, Garner, and Fagan, 2001; Sontag, 2002; Barner and Carney, 2011; and Buzawa, Buzawa, and Stark, 2011).

The "preserve-the-family" approach to handling domestic violence was favored during the 1950s and 1960s. It proposes that the objective of outside intervention should be to restore harmony to the marriage. That means salvaging the relationship, keeping the family intact, healing its wounds, and restoring its potential as a source of nurturing. Couples locked into ongoing bitter conflicts need to see counselors who could mediate disputes and build on the underlying strengths of their relationships. Advocates of this therapeutic, nonadversarial, pro-reconciliation approach presume that many battered women are partly to blame for being the first to resort to force, or at least for provoking their husbands' ire. Such cases of shared responsibility are not well handled by the courts, with their emphasis on total guilt or complete innocence, conviction or acquittal, and victory or defeat. But seeking professional assistance is a long-term approach that seems

promising only if a strong underlying bond persists, the women are not afraid to be candid during therapy sessions, and the aggressors are motivated and committed to voluntarily participating and to reforming their behaviors. Also, this reliance on social service agencies and mediation has been criticized for trivializing or condoning what might be serious criminal violence, for assuming shared responsibility, and for disregarding glaring inequalities in power relations between the two parties in their negotiations. Because their instability is deemed to be individual, personal, and peculiar, the approach downplays the seriousness and pervasiveness of wife beating as a social problem inextricably connected to family life, contemporary culture, and gender relations.

The "rely-upon-the-legal-system" approach has been in favor since the 1980s. It argues that "violence is violence," regardless of who the offender is and what his relationship with the target of his wrath might be. Criminalizing spouse abuse entails arresting the wrongdoer, and, if he is convicted, following up with a fine and/or a jail term, coupled with compulsory treatment in a batterers' anger management therapy group during a period of probation. The approach rests on these tenets: Separate the parties, rescue and protect the injured, and punish but also rehabilitate the aggressor. The philosophical underpinnings of the legalistic approach are that the state has a responsibility to enforce public morality as codified in law, and that the government has a duty to intervene when vulnerable individuals are in danger and they reach out to the authorities for help. Adherents of this approach fault the criminal justice system for not taking violence between intimates as seriously as violence between strangers. Too often assailants are not arrested; or if the police take them into custody, charges are not filed or are later dropped; or if prosecutors achieve convictions, judges impose very lenient sentences (see Davies, Lyon, and Catania, 1998 and Barner and Carney, 2011).

Traditionally, strategies intended to address the problem of domestic violence have been focused on ways of helping females recognize warning signs that they are becoming involved with violence-prone males, aiding them to disengage from existing relationships with abusers, and devising means of physically protecting them. New criminal justice policies aimed at abusers signal a social commitment to take the problem more seriously and to try to break the cycle that perpetuates the use of violence within families transmitted by parents who are negative role models to their imitative children. But criminal justice strategies that rely on arresting abusers and compelling them to enter into treatment often are ineffective because of a lack of coordination, close supervision, vigorous enforcement, and follow-through by service providers, police forces, prosecutors' offices, judges, probation departments, and parole authorities (Kennedy, 2004).

The Police Response Police officers always have found breaking up fights between husbands and wives to be unpleasant, thankless, and dangerous assignments. In the past, departmental policies governing domestic disturbances stressed preserving the peace. The preferred course of action for officers who responded to calls about lovers' quarrels was to pressure the participants to call a halt and then "kiss and make up." If that failed, the officer might have insisted that the enraged man vacate the premises until he regained his composure. If the household was known to have been the site of a ruckus in the past, the couple might have been referred to counseling. Officers routinely failed to advise victims of their rights to file complaints because they identified with their male counterparts and assumed that the females either provoked the fights or subconsciously enjoyed the beatings. Only as a last resort—if the women's injuries were so severe as to require surgical sutures (the "stitch rule")—would officers make an arrest (Rhode, 1989).

A field experiment conducted in Minneapolis, Minnesota, during the early 1980s aimed to find out which course of action produced the lowest recidivism rate. Officers followed a randomly selected option—either compel the batterer to take a walk and cool off, refer the couple to counseling, or arrest the aggressor—before they rang the doorbell (unless they discovered clear evidence of a felonious assault). For the next six months, researchers surveyed the victims by telephone about any further fighting and monitored that address for additional domestic disturbance calls. The social experiment's findings indicated that arrested offenders were about half as likely to assault their partners again (13 percent did during the follow-up period) as those men who only were forced to leave their homes to cool off (26 percent of them were recidivists). Those couples who were referred to counseling suffered a relapse rate in between these two extremes (18 percent had another violent fight). These results led the researchers to conclude that police departments should adopt a "presumption of arrest" policy unless good reasons convinced the officers at the scene that taking the assailant into custody would be counterproductive (Sherman and Berk, 1984).

As the findings of this social experiment became widely publicized, many police departments shifted away from their past practice of selective enforcement based on the officers' exercise of discretion toward an officially announced policy of full enforcement without discretion. They issued **mandatory**, or at least **pro-arrest directives**, even though the researchers did not go that far and had recommended only a presumptive or "preference-for-arrest" stance. Furthermore, the same result—a lower recidivism rate for arrested men—did not materialize when the Minneapolis Domestic Violence Experiment was replicated in other cities (as it must be in social science to establish **external validity**, which means that the findings can be generalized with confidence to other situations). In fact, the results from five replication sites suggested that arresting certain men (who were poor, unemployed, and without much of a stake in conforming to societal standards) may cause them to behave worse toward their mates in the future. Only batterers who were employed, well educated, and married to their partners (not just living together) seemed to be shaken and deterred by being arrested (see Berk et al., 1992; and Sherman, Berk, and Smith, 1992).

The widespread adoption of pro-arrest policies required retraining officers and a change in state laws. Police officers are empowered to make a probable cause warrantless arrest for a domestic violence misdemeanor not committed in their presence only in these situations: There are visible signs of injury, a dangerous weapon was involved, the officers believe the violence will continue after they depart, the police have prior knowledge of the offender's predilection for violence, or an order of protection was violated (Bouza, 1991).

In many states, officers must write a complete report, transport wounded people to a nearby hospital, supervise the eviction of abusers from their strife-torn homes, and inform the injured parties of their legal rights by reading or presenting a written list. The woman does not have to be married to the offender to receive these forms of protection (Hendricks, 1992). Some police departments have appointed special domestic violence prevention officers who are responsible for assisting battered women with safety planning in general, and in particular increasing their security in the vicinity of their homes and workplaces.

The Prosecutorial Response After deciding whether to call the police, the next dilemma a battered woman faces concerns prosecution: Should she keep up the pressure and get him into further trouble, thereby jeopardizing the relationship? Or should she withdraw her complaint and permit her violent mate to come home?

Historically, prosecutors have discouraged women from pressing charges because they are concerned about their office's conviction rates and don't want to pursue cases that are likely to fall apart. Also, they have traditionally viewed domestic violence cases as private matters that don't merit expenditures from their tight budgets. Lovers' quarrels ought to be diverted into mediation, assuming that both parties share responsibility for these ugly disputes and want to salvage their relationship, prosecutors traditionally believed.

In many jurisdictions, most domestic violence cases are dismissed. Of the remainder, most are negotiated down to lesser offenses, and these convictions usually result in a sentence of probation, perhaps coupled with mandatory participation in an anger management or aggression control program. In other jurisdictions where spouse abuse is handled more seriously, prosecutors have simplified procedures for filing complaints, set up special units

staffed with trained assistant district attorneys, provided supportive victim–witness assistance programs and advocates, and devised more sentencing options. The goal is to better deal with what they call "flip-flopping" victims whose frantic 911 calls about a drunken abuser on a Saturday night give way to a Monday morning's reconsideration about the batterer as a breadwinner (Hubbard, 2006).

A woman might bail out the man the police arrested because she fears punishing her mate would be counterproductive, resulting in further harm to her and their children in the long run. Also, she may anticipate his fury when he is ultimately released, or she may prefer that he receive treatment at a social program rather than punishment in the form of incarceration. The following worst-case scenario of a murder/suicide illustrates the gravity of this decision:

A single mother unwittingly seals her fate by bailing out her abusive boyfriend who is in jail for violating an order of protection. After the freed prisoner argues with his parents over the phone, he goes on a rampage. When he barges into their apartment, she tries to flee in their car with her four-year-old daughter in tow. But as she puts the key into the ignition, he shoots her in the face. Then, while her daughter screams, he fires a bullet into his own head.
(Livingston and Fagen, 2007)

Because many women change their minds about pressing charges or are manipulated or intimidated by their violent mates to drop the charges, prosecutors in some jurisdictions have established procedures to go forward without the complainant's cooperation as a key witness for the state. The available evidence in these cases without complainants can consist of 911 recordings of calls for help, eyewitnesses' accounts, police officers' testimony, hospital emergency room reports, photos of bruises, plus any incriminating statements by the defendant. Certain jurisdictions adopting this **no-drop** approach (also referred to as victimless prosecutions) have gone as far as mandating cooperation and threatening complainants with contempt-of-court proceedings if they set the legal machinery into motion and then decide they don't want to follow through and testify. Civil libertarians and defense attorneys are concerned that in proceedings involving these forms of hearsay evidence, the defendant is not permitted to ask questions of the accuser, in apparent violation of the Sixth Amendment's confrontation clause. However, the absence of the accuser in court still often results in dropped charges, dismissed cases, or acquittals (Bemiller, 2009; Bouza, 1991; Cahn and Lerman, 1991; Ferraro, 1992; Ford, 2003; O'Sullivan et. al, 2007; Dempsey, 2009 and Barner and Carney, 2011). Some victim advocates insist that the battered woman ought to be permitted to remain in control of "her" case and "their" future. The question of which approach works best to prevent future beatings requires impartial evaluations by researchers committed to objectivity.

Most IPV cases (nearly 85 percent) prosecuted in state courts involved charges filed against a male defendant by a woman. The overwhelming majority (almost 80 percent) concerned accusations of misdemeanor assault, and many of the rest involved the felony of aggravated assault (more than 10 percent). Close to half (46 percent) of the defendants had a history of previously abusing that same person. More than half were convicted, and most of them (over 80 percent) were sentenced to serve time in jail or prison (for the aggravated assaults), according to a study of prosecutions in large cities (Smith and Farole, 2009).

The Judicial Response   The final set of obstacles facing victims arises from their attempts to get the courts to act in their best interests. Judges seeking to dispose of cases and clear their calendars are reluctant to clog up their courtrooms with long and drawn-out spouse abuse cases. But judges can take several steps to assist those who were hurt: accede to their wishes that bail either be made low, kept high, or revoked if reprisals occur; speed up case processing by avoiding continuances; and issue **orders of protection** or **restraining orders**, which are intended to shield injured parties from further attacks. These court orders are supposed to grant immediate relief by enjoining abusers from entering the battered women's sphere of activity.

A judge's order can evict and bar an assailant from their shared residence; prohibit contacts, threats, harassment, or stalking (and even emailing and texting); limit communication to matters like supervised child visits; require him to stay away (usually at least 300 feet); insist that he pay child support; compel him to enter treatment; and force him to surrender any guns he owns (Findlaw, 2014). In the interest of the complainant's immediate safety, a temporary order of protection can be handed down in the defendant's absence if there is insufficient time to grant notice and hold a hearing. (After a proceeding where both parties have an opportunity to present their versions of events, the temporary order might be extended for up to a year.)

Because the orders are issued in civil court, the aim is separation of the disputants and not punishment. The standard of proof is a preponderance of the evidence, not guilt beyond a reasonable doubt. Violating a court order of protection can be a civil or criminal offense that subjects the trespasser to immediate arrest. However, criminal justice officials and advocates for battered women have serious doubts whether orders of protection currently are, or can ever be, truly effective. In theory, stay-away orders straddle the middle ground between inaction (no arrest, dropped charges) and overreaction (incarceration that results in escalating tensions, a criminal record, diminished job opportunities, and reduced financial support for the family).

In practice, the greatest problem is that civil orders are not vigorously enforced by many police departments, especially in high-crime urban areas (see Finn, 1991; Ferraro, 1992; and Buzawa and Buzawa, 1996). A restraining order is often disparaged by critics as nothing more than a piece of paper that can not guarantee security unless it is taken seriously (Kristof, 2014a). The limits of the depend-on-the-courts approach are illustrated by this worst-case scenario:

A former police officer with a prior history of abusing an ex-girlfriend gets married and then repeatedly beats his wife. He is arrested several times over the years. Eventually the mother of his four children files for divorce and gets an order of protection against him.

*But he barges into their home, kills her, and dumps
her body in the woods. He is arrested at his mother's
apartment and charged with murder.* (Paddock,
Shapiro, and Siemaszko, 2011)

However, the overwhelming majority of
women who had received a temporary or permanent order of protection reported that they felt better about themselves and felt safer. After obtaining
the order, they also were less likely to have experienced unwanted contact from the abuser and less
likely to have suffered injuries, according to a survey conducted in the mid-1990s (Keilitz et al.,
1997; see also Heisler, 2004).

To facilitate the application process, domestic
violence protective order packets are provided to
battered women, victim advocates, prosecutors'
offices, and private attorneys, and are also available
online. The simple instructions in the kits are written in a number of languages (Lippincott, 2006).
The stay-away stipulation of restraining orders is
enforced using cell phones, electronic ankle bracelets,
and alarm systems in some jurisdictions (Herszenhorn,
1999). The Violence Against Women Act, passed by
Congress in 1994 and renewed in 2000, requires that
every state fully recognize and enforce protective
orders issued in a different state.

Specialized domestic violence courts have been
set up to encourage battered women to call the
police, file complaints, press charges, testify as witnesses for the state, seek orders of protection, and
see cases through to completion. Judges in these
integrated services courts preside over domestic violence cases exclusively and are authorized to implement no-drop policies that allow cases to go
forward using 911 calls and police reports in place
of the testimony of reluctant victims. Dismissal rates
reportedly have fallen, and conviction rates have
risen due to increased guilty pleas from batterers,
who are often compelled to enter anger management programs as a condition of probation. Every
complainant is assigned an advocate in these experimental specialized courts so that more victims will
have faith in the effectiveness of the criminal justice
system. An estimated 300 domestic violence courts
were operating in 23 states at the start of the

twenty-first century (Gettleman, 2005), but a later
study located only around 210 of these narrowly
focused courts. A survey of key personnel determined that holding offenders accountable and
keeping victims safe by issuing orders of protection
were their highest priorities. Most courts or the
prosecutors' offices that diverted cases to them
employed victim advocates whose job was to
accompany complainants throughout the process,
counsel them, and make referrals to help them
with matters like seeking housing. And yet substantial proportions of these courts did not furnish
escorts to the building (50 percent), lacked separate
waiting areas (40 percent), and were unable to
provide childcare (75 percent), largely because of
limited resources (Labriola et al., 2010).

The Legislative Response Over the decades
since the "silent crisis" was rediscovered, lawmakers
at federal, state, county, and municipal levels have
passed numerous statutes that are intended to provide special solutions to the unique problems faced
by victims of domestic violence. As a consequence,
the response of the legal system has improved in
some ways. For example, during custody battles in
family court, husbands accused of violence may
claim that their former wives are poisoning the
minds of their children against their fathers. The
use of this argument, known as "parental alienation
syndrome," has been restricted by law in custody
cases in several states (Childress, 2006). Another
new regulation stipulates that landlords cannot
penalize a battered woman who breaks her lease
before the rental arrangement expires if she must
quickly move away to a new address unknown to
the abuser. When abusers are locked up, the targets
of their wrath are entitled to be kept posted about
their whereabouts within the correctional system
and to get advance notice if their assailants are
about to be released from custody (on bail, from
jail, or on probation). In many states, when domestic violence offenders are released, they must wear
electronic monitoring devices that use global posi-
tioning satellites to track their locations so that their
former victims can be assured that their estranged
partners are a safe distance away (Higgins, 2013).

Civil orders of protection used to be restricted to victims who were legally married or who had a child in common with their abuser. These stay away orders are now available for unmarried couples involved in domestic partnerships, whether they are heterosexual or homosexual. Also, in many states, a person—even a law enforcement officer—restrained by a domestic violence court order is prohibited from possessing a firearm while the order is in effect. This is a crucial matter because some men tend to reach for their guns right after women take out restraining orders, so to protect these complainants the firearms must be confiscated at the same time that the order of protection is issued. But in many states, a gun does not have to be handed over when a judge issues only a temporary restraining order, since the opposing party has not had a chance to present his version of events. **Gun surrender laws** remain a subject of great controversy, since they pit the rights of a fearful complainant against the gun ownership rights of the accused. The laws seem to be working effectively in only a few states, and federal provisions intended to disarm abusive spouses are difficult to enforce. Firearms confiscation provisions, when actually carried out, were correlated with fewer IPV murders of women, according to a study of files from large cities (Heisler, 2004; Zeoli and Webster, 2010; Luo, 2013; and Editors, New York Times, 2014).

THE REDISCOVERY OF BATTERED HUSBANDS AND BOYFRIENDS

The attention paid to wife beating led inevitably to the rediscovery of husband beating. Starting in the late 1970s, several social scientists began to challenge the stereotype that men almost always were the initiators of violence and the obvious victors in lovers' quarrels. They reported that their data on family violence had uncovered an overlooked problem—husband battering. Survey findings revealed that there was some truth to the old cartoon images of women slapping men's faces, or wives chasing husbands with rolling pins or throwing dishes at them.

Some studies indicated that women attacked their intimate partners (by slapping, kicking, biting, punching, throwing something, or threatening with a weapon) about as often as men assaulted women (see Steinmetz, 1978a; Straus and Gelles, 1986; Mignon, 1998; and Straus, 1999).

A meta-analysis of journal articles concluded that about 28 percent of females and 22 percent of males reported that they had perpetrated physical violence in intimate relationships; this finding underscored the need to acknowledge the use of force by girlfriends and wives (Desmarais et al, 2012).

Researchers referred to the possibility that women were the offenders in intimate partner abuse about as often as men as "gender symmetry" (see Belknap and Melton, 2005). But that contention set off a debate. Skeptics argued that the full story or entire sequence of events, and the social context surrounding the history of violence in tumultuous relationships, was not recorded in these surveys and studies. Much of the self-reported violence acknowledged by these women probably was carried out in self-defense and did not qualify as aggressive initiatives. When women do perpetrate violence that goes beyond self-defense, their resort to physical force usually is a means of releasing pent-up anger and resentment and constitutes a response to male provocations or an act of retaliation to avenge past abuse. Women don't use physical force to control or intimidate their partners, as men try to do. Because men tend to be bigger than their partners, their use of brute strength is far more likely to be intimidating and injurious (Langhinrichsen-Rohling, 2005). Many female combatants were previously victims. And the overwhelming majority of instances of severe aggression in which someone winds up in an emergency room are male-on-female offenses. Therefore, husband abuse should not be mistakenly equated with wife abuse, and a recognition that men can be injured too should not be used to undercut the urgency of tackling the much more pressing issue of women battering, feminists argued (see Pleck et al., 1978; Lewin, 1992; Cose, 1994; and Belknap and Melton, 2005). The insistence by men's rights groups that intimate partner violence cuts both ways represents a depoliticized gender-neutral view that lacks social context and harkens back to the old individual pathology explanation, which ignores feminist insights about unequal power relationships (Dragiewicz, 2011).

Actually, statistics from official sources do not show females to be as violent as males. On the contrary, about 80 percent of all victims of partner violence were girls and women, according to a massive study of *NCVS* findings from 1994 to 2010. The victimization rate for females was about five times higher than for males over those years (Catalano, 2012). Gender-neutral mandatory arrest policies targeting the "primary physical aggressor" led the police to take women into custody in about one-quarter of all domestic disturbance cases in some jurisdictions (see Goldberg, 1999; and Young, 1999). Similarly, less than 15 percent of the defendants charged with misdemeanor and felonious assault against intimate partners were females, according to a study of cases prosecuted in state courts in large cities (Smith and Farole, 2009). Surprisingly, battered men seem more inclined to call the police than battered women. About 70 percent of men assaulted by an intimate partner (who was also a male in 20 percent of these cases) reported the attack to the authorities, compared to just about 50 percent of the females who suffered IPV in 2008 (Catalano et al., 2009).

But pro-arrest policies can hurt the same individuals the criminal justice system is supposed to protect. Mistakenly condemned as aggressors, some women are compelled to attend batterer intervention programs originally designed to rehabilitate violent men. This is an unintended consequence of relying too heavily on arrest and prosecution as a means of quelling intimate partner violence. The superficial gender neutrality of the criminal justice process actually leads to "gendered injustices" when women who really are not belligerent are treated the same way as violence-prone men (Miller, 2005).

Battered men report hostile reactions when they seek solace and support from domestic violence hotlines (see Douglas and Hines, 2011). These men face several unique problems. First of all, those who report their plight to the authorities do so with great reluctance. If they call the police, they face either disbelief or mockery and scorn. Deep skepticism can cause officers to act on the basis of negative stereotypes, presume these males actually were the initiators, and arrest them. Because males traditionally are supposed to be physically adept and to "take charge of situations," for battered husbands/boyfriends to publicly admit their wives/girlfriends won the lovers' quarrels is to confess that they are not living up to manly standards. They face ridicule for not being able to control their mates (unless the battered men are elderly or physically infirm). Their failure to measure up to the prescription to be the head of the household might add to their confusion and distress. This special stigma might inhibit them from seeking help and can only contribute to their sense of isolation. Second, if they overcome their feelings of inadequacy, self-loathing, and shame, and dare to come forward, they do not have access to the same resources now available to battered women, especially support groups, professional counseling, and temporary shelters. The first sanctuary for battered men was established in 1993 in St. Paul, Minnesota, where the first women's shelter had been set up more than 20 years earlier. It housed at least 50 men in its first six months. In most cases, however, battered husbands have one crucial advantage over battered wives: Their ability to support themselves financially encourages many of them to leave their troubled relationship. Furthermore, when they separate, they are rarely stalked, brought back, and beaten again (Chavez, 1992; Lewin, 1992; Cose, 1994; Straus, 1999 and Hines et al., 2013).

VICTIM PROVOCATION AND MURDER: WHEN IS THE SLAYING OF A WIFE BEATER JUSTIFIED?

A sergeant in a crime scene unit, known as a "nice guy" and "family man" who coached Little League and was active in his church, retires from the police department after 20 years of service. But on the morning after he breaks his wife's nose, as he is shaving in preparation for a vacation, she says she will not accompany him. She then shoots him five times with his .38-caliber service revolver and then six more times with his second gun, a high-powered Glock. Although police records do not show any history of domestic disturbances at their address, he repeatedly beat her viciously, according to their grown children, members of their extended family, domestic violence counselors, and medical records. Both the son and daughter say that they feared he would murder their mother, and feel liberated by their abusive father's death; they don't attend his funeral. She is not convicted. (O'Shaughnessy, 2008; and Dwyer, 2011)

■ ■ ■

A woman is raped on her way home from work. Twenty years later she marries a wealthy widower, but soon discovers he served two years in prison for murdering his first wife. For 10 years, this jealous, possessive man controls her every movement, beats her, makes unreasonable sexual demands, and mocks her lingering rape trauma by repeatedly sneaking up from behind and grabbing her. One day he threatens to do to her what he did to his first wife. After he falls asleep, she shoots him in the head. She is convicted of second-degree murder and sentenced to five years in prison. But with a new lawyer, she appeals, is granted a second trial, and presents a defense of extreme psychological impairment. After the jury becomes deadlocked, she pleads guilty to manslaughter, and the judge sentences her to probation. (Abramson, 1994)

■ ■ ■

A woman tries to cover up her black eye and bruises when she goes to the office. She tells her co-workers that her arm is in a sling because she fell down the stairs. One night her alcoholic boyfriend throws beer cans at her, begins to beat her, and threatens to kill her. She runs into the kitchen to call 911 but he reaches the phone first and clubs her with it. She frantically reaches into a kitchen draw to find something to use to fend him off. She grabs a knife, stabs him with it once, and he dies. Jailed and charged with murder, a women's resource center mobilizes to *support her. She is allowed to plead guilty to involuntary manslaughter and is sentenced to probation.* (Kristof, 2014a)

Intimate Partner Homicides and the Criminal Justice System

When a battered woman kills her batterer, the public reaction at first seems hard to fathom: A significant part of the victims' rights movement is deeply concerned about the plight of these "murderers." For decades, the movement has raised money to pay the fees of defense attorneys, packed courtrooms to demonstrate solidarity with the accused, and held rallies outside prison gates demanding new trials, parole, pardons, or clemency for some of the killers within (Schechter, 1982; Johann and Osanka, 1989; and Gross, 1992).

From the standpoint of the law, the dead man is the victim, and the woman who took his life is the offender. But from the perspective of groups advancing the interests of battered women, the official designations of offender and victim are misleading. The female convicts behind bars are not really criminals and don't deserve confinement. The mortally wounded husbands or boyfriends are not bona fide victims but actually are dead aggressors. The battered women who ended these vicious men's lives are the genuine victims, not offenders.

Victim-blaming and victim-defending viewpoints lead to opposite conclusions regarding the tragic endings of these tortured love affairs.

Arguments Stressing That the Brutal Man Did Not Deserve to Die

Victim defending means siding with the dead man and arguing that his provocations, outrageous as they might have been, were not sufficient to justify the woman's overreaction, and that what she did cannot be condoned. Victim defending leads to offender blaming: She must be punished for the terrible crime she committed.

Victim-defending arguments on behalf of the deceased are put forward most directly by the detective who arrests the battered woman and by the prosecutor who presses charges against her. Their reasoning goes as follows: His fits of temper and violent outbursts were wrong, even criminal in nature, but so was her escalation of the level of conflict. She went too far, using criminal violence to halt criminal violence. She did not explore and exhaust all other options open to her before she chose to resort to deadly force. In particular, she should have fled their home, escaped his clutches, and dissolved their relationship. The battered woman did not fulfill her legal duty to retreat (and flee) but instead stood her ground and engaged in mutual combat. Cases in which brutal men were shot while asleep or unconscious from too much drinking were clearly acts of vengeance, motivated more by fury than fear. Such actions in retaliation for alleged wrongs cannot be stretched to fit an expanded definition of self-defense predicated upon standards of a reasonable response to an imminent threat. In the final confrontation that ended their stormy relationship, the battered woman retaliated in kind, getting even with her husband for past abuses. She struck back to settle old scores and to punish her husband for tormenting her. Such attempts by a woman to be the judge, jury, and executioner of an abusive husband, by taking the law into her own hands to deliver a dose of vigilante justice, cannot be permitted. His death must not go unpunished, and she must not get away with murder (see Rittenmeyer, 1981; and Dershowitz, 1988).

Victim defending asserts that the truth about their relationship will never be known. The dead man's side of the story cannot be told, and the woman's version of the events stands largely unchallenged. Her account of what happened between them over the years is self-serving: He is depicted as uncontrollably, irrationally, chronically, and savagely violent. In her view, the couple's problems were entirely his fault. This impression is reinforced by her use of the terms *batterer*, *initiator*, and *aggressor* to describe him, and *target*, *object*, and *victim* to refer to herself. The explanations of the survivor unrealistically place the burden of responsibility solely on the deceased party (see Neidig, 1984).

Victim defending concludes with several observations. First of all, courtroom testimony should focus on the woman who did the killing. The deceased whose reputation is being vilified is not on trial and cannot counter the negative portrait she is painting. Second, there must be better ways for a decent society to express its outrage at the brutality some women are forced to endure than to symbolically condone revenge killings and excuse lethal preemptive strikes. Not prosecuting wrongdoers, or acquitting defendants who clearly broke laws to retaliate for past beatings, or granting clemency to convicts only encourages others to pursue these same drastic courses of action (see Caplan, 1991; Bannister, 1992; Frum, 1993; and Gibbs, 1993b).

Arguments Emphasizing That the Brutal Man Provoked the Lethal Response

Victim-blaming arguments proceed from the premise that the departed was responsible for his own demise. The wife or girlfriend who emerged as the victor was reluctant to fight at the outset. In his final moments, however, the husband or boyfriend became a casualty because he incited his law-abiding mate through inflammatory insults, challenges, threats, gestures, and physical assaults that no longer could be ignored, endured, or evaded. Under attack and facing serious bodily harm, the female repelled his aggression with self-protective measures. The male expired as a result of an act of self-defense and not revenge. In these incidents, the party that should be faulted is the dead man who was the loser in a battle he started. He drove her to kill him in order to save her own life at a point when he was on the verge of murdering her. In a sense, the man got what he deserved by setting up a life-and-death struggle from which the woman could extricate herself only by resorting to lethal force. The killing should be classified by the police and prosecutor as a justifiable homicide and not a murder. He is not a genuine victim but an offender who died during his final assault.

Victim blaming asserts that these slain males are different from other men and that their extreme attitudes and behaviors are the causes of their demise. If they had changed their ways when they had a chance, they never would have met such a fate. Specifically, the men who provoke their intimates to slay them are more abusive than the typical batterer. They attack their partners more often and more viciously and are more likely to carry out sexual assaults. They tend to drink more heavily and to use illicit drugs more frequently than other batterers. Also, they are more inclined to threaten to kill their partners and to drive them to harbor suicidal fantasies and self-destructive impulses, according to an analysis of 41 cases (Browne, 1987).

In a study of 100 battered women who killed their violent mates compared to 100 who didn't, those who struck back were more isolated socially and economically. They had suffered more severe beatings, their children were more likely to have been physically abused, and their partners were heavier drinkers and drug takers (Ewing, 1987). Additional studies confirmed that compared to other battered women, abused women who kill their tormentors have suffered more severe attacks, have experienced an escalation in the level of violence, felt trapped because they had fewer resources to be independent in terms of education and employment, were involved in more traditional relationships (legally married, together for many years, raised children), and had turned to the police for help after previous assaults (Block, 2003).

Husband-blaming arguments point out that for many battered wives, escape was not a realistic option, or they tried to leave but failed. The question presupposes that fleeing her home would put an end to the dangers she faced. But in many cases the possessive husband would not tolerate her departure. Although she felt she could no longer live with him, he felt he couldn't let her live with someone else or on her own. He became infuriated by what he perceived to be rejection, abandonment, or desertion. With that mind-set, he was likely to stalk his wife, track her down if she was hiding, and use force to bring her back. As a result, the battered woman actually was held captive, trapped in a no-win situation she couldn't end.

An understanding of the battered woman syndrome helps explain why some women seem stuck in destructive relationships. The assaults inflict a type of posttraumatic stress disorder of learned helplessness that undermines her self-esteem and sense of control. Gripped by fear, with beatings following a predictable pattern, the woman can believe she is in constant danger even when the man is not on the offensive (Walker, 2009). As a result, the demoralized and terrorized woman might choose to fight back at a moment when he is not acting in a threatening manner. This can explain why she might seize the element of surprise and strike with whatever weapon is at hand when he is distracted, asleep, or has passed out from drinking or drug taking.

The battered woman syndrome is recognized as a legitimate defense in court proceedings. Presenting this cycle of tension, conflict, and temporary reconciliation as an explanation of her reactions is explicitly permitted by laws passed in various states and by Congress and is admissible subject to the judge's discretion elsewhere. Expert testimony during a trial about the cumulative psychological consequences of periodic beatings can help explain why a woman killed a violent mate who was not advancing menacingly at the time of his death (Kristal, 1991; Sargeant, 1991; Gibbs, 1993b; Stevens, 1999; and Schneider, 2000). A content analysis of the media coverage surrounding cases of battered women killing their tormentors determined that many of the articles at first medicalized and then criminalized her actions in an attempt to explain what happened: she went mad and then turned bad (Noh et al., 2010). Relying on expert testimony about the battered woman's syndrome places an emphasis on her learning to become helpless and her subsequent personal pathology. However, in certain cases, expert witnesses could advance a different explanation and successfully argue that her resort to lethal force was reasonable and justifiable under the circumstances (Terrance et al., 2012).

Legal Questions If the battered woman is believed by authorities to have acted in self-defense in a kill-or-be-killed showdown, then no charges will be pressed against her. However, if she appears to have shot or stabbed him after deliberation or premeditation at a time when she was not in imminent danger, then she can be indicted for first-degree murder. If there was no evidence of advance planning, but she did act with malicious intent at the crucial moment, then she may be indicted for the lesser crime of second-degree murder. If the prosecution believes that the dead man's provocations caused her to kill him in a spontaneous fit of rage or in sheer terror, then she could face the less serious charge of voluntary manslaughter. If the death of the man appears to be merely the outgrowth of her reckless disregard for his well-being, then the charge will probably be involuntary manslaughter, which carries the lowest penalty, perhaps just probation (Austern, 1987; and Bannister, 1992).

The possible outcomes in these cases range from no arrest, to no indictment, to an acquittal by a jury of all charges, to conviction for murder or manslaughter and a lengthy term of imprisonment. Usually, the case is resolved when the woman's lawyer strikes a deal with the prosecutor to allow her to plead guilty to a lesser charge, with the understanding that the judge will hand down a reduced sentence. In a small proportion of cases, the women elect to stand trial; of those, most argue that they suffered from diminished capacity or temporary insanity at the time of the confrontation. The bolder alternative is to raise an affirmative defense against the murder or manslaughter charges and assert that the women were compelled to lash out in self-preservation and should not be punished (Browne, 1987).

When female defendants claim they are not guilty by reason of diminished capacity or temporary insanity, they are offering an excuse for the act. By using such a defense, the woman concedes that taking the man's life was wrong. But she argues that she should not be punished for killing him because her mental state was so impaired at the time that she was unable to form criminal intent. Temporary insanity pleas seem most appropriate in cases involving defendants who cannot recall their actions and who are found to be dazed and confused in the aftermath of the confrontation. If acquitted, she need not be

confined in a mental institution because she poses no danger to the community or to herself; the irritant that provoked her out-of-control response has been eliminated (see Bernat, 1992). However, legal strategies that rely on convincing a jury of the woman's irrational and pathological behavior shift attention away from the man's provocations and her right to self-protection (Schneider, 1980).

A plea of self-defense is the alternative to one of temporary insanity. A victim-blaming argument interprets her resort to deadly force as defensive, even if it does not appear so by traditional standards. The legal doctrine of self-defense was developed by men to apply to fights between men and is usually debated and interpreted by men. The classical model posits a clash between two males of roughly equal strength who are strangers. Self-defense is accordingly defined as the justifiable use of an appropriate amount of force against an adversary by an individual who reasonably believes that he is in imminent danger of unlawful bodily harm, and that the use of such force is necessary to prevent serious injuries from being inflicted.

But this highly subjective male-oriented model, with its assumptions and prescriptions, needs to be modified when applied to clashes between males and females. For example, a woman can be considered to be acting in self-defense if she uses a weapon like a knife or gun against a man who is unarmed. The rationale is that his hands and feet can be viewed as deadly weapons because women—especially battered wives—have been beaten to death by unarmed men. Because women are generally less skilled in combat and tend to be smaller in stature, the use of a lethal weapon is a way of matching but not necessarily exceeding his level of violence. A battered woman who resorts to deadly force during the phase of the cycle when the husband is threatening harm, but not yet physically attacking, can also be considered to be acting in self-defense. Unlike a person confronted by a stranger, she is in a position to know from bitter past experience that his threats are real and will be carried out. The battered woman learns to recognize the cues signaling that a beating is imminent, such as subtle changes in the man's voice or facial expressions. Similarly, the wife who strikes out against her assailant during a lull in the ordeal or after an outbreak has peaked can also be considered to be acting in self-defense because she knows the predictable patterns of his attacks (see Jones, 1980; Schneider, 1980; Bochnak, 1981; Thyfault, 1984; Kuhl, 1986; Saunders, 1986; Browne, 1987; Ewing, 1987; Gillespie, 1989; Bannister, 1992; Richie, 1996; and Leonard, 2001).

Victim-blaming arguments are most convincing to detectives, prosecutors, and juries when many of the following elements are present: The battered woman had been threatened many times, beaten repeatedly, rescued by the police from his wrath on several occasions, and granted an order of protection. She had testified in court after pressing charges, sought marital counseling, attempted to escape, separated from him, and filed for divorce. Also, she had visible and severe injuries at the time of her arrest, and suffered permanent damage from the wounds he inflicted during their final confrontation. If a "psychological autopsy" or courtroom reconstruction of the tormentor is presented effectively by a defense attorney using an expert witness, the jurors could become so inflamed that they will want to "dig up the bully's corpse and kill him all over again" (see Sargeant, 1991).

The clash between victim-blaming and victim-defending perspectives illustrates, among other things, that all crimes are socially defined. No act is inherently criminal, even the taking of a life. Each killing of one person by another must be examined and interpreted within its context and cultural framework by detectives, prosecutors, defense attorneys, judges, jurors, the media, and the general public. Certain slayings of wife beaters by the targets of their wrath just might be deemed justifiable homicides.

But when battered wives become widows by their own deeds, parceling out blame should not be limited to just one spouse or the other. If domestic disturbances are to be prevented from escalating to such explosive levels, then effective outside intervention is necessary. Murders within marriages or domestic partnerships reflect failures of both criminal justice and social service agencies: to provide adequate protection for the victim who ultimately becomes the perpetrator and to provide timely treatment for the abuser who eventually loses his life. Some responsibility for these tragedies also falls on those officials who assign a low priority to cases of lover's quarrels, who cling to a "hands-off, settle it yourselves" doctrine, and who discourage the development of adequate refuges for battered women and the establishment of sufficient therapy programs to rehabilitate abusive men. In addition, members of each succeeding generation need to reexamine and reconsider for themselves both prevailing and alternative views about gender roles, independence and dependence, romantic relationships, marriage, decision making within families, and intervention into other intensely personal matters by the government and outsiders (see Yllo and Bograd, 1988; Websdale and Johnson, 1997; and Chornesky, 2000).

THE REDISCOVERY OF OTHER VICTIMS OF BEATINGS

When violence in intimate relationships began to be recognized as pervasive, several other rediscoveries became inevitable. First, battering can emerge during dating and courtship, when the ties that bind the couple are not so strong. Second, violence by adolescents can be directed at their parents. Third, adults can become physically and psychologically abusive toward frail, elderly people, including their closest relatives. Finally, partner abuse is not limited to heterosexual couples; violence can also break out in intimate relations between members of the same sex.

Dating Violence

A high school senior begins dating a classmate who is known to have a bad temper. At first, she is so thrilled to have a boyfriend who seems to really care for her that it doesn't bother her that he constantly checks up on her and gets angry when she spends time with other friends. But one night, when she announces she is going away for the weekend with her friends, he flies into a rage, grabs her by the arm, and throws her against a wall. He warns her never to make arrangements without his permission. She is stunned and terrified to find out he is so controlling. (Joyce, 2004)

After the plight of battered women became well known, along with the problem of acquaintance and date rape (see the next chapter), a growing number of researchers explored the phenomenon of physical violence during courtship (see Makepeace, 1981; Laner and Thompson, 1982; Allbritten and Allbritten, 1985; Stets and Pirog-Good, 1987; Demarais, 1992; Follingstad et al., 1992; O'Keefe and Trester, 1998; and Joyce, 2004). Dating violence can have a significant impact on a student's mental and physical health as well as performance in school (see Coker et al., 2014).

Incidence estimates about this kind of intimate partner violence include the survey finding that about 10 percent of students nationwide report that they were physically hurt (such as being slapped or hit on purpose) by a boyfriend or girlfriend in the past 12 months (CDC, 2010). A large scale survey of around 14,000 high school students yielded slightly higher estimates. About 13 percent of the teenage respondents disclosed that they had been hit, slapped, or otherwise physically hurt on purpose during their partner over the past year; girls were as likely as boys to have experienced these assaults (Coker et al., 2014). As for prevalence estimates, from 20 percent to 33 percent of teenagers report that they have experienced violence in a dating relationship, and between 50 percent and 80 percent say that they know others who were caught up in dating violence, according to one study (NCVC, 2011a). Another survey-based study yielded lower prevalence rates of about 9 percent for both male and female high school students, with no appreciable changes over a 12-year period ending in 2011 (Rothman and Xuan, 2014).

As for college students, the estimated proportion who have experienced dating violence ranges from 10 percent to 50 percent. Besides physical injuries, the negative consequences of these unhealthy relationships include depression, anxiety, and loss of self-esteem. Dating violence appears to be correlated with heavy drinking, drug use, sexual risk taking, and academic disengagement. (absenteeism, dropping classes, failing courses, and withdrawing from school) (Kaukinen, 2014).

Maximalists could point out that the *NCVS* has established over the years that teenagers in general are less likely to report any category of crimes committed against them, so dating violence is surely severely underreported. Most teens tell no one; if they do talk about the incident, they are more inclined to share their secrets with a peer than with a parent (see Joyce, 2004). Minimalists could argue that some studies of "unhealthy" relationships and dating "abuse" use definitions that include acts that do not qualify as criminal or delinquent behavior. Abuse is sometimes broadly defined as having non-criminal verbal and emotional/psychological dimensions and could take the form of jealous, possessive, bullying, and domineering behaviors, such as telling a partner what to wear, who to interact with, and to acquiesce to unwanted sexual acts. Some recent studies of abuse even count electronic "stalking" (examined in Chapter 11) in the form of unwelcomed phone calls, texts and photos (see CDC, 2010; NCVC, 2011a; Office on Women's Health, 2011; Texas Advocacy Project, 2011; also see Coker et al., 2014).

Courtship is considered to be the training ground for marriage, so controlling behaviors (like slapping, grabbing, shaking, kicking, choking, threatening with a weapon, and throwing things) that begin during dating may persist, and perhaps escalate, after a couple weds. But in several crucial ways, violence during courtship differs from violence within marriage. First of all, less force is used over shorter periods of time. Second, young women are more likely to initiate violence against their dates/boyfriends/fiancés than wives are against their husbands. Perhaps the young women feel they can assert themselves more freely because they are not trapped in a day-after-day cohabitation situation and can break off the relationship if the spiral of violence gets out of hand. Of course, much of the physical force exerted by females can, in all fairness, be classified as examples of fighting back—acts of immediate self-defense, of retaliation for earlier male aggression, or even as preemptive strikes to forestall impending assaults (see Langhinrichsen-Rohling, 2005).

Some possible signs that a teenager might be subjected to dating violence include emotional outbursts, mood swings, personality changes, unexplained scratches and bruises, failing grades, truancy, dropping out of high school, substance abuse and heavy drinking, and an unwanted pregnancy. Teenage girls often believe that abuse is normal because their friends experience it too; their boyfriend's controlling behaviors and use of force is actually an expression of romantic interest; there is no one they can turn to for help; and they must solve their relationship problems on their own (ACADV, 2011). Victims often blame themselves and feel anxious, angry, depressed, isolated, confused, helpless, humiliated, and frightened about an escalation in the use of force (NCVC, 2011a).

When young women are seriously harmed, once again the question arises, "Why does she stay?" Clearly, some reasons married women cite as most important do not apply to dating: remaining together for the sake of the children, depending on the husband financially, or believing that a failed marriage is shameful and divorce is wrong. So other explanations need to be tested. Perhaps some young women tolerate abuse because rules and behavioral limits in romantic relationships currently are in a state of flux as traditional norms are challenged and rejected. Other women battered during courtship may interpret fits of jealous rage as signs of his intense feelings and deep devotion. Still others may consider violence within intimate relationships to be acceptable because they were mistreated as children or their parents behaved abusively toward each other. A small percentage might even feel comfortable being dominated by a "virile" young man.

Even when the female is the aggressor and the male is the target, or when mutual combat breaks out, the adversaries are not evenly matched, and it is not a fair fight. Young men have several advantages—larger size, greater strength, and better hand-to-hand combat skills—that protect them from serious harm and endanger their girlfriends' well-being. Because male-initiated violence is more frequent and more serious, it is not the female's problem alone. Prevention and education programs involving discussions, role playing, and decision-making exercises are presented in high schools and teen centers. Serious incidents caused by dysfunctional behaviors lead to group counseling for troubled couples and ultimately problems with the authorities for the aggressors (see Makepeace, 1981; Laner and Thompson, 1982; Allbritten and Allbritten, 1985; Stets and Pirog-Good, 1987; Demaris, 1992; Follingstad et al., 1992; O'Keefe and Trester, 1998; Joyce, 2004; and Cornelius and Ressiguie, 2007).

Abuse of Parents by Adolescents

When teenagers batter their parents, the fathers and mothers tend to feel ashamed and usually wish to keep the matter private, so severe underreporting confounds attempts to estimate the scope of the problem. In many cases, the use of force directed at parents can be seen as retaliation for the violence these caretakers previously visited upon their children. In that sense, an intergenerational cycle of violence has been set into motion.

Mothers and stepmothers are more likely to be injured than fathers or stepfathers. But male parents are more likely to be the targets of extreme violence, perhaps as revenge for previous abuse or in self-defense as the attack escalates. Physically aggressive fathers with drinking problems are the most common victims of severe injuries or even lethal force by sons who view themselves as protectors of their mothers and siblings. In the rare cases in which a daughter is involved in the murder of a parent, the actual killer is usually a male she recruited to carry out the deed (see Steinmetz, 1978b; Straus, Gelles, and Steinmetz, 1980; Lubenow, 1983; Pagelow, 1989; Mones, 1991; and Ewing, 1997).

Elder Abuse

A very popular actor is at the height of his career in 1940. Over the decades, he has trouble managing his money and private life. But he appears in more than 70 movies and regains his fortune. In 2011, he testifies before a congressional committee on aging that he was being subjected to elder abuse by his stepson (who was managing his financial affairs) and his stepson's wife. He tells the senators, "...my daily life became unbearable. I felt trapped, scared, used and frustrated. But above all, I felt helpless." He files a lawsuit alleging that the couple stole his money for their own enjoyment, kept him in the dark about his own finances, threatened and verbally abused him, and refused to provide him with basic necessities, including food and medicine. He wins a judgment against them and then dies shortly afterward at the age of 93. (Gjertsen, 2014)

In general, victimization rates for elderly persons are lower than for persons in younger age groups. People over age 65 make up about 20 percent of the population (age 12 or older) but they comprised only 2 percent of all victims of interpersonal violence. Therefore, older persons enjoy disproportionately low risks of getting hurt physically. Between 1994 and 2013, their victimization rate for crimes of violence dropped by over 40 percent, from 7.4 to just 4.4 casualties (many were not really injured physically) for every 1,000 older persons per year. Murders of senior citizens dropped by almost 45 percent, from 3.7 homicides per 100,000 in 1993 down to 2.1 in 2011. Their property crime victimization rate fell even more dramatically (almost 50 percent) during those two decades from 141 down to 74 per 1,000 households per year, according to *NCVS* data (Morgan, 2014). Elderly people are the least likely of any age group to become victims of violence and household crimes, largely because of the precautions they take (BJS, 1994a; and Klaus, 1999b).

But starting in the 1970s, victimologists and advocates for senior citizens began to delve into other ways that older people are made to suffer by younger people. As a result, **elder abuse** was rediscovered as another expression of conflict within families, along with child abuse and spouse abuse. Once the term was coined, the problem began to receive the attention it merited from geriatric social workers, care providers, and law enforcement professionals, as well as researchers

(see Goldsmith and Goldsmith, 1976; Boston, 1977; Center, 1980; Hochstedler, 1981; Quinn and Tomita, 1986; Breckman and Adelman, 1988; and Steinmetz, 1988).

To begin to address this rediscovered problem, Congress passed the Older Americans Act in 1965 and Title VII: Vulnerable Elder Rights Protection Activity in 1992. In 2010, the Elder Justice Act was approved as part of a larger health reform package, but it was not adequately funded to sponsor its research and evaluation agenda. The federal government also set up an Administration on Aging that is responsible for developing effective policies to reduce elder abuse. All 50 state legislatures have passed laws that require mandatory reporting of cases of suspected abuse as a step toward improving the detection, prosecution, and prevention of elder abuse (Fryling, 2009). Just as child abuse allegations are investigated by local child protective services agencies, suspected cases of elder abuse are looked into by **adult protective services agencies**. These agencies are usually part of state health and human service departments and bridge the gap between social service organizations and the criminal justice system. Adult protective service investigators can respond to medical, psychiatric, and financial crises by seeking an order of protection, contesting guardianship, or filing criminal charges—but the elderly person retains the right to refuse these possible interventions (Kosloski, 2009).

Definitions of elder abuse vary but usually include both acts of commission (physical assaults, unwanted sexual contacts, unreasonable confinement, and/or financial exploitation in the form of outright theft, extortion, fraud, embezzlement, or misuse of income or savings) as well as acts of omission (complete abandonment or failure to provide medical care, food, clothing, and shelter; failure to protect from health and safety hazards; and failure to assist with personal hygiene) by caretakers responsible for the older person's well-being. Therefore, abuse is equivalent to maltreatment and encompasses gross neglect as well as acts of intentional harm (House Subcommittee, 1992; and CDC, 2011a).

Domestic elder abuse can be perpetrated by people who provide care to older people who live at home. The offender is most commonly a close relative, especially a grown child, spouse, or sibling. Less often, the abuser is a son- or daughter-in-law, grandchild, niece, nephew, friend, or neighbor. The typical target is a frail, ailing woman more than 70 years old. In most cases, the elder and the abuser live in the same household in social isolation from friends, neighbors, and kin who might otherwise informally deter the wrongdoing. The abusers usually are overburdened caregivers who become depressed and hostile at the long-term prospects of tending to a mentally and physically impaired and dependent individual. When homebound parents are physically beaten or financially exploited, sons are the most likely culprits. When daughters and daughters-in-law are abusive, their maltreatment usually takes the form of emotional and physical neglect. Mistreatment by home health aides is also suspected to be common (Pagelow, 1989).

Institutional elder abuse is committed by non-relatives, such as employees of nursing homes, who have a contractual obligation to tend to the needs of older people (McGrath and Osborne, 1989; and Orel, 2010). Allegations of physical and even sexual abuse against the residents of nursing homes across the United States are not promptly reported or acted upon, and arrests and prosecutions are rare. Nursing home operators, fellow staff members, and relatives of the victim have self-serving reasons to be reluctant to bring charges about abusive employees to the attention of authorities (Pear, 2002; and Orel, 2010).

The odds of being abused are determined by a combination of individual, relationship, community, and societal factors. Older people who face the greatest risks are burdened by mental illness and physical frailties that make them highly dependent. The caregivers they count upon are more likely to abuse them if these younger persons harbor high levels of hostility, are poorly trained, were compelled to assume responsibilities at a relatively early age, have inadequate coping skills, lack social support, and were mistreated themselves when they were growing up (CDC, 2011c). Elderly females

are at greater risk than their male counterparts, people 80 or older are especially vulnerable, and the perpetrators are most often spouses or grown children. Male perpetrators are most likely to abuse elders financially, emotionally, and physically. Females are more likely to neglect their elders (Fryling, 2009).

As with child abuse and intimate partner abuse, elder maltreatment is difficult to establish and accurately measure. A National Elder Abuse Incidence Study estimated that nearly 450,000 adults over 59 were abused or neglected in domestic settings (not counting institutions like nursing homes) in 1996. As for prevalence, between 1 and 2 million Americans aged 65 or older have been exploited, injured, or mistreated by someone on whom they depended for care or protection. That translates to a frequency of from 2 percent to 10 percent of all senior citizens (National Center on Elder Abuse, 2005).

Maximalists could argue that the known cases are only the tip of the iceberg because of severe underreporting. Congressional investigators estimated that only about 16 percent of abused elders dared to bring their plight to the attention of the proper authorities (House Subcommittee, 1992).

Minimalists could argue that some overly broad definitions overstate the problem because they may include people as young as 60 or even 50, not 65, as "elders"; some cases supported by evidence are civil matters but do not reach the threshold of criminal acts; and many reports of abuse are not proven. Only about 20 percent of the abusive situations that were brought to the attention of adult protective service agencies in the mid-1990s were substantiated (National Center on Elder Abuse, 2005).

Many reasons explain the reluctance of victims to complain about their predicaments. The offender is most likely a family member who is depended upon for daily care. Abused elders might see their situations as cause for shame or as private family matters. Some might feel they provoked the abuse; others may not even be aware of the wrongdoing—particularly financial exploitation. Mandatory reporting laws similar to those that require disclosure of suspected child abuse have been imposed on health care professionals, especially doctors, generating upwardly spiraling statistics and overwhelming caseloads for geriatric social workers. However, as in child abuse cases, many allegations are not thoroughly investigated and wind up classified as unsubstantiated (Wolf and Pillemer, 1989; Editors, *New York Times*, 1991; and Tatara, 1993).

Investigation, arrest, and prosecution are important strategies, but they only address part of the problem. Abusers need to be educated about how to care for the elderly, and victims need social services and medical assistance. Since the Bureau of the Census predicts the population of Americans older than 65 will grow dramatically by 2030 as baby boomers reach and exceed retirement age, it is likely that the problem will intensify in coming years. The U.S. Administration on Aging has set up a national clearinghouse of information about the many ways the nation's elders may suffer physical, psychological, sexual, and financial abuse (National Center on Elder Abuse, 2011).

Battering Within Same-Sex Relationships

Because of a growing openness about homosexuality, a predictable rediscovery was that physical fighting can mar the intimate relationships between gay men and also between lesbians. Violence in gay and lesbian couples is suspected to occur about as frequently as within heterosexual relationships, afflicting between 25 percent and 35 percent of same-sex couples (McClennen, 2005; see also Little and Terrance, 2010). Similarly, teens in same-sex relationships experience violence at levels comparable to heterosexual teenagers. About 10 percent report sustaining physical assaults by a dating partner (Futures Without Violence, 2011). Across the country during 2011, 2012, and 2013, about 20 people known to be involved in lesbian, gay, bisexual, and transgender relationships were murdered by an intimate partner. Most (about 75 percent) of the deceased were gay men (NCAVP, 2014).

Violence within lesbian, gay, bisexual, and transgender couples often is unacknowledged and underreported. Victims might be reluctant to turn to the authorities for help because they fear being "outed." As a result, they might have to turn to programs intended to assist victims of hate crimes

such as gay bashings committed by strangers. Often, police departments don't train their officers to intercede effectively when same-sex couples quarrel. When members of the gay/lesbian/bisexual/transgender community filed complaints about assaults by their intimate partners, only about half considered the officers' responses to be "courteous"; about one-fifth characterized the police as revealing "hostile" attitudes, and the rest described the reaction they received as "indifferent." Of the battered lesbians seeking shelter, one-fifth were turned away, according to a 2013 survey by an anti-violence coalition (NCAVP, 2014). In general, when compared to the experiences of heterosexual women, violence within lesbian relationships is less likely to be reported, less likely to be prosecuted, and more likely to be disregarded by service agencies as well as the general public (see Little and Terrance, 2010).

However, some progress has been made to enable injured parties to come out of the closet and identify themselves to the authorities in order to receive the protection and assistance they are entitled to: Anti-sodomy laws that criminalized certain acts between same-sex couples have been repealed in most jurisdictions, and domestic violence statutes in most states have been reworded to a gender-neutral formulation that applies to all intimate partners seeking governmental help (Tesch et al., 2010; and English, 2011).

Understandably, the LGBT community initially was reluctant to publicly concede that partner abuse took place for two reasons. Some feared that revealing the prevalence of the problem would feed negative stereotypes and fuel homophobia. Others were concerned that the discovery of violence in female–female relationships (as well as male–male relationships) would undercut the women's movement's continuing struggle for equality and justice because it would necessitate a rethinking about the root causes of violence against women. Battering by partners could no longer be viewed as simply the result of deep-seated and long-standing gender inequalities derived from patriarchal traditions of male dominance over females. Violence between intimates would have to be reconceptualized as an outgrowth of the way power and privilege are exercised in any and all romantic relationships (see Island and Letellier, 1991; Renzetti, 1992; King, 1993; Haugrud, Gratch, and Magruder, 1997; Burke, 1998; Cruz and Firestone, 1998; Jackson, 1998; McClennen, 2005; and Tesch et al., 2010).

PREVENTING BATTERING

Preventing battering means halting any further abuse of those who have already suffered beatings, as well as heading off the eruption of violence before it starts.

Occasional outbursts of physical abuse by husbands or boyfriends, and sometimes by wives or girlfriends, is considered ordinary. For this type of relationship aggression, **secondary prevention programs** attempt to teach high-risk couples negotiation skills and anger management techniques.

To rescue women from men who consistently use force to maintain control over them is more difficult and dangerous and requires much more than just couples counseling. Battered women's shelters and orders of protection are needed for the victims, and arrest and prosecution are necessary interventions to restrain the assailants. As always, reliance on criminal justice solutions may bring about temporary relief in certain abusive relationships and might even solve particular conflicts within some families. But working to cure abusers one at a time and helping each of their victims to recover does not address the root causes of the problem. **Primary prevention programs** are intended to head off a resort to physical force by refuting myths, challenging stereotypes, and changing the attitudes held by large numbers of potential victimizers and victims, starting with high school students (see Arriaga and Capezza, 2005; and Rhatigan, Moore, and Street, 2005). Unfortunately, many existing prevention programs, as well as other apparently pro-victim measures such as mandatory arrest policies and aggressive prosecution, have not been effective, according to the many evaluations carried out by criminologists and victimologists (see Mears and Visher, 2005).

SUMMARY

Victims of domestic violence face many special problems that require special solutions. They still have to contend with old-fashioned views that what goes on behind closed doors between lovers is nobody else's business. The most obvious special problem is that intimate partners are exposed to constant danger because they live in the same homes as their attackers, are usually emotionally and financially dependent upon them, and often are raising children together. Assailants are often viewed as otherwise law-abiding and upstanding members of the community, so victims are likely to be blamed or to fault themselves for the ugly flare-ups. If they have children in common, battered women run the risk of losing parental control over them if the violence takes place in front of them, or if the estranged father is better off financially and seeks joint custody or even sole custody. If the conflict festers, it may escalate to the point that one partner or the other gets seriously injured or killed.

Researchers are investigating controversial contentions: that the injured parties did something provocative that incited the violent outburst, that low-income families are troubled at a higher rate than higher-income couples, and that the degree of suffering couldn't be too serious because many victims don't try to leave the abusive relationship.

Reliable statistics about the incidence and prevalence of being beaten by a lover are lacking, so a maximalist–minimalist debate rages over the true extent and seriousness of the problem. The debate has become politicized because so much is at stake: relations between the sexes; courtship practices; ideas about romance and marriage; views about the proper role of government intervention; and clashing perspectives about which policies are genuinely "pro-family" and "pro-woman."

Special problems always require special solutions. To reduce intimate partner violence, shelters have been set up across the country as places of refuge for women and their young children. Specialized domestic violence courts have been established in some jurisdictions. The judges who work there are experts in diagnosing the problems and are familiar with the available range of protective and treatment options. Courts can issue restraining orders, and physically abusive mates can be arrested and sent to anger management programs. Special problems faced by parents harmed by their adolescent children, elderly people abused and exploited by their grown children, and gay or lesbian victims assaulted by their lovers require even more creative solutions.

Primary prevention and secondary prevention programs are intended to help reduce outbreaks of violence between intimates.

KEY TERMS DEFINED IN THE GLOSSARY

adult protective services agencies, 319

battered-woman syndrome, 300

clinical fallacy, 301

domestic chastisement, 289

domestic disturbances, 287

domestic tranquility, 288

elder abuse, 319

external validity, 306

gun surrender laws, 310

intimate partner violence (IPV), 287

mandatory, or pro-arrest, directives, 306

moderate correction, 289

no-drop prosecutions, 307

normative ambiguity, 293

order of protection, 308

patriarchy, 289

primary prevention programs, 322

restraining order, 308

rule of thumb, 289

secondary prevention programs, 322

shelters, 303

speak-outs, 292

unnatural severity, 289

QUESTIONS FOR DISCUSSION AND DEBATE

1. Why does terminology matter? Discuss the confusion that can arise when the following terms are used interchangeably: domestic violence; domestic disturbance; spouse abuse; intimate partner abuse; and intimate partner violence.

2. Discuss the pros and cons of officers following a mandatory or pro-arrest-the-aggressor directive at the scene of domestic disturbances, and of a prosecutor's office following a no-drop policy for IPV arrests.

3. Present convincing answers that explain why many battered women do not leave their abusive mates.

4. Under what circumstances, if any, could the killing of a vicious wife beater by his victim be ruled a justifiable homicide, in your opinion?

CRITICAL THINKING QUESTIONS

1. If beatings take place in same-sex relationships as well as among heterosexual couples, and during dating as well as during marriage, then what really is the root cause of violence between intimates?

2. Give possible reasons why the number of murders of husbands by wives has dropped more sharply over recent decades than the murders of wives by husbands.

3. Give possible reasons why the number of murders of spouses has dropped so sharply over recent decades, while the slaying of girlfriends and boyfriends actually has gone up.

4. Why do some teenage girls endure courtship violence when they are merely dating and they do not have to rely on their boyfriends for financial support, and they are not living together and not raising children together?

5. How come some surveys seem to show that females are more likely to initiate violence in intimate relationships than males?

SUGGESTED RESEARCH PROJECTS

1. Compile a comprehensive list of the policies (such as mandatory arrest of the aggressor) and the opportunities for assistance (such as shelters) that can be offered by government, nonprofit, self-help, and charitable organizations to ease the plight of battered women. Find out from local criminal justice officials, women's organizations, and others in the helping professions which of these pro-victim policies and forms of support are currently available in your hometown.

2. Locate some recent cases in databases of newspaper and magazine articles in which women were prosecuted for killing their abusive mates. Gather details about the slayings, the couples' lives together before the final confrontation, and the outcomes of these cases in court.

3. Carry out a strictly anonymous and confidential survey of some acquaintances to find out if they ever experienced physical abuse during a dating relationship that has ended.

4. Look through a database of newspaper and magazine articles to discover some actual cases of elder abuse that have been uncovered in your state.

10

Victims of Rapes and Other Sexual Assaults

LEARNING OBJECTIVES

To become aware of the way the plight of rape victims was rediscovered.

To understand the distinctions between stranger rapes, acquaintance rapes, date rapes, and other sexual assaults.

To become familiar with the way girls and women who reported their plight and sought help in the past were mistreated.

To recognize victim-blaming arguments and victim-defending points of view.

To appreciate the progress made by the several components of the criminal justice system in handling rape cases, as well as the problems that continue to burden victims needlessly.

SEXUAL ASSAULTS AND RAPES: THE SOCIAL REACTION

It is up to all of us to ensure victims of sexual violence are not left to face these trials alone. Too often, survivors suffer in silence, fearing retribution, lack of support, or that the criminal justice system will fail to bring the perpetrator to justice. We must do more to raise awareness about the realities of sexual assault; confront and change insensitive attitudes wherever they persist; enhance training and education in the criminal justice system; and expand access to critical health, legal, and protection services for survivors. (President Barack Obama, 2012)

A paradox surrounds the crime of rape. On the one hand, a victim's allegations sometimes are sneered at and even can become the subject of crude, snarky jokes. On the other hand, some assailants are punished so severely that forcible rape ranks as one of the most terrible and strictly forbidden interpersonal crimes. Today, who the offender is, who the injured party is, and how they acted before and during the attack determine the legal system's response to the crime. Public reactions are shaped by social attitudes

as much as by legal codes, and both attitudes and laws have been changing in recent decades.

The problem of violence by men and boys against women and girls has been caught up in sexual politics. Bitter controversies and strong emotions intrude upon attempts by victimologists and criminologists to objectively determine precisely how many people have been harmed by rapes and sexual assaults; how frequently—or infrequently—the violations of personhood are reported to the authorities; how well—or poorly—the criminal justice system handles these cases; how often the charges lodged by the complainant are completely baseless or highly exaggerated; and who or what is to blame for this age-old problem that continues to fester and claim new victims.

Even the language used to describe this type of criminal behavior is subject to dispute and consequently has been evolving. If the formulation is that "a woman got raped," the implication is that it is her problem and perhaps even her fault for arousing unstoppable desires. If the phrasing is more active and direct, that men rape women or that this is a crime by males against females, then the onus shifts and falls on the aggressors in the "battle of the sexes"—not their targets—and on those aspects of the culture that could encourage the coupling of violence with sexuality. But when the possibility of a man raping another man (or boy) is taken into account, it triggers a rethinking that inevitably leads to a deeper understanding that the crime is largely about power and control, domination and subjugation, and conquest and defeat as expressed through forceful sexual acts.

The word *rape* comes from the Latin *rapere*, which means "to seize or take by force." In English common law, the crime was called unlawful **carnal knowledge**. By definition, the unwanted intrusion could be committed only by a male against a female who was not his wife. But the old common law definition has been updated by new legislation in each state. First of all, the crime is now gender-neutral, which means that males also can be targets (almost always of other men). Second, completed intercourse is not the only punishable activity.

Other unwanted invasions of the body and forced submission to sexual acts are outlawed as well by statutes prohibiting sexual assaults and sexual battery.

One element of the crime remains the same: Forcible rape implies that the person treated as an object for the offender's gratification reasonably fears bodily harm if she or he refuses to acquiesce. Lack of consent therefore remains the key factor that distinguishes a sexual assault from an unpleasant sexual experience imposed by an overly assertive partner.

Aggravated rape is penalized more severely because it involves more than one assailant, and/or the use of a weapon, and/or the infliction of additional wounds besides unwanted penetration. Sexual assaults short of rape (for example, unwelcome sexual contacts like groping or fondling) carry a lesser penalty. Taking sexual advantage of a person who is mentally retarded or unable to give meaningful consent because she or he is drugged, drunk, or unconscious (whether or not this altered state was induced by the offender) also is illegal. Besides forcible rape, **statutory rape** also is against the law, but the penalties are not as severe. When a minor below the legal age of consent voluntarily engages in sexual intercourse, the act automatically is considered to be exploitative because a young person is considered not mature enough to make such an important decision. By definition, statutory rapes do not involve violence or the threat of force (refer back to Chapter 8).

THE REDISCOVERY OF THE PLIGHT OF RAPE VICTIMS

Forcible rape is surely one of the most heinous violent crimes imaginable, and yet for centuries the social reaction to this offense showed little regard for the well-being of the victim. In the distant past, rape was handled as an offense that harmed the interests of a man—either a father or husband—rather than a violation of personhood that threatened the emotional and physical health of the daughter or wife. Some rapists were punished

severely, but others went unprosecuted, depending on the status of both the accused offender and the female he harmed.

In biblical times, a man could be put to death for the rape of an innocent virgin. But if a married woman was raped, she could be executed too because she was considered blameworthy (unless her husband intervened on her behalf). During medieval times, a man seeking upward mobility might engage in **heiress stealing**—abducting and then raping a young woman from a wealthy family in order to compel her parents to agree to let her be his bride. As feudalism evolved, only the rape of a noblewoman was punishable; forcing a peasant woman to submit was not considered a crime. During warfare, over the ages, the enemy's women were taken by conquering soldiers as spoils of victory; the triumphant army symbolically demonstrated to the soldiers on the losing side that they were so badly defeated that they could not even protect "their own" women. Rapists in military units around the world and through the centuries were rarely arrested, prosecuted, or punished during wartime (see Brownmiller, 1975; and Siegel, 1998).

Rapes involving people of different races become particularly controversial and polarizing. From the days of slavery up until the 1950s, black men who merely were accused of raping white women were in danger of being lynched by angry mobs without even being put on trial, especially in the Deep South. When rapists were executed after being convicted in state courts, most were black men found guilty of sexually assaulting white women. But white men were not put to death for raping black women. As a result of this imbalance, in 1977, the Supreme Court (in *Coker v. Georgia*) ruled that capital punishment was an excessive penalty for rape. Consequently, life imprisonment became the maximum sentence. In 2008, the Supreme Court (in *Kennedy v. Louisiana*) struck down capital punishment for the forcible and aggravated rape of a child.

These examples illustrate the point that in the past certain rapes were taken very seriously while others were reacted to very differently. But in most cases, the wishes and well-being of the injured party either were not taken into account or were assigned a low priority by the men who determined a rapist's fate. Clearly, when a rape took place, the offender became the focus of attention while the best interests of his victim largely were overlooked.

At the start of the 1970s, feminists fighting for the rights of women to control their own bodies (particularly reproductive rights via contraception and abortion) called attention to the plight of rape victims. Instead of being regarded as some man's "damaged goods," feminists insisted that these girls and women should be recognized as individuals suffering from terrible violations of their personhood who deserved respect, support, assistance, empowerment, and protection from further harm. This pro-victim, antirape movement exposed a legacy of injustice, institutionalized neglect, and routine abuse. Because of class, race, and gender discrimination, most women did not report such offenses to the authorities, and of the incidents that were reported, most went unpunished.

Feminists argued that rape was more than a personal tragedy: It was a social problem and a political issue. They interpreted sexual assaults as skirmishes in what had been referred to traditionally as the unending battle of the sexes. Forcible rapes functioned as acts of terrorism that intimidated all women and served to keep them in their "proper place"—subordinate to males (dependent upon "good" men for protection against "bad" men) and outside of male territorial preserves. A sexual assault symbolized how "it's a man's world"—a male could exploit his power differential (his superior physical force) to have his way.

The way rape cases were handled dramatized how the men who ran the criminal justice system could not be trusted to act on behalf of victimized girls and women. Invariably, when accusations about rape were lodged, the all-male police, prosecution, judiciary, and juries scrutinized the relationship between the two parties (especially their social class, race/ethnicity, prior contacts, and her alleged blameworthiness). These men often lost sight of the violence inflicted upon the target during the sexual assault (see Russell, 1975; Griffin, 1979; Rhode, 1989; and Muehlenhard et al., 1992).

Through books, articles, dissertations, discussions at consciousness-raising groups, demonstrations at trials, and public "speak-outs," the antirape movement supported by feminist legal scholars worked to redefine the prevailing image of the crime and to rediscover its victims. Their outreach campaigns triggered public and private discussions about previously unnamed types of violations such as date rape, acquaintance rape, marital rape, serial rape, and male rape. Their aim was to shatter the myths surrounding the crime (see Koss, 2005). Since then, federal and state laws have been rewritten and victimization surveys have been reworded to recognize the possibility that the attacker was not a stranger (see Fisher, Cullen, and Daigle, 2005).

THE CONSEQUENCES OF BEING SEXUALLY ASSAULTED

Victimologists have studied the plight of rape victims intensively for several decades. Researchers aim to assess the nature of the suffering and to discover ways to speed the recovery process (see McCahill, Williams, and Fischman, 1979; Girelli et al., 1986; Burt and Katz, 1987; Allison and Wrightsman, 1993; Wiehe and Richards, 1995; Giannelli, 1997; and Zinzow et al., 2012).

Being raped is almost always a life-altering experience and may haunt the survivor for the rest of her life. The ordeal itself and the turmoil that follows challenges and may even transform her identity and the assumptions she makes about the world. The emotional impact is manifested largely as fear, anxiety, depression, sexual dysfunction, and feelings of isolation. The mental toll shows up as the loss of illusions about invulnerability and immortality, the destruction of a sense of predictability within her environment and of the meaning of events in her life, and a diminution in her sense of self-worth. Other terrible consequences can include chronic physical pain, a substance abuse habit, and the contraction of a venereal disease or, in rare instances, HIV/AIDS infections (Campbell and Wasco, 2005; and Marx, 2005).

The distress from being treated as an object instead of a person may plunge her into a **rape crisis syndrome**. The acute initial phase lasts for two or three weeks immediately following the sexual attack. Typical short-term reactions include revulsion, shock, anger, fury, self-recrimination, fear, sorrow, and total disorientation. She often suffers nausea, tension headaches, and an inability to sleep. The second phase, in which the individual's personality reintegrates, can last much longer and is characterized by recurring nightmares, defensive reactions, and strains in relationships with men. Many try to reorganize their daily lives by changing jobs, moving to a new location, dropping out of college, and limiting personal contacts. Lingering effects often include loss of sexual desire and the development of fears: of being confined indoors, about going outdoors among strangers, of being alone as well as being in crowds, and of people stealthily approaching from behind (Burgess and Holmstrom, 1974; Giannelli, 1997; and Resick and Nishith, 1997).

Like others who are stunned by an unexpected, life-threatening ordeal, individuals who were raped can suffer from **posttraumatic stress disorder** (PTSD) during the crime's immediate aftermath. They may re-experience the attack repeatedly in daydreams, flashbacks, or nightmares. Other symptoms include feeling different; wanting to avoid things that serve as reminders of the trauma; and suffering a general lack of interest or enthusiasm, an inability to concentrate, and increased irritability (Williams, 1987; and Zinzow et al., 2010). A recognition of the severe consequences of the crime for the person abused as someone else's sex object should dispel any notions that rape is an act of passion rather than of subjugation and ought to demolish any beliefs that the unwilling target somehow secretly desired or enjoyed being handled so violently.

Even though most rapes are not completed (according to the yearly *NCVS* surveys, about two-thirds are not), females who thwart their assailants' intentions can still suffer serious psychological scars. In fact, women who endured attempted rapes were more likely to contemplate suicide and even to try to kill themselves than women who suffered

completed rapes, according to the results of a telephone survey (Kilpatrick, 1985).

Women who live through gang rapes by multiple offenders generally suffer more than victims of single offenders, in the form of physical injuries, PTSD, and suicide attempts. Those subjected to gang rapes were more inclined to disclose their problems to the police, medical providers, and mental health programs but shockingly reported that they frequently received negative reactions from these people to whom they turned for help (Ullman, 2007).

One potential negative consequence of being raped is becoming pregnant. Periodically, the number of pregnancies arising from rapes—and what the victims should be allowed or encouraged to do about them—becomes a divisive high-profile issue because it is linked to the debate over abortion. Some anti-abortion legislation promoted by the pro-life movement does not allow for any exceptions, even for unwanted pregnancies resulting from incest or rape (see Editorial Board, *New York Times*, 2014). One study projected that over 30,000 pregnancies a year in the United States result from rapes (see Dellorto, 2012). An awkward, if not painful, situation can develop if the rapist doesn't get into legal trouble: In most states, he can sue for visitation and even custody rights.

THE CONTROVERSY SURROUNDING QUESTIONS OF SHARED RESPONSIBILITY

Despite whatever progress has been made in the way rape cases are viewed in general and how they are handled by the legal system on a daily basis, a number of unresolved controversies still erupt when actual cases make the news and lead to complaints and arrests. One issue that triggers heated debates is whether the victim can be faulted in any way for sharing responsibility with the offender for the crime. This divisive issue has been examined earlier for cases of homicides, robberies, burglaries, vehicle thefts, and identity thefts (refer back to Chapters 4 and 5). But there can be no doubt that the stakes are higher and the level of partisanship is greater when victim-blaming viewpoints are pitted against victim-defending arguments in certain real-life cases of rape and sexual assault.

"Real Rapes" as Compared to "Acquaintance Rapes" and "Date Rapes"

Early one morning, a recent college grad is waiting on a corner for a lift from her principal to her first day at a new "dream job" as an elementary school teacher. A drunken man comes up to her using the pretext of asking for directions, and then pulls out a gun, threatens to kill her, and drags her into an alley. He violates her "in every way imaginable." A person in a nearby building hears a commotion and looks out the window, witnesses the attack, and calls the police. The assailants DNA is found on her clothing, and an emergency room doctor testifies he found evidence that force was used. The jury convicts the 28-year-old drunk (who, it turns out, was an off-duty police officer) and the judge sentences him to 75 years to life. (Lovett, 2013)

●●●

A college student claims that a star quarterback of the football team raped her. He is arrested and charged with one count, of "sexual intercourse without consent" which carries a penalty of from two years to up to one hundred years in prison, plus a lifetime of stigmatization as a registered sex offender. She takes the stand and testifies that while watching a movie, at first they kissed and took their shirts off, but then she said no to any further sexual advances. But the 6-foot-1,200-pound athlete kept going, taking off her leggings and underwear, pinning her to the bed and then forcing her to submit, she insists. "He just changed—changed into a totally different person," she laments. She did not scream to friends in the house for help because she was "terrified and in shock." But afterwards she texts a friend, "Omg ... I think I might have just gotten raped ... he kept pushing and pushing and I said no but he wouldn't listen ... I just wanna cry ... Omg, what do I do!" The prosecutor tells the jury that the following day, she went to the university's Student Assault Resource Center and had a medical exam, which noted injuries to her head, clavicle, chest and genitals.

Then the accused takes the stand and insists the sex was consensual, asserting "I would never do that to anyone," "If somebody says no, you stop. You respect that." The defense attorney argues that the woman wanted to be with the football player but turned on him when she realized that a relationship was not part of the deal. After three weeks of testimony that rivets the attention of the college town and divides the campus community, the seven-woman, five-man jury deliberates for two and a half hours and then acquits the young man. (Robbins, 2013)

Sexual crimes involve coercion of an unwilling person, according to the law. But not all sexual assaults qualify as "real rapes" in the court of public opinion (see Estrich, 1986). There surely would be a consensus that the first case cited above constitutes a real rape. But controversy still surrounds certain incidents, such as the second one cited above. Many people have trouble distinguishing imposed intercourse from willingly engaging in sex. As a result, when a woman claims to have been penetrated against her will, some people might conjure up images of "having sex" or even "lovemaking" rather than "forcible bodily invasion" if the two were acquaintances, and especially if they were dating or had been intimate partners in the past.

Real rapes or "classic rapes" (in the language of sociology, **ideal types** in the sense that they are the clearest examples) are readily identifiable and raise few legal questions or moral doubts. Real rapes have several defining features: They are perpetrated against unsuspecting females who are ambushed in blitz attacks. The offender is a complete stranger. He is armed with a weapon and pounces out of the darkness to surprise his quarry. The injured party is virtuous and above reproach—she is too young, too old, or too inexperienced to be faulted for attracting his attention and arousing his desires. At the time of the attack, she is engaged in a "wholesome" activity that is above criticism. Even though she faces grave dangers, she dares to fight back, resists to her utmost, and suffers severe injuries in a futile attempt to fend him off. Eyewitnesses glimpse parts of the struggle and hear her cries for help. As soon as she escapes from his clutches, she reports the crime to the police. Detectives find forensic evidence that backs up all her charges of being caught off guard, confronted with a weapon, brutally assaulted, physically overpowered, and helplessly compelled to submit to his demands. Finally, the assailant, who is obviously deeply disturbed, quickly confesses when captured.

Few people would have any difficulty conceding that a rape that mirrors many of these characteristics is one of the worst experiences that a woman can suffer. Today, detectives, prosecutors, juries, and judges agree that girls or women harmed in such heinous attacks deserve to be treated with dignity and sensitivity within the criminal justice process and that the vicious sexual predators who prey upon them must be removed from society and severely punished (see Estrich, 1986).

The problem for most rape victims is that the facts in their cases usually fall short in one way or another of the unambiguous standards that characterize brutal "real rapes" committed by complete strangers.

Acquaintance rapes (by relatives, neighbors, classmates, colleagues from work, casual dates, and intimate partners) are quite distinct from real rapes by complete strangers. The nature of the victim–offender relationship is different as are their interactions before forced sexual submission took place. In cases of acquaintance rape, doubts about her version of the facts quickly surface if some other crucial defining features of real rapes are missing. Perhaps she fails to meet the old-fashioned criterion of being "virtuous," or she does not report the attack promptly. Maybe the assailant did not brandish a weapon, or he did not inflict serious physical injuries. If there was no ferocious struggle or she did not scream for help, some will reject her contention that she was unwilling. If there is no corroboration by eyewitnesses or from forensic tests, the case may boil down to her word against his. When the accused rapist is a date or a person with whom she has previously been intimate, then the teenage girl or woman will have an even tougher time convincing the authorities that she was violated against her will and that he should be arrested, prosecuted, and punished (Estrich, 1986).

Until the late 1980s, most prosecutors were reluctant to move forward, press charges, and go to trial when the accused man was not a complete stranger, if there were no eyewitnesses, no bruises from a beating, and no signs of a fierce struggle. Yet forced submission arising out of a romantic encounter meets the legal definition of rape—the use of physical coercion against a nonconsenting person—and does not hinge on the prior relationship of the accuser and the accused (see Estrich, 1993a; and Spears and Spohn, 1997).

Some would argue that if forced intercourse is preceded by a series of consensual acts with sexual overtones, her "contributory behavior" makes the nature of the crime less serious, and it should be penalized less severely than an ambush of an unsuspecting and depersonalized target. Others insist that it makes no difference if the victim and the offender knew each other and interacted warmly, even passionately, before the incident. The encounter cannot be written off as a case of "miscommunication," a "terrible misunderstanding," or an instance of a woman having regrets for the way she behaved the night before. What counts is that she was stripped of control, denied the right to make a crucial decision, and compelled to submit to someone else's sexual demands (Gibbs, 1991).

These sharply contrasting interpretations lead to a victim-blaming versus victim-defending debate over who or what is at fault and what should be done.

The conflict between victim blaming and victim defending is particularly bitter when it comes to rape. If auto theft provided a clear illustration of a crime for which there are well-organized interests with a stake in promoting motorist blaming, then rape serves as the best example of a crime for which there is a vocal and deeply committed victim-defending community. The controversy erupts over whether certain instances of rape should be viewed as victim-precipitated acts of uncontainable male sexual desire or whether all instances of forced sex are inexcusable acts of brutal domination always imposed upon unwilling, objectified targets.

A great deal is at stake in the battle for public support between victim-blaming and victim-defending viewpoints. People must choose between two distinct courses of action. Who or what has to change: How females behave in the company of males, as victim blaming contends; or how boys and men relate to girls and women, as victim defending emphasizes? Accepting victim-blaming arguments might lead to the acquittal of certain defendants, but the more socially significant consequence is that this line of reasoning excuses institutions and traditions that can be viewed as demeaning to women. According to victim defenders who blame the system, to reduce the threat of rape it is necessary to root out antifemale biases found within rigid sex roles, to rethink prevailing definitions of masculinity and femininity that infuse popular culture, to end antifemale practices within the job market and the economy, and to reform existing laws and criminal justice procedures (see Hills, 1981).

Victim-Blaming Viewpoints

Late one night, a 22-year-old mother of two enters a bar filled with men. She has a few drinks and flirts with some of the patrons. Suddenly, she finds herself held down on a pool table. Six young men force themselves on her as onlookers cheer and she screams and curses. The six men are arrested and put on trial for aggravated rape. Their defense is that she acted seductively and "led them on." The prosecution argues that a sexual assault begins whenever a man continues after a woman has said no. The jury concludes that she did not consent to what they did to her and convicts four of the six defendants. The judge sentences them to terms of 6 to 12 years in prison. At a rally held on behalf of the victim, speakers hail the outcome as a symbol that gang rape will not be tolerated as a spectator sport. But at a demonstration protesting the verdicts and sentences, speakers sympathetic to the young men contend, "She got herself raped," and "She should have known what she was getting herself into." They hold her largely responsible for enabling the men "to take advantage of her." A movie is made about her ordeal, the trial, and the public's reactions. (Schanberg, 1984, 1989)

■■■

A man is on trial for rape. His lawyer points out that the alleged victim was wearing a tank top, a lacy miniskirt, and no underpants. The defendant is found not guilty because, as one juror explains,

"We felt she asked for it." The failed prosecution inspires the state legislature to amend the laws governing rape trials to bar defense attorneys from asking complainants about the clothes they were wearing at the time of the assaults. (Merrill, 1994)

Both of these often-cited real-life cases illustrate the clash between two competing perspectives.

The victim-blaming viewpoint contends that some rape victims differ in their attitudes and actions from other females who are able to avoid sexual assault. Allegedly, there are certain kinds of women who go around "asking for trouble," "single themselves out from the pack," and eventually "get themselves raped." Such harsh condemnations rest on two premises: that the male was overwhelmed by sexual desire and lost his self-control and that the female somehow facilitated the assault (perhaps by weakening herself by taking drugs or alcohol), thoughtlessly precipitated it (by making rash decisions that put her in a temptation–opportunity situation), or even provoked his overpowering response (by suggestive and seductive utterings or deeds) (see Gibbs, 1991). Those who believe in the "just world" theory, in which people get what they deserve during their lifetimes, are more inclined to blame rape victims, even if the attacker is a complete stranger (Stromwall et al., 2013).

Victim blaming chastises women who suffer sexual assaults for acts of omission (not being cautious) as well as acts of commission, such as hitchhiking (see Amir, 1971). Even worse, the female might be castigated for secretly harboring fantasies of being ravished and then enabling such scenarios to take place (see MacDonald, 1971). The victim-blaming interpretation of date rape characterizes the incident as a terrible misunderstanding in "he said/she said" terms: He says she wanted to and didn't really object, while she says he intimidated her and forced her to yield. Miscommunication results when a female sends mixed messages, fails to make her true intentions clear, and doesn't protest unwanted sexual advances vehemently enough—a common problem during this period of rapid changes in the rules of the "dating game," with its courtship rituals and shifting sexual mores (see Warshaw, 1988; and Muehlenhard et al., 1992).

The most widely cited (and most heavily criticized) study of victim precipitation in rape was based on data drawn from the files of the Philadelphia police concerning cases reported in 1958 and 1960 (Amir, 1971). The researcher considered "precipitation" to have occurred either whenever a girl's or woman's behavior was interpreted by a teenage boy or man as a direct invitation to engage in sexual relations that was later retracted (she agreed and then changed her mind, according to him) or when she signaled that she would be amenable if he persisted in his demands (she was saying no but meant yes, in his opinion). Included in this researcher's working definition of a precipitated rape were acts of commission such as drinking alcohol, hitchhiking, or using what could be taken as indecent language or gestures. Acts of omission, such as failing to object strongly enough to his sexually charged overtures, also counted against her. The offender's interpretation was considered to be the crucial element in recognizing instances of precipitation. Even if the male was mistaken in his beliefs about her intentions, his perceptions led to actions, and that was what really mattered.

In the police department's files, specific indicators of precipitation were statements by the offender, witnesses, or detectives claiming that "she behaved provocatively," "she acted seductively," "she was irresponsible and endangered herself," or "she had a bad reputation in the neighborhood." Using these criteria, the researcher deemed 19 percent of Philadelphia's forcible rapes to be precipitated. Comparing precipitated rapes with nonprecipitated ones, it was found that alcohol consumption was more likely to have taken place and that the offender was more inclined to sexually humiliate his victim. Precipitating victims included higher percentages of females who were white, teenagers, and casual acquaintances of the males they first met at bars or parties (Amir, 1971).

The victim-blaming perspective contends that some young women precipitate rapes because of their lifestyles. They do not understand (or choose to ignore) the risks involved in certain situations, such as going to bars unescorted or accepting rides home with men they hardly know. They are unaware, naive, or gullible in their dealings with males. They wear clothing or use language that men stereotype as signaling sexual availability. They ignore the dangers that might arise if they are suddenly confronted with a weapon or are overpowered while under the influence of alcohol or some other drug. For some teenage girls, their reckless behavior is considered a form of acting out. These adolescents—especially if they come from poverty-stricken homes and suffer parental rejection—are said to be seeking protection, attention, love, intimacy, and status through precocious sexuality. As a result, they get involved with older male casual acquaintances and find themselves in situations in which they are forcibly exploited (see Amir, 1971; and Dean and de Bruyn-Kops, 1982).

Two sets of consequences follow from the acceptance of victim-blaming arguments. First, if the female shares some responsibility, then the male can be considered less culpable and less deserving of severe punishment. Second, girls and women must be educated to behave more cautiously and avoid any miscommunication about their real desires.

If the victim's behavior can be criticized, then the "tragic misunderstanding" is not entirely the offender's fault. The legal principle involved is that the female assumed the risk of attack when she voluntarily participated in potentially dangerous events that led up to the rape, such as drinking heavily or agreeing to enter an isolated area away from potential rescuers. Even though the male remains subject to arrest, her contributory behavior can provide grounds for granting him the benefit of the doubt. This line of reasoning can influence every stage of the criminal justice system's handling of these cases.

Anticipation of harsh interrogation might discourage a victim from bringing her problem to the attention of the authorities. If, after thoroughly questioning the complainant to determine her background, reputation, actions, and possible motives, the police believe that she contributed to her own victimization, charges might not be pressed. If the police do make an arrest, the prosecutor might decide that the case is unwinnable and therefore might drop the charges. If the case is brought to trial, jurors may exercise their discretion in interpreting the facts and may find the assailant guilty of a lesser charge than forcible rape (sexual assault, for example). If the defendant is convicted, the judge may hand down a lenient sentence in view of the mitigating circumstances—her misleading seductiveness might have been taken as a sign of **implied consent** (for additional references, see Schur, 1984; and Marciniak, 1999).

The other major consequence of accepting the victim-blaming point of view is that the burden of preventing rape is shifted away from aggressive males, the police, or the prevailing culture, and onto the potential targets. Girls and women are admonished that they might unwittingly be courting disaster and that it is their obligation to constantly review their lifestyles and do what they can to minimize their risks and maximize their safety. Because controlling the actions of offenders is so difficult, victim blaming seeks to reduce the incidence of rape by constraining the behavior of the potential targets. Females are warned to be careful whom they associate with, what they say in conversations, where they go, and how they dress. They are urged to communicate clearly, to signal their true intentions, and to avoid teasing or taunting males. They are held personally accountable for their own security and are pressured to follow crime prevention tips derived from the mistakes made by other females. Just as the threat of punishment is intended to make would-be rapists think twice before breaking the law, the public humiliation of victim blaming is meant to pressure females to think twice before stepping out of traditional, sheltered, family-centered roles and activities.

Teenagers and young adults are especially likely to hold these traditional beliefs about the female's responsibility for precipitated rapes. Surveys reveal that between one-quarter and one-half of all adolescents express agreement with some statements that pin blame on victims because of their demeanor, clothing, or prior actions (see Marciniak, 1999). A sizable proportion of female college students also hold victims accountable for their "mistakes" (Cowan, 2000; Bondurant, 2001; and Carmody and Washington, 2001).

In many acquaintance rape cases, the male, the female, or both were drinking alcohol or taking drugs before the confrontation. Several studies have generated the finding that about half of all men

arrested for rape disclosed that they had been drinking before the crime, and about half of all women who were raped concede they had been drinking preceding the assault (Kilpatrick et al., 2007). (However, these figures don't indicate how much they drank or how intoxicated either person was [see Abbey et al., 2004].) Girls and women who voluntarily get drunk and consequently become easy to subjugate often are singled out for particularly harsh condemnations. They are faulted for recklessly getting so high that they became unaware of developments taking place around them, unable to think clearly enough to give meaningful consent or to vehemently object, and incapable of physically warding off unwanted advances. Whereas males may use alcohol as a way to erode their "partner's" will to resist, females are condemned for getting drunk enough to dissolve their inhibitions and provide themselves with a convenient excuse afterward (see Corbin, Bernat, and Calhoun, 2001; and Falck, Wang, and Carlson, 2001). The following highly publicized case touched off an acrimonious debate over whether the victim was partly responsible for her own "downfall" and how the justice system ought to handle alcohol-fueled "date rape" cases.

A high school student tells her parents she is going to sleep over at a girlfriend's house, but after they drop her off she gets some Vodka and brings it to a party attended by about 50 beer and liquor drinking classmates, with no adults around. After that party breaks up, she vomits but insists to friends that she is intent on going to another get-together and drives off in the company of two football players, ages 16 and 17. After parents at that location close that party down, she throws up again, passes out, and is lifted and carried off by the two athletes. Six hours later, she wakes up naked in a basement in their presence, but she can't find her shoes, underwear, or cell phone. "I was embarrassed and scared, and I did not know what to think because I could not remember anything," she recalls. Over the next few days, she pieces together what had happened with the help of friends who showed her a video posted on YouTube and a picture of her lying naked. When her outraged parents file a complaint and hand over to the police a flashdrive full of videos, Facebook postings, Instagram pictures, and tweets they compiled as evidence, the events come out of the shadows and into the glare of spotlights. The case divides the small town, with devotees of the football team charging the girl, her supporters, and the national news media of blowing an episode of drunken teenage misbehavior all out of proportion. Others, especially outsiders and adults, are appalled at the evidence indicating that so many adolescents seem to accept a "rape culture" that condones or even extols forceful acts that degrade females. The two boys face very serious charges in juvenile court because the law in that state considers digital penetration to be a form of rape, but the teammates who were amused onlookers and photographed the attack do not get into legal trouble. During the widely publicized proceedings in front of a judge, two former friends testify that she has a reputation as a liar, and an expert witness contends that she drank enough to have a memory lapse, and perhaps that is why she can't recall that she granted consent to the boys to engage in sex. Prosecution witnesses include a classmate who saw the penetration take place in the back seat of the car, and another who witnessed penetration of the unconscious girl in the basement. Text messages to her the next day from one of the defendants are entered into evidence, in which he pleaded with her not to tell the police and ruin his athletic career. Both boys are "adjudicated delinquent"—the equivalent of a guilty verdict in adult court. The judge sends one athlete to a year in juvenile detention; his teammate is found responsible for both rape and disseminating child pornography, gets two years, and is ordered to register as a sex offender for twenty years. (Oppel, 2013; and Levy, 2013)

An advertisement intended to raise awareness that a bout of heavy drinking could facilitate a sexual assault caused such a controversy about whether it encouraged victim blaming that it was removed:

A state liquor control board launches a campaign to educate the public about the link between excessive drinking and alcohol poisoning, drunken brawls, and car crashes. But one ad that sparks an outcry features an image of a woman's legs on a bathroom floor with her underwear pulled down to her ankles, with the

caption, "She didn't want to do it, but she couldn't say no." Critics argue that the ad suggests that victims are to blame. Supporters say that it will encourage frank conversations about how to prevent sexual assaults. The ad is dropped from the campaign. (Begos, 2011)

Victim-Defending Perspectives

"Our daughters, our sisters, our wives, our mothers, our grandmothers have every single right to expect to be free from violence and sexual abuse. No matter what she's wearing, no matter whether she's in a bar, in a dormitory, in the back seat of a car, on a street, drunk or sober—no man has a right to go beyond the word 'no.' And if she can't consent, it also means no." (Vice President Joe Biden, 2014 [quoted in Editors, *New York Times*, 2014a])

Victim-blaming views became controversial during the 1970s and have been strongly condemned ever since then. Victim-defending arguments, originally developed by feminists in the women's rights movement, challenge this conventional wisdom handed down from generation to generation and provide alternative explanations for why some men force themselves upon women.

Over the ages, rape had been pictured as an act of lust and an outpouring of uncontrollable sexual urges. This old view seems plausible only if the vicious physical injuries and devastating emotional pain sustained by the "objects of desire" are ignored. Threats of violence and the use of force surrounding the sexual assault—before, during, and after—betrays its true nature: an attack upon the victim's dignity and personhood for the purposes of conquest and degradation. According to this new view, rape is really all about power and control. In essence, victim blaming arises from the old view whereas victim defending rests upon the newer interpretation.

Victim defending rejects as a myth the notion that rapes are acts of lust or outpourings of uncontrollable passion. Sexual assaults are reinterpreted as outbursts of aggression fueled by anger and hatred. Through sexual acts, assailants express their intentions to dominate, subjugate, and humiliate females in general and their target in particular. The assailant reveals his contempt for females—certainly not "passion" or "love" for a particular girl or woman. Nothing suggestive, flirtatious, or erotic on the victim's part could justify such hostile and degrading reactions from a stranger, acquaintance, intimate, or even a spouse (Russell, 1975; Clark and Lewis, 1978; and Griffin, 1979).

Using force to compel an unwilling partner to submit and be controlled as a depersonalized object should never be confused with "making love" or even "engaging in sex." Victim defending questions the applicability of the concept of precipitation, which was originally developed to describe the blameworthy, aggressive initiatives taken by men who start and then lose fights. Although some homicides might be deemed justifiable (cases of self-defense; see Chapter 13), there is no such thing as a justifiable rape (see Amir, 1971). In victim-precipitated homicides, the person who died was the first to escalate the level of conflict by resorting to physical strength or a weapon; then the survivor reacted to the assault by fighting back with deadly force. Violence incited retaliatory violence. Because the woman does not physically assault the man before he attacks her, the only way to apply the concept of precipitation to rape is to consider the incident as primarily a sexually charged encounter. Only then can real or presumed teasing and sexual advances by the female be considered triggering mechanisms. But there is no justification for his resort to force, no matter what she wore, said, did, or promised. Furthermore, there is great confusion and disagreement over what constitutes a sexual overture. Because the female's behavior can be subjected to a wide range of interpretations, whose perceptions should be accepted when deciding if there was precipitation on her part: his, hers, the police's, the jury's, or the researcher's? (See Silverman, 1974; Chappell, Geis, and Geis, 1977; McCaghy, 1980; and Muftic and Foster, 2010.)

Therefore, the belief that certain rapes are precipitated has been dismissed as a personification and embodiment of rape mythology, cleverly stated in academic-scientific terms (Weis and Borges, 1973), as a scholarly endorsement of the rapist's point of view that provides an excuse for blaming the injured party (Clark and Lewis, 1978), and as an *ex post facto* interpretation that fails to take into account the female's version of events (LeGrande, 1973).

As for date rapes, victim defending asserts that whenever unwanted intercourse occurs, a real rape has been committed, and not a seduction as the culmination of a romantic courtship ritual. Nor is the rape a terrible misunderstanding stemming from miscommunication. The boy or man has used coercion to take from her what he wanted and intended to get all along, while violating her personhood in the process (Estrich, 1986; and LaFree, 1989). If she was silent and passive and yielded without a struggle, this behavior should not be taken to mean acquiescence. Such an interpretation overlooks the paralyzing effects of the aggressor's overwhelming physical strength, his use of force at the outset, his tactics that caught the victim by surprise, or the implied threat posed by the presence of a weapon (see Estrich, 1986; and LaFree, 1989).

Victim defending also dismisses as "ideologically tainted" the crime prevention tips girls and women are supposed to follow in order to survive in a "man's world." Females who did not scrupulously observe these precautions are unfairly set up for blame and even berate themselves ("If only I had...."). A woman who abides by the long and rapidly growing list of recommended self-protection measures (given heightened concerns about drug-facilitated date rape—see below) ends up resembling the proverbial "hysterical old maid armed with a hatpin and an umbrella who looks under the bed each night before retiring." For years a laughable stereotype of prudery, she has become a model of prudence (Brownmiller, 1975).

Adhering to crime prevention tips means forgoing many pleasures and privileges to which men are accustomed, such as taking a walk alone on a deserted beach or strolling through the park at night. Warding off would-be rapists requires women to engage in an extraordinary amount of pretense and deception (pretending a boyfriend, husband, or father is nearby). Furthermore, seeking the protection of "trustworthy" men to fend off unwanted advances by predatory males undermines the efforts of women to develop their own strengths, self-confidence, self-reliance, and independent networks of mutual support.

The clash between victim-blaming outlooks and victim-defending counterarguments sharpened in 2011 when a Canadian police officer lectured a group of college women that if they wanted to avoid attracting assailants, they should not dress like "sluts." This advice sparked an angry protest that went viral, leading to demonstrations in 70 cities across the globe. At these "SlutWalks," some young women marched along defiantly wearing bras, halter tops, and garter belts. Feminists were divided: Some cheered them on for challenging the belief that women who appear alluring are asking to be hit on, sexually harassed, or assaulted, since so many victims were not dressed provocatively when attacked. But others fretted that the well-intentioned scantily clad demonstrators actually were insensitive to how divisive matters pertaining to age, race, class, lifestyle, and body image can be to the women's movement (Traister, 2011). Slutwalks have continued as part of a campaign to condemn the persistence of both victim blaming and rape culture.

Victim defenders do not portray females as naive, gullible, helpless, dependent, and vulnerable targets who require strict supervision to keep them out of trouble. Women, like men, exercise **agency** and ultimately are responsible for their own choices and fate. But victim defenders insist that rape prevention campaigns should not solely be aimed at females, but should educate and enlighten potential male aggressors too, as well as to pressure and threaten them to do the right thing when relating to the "opposite sex." In sum, victim defending aims to dispel "rape myths" that shift the burden of responsibility from the perpetrators on to the women they attack. Not surprisingly, a meta-analysis of studies examining rape myth acceptance concluded that boys and men are more likely than girls and women to endorse these blame-the-victim views (Suarez and Gadalla, 2010) (see Box 10.1).

Victim defenders argue that those who believe rape myths are internalizing traditional cultural

BOX 10.1 The Controversy Surrounding Widely Held Rape Myths

From a victim-defending standpoint, certain victim-blaming arguments about acquaintance rapes are deemed to be "rape myths." These widely held and frequently voiced points of view tend to dismiss the seriousness of the violation of the woman's dignity and personal integrity, or even imply that nothing illegal took place (Schwendinger and Schwendinger, 1974).

Two fundamental assumptions made by victim blamers are dismissed as myths by victim defenders (see Roger Williams University, 2011):

(a) Rape arises from uncontrollable sexual urges that well up in a man who desires sexual gratification. In reality, rape is not motivated by lust but actually is a violent assault driven by a desire to dominate.

(b) Young women provoke rapists' interests by appearing sexually attractive. In reality, assailants attack females who range from the very young to the very old, as long as they are accessible and vulnerable.

Six familiar beliefs, four that blame the victim and two that defend the perpetrator, also have been labeled as myths

that reinforce narrow stereotypes, distort reality, and interfere with the process of separating fact from fiction (see Burt, 1980; Lonsway and Fitzgerald, 1994; Franiuk et al., 2008; and Roger Williams University, 2011). Researchers adopting a victim-defending stance measure how many people believe:

1. "She is lying" for some ulterior purpose.
2. "She asked for it" by doing things that seemed to imply consent, such as drinking alcoholic beverages or accompanying the man to his home.
3. "She wanted it at the time" but changed her mind and then altered the story line and cried "rape!"
4. "She is the kind of female who gets raped." Only "certain" women get raped: promiscuous ones who place themselves at great risk.
5. "He didn't mean to cross the line." The whole incident arose from miscommunication and a terrible misunderstanding. He thought her "no" actually meant "yes" if he persevered, so his behavior is excusable.
6. "He is not the type to commit a rape." The accusations must be unfounded because only sex-crazed psychopaths use physical force to have their way.

stereotypes that may cause men to excuse or even justify their own sexually aggressive behavior. People who embrace rape myths tend to be reluctant to label an incident as a sexual assault even when it meets the legal criteria for a violation of an existing law. If rape myths are believed by hospital personnel, detectives, prosecutors, judges, and jurors, then the negative reactions of these influential people will deter other females who submitted to acquaintance rapes from reporting the crimes, pressing charges, and testifying at trials, victim defenders point out (see Schwendinger and Schwendinger, 1974; and Franiuk et al., 2008).

ESTIMATES OF THE INCIDENCE, PREVALENCE, AND SERIOUSNESS OF RAPE

Nearly 80,000 girls and women across the country notified the police that they had been forcibly raped, or an attempt was made to do so, during 2013 (about 50 females for every 100,000 inhabitants), according to the *UCR* (FBI, 2014). Almost 175,000 persons (of whom a small percentage was males) disclosed to *NCVS* interviewers that they had been raped or sexually assaulted in some other way during 2013 (a rate of about 110 for every 100,000 residents) (Truman and Langton, 2014). In another government-sponsored survey, about 1.6 percent of female respondents revealed that they had been raped during 2011, and almost 20 percent said they had been raped at least once during their lifetimes; as for men, 1.7 percent disclosed ever having been sexually assaulted (Breiding, 2014).

Both victimologists and criminologists will agree with the maximalist assertion that official statistics usually do not accurately indicate how many crimes actually are committed each year, mainly because so many people do not report completed and attempted rapes and other sexual assaults to the police. Therefore, *UCR* figures surely are an undercount. Similarly, respondents may also fail to disclose their painful experiences to interviewers, undermining the accuracy of the *NCVS*. Surely, some girls and women are very reluctant to speak openly and frankly about such incidents, especially in the presence of other family members. Some respondents might feel uncomfortable delving into such a sensitive subject with any stranger, especially a male interviewer, particularly if his age, class, or ethnicity differed from that of the respondent.

Furthermore, some incidents that could be legally classified as rapes might not be defined as crimes by the females who experienced them, especially if the aggressor was an acquaintance, and he issued threats but was not brutally violent. Before 1992, *NCVS* screening questions were worded in roundabout ways; the term *sexual attack* was used but was not spelled out sufficiently in graphic detail, and respondents were not given clear-cut examples. The survey's working definition excluded marital rapes, acts of forcible sodomy to other parts of the body, and incidents in which the perpetrator took advantage of a person's intoxicated state, mental illness, or mental retardation. Finally, **series victimizations**—repeated rapes, generally by an intimate or acquaintance—were not counted as separate incidents (Koss, 1992; and Bachman, 1998).

In 1992, the BJS redesigned the survey's questionnaire and changed the project's name from the *National Crime Survey* to the *National Crime Victimization Survey*. The original set of questions never bluntly asked about rapes because the subject was considered too personal, delicate, and sensitive to address directly. Interviewers found out about these incidents only if the respondent volunteered the information while thinking about physical attacks and threatened assaults. In the redesigned questionnaire, the interviewer asks, "Has anyone attacked or threatened you in any of these ways: any rape, attempted rape, or other type of sexual assault?" The interviewer follows up by saying, "Please mention it even if you are not certain it was a crime…. Incidents involving forced or unwanted sexual acts are often difficult to talk about. Have you been forced or coerced to engage in unwanted sexual activity by someone you didn't know before, or a casual acquaintance, or someone you know well?" Once this battery of questions was implemented (used on half of the sample), the *NCVS* estimate of the number of rapes and other sexual assaults suffered during 1992 jumped more than 150 percent (Kindermann et al., 1997).

To address some of the methodological criticisms leveled by researchers against the way the FBI's *UCR* measured rape, its data collecting systems were changed. In 1991, a National Incident Based Reporting System (NIBRS) definition of rape replaced the narrow *UCR* guideline of "carnal knowledge of a female forcibly and against her will." The FBI's NIBRS now counts sexual assaults directed against males and broadens the definition to keep track of incidents in which the person was not violated by force but was unable to give consent because of either a temporary or permanent mental or physical incapacity (for example, alcohol-induced unconsciousness). In addition, the NIBRS counts acts of "forcible sodomy" other than vaginal intercourse, sexual assaults carried out with an object, and forcible fondling. However, most police departments across the country have not switched to NIBRS yet, so the older way of recording rape incidents solely against females is still retained in annual *UCRs* under the heading "legacy definition."

Despite well-intentioned efforts to persuade more victims to come forward for help, rape continues to be underreported. Police detectives and emergency room personnel have received sensitivity training, sexual assault nurse examiners have been certified, hotlines have been set up, crisis centers have been established (including on college campuses), court advocates have been hired, and laws have been reformed—yet many victims still are reluctant to disclose the facts about sexual assaults they have endured.

Even if the official figures are routinely undercounts, what changes over time can be discerned? When annual estimates of rapes, as measured by the *NCVS* and the *UCR*, are plotted on the same set of axes, the trend lines on the graph diverge and become a source of confusing and contradictory impressions until the 1990s (see Figure 10.1). According to the *UCR*, reports of sexual violence unleashed by men against women reached a record high in 1992, but

FIGURE 10.1 Trends in Rape Rates, United States, 1973–2013

NOTES: The *UCR* counts female victims only from 1973 to 2013 (legacy definition).
NCVS rates were adjusted by the BJS for compatibility with the redesigned 1992 survey.
SOURCES: FBI's *UCR*, 1973–2013; BJS's *NCVS*, 1973–2013.

after that the rape rate steadily declined (as did the rate of all other index crimes, including murder, robbery, assault, burglary, and motor vehicle theft). The number of reported rapes in 2013 reached its lowest point since the late 1970s, according to *UCR* figures based on formal complaints to the police.

According to the *NCVS*, rape rates generally have trended downward since the late 1970s. But during the twenty-first century, *NCVS* rates remained roughly steady (and after hitting a record low in 2009 even crept back up from 2010 to 2012) and thus did not mirror the year-after-year decline indicated by *UCR* figures (compare the two lines in Figure 10.1). However, the take-away message from both government-run monitoring systems was the same: sexual violence was becoming less of a threat to girls and women.

WHO FACES THE GRAVEST DANGERS? DIFFERENTIAL RISKS OF BEING SEXUALLY ASSAULTED AND RAPED

Even though the *NCVS* figures are underestimates, the differential risks derived from yearly surveys are worth analyzing. The findings confirm the stereotype that virtually all of the assailants of females were males, as were nearly all of the assailants of males. The findings also support the belief that certain categories of girls and women face higher levels of danger than others. The gravest risks of being raped were borne by females in their late teens or early twenties, unmarried, living in low-income families, unemployed, black, and residing in large cities. Females who faced the smallest risks were over age 50, white, married or widowed, affluent, and living in rural areas, according to a statistical portrait drawn from a huge database of *NCVS* interviews conducted between 1973 and 1987 (Harlow, 1991).

More recent findings from a giant *NCVS* database collected from 1995 to 2010 painted a slightly different picture. One positive trend, cited above, was the sharp decrease in the victimization rate from 1995 until about 2005, especially for completed rapes and assaults (as distinct

from attempts and threats, which remained largely unchanged). One disturbing shift over the decades was that the percentage of females who were injured by the assailant and needed medical treatment went up. Another negative trend concerned differential risks: by the early years of the twenty-first century, the age group facing the gravest dangers turned out to be girls between the ages of 12 and 17. As during previous decades, young women from 18 to 34 years old also faced high risks. As for race and ethnicity, Native Americans were victimized the most, and Hispanic/Latina females the least. Single women who were divorced and separated or never married were sexually assaulted much more often than married or widowed (usually older) women. Low-income women faced much higher odds than those in the middle-income category. One other shift was that women living in cities and suburbs experienced such a welcomed drop in risks since the 1990s that now rural dwellers are more likely to suffer sexual assaults, according to the *NCVS* (Planty and Langston, 2013). Other studies have confirmed the disturbing finding that youngsters face particularly grave dangers. Nearly half of all female victims were sexually assaulted before they turned 18, and over one quarter of all male victims suffered their sexual abuse before they were 10 years old. Several additional high-risk groups have been identified: people with disabilities, prisoners, homeless persons, undocumented immigrants, and members of the LGBT community (White House Council on Women and Girls, 2014).

One issue that concerns many people also has received attention from victimologists—whether strangers or nonstrangers pose a greater threat to girls and women. The answer is not clear from official statistics, largely because so many victims do not want to discuss the incidents with anyone—not detectives and not survey interviewers. The attacker was a stranger more than half the time (55 percent), according to an analysis of attempted and completed rapes disclosed to *NCVS* interviewers from 1982 to 1984 (Timrots and Rand, 1987). However, a comparable analysis of *NCVS* data from 1987 to

1991 yielded a somewhat lower figure of 44 percent for sexual assaults by strangers (Bachman, 1994). Strangers were responsible for 25 percent of all attacks disclosed in 1998, 30 percent in 2001 and 2005, 39 percent in 2006, and just 25 percent in 2010 (Truman, 2011). For the six-year period from 2005 to 2010, only 22 percent of the offenders were not family members, intimate partners, friends, or acquaintances (Planty and Langston, 2013). Therefore, in terms of victim–offender relationships, the risks posed by stranger danger appear to be declining. Consequently, those who face the gravest risks are females who cannot completely trust the men they know.

HOW THE CRIMINAL JUSTICE SYSTEM HANDLES RAPE VICTIMS

Before public consciousness was raised by the antirape movement, complainants who courageously reported sex crimes frequently found themselves socially stigmatized. An old-fashioned notion of "Good girls don't get raped" prevailed, so those who did get raped must have done something to deserve their fate. Even if an unquestionably innocent victim was taken against her will, she was callously looked down upon as being "defiled" and "devalued" by the experience. Those who dared to press charges were often told that their cases were unwinnable, given the unreasonably stringent legal standards required for conviction.

The laws passed over the centuries and amended by judges' case-by-case decisions were not intended and never functioned to guarantee women's safety, freedom of movement, and peace of mind. The use of terms such as *fallen*, *ravaged*, and *despoiled* to describe rape victims betrayed antiquated attitudes of men toward girls and women: that they were the "property" of their fathers or husbands who lost "market value" and became "damaged goods" if they were "violated." Rape laws reflected and reinforced prevailing double standards regarding appropriate forms of sexual conduct and sex-based roles for females and males (LeGrande, 1973).

The account presented in Box 10.2 illustrates how the system routinely mistreated women who were raped in the "bad old days" before the victims' rights movement raised objections and brought about meaningful reforms. This fictional composite sketch illustrates everything that possibly could go wrong. It was compiled by the President's Task Force on Victims of Crime from testimony about real-life ordeals brought to their attention at the start of the 1980s. Because this worst-case scenario provides a virtual checklist of nearly all the possible problems, frustrations, and abuses that can arise, it can serve as a standard for comparison with current case handling to identify how much progress has been made and exactly what remains to be accomplished.

The narrative follows one woman's plight as her case is processed. The presidential task force pinpointed why victims find themselves pitted against the police, the prosecuting attorney working for the government, the defense lawyer acting on behalf of the accused, the judge presiding over the case, the jury sitting in judgment, and the parole board determining the convict's future. This excerpt accentuates the negative by emphasizing the mishandling of rape cases at every level because victims of sexual assaults were—and still are—the most mistreated of all those who seek help from the criminal justice system (see Box 10.2).

The account presented in Box 10.2 identified and dramatized all the antivictim practices and procedures that had accumulated within the criminal justice system over the centuries. One by one, they have been addressed by the antirape movement. Many policies and practices have been reformed over the past few decades, including the basic legal statutes that govern court procedures.

And yet 25 years after the President's Task Force issued recommendations for reform (based on this collection of horror stories), a coalition against sexual assault released a report that concluded that rape victims often still suffered mistreatment in New York City. The study, based on interviews with 65 male and female victims, determined that only one-third were asked whether they had a safe place to return to in the aftermath of the

B O X 10.2   The System's Shortcomings from a Victim's Point of View

The Crime

You are a 50-year-old woman living alone. You are asleep one night when suddenly you awaken to find a man standing over you with a knife at your throat. As you start to scream, he beats you and cuts you. He then rapes you. While you watch helplessly, he searches the house, taking your jewelry, other valuables, and money. He smashes furniture and windows in a display of senseless violence. His rampage ended, he rips out the telephone line, threatens you again, and disappears in the night.

At least you have survived. Terrified, you rush to the first lighted house on the block. While you wait for the police, you pray that your attacker was bluffing when he said he'd return if you called them. Finally, what you expect to be help arrives.

The police ask questions, take notes, dust for fingerprints, and take photographs. When you tell them you were raped, they take you to the hospital. Bleeding from cuts, your front teeth knocked out, bruised and in pain, you are told that your wounds are superficial, that rape itself is not considered an injury. Awaiting treatment, you sit alone for hours, suffering the stares of curious passersby. You feel dirty, bruised, disheveled, and abandoned. When your turn comes for examination, the intern seems irritated because he has been called out to treat you. While he treats you, he says that he hates to get involved in rape cases because he doesn't like going to court. He asks if you "knew the man you had sex with." The nurse says she wouldn't be out alone at this time of night. It seems pointless to explain that the attacker broke into your house and had a knife. An officer says you must go through this process, and then the hospital sends you a bill for the examination that the investigators insist upon. They give you a box filled with test tubes and swabs and envelopes and tell you to hold onto it. They'll run some tests if they ever catch your rapist.

Finally, you get home somehow, in a cab you paid for and wearing a hospital gown because they took your clothes as evidence. Everything that the attacker touched seems soiled. You're afraid to be in your house alone. The one place where you were always safe, at home, is a sanctuary no longer. You are afraid to remain, yet terrified to leave your home unprotected.

You didn't realize when you gave the police your name and address that it would be given to the press through police reports. Your friends call to say they saw this information in the paper, your picture on television. You haven't yet absorbed what's happened to you when you get calls from insurance companies and firms that sell security devices. But these calls pale in comparison to the threats that come from the defendant and his friends.

You're astonished to discover that your attacker has been arrested, yet while in custody he has free and unmonitored access to a phone. He can threaten you from jail. The judge orders him not to annoy you, but when the phone calls are brought to his attention, the judge does nothing.

At least you can be assured that the man who attacked you is in custody, or so you think. No one tells you that he is released on his promise to come to court. No one asks you if you've been threatened. The judge is never told that the defendant said he'd kill you if you told or that he'd get even if he went to jail. Horrified, you ask how he got out after what he did. You're told the judge can't consider whether he'll be dangerous, only whether he'll come back to court. He's been accused and convicted before, but he always came to court, so he must be released.

You learn only by accident that he's at large; this discovery comes when you turn a corner and confront him. He knows where you live. He's been there. Besides, your name and address were in the paper and in the reports he's seen. Now nowhere is safe. He watches you from across the street; he follows you on the bus. Will he come back in the night? What do you do? Give up your home? Lose your job? Assume a different name? Get your mail at the post office? Carry a weapon? Even if you wanted to, could you afford to do these things?

You try to return to normal. You don't want to talk about what happened, so you decide not to tell your co-workers. A few days go by and unexpectedly the police come to your place of work. They show their badges to the receptionist and ask to see you. They want you to look at some photographs, but they don't explain that to your co-workers. You try to explain later that you're the victim—not the accused.

The phone rings, and the police want you to come to a lineup. It may be 1:00 A.M. or in the middle of your work day, but you have to go; the suspect and his lawyer are waiting. It will not be the last time you are forced to conform your life to their convenience. You appear at the police station and the lineup begins. The suspect's lawyer sits next to you, but he does not watch the stage; he stares at you. It will not be the last time you must endure his scrutiny.

Charges Are Pressed Against a Defendant

You have lived through the crime and made it through the initial investigation. They've caught the man who harmed you, and he's been charged with armed burglary, robbery, and rape. Now he'll be tried. Now you expect justice.

You receive a subpoena for a preliminary hearing. No one tells you what it will involve, how long it will take, or how you should prepare. You assume that this is the only time you will have to appear. But you are only beginning your initiation in a system that will grind away at you for months, disrupt your life, affect your emotional stability, and certainly cost you money; it may cost you your job, and, for the duration, will prevent you from putting the crime behind you and reconstructing your life.

Before the hearing, a defense investigator comes to talk to you. When he contacts you, he says he's "investigating your case," and that he "works for the county." You assume, as he intends you to, that he's from the police or the prosecutor's office. Only after you give him a statement do you discover that he works for the man who attacked you.

This same investigator may visit your neighbors and coworkers, asking questions about you. He discusses the case with them, always giving the defendant's side. Suddenly, some of the people who know you seem to be taking a different view of what happened to you and why.

It's the day of the hearing. You've never been to court before, never spoken in public. You're very nervous. You rush to arrive at 8 A.M. to talk to a prosecutor you've never met. You wait in a hallway with a number of other witnesses. It's now 8:45. Court starts at 9:00. No one has spoken to you. Finally, a man sticks his head out a door, calls out your name, and asks, "Are you the one who was raped?" You're aware of the stares as you stand and suddenly realize that this is the prosecutor, the person you expect will represent your interests.

You speak to the prosecutor for only a few minutes. You ask to read the statement you gave to the police, but he says there isn't time. He asks you some questions that make you wonder if he's read it himself. He asks you other questions that make you wonder if he believes it.

The prosecutor tells you to sit on the bench outside the courtroom. Suddenly you see the man who raped you coming down the hall. No one has told you he would be here. He's with three friends. He points you out. They all laugh and jostle you a little as they pass. The defendant and two friends enter the courtroom; one friend sits on the bench across from you and stares. Suddenly, you feel abandoned, alone, afraid. Is this what it's like to come to court and seek justice?

You sit on the bench for an hour, then two. You don't see the prosecutor; he has disappeared into the courtroom. Finally, at noon he comes out and says, "Oh, you're still here? We continued that case to next month." You repeat this process many times before you actually testify at the preliminary hearing. Each time you go to court, you take leave from work, pay for parking, wait for hours, and finally are told to go home. No one ever asks if the new dates are convenient to you. You miss vacations and medical appointments. You use up sick leave and vacation days to make your court appearances. Your employer is losing his patience. Every time you are gone his business is disrupted. But you are fortunate. If you were new at your job, or worked part-time, or didn't have an understanding boss, you could lose your job. Many victims do.

The preliminary hearing was an event for which you were completely unprepared. You learn later that the defense is often harder on a victim at the preliminary hearing than during the trial. In a trial, the defense attorney cannot risk alienating the jury. At this hearing there is only the judge—and he certainly doesn't seem concerned about you. One of the first questions you are asked is where you live. You finally moved after your attack; you've seen the defendant and his friends, and you're terrified of having them know where you now live. When you explain that you'd be happy to give your old address the judge says he'll dismiss the case or hold you in contempt of court if you don't answer the question. The prosecutor says nothing. During your testimony, you are also compelled to say where you work, how you get there, and what your schedule is.

Hours later you are released from the stand after reliving your attack in public, in intimate detail. You have been made to feel completely powerless. As you sat facing a smirking defendant and as you described his threats, you were accused of lying and inviting the "encounter." You have cried in front of these uncaring strangers. As you leave no one thanks you. When you get back to work they ask what took you so long.

You are stunned when you later learn that the defendant also raped five others; one victim was an eight-year-old girl. During her testimony, she was asked to describe her attacker's anatomy. Spectators laughed when she said she did not understand the words being used. When she was asked to draw a picture of her attacker's genitalia, the girl fled from the courtroom and ran sobbing to her mother, who had been subpoenaed by the defense and had to wait outside. The youngster was forced to sit alone and recount, as you did, each minute of the attack. You know how difficult it was for you to speak of these things; you cannot imagine how it was for a child.

Now the case is scheduled for trial. Again there are delays. When you call and ask to speak with the prosecutor, you are told the case has been reassigned. You tell your story in detail to five different prosecutors before the case is tried.

(Continued)

BOX 10.2 Continued

Months go by and no one tells you what's happening. Periodically you are subpoenaed to appear. You leave your work, wait, and are finally told to go home. Continuances are granted because the courts are filled, one of the lawyers is on another case, and the judge has a meeting to attend or an early tennis match. You can't understand why they couldn't have discovered these problems before you came to court. When you ask if the next date could be set a week later so you can attend a family gathering out of state, you are told that the defendant has the right to a speedy trial. You stay home from the reunion and the case is continued. The defense attorney continues to call. Will you change your story? Don't you want to drop the charges?

Time passes and you hear nothing. Your property is not returned. You learn that there are dozens of defense motions that can be filed before the trial. If denied, many of them can be appealed. Each motion, each court date means a new possibility for delay. If the defendant is out of custody and fails to come to court, nothing can happen until he is reapprehended. If he is successful in avoiding recapture, the case may be so compromised by months or years of delay that a successful prosecution is impossible.

For as long as the case drags on, your life is on hold. You don't want to start a new assignment at work or move to a new city because you know that at any time the round of court appearances may begin again. The wounds of your attack will never heal as long as you know that you will be asked to relive those horrible moments.

No one tells you anything about the progress of the case. You want to be involved, consulted, and informed, but prosecutors often plea bargain without consulting victims.

You're afraid someone will let the defendant plead guilty to a lesser charge and be sentenced to probation. You meet another victim at court who tells you that she and her family were kidnapped and her children molested. Even though the prosecutor assured her that he would not accept a plea bargain, after talking with the attorneys in his chambers, the judge allowed the defendant to plead guilty as charged with the promise of a much-reduced sentence. You hope that this won't happen in your case.

The Trial

Finally the day of trial arrives. It has been 18 months since you were attacked. You've been trying for a week to prepare yourself. It is painful to dredge up the terror again, but you know that the outcome depends on you; the prosecutor has told you that the way you behave will make or break the case. You can't get too angry on the stand because then the jury might not like you. You can't break down and sob because then you will appear too emotional, possibly unstable. In addition to the tremendous pressure of having to relive the horrible details of the crime, you're expected to be an actress as well.

You go to court. The continuances are over; the jury has been selected. You sit in a waiting room with the defendant's family and friends. Again you feel threatened, vulnerable, and alone.

You expect the trial to be a search for the truth; you find that it is a performance orchestrated by lawyers and the judge, with the jury hearing only half the facts. The defendant was found with your watch in his pocket. The judge has suppressed this evidence because the officer who arrested him didn't have a warrant.

---

attack, less than half were told about opportunities for counseling, and only half were informed about the availability of a vaccine to reduce the risks of contracting HIV/AIDS (Boyle, 2007). The report included a real-life experience that bore a disturbing resemblance to the worst-case scenario compiled by the President's Task Force decades ago:

> An intruder creeps into a 40-year-old librarian's bedroom and rapes her. She runs to a neighbor's home, wearing nothing but an overcoat. When the police arrive, they do not immediately race next door to investigate the crime scene. Eventually, she is transported to a hospital, but is left alone in a room because no victim's advocate is on duty. Two male detectives ask her to recount the series of events in great detail three times. After being tested for traces of DNA, she is totally naked because her coat was taken as evidence. When she finally is allowed to leave she has to track down a male orderly to get something to wear, and has to plead with the hospital's staff to arrange for a taxicab to take her home. (Boyle, 2007)

The dramatization in Box 10.2 of everything that can go wrong in the aftermath of a rape and during the case's processing by the criminal justice system can be useful to antirape activists today.

Your character is an open subject of discussion and innuendo. The defense is allowed to question you on incidents going back to your childhood. The jury is never told that the defendant has two prior convictions for the same offense and has been to prison three times for other crimes. You sought help from a counselor to deal with the shattering effect of this crime on your life. You told him about your intimate fears and feelings. Now he has been called by the defense and his notes and records have been subpoenaed.

You are on the stand for hours. The defense does its best to make you appear a liar, a seductress, or both. You know you cannot relax for a moment. Don't be embarrassed when everyone seems angry because you do not understand. Think ahead. Be responsive. Don't volunteer. Don't get tired.

Finally, you are finished with this part of the nightmare. You would like to sit and listen to the rest of the trial but you cannot. You're a witness and must wait outside. The jury will decide the outcome of one of the major events of your life. You cannot hear the testimony that will guide their judgment.

The verdict is guilty. You now look to the judge to impose a just sentence.

The Sentence

You expect the sentence to reflect how terrible the crime was. You ask the prosecutor how this decision is reached and are told that once a defendant is convicted he is interviewed at length by a probation officer. He gives his side of the story, which may be blatantly false in light of the proven facts. A report that delves into his upbringing, family relationships, education, physical and mental health, and employment and conviction history is prepared. The officer will often speak to the defendant's relatives and friends. Some judges will send the defendant to a facility where a complete psychiatric and sociological work-up is prepared. You're amazed that no one will ever ask you about the crime, or the effect it has had on you and your family. You took the defendant's blows, heard his threats, and listened to him brag that he'd "beat the rap" or "con the judge." No one ever hears of these things. They never give you a chance to tell them.

At sentencing, the judge hears from the defendant, his lawyer, his mother, his minister, and his friends. You learn by chance what day the hearing is. When you do attend, the defense attorney says you're vengeful, and it's apparent that you overreacted to being raped and robbed because you chose to come and see the sentencing. You ask permission to address the judge and are told that you are not allowed to do so.

The judge sentences your attacker to three years in prison, less than one year for every hour he kept you in pain and terror. That seems very lenient to you. Only later do you discover that he'll probably serve less than half of his actual sentence in prison because of good-time and work-time credits that are given to him immediately. The man who broke into your home, threatened to slit your throat with a knife, and raped, beat, and robbed you will be out of custody in less than 18 months. You are not told when he will actually be released, and you are not allowed to attend the parole release hearing anyway.

SOURCE: Excerpted from the report of the President's Task Force on Victims of Crime, 1982, pp. 3–11.

Box 10.2 provides a set of benchmarks or even a checklist that can be used to evaluate how much progress has been made in any given jurisdiction, and how much more work remains to be accomplished in the quest for justice.

The Controversy over Unfounded Accusations

Rape always has been in a class by itself in one peculiar way: The complainant immediately confronts a credibility issue. For hundreds of years, it has been asserted that spiteful women "cry rape" to get revenge against men who spurned them. Deep concerns about the danger of false accusations against innocent men led to the insertion into the legal system of special safeguards to protect male defendants—which female accusers had to surmount. Knowingly and maliciously filing a false complaint with the police and testifying dishonestly are punishable acts no matter what the crime, but fears about maliciously concocted charges arise almost automatically in rape cases (see MacDonald and Michaud, 1995; and Lisak et al., 2010).

Two errors are possible: One type is honest mistakes in which victims accidentally misidentify assailants and innocent men get arrested, put on trial—and if the mistake is not caught—even convicted and imprisoned. The other type of error is inexcusable: knowingly lodging a false complaint against an innocent male.

A complainant acting in good faith may identify the wrong person—especially a complete stranger—as the perpetrator (this would not be a problem in acquaintance and date rapes). DNA tests make it possible to scientifically eliminate some male suspects and to rectify preexisting miscarriages of justice by casting aside convictions and freeing wrongfully convicted men from their prison cells (for example, see Thompson-Cannino and Cotton, 2010). By 2013, about 220 men had their rape convictions overturned based on an analysis of DNA evidence (National Registry of Exonerations, 2014).

Besides the possibility of honest mistakes, fraudulent accusations are another area of legitimate concern. A girl or woman could attempt to deceive authorities by lodging a fake charge against an innocent boy or man for one of many ulterior purposes: perhaps to arouse sympathy or to gain attention; to punish a former lover; to provide a "don't blame me" explanation for contracting an embarrassing venereal disease or for becoming pregnant as well as for seeking medical treatment for these conditions; to justify a suspicious absence to a parent or a significant other; or to hide the truth for another reason (see Dedel, 2011).

Widely held negative stereotypes and suspicions about manipulative or vengeful women fuel these fears. Highly publicized real-life examples give renewed life to traditional doubts that cast a cloud of suspicion over the credibility of all genuine victims who demand to be taken seriously. False accusations of sexual assault lodged by dishonest complainants posing as victims also send shock waves within the criminal justice process and threaten to undermine much of the progress made by the antirape movement. Well-known cases like these three are often cited to justify the skepticism that complainants routinely encounter in press coverage, police stations, prosecutors' offices, and courtrooms:

A 22-year-old woman gets drunk and ditches her girlfriends to get into a car with a 27-year-old man she just met. When she returns they are so furious with her that they beat her, so to gain their sympathy she claims that he raped her at knifepoint. She testifies that she is "110 percent sure" before a grand jury and at a trial against the man, who has a rap sheet of violent assaults. He is convicted and serves nearly four years before she confesses to a priest, submits to a DNA test that clears him, and recants her perjured testimony. The falsely imprisoned man is released and the judge sentences her to three years in prison for framing him. "I can honestly tell you that to this date I have no idea how I got myself into this mess … I want him to know I will carry this guilt for the rest of my life," she says, pleading for mercy. (Italiano, 2010)

● ● ●

A 15-year-old black girl is discovered in an apparent state of shock curled up in a plastic garbage bag, smeared with feces and with racial slurs scrawled on her body. She does not say much to police officers or doctors but according to her relatives and her advisors, she had been kidnapped and repeatedly raped for several days by four white men who appeared to have law enforcement affiliations. Her explosive charges divide the public along racial lines. A special grand jury is impaneled by the state's attorney general to look into the inflammatory accusations and to explore the possibility of an official cover-up. It concludes that there is insufficient evidence to charge anyone with a crime. Months later, the girl's boyfriend claims that she told him that she and her mother made up the whole story so that her violence-prone stepfather (who served time for killing his first wife) would not beat her for staying out late. Unfortunately, an aunt who believed the story contacted the news media, which sensationalized the concocted allegations into headlines for months. Years later, one of the maligned men, an assistant district attorney, sues the supposed victim and her advisors in civil court for defamation of character and wins a monetary judgment against them; her advisor becomes the host of a television talk show but her lawyer is disbarred; she goes to college, undergoes a religious conversion, changes her name, and moves to a small town. Her mother still insists a rape took place and urges the governor to reopen the case. Unapologetic, the hoaxer very slowly pays off the judgment through garnisheed wages to the former prosecutor she slandered. (Payne, 1989; Taibbi and Sims-Phillips, 1989; Schaye, 1998; Block, 2007; and Gartland, 2013)

■■■

Two women are hired as strippers to perform at a party for the young men of a university lacrosse team. One of the dancers says she was hustled into a bathroom and sexually assaulted by three players. Three members of the team are arrested and indicted for rape, sexual offense, and kidnapping, even though highly sensitive genetic tests do not reveal any DNA trace evidence from them, and she is unable to identify her attackers from team pictures. The university president cancels the remainder of the lacrosse season, the coach resigns, and the three players are suspended pending a trial. The highly publicized case touches off scathing commentaries about the sense of entitlement privileged young white men feel toward exploiting poor young black women. But then the case unravels, the mentally troubled exotic dancer becomes uncertain about what really happened, and the veteran prosecutor who had just been reelected resigns in disgrace and is disbarred. The young men who were falsely accused, publicly humiliated, and traumatized by the prospects of 30-year sentences file lawsuits against the former prosecutor, the police department, the DNA lab, and the city, charging them with premeditated police, prosecutorial, and scientific misconduct. Five years later, the woman who lodged the false accusations graduates from college and writes a memoir, but then is arrested twice for armed attacks against two different boyfriends. (Brooks, 2006a; Nizza, 2007; Wilson, 2007; and Rodriguez, 2011)

The 1931 "Scottsboro Boys" case stands out in history as the most notorious example of a false accusation of rape for a malicious purpose. The apparently trumped-up charges—that eight young black men gang-raped two white women riding with young white men in a boxcar of a freight train—were lodged for political reasons. In the

Old South, white women were often pressured by white men to accuse black men of rape so that the alleged suffering of the victims could be seized upon to justify the execution or lynching of the accused individuals, and by extension to legitimize the segregation and repression of all black men (Sagarin, 1975). The controversy surrounding the way the defendants in this case of Southern "racial justice" were "railroaded in a kangaroo court" without lawyers and sentenced to die led to a Supreme Court decision (*Powell v. Alabama*, 1932). This landmark ruling established the right of indigent people accused of capital crimes to be represented by competent counsel provided by the government at no cost (later decisions extended this right to all defendants).

The task confronting detectives and prosecutors is to weed out the very small number of false claims (about a consensual act that is later characterized as forced, or about a totally fabricated incident that never took place) from the overwhelming majority of genuine charges. The dishonesty of a few does not justify routinely mistreating all complainants as possible liars (Fairstein, 1993). This issue of victim credibility can become very polarized and emotional when those who believe in "lying women" debate those who trust that "women wouldn't lie about a matter as serious as this." The task for criminologists and victimologists is to determine how often completely baseless charges are lodged and whether false accusations really are more of a problem in rape cases than in other crimes such as robberies or car thefts (see MacDonald and Michaud, 1995).

From the outset, careless phrasing and imprecise language and terminology can cause great confusion. What is the exact definition of a false allegation? Policies adopted by law enforcement agencies state that a determination of whether or not a complaint is false—meaning that no crime was committed or even attempted—can be made only after a thorough investigation. A basis for concluding that a sexual assault never took place could include physical evidence or statements from credible witnesses that clearly contradict what the complainant asserts. But unearthing evidence that undermines the accuser's credibility (for example, that she delayed filing a complaint; or gives inconsistent accounts of events; or changes her mind and stops cooperating; or leaves out embarrassing details like being intoxicated) does not definitively mean that the incident never happened. If an investigation fails to dig up solid evidence that a sexual assault occurred, then the charge is to be classified as "unsubstantiated" but that is not the same as "unfounded" or "deliberately false" (see Lisak et. al, 2010).

Given these complications, reliable statistics about the percentage of complaints that turn out baseless are hard to find. Social workers at a hospital and a police sex crime unit estimated their false complaint rates to be less than 2 percent (Bode, 1978). The prevalence of false allegations ranges from 2 percent to 10 percent of all charges, according to a review of previous studies plus an analysis of university records over a 10-year period (Lisak et al., 2010). But a controversial study concluded that 40 percent of more than 100 complaints turned out false—the woman recanted her original charges when told that she faced a stiff fine and a jail sentence—according to records from 1978 to 1987 of a police department in a small Midwestern city (Kanin, 1994). But some victims under intense pressures might recant charges that actually are true (see McArdle, 2014).

The FBI's *UCR* reported that in 1966, after a preliminary investigation, police forces across the country had declared 20 percent of all rape complaints unfounded. Ten years later, the *UCR* stated that 19 percent had been closed as unfounded. The *UCRs* for 1996 and 1997 stated that about 8 percent of all rape complaints were classified as unfounded by local police departments, compared to 2 percent of complaints about other index crimes. No such figures have appeared in the *UCRs* since then. Note that the designation *unfounded* is not synonymous with "patently false." Some cases in this category were deemed unsubstantiated after an inconclusive investigation or unprovable in court in the opinion of detectives. But that doesn't mean the allegations were baseless or that accusers were deliberately committing

perjury or imagining situations that didn't really happen (Archambault, 2005).

Police departments that consider too many sexual assault complaints to be unfounded or untrue can find themselves under scrutiny. For example, in Baltimore, reported rapes tumbled so dramatically that investigative reporters looked into the matter and discovered that for about 10 years official statistics were suspiciously low. It appears that officers often refused to accept complaints at crime scenes, or that detectives asked such hostile and confrontational questions that complainants stopped cooperating. Because the sex crime unit declared about one-third of all complaints to be unfounded each year, it became the target of an investigation (Fenton, 2010).

In the past, detectives often presumed that false cries of forcible rape were the rule and not the exception. They were especially suspicious if the woman did not report the attack immediately or didn't seem upset by her injuries. Her credibility was questioned if she was either extremely vague about the details or unusually precise, or was reluctant to describe the assailant or the exact location. Their disbelief of her story escalated if she was intoxicated at the time, had filed complaints before, or had a history of emotional problems (Jordan, 2004; and Archambault, 2005).

Consequently, many police departments routinely administered lie detector tests to check a complainant's credibility. Unfortunately, submitting to the questionable reliability of a polygraph looms as an added indignity and served as a further deterrent to reporting crimes and pressing charges. Groups in the antirape movement—who are convinced the problem of false allegations is greatly exaggerated—went to court to get injunctions against the practice. The President's Task Force on Victims of Crime (1982) recommended that procedures that reflected automatic distrust of complainants be abandoned, and a number of states have specifically outlawed polygraph testing of complainants. The Violence Against Women Act reauthorization in 2005 stipulated that subjecting rape complainants to polygraph testing could jeopardize a department's eligibility for federal aid.

However, reports surface periodically that police departments still administer polygraphs and other truth verification tests such as computerized voice stress analyzers to certain categories of sexual assault victims ("Report exposes lie detector tests…," 2003; see also Lisak et al., 2010).

Because of the credibility issue, very stringent standards of proof were crafted into rape laws to make it particularly difficult to secure convictions. The men who wrote the laws and administered the legal system considered these difficult-to-surmount hurdles to be safeguards against miscarriages of justice. But from the standpoint of a genuinely innocent victim, the safeguards posed major obstacles that discouraged and thwarted her pursuit of justice. From a feminist perspective, truth tests represented a clear case of institutionalized discrimination against female complainants. The exceptionally high standards of proof took several forms: demands for evidence that the accuser did not willingly consent to engage in sex, a requirement that her testimony be corroborated (backed up independently), and a tradition that she undergo a particularly vigorous cross-examination by a defense attorney during the trial. After both sides rested their case, a judge often delivered a "cautionary instruction" to the jurors before they began their deliberations, paraphrasing an English jurist's warnings from 1671 that it is easy to accuse a man of rape but hard to prove the charge, but it is even harder for an innocent man to defend himself and clear his name.

The Accuser Versus the Accused

Rape prosecutions directly pit the rights of the accused male against the rights of the female complainant. He has the Sixth Amendment right to wage a vigorous defense through his attorney. She has a right to be taken seriously and treated with respect on and off the witness stand, according to recent victims' rights legislation and rewritten rape laws. Honoring the rights of both parties requires a delicate balancing act that has yet to be resolved.

Advocates for rape victims argue that when the rights of one party are pitted against the other, her needs trump his. For example, a victim can contract HIV/AIDS from an assailant, especially if the intrusion is violent and bloody. Therefore, state laws mandating that accused rapists must quickly undergo HIV testing would seem to be "pro-victim" at the expense of the privacy of males who are suspects but not yet indicted or convicted. If court-ordered testing determines that he is not infected, this news might allay some of her fears.

However, experts insist that a genuinely "pro-victim" approach would not necessarily involve a loss of the arrested person's privacy rights. What if he is actually within the window period during which a person recently infected with the virus tests negative? What if he is not the assailant? What if no one is quickly apprehended? A safer course of action would be to guarantee that victims of sexual assaults be informed immediately about the availability of a treatment called postexposure prophylaxis—which involves taking retroviral medications for 28 days—and be entitled to this urgent care at no cost (Hofmann, 2007). Criminal transmission of the AIDS virus is a separate punishable offense, but it also can be the reason for sentencing an attacker who knows he is infected more harshly (Myers and Jacobo, 2006).

Criminal court is the arena where the two parties will be pitted against each other. The accused man can pursue one of several possible defense strategies. The first is to argue that the complaining witness has made a terrible but honest error, picking an innocent man out of a lineup (the "mistaken identity" defense). The second is to deny that he engaged in sexual acts with her (the "it-never-happened" defense). This requires a direct attack on the alleged victim's credibility and motivation by charging that she made up the false story for some deceptive reason. The third defense is to concede that he had sexual intercourse with her but that she agreed at the time; afterward, she changed her mind, considered it a rape, and had him arrested (the "consent" defense) (see Toobin, 2003).

Built-in antivictim biases that shaped the way cases were investigated and prosecuted were most evident in the corroboration rule, the resistance requirement, and the practice of inquiring into the complainant's sexual history in order to discredit her testimony. However, as public alarm grew about an apparent upsurge in sexual violence, legislators became more willing to change sexist practices that reflected the moralistic assumptions of the distant past. Beginning with Minnesota and Michigan in 1974, statutes were rewritten state by state as the analysis put forward by feminists gained acceptance and as more women became lawyers and legislators and reformed the legal system from within as well as pressuring it from without (Largen, 1987).

The issue of consent is central to any rape complaint because willingness or at least voluntary compliance is what distinguishes engaging in sexual relations from being sexually assaulted. The injured party must convince the police, the prosecution, and ultimately a jury that she did not agree freely to participate in sex acts but was forced to submit by her attacker. The burden of proof shifts to the woman, who must present a compelling account that she was violated against her will. The prosecution must establish beyond a reasonable doubt that she was forced—hit, knocked down, pinned down, overpowered, or threatened with serious bodily harm. The prosecution must also show that she is a woman of integrity and good character, who has no motive to distort the truth and ought to be believed. To stir up reasonable doubts, the defense will pursue a strategy of impeaching her credibility by attacking her virtue. The goal is to sow the seeds of doubt among jurors by asserting that she consented at the time but later regretted her decision and then lodged false charges. To undermine her credibility as the key prosecution witness, the defense attorney often pursues a "nuts and sluts" strategy, portraying her as a mentally unstable liar and/or a sexually promiscuous, willing partner to many others.

To counter such personal attacks, the prosecution must argue that the defense attorney is turning the tables and is putting the victim on trial and humiliating her once again, this time in front of the jury. From the complainant's point of view, some reasonable limits should be placed on the defense's cross-examination so it doesn't become a degrading spectacle. But from the defendant's point of view, it is only fair that she answer probing questions about her sexual involvements in the past and her mental health. Only then can he have a fighting chance to clear his name and expose the falseness of her charges against him in this credibility contest (see Estrich, 1993b; and Vachss, 1993).

Unwanted Publicity and Negative Media Portrayals

A high-profile case is often tried in the court of public opinion, based on selective leaks of "evidence"presented in media accounts, long before the accused and the accuser actually appear before a judge (see Chancer, 2005). Fears about intrusive press coverage, unwanted publicity, and victim blaming discourage some people who were sexually assaulted from turning to the criminal justice system for help.

Since the middle of the 1800s, newspapers have regularly featured stories about violent crimes, but they rarely covered rapes until the two trials of the Scottsboro Boys in the 1930s. For a number of years, the only cases that aroused media interest were those that resulted in lynchings, when a black man accused of raping a white woman was murdered by a white mob. To this day, mainstream media outlets remain preoccupied with the rape of white women, continue to sensationalize interracial cases involving a black defendant, and rarely devote comparable attention to sexual assaults committed against black women. Journalists tend to stereotype women as either "virgins" (pure and innocent who are ravaged by bestial males) or "vamps" (wanton and sexually provocative temptresses who arouse male lust). She is likely to be portrayed as a vamp if the defendant is an acquaintance and no weapon was brandished; if they are both from the same ethnic group and social class; and if she is young, attractive, and doesn't live with her family. By assigning blame to one party or the other, crime reporters improperly take on the responsibilities of judges and juries, according to a content analysis of the way the news media covered several highly publicized rapes (Benedict, 1992).

The following case about an inter-racial encounter became a media spectacle that illustrated the interplay of these factors:

A 19-year-old college student working in a hotel meets a famous 24-year-old married professional basketball player and willingly goes to his room. She claims that after they flirted and kissed, the athlete used force to bend her over and to make her submit to sex acts. She has him arrested for felony sexual assault. The basketball player reluctantly concedes the acts took place but insists they were consensual. News accounts do not mention the accuser's name. But the press coverage describes her appearance, reveals her e-mail address, discloses her hometown and the college she attends, and recounts salacious stories about her sex life told by people describing themselves as her friends. After a while, her name and picture circulate on the Internet. She is vilified by his fans, and receives threats that lead to arrests. The prosecution's case falls apart when the young woman declares she will not testify because she anticipates that many of the distortions that were leaked will be used to discredit her during cross-examination. Her civil lawsuit is settled amid threats from both sides about disclosing damaging information—about her medical, psychological, and sexual history, and about his sexual past. The famous athlete offers a public apology to his accuser, acknowledging that he understood how she might have had a different interpretation of their encounter. (Zernike, 2003; Johnson, 2005; and Franiuk et al., 2008)

When a girl or woman lodges charges of sexual assault against a boy or man, like any other complainant of any other crime, her name appears in police files and court documents. The question then arises as to whether her identity should be revealed in media accounts. Laws prohibit the press from publishing the name of the victim of a sex crime in a number of states. Elsewhere, most newspapers, magazines, and radio and television stations have adopted a policy of self-restraint that shields the injured person from unwanted public exposure.

The arguments in favor of keeping the complainant's name out of the media center on the potential for inflicting additional suffering on a person who is already hurt and on the chilling effect the unwanted publicity surrounding her case will have on other victims who are considering going to the authorities for help. The longstanding ethical norm of concealing a complainant's name developed from a realization that rapes are not like other crimes. Victims are more likely to be emotionally fragile and afflicted by posttraumatic stress, nervous breakdowns, and suicidal impulses. Publicly identified rape victims have always been discredited, stigmatized, scandalized, mocked, scorned, and even harassed. Revealing a complainant's name is a humiliating second violation that is likely to prolong her suffering. Furthermore, other rape victims, who see how powerless she was to prevent her name and intimate details about her life from being circulated, might be deterred from going to the police. Media self-censorship is a way to respect a victim's privacy rights unless she chooses to go public and speak out about the attack (Pollitt, 1991; and Young, 1991).

Arguments in favor of disclosing victims' names appeal to the principles of the public's right to know, the defendant's right to a fair trial, and the news media's right to be free from censorship. Media outlets have an obligation to disseminate all relevant and newsworthy facts. Accusations from anonymous sources are contrary to American jurisprudence. The accused, who must be presumed innocent unless proven guilty, endures humiliation from the publicity surrounding the arrest. The accuser's name should be revealed as well to deter untrue allegations. Potential witnesses with knowledge about her credibility might come forward with information about her background and character that could aid in the defense of a falsely accused man. Finally, shielding complainants from exposure implies that being forced to submit to a sexual act is a shameful, "dirty secret," when it actually should not be a cause of public humiliation. In the long run, routinely giving faceless victims a human identity might diminish the stigma that still surrounds being raped (see Dershowitz, 1988; Cohen, 1991; and Kantrowitz, Starr, and Friday, 1991).

Rape Shield Laws

During the mid-1970s to the mid-1980s, the anti-rape movement successfully convinced legislatures in almost every state to pass laws prohibiting improper cross-examinations. Generally, **shield laws** stipulate that the defense cannot introduce evidence about an accuser's past sexual conduct unless the woman has been convicted of prostitution, has had consensual sex before with the defendant, or has an obvious incentive to lie. Procedural guidelines provide for a hearing to be held in the absence of the jury, spectators, and the press. The aim is to permit the judge to determine whether the defense counsel's allegations about the woman's past are relevant and should be aired in open court.

Staunch supporters of shield laws want more restrictions placed on the ability of defense attorneys to assassinate the complainant's character as a way of impeaching her credibility. They cite several justifications: to encourage victims to go to the authorities for help by assuring them their privacy will be respected; to spare complainants the embarrassment of having intimate details of their sex lives made public and used against them in court; to dispel the fallacy that "if she consented in the past she probably consented this time, too"; and to prevent juries from being distracted by allegations about the complainant's past affairs when they should be focusing on the issue of the defendant's use of force.

Critics of shield laws want fewer restrictions on the line of questioning a defense attorney can pursue. Limitations impair the ability of the accused to confront his accuser effectively, and therefore to have a fair trial on a "level playing field" (Stark and Goldstein, 1985; Austern, 1987; and Lewin, 1992). Higher court decisions generally have upheld shield laws, concluding that most inquiries into an accuser's reputation for chastity have little relevance for determining consent. Furthermore, shield laws may not actually be working to protect the privacy concerns of rape victims. During trials, prosecutors may not object strenuously enough about what they consider irrelevant questions by defense attorneys that "merely" damage their clients' reputations, and judges

may err on the side of the defendants in order to prevent subsequent convictions from being overturned on appeal (Spohn and Horney, 1992).

When complainants turn to detectives and prosecutors for guidance, understandably they often ask how many people they will have to tell their account to, and whether their identities will be revealed in media coverage and court proceedings. Fears that extremely personal matters might be made public surely are heightened by cases like this one:

> *A young woman accuses two police officers of taking advantage of her after they brought her back to her apartment because she was too drunk to return home on her own. At the rape trial of the two officers, in a courtroom packed with over 100 people, she is compelled to confirm that she knows how it feels to be penetrated in one manner rather than another; a forensic evidence expert testifies that traces of three other men were found in her bed; and a close-up picture of her cervix is projected on a screen while the dueling attorneys debate the causes of redness. The officers are acquitted of rape but convicted of official misconduct misdemeanors, and are fired from the police department. The accuser files a lawsuit against the city and the officers for $57 million (Eligon and Baker, 2011a, 2011b).*

Issues Surrounding Force and Resistance

In the not-so-distant past, in order to convict a rapist, a woman had to convince a jury that she forcefully resisted to her utmost and ceased struggling only because she feared she would be killed or seriously injured. The justification cited for requiring such proof of fierce resistance was that signs of a struggle indicated the victim's state of mind (unwillingness) and refuted the defendant's claims that he reasonably believed his partner was feigning reluctance and was agreeing to engage in sex. Most state laws no longer require that the woman who wants to press charges must prove that she risked her life to fend off her attacker. A **reasonableness standard** stipulates that the degree of resistance that expresses lack of consent can depend on the circumstances. A strong verbal statement or an unambiguous physical act is sufficient to show lack of consent in the face of overwhelming force or an intimidating weapon. The woman does not have to fight back, scream, or try to flee. Evidence that the accused possessed a weapon or that the complainant was physically injured also is sufficient to establish nonconsent (Robin, 1977; Stark and Goldstein, 1985; and Austern, 1987).

Although they may be emotionally devastated, most females who were sexually assaulted were not so severely injured that they needed to seek some type of treatment for their wounds. However, a disturbing trend was detected: A little over 25 percent sought medical care during the period 1994–1998, but 35 percent needed to see a doctor from 2005 to 2010, according to a study of *NCVS* findings (Planty and Langton, 2013).

How a victim reacts during the sexual assault can profoundly influence the outcome in terms of her injuries. Her behavior—either submission or resistance—affects the attacker's decisions whether to try to complete the act and about how much force to use to subdue her. Most assailants were unarmed: Only about 10 percent had a gun, knife, or other weapon, according to an analysis of *NCVS* findings from 2005 to 2010 (Planty and Langton, 2013). (Roughly two decades earlier, about 20 percent of all assailants had guns, knives, or other sharp instruments, according to an analysis of *NCVS* data from 1987 until 1992 [Bachman, 1994].)

Most women who took some type of self-protective action, such as yelling for help or fighting back, told survey interviewers that they believed it helped their situation (61 percent) rather than made it worse (17 percent) (Bachman, 1994). Women who resisted improved their chances of thwarting the rapists' aims of completing the act, but unfortunately they also increased their risks of suffering a physical injury. One-third of the nonresisting victims were wounded in addition to being sexually assaulted. In contrast, two-thirds of victims who applied self-defense measures were physically hurt—bruised, cut, scratched, even stabbed or shot—according to a study of *NCVS* data from the late 1970s (McDermott, 1979).

Studies assessing the relative effectiveness of various responses have generated mixed, confusing, and perhaps impractical recommendations. It is impossible to predict the outcome of a particular assault, given the complex web of factors involving the offender, his intended victim, and their situation at that moment. One study of 125 victim's responses concluded that the best strategy turned out to be a **dual verbal defense** of calling out for help while simultaneously attempting to reason with, plead with, or threaten the attacker. Nearly all of the women who physically resisted their assailants reported that their actions made the men angrier, more vicious, and more violent (Cohen, 1984).

But at least one factor in the equation has changed to the advantage of those under attack. Whether or not fiercely resisting "within reason" is the best strategy under all circumstances, it is no longer required to justify an arrest and prosecution.

The apparent acquiescence of some victims can be readily explained. The primary reaction of nearly all intended targets is to fear for their lives, according to interviews conducted at a hospital emergency room (Burgess and Holmstrom, 1974). Therefore, some females are simply immobilized by terror, shock, and disbelief. Faced with the prospect of death or severe physical injury, many conclude that their only way out is to strike a bargain or work out a tacit understanding with the attacker and trade submission for survival (that is, to endure sexual violation in return for some sort of pledge that they won't be killed, savagely beaten, or cruelly disfigured). There is, of course, no guarantee that compliance will minimize physical injury. Rapists do not have to keep their promises (Brownmiller, 1975).

The Need for Corroboration

In the past, one aspect of the law in most states that made rape charges very difficult to prove beyond a reasonable doubt was the **corroboration** requirement, which demanded that the prosecution discover independent evidence to back up the key elements of the complainant's account. Derived hundreds of years ago from the evolution of English common law, the corroboration requirement assumed that serious charges carrying dire consequences were not credible without some other substantiation. The belief that the woman's word alone is not enough to secure a conviction in court is based on several legitimate concerns: that the male is entitled to the presumption of innocence, that certain females might somehow gain something by committing perjury, that defendants charged with rape are immediately—and possibly permanently—stigmatized even if they are later acquitted of all charges, and that conviction carries very severe penalties including, until the 1970s, execution.

Corroboration could take the form of obvious physical injuries; medical and forensic evidence gathered by a doctor; torn clothing; other signs of a struggle; or the testimony of an eyewitness or a third party such as a police officer, family member, or friend who had been promptly told about the assault. But the corroboration requirement was criticized as being patently unfair for putting those who endured sexual assaults in the unique position, compared to complainants about other kinds of assaults, of being automatically distrusted without additional "real proof." To strike a balance, most state laws have been reformed and no longer require corroboration unless the victim is a minor, was previously intimate with the accused, did not promptly report the crime to the authorities, or provides a version of events that is inherently improbable and self-contradictory (Robin, 1977; Stark and Goldstein, 1985; and Austern, 1987).

Rape Victims and the Police: Reporting Rates and Solution Rates

In order for a crime to be solved and processed by the justice system, it must first be brought to the attention of the police. But during most years, less than half of all rapes are not reported, according to the annual findings from the *NCVS*. The highest reporting rates were recorded in 2002 and 2003, at 55 percent. The lowest rates, a mere 25 percent or so, were discovered by the *NCVS* in 1995, 1997,

1999, 2009, and 2011. The reporting rate was 28 percent in 2012 and 35 percent in 2013. In sum, over the years, most of the teenage girls and women who told the *NCVS* about sexual assaults never informed the police (BJS Victimization Analysis Tool, 2014). Furthermore, no sustained improvement toward higher rates of reporting can be discerned from the annual *NCVS* surveys (refer back to Table 6.1). Despite many public relations campaigns to encourage victims to come forward (such as circulating posters and setting up special hotline numbers) and several reforms (such as safeguarding a woman's privacy by not publicly identifying her and providing intermediaries and advocates at rape crisis centers at hospitals and on college campuses to accompany complainants), the problem of nonreporting persists.

Girls and women told *NCVS* interviewers that they did not report sexual assaults to the authorities because of these reasons: They lacked proof that they were violated against their will; they considered the incident to be a private or personal matter not serious enough to bring to court; they are not sure the perpetrator intended to harm them; they are too embarrassed or ashamed to reveal what happened to them; they fear they will be stigmatized because of widely held victim-blaming rape myths; they are afraid of reprisals from the assailant; and they anticipate a "second wound" if they are demeaned, belittled, or entirely disbelieved by people who are supposed to assist and support them. Some might also believe the violation was partly their fault or feel compromised if they were engaged in wrongdoing, such as underage drinking, drug taking, or prostitution. If they tell anyone, that individual is more likely to be a friend rather than an authority figure, family member, or lover. Many specifically did not want their family or other people to know about what happened to them (see Fisher, Daigle, and Cullen, 2008; Brody, 2011; and Cohn et al., 2013).

Women who report offenses to the police most often say that they do so to be rescued from an assailant, to prevent the rapist from harming them again or from attacking someone else, and to get him in trouble so that he will be punished.

Women are more likely to go to the authorities if the perpetrator used a weapon, if they are physically wounded and require medical care for their injuries, if they actively resisted and put up a struggle, and if they were forced to endure a particularly vicious and depraved assault (Dedel, 2011). Surprisingly, whether or not the offender was a complete stranger, an acquaintance, or an intimate does not seem to affect the decision whether to report the crime, according to *NCVS* findings.

The next question to be answered with the help of data is, "How successful are the police in solving the sexual assaults reported to them?" Rape clearance rates for police departments across the nation show a disturbing decline over the past few decades, according to the FBI's *UCRs*. The percentage of reported rapes that were cleared by an arrest hit an all-time low of 40 percent in 2010 and remained stuck at that unsatisfactory level in 2013 (refer back to Table 6.3). This lack of progress is surprising and disappointing, considering that increasing numbers of easily "solved" acquaintance rape cases (in which the suspect's identity and whereabouts are known) presumably are being brought to the attention of the local authorities as the stigma diminishes (see Kanin, 1984; and Estrich, 1986).

When low reporting rates are combined with low solution rates, an even more discouraging statistic emerges. Only about 12 percent of all the sexual assaults and rapes disclosed to the *NCVS* between 2005 and 2010 resulted in an arrest at the scene of the crime or after a follow-up investigation (Planty and Langton, 2013).

To prevent victims from being deterred from pressing charges by the prospect of insensitive handling, some police departments have set up sex crimes squads or special victims units staffed with specially trained female detectives. Nearly 90 percent of all departments have gone even further and participate in collaborative programs known as **sexual assault response teams**. These SARTs coordinate the efforts of the detectives, the local prosecutor's office, nurse examiners who collect forensic evidence, and victim advocates; however, sometimes they don't work as effectively as they should (PERF, 2012).

Although acquaintance rape cases are easily "solved" because the accused person is known to the accuser, convictions are more difficult to secure than in cases of stranger rapes. Attrition rates for acquaintance rape cases are substantially higher. Victims are more inclined to ask that charges be dropped. Also, prosecutors are less willing to press forward because they fear the jury will find "reasonable doubts" about her insistence that she did not consent, and therefore will not convict the defendant (LaFree, 1989; Mansnerus, 1989; and Bachman, 1998). This problem has been documented by detailed data from the FBI's NIBRS reporting system, which shows that of the mere 35 percent of all rape cases "solved" by an arrest in 2011, the case was closed and charges were dropped in nearly 15 percent of them because the victim refused to cooperate further; and were dismissed in about 25 percent of them because prosecutors declined to press charges (Office for Victims of Crime, 2014b).

More cases could be solved if greater efforts were made to collect and analyze evidence. Forensic evidence can corroborate a woman's claim that sexual intercourse took place and that the assailant injured her during the assault. At some hospitals, specially trained sexual assault nurse examiners (SANE) are ready to accompany victims throughout the evidence-gathering medical procedures that are grueling and invasive processes that can last as long as six hours (see Little, 2001; and Kristof, 2009). Understandably, anger is sure to erupt whenever the public discovers that this painstakingly collected biological evidence languishes untested in some storage area of a police station or crime lab (see Box 10.3).

Rape Victims and Prosecutors

To increase the conviction rate, some district attorneys have established sex crimes prosecution units with specially trained lawyers. Traditionally, prosecutors whose performance was judged on the basis of their won/lost records preferred offering lenient pleas rather than risking defeat by going to trial. Prosecutors prefer to negotiate an out-of-court

BOX 10.3   The Problem of Untested Rape Kits

A **rape kit** is a collection of evidence gathered by a doctor or a sexual assault nurse examiner (SANE). Over the course of about four to six hours, hairs, saliva, blood, and semen are collected from the victim's bodily fluids, skin, nails, clothing, mouth, and genitals. As part of the medical exam, a test for sexually transmitted diseases might be conducted and a pill to prevent pregnancy might be offered.

When scientifically tested, forensic evidence can identify an assailant who was a stranger, even in cold cases from years ago, or confirm that an accused acquaintance indeed had physical and sexual contact with the complainant (but cannot answer the question of consent). The material in the kit can link the suspect in one case to other unsolved sex crimes, and it can exonerate men who insist on their innocence. Since the late 1990s, the evidence from the victim's body can be tested to see if it matches the DNA of a suspect contained in the FBI's Combined DNA Index System (CODIS). Departments that test the evidence in kits often discover "cold hits" that lead to arrests of suspects whose DNA is on file in databanks, and consequently achieve higher solution rates (Herbert, 2002; Kristof, 2009; and AP, 2011b). When about 8,000 kits that had accumulated from police departments in Ohio over the years were finally tested, nearly 1,500 hits provided important clues for detectives to investigate (AP, 2014).

A problem arises whenever either police departments don't send rape kits off to crime labs for testing or the labs allow large backlogs to develop.

In 2006, the Justice Department estimated about 180,000 unutilized kits languished in storage facilities across the country. By 2014, that estimate of the backlog had grown to 400,000. In nearly 20 percent of all sexual assault cases between 2002 and 2007, forensic evidence was collected but was not sent off to be lab tested (Chemaly, 2014). A National Institute of Justice study concluded that the actual number of unopened kits could not be determined because so many police departments have "antiquated" noncomputer-based systems of cataloging and tracking forensic evidence (White House Council on Women and Girls, 2014). An audit of police departments in Texas discovered about 20,000 untested kits sitting on shelves in evidence storage areas in 2012 (Grissom, 2013). A lawsuit filed against the police in Memphis, Tennessee, claimed the department threw away as many as 15,000 kits or allowed the evidence in them to spoil over several decades (Lessmiller, 2013).

The evidence in kits stored by law enforcement agencies and prosecutors' offices often goes unanalyzed for several reasons: inadequate government financing to pay for all this testing (each analysis costs from $800 to about $1,500); certain sexual assault cases are assigned a low priority because they are likely to end with an acquittal (especially those involving acquaintances, heavy drinking, or complainants who have decided to stop their cooperation); DNA collected from murders, robberies, and burglaries are given higher priorities; the prosecutor's office didn't ask the police department to have the evidence tested; and the understaffed and overworked crime labs that have limited storage space already are unable to process the growing number of requests in a timely manner and would be completely overwhelmed by the arrival of all the kits departments have accumulated (White House Council on Women and Girls, 2014).

The consequences of the accumulation of huge backlogs are that assailants escape apprehension and may strike again, and victims don't achieve closure and a sense that their complaint was taken seriously and acted upon so that justice could be served.

Once a kit is processed, the DNA profile can be used by the prosecution to get a "John Doe" warrant that can keep the manhunt going until the statute of limitation expires. As of 2014, in 34 states the statute of limitations on filing charges of sexual assault or rape ranged from 3 to 30 years. However, in 27 states the time limit could be extended or even suspended if DNA evidence already has led to a hit (matches the DNA of a suspect in the CODIS database) but not an arrest yet (Smith, 2014).

The solution to the backlog problem, according to advocates, is to require departments to monitor how many kits remain untested and then to find sufficient resources to process the evidence at the labs in a timely manner. In 2010, Illinois became the first state to require its police departments to send all kits to crime labs (Human Rights Watch, 2010). Houston, Texas, passed an ordinance enabling the city to collect a fee from strip club patrons and earmarks that money to pay for kit testing (Grissom, 2013). In 2013, Congress passed the Sexual Assault Forensic Evidence Reporting (SAFER) Act that requires law enforcement agencies to audit and make public the size of their backlogs. The bill also provided additional funding to pay labs to test the kits (RAINN, 2014b). In 2014, Congress provided still more resources to test kits when it reauthorized the "Debbie Smith DNA Backlog Grant Program" (Cox, 2014).

An untested kit symbolizes that solving a particular case has not been assigned a high priority. If victims had the right to be kept posted about developments in their cases, then they would know if police departments were allowing their untested kits to languish in storage lockers.

settlement unless the complainant fits the narrow stereotype of the kind of victims who are believed by jurors and elicit their sympathy: wives and mothers who are well educated, articulate, visibly upset but not hysterical while testifying, and attractive but not too sexy (Vachss, 1993).

Even though more rape cases go to trial than any other type of charge except murder and aggravated assault, the overwhelming majority of cases are still resolved through plea negotiations. The percentage of rape cases that go to trial varies greatly by jurisdiction (Boland and Sones, 1986). About 10 percent of all rape cases were resolved by a trial, with the prosecution victorious about 70 percent of the time, in the 75 largest counties during 1994 (Reaves, 1998). Fifteen years later not much had changed: Trials were held in only 8 percent of all rape cases, of which about 70 percent led to a conviction (Reaves, 2013).

A negotiated plea is often justified on the grounds that it spares the accuser from having to recount under oath with great specificity exactly what happened to her. If she serves as a witness for the prosecution, she also faces the prospect of a tough cross-examination intended to undermine her credibility. It is widely assumed that testifying at a trial months or years later would lead to retraumatizing the victim. But a study of the experiences of nearly 140 women who had testified about rapes and other sexual assaults committed against them did not turn up clear evidence that symptoms of PTSD burdened them once more (Orth and Maercker, 2004).

Besides creating special investigation and prosecution squads, a number of other reforms have been enacted to try to improve arrest, prosecution, conviction, and incarceration rates. In most jurisdictions, the chances of conviction in sexual assault cases have been enhanced by new legal codes and sentencing structures that specify graded levels of seriousness from improper sexual contact to forcible rape, each carrying a corresponding penalty (Bienen, 1983; and Largen, 1987). In many courtrooms, evidence of rape trauma syndrome can be introduced during trials to account for any questionable behavior on the victim's part (concerning

reporting delays or failure to actively resist) that in the past would have undermined her credibility.

And yet despite many reforms and attempts at improving the criminal justice system's handling of rape cases, most attackers still are never arrested, prosecuted, convicted, and certainly not incarcerated (see Lisefski and Manson, 1988; and Senate Judiciary Committee, 1993). By the end of the adjudication process in state courts, of all the defendants arrested for rape, 61 percent were convicted, 58 percent of felonies and 3 percent of misdemeanors, according to a nationwide study of 75 large counties (Reaves, 1998). Fifteen years later, the conviction rate in large counties had risen to 68 percent, with about the same proportion (57 percent) guilty of felonies; the improvement in the conviction rate was due to a rise in the number (11 percent) pleading guilty to mere misdemeanors (Reaves, 2013). The following example illustrates how convicted rapists might receive lenient sentences for a misdemeanor:

> A 15-year-old girl is lured to the home of an 18-year-old young man on the pretext of helping him work on his MySpace page. Suddenly, his 17-, 18-, and 19-year-old friends barge in, encircle her, and take turns raping her. All four assailants plead guilty to first-degree rape, but only the ringleader who masterminded the plot gets a sentence of four years in prison. The three others will each serve a year in jail. The prosecution justifies the negotiated plea as a way of sparing the high school sophomore the ordeal of being subjected to four separate cross-examinations at the trial. But the girl tells reporters that the one year jail sentences are "nothing" as she is escorted by police from the courtroom amid catcalls, taunts, and threats from the young convicts' relatives.
> (Bode, 2007)

Optimists emphasize how much progress has been made over the past several decades by the pro-victim, antirape movement. It has tried to eliminate unfair roadblocks on the path to justice by dismantling the institutionalized expressions of discrimination that put victims at such an unusual disadvantage in the not-too-distant past (see Fairstein, 1993). Pessimists, however, point out how many antivictim practices persist within the legal system.

The degree of success achieved by the antirape movement could be evaluated by examining a number of criteria. One sign of success would be gains in the willingness of complainants to report the crimes and to press charges. Additional indicators of progress would be decreases in the number of complainants who conclude that the entire fact-finding and decision-making process was emotionally painful and degrading. Of course, hard evidence would be necessary to back any claims that the way the criminal justice system handles rape cases is better now than in the "bad old days": statistics indicating increases in the percentage of cases solved by making arrests, cases prosecuted rather than dropped or dismissed; defendants convicted rather than acquitted, and rapists incarcerated and then rehabilitated rather than freed to become recidivists (see Goldberg-Ambrose, 1992; Spohn and Horney, 1992; and Bachman and Paternoster, 1993).

CRISIS CENTERS: PROVIDING EMERGENCY ASSISTANCE

No matter how poorly (or how well) the criminal justice system handles rape cases in the long run, sexual assault victims need immediate aid.

Starting in 1972, feminist activists began to provide emergency assistance to women who had just been raped. The first crisis centers, also known as distress or relief centers, were set up in Berkeley, California, and Washington, D.C. These independent self-help projects were intended to provide an alternative to the very limited services available from the police, at hospital emergency rooms, and through mental health centers. These centers also became bases to organize support for the nationwide antirape movement.

Rape crisis centers provide a variety of services. Usually, a 24-hour telephone hotline puts victims in contact with advocates who are standing by to help. The center's staff members are available to accompany women to emergency rooms where forensic evidence is collected and first aid is received, and to police stations or prosecutor's offices where complaints are filed and statements are made. Individuals may receive peer counseling and are invited to participate in support groups. Complainants are referred to other community agencies that provide social services. Some centers conduct in-service training to sensitize doctors, nurses, police officers, and assistant district attorneys about the needs and problems of the survivors they encounter. Most undertake educational campaigns to raise public consciousness about the myths and realities surrounding sex crimes and the victims' plights. Frequently, centers offer self-defense courses for women and children.

Many staff members at the original crisis centers are former victims who shared a commitment to themes embodied in the protest movements of the 1960s and early 1970s. Feminist activists put forward the analysis that rape was primarily a women's issue, best understood and more effectively dealt with by women than by men in positions of authority. A distrust of remote bureaucracies and control by professionals who claim to know what is best for their clients was derived from the youthful counterculture with its "crash pads" (emergency shelters), drop-in centers (for counseling and advocacy), and free clinics (for drug-related health crises) in "hippie" neighborhoods. The New Left's emphasis on egalitarianism, volunteerism, and collective action led to grassroots, community organizing projects stressing self-help and peer support, and to symbolic confrontations with the power structure: protest demonstrations at police stations and courtrooms.

With the passage of time, however, rifts developed within many rape crisis centers. More pragmatic and less ideological staffers softened the staunch stands taken by these nonprofit, nonhierarchical, nonprofessional, and nongovernmental organizations. They pressed for a more service-oriented approach that would avoid militancy and radical critiques, improve chances for funding, increase referrals from hospitals and police departments, and permit closer cooperation with prosecutors. To the founders of the centers, such changes represented a cooptation by the establishment and a retreat from the original mission (see Amir and Amir, 1979; and Largen, 1981).

For the staff members and volunteers at crisis centers and at domestic violence shelters too, the biggest problems in their emotionally exhausting jobs are vicarious traumatization, secondary traumatic stress, and burnout from constant exposure to the adverse reactions and suffering of their clients (Baird and Jenkins, 2003; and Campbell and Wasco, 2005).

THE REDISCOVERY OF MORE VICTIMS OF RAPES AND SEXUAL ASSAULTS

Drug-Facilitated Sexual Assaults

During the 1990s, drug researchers and advocates who assisted rape victims began to receive anecdotal reports about drug-facilitated acquaintance rapes. The charge was that certain predatory men were escalating their aggressive tactics and going beyond weakening their prey by plying them with alcohol. They were secretly spiking the drinks of the young women they were targeting with chemical substances that were far more effective than just beer, wine, or liquor.

To overcome female resistance, the unscrupulous males would surreptitiously administer certain club drugs that were popular among partygoers: primarily Rohypnol ("roofies") and GHB ("liquid ecstasy"), but also MDMA ("ecstasy") and ketamine ("special K"). Large doses of these controlled substances rapidly induce sedation and temporary amnesia, and drinking alcohol magnifies those effects. Odorless and colorless, the drugs can be dropped into a drink, and the unsuspecting quarry either feels paralyzed or loses consciousness and the ability to recall events (Ottens and Hotelling, 2001; and Pope and Shouldice, 2001).

Despite the attention paid to drug-facilitated sexual assaults in recent years, the true scope of the problem remains unknown because of the absence of reliable estimates of incidence and prevalence rates. The situation becomes especially complicated because voluntary and involuntary drug taking and drinking often are intertwined. One forensic analysis of the bodily fluids of nearly 150 sexual assault complainants who went to clinics established that about 4 percent had been victims of surreptitious drugging; an additional 30 percent voluntarily ingested these controlled substances (Negrusz et al., 2005). A phone survey discovered that of the women who considered themselves to be incapacitated before they were violated because of either drugs or alcohol, about 95 percent believed that alcohol, not other drugs, were the cause (Kilpatrick et al., 2007). Another phone survey determined that about 2 percent of the sample believed that they had suffered a drug-facilitated rape, but of these women, nearly 80 percent of the assaults began with voluntary substance use (Zinzow et al., 2010).

A maximalist viewpoint and a competing minimalist viewpoint can be discerned whenever the following questions arise: "How many rapes actually were drug facilitated?" And also, "How should the rapists' preferred targets respond to this threat?"

According to maximalists, the problem is serious because the overwhelming majority of drug-facilitated rapes go unreported, and those that are reported end up unsubstantiated by lab tests. Furthermore, teenage girls and women might not even be aware that they were intentionally drugged and then violated. When they wake up, they might not realize that they were mentally and physically incapacitated for up to several hours, unless they find themselves in compromising circumstances or bruised and sore from rough sexual intrusions. Maximalists believe that sexual predators quickly learned to use these "liquid poisons" to subdue their prey as soon as the drugs became widely available and popular among partygoers during the early 1990s. Law enforcement officials lamented that GHB-fueled rapes are a "perfect" crime because females who were "roofied" usually can't prove it. If they don't notify the authorities immediately, and if hospital and laboratory personnel don't perform chemical tests quickly, the traces of the drugs disappear from the target's blood and urine within hours or days of ingestion (depending on the specific substance). As a result, police investigations involving complainants who suspect they were surreptitiously drugged usually turn out to be inconclusive because the window of opportunity for testing their bodily fluids has passed, or because local law enforcement agencies do not have the forensic laboratory expertise to collect and preserve this evidence, which does not show up in routine screening procedures Without toxicological evidence indicating foul play, the accused male merely can insist that the woman had not been comatose but had consented to the sex acts that took place. Even if traces of club drugs are found in lab results, the defendant still can claim that she willingly took the drugs to achieve a pleasurable high. Females incapacitated by the drugs will have difficulty recalling specific details of the assault and will tend to be less effective as complainants in police stations and as prosecution witnesses in court (Ottens and Hotelling, 2001; Pope and Shouldice, 2001; Smalley and Mnookin, 2003; Fitzgerald and Riley, 2005; and Jordan, 2005).

Maximalist concerns about a surge in these insidious attacks have brought about a number of responses by government, colleges, and even drinking establishments. Congress passed the Drug-Induced Rape Prevention Act of 1996, which imposed stiff penalties for selling or even possessing some of these controlled substances. In 2000, Congress increased the punishments for dealers and users of GHB, which had been banned by the FDA in 1990. The Department of Justice's Office for Victims of Crime has provided training and technical assistance to improve the detection abilities of medical examinations seeking evidence of traces of drugs in the aftermath of sexual assaults. A Los Angeles County task force pioneered the use of a forensic evidence kit specifically in cases when drug-induced paralysis and amnesia is suspected. The U.S. Drug Enforcement Administration collaborated with antirape organizations to sponsor campaigns that alert women about this presumably growing threat and dedicated increased resources to investigations of predatory drug rings. College administrations have undertaken "Watch That Drink" campus awareness events. Students are urged to pay close attention to risk factors that heighten their vulnerability: Never leave their beverages unattended; only

accept drinks directly from waiters and bartenders; never drink from a punch bowl, keg, or bottle that is being passed around; and, of course, never accept drinks from people they don't completely trust. Of course, the potential for victim blaming and self-blame arises whenever a woman who believes she has suffered a drug-facilitated rape concedes that she did not scrupulously follow all of these precautions (see Abramovitz, 2001; Drug Enforcement Administration, 2003; Office of National Drug Control Policy, 2003; Bergfeld, 2005; and Fitzgerald and Riley, 2005).

By 2003, thousands of bars and at least 40 universities distributed chemically impregnated cardboard coasters that turn colors when doused with a few drops of a beverage laced with club drugs like GHB. The manufacturer of this drug detection device planned to market it to more than 1,000 college campuses nationwide, although critics warned it was far from foolproof. A straw and a cup that changes colors when in contact with date rape drugs is also being marketed (Mason, 2002; Ellin, 2003; Smalley and Mnookin, 2003; Maddalenna, 2005; and Lear, 2013).

The minimalist viewpoint proceeds from the observation that the number of reports to police departments of suspected drug-facilitated assaults is low, and stories in the press about successful prosecutions that prove conclusively that surreptitious drugging took place are very hard to find. A search of newspaper articles using the keywords "date rape drug" will turn up many warnings in articles and on blogs about the potential dangers to women posed by predatory men who might use powerful chemical substances to immobilize their prey. Past news items centered on men arrested for possession of date rape drugs, individuals who suffered from self-induced overdoses, some criminal cases handled in other countries, and stories about young women who suspected that they had been drugged. But only a few actual cases can be found about men arrested, prosecuted, and convicted for carrying out drug-facilitated sexual assaults such as this one:

A 17-year-old girl meets a man in a bar and then goes to his apartment. She complains of a headache so he gives her a white pill. She wakes up periodically over the next six hours but is unable to move a muscle as he repeatedly takes sexual advantage of her. A week later she goes to the police but can provide no medical or toxicological evidence to corroborate her complaint. But when four other women make strikingly similar charges against the same man over the next two years, a prosecutor of a special victims unit convinces a judge to consolidate the cases. The man is convicted of sexually assaulting four of the five women and is sentenced to a minimum of 30 years in prison. (Warkentin, 2006)

The minimalist viewpoint argues that the alarming warnings about the size of the problem that are circulated by persons holding the maximalist viewpoint are not based on solid evidence. For example, minimalists would cite the findings of a survey of over 5,000 women in college in which only 0.6 percent believed that they had been given a drug (not alcohol) without their knowledge or consent before being sexually assaulted (Krebs et al., 2009).

A skeptical perspective that questions widespread concerns about this "terrifying scourge" of drink tampering has taken root in other English-speaking societies but has not gained traction yet in the United States (but see Bliss, 2013). The skeptical stance first emerged when a British tabloid published the results of a controversial study. It challenged the message of a "Watch Your Drink" campaign emanating from an "anti-drink-spiking" organization that innocent and unsuspecting young women were being slipped a dose of an "anesthesia" drug at pubs and clubs. A forensic analysis of samples collected in the United Kingdom from more than 1,000 women who alleged drug-facilitated rape did not find traces of Rohypnol in a single specimen. The lab tests did find that a large proportion of the young women had been binge drinking or using recreational drugs, or had taken heavy doses of both. A similar investigation by British doctors of evidence collected from 75 women seeking medical treatment because of fears of drink spiking also concluded that not one tested positive. Similarly, an analysis in

Australia of nearly 100 hospital emergency room files of persons who thought they were victims of spiking found no traces of illegal drugs. Skeptics in these countries concluded that the threat posed by insidious predators on the prowl, promoted by alarmists, was greatly exaggerated. To minimalists, the presumed rash of drug-induced rapes seems to be largely based on anecdotal evidence from rape crisis centers and hotlines, victims' suspicions, and a spate of newspaper articles about arrests but not convictions. What keeps this "urban legend" (as minimalists might call it) going is not forensic evidence and court cases but rather the several useful functions it plays. The focus on controlled substances draws attention away from the primary drug of choice of rapists for eroding resistance: alcohol. Believing that she was surreptitiously drugged by some evil man enabled a woman to "play the victim" rather than to take responsibility for drinking herself into a stupor. It was more socially acceptable to demonize spiking than to condemn binge drinking. The specter of stranger danger enabled parents to impart "safety advice" without engaging in frank and unpleasant discussions with their daughters about alcohol and sexuality. Various rituals to protect drinks from being contaminated allowed women to bond and form alliances to take care of each other when out partying. Of course, focusing on women's behavior and blaming them for making themselves so utterly vulnerable doesn't excuse the men who imposed themselves on a semicomatose "partner" incapable of granting consent: The male exploiters of weakness were still breaking the law by committing sexual acts without the other party's permission (see Platell, 2005; Weathers, 2005; Hope, 2007; Adams, 2009; Burgess et al., 2009; White, 2009; and Brooks, 2011).

THE REDISCOVERY OF MORE RAPE VICTIMS

Because of the renewed attention paid to sexual assault by the antirape movement over the past three decades, the plight of other groups soon was rediscovered: sexual assaults on campuses, in the military, between men, behind bars in jails and prisons, and within marriages.

Sexual Assaults on Campus

For decades, sexual assaults on college campuses were a real but largely overlooked problem. Students often found their complaints were greeted with doubts or were largely disregarded. If they persevered, the classmates they accused might eventually be chastised or mildly penalized by administrators. As a result of this insensitivity and mishandling, some victims became activists and banded together in organizations to form a social movement fighting for reforms.

A bitter maximalist versus minimalist controversy surrounds the incidence and prevalence of acquaintance rape on college campuses. The sharp disagreement over the seriousness of the problem first surfaced in the late 1980s and erupted when Congress passed the federal Campus Sexual Assault Victims' Bill of Rights in 1992, which imposed procedures outlining how college administrations ought to handle rape complaints. But the dispute never was resolved. It simmered for two decades and then flared up again in 2014. About 12 million young women attended college in the United States, along with about 9 million young men, in 2014. But it is far from clear how many actually were victims and how many were perpetrators (see Warshaw, 1988; Schreiber, 1990; Bohmer and Parrot, 1993; Faludi, 1993; Leone and de Koster, 1995; Sampson, 2004; Koss, 2008; MacDonald, 2008a, 2008b; Fisher, Daigle, and Cullen, 2010; McFadden, 2010; Bernstein, 2011; Rennison and Addington, 2014; and Yoffe, 2014).

Maximalist Versus Minimalist Perspectives

Campus antirape activists took a maximalist stance based on their belief that they had uncovered statistical evidence that sexual assault was a widespread but severely underreported problem. It was well known from the annual findings of the *NCVS* that young women in their late teens and early twenties faced the gravest risks of being sexually assaulted. It became clear that attacks by complete strangers in deserted

areas of campuses (such as unlit parking lots or isolated offices) were unusual. But it was a shock to find out that unexpected acts of sexual aggression by dates and even mere acquaintances were so common. Maximalists pointed out that the term *date rape* framed the issue too narrowly because assailants often were classmates, friends, and other acquaintances and not strictly boyfriends or ex-boyfriends, and that the forced sex took place on occasions other than formal dates (such as study sessions and parties).

The maximalist viewpoint is based on findings from surveys. One widely cited survey of more than 3,000 female students at 32 colleges presented the young women with scenarios that described what recently reformed state statutes would legally designate as sexual assaults. Respondents could identify elements of the crime that resembled their own experiences, such as being plied with liquor until their judgment was so impaired that "consent" was meaningless, or being physically held down, or being forced to submit after painful arm-twisting. Based on the survey's findings, the researcher estimated that about 166 out of every 1,000 female students (about 17 percent) suffered one or more attempted or completed acquaintance rapes per year. Fewer than 5 percent reported the assault to police, about 5 percent sought solace at rape crisis centers, and almost half told no one what happened. In nearly 85 percent of the cases, the victim knew the offender; and in over 55 percent he was a date. Projecting a yearly incidence estimate into a lifetime prevalence estimate, perhaps as many as one in four college-aged young women might have experienced an attempted rape or a completed rape since she was 14 years old (Koss, Gidyez, and Wisniewski, 1987; Koss and Harvey, 1991; Koss and Cook, 1998; and Koss, 2008).

Similar findings emerged from a telephone survey of a national sample of nearly 4,500 women attending two- and four-year colleges during 1996. The researchers discovered that almost 3 percent of the female students suffered a completed or attempted rape during the nine-month academic year. Projecting that number on to an enrollment of 10,000 female students, nearly 300 will be harmed over two semesters. Over the course of an entire calendar year, as many as 5 percent of young women will experience a completed or attempted sexual assault. Because students often take an average of five years to complete their degrees, between 20 and 25 percent of young women may be raped during their college years. In the overwhelming majority of these attacks, the women knew the assailants. About 90 percent were boyfriends, ex-boyfriends, classmates, coworkers, friends, and casual acquaintances. Faculty members were not identified as perpetrators of any rapes or sexual assaults but were cited in a small percent of incidents as imposing unwelcome sexual contacts. Most incidents took place off campus. Furthermore, the study confirmed the results of earlier research projects—that hardly any (just 5 percent) of the sexual assaults were brought to the attention of local law enforcement agencies or even the campus police. These victims also did not seek medical care or professional counseling services (Fisher, Cullen, and Turner, 2000; and Karjane, Fisher, and Cullen, 2005).

Another survey of over 5,000 women in college led to a very similar estimate that one in every five students will be sexually assaulted during their years at an institution of higher learning (Krebs et al., 2007). The continuing problem of underreporting also was confirmed by additional surveys. One study estimated that only 12 percent of college women reported their sexual assaults to the police (Kilpatrick et al., 2007).

Survey findings also shed light on when and how the attacks took place. Many of the "incapacitated" assaults directed at young women who were drunk, under the influence of drugs, or who had passed out were perpetrated during parties. The first few weeks of the freshman and sophomore years seem to be a period of greatest vulnerability; the first few days of the freshman term in particular are fraught with danger. Most incidents took place off campus after 6 P.M. and especially after midnight. In only about 20 percent of the assaults did the young women suffer physical injuries, such as bruises, cuts, swellings, black

eyes, and chipped teeth. Slightly more than half of these targets of male aggression fought back physically. Most tried at least one resistance strategy, including running away, begging, using force, screaming, and yelling "Stop." Some of the assailants could be considered serial offenders because they admitted that they had abused a number of women during their years at college (Sampson, 2004; and Krebs et al., 2009).

Maximalists argued that students, college administrators, and parents didn't realize that an epidemic of sexual assaults in dorms, fraternity houses, and off-campus apartments was taking place because of the extremely low reporting rate. The crisis remained under the radar screen because young women were reluctant to bring their troubles to the attention of the campus security force or to the local police for a long list of reasons: They may fear unwanted publicity and exposure; they may feel embarrassed and humiliated; and they may blame themselves for getting drunk or for going to a secluded spot. Also they may anticipate that they won't be believed by detectives or prosecutors or juries; they may not want their former friends or dates to be severely stigmatized and punished as "rapists"; they may have little faith in the on-campus judicial system; and they could worry about reprisals from the assailant and social ostracism by his friends and maybe even their own friends. Additionally, they may be concerned that their family will find out and may dread that they will be harshly judged, condemned, and slandered for allegedly "precipitating" the young man's out-of-control outpouring of "lust" (see Sampson, 2004; and Cohn et al., 2013).

But minimalists wondered whether the problem was really as alarming as maximalists pictured it to be. These skeptics did not accept the often cited figures of "1 out of every 5" or "1 in 4" that maximalists circulated. In particular, they argued that the maximalist definition was too broad, vague, and inclusive. Applying the very serious terms *forcible rape* and *sexual assault* to instances of sexual harassment (which are not a criminal matter), verbal threats, unwanted kisses, and acts involving groping and fondling resulted in inflated estimates of risks.

Also, ambiguous sexual encounters that involved coercion or deceit without threats of bodily harm or actual violence led to even more frightening but unrealistic estimates. Some disturbing and confusing sexual experiences might fall into a gray area, and hence should be referred to as *gray rapes*. An outgrowth of flirting, partying, binge drinking, and mutual desires, gray rapes blur the boundaries between the clear black-and-white alternatives of enthusiastic consent versus vehement objection (Stepp, 2007). Consequently, maximalists were mistakenly counting incidents in which a young woman felt pressured into agreeing to engage in sex, or had lost good judgment because of excessive drinking or drug taking, or had wanted to say "No!" but was not assertive enough to stop the young man's advances. If the young woman drank alcohol or took drugs provided by the man before intercourse, that does not mean she was "intentionally incapacitated." Verbal coercion, manipulation, deception (about being in love), false promises (of a long-term relationship or marriage), and betrayal of trust—all nonviolent tactics in the male arsenal of seduction—were erroneously being equated with "being forced to give in." Most of these women deemed "victims" by maximalist researchers did not consider themselves to have been raped, and explained to interviewers that they did not file complaints because their experiences were "personal matters" or not "serious enough" to report—a judgment that seems unlikely from a person who suffered a "real" rape, minimalists concluded. In fact, more than 40 percent of the women dated their supposed assailants again and engaged in intercourse with them again, surveys revealed. By overestimating the date rape problem, maximalists were manufacturing a crisis to further their social agenda of unfairly portraying male–female relationships as inherently antagonistic and fraught with danger. Promoting such a negative image of sexuality stigmatized normal heterosexual intercourse as bordering on criminal conduct unless explicit, unambiguous consent had been secured from the female partner before each escalation in intimacy. The presumed adversarial model of bold male initiatives and token female resistance denies the reality of female desires and portrays women as naive, helpless, vulnerable, and more in need of strictly enforced protective codes of appropriate sexual behavior than of equal rights, minimalists insisted. Overestimates unnecessarily alarmed young women, overshadowed those "real" rapes that are genuinely brutal, and undermined the credibility of "real" complainants. The underlying politics of the antiacquaintance rape movement actually sets back the cause of women's equality, adherents of the minimalist position insisted (see Eigenberg, 1990; Gilbert, 1991; Podhoretz, 1991; Crichton, 1993; Hellman, 1993; Roiphe, 1993; MacDonald, 2008a, 2008b; and Yoffe, 2014).

Minimalists pointed out that despite many rape awareness activities launched by maximalists, campus rape crisis centers never became overwhelmed by a flood of new cases. FBI statistics monitoring crime on college campuses revealed that very few women filed complaints. If such attacks were rare and isolated, maintaining a rape crisis center was an unnecessary expense and engendered needless anxiety and tension. Skeptics charged that alarmists in the campus antirape movement have morphed into an "industry" that was preoccupied by the limited use by female students of rape crisis centers, sexual assault disciplinary committees, and emergency hotlines (see Eigenberg, 1990; Gilbert, 1991; Podhoretz, 1991; Crichton, 1993; Hellman, 1993; Roiphe, 1993; and MacDonald, 2008a, 2008b).

Minimalists also scoffed that if it truly were the case that large numbers of "forcible rape victims" graduated from college each year burdened by serious emotional scars inflicted by male students, their parents would have demanded action, and alternative academic institutions would have sprung up to guarantee young women a safer environment in which to live and learn. These skeptics offered a solution that is direct and blunt: The simplest and surest way to prevent these alleged sexual assaults is for college women to reject the "booze-fueled hookup subculture of casual couplings and one-night stands" by exercising more prudence, modesty, and restraint in their interactions with testosterone-charged young men. Skeptics asserted that this advice was consistent with the theme of female empowerment and recognized that young women are able to control their fates and take the lead in solving the problem of rape on campus (see MacDonald, 2008a, 2008b; Stepp, 2008; Franklin, 2011; and Yoffe, 2013).

Addressing Sexual Misconduct on Campus
Whether the problem is as widespread as maximalists believe, or is more limited, as minimalists suspect, student-on-student sexual assaults surely are a campus issue that college administrations must address. The women who are sexually assaulted suffer academic consequences: Their grades are likely to plunge, they may stop attending or drop certain classes, transfer to another college if their concerns escalate about encountering their assailant on campus, feel alienated from former classmates, and even interrupt their education for several terms or years.

Some activists insist that a genuine solution requires much more than a victim-blaming "Just say no to partying and the subsequent casual sex!" approach or an offender-blaming emphasis on punitive solutions. If acquaintance rape on campus truly has reached epidemic proportions, its roots can be traced to a hypermasculine subculture that emanates from some fraternities and some college athletic teams, whose members are encouraged to devalue and degrade women as objects to be toyed with, sexually exploited, and then discarded. Young men have to organize against their socialization into the prevailing campus rape culture and in the process redefine what genuine masculinity really entails (see Schwartz and DeKeseredy, 1997; Benedict, 1998; Benedict and Klein, 1998; Martin and Hummer, 1998; Sampson, 2004; and Sanday, 2007).

College men and women need to discuss and rethink the issue of explicit consent. To reduce the threat of assault, college administrations need to sponsor workshops about dating and intimacy during freshman orientation week, complete with reenactments of dangerous situations and role-playing exercises to encourage bystander intervention (see itsonus.org, 2014). Student governments ought to issue reader-friendly, easily accessible,

and widely distributed guidelines and handbooks that clarify and define completely what characterizes consensual sexual conduct. Administrations should issue no-contact orders to protect complainants from harassment and warn that sexual misconduct and acts of retaliation against those who press charges are punishable by expulsion from the community by a campus judicial committee. Campus rape crisis centers should encourage students to seek help by devising confidential, third-party, and even anonymous ways of reporting incidents, and by listing the properly trained people to turn to for counseling, medical care, legal advocacy, protection, and other forms of assistance on campus and in the surrounding community (Crichton, 1993; Bohmer and Parrot, 1993; and Karjane et al., 2005).

In 2011, the Civil Rights Office of the U.S. Department of Education issued guidelines that pressured colleges to adopt a zero-tolerance stance toward both sexual harassment and sexual assaults on campus. Colleges were supposed to guarantee equal protection by granting both the accuser and the accused the same rights. College officials were not allowed to try to dissuade accusers from also reporting the incident to the local police and were compelled to implement violence prevention programs that included training for residence hall counselors and coaches. Institutions of higher learning that failed to implement these measures would risk losing federal funding and could face legal sanctions (Editors, *New York Times,* 2011b).

In 2013, Congress passed the Campus Sexual Violence Elimination Act, requiring that incidents of dating violence, sexual assault, and stalking be included in annual campus crime statistics reports. In 2014, the Obama administration created a task force to coordinate federal efforts to identify the best practices implemented on various campuses across the country so that other college administrations could more effectively prevent sexual assaults and handle cases brought to their attention. Federal agencies would get involved and penalize college administrations that were unable to bring the perpetrators to justice (Calmes, 2014). The task force recommended that colleges carry out anonymous surveys of student opinion about the problems on their campus periodically. Questions could focus on feelings about safety on campus; prevailing attitudes about sexual assaults, victim-blaming, and miscommunication; and direct queries about actually experiencing unwanted sexual contacts involving force, threats, or incapacitation during the school year. A website was set up to inform students about their rights, about what progress is being made at other colleges, and how to file a complaint and access supportive services (Notalone, 2014). Campus activists launched campaigns to raise student awareness about their rights and the U.S. Department of Education made public a long list of nearly 90 colleges that were being investigated for allegedly mishandling student-on-student sexual assault cases (Hanna et al., 2014; and Yoffe, 2014).

California in 2014 became the first state to go beyond the "no means no" formulation and pass "yes means yes" legislation requiring its colleges to adopt standards of affirmative sexual consent in which the initiator must get his partner to agree consciously, unambiguously, and voluntarily to proceed to the next step in order to later avoid charges of sexual assault.

Campus disciplinary boards composed of administrators, professors, and members of the staff handle certain cases, whether or not they are also investigated by the police and prosecuted in the courts. The judicial machinery set up by administrations has been criticized as ineffective and unsatisfactory: insensitive to the complainants whose lives are disrupted, and also unduly lenient toward the perpetrators who often are not expelled but go on to graduate even after being found culpable. Students whose complaints about alleged sexual assaults have been rejected sometimes sue the university. But the judicial process also is faulted, for branding and even blacklisting students as sexual exploiters when in fact no assault took place. Students who insist on their innocence and assert that they have been falsely and mistakenly determined to be guilty also sue universities. Administrations are condemned for being so protective of and preoccupied with the institution's reputation that a "culture of indifference" seems to prevail on campus (Center

for Public Integrity, 2010; and Rubenfeld, 2014). This horror story is often cited to demonstrate the consequences of mishandling a case:

> *A student at a small religiously oriented college in a rural setting is returning to her dorm room after celebrating and drinking at an end-of-year party. Appearing disoriented, she is led into another room by two members of the basketball team. She is penetrated by the two athletes and another man, while several other students stand in the hallway, peer in, and high-five each other. One of the aggressors walks up to a security camera in the corridor and holds up a handwritten note purportedly signed by the young woman that reads, "I want to have sex." The next morning, she spots blood on her underwear, tells her roommate, reports the incident to the police as well as administrators, and travels to a hospital for a forensic exam. But the authorities are unsure about whether she actually consented, so no action is taken. Disturbed that her exploiters might still be on campus, she drops out (actually, they chose not to re-enroll but the unsupportive administration never informed her). Seven months after the incident, listless and depressed at home, she locks herself in her room, places a plastic bag over her head, and commits suicide. Her mother sues the college, claiming it lulled parents into a false sense of security by systematically undercounting sexual assaults, and also violated federal antidiscrimination regulations by failing to conduct a fair and thorough investigation.* (Myers, 2009; and McFadden, 2010)

■ ■ ■

> *A sophomore is forced by her date to submit to a sex act that she desperately does not want to allow. The scene of the violation is her bed in her dorm, so after 3 months of turmoil, she turns to the campus judicial board for redress. Even though she is the third undergraduate to file a complaint against this student, the board finds him "not responsible" and upholds its decision after she appeals. To dramatize what she endured and to call attention to the larger issues, she carries her mattress around the campus. Her "performance art" serves as an act of protest which successfully draws media attention to the problem of*

inadequate procedures and policies by college administrations. Soon 22 other sexually assaulted students join her in a lawsuit against the Ivy League university for violating federal regulations. (Bogler, 2014)

However, on other occasions, the campus judicial machinery might not underreact to well documented charges but overreact to unsubstantiated allegations, as this case illustrates:

An undergrad accuses a freshman on a full scholarship of raping her. The Ivy League university's administration quickly pressures him to withdraw, even though she does not inform the police or press charges. She goes on to graduate; he transfers and obtains his degree from a different college. But he sues the university, his accuser, and her father, who is a wealthy alumnus and a substantial donor to the university, alleging that her father used his status to convince the administration to take unjustifiably swift action against him. The lawsuit claiming false allegations is settled in his favor. (The Ticker, 2011)

The above examples indicate the complexity of the situation and the potential pitfalls that can plague efforts to achieve justice. The proper ways that allegations about sexual misconduct on campuses are supposed to be handled are outlined in Box 10.4. However, law professors have criticized these recommended "best practices" as unfairly tilting too far in favor of the accuser and thereby violating procedural safeguards intended to protect the accused men from false, mistaken, and malicious charges (see Rubenfeld, 2014).

If a student decides to lodge a rape accusation against a male student with a judicial board or if she turns to the local criminal justice system for redress, the strength or weakness of her "no weapon and no physical injuries, he said/she said" case will hinge

---

BOX 10.4 Guidelines for the Proper Handling of Allegations of Sexual Misconduct on Campuses

The U.S. Department of Education's Office for Civil Rights issued procedural guidelines in 2014 that ought to be followed when handling complaints about sexual misconduct on college campuses. Title IX prohibits discrimination on the basis of sex, so if the campus judicial machinery violates this stature and the college refuses to admit wrongdoing, it could lose federal funding. A number of best practices drawn from the successful experiences of various college student disciplinary boards should guide the adjudication process:

- Each college should define the boundaries of prohibited sexual misconduct in terms of failing to secure voluntary, explicit, and unambiguous affirmative consent before proceeding. Silence, confusion due to intoxication, or failure to resist does not indicate willingness to engage in sex.

- The adjudication process should be equitable and impartial. The reporting process should be streamlined. Complainants should be able to present their version of events through testimony, witnesses' statements, perhaps with cross-examination and legal representation.

- Colleges should provide victim services that are comprehensive and holistic, which address the complainants' medical, emotional, and academic needs.

- A "single investigator" from the administration ought to play the role of prosecutor, judge, and jury, and make a determination about whether the accused bears responsibility or not for a violation of the college's policies. Confidentiality and anonymity should be respected at all student disciplinary hearings.

- The proceedings are civil, not criminal, so the standard of proof should be "preponderance of the evidence" that translates to "more likely than not" (a certainty in excess of 50 percent). This is a lower standard than "clear and convincing evidence" and is much easier to achieve than the required proof in criminal proceedings, which is "beyond a reasonable doubt."

- After a prompt resolution, penalties can include suspension and even expulsion from the college.

- If the accused person is found "responsible" for sexual misconduct, that finding can be appealed. If the accused is found not responsible, then the accuser can appeal this decision.

- Students at public universities must be accorded certain due process rights. At privately run colleges, the students must be granted certain contractual rights.

SOURCES: Notalone, 2014; Rubenstein, 2014; Yoffe, 2014; and Shulevitz, 2015.

on a number of factors, some of them in contradiction with the others. In terms of consent, she will have to convince those who sit in judgment that she said "No!" and meant it, or clearly did not give permission. The man's defense will be more credible if he did not hear that "No!" or had reason to believe it was part of a game or traditional script. If witnesses testify that they saw and heard her resist his advances, it supports her case. If witnesses observed her acting provocatively and seductively, that undermines her version of events leading up to the alleged assault. As for her immediate reactions, if she quickly got up and left the premises, called the police, or at least disclosed her distress to someone else, her charges seem more credible. But if she stayed the night, had breakfast with him, and continued to date him, that undermines her later reassessment that whatever took place that evening violated her wishes. If she engaged in heavy drinking, the accuracy of her memory of events might be challenged on cross-examination. But her accusation that she was taken against her will could be believable if there is evidence that he plied her with liquor until she was too drunk to actually give consent (Banfield, 2007).

To put the problem into perspective, it is worthwhile to compare the risks faced by college women to their non-student counterparts between the ages of 18 and 24. An analysis of a huge *NCVS* database of survey findings from 1995 to 2013 revealed that young women lived slightly safer lives if they were involved in higher education during those high risk years. The rate of rape and sexual assaults suffered by nonstudents were a little higher (1.2 times more, 7.6 per 1,000 for nonstudents compared to 6.1 per 1,000 for students). About 33 percent of nonstudents shared their problems with the police, whereas only 20 percent of college women did. Otherwise, few differences could be discerned. About 20 percent of both groups feared reprisals if they informed the police about what happened. Both groups knew their assailants in about 80 percent of the sexual assaults; and the offenders used a weapon against the nonstudents as well as the students in only 10 percent of the attacks (Sinozich and Langton, 2014). In sum,

there is no evidence that college is a more dangerous place to spend the high risk years of the late teens and early twenties than in the "real world" beyond the campus gates.

Sexual Assaults Within the Military

Accusations from female soldiers, plus concerns voiced by elected officials, have caused the Pentagon to investigate domestic violence and sexual misconduct in the military and to issue sweeping policy reforms 18 times over 16 years (see Office of the Inspector General, 2003; Corbett, 2007; Herbert, 2009; Myers, 2009; and Parker, 2011). Besides sexual assaults in the barracks on military bases, the problem has involved cadets at military academies and patients at mental health clinics run by the Department of Veterans Affairs (Walsh, 2011).

Technically, in the military, "sexual assault" investigations refer to a range of crimes, including rape, aggravated sexual assault, nonconsensual sodomy, aggravated sexual contact, abusive sexual contact, wrongful sexual contact, and attempts to commit these offenses, as defined by the Uniform Code of Military Justice. Many of the assaults are of the less serious contact types. The accused "subjects of investigation" are interrogated by military police officers of that branch of the service (Brown, 2013).

The size of the problem is measured in two ways. One is by monitoring the number of complaints and the other is by periodically surveying a sample of the nearly 1.5 million members of the U.S. armed forces. According to the survey, an estimated 19,000 men and women suffered sexual assaults in 2010. That figure rose to 26,000 in 2011. The stereotype of a female enlistee being forced to submit to the demands of a superior officer, especially a drill sergeant during basic training, has some truth to it. Women are only 15 percent of all members of the service but account for nearly half of all the respondents disclosing that they suffered an assault. However, more than half (53 percent) of the respondents describing unwanted sexual contacts—or worse—were men and the alleged perpetrators were other men taking part in bullying or hazing. Most male victims are too ashamed or too fearful (of being punished, ignored, or ridiculed) to report what happened to them. As for formal complaints, about 3,500 were filed during a nine-month period ending in June 2013 (Dao, 2013; and Steinhauer, 2013).

Offenders can receive reductions in rank or dishonorable discharges and could be imprisoned. But a number of issues make it difficult for victims to get the machinery of the court martial system to deliver justice. Commanding officers control whether or not a case moves forward to prosecution, and some seem inclined toward covering up what goes on in their units. Some of the accused are superior officers who take advantage of their rank and can retaliate against those who dare to file charges against them. Some soldiers are deterred from lodging complaints because they are subject to harsh cross-examinations at "Article 32" pretrial hearings (Steinhauer, 2013).

In recent years, the Pentagon has reformed the nature of the training commissioned officers and enlisted personnel receive right at the outset of their service and has established "Special Victims Units". A Senate bill to remove cases from the chain of command and give prosecutors more power to pursue them was rejected in favor of a bill that assigned lawyers to complainants and removed the authority of commanding officers to overturn jury verdicts. Some would attribute the sexual assault problem to allowing women into the previously all-male world of the armed forces or to ending the "don't ask, don't tell" ban on openly gay soldiers. But the large number of male-on-male attacks due to bullying and hazing indicates that the problem goes deeper and started earlier and is rooted in the centuries-old macho norms of traditional military culture (Brown, 2013; and Dao, 2013).

Sexual Assaults Between Males

The forcible rape of a male by a female is presumed to be rare (as distinct from cases of seduction and statutory rape of boys by mature women), and the imagery usually arouses smirks rather than alarm.

When women are arrested in sexual assault cases, they usually were acting as the accomplices of domineering men. But the molestation of little boys by men (see Chapter 8) has been of great concern for a long time (see Maghan and Sagarin, 1983; and Porter, 1986).

More recently, the rape of a teenage boy or a young man by another male or by a gang of males was recognized as more than just a theoretical possibility. Yet this had been such a taboo subject that many state laws had ignored this possible victim–offender relationship and had defined rape strictly as a crime perpetrated by males against females. In 1986, however, Congress passed a bill revising federal rape statutes (governing the handling of sexual assaults committed on federal property). Among other changes, the law redefined rape as a gender-neutral offense, so both victims and perpetrators could be of either sex ("Federal Rape Laws," 1986). This official recognition that males also could be rape victims paved the way for their rediscovery, including efforts to estimate the scope of the problem and to devise effective ways of easing their suffering.

The first rough estimates about sexual assaults attempted or completed against males (teenagers and adults) were derived from the findings of annual *NCVS* surveys. Between 1973 and 1982, the number of male rape victims was projected to be almost 125,000, corresponding to about one-twelfth of the problem females faced (Klaus et al., 1985). The 2010 *NCVS* estimated that about 15,000 males over the age of 11 were victims of sexual assaults, but only about 1,200 of these attacks were carried out by complete strangers (Truman, 2011). As for rapes reported to the police, only 9 percent in three states during 1991 were male-on-male (0.8 percent were female-on-female and 0.2 percent were female-on-male), according to an analysis of more detailed data in the FBI's NIBRS (Reaves, 1993). As for lifetime prevalence rates, about 3 percent of all males probably have suffered a sexual assault, most occurring before age 18 (Tjaden and Thoennes, 2006).

Males who are raped are highly unlikely to report the offense and seek medical attention or counseling unless they are severely injured. When they do identify themselves as having been sexually assaulted, it is usually years later. They have fewer places to go to seek solace and treatment for acts that undermine their sense of personhood, masculinity, and sexual identity (Tewksbury, 2009).

Records kept by rape crisis centers indicated that about 1 of every 10 callers was a male. Male rape victims are subjected to the same disbelief, scorn, and insensitive treatment today that females routinely endured in the not-so-distant past. They are often blamed for their misfortunes, stereotyped as homosexual (the majority are exclusively heterosexual), disparaged as not being "real men" for not resisting to the utmost and for not thwarting their attackers, and accused of secretly enjoying the experience. Although males and females suffer in similar ways, experiencing bouts of depression, flashbacks, recriminations, nightmares, and an overwhelming sense of vulnerability, males are more visibly angry and more preoccupied with fantasies of revenge. A few large cities have set up support groups for these men. The available evidence indicates that male rape victims experience more force and brutality, are held captive longer, and are subjected to more acts of sexual humiliation. Evidently, sexual assaults against both males and females are expressions of culturally induced drives toward domination and subjugation within a society that prizes exercising power over other people (Krueger, 1985; and White and Wesley, 1987).

Any *NCVS* projections about the incidence of male-on-male rapes are probably gross underestimates because they exclude the sexual assaults committed in dangerous institutional settings such as jails, prisons, and reform schools.

Sexual Assaults Behind Bars

Sexual violence among inmates was rediscovered and documented as a serious problem decades ago (see Lockwood, 1980). The rape of weaker inmates by stronger prisoners, once a taboo topic, has been written about and depicted in movies for decades (see MacNamara, 1983). Rapes are periodically pictured in movies about prison life—sometimes

mockingly—and are tacitly condoned as an additional form of deterrence in warnings issued by hardened convicts to delinquents in "Scared Straight"–type programs. Older and stronger "wolves" compel younger and weaker inmates to be their sex slaves in return for protection from gang rapes that would stigmatize them as easy pickings and as the "girl" of the institution.

Several court cases in the 1980s and 1990s raised the issue of how female inmates were sexually exploited by male guards. In the late 1990s and the early years of the new century, advocacy groups charged that the authorities showed deliberate indifference to the systematic sexual abuse and exploitation that stronger prisoners imposed on weaker ones who had no avenue for escape. Their investigations also unearthed evidence that corrections officers and other staff sexually abused vulnerable delinquents and female inmates. The groups' reports called for a greater emphasis on prevention strategies to stop prison rape, including more carefully classifying inmates to cellblocks and cells by risk levels, and increasing the size of the custodial staff. Other recommendations focused on improving means of redress, including safer reporting procedures, and stepped up arrests and prosecutions (Mariner, 2001; and Fink, 2011).

But it was not until 2003 that those who endured sexual assaults while incarcerated were rediscovered officially when Congress unanimously passed the Prison Rape Reduction Act. Public Law 108-79 promulgated a zero-tolerance policy and mandated that preventing, detecting, and prosecuting sexual attacks become a top priority in each federal, state, and local correctional institution in order to protect the Eighth Amendment rights of individuals subjected to the government's care and custody. Wardens were put on notice that they would be held responsible for failures to reduce sexual assaults behind bars ("What sheriffs need to know…," 2004).

Acknowledging that there was insufficient solid research and data about the extent and seriousness of sexual aggression behind bars, the legislation assigned the task of administering a survey to the Bureau of Justice Statistics to determine the frequency and consequences of inmate-on-inmate sexual contacts, both nonconsensual and consensual. The National Prison Rape Elimination Commission's first national survey in 2007, based on a representative sample of state and federal prison inmates, yielded an estimate that nearly 5 percent (about 70,000 individuals) had endured sexual violence during a single year (NPREC, 2008). During 2008–2009, 3 percent of jail inmates and over 4 percent of prison inmates alleged they had been sexually victimized one or more times within a year, either by another inmate or a member of the staff. Female inmates, whether in jail or prison, were more than twice as likely as males to be sexually victimized. The male inmates of jails and prisons were more likely than females to have been sexually abused or assaulted within the first 24 hours after admission (Beck and Harrison, 2010).

The most vulnerable of all inmates are teenagers confined in juvenile institutions. Over 12 percent of these young prisoners reported experiencing one or more incidents of sexual victimization in the course of a year. Almost 3 percent said the assailant was another young inmate, while about 10 percent claimed the perpetrator was an adult member of the staff (sometimes a woman). Homosexual boys and teenage girls suffered the most victimizations, and the sexual violence in some facilities was much worse than in others, according to a National Survey of Youth in Custody carried out in 195 facilities during 2008–2009 (Beck et al., 2010).

But determining the true scope of the problem is difficult. Many inmates conceal their ordeals from the authorities because they fear retaliation or don't want to be labeled as a "snitch," since maintaining confidentiality behind bars is extremely difficult. Other prisoners may lodge false accusations in order to get an enemy into serious trouble, or to justify a transfer to a more favorable setting. The high turnover in jail populations makes it very difficult to make accurate measurements, but short-term detention facilities are suspected to be more dangerous places than prisons where inmates are confined for years.

The National Prison Rape Elimination Commission holds annual hearings to identify the common characteristics of both perpetrators and victims, and to examine why some facilities have had more success in reducing sexual violence than others. The commission believes it is in the enlightened self-interest of law-abiding citizens to be concerned about sexual violence behind bars: Young men who have been gang-raped when corrections officers weren't present to intervene are likely to suffer from deep-seated rage, intense shame, low self-esteem, self-loathing, and an inability to trust others. They are prone to substance abuse and a return to criminal behavior upon release ("What Sheriffs Need to Know...," 2004; and Parsell, 2005). Yet in most correctional institutions, inmates who have suffered sexual assaults still cannot find safe, reliable, and responsive ways to report these attacks, nor are they are able to access adequate and timely medical and mental health services behind bars (McFarland, Ellis, and Chunn, 2008). A stricter enforcement of the new standards will spare hundreds of thousands of inmates from these ordeals in coming years, but the Justice Department's monitoring of compliance in some institutions needs improvement (see Kaiser and Stannow, 2011). One procedure that continues to generate complaints about sexual abuse by staffers is the pat downs and strip searches routinely carried out to prevent inmates from smuggling in drugs and weapons (Virella, 2011).

In the pumped-up, heavily tattooed, hypermasculine world of prison life, males who are stripped of autonomy and compelled to obey orders as if they were little boys, try to regain their sense of manhood by forcing weaker inmates to submit to sexual demands as if they were females. Ironically, antirape education programs have discovered that the specter of being taken forcefully by another man might be an effective way to reach and sensitize domineering males who otherwise belittle or justify their sexual aggression toward females (Sabo, 1992; and Beirne and Messerschmidt, 2000).

Sexual Assaults Within Marriages

Under English common law, rape within marriage had been considered impossible, by definition. For centuries, the leading figures in jurisprudence contended that under the marriage contract, a wife consented to yield to her husband's desires wherever and whenever he wished. But during the 1970s, the antirape movement argued that all forced sex should be outlawed, no matter who the aggressor is and what his relationship to the victim might be. Hence, marital rape was "rediscovered" when the feminist perspective became widely accepted: that a wife retains the right to say "no" to her husband despite the license issued by the government, the wedding vows to "love, honor, and obey," and religious teachings about submitting and performing wifely duties.

The forcible rape of a spouse first became officially recognized as a crime in 1975, when South Dakota legislators rewrote the state's statutes and rejected the common law exception that exempted husbands from arrest and granted them the "right" to unlimited sexual access (Russell, 1982). By 1990, in every state, that immunity no longer applied if his wife had separated from him and filed for divorce (Russell, 1990). By 1993, marital rape was a crime in all 50 states. By 2005, all spousal exemptions had been removed in 20 states. But in the remaining 30, husbands might be subjected to lesser charges and lower penalties than nonspouses, and wives had to report the offense more quickly (Hui, 2009).

Wives whose husbands force them to submit to unwanted degrading acts are the least likely sexual assault victims to report incidents, to be believed by the authorities, to have their cases adjudicated, and to secure convictions. The first known case of a husband prosecuted for raping his wife who still lived with him took place in 1978, but he was acquitted. Between 1978 and 1985, only 118 husbands were prosecuted across the country, although 104 of them (90 percent) were convicted, according to a report by a national clearinghouse on marital rape (Barden, 1987).

Estimates about the incidence and prevalence of marital rape do not rest on a solid empirical foundation because the problem is still shrouded in secrecy. In 1978, a survey revealed that 14 percent of all wives confided that had been sexually assaulted by their husbands, a rate that was twice the nonspousal rate (Bui, 2009). According to

projections from a telephone survey, more than 1 million married women had been forced to perform unwanted sexual acts one or more times by their husbands (Crime Victims Research and Treatment Center, 1992). The prevalence rate of marital rape during the course of a marriage was thought to range from as low as 8 percent (Russell, 1990) to as high as 25 percent (Bergen, 1998). A troubling proportion of women, ranging from 15 percent to 25 percent, reported that they were raped by an estranged or ex-husband or former live-in lover (Finkelhor and Yllo, 1985).

Raped wives endure problems similar to women who were sexually assaulted by nonintimates. They are physically injured, psychologically scarred, and personally humiliated (Bowker, 1983). Raped wives also are battered wives in most cases. They are beaten periodically and raped repeatedly over years, and both the physical attacks and sexual assaults symbolize his need to dominate and subjugate her (Peacock, 1998).

THREE COMPETING APPROACHES TO REDUCING THE PROBLEM OF FORCIBLE RAPE

Over the years, three approaches have been developed to address the problem of sexual assault. The oldest (now subject to vehement denunciation) is the blame-the-victim approach, which faults the attitudes, words, and actions of the person attacked. Following the logic of this approach, females must change their ways and take precautions to avoid facilitating sexual assaults through careless, reckless, or even provocative behavior. Because teenage girls and young women are more likely to be targeted than others, risk reduction strategies should focus on behaviors and situations that researchers have been identified as heightening their vulnerability to attack. Consuming alcoholic beverages to the point of intoxication, associating with males who are heavy drinkers, and spending large amounts of time in bars, clubs, fraternity houses, and parties raise the odds of being sexually assaulted. Techniques to resist advances verbally and then physically if necessary can reduce the chances of a completed rape. Interventions proven to be effective include rape awareness programs; campaigns against binge drinking; self-defense, assertiveness, and resistance training; establishing support networks among friends; and providing health care services such as medical treatment and psychological counseling (see Fisher et al., 2008; and Erdely, 2014).

An alternative perspective is the blame-the-offender approach, which views sexual assaults as pathological acts by mentally disturbed individuals. If deranged sexual predators are the source of the problem, then the solutions lie in criminal justice strategies that remove these dangerous deviants from circulation (incapacitation via incarceration, followed by treatment, compulsory if necessary during a period of postprison civil commitment). Because the public can't be sure a released sexual predator has been cured completely, community notification laws are needed to alert neighbors whenever an ex-convict moves nearby so that female family members can remain vigilant and take defensive measures. Various technological devices are now used to monitor the whereabouts of former sex offenders.

In theory, deterrence through punishment attempts to teach the offenders who are not mentally disturbed a lesson they won't forget and to make transgressors into negative role models to serve as warnings to other men so they will think twice, consider the likelihood of imprisonment, and decide not to act out their vicious fantasies. But deterrence and incapacitation are ineffective strategies as long as many rapists are not complained about, caught, and convicted, thereby escaping the sentences mandating the punishment and treatment that they need. At best, an efficient criminal justice system weeds out assailants and brings them under control one at a time, after they have struck and caused a great deal of harm. At most, criminal justice "solutions" can only keep a lid on situations that breed new crops of assailants.

In the debate over the causes of forcible rape, victim blaming, victim defending, and offender blaming focus too narrowly on the attitudes and actions of the male aggressors and their female targets. These points of view tend to ignore crucial insights about prevailing cultural themes surrounding ideas about masculinity and femininity, sex roles, romance, eroticism, seduction, domination, and prestige. According to the institution-blaming perspective, a serious examination of the roots of the problem of forced sex would focus upon the economic, political, and social inequalities between males and females and the cultural supports for rape in contemporary culture. But these larger issues get lost when the analysis is limited to a deconstruction of the "he said/she said" interaction by victim blamers and victim defenders.

Antirape activists have sought not only to defend victims but also to place the burden of blame for recurring outbreaks of male "sexual terrorism" on key social institutions, especially the family, the economy, the military, religion, and the media. Asserting that "the personal is political," they have stressed that apparently private troubles need to be seen as aspects of larger social problems besetting millions of people. Collective solutions that get at the social roots of male-against-female violence hold greater promise in the long run than any reliance on individual strategies of risk reduction and self-defense. Attitudes and myths that tacitly belittle, normalize, or excuse date rape and acquaintance rape must be countered. And more men must realize that rape is a problem they too should be concerned about and strive to solve (see Buchwald, Fletcher, and Roth, 1993; Smith and Welchans, 2000; Ottens and Hotelling, 2001; Price and Sokoloff, 2003; Abbey, 2005; Koss, 2005; Sanday, 2007; Fisher et al., 2008; Brown and Walklate, 2011; Burleigh, 2014; and Erdely, 2014).

President Obama advocated this approach when he urged more men to intervene when they witness a crime in progress, and to report the attack afterwards, declaring "I want every young man in America to feel some strong peer pressure in terms of how they are supposed to behave and treat women" (quoted in Calmes, 2014). Vice President Biden elaborated on this theme, noting, "Men have to take more responsibility; men have to intervene. The measure of manhood is willingness to speak up and speak out, and begin to change the culture" (quoted in Calmes, 2014).

SUMMARY

Rape and sexual assault victims face a host of special problems. The nature of the attack can be emotionally devastating, with severe consequences that can spoil any future enjoyment of sexuality. Because of long-standing attitudes toward sexuality, public airing of details is embarrassing. Due to old ideas and traditional cultural themes, a woman's violation will be widely regarded as a loss of status. Her accusations may be disbelieved as entirely unfounded (it never happened) or exaggerated (she gave consent at the time but later cried rape) or she may be blamed as sharing responsibility with the male for the terrible miscommunication and misunderstanding that unfolded. Filing a complaint and pressing charges will cause the most intimate aspects of her life to become an open book. She will feel as if she, and not the male she accuses, is on trial. Even a conviction will not bring closure if she is emotionally scarred and suffers from lingering phobias and recurrent flashbacks or anxiety attacks.

Special solutions have been devised to address these problems. Starting in the 1970s, feminists in the antirape movement brought about significant changes in the way the criminal justice system and the larger society respond to these attacks. The complainant can seek immediate solace and advice at a rape crisis center. The victim's name is not publicized. Trained detectives and prosecutors, many of them females, handle sex crimes cases. The collection of forensic evidence is carried out by the police and medical personnel more scientifically and thoroughly. The laws of evidence have been changed to make corroboration less difficult, and arguments smearing her as a willing participant based on her past sexual experiences are less likely to be admissible in court because of shield laws. She does not have to struggle to her utmost to prove that what happened to her was against her will.

And yet, serious problems persist: reporting rates, clearance rates, prosecution rates, conviction rates, and incarceration rates remain stubbornly low.

Sexual assaults have been exposed as a festering problem on college campuses, on military bases, in jails and prisons, and even in some dysfunctional marriages.

Strategies to reduce rape include focusing on educating girls and women to take precautions, on controlling known offenders, and on eradicating what are believed to be institutional supports and cultural encouragements for sexual aggression.

KEY TERMS DEFINED IN THE GLOSSARY

acquaintance rapes, 331

agency, 337

carnal knowledge, 326

corroboration, 353

dual verbal defense, 353

heiress stealing, 327

ideal types, 330

implied consent, 334

posttraumatic stress disorder, 329

rape crisis syndrome, 329

rape kit, 356

reasonableness standard, 352

series victimizations, 338

sexual assault response teams, 355

shield laws, 352

statutory rape, 327

QUESTIONS FOR DISCUSSION AND DEBATE

1. Compile a list of all the ways rape victims were handled insensitively and improperly in the past, as described in Box 10.2. Discuss how each problem is supposed to be handled today.

2. Explain why the concepts of victim facilitation and precipitation are so controversial today when applied to sexual assaults and rapes.

3. Under what circumstances, if any, should the identity of a woman who has been raped be made public? Should the man's name always be released to the press?

4. Discuss the pros and cons of trying to reduce rapes by trying to convince girls and women to alter their behavior.

CRITICAL THINKING QUESTIONS

1. If rapes take place in jails and prisons among men, then what are the root causes of sexual violence?

2. Speculate about the possible reasons why the proportion of rapes reported to the police has not improved over the decades, according to *NCVS* figures.

3. Speculate about the possible reasons for the decline in rape clearance rates over the decades, according to *UCR* figures.

4. What should preadolescent boys be told about rape victims? Should preadolescent girls be told the same information about rape victims?

5. Go over each of the rape myths in Box 10.1 and argue that these beliefs are not myths but realities. Why are these beliefs so controversial?

SUGGESTED RESEARCH PROJECTS

1. Compile a list of policies (such as setting up a sex crimes squad) and opportunities for assistance (such as establishing a rape crisis center) that can be offered by government, nonprofit, self-help, and charitable organizations to ease the plight of sexual assault victims. Then check with local criminal justice officials, women's organizations, and others in the helping professions to see which policies and services on the list are available in your hometown.

2. Find out how allegations of sexual misconduct are handled on your campus. Discover where to go to file a complaint; analyze any forms that have to be filled out; establish what rights the complainant and the accused are supposed to be able to exercise; examine the annual campus crime reports for the past few years to see if any sexual assaults and rapes have been reported to the administration; and determine if a campus climate survey has been conducted and what its findings were.

3. Search databases of newspaper and magazine articles to find accounts of recent arrests, trials, and convictions of men for surreptitiously slipping date rape drugs to unsuspecting girls and women. Summarize the cases that seem the most solid and convincing, in terms of assessing the seriousness of the threat of drug-facilitated rapes.

4. See if your local police department makes public the number of sexual assault reports they receive each year and the clearance rate that reflects their ability to solve these crimes. Interview detectives and prosecutors who handle these investigations to determine how they view the problems of low reporting rates, low solution rates, and low conviction rates.

11

Additional Groups of Victims with Special Problems

LEARNING OBJECTIVES

To appreciate the difficulties faced by individuals who are being stalked.

To become aware of the risks of violence and theft facing students in middle and high school.

To become more knowledgeable about the dangers facing students on college campuses.

To discover whether workplace violence is growing or diminishing.

To derive an accurate picture of the targets of hate crimes.

To appreciate the dangers of life behind bars.

To recognize the most risky assignments in police work.

To develop a realistic assessment of the threat of terrorist attacks within the United States.

This chapter examines additional groups of victims whose plights have been rediscovered in recent years: individuals hounded by menacing persons, students harmed in schools and on college campuses, individuals targeted by hate-filled offenders, prisoners attacked by other inmates, workers injured or murdered while doing their jobs, police officers wounded or slain in the line of duty, and innocent persons within the United States harmed by terrorist attacks. To some unavoidable extent, these categories overlap. For example, some of the persons injured by workplace violence were women who had been stalked by ex-lovers. Now that these groups are receiving the long overdue attention they deserve, the criminal justice system needs to improve how it handles their cases and addresses their needs.

INDIVIDUALS MENACED BY STALKERS

Stalking: A New Word for an Old Problem

Stalking is a serious and pervasive crime that affects millions of Americans each year.... This dangerous and criminal behavior is still often mischaracterized as harmless.... Persistent stalking and harassment can lead to serious consequences for victims, whose lives may be upended by fear. Some victims may be forced to take extreme measures to protect themselves, such as changing jobs, relocating to a new home, or even assuming a new identity. (President Barack Obama, 2010)

Terrorists, political assassins, mob hit men, and kidnappers always have trailed and hunted down their prey before finding an opportune moment to strike. But it was not until the 1980s that the term **stalking** was coined and entered into everyday language. The media began to use it in the aftermath of a widely publicized attack in 1982 when an actor was repeatedly stabbed near her home by an obsessed fan; she made a movie about her ordeal to raise consciousness about this unrecognized danger. Another young actor was shot to death when she opened her door by a jealously deranged admirer in 1989. Since then, this long-standing problem plaguing celebrities and public figures, but also everyday people who are locked in conflict with particular individuals, has been rediscovered as a confrontational crime that could potentially escalate into a sexual assault, a beating, or on rare occasions even a murder.

Stalking is defined as a pattern of criminal conduct inflicted by an offender on an unwilling target who becomes fearful for his or her own safety. The illegal acts include certain intimidating, harassing, and threatening behaviors that would make a reasonable person afraid of an impending attack that could inflict bodily harm. Confusion and controversy can arise because a neutral observer may consider certain perfectly legal acts as nonthreatening, such as repeated phone, e-mail, and text messages and unwanted "gifts" and unwelcome "chance" encounters that evolve into face-to-face confrontations. Other acts clearly could be interpreted as ominous: following at a short distance, spying on someone and taking photos or videos, tracking a person through some hidden GPS device, and contacting the target's family, friends, or employers. Before an appropriate expression was devised to capture the essence of these intolerable intrusions into another's daily life, individuals who were stalked faced a special problem: Being shadowed, hounded, and bombarded with one-sided communications was not taken seriously by the authorities unless and until physical injuries were sustained. Even though threatening behavior is hard to prove and difficult to stop, in 1990 California's legislature was the first to criminalize these unnerving situations. Soon after, the Los Angeles Police Department established a Threat Management Unit, the first squad specifically set up to investigate calls for help from people sensing that they were targets of an impending attack.

Two types of victim–offender relationships account for most complaints. In celebrity stalking, the first category, a well-known person (often a pop star, media personality, professional athlete, or political figure) experiences continual, unwanted interference from either a "secret admirer" or an outright enemy. These nuisance cases become highly publicized if an attack followed by an arrest takes place. In the second, more common, type, the target knows and is repeatedly contacted by the aggressor in a frightening way. This kind of prior-relationship stalking can materialize between professionals and their clients, employers and their employees, or former intimate partners. It can begin with benign contacts but escalate as the undesired attention becomes a distressing reminder of unresolved personal issues and growing hostility. Stalkers shadow their targets as they engage in routine activities and linger in front of their homes, schools, or workplaces. They also might vandalize their target's property, harm their pets, approach their children, steal their mail, and seek to get them in trouble with the law, friends, kin, landlords, and employers.

Victims can suffer in a number of ways. If they are hunted and haunted, they may experience anxiety, panic attacks, depression, sleep disturbances, nightmares, memory lapses, and weight loss, among other emotional and physical symptoms. Financially, the harassment may inflict costs because of damaged possessions, lost earnings from missing work, and in extreme cases, moving expenses to relocate (OJP, 2008b).

The Scope of the Problem

Stalking is usually measured by researchers by interviewing or surveying members of the general public. Respondents are categorized as stalking victims if they disclose that they were contact many times by the same person in the same way, or if they experienced a number of different kinds of unwanted contacts by the same person, and then became very fearful that they, or someone close to them, subsequently would be harmed or killed (Breiding et al., 2014).

Using this methodology, over 5 million women disclosed that they were stalked in 2011, which corresponded to an incidence rate of 42 per 1,000. For males, the rate was half as serious, at about 21 per 1,000. Taken together, nearly 7.5 million people were stalked during 2011. This study projected a lifetime prevalence rate of about 15 percent for women and nearly 6 percent for men, based on a national telephone survey (Breiding et al., 2014).

But these findings were much higher than the estimates derived from the first national phone survey carried out about 15 years earlier. This study concluded that 1.4 million people (about 1 million of whom were females) considered themselves to be victims of stalking in one year in the mid-1990s. The estimated prevalence rate of being stalked at some point in their lives for women was about 8 percent and about 2 percent for men (Tjaden and Thoennes, 1998).

A special survey by the *NCVS* yielded findings that were in the middle of this range. About 3.3 million people age 18 or older identified themselves as having experienced stalking (which was broadly defined) during 2006. That translated into an incidence rate of 15 per 1,000. Almost half received an unwanted contact once a week, and about one-tenth endured five years or more of unwelcomed intrusions into their lives. Most of the unwanted contacts that made the recipients fearful were phone calls and messages, but about a third of the sample said that the wrongdoer followed or spied on them. About 7 out of 10 respondents knew their stalker in some capacity. About one in eight who had jobs missed work as a result of the trouble they experienced. About one in seven moved to escape their tormentors. As for differential risks, separated and divorced persons experienced the highest rates, at 33 per 1,000, as did low-income people. In terms of age, risks were highest for 18- to 24-year-olds, and then dropped off among older groups. Women were at greater risk than men, but both sexes reported their problems to the police at roughly equal rates (about 40 percent) (Baum et al., 2009; and Catalano, 2012a).

A study of college women yielded a much higher victimization rate because it used an even broader definition of stalking. Its screening question was posed as follows: "Since the school year began, has anyone from a stranger to an ex-boyfriend repeatedly followed you; watched you; or phoned, written, or e-mailed you in ways that seemed obsessive and made you afraid or concerned about your safety?" About 13 percent of the college women in the sample answered "Yes." However, the percentage answering "Yes" dropped to only about 2 percent when the question was rephrased to ask whether the person who was the source of the unwanted attention actually threatened harm, which is the definition used in many state statutes. Almost one-third of college women disclosed that they suffered emotionally because of a campus stalking incident (Fisher, Cullen, and Turner, 2000).

Although most stalkers do not become physically abusive, their unnerved targets worry that the unwanted intrusions might escalate into a beating, a kidnapping, a sexual assault, or even a murder. An FBI study discovered that 30 percent of slain women had been stalked by their former boyfriends or husbands before the former intimates murdered them (Office of Justice Programs, 1998). An inquiry that focused solely on females killed by their intimate partners revealed that most (76 percent) had been stalked by these murderous men before the fatal encounter (McFarlane et al., 1999). In general, intimate partners or former intimates issue more serious warnings, are more persistent, are more likely to escalate the frequency and intensity of their ominous contacts, and are more likely to follow through on those threats, often by using weapons, against their former lovers, their property, or even third parties close to them. Former intimate partners are also more likely to know their targets greatest fears and vulnerabilities and to reoffend, even after a court issues an order of protection (see Logan, 2010). Targets of nonsexual obsessions are more likely to be harassed by mentally ill but less dangerous offenders (Farnham, James, and Cantrell, 2000).

The most common tactics stalkers use against their victims include unwanted phone calls and messages but also physical surveillance (shadowing around, showing up at places of work, etc.) and property invasion (trespassing). **Proxy stalking**, carried out in behalf of the perpetrator, takes place when the target is closely watched by a family member, friend, new intimate partner, or even a private investigator hired to maintain surveillance.

Turning to the Criminal Justice System for Relief Spurred on by victims' rights groups, by 1994 all 50 states had criminalized the practice of willfully, purposefully, maliciously, and repeatedly

pursuing and harassing someone. Congress passed a comparable Interstate Stalking Act in 1996, making it a felony to travel across state lines with the intent to kill, injure, harass, or intimidate someone who, as a result of these actions, reasonably fears death or serious bodily injury. Antistalking laws fill a void in the patchwork of statutes forbidding menacing, trespassing, and threatening behavior and allow the authorities to take action before the object of the unwanted attention is seriously hurt.

To permit the police to arrest a stalker before an attack is actually carried out, many state laws focus on the victim's state of mind as well as the offender's intentions. These laws take context into account and require that the targeted individual has a reasonable fear of death or grave bodily injury that arises from a credible threat of violence made by the aggressor. In some jurisdictions, stalking is a misdemeanor, while in others it is a felony. Most states have laws that distinguish misdemeanor from felony stalking depending on how ominous the threat is. First offenses usually are prosecuted as misdemeanors. Stiffer punishments for felonies can be imposed if the offender actually causes bodily harm or confines or restrains the person being pursued, or if there are aggravating factors (such as brandishing a weapon, harassing someone under 16 years of age, disregarding an order of protection, or violating the restrictive conditions of probation or parole) (Beck et al., 1992; Hunzeker, 1992; Kolarik, 1992; Wright et al., 1996; and Stalking Resource Center, 2009).

Of the incidents that are reported to the police, less than a quarter lead to prosecution. Only about half of the prosecutions result in convictions, usually not for stalking per se, but for other minor crimes such as disorderly conduct, harassment, menacing, intimidation, trespassing, vandalism, simple assault (and in the more serious instances, breaking and entering or robbery). Many stalkers violated orders of protection that their intended prey had obtained in court (Tjaden and Thoennes, 1998; Dunn, 2002; and Jordan et al., 2003).

Individuals who just want to be left alone will have a tough time convincing the authorities to take action if the police officers are not adequately trained to recognize the various forms that the outlawed behavior might take. Furthermore, targets often find it unreasonably difficult to document that they are being subjected to meaningful threats. The burden of proof is so high that very few stalkers are found guilty, and most of these misdemeanants are jailed for just a few weeks. For these reasons, victim advocates proposed an updated model stalking code for state legislatures to consider, which closed loopholes in existing laws. It would make the following additional behaviors punishable: engaging in obsessive and controlling actions; targeting third parties (family members, children, friends) in order to instill fear; harassing a person when exercising visitation or custody rights; misusing the court system to file motions and suits ("litigation abuse"); applying sophisticated surveillance technology to monitor movements; impersonating a target to ruin credit or interfere with employment; and posting and disseminating inaccurate and embarrassing information or humiliating photographs (NCVC, 2007).

Whereas some people consider existing laws to be so limited as to be ineffective, civil libertarians consider the wording to be so vague and overly broad as to be unconstitutional. Some improper conduct that could be misconstrued as constituting stalking should not be outlawed, they say. Alleged stalkers may believe that their repeated activities are allowed under First Amendment free speech protections. These persistent people don't realize that they could find themselves as defendants in criminal and civil courts. Also, some hastily crafted statutes may grant too much discretion to law enforcement agencies, opening the door to arbitrary enforcement (see Endo, 1999; and Reno, 1999).

Reducing Risks   Not surprisingly, stalking victims sometimes find themselves being faulted for enabling their predicament to develop. Victims can be blamed for facilitating (through carelessness), precipitating (through rash conduct), or even provoking (through intentional incitements) a stalker's preoccupation with initiating or reviving a relationship. Victims' fears sometimes are belittled. Female targets in particular are told that they are imagining

that harmless messages foreshadow impending doom, or that they should be flattered by the attention, or that they are somehow encouraging the unwanted contacts through bad judgment. Victim blaming insists that the behavior of the targets is at the root of the problem and that they should examine their own responses and then change how they react (see Meloy, 1998).

To head off serious trouble, the following suggestions have been offered: Tell the offender to desist just once and then break off contact; keep a log or journal documenting acts of harassment and intimidation; formulate plans that will enhance safety at home, when traveling, and while at work; and fully exercise the options for protection and prosecution offered by the criminal and civil justice systems (Spence-Diehl, 1999; and Day One, 2011). Research by victimologists is needed to determine whether this advice is sound and genuinely effective.

Stalking victims can take many self-protective measures. In addition to reporting the crime and preserving corroborating evidence, they can go to court for a restraining order, sign up for an unlisted phone number (and a trap to tape incoming calls), change locks, vary their daily routines, practice self-defense techniques, seek the company of trustworthy protectors, and pack an emergency suitcase for a temporary escape to a more secure place. In extreme cases, terrorized people can move away to an undisclosed location and even change their identities to enhance their safety and the wellbeing of their families.

Unfortunately, stalkers are discovering new high-tech ways to track the movements of their victims, such as by secretly placing a tracking device on a target's car or by surreptitiously installing spyware to reveal e-mails written and websites visited by the people they are hounding ("When technology gets diabolical...," 2005). GPS technology linked to smartphones also can be used to facilitate stalking. Tracking programs have assisted motorists who are hopelessly lost, or helped parents keep tabs on their children, and even enabled detectives to locate kidnap victims or arrest suspects on their most wanted lists. But those same services offered by cellular carriers also empower stalkers to monitor the whereabouts of their targets, often within a tight radius of less than 100 feet. To thwart this high-tech threat, some shelters that house battered women insist that their cell phones—which the victims assumed were a source of protection—be decommissioned while they take refuge at these secret locations (Scheck, 2010). About 10 percent of survey respondents in 2006 who said they were stalked reported being tracked by a GPS device, and 8 percent said they had been monitored through listening devices or with video or digital cameras (Baum et al., 2009).

Like spouse abuse and forcible rape, stalking seems to be an offense that is usually motivated by desires for domination and subjugation. Most frequently, the terrorized party is a woman who is being followed by a jealous, possessive, violence-prone ex-boyfriend or ex-husband who refuses to accept her decision that their romantic relationship is over. However, many variations on the themes of "fatal attraction," "murderous obsession," or "erotomania delusions" are possible: A young man's new girlfriend can be trailed and threatened by his old girlfriend, a therapist can be besieged by a former patient who feels abandoned and betrayed after an affair, or a boss might be chased after by a disgruntled worker who was subjected to intense sexual harassment, then sexually exploited, and fired afterward. Most stalkers, according to clinical studies, are primarily motivated by vengeance and hatred of the victim, as opposed to genuine affection or romantic inclinations. They desire to exert power or to regain control over their targets, whom they blame for the falling out (Meloy, 1998).

Cyberstalking: A New Word for a New Problem

A young woman goes to court and gets a no-contact restraining order against a 28-year-old man who is harassing her. In retaliation, during the course of more than a year, the man posts her name and address on popular Internet websites including MySpace, Facebook, and Craigslist, inviting men to visit her home for "sexual gratification." At the same

time, he e-mails death threats to her, according to the indictment in federal court that charges him with cyberstalking. (Wood, 2008)

Before the Internet, the prospect of being chased through cyberspace and getting bombarded with unwanted messages didn't exist. When the potential for abuse was first recognized—that obsessive assailants and sexual predators had a new way to discover and pursue their targets—there wasn't an adequate phrase to characterize this disturbing situation. At first, the problem was referred to as "online abuse," "online harassment," or even "cyber harassment." Those who became alarmed about inappropriate and worrisome communications they were receiving via instant messaging, in their e-mail accounts, in chat rooms, and on widely accessed social networking websites faced a special problem. The authorities to whom they turned for help in moments of despair merely advised them to shut off their computers. Often they were told that the vile suggestions and ominous threats awaiting them when they logged on, or that were posted about them on others' webpages, did not rise to the level of criminal activity.

The first anguished complainants got the runaround from law enforcement officials because it was unclear which agency, if any, had jurisdiction—local police, state police, the local prosecutor, the state attorney general's office, or a branch of the federal government. Geographically, the jurisdiction question was whether the crime took place within the sender's area or within the recipient's area. Internet service providers generally were not cooperative with investigators because of concerns about respecting the privacy of their subscribers (Hitchcock, 2002).

By the turn of the century, the term **cyberstalking** was coined to describe this potentially dangerous conduct. Within a few years, most states added provisions to their stalking and harassment statutes to outlaw the misuse of computers and electronic communications to pass along threats. The criminal justice system is becoming more responsive as police departments set up units to investigate computer crimes (as the NYPD did in

1995), and county prosecutors establish stalking and threat assessment bureaus (as in Los Angeles) or use the staffs of existing sex crimes divisions.

However, many law enforcement agencies do not have enough adequately trained officers and prosecutors and sufficient state-of-the-art technology to successfully pursue these kinds of cases. Furthermore, the threats might not be taken seriously if the authorities judge the likelihood of an actual physical confrontation to be remote, especially if the harasser lives far away in another region or a different country. Self-help and support groups have sprung up on the Internet to assist and advise those who feel distressed, frustrated, and powerless to stop the unwanted communications. Voluntary online surveys filled out at these websites indicate that the majority of victims of cyberstalking are female, especially teenage girls and young women, and that most of the perpetrators are male. Many offenders seem to be complete strangers, which can be particularly unnerving because their appearances and whereabouts, as well as the credibility of their threats, are unknown (Hitchcock, 2002; Riveira, 2002; and D'Ovidio and Doyle, 2003).

Of all the persons who identified themselves as stalking victims in a *NCVS*-based survey in 2006, about one-fourth disclosed that they had experienced cyberstalking, either via their e-mail accounts (83 percent) and/or by instant messaging (35 percent) (Baum et al., 2009). As for pursuing a reported case of stalking in cyberspace, during 2001 only 16 percent of prosecutors' offices nationally (but 77 percent of those serving large cities) handled an e-mail cyberstalking case (DeFrances, 2002). By 2005, 36 percent of prosecutors' offices nationwide (with 82 percent of those serving more than 1 million residents) had pursued a cyberstalking case (Perry, 2006).

A comparison of victims of stalking compared to cyberstalking discerned that those who experienced cyberstalking found that the harassment didn't last as long, and they were not as fearful. However, they were a little more likely to report the disturbing contacts and to take self-protective measures like changing their e-mail addresses, taking time off from school or work, or avoiding certain people, according to a detailed analysis of *NCVS* data (Nobles, et al., 2014).

The lifestyle-exposure and routine activities theory has been applied to the problem of being pursued through cyberspace. It appears that adding strangers as friends on social media sites, harassing other people online, attempting to hack into other people's social network accounts, and associating with "deviant peers" online (for example, engaged in sending sexually explicit images or advances) are associated with higher odds of becoming a cyberstalking victim, according to a web-based survey of college students' experiences (Reyns et al., 2011).

VICTIMS OF CRIMES COMMITTED AT SCHOOL

Threats Facing Middle and High School Students

Teenage students face a special problem. Compulsory education laws compel them to attend their local high school, unless their parents can afford a private or parochial school or are able to home-school them. By entering into the mainstream of high school activities, they are forced to interact with potential victimizers. The resulting experiences may be aggravating, terrifying, and even deadly. On rare occasions, bullied students turn the tables on their tormenters, unleash retaliatory violence, and in the process become assailants themselves. Unfortunately, in an environment burdened by threats of attacks, counterattacks, security procedures, and other potential disruptions, teachers will find it difficult to stick to lesson plans, and distracted targets and their classmates will have trouble learning what they need to know.

To measure the relative safety of various schools and school systems, several federal government agencies monitor reports of incidents of violence and theft. Statistics from the BJS's annual *NCVS* reveal how many adolescents between the ages of 12 and 18 suffer acts of violence and theft that they are willing to disclose to interviewers, whether or not these negative experiences were reported to the school authorities or the police. The statistics permit a comparison of the risks students faced on school property as distinct from other places, including their own homes and neighborhoods (see Table 11.1).

The data assembled in Table 11.1 from the *NCVS* shows one reassuring finding that should not be a surprise: The victimization rate for students in middle/junior high schools and high schools dropped sharply from 1992 to 2012, a trend that mirrored a general decline in crime rates burdening Americans of all ages and at all locations. Property crimes vastly outnumber serious violent crimes both inside and outside of schools. But while 12- to 18-year-olds were on school grounds, they suffered more thefts than at home or in their neighborhoods. Over the 20-year span, theft rates in both settings dropped sharply and the "at school/away from school" gap narrowed. As for serious acts of violence (not counting simple assaults like fistfights), the worst year was in 1992 outside of school and 1996 inside of schools. Over two decades, the combined rate of rapes, sexual assaults, robberies, and aggravated assaults committed against students inside schools subsided considerably while out on the streets it dropped even more dramatically. In sum, while under the supervision of responsible adults, students are less likely to suffer serious violence in the classrooms, lunchrooms, stairwells, corridors, and school yards than when they are out on the streets or back at home. Even though school safety improved impressively from 1992 to 2012,

the level of violence in the students' communities subsided even more dramatically. And school grounds still were the scenes of more thefts of personal items in 2012 than the suddenly safer streets (see the bottom row of Table 11.1).

However, as with all databases, the accuracy of school crime statistics must be examined objectively. Occasionally claims appear in the news media that middle and high school safety officers (sometimes called school resource officers), principals, and even top school system administrators may seek to suppress initial reports or the eventual official records of particular incidents to make schools seem safer than they really are. Principals may be acting in good faith, and certain disruptive behaviors surely fall into a gray area where discretion legitimately can be exercised. But intentional statistical manipulation and underreporting of victimizations violates federal No Child Left Behind legislation. It also does a disservice to students, parents, and members of the staff because if a school does not get the attention and resources that it deserves, everyone inside it will be at greater risk (Gootman, 2007).

As always, murders are the most accurately counted of all crimes. Fortunately, there are not many of these tragedies on school property to count. The graph in Figure 11.1 shows data about slayings of youths between the ages of 5 and 19 since the start of the 1990s, when school-based data collection and reporting systems were first established (note that murders of teachers, staff,

T A B L E   11.1   Victimization Rates per 1,000 Students, 12 to 18 Years Old, at School Compared to Away from School, 1992–2012

Type of Crime and Location	Serious Violence at School	Serious Violence Away from School	Thefts at School	Thefts Away from School
Year				
1992	8	44	114	78
1996	14	33	85	60
2000	8	15	49	45
2004	4	10	41	27
2008	5	10	25	19
2012	3	7	24	18

NOTE: Serious violence includes forcible rape, sexual assaults, robberies, and aggravated assaults but excludes simple assaults.

SOURCE: *NCVS* findings, compiled by the NCES, Indicators of School Crime and Safety, 2013, adapted from Table 2.1.

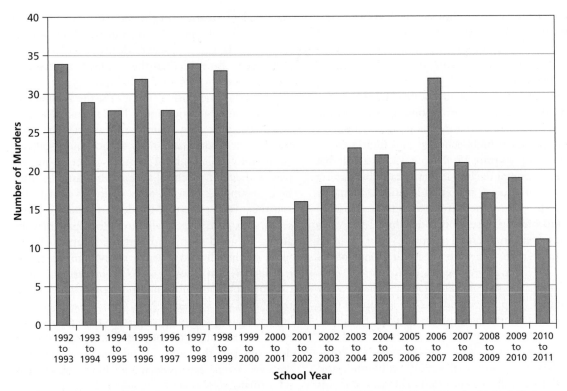

FIGURE 11.1   Trends in Murders of Students at Elementary, Middle, and High Schools, United States, School Years 1992 to 2011
SOURCES: National Center for Educational Statistics, 2013.

and parents on school grounds are not included in these body counts).

Often a single horrific outbreak of mass murder accounts for most of the deaths of students in a given year. The vicious mass shooting of 20 elementary school children (and six adults) by a severely disturbed young man (who had access to his mother's arsenal) in Sandy Hook, Connecticut, is a sad example that will cause the death toll for the 2012–2013 school year to spike (not shown in Figure 11.1). The trend line shows that school security has improved to some degree. The number of rare yet tragic murders remained relatively constant during most of the 1990s, even though killings between adolescents beyond school grounds declined during this time. At the end of the 1990s, a substantial drop in slayings on school grounds took place, and this reduced level of lethal violence was maintained during most of the first decade of the twenty-first century, except for the 2006–2007 school year (see Figure 11.1).

Unfortunately, a spate of school shootings has overshadowed that positive trend in public discourse and in the minds of concerned parents. Although they are highly unusual, these sudden and senseless outbursts of gunfire directed at fellow students, teachers, and administrators by distraught and often suicidal assailants have permanently changed the environment of the nation's elementary, middle, and high schools. To curb violence and theft on school grounds, many superintendents and principals now take security considerations much more seriously. Reports about threats issued by disgruntled students usually are checked out. Many schools have beefed up security by hiring more school safety officers, arming them, carrying out searches of backpacks, installing surveillance cameras and metal detectors at their front doors, devising lockdown procedures, and instituting conflict resolution and antibullying programs. To put the problem of school violence into perspective, it is important to note that each year the proportion of youngsters slain on school grounds is less than 2 percent of all youth killings. In other words, more than 98 percent of children who are murdered are killed in settings other than school. Therefore, statistically speaking, even turbulent high schools remain relatively safe compared to nearby streets, parks, and homes. Put another way, students are close to 50 times more likely to be murdered away from school than on school grounds (NCES, 2008; 2013).

Threats Facing College Students

In the not-so-distant past, the ivy-covered buildings on academic quadrangles were pictured as sanctuaries that were shielded from the problems of the "real world." But a growing stream of stories about college students killed, raped, and robbed on campus has shattered that myth. Undergraduates and graduate students can be hurt by other students, or by outsiders who enter their buildings and grounds, or by local residents when students venture outside their gated communities. An abundance of bicycles, electronic devices, and computers in an open, unguarded environment attracts burglars and thieves to dormitories and cafeterias. Special types of interpersonal violence can break out too, taking the form of assaults (including brutality against fraternity pledges during hazing), drunken brawls after sports events, hate crimes (gay bashings and racial attacks), gang rapes (at parties), and date rapes, especially after heavy drinking.

The Extent of Crime on Campus America's nearly 8 million part-time and full-time college students face a special problem. Most undergraduates are between the ages of 18 and 24—precisely at the stage of life when the dangers of engaging in violence and theft reach their peak. Simultaneously, people in that same age range face the gravest risks of being harmed by physical attacks and stealing. Demographically speaking, college campuses contain a volatile mix of potential offenders and victims. Drug taking and drinking raise the odds of trouble breaking out. But what is the reality?

It should come as no surprise that college students turn out to be less likely to experience violence than their nonstudent counterparts. For example, a large proportion of killings that take place on the meanest streets of the nation's toughest neighborhoods involve young men between the ages of 18 and 24 as a perpetrator, a victim, or both. But rarely is either party enrolled at an institution of higher learning. Similarly, young men who were not students were robbed much more often (about 12 per 1,000 per year) than undergrads (just 7 per 1,000). Nonstudents 18–24 years old also were subjected to aggravated assaults and simple assaults more often than their college counterparts. Most of the assailants of college students were strangers (58 percent) rather than acquaintances. Most of these attackers (66 percent) did not use a weapon, and only a small proportion (9 percent) pulled out a gun. College students were less inclined to report these incidents to the police than nonstudents (35 percent filed complaints compared to 47 percent). Not surprisingly, the overwhelming majority of attacks were carried out off-campus (93 percent), and after dark (72 percent), according to an analysis of *NCVS* findings from 1995 to 2002 (Baum and Klaus, 2005).

A more recent study that focused only on women between the ages of 18 and 24 found that nonstudents were robbed at a much higher rate than students (6 compared to 3 per 1,000 per year). Nonstudents also suffered from aggravated assaults more frequently than college women (13 compared to 8) as well as from simple assaults (47 compared to 29). Female nonstudents were sexually assaulted a little more often (8 compared to 6), suffered completed rapes more often, and were more inclined to report what happened to them to the police than college women (32 percent in contrast to 20 percent), according to an analysis of a massive *NCVS* database covering the period 1995 to 2013 (Sinozich and Langton, 2014).

Despite the relative safety of college campuses, serious crimes, even murders, can and do take place on the grounds of institutions of higher learning on occasion. This case led to federal legislation that imposed reporting requirements on college administrations:

> *Early one morning, a student with a history of drug and alcohol abuse wanders through a campus dormitory, passing through a series of three propped-open doors that should have been locked. He invades the room of a young woman and proceeds to torture, sodomize, rape, and ultimately kill her. He is caught, convicted, and sentenced to die. But her parents discover that crime on campus is "one of the best-kept secrets in the country." The callousness, stonewalling, and cover-up by the college's administration intent on protecting the institution's public image causes the grieving parents to launch a lawsuit charging negligence and failure to warn of foreseeable dangers. The college offers a settlement, and the parents use the money to set up the first national not-for-profit organization dedicated to preventing campus violence and assisting victims. The parents also lead a movement to force colleges to reveal to current and prospective students information about incidents taking place on campus. After nine states pass laws requiring disclosure of crime data within just a few years, Congress passes the Crime Awareness and Campus Security Act of 1990.* (Clery and Clery, 2001)

A handful of highly publicized shootings and rapes, as well as a spate of negligence lawsuits filed by distraught parents, have compelled administrators, faculties, and student governments to address threats to personal safety on college and university campuses. Image-conscious administrators initially devised ways to downplay the risks that their students actually faced for fear that such revelations would damage their schools' reputations, scare away potential candidates from applying for admission, and hurt fundraising campaigns seeking donations from alumni. Despite continued opposition by administrators, Congress extended the themes of its 1990 student right-to-know legislation by passing the Higher Education Act in 1992. It mandated

that colleges establish sexual assault prevention programs and grant procedural rights to rape victims.

Congress imposed even tougher right-to-know regulations in 1998 with the enactment of the Jeanne Clery Disclosure of Campus Security Policy and Campus Crime Statistics Act (named after the young woman murdered in her dorm in the incident cited above). It required institutions receiving federal aid to maintain detailed crime logs and issue comprehensive annual crime reports. All institutions of higher learning must compile and disclose the nature, date, time, and location of incidents brought to the attention of campus security officers as well as the local police. Crimes committed in residential housing, off-campus buildings, parking areas, and adjacent streets must be included. The log must be made available to the public—especially students, parents, employees, and journalists—during normal business hours. These statistics can be posted online as well. Timely warnings must be issued to alert the campus community about ongoing threats to personal safety. Administrations face a fine of $25,000 for each willful violation of the reporting requirements (Carter, 2000; and Sampson, 2004). In 2014, amendments to the Clery Act went in to effect that were monitored by the U.S. Department of Education. College administrations were required to start collecting and disclosing data about incidents of domestic violence, dating violence, sexual assault, and stalking on campus; to offer programs to incoming students and employees designed to prevent these four kinds of criminal activity; and to improve their responses to these offenses by offering assistance to victims to change their academic, living, working, and transportation arrangements, and by notifying them about their rights (Clery Center, 2014).

Each year, reports of property crimes on college campuses are much more numerous than violent crimes, according to the extensive database maintained by the U.S. Department of Education (see Table 11.2). Larcenies top the list, but some of these thefts are of school property from offices or labs or items from the bookstore rather than students' possessions (and therefore do not appear in Table 11.2).

TABLE 11.2   Crimes Committed on College Campuses, United States, 2001–2011

Type of Crime	Number of Incidents per Year						
	2001	2003	2005	2007	2009	2011	2013
Murders	17	9	11	44	16	17	24
Forcible sex offenses	2,200	2,600	2,670	2,700	2,540	3,440	5,050
Robberies	1,660	1,630	1,550	1,560	1,410	1,650	1,570
Aggravated assaults	2,950	2,830	2,660	2,600	2,330	2,500	2,300
Burglaries	26,900	28,640	29,260	29,490	23,080	20,230	16,000
Motor vehicle thefts	6,220	6,290	5,530	4,620	3,980	3,620	3,260

NOTE: Numbers of reported incidents, except for murders, are rounded to the nearest 10.
Figures for 2001–2009 are from a slightly different DOE database.

SOURCES: U.S. Department of Education, Indicators of School Safety, 2013, On-Campus Crimes, Table 22.1; and U.S. Department of Education Campus Safety and Security Data Analysis Cutting Tool (2014).

Burglaries (again, not solely of student lockers or dorm rooms) take place more frequently than vehicle thefts from nearby lots and streets. As for violent offenses, aggravated assaults outnumber robberies and rapes. In terms of trends from 2001 to 2013, the numbers of reported aggravated assaults, burglaries, and motor vehicle thefts have declined. Reports of robberies have not improved much and complaints to the police or to campus security departments of forcible rapes and other sexual assaults have risen over the years.

Murders on college grounds are relatively rare, unlike on the contested turf of poor neighborhoods, where thousands of 18- to 24-year-olds lose their lives every year. Killings on campus, presented in the first row of Table 11.2, do not show a consistent trend. In 2007, a deranged undergraduate slaughtered 33 people, and another shooting rampage by a graduate student took place in 2008, snuffing out five lives, reversing any short-lived improvements in campus security (see Hauser and O'Connor, 2007; and Nizza, 2008). During 2013, over 25 shootings took place on or near college campuses, claiming the lives of 18 people and wounding many others (Kingkade, 2014). The total loss of life in 2013 stood at 24.

Most campus slayings involved firearms and could be characterized as student-on-student, but some casualties included administrators, staff, and professors. (However, college teaching remains one of the safest occupations.) Box 11.1 lists some of the bloodiest high-profile shootings, mostly by undergraduates and graduate students, that broke out over the decades on campuses both large and small, in urban and rural settings claiming many innocent lives.

In the aftermath of bloody rampages, classes are cancelled, students build shrines and post messages of consolation online and organize memorials. Administrators set up scholarship funds in the names of the victims and offer crisis and grief counseling to distraught members of campus communities. But the reactions go far beyond those immediate responses. Campus police forces and local law enforcement agencies engage in "threat assessment" when necessary: a process that involves identification of troubled students and evaluation of verified facts about them, determining their threat level and devising an effective response (Booth et al., 2011). The FBI has encouraged administrators to involve the campus community in "active shooter" drills. These exercises are intended to limit the bloodshed when a mentally unbalanced person opens fire on unsuspecting targets. Many administrations are enhancing the mental health services offered at counseling centers especially to recognize red flags and identify potentially explosive members of the campus community. Simultaneously, they are arming their security forces and devising lockdown procedures to seal off buildings. In accordance with a 2008 federal law, campuses are signing up students and faculty to receive immediate emergency notification alerts via e-mail and text messages about incidents as soon as possible after they take place (Sander, 2011).

B O X   11.1   A Timeline of Some of the Worst Campus Shootings

Year	Campus	What Happened and Who the Casualties Were
1966	University of Texas	A student climbs a tower and opens fire, killing 16 and wounding 31.
1968	South Carolina State College	State police officers kill three students and wound 27 others during a protest against desegregation.
1970	Jackson State College	Highway Patrol officers kill two students and wound nine others by shooting into a crowd.
1971	Kent State University	National Guard troops open fire on antiwar demonstrators, killing four students and wounding nine.
1991	University of Iowa	A grad student slays three professors, an administrator, a student, and then himself.
1996	San Diego State	A grad student murders three professors during his thesis defense.
2002	Appalachian School of Law	A grad student who flunked out of school slays a dean, a professor, and a student and wounds three others.
2002	University of Arizona	A failing student kills three instructors and then himself.
2007	Virginia Tech University	An undergrad shoots to death 30 students and two professors and wounds 24 others in a rampage that begins in a dorm and ends in a classroom, before he takes his own life.
2008	Northern Illinois University	A grad student opens fire in a lecture hall, murdering five students and injuring 18 others before committing suicide.
2010	University of Alabama-Huntsville	A science professor who is turned down for tenure methodically shoots six members of her department at a meeting, killing three colleagues and wounding the others.
2011	Virginia Tech University	A gunman murders a campus police officer and then kills himself.
2012	Oikos University	A student suffering from paranoid schizophrenia shoots seven students to death and wounds three others.
2013	Santa Monica College	A student slays two family members and then goes on a shooting rampage near the college, killing five and wounding four others before dying from police bullets.
2014	University of California, Santa Barbara	A former student stabs to death his three roommates, fatally shoots two women in front of a sorority house and one man in a store, and injures 13 other people before engaging the police in a shootout and then ending his own life near the campus.

SOURCES: Wicker, 1970; Associated Press, 2008b; Dewan and Zezima, 2010; Sander, 2011; and Kingkade, 2014.

In the wake of the mass shootings listed in Box 11.1 above, some parents and students called for stricter gun control legislation and lobbied to designate campuses as gun-free zones (Mash, 2013). However, others took an opposite stance and argued that the problem was not too many guns on campus, but too few. Guns enthusiasts convinced legislatures in eight states to pass "licensed campus carry" laws (Burnett, 2011; and keepgunsoffcampus, 2014) (for a discussion of arming for self-defense, see Chapter 13). Meanwhile, hundreds of colleges have paid for a training program that encourages students to dispel feelings that they are defenseless and to take advantage of their superior numbers and to fight back with improvised weapons, from backpacks to laptops, to subdue a deranged gunman (Zagier, 2008). Even though the streets around urban universities and campus buildings and grounds are much safer than they were at the start of the 1990s, self-defense classes for students are growing in popularity. Some colleges offer credit for these courses; some are coed and others are designed to empower women. The syllabus not only centers on physical skills but also teaches about responsible decision making and the dangers of drinking to excess as well as everyday risk avoidance tactics (Schwab, 2008).

Because parents and prospective students understandably are concerned about campus security, it is tempting to try to calculate the victimization rates for various campuses to identify the safest and the most dangerous ones in the nation. But comparisons of relative safety can be misleading. The composition of the student body—undergrads compared to grad students, the ratio of men to women, and dorm residents versus commuters—varies dramatically. Also, campus student bodies change in size from day sessions to evening classes to nighttime residence hall populations. Furthermore, some colleges are situated in idyllic rural settings; others are located in densely populated urban neighborhoods or have several scattered satellite centers, branches, or affiliated teaching hospitals. It may even be downright unfair to compare security measures at minimally funded community colleges to those at well-endowed Ivy League universities, and to rank safety levels at large public urban institutions against small, sheltered, private, or religiously based colleges.

Usually, incidents that take place in the immediate vicinity of the campus that would boost the dangerousness ratings are caused by conditions that are beyond the college administration's ability to improve or control. Nonreporting to the campus security force or the local police may be a larger problem on certain campuses than others, so calculations of victimization rates can be inaccurate and misleading for this reason as well. Finally, published figures may be inaccurate and misleading for institutions whose administrations manipulate the numbers to make their campuses appear safer than they really are to attract security-minded applicants. An example of this would be downgrading burglaries—crimes involving intruders that should be reported to the U.S. Department of Education's National Center for Educational Statistics recording system—to larcenies not resulting from trespassing, which aren't counted by the NCES and don't have to be publicized to the college community, but are disclosed in the FBI's *UCR* (see Seward, 2006).

In 2005, Congress designated September as National Campus Safety Awareness Month (Feingold,

2005). To prevent incidents, most campuses now have gates and checkpoints, ID systems, electronic card-key entry systems to buildings, better locking devices, message boards, professional security forces, stepped-up patrols, extensive monitoring via video surveillance cameras, better lighting, indoor and outdoor emergency phones, evening shuttle buses, student escorts, crisis counseling centers, crime blotter columns in campus newspapers, and workshops on date rape and crime prevention as part of first-year orientations. Colleges are now rated in terms of the number and kinds of security measures they have implemented to protect their campus communities. By 2005, most public colleges had sworn officers with firearms and full arrest powers, but many private institutions of higher learning still had only unarmed security guards, according to a federal survey (Purdum, 1988; Smith, 1988; Graham, 1993; Mathews, 1993; Whitaker and Pollard, 1993; Lederman, 1994; Molotsky, 1997; Ottens and Hotelling, 2001; and Reaves, 2008).

Unfortunately, the relaxed and open atmosphere of academia, which was based on freedom of movement and free expression of ideas, is being sacrificed in the name of enhanced campus security (see Fox and McDowall, 2008; and Mathias, 2008). Despite the shocking and tragic outbreaks of violence at universities listed in Box 11.1, the special solution—and the best overall risk reduction advice—for the millions of college students seeking to avoid trouble, whether they are commuters or live in dormitories, is to spend as much time as possible on campus, because the buildings and grounds of the nation's nearly 3,700 institutions of higher learning still are among the safest locales in the country.

The Controversy over Hazing on Campus

A 26-year-old drum major in a marching band known for combining technical brilliance with innovative showmanship dies of hemorrhagic shock from being punched repeatedly during an initiation ritual. Because the marching band has a reputation for tolerating physical hazing, the board of trustees puts the band's leader on administrative leave and reprimands the college's president. The ringleader of the brutal ritual is convicted of manslaughter and felony hazing. (Taylor, 2011; and Hightower, 2014)

Hazing is a widespread practice that can be part of the process for selecting and inducting new members into an exclusive, highly sought, and cohesive group. A contradiction surrounds hazing. On the one hand, administrators, professors, parents, alumni, law enforcement officials, and legislators condemn it and try to suppress it. Hazing has been officially outlawed but continues to happen under the radar unless outrageous incidents make the news, triggering investigations and arrests, and ultimately lawsuits. On the other hand, these long-standing and widespread traditions are tolerated, perhaps accepted, sometimes defended, and even celebrated by undergraduates as an integral part of campus culture.

Hazing can be viewed as an expression of organized and institutionalized bullying, a rite of passage in which existing members subject new members to a period of probation while they are socialized into the group's mores—surely a necessary step to create group solidarity and maintain internal discipline. But in extreme cases, it can force would-be members to submit to conduct that can be dangerous and potentially illegal.

A nationwide survey of over 14,000 undergrads at more than 50 colleges and universities carried out in 2008 accentuated the negative, defining hazing as any activity imposed on someone seeking to join a group that humiliates, degrades, abuses, or endangers the pledge, regardless of his or her willingness to participate. Using this broad definition, the survey established that hazing not only permeates varsity athletics as well as fraternities and sororities but is also practiced in other student organizations like marching bands and performing arts groups. Alcohol consumption, public humiliation, isolation, sleep deprivation, and sex acts are common practices. More than half of all college students involved in clubs, teams, and organizations experienced hazing. Almost half of all respondents had already been through hazing by the time they entered their freshman year. Most significantly, 9 out of 10 students who had been through hazing did not consider themselves to have been abused. Ninety-five percent did not report their experiences to college officials. But about one-quarter of all coaches, advisors, and alumni were aware of the hazing that went on in the activities they supervised (Allan and Madden, 2008).

Just like abused children are at greater risk of becoming abusive parents and violence-prone persons, students who endure severe hazing and then become full-fledged members may be inclined to inflict harsh punishments on newcomers. To break this vicious cycle, institutions of higher education adopt a punitive zero-tolerance approach that calls for expelling the ringleaders and suspending the entire chapter whenever incidents come to light. If serious injuries result, college administrators hand the case over to the criminal justice system and prepare their defense against lawsuits launched by distraught parents. Despite these efforts to suppress hazing first implemented decades ago, the problem seems merely to have been driven underground (see Gose, 1997). A victim-blaming perspective suggests that to discourage the persistence of this banned practice, students who voluntarily and knowingly undergo hazing also should be subjected to disincentives such as having to attend counseling or perform community service (Taylor, 2011).

CASUALTIES OF WORKPLACE VIOLENCE

Fearing that he is about to be fired, a part-time letter carrier barges into the back room of his local post office and starts shooting wildly. He guns down 14 people and then kills himself. (Rugala, 2004)

■■■

A military reservist with a top secret clearance who was working for a defense contractor is waved through the checkpoint of a Navy base. Concealing a sawed-off shotgun, he walks around firing at unsuspecting people, slaying twelve and wounding four others for an hour and a half until the police kill him. A review by the Department of Defense concludes that his employer overlooked red flags in his troubled history indicating mental instability, and that the Navy was too focused on keeping a secure perimeter against outside threats and not concerned enough about the dangers posed by insiders granted clearance to enter military installations. (Cooper, 2014)

Shocking massacres like these serve as vivid reminders that workers can become injured or murdered while doing their jobs under conditions determined by their employers. In the wake of a spate of mass shootings during the 1980s and 1990s similar to the cases described above, the phrase *going postal* entered everyday conversations (see Ames, 2005). (However, a U.S. Postal Commission study concluded in 2000 that the derogatory expression was misleading and unfair because post office employees actually were less likely to be assaulted or killed on the job than other workers [see Rugala, 2004].)

Disgruntled or emotionally disturbed employees have attacked bosses or coworkers for many years, but the problem was not monitored or analyzed until its rediscovery in 1989, when the term *workplace violence* was coined. The U.S. Occupational Safety and Health Administration (OSHA) describes its scope as including any act or even any threat of harassment, intimidation, or physical assault or other disruptive behavior that takes place at a work site. According to OSHA's broad definition, even noncriminal matters (like verbal abuse) count, and the potential victims are not limited to employees but can also include customers, clients, and even visitors. Although this government agency warned that workplace violence can strike "anywhere, anytime, and no one is immune," it identified a number of risk factors: working in a position where handling cash is part of the duties; interacting with volatile and unstable people (as in a mental hospital); being employed in places where alcohol is served; performing tasks alone (such as cab drivers) or in isolated areas; and working late at night (as in convenience stores), especially in high-crime neighborhoods (OSHA, 2014).

On-the-job injuries and deaths certainly are not new: Recall images of pirates killing sailors when boarding ships on the high seas, and robbers shooting stagecoach drivers and crews on steam locomotives in the Old West. Now that monitoring systems are in place, it is possible for criminologists and victimologists to determine whether an upsurge in attacks and multiple slayings truly is taking place at job sites or whether more attention is being paid to scattered tragedies. The evidence-based answer is that the shootings that attract sensational media coverage are relatively rare events. The most common on-the-job threats that cause business owners, administrators, and supervisors concern about their employees' ability to focus on the tasks at hand are crimes that are quite mundane—robberies, assaults, stalkings, and acts of intimidation, plus potentially disruptive noncriminal matters such as abusive bullying relationships and sexual harassment (Rugala, 2004).

During the 1990s, the rate of workplace violence declined just as the rate of violent crime did both before and after work across the country. Incidents at work on average made up about 18 percent of the violent crimes committed each year from 1993 to 1999, according to the *NCVS*. The survey identified the characteristics of typical victims. It discovered that nonfatal violence harmed males more often than females, and younger workers (20–34 years old) more often than older workers—patterns that were the same as for similar crimes outside of work. But whites suffered a higher rate of assault than blacks (13 compared to 10 victims per 1,000 workers per year), which was the opposite of the pattern for nonworkplace violence. People employed by the government were harmed at about the same rate as employees in the private sector (Duhart, 2001).

Casualties While on the Job

Certain jobs are far more dangerous than others. For example, injuries and deaths arising from robberies are a real possibility for cashiers in convenience stores, gas station attendants, and taxi drivers.

Taxi drivers and chauffeurs of limousines and car services suffer the highest rate of workplace homicides of any occupational group: 18 murders for every 100,000 workers per year. These drivers make up only 0.2 percent of the workforce, but their deaths account for 7 percent of on-the-job killings. The actual danger of being murdered during a robbery is even higher for cabbies collecting cash fares from passengers who are strangers than for chauffeurs for limousine services handling credit card transactions. Besides intentional slayings, taxi drivers face additional risks of injury and death from automobile accidents. Police officers and detectives who arrest suspects face high risks of assault and suffer the second highest on-the-job murder rate, more than 4 fatalities for every 100,000 law enforcement agents per year. They too face additional risks from car crashes. Private security guards carry out assignments that are almost as dangerous, and nearly 4 per 100,000 die each year as a result (Sygnatur and Toscano, 2000).

In general, employees engaged in law enforcement (including corrections officers in jails and prisons) faced the highest risks of attack while carrying out their duties, followed by workers in the mental health field. People employed in transportation, medicine, retail sales, and teaching faced much lower risks. Police officers experienced the highest rate of physical assaults (about 260 per 1,000 officers per year), while college teachers enjoyed the safest job of all (just 2 attacks per 1,000 professors per year) (Duhart, 2001). In terms of differential risks, disproportionate shares of work-related deaths were suffered by men, immigrants, and minorities (African-Americans, Hispanics, and Asians) (Sygnatur and Toscano, 2000).

As for trends, a positive development has taken place since the 1990s, as Figure 11.2 shows. On-the-job homicides declined across the country, just as they did before and after work. By 2004, deadly assaults at workplaces had declined so substantially that violence at job sites was less likely to claim lives than motor vehicle accidents, falls, or being struck by a heavy object. Job-related homicides mostly (80 percent) result from gunfire, according to the BLS's Census of Fatal Occupational Injuries (Department

of Labor, 2011; and Botelho, 2014). The nearly 400 workplace homicides in 2013 accounted for less than 10 percent of all on-the-job fatalities. Workers were more likely to die because of transportation accidents, trips and falls, or from being hit by equipment or some object.

Impressions derived from media coverage about the nature of workplace violence can be misleading. More than 67 percent of on-the-job slayings stemmed from robberies, not outbursts of fury by coworkers (13 percent); by customers or clients (7 percent); or by intimates and relatives (9 percent), according to an analysis of the murders at workplaces between 1992 and 1998 in which a victim–offender relationship could be established. Also, except for the killings of taxi drivers and store cashiers, most murders do not take place late at night: Midnight to 8 A.M. is the time period with the fewest slayings (Sygnatur and Toscano, 2000).

Violence by students directed toward other students was focused upon earlier in this chapter (see above). But teachers (as well as administrators and other school personnel) can also be the targets of students' physical attacks (about 4 per 1,000 were assaulted in 2008). Teachers who worked at elementary schools were less likely to suffer acts of violence or theft than those who taught at middle/junior high schools and high schools. Not surprisingly, teachers in urban schools experienced more violent incidents than their suburban and rural counterparts, which closely reflected the geographic distribution of crimes committed off school grounds. Public school teachers were subjected to more assaults than those employed by private schools, and male staffers sustained more injuries than females (NCES, 2011a).

Employees have a right to perform their assigned duties in a safe workplace. By law, employers must strive to maintain working conditions that are free of known dangers. Employers cannot retaliate against workers who voice concerns about their own safety or report on-the-job injuries from acts of violence by supervisors, coworkers, subordinates, customers, visitors, or intruders (such as robbers or angry former intimate partners).

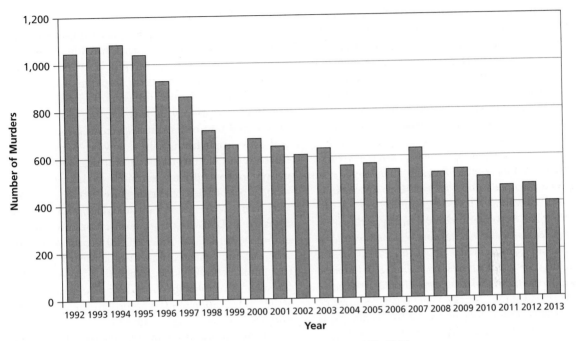

FIGURE 11.2 Trends in Work-Related Murders, United States, 1992–2013
SOURCE: Bureau of Labor Statistics, Census of Fatal Occupational Industries, 2013.

During the decades since the rediscovery of workplace violence, a cottage industry of security consulting firms offering threat assessment and risk management services has emerged, offering ways to reduce the chances of violence erupting at factories, offices, and other job sites—both to enhance worker safety as well as to fend off lawsuits charging employer negligence. Four kinds of threats must be addressed by high-tech equipment, preventive measures, training sessions, company regulations, and emergency procedures. The first is to prevent an intruder from slipping or barging into the workplace to rob or rape someone. The second is to prevent personal disputes from escalating within the workplace (such as when a man invades an office to confront his former girlfriend). The third is to protect employees who must deal with irate customers, angry clients, unruly students, disturbed patients, or dangerous inmates. The fourth is to safeguard workers, bosses, and owners from disgruntled current or former employees (Rugala, 2004).

TARGETS OF HATE CRIMES

Rediscovering a Very Old Problem

A 15-year-old boy comes out and tells classmates that he is a homosexual. When he begins to wear makeup and jewelry, he has to endure teasing and bullying from some of the boys at the junior high school. During a computer lab, in front of 24 other eighth graders, a 14-year-old pulls out a gun and shoots the boy in the head. The prosecutor charges the teenage killer with a hate crime, arguing that he was motivated by homophobia and white supremacist views. The youth pleads guilty to second degree murder and is sentenced to 25 years behind bars. (Cathcart, 2008; and Lovett, 2011)

■■■

After drinking in a park, seven high school students go hunting for a "Mexican" to attack (a "sport" they call "beaner hopping"). They chase several young Hispanic men before closing in on a

37-year-old recent immigrant from Ecuador who works at a dry cleaning shop and stab him to death. After the slaying, a number of Hispanic residents come forward and report incidents of harassment and assault. The police department is the subject of a federal investigation but pledges to repair its strained relations with recent immigrants. The hate crime so shocks the conscience of the community that the leading local elected official, known for his tough stance against illegal immigration, declares "that this brutal killing of an innocent, hardworking man for no other reason than he was Hispanic ... can be the spark for all of us—yours truly included—to admit our faults, to work more closely with one another, to pay more attention to what our children are doing, and to pay more attention to what we say." The group's ringleader, who has a Hispanic girlfriend and claims that a friend paid for a swastika tattoo on his leg "as a dare" and "as a joke," is convicted of manslaughter as a hate crime and is sentenced to 25 years in prison. The victim's family sues the police force, arguing that it failed to accord equal protection to Hispanics, since the teenage mob had been questioned by officers about earlier assaults that night but released before the stabbing took place. (Applebome, 2008; and Fernandez, 2010)

During the 1980s, a long-standing problem finally began to receive the attention it deserved: violence and vandalism motivated by the offender's hatred of the victim's "kind" of person, in terms of race, ethnicity, religion, or sexual preference. Throughout world history, assailants from one group have attacked such "enemies" and suffered counterattacks as reprisals. An examination of U.S. history reveals that significant proportions of murders, assaults, and acts of vandalism and desecration were fueled by bigotry. Intergroup tensions break out periodically in mob actions, race riots, lynchings, looting, intentionally set fires, street battles, and even vicious schoolyard fights. Some bias-driven attacks have been spontaneous and isolated while others were planned by organized hate groups as part of a campaign of political intimidation.

Usually, aggressors went after members of groups that lacked social and political influence. In the past, the suffering of these individuals and the fears that others who identified with them shared did not often arouse public sympathy or attract media attention. Law enforcement officials did not assign a high priority to investigating these breakdowns in intergroup relations, catching the culprits, and preventing further shockwaves. Many victims felt reluctant to turn to the authorities for help, and many police departments failed to keep accurate records of the incidents that were brought to their attention. Without a standard definition and an appropriate label for this type of crime, no government agency could issue official estimates of the scope of the violence and destruction of property that fell into this category. Therefore, no one knew for sure which groups were being singled out for attack most often and whether this rediscovered problem was growing or subsiding.

That situation changed during the 1980s. Organizations representing constituencies that perceived that they were being targeted (such as racial and religious minorities) began to compile their own statistics and to issue reports. These political activists asserted that the problems of victims of hate-fueled crimes merited special solutions. They advanced the following argument: Recognizing **bias crime** or **hate crime** as a distinct category implies that its impact on the victim and on the community at large goes far beyond the specific harm inflicted. In other words, burning a cross on the lawn of a home that was just purchased by a black family in a predominantly white neighborhood is more than mere criminal mischief; spray painting a swastika on the wall of a Jewish synagogue is much more than a minor act of vandalism; and an unprovoked gang attack on a gay couple symbolizes more than simply a random assault by complete strangers.

In 1990, the rediscovery process was propelled forward when Congress enacted the Hate Crime Statistics Act to generate data that might dispel misperceptions about patterns and trends. The federal legislation authorized the U.S. attorney general to preside over the collection of the data. The attorney general delegated that responsibility to the FBI; its Uniform Crime Reporting Program has issued annual reports on hate crimes reported to the police since 1992. Because hate crimes are not different from ordinary street crimes except for the perpetrator's motive, yearly compilations monitor the same set of offenses as the *UCR*: murder and manslaughter, forcible rape, aggravated and simple assault, robbery, burglary, theft, motor vehicle theft, and arson.

The reporting system also closely tracks crimes of intimidation (threats that place the recipient in reasonable fear of physical injury) and vandalism (damage to and destruction of property, including defacing surfaces with graffiti). **Bias incidents** that involve constitutionally protected speech, such as handing out hate-filled leaflets, no matter how offensive and insulting, don't qualify as criminal activity and are not reported or counted. In 1994, Congress instructed law enforcement agencies to not only keep track of ordinary crimes that were fueled by the offender's bigotry against the victim's race, ethnicity, religion, national origin, or sexual orientation but also to monitor attacks on individuals because of perceived mental and physical disabilities (Harlow, 2005). In 2009, the Hate Crime Statistics Act was amended a second time to now include acts driven by the perpetrators' prejudices against the targets' gender or gender identity (Langton and Planty, 2011).

Before the government took on this responsibility, civil rights organizations and human relations commissions solicited reports from victims, collected information from police sources, and scanned news media accounts for new cases. When Congress first debated the issue of compiling a national data bank of hate-fueled incidents in 1985, the FBI initially resisted the assignment mainly because of the additional expenses it would impose. Local police departments also wanted to opt out because of unreimbursed start-up costs and administrative overhead ("Lukewarm Reception," 1988). The FBI began to issue reports in 1997.

Hate crimes are assumed to have more profound and enduring consequences than comparable "ordinary" offenses. Hate crimes can be interpreted as

symbolic affronts to members of the victim's racial, ethnic, religious, or sexual preference group. People who share the same characteristics as the targets of bias crimes might sense that they are vulnerable too, and even may feel directly harmed themselves. Thus, they tend to identify with and rally around the victim. If other people side with the aggressor, then the community, or even the entire society, becomes polarized. At that point, intergroup relations, which are delicately balanced in a pluralistic society in the best of times, quickly become strained. The resulting rifts could trigger a cycle of aggressive initiatives and violent responses, and perhaps a dangerous escalation in the level of force used in retaliatory attacks. The original act also can inspire copycat crimes by members of the offender's group, which, in turn, could touch off acts of vengeance by members of the victim's group. Therefore, when bias is recognized as a motivation behind an offense, the police and prosecutors must assign a high priority to resolving the case before the situation spirals out of control. Members of the victim's group and of the community at large could misinterpret the authorities' apparent indifference, skepticism, or tendency to blame the victim as tacit official approval of the offender's spiteful actions. The opposite response—taking the crimes very seriously—indicates the government's resolve to provide what the constitution pledges: equal protection under the law (Wexler and Marx, 1986; and Anti-Defamation League, 2003).

Pressures from below finally compelled those at the helm of the criminal justice system to confront this challenge by taking a series of steps: initiating efforts to monitor and measure the frequency and intensity of incidents motivated by raw bigotry; improving the response of police and prosecutors to the victims' plights; and developing community level solutions to head off or at least defuse these polarizing events.

How Much Hate?

Bias crimes are motivated in whole or in part by the perpetrator's hatred of the victim's entire group. Those on the receiving end of bigots' wrath usually are members of negatively stereotyped out-groups, in terms of race, ethnicity and national origin, religion, or sexual orientation. Aggressors generally belong to what they consider in-groups. Targets of outbursts of group hatred may be individuals and their personal possessions; commercial property such as stores; or institutional property such as houses of worship, religious schools, and cemeteries. The offenses range from beatings to murders and from criminal mischief to arson and bombings. The perpetrators may be isolated individuals, spontaneously formed mobs, groups of teenagers, loosely structured gangs, or organized hate groups immersed in a subculture built around intense and explicit antagonism directed at their "enemies." Hate crimes often stand out from ordinary acts of interpersonal violence in several ways: The level of brutality can be extreme or excessive, the target is frequently a stranger singled out at random for being "one of them," and offenders often prowl around and lash out in a group rather than as isolated bigots (Levin and McDevitt, 2003).

Data about people who have been subjected to bias crimes can indicate the intensity of racist, anti-Jewish, anti-Muslim, homophobic, and other bigoted sentiments at various times and places. Rough estimates about bias crimes can serve as an early warning system for pinpointing areas where relations are strained and trouble is brewing; they can also serve as criteria for evaluating the effectiveness of outreach efforts to defuse potentially explosive intergroup conflicts. But measuring victimization rates reliably and calculating differential risks for experiencing bias crimes is difficult for several reasons. First, many victims still do not report such incidents to the authorities. Second, not all police departments are as yet committed to keeping records of the numbers and types of bias crimes reported to them. Entire states still do not report hate crimes to the FBI. Third, some attacks inspired by bigotry might not be recognized as such by detectives who do not thoroughly investigate suspected cases to discern the offenders' motives (Southern Poverty Law Center, 2001).

The general reluctance of injured parties to : offenses to the police might be magnified

when it comes to hate crimes because of the widespread perception that officials will respond with indifference or hostility. People singled out for attack because of their true or assumed sexual preference (victims of "gay bashing") might be especially reticent to press charges and thereby publicize the incident (Maghan and Sagarin, 1983). Sometimes victims who are unwilling to disclose such incidents to the police will provide the information to civil rights groups defending their interests.

Establishing motivation (for purposes of investigation, classification, and record keeping, and later as the basis for harsher sentences after successful prosecutions) can be quite difficult. People who have been targeted for bias crimes might not know why their assailants singled them out. Mere differences in skin color, ethnicity, religion, or sexual preference between offender and victim are not necessarily indications of bigotry, of course. The police and the prosecution, with the assistance of the injured party, must discover the underlying basis for the offender's actions. The clearest evidence would be explicit utterances during the attack or the scrawling of graffiti containing slurs against the victim's group by the offender before the assault, or the perpetrators' use of well-known symbols of hate such as a burning cross, a swastika, or the initials KKK.

Another clue to the offender's motivation might be that the target was a prominent figure in promoting or defending the interests of his or her group, or the offender was active in an organized hate group. Perhaps the incident occurred on a day of special significance to the victim's or the offender's group, such as an anniversary or holiday. The incident might have broken out at a symbolic location, such as a gay bar, a house of worship, or a park frequented by members of a certain group. The target might be one member of a small group vastly outnumbered by members of the offender's group in the immediate area of the crime scene. The person singled out for negative treatment might have received warnings or endured prior acts of harassment or intimidation. Otherwise, the investigators must concentrate on issues such as ongoing neighborhood tensions, patterns of previous incidents, ways the victim stands out from other potential targets, statements made about the offender's behavior by witnesses, or an absence of any other logical motivation such as economic gain (Wessler and Moss, 2001; Turner, 2002; Nolan, McDevitt, and Cronin, 2004).

The difficulty in establishing the offender's motive and whether a reported incident is a hate crime was dramatized when an independent group, the National Coalition of Anti-Violence Programs (NCAVP) issued annual reports for 2003 and 2004 covering incidents reported to its chapters in certain metropolitan areas (where a little more than 25 percent of the population of the United States resided). The NCAVP, which closely monitors attacks against people who are gay, lesbian, bisexual, and transgendered, considered 18 murders in 2003 to embody antihomosexual bias, whereas the FBI's annual hate crimes report cited six. For 2004, the discrepancy was greater: The NCAVP deemed 20 killings to be antigay. But the FBI reported that a mere five murders across the entire country were considered by detectives at local police departments to be fueled by any kind of bias—race, religion, national origin, mental or physical disability, or presumed sexual preference (Patton, 2005). Starting in 2014, police departments began to identify attacks motivated by the offender's bias against the victim's gender identity, as required by the Mathew Shepard and James Byrd Jr. Hate Crime Prevention Act.

According to the FBI's annual report on hate crimes for 2012, over 14,000 law enforcement agencies voluntarily participated in the program but only 1,730 agencies actually sent in information about close to 5,800 incidents (down from close to 6,600 in 2010). Nearly 4,000 offenses were directed at persons (many of the other hate crimes were acts of vandalism directed against property or houses of worship, gravestones, and other symbolic targets). Only 10 murders (up from 7 in 2010) were attributed to the offender's hatred of the victim's "kind," as were 15 forcible rapes (way up from just 4 two years earlier). Over 850 people were hurt in aggravated assaults. But most of the interpersonal

violence took the form of acts of intimidation or simple assaults. As for the offenders' reasons in 2012, almost 50 percent of all offenses against persons or their property were motivated by racial animosity, nearly 20 percent by religious prejudices, and close to 20 percent by biases surrounding sexual orientation, the same proportions as in 2010. The remainder seemed to be reflections of the perpetrators' dislike of their targets' nationality or ethnicity. Almost 2 percent was motivated by a disdain for physical or mental disabilities (FBI, 2013a).

Of the offenses motivated by racial bias, nearly 67 percent were directed at Americans of African descent. Bias against whites fueled a little over 20 percent of the cases, and anti-Asian prejudices inflamed close to 4 percent of the incidents (the remainder were hard to categorize.). As for national and ethnic backgrounds, Hispanics were the main targets (close to 60 percent) of other people's wrath. Of the victims of crimes driven by religious intolerance, the majority (60 percent) were Jewish Americans. About 13 percent of targeted individuals were followers of Islam, 7 percent were Catholics, and 3 percent were Protestants. The remainder of the cases reflected hatred for adherents of various other religions and atheists (FBI, 2013).

Over the years, racial animosity consistently has been the leading motivation, followed by religious intolerance, with hatred of the victim's sexual orientation coming in third. Nearly all the cases embodying the offender's bias against the victim's perceived sexual orientation were attacks by heterosexuals on homosexuals, mostly directed at gay males rather than at lesbians.

Besides the FBI's *UCR*, the BJS's *NCVS* (since 2000) also can be used to gauge the extent and seriousness of certain hate-driven activities. Whereas the *UCR* measures incidents that detectives considered to be bias-motivated, the *NCVS* takes the victims' perceptions at face value. Most of the respondents who felt that they were victims of bias crimes based their impression on the derogatory slurs their attackers uttered, or far less often, the symbolic evidence (for example, graffiti) that vandals left behind in hate-fueled property crimes. Using these criteria, an analysis of *NCVS* data for the period 2004–2012 revealed that in most of the incidents, the injured party believed the offender was motivated by racial or ethnic (ancestral, cultural, nationality) hatred. Religious intolerance and disdain for the victims' sexual orientation or disabilities were less common motivations. About 33 percent of all bias-driven violent incidents were reported to the police. As for trends in hate crimes, analyses of *UCR* data and *NCVS* statistics did not lead to the same conclusion. Whereas *UCR* figures indicated a decrease in hate crimes reported to the police from 2004 to 2012, *NCVS* findings showed no significant change in total victimizations per year and actually indicated an increase in acts of bias-driven violence (Langton and Planty, 2011; and Wilson, 2014).

Criminal Justice System Reforms

Bias crime victims and their supporters have been able to improve the response of the criminal justice system in many ways: securing the passage of new laws penalizing hate-motivated acts more severely; spurring police departments to take special steps to investigate and solve these kinds of crimes; and encouraging district attorneys to prosecute hate crimes vigorously.

Starting in the 1980s, a number of state legislatures enacted statutes that applied stiffer penalties to hate crimes to discourage attacks against people considered by bigots to be of the "wrong" race, ethnic group, religion, or sexual orientation. (In the 1980s, many state legislators and congressional representatives opposed the inclusion of sexual preference as a protected category, fearing that specifically prohibiting assaults against homosexuals could be viewed as an endorsement of that lifestyle.) In 1984, California became the first state to amend an existing hate crime statute to include attacks against gays and lesbians—as well as people singled out for their age or disability (Gutis, 1989).

Most recent state laws have civil lawsuit provisions that make it easier for plaintiffs to sue bigots who interfere with the exercise of their constitutional rights. Victims can recover out-of-pocket expenses, can collect punitive damages

and reimbursement for attorney's fees, and can secure injunctive relief: court orders of protection.

Because many offenders are teenagers who are processed by the juvenile justice system, most states have passed laws that enable injured parties to hold the wrongdoer's parents liable for up to several thousand dollars in damages (Pfeiffer, 2007).

The police department in New York City established the country's first specialized unit to investigate possible bias crimes in 1980. Police forces in Baltimore, Boston, San Francisco, and Nassau and Suffolk counties in New York also set up hate crime squads during the 1980s. By 1990, 34 percent of police departments in large cities had established full-time units. However, by 2000, that percentage dropped to 26 percent, although 71 percent of local law enforcement agencies had some officers assigned to investigate bias crimes on a part-time basis (Reaves and Hickman, 2002). When neighborhood tensions soar, these squads can maintain surveillance and monitor people and places judged to be likely targets. They can send police officers as decoys to pose as vulnerable victims to entice would-be offenders to attack—and then be arrested immediately by backup teams lying in wait (Scott and Williams, 1985; and Wexler and Marx, 1986).

When bias crime victims come forward and request help, the police can serve them in many ways. They can respond promptly, be sensitive when questioning them (and not dismiss the incident as a prank, betray skepticism about whether the event occurred, or imply it was somehow provoked), and make arrests quickly. Detectives can keep victims informed about progress in their cases; can "read them their rights" about opportunities for restitution, compensation, and civil lawsuits; and can try to discourage the news media from revealing names and addresses of complainants. If victims are in continuing danger, the department can provide extra security from reprisals or temporarily relocate them to safer surroundings. Officers also can refer bias crime victims to community organizations offering hot lines, crisis intervention services, and support groups (Scott and Williams, 1985).

Supporters of a get-tough stance against hate-motivated crimes concede that harmony and mutual respect among people of different races, ethnic groups, religions, and sexual preferences cannot be brought about through legislation. But they believe that the threat of thorough investigations, vigorous prosecutions, and extra severe sanctions might deter conscious attempts to provoke intergroup strife. Critics of these measures question whether an aggressor's alleged motive—to express his animosity toward an entire group—can ever be established beyond a reasonable doubt in court. Those critics suggest that the harm inflicted rather than the attacker's personal reasons should be the basis for determining the degree of punishment (Klurfeld, 1988; see also Jacobs and Potter, 1998).

The rediscovery of hate crime victims and the emerging consensus that these offenses must be taken very seriously can be seen as a positive development because highly publicized incidents have the potential to sabotage the ongoing social experiment of fostering an acceptance of a post-racial multiculturalism in the United States—at a time when full participation in a global economy requires tolerance by individuals and entire societies toward diversity in religious beliefs and ethnic identities.

VIOLENCE BETWEEN PRISONERS

Inmates who are attacked by other inmates face several unique problems: They are captives held against their will in the company of others who also desperately would like to be somewhere else. Yet the predicament facing nonviolent inmates is that they can't escape interacting with dangerous persons under very difficult circumstances and adverse conditions. Also, injured parties generally are reluctant to report what happened to them to the officers guarding them for fear of being branded a "snitch." "Squealing" is strictly forbidden by the inmate code, a subculture that engulfs members of this society of captives. The penalty for informing on others can be death.

Worse yet, inmate-on-inmate resentment leading to violence is often motivated by the lowest common denominator, which is an unchangeable characteristic: race/ethnicity. As a result, prisoners band together in race-based gangs for self-protection against each other. Added to this "watch your back" struggle to survive are other exacerbating factors: overcrowding; indifference or even hostility from corrections officers toward certain inmates or groups; cellmates suffering from mental illness; and cell blocks populated by angry people with violent tempers, short fuses, and histories of violence.

It is well known that when large numbers of criminally inclined men are held against their will, they vent their anger and frustration on each other. Inmates target one another in a number of ways, including thefts of their meager possessions, extortion, assaults with homemade weapons, and gang fights (see Silberman, 1995; Schneider, 1996; and O'Connell and Straub, 1999). But the worst expressions of violence born of frustration—sexual assaults and murders (fatal beatings and stabbings)—are receiving renewed attention from corrections administrations intent on running orderly institutions. It is in the public's enlightened self-interest to quell and prevent inmate-on-inmate violence, and to offer programs and services for self-improvement while they are in the government's custody. Most individuals kept behind bars will be released someday. If formerly incarcerated persons receive the assistance they need during reentry, they have a chance at leading productive and law-abiding lives. If they are more bitter and hostile when they leave jails and prisons than when they entered, their recidivism will create another wave of victims.

Even worse than being forcibly raped (refer back to Chapter 10) is to be murdered while ostensibly under the government's care and control. Controversies often break out when suspects, defendants, and convicts die while in the custody of law enforcement agencies (police station lockups), the courts (holding pens), or the correctional system (jails, prisons, and juvenile facilities). Some deaths might be attributed to medical conditions (heart attacks and strokes), drug abuse (overdoses or adverse reactions), suicides, or the use of necessary force by officers during an escape attempt. But some of the deceased were killed by fellow inmates over some personal "beef" or as a result of gang rivalries carried over from the streets but heightened by the frustrations of confinement. Researchers were unable to estimate the comparative risks of death from illnesses, suicides, and violence until Congress officially rediscovered the existence of homicides behind bars and passed the Deaths in Custody Reporting Act of 2000.

The Bureau of Justice Statistics was assigned the task of maintaining a database about all fatalities while in custody, whether under suspicious circumstances or not. The information includes the gender, race/ethnicity, and age of the deceased; the date, time, and location of the incident; and a brief narrative about the circumstances. Focusing on homicides (as opposed to the major causes of deaths—illnesses and suicides), a compilation of records from jails across the country for the years 2000–2012 revealed that the number of deaths from inmate-on-inmate violence ranged from a low of 15 in 2003 to a high of 36 in 2006. During 2012, 22 jail inmates were victims of homicide, which comprised only about 2 percent of all deaths in jails that year and yielded a mortality rate of about 3 per 100,000. (Suicide was the leading cause of death of persons kept for up to a year in jails, claiming 40 lives out of every 100,000 inmates.) As for persons incarcerated in state prisons, the death toll for the period 2001–2012 was a little over 670; slightly more than 100 were slain in penal institutions run by the federal government. The body count ranged from a low of 39 in 2001 to a high of 85 in 2012, indicating a disturbing upward trend in lethal violence. Those 85 inmates murdered by fellow prisoners accounted for less than 3 percent of all deaths of felons behind bars that year (most died from illnesses or suicide). But the 2012 homicide rate of about 7 per 100,000 per year was the highest recorded since the monitoring program began in (Noonan and Ginder, 2014).

As always, location plays a role in determining differential risks. The level of violence within the institutions' walls varied greatly from state to state. For the years from 2001 to 2012 combined, the homicide rate for all state prisons averaged out to 4 inmates slain for every 100,000 confined per year; for the federal penitentiaries, it was 5 per 100,000 annually. The most dangerous state prison systems for the years from 2001 to 2012 were located in Oklahoma (14 homicides per 100,000 inmates annually), Maryland (11), New Mexico (9), Tennessee (9), South Carolina (8), Maine (8), and California (8). The safest states to be locked up in were in Minnesota, North Dakota, New Hampshire, Vermont, Wisconsin, and Wyoming (all with virtually zero) (Noonan and Ginder, 2014). To put these figures into context, the numbers ought to be close to zero, since the government is responsible for the well-being of the people it confines against their will. On the other hand, the murder rates of incarcerated persons were somewhat lower than the homicide rate for "average Americans" in the rest of the country each year until 2012. Slayings behind bars appear to be the only kind of murders that currently are on the rise in the United States.

As for the demographics of the local jail inmates who were stabbed or beaten to death or killed in other ways, almost all were males (270 of the nearly 275 victims between 2000 and 2012). The highest risks of being slain were faced by men over 45, and especially over 55. Victimization rates by race and ethnicity were virtually the same. Most disturbing of all was their legal status: Nearly 200 (almost 75 percent) of the inmates killed while in jail had not yet been convicted of any crime; they were technically innocent and were being detained awaiting their trial. As for the demographics of the convicted felons slain while serving time in prisons, the highest murder rates were suffered by inmates beyond the age of 45, and particularly those older than 55, and the lowest by prisoners between the ages of 18 and 24. Only 4 of the approximately 670 victims were females; differences in rates by race and ethnicity were minor (Noonan and Ginder, 2014).

When convicts are sentenced to prison, the administration classifies them in terms of their propensity to commit new acts of violence while incarcerated, and wardens supervise them in either maximum, medium, or minimum security facilities. But all inmates also could be rated in terms of their vulnerability to violent victimization while they are locked up. A risk assessment scale based on an actuarial type of statistical analysis has determined the following factors to be the best predictors of being attacked, beaten, or stabbed: having ever been placed in segregation as a punishment, having been convicted of certain sex offenses, suffering from a mental illness, instigating others to engage in misconduct behind bars, holding other inmates in low regard, and turning to drugs to cope with stress. These factors were better predictors of becoming a target for physical assaults than age, race, marital status, education, or having a history of acting violently. Inmates with high scores on this risk assessment instrument need special supervision and protection if they are to avoid violent victimization and undergo successful rehabilitation and treatment while in confinement (Labrecque et al., 2014). Similarly, large jail systems with high turnover rates need to do a better job of rapidly identifying vulnerable inmates before they are attacked or slashed, especially since an increasing number of people in short-term confinement have undiagnosed and untreated mental problems that cause them to respond to tense situations defiantly or erratically (see Schwirtz, 2014).

More detailed statistical profiles of the deceased inmates and their killers are needed to figure out where, when, and why these slayings happen to determine the circumstances that would heighten the risks that a prisoner will be beaten or stabbed to death with homemade weapons, either by vindictive or deranged individuals or by ethnically based, organized prison gangs, and to examine what specifically can be done in the future to prevent such needless loss of life of convicts but also especially of detainees awaiting trial while under governmental custody, who under the law are to be considered innocent unless proven guilty beyond a reasonable doubt.

LAW ENFORCEMENT OFFICERS INJURED AND SLAIN IN THE LINE OF DUTY

Officers who work for law enforcement, probation, parole, or corrections agencies at local, state, and federal levels face special challenges. They must seek out and interact with known criminals on a daily basis—just the opposite of what risk reduction strategies would recommend. The police have the most perilous tasks of all: As people scatter at the sound of gunfire, officers must race toward the disturbance to subdue troublemakers who are armed and dangerous. They patrol the meanest streets of the toughest neighborhoods, break up crimes in progress, search suspicious people, track down fugitives, and guard prisoners. Because badges and uniforms are symbols of governmental authority, officers face the additional risk of being ambushed by those who oppose what agents of officialdom represent. As the first line of defense for a social order, law enforcement agents serve as lightning rods, attracting and absorbing the bolts of discontent from alienated individuals and hostile groups within society.

Killing a police officer is one of the most heinous of crimes. In most states, it is punishable by death. The National Law Enforcement Officers Memorial Fund keeps track of those who made the ultimate sacrifice to protect the public, as does the FBI's Uniform Crime Reporting Division in its annual analysis, *Law Enforcement Officers Killed and Assaulted* (LEOKA). Fortunately, deadly attacks on officers have been declining, according to records kept by these two sources. Over the decades, policing has become a safer occupation, as the graph of trends in line-of-duty deaths shows (see Figure 11.3). Murders peaked in 1973, dropped during the early 1980s, and since then have been fairly stable, even though many more people now are engaged in law enforcement duties. Smaller numbers of deadly assaults took place during 1999 and 2008 (note that the 72 law enforcement officers killed in New York and the Pentagon on September 11, 2001, were not included by the FBI in its

LEOKA statistics). Disturbingly, deadly felonious assaults crept back up in 2009 and 2010. But then the number of officers who perished from injuries inflicted by criminals tumbled to an all-time low in 2013. Only four of the slain officers in 2013 worked for large urban departments serving populations of more than 250,000. Apparently, being a big city cop suddenly became a much safer occupation in 2013, which was a much-welcomed development (see Figure 11.3). Adding together murders, accidental deaths, and losses of life from acts of heroism, the 2013 combined body count for line-of-duty-deaths was the lowest since 1944 (Stockton, 2014). However, that brief respite in the number of officers cut down was short lived: Preliminary unofficial figures for 2014 indicated that about 50 were murdered by gunfire and another 5 were intentionally run over by attackers (about 5 more were accidentally rammed by drunk drivers; these killings

were not counted as fatal felonious assaults) (Groeninger, 2014; and Officer Down Memorial Page, 2015), which was a little above the annual average of around 50 slayings per year that prevailed during the 10 years from 2004 to 2013.

Who, Where, What, When, How, and Why?

The FBI closely monitors line-of-duty deaths and assaults to determine the profile of a typical officer who suffered fatal wounds. In order to develop insights that can improve training and tactics that will reduce casualties, it is necessary to discover how, when, and where the attacks took place; and what the most dangerous situations were during their daily routines. To derive answers to these questions, the FBI carefully analyzes the murders and assaults over a 10-year period to discern patterns and trends.

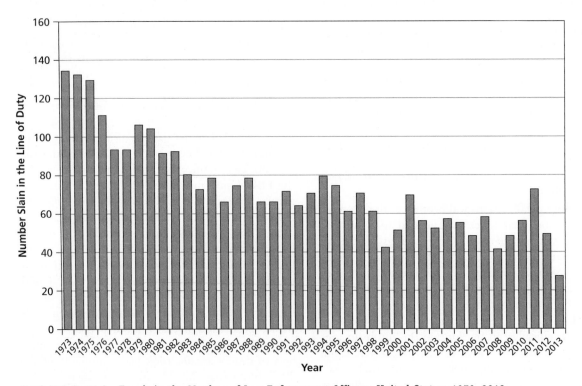

FIGURE 11.3   Trends in the Murders of Law Enforcement Officers, United States, 1973–2013

72 deaths resulting from the September 11, 2001, terrorist attacks are excluded.
Law Enforcement Officers Killed and Assaulted (LEOKA), 2013 (FBI, 2014e).

In 2013, the FBI gathered data from over 11,000 local, county, state, and federal (including public campus and tribal reservation) law enforcement agencies that employed over 625,000 officers. That year, 27 were slain (a little more than 4 out of every 100,000) and almost 50,000 were assaulted (a rate of about 9 percent of every 100 sworn officers). However, only about 30 percent of the assaulted officers sustained physical injuries. Over a 10-year period from 2004 to 2013, 511 officers died from the injuries felons inflicted upon them (FBI, 2014e).

As for what the 511 officers were doing at the time they were murdered, the most perilous assignments were making arrests, responding to disturbances (mostly family quarrels and bar fights), and carrying out traffic stops and pursuits. Some officers were slain while investigating suspicious people and situations. The assignments that were less likely to result in loss of life were handling prisoners and emotionally disturbed persons. No officers were killed during civil disturbances and riots. Over 20 percent of the slayings from 2004 to 2014 were ambushes (FBI, 2014e).

As for where the 511 officers were slain, almost half were working on the streets and highways in the southern states. About one-fifth were employed by departments in big cities of over 250,000 inhabitants. As for when the killings took place, the most dangerous time to be on patrol was between 6 P.M. and 2 A.M. Thursdays, but also Fridays and Saturdays were the most violent days of the week, while Sundays had the lowest body counts. Augusts and Decembers were the months with the most line-of-duty deaths, and Octobers had the fewest. About 40 percent of the officers were working alone when they were slain. Roughly 10 percent were off duty when they intervened to stop a crime-in-progress and were murdered (FBI, 2014e).

A profile of the 511 fallen officers showed that 95 percent were males; about 85 percent were white and 12 percent were black (FBI records don't provide breakdowns for Hispanics as a separate category). During the 10-year period from 2004 to 2013, most were between 25 and 40 years old (38 was the average age) and had been on the job for about 11 years. Practically all (93

percent) were killed with firearms, mostly handguns. Being intentionally run over or rammed by a vehicle ranked a distant second as a cause of fatalities. Hardly any officers were stabbed to death over those 10 years. Only about 25 percent fired their own weapons in self-defense in the final confrontations that ended their lives.

As for the nearly 565 cop killers, 98 percent were males, a little over 50 percent were white, and a disproportionately high 43 percent were black. Over 60 percent were between 18 and 30 years old, and 31 was their average age. More than 80 percent had a criminal record of prior arrests, and about 25 percent were under some sort of judicial supervision (on probation or parole, out on bail, or escapees) at the time of the deadly confrontation. Hardly any of the cop killers got away with murder, according to an analysis of the fates of 607 murderers during the 10 years from 2002 to 2011. Nearly 70 percent (420) were arrested, only 4 remained at large as fugitives, and about 30 percent (185) were not arrested because they perished. Of those 185 alleged killers, about 65 percent (120) were "justifiably killed," either by the dying officer (40) or by other officers or civilians (80). Around 30 percent (55) committed suicide rather than being captured, and 7 died under other circumstances. Of the 420 who were arrested, over 60 percent (260) were found guilty of murder, of which nearly 70 were sentenced to die and almost 150 received a sentence of life imprisonment. Most of the remaining cases led to convictions for lesser crimes with lower penalties. But only about 8 percent were acquitted or had their charges dismissed (FBI, 2014e).

Only 2 percent (11) of the law enforcement agents murdered during the first decade of the twenty-first century worked for federal agencies. Since these line-of-duty deaths were so infrequent, it is not possible to determine the homicide victimization rates faced by officers of different federal agencies. But an earlier comparative study yielded some surprising findings: Agents for the Internal Revenue Service, an unpopular branch of government, enjoyed the lowest risks of being attacked on the job. And contrary to widespread impressions and media images, the federal law enforcement officers who faced the greatest statistical risks of injuries from assaults did not work for the FBI, Drug Enforcement Administration (DEA), U.S. Marshals, the Bureau of Alcohol, Tobacco, and Firearms (BATF), or branches of what is now part of the Department of Homeland Security. They worked for the U.S. Department of the Interior's National Park Service (Reaves and Hart, 2001). Although the 1,000 rangers stationed across the country suffered a high assault rate, only 9 have died in the line of duty since the national park system was established in 1916 (see Yardley and Raftery, 2012).

Media images of gun fights as a frequent aspect of police work are misleading. The average officer goes through a 20-year career without ever firing a shot except for target practice. However, undercover officers face a much greater chance than their uniformed colleagues of shooting at suspects and of being shot. African-American officers in undercover and plainclothes assignments run an additional risk of being hit by "friendly fire"—officers who mistake them for armed criminals (Geller, 1992). Friendly fire in all kinds of situations—mistaken identity, training exercises, and accidental discharges—during more than a century of policing from 1893 through 2006 has claimed the lives of nearly 200 officers (O'Connor and Pacifici, 2007).

Tragically, officers die by suicide more often than at the hands of assailants (Cowan, 2008; and Clark et al., 2012). Unfortunately, accidents also claim more lives than felonious assaults. For example, during 2013, 49 law enforcement officers died from on-the-job accidents (such as car crashes) while 27 were murdered by criminals. Over the 10-year span ending in 2013, 636 officers died accidentally while 511 were killed intentionally (FBI, 2014b). However, statistically speaking, policing is not the most dangerous job of all in terms of intentional plus accidental injuries and deaths—taxi driving is.

Making the Job Safer   The leading reasons for the decline in line-of-duty deaths noted in Figure 11.3 include regulations requiring officers to wear bullet-resistant vests, better training, improved weaponry, ⸱ ⸱⸱ailability of stun guns that can substitute for o-hand combat, the use of specially-trained

SWAT teams to handle extremely dangerous situations, restrictions on the private ownership of deadly weapons, and a diminishing amount of interpersonal violence across the country (Butterfield, 1999; and Lee, 2015). To improve the chances that officers will complete each tour of duty without getting hurt, the Department of Justice has fostered a number of initiatives, including the establishment of an Officer Safety and Wellness Working Group to develop "best practices," a Preventing Violence Against Law Enforcement and Ensuring Officer Resilience and Survivability (VALOR) program that provides training and technical assistance, and the creation of an "Officer Safety Toolkit" that furnishes advice about how to anticipate and survive violent encounters. The federal government also gives financial assistance to local departments to purchase the latest bulletproof and stab-resistant vests (Holder, 2011; and Stephens and Matarese, 2013).

Other peace officers also face grave risks of bodily harm. To reduce probation and parole officers' vulnerability to assault, robbery, and car theft when carrying out supervisory tasks and home visits, a growing number of agencies are providing them with firearms, bulletproof vests, alarms, armed escorts, and training in self-defense tactics and crisis management techniques (Lindner and Koehler, 1992; Del Castillo and Lindner, 1994).

Showing Solidarity

As long ago as 1894, an association was established in New York City to take care of the widows and orphans of fallen officers. But over the next 100 years, families of law enforcement agents mistakenly were assumed to be stronger emotionally and better prepared than civilians to cope with losses and grief because they are part of a tightly knit community that "takes care of its own." The inadequate responses of many police departments brought about the establishment of counseling units, death notification training, and peer support groups for injured and disabled officers (see Sawyer, 1987; Stillman, 1987; Martin, 1989; and "Does Your Agency Measure Up?" 1999).

A national self-help group with many local chapters that is dedicated to addressing the concerns of survivors (mostly young widows and their children) offers many forms of concrete aid and emotional support (for example, advice about sleep problems while grieving and ways of coping with depression during major holidays). The scope of their services ranges from monitoring the trials of accused cop killers and opposing their eventual parole to erecting memorials for those who gave their lives to protect the public. The organization provides training to alert officers about dangerous situations that are preventable; offers peer-support retreats for grieving spouses and coworkers; delivers emotional support via counseling, group outings, publications, and websites; holds seminars about proper methods of death notification and ways of obtaining all the benefits the next of kin are entitled to; and raises money through walks, contests, and tournaments for scholarships and special events (such as summer camps for the slain officers' children) (see Gregory, 2011; and Bernhard, 2014). These activities demonstrate how an entire caring community—in this case, the "police family"—can work together to ease the suffering of those who have lost a loved one.

Law enforcement agents demonstrate another kind of solidarity when "one of their own" is murdered. They are relentless in their pursuit of the killers of "their brothers in blue" until they are all "brought to justice." As noted above, only 4 fugitives escaped the long arm of the law out of the roughly 600 persons wanted for slaying cops in the line of duty. Therefore, the clearance rate for murders of officers was about 99 percent, as compared to a clearance rate of around 65 percent for murders of civilians during the 10 years between 2002 and 2011.

CASUALTIES OF POLITICALLY INSPIRED VIOLENCE AND TERRORISM

Terrorism predates organized warfare. Lone individuals and small bands surreptitiously attacked their enemies long before armies of men were thrown into battle. Terrorism took the form of killing leaders or potential challengers to a throne and of spreading panic by carrying out barbaric acts.

Although the means and the goals have evolved over the centuries, terrorism still involves the unlawful use of force against persons or property in order to intimidate a government, frighten a civilian population, or coerce a segment of the public to surrender to political or social demands. Unlike common criminals, terrorists do not commit violent offenses to line their pockets. They intend to advance their social, religious, or political cause and seek publicity for their dramatic deeds to score propaganda victories. They attack certain targets to gain the attention of a third party—the audience they are desperately trying to influence. By relying upon stealth and deception, terrorists can disrupt and demoralize more powerful adversaries who would easily defeat them in conventional warfare. Terrorist violence includes bombings, suicide missions, assassinations, airplane hijackings, kidnappings for ransom, and hostage taking to arrange prisoner exchanges or to negotiate from a position of strength. But modern forms can also encompass new tactics, such as cyberattacks, to sabotage and disrupt computer operations (FBI, 2001).

Focused terrorism is aimed at specific targets and symbols such as corporate headquarters and government officials. Indiscriminate acts of violence inflict casualties on innocent, randomly selected targets of opportunity who just happen to be at the wrong place at the wrong time. Usually, those who are wounded or murdered have no special connection to, substantial influence over, or particular responsibility for the political, social, and religious conflicts that motivated the terrorist attack. The injured parties are pawns or bargaining chips in high-stakes power struggles and fear campaigns designed to spread panic and undermine confidence in the government.

The public can be affected indirectly in several ways. People may become cynical and pessimistic either about the enemy or about their own side's widely proclaimed lofty ideals and may lose faith in the ability of their government and its criminal justice system to protect and serve them. Indirect victims are not personally involved in an attack but suffer the adverse consequences of it (for example, their livelihoods are linked to the fortunes of the tourism industry, which experiences business losses in the aftermath of a disruptive event). Besides fearing the terrorists, sectors of the public may also become frightened of their own law enforcement agencies if onerous national security restrictions are imposed and cherished civil liberties are sacrificed in the quest to root out hidden terrorist cells and disrupt clandestine networks conspiring to strike again (Kratcoski, Edelbacher, and Das, 2001).

Assessing the Threat of Terrorism

To determine the number of people harmed by terrorist attacks, and to discern whether or not the threat is growing or subsiding, criminologists and victimologists need a definition for "terrorism" that clearly spells out which incidents should be counted and which belong in other categories (like hate crimes or ordinary street crimes).

Several measurement issues confound efforts by criminologists and victimologists to gauge the threat of terrorist attacks accurately. First, terrorist groups don't always claim responsibility for their violent deeds. Unless arrests are made, the unsolved incidents are recorded by the FBI as **suspected**, as opposed to **confirmed terrorist attacks**. Some definitional problems add to the confusion. The FBI (2004b) follows the Code of Federal Regulations that categorizes terrorism as "the unlawful use of force and violence against persons or property to intimidate or coerce a government, the civilian population, or any segment thereof, in furtherance of political or social objectives." The FBI distinguishes terrorism as either **domestic** or **international**, depending upon the group's origins, base of operations, and objectives. Domestic terrorism encompasses activities that involve acts dangerous to human life such as assassination, kidnapping, or unleashing weapons of mass destruction within the United States and Puerto Rico, in violation of state or federal law, by groups or individuals with no foreign ties. But applying these criteria to real-life situations often raises complications.

The biggest obstacle to consistently categorizing events is establishing motivation. For example, the many letter bombs mailed by the "Unabomber" from 1978 until his capture in 1995 killed 3 people and maimed 22, including college professors he had never met. But his repeated depredations that frightened the campus community were not counted as acts of terrorism by the FBI because this federal prison inmate's motivation remains unknown and unclear despite his rambling manifestoes, and may have reflected either random selection or a peculiar personal vendetta against his unsuspecting targets.

Another complication is that some politically motivated attacks overlap a gray area between terrorism and bias-driven hate crimes. The acts must be counted as either one or the other—but not both. For instance, in 1999 when a member of a white supremacist group went on a rampage, shooting at 32 complete strangers (some of them Jewish worshippers leaving a synagogue), killing 2 (one was African-American, the other Asian-American) and wounding 8, the FBI categorized the incident as an act of domestic terrorism and not a hate crime. Similarly, when a distraught gunman with no known ties to any group opened fire at a ticket counter in an airport, killing a representative of an Israeli airline and one bystander and wounding another before being shot to death by security officers in 2002, the FBI initially considered the murders to be a hate crime. But later, it classified the incident as international terrorism because the killer was an immigrant from the Middle East. Yet the FBI categorizes assaults and slayings of doctors who perform abortions by extremists in the antiabortion movement as hate crimes, not as acts of domestic terrorism.

To further complicate the issue of threat assessment, attempted acts are counted. But what about planned attacks that are foiled? The FBI tabulates these separately as **preventions**, in which law enforcement agencies thwart a terrorist plot (it is "successfully interdicted through investigative activity") before anyone is hurt or any damage is done (FBI, 2001: 15–27; 2007b: iv–v).

The FBI formally began monitoring terrorist attacks in the United States in the mid-1970s (see Figure 11.4). First of all, note that nobody on U.S.

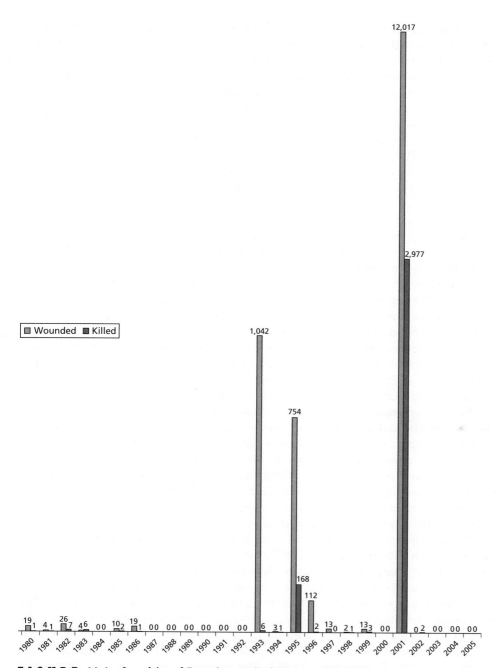

FIGURE 11.4   Casualties of Terrorism, United States, 1980–2005

NOTES: The FBI uses 12,017 as an estimate for the number of those injured as a result of the September 11 attack; the exact number is unknown. Seventeen persons were infected by and recovered from exposure to the anthrax mailings during September–November 2001.

SOURCE: FBI's *Terrorism in the United States*, 2005 (FBI, 2007b), p. 31.

soil was hurt or killed during a number of years (1984, 1987–1992, 2000, and 2003–2005). Based on its database, the FBI attributed 327 incidents within U.S. borders from 1980 to 1999 to the work of terrorists. Of these suspected and confirmed acts, 239 (73 percent) were carried out by domestic terrorists; the rest were inflicted by groups with international ties. Even before September 11, 2001, two trends had emerged: The number of specific attacks was decreasing, but the average seriousness of the strikes (in casualties and property destroyed) was increasing. During the 1980s, 267 incidents that took place on U.S. soil claimed 23 lives and injured 105 people. During the 1990s, 182 people were murdered and 1,932 were wounded in just 60 attacks. Overall, the FBI attributed 205 deaths and at least 2,037 injuries to terrorist attacks between 1980 and 1999. Also, during these two decades law enforcement agencies claimed credit for preventing or aborting 130 terrorist plots, of which 47 (36 percent) were planned by foreigners (FBI, 2001: 15–27). After 2005, the FBI discontinued the updating of this graph.

The characteristics of terrorist attacks, the beliefs or political causes fueling them, and the people and places that were targeted have changed dramatically over the decades. Starting in the late 1960s, extremists in the antiwar movement and the Puerto Rican independence movement engaged in bombings, and militants in the black power movement carried out assassinations of police officers. By the mid-1980s, these outbreaks of leftwing terrorism had faded into insignificance and the groups responsible for them had disbanded. Soon terrorism from far right fringe groups emerged as the more serious threat. White racists, neo-Nazis, and extremists among antitax, antiabortion, and survivalist groups and the militia movement were behind a series of random shootings, targeted assassinations, bank robberies to raise money, and abortion clinic bombings. Right wing terrorist attacks peaked in 1995 with the blast in Oklahoma City that toppled a federal building and claimed the lives of 168 people, including 19 children in a day care center, and injured 642 others. A homemade car bomb was set off on the

second anniversary of the fiery massacre that ended the standoff between the FBI and a besieged, heavily armed religious cult in Texas. The two perpetrators were hostile to the FBI and BATF and had indirect ties to the militia movement. Right wing terrorism diminished to some degree after that devastating explosion, but what the FBI terms special-interest terrorism—especially by extremists in the animal rights and environmental movements—became noticeable in the latter part of the 1990s. The only significant attack carried out by international terrorists was the 1993 truck bombing by a small cell of Middle Eastern Islamic extremists at downtown Manhattan's World Trade Center. The blast failed to topple the twin towers, but the explosion resulted in six deaths and more than a 1,000 injuries.

Looking back over the 1980s and 1990s, about half of the targets of domestic terrorists were civilian or commercial. The remaining attacks were directed at government buildings or the embassies and other properties of foreign governments (especially of Cuba and of the former Soviet Union) or military sites (FBI, 2001: 15–27).

During 2000, the FBI investigated eight terrorist incidents perpetrated by extremists within the animal rights and environmentalist movements; no deaths or serious injuries resulted. The FBI also prevented one attack on a federal building by a right wing extremist. During 2001, 13 incidents took place, mostly minor fires and raids by animal rights and environmental extremists; two bank robberies were carried out by an antiabortion extremist (FBI, 2004). But the relative quiet on the domestic front was shattered on September 11, 2001.

The worst suffering due to terrorism in U.S. history unfolded when 19 hijackers from the Middle East with links to Al Qaeda crashed two airplanes into Manhattan's World Trade Center towers, causing their collapse. The inferno killed 2,838: This included people inside the aircraft and the skyscrapers as well as police officers and firefighters working as rescuers. The hijackers smashed another plane into the Pentagon, killing 189 people working for the Department of Defense. A fourth hijacked plane hit the ground and exploded in

Pennsylvania, claiming 44 lives; some of the passengers and crew fought back against the men who had commandeered it (see Arias and Smith, 2003). The FBI estimated that about 12,000 people were injured that day, although hospital emergency rooms in New York City treated very few wounded survivors. (Stories that circulated about orphans who needed to be adopted after the attacks killed their parents turned out to be urban myths [Bernstein, 2001].)

In the immediate aftermath of the September 11 hijackings, what appeared to be the first major bioterrorist attack in American history was launched. The widespread fears it engendered about terrorists unleashing "weapons of mass destruction" and "germ warfare" surely contributed to the public's initial support for the war waged by the Bush administration against Saddam Hussein's Iraq (see Greenwald, 2008). However, when the case was "officially solved" years later, it seemed that those who had perished were not victims of terrorist acts:

A spate of letters to prominent people that are contaminated with deadly anthrax spores kill five people, sicken 22 others, disrupt mail deliveries, force the evacuation of government buildings, and lead to numerous "white powder" scares. One poisonous letter to a TV newscaster explicitly links the anthrax attacks to Islamic terrorism, stating "Death to America, Death to Israel, Allah is great." However, after a lengthy investigation, the FBI concludes that a prominent but mentally disturbed U.S. Army microbiologist with no ties to the Middle East is behind these mailings for a tangled mix of personal and professional career reasons. But he commits suicide before being arrested, so doubts linger about the real identity of the perpetrator and his true motive. (CFR, 2004; Shane and Lichtblau, 2008a; 2008b; and Editors, New York Times, 2011c)

Ironically, after the anthrax-laced letters, domestic terrorism for most of the first decade of the twenty-first century reverted to the pattern that prevailed before September 11. Most of the incidents inflicted minor damage on commercial and government property and nearly all were attributed to the efforts of extremists in the animal rights and environmental movements. The slaying

of two people in 2002 by a distraught individual from the Middle East acting alone was originally considered a hate crime but was later reclassified as an act of terrorism by a "lone wolf" (see FBI, 2008b; and National Consortium, 2012).

During the years since 9/11, a number of attacks by "homegrown violent extremists" (HVEs) holding political beliefs connected to the far right of the political spectrum have injured and killed a number of innocent people, including a manager in an IRS building hit intentionally by a pilot of a small airplane; a guard at the Holocaust Museum in Washington, D.C.; minority passersby on the street; worshippers in a Unitarian church and a Sikh temple; and dozens of police officers. Fortunately, some extremists bungled their attempted bombings. As for preventions, law enforcement authorities have foiled many plots by would-be terrorists of American far right groups as well as by individuals inspired by Islamic extremism (see cases listed in the Office of Intelligence and Analysis Assessment, 2009; Beutel, 2011; and START, 2014). But which of these acts should be categorized as hate crimes or else dismissed as the work of twisted "lone nuts," and which constitute "genuine" terrorist attacks remains a subject for debate (see Shane, 2010; and Rich 2010)?

The most terrible incident carried out in the United States from 2001 up to 2013 that could have been classified as either an act of terrorism or as a hate crime would be this mass shooting, the worst attack on a military installation in the United States in recent history:

An increasingly unhinged Army doctor is investigated but considered fit for continued duty. He goes to a gun shop and purchases a technologically advanced semiautomatic pistol that holds many bullets in its magazine. One day, he enters his workplace, the Soldier Readiness Processing Center at Fort Hood, Texas, the most populous U.S. military base in the world, and opens fire, getting off more than 200 shots. He kills one civilian and 12 soldiers and wounds another 32 people. Civilian police officers respond to the emergency and he shoots at them, wounding one officer. The assailant is shot, captured, and paralyzed from the chest down after being shot in the back by an officer. He is charged with 13 counts of premeditated murder and 29 counts of attempted murder. No terrorist group claims responsibility for the massacre, and it appears the mentally disturbed psychiatrist carefully planned his attack but acted alone, apparently motivated by his jihadist beliefs. The major is put on trial for murder, and 20 victims and relatives of the deceased testify during the court martial. Acting as his own attorney, he makes an opening statement in which he takes responsibility for the mass killing because he "switched sides" in what he believed was a "war against Islam," and then rests his case without calling a single witness in his behalf, and without making any closing argument. He is convicted by a panel of 13 senior military officers and is sentenced to die. He will be the first soldier executed under the military code of justice since 1961. (Kenber, 2013)

However, this bloody rampage was not classified by the authorities as either a terrorist attack or as a hate crime. It was officially declared to be an act of workplace violence. The significance of that controversial categorization was that it prevented the victims from receiving combat-related benefits and Purple Hearts (Fernandez and Blinder, 2014).

But another incident caused by two brothers who were not affiliated with any domestic or international group actually was declared an act of terrorism by President Obama: the setting off of two bombs at the finish line of the Boston Marathon in 2013:

Thousands of spectators gather near the finish line of a famous long distance race. Suddenly a homemade pressure-cooker bomb made from fireworks, hidden in an abandoned backpack, explodes, and then another is detonated. A college student, another young women, and a little boy die from the blast and more than 260 are injured, many losing feet and legs. Pictures and videos of the crowd before the explosions that were taken by onlookers using smartphones are shown on television, eliciting tips from the public that enable the FBI to identify two suspects, who were apparently motivated by a desire to avenge the suffering inflicted on Muslims in Chechnya, in southern Russia. One is a 26 year old amateur boxer and the

other is a 19 year old sophomore majoring in marine biology at a nearby college. Trying to flee, the pair shoots a 26 year old campus officer to death, and then carjack a SUV. A manhunt leads to a car chase, with the brothers hurling makeshift explosives at the pursuing police cars. The older brother dies after a gun battle, and one officer is seriously wounded. Although thousands of state and local police as well as federal agents lock down the surrounding area and shut down the mass transit system and warn the public to stay indoors, the younger brother flees on foot and eludes the authorities until a suburban homeowner spots him hiding in his powerboat trailered in his backyard. Weak and bleeding from gunshot wounds, the 19 year old is captured and held in solitary confinement without bail at a federal facility, facing 30 counts, of which 17 carry the death penalty. (Warrick and Horwitz, 2013; and McPhee, 2014)

In order to carry out a threat assessment, criminologists and victimologists begin by counting the number of people who have been harmed. It is difficult to assess the true scope of the danger of domestic terrorism to people living within the borders of the United States because, as the discussion above shows, there is no official consensus about the criteria for classifying an incident as an act of terrorism. The standards differ, seem inconsistent, and may even shift, depending on political considerations. It appears that not a single person has been killed or wounded on U.S. soil in a "genuine 9/11-type terrorist attack planned and executed by agents of some foreign movement or members of an international organization" since September 11, 2001. If attacks by independent, unaffiliated, self-directed, homegrown, and often deeply disturbed "lone wolves" of various political persuasions are not counted, then this excellent safety record makes it very difficult to assess the true dimensions of the global terrorist threat against people and property within the United States.

However, politically inspired violence surely is on the rise in other countries. For example, a Global Terrorism Database contains information on over 125,000 terrorist attacks carried out around the world between 1970 and 2013 (START, 2014). The worldwide death toll due to acts of domestic and international terrorism by disaffected groups in each country has been monitored since 2005 by the Worldwide Incidents Tracking System (WITS) under the auspices of the FBI's National Counterterrorism Center (NCTC). That body count surely is rising rapidly as many nations take part in the stepped-up war against global terrorism. The specter of terrorists unleashing weapons of mass destruction (biological and chemical agents and radioactive dirty bombs that sicken, injure, and kill huge numbers of people) conjures up scenarios of incalculable damage, which underscores how the potential threat posed by terrorism is of a far greater magnitude than ordinary street crime.

Assistance and Recovery

After a traumatic disaster such as a politically inspired bombing, victims are likely to be overwhelmed by intense emotions of shock, anxiety, confusion, sorrow, and grief. Some are immediately beset by outrage and revenge fantasies, or even guilt for surviving, while others undergo delayed reactions. As the unfocused anger dissipates, depression and loneliness may set in. Sleep disorders, panic attacks, sudden weight gains or losses, and abuse of alcohol and prescription drugs are common symptoms of inner turmoil. Sensing that no one understands what they have endured, some might even contemplate suicide. Professional counseling, spiritual support, and membership in a self-help group might stave off the most serious consequences of experiencing this ordeal (Office of Victims of Crime, 2001). However, the "debriefings" during counseling sessions frequently offered to traumatized survivors of disasters, such as the September 11 attacks, may be ineffective at best or even counterproductive, according to two recent studies. Researchers turned up scant evidence that the recipients of trauma counseling fare better, in terms of their long-term mental health, than victims who get no professional care, or those who just talk to friends and family members (Van Emmerik et al., 2002).

Victimologists interested in survivorology could study a number of real-life examples of the exemplary resilience shown by some of the spectators wounded at the Boston Marathon bombing, such as these:

A 27 year-old newlywed undergoes 17 surgeries to try to salvage her leg, which was severely mangled by the bomb blast. Eventually, doctors conclude, and she agrees, that amputation is the best course of action. She hosts a "last supper" party for her limb and posts pictures about it on her Facebook page, writing to it, "I'm sure it won't come as a shock to you when I say that we've grown apart. The love that we once had has dwindled, and this relationship has become a real burden on my life." Then the courageous young mother goes under the knife, and the surgeon declares the operation a success. From her hospital bed, she tells her supporters that this marks a new beginning and signs the message with a new last name, "Unleashed." (Walsh, 2014)

∎ ∎ ∎

Two brothers, 32 and 34 years old, both construction workers, are watching marathon runners cross the finish line when the bombs explode. Each brother loses a leg from the blast and the shrapnel. After lengthy hospitalizations and a total of 50 surgeries between them, both now are able to walk with their prosthetic legs. A compensation fund for the bombing victims awards each of them over a million dollars, but they wisely put the money into a savings account to pay for future medical bills. After suffering bouts of depression and suicidal impulses, they recuperate, move out of their family's house, move in with their girlfriends, and make plans for a wedding and for starting a roofing business. After they appear on panel discussions and television interviews, complete strangers walk up and tell them they are "an inspiration." "Maybe I am helping them in some way," one brother speculates. (Seelye, 2014)

To help victims recover from the financial losses and the side effects of politically driven attacks overseas, the Department of Justice's Office for Victims of Crime established an International Terrorism Victims Compensation Program. The Justice

Department also operates a Terrorism and International Victims Unit, and the FBI set up an Office for Victim Assistance in 2002 (Office of Victims of Crime, 2002).

The federal 9/11 Victim Compensation Fund distributed about $7 billion to the several thousand families of those killed and wounded in the second World Trade Center attacks (the casualties of the first World Trade Center underground garage truck bomb explosion were not compensated so adequately). Its formula focused on calculations of lost income, so the families of victims who were making high salaries received the largest payments. For example, more than $6 million was awarded on average to each of the four families who lost a breadwinner making $4 million or more a year. About $1 million was awarded on average to each of the roughly 160 families who lost a member who was earning less than $25,000 a year. As for the injured, 40 survivors who were badly burned received awards averaging about $2 million each (Chen, 2004).

Congress's hasty appropriation of a relatively large amount of money for a 9/11 Victim Compensation Fund set off a firestorm of debate and soul searching concerning the weighty moral and philosophical issues surrounding the proper societal response to victimization due to terrorism. Confusing precedents were set, and conflicting principles remain unresolved. Should murders inflicted by terrorists be taken more seriously than slayings committed by robbers or deaths caused by drunk drivers? Should compensation amounts be higher for the survivors of heroic rescuers such as police officers and firefighters who died in the line of duty than for the next of kin of average civilians caught up in a disaster? Conversely, is it fair to repay families based on the victim's lifetime earnings potential, which means that wealthy families who lost highly paid executives would receive much more than the families of workers? How much compensation ought to be awarded to the families of immigrant workers who had entered the country illegally, the relatives of single people without dependents, and to the children and domestic partners of victims who were not officially

married? Would standard flat amounts for everyone, regardless of status, be fair? Why were the several thousand families of the victims of the attacks on the World Trade Center in 2001 repaid from a special federal fund, whereas the six families who lost loved ones in the 1993 terrorist bombing of the same buildings for roughly the same motives were not? Why were the families of the over 3,000 9/11 victims of foreign religious extremists given more financial compensation than the families of the 168 victims of domestic right-wing extremists in Oklahoma City? Should attacks that take place within the United States evoke more generous outpourings of economic assistance than attacks on Americans on foreign soil? Most importantly, can money really serve as an adequate surrogate or metaphor for other significant public and governmental responses and expressions of collective emotions, such as compassion, support, respect, honor, regret, sorrow, obligation, and appreciation, that are intended to help victims and their loved ones cope with the special problems terrorism imposes? And finally, will such special arrangements for payouts be implemented every time terrorists inflict casualties in the future (Belkin, 2002)? (Until 9/11, people injured by terrorist attacks and the next of kin of those who died in the attacks applied for financial assistance from their state victim compensation funds, which have very limited resources set aside to reimburse individuals who get wounded in ordinary street crimes. See Chapter 12 for a full discussion of the legislation establishing government-run compensation funds.)

In the aftermath of the vicious Boston bombing, similar but not identical thorny questions were raised: Where should the funds to help victims recover primarily come from, the government at the local, state, or federal level, or private sources, or a mix of both? How much aid should each totally innocent person who was in the wrong place at the wrong time get? What would it take to try to make each individual "whole again"?

The task of compensating the many wounded spectators and the next of kin of the four who were murdered largely fell to private charitable organizations, especially One Fund Boston, not the city of

Boston, the state of Massachusetts, or the federal government. This charity, rapidly set up to assist the victims of this particular bombing, distributed over $60 million and planned to parcel out an additional $20 million to the over 200 casualties and the families of the three who perished plus the officer who was slain during the bombers' attempts to get away. Its basic formula was to give priority to people who face a lifetime of medical and psychological care because they needed amputations or treatments for severe injuries to their limbs. The highest payouts, over $2 million per person, went to the families of those who were murdered or suffered double amputations. Others received payouts based on whether the amputation was above or below the knee; the severity of the injuries to their remaining limbs; the number of surgeries they underwent; and their age. But some of the younger amputees expressed concerns that the seemingly generous awards actually would not cover a lifetime of medical expenses. Others who were wounded questioned a payment formula that based allotments on the number of days they spent in a hospital. Those with traumatic brain injuries (as well as hearing loss, PTSD, and blast-related phobias) felt that they did not receive sufficient "cash gifts" as they were called—only about $8,000 each—from the fund's medical advisory board to cover the treatment of their permanent yet invisible wounds (Abel, 2014; and Bernstein, 2014).

Civil lawsuits for damages are another avenue for financial recovery that can be pursued by people injured by terrorists, and for the families of those who perish from their wounds. The obvious targets for these lawsuits are the evildoers themselves. But terrorists rarely have assets that can be confiscated, sold, and divided up. An alternative strategy is to sue some other party that can reasonably be proven to be partly responsible for the injuries and losses. (See Chapter 12 for a detailed discussion of these third-party lawsuits.)

Concerns about the need to enhance security at potential targets predated the 1993 bombing of the World Trade Center. Therefore, shortly after that attack, more than 400 plaintiffs (injured office workers and the families of the six who were fatally wounded, plus some owners of businesses in the building) sued the Port Authority of New York and New Jersey, the governmental body that built and operated the Twin Towers, for negligence for failing to safeguard a likely target. Twelve years later, a six-person civil jury unanimously ruled in the plaintiffs' favor. In a historic decision, the jurors accepted the victims' argument that the agency should have realized that the commercial center symbolized American capitalism and consequently ought to have foreseen the likelihood of a terrorist attack and should have taken steps to prevent it. Specifically, the management did not heed the warning about the vulnerability of an underground garage that was flagged by a 1985 security study that it had commissioned in the wake of a spate of bombings in Europe and the Middle East. However, New York's highest court reversed the 2005 decision in 2011 and ruled by a 4–3 vote that the Port Authority was not liable for the damages inflicted by the 1993 truck bombing on the 400 plaintiffs (Weiser, 2011).

The survivors of the September 11 attacks and the families of those who perished also have used third-party lawsuits as a means of empowerment and redress. Because there were so many victims drawn from such diverse backgrounds, more than 20 groups sprung up to represent them (Voboril, 2005). In their search for the truth about the events leading up to the attacks, they have pursued a wide range of targets in civil court, from terrorist groups and foreign governments that may have harbored them to businesses and charities that may have served as fronts for terrorist fundraising (CNN, 2002). Some survivor organizations also have supported whistleblowers who publicly reveal government blunders and weaknesses in national security strategies (American Civil Liberties Union, 2005).

People concerned about becoming victims of future acts of terrorism can take out insurance backed by the federal government. When Congress passed the Terrorism Risk Insurance Act of 2002, it authorized the secretary of the treasury, in concurrence with the secretary of state and the U.S. attorney general, to determine whether any act inflicting casualties and losses on American soil, or to U.S. airplanes or ships, was committed on behalf of any foreign person or interest. If it decides the injuries and damage was due to international terrorism, then the U.S. Treasury will pay 90 percent of the covered losses beyond what the insurance companies must reimburse to their policyholders. Ways of repaying victims of any and all crimes is the subject of the next chapter.

SUMMARY

Groups of victims who face special problems that require special solutions have received a lot more attention in recent years. Victims of stalking, until recently, had a difficult time convincing the authorities to take seriously their concerns about being in danger. New legislation, improved law enforcement responses, support groups, and self-protection tactics now help ease their plight. Meanwhile, the problem of cyberstalking is growing. Fortunately, the number of officers slain in the line of duty is declining thanks to improved training and better equipment. Victims of bias-motivated hate crimes need social support from well-meaning people who are trying to make the ongoing experiment in multiculturalism in America succeed. Worker safety, including protection from violence, requires greater attention on the part of employers. Inmates in jails and prisons face grave dangers from their cellmates and rivals but the violence they inflict on each other no longer is overlooked or tolerated. Police officers face unusual dangers because of their special mission: They confront people known to be armed and dangerous on a daily basis—just the opposite of what risk reduction strategies would recommend. To enhance their on-the-job safety, they need better training and improved equipment, but new initiatives also must target suicide and accidents, which claim more lives. In the aftermath of the September 11 attacks, difficult questions arose that still have not been resolved about the proper principles to follow to financially support the casualties of terrorism. A spate of school shootings have focused attention on the dangers that students face while at school, but school grounds still are much safer than the streets of surrounding communities. The myth of college campuses as crime-free sanctuaries also has been shattered, but campuses remain among the very safest places for 18- to 24-year-olds to spend their high-risk years.

KEY TERMS DEFINED IN THE GLOSSARY

bias crime, 394	cyberstalking, 381	international terrorism, 406	stalking, 377
bias incidents, 395	domestic terrorism, 406		suspected terrorist attacks, 406
confirmed terrorist attacks, 406	hate crime, 394	preventions, 406	
		proxy stalking, 379	

QUESTIONS FOR DISCUSSION AND DEBATE

1. Describe the particular problems faced by persons who experienced hate crimes.

2. How serious is the problem of cyberstalking, in your opinion?

3. Why should law-abiding people care about inmate-on-inmate violence?

CRITICAL THINKING QUESTIONS

1. What is the difference between an assassination or a bombing carried out by an organized hate group and a domestic terrorist attack?

2. Devise some scenarios in which an individual might feel threatened and falsely accuse someone of stalking when no real harm was intended by the alleged stalker.

3. If police departments can solve nearly all murders of officers, then why can't they solve almost as high a proportion of murders of "civilians."

4. Develop your own answers to the difficult questions that arose when the victims of the September 11, 2001, terrorist attacks received more financial compensation than the victims of the 1993 World Trade Center bombing and the 1995 Oklahoma City federal building bombing.

SUGGESTED RESEARCH PROJECTS

1. Find out how many police officers have been killed in the line of duty in recent decades in your hometown or state. Try to ascertain the circumstances under which they were fatally assaulted, and what happened to their murderers. Collect the information by accessing online databases about murdered officers and then follow up by finding newspaper articles about their deaths and the trials of their killers.

2. Access the Census of Fatal Occupational Injuries report issued each year by the Bureau of Labor Statistics. Look up careers that interest you, and see how often people holding these jobs were murdered while at work and how frequently they died from accidents.

3. Obtain summaries about criminal incidents reported on your campus similar to the data presented in Table 11.2. Compare these figures to reported crimes posted online at other college campuses of interest to you.

4. Find out more details about the victims of campus shootings listed in Box 11.1. How were the victims and their next of kin given support by the college or the government?

5. Draw up a checklist of the possible security measures and risk reduction strategies that could be implemented either at your workplace or on your college campus. Determine how many actually have been implemented, and suggest additional measures to make these sites even safer.

6. Investigate whether hazing goes on at your college, and determine whether the practices are really dangerous for the pledges, and whether antihazing policies effectively limit their risks.

12

Repaying Victims

LEARNING OBJECTIVES

To recognize the many costs imposed by criminal activities.

To identify the different ways that injured parties can get reimbursed for their losses.

To understand the various rationales for imposing restitution obligations on offenders.

To become familiar with the arguments in favor of and in opposition to state-run compensation funds.

To recognize the opportunities and drawbacks of civil lawsuits.

To realize the limitations of insurance coverage as a means of recovery.

To appreciate the reasons for favoring and for opposing notoriety-for-profit laws.

The costs of victimizations cannot be measured solely in monetary terms. Mental anguish and physical suffering cannot easily be translated into dollars and cents. Nevertheless, repairing the damage to a victim's financial standing is an achievable goal and a necessary step toward recovery.

Out-of-pocket expenses can be regained in many ways. Making the offender pay is everyone's first choice, as it embodies the most elemental notion of justice. In criminal court, judges can order convicts to make restitution, generally as a condition of either probation or parole. Insurance coverage also can be a source of repayment. In some cases, financial aid can be forthcoming from a government-run state compensation fund set up to cover certain crime-related expenses. Note that restitution and compensation are alternative methods of repaying losses. Restitution is the responsibility of blameworthy offenders. Compensation comes from blameless third parties, either government-run funds or private insurance companies. In civil court, judges and juries can compel wrongdoers to pay monetary damages. Another possible source of reparations might come in the form of a civil court judgment against a grossly negligent third party, such as a commercial enterprise or a governmental agency that is considered to bear some responsibility for the criminal incident. Finally, in rare instances, victims might be able to deprive offenders of any profits gained from selling a sensationalized "inside story" of their shocking exploits.

This chapter explores all of these means of economic recovery: court-ordered restitution, lawsuits for damages, third-party civil suits, private insurance policies, government compensation plans, and legislation prohibiting criminals from cashing in on their notoriety.

THE COSTS OF VICTIMIZATIONS

The social costs of crime-related expenditures are staggering, according to economists' estimates. The losses people suffer can be identified as either intangible or tangible. Intangible costs are hard to translate into dollars and cents but refer to the pain,

suffering, and reductions in the quality of life individuals endure when they are shaken or even traumatized by negative events. Direct tangible economic losses are relatively easy to measure monetarily whenever offenders take cash or valuables; steal, vandalize, or destroy property; and inflict injuries that require medical attention and recuperation that interferes with work. Theft and fraud bring about the direct transfer of wealth from victims to criminals. Murders terminate lives prematurely, resulting in lost earnings. Nonfatal wounds trigger huge expenses for medical care—bills from doctors, emergency rooms, hospitals, pharmacies, nursing services, occupational therapists, and dentists. The old saying "It's only money" might underestimate how even modest losses from a robbery or theft can impose serious hardships for individuals living from paycheck to paycheck, as this case demonstrates:

> A knife-wielding robber steals the purse and jewelry of a retired woman scraping by on disability payments. It takes at least six weeks to replace the ID cards and Social Security check in her stolen wallet. In the meantime, she has no cash, no bus pass, and no way to pay for her many prescription drugs, or even dog food for her pet. None of the social service agencies on the list provided by the big city police department offers emergency financial assistance. Finally, she discovers a faith-based charity that is willing to pay her rent and electric bill and give her food vouchers and $50 in cash. "If not for them, I could not have gotten my heart medication, and I'd be going to bed hungry," she tells a reporter. (Kelley, 2008)

Serious injuries may also inflict emotional suffering that requires psychological care for intense feelings of fear, grief, anger, confusion, guilt, and shame. Possible long-term consequences include mental illness and suicide, as well as alcohol and drug abuse. Some may get their lives back in order rather quickly, but others could be haunted by disturbing memories and burdened by phobias and by posttraumatic stress disorder (PTSD) for long periods of time. Overall, the lifetime risk of developing PTSD is much higher for those who suffer attacks than for the general public. Rates of experiencing episodes of major depression and generalized anxiety also are greater. Furthermore, the effects of the victims' emotional turmoil are likely to spill over on to family members, close friends, and even neighbors. An outbreak of crime can have a negative impact on an entire community, stoking a fear of strangers, undermining involvement in activities outside the home, eroding a sense of cohesiveness, and driving out some of the most productive residents (Herman and Waul, 2004).

Even those who are not directly connected to the injured parties may suffer a psychic toll from the ever-present fear that permeates a crime-ridden community. The result is that people are willing to pay substantial amounts of money in the form of taxpayer-funded government actions plus private expenditures in their search for greater security and an improved quality of life. Expenses arise from the crime-induced production of goods and services that would not be necessary if illegal activities were not such a grave problem. For example, the time, money, and resources spent on manufacturing protective devices (locks, surveillance cameras, and alarm systems) are crime-induced outlays, as are private security forces and theft insurance. Similarly, local, state, and federal government funds are consumed pursuing the "war on crime," the "war on drugs," and the "war on terror." That translates into huge expenditures for investigating illegal activities by law enforcement agencies and running court and prison systems (including prosecutors' offices, indigent defense, incarceration, treatment programs, probation, and parole). All of these governmental expenditures can be considered to be a net loss of productive resources to society. If the risks to life and health from criminal activity were not so great, these corporate, governmental, taxpayer, and personal expenditures could have been used to meet basic needs and improve living standards for the law-abiding majority (Anderson, 1999).

Some studies that attempt to estimate the costs of crimes focus on what victims lose, but others highlight how much society loses when an offender

becomes enmeshed in a criminal career. For example, one group of researchers projected that every murder of an adult (in Pennsylvania in the late 1990s) cost the entire society about $3.5 million. Another group of researchers devised a formula for monetizing a criminal career in order to determine its "external costs" to others over a lifetime and came up with even larger estimated societal outlays. For example, each murder inflicted about $4.7 million in victim costs, over $300,000 in justice system expenditures, and nearly $150,000 in offender productivity losses, for a total cost of over $5 million. Each armed robbery imposed costs of nearly $50,000, and the average burglary inflicted losses of about $5,500 (De Lisi et al., 2010). A study using a different method of defining and measuring tangible and intangible losses and expenses yielded estimates that each murder cost over $8.4 million, each robbery about $25,000, and each burglary over $1,650. Rapes were second only to murder in the size of losses, costing over $200,000. These estimates need to be incorporated into cost-benefit analyses when discussing appropriate funding levels for criminal justice outlays, such as for police departments or drug treatment programs (McCollister et al., 2010).

GAINING RESTITUTION FROM OFFENDERS

Back to Basics

A renewed interest in restitution developed during the 1970s. Restitution takes place whenever injured parties are repaid by the individuals who are directly responsible for their losses. Offenders return stolen goods to their rightful owners, hand over equivalent amounts of money to cover out-of-pocket expenses, or perform direct personal services to those they have harmed. **Community service** is a type of restitution designed to make amends to society as a whole. Usually it entails offenders working to "right some wrongs," repairing the damage they are responsible for, cleaning up the mess they made, or laboring in order to benefit some worthy cause or group. **Symbolic restitution** to substitute victims seems appropriate when the immediate casualties can't be identified or located, or when the injured parties don't want to accept the wrongdoers' aid (Harris, 1979). **Creative restitution**, an ideal solution, comes about when offenders, on their own initiative, go beyond what the law asks of them or their sentences require, exceed other people's expectations, and leave their victims better off than they were before the crimes took place (Eglash, 1977).

As a legal philosophy, assigning a high priority to restitution means the financial health of victims will no longer be routinely overlooked, neglected, or sacrificed by a system ostensibly set up to deliver "justice for all." Criminal acts are more than symbolic assaults against abstractions like the social order or public safety." Offenders shouldn't be prosecuted solely on behalf of the state or the people. They don't only owe a debt to society. They also have incurred a debt to the flesh-and-blood individuals who suffer economic hardships because of illegal activity. Fairness demands that individuals who have been harmed be made whole again by being restored to the financial condition they were in before the crime occurred (see Abel and Marsh, 1984).

In about one-third of the states, judges are required to order felons convicted of violent acts to pay restitution as part of their sentences. Restitution can be imposed for out-of-pocket (unreimbursed) losses directly stemming from the crime, including charges for medical expenses, prescription drugs, counseling, and therapy; lost earnings from missing work; replacement or repairs for stolen or damaged property; bills for crime scene clean-ups; expenses from participating in the criminal justice process (such as for transportation and child care); and money to cover insurance policy deductibles (NCVC, 2004).

Usually, wrongs can be righted in a straightforward manner. Adolescent graffiti artists scrub off their spray-painted signatures. Burglars repay cash for the goods they have carted away. Embezzlers return stolen funds to the business they looted. Occasionally, client-specific punishments are imposed,

tailored to fit the crime, the offender, and unmet community needs. For example, a drunk driver responsible for a hit-and-run collision performs several months of unpaid labor in a hospital emergency room to see firsthand the consequences of his kind of recklessness. A teenage purse snatcher who preys on the elderly spends his weekends doing volunteer work at a nursing home. A lawyer caught defrauding his clients avoids disbarment by spending time giving legal advice to indigents unable to pay for it. Such sentences anger those who are convinced that imprisonment is the answer and fervently believe, "If you do the crime, you must do the time." But imaginative dispositions that substitute restitution and community service for confinement are favored by reformers who want to reduce jail and prison overcrowding, cut the tax burden of incarceration, and shield first-time and minor offenders from the corrupting influences of the inmate subculture ("Fitting Justice?," 1978; "When Judges Make the Punishment Fit the Crime," 1978; and Seligmann and Maor, 1980).

The Rise, Fall, and Rediscovery of Restitution

The practice of making criminals repay their victims is an ancient one. Spontaneous acts of revenge were typical responses by injured parties and their kin before restitution was invented. Prior to the rise of governments, the writing of laws, and the creation of criminal justice systems, the gut reaction of people who had been harmed was to seek to "get even" with wrongdoers by injuring them physically in counterattacks and by taking back things of value. But as wealth accumulated and primitive societies established rules of conduct, the tradition of retaliatory violence gave way to negotiation and reparation. For the sake of community harmony and stability, compulsory restitution was institutionalized in ancient societies. Reimbursement practices went beyond the simplistic formula of "an eye for an eye and a tooth for a tooth." Restitution was intended to satisfy a thirst for vengeance as well as to repay losses. These transactions involving goods and money were designed to encourage lasting set-tlements (**composition**) between the parties that would head off further strife (Schafer, 1970).

In biblical times, Mosaic law demanded that an assailant repay the person he injured for losses due to a serious wound and required that a captured thief give back five oxen for every one stolen. The Code of Hammurabi granted a victim as much as 30 times the value of any possessions stolen or damaged. Under Roman law, a thief had to pay the victim double the value of what he stole if he was caught in the act. If he escaped and was caught later, he owed the victim three times as much as he took. And if he used force to carry out the theft, the captured robber had to repay the injured party four times as much as he stole. Under King Alfred of England in the ninth century, each tooth knocked out of a person's mouth by an aggressor required a different payment, depending upon its location (Peak, 1986).

In colonial America before the Revolution, criminal acts were handled as private conflicts between individuals. Police departments and public prosecutors did not exist yet. A victim in a city could call upon night watchmen for help, but they might not be on duty, or the offender might flee beyond their jurisdiction. If the injured party sought the aid of a sheriff, he had to pay a fee. If the sheriff located the alleged perpetrator, he would charge extra to serve a warrant against the defen-dant. When the suspect was taken into custody, the complainant had to hire a lawyer to draw up an indictment. Then the complainant either prose-cuted the case personally or hired an attorney for an additional fee to handle the private prosecution. If the accused was found guilty, the person he harmed could gain substantial benefits. Convicted thieves were required to repay their victims three times as much as they had stolen. Thieves who could not hand over such large amounts were com-pelled to be servants until their debts were paid off. If the victims wished, they could sell these inden-tured servants for a hefty price, and they had one month in which to find a buyer. After that, victims were responsible for the costs of maintaining the offenders behind bars. If they didn't pay the fees,

the convicts were released (Geis, 1977; Jacob, 1977; McDonald, 1977; and Hillenbrand, 1990).

In the years following the American Revolu-tion, the procedures that the British had set up in the colonies were substantially reorganized. Refor-mers were concerned about the built-in injustices afflicting a system in which only wealthy victims could afford to purchase "justice" by posting rewards and hiring sheriffs, private detectives, bounty hunters, and prosecuting attorneys. Crimes were redefined as acts against the state. Settling individual grievances was no longer regarded as the primary function of court proceedings. To pro-mote equal handling and consistency, local govern-ments hired public prosecutors. State agencies built prison systems to house offenders. A distinction developed within the law between crimes and torts. Crimes were offenses against the public and were prosecuted by the state on behalf of "the people." **Torts** were the corresponding wrongful acts that harmed specific persons. Criminals were forced to "pay their debt to society" through fines and periods of confinement. But injured parties who wanted offenders to repay them were shunted away from criminal court and directed to civil court, a separate arena where interpersonal conflicts were resolved through lawsuits (McDonald, 1977).

The modern rediscovery of restitution in the United States began in 1967, when the President's Commission on Law Enforcement and the Adminis-tration of Justice recommended the revival of this old practice that had fallen into disuse. Since the 1970s, opinion polls have indicated widespread public support for its restoration. A greater reliance on resti-tution also was endorsed by the American Law Insti-tute, the American Bar Association, the American Correctional Association, the National Advisory Commission on Criminal Justice Standards and Goals, the Supreme Court, the National Association of Attorneys General, the Office for Victims of Crime of the Justice Department, and reformist groups such as the National Moratorium on Prison Construction. The Federal Victim/Witness Protection Act of 1982 removed restrictions that had limited restitution to simply a possible condition of probation within the federal judicial system.

Also in 1982, the President's Task Force on Victims of Crime noted that it was unfair that people suffering serious injuries had to liquidate their assets, mortgage their homes, get along without adequate health care, or cut back on tuition expenses while criminals escaped financial responsibility for the hardships they inflicted. The task force recommended that judges routinely impose restitution or else clearly explain their specific reasons for not doing so. The Violent Crime Control and Law Enforcement Act passed by Congress in 1994 made restitution mandatory in federal cases of sexual assault or domestic violence. The enactment of the Mandatory Victim Restitution Act of 1996 imposed repayment obligations on all violent offenders in the federal system. The Federal Bureau of Prisons created a payment collection program in the late 1980s that many state correctional authorities have copied. The growing use of alternative, creative, or constructive sentences reflects the rediscovery of restitution by judges (Leepson, 1982; Harland, 1983; Herrington, 1986; McDonald, 1988; National Victim Center, 1991b; Galaway, 1992; and Office of Justice Programs, 1997).

In the juvenile justice system, restitution has been ordered more often and for a longer period of time. The oldest existing repayment program for people who have been harmed by delinquents was initiated in Florida in 1945. The earliest community service program was set up in South Dakota in 1965. A Minnesota program established in 1972 was the first to allow youthful offenders to perform direct services for victims instead of paying them in cash. It also pioneered the use of mediation sessions between the two parties to foster a spirit of reconciliation. Hundreds of juvenile restitution projects were set up during the 1970s and 1980s (Warner and Burke, 1987; Klein, 1997; Bradshaw and Umbreit, 1998; and Roberts, 1998).

Divergent Goals, Clashing Philosophies

Even though support for restoring restitution to its rightful place in the criminal justice process is growing, its advocates do not agree on priorities and purposes. Some advocates have been promoting this ancient practice as an additional form of punishment, while others tout it as a better method of rehabilitation. Still other champions of restitution emphasize its beneficial impact on the financial well-being of victims and its potential for resolving interpersonal conflicts. As a result, groups with divergent aims and philosophies are all pushing restitution but are pulling at established programs from different directions (see Galaway, 1977; Klein, 1997; and Outlaw and Ruback, 1999).

Restitution as a Means of Repaying Victims Those who advance the idea that restitution is primarily a way of helping victims (see Barnett, 1977; and McDonald, 1978) argue that the punitively oriented criminal justice system offers victims few incentives to get involved. Those who report crimes and cooperate with the police and prosecutors incur additional losses of time and money for their trouble (for example, from missing work while appearing in court). They also run the risk of suffering reprisals from offenders. In return they get nothing tangible, only the sense that they have discharged their civic duty by assisting in the apprehension, prosecution, and conviction of a dangerous person—a social obligation that goes largely unappreciated. The only satisfaction the system provides is revenge. But when restitution is incorporated into the criminal justice process, cooperation really pays off.

If the primary goal of restitution is to ensure that victims are repaid, then they should be able to directly negotiate arrangements for the amount of money and a payment schedule. Reimbursement should be as comprehensive as possible. The criminal ought to pay back all stolen cash plus the current replacement value of lost or damaged possessions, outstanding medical bills from crime-related injuries (including psychological wounds attended to by therapists), wages that were not earned because of absence from work (including sick days or vacation time used during recuperation or while cooperating with the investigation and prosecution), plus crime-related miscellaneous expenses (such as the cost of renting a car to replace one that was stolen or the cost of child care when a parent is testifying in court). Repayment on the installment plan should begin as promptly as possible because victims must foot the entire bill in the interim.

Restitution as a Means of Rehabilitating Offenders
Advocates of restitution as a means of rehabilitation (see Prison Research, 1976; and Keve, 1978) argue that instead of being punished, wrongdoers must be sensitized to the disruption and distress that their illegal actions have caused. By expending effort, sacrificing time and convenience, and performing meaningful tasks, they begin to understand their personal responsibilities and social obligations. By making fiscal atonement or doing community service, they can feel cleared of guilt, morally redeemed, and reaccepted into the fold. Through their hard work to defray their victims' losses, offenders can develop a sense of accomplishment and self-respect from their legitimate achievements. They may also gain marketable skills, good work habits (such as punctuality), self-discipline, and valuable on-the-job experience as they earn their way back into the community.

If restitution is to be therapeutic, offenders must perceive their obligations as logical, relevant, just, and fair. They must be convinced to voluntarily shoulder the burden of reimbursement because it is in their own best interest as well as being "the right thing to do." However, offenders probably will define their best interests as minimizing any penalties for their lawbreaking. This includes minimizing payments to injured parties, even if restitution is offered as a substitute for serving time behind bars. Offenders most likely will underestimate the suffering they have inflicted, while those on the receiving end may tend to overestimate their losses and want to extract as much as they can (see McKnight, 1981). The sensibilities of wrongdoers must be taken into account, because their willingness to make amends is the key to the success of this "treatment."

Restitution as a Means of Reconciling Offenders and Their Victims Some advocates of restitution view the process primarily as a vehicle for reconciliation. After offenders have fully repaid the individuals they hurt, hard feelings can dissipate. Also,

reconciliation between two parties who share responsibility for breaking the law can be achieved after face-to-face negotiations. In situations without a clearly designated wrongdoer, restitution might be mutual, with each of the disputants reimbursing the other for damages inflicted during their period of hostility. Both parties have to consider the restitution agreement to be fair and constructive if a lasting, peaceful settlement is to emerge. (The philosophy and operating principles of restorative justice, which relies heavily on restitution, are discussed in Chapter 13.)

Restitution as a Means of Punishing Offenders
Those who view restitution primarily as an additional penalty (see Schafer, 1977; and Tittle, 1978) argue that for too long offenders have been able to shirk this financial obligation to their victims. First, convicts should suffer incarceration to pay their debt to society. Next, they should undertake strenuous efforts to repay the specific individuals they harmed. Only then can their entanglement with the criminal justice system come to an end.

Reformers who promote restitution as a means of repaying victims, as a way of rehabilitating offenders, or as the basis for bringing about mutual reconciliation can come into conflict with crime control advocates who view restitution as an additional means of punishment and deterrence. The problem with imposing restitution as an extra penalty following incarceration is that it delays repayment for many years. Because few convicts can earn decent wages while behind prison walls, the slow process of reimbursement cannot begin until their period of confinement is over, either when the sentence expires or upon the granting of parole. When punishment takes priority over reimbursement, the victims' financial needs, the offenders' therapeutic needs, and the community's need for harmony are subordinated to the punitive interests of the state. As long as prison labor remains poorly paid, restitution and incarceration will be incompatible.

The major argument against prioritizing reimbursement is that the operations of the criminal justice system are intended to benefit society as a whole and not just the injured party. Other considerations should come first: punishing criminals harshly to teach them a lesson and to deter would-be lawbreakers from following their example, treating offenders in residential programs so that they can be released back as rehabilitated and productive members of the community, or incapacitating dangerous persons by confining them for long periods of time. Subordinating these other sentencing objectives to restitution would reduce the legal system to a mere debt collection agency catering to victims, according to a 1986 Supreme Court decision (Triebwasser, 1986).

Opportunities to Make Restitution

Restitution is an extremely flexible sanction that is not being used to its full potential. It can be applied at each stage in the criminal justice process, from the immediate aftermath of the crime up until the final moments of parole supervision following a period of imprisonment. Figure 12.1 illustrates how restitution can be an option at every decision-making juncture.

As soon as a suspect is apprehended, an informal restitution arrangement can settle the matter. For example, a storekeeper might order a shoplifter to put the stolen item back on the shelf and never return to the premises, or parents might offer to pay for their son's spray painting of a neighbor's fence. In most states, however, serious offenses cannot be resolved informally. It is a felony for an injured party to demand or accept any payment as "hush money" to cover up a major violation of the law, in return for not pressing charges, or as a motive for discontinuing cooperation with the authorities in an investigation or prosecution. A criminal act is an offense against the state in addition to a particular person and cannot be settled privately (Laster, 1970).

After a suspect is arrested, a restitution agreement can be worked out as an alternative to prosecution (diversion). If a defendant is indicted, the district attorney's office can make restitution a condition for dismissing formal criminal charges. Once prosecution is initiated, restitution can be part of a plea bargain struck by the defense lawyer and the district attorney, wherein the accused concedes

guilt in return for lesser penalties. Restitution is particularly appropriate as a condition of probation or of a suspended sentence. If incarcerated, an inmate can try to begin to repay the injured party from the meager wages he earns from labor in prison, but he will be more capable of putting money aside if he gets a real job while he is on work release or when he resides at a halfway house. After serving time, restitution can be included as a condition of parole. Restitution contracts can be administered and supervised by various parties concerned about the crime problem: community groups, private and nonprofit charitable and religious organizations; juvenile courts; adult criminal courts; probation departments; corrections departments; and parole boards.

Yet as promising as restitution seems to be, it is not the answer for most victims. Only a small percentage will ever collect anything. The problem is directly parallel to the quest for emotional satisfaction from retribution. Just as most criminals escape punishment, most also evade restitution. The phenomenon of case attrition has been labeled **funneling**, or **shrinkage**, and has been likened to a "leaky net." At the outset, many cases seem appropriate for restitution. But at the end of the criminal justice process, only a relative handful of injured parties receive even partial restitution. All the other cases (and offenders) have slipped through holes in the net. Figure 12.2 explains how and why so many escape their financial obligations.

First of all, a large number of offenders will never have to make amends because their victims do not report the incidents to the police (refer back to Table 6.1). Next, the majority of offenders get away with their crimes because the police cannot figure out who the perpetrators are (clearance rates are especially low for the most numerous property crimes: burglaries, car thefts, and other forms of stealing; refer back to Table 6.3). Hence, right away most of the people who have suffered harm already have been eliminated from any chance of receiving reimbursement. For example, only about one-half of all robberies are reported, and only one-quarter are solved, so only one out of eight robbery cases enters the system.

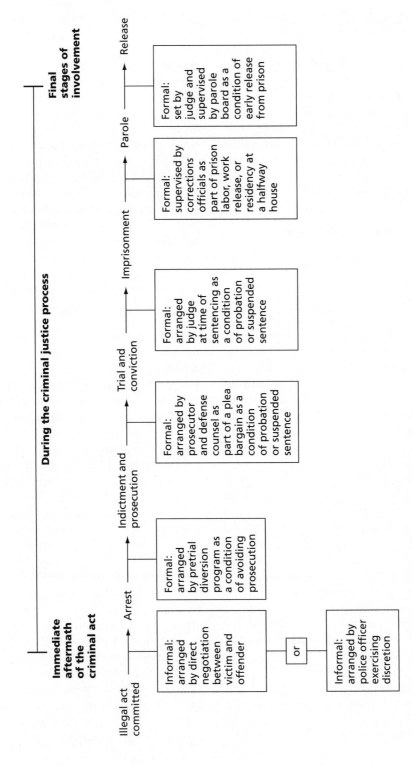

FIGURE 12.1 Opportunities for Offenders to Make Restitution
© Cengage Learning®

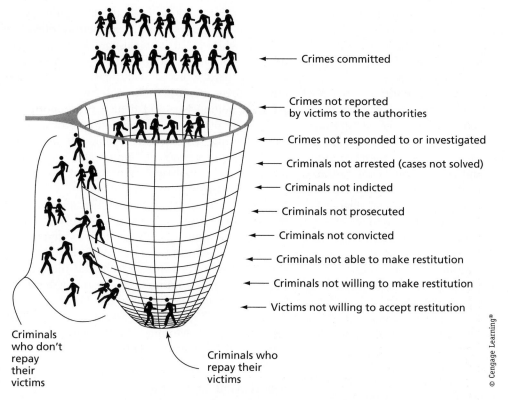

FIGURE 12.2 Case Attrition, Funneling, or Shrinkage: The Leaky Net

Of the relatively small number of crimes that are solved by an arrest, additional problems can arise during the adjudication process. The overwhelming majority of cases (upwards of 90 percent in many jurisdictions) are resolved through plea negotiations that involve dropping charges or counts. Many complainants are eliminated from consideration if offenders do not admit to hurting them. Some cases that go to trial result in acquittals, and some convictions are reversed on appeal. Of those who are convicted or who plead guilty, many are unwilling or unable to shoulder financial obligations. Judges may not order convicts to repay the people they harmed. Inmates usually cannot earn substantial amounts of money. Prisoners granted parole have difficulty finding any work, let alone a job that pays enough to allow them to set aside meaningful amounts after all their other deductions.

Finally, many jurisdictions lack both a tradition of ordering restitution and a mechanism for monitoring and enforcing such arrangements. Actually collecting the funds in a timely manner remains a major challenge for victims (Harland, 1983; McGillis, 1986; and Davis and Bannister, 1995).

Obstacles Undermining Restitution

Economic realities limit the ability of many convicts to meet their restitution obligations. Because the street crime problem is in large part an outgrowth of poverty and the desperation it breeds, restitution obligations collide with competing claims for the same earnings. Ex-offenders have more pressing expenses and other debts. Furthermore, restitution is predicated on work that pays a living wage. Offenders must have, must be helped to find, or must be given reasonably well-paying jobs. These jobs need to pay far more than the minimum wage to permit installments for victims to be deducted from total after-tax earnings. But the U.S. economy cannot provide decent jobs for all who want to earn a living, even during the best of times.

Many dilemmas arise when restitution obligations are considered within the context of intense competition for the limited number of well-paying jobs convicts are capable of doing. If a position is found or created for an ex-offender, then the prospects for the successful completion of the restitution obligation are increased. Otherwise, those hurt by down-and-out street criminals are denied a realist chance to get repaid. If the job pays low wages, then the repayment process cannot be completed within a reasonable amount of time. If nearly all of the ex-offender's earnings are confiscated and handed over to the victim, it would jeopardize the wrongdoer's commitment to the job and to repaying the debt. If the job is demeaning, then its therapeutic value as a first step in the direction of a new lifestyle built on productive employment is lost. If the job is temporary and only lasts for the duration of the restitution obligation, then the risk of returning to a career of crime is heightened.

But if a job found or created for an ex-offender is permanent and pays well, then some observers might object that criminals are being rewarded, not punished, for their misdeeds. Law-abiding people desperately seeking decent jobs will resent any policy that seems to put offenders at the front of the line. Trade union members rightfully will fear that convict labor could replace civilian labor over the long run. But if inmates are put to work in large-scale prison industries, then business interests and labor unions justifiably will complain about unfair competition. If adolescents owing restitution are too young to receive working papers, then a job in private industry would violate child labor laws. Only unpaid community service would be permissible—but then the direct victims get nothing.

When the injured parties are hard-pressed to make ends meet, restitution seems appropriate and fair. But if indigent offenders must hand over money to affluent victims, then restitution smacks of exploitation—taking from the poor and giving to the rich. Conversely, if prosperous offenders (such as white-collar criminals) are allowed to pay off their obligations from their bank accounts and not with hard work, it will appear that they are buying their way out of trouble. If poor people are kept behind bars and denied the opportunity to make restitution as a condition of probation or parole because they lack marketable job skills, such discrimination against an entire class of people seems to be a violation of the equal protection clause of the Fourteenth Amendment.

Yet in jurisdictions where the criterion for release from confinement was a perceived ability to repay, a typical participant in a restitution program turned out to be a white, middle-class, first-time property offender, and the most common recipient of reimbursement was a business, studies showed (see Galaway and Hudson, 1975; Edelhertz, 1977; Hudson and Chesney, 1978; Gottesman and Mountz, 1979; Harland, 1979, 1981a; and Outlaw and Ruback, 1999).

Restitution in Action

Courts in every state now have the authority to order restitution. Victims are promised a right to restitution in some states that have adopted pro-victim constitutional amendments. In many states, judges are supposed to impose restitution obligations on convicts whenever possible and if appropriate, unless there are compelling or extraordinary circumstances (which must be entered into the record in writing). Restitution should routinely be part of the sentence after either negotiated pleas or trials. Often, judges are specifically directed to order reimbursement in cases of child abuse, elder abuse, domestic violence, sexual assault, identity theft, drunk driving, and hate crimes. The repayment can cover outlays for medical expenses, counseling bills, replacing property that was damaged or destroyed, lost wages, other direct costs, and even funeral expenses (National Center for Victims of Crime, 2002d).

Statistics compiled by the federal government shed light on the actual rate of ordering convicts to make restitution in state courts around the country.

The national data compiled in Table 12.1 (up to 2006, the latest year available) reveals that, in general, judges have not been imposing restitution obligations on most offenders. Judges ordered felons to repay their victims in addition to another sentence (usually a term of incarceration, but sometimes a fine or compulsory treatment) in only a fraction of all convictions for either violent crimes or property crimes. Restitution was part of the sentence in a larger percentage of felony convictions for burglary, larceny, motor vehicle theft, and fraud than it was for murder, rape and other sexual assaults, robbery, and aggravated assault. People who commit fraud are the most likely to have to pay back those they fleeced (who might be businesses rather than individuals). Murderers are the least likely of all felons to be forced to take financial responsibility for the losses they inflicted (presumably to the families of the people they killed).

As for changes over time, the imposition of restitution by judges may have been creeping upward during the late 1990s but slipped backward during 2002. However, by 2006, the ordering of repayment in state courts rebounded and reached new highs that surely were still disappointingly low to those who firmly believe in restitution as an important component of criminal justice. The trends in Table 12.1 were derived from a court monitoring system operated by the Department of Justice that tracks dispositions in nearly 1 million cases every two years in the nation's 75 largest jurisdictions (see Langan and Graziadei, 1995; Durose, 2004; BJS, 2008c; and Rosenmerkel et al., 2010).

Another set of figures from this federal database is worth examining for national trends (see Table 12.2). In theory, making restitution is more feasible if a convict is on probation rather than behind bars. In practice, restitution doesn't materialize most of the time. Of felons who were fortunate enough to be sentenced to probation for violent acts, only about one in seven was ordered by a judge in state court to try to reimburse those they harmed as one of the conditions they must obey; and in 2006 this fraction plunged to merely 1 in 11, as second row in Table 12.2 shows. However, in 2009, this proportion shot up to over 20 percent, which is a hopeful sign. The third row reveals that felons on probation for property crimes are ordered to make restitution at a higher rate. But not much changed over a 15-year period. The highest proportion was achieved in 1996, when about two-fifths of all probationers were ordered to work off their debt. After drifting downward, nearly the same percentage was reached in 2009. This lack of an upward trend toward greater use of restitution in property crimes (seemingly the easiest and most appropriate cases) is another disappointment to people who believe in the potential of restitution as a means of reimbursement.

The three most frequently cited reasons for judges failing to impose restitution are that victims didn't request reimbursement, they failed to document their losses, or they were unable to calculate their exact expenses. Often, judges felt that restitution obligations would be inappropriate if convicts also had to repay society by serving time behind bars or if they had a very limited potential to earn a living wage.

T A B L E   12.1   Percentages of Convicted Felons Sentenced to Restitution as an Additional Penalty in the 75 Largest Jurisdictions Nationwide, Selected Years, 1996–2006

Convicted for:	1996	1998	2000	2002	2004	2006
Murder	9	10	11	7	14	13
Rape and sexual assault	9	11	11	10	16	18
Robbery	11	13	13	10	16	18
Aggravated assault	14	14	13	11	15	18
Burglary	21	23	24	20	24	27
Larceny	22	21	25	19	26	26
Vehicle theft	22	21	27	19	37	28
Fraud	32	29	31	24	30	29

SOURCES: Rosenmerkel, S., Durose, M., & Farole, D. (2010, November). Felony sentences in state courts, 2006, (revised). BJS National Judicial Reporting Program. Washington, DC: U.S. Department of Justice.

T A B L E   12.2   Percentage of Convicted Felons Placed on Probation Who Have Restitution Obligations in the 75 Largest Jurisdictions Nationwide, Selected Years, 1994–2009

	1994	1996	2000	2002	2004	2006	2009
On Probation for: Violent crimes	15	15	14	15	15	9	22
Property crimes	34	40	33	32	26	24	37

SOURCES: Reaves, 1998; Hart and Reaves, 1999; Rainville and Reaves, 2003; Cohen and Reaves, 2006; Kyckelhahn and Cohen, 2008; Cohen and Kyckelhahn, 2010; and Reaves, 2013.

Despite these obstacles, limitations, conflicting priorities, dilemmas, and ironies, restitution is under way in many jurisdictions. Probation departments run most (75 percent) supervision and collection programs (Office of Juvenile Justice and Delinquency Prevention, 1998a, 1998b).

When criminologists and victimologists evaluate the effectiveness of these programs, the challenge is to identify the specific goals and to devise appropriate criteria to measure degrees of success and failure. Victim-oriented goals involve making the injured parties whole again by enabling them to collect full reimbursement and to regain peace of mind (recovery from emotional stress and trauma). Offender-oriented goals are achieving rehabilitation and avoiding recidivism. System-oriented goals include reducing case processing costs, relieving taxpayers of the financial burden of compensating people who have been harmed, alleviating jail and prison overcrowding through alternative sentences, and improving citizen cooperation by providing material incentives to injured parties for participating in the criminal justice process. So many different aims and touted benefits coexist that no sweeping conclusions can be drawn about the effectiveness of the programs now in operation (for example, see McGillis, 1986; Butts and Snyder, 1992; Davis, Smith, and Hillenbrand, 1992; and Jacobs and Moore, 1994).

To improve the chances that convicts will make at least partial restitution, notification laws could be strengthened to ensure that victims are advised of their rights. Prosecutors could bear the routine responsibility of requesting restitution, or restitution could be considered mandatory unless the judge specifically excuses the offender from this obligation. Presentence investigation reports and victim impact statements could be used as a standard form to document claims for repayment (NCVC, 2002c). To better enforce restitution orders, judges could routinely investigate the assets of convicts before crafting a workable payment plan. To decrease the likelihood of default, prosecutors could obtain injunctions to prevent defendants from hiding or quickly spending their assets (cash, savings, investments, homes, vehicles, valuable possessions), and probation and parole departments could more closely monitor these court-ordered payments, and either revoke or extend periods of probation and parole if the convict willfully refuses to make timely payments. The money to be handed over can be deducted from inmates' wages from prison labor, state and federal income tax refunds, lottery winnings, inheritances, trust accounts, and collateral used for bail. If convicts default, private collection agencies can be called, and unpaid balances can be converted into civil judgments enforced by seizures of property by sheriffs' departments (NCVC, 2002b).

However, for those who become impatient and dissatisfied with the slow pace of improvement in restitution ordered by judges in criminal courts, another avenue for reimbursement can be pursued: lawsuits in civil courts.

WINNING JUDGMENTS IN CIVIL COURT

The Revival of Interest in Civil Lawsuits

A famous retired football player is put on trial for the murder of his ex-wife and her friend, but he is acquitted by a jury that is not convinced of his guilt *beyond a reasonable doubt by the prosecution's extensive but extremely complicated forensic evidence. The outraged families of the murder victims sue him in civil court. A jury finds him liable for the wrongful deaths and awards the two families more than $33 million in compensatory and punitive damages. When he announces that he is writing a book entitled "If I Did It, Here's How It Happened," the two families are divided over whether to go after the royalties to speed up the slow payment of the judgment. Thirteen years to the day after he was acquitted of murdering his former wife, he is convicted of taking part in an armed robbery of sports memorabilia by a group of men in a hotel room and is sentenced to prison. He appeals the conviction, arguing that his attorneys were improperly barred from asking prospective jurors about their knowledge of his previous acquittal in criminal court and the subsequent judgment against him in civil court, but his lengthy sentence is upheld.* (Ayres, 1997; and Martinez, 2010)

■■■

The wife of a well-known television and movie star is shot while she sits in their car outside of a restaurant. He is put on trial but acquitted. The district attorney angrily brands him, "guilty as sin" and denounces the jury as "incredibly stupid." The wife's four grown children decide to sue the actor in civil court, contending that either he killed her himself or hired someone to do it. Although he did not testify at his murder trial, he is compelled to take the stand and answer questions in civil court. Ten of the twelve jurors conclude that he was involved in the slaying, and the judge orders him to pay $30 million to his dead wife's four children. He declares bankruptcy and appeals the judgment. Several years later, a judge halves the damages he owes her children but rules that the jury did not act improperly when it discussed "sending a message" to celebrities that they can't get away with murder, as they may have in other cases. (Associated Press, 2005; BBC, 2008; and Morrison, 2010)

A growing number of victims are no longer content to just let prosecutors handle their cases in criminal court, especially if convictions are not secured. They have discovered that they can go after their alleged wrongdoers and pursue their best interests in a different arena: via a lawsuit in civil court.

Criminal proceedings are intended to redress public wrongs that threaten society as a whole. As a result, the economic interests of injured parties seeking restitution from convicts routinely are subordinated to the government's priorities, whether probation, incarceration, or execution. Injured parties seeking financial redress are directed to civil court. In that venue they can launch lawsuits designed to remedy torts—private wrongs—arising from violations of criminal law. Under tort law, **plaintiffs** (victims) can sue **defendants** and win **judgments** for **punitive damages** (money extracted to punish wrongdoers and deter others) as well as **compensatory damages** (to repay expenses).

Activists and advocates like to call attention to these often-overlooked legal rights and opportunities. Guilty verdicts in criminal courts cost offenders their freedom; successful judgments in civil courts cost offenders their money. Lawsuits can be successful even if charges are not pressed or if the alleged perpetrator is found not guilty after a trial in criminal court. Centers for legal advocacy and technical assistance have sprung up in many cities to make lawsuits an occupational hazard and a deterrent for habitual criminals (Barbash, 1979; Carrington, 1986; Carson, 1986; and National Victim Center, 1993).

The Litigation Process

Civil suits can involve claims for punitive damages as well as compensatory and **pecuniary damages**. Awards for compensatory damages (repayment of expenses) and pecuniary damages (to cover lost income) are supposed to restore victims to their former financial condition (make them "whole" again). They can receive the monetary equivalent of stolen or vandalized property, wages from missed work, projected future earnings that won't materialize because of injuries inflicted by the offender, and outlays for medical and psychiatric care (hospital bills, counseling expenses) plus recompense for physical pain and mental suffering (resulting from loss of enjoyment, fright, nervousness, grief, humiliation, and disfigurement). Punitive damages might be levied by the court to make negative examples of lawbreakers who deliberately act maliciously, oppressively, and recklessly (Stark and Goldstein, 1985; and Brien, 1992).

In civil courts, injured parties and their kin can sue offenders for certain intentional torts. **Wrongful death** suits enable survivors to collect compensation for the loss of a loved one without justification or legitimate excuse and for assault, which covers acts sufficiently threatening to cause fear of immediate bodily harm. Suits for **battery** involve intentional, harmful, physical contact that is painful, injurious, or offensive. Suits charging **trespass** center upon the intentional invasion of another person's land. **Conversion of chattel** suits accuse defendants of knowingly stealing or destroying the plaintiffs' possessions or property through theft or embezzlement. Suits alleging **false imprisonment** contend that the offender held the plaintiff against his or her will, even if for a brief period of time, such as during a hostage taking or rape. Charges of fraud can arise from white-collar crimes if intentional misrepresentation and deception can be established. Finally, suits can allege that the defendant intentionally or recklessly inflicted emotional distress through extreme or outrageous conduct, such as by stalking the plaintiff (Stark and Goldstein, 1985; Brien, 1992; and National Crime Victims Bar Association, 2007).

Civil actions commence when the plaintiff (also called the **second party**) formally files a complaint (also referred to as a **pleading**). This document includes a brief statement of the legal jurisdictional issues, a summary of the relevant facts of the case (the **causes of action** that show how the harm to the victim was a "direct and proximate result" of the alleged wrongdoer's behavior), and a request for relief for the injuries and damages sustained (monetary compensation). The victim's attorney brings the complaint to civil court and pays a fee. A deputy sheriff (or a privately retained **process server**) must physically hand this written document to the defendant (also called the **first party**), along with a summons requiring a response to the allegations within a stated period of time (usually one month). The accused wrongdoer submits an answer either admitting to the charges or, more likely, contesting them and issuing a defense (or perhaps even launching a countersuit).

In preparing for a trial to resolve the competing claims, both parties engage in a process called **discovery**, in which they exchange written replies to questions, documents, and sworn statements of eyewitnesses (including police officers). Just as in criminal proceedings, the typical outcome is a negotiated compromise agreement. But if an out-of-court settlement cannot be reached, the accused exercises his Seventh Amendment right to a trial, and the injured party has to prove the allegations in court. After considerable delays because of congested court calendars, the trial is held before 12 (or, in some states, six) jurors or perhaps only in front of a judge (Stark and Goldstein, 1985).

In civil proceedings, the defendant in third-party lawsuits is likely to allege contributory negligence (the injured party was partly responsible for what happened). In battery cases, the rebuttal might be victim provocation (leading to responses necessary for self-protection). In other lawsuits, the defense might argue that the plaintiff knowingly and voluntarily "assumed the risk"; for example, a woman alleging rape was drinking heavily and agreed to go to the man's apartment (Stark and Goldstein, 1985; and National Crime Victims Bar Association, 2007).

Following opening statements presented by attorneys for each side, witnesses testify and are cross-examined, and physical evidence is introduced. **Interrogatories** (lists of questions for the other side to answer), **depositions** (answers to the opposing lawyer's questions), and requests for documents may generate important evidence. Then each party's attorney sums up, and the jury retires to deliberate. The jury votes and then renders its verdict on which of the two versions of events seems more truthful. The jury awards compensatory and perhaps punitive damages if it finds for the plaintiff and rejects the defendant's arguments. The losing party is likely to appeal the decision, and a higher court can overturn the trial court's verdict if errors in procedural law are discovered or if the jury acted contrary to the evidence. Appeals may take many years to be resolved (Stark and Goldstein, 1985).

Litigation in civil court usually follows rather than precedes adjudication in criminal court. People who have been badly hurt usually wait to proceed with litigation because the evidence that is introduced during the criminal proceedings can be used again in the lawsuit and generally is sufficient to establish that a tort occurred. Furthermore, if the civil action is filed too early, the defense attorney will use this fact to try to undermine the complainant's credibility as a witness for the prosecution, claiming that the testimony is motivated by potential financial gain. But if the civil action is not filed for years, the **statute of limitations** might run out, and it will be too late to sue the defendant. For example, in most states, lawsuits alleging assault must be filed within two years, before complainants' and defendants' memories fade and material evidence is lost or destroyed (Brien, 1992).

Possibilities and Pitfalls Injured parties who are considering civil litigation must weigh the advantages and disadvantages of this course of action. One reason civil lawsuits are relatively uncommon is that most victims conclude that the benefits are not worth the costs. In addition, many people are unfamiliar with this option.

Civil lawsuits have several attractions. First and foremost, victims can seize the initiative, haul their assailants into court, bring them to the bar of justice, and sue them for all they can get. In criminal cases, prosecutors exercise considerable discretion and make all the important decisions, even in jurisdictions where victims have the right to be informed and consulted. In civil cases, victims can regain a sense of control and feel empowered. They are principal figures entitled to their day in court, are aware of all the facts surrounding the case, and can't be excluded from the courtroom. It is up to them to decide whether to sue and whether to

accept a defendant's offer of an out-of-court settlement. (In small-claims courts, plaintiffs don't even need an attorney. They can present their own cases using simplified procedures designed to expedite trials, because not much money is at stake.)

Plaintiffs seeking large awards must hire attorneys of their own choosing and can participate in developing a strategy and preparing the case in anticipation of the trial. Victims can achieve full reimbursement, perhaps even more money than they lost, through lawsuits. They can collect punitive damages far in excess of actual out-of-pocket expenses and can receive compensation for the mental pain and emotional suffering they endured. Defendants' assets, including homes, cars, savings accounts, investments, and inheritances, can be **attached** (confiscated), and their wages can be **garnished**. Most attorneys practicing civil law accept cases on a contingency basis and don't charge a fee unless they win. Suits can be brought by the victims' family (parents, children, spouse, or siblings) if an injured party is too young, mentally incapacitated, or dies (Stark and Goldstein, 1985; Brien, 1992; and National Crime Victims Bar Association, 2007).

Winning a judgment in civil court is easier than securing a conviction in criminal court—the standard of proof is lower and less demanding. In lawsuits, conflicting claims are decided by a **preponderance of the evidence** (the winning side is the one that presents the more convincing arguments, translated as "more likely than not" or "51 percent"), not by guilt beyond a reasonable doubt (proving the charges to a moral certainty). Therefore, a civil suit following a conviction in criminal court is likely to succeed because the same evidence and testimony can be used again in front of a second jury that does not have to reach a unanimous agreement and does not have to be convinced beyond a reasonable doubt. An acquittal in criminal court does not rule out civil action, because a jury still might decide in favor of a plaintiff who presents a more persuasive case than the defendant. Even if the prosecutor drops the criminal charges that were initially lodged by the police, a plaintiff might win if the evidence that came to light during the police investigation is presented in civil court. If plaintiffs win awards but defendants are unwilling to pay up voluntarily, sheriffs and marshals can be enlisted to enforce the courts' judgments by seizing contested assets or property, which can be sold at public auctions to raise cash.

Because defendants in civil court do not face imprisonment or execution, constitutional protections are less stringent than in criminal court. Defendants cannot ignore lawsuits for more than 30 days, or else they automatically lose (a **default judgment**). Nor can the accused plead the Fifth Amendment and refuse to testify on the grounds of self-incrimination. Defendants must reply to the questions put to them or risk a quick defeat. Rules of evidence are more flexible and, for example, allow the plaintiff to reveal the defendant's prior convictions for similar acts, a disclosure that usually wouldn't be permissible in criminal court (Stark and Goldstein, 1985; and Brien, 1992).

Successful suits can make victims feel vindicated: The judges and jurors sided with them, accepted their version of events, and rejected the defendants' denials, excuses, or justifications. Victims teach perpetrators the lessons that crime does not pay and that wrongdoers ultimately will be held liable for their misdeeds. Reimbursement is soothing, and revenge is sweet. Civil suits are the only means of redress when the entire injury and loss is intangible and subsumed under the heading of **pain and suffering**.

Despite the prospect of financial reimbursement, several drawbacks deter most victims from pursuing civil actions. Civil proceedings are independent of criminal proceedings. The entire case must be fought all over again in the courtroom, this time at the victim's expense without the backing of the government and its enormous resources. A statute of limitations may have run out—the time limits for filing a lawsuit vary by crime and by state; those with recovered memories of abuse during childhood may be entitled to extra amounts of time. Victims have to put their lives on hold for years while the litigation process slowly drags on.

Cases involve motions, hearings, conferences, negotiations, trials, and appeals. In the meantime, plaintiffs (and defendants as well) undergo a long, drawn-out ordeal punctuated by moments of suspense, anxiety, frustration, despair, and humiliation. Despite their opposing interests and simmering mutual hostility, the warring parties must keep in contact (at least through their respective lawyers) for months or even years after criminal proceedings end. If negotiations fail and last-minute, out-of-court settlements are beyond reach, victims must take the stand and once again relive the incident in painful detail. After testifying, victims must submit to a withering cross-examination by the defense attorney that could raise questions of shared responsibility, damage the victims' reputation, and expose the most intimate details about lifestyles, injuries, losses, and suffering. The backlogs and delays in civil court are worse than those in criminal court because litigation has become such a popular way to settle disputes. Win or lose, civil suits drag on for years before they are resolved, forestalling closure for victims who want to get on with their lives. Furthermore, the injured parties run the risk of being sued themselves. Countersuits by defendants against plaintiffs fit into a strategy of harassment and intimidation intended to force victims to drop certain charges, or to withdraw their suits entirely, or to accept unfavorable out-of-court settlements (see Stark and Goldstein, 1985; Brien, 1992; and National Crime Victims Bar Association, 2007).

In the adversary system of civil proceedings, top-notch lawyers are said to be as important a factor as the facts of the case. Unfortunately, they probably won't be interested unless great sums of money are at stake. Their **contingency fees** can range as high as one-third to one-half of the money awarded to plaintiffs, if they are victorious. Even victims who win may have to pay for most litigation expenses other than their attorney's fees, such as filing fees, deposition costs, and expert witness fees.

Most discouraging of all is the problem of collecting the debt. Even in victory there can be defeat. If the offenders have spent or hidden the spoils of their crimes, it will be difficult for the plaintiffs' attorneys to recover any money without incurring great expenses. Most street criminals don't have what lawyers call **deep pockets** (assets like homes, cars, jewelry, bank accounts, investments in stocks and bonds, or business interests). On the contrary, many are virtually **judgment-proof**—broke and with no prospects of coming into money from work or inheritances (see Stark and Goldstein, 1985; and Brien, 1992).

No government agency systematically compiles records about the successes and failures of plaintiffs who have sued defendants in civil courts. The actual dollar amounts of some out-of-court settlements are kept confidential. Nevertheless, advocacy groups urge victims to consider exercising their civil court option, especially if the identity and whereabouts of the offender are known, if restitution is not forthcoming from criminal court proceedings, and if compensation is not available from insurance companies or government-administered funds.

Recognizing that few street criminals who commit acts of violence or theft have substantial assets or incomes, attorneys within the victims' rights movement have developed a strategic alternative: lawsuits against financially sound third parties.

Collecting Damages from Third Parties

Even when the perpetrators of a crime are known to be judgment-proof, victims still have a chance to recover their losses. Instead of suing those who inflicted their injuries directly and intentionally, plaintiffs can go after **third parties**: individuals or entities such as businesses, institutions, or government agencies. The twist in these civil suits is to allege that a third party is partly to blame for the victim's misfortunes.

The legal theory behind third-party suits parallels traditional notions of **negligence**. The plaintiff argues that the defendant (the third party) had a duty or obligation, that there was a breach of this duty, and that this breach proximately caused injury to the plaintiff. The plaintiff tries to prove that the third party's gross negligence put the criminal in a position to single him or her out for harm (Carrington, 1977). For example, in the aftermath of a spate of massacres on school grounds, families of youngsters who were killed or wounded filed lawsuits against the parents of the students who went berserk, the people who inadvertently were

the sources of the weapons, the school district, and the manufacturers of the guns (Lewin, 2001).

There are two types of third-party liability suits. The first is directed against enterprises such as private businesses (for example, firearms dealers who failed to take adequate steps to prevent their handguns from being sold illegally to teenage gang members). The second type is aimed at custodial agencies and officials of the criminal justice system (such as municipal police departments, prison wardens, and directors of mental institutions). Whereas suing offenders is reactive, third-party civil suits can be both reactive and proactive. If for no other motive than their own enlightened self-interest, the private enterprises and governmental bodies that are the targets of these kinds of suits are compelled to take reasonable and necessary precautions to prevent further incidents for which they could be sued again. By discouraging the indifference and negligence that facilitate predatory acts, third-party civil suits contribute to security consciousness and crime prevention (Carrington, 1986). A National Crime Victim Bar Association (2007) encourages injured parties to seek redress through civil actions and provides names of attorneys who specialize in lawsuits.

Suing Private Enterprises   Several successful suits during the 1970s have served as landmark cases for many subsequent claims:

> A well-known singer is raped in a motel by an unknown assailant who entered her room by jiggling the lock on the sliding glass terrace doors. Badly shaken by the experience and unable to appear on stage, the singer sues the motel chain for loss of earnings. Her attorney argues that the motel showed gross negligence by failing to maintain secure premises for its guests. A jury renders a verdict in her favor of $2.5 million. The motel chain agrees to a settlement by not appealing the verdict and pays her $1.5 million. (Barbash, 1979; and Rottenberg, 1980)

■ ■ ■

> A security guard at a drive-through hamburger stand is shot in the head during a robbery. He doesn't sue the offender or his employer (the restaurant). Instead,

his attorney argues successfully that the chain store that sold the robber the bullet is guilty of gross negligence. The guns and ammunition department routinely ignored an obscure state law that requires two citizens to vouch for the identity of the purchaser of bullets. (Barbash, 1979; and Rottenberg, 1980)

Third-party lawsuits against businesses have established new definitions of corporate responsibility and financial liability. The suits never accuse the defendant (business) of intentionally harming the plaintiff because the executives in charge probably never met either the victim or the offender and were two or three steps removed from the criminal action. What is alleged is that the defendant's gross negligence and breach of responsibility created a climate that made the criminal's task easier and the incident predictable (Carrington, 1977, 1978).

Third-party suits against private enterprises can take several forms. Lawsuits can allege that landlords are responsible for crimes committed against their tenants because of inadequate lighting or locks. Hotels and motels may be liable for assaults and thefts committed against guests because of lax security measures (such as failure to install closed-circuit television monitors, store room keys safely, or hire guards). Banks, stores, shopping malls, and theaters can be held accountable for failure to provide ordinary care to protect customers from robbers and thieves. "Common carriers" (bus, train, or airplane companies) might be liable for failure to furnish customary forms of protection for passengers on vehicles or at stations and platforms. Employers who negligently hire known felons and put them in positions of trust might be partly to blame if the ex-cons break laws during the course of their assigned duties. Even college administrations could be responsible for failing to correct security lapses that a reasonable and prudent individual would realize endanger students in campus buildings and dormitories (Austern, 1987).

Plaintiffs can win if they can prove in civil court that the third party did not take sufficient actions to prevent a reasonably foreseeable crime. To prevail, the attorney must convincingly demonstrate that the defendant chronically disregarded complaints, did not post warnings, chose not to rectify conditions and improve security, and did not offer the degree of protection expected by community standards. Most claims fail to meet this test, but the few that succeed can contribute to the improvement of public safety in places like shopping centers, bus terminals, parking lots, hotels, and apartment complexes (Brien, 1992), as well as airports and on airplanes, as these two suits demonstrate:

> *A third-party lawsuit alleging wrongful deaths and injuries is filed in 2002 in behalf of 85 people who were killed and 11 who were injured when a hijacked plane crashed into one of the towers in New York's World Trade Center on September 11, 2001. The plaintiffs allege that the airline and the airport security company it hired to screen passengers showed gross negligence in allowing five terrorists to board the plane with knives and a canister of Mace which they used to take command of the aircraft from the crew. The defendants argue that an airline and a security company could not be held liable "for not stopping an attack that the entire federal government was unable to predict, plan against or prevent." Before a civil trial begins, most of the plaintiffs accept an out-of-court settlement in 2009; the remaining family agrees in 2011. (Thousands of other victims were not covered by the suit because they opted for relatively quick and uncontested settlements from a special compensation fund created by Congress.) In a parallel case, a major financial firm in 2004 files a nearly $950 million gross negligence lawsuit against a different airline whose plane was hijacked by a cell of 5 terrorists and then crashed into the other tower. After nearly 10 years, the firm, which had been located near the top of the skyscraper, agrees to accept a settlement of $135 million from the airline that covers business losses, but does not provide compensation for the death of all of its 660 employees working in their offices that day.* (Weiser, 2011; and Larson, 2014)

Because many lawsuits against property owners are settled out of court, reliable figures about their rate of occurrence and success are hard to find. One estimate from a sample of court records turned up 186 suits against property owners from 1958 to

1982. A later study established that the rate had increased, locating 267 third-party suits from 1983 to 1992. Almost half of all the suits were launched by women who had been raped (Deutsch, 1994). As attorneys hone their skills at security litigation seminars, landlords and businesses attempt to make their premises or products as suit-proof as possible, even if they cannot make them crime-proof (Purdy, 1994).

In recent years, one type of third-party lawsuit has become extremely controversial. People wounded by gunfire have filed many claims against the firearms industry over the years. One example of a successful suit took place after a pair of snipers terrorized the Washington, D.C., area in 2002. Eight people who were wounded and the next of kin of those who were murdered eventually won a $2.5 million legal settlement from the manufacturer of the high-powered rifle and from the gun dealer who improperly sold it. In reaction, a lobbying campaign by the National Rifle Association convinced Congress in 2005 to pass "shield legislation (similar to the existing laws in 33 states). The Protection of Lawful Commerce in Arms Act prohibits third-party lawsuits against firearms and ammunition manufacturers and dealers as long as their products function as designed and intended. Victorious backers of the gun lobby's measure said it was needed to preserve the Fourth Amendment's constitutional right to bear arms and also to keep the American arms industry in business in the face of "frivolous" but costly negligence lawsuits. Disappointed opponents argued that firearms are a uniquely hazardous product that can cause foreseeable harm to others if reasonable steps are not taken to prevent their misuse. By passing the shield law, Congress deprived wounded people and the next of kin of murder victims (as well as entire municipalities, such as New York City, that incur huge expenses from gun violence) from pursuing a legitimate avenue for financial recovery. Since 2005, most third-party lawsuits have been dismissed by the courts. Lawsuits seeking to hold gunmakers accountable when their weapons are used to commit crimes like mass shootings of innocent people have a chance of success only if the civil litigants can

prove that grossly negligent behavior on the part of manufacturers or distributors enabled powerful weapons to get into the hands of known criminals prohibited from owning them (for example, due to a licensed dealer knowingly filing false paperwork about a sale) (Stolberg, 2005; Fisher, 2012; Morgenthau, 2013; and Hamburger et al., 2013).

Suing Governmental Bodies   Successful third-party lawsuits against criminal justice agencies and custodial officials, like the two 1970s landmark cases described below, are less common than suits against private enterprises:

> *A 14-year-old girl is abducted from a private school, tied to a tree, molested, and then left to freeze to death. The man who kills her had previously attacked another girl from the same school in the same way. He had been committed for treatment while under confinement at a nearby psychiatric institute. The victim's parents sue the mental hospital, a psychiatrist, and a probation officer for arranging the release of the offender into an outpatient program without first receiving court approval. They win a judgment of $25,000. (Carrington, 1977, 1978)*

...

> *An inmate with a record of 40 felony convictions and 17 escape attempts is permitted to participate in a "take-a-lifer to dinner" program. After eating at the home of the prison's baker, he breaks loose, commits an armed robbery, and kills a man. The victim's widow sues the warden both personally and in his official capacity, in addition to the state prison system, for gross negligence. Her attorney argues that the warden didn't have legislative authority or administrative permission from his superiors to let the inmate out that night. She wins a judgment of $186,000, which the state does not appeal. (Barbash, 1979; and Rottenberg, 1980)*

The basic charge in civil actions against the government once again is gross negligence. The plaintiffs allege that public officials severely abused their discretionary authority. The crimes are said to have happened because official inaction or incompetence facilitated the offenders' inclinations to harm innocent parties. In a few states, governmental bodies cannot be sued even when the negligence of officials clearly contributed to the commission of crimes; the agents and agencies are protected by the English common law doctrine of **sovereign immunity**. Most states and the federal government permit citizens to sue but impose limitations (for example, financial caps and exemption from punitive damages) and invoke special procedures (Carrington, 1978; and Austern, 1987).

Specific charges in third-party liability lawsuits against governmental agencies and officials fit under a number of headings (Austern, 1987). Claims against the police can allege **nonfeasance**: that officers failed to act to protect individuals to whom they owed a special duty, such as witnesses for the prosecution. Claims can also allege police **malfeasance**: that officers acted carelessly or inattentively as victims were hurt, as in the following often-cited case:

> A woman is stabbed by her husband 13 times. Nearly 30 minutes later, the police arrive in response to her earlier call for help. As the husband wanders around screaming, he kicks her in the head, then drops their son on her unconscious body and kicks her again. Finally, the police restrain him and take him into custody. After eight days in a coma and several months in a hospital, the woman sues the city, three police chiefs, and 29 officers. Her lawsuit alleges that because the assailant was her husband, the police failed to provide her with equal protection under the law, as guaranteed by the Fourteenth Amendment, by handling her numerous calls for help over the years differently than cases of assaults by strangers. A jury finds the police department negligent for failing to protect her and awards her $2.3 million. The city appeals, and she settles for $1.9 million out of court. (Gelles and Straus, 1988)

When prisoners are not supervised adequately or are released as a result of an administrative error and then inflict harm, suits can allege **wrongful escape**. When dangerous convicts are released and they injure people whom they had previously publicly threatened, suits can be filed for **failure to warn**. Claims can also allege **wrongful release**

when, through gross negligence on the part of officials, a high-risk inmate is granted conditional release (probation, parole, or furlough) from a jail, prison, or mental institution and then commits a foreseeable act of lawlessness. The following cases illustrate these problems:

> A 24-year-old graduate student in criminal justice is drinking alone at a fashionable club at closing time. The bar's bouncer lures her into his van, binds her, drives to a deserted spot, sexually assaults her, and then kills her. He is caught, convicted, and sentenced to life imprisonment. The murdered student's family sues the 44-year-old bouncer, the bar, and the U.S. Probation Service. The bouncer is penniless, and the bar settles its suit for $375,000. The suit seeks $100 million, charging that the U.S. Probation Service was guilty of gross negligence for failing to monitor the bouncer, who was on probation at the time of the slaying and was known to be a violent ex-convict who was not eligible to work in a drinking establishment. Federal Probation is represented by the U.S. attorney in that district and argues that it cannot be sued. But the agency consents to a settlement of $130,000, of which almost half goes to the three lawyers representing the family (they get a 25 percent contingency fee and the rest covers expenses). Most important to the family, the U.S. Probation Service names its probation-tracking program in her honor. (Italiano and Mangan, 2011)

■ ■ ■

> An 11-year-old girl is snatched off the street, raped periodically, and held captive for over 18 years in tents and sheds in the backyard of a convict who had previously served time for kidnapping and rape. As the girl grows up, she is impregnated twice and bears two daughters. She is finally rescued at the age of 30, along with her children, now 12 and 15 years old. The three females sue the Department of Corrections and Rehabilitation for gross negligence in supervising the known sex offender, since parole officers making home visits failed to detect their presence in the backyard for about 10 years of her captivity. The state's inspector general issues a report lambasting the agency's operations, and as a result parole officers are

given smaller caseloads and closer supervision, and high-risk offenders are watched more carefully. Even before the man is convicted, the state legislature votes nearly unanimously to quickly settle the suit for $20 million, even though the government is in the throes of a fiscal crisis. The money will be used to buy the family a home, ensure their privacy, pay for the mother's and daughters' education, compensate for lost income, and cover years of psychotherapy. (Thompson, 2010)

Suits against custodial officials and probation and parole agencies raise important issues. The Supreme Court ruled in 1980 *(Martinez* case) that neither the Constitution nor the Civil Rights Act of 1964 gave the survivors of a person who was murdered the right to sue a state parole board (Carrington, 1980). In upholding the doctrine of sovereign immunity from liability, the justices of the Court argued that government has a legitimate interest in seeking to rehabilitate criminals. Every treatment alternative to totally incapacitating convicts through maximum-security confinement involves taking risks with the public's safety. Halfway houses, therapeutic communities, work release, educational release, furloughs, probation, and parole all grant conditional liberty to known offenders who may pose a continuing threat to community safety. Underlying a charge of **abuse of discretionary authority** and gross negligence is the assumption that danger can be predicted—but it usually cannot be with any statistical certainty. Some patients and inmates thought to be dangerous turn out to be well-behaved (**false positives**), and some out on probation or parole enjoying conditional liberty who were rated as posing a low risk may suddenly act viciously (**false negatives**).

What is predictable is that successful third-party lawsuits by victims against custodial officials and agencies will have a chilling effect on wardens, psychiatrists, parole boards, and others who make decisions regarding confinement versus release. What might develop in these therapeutic relationships is a type of defensiveness comparable to the defensive medicine practiced by doctors afraid of malpractice suits. Fear of legal and financial repercussions could dominate professional judgments and record keeping. Rehabilitation programs could be severely constrained. Eligible convicts could be barred from such programs because administrators wouldn't want to jeopardize their careers by releasing them from total confinement. Qualified professionals could be deterred from taking jobs as custodial officials because of exposure to personal liability lawsuits, unless states protect such employees under a doctrine of sovereign immunity.

On the other hand, vulnerable members of the general public need lawsuits as a vehicle to exert some leverage over justice officials and unresponsive bureaucracies. Also, aggrieved parties need a way to hold grossly negligent agency officials accountable, as well as a mechanism to recover losses inflicted by dangerous people who should not have been left unsupervised. Third-party lawsuits can serve as an appropriate remedy to establish a proper balance between two conflicting policy objectives: lowering the crime rate in the long run by rehabilitating offenders through the judicious granting of conditional liberty and maintaining public safety in the short run by incapacitating and incarcerating individuals believed to be dangerous to the community (Carrington, 1980).

COLLECTING INSURANCE REIMBURSEMENTS

Private Crime Insurance

Private insurance companies are innocent third parties that can quickly and routinely provide reimbursement for losses. The positive aspect is that a prudent policyholder can be repaid without too many complications as long as a formal complaint is filed with the police. The drawbacks are that a potential target must have the foresight to purchase protection in advance, a company must be willing to issue a policy (some people and businesses in high-crime areas have trouble finding an insurer), premiums for the coverage must be affordable (many people are aware of life's dangers but do not have the disposable income to pay for the "luxury" of insurance), and exclusions of relatively minor losses (because of **deductible clauses**) impose serious financial hardships on low-income families (Sarnoff, 1996).

Cautious individuals can protect themselves against a variety of hazards (see Miller, Cohen, and Wiersema, 1996). Life insurance policies can pay sizable sums to the survivors of loved ones who were murdered. Some policies (which cost more) contain a **double indemnity clause** that grants survivors twice as much if the policyholder dies unexpectedly from an accident or a criminally inflicted injury. Coverage can also be purchased to offset lost earnings (income maintenance) and expenses due to medical bills (health insurance). Property can be insured against loss or damage. Car and boat insurance covers expenses imposed by theft, vandalism, and arson. Home insurance protects against losses due to burglary, some larcenies (items left on porches or in yards, for example),

vandalism, arson, and robbery if the confrontation occurs within the dwelling. Some companies sell robbery insurance that reimburses policyholders for lost valuables such as jewelry or cameras no matter where the crime occurs. A few companies offer protection to businesses whose executives might be kidnapped and held for ransom.

In order for burglary victims to collect reimbursements under homeowner policies, documentation requirements, deductibles, exclusions, limits, depreciation of value due to age and wear, plus optional rider clauses (for example, to cover the theft of very expensive jewelry) make complete recovery unlikely (Weisberg, 2008). If detectives determine that the intruder committed a theft due to a victim-facilitated "no force entry" (see Chapter 5), a careless policyholder's claim could be reduced or rejected (Reeves, 2006). Obstacles to collecting insurance reimbursement like these are listed in Box 12.1.

B O X 12.1 Challenges Facing Burglary Victims Who Seek Insurance Reimbursement

Many hurdles have to be surmounted before crime-conscious individuals who have taken out renters or homeowners insurance can collect money to cover their losses inflicted by intruders who stole their valuable possessions. Here are some issues that can arise, step-by-step:

- The crime scene should not be disturbed until detectives arrive.
- A police report must be filed in a timely manner.
- An inventory must be prepared of the items that were in the home that now are missing or damaged (broken locks, smashed windows).
- Having an updated home inventory list to work from will be useful. Receipts, photographs, and appraisals that verify the value of stolen items will be necessary to document major losses.
- If the policy language reads "actual cash value," then the amount of reimbursement will be only a fraction of the original costs because of depreciation. If it reads "replacement value" (which requires higher premiums before the crime occurs), the reimbursement will be greater in order to pay current prices.

- The insurance company may send a claims adjustor to the home to assess the size of the loss.
- If the total value of the items that were stolen adds up to less than the amount of the policy's deductible, then no reimbursement will be forthcoming.
- If the grand total far exceeds the cap or limit, then only partial reimbursement will take place.
- If the claim is for a substantial amount, the cost of subsequent years' premiums could be increased.
- The company will take weeks to process the claim before sending a check.
- Unjustified delays, gross negligence, or dishonesty on the victim's part could cause the claim to be reduced or rejected, as noted in the policy's fine print.
- Claims for the loss of big ticket items filed by persons undergoing financial hardships will raise suspicions about possible insurance fraud.
- Too many claims can cause the policy to be cancelled, and it may be difficult to find another company that will offer homeowner's or tenant's insurance for a dwelling that is classified as high risk.

SOURCE: (Adapted from Siedsma, 2012).

Patterns of Loss, Recovery, and Reimbursement

Statistics derived from the National Crime Victimization Survey confirm some commonsense predictions about insurance coverage and recovery. First, some types of coverage are more common than others. More people are insured against medical expenses than against property losses. Medical and dental costs are potentially more devastating than theft or vandalism of tangible goods, and health coverage often is provided by an employer as a fringe benefit of full-time jobs. Second, high-income individuals are more likely to buy crime insurance than low-income people (even though the poor are exposed to greater risks and suffer higher victimization rates). Third, larger losses are more likely than smaller ones to be reimbursed through insurance claims. The households that are most likely to receive cash settlements are those whose cars are stolen. Only a small proportion of families who suffer burglaries and larcenies are reimbursed. An even smaller fraction of people who are robbed or pickpocketed are insured against such losses. Most policies have deductible clauses that stipulate that the victim must absorb the first $500 (or some other sum) of the losses and cannot file a claim unless out-of-pocket expenses exceed this figure. Hence, most crime-imposed losses (which usually are small) cannot be recovered (Harland, 1981a).

Studies concerning actual patterns of burglary loss, coverage, and recovery are rare. One revealed that both the average amount stolen and the percentage of victims who are insured are positively correlated with family income. That means that wealthy families lose more to burglars but also are more likely to be insured than low-income households. In one study during the 1970s, only 1 family in 10 had purchased burglary insurance in the lowest income category, but about half the families in the higher-income category were covered. (Presumably, the rich were fully insured, but those data was unavailable.) In sum, although a small number of families recover substantial amounts, insurance provides relief for relatively few burglary victims (Skogan, 1978; and

Harland, 1981a). Some more recent data is available from the *NCVS*. It indicated that the bigger the loss, the more likely the victim was to report the burglary to the police and to an insurance company as well. In 1994, just about 40 percent of households suffering a loss to burglars of $1,000 or more informed an insurance company about their misfortunes. In 2003, that figure dropped to 33 percent. By 2011, it stood at 35 percent of households losing $1,000 or more (Walters et al., 2013). It appears that fewer people currently have burglary insurance coverage for major losses than in previous years.

As for medical insurance coverage for expenses arising from hospital care, doctors, and medicines due to injuries resulting from violent crime, women were more likely to receive reimbursement (73 percent) than men (57 percent). The lowest income grouping (61 percent) and the highest income grouping (95 percent) were much more likely to get their out-of-pocket costs paid by health insurance (from the government in the case of the poor; from private companies in the case of the affluent) than the working poor (45 percent) who usually earn too much for Medicaid but too little to afford their own policies. All senior citizens received coverage of their bills under Medicare, but less than half (45 percent) of injured individuals between 20 and 24 years of age had health insurance coverage, according to the *NCVS* for 2006 (BJS, 2008d). As various phases of the federal Affordable Care Act go into effect, these percentages ought to improve.

Federal Crime Insurance

Insurance companies make profits in two ways: They adjust their rates continuously so that they take in more money in premiums than they pay out in claims, and they invest the money paid by policyholders in order to collect interest, dividends, and rents. To contain costs and limit payouts, companies raise their rates, place caps on reimbursements, impose sizable deductibles, and exclude certain kinds of losses. One irony of the for-profit insurance business is that those who face the greatest risks and therefore need coverage the most are sometimes either denied policies outright or charged exorbitant premiums that they can't afford.

The insufficiency and unfairness of private insurance underwriting practices first received public attention during the late 1960s. The National Advisory Panel on Insurance in Riot-Affected Areas (part of the National Advisory Commission on Civil Disorders) in 1967 examined the plights of inner-city residents and businesses that had suffered losses due to looting and arson during ghetto rebellions. The panel cited a general lack of insurance availability as a factor contributing to urban decay: the closing of businesses, the loss of jobs, the abandonment of buildings, and the exodus of residents from high-crime areas.

In 1968, Congress followed some of the panel's recommendations and granted relief to those who suffered from insurance **redlining** (an illegal, discriminatory practice that results in denial of coverage). The Department of Housing and Urban Development Act set up Fair Access to Insurance Requirements plans to make sure that property owners were not denied fire damage coverage solely because the neighborhood had a high rate of arson cases. In 1970, Congress amended the 1968 act to permit the federal government to offer affordable burglary and robbery insurance directly to urban homeowners, tenants, and businesses in areas where such coverage from private companies was either unavailable or unreasonably expensive. Federal intervention into the insurance market to assist actual and potential crime victims was viewed as a last resort (Bernstein, 1972). The Federal Emergency Management Agency currently runs the Federal Insurance Administration.

Once the government began to sell insurance coverage, it became reasonable to ask whether public funds could be set up to bail out families that faced economic ruin because they were not willing or able to pay for private insurance policies, or were inadequately protected, especially against huge medical bills and lost earnings. Public insurance plans are called crime victim compensation programs.

RECOVERING LOSSES THROUGH VICTIM COMPENSATION PROGRAMS

Most street crime victims never receive criminal court-ordered restitution for one obvious reason: The offenders are not caught and convicted. For a parallel reason, most victims never collect court-ordered civil judgments: The perpetrators cannot be identified or located and then successfully sued. Furthermore, rarely can a third party be held partly responsible for the incident and sued for gross negligence. Given the inadequacy of most private insurance coverage when major disasters strike, the only remaining hope for monetary recovery lies with a different sort of third party: a state compensation fund. Reimbursement from a government fund appears to be the only realistic method for routinely restoring individuals to the financial condition they were in before the crime occurred. The shortcomings of restitution were dramatized by this classic case:

> A middle-aged man is blinded by assailants, who are later caught, convicted, and imprisoned. Upon their release, they are ordered by the court to pay restitution to the injured man for the loss of his eyesight. Under the arrangement, it will take 442 years for the man to collect the full amount due him. (Fry, 1957)

The following situation, which unfolded in the mid-1960s when mothers generally did not work unless their family relied on their earnings, underscored the need for government programs to furnish assistance to innocent people who suffered devastating losses. Editorials about this tragedy generated public support that led elected officials to set up a state-funded compensation program:

> An onlooker comes to the aid of two elderly women who are being harassed by a drunken youth on a subway train. As his wife and child watch in horror, the Good Samaritan is stabbed to death by the drunk. The killer is captured and sentenced to 20 years to life in prison. The widow is forced to send her child to live with her mother while she goes to work in order to pay her bills. (Editors, New York Times, 1965)

The next case, which describes a settlement from a state-run fund, illustrates the kinds of aid that these government boards now provide:

> *A gunman barges into a building and goes on a shooting rampage. Eleven immigrants taking a course to learn English, their teacher, and a case-worker are shot to death before the killer takes his own life. The crime victims fund sets up a toll-free number, provides on-site assistance, distributes emergency awards of up to $2,500 to the families of the deceased, and pays for medical and funeral expenses as well as compensation for lost wages and counseling services.* (Stanford, 2011)

Compensation is the easiest, simplest, and most direct way of speeding a victim's recovery and of institutionalizing the notion of helping someone in desperate need of emergency financial support.

The History of Victim Compensation by Governments

The earliest reference to governmental compensation for crime victims can be found in the ancient Babylonian Code of Hammurabi, which is considered to be the oldest written body of criminal law (about 1775 BC). The code instructed territorial governors to replace the lost property of someone who was robbed if the criminal was not captured. In the aftermath of a murder, the governor was to pay the heirs a specific sum in silver from the treasury. In the centuries that followed, restitution by the offender replaced compensation by the state. But during the Middle Ages, restitution also faded away. Victims had no avenue of redress except to try to recover losses by suing offenders in civil court.

Interest in compensation revived during the 1800s, when the prison reform movement in Europe focused attention on the suffering of convicts and in doing so indirectly called attention to the plight of their victims. Leading theorists in criminology endorsed compensation and restitution at several International Penal Congress meetings held at the turn of the century. But these resolutions did not lead to any concrete actions. Legal historians

have uncovered only a few scattered instances of special funds set aside for crime victims: one in Tuscany after 1786, another in Mexico starting in 1871, and one beginning in France in 1934. Switzerland and Cuba also experimented with victim compensation (Silving, 1959; Schafer, 1970; and MacNamara and Sullivan, 1974).

An English prison reformer sparked the revival of interest in compensation in the late 1950s. Because of her efforts, a government commission investigated various reparations proposals and set up a fund in 1964 in Great Britain. Several Australian states and Canadian provinces followed suit during the next few years. New Zealand offered the most complete protection in the Western world in 1972, when it abolished the victim compensation program it had pioneered in 1963 and absorbed it within a universal accident insurance system. Everyone in New Zealand was covered for losses arising from any type of misfortune, including criminal acts. The nature of the event, the reason it occurred, and the person responsible for it did not affect compensation decisions (European Committee on Crime Problems, 1978; and Meiners, 1978).

The Debate over Compensation in the United States

In the late 1950s, the question of compensation surfaced in American law journals. Initially, distinguished scholars raised many objections to the idea of having the government provide financial assistance to innocent individuals wounded or slain by criminals. But support for the notion of compensation grew when a Supreme Court justice argued that society should assume some responsibility for making whole again those whom the law had failed to protect. Soon, well-known political figures of the period came to accept the proposition that special funds should be set up to repay victims. Their enthusiasm was in accord with the liberal political philosophy embodied in President John F. Kennedy's New Frontier and President Lyndon Johnson's Great Society: Government should develop programs to try to ameliorate persistent social problems.

The proposals of elected officials, the suggestions of legal scholars and criminologists, and the pressures of coalitions of interest groups were necessary but not sufficient to trigger legislatures to take action. Widely publicized brutal and tragic incidents supplied the missing ingredient of public support in the first few states to experiment with compensation schemes. In 1965, California initiated a repayment process as part of its public assistance system. In 1966, New York created a special board to allocate reimbursements. In 1967, Massachusetts designated certain courts and the state attorney general's office as granters of financial aid to victims.

Starting in 1965, Congress began to debate the question of encouraging and aiding state compensation programs. No lobby emerged to pressure elected officials to vote against compensation plans. Even private insurance companies did not feel threatened by the potential loss of business. At the hearings, the idea of compensation was endorsed by the American Bar Association, International Association of Chiefs of Police, National District Attorneys' Association, U.S. Conference of Mayors, National League of Cities, National Conference of State Legislatures, existing state compensation boards, judges' organizations, senior citizens' groups, and the National Council on Crime and Delinquency ("Crime Control Amendments," 1973; Edelhertz and Geis, 1974; "Crime Victims' Aid," 1978; and Meiners, 1978). The arguments over the pros and cons of governmental compensation raised many important political, philosophical, and pragmatic issues (see Childres, 1964; Schultz, 1965; Wolfgang, 1965; Brooks, 1972; Geis, 1976; Meiners, 1978; Carrow, 1980; U.S. House Committee on the Judiciary, 1980; Gaynes, 1981; and Elias, 1983a).

The most compelling rationales advanced by advocates presented compensation as additional social insurance, or as a way of meeting an overlooked governmental obligation to all citizens, or as a means of assisting individuals facing financial ruin. Proponents of the **shared-risk rationale** viewed compensation as part of the "safety net" of the comprehensive social insurance system that had been developing in the United States since the Great Depression. All public welfare insurance programs are intended to enable people to cope with the hazards that threaten stability and security in everyday life. Health expenses are addressed by Medicaid and Medicare, disability and untimely death by Social Security, on-the-job accidents by workers' compensation, and loss of work and earnings by unemployment compensation. The premiums for these state-run compulsory insurance plans are derived from taxation. Criminal injury insurance, like the other types of coverage, provides equal protection against dangers that are reasonably certain to harm some members of society but are unpredictable for any given individual. All taxpayers contribute to the pool to spread the costs, and therefore everyone is entitled to reimbursement.

The **government-liability rationale** argues that the state is responsible for the safety of its citizens because it monopolizes, or reserves for itself, the right to use force to suppress crime and to punish offenders. Because individuals are not allowed to routinely carry deadly weapons around for their own defense wherever they go, the government has made it difficult for law-abiding people to protect themselves. Therefore, within the social contract, the state becomes liable for damages when its criminal justice system fails to fulfill its public safety obligation to its citizens. By the logic of this argument, innocents who have been harmed ought to have a right to compensation, regardless of their economic standing and the type of loss they have suffered.

Those who take a **social-welfare approach** believe that the state has a humanitarian responsibility to assist victims, just as it helps other needy and disadvantaged groups. The aid is given as a symbolic act of mercy, compassion, and charity—and not as universal insurance coverage or because of any legal obligation. According to this theory, receiving compensation is a privilege, not a right, so eligibility and payment amounts can be limited.

Besides these three rationales, several additional arguments were advanced to encourage public acceptance of compensation. Some sociologists and criminologists put forward a **social-justice rationale**. It contended that the "system" (the institutions, economic and political arrangements, and prevailing relationships within society) generates crime by perpetuating intense competition, discrimination, unemployment, financial insecurity, and poverty, which in turn breed greed, desperation, theft, and violence. Therefore, society owes compensation through its governmental agencies to people who are harmed through no fault of their own.

Other advocates contrasted the attention accorded to criminals with the neglect shown toward their innocent victims. They charged that it was blatantly unfair to attend to many of the medical, dental, emotional, educational, vocational, and legal needs of wrongdoers (albeit minimally and sometimes against their will) at public expense while at the same time abandoning injured victims to fend for themselves. Compensation partly corrected this "imbalance." Finally, some pragmatists anticipated that the prospect of monetary rewards would induce more individuals to cooperate with the authorities by reporting incidents, pressing charges, and testifying against their assailants.

Skeptics and critics objected to the notion of government intervention on both philosophical and practical grounds. The earliest opponents of importing this British Commonwealth practice to the United States denounced what they considered to be the spread of "governmental paternalism" and "creeping socialism." They contended that taxpayer-funded crime insurance undermined the virtues of rugged individualism, self-reliance, personal responsibility, independence, saving for emergencies, and calculated risk taking. They considered an expansion of the "welfare state" and the growth of new, expensive, and remote bureaucracies to be greater evils than the fiscal neglect of victims. They contended that, unlike governmental bodies, private enterprises could write more effective and efficient insurance policies for families that had enough prudence and foresight to purchase protection before tragedy struck. Other opponents worried that criminal-injury insurance—like fire, auto, and theft coverage—was vulnerable to fraud. Deserving applicants would be hard to distinguish from manipulators who staged incidents, inflicted their own wounds, and padded their bills.

Finally, certain critics did not dispute the merits of compensation programs but objected to their establishment and expansion on financial grounds. They argued that it was unfair to compel taxpayers to repay victims' losses, as well as to foot the bill for the costs of the police, courts, and keeping convicts in prisons. To accommodate this objection, state programs have come to rely more heavily on raising money from penalties imposed on lawbreakers of all kinds, including traffic law violators, rather than taxpayers (see Childres, 1964; Schultz, 1965; Wolfgang, 1965; Brooks, 1972; Geis, 1976; Meiners, 1978; Carrow, 1980; U.S. House Committee on the Judiciary, 1980; Gaynes, 1981; and Elias, 1983a).

A statistical analysis of congressional votes on bills between 1965 and 1980 revealed that Democrats (particularly liberal Democrats) tended to favor allocating federal aid to reimburse crime victims; Republicans (especially conservative Republicans) tended to oppose spending federal tax dollars on state compensation programs. The usual exceptions to these patterns were conservative Democrats (generally from southern states) who sided with conservative Republicans against compensation plans and some liberal Republicans (often from northern states) who joined with liberal Democrats in support of these pro-victim legislative initiatives. In other words, ideology proved to be a better predictor of voting behavior than party affiliation (Karmen, 1981b).

In 1984, Congress finally reached a consensus about the appropriate role for the federal government on the question of compensation and passed a Victims of Crime Act (VOCA), ending nearly 20 years of floor debates, lobbying, political posturing, maneuvering, and last-minute compromises. VOCA established a fund within the U.S. Treasury, collected from fines, penalties, and forfeitures. Administered by the attorney general, the money was earmarked to subsidize state compensation funds and victim assistance services, and to aid victims of federal crimes (Peak, 1986). In 1989, VOCA guidelines were revised to encourage state programs to expand coverage and to resemble each other more closely. Providing federal matching funds worked out as intended: Every state had set up a compensation program by 1993 (Maine and South Dakota were the last to participate).

How Programs Operate: Similarities and Differences

In all states plus the District of Columbia, Puerto Rico, Guam, and the U.S. Virgin Islands, the question of whether to compensate victims has been answered for the time being. But the programs vary in many ways, reflecting the diversity in the traditions, populations, crime rates, and resources of the states and the differing rationales on which the programs were based.

Certain requirements are the same in each state (see Parent, Auerbach, and Carlson, 1992). All of the programs grant reimbursements only to "innocent" victims. Compensation board investigators always look for evidence of contributory misconduct. If it is established that the individual was partly to blame for getting hurt, the grant can be reduced in size or disallowed entirely. For example, applicants would not be repaid if they were engaging in an illegal activity when they were wounded (such as being shot while holding up a liquor store, being stabbed while buying drugs, or being beaten after agreeing to perform an act of prostitution). Most boards would rule injured parties in barroom brawls ineligible if they had been drinking, uttered "fighting words," and provoked the fracas in which they were seriously hurt. However, applicants could appeal claims that were denied.

Another common feature is that the programs deal only with the most serious crimes that result in physical injury, psychological trauma, or death: murder, rape, assault, robbery, child sexual abuse, child physical abuse, spouse abuse, other types of domestic violence, and also hit-and-run motor vehicle collisions caused by drunk drivers. Most do not repay people for property that is damaged or lost in thefts, burglaries, or robberies (unless they are elderly or their possessions are essential, such as hearing aids or wheelchairs). Only out-of-pocket expenses are reimbursed: bills not paid by collateral sources such as Medicaid or private insurance such as Blue Cross. Payments can be for medical expenses, mental health services, dental bills, and earnings lost because of missed work. Families of individuals who succumb to their wounds are eligible for assistance with reasonable funeral and burial costs; dependents can qualify for a death benefit or pension to compensate for their loss of financial support. Some states go further and pay for the services of home health aides and housekeepers, child care, transportation costs for medical treatments and court appearances, and even for relocation when necessary (New Jersey Victims of Crime Compensation Agency, 2008). Each program requires that all parts of a claim be fully documented with bills and receipts. Every program prohibits double recoveries. Money collected from insurance policies or other government sources (such as Veteran's Benefits) is **subrogated** (subtracted) from the compensation board's final award. In the statistically unusual cases in which offenders are caught, found guilty, and forced to pay restitution, this money is also deducted from the award. For a claimant to be repaid, the assailant does not have to be caught and convicted. But in every state, the applicant must report the crime promptly to the police and cooperate fully with any investigation and prosecution to remain eligible.

Despite sharing these basic features, the 50 state programs differ in many ways: How long victims can wait before telling the police about the crime (from one day to three months, with a mode of three days); how long victims can take before applying for reimbursement (from six months to three years, with a mode of one year); how much claimants can collect (maximum awards of $1,000 to $50,000 plus limitless medical expenses, with modes at $10,000 and $25,000); whether the program will grant an emergency loan before fully investigating a case; and whether lawyers can be hired to help present cases and collect fees. Eligibility rules differ slightly from state to state. For example, survivors of those who are slain can include parents, siblings, and in-laws in some programs, but most states limit coverage only to children and spouses (NACVCB, 2011).

In 1988, amendments to the Victims of Crimes Act mandated that eligibility in all states be extended to innocent family members injured by domestic violence, people hurt by drunk driving crashes, and nonresidents (visitors and commuters). Some states have gone further in expanding the list of covered individuals and offenses. For example, besides victims of violence such as kidnappings and carjackings, New Jersey compensates individuals injured in hit-and-run collisions, people sickened by drug and food tampering, bystanders hurt by criminals trying to elude the police, and people brought in to the state by human traffickers (New Jersey Victims of Crime Compensation Agency, 2008). New York's Victim Compensation Board will consider claims from individuals who were not physically injured if they were Good Samaritans or suffered from stalking, harassment, menacing, unlawful imprisonment, or even frivolous counterlawsuits by offenders. The board covers the expenses of those subjected to sexual assaults for forensic examinations at hospitals (to collect evidence for "rape kits") and for people who incur losses from attempted strangulations, whether or not physical injuries result (Stanford, 2011).

On the other hand, entire groups of people may be ruled ineligible. In each state, the list varies. Law enforcement officers and firefighters injured in the line of duty generally are excluded because they are covered by workers' compensation. In some jurisdictions, prison inmates, parolees, probationers, exconvicts, and members of organized crime are automatically eliminated from consideration (National Institute of Justice, 1998). In eight states, all persons with a felony conviction are ineligible for aid, even if their current predicament has nothing to do with their past illegal activities (Mitchell, 2008).

Many trends in compensation regulations are worth noting. One change over time has been to broaden coverage to include the cost of cleaning up a crime scene and replacing essential personal property such as eyeglasses and false teeth. In just a handful of states, money is available to offset pain and suffering. Some programs extend eligibility to include individuals who suffered incest as children, people who were sexually assaulted but escaped

without physical injuries, the elderly whose homes were burglarized, and parents of missing children.

Initially, the money given out by compensation programs came from general revenues, which essentially means from taxpayers. Since the 1970s, the trend has been to rely more heavily on funds derived from **penalty assessments** or abusers' taxes (more than half of the programs get all or part of their money this way). These funds are raised from fines and surcharges levied on persons convicted of traffic violations, misdemeanors, and felonies. Some states impose taxes on the earnings of offenders on work release and from collateral forfeited by defendants who jump bail. Offender-funded compensation programs reflect a larger trend that compels convicts in some jurisdictions to shoulder all kinds of financial obligations, including restitution, charges for room and board, fines, court costs, and supervision fees. By the start of the twenty-first century, 90 percent of state and federal funding came from money extracted from offenders. Taxpayer dollars supplemented these limited and unpredictable revenues in only 13 states. Although making wrongdoers pay their collective debts has symbolic value as a form of group restitution, albeit indirect and impersonal, this is an insufficient source of money to meet all the critical needs of the eligible and worthy claimants seeking financial aid (Herman and Waul, 2004). For example, in Idaho, every person convicted of a misdemeanor has to pay a fine of $37, and of a felony, $74. Convicted sex offenders must send in $300 to the state compensation fund (Nelson, 2014).

Before the 1980s, in about one-third of the states, only claimants who faced severe financial hardships could pass a **means test** to become eligible for reimbursement. The others were told they could afford to absorb their losses. By the end of the 1980s, only 11 programs still required their applicants to establish a dire fiscal need before receiving an award. Encouraged by VOCA's financial support, some states have raised the upper limits for awards because of substantial hikes in the cost of living over the years. Minimum loss requirements and deductible provisions (usually of $100) designed to eliminate minor claims have been scrapped and persist in less than half the states (NOVA, 1988; Parent et al., 1992; NIJ, 1998; and NACVCB, 2011). However, many states have frozen maximum benefits (still usually capped at $25,000, even after years of rising prices), so compensation payments fail to keep up with the rate of inflation year after year. For example, in Georgia, the maximum amount any one victim can receive is $25,000. Breaking that down, medical expenses can't exceed $15,000, economic aid is capped at $10,000, and $3,000 is the limit for counseling costs (West, 2014).

Monitoring and Evaluating Compensation Programs

Many arguments about the rightness of compensation hinge on judgments about the type of financial help victims require and on assumptions about the ability of programs to meet these needs. Because many states have operated programs for several decades, a substantial body of data is available for analysis. The differences between state programs can be considered an asset: Each jurisdiction can be regarded as a social laboratory where an experiment is in progress. From this viewpoint, various approaches to achieving the same ends are tested to determine which works best. Evaluation is especially important as a means of improving service delivery during periods when the public clamors for additional government aid but is unwilling to pay higher taxes for it.

Program evaluations reveal how well compensation boards are meeting their goals. But assessing whether they are succeeding or failing in their mission requires a clear statement of goals. In the 1960s, the early advocates of reimbursing victims from government-administered funds had ambitious expectations and made optimistic (and perhaps unrealistic) pronouncements. Their noble, charitable, and humanitarian aims of substantially alleviating the economic suffering of injured parties generally have not been realized. Statistics that either support or refute other contentions can be derived from two assessments: process evaluations and impact evaluations.

Process Evaluations: Uncovering How Programs Work   Process evaluations focus on the programs' internal operations and monitor variables such as productivity, overhead costs, and decision-making patterns. Assessments of the efficiency of administrative practices contribute to efforts to eliminate delays, minimize overhead, and iron out inequities. Process evaluations also develop profiles of the typical claimants and recipients of awards. Analyzing data bearing on these questions allows evaluators to provide useful feedback to administrators and board members about trends and patterns that characterize their efforts.

Two process evaluations of a sample of the 50 state funds in operation at the end of the 1980s (Parent et al., 1992) and the start of the 1990s (Sarnoff, 1996) shed light on aspects of how compensation programs actually work. The programs in the survey's sample granted aid to about two-thirds of the applicants. Most of the funds' revenue was raised from fines and penalty assessments levied on all kinds of law violators (including drivers who committed traffic infractions), with the rest derived from general appropriations (taxes) and from the federal government in grants from VOCA. Most claims concerned drunk driving crashes, homicides, rapes, robberies, aggravated assaults, and child abuse cases. Very few claims arose from spouse abuse. The volume of cases handled per year varied dramatically by population size and crime rate. Case processing time (how long it took to resolve a claim) ranged from one month to two years, with a mean of 18 weeks. To aid victims during the interim, most states granted small emergency awards. Some programs were run more efficiently than others, in terms of administrative costs as a percentage of total expenditures.

As for decision-making patterns, denial rates indicated that some boards were much stricter than others. Denials can be issued for technical reasons, such as failure to supply sufficient documentation of expenses; and for fault, such as the stigmatizing moral judgment that the claimant was guilty of contributory misconduct. Some boards seemed more generous, while others were determined to refute the charges that they "gave money away" and were vulnerable to fraud and abuse.

The average award ranged from a low of nearly $700 to a high of roughly $9,000 (in a state where attorney's fees were covered). The rate of compensation, calculated as a proportion (crimes that were compensated compared to reported crimes committed in that state that year that potentially could have been eligible for compensation), also showed tremendous variation. It ranged from a low of 1 percent to a high of 91 percent and averaged 19 percent. The number of "unserved" victims a year in the late 1980s was estimated to be 55 percent of all potentially eligible persons (innocent, injured, suffering out-of-pocket expenses). In other words, despite outreach efforts (such as public service announcements and posters in police stations and hospital emergency rooms), more than half of all possible beneficiaries did not know their rights and/or did not even file a claim. Some state program administrators estimated that 67 percent, maybe even 95 percent, of eligible victims did not apply for financial aid. Of course, if more eligible people had been aware of their rights and sought reimbursement, their claims would have taken even longer to process. Also, the boards either would have had to cut back on the average size of awards or turn down a greater proportion of applicants, unless the directors could somehow raise more money (Parent et al., 1992; and Sarnoff, 1996). Setting up storefront offices to accept claims from people living in high-crime areas helps achieve the objective of reaching the maximum number of deserving individuals in the most effective and efficient manner possible (McCormack, 1991). Reading victims their rights is the most effective form of outreach. In North Carolina, police departments are required within 72 hours to tell victims about the resources available to them, including financial assistance through its state compensation program (Hinchcliffe, 2014).

The findings from process evaluations about insufficient funding and inadequate outreach confirm that compensation plans are failing to live up to their humanitarian commitments. Because of their limited budgets, many boards maintain low

profiles or even face prohibitions against advertising. Lack of interest on the part of police, prosecutors, and hospital emergency room personnel might also be a continuing problem. Some injured parties might be deterred by complex filing procedures and detailed probes into their personal finances (to prevent fraud). Others are discouraged when they hear about high rejection rates, long waits, and disappointingly small awards. On one hand, even with low rates of applications and awards, underfunded programs can run out of money before the year is over (McGillis and Smith, 1983; and Sanderson, 1994). On the other hand, inadequate outreach efforts can result in surpluses if injured parties don't realize that they can be reimbursed for expenses such as crime scene cleanups, counseling, and rehabilitation services ("New Jersey," 2002).

In 1995, state compensation programs across the country paid nearly $250 million to about 120,000 people harmed by violent crimes. Victims of assault (47 percent) and child abuse (especially sexual abuse) (12 percent) were the most numerous recipients. Almost half of the money went to cover medical expenses, and most of the rest was reimbursement for lost wages, mental health treatment, and funeral expenses. The national average for an award was close to $2,000. By 2010, even though crime rates were substantially lower, the number of recipients had risen to more than 200,000, and the total payout had climbed to close to $500 million. Most of this money from the 50 state programs came from offenders rather than taxpayers. Federal funding provided about 35 percent of the benefits the states disbursed, but fines and assessments imposed on those convicted in federal courts were the sole sources of this aid from Washington. Reimbursements often were for medical expenses, and millions were spent on covering the costs of forensic examinations for persons who had been sexually assaulted. Abused children received nearly 30 percent of the financial aid, families of murdered persons received about 10 percent, and those who were sexually assaulted received about 8 percent. Individuals who were physically assaulted (especially from acts of domestic violence) continued to be the largest group getting monetary help (adding up to about half of all successful claimants) (NACVCB, 2011). Of course, not all claimants deserve compensation, or meet the eligibility requirements, or can document their losses. In Delaware, the approval rate was a little over 75 percent in 2013 (Anderson, 2014). Eligibility rules can be rather strict. For example, in North Carolina, a claim can be turned down if the injured party was convicted of a serious felony in the three years prior to the victimization (Hinchcliffe, 2014).

Impact Evaluations: Measuring the Effects of Programs   Impact evaluations are carried out to compare a program's intentions with its actual accomplishments. The studies reveal the consequences of a program for its clients and the community. To determine whether compensation really eases financial stress, the ratio of award payments to submitted losses can be calculated. To assess a program's impact on the participation of compensated complainants in the criminal justice system, those who did and did not receive aid can be compared, in terms of their attendance rates as witnesses in police lineups and court proceedings. The diversity of structures and procedures in different state programs provides opportunities to test which arrangements work best under what conditions.

The findings of research and evaluation studies can have important consequences for the future of compensation. Determining successes and failures can help resolve the ongoing debates over the pros and cons of compensating crime victims with public funds and the merits and shortcomings of particular rules and practices (Chappell and Sutton, 1974; Carrow, 1980; and NIJ, 1998).

The findings of several impact evaluations do not support the hypothesis that the prospect of reimbursement would increase the public's degree of cooperation with law enforcement. In the 1970s, when reporting rates for violent crimes in states with programs were compared with the rates in states without programs, no appreciable differences were found (Doerner, 1978). Comparing the attitudes of claimants in Florida who were granted awards to those whose requests were denied

revealed that being repaid did not significantly improve a victim's ratings of the quality of performance of the police, prosecutors, or judges (Doerner and Lab, 1980).

More information is needed about the impact of board decisions on the psychological and economic well-being of physically injured applicants. Those who were rejected because of what they perceived to be mere technicalities (such as waiting too long before filing) might feel cheated. Insensitive treatment, lengthy background investigations, extensive delays, and partial reimbursements can make even successful claimants feel victimized once again (McGillis and Smith, 1983).

One researcher who evaluated the New York and New Jersey programs concluded that claimants ended up more alienated from the criminal justice system than nonclaimants. Instead of reducing public discontent with the police and courts, compensation programs provoked additional frustrations. Applicants' expectations probably rose when they first learned about the chance of reimbursement, but these hopes were consistently frustrated when most claimants, for a variety of reasons, were turned down or awarded insufficient funds to cover their documented expenses. Three-quarters indicated that they would not apply for compensation again if they were victimized a second time, largely because of their displeasure over delays, eligibility requirements, incidental expenses, inconveniences, their treatment by program administrators, and, ultimately, the inadequacy of their reimbursements (Elias, 1983a).

The enactment of compensation programs might have been merely an exercise in "symbolic politics." This judgment accuses certain manipulative politicians of voting for programs that look impressive on paper because they want to appear to be doing something for victims, but these elected officials fail to allocate the necessary resources to make the promise a reality. Nevertheless, the public is favorably impressed by the foresight and concern shown by policymakers and legislators toward victims. Unaware that the majority of claimants are turned down and that the remainder are largely dissatisfied, voters are led to believe that an effective safety net has been set up to cushion the blows of violent crime (Elias, 1983b, 1986).

In sum, four longstanding problems undermine the effectiveness of these programs. First, outreach is inadequate: Too many injured parties are unaware that they are eligible for reimbursement. Only 4 percent of violent crime victims nationwide applied for compensation from state programs in 2002. Second, eligibility is too restrictive: Too many claimants are turned down because of overly strict requirements. Third, the awards that successful applicants receive too often are not enough to bail them out of their financial predicaments. And fourth, money derived from penalizing and fining lawbreakers never is sufficient to meet critical needs (Herman and Waul, 2004).

And yet, the swift action by Congress to establish the September 11th Victim Compensation Fund demonstrates that governmental organizations are capable of taking creative, resourceful, sustained, compassionate, and generous steps to help people rebuild their lives. Could those same unprecedented efforts that aided the more than 4,400 individuals directly injured by the terrorist attacks and the nearly 3,000 survivor families be mobilized on a routine basis to assist the 23 million people harmed annually by "ordinary" crimes, advocates ask?

Inspired by the September 11th fund, victim advocates called for many reforms. All innocent parties should be eligible for compensation, not only people injured by violence. All crime-related losses should be reimbursed, and time limits shouldn't be imposed on ongoing problems (such as PTSD). Everyone who files a complaint with the police should be informed about and helped to fill out a claim. The process of granting aid should be fair, respectful, efficient, and easy to understand. Income tax relief should be granted to offset victims' losses (currently most do not lose enough money to qualify for tax deductions). Tax revenue should supplement the inadequate funding raised from offender penalties. Legislatures should determine the best practices already implemented in the various states, as well as in compensation programs in other countries, advocates suggest (Herman and Waul, 2004).

CONFISCATING PROFITS FROM NOTORIOUS CRIMINALS

Six people are shot dead in ambushes and many others are wounded by a lone gunman who describes himself in letters to a journalist and notes left at crime scenes as a monster who is being driven by demons communicating through dogs to kill young women . Dubbed the "Son of Sam" as well as the ".44-Caliber Killer" by the media, he is eventually caught, convicted, and sentenced to a lifetime behind bars. From his cell, he grants interviews to writers and accumulates about $90,000 in royalties from publishers. The individuals he wounded and the families of the people he murdered sue him to prevent him from cashing in on his notoriety. Eight years later, his attorneys arrive at a settlement: all the money he gained will be divided among those he harmed, and they will share any additional earnings this serial killer might receive. (Associated Press, 1984)

■ ■ ■

Four employees are taken hostage by a man who bungles his attempt to rob a bank. The police block his escape route and a lengthy siege ensues. Eventually, the four captives are released, and he is captured, convicted, and imprisoned. Hollywood producers pay him $100,000 for the rights to depict his exploits in the movie Dog Day Afternoon. *The money is seized by the New York State Crime Victims Board and doled out to his kidnap victims, his lawyers (to whom he owed fees), and his former wife (for alimony and child support payments). (Roberts, 1987)*

One additional option for recovering losses remains open to just a handful of victims or their next of kin: going after the profits made by offenders who sell their firsthand accounts of how and why they committed their high-profile crimes. Cases such as the two well-known lawsuits cited above dramatize how victims can fight back when convicts seize opportunities to make a fortune from the sensationalism surrounding their well-publicized exploits. The practical issue that arises is when and how victims can take these "fruits of crime" away from the perpetrators of violence and mayhem.

Writing and Rewriting the Law So That Crime Doesn't Pay

In 1977, the New York State legislature passed a forfeiture of assets bill to prevent a vicious serial killer (cited in the first example above) from being showered with lucrative offers for book contracts, movie rights, and paid appearances to tell his inside story. The law stipulated that whenever an offender signed a contract to receive profits from recounting his illegal acts, the company receiving the profits had to turn them over to the government for disbursement to the immediate victims or to merge the proceeds into the state's compensation fund. The principle behind the law was that it was contrary to the public's interest to enable violent offenders to make money from retelling their exploits at the same time that the parties they injured struggled financially and suffered renewed emotional pain from the additional wave of publicity. In the next few years, 42 states and the federal government followed New York's lead and enacted similar "Son of Sam" laws (NCVC, 2011b). Public opinion backed this legislative trend. In one poll, 86 percent of the respondents favored a law that would take away profits gained by notorious criminals and distribute this money to their victims (National Victim Center, 1991a).

These statutes went after financial windfalls: fees, advances, and royalties from reenactments of the heinous deeds in movies, memoirs, books, magazine articles, tape recordings, records, radio programs, television shows, or other forms of entertainment. If offenders (whether accused or convicted) were paid for expressing their thoughts, opinions, or feelings about their depredations, or for giving graphic descriptions about these vicious acts, their income could be seized by the government and placed in an escrow account before they could spend it.

The law operates somewhat differently in each state. In most states, the injured parties must first successfully sue the offender for damages in civil court and obtain a judgment in order to be eligible to claim a portion of the profits. In other states, victim compensation programs handle the claims and dole out the accrued profits. It usually doesn't matter if the perpetrator is convicted at a trial or admits guilt after plea negotiations. Those who are not convicted on the grounds of insanity and even defendants under indictment also can be compelled to turn over their profits in some states. For up to five years until a statute of limitations runs out, individuals who had incurred direct physical or mental injuries or financial losses could argue in civil court that they were entitled to a portion of the money held by the state in an escrow account. In some states, leftover funds not awarded in damage lawsuits could revert back to the offenders. But in other jurisdictions, any remaining money could be used to cover unpaid attorneys' fees plus the court costs arising from the prosecution or to replenish the state's victim compensation fund (Stark and Goldstein, 1985; NOVA, 1988; and NCVC, 2011b). However, whenever a notorious offender was found guilty of a political crime, or a white-collar swindle, or a vice offense such as running a lucrative prostitution ring or trafficking in drugs, the legal issue of exactly which individuals were entitled to carve up these ill-gotten gains became very complicated.

Notoriety-for-profit laws were primarily symbolic gestures intended to drive home the message that "crime doesn't pay." They also were designed to facilitate handing over money to injured parties—but from the outset, these laws were controversial. Critics argued that the confiscation of payments by government had a chilling effect on the First Amendment's guarantee of freedom of expression. In 1991, the justices of the Supreme Court agreed and by a vote of 9 to 0 struck down New York's law and all the others like it in various states. In its unanimous opinion (*Simon and Schuster v. New York State Crime Victims Board*), the Court recognized that states had an undisputed compelling interest to deprive felons from profiting from recounting their illegal activities and were pursuing a worthwhile goal in trying to transfer the proceeds from criminals to their victims. In this case, a leading publisher was about to release a book that was going to be made into a movie in which a Mafia wiseguy narrates how he pulled off daring robberies and grisly murders until the law finally caught up with him. However, the justices argued that enacting these overly broad state laws unfairly singled out a convict's "speech derived income" for a special tax burden and thereby established an inhibiting financial disincentive to create or publish works with a particular content. Publishers, filmmakers, and civil libertarians hailed the Court's landmark ruling as a victory that preserved the constitutional right to free expression and protected authors and their audiences. They noted that a substantial body of worthwhile literature and redeeming commentary by notable prisoners might never have been written if those laws were in force years ago.

But others denounced the Court's decision as a blow to victims' rights. They undertook the task of redrafting provisions about lawsuits, statutes of limitation, fines, forfeitures, and escrow accounts so that they would meet constitutional standards. Soon, state legislatures passed revised "Son of Sam" laws that do not single out royalties from books or movies but target any and all assets these convicts accrue (Fein, 1991; and Alexander, 1992). Several states have gone even further and prohibit law enforcement officials (such as detectives, prosecutors, defense attorneys, judges, and witnesses) from making money by telling about their roles in high-profile cases from the time of indictment until the completion of appeals (NCVC, 2011). However, several state court decisions have struck down "Son of Sam" laws on First Amendment grounds, signaling that these statutes must be narrowly crafted to survive constitutional challenges. But even if notoriety for profit laws don't serve their intended purpose to make sure that "crime doesn't pay," victims still can seek restitution from offenders' assets through traditional tort suits and general civil forfeiture actions (Hudson, 2012).

Injured parties and close relatives of murder victims still face an uphill battle to collect what they believe is due them, as the following widely discussed account illustrates:

A prisoner writes a book about the nightmare of growing up behind bars in juvenile institutions and state prisons. The inmate's insightful life story sells so well that it becomes the basis for a play, and well-known writers help him get parole. But just six weeks after he is released, he becomes embroiled in an argument with a waiter over the use of the restaurant's restroom, and stabs him to death. After he is sentenced to prison for manslaughter, the waiter's young widow sues him in civil court. The inmate, representing himself, asserts that the waiter's life "was not worth a dime," but the jury awards her more than $ 7.5 million. Over the next decade or so, the inmate earns about $115,000 in royalties from his several books and plays, yet the widow collects less than $50,000. In the meantime, he launches two counter lawsuits against her. Exercising her right to appear before the parole board, she argues against his early release. When he is turned down, the infamous convict–author hangs himself in his cell. "After what he put us through," the widow asserts, "it's more than a relief, it's fresh air. What goes around comes around." (Halbfinger, 2002)

On rare occasion, victims and their families can receive some proceeds from the sale of "murderabilia"—the artifacts of notorious killers. For example, the United States Marshals Service auctioned off 58 lots of possessions seized from a demented critic of technology (imprisoned for the rest of his life) who sent letter bombs to professors and others during a 17-year terror spree. The online auction, ordered by a federal judge many years after the trial, raised over $230,000 from the sale of items deemed to be of some monetary value by private collectors who paid top dollar to purchase them. The proceeds were divided up by the next of kin of the three people he had killed and the 23 who had been injured by his bombs. But most of the time, the sale of murderabilia merely enriches the speculators who buy and sell artifacts in a ghoulish trade that glorifies the criminal and rekindles the grief of injured parties. Making a profit from the sale of murderabilia is prohibited by law in eight states (Vinciguerra, 2011).

SUMMARY

Victims can try to recover their financial losses in several ways. Restitution payments directly from the offender's earnings seem to be a fair and appropriate method of reimbursement and may provide a solid foundation for redemption and eventual reconciliation. Restitution may be viewed as an additional penalty but also as a way to sensitize and rehabilitate lawbreakers. Unfortunately, many victims never receive any money because their offenders are not caught, convicted, and sentenced to restitution or are unable or unwilling to earn adequate amounts of money to pay meaningful installments.

Victims can attempt to sue their offenders in civil court for compensatory and punitive damages. As plaintiffs, they have a better chance of winning against defendants than in criminal court because the standard of proof—a preponderance of the evidence—is easier to meet than guilt beyond a reasonable doubt. However, only offenders who are identified and who have substantial exposed assets can be sued successfully. If criminals are not caught or have no tangible assets, victims might be able to launch lawsuits against third parties such as businesses or criminal justice agencies that acted with such gross negligence that innocent parties were harmed in predictable ways by dangerous individuals.

Private insurance coverage can repay losses from assaults, car thefts, burglaries, robberies, and slayings. But many victims could not afford the premiums, did not have the foresight to take out a policy, or could not find a company that would sell them coverage at reasonable rates.

Victim compensation funds have been set up in most states since the 1960s, although they initially met considerable political resistance. Injured parties may receive reimbursement even if the perpetrators are not caught and convicted. However, only innocent victims of violent crimes, not people who have suffered losses from property crimes, currently are eligible for financial aid that covers lost earnings and out-of-pocket medical expenses. Many state funds do not have enough money from penalty assessments and the general treasury to quickly and adequately reimburse all eligible applicants.

A small number of individuals might be able to launch lawsuits to claim a portion of the money that certain convicts who viciously harmed them made by cashing in on their notoriety.

KEY TERMS DEFINED IN THE GLOSSARY

QUESTIONS FOR DISCUSSION AND DEBATE

1. Explain how restitution can serve many distinct purposes.
2. Review both the advantages and the disadvantages victims face when they sue offenders in civil court.
3. Why are third-party lawsuits potentially lucrative to victims but also highly controversial?
4. Summarize the arguments that favor the establishment of victim compensation funds by state governments using tax revenue. Then present arguments that taxpayers' money should not be used to provide financial reimbursement to victims.
5. Why is there so much controversy surrounding laws that compel criminals to repay their victims from any profits they gain from their notoriety?

CRITICAL THINKING QUESTIONS

1. Argue that reimbursement is a necessary step to enable recovery. Then grapple with this issue: To what extent can pain and suffering be translated into dollars and cents?
2. Even though many possible sources of reimbursement exist—court-ordered restitution, private insurance coverage, state compensation funds, civil lawsuits, and "notoriety-for-profit" laws—why do so many victims still fail to receive any repayment of their losses and expenses?

SUGGESTED RESEARCH PROJECTS

1. Locate articles in a news database about civil lawsuits on behalf of victims. Find out about their victories and defeats. Were any of the suits against third parties? Summarize the details.
2. Locate and interview a few insurance agents in your area who have handled burglary and vehicle theft claims. What kinds of losses did these policyholders incur. Were these customers fully reimbursed for losses and expenses? If not, why not?
3. Look up information on the Internet about the state compensation fund in your hometown or in the jurisdiction of your college. Examine its annual report. What are the eligibility requirements? What are the caps that limit payments, and what proportion of applicants received awards? What was the average amount of compensation that successful applicants were granted, and for what kinds of expenses were they reimbursed? How long did the process take, on average?

13

Victims in the Twenty-First Century: Alternative Directions

LEARNING OBJECTIVES

To understand the principles and rationales behind laws governing the use of force in self-defense.

To become conversant with the arguments of both sides in the debate over arming for self-protection.

To be able to recognize instances of retaliatory violence and vigilantism.

To become familiar with the principles and rationales of restorative justice.

To be able to compare and contrast restorative justice with retributive justice.

To become familiar with how restorative justice programs operate.

To become aware of the pros and cons of resolving more cases at restorative justice programs.

How will victims fare during the rest of the twenty-first century? The answer to that question depends on how several of today's contradictory tendencies work themselves out. On the one hand, the victims' movement is waging a successful campaign to gain additional formal legal rights within the criminal justice system. Activists and advocacy groups want to empower victims so they can be treated with fundamental fairness and exercise greater influence over how their cases are resolved. The rights victims have gained within the formal criminal justice process, and the remaining shortcomings in the way the system currently handles cases, were discussed in detail in Chapter 7.

On the other hand, some individuals and groups are moving away from the arena of formal legal rights to explore other alternatives. Within this tendency toward informal case handling are two opposite currents. One is to return to an earlier, more forceful method of settling conflicts: drawing a gun, threatening to use it, and firing if necessary. This solution is grounded in two rights: the constitutional right to bear arms, as granted by the Second Amendment, and also the right to resort to force in self-defense, which many see as an inalienable natural right that precedes the intervention of governmental authority.

The distinct alternative to stressing this "fight fire with fire" on-the-spot "solution" to the threat of interpersonal violence is to emphasize the need for an informal forum in which to resolve conflicts between people embroiled in disputes. This idea presupposes relying on the formal criminal justice system but only up to a point. The police must be brought in so that the crime can be verified and solved and the defendant identified. But after that, the wrongdoer and the injured party have to search for ways to settle their differences that are not as adversarial and legalistic. In this new paradigm of restorative justice, victim–offender reconciliation is the goal, restitution arranged through mediation is the method, and a community-based program is the setting. This search for another forum to resolve disputes is spurred on by a belief that it is unrealistic to attempt to compel a criminal justice system controlled by powerful interests and entrenched bureaucracies to become more responsive and accountable to the ostensible "clients" or "consumers" of its services.

The situation of victims in the years ahead will be shaped by the interaction of these three distinct tendencies: relying on the formal justice system, relying on weapons when under attack, and seeking peacemaking opportunities to rectify the fallout from interpersonal violence and theft.

TOWARD COUNTERING CRIMINAL VIOLENCE WITH FORCEFUL RESPONSES

The Legitimate Use of Force in Self-Defense

A sixth-grader is going door to door, selling chocolates for a school fundraiser. A man sitting on his porch agrees to buy some candy and invites the girl inside while he gets some money. But then he whips out a knife and threatens to kill the 11-year-old if she doesn't undress. As he throws her on a couch, she snatches the knife away from him, slashes him on the hand, kicks him in the stomach, and bolts out the front door. Within minutes, the man, who had served time for raping a 10-year-old relative, is placed under arrest for attempted aggravated sexual assault, kidnapping, and assault with a deadly weapon. (Smith, 1994)

■■■

An emergency room nurse returning home from work opens her door and is confronted by an intruder armed with a hammer. They clash, and she strangles him with her bare hands. Detectives determine that she acted with reasonable force to protect herself in her dwelling, as permitted by state law, so the prosecutor does not bring this homicide of a convicted felon with an extensive criminal record before a grand jury. (AP, 2006)

The ultimate right of an individual facing immediate danger is to resist victimization. People under attack are entitled by law to use proportional force to protect themselves. Self-preservation is a basic human right.

Statutes governing fighting back in self-defense are not worded the same in each state because they have been shaped by four distinct rationales. According to a **punitive rationale**, using force against an attacker is permissible because any injuries the aggressor suffers are deserved. Under the **rationale of necessity**, the use of violence is excused when a victim fearing great harm has no choice but to resort to force as a means of self-protection. According to the **individualist rationale**, a citizen does not have to yield or concede any territory to those who would encroach on his or her autonomy. Under the **social rationale** for self-defense, resistance to attack is justified as a way of preserving law and order (Fletcher, 1988).

By definition, the **right to self-defense** is the permissible use of appropriate force to protect one's life or that of an innocent third party from an adversary whom one reasonably believes is threatening harm. If a person who meant no harm is hurt or killed, the individual who thought he was in grave peril has made a terrible mistake and can be held responsible for assault or murder. Five qualifications within the law are intended to restrain victims in order to discourage needless escalations of hostilities that can increase danger or imperil bystanders and to prevent tragic misunderstandings that can cause innocent people to be mistaken for dangerous offenders. First, the threat posed by an aggressor must be imminent. A frightened individual may not use force if the would-be aggressor issues a conditional threat ("If I ever catch you, I'll …") or a future threat ("The next time I catch you I'll …"). Second, if the assailant retreats, removing a victim from imminent danger, force may no longer be used. In some states, the intended target must try to evade a confrontation or attempt to escape before resorting to deadly force. Third, the target's belief that harm is imminent must be reasonable. A reasonable person takes into account the size of the adversary, the time of day, the setting, the presence or absence of a weapon, and similar factors. Fourth, the degree of force the target uses to repel the attack must be in proportion to the threat of injury or death posed by the aggressor. And fifth, the timing of the target's action must be appropriate. A preemptive strike initiated before the presumed attacker makes his or her intentions known (too soon) is illegal. A retaliatory strike made after the clash is over (too late) also exceeds the limits of self-defense (see Austern, 1987; and Fletcher, 1988).

In every jurisdiction, the law permits law-abiding people to use deadly force to protect themselves from serious bodily harm, and it spells out the circumstances under which victims of particular crimes can try to wound or kill their adversaries. For example, whether or not citizens are entitled by law to unleash deadly force to protect their homes and property varies substantially from state to state. In most jurisdictions, intruders guilty of forcible entries into dwellings can be shot. In some states, however, residents must be threatened or actually attacked before they can use lethal force against criminals who invade their homes. Trespassers generally are not considered to pose a grave peril and therefore cannot be shot on sight. Only a few states authorize private citizens to use some degree of physical force to safeguard their property from thieves (BJS, 1988).

A number of guidelines that suggest when victims under attack can legally resort to deadly force in self-defense appear in Box 13.1.

Would Victims Be Better Off if They Were Armed?

People buy firearms for a number of reasons: to collect them, to use them for target practice and sport shooting, to hunt game, and for self-protection. Gun culture is deeply rooted in the American experience, beginning with the day the first settlers arrived to clear and colonize the land. But ever since the 1960s, when the waves of street crime and social unrest became divisive issues and public concerns, many people have told pollsters that their primary reason for owning a gun is for self-defense. They believe that they are improving their odds of surviving a felonious assault by possessing firearms and having them loaded and handy, just in case (see Baum, 2013).

BOX 13.1   What Armed Citizens Under Attack Must Consider Before Pulling the Trigger

Some issues that armed citizens who find themselves under attack must grapple with before they open fire were raised in a book review in the official publication of the National Rifle Association:

1) *Be reasonable*

In all states, a claim of self-defense in the aftermath of a confrontation that resulted in an injury or a fatality will be judged by whether the defender's perceptions and actions were those of a reasonable person.

Ideally, the image of a reasonable person is someone who is cautious, responsible, sober, and slow to anger.

Before any trouble occurs, a reasonable person would be known for walking away from fights, regardless of insults and other provocations, if possible, and for being nonaggressive, honorable, and reliable.

After a clash ending in bloodshed, a reasonable person would demonstrate "consciousness of innocence" by retreating to a safe location, quickly notifying the police, and cooperating with their investigation.

2) *Be innocent*

A person who starts or escalates a fight could be viewed as precipitating or provoking a physical confrontation. Such a person will find it difficult, if not impossible, to successfully claim that the use of force was an act of self-defense.

3) *Be sure the threat is imminent*

An armed citizen must ask, "Is an attack about to take place right now unless action is undertaken immediately?" Three conditions must be met: Ability (is the assailant really dangerous?), opportunity (can the attacker reach his intended target?), and jeopardy (is there some indication that the opponent will use the ability and opportunity to inflict harm?).

4) *Be sure the counterforce is in proportion to the threat*

A forceful reaction, such as pulling a trigger, must match the seriousness of the attacker's intentions and capabilities.

5) *Be sure the confrontation is unavoidable*

A victim has no duty to retreat before resorting to force to repel an attack if it is unfolding in a place where he or she has a right to be, but only if that jurisdiction has adopted a "stand your ground" rule. In other locations, an innocent person must first try to retreat, if it is possible to do so safely.

SOURCES: Adapted from Branca, 2013; and Frazer, 2014.

Almost one-third of respondents (30 percent) in a 2013 poll answered yes to the question, "Have you, or any close personal friends or relatives of yours, ever been a victim of a crime involving a gun or not?" (ABC News/*Washington Post*, 2013). Clearly, the issue of gun violence has touched many people's lives and stimulated a lot of fear, thought, and debate about this issue.

Purchasing and Using Firearms for Self-Protection: The Maximalist Versus Minimalist Debate

There are a number of ways of framing the issues underlying the debate over whether or not potential victims would be better off going around carrying loaded guns (whether concealed or openly visible) in their everyday lives. One way is to recognize that the debate incorporates some elements of a maximalist versus minimalist disagreement over the facts and the risks.

Some of the people advocating armed self-defense take a maximalist point of view and make alarming assumptions. They contend that an individual must always be prepared, on guard, and vigilant. An attacker could strike anytime, anywhere, and without warning. Law-abiding people ought to be allowed to take a gun with them wherever they go. Robbers or rapists might appear out of nowhere. When commuting, an aggressive driver may instigate a road rage incident. While on the job or when shopping, an employee or customer might spark an outburst of workplace violence. When taking college classes, a deranged member of the campus community could open fire and a mass shooting could break out . While relaxing at a bar or club, a vicious brawl could erupt. When dining in a restaurant, the tranquility suddenly can be upset by an assailant. While a family is asleep, an armed intruder may invade the sanctity of their home. Even while attending a religious service, some outsider might barge in with a knife or gun.

Many cases could be cited to illustrate each of these threats. Therefore, law-abiding gun owners should be permitted to carry concealed weapons with them at all times, if they so choose, so they will be prepared to defend themselves, their families, and other innocent bystanders at a moment's notice, as best they can (for example, see Cox, 2009). In the aftermath of some vicious attack on unarmed persons, maximalists often say wistfully, "If only there was a 'good guy' with a gun at the scene while the crime was in progress, the outcome could have been very different."

Minimalists contend that these hypothetical scenarios put forward by maximalists are too unlikely, statistically speaking, to justify routinely going around armed. They add that the alarmist policy recommendation that guns can and should always be present if owners so choose is counterproductive because the introduction of a firearm can lead to less desirable outcomes than the best-case scenarios predicted by maximalists.

The gun-enthusiast side in this debate sees these weapons as **equalizers** that can save innocent lives and works for policies that provide ready access to firearms for responsible, law-abiding mature adults. The disarmament side seeks to further restrict gun availability to all persons. But they are especially concerned about military-style semi-automatic assault weapons with high-capacity ammunition magazines, as well as handguns, falling into the "wrong hands" (particularly known criminals, drug law violators, teenagers, and mentally unbalanced persons). That concern arises because firearms are seen as **facilitators** that enable lawbreakers to gain powerful advantages over their intended targets. Having a gun handy also can cause everyday conflicts to escalate into deadly showdowns. Both sides in the debate admit that there is a trade-off between legitimately using a gun for self-defense and improperly using a gun to commit crimes, but the two opposing camps differ sharply on whether the costs outweigh the benefits (see Kleck, 1997).

The different assumptions and policy proposals of the two opposing camps were clarified when a gun control organization sponsored a television advertisement right before congressional hearings were held about disarming individuals who are the subject of restraining orders after misdemeanor convictions for domestic violence:

> *A mother and her child are alone at home when a man begins to pound on the door and demands to be let in. The woman calls 911 and explains that she has an order of protection against her "ex" but he is trying to enter her home. While she is still on the phone, he barges in and grabs the child. She tries to stop him but he pulls out a gun. As the screen fades to black, a gunshot rings out.* (NRA-ILA, 2014)

To the sponsors of the ad, the message was clear: Belligerent offenders ought to be compelled to surrender their firearms as soon as judges grant orders of protection. Dangerous situations could be defused if fewer people had access to deadly weapons that facilitate an escalation of disputes, leading to serious injury or death. But to advocates for armed self-defense, the ad inadvertently supported their opposite interpretation of the facts: Victims need guns as equalizers so they won't easily be dominated and wounded or killed by more powerful adversaries (NRA-ILA, 2014).

It is worthwhile to investigate a number of victim-centered aspects of arming for protection (but not the hot button issues of political philosophy about armed citizens as a bulwark against governmental tyranny or enemy invaders, or what the Founding Fathers intended when they phrased the Second Amendment). In this emotionally charged and highly politicized debate, unbiased researchers need to answer these questions: How many guns are held in private hands today? How many people or households own firearms and have permits to carry them around with them in everyday life? How often are armed victims confronted by robbers, rapists, intruders, and other assailants? How often are armed victims triumphant in warding off an attack, subduing an assailant, or slaying an opponent in a life and death struggle? How often are they vanquished by a better armed or more ruthless opponent? And how often are armed victims responsible for terrible mistakes, tragic accidents, and needless bloodshed?

None of these questions can be answered definitively and decisively, but some data can be unearthed to shed light on certain aspects of this pro-arming versus pro-disarming debate with maximalist versus minimalist undercurrents.

Arguments Advanced by Proponents of Arming for Self-Protection

1) *Reaching for a gun can save a victim's life*

Gun ownership advocates consider keeping a firearm at home or at work (especially in stores) as well as routinely carrying around a legally registered concealed handgun to be a rational and reasonable means of protecting an individual from the constant yet unpredictable threat of violent crime. Advocates of armed self-defense tend to cite examples such as these three, which illustrate how lawfully owned guns can be wielded to successfully protect life and property:

> A 34-year-old man breaks into a home but the occupant fights back, causing the intruder to flee empty handed. The suspect then shows up a few miles away, and knocks on a door saying he was just assaulted and needs help. As soon as a 72-year-old woman lets him in, he throws her to the floor and begins choking her. Her grown son hears the commotion and runs to his bedroom to grab his legally owned gun. The home invader follows him and lunges towards him. The son fires and kills the intruder; the mother and her son sustain only minor injuries. (Walsh, 2014)

...

> A man taking his girlfriend to dinner steps out of his car in a restaurant parking lot. A concealed-carry permit holder, he usually leaves his handgun in his vehicle, but this time he takes it with him. A few moments later, a masked man rushes up to his girlfriend with what appears to be a gun. The man tells his girlfriend, "Get down, get down!" and fires four shots, wounding the assailant, who is arrested after being discharged from a hospital. His girlfriend tells a reporter, "I don't know what

> would have happened if he hadn't had the gun," and calls him her hero. (Nipps and Lang, 2011)

...

> A 64-year-old man waiting for a bus is accosted by a 50-year-old stranger with a knife. The robber stabs him repeatedly in an attempt to steal his possessions. The older man screams, "I don't have any money! Leave me alone!" A man driving by witnesses the attack and intervenes in behalf of the victim by pulling out a concealed handgun he was legally carrying. The armed onlooker detains the robber at gun point until the police arrive. Besides robbery, the attacker is charged with attempted first degree murder. The victim is treated at a local hospital and is expected to survive his severe wounds. (Stennett, 2014)

Advocates of arming for self-protection cite cases like these as evidence to demonstrate how firearms can serve as "equalizers" that enable otherwise disadvantaged victims or courageous bystanders to emerge victorious from life-and-death struggles with stronger and ruthless foes.

2) *Gun ownership instills peace of mind*

Advocates believe that people armed with guns at home and concealed handguns when venturing outside will feel more confident to go about their daily business without being fearful. Although Americans own guns for a number of reasons, self-protection is becoming a more frequently voiced reason.

When asked if gun ownership does more to protect people from becoming victims of crime or does more to put people's safety at risk, the majority of respondents (57 percent) chose "protects people" while far fewer (38 percent) indicated "puts safety at risk," with a very small proportion (5 percent) unsure in 2014 (Pew Research Center, 2014; Doherty, 2015).

A growing number of Americans believe that having a gun in a home makes it a safer place to be. A poll in 2014 showed that nearly 65 percent of respondents felt that a gun makes a home safer, up sharply from just 35 percent in 2000 (McCarthy, 2014).

3) *Would-be criminals might think twice before attacking a target who could turn out to be armed*

Advocates advance a deterrence rationale: Just the prospect that the intended targets would be prepared for battle might dissuade some potential predators from trying to start trouble. Would-be assailants might become reluctant to accost anyone since they do not know who is actually legally carrying a concealed handgun. The general public consequently will benefit from a reduced victimization rate. Advocates assert that firearms are used by intended victims for self-defense more often than they are used by predators to commit crimes. Advocates suspect that the number of lives saved by guns might exceed the number of lives lost to bullet wounds annually. The crime-inhibiting effect of gun ownership by potential targets counterbalances the lawbreaking of gun-toting criminally inclined persons (see Kleck, 1991, 1997; Will, 1993; and Witkin, 1994; and "Concealed Guns," 2012). Proponents believe that communities known to be heavily armed won't be viewed by burglars and robbers as attractive places to operate, and that a well-armed populace can serve as an effective backup for local law enforcement (Reynolds, 2007). Gun proponents claim the growing presence of armed citizens has helped to deter crime ever since the second half of the 1990s (sloganized as "more guns, less crime") (see Lott, 1998; and NRA, 2012). (But a blue ribbon commission found no conclusive evidence that the passage of "shall carry" laws had any impact on local crime rates in the states that had adopted this approach [Vines, 2004].)

4) *Just brandishing a gun may be sufficient to cut short an attack*

Advocates argue that if an assailant begins to approach what he anticipates will be an easy mark, the mere sight of a firearm in the hands of the target might intimidate this offender into retreating and aborting his plans. The crime will be categorized as an attempt and not a successfully completed act.

5) *Firing a gun may save a victim's life*

In a life-or-death struggle, a gun can improve the victim's odds of surviving a battle with an armed and dangerous, more physically powerful foe, proponents of carrying concealed weapons insist. Furthermore, a law-abiding citizen could wound, capture, and hold an assailant at bay until the police arrive and thereby successfully "solve" his own case (see ProCon, 2012).

It is difficult to find estimates of the number of assailants that victims felt they had to shoot during crimes in progress in order to protect themselves. The FBI tracks the number of violent felons killed by victims that were deemed legally permissible by the police and, if necessary, the courts. In 2013, private citizens under attack had to resort to deadly force to prevent grave bodily harm or even to save their lives in over 280 incidents. In nearly 225 (about 80 percent) of these kill-or-be-killed confrontations, the victims fired guns (as opposed to dispatching their foes in other ways) according to the *UCR* (FBI, 2014) (see the discussion of "justifiable homicides").

6) *People ought to take responsibility for their own safety and prepare to defend themselves and their families from criminals.*

Self-reliance is necessary to supplement the basic protections provided by the police. Officers cannot effectively reach everyone under attack in time during crimes in progress, especially in the midst of crisis situations. The government can never guarantee the safety of all of its citizens at all times and places. Consequently, protecting oneself and one's family is not just a right but an obligation. Some advocates of armed self-defense as well as self-reliance go as far as to argue that intended targets have a "moral responsibility" to fight back if their property, lives, families, and communities are in danger. To do this effectively, law-abiding citizens need to be trained and to be equipped with guns as equalizers. The existence of police departments does not relieve individuals of their obligations to protect themselves, and officers cannot be depended upon to serve as personal bodyguards. Readiness to resist an assault on one's dignity is a prerequisite for self-respect, as well as a deterrent to crime (see Snyder, 1993; and Will, 1993).

A small town in Georgia has had an ordinance in effect since 1982 that requires every household to possess a gun for self-defense (Gray, 2013).

Counterarguments Advanced by Critics Opposed to Arming for Self-Protection

A number of groups and organizations can be considered to be part of a movement to promote the view that gun ownership is risky and needs to be discouraged or at least more tightly controlled. They point out that over 30,000 lives were lost because of bullet wounds in 2010. For every person who dies, two others survive their wounds, leading to an overall toll that approaches 100,000 Americans injured or killed due to firearms per year. Over the years from 2005 to 2010, despite the drop in crime rates, on average 33 people a day were murdered by gun-wielding assailants. Nearly 50 people a day committed suicide during those years by using guns. And about two people died accidentally each day from gunfire (Law Center, 2012). In response to all this bloodshed, the movement in opposition to arming for self-protection cites a number of reasons for rejecting going around armed as a means of self-protection: More deadly weapons in private hands will lead to more suicides, accidental injuries and deaths, minor disputes spiraling out of control into shootings, and needless suffering (see Fox and McDowall, 2008; Luo, 2011b; and ProCon, 2012). Specifically, the opponents of arming for self-protection put forward the following arguments.

1) *There are far too many guns in circulation already. Further production and purchases by fearful people should be discouraged and restricted in order to improve public safety.*

Estimates differ over how many guns are in the hands of private citizens (excluding members of the armed forces and law enforcement agencies) and how many people own a firearm. But it appears that a shrinking number of Americans own two-thirds of the nation's firearms, and although they constitute less than 1 percent of the world's population, this heavily armed group might possess as many as one-third of all the guns in circulation across the globe (Brennan, 2012).

At the start of the twenty-first century, about 75 million Americans owned an estimated 200 million to 250 million guns, of which about 70 million were handguns (Riczo, 2001; and Kohn, 2005). By 2011, the estimated number of privately owned firearms approached 300 million, of which nearly 100 million were handguns, and tens of millions were extremely lethal "assault weapons" that for a time (1994–2004) had been banned by federal law. This arsenal stockpiled by 80 million owners set an all-time record. The number of firearms in circulation is much larger than it was in 1970, when federal gun control laws first became a hotly debated political issue (Morganthau and Shenitz, 1994; Witkin, 1994; Cook and Ludwig, 1997; Riczo, 2001; and NRA-ILA, 2011; 2012). Gun sales and federally mandated background checks increased from 2008 to 2012. On "Black Friday" in 2012, licensed firearms dealers requested over 150,000 background checks from the FBI for shoppers seeking to purchase handguns, rifles, and shotguns that day (Oatman and Gordon, 2012).

The proportion of households in which there is a gun remains unclear, along with trends in gun ownership. The answer depends on which survey organizations are cited. Gallup Polls over the decades from the late 1950s through 2014 revealed that during most years, less than half of all American households possessed at least one gun. The highest figure for gun ownership was 54 percent in 1993, and the lowest was 43 percent in 2013. In 2014, interviewers were told that a gun was owned by 44 percent of all households (note that this question counts guns kept in the home plus in other places like garages, barns, or vehicles). In terms of trends, a slight decrease can be discerned over the years, but with no substantial changes since the mid-1990s (McCarthy, 2014).

But according to the widely used General Social Survey, the highest level of household gun ownership was registered in 1977 at 54 percent. Over the decades since then gun ownership has steadily declined, and hit an all-time low in 2010 at less than 33 percent. From 1985 to 2010, the number of Americans who claimed that they personally owned a gun (as opposed to their family in general) dropped by nearly one-third, ending up at roughly one in every five people. Only 1 in every 10 women and one in every three men told interviewers they owned a gun in 2010. Several reasons (not directly related to the question of self-protection) might explain the decline: the end of military conscription and the decline of participation in military service, a loss of interest in gun ownership by younger people, an increase in single-parent households headed by women, and growing restrictions on hunting lands and shooting ranges (VPC, 2011; and Tavernise and Gebeloff, 2013).

Gun ownership generally was higher among men than women, whites than blacks, older people than people under 50, higher-income than lower-income families, Southerners than inhabitants of other regions, residents of rural rather than urban areas, and Republicans rather than Democrats (Roper, 2004; and McCarthy, 2014).

Critics worry that many of the millions of guns owned by "law-abiding" citizens fall into the wrong hands when burglars steal them. Over 230,000 guns were stolen each year from homes during the time period of 2005–2010 (VPC, 2013).

2) *Very few victims draw a weapon in their own defense when under attack.*

One of the most controversial aspects of using a gun as a means of protection concerns how often it actually happens. How many persons under attack draw their own weapons and fight back? Advocates of guns for self-protection routinely circulate claims that millions of victims successfully use firearms to ward off dangerous assailants, or shoot at them, or wound them, or, if necessary, kill them each year. Opponents of arming for self-defense take a minimalist stance and are highly skeptical of those estimates.

Self-protection measures can be defined broadly and are not limited to pulling out a knife or gun (or other weapons like mace or pepper spray) during a showdown. NCVS findings reveal that people under attack took measures to protect themselves in roughly 60 percent of all violent offenses (robberies, simple and aggravated assaults,

and sexual assaults and rapes). However, not all of their self-defense tactics involved the use of physical force. Their nonforceful reactions included screaming for help, running away, and reasoning with or threatening the offender as well as trying to capture the assailant and counterattacking with or without a weapon. Willingness to take self-protective measures did not vary dramatically by race, sex, or prior relationship (stranger or nonstranger) but was slightly dependent upon age (older victims were less likely to put up a struggle). Males were more inclined to fight back to resist and capture an assailant, while females were more prone to call for help or threaten the attacker verbally. Most respondents reported that their self-protective measures helped the situation (by enabling them to avoid injury altogether or at least to prevent further wounds, or to escape or scare off the offender) rather than hurt it (by making the aggressor more violent). Just about 2 percent of persons embroiled in violent confrontations claimed that they counterattacked by drawing their own weapon (other than a firearm). Less than 1 percent told interviewers they drew a gun and threatened to shoot, or did fire in self-defense, according to the 2010 NCVS (Harrell, 2011).

Estimates of "defensive gun uses" (abbreviated as DGUs by researchers and activists) are a hotly contested statistic that can sway public opinion in favor of arming for self-defense if they are very large. (Note that brandishing a gun does not necessarily lead to pulling the trigger, and a crime that is attempted but not completed or a confrontation that winds down because of a DGU may not be reported by the victim.) DGUs numbered a mere 235,000 or so over a five-year span from 2007 to 2011, according to *NCVS* findings. Yet, during those same five years, nearly 30 million violent crimes were attempted or completed (VPC, 2013). (But gun ownership advocates dismiss this official estimate as misleadingly low and suspect that many respondents are reluctant to tell interviewers working for the government the full story of how they repelled an attacker, possibly by drawing a gun that was not obtained legally [Bell, 2012].) Estimates of defensive uses of guns by people about to be victimized range from a low of

100,000 or even 32,000 (see Cook and Ludwig, 2003) to a maximum of 1.5 million or even 2.5 million (see Kleck and Gertz, 1995; and Kleck and DeLone, 1993) due to different methodologies and assumptions.

3) Getting a gun for protection actually puts its owner in greater danger

Although many people conjure up fantasies about how drawing a gun will save them, the reality is that gunfire is more likely to claim an innocent life or their own. Owning a firearm for personal safety could actually heighten risks and lead to a false sense of security, gun control advocates insist. They point to studies that seem to show that keeping a gun at home, instead of safeguarding the lives of members of a household, increases the likelihood that someone will be killed there in a moment of rage. Loaded guns are more likely to be used to slay family members than intruders. The availability of handguns causes ordinary fights between family members, former friends, and neighbors to evolve into deadly showdowns. According to an analysis of 420 homicides committed in the homes of victims who had access to guns, the majority of the deceased were not murdered by an armed intruder. On the contrary, about three-quarters (77 percent) were slain by a spouse, other family member, or someone else they knew. Only a small proportion (4 percent) was murdered by a complete stranger. The remaining cases (19 percent) were not solved. The highest risks of being shot to death at home are faced by people who keep one or more guns handy, reside in a rental unit, and either live alone or with someone who was previously arrested, uses illicit drugs, assaults others, or was hurt in a family fight (see Leary, 1993).

4) Introducing a gun into a conflict is likely to lead to an escalation of hostilities

Critics believe that carrying around a deadly weapon increases the likelihood that a minor argument will turn into a life-threatening showdown. The chances of a needless tragedy breaking out are heightened when gun owners are tired, frightened, intoxicated, and untrained. Ready access to a gun facilitates the escalation of everyday disputes into high-stakes confrontations, as this example demonstrates:

> One Sunday morning, a man is bicycling with his four-year-old son strapped in behind him. An SUV pulls alongside him, and the driver begins to curse at him for riding on a highway and slowing down traffic. They exchange words, and the driver pulls out a gun, warning, "I'll shoot you! I'll kill you!" The father turns away, but hears a deafening bang as a bullet grazes his bike helmet. The driver, a 42-year-old firefighter, is captured and pleads guilty to assault with a deadly weapon with intent to kill. (Luo, 2011b)

5) Some so-called "law-abiding citizens" who own guns for protection might actually use firearms to commit crimes

People who have been issued permits do not always remain law-abiding upstanding citizens. Proponents of armed self-defense frequently assert that citizens who get right-to-carry permits are law-abiding, upstanding community leaders who merely seek to exercise their right to self-defense, and that fears about them engaging in shooting rampages are baseless. But opponents point out that an unknown fraction of permit holders do commit crimes. Over 670 concealed carry killers have been identified from news reports and court records by a gun control organization that has been maintaining an admittedly incomplete database since 2007. As of 2013, nearly 30 of these concealed carry killers had perpetrated mass shootings, and 17 had murdered law enforcement officers (VPC, 2014a), as these two examples illustrate:

> A 39-year-old man with no known history of violence or mental illness takes a two-hour training course and a four-hour safety course in order to qualify for a concealed weapons permit for his $600 9 mm semiautomatic Glock pistol. Three years later, he lights a fire in his apartment by setting about $10,000 in cash ablaze with a combustible liquid. He shoots to death two building managers who see the smoke and come to investigate. Then he stands on his balcony and fires up to 20 shots indiscriminately into the parking lot, gunning down a bystander.

After that spree, he goes down one flight of steps, kicks in a door, and shoots a couple to death. Their 17-year-old daughter hides in the bath tub, but he discovers her cowering there and slaughters her too. He begins to fire randomly until the police arrive at the bullet-riddled apartment building. They engage him in a running gun battle so he takes two people hostage. Negotiators try to talk him into surrendering, but eventually a heavily armed SWAT team has to be sent in to free the hostages by killing the crazed gunman. (Flor and Ovalle, 2013)

∎∎∎

A pharmacist is stopped by a police officer for speeding. After the officer fills out the ticket, the video camera from his patrol car shows him briefly speaking to the driver. Then, without saying a word, the pharmacist pulls out his licensed concealed handgun and fires one shot, striking the officer in the face. The driver flees the scene, abandons his car, and attempts to break into another vehicle. He notices an onlooker and brandishes his revolver, chasing the bystander away. Then he calls his brother, a police officer, who picks him up, and convinces him to surrender to the authorities. The pharmacist's defense, that he is burdened by mental disorders, is rejected by a jury, and he is sentenced to death by lethal injection for murdering an on-duty police officer during a traffic stop. (Wagner, 2011)

Perpetrators of domestic violence, even misdemeanor assaults, are supposed to lose their right to own firearms in many jurisdictions. And yet many offenders remain a threat to their partners and to public safety because their guns frequently are not confiscated by local law enforcement agencies (Connelly and Luo, 2011). Only a handful of states have enacted legislation that requires that guns be surrendered when a victim takes out an order of protection against a former intimate partner (Luo, 2013).

6) *People who own guns for protection might turn their weapons on themselves*

Impulsive suicides in moments of despair are disturbingly common. Suicides by gunfire outnumber gun murders each year (Miller and Hemenway,

2008). In 2011, just about 20,000 people ended their lives with firearms. Murderers dispatched about 11,000 individuals using bullets that year (CDC, 2013b). So Americans were almost twice as likely to die by their own hands as to be shot dead by a criminal that year. When police officers decide that they want to die, they know that "eating the gun" and then pulling the trigger will not fail to meet their goal.

7) *Guns owned for protection can accidentally discharge and claim a significant number of lives and mar many others*

During 2011, almost 600 people perished from accidental discharges of firearms. Many more were wounded by bullets from loaded guns that went off unexpectedly (CDC, 2013b). Over 135 of these accidental deaths by gunfire were of children and teenagers (Brady Center, 2013a). These troubling figures turn out to be underestimates. Investigative journalists reviewing deaths of children from firearms discovered that such fatal accidental shootings took place roughly twice as often as the official records indicate because of inconsistencies in the ways authorities classify these cases (Luo and McIntre, 2013). Some of these unintentional deaths from stray bullets are particularly poignant if not outrageous:

> *A licensed security guard is showing his permitted concealed handgun to another member of his congregation who is interested in buying a gun for his 21st birthday. The guard thinks the gun is unloaded, but he forgets that one bullet is still in the chamber. The gun discharges accidentally, and the bullet penetrates the wall of a room in the church before striking the pastor's 20-year-old daughter in the head. After a week in the intensive care unit, the young woman, who is the girlfriend of the young man shopping for a weapon, perishes in the hospital.* (Daily Mail Reporter, 2012)

∎∎∎

A mother is in a department store with her two-year-old son and her three other children. Left alone for a moment in a shopping cart, the toddler reaches into his mother's purse. He discovers a small caliber handgun, for which she has a concealed weapons permit. He plays with it and it discharges one time, striking and killing his 29-year-old mother. (Geranios, 2014)

Besides these terrible accidents, gun control advocates bring up horror stories like the following incidents to illustrate how individuals who mistakenly perceive themselves to be in grave danger might fire their guns in error, causing avoidable tragedies:

Two teenage boys play hooky from high school. When the father of one of the boys returns home unexpectedly in the early afternoon, they quickly hide in a closet. The father hears muffled noises, mistakes the boys for burglars, grabs his gun, and fires through the closet door. After the 15-year-old friend dies from his wounds, the father is arrested and charged with assault, reckless endangerment, and criminal possession of a weapon, even though the victim's parents did not want to press charges. (Friefeld, 2000)

■ ■ ■

Two teenage boys, 15 and 16, take a shortcut across a neighbor's yard at night. A 74-year-old neighbor sees the shadowy figures, opens a window, and fires his handgun at what he suspects are burglars about to break into his home. One boy is wounded in the arm, and they both run home. The injured teen's mother frantically drives them to the hospital and is involved in a head-on collision. She is killed and they sustain further injuries. The elderly man is indicted on charges of aggravated assault and faces up to 20 years in prison. (Thornburgh, 2008)

Overall, the rate of fatal shootings of children under 15 years of age, another important indicator of misuse and misjudged risks, is more than 10 times higher in the United States than in 25 other industrialized countries combined (Children's Defense Fund, 2005). A child is hospitalized from a bullet wound every hour; and a child is killed by gunfire every other day (Goldstein, 2014).

8) *Victims might lose shootouts against better armed, more ruthless opponents*

In gun battles with armed offenders, victims probably lose more often than they win, skeptics

believe. In some confrontations, attackers may wrest the gun away and shoot victims with their own weapons—this even happens to well-trained, physically fit police officers. In many other confrontations, gun possessors don't even get the chance to draw their weapon, or they hesitate to shoot their armed adversary. However, hard data is not available to back up these claims.

In sum, in the ongoing "domestic arms race" between "good guys" and "bad guys," critics are convinced that encouraging more people to reach for their guns is a recipe for disaster that will further endanger everyone. On balance, the risks that arise from gun availability substantially outweigh the benefits (see Wright, Rossi, and Daly, 1983; Kates, 1986; Green, 1987; Witkin, 1994; and Butterfield, 1999).

Gun Laws Directly Affecting Victims

Gun laws (like drug laws and capital punishment statutes) are matters for state legislatures to determine, so they vary considerably across the country. Gun laws represent the clearest example of how legislation has been crafted by special interests: lobbyists representing the firearms industry and gun enthusiasts who engage in political battles with lobbyists representing gun control organizations and their supporters. State and local (county and municipal) gun laws address a number of contentious issues that directly affect victims and people worried that they could become victims. The most divisive issues concern the right to keep (own) a firearm in one's home; the way firearms are stored in the home (loaded, unlocked, and handy vs. unloaded and locked away); the right to bear arms outside the home (carry around a concealed handgun); and under what circumstances it is legal to use (discharge) firearms in self-defense ("castle doctrine" and "stand your ground" provisions). Other highly controversial issues that have implications for victims and crime-conscious people arming for self-protection center on whether military-style assault weapons ought to be banned again, whether longer waiting periods ("cooling off" periods) should be imposed, whether guns or even bullets ought to be registered with local law enforcement agencies, whether armor-piercing Teflon-tipped "cop killer" bullets should be sold to the public, whether the number of guns purchased per month should be restricted, whether the "gun show loophole" for purchasing firearms from unlicensed sources should be closed, and whether the prohibition on third-party lawsuits against gunmakers and licensed firearms dealers alleging gross negligence should be lifted.

Most states do not require residents to obtain a license in order to keep a firearm at home for protection. Some states allow residents to openly carry guns in public. However, advocates of armed self-defense have focused most of their energies in recent decades on expanding the number of states that give permission to citizens to carry concealed handguns around in their everyday travels (Luo, 2011b).

Gun proponents hail the spread of "right-to-carry" permit systems ("shall carry" or "shall issue" legislation) that authorize citizens to take concealed handguns along in everyday life. Every state except Illinois (and the District of Columbia) has adopted a law that allows non–law enforcement personnel (the general public) to carry concealed handguns under certain clearly spelled out circumstances. In three states (Alaska, Arizona, and Vermont), residents who are eligible to buy a handgun under federal law do not need any further permission to carry it around in a concealed manner. In the 39 "shall issue" states, permits are easily obtainable without special permission from the police, provided that the applicant meets the minimum age requirements, is "of good character," and doesn't have a record of arrests and convictions for felonies or drug abuse or a documented history of mental illness. In seven other states, discretionary "may issue" laws require citizens to prove that they have a compelling need to be armed, and local police chiefs, sheriffs, and judges decide who gets the limited number of permits. A complex patchwork of county and municipal regulations governs the permit process. Specifically where gun owners are allowed to carry their concealed weapons is a subject of dispute and therefore varies from place to

place. Advocates of armed self-defense seek to secure the right to take their concealed handguns with them to work, college campuses, restaurants, houses of worship, and local, state, and national parks. The most intense controversies have to do with demands to carry guns into schools, government buildings, and places where alcohol is served. Another contentious issue is whether people who have permits from their home state can take along their concealed handguns when they travel to other states (called the national right to carry reciprocity) (see LaPierre, 2008; Cox, 2011; and Luo, 2011a; 2011b).

Proponents of arming for self-protection work to pass "defense of habitation" and "stand your ground" state laws that authorize people to use deadly force—without first trying to back away from a showdown ("duty to retreat")—against intruders who threaten them. "Stand your ground" laws are based upon a "castle doctrine": People's homes are their castles, where they have a right to defend their lives and property against robbers and burglars (NRA, 2008; Perrusquia, 2008; and Thornburgh, 2008). Some "stand your ground" laws go beyond the castle doctrine, which centers on home invasions, and apply to confrontations in other locations. For example, in Texas, the castle doctrine presumes that the apparent target who feels threatened is acting reasonably if he or she unleashes deadly force against someone who, illegally and with force but without provocation, is entering an occupied home, car, or workplace. The target of what appears to be an imminent attack no longer has a "duty to retreat" if he or she has a right to be there and is no longer liable to a civil lawsuit by the person who is shot, even if it turns out to be a mistake or tragic misunderstanding. Thirty states have adopted some variation of the castle doctrine (Thompson, 2008; Thornburgh, 2008; and NRA, 2012).

Overall, the states with the most strongest or most restrictive laws governing firearms (such as compulsory reporting of lost or stolen guns, requiring background checks on would-be buyers, imposing waiting periods of several days before pick-up, and prohibiting dangerous persons from purchasing guns) are largely in the northeast: New York, New Jersey, Connecticut, Delaware, Maryland, Massachusetts, and Rhode Island, but also Hawaii, California, and Illinois. The states with the least restrictive laws are Alaska, Arizona, South Dakota, and Wyoming (Brady Center, 2013b).

As for trends in public opinion, voters' support for gun control measures to limit firearms ownership and restrict legal handgun carrying is losing ground. In 1959, before crime became a highly politicized social problem, a majority of respondents (60 percent) told pollsters they would support a ban on handgun ownership. By 2014 a huge shift had taken place: Almost three-quarters (73 percent) of respondents opposed a ban on handguns. Less than half of all respondents (47 percent) said they favored stricter gun laws (down from 62 percent in 2000); respondents favoring less restrictive laws increased (to 14 percent from a low of 5 percent in 2000); and the proportion of the sample believing existing state laws should be "kept as is" stood at 38 percent in 2014 (Swift, 2014).

Nevertheless, gun control advocates insist that restrictive state laws are more effective ways of controlling firearm violence than lenient ones. Genuine public safety can be better maintained by insisting that residents go about their daily routines unarmed and by relying upon the police for protection (see Goodnough, 2005; Editors, *New York Times*, 2007; and Alvarez, 2012).

For example, in New York City, murders declined from nearly 2,250 in 1990 to less than 330 in 2014. Yet this dramatic reduction in lethal violence came about without allowing the law-abiding populace to arm for self-protection. In New York State, individuals do not have a right to own a gun, even to defend their homes. State law regards a "premise license" as a privilege that can be denied by local law enforcement authorities to persons who lack "good moral character." Homeowners with licenses can fire in self-defense only if they reasonably believe they are protecting the people within from burglary (home invasion) or arson; deadly force can't be unleashed on mere trespassers or thieves. In New York City, law-abiding applicants for a permit to

carry a gun around are routinely turned down unless they can demonstrate that they are in extraordinary personal danger (only relatively few prominent persons and celebrities qualify). Having been a victim of violence and living or working in a high-crime neighborhood does not meet the standard of establishing proper cause for a special handgun license (Wasserman, 2008).

Victimologists can conduct research to help resolve the heated debate over whether arming for self-defense makes people safer or puts them at greater risk of being wounded or shot to death. Anecdotal evidence, such as the real-life examples presented earlier, is not sufficient. Researchers need to assemble an accurate and comprehensive database about all kinds of shootings, whether accidental or intentional. The *NCVS* and the *UCR* contain information about offenders pulling out guns and shooting them but not about the circumstances under which victims felt compelled to reach for a gun. How many of these confrontations involving armed victims in which a firearm was visibly brandished but not discharged aborted a situation of impending danger and persuaded the wrongdoer to run away? How often does the presence of a deadly weapon in "the right hands" lead to the capture, wounding, or even justifiable killing (if absolutely necessary) of someone armed and dangerous; and how often is there a tragic ending or a terrible misunderstanding leading to the shooting of the wrong person? Such a database should include the demographic characteristics and criminal histories of the assailants and their intended targets, the settings and specific locations, the circumstances that precipitated the gunfire, the kinds of weapons involved, and the outcomes. This kind of information currently is scattered in the files of police detectives, prosecutors, medical examiners' and coroners' offices, hospital emergency rooms, health department death certificate records, and forensic lab reports (see Barber et al., 2000). Unfortunately, funding for research into these matters has been undermined by the "gun lobby," gun control advocates suspect (see Luo, 2011a).

Victimologists interested in contributing to the field of survivorology could study the reactions of persons who drew legally owned firearms to fight back and emerged from deadly confrontations unscathed, as well as those who pulled guns and still sustained serious injuries. Compared to a third group, unarmed victims who were shot, which group showed the greatest progress in recovering from these harrowing experiences? Did the presence or absence of a gun in the victims' hands at the time of the crime make a difference in the rate and degree of their recovery, physically and emotionally?

Justifiable Homicides Carried Out by Victims and Law Enforcement Officers

One measure (of questionable reliability) of how frequently Americans resort to deadly force to protect themselves is the annual body count of deaths resulting from **justifiable homicides**. Justifiable homicides take place when peace officers in the line of duty are compelled to shoot dangerous felons, or when private citizens during the commission of a violent felony have to protect themselves by killing their attacker. These slayings are not classified by the FBI as murders or manslaughters because they are legally excusable. Since 1988, the FBI's UCR has been keeping track of two categories of justifiable homicides: by victims acting in self-defense who had to kill criminals posing an imminent threat of severe bodily harm or death and by law enforcement officers shooting suspects considered to be armed and dangerous to them or to others in their path.

The yearly data assembled in Figure 13.1 shows a pattern in which officers each year slay more criminals than civilians do. Officers and victims combined put an end to the lives of more than 800 attackers in 1993, and again in 1994, as Figure 13.1 shows. Compared to the number of Americans who were murdered during those high-crime years, justifiable homicides accounted for about 4 percent of all violent deaths nationwide. Most of these nonpunishable deaths of persons deemed to be dangerous felons resulted from gunfire (99 percent of those killed by officers, 83 percent of assailants slain by civilians, in 2013), the UCR revealed (FBI, 2014).

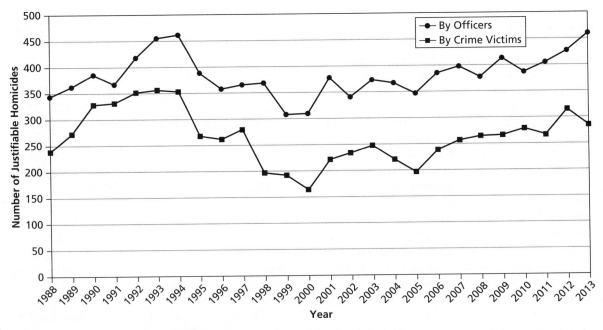

FIGURE 13.1 Trends in Justifiable Homicides, United States, 1988–2013
SOURCES: FBI, UCR, 1988–2013.

Unfortunately, the data may not be reliable because of incomplete participation by police departments and inadequate record-keeping by departments that do take part in the annual body count. Investigative reporters uncovered more than 550 police-involved killings between 2007 and 2012 that were missing from the SHR reports sent in to the *UCR* by over 100 of the country's largest police departments. Consequently, they concluded that it is not clear how many people are killed by officers each year under circumstances that are deemed justifiable (Barry and Jones, 2014). The completeness of *UCR* statistics about justifiable homicides carried out by victims under attack is not known.

A study based on SHRs discovered that race appears to play a role in influencing whether a fatal shooting is considered by the police to be a justifiable homicide or not. If the shooter was white and the person who was shot was white, then the homicide was considered to be justifiable in about 2 percent of all cases examined. If the shooter was black and the deceased person was white, then only 1 percent were deemed to be justifiable. But if the shooter was white and the dead person was black, then the homicide was deemed to be justifiable in almost 10 percent of the cases in states without "stand your ground" laws and in 17 percent of the confrontations that unfolded in states with "stand your ground" statutes (Roman, 2013).

As for trends, as the level of lethal violence increased throughout the United States from the late 1980s into the early 1990s, the number of justifiable homicides climbed as well. When the murder rate dropped sharply as the twentieth century came to a close, the body count from the defensive use of deadly force unleashed by victims and by law enforcement officers subsided too. Justifiable homicide by police officers peaked in 1994 but tumbled to its lowest level just six years later. Killing in self-defense by civilians showed basically the same trend, with the death toll topping out in 1993 but then subsiding to its lowest level in 2000. However, during the first decade of the twenty-first century, this statistical relationship and correlation reversed. The number of murders (and other violent offenses) across America fell substantially from 2000 to 2013,

but justifiable homicides carried out by victims of violence and by police officers went up considerably, as Figure 13.1 shows. In other words, prior to 2000, there was a direct relationship and a positive correlation between the level of violence in U.S. society and the forceful response by the authorities and by victims under attack. The lines rose and fell in tandem with the crime rate (not shown in Figure 13.1). After 2000, the situation reversed, an inverse relationship developed, a negative correlation emerged, and the lines reflecting justifiable homicide body counts by officers as well as by victims rose even though the rate fell for violent crimes in general (refer back to Figure 3.2) and for murders in particular (refer back to Figure 4.1).

The Vague Line Between Victims Acting in Self-Defense and Using Excessive Force

Five young men board a subway train late at night after drinking at a baby shower. They sit across from a number of other young men who had been drinking at a bar and are loud and raucous, and harassing other passengers. One of these men throws a bag of garbage toward the door but it misses, and it is tossed back to him. The two sides curse each other out, and a fight ensues. A 24-year-old hits a 19-year-old student majoring in criminal justice over the head with a beer bottle. The student falls to the floor and the group pounces on him. He pulls out a four-inch folding knife that he had been carrying around since being attacked twice over the previous few years. He lashes out and fatally stabs two of his assailants. The student and his friends jump off the train at the next stop and flee. He is later arrested, charged with second degree murder, and held in jail. In a newspaper story, he is branded "the knife-wielding butcher in the horrific subway slaughter" who "went berserk," and the two deceased persons are portrayed in a sympathetic light. But a grand jury does not indict him, deciding that because he feared for his life and was unable to escape, he was actually a victim and his use of a concealed weapon was an excusable act of self-defense. (Eligon and Baker, 2010; and Parascandola et al., 2010)

...

Around five in the morning, a woman hears an alarm go off, looks out the window, and spots 3 men trying to pry out the radio from their car in their driveway. She awakens her husband, an FBI agent who works undercover assignments, who grabs his service pistol. When banging on the window and yelling doesn't stop the trio of thieves, and one appears to be reaching for a weapon, the agent fires a single shot from his second floor perch, hitting that man in the back. They are soon captured at the hospital. But weeks later all four agree not to testify against each other. Misdemeanor charges are dropped against the thieves, and the agent's possible felony isn't brought before a grand jury. The FBI pledges that it will conduct a thorough and independent investigation of the incident, since the Bureau's guidelines clearly state that an agent can resort to deadly force only if he believes that a suspect poses an imminent danger of death or serious physical injury to him or another person. (Celona et al., 2012)

As the above examples show, sometimes victims cross a vague line and face charges of overreacting to a crime in progress. Self-defense involves the use of force to prevent a violent crime from being completed or to rescue an intended victim from harm. In certain cases, however, the explosive violence unleashed by victims might seem to be a response that is out of proportion to the initial threat and therefore is more force than the law permits under the doctrine of self-defense. But such distinctions are more easily drawn in classrooms and in textbooks than in real-life confrontations. In actual cases, difficult questions must be resolved: Was the victim still in imminent danger? Did the victim still reasonably fear serious bodily harm, or even death? Was the response proportionate to the perceived threat, or did the victim overreact?

Police officers are the first to grapple with these questions when they decide whether to make an arrest. Prosecutors confront these issues when they determine what charges, if any, to lodge against an intended target who emerged victorious from a battle with an aggressor. If the case goes to trial, jurors, acting as the conscience of the community, must arrive at a verdict by answering such hypothetical

questions as: What would I have done under similar circumstances? Does the abuse the victim endured excuse his or her excessive reaction? Did the assailant get what was coming to him? What message does the verdict send to the public? Juries retain the right to nullify legal principles, disregard the limits imposed by the law, and render a collective decision based on their own interpretations of what is reasonable and appropriate under particular circumstances (Dershowitz, 1988).

Difficult "judgment call" cases like these illustrate the sociological insight that no act is inherently criminal, and that all crimes are socially defined. Even when one person slays another, the killing may not be a murder punishable by many years of imprisonment. The survivor could argue that the nature of the confrontation was a matter of life and death, and that the deceased person should not be viewed as a victim but as a would-be offender who was vanquished in a kill-or-be-killed struggle. The way this death is handled is socially defined: It is up to the police to determine whether to make an arrest and to the prosecutor and a grand jury whether to press charges. If the person arguing that he killed in self-defense is arrested and put on trial, then it is up to the jury and perhaps even the judge to decide the validity of this claim. If the survivor of the showdown is convicted and sent to prison, then a parole board ultimately can shape his fate. All throughout the process of deciding what to do about the killing, public opinion, media coverage, and the reactions of elected officials and lawmakers play a role in shaping the social definition of what happened and how similar cases should be handled in the future.

Victims and Bystanders Sometimes Engage in "Retaliatory Justice"

A nine-year-old girl is allegedly raped on two occasions by her uncle. Her uncle's son allegedly molests her older brother. Their mother reports these allegations to the police and a bitter family feud ensues. One day, the mother drives to the uncle's workplace and directly confronts him. She claims the uncle laughs and says, "What are you going to do about it?" She responds by shooting him five times, reloads her revolver, and pumps five more rounds into him. Then she turns herself in, sobbing, "He raped my baby." In her first trial, the jury acquits her of first-degree murder but is deadlocked over the charge of second-degree murder. In her second trial, the jury acquits her of second-degree murder but finds her guilty of voluntary manslaughter. She is sentenced to four years in prison, but on appeal, her punishment is reduced to just six months behind bars. (Francescani, 2007)

■■■

A police officer's wife approaches a 22-year-old man as he watches a basketball game. Believing that he had groped her 13-year-old daughter two weeks earlier, she pulls out a gun and shoots him in the chest, yelling, "That's what you get for messing with my children!" The 41-year-old mother is arrested and charged with murder and criminal possession of a weapon. But when the dead man's pal declines to "snitch" and refuses to testify against her, the prosecution drops all charges against her. (Ginsberg, 2009)

■■■

Violent retaliation and vigilantism should not be confused with the legitimate use of force in self-defense. Retaliatory violence embodies the use of force to punish an offender after a crime has been completed. Once the immediate threat has passed, the victim—or the victim's protectors—may not use violence to exact revenge. Their "do-it-yourself" vengeance has been labeled **retaliatory justice**. This outlawed alternative to formal case processing within the criminal justice system in common parlance is dubbed back-alley justice, curbstone justice, street justice, or frontier justice. The victim's forceful response exceeds the limits of what the laws of self-defense permit. When innocent victims gain the upper hand during confrontations, they may overreact, not only to subdue their attackers but also to make them pay on the spot for their attempted crimes.

Bystanders also can get swept up by the contagious urge to meet out on-the-spot retaliatory justice and transform in an instant from good Samaritans to "bad Samaritans." These onlookers who spontaneously intervene to break up a crime in progress, to rescue a person in trouble, and to catch an assailant can get caught up by a mob mentality or crowd psychology and feel compelled to "get in a few good licks" to punish the offender right then and there, as in these two cases:

A 26-year-old man forces his way into an unlocked apartment where a 22-year-old mother is playing with five children. Brandishing a knife, he sexually assaults her while some of the children flee. Later, as he gets dressed, the victim escapes and runs to her boyfriend. The boyfriend, in front of a gathering crowd, confronts the accused rapist in the apartment building, and a fight ensues. The melee spills over into the parking lot. Someone in the mob beats the alleged rapist with a bat and another man shoots him in the head. "He got what he deserved," a neighbor says. (AP, 2008c)

■■■

A 17-year-old fires a semiautomatic pistol at a group of young men milling about the grounds of a housing project. He fails to hit anyone, and when he runs out of bullets, his intended targets start to chase him. After about seven blocks, a mob of between ten to fifteen young men and a few women catches up with him and starts beating him. They stomp on him for about five minutes until someone finishes him off by smashing him in the head with a large rock. Two of the young men are arrested for murder, but a resident says, "He got street justice. You live by the gun, you die by the gun." (Schwirtz, 2013)

To government officials, criminologists, and victimologists, street justice is the modern-day expression of an old-fashioned crowd impulse called **vigilantism**. Clear-cut examples usually attract extensive media coverage and become well known. Most reported incidents fit into one of three categories (see Shotland, 1976): victims avenging an earlier incident (a common reason for drive-by shootings); retaliatory actions carried out on behalf of victims by family members or close friends; and spontaneous mob actions in which a crowd gets carried away when responding to a victim's call for help, beating or killing suspects, which represents vigilantism by bystanders.

Vigilantism's Frontier Origins

Vigilantism has a long and ugly history, especially in the Old West and the Deep South. It began in colonial times as a reaction to marauding bands of desperadoes operating along the frontier. In Virginia in the late 1700s, a vigilance committee led by Colonel William Lynch developed a reputation for the public whippings it staged. Its escalating violence against lawbreakers gave rise to the terms *lynch law* and **lynchings**. From 1882 until as recently as 1951, lynch mobs killed 4,730 people. Many targets of these murderous crowds seeking vengeance on behalf of victims, particularly in Southern rural areas, were black men accused of harming white women (Hofstadter and Wallace, 1970; see also EJI, 2015).

Over the course of American history, vigilantism, just like lynching, often has arisen as a response to victimization. Vigilantes called for action whenever "honest, upright citizens" became terrified and enraged about what they considered to be an upsurge of criminality and a breakdown of law and order. Pointing to the plights of victims, vigilantes feared that they would be next if they didn't take drastic measures. Hence, "red-blooded, able-bodied, law-abiding" men banded together and pursued outlaws who threatened their families, property, and way of life. Vigilance committees led by individuals from the local power elite (with a solid middle-class membership) tended to go after people at the bottom of the hierarchy and the margins of society. They lashed out at alleged cutthroats, bushwhackers, road agents (robbers), cattle rustlers, horse thieves, and desperadoes of all kinds. They also crusaded against people they branded as parasites, drifters, idlers, sinners, loose women, uppity members of subjugated groups, outside agitators, and subversives with anarchist and communist

leanings. The targets of their wrath were blacklisted, banished (run out of town), flogged, tarred and feathered, mutilated, and in some instances slaughtered (Burrows, 1976). From 1767 to 1909, 326 short-lived vigilante movements peppered American history (mostly as Western frontier phenomena), claiming 729 lives (Brown, 1975).

Vigilantes portrayed themselves as true patriots and dedicated upholders of moral codes and sacred traditions. The manifestos of vigilance committees were crowned with references to "the right to revolution," "popular sovereignty," and personal survival as "the first law of nature." Just as they held criminals fully accountable for their transgressions, these rugged individualists held themselves personally responsible for their own security. If duly constituted authority could not be relied on for protection, they would shoulder the burden of law enforcement and the obligation to punish offenders.

The vigilante credo boiled down to a variation of "the end justifies the means": To preserve the rule of law, it is necessary to break the law. Most vigilantes defended their violence in terms of avenging victims and punishing common criminals. Very few of these self-appointed guardians of virtue ever got into legal trouble for their lawless deeds. Teaching lawbreakers a lesson and making an example out of them to deter other would-be offenders was the goal the men in the mob attacks cited to rationalize their own criminality. Surely, vigilantes had ulterior motives as well, and, in retrospect, other reasons may have been paramount: to quash rebellions; to reassert control over rival racial, ethnic, religious, or political groups; to intimidate subordinates back into submission; and to impose the dominant group's moral standards on outsiders, newcomers, and defiant members of the community (Brown, 1975).

Currently, vigilantism is argued about much more often than it is carried out. The label "vigilante"—a term formerly accepted with pride but now hurled as an epithet—crops up occasionally in news accounts and political debates. Usually, the word is used for shock value by journalists and public officials. When "survivalists" fortify their homes and stockpile weapons, that is not vigilantism—although some of these heavily armed persons warn that they will resort to force if a crisis develops and the government becomes paralyzed or collapses. When neighbors organize citizen patrols and serve as additional eyes and ears for the police, that's not vigilantism, either. (The first such crime-watch patrol in 1964 in a Brooklyn community was dubbed a vigilante group by the authorities, but this overreaction quickly subsided. Ever since, federal money has sponsored local efforts to supplement law enforcement, and police departments have provided training and equipment to civilian anticrime patrols.) Tenant and subway patrols such as the "Guardian Angels" also have been mischaracterized as vigilante groups. They do not fall into this category as long as they confine their activities to reporting incidents, attending to injured victims, and making citizen's arrests of suspects, and do not cross the line to dish out back-alley justice (Marx and Archer, 1976).

The Appeal of Retaliatory Justice

Once in a while, a case that appears in the news serves as a reminder that victims and their allies can go too far and unleash violence to avenge past wrongs—and still garner public support for their misdeeds:

A man in court is accused of molesting several young boys at a camp. Detecting a smirk on his face as he walks forward to take the witness stand, the mother of one of the boys pulls out a gun and shoots him in the back of the head five times. When she is put on trial for murder, some people rally to her side. Picturing her as a heroic figure who rose up in righteous indignation in defense of her child, they send telegrams offering support and raise money for her defense. But others are skeptical of her portrayal as an anguished parent pushed to the breaking point by an arrogant offender who was about to be coddled by an ineffectual judicial system. When they learn that she waited two years for the chance to shoot the alleged molester, was high on methamphetamine that day, and had a past conviction for auto theft,

they view her more as a drug-addled ex-con with a score to settle. Convicted of voluntary manslaughter, she is sentenced to 10 years in prison by a judge who categorizes her courtroom gunplay as an execution that was an intentional and intolerable assault on the justice system. The sentence is hailed by the prosecutor who interprets it as affirming the message that victims must not dish out street justice. But her supporters urge clemency so she can be freed to lead a crusade to toughen the way child molesters are handled by the legal system. After three years, her sentence is overturned and she is released. A movie is made about her case, but she does not become a reformer. Several years later, she is imprisoned again, this time for selling methamphetamine. Her son, who was molested at age 6, turns 23, stomps a man to death, and is sentenced to 25 years to life. (Kincaid, 1993; and Associated Press, 2008d)

●●●

A 48-year-old auto body repairman harasses and bullies his neighbors for two years, tailgating and threatening to ram their cars, and terrorizing them with taunts like, "I know where you live." Residents organize a "safe streets action group" and send complaints to elected officials, documenting more than 150 incidents affecting 42 people. Eventually, he is prosecuted for assault but is acquitted. A retired navy commander who has played a major role in collecting evidence for the community group confronts the bully one day near his home. The veteran testifies that the bully drives by and then boasts, "You and your family are as good as dead." Those are the last words he ever utters. The 51-year-old man pulls out a revolver, opens the passenger side window of his car, starts shooting, reloads, and fires a total of 13 rounds, killing his feared but unarmed opponent. Although many callers to talk radio shows during his nationally televised trial support his actions, saying things like, "He should get a medal," and "Put me on that jury, and he'd get off," the retired commander is convicted of second-degree murder. His wife writes to the judge, arguing that her husband is "neither a vigilante nor a hero." The judge, declaring that the deceased got what was coming to him, overturns the jury's verdict, reduces the conviction to manslaughter, and cuts the shooter's sentence in half. He is released from prison after nine years. (Jones, 2004)

■■■

A man calls 911 and tells the dispatcher about two men who appear to be breaking into his neighbor's home. He says he has a shotgun, but the emergency operator urges him to stay indoors, declaring "Ain't no property worth shooting somebody over, okay?" The dispatcher insists that officers will arrive on the scene soon and warns the man, "You're going to get yourself shot." The man replies, "You wanna bet? He then goes out his door, yells out, "Move, you're dead!" and unleashes three shotgun blasts at the duo, hitting them in their backs as they retreat across his lawn with a bag of stolen goods. The police arrive 80 seconds after the 911 call ends. The 62-year-old neighbor who intervened to prevent burglars from getting away is hailed as a hero by many local residents. When a small group assembles near his home to protest the killings as an act of vigilantism, they are shouted down and driven away by neighbors and bikers chanting, "U.S.A.! U.S.A.!" A grand jury declines to indict him for the slayings of the men, who turn out to be "illegal aliens" with false IDs and criminal records. (Thornburgh, 2008)

■■■

A father and his two sons are pushing their truck along a country road because it ran out of gas. A drunken 20-year-old plows into them, killing both boys, ages 12 and 11. Shortly after the crash, someone shoots the drunk driver. The father is put on trial for murder because, according to the prosecution, he allegedly ran to his nearby home to get his gun so he could carry out a "roadside execution" of the man who killed his sons. But the murder weapon is never found, and the ballistic and forensic evidence is inconclusive, so the jury deliberates for a mere three hours before acquitting the father. (Lozano, 2014)

Retaliatory violence seems to appeal to many people on a gut level. A steady stream of extremely popular movies have capitalized on the theme of personal vendettas and getting even. Even though the plots are transparent and the thirst for revenge is quenched by the end of the story, audiences stand up and cheer for the victims who strike back and make vicious thugs pay in blood for their cruel misdeeds.

No statistics purporting to measure the prevalence of retaliatory violence are available—no government agency or private research group keeps track of such outbreaks. Cases of vigilante violence seem to be relatively infrequent. But if vigilantism is defined broadly as "taking the law into one's own hands" by physically punishing suspected transgressors, then it may be more common than initially realized. Many, if not most, instances of vigilantism are never detected, recorded, investigated, or prosecuted because victims and their allies (relatives, accomplices, or members of a crowd) don't want the authorities to find out their real motives. Additionally, many schoolyard fist-fights and barroom brawls probably are touched off by a victim's desire to settle a score with some bully or aggressor. Surely, some incidents of domestic violence are fueled by a yearning for personal vengeance. Some battered wives who fight back or even kill their tormentors go beyond the legal limits of self-defense by launching preemptive strikes to forestall another beating or by unleashing retaliatory violence to get him back for a previous assault. A few cases even have come to light in which physically and sexually abused children grow up and slay their parents. Perhaps some incidents in which officers use excessive force to take resisting or unruly suspects into custody (commonly referred to as police brutality) might really be outbreaks of "police vigilantism" (Kotecha and Walker, 1976).

Criminals act as vigilantes all the time: They routinely resort to brute force to settle their disputes precisely because they cannot bring their personal problems and business quarrels to the police, prosecutors, and courts without incriminating themselves. Vigilantism breaks out whenever street gangs engage in drive-by shootings to retaliate for an ambushing of one of their members, when mobsters hire hit men to "whack" some rival or "rat," or when drug dealers eliminate someone who cheated or stole from them.

Vigilantism also has an overtly political side. It has been part of the ideology of right-wing extremist groups—such as the Ku Klux Klan, neo-Nazis, racist skinheads, and certain militia movement groups—that openly proclaim their intention to "rid society of undesirable elements," "troublemakers," and "traitors" (see Madison, 1973; Burrows, 1976; Lasch, 1982; King, 1989; and Dees and Corcoran, 1997).

The emotional attraction of the vigilante solution to street crime rests on the notion that retaliation-in-kind is what justice is all about. Offender rehabilitation, restitution, and reconciliation are out of the question. Because the legal system cannot impose far-ranging punishments that directly match the suffering inflicted by offenders, it consistently fails to deliver payment in blood. As the gulf widens between the harsh punishments some people call for and the incarceration penalties the system metes out, street justice gains appeal in some circles as being more appropriate than the sentences imposed by judges.

When individuals accused of retaliatory violence are not arrested, not vigorously prosecuted, or acquitted by a jury after a trial, commentators try to decipher the meaning or symbolism: Was the person who allegedly dispensed street justice vindicated by public opinion as doing the right thing? Was the prosecution, representing the criminal justice system and the government, repudiated? Were the laws restraining the use of force rejected? Various interpretations are possible when those charged with retaliatory violence are not held accountable for their questionable deeds (see Bahr, 1985; and Dershowitz, 1988).

The impulse toward vigilantism is held in check by two counterideologies. Law enforcement officials and responsible figures in government, embracing the tenets of professionalism, reject vigilantism from the conviction that experts, not ordinary citizens, ought to control the criminal justice process. They urge citizens to allow the proper

authorities and courts to handle cases and to reject any do-it-yourself impulses.

Civil libertarians marshal even stronger arguments. They insist that due process safeguards and constitutional guarantees must be adhered to faithfully to make sure that innocent individuals are not falsely accused and then subjected to the passions of mob rule. "On-the-spot justice" has been criticized as too swift, too sure, and too informal. Victims and their accomplices dispense with all the rules of the criminal justice game. They assume the roles normally played by the police, prosecutor, judge, jury, and ultimately, executioner. The delicate balance between the rights of victims and of accused persons, hammered out through centuries of competition and compromise, is overturned, and suspects are presumed guilty, no matter how much they assert their innocence. The history of vigilantism is filled with cases of mistaken identity, when the wrong person was made to pay for someone else's misdeeds, as the following four worst-case scenarios show:

> *A furious father corners a 17-year-old boy whom his 14-year-old daughter claims raped her on the roof of their apartment building. The father shoots the teenager and then bashes his head with a hammer. But later the girl admits she lied about key parts of her unfounded rape charge. The father is convicted of first-degree manslaughter and is sentenced to 7 to 14 years in prison for his terrible over-reaction.* (Barrett, 1998)

■ ■ ■

> *A wife on vacation with her children telephones her husband, who is a lawyer, and tells him that their 2-year-old daughter claims that the man next door touched her inappropriately and exposed himself. The 30-year-old lawyer grabs several knives, walks across the driveway, bursts into the adjoining house, and stabs his 59-year-old neighbor to death in front of his elderly parents. He is initially charged with first-degree murder. But his "extreme emotional disturbance" is taken into account as a mitigating factor, and he is allowed to plead guilty to first-degree manslaughter and receives a sentence of 12 years in*

prison. According to a police investigation, the wife's claim about child molestation was bogus: the neighbor had never even been in their home. The elderly parents of the murdered man sue the lawyer and his wife in civil court. (Stowe, 2007)

●●●

A crowd of 50 teenagers gather in response to a rumor that a classmate from their suburban high school has been raped. Intent on retaliating, they pile into cars and cruise an adjoining neighborhood, spoiling for a fight. Several fistfights break out, and some youths are injured by rocks and bottles. Then the teenagers, armed with baseball bats, corner about 15 boys from a parochial high school and beat one to death. Six students from the mob, who don't know each other and have not been in serious trouble before, are arrested, charged with murder, and tried as adults. All six are convicted of conspiracy to commit murder, and three are found guilty of third-degree murder. The rumor about the rape of a teenage girl that triggered the mob action later proves to be false. (Janofsky, 1994; and "Mixed Verdict," 1996)

●●●

An 11-year-old girl is walking to school when a young man accosts her, threatens to shoot her, and then takes her to a nearby backyard and rapes her. When police circulate a poster about a "person of interest," neighborhood residents go hunting for him. Even local drug dealers ask to see a picture of the suspected child rapist. A group of men catch the suspect and pummel him until the police arrive. After the suspect is released from a hospital, he is arrested, beaten by guards in jail, and then convicted and sentenced to up to 66 years behind bars. (At the trial it is discovered that he was born addicted to heroin, beaten by his mother, and rented out to strangers for sex.) But no charges are filed against those who beat him. In fact, the police commissioner and the mayor remark that the reaction was understandable, considering the heinous nature of the crime. Meanwhile, on the day of the rape, another group of men close in on someone who has the same nickname as the suspect. When a woman begins to scream that he is a rapist, he calls out that he is innocent, but several men in the

gathering crowd kick and beat him with a stick and a bat, yelling, "That's what you get for raping little kids" before calling 911. This victim of mistaken identity tells the press, "I'm still traumatized" and presses charges against his assailants. He also sues the police department and the city, alleging that officers circulated his photo in the neighborhood and suggested that residents should use any means necessary to detain this suspected child rapist until the police arrive, thereby encouraging them to engage in vigilante justice. A civil court judge rejects the city's motion to dismiss the lawsuit. (Gambacorta, 2009; Aguiluz, 2011; Fry, 2012; and COTWA, 2013)

Do-it-yourself street justice also has been denounced as far too harsh. Physical punishments, including death, are imposed in the heat of the moment for offenses that merit lesser penalties under the law. The vigilante's intent is to settle matters in a manner that mirrors the original act—forcefully—but with the roles reversed.

The widely used phrase "taking the law into one's own hands" does not capture the essence of this reaction to crime. Vigilantes don't take the law; they break the law. They don't use force in self-defense, which is legal; they unleash retaliatory violence in order to inflict physical punishment, which is illegal. Their disdain for the technicalities of due process mocks the entire criminal justice process. Unleashed in the name of restoring law and order, vigilantism undermines the legal system and sends shock waves through the social order by trampling the Bill of Rights. In trying to vindicate victims, overzealous vigilantes create new ones.

From an academic standpoint, the study of revenge killings and retaliatory justice leads victimology full circle, back to its ancestral origins in criminology. Through vigilantism's role reversals, victims become lawbreakers, physically harming individuals whom they believe made them suffer. Offenders, formerly enjoying the advantage within the oppressive relationship, are compelled to experience firsthand what it is like to be on the receiving end of criminal violence. But trading places—transforming victims into offenders and offenders into victims—is no solution to the crime problem.

In an ironic twist, by striking out against the wrong person or by unleashing excessive force, vengeful victims open themselves up to the risk of being prosecuted in criminal court and sued in civil court. There are too many aggressors out there already. Encouraging do-it-yourself retaliatory justice would just add to their ranks.

TOWARD RESTORATIVE JUSTICE

What might happen if victims met with their victimizers or people closely related to their offenders? Could anything constructive come from these encounters? A social movement advocating restorative justice believes victims would be better off if they explored the healing potential of such meetings in order to get past the understandable sorrow and bitterness that invades and then engulfs their lives. From the standpoint of survivorology, a face-to-face encounter with the offender might be an important step that helps the victim to heal emotionally and to rebuild a shattered life. Consider what seems to have been achieved in these cases:

A 16-year-old girl has an affair with a married 38-year-old man who owns an auto repair shop. The love-struck teenager shoots the man's wife in the face. The young assailant is quickly captured, pleads guilty to first-degree assault, and is sentenced to a 5- to 15-year prison term. The wife survives, but the bullet remains lodged in her brain, interfering with her eating and drinking and causing her constant pain. The husband pleads guilty to statutory rape and serves six months in jail before becoming a talk show host. Nearly seven years later, the shooter comes up for parole. She tells the woman she tried to kill, "It was my fault, and I'm sorry." The wife recommends to the parole board that they release her, and they do. Years later, the wife undergoes successful facial reconstructive surgery but declines an invitation to "reunite" at a staged event with her former husband and former attacker who continue to lead troubled lives and periodically engage in publicity stunts. "I don't want to go back there with those two …

I have moved on with my life," she declares. She remarries, writes a best-selling book about her experiences, and speaks to college audiences about avoiding entanglements in toxic relationships. (Associated Press, 1999a; Winfrey, 2006; and Buttafuoco, 2012)

∎∎∎

A 78-year-old widow is visiting the grave of her husband of sixty years, who died two weeks earlier. A man takes advantage of her preoccupation and runs off with her handbag containing $700. But the purse snatcher is quickly caught and his mug shot is shown on the local TV station as part of a news story about the cruel crime. A 15-year-old boy recognizes the man in the picture as his father, who abandoned the family when he was a toddler and is periodically in and out of jail. The father occasionally drifts back into his son's life, and he just gave him $250 in cash to pay for a special long-awaited trip. The son contacts the widow and they meet in a church parking lot. He says he is sorry for what happened. "If I didn't apologize, who would?" he tells her. Then he insists that she take the $250, confiding that "I'm not sure if it was yours … but I'd feel bad if I didn't give it to you." She takes the cash but quickly hands it right back to the boy, saying, "I want you to take your trip.... I feel more like my life still has a purpose," the elderly widow declares. (Hartman, 2013)

∎∎∎

A 19-year-old shoots a 21-year-old police officer, permanently damaging his right arm. The assailant is released on bail but flees to Canada and lives a conventional life, becoming a husband, father, and librarian. Thirty-five years later the authorities arrest and extradite him. Facing up to 23 years in prison, his attorney negotiates an unusual plea with the officer's approval. He is sentenced to 30 days in jail, two years on probation, and to make restitution payments that will add up to $250,000 to a foundation that assists families of injured police officers. The officer declares, "Something good had to come of this. The easy way out would have been to have a trial, and cost this county hundreds of thousands of dollars ... and cost the prison system hundreds of thousands of dollars." (Einhorn, 2008)

■■■

A young woman is mortally wounded from a shot-gun blast by her distraught and suicidal fiancé. Her deeply religious parents make the gut-wrenching decision to remove her from life support and then make a highly unusual request of the prosecutor: to allow them and their minister to meet with the fiancé and his parents. The prosecutor reluctantly agrees. The group assembles during a pre-plea conference, which is normally limited to the prosecutor and the defense attorney so that they can try to negotiate a mutually acceptable resolution of a case. The murdered woman's parents are determined to transform her demise into the seeds of something transcendent. They declare their forgiveness at the outset but then ask tough questions, including, "How could this have possibly happened? What were our daughter's last words? How can you redeem yourself?" The fiancé confesses his guilt, and accepts the possibility of a lengthy period of incarceration, followed by parole with anger management and domestic violence counseling as well as an obligation to speak to students about dating violence and to perform volunteer work that the young woman would have done. The victim's father suggests a sentence of 10 to 15 years in prison, and her mother urges no less than 5 but no more than 15 years. The prosecutor takes their views into consideration, and several weeks later offers the defense attorney a relatively lenient sentence of a minimum of 20 years, followed by all the agreed-upon community service obligations. The young killer accepts the negotiated plea. (Baliga, 2012)

■■■

A reclusive 20-year-old with mental problems kills his mother, arms himself from her arsenal of military-style weapons, drives to a nearby elementary school, barges in, and proceeds to gun down 20 pupils and 6 educators before killing himself as the police arrive. The parents of one of the slain first graders ask to meet with the gunman's father, explaining that they want to be able to draw some lessons from the killing spree that claimed the life of their 6-year-old daughter, and that his cooperation was vital since he was the only person who could answer the questions that troubled them. During the emotional get-together that lasts for over an hour, they share their condolences and talk about their deceased children. Afterward, the father of the murdered 6-year-old refers to his two remaining daughters, ages 3 and 5, declaring, "... anger towards somebody or trying to point blame at anybody seems like a waste of time and energy that we can use to be better parents to our girls." (AP, 2013)

Even in these jaded and cynical times, when calls for rehabilitating criminals are greeted with skepticism and demands for severe punishment receive enthusiastic support, a new approach that assumes the best about people is gaining ground. It is attracting a growing proportion of victims who don't want to use their leverage within the legal system to make their offenders suffer. They are taking advantage of the chance to actively participate in a process whose goals are victim recovery, offender sensitization to the harm caused, a cessation of mutual hostilities, and a sense of closure, in which both parties put the incident behind them and rebuild their lives.

These are the aims of **restorative justice**, a rapidly evolving way of reconceptualizing the crime problem that many enthusiastic adherents find promising. It draws upon nonpunitive methods of peacemaking, mediation, negotiation, dispute resolution, conflict management, and constructive engagement. These strategies could bring about mutual understanding, offender empathy for the victim's plight, victim sensitivity about the causes of the offender's problems, and lasting settlements that reconcile tensions between the two parties as well as within their community. But frustration with inaction and gridlock is causing some activists to abandon their efforts at reforming the bureaucratic process and to redirect their energies into developing a venue for **informal justice** where injured parties can be central figures who play hands-on roles and take charge of the way their cases are resolved. These activists urge victims to arrange to meet their offenders face-to-face in the presence of mediators, demand an explanation, and insist that the wrongdoers take responsibility and make amends for the damage and hardships they have inflicted.

A Brief History of Restorative Justice

Restorative justice embraces themes important to the victims' rights movement, especially notification, empowerment, direct involvement, offender accountability, and receiving restitution. This emerging challenge to the prevailing punitive paradigm incorporates some traditions that helped blunt crime's negative repercussions centuries ago, before the state asserted its authority to dominate the justice process. In the distant past, legal systems were victim-focused and restitution-oriented. Detailed lists specified how much a wrongdoer had to pay an injured party for each kind of wound or loss.

But priorities shifted dramatically in most societies when the upper class discovered that the legal apparatus could be used to control the populace. The government symbolically displaced the wounded person as the injured party, and the courts were transformed from a forum to settle disputes between specific individuals into an arena for ritualized combat between representatives of the state and of the accused. If the prosecution succeeded, the state inflicted pain upon its vanquished opponents in order to teach them not to break the law again (specific deterrence) and to make negative examples of them to serve as a warning to others (general deterrence). Later, prisons were invented to serve these purposes as well as to take troublemakers out of circulation to protect the public (incapacitation) and to force maladjusted people to undergo compulsory treatment (rehabilitation).

In addition to the suffering caused by the deprivation of liberty and the imposition of harsh conditions (retribution), the government often extracted a fine or seized property from convicts, but it never shared the spoils with victims. The overriding concern of the authorities was to impose the appropriate punishment, not to help rebuild the victim's emotional and economic well-being. This paradigm shift to **retributive justice** resulted in a process that was state-centered, offender-focused, and punishment-oriented rather than injury-centered, victim-focused, and reparation-oriented (see Sullivan and Tifft, 2001).

Centuries later, reformers in a worldwide social movement are promoting another paradigm shift by working to revive the ancient insight that achieving genuine justice requires that something be done *for* the victim and not simply *to* the offender. Street crimes—acts of interpersonal violence and theft—are viewed as conflicts between individuals more than as affronts to abstractions such as "society's norms" or the "state's authority" or "law and order" (see Christie, 1977).

The differences between retributive justice and restorative justice are highlighted in Table 13.1.

Starting in the 1970s, innovative activists began to promote dispute resolution as a way to resolve conflicts that involved shared responsibility. They argued that calling the police, pressing charges, prosecuting in court, and seeking vindication through conviction were inappropriate for handling minor violations of the law, especially if they stemmed from ongoing relationships in which each party did something to antagonize, provoke, and harm the other.

In addition, proponents of dispute resolution argued that the adversary system underlying both criminal and civil proceedings is essentially a zero-sum game. At each stage, one party gains points at the expense of the other. Strict rules of evidence may prevent the disputants and witnesses from telling the whole story. Both sides are preoccupied with issues of blame, guilt, and liability. At the end of the contest, there must always be a winner and a loser. The victorious side is pleased with the outcome, while the defeated side is angry and disappointed. The two parties may leave court just as they arrived, locked in conflict and seething with hostility, and sometimes even more alienated, bitter, and polarized than at the outset (Wright, 1985, 1989; and Cooper, 2009).

T A B L E   13.1   Comparing and Contrasting Retributive and Restorative Justice

Issue	Retributive Justice	Restorative Justice
Nature of crime	A violation of the state's rules	An act that harms specific individuals
Jurisdiction	Handled by the criminal justice system's agencies and officials	Resolved by community members
Goals	Conviction and punishment for the purpose of retribution, deterrence, and incapacitation	Recovery of victim, rehabilitation of offender, restoration of harmony
Methods	Adversary system, establish guilt according to strict rules of evidence	Mediation, negotiation, frank discussion, consensus, restitution
Victim's role	Limited to complainant and witness for the prosecution	Central figure, direct participant
Offender's role	Must accept blame, suffer consequences	Must accept responsibility, make amends
Orientation	Past wrongful acts, prevention via fear of consequences	Past harm and future recovery, rehabilitation

SOURCES: Adapted from OJP, 1997; Crowe, 1998; and Zehr, 1998.

The development of methods of **alternative dispute resolution (ADR)** around the globe stimulated interest in reconciliation programs within the United States. **Mediation** lies at the center of a continuum bounded by conciliation and arbitration.

It requires direct negotiations between disputants with a neutral person, a mediator, who helps the feuding parties arrive at a mutually acceptable compromise by promoting discussion, soliciting viewpoints, and discovering areas of common interest. **Conciliation** simply requires a go-between to facilitate the flow of information from one disputant to another. In **arbitration**, a neutral individual is called in to break a deadlock. The arbitrator plays an active role as fact finder and then, after hearing presentations from both sides, imposes a fair, final, and legally binding decision. Using ADR was viewed as preferable to adjudication because it could lead to a compromise settlement that might satisfy both sides and resolve their dispute with some degree of finality.

These alternative ways of settling conflicts were made available at places called **multidoor courthouses** or **neighborhood justice centers**. Disputants took their cases to an intake/diagnosis/referral unit, where a screening specialist decided on the most appropriate method of resolving the matter: conciliation, mediation, arbitration, or adjudication within the criminal justice system.

At neighborhood justice centers practicing ADR techniques, hearings were scheduled at the convenience of the participants, not the staff. The use of private attorneys was discouraged. The rules governing the introduction of evidence were minimized. Witnesses were not sworn in. Mediators did not wear robes or sit above and apart from the others. Nontechnical language was used, and only limited records of the proceedings were kept. This moot model of informal justice avoided the constraints of a guilty/innocent, wrong/right, and pin-the-blame/deny-responsibility framework. With the mediator acting as a referee, the disputants educated each other by presenting their own versions of their conflict. The intent was to look to the future rather than to dwell on the past. The ultimate goals were to reconcile the estranged parties and repair rifts within their community (Prison Research, 1976; Roehl and Ray, 1986; and Wright, 1991).

Neighborhood justice centers were not sought by activists when the victims' rights movement first emerged during the 1970s. Originally, the idea of relying on informal negotiations to settle criminal matters conjured up the unfavorable image of an unwilling, trembling victim being forced to shake hands with a smirking, unrepentant offender. The impetus for developing this additional forum came from other constituencies.

Attempting to streamline the judicial process, court administrators sought ways to remove the minor criminal cases that clogged their calendars. Judges, including the justices of the Supreme

Court, encouraged experiments in conflict resolution so that settling disputes in criminal and civil court at great public expense would become a last resort. Police and prosecutors endorsed weeding out what they considered "junk" cases from their workloads. From their viewpoints, too many people wasted the time of public agencies trying to resolve private matters. They argued that the complex machinery of criminal justice should be reserved for "real" crimes involving large financial losses and serious injuries inflicted by strangers. The limited resources of the court system should not be used to attempt to settle petty squabbles between people with prior relationships. Prosecutors complained that a great many complainants decided to drop charges or failed to appear in court to testify when the defendants were family members, lovers, former friends, classmates, fellow workers, or neighbors. Anticipating that these complainants would change their minds shortly after an arrest, prosecutors disposed of their "garbage" cases quickly, either by dropping the charges completely or by plea bargaining them down (Silberman, 1978; Ray, 1984; and Umbreit, 1987).

The first experiments with ADR techniques for resolving civil and criminal conflicts were launched at the start of the 1970s in Philadelphia and in Columbus, Ohio. The Law Enforcement Assistance Administration provided seed money to cover the start-up costs of other programs. Most experiments were sponsored by and attached to a criminal justice agency such as a court or prosecutor's office; others were run by private nonprofit organizations, a community group (such as the local bar association), or a county or municipal governmental body. The kind of sponsorship behind a center shaped the way it conducted its business and the types of cases it accepted (Alper and Nichols, 1981; Freedman and Ray, 1982; McGillis, 1982; Goldberg, Green, and Sander, 1985; and Harrington, 1985).

Pilot programs to test whether mediated restitution arrangements could lay the groundwork for reconciliation were pioneered in Canada in the mid-1970s and in Elkhart, Indiana, in 1978. Members of the Mennonite religious sect were among the first enthusiastic supporters of this healing process. Their experimental project became a model for others to replicate and modify, just as the penitentiary (invented by the Quakers in the early 1800s as a nonviolent alternative to corporal and capital punishment) was copied by governments worldwide.

In 1980, Congress passed the Dispute Resolution Act, authorizing the creation of a national clearinghouse to conduct research and disseminate information about "storefront" justice. In 1981, New York became the first state to fund new and existing programs. The entire branch of social science known as **conflict resolution** received much-needed recognition, legitimation, and support in 1984 when Congress earmarked money within the military budget to establish the United States Institute of Peace. Courses on the techniques, strategies, and philosophies of conflict resolution and peacemaking are now offered routinely in schools and colleges, and in training programs for lawyers, police officers, and other criminal justice personnel (Cooper, 2000; and Volpe, 2000).

By the early years of the twenty-first century, statutes authorizing victim–offender mediation were on the books in 29 states. In some states, the possibility of mediating a conflict was simply listed as one of many sentencing alternatives, but in others, detailed provisions addressed liability issues, expenditures, the confidentiality of proceedings, training requirements for mediators, and methods for evaluating these programs (Lightfoot and Umbreit, 2004).

In 2002, the United Nations urged member countries to consider setting up experimental programs in restorative justice.

The Peacemaking Process: How Reconciliation Programs Work

Restorative justice projects are experimenting with four different approaches (see Dzur, 2011; and Armour, 2012). The most numerous is **victim–offender mediation**. Both parties engage in a structured dialogue that is facilitated by a trained mediator. This intermediary is more often a trained volunteer than a criminal justice professional. The mediator's goal is to assist the disputants to arrive at a mutually acceptable settlement that heals their strained relationship. A second approach involves a community board, a small group of local residents, who meet with victims and offenders separately, in search of common ground. Two additional approaches draw upon traditional ways of bringing estranged parties together: peacemaking circles and family group conferencing. The use of overlapping **peacemaking circles** (also called "sentencing circles" or "repair of harm circles") is derived from Native American tribal culture in the United States and Canada. Frank discussions take place between the victim and his support system, the offender and his family, and community members. Each person in turn speaks about what led up to the violation of a law. Then the groups merge into a disposition circle that develops a consensus about how to restore harmony to the afflicted individuals, their relatives, and their neighbors. A follow-up circle monitors the wrongdoer's progress in making amends (OJJDP, 1998b; Zehr, 1998; Pranis, 1999; and Armour, 2012).

Family group conferencing is the fourth means of conflict resolution that is gaining adherents. Originally, it was developed by the Maori, the indigenous people of New Zealand. It has been adapted to resolve juvenile delinquency cases there and in Australia. Run by a trained facilitator, the conference begins with the wrongdoer undergoing reintegrative shaming by describing the incident to an assembly of relatives, friends, and neighbors. Then the victim explains how this event caused distress, injuries, and losses. Other members of the community fill in details about the impact on their lives. The offender begins to realize how his actions caused hardships and accepts responsibility for taking steps to repair the damage. After the victim suggests desired outcomes, the entire group discusses ways to solve the problem. By the end of the conference, a written settlement sets forth the community's expectations about the constructive actions the wrongdoer is obliged to undertake to undo the harm he inflicted on others (Bradshaw and Umbreit, 1998; and Zehr, 1998). In

cases where the victim has suffered a burglary or robbery and the offender is a teenager caught up in the juvenile justice system, family group conferencing might also involve a representative from the police department and the local prosecutor's office as well (Baliga, 2012).

Making restitution, in monetary payments from earnings or by performing direct personal services, is a symbolic gesture that is a prerequisite for reconciliation and reacceptance into the community. Reparations not only help victims recover from the aftershocks of predatory incidents but also provide the basis for forgiveness. The government—through its criminal justice agencies—can strive to maintain order and protect lives and property, but only the community—through its local institutions and traditions—can encourage reintegration. A neutral third party can facilitate and oversee the process of restoring harmonious relations better than an agent of the state—such as a prosecutor, judge, or probation officer who coerces both parties to agree to certain terms (Umbreit, 1989, 1990; Van Ness, 1990; Wright, 1991; and OVC, 1997).

The kinds of cases considered appropriate for mediation and conflict resolution have grown steadily since the first projects were initiated. Originally, guidelines restricted the types of matters that were referred to neighborhood justice centers to noncriminal quarrels between people with ongoing relationships. Then the scope of eligible cases was broadened to include such misdemeanors as harassment, simple assault, petty larceny, and vandalism, in which the disputants had committed retaliatory acts against each other as part of a simmering feud. Such cases of shared responsibility were not suitable for criminal justice processing because the adversary framework imposed a winner take-all format that resulted in an undeserved victory for one party and an unjust defeat for the other.

Over the years, the nature of the relationship between the injured party and the offender rather than the nature of the offense became the single most important criterion for diverting cases out of the criminal justice system. Neighborhood justice centers began to handle acts of violence unleashed by offenders who knew their victims. Eventually, even violent incidents perpetrated by complete strangers were considered appropriate cases for face-to-face meetings. Some programs go as far as bringing together for group sessions victims whose cases were never solved and offenders convicted of harming people who don't wish to participate (Umbreit, 1989; and Wright, 1989, 1991).

Most programs treat reconciliation as the desired outcome of a process that has four distinct phases: case selection, preparation, mediation and negotiation, and monitoring during the follow-up period. The healing process begins when a case manager selects cases that seem suitable. Next, a trained mediator (either a staff member or a volunteer) contacts the complainant and then the accused to explain the mechanics of the program, discuss the nature of the charges, and test their willingness to participate in a face-to-face encounter. If they both agree, the mediator meets with each side separately and then brings the two disputants together—at the victim's home, at the jail where the defendant is being detained, or at the program's office. At their conference or dialogue, both parties vent their emotions and share their reactions to the crime and the way it was handled by the criminal justice system. After that, they focus on the damage that was done. They attempt to hammer out a mutually acceptable arrangement in which the offender pledges restitution to cover the injured person's expenses. After the meeting, the mediator remains in contact with both parties, supervising and verifying that the written contract is being completely fulfilled. The agreement usually requires that the wrongdoer make payments from earnings, perform useful and needed personal services, or undertake community service work to benefit a charity (Galaway, 1987; Coates, 1990; Umbreit, 1990, 1994; and OJJDP, 1998b).

The heart of the process is the encounter between the person who was hurt and the person who harmed him; it takes place in a structured and secure setting—often at the program's headquarters, a community center, library, or house of worship but occasionally in a courtroom or the victim's home. Usually, each side has met individually with the mediator. The mediator, typically an uncertified volunteer with at least 30 hours of training and experience, tries to make both parties feel comfortable, facilitates their dialogue, and assists them to find common ground.

At the outset, the injured party describes how the illegal act inflicted emotional, physical, and financial harm, and asks questions like, "Why me? What did I ever do to you?" and "How could I have avoided this?" The wrongdoer then tells his side of the story, often in the presence of his parents. By the end of the exchange, the wrongdoer comes to appreciate the error of his ways, accepts responsibility, expresses genuine remorse, apologizes, and agrees to try to restore the person who was harmed to the condition he was in before the crime occurred. The mediator, the program's staff, or a probation officer supervises the repayment process during the follow-up period. In cases where compliance lags, continued contacts and renegotiation of the settlement may become necessary. After restitution obligations have been fulfilled, reconciliation becomes a real possibility (see Umbreit and Greenwood, 1998; and Price, 2002).

The majority of victim–offender reconciliation programs are run by private nonprofit organizations rather than criminal justice agencies, according to a survey carried out during the mid-1990s. Programs administered by private, community-based groups made up the largest single category (more than 40 percent). Nearly 25 percent were overseen by religious organizations. Criminal justice agencies ran the remainder: probation departments (about 15 percent), corrections departments (nearly 10 percent), and police forces and prosecutor's offices (a few percent each). Almost half of all programs dealt with both juvenile and adult offenders; about 45 percent handled only delinquency cases; and nearly 10 percent only supervised adult lawbreakers (Umbreit and Greenwood, 1998).

Local and state governments were the most frequent primary sources of funding. The federal government, faith-based organizations, foundations, private charities, and individual contributors also helped to pay for operating expenses. A typical program had a relatively small budget of just over $50,000, employed two full-time staff members, and relied on 35 or more volunteers to carry out its mission. On average, a program handled about 135 cases concerning juvenile offenders and supervised around 75 involving adults. Roughly 33 percent of the offenses were felonies, and the remaining 67 percent arose from misdemeanors. The most common crimes were vandalism, minor assaults, thefts, and burglaries. But about 33 percent of the programs reported that they occasionally handled more serious offenses, such as attacks leading to physical injuries and assaults with a deadly weapon. Some programs even dealt with sexual assaults by strangers, attempted murders, negligent homicides, and manslaughter. Probation officers, judges, and prosecutors referred all kinds of cases to mediation (Umbreit and Greenwood, 1998).

In every program, victims participated voluntarily, and they could quit at any time. In about 20 percent of the programs, offenders had to take part if the people they harmed wanted them to, and they had to admit their guilt before proceeding in 65 percent of the programs. About 33 percent of all wrongdoers were participating as a condition of diversion before adjudication. A little more than 25 percent had been found guilty in court but had not been sentenced yet, and an equal percentage was attending as part of their sentence. Of the cases in which victims and offenders met in the presence of a mediator, nearly 90 percent were settled by a written agreement, and the overwhelming majority of offenders completed their obligations successfully. However, program directors reported that a variety of problems plagued their operations. Securing adequate funding from private and public sources presented a continuing challenge. Receiving a steady flow of appropriate referrals from criminal justice agencies required maintaining good working relationships. Cultivating support within the community demanded an ongoing dialogue with the advocates of retributive justice. Similarly, convincing angry victims to give restorative justice a chance required patience to overcome their initial resistance (see Umbreit and Greenwood, 1998).

Advocates for restorative justice place a great deal of emphasis on the specific interactions and actual processes that take place when the offender encounters the victim. For example, eye contact can express a more profound apology than words, and facial expressions and body language can be very revealing. Videotaping the dynamics of conferences allows practitioners to analyze the dialogue, spot turning points and emotional breakthroughs, and to discover why some conferences achieve mutually agreed-upon settlements that will stand the test of time while others don't (Wright, 2014).

In the United States, there are nearly 400 programs based on victim–offender mediation, more than 225 community board programs, close to 100 family group conferencing programs, and fewer than 20 sentencing circles in operation in various jurisdictions. The states with the greatest number of restorative justice programs are California, Pennsylvania, Minnesota, Texas, Colorado, Arizona, Ohio, New York, Alaska, and Vermont. However, restorative justice is not an option in about 85 percent of all counties within the United States (Dzur, 2011).

Evaluating Efforts at Reconciliation

In theory, victim–offender reconciliation offers advantages both to parties and to their crime-plagued communities. A number of criteria for success can serve as the focus of evaluation research. Victims ought to have opportunities to release pent-up feelings and get answers to troubling questions. In addition to emotional catharsis, victims should be able to leave the negotiations with a satisfactory restitution agreement in hand. For offenders, the encounter offers an occasion to accept responsibility, express remorse, and ask for forgiveness. Probably more important to most perpetrators is the chance to substitute restitution obligations for time behind bars. For the community, the pragmatic benefit is that negotiated settlements relieve court backlogs as well as jail and prison overcrowding and eliminate the need to build more cells to confine greater numbers of convicts at the taxpayers' expense. A less tangible but significant spiritual dividend is the fostering of an atmosphere of tolerance, understanding, and redemption within the community (Coates, 1990; Umbreit, 1990; Viano, 1990b; and Sullivan and Tifft, 2001).

Evaluations of different programs highlight many important issues. Offender recidivism rates may not be any lower for adult participants in restorative justice experiments (see Niemeyer and Shichor, 1996; and Hansen, 1997), but juveniles may benefit from making restitution. Youthful offenders who passed through mediation committed fewer and less serious offenses than a control group of their peers during the one-year follow-up period (Umbreit, 1994). As for the willingness of people who suffered harm to meet with juveniles placed on probation for property crimes, the percentages ranged from 54 percent to 90 percent. Reportedly, nearly 95 percent of the meetings led to a mutually acceptable agreement. The average amount of money the adolescents pledged to pay their victims ranged from about $175 to $250. The proportion of the contracts that were carried out to the victims' satisfaction ranged from a low of 52 percent in one program to a high of 91 percent in another. In general, research findings show that many victims volunteer to participate in face-to-face confrontations, very few mediation sessions become emotionally explosive, and most victims are not vindictive and do not make unreasonable demands (Galaway, 1987).

Another evaluation of four mediation projects attached to juvenile courts uncovered high levels of client satisfaction, approaching 80 percent of the victims and nearly 90 percent of the offenders. Roughly 85 percent of the participants felt that the process of mediation was fair to both parties. Before meeting their offenders in person, nearly 25 percent of the victims confided that they were afraid of being preyed upon again by the same individual; after the mediation session ended, only 10 percent still harbored that fear. More than 80 percent of the delinquents successfully completed their negotiated restitution arrangements, compared to less than 60 percent of similar offenders ordered to make restitution by juvenile court judges who didn't directly involve victims or use mediation (Umbreit, 1994). Victim dissatisfaction surfaced in those programs that failed to follow up to see to it

that restitution pledges were fulfilled (Coates and Gehm, 1989).

Mediators received higher ratings for fairness than judges, according to several evaluations that compared cases handled at selected ADR programs to similar cases adjudicated in court. Most disputants reported that they left the neighborhood justice centers believing that their differences had been settled. The compromise solutions worked out at centers were adhered to more faithfully than dispositions imposed by criminal or civil court judges (Cook, Roehl, and Sheppard, 1980; Davis, Tichane, and Grayson, 1980; and Garofalo and Connelly, 1980). Similarly, meetings between victims and juvenile delinquents and their parents that were facilitated by trained police officers received high satisfaction ratings from all parties (McCold, 2003).

Proponents of mediation in pursuit of reconciliation interpret these findings as evidence of a solid, positive track record. They conclude that the experimental stage can be judged a success and that the time has come for a substantial reallocation of resources that would enable these programs to handle many more cases. They point to polls that demonstrate that considerable public support favors restitution as an alternative to imprisonment, at least for cases involving property crimes and minor assaults (Galaway, 1987, 1989).

Pros and Cons from the Victim's Point of View

A father is brutally murdered. After 20 years his killer comes up for parole. The victim's family is consumed by intense feelings of anger, vulnerability, and insecurity. They avail themselves of their right to address the parole board, and the convict is not released. But a daughter, now a young mother, asks to meet the man who killed her father, in order to try to find peace within herself and for her family. The convict feels deep remorse for his terrible crime and agrees. When they are brought together within the prison, she sobs a great deal but eventually is able to tell her story of trauma, loss, and yearning for healing. The inmate explains his actions, how his life was ruined, and the enormous shame he endures. After five hours, the daughter looks directly at the convict and declares she forgives him for killing her father because this will free her from the pain that has burdened her for 20 years. (Overland, 2011)

Practitioners who work with victims in restorative justice programs believe that forgiveness achieved through victim–offender dialogues can play a crucial role in the recovery process (see Fehr et al., 2010). In the aftermath of serious crimes, victims can tell offenders in their own words exactly how they suffered physically, financially, and emotionally. They can ask troubling questions that only the offender can answer (such as "How did you get in?" or "Were you following me?"), which might finally lead to peace of mind and closure. If they dread the public spectacle of testifying and of being cross-examined in open court, they will be relieved to take part in a low-key proceeding behind closed doors. Informal justice has proven to be speedier, cheaper, and more accessible than formal hearings and trials. Cases are handled sooner, are heard at times and places convenient to the participants, and cost less in terms of time, money, and stress. People who have been harmed can feel a sense of empowerment by representing themselves rather than accepting the services of a prosecutor who primarily looks after the state's interests or, in civil court, a private attorney who is after a share of the judgment awarded to the plaintiff. The settlement can be seen as a vindication if the other party apologizes in writing and undertakes restitution as an admission of responsibility. Such agreements can provide a sound basis for reconciliation for people who want to—or have to—learn to—get along with each other in the future within their community. Smoldering tensions that might flare up again and result in violence and retaliation can be smothered (see Price, 2002). From the standpoint of survivorology, restorative justice programs might provide the opportunities that are necessary for resilient victims to take advantage of so that they can recover from their ordeals.

Civil libertarians have some reservations about the way restorative justice is carried out. They are concerned that the emphasis on healing and redemption undermines the presumption of innocence and other legal practices in adversarial proceedings (such as remaining silent) that protect the accused from the power of the state. Suspects and defendants are being pressured to give up their due process rights and readily admit guilt in order to negotiate restitution arrangements and get out of the grip of the punitive system. Offenders from more privileged backgrounds may be more able to buy their way out of trouble or work off their debts than disadvantaged wrongdoers with few marketable skills. Sentence disparity grows because the consequences for committing the same crime vary substantially, depending entirely upon the input from the particular victim and whatever community members take part in the unstructured conferencing process. Whereas court proceedings are generally open to the public to ensure that rules are properly followed, conferencing usually takes place behind closed doors. Also, the willingness of programs to deal with even the most minor infractions stimulates the criminal justice system's appetite for **widening the net**—intervening more intrusively into private matters that previously would have been off-limits to outsiders (see Butler, 2004b).

But from the victims' viewpoints, other drawbacks persist. As with criminal court-ordered restitution, the opportunity for a mediated settlement arises only in cases where a suspect has been apprehended but not necessarily formally convicted. Statistically, that prerequisite excludes most property crime victims. As for violent crimes, the harm inflicted in a moment can last a lifetime. Injuries and losses might be so great that they add up to expenses that far exceed what the offender is able to repay and what a small community can afford to reimburse. The limited capacity of the offender and the community to provide resources might serve as a cap that prevents a seriously wounded person from fully recovering all expenses (Herman, 1998).

For victims of minor offenses who are embroiled in ongoing conflicts for which they admittedly bear some responsibility, alternative dispute resolution offers several advantages over adjudication in criminal or civil court. If the injured parties don't want an arrest to be made or charges to be pressed, they now have the additional option of bringing their problems to a neighborhood justice center. Incidents that otherwise would be too trivial to interest the police or prosecutors can be addressed (see Cooper, 2000).

A completely innocent victim might find informal justice unsatisfactory. If the process consciously abandons the presumptions of guilt and innocence that underlie the labels *offender* and *victim* and terms both parties *disputants*, then the complainant's conduct is open to scrutiny, especially in the absence of rules governing evidence and cross-examination. The notion of shared responsibility is frequently invoked by mediators who view disputes as outgrowths of misunderstandings and the pursuit of narrow self-interest by both parties. To reach a compromise, complainants might be pressured to concede more responsibility, fault, or involvement than they feel they should. The entire notion of a compromise solution as a means of achieving reconciliation rests on the practice of both parties giving in, to varying degrees, from their original demands. Complainants who insist that they are absolutely blameless can feel cheated. When their case was diverted from the criminal justice system, that reassignment symbolized a withdrawal of governmental support (prosecutorial backing) from their side. They may feel that they were coerced to give in to a preordained outcome—reconciliation—even if their legitimate feelings of anger and hostility have not dissipated.

For victims intent on revenge, the greatest drawbacks of mediation and restitution are that these processes are not punishment-oriented. Neighborhood justice centers and victim–offender reconciliation programs are not authorized to convict offenders, publicly humiliate them with the stigma of the label of *criminal*, impose stiff fines, or confine them in a penal institution (Garofalo and Connelly, 1980; Butler, 2004b).

The Future of Restorative Justice

In the near future, the number of cases directed to neighborhood justice centers and victim–offender reconciliation programs will grow because there is a movement toward informality throughout the criminal justice system. In practice, informality is marked by a preference for unwritten, flexible, commonsense, discretionary procedures tailored to fit particular cases. As an ideology, informality is characterized by an antipathy toward rigid hierarchy, bureaucratic impersonality, and professional domination.

The growing interest in informal justice is fostered by several beliefs. One is that centralized governmental coercion has failed as an instrument of social change. Consequently, people must solve their own problems in decentralized, community-controlled settings. Another belief is that nonstranger conflicts ought to be diverted from the formal adjudication process whenever possible. The third contention is that both punishment and rehabilitation efforts behind bars have failed to "cure" offenders, largely because criminal justice officials and agencies primarily serve the state's interests (or their own), to the detriment of both offenders and victims. Enthusiasm for informal alternatives is fed by perceptions that the criminal courts are paralyzed by huge caseloads, civil courts are swamped with frivolous lawsuits, and prisons and jails are dangerously overcrowded. As a pragmatic response to such economic and political realities, informality beckons as a solution to the government's fiscal crisis. Neighborhood justice centers and victim–offender reconciliation programs can relieve the overburdened criminal justice system at a time when calls for increased services are colliding with demands for reduced taxation (Able, 1982; and Van Ness and Strong, 1997).

Several potential problems could plague the extrajudicial approaches of family group conferencing, alternative dispute resolution, and victim–offender reconciliation programs. If caseloads grow too large, mediators might be inclined to adopt an assembly line approach to speed up the process and avoid backlogs. Worse yet, overworked staff members might be tempted to eliminate the face-to-face mediation session entirely to dispose of a large caseload more quickly.

Originally, the cases considered suitable for mediation, restitution, and reconciliation involved petty, nonviolent offenses against property. Program staff members acceded to this limitation to perfect their techniques, avoid controversy, and maintain funding and referral sources. But now legislators and judges seem increasingly willing to send conflicts marred by violence between strangers to mediation. Some of these more serious cases don't fit the mediation format, and the harm cannot be repaired through restitution. And other tough cases will require more time to resolve, professional mediators, a greater commitment of resources, and more support from social service and criminal justice agencies (Coates, 1990; Umbreit, 1990; Johnstone, 2001; and Wemmers, 2002). The risks of revictimization must be weighed against the prospects for reconciliation when, for example, mediators facilitate victim–offender dialogue in father–daughter incest cases (Wilson, 2008).

In terms of political support, conservatives favoring small government might welcome the diversion of a larger number of cases to restorative justice programs as a way of saving taxpayer money, as long as individuals accept responsibility for their misdeeds and public safety is not endangered. Deeply religious people may find very appealing the emphasis on the offender admitting guilt and seeking redemption. Liberals generally support alternatives to mass incarceration that feature reintegration and a greater focus on the social problems that breed criminal activity (Belden, 2012).

Signs of conflict already have emerged within the restorative justice movement between practitioners and advocates over the accusation that some programs have strayed too far from the original victim-centered focus of repairing the harm done to individuals by making wrongdoers accept responsibility for their misdeeds. Offenders must show genuine remorse, exhibit empathy, and sincerely apologize in order to elicit the forgiveness response that they seek. Overly enthusiastic staff members and mediators can pressure reluctant victims of serious violence to participate in a dialogue, but then insensitively impose simplistic, moralistic, or religious formulas on them: "Forgive and forget; learn to move on; reconciliation brings healing" (see Umbreit et al., 2004; Wilson, 2005; and Armour and Umbreit, 2006).

Furthermore, restorative justice can be oversold as a nonpunitive, redemption-oriented cure-all that can handle most criminal matters. It appears to be the humane and politically progressive alternative to mean-spirited retributive justice. Its popularity arises in part from the imposition of "compulsory compassion" on both good-natured victims and "sinners" seeking redemption (Acorn, 2004). Enthusiasm for other sweeping reforms in the past quickly led to disillusionment when they failed to live up to their potentials. Unfounded optimism greeted the substitution of supposedly rehabilitative reformatories in place of harsh corporal and capital punishment and of ostensibly treatment-oriented juvenile institutions to supplant a punitive adult court and prison system. A number of other highly touted innovations ultimately disappointed their advocates: The replacement of fixed terms of incarceration with indeterminate sentences that provided incentives for self-improvement; the use of scared-straight visits to prisons to shock delinquents into changing their ways; and the proliferation of boot camps as places to break youthful offenders of bad habits and build self-disciplined, law-abiding young men. Restorative justice programs may fall short too, but promising experimental programs that divert first-time, teenage, and nonviolent offenders into mediation conferences certainly merit an expanded role in the justice system of crime-ridden metropolitan areas.

SUMMARY

During the twenty-first century, victims will pursue three very different courses of action. Most will seek to exercise their recently granted rights within the formal criminal justice process.

Another course of action that many victims and potential victims rely upon is armed self-defense. Gun laws have evolved over the years and now authorize greater proportions of residents of most states to obtain firearms and carry around concealed handguns for self-protection. Victims under attack have greater backing from the law in those states that have adopted stand your ground or castle doctrines. Unfortunately, some distraught victims will pursue what can best be described as retaliatory justice or even vigilantism. This do-it-yourself approach has a long and bloody history. It arises from a preoccupation with exacting revenge and a frustration with the cumbersome criminal justice process. As opposed to legitimate self-defense, retaliatory violence visited upon suspected predators causes a role reversal: Victims become offenders, and offenders become victims.

Some victims will direct their energies toward developing more restorative justice programs, which at the start of the twenty-first century handled only a small, but growing, fraction of cases. Restorative justice rejects retributive justice's emphasis on conviction and punishment, and instead substitutes mediation, restitution, and reconciliation. Its goal is to enable the two parties to work out a lasting settlement that restores harmonious relations within a community.

KEY TERMS DEFINED IN THE GLOSSARY

alternative dispute resolution (ADR), 480

arbitration, 480

conciliation, 480

conflict resolution, 481

equalizers, 458

facilitators, 458

family group conferencing, 482

individualist rationale, 456

informal justice, 478

justifiable homicides, 468

lynchings, 472

mediation, 480

multidoor courthouses, 480

neighborhood justice centers, 480

peacemaking circles, 482

punitive rationale, 456

rationale of necessity, 456

restorative justice, 478

retaliatory justice, 471

retributive justice, 479

right to self-defense, 456

social rationale, 456

victim–offender mediation, 481

vigilantism, 471

widening the net, 486

QUESTIONS FOR DISCUSSION AND DEBATE

1. Present the major arguments of both sides of the debate over whether victims would be better off if they were armed.

2. What is the difference between using force in self-defense and unleashing retaliatory violence? Make up some scenarios that clearly illustrate this distinction.

3. Compare and contrast the principles of retributive justice and restorative justice.

4. From a victim's point of view, what are the potential benefits and drawbacks of participating in a victim–offender reconciliation program?

CRITICAL THINKING QUESTIONS

1. Does a victim "own his or her case" and therefore have a valid justification to try to control its outcome? If cases of burglary or robbery handled at victim–offender reconciliation programs are settled with agreements that are very inconsistent, and also very different from the sentences imposed in criminal courts, is that a serious problem? Why or why not?

2. Is reconciliation always a worthy goal? Make up some scenarios that would be inappropriate for a mediated dialogue between an offender and an injured party, in your opinion.

3. Should victims be punished if they carry out acts of retaliatory justice? Why or why not? If yes, how severely?

SUGGESTED RESEARCH PROJECTS

1. Look through a database of newspaper and magazine articles and assemble some accounts in which a victim under attack pulled out a gun and as a result escaped serious bodily harm. Then find articles that describe how armed victims suffered serious injuries or were murdered, either by the offenders' weapon, or by the offender taking away their weapon and using it against them.

2. Look through the accounts of victim–offender mediation programs and assemble some cases in which clever and creative solutions were worked out to settle bitter conflicts.

Glossary

abuse To maltreat, exploit, take advantage of, harm physically, hurt emotionally.

abuse of discretionary authority When a person, acting in an official capacity, takes unfair advantage of an ability to make choices and thereby violates the rights of victims or offenders.

acquaintance rapes Sexual assaults or coerced acts against the target's wishes imposed by a non-stranger such as a friend, classmate, co-worker, or neighbor.

adult protective service agencies Investigative bodies, often run by county governments, that look into charges of abuse, severe neglect, and exploitation of seniors older than 65 or other adults who are disabled or otherwise unable to take full responsibility for their own well-being.

advocates People who represent the best interests of victims and speak, write, or plead on their behalf.

agency The ability of a victim to make choices, seize opportunities, and regain control of his or her future; also, a government bureau.

allocution The chance to speak out and advocate for oneself in court, now available to victims as well as defendants at sentencing hearings.

alternative dispute resolution (ADR) An option available to victims who are willing to settle conflicts through the use of conciliation, mediation, and arbitration instead of criminal proceedings.

Amber Alert A notification system that uses various means of mass communication such as highway message boards, radio announcements, and text messages to inform and mobilize the public to help search for a kidnapped child.

arbitration A process in which, when two parties are deadlocked, a neutral person engages in fact-finding and then imposes a legally binding, fair settlement of a dispute.

assault In criminal law, an attack intended to inflict bodily harm.

assistant district attorney A lawyer working for the prosecution, who handles cases in court representing the interests of the victim, but also the government and society at large.

attached To seize earnings and hand them over to victims as part of a restitution obligation.

attractiveness How appealing a potential target is to a criminally inclined person.

avoidance strategies Precautions that crime-conscious individuals can follow to reduce their risks of being accosted by criminally inclined persons.

battered-child syndrome Physical and emotional suffering caused by deliberate repeated attacks; also, a defense against criminal charges in which the perpetrator argues that the illegal behavior arose as a result of serious abuse by parents or caretakers that was suffered during childhood.

battered-woman syndrome Physical and emotional suffering caused by deliberate, repeated attacks; also, a defense against criminal charges in which the perpetrator argues that her retaliatory violence arose as a result of repeated physical abuse by a partner.

battery In both criminal and tort law, an unlawful use of force intended to be offensive or harmful to the recipient.

bedsheeting A harsh practice of charging a defendant with every possible crime that may have been committed during a single incident.

best practices A collection of recommended procedures that have been proven effective by evaluation research.

bias crime An act of violence or an attack on property that is motivated by the offender's hatred of the victim's kind of person.

bias incident An act that is not illegal but is an expression of the aggressor's hatred of the victim's kind of person.

bifurcated capital trials A two-stage proceeding in which, after the conviction and during the penalty phase, the murder victim's next of kin can testify and recommend a sentence.

big picture A general overview that reveals patterns and trends in an area that is assembled by putting together statistical reports about specific crimes from particular localities. The big picture shows what is going on now and forecasts emerging developments.

blame-the-offender approach A perspective that holds the wrongdoer solely responsible for committing the illegal act.

blame-the-system approach A perspective that holds certain social institutions and conditions partly responsible for causing the illegal act.

blame-the-victim approach A perspective that holds the injured party partly responsible for causing the illegal act.

blind justice An ideal situation in which the victim's characteristics as well as the offender's characteristics do not influence legal proceedings.

boost explanation A theory holding that repeat victimizations occur because the offender gains important knowledge about the target during the initial crime.

Brady Bill A federal statute named after James Brady, the White House press secretary who was shot during an assassination attempt on President Reagan that imposes a background check and a waiting period on purchasers of firearms.

burnout Physical and emotional exhaustion caused by stress.

bystanderology A term that could characterize studies that focus on the responses (or lack of action) of onlookers who witness a crime in progress, which is an aspect of the social reaction to victimization.

caller ID phone spoofing A fraudulent practice used by identity thieves to deliberately falsify the telephone number and/or name that appears in the caller ID information box in order to deceive the recipient of the phone call into revealing important information.

carjacking A robbery in which the offender threatens or attacks a motorist and then drives away in the vehicle.

carnal knowledge An old-fashioned legal term for imposed sexual intercourse by a male in violation of the law.

causes of action In civil lawsuits, the allegation that the harm suffered by the plaintiff (victim) was a direct and proximate result of the defendant's behavior.

character contest A situation in which a slur or insult leads to a confrontation that escalates into a fight because each party wants to save face by not backing down.

child lures Deceitful tactics used by molesters to attract and isolate their victims.

children's rights group A coalition that advances reforms to prevent the exploitation, oppression, and abuse of youngsters, including those who are juvenile delinquents as well as young victims of crimes.

citizen's arrest A warrantless arrest carried out by a private citizen, such as the victim or a bystander, in the immediate aftermath of a crime.

civil court An arena in which lawsuits surrounding torts (private wrongs) are settled by a preponderance of the evidence in accordance with civil law.

civil liberties movement A coalition that advances reforms that preserve constitutional rights and due process guarantees placing limits on what a government can do to its citizens, especially those accused of committing crimes.

civil rights movement A coalition that advances reforms intended to prevent acts of hatred and discrimination on the basis of race, ethnicity, religion, sex, or sexual preference, including prejudicial decisions made by criminal justice officials.

claims-making Estimates of the seriousness of the problem, demands for credit, and explanations that appear to be self-serving.

classical school A philosophy developed by Beccaria and Bentham that emphasizes the rational choices facing individuals and the consequences they must accept for making mistakes.

clearance rate The percentage of reported incidents of a particular category of crime, which the police consider to be solved because they have arrested at least one suspect.

clinical fallacy Making the mistaken assumption that people who come in for treatment are very similar to those who do not seek help.

Code Adam An emergency procedure to lockdown a facility, such as a department store, to prevent a kidnapper from escaping with a captive.

cold case squad A special unit of detectives whose assignment is to reopen, reexamine, and resolve unsolved cases.

community service An alternative sentence that compels offenders to pay back society as a whole, rather than the specific individuals they directly harmed, by performing useful labor.

community policing An approach that emphasizes the importance of maintaining a close working relationship or partnership with neighborhood residents.

comparative risks Weighing the relative statistical odds of experiencing different kinds of misfortunes, such as crimes, accidents, and diseases.

compensatory damages A judgment won in civil court in which a plaintiff (victim) is to be repaid by a defendant for the injuries and losses sustained during a crime.

composition An ancient practice in which the payment of money or goods to a victim by an offender's family was intended to permanently settle a dispute.

Compstat A system of police management pioneered by the NYPD during the mid-1990s that closely monitors victimization patterns and statistical performance indicators and holds precinct commanders accountable for any failure to address problems in their jurisdictions.

conciliation A procedure in which disputants negotiate by communicating through a neutral third party.

confirmed terrorist attacks Incidents in which law enforcement agencies have identified the group responsible and its political motive.

conflict approach An orientation that focuses on laws and policies that reflect opposing interests and clashing goals due to struggles for resources and power.

conflict resolution An informal method that seeks compromise settlements through negotiations and avoids notions of guilt and innocence.

consideration Concessions offered by the prosecution during plea negotiations to induce defendants to admit guilt and forgo their constitutional right to a trial by a jury of their peers.

constructionist approach A perspective that focuses on how powerful elites try to impose their definitions of reality on other individuals and groups.

Consumer Sentinel Network A program of the Federal Trade Commission (FTC) that enables law enforcement agencies to access information in consumer complaints voluntarily filed with the government about white-collar crimes like fraud and identity theft.

contingency fees A financial arrangement in which the attorney representing the plaintiff (victim) in a civil lawsuit is paid an agreed-upon share of the judgment (monetary award), but only if the plaintiff is successful.

conversion of chattel In civil law, the tort of knowingly stealing or destroying a victim's possessions.

co-orientation A stage during a robbery in which the offender orders the victim to surrender and comply with instructions or else suffer severe consequences.

cop a plea Slang meaning to admit guilt during negotiations in return for "consideration" (concessions) by the prosecution that might disappoint a punitively oriented victim.

co-presence A stage during a robbery where the offender moves within striking distance without arousing either a flight or fight reaction from the target.

correlation An indication that there is some degree of association, connection, and perhaps a statistical relationship between two variables.

corroboration Evidence that supports or confirms a victim's accusations.

cost–benefit analysis A process that weighs the advantages versus the disadvantages (pros and cons) of adopting a certain policy.

creative restitution A situation in which the offender pays the victim back more than was required or expected.

Crime Clock A device used by the FBI in its *Uniform Crime Report* to illustrate how frequently a particular crime is committed within the entire United States.

crime conscious A person who is aware of the risks and ways of becoming a victim.

crime control An outlook that emphasizes the need for a firm and efficient criminal justice system as a means of protecting the law-abiding majority.

crime crash An expression that describes an unanticipated, dramatic drop in the crime rate; the opposite of a crime wave or spike.

crime prevention A collective political and economic strategy intended to eradicate the social conditions that are thought to generate criminal behavior.

crime prevention through environmental design (CPTED) A specific set of architectural features that are intended and expected to make it more difficult for offenders to carry out their illegal acts.

crime resistance Strategies and techniques undertaken by the victim to make the offender's tasks more difficult.

crime crash A sudden, sharp drop in the victimization rate, a much welcomed surprise.

crime wave A sudden, sharp rise in the victimization rate; the opposite of a crime crash.

criminology The scientific study of crimes, offenders, victims, criminal laws, the operations of the criminal justice system, and the social reaction to illegal behavior.

cruelty to children An old-fashioned expression that was parallel to cruelty to animals and that gave rise to the recognition of child abuse.

cumulative risks The chances of becoming a victim over the course of a lifetime.

cyberstalking The use of e-mail, postings on Internet websites, and other web-based and mobile social media of communication to threaten and harass someone.

deductible clause An agreement in an insurance policy that the company will not reimburse victims for relatively minor losses and expenses.

deep pockets An expression used in civil court to refer to persons and entities that have substantial assets that could be taken away if a plaintiff's (victim's) lawsuit succeeds.

default judgment A victory that is won in civil court because the other party fails to present a case.

defendants In criminal and civil court, individuals accused of being victimizers and violating laws.

defounding A process in which, after an investigation, the police downgrade the complainant's original accusations into less serious charges.

depositions In civil lawsuits, a witness's sworn testimony that is taken out-of-court, often as part of the discovery process; may be used under limited circumstances, at a trial.

deterrence theory A widely held belief that if individuals are punished they will learn a lesson not to behave that way again (specific deterrence); and that the suffering of punished persons will serve as a warning to others (general deterrence).

deviant lifestyles Routines and unconventional everyday patterns of behavior that generally elicit social disapproval, often centering on sexual activities, drug-taking, heavy drinking, and gang fighting.

deviant place factor An explanation for a geographic concentration of incidents that focuses on areas that attract criminally inclined people.

differential access to justice The accusation that criminal justice officials are not yet blind to the wealth, power, and prestige of specific victims and offenders, and consequently handle cases differently.

differential handling The accusation that some people receive better treatment in the criminal justice system than others because of sex, race, or class.

differential reporting rates Substantially different risks of being harmed are faced by individuals who fall into various groupings.

differential risks An observation that people in a particular group experience much higher or much lower rates of victimization than people who do not share this trait or factor in common.

direct or primary victims Individuals who suffer physical, economic, or emotional harm firsthand.

discovery In a civil lawsuit, a process in which each side demands information and answers from the other before the trial.

district attorney Chief of the government's prosecution unit within a jurisdiction; usually elected, and ostensibly representing victims as well as the organization and the public interest.

domestic chastisement A privilege formerly accorded to husbands to discipline their wives by using reasonable force.

domestic disturbances A phrase used by police departments to refer to calls for service involving violence between family members or intimate partners.

domestic terrorism Attacks to advance a political cause launched by groups within a country.

domestic tranquility A widely held illusion that women were safe when at home.

double indemnity clause A provision in a life insurance policy that pledges a payment of twice the normal amount if the covered individual dies accidentally or is murdered.

dual verbal defense A strategy of victims under attack that involves calling for help while simultaneously reasoning with, pleading with, or threatening the assailant.

due process A series of steps that must be followed in order to respect, guarantee, or safeguard the rights of a person in the criminal justice system.

dumpster diving A practice engaged in by identity thieves in which they retrieve important personal information thrown away by their intended victims.

elder abuse Harming older people physically, stealing from them, exploiting them financially, or neglecting them emotionally.

English common law The original source of most laws enacted in colonial America; a system of laws not formally written down but supposedly applicable to everyone.

equal protection under the law A pledge derived from the Fourteenth Amendment to the Constitution that promises that criminal justice decision makers will disregard a victim's or a defendant's social class, race, national origin, gender, sexual preference, age, or religion when making discretionary procedural decisions.

equalizers A view that firearms would protect victims under attack from assailants who have initial advantages such as larger size or greater numbers and the element of surprise.

equivalent group An outlook that emphasizes that victims often share many characteristics with their assailants.

exposure A risk factor that emphasizes how individuals and their possessions may be left unguarded and vulnerable to attack by would-be offenders in the vicinity.

external validity The extent to which the results of a research project can be generalized to other groups of people or other situations beyond those directly studied.

facilitation Careless or thoughtless behavior that makes a criminal's tasks easier, especially when perpetrating a theft of some kind.

facilitators A view that the presence of firearms makes it more likely that minor quarrels can escalate into shootings over disputes that should not be matters of life and death.

failure to warn An accusation in a civil lawsuit that a third party was grossly negligent by not notifying a person that he or she was in grave danger.

false imprisonment The unlawful detention or incarceration of an innocent person based on a false arrest, possibly due to a mistaken identification by a complainant.

false memory syndrome A condition that causes some individuals to believe they can recall abusive events that never took place.

false negatives People who are predicted to pose a low risk of criminal behavior but end up acting illegally.

false positives People who are predicted to pose a high risk of criminal behavior but apparently behave legally.

family group conferencing A method of implementing restorative justice that involves members of the community in negotiations to resolve a conflict and to repair the harm suffered by the victim.

first party The defendant in a lawsuit who is accused of harming the plaintiff (victim).

flag explanation A theory proposing that repeat victimizations occur because a target has permanent characteristics that attract criminals, such as being at a vulnerable location.

forward telescoping A tendency to believe that an offense occurred more recently than it actually did; a memory problem that is a source of inaccuracy for respondents in the *NCVS*.

free will A philosophical or religious concept that emphasizes the ability of individuals to make their own decisions and to choose among different courses of action.

funnel model Best pictured as a leaky net: many crimes take place but by the end of the adjudication process substantial case attrition has occurred and relatively few guilty parties end up behind bars.

funneling or shrinkage The reduction in the volume of cases for a number of reasons during the adjudication process.

garnish To seize a portion of a wrongdoer's earnings and give it to the victim as restitution.

going rate A shared notion among members of the courtroom workgroup about the appropriate punishment for conviction of a specific offense at a particular time and place.

government–liability rationale A belief that the state is obligated to pay compensation to violent crime victims because it prohibits law-abiding citizens from going around armed.

gross negligence A basis for a lawsuit that charges a third party with failing to provide adequate protection to a person who was harmed by a criminal in a foreseeable manner.

guardian ad litem (GAL) A court-appointed advocate who is responsible for pursuing the best interests of a child when an abusive or neglectful parent cannot fulfill that role.

gun surrender laws Legislation requiring individuals who are convicted of a crime or who are the subject of an injunction or restraining order to hand over any firearms in their possession to local law enforcement agencies.

hate crime An offense that is committed because of the perpetrator's hatred of people who are similar to the victim.

heiress stealing An old-fashioned practice of raping a young woman in order to force her and her parents to agree to a marriage with the assailant.

hot dots Individuals who are preyed upon repeatedly.

hierarchy rule An instruction from the FBI's Uniform Crime Reporting Division to local police departments to classify each incident in which several laws were broken solely in terms of the most serious offense that was committed.

hot spots Locations where crimes repeatedly take place and police are frequently summoned.

House of Refuge movement A coalition in the early 1800s that tried to salvage the lives of abused children by sending them to institutions that also housed delinquents.

ideal types A sociological term meaning the clearest cases and best examples for comparison purposes.

identity theft A white-collar crime in which an imposter obtains key bits of confidential personal information, such as a Social Security number, in order to impersonate someone else, usually in order to take out loans or obtain credit cards and run up charges or fees for services that the victim will be responsible for.

ideology A set of ideas and beliefs that guides the decisions and outlooks of political parties and social movements.

implied consent An assumption on the part of a male that a female's behavior indicated that she was willing to engage in sexual intercourse.

incidence rate A research-based estimate of the number of individuals who suffer a particular type of victimization in a particular year.

index crimes The eight crimes (seven if arson is excluded) in Part I of the *UCR* that are closely tracked and whose reported incidents are added together to calculate the total crime index for a particular year: murder, forcible rape, robbery, aggravated assault, burglary, larceny, and motor vehicle theft.

indirect or secondary victims Individuals who were not directly attacked but also suffer financially and emotionally, such as members of the injured party's family.

individualist rationale A view of self-defense that argues that a person under attack does not have to retreat from an aggressor.

informal justice An alternative approach to resolving cases that does not rely upon arrest, prosecution, and the exercise of formal rights by victims; includes both retaliatory violence and restorative justice.

institution blaming An approach that argues that deep-seated problems in a society's basic structures and fundamental relationships (its "system") are partly to blame for criminal activity and the resulting victimization.

instrumental coercion Using force to achieve a specific purpose.

international comparisons Compilations of statistics showing victimization rates in various countries and foreign cities during the same time period.

international terrorism Politically motivated attacks carried out by groups based in or originating from foreign countries.

interrogatories A set of written questions that must be answered as part of a lawsuit.

intimate partners People who currently are or formerly were lovers.

intimate partner violence (IPV) Repeated acts of violence by one person against another during or after a romantic relationship, whether or not they are living together.

inveiglement Enticement, persuasion to do something wrong.

judgment A victorious outcome providing relief for the plaintiff (victim) as a result of a jury verdict or a judge's decision in a civil lawsuit.

judgment-proof A defendant who is "financially insolvent" and has no assets or earnings and thus cannot be compelled to make payments after losing a civil lawsuit.

just deserts A philosophy that argues that offenders have "earned" their punishments and ought to suffer in ways that are in proportion to the seriousness of the harm they have inflicted on others.

just world outlook A victim-blaming belief that bad things happen only to bad people; those who suffer must have done something to deserve their fate.

justifiable homicide A legal ruling that a killing does not merit punishment, usually because it was the result of an act of self-defense in a perilous kill-or-be-killed confrontation.

law-and-order movement A coalition of victims, elected officials, and politically conservative organizations that since the 1960s has pressed for harsher punishments and an end to what they consider to be unwarranted leniency ("permissiveness").

lifestyle How a person spends his or her leisure time and disposable income.

lifetime likelihood A research-based projection of the proportion of a population that will probably experience a particular type of victimization during the course of their lives, based on current incidence rates.

likelihood or probability A statistical term assessing the odds or chances of something happening, ranging from 0 (impossible) to 1 (certainty).

lynching A violent mob action against a suspect or defendant accused of committing a serious crime, often instigated by vigilantes. The individual is brutally murdered, usually by being hanged by the neck.

macroscopic A view that looks at the larger picture at the expense of overlooking particular details.

malfeasance Carrying out required tasks ineptly.

maximalist An alarmist perspective that assumes the worst and calls for drastic measures to address a crisis.

means test A qualification in compensation program eligibility guidelines that eliminates from reimbursement those who are considered able to absorb or "afford" the loss without financial assistance.

mediation A method of resolving conflicts that counts on the effective intervention of a neutral third party who works with the disputants.

Megan's Law A statute named after a New Jersey girl murdered by a child molester that requires registration of sex offenders and community notification.

memory decay A problem of forgetfulness on the part of respondents that undermines the accuracy of the *NCVS*.

microscopic A view that looks closely at specific details at the expense of overlooking the larger picture.

minimalist A skeptical point of view that assumes many statistics are inflated and that their interpretation by maximalists exaggerates the true scope and seriousness of the crime problem.

misprision of a felony A deliberate and illegal attempt to cover up the fact that a serious crime was committed; a concealment of the facts that goes beyond a mere failure to report an offense to the authorities.

missing children A catch-all phrase popularized by the media to refer to the huge number of youngsters whose whereabouts are unknown to their caretakers at any given moment.

moderate correction The permissible use of reasonable force on occasion by a husband who felt compelled to "discipline" his wife.

muggability ratings An assessment by robbers of the attractiveness and vulnerability of specific potential targets.

muggings Unarmed robberies, also called in the past "strong-arm" or "yokings."

multidoor courthouse A neighborhood justice center that offers conciliation, mediation, and arbitration as ways of settling disputes that might otherwise be sent to civil or criminal court.

National Crime Victimization Survey (NCVS) An annual undertaking since 1973 that attempts to determine how frequently certain crimes take place, who suffers and to what degree, and what proportion of victims report the incidents to the police; originally called the *National Crime Survey (NCS)*.

needs assessment A research-based report that outlines the kinds of help victims require in order to recover from the financial, physical, and emotional damage they suffered.

negligence Grounds for a lawsuit; doing something without the care required by circumstances as foreseen by a prudent person, or not taking any action, resulting in harm to an innocent person.

neighborhood justice center A place offering a variety of alternatives to settle minor conflicts that otherwise would be resolved in civil or criminal court.

no-drop prosecution A practice adopted by some district attorneys to press assault charges in domestic violence cases even if the battered woman decides to discontinue her cooperation.

nonfeasance Grounds for a lawsuit; not taking action or not doing what is required.

normative ambiguity A situation in which conventional standards of behavior and recommended courses of action differ considerably from the beliefs of a particular group, such as a street gang.

objectivity A stance of neutrality, evenhandedness, and open-mindedness that is desirable in victimology to avoid either pro-victim or antivictim biases.

offender blaming An approach that rejects both system blaming as well as victim blaming, and holds a wrongdoer solely responsible for harming a victim.

offenderology A critique of criminology that condemns its alleged preoccupation with or exclusive focus on wrongdoers and its systematic inattention to victims.

official statistics Measurements and data disseminated from government agencies.

operationalize A step in the data gathering process in which the researcher decides what to include and exclude when making measurements.

order of protection A restraining order issued by a judge that forbids a specific person from having contact with a particular victim.

outlet-attractor perspective An explanation that accounts for an outbreak of crimes concentrated near certain bars and clubs, or other sources of alcoholic beverages.

overcharging An abusive practice in which prosecutors lodge all plausible charges against a defendant including ones that are not well supported by the available evidence.

pain and suffering A basis for seeking a judgment in civil lawsuits; an attempt to determine an appropriate amount of monetary compensation for the emotional damage as well as from the physical injuries endured by a plaintiff due to the defendant's criminal behavior.

Part I crimes The FBI's Uniform Crime Report designation for four crimes "against the person" (murder, forcible rape, robbery, and aggravated assault) and four crimes "against property" (burglary, larceny, motor vehicle theft, and arson) that are closely monitored.

Part II crimes The FBI's Uniform Crime Report designation for a grouping of over twenty types of crimes for which the number of arrests are tabulated.

patriarchy A system in which men (in their roles as fathers and husbands) rule over women and girls; the justification for the subordination of females is based on beliefs about male supremacy.

patterns Regularities and predictable relationships that emerge during the analysis of victimization data.

peacemaking circles An approach within restorative justice that attempts to draw a number of interested parties into the process of settling a conflict.

pecuniary damages A basis for civil lawsuits that focuses on financial harm.

penalty assessments A mechanism that enables state governments to raise money to pay for compensation programs by levying fines on all sorts of lawbreakers ("abusers' taxes").

performance measures Statistical indicators revealing the degree to which organizations, such as police departments, are meeting the goals they have set.

pharming A hacker slang term referring to a deceitful practice in which unsuspecting computer users are redirected from legitimate websites to fraudulent ones so that their confidential data can be stolen by identity thieves.

phishing A deceitful practice intended to obtain confidential information from unsuspecting computer users, usually by sending an email that looks as if it is from a legitimate organization, such as a bank or credit card company, which contains a link to a fake website that appears to be genuine.

plaintiff A person who feels victimized and who files a lawsuit in civil court against a defendant or a negligent third party.

plea bargain An out-of-court settlement negotiated by a prosecutor and a defense attorney, in which the accused admits guilt and forfeits the right to a trial by jury in return for some concession by the government.

plea negotiation A longstanding practice in which the prosecution offers some concessions to the defense to convince the accused to admit guilt and settle the case without going to trial.

pleadings Formal arguments about claims and defenses put forward by both parties in a civil suit.

post-traumatic stress disorder (PTSD) A persistent, recurring, intense emotional reaction that is triggered by a highly unusual and potentially serious crisis such as a violent crime.

precipitation A situation in which the person who is targeted may be considered partly at fault for attracting the offender's interest or attention prior to an attack.

preponderance of the evidence The burden of proof in civil proceedings in which the side that presents the slightly more impressive, truthful, or convincing case wins.

presentence investigation report An investigation conducted by an officer of the probation department to bring to the judge's attention information about the convicted person, the crime, and the degree of harm suffered by victims.

prevalence rate A research-based estimate of the proportion of the population that has ever experienced a particular type of victimization during their lifetimes up to that point in time; as distinct from cumulative risk or lifetime likelihood, which is a prediction about future events.

preventions An FBI term to describe terrorist plots that were thwarted.

primary prevention programs Before any violence breaks out, training high-risk potential victimizers and victims (such as intimate partners) how to work out compromises and avoid resorting to force to settle their disputes.

principle of homogamy An observation that the offender and the victim, such as in instances of road rage, have a great deal in common.

private prosecution An unusual arrangement permitted in a few jurisdictions in which a victim is entitled to hire a lawyer and press charges in criminal court.

mandatory, or pro-arrest, directive A departmental policy that instructs officers to tend to arrest the person who appears to be the aggressor in domestic disturbances.

process server A person hired to officially inform a defendant that a plaintiff has filed a lawsuit in civil court against him or her, claiming to be harmed and seeking compensation.

profiles Statistically based portraits of the characteristics most offenders or victims share in common.

provocation An act that triggers, instigates, or incites someone who was not criminally inclined to commit an unlawful attack.

proximity Being within striking distance of an offender.

proxy stalking The recruitment of a third party by a stalker to carry out the actual surveillance and shadowing of the target.

pseudomemories Recollections of events that never happened.

public prosecutors Lawyers working for the government who represent the interests of victims but also their agency as well as society at large.

punitive damages A part of a lawsuit that requests additional money beyond mere reimbursement of expenses for the plaintiff as a way of punishing a defendant for committing a crime.

punitive rationale An argument justifying the use of force in self-defense that rests on the social and moral necessity of punishing wrongdoing.

range (confidence interval) A statistical notion that predicts that the true but unknown answer is very likely to fall somewhere between the minimum and maximum value; an issue that arises when interpreting the findings of any survey, including the *NCVS*.

rape crisis syndrome An intense emotional reaction to being violated that repeatedly burdens a victim in the aftermath of a sexual assault.

rape kit A collection of samples of forensic evidence (such as blood, hairs, and DNA) collected directly from the victim's body, which could be tested at a crime lab in order to try to identify the assailant.

rates A way of expressing risks or odds by comparing the number of victims out of every 1,000 individuals, or per 100,000 people or households, in a single year; the use of rates makes it possible to compare the experiences of groups or populations of different sizes.

rational choice theory An explanation for behavior that presumes that would-be lawbreakers (or potential victims) mull over their decisions and weigh the costs and benefits of their conduct before they act.

rationale of necessity A justification for using force as a means of self-protection to prevent serious injury.

raw numbers The actual number of victims, such as a body count or death toll in murders, as opposed to the rate per 100,000 per year.

reasonableness standard An argument that rests on the assumption that most rational people would arrive at the same conclusion.

red carpet or VIP treatment A situation in which victims receive preferential handling by criminal justice officials that is clearly superior to what others experience.

redlining An illegal practice in banking and insurance that involves discrimination against all the disadvantaged people who live in a troubled neighborhood, usually by denying them coverage or charging exorbitant rates.

reform A change for the better in the opinion of supporters, although people holding opposing views would disagree.

restorative justice An approach to resolving criminal cases that rejects inflicting punishment and pursuing retribution in favor of seeking restitution followed by victim–offender reconciliation.

restraining order An order of protection issued by a judge that forbids a specific person from having contact with a particular victim.

retagging Stealing a car and then falsifying its paperwork so that it can be sold as a used car.

retaliatory justice A violent response that emphasizes that the offender must suffer physically at least as much as the victim suffered; usually meted out informally on the spot as "curbstone" or "street justice."

retributive justice A punitive approach that emphasizes the necessity of an offender "paying a debt to society" by serving time behind bars.

right to self-defense The philosophy that victims under attack are justified to use as much force as necessary to protect themselves and their property from harm.

risk–benefit analysis An approach that weighs the pros and cons, or potential losses and gains, of a possible course of action.

risk-management tactics Ways to protect oneself against the dangers of being victimized while carrying out unavoidable activities.

risk-reduction activities Ways to limit exposure to dangers and of hardening targets that are likely to be attacked, to improve the odds faced by potential victims.

road rage An outburst of violence triggered by an incident while driving.

routine activities Everyday responsibilities and behaviors that shape lifestyles and determine risks; part of a theory that predicts patterns of victimization based on the presence of motivated offenders, the absence of suitable guardians, and the availability of attractive targets.

rule of thumb A term in architecture; and possibly centuries ago, a restriction that limited husbands to using sticks no thicker than their thumbs when beating their wives.

safe haven law A provision that enables a new mother to permanently relinquish her parental rights to an unwanted newborn baby, by carefully dropping it off at an authorized location, without penalties.

SAID syndrome An accusation that false charges are being lodged in family court; voiced during a bitter child custody battle following a divorce; the claim is that one party (usually the wife) is dishonestly charging the other party with sexually abusing their child in order to discredit a parent seeking joint custody or visitation rights.

second party The plaintiff (victim) who pursues a lawsuit against the first party (the defendant).

second wound Additional emotional suffering inflicted on a victim by insensitive caregivers and family members; usually arising from victim-blaming accusations.

secondary prevention programs Training couples who have engaged in intimate partner violence to use negotiation and anger management techniques to settle disputes without resorting to force; also, teaching abusive parents how to properly raise their children.

second-class treatment Recognized as part of differential handling; inferior treatment of certain victims by government officials; as opposed to red-carpet or VIP treatment.

selective-disinhibition perspective An explanation for misbehavior due to intoxication.

self-help movement A coalition of individuals and organizations who know from their own direct, firsthand experience just how a victim is suffering.

self-report survey A research tool that depends upon respondents revealing their experiences as victims or as offenders.

sensationalism A tendency to exaggerate or distort aspects of a crime to attract greater media coverage for personal and commercial gain; an exploitive attention-grabbing practice engaged in by television, radio, and newspaper reporters, editors, and headline writers.

sentence disparity Sharp differences in punishments imposed on people who committed the same crime.

series victimizations Repeated incidents of a similar nature suffered by the same person.

sexual assault Rape or other unwanted forceful sexual contacts and physical impositions against the victim's will.

sexual assault response teams Joint efforts by police departments, prosecutor's offices, and hospitals to provide more coordinated and comprehensive services to rape victims.

shared responsibility The perspective that the offender does not bear total responsibility for the criminal act, and that some of the blame falls either on the victim or the social system, or both.

shared-risk rationale The belief that funds set aside for compensating victims should be accumulated in a way that is similar to the collection of insurance premiums, so that reimbursement is feasible when disaster strikes.

shelters Safe houses where battered women and their young children can flee to and take temporary refuge during a crisis.

shield laws Provisions prohibiting the introduction of evidence or cross examination about the past sexual experiences of a rape victim if a judge considers this information to be irrelevant to the question of guilt or innocence of the alleged assailant.

shoulder surfers Identity thieves who attempt to spot passwords and other confidential information.

situational crime prevention A strategy that depends on reducing the opportunities for criminals to commit crime by making it appear less rewarding, more difficult, and riskier.

situational factors Outside elements that can influence behavior, including encouraging or discouraging attempts to victimize others.

skimmers Mechanical and electronic devices that enable identity thieves to capture an individual's credit card, debit card, and personal identification numbers (PINs).

social construction A view that influential people and powerful groups determine which specific individuals are defined as legitimate victims deserving of support.

social ecology of victimization An attempt to identify under what circumstances, where, and when various groups face the greatest risks of suffering interpersonal violence and theft.

social rationale A justification for compensating innocent victims because of the social system's inability to eradicate the social roots of crime that predictably result in outbreaks of violence.

social-justice rationale A justification for using force in self-defense as a way of preserving law and order in the community.

social-welfare approach A justification for compensating innocent victims of violent crimes because the government has a humanitarian obligation to provide a safety net to help needy and disadvantaged persons who are suffering from devastating criminal acts.

sovereign immunity The protection of certain government officials such as judges or members of a parole board from civil lawsuits challenging the exercise of their discretion after they mistakenly release an offender from custody who then commits an unforeseeable violent crime.

speak-outs Events at which victims reveal the details of their plight.

spin A slanted or biased way of looking at a situation or interpreting a statistic that can be challenged or questioned.

stalking The carrying out repeatedly of specific unwanted harassing and ominous behaviors that threaten bodily injury by one person against another, who can be a complete stranger, an acquaintance, or even a former intimate partner.

statistics Important numbers that can be used as evidence to confirm or undermine some argument.

statistical portrait A mathematic picture of what is typical or usual about victims.

statute of limitations A provision in the law that states that a person can no longer be held criminally responsible after this amount of time has expired.

statutory rape Consensual sex involving a minor considered too young and immature to make such an important choice as granting consent.

stigma contests Struggles to shape public opinion involving attempts to discredit certain persons versus their attempts to gain respectability and sympathy.

Stockholm syndrome Behavior by a hostage during and after the period of captivity that appears to be unduly sympathetic or supportive of the situation of the kidnapper.

street crimes A broad category that usually refers to acts of interpersonal violence and theft.

strong-arm robberies Unarmed robberies in which no weapon is used.

subculture of violence The way of life of a group that appears to condone or even approve of the use of force to settle disputes.

subintentional death Provocative behavior that can cause a victim, who harbors self-destructive impulses to get killed in a confrontation with a powerful adversary.

subjective approach In contrast to the objective approach, reactions to victimizations that are based on emotions and allegiances.

subrogated A legal term meaning substituted for, or subtracted from.

Supplementary Homicide Report (SHR) A form police departments fill out and send to the FBI's Uniform Crime Reporting Division that contains whatever details are known about the murder.

survivors The next of kin of murder victims; also, a term of respect applied to those victims who have undergone traumatic experiences and ordeals.

survivorology An emerging branch of victimology that focuses on individual character traits and other sources of resiliency that enable certain victims to recover from their ordeals in exemplary ways.

suspected terrorist attacks An FBI categorization about unsolved offenses in which the perpetrator's motives cannot be confirmed.

symbolic restitution Made by offenders, partial repayments or token amounts delivered to individuals or organizations that substitute for actual victims.

system blaming A viewpoint that does not hold either the offender or the victim fully culpable for what happened, but places some of the responsibility on a society's social institutions and economic and political arrangements.

target hardening A strategy that relies on making the offender's tasks even more difficult and discouraging; the opposite of facilitation.

techniques of neutralization A social theory, which proposes that offenders have learned certain pat answers that neutralize their guilt over harming others.

theoretical explanations Attempts to account for the reasons why certain people, including offenders or victims, think and act as they do.

third parties People, businesses, or organizations that are neither victims nor offenders but are accused of gross negligence and are sued in civil court for monetary damages for allegedly inadvertently contributing to the harmful incident.

throwaways Children expelled from their homes by their parents or guardians.

tort law Civil law governing the redress of private wrongs through suits in courts.

torts Ways individuals can suffer harm that can be redressed in civil court through monetary judgments.

trafficking in human beings Often considered a type of modern day slavery, an illegal trade in smuggled persons who are held against their will or subjected to various forms of coercion so they don't seek help from the authorities after their sexuality or labor has been exploited.

trend analysis Discerning upward or downward changes that take place over the years by compiling data in a table or drawing a graph.

trends Increases or decreases in a variable over time.

trespass In criminal and civil law, an intentional invasion of another person's space or land.

truth-in-sentencing rule Laws passed ostensibly to give victims and the general public realistic notions of how long an offender will be incapacitated; in reality, laws designed to keep convicts incarcerated for longer periods of time before becoming eligible for release on parole.

typology A classification system that attempts to sort each case into some category.

unfounded report A complaint that the police reject as untrue or unsupported by sufficient evidence.

unfounding A process in which detectives decide that there is insufficient evidence to justify continuing an investigation of a complainant's allegations.

Uniform Crime Report (UCR) An annual, national compilation based on a total number of crimes known to local police departments.

unnatural severity An old-fashioned term for child abuse; overly strict parenting.

valve theory of crime shifts The belief that protecting one type of target deflects criminally inclined people toward a comparable but more vulnerable type of target.

victim A person who suffers physical, emotional, and/or financial harm because of illegal activity.

victim blaming An approach that holds an injured party partly responsible for what happened.

victim defending A perspective that denies that an injured party should be held partly responsible for what happened; the belief that the blame falls solely on the offender, or the social system, or both.

victim impact statement A document about losses and injuries used by the judge in court to help determine the severity of the sentence meted out to a person convicted of a crime.

victim–offender mediation A process that enables both parties to meet, discuss, and negotiate a mutually agreed-upon and hopefully permanent settlement of their conflict.

victimism An outlook that traces deleterious consequences of past injustices right up to the present; often confused with the scientific study of the suffering experienced by crime victims.

victimization An asymmetrical relationship that is abusive, painful, destructive, parasitical, and unfair.

victimization prevention Specific precautions taken by particular individuals intended to increase their personal safety, in contrast to crime prevention, which is societal in scope.

victimization rates The chances of becoming harmed by a particular crime, usually expressed as "for every 1,000 persons age 12 and older per year" (in the *NCVS*) or "per 100,000 inhabitants per year" (in the *UCR*).

victimology The scientific study of the victim's plight, the criminal justice system's responses, and the public's reactions; usually viewed as a branch of criminology.

victims' rights Pledges as well as guarantees concerning how an injured party will be handled by officials and agencies during the criminal justice process.

victim/witness assistance programs (VWAPs) Programs run by prosecutors' offices to provide tangible services and protection from reprisals to victims and other witnesses for the state.

video portraits Projections of how a missing child might look as time passes.

vigilantism Retaliatory violence vented by victims and their supporters against individuals suspected of being offenders.

vulnerability A prediction about the degree of susceptibility of a target to attack.

widening the net A tendency within criminal justice to intervene in situations that in the past had been overlooked or left alone.

women's movement A coalition guided by the ideology of feminism that seeks reforms, equal rights, and the empowerment of girls and women to reduce their vulnerability and suffering, especially victims of intimate partner violence, sexual assaults, incest, and stalking.

working definition A decision by a researcher about what to include and what to exclude when making measurements.

wrongful death The basis of a civil lawsuit by the family of a murder victim.

wrongful escape The basis of a civil lawsuit by a plaintiff (victim) that alleges gross negligence on the part of a third party in a department of corrections considered responsible for the harm caused by an escaped inmate.

wrongful release The basis of a civil lawsuit by a plaintiff (victim) against a third party in a department of corrections considered grossly negligent for improperly allowing a dangerous inmate to leave confinement.

yokings Unarmed robberies; muggings.

zero-sum game model An approach that assumes that the gains made by one party come at the expense of losses experienced by the other party.

References

ABA. *See* American Bar Association.

Abbey, A. (2005, January). Lessons learned and unanswered questions about sexual assault perpetration. *Journal of Interpersonal Violence, 20,* 39–42.

Abbey, A., Zawacki, T., Buck, P., Clinton, M., & McAuslan, P. (2004, May–June). Sexual assault and alcohol consumption. *Aggression and Violent Behavior, 9,* 271–303.

Abby-Lambertz, K. (2014, August 8). Theodore Wafer found guilty of second-degree murder in death of Renisha McBride. *Huffington Post.* Retrieved August 10, 2014, from http://www.huffingtonpost.com/2014/08/07/theodore-wafer-guilty-renisha-mcbride_n_5655163.html.

ABC News/Washington Post Poll. (2013, April 11–April 14). Experience as a victim of gun crime. Retrieved December 22, 2014, from http://www.pollingreport.com/guns.htm.

Abel, D. (2013, October 15). First responders still in grip of Marathon's horror. *Boston Globe.* Retrieved September 20, 2014, from http://www.bostonglobe.com/metro/2013/10/14/coping-with-aftermath-marathon-bombings-some-first-responders-struggle/P4u35gXwcFlNZcYd3eLnzH/story.html.

———. (2014, June 20). Marathon bombings survivors seek more aid. *Boston Globe.* Retrieved December 19, 2014, from http://www.bostonglobe.com/metro/2014/06/20/marathon-bombing-survivors-question-one-fund/mbSvBh251ZrlgoG6F8YVaP/story.html.

Abel, C., & Marsh, F. (1984). *Punishment and restitution: A restitutionary approach to crime and the criminal.* Westport, CT: Greenwood Press.

Able, R. (1982). *The politics of informal justice: Vol. 1. The American experience.* New York: Academic Press.

Abraham, Y. (2014, August 9). For victims of domestic violence, each day carries danger. *Boston Globe.* Retrieved September 10, 2014, from http://www.bostonglobe.com/metro/2014/08/09/for-victims-domestic-violence-each-day-carries-danger/3NBK4TZqLMWq0vLWYXAl6H/story.html.

Abramovitz, M. (2001, March). The knockout punch of date rape drugs. *Current Health, 27,* 18–22.

Abramovsky, A. (1992, Fall). Victim impact statements: Adversely impacting upon judicial fairness. *St. John's Journal of Legal Commentary, 8,* 21–35.

Abrams, A. (1987, December 21). Sharing sorrow: Shelter helps turn victims into survivors. *New York Newsday,* pp. 2, 40.

Abramson, L. (1994, July 25). Unequal justice. *Newsweek,* p. 25.

Achimovic, L. (2003). *Parent alienation syndrome revisited.* Canberra, Australia: Australian Institute of Criminology.

ACF. *See* Administration for Children and Families.

ACLU. *See* American Civil Liberties Union.

Acohido, B. (2014, February 10). Point-of-sales systems targeted in retailer data thefts. *USA Today.* Retrieved December 1, 2014, from http://www.usatoday.com/story/cybertruth/2014/01/13/point-of-sale-systems-targeted-in-retailer-data-thefts/4457279/.

Acorn, A. (2004). *Compulsory compassion: A critique of restorative justice.* Vancouver, Canada: UBC Press.

ADL. *See* Anti-Defamation League.

Adame, J. (2014, February 24). Are domestic violence homicides preventable? *The Crime Report.* Retrieved November 21, 2014, from www.thecrimereport.org.

Adams, S. (2009, October 27). Date rape drink-spiking an "urban legend?" *The Telegraph.* Retrieved December 20, 2011, from www.telegraph.co.uk.

502

Adler, J. (1994, January 10). Kids growing up scared. *Newsweek*, pp. 43–50.

Administration for Children and Families (ACF), U.S. Department of Health and Human Services. (2010). Fourth national incidence study of child abuse and neglect. *ACF.gov*. Retrieved December 9, 2011, from http://www.acf.hhs.gov/programs/opre/resource/fourth-national-incidence-study-of-child-abuse-and-neglect-nis-4-report-to.

———. (2013). Child maltreatment 2012. *ACF.gov*. Retrieved November 9, 2014, from http://www.acf.hhs.gov/sites/default/files/cb/cm2012.pdf.

Aguayo, T. (2006, July 1). Confession barred because of request for lawyer. *New York Times*, p. A18.

Aguiluz, E. (2011, March 23). Mob attack: Michael Zenquis wrongly beaten and accused of rape. Retrieved January 20, 2012, from www.philadelphiacriminallawnews.com.

Aguirre, A., Davin, R., Baker, D., & Konrad, L. (1999). Sentencing outcomes, race, and victim impact evidence in California. *The Justice Professional*, 11(3), 297–310.

Ahrens, J., Stein, J., & Young, M. (1980). *Law enforcement and victim services*. Washington, DC: Aurora Associates.

Ai, A., & Park, C. (2005, February). Possibilities of the positive following violence and trauma. *Journal of Interpersonal Violence*, 20, 242–250.

AIUSA. *See* Amnesty International, USA.

Akiyama, Y. (1981, March). Murder victimization: A statistical analysis. *FBI Law Enforcement Bulletin*, 50(3), 8–11.

Alabama Coalition Against Domestic Violence (ACADV). (2011). Dating violence. Retrieved October 21, 2011, from www.acadv.org.

Albanesius, C. (2011, July 11). Sony extends PlayStation ID theft protection. Retrieved October 31, 2011, from www.pcmag.com.

Albrecht, B., Albrecht, C., & Tzafrir, S. (2011). How to protect and minimize consumer risk to identity theft. *Journal of Financial Crime*, 18(4), 405–414.

Alexander, M. (2012). *The new Jim Crow: Mass incarceration in the age of colorblindness*. New York: New Press.

Alexander, R. (1992). Victims' rights and the Son of Sam law: Implications for free speech and research on offenders. *Criminal Justice Policy Review*, 6, 275–290.

Allan, E., & Madden, M. (2008, March). Hazing in view: College students at risk. Retrieved December 27, 2011, from www.hazingstudy.org.

Allbritten, R., & Allbritten, W. (1985). The hidden victims: Courtship violence among college students. *Journal of College Student Personnel*, 26, 201–204.

Allen, H., Friday, P., Roebuck, J., & Sagarin, E. (1981). *Crime and punishment: An introduction to criminology*. New York: Free Press.

Allen, N. (1980). *Homicide: Perspectives on prevention*. New York: Human Sciences Press.

Allison, J., & Wrightsman, L. (1993). *Rape: The misunderstood crime*. Newbury Park, CA: Sage.

Allredge, E. (1942). Why the South leads the nation in murder and manslaughter. *Quarterly Review*, 2, 123–134.

Almanzar, Y. (2008, December 16). 27 years later, case is closed in slaying of abducted child. *New York Times*, p. A17.

Alper, B., & Nichols, L. (1981). *Beyond the courtroom*. Lexington, MA: Lexington Books.

Altman, R., & Aguayo, T. (2006, August 27). Here illegally, Guatemalans are prime targets of crime. *New York Times*, p. A12.

Anderle, M. (2013, July 26). Cruise ship crimes: 928 cases withheld despite transparency law. *Newsmax*. Retrieved September 30, 2014, from http://www.Newsmax.com/TheWire/cruise-ship-crimes-withheld/2013/07/26/id/517225/#ixzz3ErBk49qr.

Anglen, R. (2014). New law would make crimes aboard cruise ships public. *Arizona Republic*. Retrieved December 29, 2014, from http://www.azcentral.com/story/money/business/consumer/call-12-for-action/2014/12/07/new-law-force-cruise-lines-reveal-crimes/20039129/.

Alvarez, L. (2012, March 21). A Florida law gets scrutiny after a killing. *New York Times*, pp. A1, A15.

———., & Buckley, C. (2013, July 13). Zimmerman is acquitted in Trayvon Martin killing. *New York Times*, pp. A1, A12.

American Bar Association (ABA) Committee on Victims. (1979). *Reducing victim/witness intimidation: A package*. Washington, DC: Author.

American Civil Liberties Union (ACLU). (2005). 9/11 victims' families and national security whistle-blowers demand an end to government silencing of employees who expose security risks. *Press Release*, January 26. Retrieved November 2, 2005, from www.aclu.org. ACLU.

———. (2008). Prisoner's rights—ACLU position paper. Retrieved May 2, 2008, from www.aclu.org.

American Rifleman. (2014, October). Bloomberg ad inadvertently portrays limits of gun control agenda. *American Rifleman*, p. 91.

Ames, M. (2005). *Going postal: Rage, murder, and rebellion: From Reagan's workplaces to Clinton's Columbine and beyond*. New York: Soft Skull Press.

Amir, D., & Amir, M. (1979). Rape crisis centers: An arena for ideological conflicts. *Victimology*, 4(2), 247–257.

Amir, M. (1967). Victim precipitated forcible rape. *Journal of Criminal Law, Criminology, and Police Science*, 58, 493–502.

———. (1971). *Patterns in forcible rape*. Chicago: University of Chicago Press.

Amnesty International, USA (AIUSA). (1999). *United States of America: Race, rights, and police brutality.* New York: Amnesty International.

Anderson, B. (2008, April 18). Dead zone of the human spirit. *City Journal.* Retrieved October 13, 2008, from www.city-journal.org.

Anderson, C. (2014, July 5). Bill helps victims' compensation fund stay solvent. *Delaware State News.* Retrieved December 13, 2014, from http://delaware.newszap.com/centraldelaware/133353-70/bill-helps-victims-compensation-fund-stay-solvent.

Anderson, D. (1999, October). The aggregate burden of crime. *Journal of Law and Economics, 42,* 611–642.

Anderson, D. (2011). Emmett Till case. Retrieved August 26, 2011, from www.emmetttillmurder.com.

Anderson, E. (1999). *The code of the streets.* New York: W.W. Norton.

Anderson, E. (2014, August 6). Jurors hear closing arguments in Wafer fatal porch shooting trial. *Detroit Free Press.* Retrieved August 21, 2014, from http://www.freep.com/article/20140806/NEWS05/308060160.

Anderson, M., & Renzetti, C. (1980, July). Rape crisis counseling and the culture of individualism. *Contemporary Crises, 4,* 323–341.

Andrews, L. (1986, December). Are we raising a terrified generation? *Parents,* 139–142, 228–230.

Angier, N. (2014, April 1). Spite is good. Spite works. *New York Times,* pp. D1, D3.

Anti-Defamation League (ADL). Hate crimes laws. Retrieved July 17, 2003, from www.adl.org/99hatecrime.

AP. *See* Associated Press.

Applebome, P. (2008, November 19). Immigrant's death overshadows a debate. *New York Times,* p. A36.

Archambault, J. (2005, January). How many rape reports are false? *The Crime Victims Report, 8,* 83–84.

Arias, E., & Smith, B. (2003, March 14). Deaths: Preliminary data for 2001. *National Vital Statistics Report* (CDC NVSS), *51,* 1–5.

Armour, M. (2012, Winter). Restorative justice: Some facts and history. *Tikkun,* 25–26, 64. Retrieved January 27, 2012, from www.tikkun.org.

Armour, M., & Umbreit, M. (2006). Victim forgiveness in restorative justice dialogue. *Victims and Offenders, 1*(2), 123–140.

Arriaga, X., & Capezza, N. (2005, January). Targets of partner violence: The importance of understanding coping trajectories. *Journal of Interpersonal Violence, 20,* 85–99.

Asbridge, M., & Butters, J. (2013). Driving frequency and its impact on road rage offending and victimization: A view from opportunity theory. *Violence and Victims, 28*(4), 602–618.

Asbridge, M., Smart, R., & Mann, R. (2003). The "homogamy" of road rage. *Violence and Victims, 18*(5), 517–540.

———. (2006, April). Can we prevent road rage? *Trauma, Violence, and Abuse, 7*(2), 109–121.

Ash, M. (1972, December). On witnesses: A radical critique of criminal court procedures. *Notre Dame Lawyer, 48,* 386–425.

Ashman, C., & Trescott, P. (1987). *Diplomatic crimes.* Washington, DC: Acropolis Books.

Asmussen, K., & Creswell, J. (1995, September). Campus response to a student gunman. *The Journal of Higher Education, 66*(5), 575–598.

Associated Press (AP). (1984, September 20). Victims to get "Son of Sam" cash. *New York Times,* p. B3.

———. (1994a, January 8). Mother gets 10 years for slaying molester suspect. *New York Times,* p. A7.

———. (1994b, June 12). Notifying the next of kin: The worst job is often poorly done. *New York Times,* p. A35.

———. (1996, July 3). Found memory murder case won't be retried. *Long Island Newsday,* p. A44.

———. (1999a, May 7). Amy Fisher wins parole after 6 years in prison for shooting. *New York Times,* p. B12.

———. (1999b, October 15). Some park visitors stroll safely, then claim robbery. *New York Times,* p. B4.

———. (2005, November 19). Actor is ordered to pay $30 million in killing. *New York Times,* p. A17.

———. (2006, August 9). Oregon nurse returning home discovers intruder, strangles him with bare hands. Retrieved October 3, 2008, from www.ap.org.

———. (2007b, June 14). Data shed light on child sexual abuse by Protestant clergy. *New York Times,* p. A12.

———. (2008a, February 10). Man beaten with baseball bat, shot after accused rape. Retrieved September 28, 2008, from www.ap.org.

———. (2008b, February 15). List of recent deadly campus shootings. Retrieved September 8, 2008, from www.ap.org.

———. (2008c, March 31). Two freeway shootings, 1 fatal, extend a string in California. Retrieved April 28, 2008, from www.nytimes.com.

———. (2008d). Vigilante killer Ellie Nesler dies at 56. *USA Today.* Retrieved January 20, 2012, from www.usatoday.com.

———. (2009, May 15). Cities with most, fewest instances of road rage ranked. Retrieved September 18, 2011, from www.ap.org.

———. (2010, November 10). Utah: An almost-rescue recounted. Retrieved November 28, 2011, from www.ap.org.

————. (2011a, May 25). Utah: Street preacher gets life sentence for abduction. Retrieved November 28, 2011, from www.ap.org.

————. (2011b, June 1). New York rape victim leads project to catch predators. Retrieved December 18, 2011, from www.ap.org.

————. (2011c, December 15). On long Island, theory of single killer divides officials. Retrieved December 18, 2011, from www.ap.org.

————. (2013, March 22). Parents meet father of gunman in Sandy Hook massacre. *New York Times*, p. A14.

————. (2014a, July 4). Ohio rape kit DNA tests yield nearly 1,500 hits. *CBS Cleveland*. Retrieved January 5, 2015, from http://cleveland.cbslocal.com/2014/07/04/ohio-rape-kit-dna-tests-yield-nearly-1500-hits/.

————. (2014b, December 18). AP examines deaths of kids known to child protective services. *Milwaukee Wisconsin Journal Sentinel*. Retrieved December 29, 2014, from http://www.jsonline.com/news/wisconsin/ap-examines-deaths-of-kids-known-to-child-protective-services-b99410970z1-286276231.html.

Astin, M., Lawrence, K., & Foy, D. (1993). Posttraumatic stress disorder among battered women: Risk and resiliency factors. *Violence and Victims, 8*(1), 17–28.

Aunapu, G., Epperson, S., Kramer, S., Lafferty, E., & Martin, K. (1993, December 27). Robbing the innocents. *Time*, p. 31.

Austern, D. (1987). *The crime victim's handbook*. New York: Penguin.

Austin Police Department. (2011). No cost precautions. Retrieved October 25, 2011, from www.ci.austin.tx.us/police.

Auto theft alert. (1994, Fall). CAR (Citizens for Auto-Theft Responsibility). *Newsletter,*p.7.

Ayar, A. (2006, Summer). Road rage: Recognizing a psychological disorder. *Journal of Psychiatry and Law, 34*, 123–133.

Ayres, B. (1994, May 22). Big gains are seen in battle to stem drunk driving. *New York Times*, pp. A1, A24.

————. (1997, February 5). Civil jury finds Simpson liable in pair of killings. *New York Times*, pp. A1, A16.

Bachman, R. (1994).*Violence against women: A National Crime Victimization Survey report. BJS*. Washington, DC: U.S. Department of Justice.

————. (1998). The factors related to rape reporting behavior and arrest: New evidence from the National Crime Victimization Survey. *Criminal Justice and Behavior, 25*(1), 8–29.

Bachman, R., & Paternoster, R. (1993). A contemporary look at the effects of rape law reform: How far have we really come? *Journal of Criminal Law and Criminology, 84*(3), 554–574.

Bahr, R. (1985, May). The threat of vigilantism. *Kiwanis*, pp. 20–24.

Baird, S., & Jenkins, S. (2003, February). Vicarious traumatization, secondary traumatic stress, and burnout in sexual assault and domestic violence agency staff. *Violence and Victims, 18*, 71–84.

Baker, A. (2011, December 30). Police tactic: Keeping crime reports off the books. *New York Times*, p. B4.

————., & Maag, R. (2011, October 25). 3 arrested in killing of woman near school. *New York Times*, p. B1.

————., & Rashbaum, W. (2011, January 6). City police ask panel to review crime statistics. *New York Times*, pp. A1, A24.

————., & Rivera, R. (2010). U.S. reviews New York police dealings who don't speak English. *New York Times*, p. A17.

————., Robbins, L., & Goldstein, J. (2011, July 13). Missing boy's dismembered body found. Suspect says he panicked. *New York Times*, pp. A1, A18.

Baldus, D. (2003, March–April). Racial discrimination in the administration of the death penalty. *Criminal Law Bulletin, 39*(2), 194–220.

Baliga, S. (2012, Winter). The day the jail walls cracked: A restorative plea deal. *Tikkun*, 22–24, 64. Retrieved January 27, 2012, from www.tikkun.org.

Balkan, S., Berger, R., & Schmidt, J. (1980). *Crime and deviance in America: A critical approach*. Belmont, CA: Wadsworth.

Banfield, A. (2007, September). His case vs. her case. *Cosmopolitan Magazine*, p. 204.

Banks, D., & Kyckkelhahn, T. (2011, April). *Characteristics of suspected human trafficking incidents, 2008–2010. Bureau of Justice Statistics Special Report*. Washington, DC: U.S. Department of Justice.

Bannister, S. (1992). Battered women who kill their abusers: Their courtroom battles. In R. Muraskin & T. Alleman (Eds.), *It's a crime: Women and justice* (pp. 316–333). Englewood Cliffs, NJ: Regents/Prentice Hall.

Barbash, F. (1979, December 17). Victim's rights: New legal weapon. *Washington Post*, p. 1.

Barber, C., Hemenway, D., Hargarten, S., Kellerman, A., Azrael, D., & Wilt, S. (2000). "A call to arms" for a national reporting system of firearms injuries. *American Journal of Public Health, 90*(8), 1191–1194.

Barden, J. (1987, May 13). Marital rape: Drive for tougher laws is pressed. *New York Times*, p. A16.

Barner, J., & Carney, M. (2011). Interventions for intimate partner violence: A historic review. *Journal of Family Violence, 26*, 235–244.

Barnett, O., & LaViolette, A. (1993). *It could happen to anyone: Why battered women stay*. Newbury Park, CA: Sage.

Barnett, O., Miller-Perrin, C., & Perrin, R. (2005). *Family violence across the lifespan* (2nd ed.). Thousand Oaks, CA: Sage.

Barnett, R. (1977). Restitution: A new paradigm of criminal justice. In R. Barnett & J. Hagel (Eds.), *Assessing the criminal: Restitution, retribution, and the criminal process* (pp. 1–35). Cambridge, MA: Ballinger.

Barrett, D. (1998, July 28). Vigilante dad sentenced in mistaken rapist slay. *New York Post*, p. 6.

Barringer, F. (1989, May 30). Children as sexual prey, and predators. *New York Times*, pp. A1, A16.

Barrow, L. (2008). *Criminal victimization of the deaf*. New York: LFB Scholarly Publishers.

Barton, L. (2011, August 22). The "missing white woman syndrome." Retrieved October 20, 2011, from www.thecrimereport.org.

Barry, R., & Jones, C. (2014, December 1). Hundreds of police killings are uncounted in federal stats: FBI data differs from local counts on justifiable homicides. *Wall Street Journal*. Retrieved December 10, 2014, from http://www.wsj.com/articles/hundreds-of-police-killings-are-uncounted-in-federal-statistics-1417577504?mod=djemalertNEWS.

Bass, E., & Davis, L. (1992). *The courage to heal: A guide for women survivors of child sexual abuse* (3rd ed.). New York: Harper Collins.

Bastian, L. (1993). *Criminal victimization 1992. BJS Bulletin*. Washington, DC: U.S. Department of Justice.

Baum, D. (2013). *Gun guys: A road trip*. New York: Vintage.

Baum, K. (2006). *National Crime Victimization Survey: Identity theft, 2004. BJS Special Report*. Washington, DC: U.S. Department of Justice.

———. (2007). *National Crime Victimization Survey: Identity theft, 2005. BJS Special Report*. Washington, DC: U.S. Department of Justice.

———., Catalano, S., Rand, M., & Rose, K. (2009, January). *Stalking victimization in the United States. BJS Special Report*. Washington, DC: U.S. Department of Justice.

———., & Klaus, P. (2005). *Violent victimization of college students, 1995–2002. BJS Special Report*. Washington, DC: U.S. Department of Justice.

———., & Langton, L. (2010, June 30). *Identity theft reported by households, 2007–statistical tables. BJS Special Report*. Washington, DC: U.S. Department of Justice.

BBC. (2008, April 27). Actor Blake loses US court appeal. *BBC News*. Retrieved January 4, 2012, from www.bbc.co.uk.

Beall, G. (1980, October). Negotiating the disposition of criminal charges. *Trial, 16*, 10–13.

Beck, A., & Harrison, P. (2010, August). *Sexual victimization in prisons and jails reported by inmates, 2008–09. BJS Special Report*. Washington, DC: U.S. Department of Justice.

Beck, A., Harrison, P., & Guerino, P. (2010, January). *Sexual victimization in juvenile facilities reported by youth, 2008–09. BJS Special Report*. Washington, DC: U.S. Department of Justice.

Beck, M., Rosenberg, D., Chideya, F., Miller, S., Foote, D., Manly, H.,et al. (1992, July 13). Murderous obsession. *Newsweek*, pp. 60–62.

Beckett, K. (1996). Culture and the politics of signification: The case of child sexual abuse. *Social Problems, 43*(1), 57–76.

Begos, P. (2011, December 8). PA. liquor board pulls ad on heavy drinking. *Associated Press*. Retrieved December 20, 2011, from www.ap.org.

Behar, R. (1993, August 16). Car thief at large. *Time*, pp. 47–48.

Beirne, P., & Messerschmidt, J. (1991). *Criminology*. San Diego, CA: Harcourt Brace Jovanovich.

———. (2000). *Criminology* (3rd ed.). Boulder, CO: Westview Press.

Belden, D. (2012, Winter). Controversies around restorative justice. *Tikkun, 27–29*, 62. Retrieved January 27, 2012, from www.tikkun.org.

Belkin, L. (2002, December 8). Just money. *New York Times Magazine*, pp. 92–97, 148, 150.

Belknap, J., & Melton, H. (2005, March). Are heterosexual men also victims of partner abuse? *National Resource Center on Violence Against Women*. Retrieved August 20, 2008, from www.vawnet.org.

Bell, L. (2012, February 21). Op Ed: Disarming the myths promoted by the gun control lobby. *Forbes Magazine*, p. 22.

Bellamy, P. (2005). The murder of JonBenet Ramsey. *Court TV's Crime Library*. Retrieved October 4, 2005, from www.courttv.com.

Beloof, D. (1999). *Victims in criminal procedure*. Raleigh, NC: Carolina Academic Press.

Bemiller, M. (2009). No-drop policies. In J. Wilson (Ed.), *The Praeger handbook of victimology* (p. 183). Santa Barbara, CA: Praeger.

Benedict, H. (1992). *Virgin or vamp: How the press covers sex crimes*. New York: Oxford University Press.

Benedict, J. (1998). *Athletes and acquaintance rape*. Thousand Oaks, CA: Sage.

——— & Klein, A. (1998). Arrests and conviction rates for athletes accused of sexual assaults. In R. Bergen (Ed.), *Issues in intimate violence* (pp. 169–179). Thousand Oaks, CA: Sage.

Bensing, R., & Schroeder, O. (1960). *Homicide in an urban community*. Springfield, IL: Charles C. Thomas.

Bent-Goodley, T. (2005, February). Culture and domestic violence. *Journal of Interpersonal Violence, 20*, 195–203.

Bergen, R. (Ed.). (1998). *Issues in intimate violence.* Thousand Oaks, CA: Sage.

Bergfeld, D. (2005, July 22). Students teach others dangers of date rape drugs at Texas Tech. *Texas Tech University Daily,* p. 8.

Berk, R., Campbell, A., Klap, R., & Western, B. (1992, October). The deterrent effect of arrest in incidents of domestic violence: A Bayesian analysis of four field experiments. *American Sociological Review, 57,* 698–708.

Berke, R. (1989, March 28). Capital offers unlimited turf to drug dealers. *New York Times,* pp. A1, A16.

Berliner, L. (1987, March). Commentary: Editor's introduction. *Journal of Interpersonal Violence, 2,* 107–108.

Bernat, F. (1992, March). Book review: "Representing battered women who kill" by Johann and Osanka. *Justice Quarterly, 9*(1), 169–172.

Bernhard, D. (2014, Fall). From C.O.P.S. executive director. *Rap Sheet,* p. 1.

Berns, W. (1994, April). Getting away with murder. *Commentary, 97,* 25–29.

Bernstein, E. (2010, Autumn). Militarized humanitarianism meets carceral feminism: The politics of sex, rights, and freedom in contemporary antitrafficking campaigns. *Signs: Journal of Women in Culture and Society, 36*(1), 45–71.

Bernstein, G. (1972). Statement. In *U.S. Senate, report on the federal crime insurance program. Committee on the Judiciary, Subcommittee on Criminal Laws and Procedures, 1st session* (pp. 521–529). Washington, DC: U.S. Government Printing Office.

Bernstein, L. (2014, June 27). Boston marathon bombing victims to get $20 million more. *Washington Post.* Retrieved December 11, 2014, from http://www.washingtonpost.com/news/to-your-health/wp/2014/06/27/boston-marathon-bombing-victims-to-get-20-million-more/.

Bernstein, N. (2001, October 26). Thousands of orphans? An urban myth. *New York Times,* pp. B1, B10.

———. (2011, November 11). On campus, a law enforcement system to itself. *New York Times,* p. A18.

Bernstein, N., & Kaufman, L. (2004, October 2). Women likelier to be slain by a partner than a stranger. *New York Times,* p. B3.

Berube, M. (2011, November 18). At Penn State, a bitter reckoning. *New York Times,* p. A33.

Besharov, D. (1987, November). Federal action urged to protect rights of parents accused of child abuse. *Crime Victims Digest,* pp. 5–6.

———. (1990). *Recognizing child abuse: A guide for the concerned.* New York: Free Press.

Best, J. (1988, Summer). Missing children, misleading statistics. *Public Interest,* pp. 84–92.

———. (1989a). Dark figures and child victims: Statistical claims about missing children. In J. Best (Ed.), *Images of issues: Imagining contemporary social problems* (pp. 21–37). New York: Aldine de Gruyter.

———. (Ed.). (1989b). *Images of issues: Imagining contemporary social problems.* New York: Aldine de Gruyter.

———. (1991, August). "Road warriors" on "Hair-trigger highways." *Sociological Inquiry, 61*(3), 327–344.

———. (1997, May–June). Victimization and the victim industry. *Society, 34*(4), 8–10.

Best, J., & Luckenbill, D. (1982). *Organizing deviance.* Englewood Cliffs, NJ: Prentice Hall.

Better Business Bureau. (2014, April 7). BBB reports home alarm system sellers ignore do not call registry and use fear tactics. *BBB.org.* Retrieved October 12, 2014, from http://www.bbb.org/connecticut/news-events/news-releases/2014/04/illegal-telemarketing-calls-mention-fbi-to-get-your-attention/.

Beutel, A. (2011). Policy report: Data on post 9-9/11 terrorism in the United States. *Muslim Political Affairs Council.* Retrieved September 16, 2011, from www.mpac.org.

Biblarz, A., Barnowe, J., & Biblarz, D. (1984). To tell or not to tell: Differences between victims who report crimes and victims who do not. *Victimology, 9*(1), 153–158.

Bienen, L. (1983). Rape reform legislation in the United States: A look at some practical effects. *Victimology, 8*(1), 139–151.

Birkbeck, C. (1983). "Victimology is what victimologists do." But what should they do? *Victimology, 8*(3/4), 270–275.

Biskupic, J. (2000, May 16). Justices reject lawsuits for rapes. *Washington Post,* p. A1.

BJS. *See* Bureau of Justice Statistics.

Bisnar and Chase Law Firm. (2011). The hit and run victims legal rights handbook. Retrieved September 29, 2014, from http://www.hitandrunreward.com/hit-run-victims-rights-handbook.html.

Black, D. (1968). *Police encounters and social organization.* Unpublished doctoral dissertation, University of Michigan, Ann Arbor, MI.

Black, M., Basile, K., Breiding, M., Smith, S., Walters, M., Merrick, M., et al. (2011, November). *The National Intimate Partner and Sexual Violence Survey (NISVS). 2010 summary report.* Atlanta, GA: National Center for Injury Prevention and Control, Centers for Disease Control and Prevention.

Blinder, A. (2013, June 28). Georgia suspends 19 state workers over delayed abuse inquiries. *New York Times,* pp. A19.

Bliss, J. (2013, October 28). Police, experts: Alcohol most common in sexual assaults. *The Tennessean.* Retrieved December 2, 2014, from http://www.usatoday.com/story/news/nation/2013/10/28/alcohol-most-common-drug-in-sexual-assaults/3285139/.

Block, C. (2003, November). How can practitioners help an abused woman lower her risk of death? *NIJ Journal, 250*, 4–7.

Block, D. (2007, November 18). Twenty years later, Tawana Brawley turns back on the past. *New York Daily News*, p. 12.

Block, R. (1981). Victim–offender dynamics in violent crime. *Journal of Criminal Law and Criminology, 72*, 743–761.

———, Felson, M., & Block, C. (1985). Crime victimization rates for incumbents of 246 occupations. *Sociology and Social Research, 69*(3), 442–449.

Blue Campaign. (2010, January). *Human trafficking indicators*. Washington, DC: U.S. Department of Homeland Security.

Blumstein, A., & Rosenfeld, R. (1998, Summer). Explaining recent trends in U.S. homicide rates. *Journal of Criminal Law and Criminology, 88*(4), 1175–1216.

Bochnak, E. (Ed.). (1981). *Women's self-defense cases: Theory and practice*. Charlottesville, VA: Michie Co. Law Publishers.

Bode, J. (1978). *Fighting back*. New York: Macmillan.

Bode, N. (2007, September 5). Rapists' kin taunt, curse victim. *New York Daily News*, p. 16.

Bogler, E. (2014, September 2). Emma Sulkowicz's performance art draws support from campus activists. *Columbia Spectator*. Retrieved January 7, 2014, from http://columbiaspectator.com/news/2014/09/02/emma-sulkowiczs-performance-art-draws-support-campus-activists.

Bohmer, C., & Parrot, A. (1993). *Sexual assault on campus: The problem and the solution*. New York: Lexington Books.

Boland, B., Mahanna, P., & Sones, R. (1992). *The prosecution of felony arrests, 1988. BJS Report*. Washington, DC: U.S. Department of Justice.

Boland, B., & Sones, R. (1986). *Prosecution of felony arrests, 1981. BJS Special Report*. Washington, DC: U.S. Department of Justice.

Bondurant, B. (2001). University women's acknowledgement of rape: Individual, situational, and social factors. *Violence Against Women, 7*(3), 294–314.

Booth, B., Van Hasselt, V., & Vecchi, G. (2011, May). Addressing School Violence. *FBI Law Enforcement Bulletin, 80*(5), 3–9.

Boston, G. (1977). *Crimes against the elderly: A selected bibliography*. Washington, DC: National Criminal Justice Reference Service.

Botelho, G. (2014, December 27). Workplace violence: Know the numbers, risk factors and possible warning signs. *CNN*. Retrieved December 22, 2014, from http://www.cnn.com/2014/09/27/us/workplace-violence-questions-answers/.

Bouza, A. (1991). Responding to domestic violence. In M. Steinman (Ed.), *Woman battering: Policy responses* (pp. 191–203). Cincinnati, OH: Anderson.

Bowker, L. (1983, June). Marital rape: A distinct syndrome? *Social Casework, 64*(6), 340–350.

Bowman, C. (1992). The arrest experiments: A feminist critique. *The Journal of Criminal Law and Criminology, 83*(1), 201–208.

Boyer, D., & James, J. (1983). Prostitutes as victims. In D. MacNamara & A. Karmen (Eds.), *Deviants: Victims or victimizers?* (pp. 109–146). Newbury Park, CA: Sage.

Boyle, C. (2007, April 13). Rape just 1st ordeal. *New York Daily News*, p. 12.

Boyle, P. (1994, April). Travel industry launches drive to protect tourists. *New York AAA Motorist, 1*, 18.

Bradshaw, W., & Umbreit, M. (1998). Crime victims meet juvenile offenders: Contributing factors to victim satisfaction with mediated dialogue. *Juvenile and Family Court Journal, 49*(3), 17–25.

Brady Center. (2013a). The truth about kids and guns. *Brady Center To Prevent Gun Violence*. Retrieved December 22, 2014, from http://www.bradycampaign.org/sites/default/files/Children-and-Guns-Report.pdf.

———. (2013b, December 9). One year after Newtown, states lead the way on gun violence prevention according to new analysis of state gun laws. *Brady Center To Prevent Gun Violence*. Retrieved December 22, 2014, from http://www.bradycampaign.org/inthenews/one-year-after-newtown-states-lead-the-way-on-gun-violence-prevention-according-to-new.

Branca, A. (2013). *The law of self-defense: The indispensable guide to the armed citizen* (2nd ed.). Maynard, MA: LLC.

Brandl, S., & Horvath, F. (1991). Crime victim evaluation of police investigative performance. *Journal of Criminal Justice, 19*, 109–121.

Breckman, R., & Adelman, R. (1988). *Strategies for helping victims of elder mistreatment*. Newbury Park, CA: Sage.

Breiding, M., Smith, S., Basile, K., Walters, M., Chen, J., & Merrick, M. (2014, September 5). Prevalence and characteristics of sexual violence, stalking, and intimate partner violence victimization—National Intimate Partner and Sexual Violence Survey, United States, 2011. *Center for Disease Control*. Retrieved November 20, 2014, from http://www.cdc.gov/mmwr/preview/mmwrhtml/ss6308a1.htm?s_cid=ss6308a1_e.

Breitman, G. (1966). *Malcolm X speaks*. New York: Grove.

Breitman, N., Shackelford, T., & Block, C. (2004, June). Couple age discrepancy and risk of intimate partner homicide. *Violence and Victims, 19*, 321–333.

Brennan, A. (2012, July 31). Analysis: Fewer U.S. gun owners own more guns. *CNN News*. Retrieved December 14, 2014, from http://www.cnn.com/2012/07/31/politics/gun-ownership-declining/index.htm.

Brents, B., & Hausbeck, K. (2005, March). Violence and legalized brothel prostitution in Nevada. *Journal of Interpersonal Violence, 20*, 270–295.

Brien, V. (1992). *Civil legal remedies for crime victims.* Washington, DC: Office for Victims of Crime bulletin, U.S. Department of Justice.

Brienza, J. (1999, May). Crime victims laws sometimes ignored. *Trial, 35*, 103–105.

Briere, J. (1992). *Child abuse trauma: Theory and treatment of the lasting effects.* Newbury Park, CA: Sage.

Briscoe, D. (2005, February 7). Mail order misery. *Newsweek,* p. 54.

Broder, J., & Madigan, N. (2005, June 14). Jackson cleared after 14-week child molesting trial. *New York Times,* pp. A1, A19.

Brody, J. (2003, January 28). Empowering children to thwart abductors. *New York Times,* p. F6.

———. (2011, December 12). The twice-victimized of sexual assault. *New York Times,* p. F8.

Bromley, D. (1991, May–June). The satanic cult scare. *Society, 28*(4), 55–66.

Brooks, D. (2006a, April 9). Virtues and victims. *New York Times,* p. E12.

Brooks, J. (1972). *Criminal injury compensation programs: An analysis of their development and administration.* Unpublished doctoral dissertation, University Microfilms, Ann Arbor, MI.

Brooks, O. (2011). Guys! Stop doing it! Young women's adoption and rejection of safety advice while in bars, pubs, and clubs. *British Journal of Criminology, 51*(4), 635–651.

Brown, J., & Langan, P. (1998). *BJS Report: State court sentencing of convicted felons, 1994.* Washington, DC: U.S. Department of Justice.

Brown, J., & Walklate, S. (2011). *Handbook on sexual violence.* London, UK: Routledge.

Brown, M. (2013, December 14). Breaking the silence. *Baltimore Sun.* Retrieved December 1, 2014, from http://data. baltimoresun.com/military-sexual-assaults/.

Brown, R. (1975). *Strains of violence: Historical studies of American violence and vigilantism.* New York: Oxford University Press.

Brown, S. (2003, April). Victims' rights legislation in the twenty-first century. *NCSL State Legislative Report, 28*(7), 1–12.

Browne, A. (1987). *When battered women kill.* New York: Free Press.

Brownmiller, S. (1975). *Against our will: Men, women, and rape.* New York: Simon & Schuster.

Brownstein, H. (1996). *The rise and fall of a violent crime wave.* Guilderland, NY: Harrow and Heston.

Bruni, F. (1989, April 3). Maureen Reagan reveals husband beat her. *New York Post,* p. 9.

Buchwald, A. (1969, February 4). Victim precipitation. *Washington Post,* p. 23.

Buchwald, E., Fletcher, P., & Roth, M. (1993). *Transforming a rape culture.* Minneapolis, MN: Milkwood Editions.

Buckler, K., & Travis, L. (2005). Assessing the news-worthiness of homicide events. *Journal of Criminal Justice and Popular Culture, 12*(1), 1–25.

Buckley, C. (2007, January 13). Safe haven laws fail to end discarding of babies. *New York Times,* pp. B1, B5. *Islamorada Free Press* (Florida), p. 30A.

Buckley, W. (1994, December 21). Excelsior the counterculture. On the Right (syndicated column). *Islamorada Free Press* (Florida), p. 30A.

Bui, H. (2009). Marital rape. In J. Wilson (Ed.), *The Praeger handbook of victimology* (pp. 163–164). Santa Barbara, CA: Praeger.

Bulletin Board. (2004, August). Victims get work leave in Hawaii. *The Crime Victims Report, 8*(3), 48.

Bultman, M., & Jaccarino, M. (2010, December 1). College student and aspiring cop gunned down by gang in mistaken identity slay. *New York Daily News,* p. 11.

Bunch, J. (2005, June 28). Justices deny mom's right to sue police; Court: Castle Rock cops couldn't have known dad would kill kids. *Denver Post,* p. A1.

Bureau of Justice Statistics (BJS). (1974–2011). *Criminal victimization in the United States* (Annual Reports). Washington, DC: U.S. Department of Justice.

———. (1988). *Report to the nation on crime and justice* (2nd ed.). Washington, DC: U.S. Department of Justice.

———. (1994a). *Elderly crime victims.* Washington, DC: U.S. Department of Justice.

———. (1994b). *Violence and theft in the workplace. BJS Crime Data Brief.* Washington, DC: U.S. Department of Justice.

———. (2008a). Intimate partner violence in the U.S. Retrieved August 20, 2008, from www.ojp.usdoj.gov/ bjs/intimate/circumstances.htm.

———. (2008b). Homicide trends in the U.S.: Intimate partners. Retrieved August 20, 2008, from www.ojp.usdoj. gov/bjs/homicide/intimates.htm.

———. (2008c). National Crime Victimization Survey – statistical tables 2006. Retrieved September 30, 2008, from www.ojp.gov/bjs/pub/cvus.

———. (2008d). State court sentencing of convicted felons – statistical tables. Retrieved September 29, 2008, from www.ojp.gov/bjs/pub/pdf/sc0001st.pdf.

———. (2011). National Crime Victimization Survey– statistical tables 2008. Retrieved September 6, 2011, from www.ojp.gov/bjs/pub/cvus.

———. (2014). Data tables generated using the NCVS Victimization Analysis Tool at www.bjs.gov. Retrieved September 15, 2014, from http://www.bjs.gov/index.cfm?ty=nvat.

Bureau of Public Affairs. (2005). *The link between prostitution and sex trafficking.* Washington, DC: U.S. Department of State.

Burgess, A., Donovan, B., & Moore, S. (2009). Embodying uncertainty. Understanding heightened risk perception of "drink spiking." *British Journal of Criminology, 49*(6), 848–862.

Burgess, A., & Holmstrom, L. (1974). Rape trauma syndrome. *American Journal of Nursing, 131*, 981–986.

Burke, C. (2009, August 31). Slime made victim key to his print shop success. *New York Post*, p. 4.

Burke, T. (1998). Male-to-male gay domestic violence: The dark closet. In N. Jackson & G. Oates (Eds.), *Violence in intimate relationships: Examining sociological and psychological issues* (pp. 161–180). Woburn, MA: Butterworth-Heinemann.

Burleigh, N. (2014, June 4). Confronting campus rape. *Rolling Stone*. Retrieved December 14, 2014, from http://www.rollingstone.com/politics/news/confronting-campus-rape-20140604.

Burnett, D. (2011, February 28). Opposing view: Decriminalize self-defense. *USA Today*. Retrieved November 6, 2011, from www.usatoday.com./opinions.

Burrows, W. (1976). *Vigilante!* New York: Harcourt Brace Jovanovich.

Burt, M. (1980). Cultural myths and support for rape. *Journal of Personality and Social Psychology, 38*, 217–230.

———. (1983). A conceptual framework for victimological research. *Victimology, 8*(3/4), 261–268.

Burt, M., & Katz, R. (1987, March). Dimensions of recovery from rape. *Journal of Interpersonal Violence, 2*(1), 57–81.

Burying crime in Chicago. (1983, May 16). *Newsweek*, p. 63.

Busch-White, L. (2002). *Identity theft victim: Help and support after the crime.* Bloomington, IL: 1st Books Library.

Bush, G. (2002). President Bush endorses Feinstein-Kyl Victims Rights Amendment. Retrieved September 3, 2005, from www.nvcap.org.

———. (2004, July 16). President announces initiatives to combat human trafficking. *White House Archives*. Retrieved September 28, 2014, from http://georgew bush-whitehouse.archives.gov/news/releases/2004/07/20040716-11.html.

Business Wire. (2014, November 17). International Cruise Victims (ICV) applauds court ruling which reinstates negligence suit against cruise line. *Yahoo Finance*. Retrieved November 17, 2014, from http://finance.yahoo.com/news/international-cruise-victims-icv-applauds-154500471.html.

Butler, D. (2004, September 17). Objection your honor. *The Ottawa Citizen,* p. B1.

Butler, K. (2006, February 28). Beyond rivalry, a hidden world of sibling violence. *New York Times*, p. A22.

Buttafuoco, M. (2012). About me. Retrieved January 19, 2012, from www.maryjobuttafuoco.com.

Butterfield, F. (1999, October 17). Guns used more for suicide than homicide. *New York Times*, p. A16.

Butts, J., & Snyder, H. (1992). *Restitution and juvenile recidivism: OJJDP Update on Research.* Washington, DC: U.S. Department of Justice, Office of Juvenile Justice and Delinquency Prevention.

Buzawa, E., & Buzawa, C. (1990). *Domestic violence: The criminal justice response.* Newbury Park, CA: Sage.

———. (1996). *Do arrests and restraining orders work?* Thousand Oaks, CA: Sage.

———., & Stark, E. (2011). *Responding to domestic violence: The integration of criminal justice and human services* (4th ed.). Thousand Oaks, CA: Sage.

Cable News Network (CNN). (2002, August 16). $116 trillion lawsuit filed by 9/11 families. Retrieved November 2, 2005, from www.cnn.com.

Caffaro, J., & Caffaro, A. (1998). *Sibling abuse trauma.* Binghamton, NY: Haworth Press.

Cahn, N., & Lerman, L. (1991). Prosecuting woman abuse. In M. Steinman (Ed.), *Woman battering: Policy responses* (pp. 95–113). Cincinnati, OH: Anderson.

Calmes, J. (2014, January 22). Obama seeks to raise awareness of rape on campus. *New York Times,* p. A10.

Campbell, J., et al. (2003, November). Assessing risk factors for intimate partner homicide. *NIJ Journal, 250*, 14–19.

Campbell, R., & Wasco, S. (2005, January). Understanding rape and sexual assault: Twenty years of progress and future directions. *Journal of Interpersonal Violence, 20*, 127–131.

Cantor, D. (2011). Divorce/custody proceedings and child molestation proceedings = False convictions. *National Child Abuse Defense and Resource Center (NDADRC).* Retrieved December 5, 2011, from www.falseallegation.org.

Caplan, G. (1991, February 25). Battered wives, battered justice. *National Review*, pp. 15–20.

Cares, A. C. (2012). *Teaching about Criminal Victimization: Guidelines for Faculty.* Lowell, MA: University of Massachusetts Lowell. Retrieved September 30, 2014, from http://www.uml.edu/docs/Faculty%20Guidelines_FINAL_SEP2012_tcm18-60976.pdf.

Carmody, D., & Washington, L. (2001). Rape myth acceptance among college women. *Journal of Interpersonal Violence, 16*(5), 424–436.

Carr, P., Lord, K., & Maier, S. (2003). Keep me informed: What matters for victims as they navigate the juvenile criminal justice system in Philadelphia. *Internal Review of Victimology, 10*(2), 117–136.

Carey, B. (2004, July 27). Payback time: Why revenge tastes so sweet. *New York Times,* p. B4.

Carrington, F. (1975). *The victims.* New Rochelle, NY: Arlington House.

———. (1977). Victim's rights litigation: A wave of the future? *University of Richmond Law Review, 11*(3), 447–470.

———. (1978, June). Victim's rights: A new tort. *Trial, 14,* 39–41.

———. (1980, February 11). Martinez ruling won't bar suits on negligent custodial releases. *National Law Journal, 26,* 12–18.

———. (1986, June). Preventing victimization through third-party victims' rights litigation. *Networks* (newsletter of the National Victims Center, Fort Worth, Texas)*, 1,* 7.

Carrow, D. (1980). *Crime victim compensation: Program model.* Washington, DC: U.S. Department of Justice.

Carson, E. (1986, September). Crime victims strike back with civil lawsuits for compensation. *NOVA Newsletter, 1–2,* 4.

———. (2014, September 14). *Prisoners in 2013. BJS Prisoner Series.* Washington, DC: U.S. Department of Justice.

Carter, S. (2000, September). Covering crime on college campuses. *Quill Magazine,* pp. 8–10.

Caspi, J. (2011). *Sibling aggression.* New York: Springer Publishers.

Cassell, P. (2010). Protecting crime victims in federal appellate courts. *Denver University Law Review, 87,* 1–34.

Cassell, P., & Joffee, S. (2011). The crime victim's expanding role in a system of public prosecution. *Northwestern University Law Review, 105,* 164–189.

Castillo, M. (2013, January 24). Many abused women may be sexual "coercion" victims. *CBS TV News.* Retrieved November 20, 2014, from http://www.cbsnews.com/news/many-abused-women-may-be-sexual-coercion-victims/.

Catalano, S. (2009, September). *Female victims of violence.BJS Selected Findings.* Washington, DC: U.S. Department of Justice.

———. (2012a, September). *Stalking victims in the United States, Revised. BJS Special Report.* Washington, DC: U.S. Department of Justice.

———. (2012b, November). *Intimate partner violence, 1993–2010. BJS Special Report.* Washington, DC: U.S. Department of Justice.

Catania, S. (2005, July 1). Breaking the silence. *Mother Jones,* pp. 8–10.

Cathcart, R. (2008, February 23). Boy's killing, labeled a hate crime, stuns a town. *New York Times,* p. A16.

Cavacuiti, C., Ala-Leppilampi, K., Mann, R., Govoni, R., Stoduto, G., Smart, R., et al. (2013). Victims of road rage: A qualitative study of the experiences of motorists and vulnerable road users. *Violence and Victims, 26*(6), 1068–1084.

Cavalieri, S. (2011). Between victim and agent: A third-way feminist account of trafficking for sex work. *Indiana Law Journal, 86,* 1409–1460.

Cawthorne, A., & Rawlins, C. (2014, February 20). Venezuela's violent crime fuels the death business. *Reuters News Service.* Retrieved October 20, 2014, from http://www.reuters.com/article/2014/02/20/us-venezuela-crime-idUSBREA1J0KM20140220.

CCRC. *See* Crimes Against Children Research Center.

CDF. *See* Children's Defense Fund.

Ceci, S., & Bruck, M. (1993). Suggestibility of the child witness: A historical review and synthesis. *Psychological Bulletin, 113*(3), 403–439.

Celock, J. (2013, February 27). Mark Warden, New Hampshire State Legislator, says people may like 'being in abusive relationships.' *Huffington Post.* Retrieved November 20, 2014, from http://www.huffingtonpost.com/2013/02/27/mark-warden-new-hampshire_n_2773889.html.

Celona, L. (2005, September 26). "Lie" detectives. *New York Post,* p. 17.

———., Margolin, J., & Fredericks, B. (2012, July 19). G-Man vigilante. *New York Post,* p. 7.

Center, L. (1980). Victim assistance for the elderly. *Victimology, 5*(2), 374–390.

Center for Disease Control, U.S. Department of Health and Human Services, National Center for Health Statistics (CDC). (1999, October). *National Vital Statistics Report, 41*(25), 27–28.

———. (2008, February). Adverse health conditions and health risk behaviors associated with intimate partner violence. *Morbidity and Mortality Weekly Report, 57,* 122.

———. (2010). Fact sheet: Understanding teen dating violence. Retrieved January 3, 2012, from www.cdc.gov/violenceprevention.

———. (2011a). Elder maltreatment: Definition. Retrieved December 10, 2011, from cdc.gov.

———. (2011b). Fact sheet: Understanding intimate partner violence, 2011. Retrieved December 20, 2011, from cdc.gov.

———. (2013a, December 20). Deaths: Leading causes for 2010. *National Vital Statistics Reports, 62*(6), 17. Retrieved October 20, 2014, from http://www.cdc.gov/nchs/data/nvsr/nvsr62/nvsr62_06.pdf.

———. (2013b). Deaths: Final Data for 2011. *National Vital Statistics Report, 62.* Retrieved October 28, 2014, from http://www.cdc.gov/nchs/data/nvsr/nvsr63/nvsr63_03.pdf.

Center for Public Integrity. (2010, February 24). *Sexual assault on campus: A frustrating search for justice.* Retrieved January 2, 2012, from www.publicintegrity.org.

Chan, S. (2007, September 18). To avoid return to Iraq, soldier arranged to be shot. *New York Times,* p. B3.

———. (2007, December 5). City Room: Legal help for immigrants, even illegal ones. *New York Times,* p. B1.

Chancer, L. (2005). *High-profile crimes: When legal cases become social causes.* Chicago: University of Chicago Press.

Chang, S. (2006, November 3). Source of inspiration. *Newsday*, p. A17.

Chapman, J., & Smith, B. (1987). *Child sexual abuse: An analysis of case processing*. Washington, DC: American Bar Association.

Chappell, D., Geis, R., & Geis, G. (1977). *Forcible rape: The crime, the victim, and the offender*. New York: Columbia University Press.

Chappell, D., & Sutton, P. (1974). Evaluating the effectiveness of programs to compensate victims of crime. In I. Drapkin & E. Viano (Eds.), *Victimology: A new focus* (Vol. 2, pp. 207–220). Lexington, MA: D. C. Heath.

Chappell, W. (2014, September 29). California enacts 'Yes Means Yes' law, defining sexual consent. *NPR News*. Retrieved September 30, 2014, from http://www.npr.org/blogs/thetwo-way/2014/09/29/352482932/california-enacts-yes-means-yes-law-defining-sexual-consent.

Charkes, J. (2008, March 22). DNA tests lead to arrest in a 25-year-old killing. *New York Times*, p. B2.

Chavez, J. (1992). Battered men and the California law. *Southwestern University Law Review, 22*, 239–256.

Chemaly, S. (2014, September 19). How many of the hundreds of thousands of untested rape kits in the US are in your city? *Huffington Post*. Retrieved December 12, 2014, from http://www.huffingtonpost.com/soraya-chemaly/how-many-of-the-uss-40000_b_5845052.html.

Chen, D. (2004, November 18). Striking details in final report on 9/11 fund. *New York Times*, pp. B1, B8.

Chicago police found to dismiss cases erroneously. (1983, May 2). *New York Times*, p. A20.

Child abuse victims get help through interior decor. (1989, May 15). *Law Enforcement News*, pp. 1, 12.

Children's Defense Fund (CDF). (2005). *A moral outrage: One American child or teen killed by gunfire nearly every three hours*. Retrieved December 20, 2005, from www.childrensdefense.org.

Childres, R. (1964). Compensation for criminally inflicted personal injury. *New York University Law Review, 39*, 455–471.

Childress, S. (2006, September 25). Fighting over the kids. *Newsweek*, p. 35.

Chilton, R. (1987). Twenty years of homicide and robbery in Chicago: The impact of the city's changing racial and age composition. *Journal of Quantitative Criminology, 3*(3), 195–206.

———. (2004, February). Regional Variations in Lethal and Nonlethal Assaults. *Homicide Studies, 8*, 40–56.

Chira, S. (1993, December 5). Sexual abuse: The coil of truth and memory. *New York Times*, p. E3.

Chornesky, A. (2000). The dynamics of battering revisited. *Journal of Women and Social Work, 15*(4), 480–501.

Christie, N. (1977). Conflicts as property. *British Journal of Criminology, 17*, 1–15.

Christie, N. (1986). The ideal victim. In E. Fattah (Ed.), *From crime policy to victim policy* (pp. 125–134). New York: St. Martin's Press.

Chu, L., & Kraus, J. (2004, May). Predicting fatal assault among the elderly using the National Incident- Based Reporting System crime data. *Homicide Studies, 8*, 71–95.

Chuang, J. (2010). Rescuing trafficking from ideological capture. *University of Pennsylvania Law Review, 158*(6), 1655–1728.

Cicchini, M., & Kushner, A. (2010). *But they didn't read me my rights!* Amherst, NY: Prometheus Books.

Cihan, A., Zhang, Y., & Hoover, L. (2012, September). Police response time to in-progress burglary: A multilevel analysis. *Police Quarterly, 15*(3), 307–327.

Clancy, S. (2005). *Abducted: How people come to believe they were kidnapped by aliens*. Cambridge, MA: Harvard University Press.

Clark, C., & Block, T. (1992, Fall). Victims' voices and constitutional quandaries: Life after *Payne v. Tennessee*. *St. John's Journal of Legal Commentary, 8*(1), 35–64.

Clark, D., White, E., & Violanti, L. (2012, May). Law enforcement suicide: Current knowledge and future directions. *The Police Chief*, pp. 6–11.

Clark, L., & Lewis, D. (1978). *Rape: The price of coercive sexuality*. Toronto: Women's Press.

Clark, R., & Harris, P. (1992). Auto theft and its prevention. In M. Tonry (Ed.), *Crime and justice: A review of research* (Vol. 16, pp. 1–54). Chicago: University of Chicago Press.

Clery Center For Security On Campus. (2014). Policy. *CleryCenter.org*. Retrieved December 1, 2014, from http://clerycenter.org/national-campus-safety-awareness-month.

Clery, H., & Clery, C. (2001). What Jeanne didn't know. Retrieved September 21, 2005, from www.securityoncampus.org.

Clinton, W. (1996, June 27). President Clinton's memorandum to Attorney General Janet Reno. White House Press Release. Retrieved August 23, 2008, from www.whitehouse.gov.

———. (2000, October 28). Statement on signing the Victims of Trafficking and Violence Protection Act of 2000. Retrieved September 28, 2014, from http://www.presidency.ucsb.edu/ws/?pid=1105.

CNN. See Cable News Network.

Coates, R. (1990). Victim–offender reconciliation programs in North America: An assessment. In B. Galaway & J. Hudson (Eds.), *Criminal justice, restitution and reconciliation* (pp. 125–134). Monsey, NY: Willow Tree Press.

Coates, R., & Gehm, J. (1989). An empirical assessment. In M. Wright & B. Galaway (Eds.), *Mediation and criminal justice: Victims, offenders, and community* (pp. 251–263). Newbury Park, CA: Sage.

Cohen, L., & Felson, M. (1979). Social change and crime rate trends: A routine activity approach. *American Sociological Review, 44,* 588–607.

Cohen, L., Kluegal, J., & Land, K. (1981). Social inequality and criminal victimization. *American Sociological Review, 46,* 505–524.

Cohen, P. (1984). Resistance during sexual assaults: Avoiding rape and injury. *Victimology, 9*(1), 120–129.

Cohen, R. (1991, April 21). Should the media name the accuser when the crime being charged is rape? *New York Times,* p. E4.

Cohen, S., Ruiz, R., & Childress, S. (2013, January 24). Departments are slow to police their own abusers. *New York Times,* pp. A1, A22.

Cohen, T., & Reaves, T. (2006, February). Felony defendants in large urban courts, 2002. Statistical tables. Retrieved September 30, 2008, from www.ojp.gov/bjs/abstract/fdluc02.htm.

———., & Kyckelhahn, T. (2010). *Felony defendants in large urban counties, 2006. Bureau of Justice Statistics.* Washington, DC: U.S. Department of Justice.

Cohn, A., Zinzow, H., Resnick, H., & Kilpatrick, D. (2013, February). Correlates of reasons for not reporting rape to police. *Journal of Interpersonal Violence, 28*(3), 455–473.

Cohn, E., Kidder, L., & Harvey, J. (1978). Crime prevention vs. victimization prevention: The psychology of two different reactions. *Victimology, 3*(3), 285–296.

Coker, A., Clear, E., Lisandra, S., Ibitola, O., Cook-Craig, P., Brancato, C., et al. (2014). Dating violence victimization and perpetration rates among high school students. *Violence Against Women, 20*(10), 1220–1238.

Cole, S. (2009). Cultural consequences of miscarriages of justice. *Behavioral Sciences and the Law, 27,* 431–449.

Collins, J., & Hoffman, S. (2004). *Identity theft victims' assistance guide: The process of healing.* New York: Looseleaf Law Publishers.

Collins, J., McCalla, M., Powers, L., & Stutts, E. (1983). *OJJDP update on research: The police and missing children: Findings from a national survey.* Washington, DC: U.S. Department of Justice.

Combined News Services. (1993, September 27). NYC man slain on Florida highway. *New York Newsday,* p. 17.

Congressional Victims' Rights Caucus. (2012). Legislation, 2011. Retrieved January 23, 2012, from http://vrc.poe.house.gov/ind.

Conklin, J. (1975). *The impact of crime.* New York: Macmillan.

Connelly, E., & Luo, M. (2011, February 6). States struggle to disarm people who've lost right to own guns. *New York Times,* pp. A1, A3.

Consumer's Union. (2008). *Notice of security breach state laws.* Retrieved July 18, 2008, from www.consumersunion.org/campaigns/Breach_laws.

Cook, P. (1985). Is robbery becoming more violent? An analysis of robbery murder trends since 1968. *Journal of Criminal Law and Criminology, 76*(2), 480–490.

———. (1987). Robbery violence. *Journal of Criminal Law and Criminology, 78*(2), 357–377.

——— & Ludwig, J. (1997). *NIJ Research in Brief: Guns in America—National survey on private ownership and use of firearms.* Washington, DC: U.S. Department of Justice.

———. (2003). *Evaluating gun policy.* Washington, DC: Brookings Institute.

Cook, R., Roehl, J., & Sheppard, D. (1980). *Neighborhood justice centers field test.* Washington, DC: U.S. Department of Justice.

Cooper, A., & Smith, E. (2011). *Homicide trends in the United States, 1980–2008. BJS, Patterns and Trends.* Washington, DC: U.S. Department of Justice.

Cooper, C. (2000). Police mediators: Rethinking the role of law enforcement in the new millennium. *Dispute Resolution Magazine, 7*(1), 17.

Cooper, H. (2014, March 8). Pentagon finds Washington Navy Yard killings could have been prevented. *New York Times,* p. A12.

Cooper, M. (2005, April 7). Racial disproportion seen in applying "Kendra's Law." *New York Times,* p. B4.

Copeland, L., & Martin, N. (2006, June 8). Police in some areas see increase in home invasions; In robberies, armed criminals violate property and people. *USA Today,* p. A4.

Corbett, S. (2007, March 18). The women's war. *New York Times Magazine,* pp. 41–57.

Corbin, W., Bernat, J., & Calhoun, K. (2001). The role of alcohol expectancies and alcohol consumption among sexually victimized and nonvictimized college women. *Journal of Interpersonal Violence, 16*(4), 297–311.

Cornelius, T., & Ressiguie, N. (2007, May–June). Primary and secondary prevention programs for dating violence: A review of the literature. *Aggression and Violent Behavior, 12*(3), 364–375.

Cornell, I. (2011, September 14). Former WABC-TV weatherperson Heidi Jones pleads guilty to faking rape story. *CBS News, New York.* Retrieved November 14, 2014, from http://newyork.cbslocal.com/2011/09/14/former-tv-weatherperson-heidi-jones-pleads-guilty-to-faking-attack-story/.

Cornell, K. (2006, November 11). Avenging angel: Make my torturer suffer too: Sliwa. *New York Post*, p. 29.

Cose, E. (1994, August 8). Truths about spouse abuse. *Newsweek*, p. 49.

Coston, C. (Ed.). (2004). *Victimizing vulnerable groups*. New York: Praeger.

COTWA. (2013, July 3). Philadelphia policy: 'Almost never' arrest false rape accusers. *Community of the Wrongly Accused*. Retrieved December 22, 2014, from http://www.cotwa.info/2013/07/philadelphia-policy-almost-never-arrest.html.

Council on Foreign Relations (CFR). (2004). *Terrorism: Questions and answers: The anthrax letters*. Retrieved October 4, 2005, from www.cfr.org.

Cowan, A. (2008, April 8). Police face a threat deadlier than any criminal's gun. *New York Times*, pp. B1, B6.

Cowan, G. (2000). Women's hostility toward women and rape and sexual harassment myths. *Violence Against Women*, *6*(3), 238–246.

Cox, C. (2009, August 26). Right-to-carry in restaurants. *National Rifle Association*. Retrieved December 1, 2014, from www.nraila.org.

———. (2011, November). In the states, gun rights are on the march. Retrieved January 22, 2012, from www.americanrifleman.com.

Cox, R. (2014, September 18). Senate passes bill to address rape kit backlog. *The Hill*. Retrieved December 14, 2014, from http://thehill.com/social-tags/debbie-smith-act.

Crew, R., Fridell, L., & Pursell, K. (1995). Probabilities and odds in hot pursuit: A benefit–cost analysis. *Journal of Criminal Justice*, *23*(5), 417–424.

Crichton, S. (1993, October 25). Sexual correctness: Has it gone too far? *Newsweek*, pp. 52–56.

Crime control amendments. (1973). *Congressional Quarterly Almanac*, *29*, 370–372.

Crime Victims Digest. (1985, August). Crime control needs citizens to do their part in helping. *Crime Victims Digest*, pp. 1–2.

Crime victims' aid. (1978). *Congressional Quarterly Almanac, 34*, 196–198.

Crime Victims Research and Treatment Center. (1992). *The national women's study*. Charleston, SC: Medical University of South Carolina.

Crouse, K. (2014, September 11). Ray Rice is an outlier: Most domestic abuse suspects play on. *New York Times,* p. D1.

Crowe, A. (1998, Summer). Restorative justice and offender rehabilitation: A meeting of the minds. *Perspectives, the Journal of the American Probation and Parole Association*, *22*, 28–40.

Crowley, K. (2007, October 24). Tiny chop-keeper kicks gunman's ax. *New York Post*, p. 3.

Cruz, J., & Firestone, J. (1998, Summer). Exploring violence and abuse in gay male relationships. *Violence and Victims*, *13*(2), 159–174.

Crystal, S. (1988, Summer). Elder abuse: The latest "crisis." *Public Interest*, *88*, 56–65.

Culhane, S., Hosch, H., & Weaver, W. (2004, December). Crime victims serving as jurors: Is there bias present? *Law and Human Behavior*, *28*(6), 649–659.

Cunningham, J., Paddock, B., & Badia, E. (2012, October 21). Good Samaritan bouncer murdered after trying to break up vicious fight outside Brooklyn club. *New York Daily News,* p. 12.

Cuomo, M. (1992, Fall). The crime victim in a system of criminal justice. *St. John's Journal of Legal Commentary*, *8*(1), 1–20.

Curry, C. (2011, November 10). Rep. Gabrielle Giffords smiling, talking 11 months after shooting. *ABC News*. Retrieved December 12, 2011, from http://news.yahoo.com.

Curtis, L. (1974). Victim precipitation and violent crime. *Social Problems*, *21*, 594–605.

Curtis, R., Terry, K., Dank, M., Dombrowski, K., Khan, B., Muslim, A., Labriola, M., & Rempel, M. (2008, December). *Executive summary: Commercial sexual exploitation of children in New York City*. Washington, DC: U.S. Department of Justice.

Dahl, J. (2011, August 3). How to solve a cold case. Retrieved August 4, 2011, from www.thecrimereport.com.

Daily Mail Reporter. (2012, February 18). Pastor's daughter, 20, dies a week after being shot in the head by a stray bullet at her father's church. *Daily Mail*. Retrieved December 6, 2014, from http://www.dailymail.co.uk/news/article-2103220/Hannah-Kelley-Pastors-daughter-accidentally-shot-head-church-dies.html#ixzz3LbiHSnyo.

Dalesio, E. (2011, September 19). Police: Trucker killed three prostitutes across South. Retrieved November 28, 2011, from www.ap.org.

Dank, M. (2014, March). Estimating the size and structure of the underground commercial sex economy in eight major US cities. *The Urban Institute*. Retrieved September 29, 2014, from http://www.urban.org/UploadedPDF/413047-Underground-Commercial-Sex-Economy.pdf.

Dao, J. (2013, June 23). In debate over military sexual assault, men are overlooked victims. *New York Times*, p. A10.

Darnton, N. (1991, October 7). The pain of the last taboo. *Newsweek*, pp. 70–72.

Davey, M., & Einhorn, C. (2007, December 8). Settlement for torture of four men by police. *New York Times*, p. A11.

Davidson, H. (1986, July–August). Missing children: A close look at the issue. *Children Today*, 26–30.

Davies, J., Lyon, E., & Catania, D. (1998). *Safety planning with battered women: Complex lives/Difficult choices*. Thousand Oaks, CA: Sage.

Davis, R. (1983). Victim/witness noncooperation: A second look at a persistent phenomenon. *Journal of Criminal Justice, 11,* 287–299.

Davis, R., & Bannister, P. (1995). Improving the collection of court-ordered restitution. *Judicature, 79*(1), 30–33.

Davis, R., Erez, E., & Avitabile, N. (2001). Access to justice for immigrants who are victimized. *Criminal Justice Policy Review, 12*(3), 183–196.

Davis, R., Henderson, N., & Rabbitt, C. (2002). *Effects of state victim rights legislation on local criminal justice systems.* New York: Vera Institute of Justice.

Davis, R., Kunreuther, F., & Connick, E. (1984). Expanding the victim's role in the criminal court dispositional process: The results of an experiment. *Journal of Criminal Law and Criminology, 75*(2), 491–505.

Davis, R., & Mulford, C. (2008). Victim rights and new remedies. *Journal of Contemporary Criminal Justice, 24*(2), 198–208.

Davis, R., & Murray, D. (1995). *Immigrant populations as victims: Toward a multicultural criminal justice system.* New York: Victim Services Agency.

Davis, R., Smith, B., & Hillenbrand, S. (1992). Restitution: The victim's viewpoint. *The Justice System Journal, 15*(3), 746–758.

Davis, R., Tichane, M., & Grayson, D. (1980). *Mediation and arbitration as alternatives to criminal prosecution in felony arrest cases: An evaluation of the Brooklyn Dispute Resolution Center (first year).* New York: Vera Institute of Justice.

Dawson, J., & Langan, P. (1994). *Murder in families: BJS Special Report.* Washington, DC: U.S. Department of Justice.

Dawson, J., Smith, S., & DeFrances, C. (1993). *Prosecutors in state courts, 1992. BJS Bulletin.* Washington, DC: U.S. Department of Justice.

Dawson, R. (1969). *Sentencing. The decision as to type, length, and conditions of sentence.* Boston: Little, Brown.

Day One. (2011). What is stalking? *Know Your Rights Guide.* Retrieved December 1, 2011, from www.dayoneny.org.

DEA. *See* Drug Enforcement Administration.

De Fabrique, N., Romano, S., Vecchi, G., & Van Hasselt, V. (2007, July 7). Understanding Stockholm syndrome. *FBI Law Enforcement Bulletin, 76*(7), 10–16.

De Koster, K., & Swisher, K. (Eds.). (1994). *Child abuse: Opposing viewpoints.* San Diego: Greenhaven Press.

De Lisi, M., Kosloski, A., Sween, M., Hachmeister, E., Moore, M., & Drury, A. (2010, August). Murder by numbers: Monetary costs imposed by a sample of homicide offenders. *Journal of Forensic Psychiatry and Psychology, 21*(4), 501–514.

De Parle, J. (1999, November 28). Early sex abuse hinders many women on welfare. *New York Times,* pp. A1, A28.

Dean, C., & de Bruyn-Kops, M. (1982). *The crime and the consequences of rape.* Springfield, IL: Charles C. Thomas.

Deane, G. (1987). Cross-national comparison of homicide: Age/sex-adjusted rates using the 1980 U.S. homicide experience as a standard. *Journal of Quantitative Criminology, 3*(3), 215–227.

Dedel, K. (2006, July). Witness intimidation. Retrieved November 20, 2011, from www.cops.usdoj.gov/files/ric/Publications/e07063407.pdf.

———. (2011). Sexual assaults of women by strangers. *Problem Oriented Policing Guide No. 62.* Retrieved November 20, 2011, from www.popcenter.org.

Dees, M., & Corcoran, J. (1997). *America's militia threat.* New York: Harper Collins.

DeFrances, C. (2002). *Prosecutors in state courts, 2001. BJS Bulletin.* Washington, DC: U.S. Department of Justice.

DeGette, D., Jenson, J., & Colomy, P. (2000). Law and policy surrounding youth violence. *Denver University Law Review, 77*(4), 615–812.

Deiters, B. (2013, September 12). Victim of 1981 rape sees justice but tells judge 'my life has been screwed up.' *Michigan Live.* Retrieved November 13, 2014, from http://www.mlive.com/news/grand-rapids/index.ssf/2013/09/victim_of_1981_rape_sees_justi.html.

Del Castillo, V., & Lindner, C. (1994). Staff safety issues in probation. *The Justice Professional, 8*(2), 37–54.

Dellorto, D. (2012). Experts: Rape does not lower odds of pregnancy. *CNN News.* Retrieved December 2, 2014, from http://www.cnn.com/2012/08/21/health/rape-pregnancy/index.html.

Demarais, A. (1992). Male versus female initiation of aggression: The case of courtship violence. In E. Viano (Ed.), *Intimate violence: Interdisciplinary perspectives* (pp. 111–120). Washington, DC: Hemisphere Publishing.

Dempsey, M. (2009). *Prosecuting domestic violence.* New York: Oxford University Press.

Dershowitz, A. (1988). *Taking liberties: A decade of hard cases, bad laws, and bum raps.* Chicago: Contemporary Books.

———. (1994). *The abuse excuse and other cop-outs, sob stories, and evasions of responsibility.* Boston: Little, Brown.

Desmarais, S., Reeves, K., Nicholls, T., Telford, R., & Fiebert, M. (2012, April). Prevalence of physical violence in intimate relationships, Part 2: Rates of male and female perpetration. *Partner Abuse, 3*(2), 170–198.

———., Pritchard, A., Lowder, E., & Janssen, P. (2014). Intimate partner abuse before and during pregnancy as risk factors for postpartum mental health problems. *BMC Pregnancy & Childbirth, 14*(1), 1–21.

DeStefano, A. (2007). *The war on human trafficking: U.S. policy assessed.* New Brunswick, NJ: Rutgers University Press.

Deutsch, C. (1994, June 3). Victims of violence increasingly hold landlords liable for crimes. *New York Times*, p. B8.

Dewan, S. (2005, July 14). Report on court killings is said to lead to firing of deputies. *New York Times*, p. A10.

Dewan, S., & Zezima, K. (2010, February 15). Eye-opening to jaw-dropping: Twists multiply in shooting case. *New York Times*, pp. A1, A13.

Dignan, J. (2005). *Understanding victims and restorative justice*. New York: Open University Press/McGraw Hill.

Dobash, R. P., & Dobash, R. E. (1979). *Violence against wives: The case against patriarchy*. New York: Free Press.

———. (1992). *Women, violence, and social change*. New York: Routledge.

Dobner, J. (2010a, November 9). Elizabeth Smart on abduction: I thought I was having a nightmare. *Associated Press*. Retrieved November 28, 2011, from www.ap.org.

———. (2010b, December 10). Elizabeth Smart's kidnapper found guilty. *Associated Press*. Retrieved November 28, 2011, from www.ap.org.

Docksai, M. (1979, August). Victim/witness intimidation: What it means. *Trial, 15*, 51–54.

Dodge, R. (1988). *The seasonality of crime. BJS Bulletin*. Washington, DC: U.S. Department of Justice.

Doerner, W. (1978). An examination of the alleged latent effects of victim compensation programs upon crime reporting. *LAE Journal, 41*, 71–80.

Doerner, W., & Lab, S. (1980). Impact of crime compensation on victim attitudes toward the criminal justice system. *Victimology, 5*(2), 61–77.

Does your agency measure up? (1999, November). *Rap Sheet* (newsletter of Concerns of Police Survivors), *6*, 4.

Doherty, C. (2015, January 9). A public opinion trend that matters: Priorities for gun policy. *Pew Research Center*. Retrieved January 13, 2015, from http://www.pewresearch.org/fact-tank/2015/01/09/a-public-opinion-trend-that-matters-priorities-for-gun-policy/.

Domestic abusers take it out on pets, too. (1999, February 28). *Law Enforcement News*, p. 6.

D'Ovidio, D., & Doyle, M. (2003, March). A study in cyberstalking: Understanding investigative hurdles. *FBI Law Enforcement Bulletin, 72*, 10–17.

Douglas, E., & Hines, D. (2011). The help-seeking experiences of men who sustain intimate partner violence. *Journal of Family Violence, 26,* 473–485.

Doyle, J., & Fredericks, B. (2011, January 4). Craigslist car-theft victim turns tables on foe. *New York Post*, p. 10.

Dragiewicz, M. (2011). *Equality with a vengeance: Men's rights groups, battered women, and antifeminist backlash*. Boston, MA: Northeastern University Press.

Dreher, R. (2001, August 21). Jesse, Sharpton, and Kwesi are problem, not solution. *New York Post*, p. 5.

Drug Enforcement Administration (DEA). (2003). *Ecstasy and predatory drugs*. Washington, DC: U.S. Government Printing Office.

Dubber, M. (2002). *Victims in the war on crime: The use and abuse of victims' rights*. New York: NYU Press.

Dugan, L., Nagin, D., & Rosenfeld, R. (2003). Do domestic violence services save lives? *NIJ Journal, 250*, 20–25.

Duhart, D. (2001). *Violence in the workplace, 1993–99. BJS Special Report*. Washington, DC: U.S. Government Printing Office.

Duncan, A. (2014, June 29). RRPD helps victims of violent crime navigate through justice system. *Albuquerque Journal*. Retrieved November 14, 2014, from http://www.abqjournal.com/421950/news/rio-rancho-news/rrpd-helps-victims-of-violent-crime-navigate-through-justice-system.html.

Dunn, J. (2002). *Courting disaster: Intimate stalking, culture, and criminal justice*. New York: Aldine de Gruyter.

Duret, D., & Patrick, R. (2004, October 24). Truck driver is shot along I-44. *St. Louis Post-Dispatch*, p. A1.

Durose, M. (2004). *Felony sentencing in state courts, 2002. BJS Bulletin*. Washington, DC: U.S. Department of Justice.

Dussich, J. (2003). History, overview, and analysis of American victimology and victim services education. In *Proceedings of the first American symposium on victimology* (pp. 4–17). Retrieved July 12, 2011, from www.american-society-victimology.us/documents.

———. (2009a). Advocates. In J. Wilson (Ed.), *The Praeger handbook of victimology* (pp. 8–9). Santa Barbara, CA: Praeger.

———. (2009b). Victimology. In J. Wilson (Ed.), *The Praeger handbook of victimology* (pp. 299–301). Santa Barbara, CA: Praeger.

———. (2011). Editorial: Considering vulnerability as a viable victimological issue. *International Perspectives on Victimology, 6*(1), 9–11.

Dutton-Douglas, M., & Dionne, D. (1991). Counseling and shelter services for battered women. In M. Steinman (Ed.), *Woman battering: Policy responses* (pp. 113–130). Cincinnati, OH: Anderson.

Duwe, G. (2000, November). Body count journalism: The presentation of mass murder in the news media. *Homicide Studies, 4*(4), 364–399.

Dwyer, J. (2011, April 27). A court battle over a husband's rage and a wife who'd had enough. *New York Times*, p. A21.

Dzur, A. (2011, December). Restorative justice and democracy: Fostering public accountability for criminal justice. *Contemporary Justice Review, 14*(4), 367–381.

Ebony. (1979, August). Black on black crime (special issue). *Ebony magazine*.

Eckholm, E. (2013, August 17). Victims' dilemma: 911 calls can bring eviction. *New York Times,* pp. A1, A12.

Eddy, D. (1990). Supreme Court decides cases involving VOCA, restitution, child witnesses, sobriety checkpoints. *NOVA Newsletter, 14*(3), 6.

Edelhertz, H. (1977). Legal and operational issues in the implementation of restitution in the criminal justice system. In J. Hudson & B. Galaway (Eds.), *Restitution in criminal justice* (pp. 63–76). Lexington, MA: Lexington Books.

Edelhertz, H., & Geis, G. (1974). *Public compensation to victims of crime.* New York: Praeger.

Editors, *New York Post.* (2006, April 3). Enough already. *New York Post,* p. 22.

Editors, *New York Times.* (1965, November 20). The Good Samaritans. *New York Times,* p. A34.

———. (1991, April 17). Growing old under siege of social workers: More funds needed. *New York Times,*p. A24.

———. (2005a, April 15). Identity thieves' secret weapon. *New York Times,*p. A18.

———. (2005b, June 30). Help for victims of sexual assault. *New York Times,*p. A14.

———. (2007, April 26). Guns and more guns. *New York Times,* p. A24.

———. (2011b, April 20). Making campuses safer. *New York Times,* p. A22.

———. (2011c, October 17). Who mailed the anthrax letters? *New York Times,* p. A24.

———. (2014a, January 25). Talking sexual violence without giving offense. *New York Times,* p. A26.

———. (2014b, April 27). Disarmament for spousal abusers. *New York Times,* pp. A22.

Edwards, C., & Riley, M. (2011, May 3). Sony data breach exposes users to years of identity theft risk. Retrieved November 1, 2011, from www.businessweek.com/news.

Egan, J. (2011, June 22). Keys in ignition: Easy target for car thieves. Retrieved October 25, 2011, from www.carin surancequotes.com.

Egger, K., & Egger, S. (2002). Victims of serial killers: The less dead. In J. Sgarzi & J. McDevitt, *Victimology: A study of crime victims and their roles* (pp. 9–32). Upper Saddle River, NJ: Prentice Hall.

Eglash, A. (1977). Beyond restitution: Creative restitution. In J. Hudson & B. Galaway (Eds.), *Restitution in criminal justice* (pp. 91–100). Lexington, MA: Lexington Books.

Eigenberg, H. (1990). The National Crime Survey and rape: The case of the missing question. *Justice Quarterly, 7,* 655–671.

Einhorn, C. (2008, February 23). Four decades after shooting, effort to make punishment fit the crime. *New York Times,* p. A10.

EJI. See Equal Justice Initiative.

Elias, R. (1983a). The symbolic politics of victim compensation. *Victimology, 8*(1), 210–219.

———. (1983b). *Victims of the system: Crime victims and compensation in American politics and criminal justice.* New Brunswick, NJ: Transaction Books.

———. (1986). *The politics of victimization: Victims, victimology and human rights.* New York: Oxford University Press.

———. (1993). *Victims still: The political manipulation of crime victims.* Newbury Park, CA: Sage.

Eligon, J. (2008, August 11). "Preppy killer" pleads guilty to selling cocaine. *New York Times,* p. B2.

Eligon, J., & Baker, A. (2010, May 22). No indictment of a man who killed 2 in the subway. *New York Times,* p. A13.

———. (2011a, May 9). Privacy disappears at a trial about rape. *New York Times,* p. A19.

———. (2011b, May 31). Officers' accuser says she was devastated by verdict. *New York Times,* p. A14.

Ellenberger, H. (1955). Psychological relationships between the criminal and his victim. *Archives of Criminal Psychodynamics, 2,* 257–290.

Ellin, A. (2003, January 12). Here's one way to turn off a date. *New York Times, Education Life Supplement, 152,* 7.

Ellis, C. (2000, September). Nation's first police shelter for victims of domestic violence. *The Crime Victims Report, 4,* 49–50.

Emily, J. (2010, April 22). Tarrant county juror in capital murder trial nearly lands in jail after not disclosing relatives were murder victims. *The Dallas Morning News.* Retrieved January 3, 2012, from www.dallasnews.com.

Endo, E. (1999, July 21). Anti-stalking bill stalled by budget. *Long Island Newsday,* p. A45.

English, P. (2011, August). Words matter: Defining victims in state domestic violence statutes. *International Perspectives in Victimology, 6*(1), 1–8.

Equal Justice Initiative. (2015, February 15). Lynching in America: Confronting the Legacy of Racial Terror. *EJI.org.* Retrieved February 16, 2014, from http://www.eji.org/files/EJI%20Lynching%20in%20America%20SUM MARY.pdf.

Erdely, S. (2014, November 19). A rape on campus: A brutal assault and struggle for justice at UVA. *Rolling Stone.* Retrieved December 19, 2014, from http://www.roll ingstone.com/culture/features/a-rape-on-campus-20141119#ixzz3RdZXw8jb.

Erdrick, L. (2013, February 26). Rape on the reservation. *New York Times,* p. A22.

Estrich, S. (1986). *Real rape.* Cambridge, MA: Harvard University Press.

———. (1993a, October 24). The sympathy defense. *New York Times*, p. E15.

———. (1993b, October 25). Balancing act. *Newsweek*, p. 64.

Eterno, J., & Silverman, E. (2012). *The crime numbers game: Management by manipulation*. Boca Raton, FL: CRC. Press.

European Committee on Crime Problems. (1978). *Compensation of victims of crime*. Strasbourg, Austria: Author.

Every Child Matters Education Fund. (2011). *Child abuse and neglect*. Retrieved December 8, 2011, from www.every childmatters.org.

Ewing, C. (1997). *Fatal families: The dynamics of intra-familial homicide*. Thousand Oaks, CA: Sage.

Ewing, P. (1987). *Battered women who kill: Psychological self-defense as legal justification*. Lexington, MA: D.C. Heath.

Fagan, J. (1988). Contributions of family violence research to criminal justice policy on wife assault: Paradigms of science and social control. *Violence and Victims, 3*(3), 159–186.

Fagan, J., Piper, E., & Cheng, Y. (1987). Contributions of victimization to delinquency in inner cities. *Journal of Criminal Law and Criminology, 78*(3), 586–611.

Fahn, M. (1991, Summer). Allegations of child sexual abuse in custody disputes: Getting to the truth of the matter. *Family Law Quarterly, 25*(2), 16–21.

Fairstein, L. (1993). *Sexual violence: Our war against rape*. New York: William Morrow.

Falck, R., Wang, J., & Carlson, R. (2001). The epidemiology of physical attack and rape among crack-using women. *Violence and Victims, 16*(1), 79–89.

Faludi, S. (1993, October 25). Whose hype? *Newsweek*, p. 61.

Farmer, A. (2008, January 25). At 101, mugging victim has her (early) day in court. *New York Times*, p. B5.

Farnham, F., James, D., & Cantrell, P. (2000, January 15). Association between violence, psychosis, and relationship to victim in stalkers. *The Lancet, 355*, 322–323.

Farrell, A., McDevitt, J., & Fahy, S. (2010, May). Where are all the victims? *Criminology and Public Policy, 9*(2), 201–233.

Farrell, G., Tseloni, A., Wiersema, B., & Pease, K. (2001). Victim careers and "Career victims?": Toward a research agenda. *Crime Prevention Studies, 12*, 241–254.

Farrell, R., & Swigert, V. (1986, November). Adjudication in homicide: An interpretive analysis of the effects of defendant and victim social characteristics. *Journal of Research in Crime and Delinquency, 23*(4), 349–369.

Fattah, E. (1967). Toward a criminological classification of victims. *International Criminal Police Review, 209*, 162–169.

———. (1976). The use of the victim as an agent of self-legitimation: Toward a dynamic explanation of criminal behavior. In E. Viano (Ed.), *Victims and society* (pp. 105–129). Washington, DC: Visage.

———. (1979). Some recent theoretical developments in victimology. *Victimology, 4*(2), 198–213.

———. (1986). *From crime policy to victim policy*. New York: St. Martin's Press.

———. (1990). Victims and victimology: The facts and the rhetoric. *International Review of Victimology, 1*(1), 43–66.

———. (1991). *Understanding criminal victimization: An introduction to theoretical victimology*. Scarborough, Ontario: Prentice Hall Canada.

———. (1992a). The need for a critical victimology. In E. Fattah (Ed.), *Towards a critical victimology* (pp. 3–28). New York: St. Martin's Press.

———. (Ed.). (1992b). *Towards a critical victimology*. New York: St. Martin's Press.

Faulk, M. (1977). Men who assault their wives. In M. Roy (Ed.), *Battered women: A psycho-sociological study of domestic violence* (pp. 119–126). New York: Van Nostrand.

FBI. *See* Federal Bureau of Investigation.

FBI NCTC (National Counterterrorism Center). (2010). *2009 report on terrorism*. Washington, DC: U.S. Department of Justice. Retrieved December 23, 2011, from www.fbi.gov.

Federal Bureau of Investigation (FBI). (1954–2014). *Uniform Crime Report: Crime in the United States* (statistics for selected years from 1953 to 2014). Washington, DC: U.S. Government Printing Office.

———. (1993). *Law enforcement officers killed and assaulted, 1992*. Washington, DC: U.S. Department of Justice.

———. (1999). *National incident-based reporting system*. Washington, DC: U.S. Department of Justice.

———. (2001). *Terrorism in the United States, 1999: Terrorism: A retrospective*. Washington, DC: U.S. Department of Justice.

———. (2004). *Terrorism 2000/2001*. Washington, DC: U.S. Department of Justice.

———. (2006, August 21). Protecting your identity: Advice from FBI agent Lanza. *FBI Stories*. Retrieved May 21, 2014, from http://www.fbi.gov/news/stories/2006/august/idtheft_082106.

———. (2007b). *Terrorism 2002/2005*. Washington, DC: U.S. Department of Justice.

———. (2008a). *Law enforcement officers killed and assaulted, 2007*. Washington, DC: U.S. Department of Justice.

———. (2008b, August). Stories: Mortgage fraud: How to avoid becoming a victim. Washington, DC: U.S. Department of Justice.

———. (2009). *Uniform Crime Reporting System Guidelines*. Washington, DC: U.S. Department of Justice.

———. (2013a). *Hate Crime Statistics, 2012*. Washington, DC: U.S. Department of Justice.

———. (2014a). It's sad but true: Here in this country, people are being bought, sold, and smuggled like modern-day slaves. *Federal Bureau of Investigation*. Retrieved September 29,

2014, from http://www.fbi.gov/about-us/investigate/civilrights/human_trafficking.

———. (2014b). 2012 National Incident-Based Reporting System. *Federal Bureau of Investigation.* Retrieved September 29, 2014, from http://www.fbi.gov/about-us/cjis/ucr/nibrs/2012/resources/nibrs-participation-by-state.

———. (2014c). A study of active shooter incidents in the United States between 2000 and 2013. Retrieved October 29, 2014, from http://www.fbi.gov/news/stories/2014/september/fbi-releases-study-on-active-shooter-incidents/pdfs/a-study-of-active-shooter-incidents-in-the-u.s.-between-2000-and-2013.

———. (2014d). NCIC Missing person and unidentified person statistics for 2013. *Federal Bureau of Investigation.* Retrieved September 20, 2014, from http://www.fbi.gov/about-us/cjis/ncic/ncic-missing-person-and-unidentified-person-statistics-for-2013.

———. (2014e). Law enforcement officers killed and assaulted, 2013. (LEOKA). *Federal Bureau of Investigation.* Washington, DC: U.S. Department of Justice.

Federal rape laws revised: Now apply to male victims. (1986, November). *Crime Victims Digest,* p. 10.

Federal Trade Commission (FTC). (2002). *ID theft: When bad things happen to your good name.* Washington, DC: U.S. Department of Commerce, FTC.

———. (2007). National and state trends in fraud and identity theft, January–December 2006. Retrieved July 15, 2008, from www.ftc.gov/idtheft/consumers.

———. (2008). About Identity theft – deter, detect, defend, avoid ID theft. Retrieved July 15, 2008, from www.ftc.gov/idtheft/consumers.

———. (2011, March 11). Consumer Sentinel Data Book, 2010. Retrieved October 29, 2011, from www.ftc.gov/sentinel/reports.

———. (2014). Consumer Sentinel Data Book, 2013. Retrieved October 2, 2014, from www.ftc.gov/sentinel/reports.

Feher, T. (1992). The alleged molestation victim, the rules of evidence and the Constitution: Should children really be seen and not heard? In E. Fattah (Ed.), *Towards a critical victimology* (pp. 260–282). Englewood Cliffs, NJ: Prentice Hall.

Fehr, R., Gelfand, M., & Nag, M. (2010). The road to forgiveness. *Psychological Bulletin, 136*(5), 894–914.

Fein, E. (1991, December 11). Decision praised as a victory for free speech rights. *New York Times,* p. B8.

Feingold, R. (2005). *U.S. Senate recognizes September as first-ever national campus safety awareness month.* Retrieved December 20, 2005, from www.securityoncampus.org.

Felson, M. (1994). *Crime and everyday life.* Thousand Oaks, CA: Pine Forge Press.

———. (1997). Routine activities and involvement in violence as actor, witness, or target. *Violence and Victims, 12*(5), 209–220.

———., & Boba, R. (2010). *Crime and everyday life* (4th ed.). Thousand Oaks, CA: Sage.

Fenton, J. (2010, July 27). City rape statistics, investigations draw concern. *Baltimore Sun,* p. 12.

Fernandez, M. (2010, November 22). Lawsuit filed by estate of the immigrant killed on Long Island. *New York Times,* p. B2.

———. (2011, September 19). Adults can help stop child sexual abuse. Retrieved December 9, 2011, from www.thecrimereport.org.

———., & Blinder, A. (2014, April 8). At Fort Hood, wrestling with label of terrorism. *New York Times,* p. A12.

Ferraro, K. (1992). Cops, courts, and woman battering. In P. Bart & E. Moran (Eds.), *Violence against women: The bloody footprints* (pp. 165–176). Newbury Park, CA: Sage.

Fierro, I., Morales, C., & Alvarez, J. (2011, March). Alcohol use, illicit drug use, and road rage. *Journal of Studies on Alcohol and Drugs, 72*(2), 185–197.

Findlaw. (2014). Domestic violence: Orders of protection and restraining orders. *Findlaw.com.* Retrieved January 4, 2015, from http://family.findlaw.com/domestic-violence/domestic-violence-orders-of-protection-and-restraining-orders.html.

Fine, L. (2001, March 28). Second high school shooting rocks a California school district. *Education Week, 20*(28), 3.

Fingerhut, L., Ingram, D., & Feldman, J. (1992, June 10). Firearm and non-firearm homicide among persons 15 through 19 years of age. *Journal of the American Medical Association, 267*(22), 3048–3053.

Fink, B. (1992). Firearm homicide among black teenage males in metropolitan counties: Comparison of death rates in two periods, 1983 through 1985 and 1987 through 1989. *Journal of the American Medical Association, 267,* 3054–3058.

———. (2011, June). The politics of prison rape. *City Limits, 35*(2), 23–24.

Finkelhor, D. (1990, Winter). Is child abuse over-reported? *Public Welfare, 48*(1), 20–30.

———. (1994). Current information on the scope and nature of child sexual abuse. *The Future of Children, 4*(2), 31, 46, 48.

———. (2008). *Childhood victimization.* New York: Oxford University Press.

Finkelhor, D., & Asdigian, N. (1996, Spring). Risk factors for youth victimization: Beyond a lifestyle/routine activities theory approach. *Violence and Victims, 11*(1), 3–20.

Finkelhor, D., Hammer, H., & Sedlak, A. (2002). *NISMART–2: Nonfamily abducted children: National estimates and characteristics.* Washington, DC: U.S. Department of Justice, Office of Juvenile Justice and Delinquency Prevention.

Finkelhor, D., Hotaling, G., & Sedlak, A. (1990). *Missing, abducted, runaway, and thrown away children in America: First report*. Washington, DC: U.S. Department of Justice, Office of Juvenile Justice and Delinquency Prevention.

Finkelhor, D., & Jones, L. (2004). *Explanations for the decline in child sexual abuse cases*. Washington, DC: U.S. Department of Justice, Office of Juvenile Justice and Delinquency Prevention.

Finkelhor, D., & Leatherman, J. (1994, March). Victimization of children. *American Psychologist, 49*(3), 173–183.

Finkelhor, D., & Ormrod, R. (2000, June). Kidnapping of juveniles: Patterns from NIBRS. *OJJDP Juvenile Justice Bulletin, 1–7.* Washington, DC: U.S. Department of Justice.

Finkelhor, D., & Ormrod, R. (2001). Crimes against children by babysitters. *OJJDP Juvenile Justice Bulletin*. Washington, DC: U.S. Department of Justice.

Finkelhor, D., & Yllo, K. (1985). *License to rape: Sexual abuse of wives*. New York: Holt, Rinehart & Winston.

Finn, P. (1991). Civil protection orders: A flawed opportunity for intervention. In M. Steinman (Ed.), *Woman battering: Policy responses* (pp. 155–190). Cincinnati, OH: Anderson.

Finn, R. (2005, October 28). Pushing past the trauma of forgiveness. *New York Times*, p. B2.

Fisher, B., Cullen, F., & Daigle, L. (2005). The discovery of acquaintance rape. *Journal of Interpersonal Violence, 20*(4), 493–500.

Fisher, B., Cullen, F., & Turner, M. (2000). *The sexual victimization of college women*. Washington, DC: National Institute of Justice.

Fisher, B., Daigle, L., & Cullen, F. (2008). Rape against women: What can research offer to guide the development of prevention programs and risk reduction interventions. *Journal of Contemporary Criminal Justice, 24*(2), 163–177.

———. (2010). *Unsafe in the ivory tower: The sexual victimization of college women*. Newbury Park, CA: Sage.

Fisher, D. (2012, December 18). Gunmaker paid up after Washington sniper killings, and may yet pay again. *Forbes Magazine*. Retrieved December 8, 2014, from http://www.forbes.com/sites/danielfisher/2012/12/18/bushmaster-paid-after-malvo-killings-and-may-yet-pay-again/.

Fitting justice? Judges try "creative" sentences. (1978, April 24). *Time*, p. 56.

Fitzgerald, N., & Riley, K. (2005). Club drugs facilitate rape. In K. Balkin (Ed.), *Club drugs: At issues series* (pp. 100–105). Westport, CT: Greenhaven Press.

Fitzpatrick, K., LaGory, M., & Ritchey, F. (1993). Criminal victimization among the homeless. *Justice Quarterly, 10,* 353–368.

Flathman, M. (1999). Trauma and delayed memory: A review of the "repressed memories" literature. *Journal of Child Sexual Abuse, 8*(2), 1–23.

Flegenheimer, M., & Rosenberg, N. (2011, December 13). Eleventh body, believed to be of a missing woman, is found. *New York Times*, p. A20.

Fletcher, G. (1988). *A crime of self-defense: Bernhard Goetz and the law on trial*. Chicago: University of Chicago Press.

Fleury, R., Sullivan, C., Bybee, D., & Davidson, W. (1998). Why don't they just call the cops? *Violence and Victims, 13*(4), 333–340.

Flock, E. (2012, July 23). President Obama unveils landmark actions to fight human trafficking. *U.S. News and World Report*. Retrieved September 29, 2014, from http://www.usnews.com/news/articles/2012/09/25/president-obama-unveils-major-actions-to-fight-human-trafficking.

Flor, E., & Ovalle, D. (2013, September 8). Hialeah police chief details tense moments of hostage rescue. *Miami Herald*. Retrieved December 22, 2014, from http://www.miamiherald.com/news/special-reports/hialeah-mass-shooting/article1953652.htm.

Flynn, E. (1982). Theory development in victimology: An assessment of recent progress and of continuing challenges. In H. Schneider (Ed.), *The victim in international perspective* (pp. 96–104). Berlin: De Gruyter.

Follingstad, D., Rutledge, L., McNeill-Harkins, K., & Polek, D. (1992). Factors related to physical violence in dating relationships. In E. Viano (Ed.), *Intimate violence: Interdisciplinary perspectives* (pp. 121–135). Washington, DC: Hemisphere Publishing.

Fooner, M. (1971, February). Money and economic factors in crime and delinquency. *Criminology, 8*(4), 311–320.

Ford, D. (2003). Coercing victim participation in domestic violence prosecutions. *Journal of Interpersonal Violence, 18*(6), 669–680.

Forer, L. (1980). *Criminals and victims: A trial judge reflects on crime and punishment*. New York: Norton.

Forst, G., & Hernon, J. (1984). *NIJ research in brief—The criminal justice response to victim harm*. Washington, DC: U.S. Department of Justice.

Forst, M., & Blomquist, M. (1991). *Missing children: Rhetoric and reality*. New York: Lexington Books.

Fox, J., & McDowall, D. (2008). Brief of professors of criminal justice as *amici curiae, D.C. vs. Heller. U.S. Supreme Court*. Retrieved October 3, 2008, from www.nraila.org/heller.

Fox, J., & Zawitz, M. (2002). *Homicide trends in the United States. BJS Special Report*. Washington, DC: U.S. Department of Justice.

Francescani, C. (2007). Murder or vigilante justice? *ABC News*. Retrieved January 22, 2012, from www.abcnews.go.com.

Franiuk, R., Seefelt, J., Cepress, S., Vandello, J. (2008, March). Prevalence and effects of rape myths in print journalism: The Kobe Bryant Case. *Violence Against Women, 14*(3), 287–309.

Frank, M. (2010). *The complete idiots guide to recovering from identity theft*. New York: Alpha Books.

Franklin, B. (1978). *The victim as criminal and artist: Literature from the American prison*. New York: Oxford University Press.

Franklin, C. A. (2011, March). An investigation of the relationship between self-control and alcohol-induced sexual assault victimization. *Criminal Justice and Behavior, 38*(3), 265–283.

Franklin, C., & Franklin, A. (1976). Victimology revisited. *Criminology, 14*(1), 125–136.

Frazer, J. (2014, May). Book Review: The law of self-defense. *America's 1st Freedom,* pp. 44–48.

Fredericks, B., (2014, July 11). Shot-in-head teen heroine. *New York Post,* p. 11.

Freedman, L., & Ray, L. (1982). *State legislation on dispute resolution*. Washington, DC: American Bar Association.

Freie Universitaet Berlin. (2014, August 30). Conflicts with teachers are risk factor for school shootings. *PsyPost*. Retrieved September 24, 2014, from http://www.psypost.org/2014/08/conflicts-teachers-risk-factor-school-shootings-27767.

Freking, K. (2011, November 15). Gabrielle Giffords interview: Congresswoman speaks, smiles in "20/20" interview. *Associated Press*. Retrieved December 8, 2011, from www.ap.org.

Frey, C. (2009). Allocution. In J. Wilson (Ed.), *The Praeger handbook of victimology* (pp. 11–12). Santa Barbara, CA: Praeger.

Freyd, P. (2011, Fall). FBI asks us to stop. *False Memory Syndrome Foundation Newsletter, 20*(4), 1–4. Retrieved December 6, 2011, from www.fmsonline.org.

Fried, J. (1982, May 2). Intimidation of witnesses called widespread. *New York Times*, p. S1.

Friedman, L. (1985, November). The crime victim movement at its first decade. *Public Administration Review, 45*, 790–794.

Friedrichs, D. (1983, April). Victimology: A consideration of the radical critique. *Crime and Delinquency, 29*(2), 280–290.

Friefeld, K. (2000, February 11). Man charged in shooting of son's hooky partner. *Long Island Newsday*, p. A35.

Frieze, I., & Browne, A. (1991). Violence in marriage. In L. Ohlin & M. Tonry (Eds.), *Crime and justice: A review of research, Volume 11: Family violence* (pp. 163–218). Chicago: University of Chicago Press.

Frum, D. (1993, January 18). Women who kill. *Forbes*, pp. 20–24.

———. (2014, June 20). The victimology of Hillary Clinton. *The Atlantic*. Retrieved September 11, 2014, from http://www.theatlantic.com/politics/archive/2014/06/the-victimology-of-hillary-clinton/373129/.

Fry, C. (2012, March 28). City may be liable for igniting street justice. *Courthouse News Service*. Retrieved December 28, 2014, from http://www.courthousenews.com/2012/03/28/45111.htm.

Fry, M. (1957, November 10). Justice for victims. *London Observer*, p. 8. Reprinted in 1959. *Journal of Public Law, 8*, 191–194.

Frye, V. (2001). Examining homicide's contribution to pregnancy-associated deaths. *Journal of the American Medical Association, 11*, 285–300.

Fryling, T. (2009). Elder abuse. In J. Wilson (Ed.), *The Praeger handbook of victimology* (pp. 83–85). Santa Barbara, CA: Praeger.

FTC. *See* Federal Trade Commission.

Fulginiti, L. (2008, January). Fatal footsteps: Murder of undocumented border crossers in Maricopa County, Arizona. *Journal of Forensic Sciences, 53*(1), 41–56.

Fuller, R., & Myers, R. (1941, June). The natural history of a social problem. *American Sociological Review, 6*, 320–328.

Fumento, M. (1998, August). "Road rage" versus reality. *The Atlantic Monthly*, pp. 18–21.

Furstenberg, F. (1972). Fear of crime and its effect on citizen behavior. In A. Biderman (Ed.), *Crime and justice* (pp. 52–65). New York: Justice Institute.

Fuselier, G. (1999, July). Placing the Stockholm Syndrome in perspective. *FBI Law Enforcement Bulletin, 68*(7), 22–25.

Futures Without Violence. (2009). The facts on housing and violence. Retrieved December 1, 2011, from www.futureswithoutviolence.org/content/action_center.

———. (2010, February). The facts on adolescent pregnancy, reproductive risk, and exposure to dating and family violence. Retrieved December 1, 2011, from www.futureswithoutviolence.org/content/action_center.

———. (2011). The facts on tweens and teens and dating violence. Retrieved December 1, 2011, from www.futureswithoutviolence.org/content/ action center.

———. (2014). The facts on the military and violence against women. Retrieved November 20, 2014, from http://www.futureswithoutviolence.org/userfiles/Military%20Factsheet%20update%2003%2003%2013.pdf.

Gado, M. (2005). My baby is missing! *Crime Library*. Retrieved October 13, 2005, from www.courttv.com.

Gagliardi, B. (2005, March/April). Corrections-based services for victims of crime. *The Crime Victims Report, 9*(1), 6.

Galaway, B. (1977). The uses of restitution. *Crime and Delinquency, 23*(1), 57–67.

———. (1987). Victim–offender mediation as the preferred response to property offenses. In E. Viano (Ed.), *Crime and its victims: International research and public policy issues* (pp. 101–111). New York: Hemisphere.

———. (1989). Prospects. In M. Wright & B. Galaway (Eds.), *Mediation and criminal justice: Victims, offenders and community* (pp. 270–275). Newbury Park, CA: Sage.

———. (1992). Restitution as innovation or unfilled promise? In E. Fattah (Ed.), *Towards a critical victimology* (pp. 347–371). New York: St. Martin's Press.

Galaway, B., & Hudson, J. (1975). Issues in the correctional implementation of restitution to victims of crime. In J. Hudson & B. Galaway (Eds.), *Considering the victim: Readings in restitution and victim compensation* (pp. 351–360). Springfield, IL: Charles C. Thomas.

———. (Eds.). (1981). *Perspectives on crime victims*. St. Louis, MO: C.V. Mosby.

Gambacorta, D. (2009, June 4). Police: Video might link Carrasquillo to high school attack. Retrieved January 20, 2012, from www. philly.com.

Garase, M. (2006). *Road Rage*. New York: LFB Scholarly Publishing.

Garbarino, J. (1989). The incidence and prevalence of child maltreatment. In L. Ohlin & M. Tonry (Eds.), *Crime and justice: A review of research, Volume 11: Family violence* (pp. 219–262). Chicago: University of Chicago Press.

Garcia, V., & McManimon, P. (2011). *Gendered justice: Intimate partner violence and the criminal justice system*. New York: Rowman and Littlefield.

Gardiner, S. (2008, May 6). NYPD inaction over a missing woman found dead sparks a historic racial-bias lawsuit. Retrieved October 1, 2008, from www.villagevoice. com.

———. (2010, June 16). Beware the "Jiggler": Thieves use bits of metal to feast on older Hondas, Toyotas. *Wall Street Journal*, p. B4.

———. (2013, March 6). No charges for FBI agent in shooting. *Wall Street Journal*, p. A8.

Gardner, R. (1990). *Sex abuse hysteria: Salem witch trials revisited*. Cresskill, NJ: Creative Therapeutics.

———. (1994). Belated realization of child sex abuse by an adult. In K. de Koster & K. Swisher (Eds.), *Child abuse: Opposing viewpoints* (pp. 217–223). San Diego, CA: Greenhaven Press.

Garfinkle, H. (1949, May). Research note on inter- and intra-racial homicides. *Social Forces, 27*, 370–381.

Garlock, S. (2007, February). Congressional victim's rights caucus offers "a voice of victims" in Washington. *The Crime Victims Report, 10*(6), 85, 89.

Garofalo, J. (1981). Victimization surveys: An overview. In B. Galaway & J. Hudson (Eds.), *Perspectives on crime victims* (pp. 98–103). St. Louis, MO: C.V. Mosby.

———. (1986). Lifestyles and victimization: An update. In E. Fattah (Ed.), *From crime policy to victim policy* (pp. 135–155). New York: St. Martin's Press.

Garofalo, J., & Connelly, K. (1980, September). Dispute resolution centers: Part 1—Major features and processes; Part 2—Outcomes, issues, and future directions. *Criminal Justice Abstracts, 12*(3), 416–610.

Gartland, M. (2013, August 4). Pay-up time for Brawley: '87 rape-hoaxer finally shells out for slander. *New York Post*, p. 14.

Gartner, A., & Riessman, F. (1980, February 19). Lots of helping hands. *New York Times*, p. A22.

Gartner, R. (1990, February). The victims of homicide: A temporal and cross-national comparison. *American Sociological Review, 55*(1), 92–106.

Garvey, M., & Winton, R. (2003, June 27). High court's term ends; those who came forward feel betrayed. *Los Angeles Times*, p. 29.

Gately, G. (2005, February 12). Baltimore struggles to battle witness intimidation; prosecutors say violence, threats hinder testimony. *Boston Globe*, p. A3.

Gates, R., quoted in Quigley, S. (2009, July 16). Gates thanks 10th mountain division for sacrifices. *American Forces Press Service*, p. 1.

Gaynes, M. (1981, November–December). New roads to justice: Compensating the victim. *State Legislatures, 11*(10), 11–17.

Gegan, S., & Rodriguez, N. (1992, Fall). Victims' roles in the criminal justice system: A fallacy of empowerment. *St. John's Journal of Legal Commentary, 8*(1), 225–250.

Geis, G. (1976). Compensation to victims of violent crime. In R. Gerber (Ed.), *Contemporary issues in criminal justice* (pp. 90–115). Port Washington, NY: Kennikat.

———. (1977). Restitution by criminal offenders: A summary and overview. In J. Hudson & B. Galaway (Eds.), *Restitution in criminal justice* (pp. 147–164). Lexington, MA: Lexington Books.

———. (1983). Victim and witness assistance programs. In S. Kadish (Ed.), *Encyclopedia of crime and justice* (pp. 1600–1604). New York: Free Press.

Geis, G., & Loftus, E. (2009). Taus v. Loftus: Determining the legal ground rules for scholarly inquiry. *Journal of Forensic Psychology Practice, 9*, 147–162.

Geller, L. (2011, October 18). Expert: Theft of truck has broad security implications. *WWBT, NBC News*. Retrieved November 3, 2011, from www.nbc12.com.

Geller, W. (1992, December 31). Put friendly-fire shooting in perspective. *Law Enforcement News*, p. 9.

Gelles, R. (1987). *The violent home*. Newbury Park, CA: Sage.

Gelles, R., & Cornell, C. (1990). *Intimate violence in families* (2nd ed.). Newbury Park, CA: Sage.

Gelles, R., & Straus, M. (1988). *Intimate violence*. New York: Touchstone Books.

George, M. (2003). Ask the FBI: The white slave trade. *Interactive Chat*. Retrieved June 19, 2000, from www.FBI.gov.

George, S. (2012, April 12). The strong arm of the law is weak. *Creighton Law Review, 45*, 563–599.

Geranios, N. (2014, December 30). 2-year-old accidentally kills his mom in Wal-Mart. *Associated Press*. Retrieved January 10, 2015, from http://news.yahoo.com/police-boy-2-accidentally-kills-mom-wal-mart-201635957.html.

Gettleman, E. (2005, July 1). A new order in the court. *Mother Jones*, p. 8.

Gewurz, D., & Mercurio, M. (1992, Fall). The victims' bill of rights: Are victims all dressed up with no place to go? *St. John's Journal of Legal Commentary, 8*(1), 251–278.

Ghandnoosh, N. (2014). Race and punishment: Racial perceptions of crime and support for punitive policies. The Sentencing Project. Retrieved September 24, 2014, from http://www.sentencingproject.org/doc/publications/rd_Race_and_Punishment.pdf.

Giacinti, T. (1973). *Forcible rape: The offender and his victim*. Unpublished master's thesis. Ann Arbor, MI: University Microfilms.

Giannelli, P. (1997). Rape trauma syndrome. *Criminal Law Bulletin, 33*, 270–279.

Giardino, A., & Giardino, E. (2010). *Intimate partner violence*. Houston, TX: STM publishers.

Gibbs, N. (1991, June 3). When is it rape? *Time*, pp. 38–40.

———. (1993a, January 18). Til death do us part. *Time*, pp. 38–45.

———. (1993b, August 16). Hell on wheels. *Time*, pp. 44–46.

Gibson, R. (2004). Most-stolen cars? It's debatable. Retrieved September 7, 2005, from www.bankrate.com.

Gidcyz, C., Orchowski, L., & Berkowitz, A. (2011, June). Preventing sexual aggression among college men. *Violence Against Women, 17*(6), 720–742.

Gilbert, N. (1991, Spring). The phantom epidemic of sexual assault. *The Public Interest, 103*, 54–65.

Gillespie, C. (1989). *Battered women, self-defense, and the law*. Columbus, OH: Ohio State University Press.

Ginsberg, A. (2005, September 20). Reliving horror at rape trial. *New York Post*. Retrieved January 3, 2012, from www.nypost.com.

Ginsberg, A. (2005, September 20). Reliving horror at rape trial. *New York Post*, p. 20.

———. (2009, September 23). Slay witness stays silent. *New York Post*. Retrieved January 7, 2012, from www.nypost.com.

Girdner, L., & Hoff, P. (1994). *Obstacles to the recovery and return of parentally abducted children. Research summary*. Washington, DC: U.S. Department of Justice.

Girelli, S., Resick, P., Dvorak, S., & Hutter, C. (1986). Subjective distress and violence during rape: Their effects on long-term fear. *Victims and Violence, 1*(1), 35–46.

Gjertsen, E. (2014, April 10). The 'double life' of Mickey Rooney. *CNBC.com*. Retrieved November 21, 2014, from www.cnbc.com/id/101568802#.

Glaberson, W. (2003, July 6). Justice, safety, and the system: A witness is slain in Brooklyn. *New York Times*, pp. A1, B18–19.

———. (2005, April 6). Sex-Trafficking pleas detail abuse of Mexican women. *New York Times*, p. B3.

Glaze, L., & Bonczar, T. (2007). *Probation and parole in the United States, 2006. BJS Bulletin*. Retrieved July 28, 2008, from http://www.ojp.usdoj.gov/bjs/pub/pdf/ppus06.pdf.

Glensor, R., & Peak, K. (2004). Crimes against tourists. *Problem-Oriented Policing Guide, No. 26*. Retrieved July 22, 2011, from www.popcenter.org.

Glover, S. (2009, April 5). FBI database links long-haul truckers, serial killings. Retrieved October 10, 2009, from www.latimes.com.

Gobert, J., & Jordan, W. (2009). *Jury selection: The law, art, and science of selecting a jury* (3rd ed.). New York: Clark Boardman Callaghan.

Goldberg, C. (1998, September 8). Getting to the truth in child abuse cases: New methods. *New York Times*, pp. C1, C5.

———. (1999, November 23). Spouse abuse crackdown, surprisingly, nets many women. *New York Times*, p. A16.

Goldberg, S., Green, E., & Sander, F. (1985). *Dispute resolution*. Boston: Little, Brown.

Goldberg-Ambrose, C. (1992). Unfinished business in rape law reform. *Journal of Social Issues, 48*(1), 173–185.

Golden, J. (2009). Defensible space. In J. Wilson (Ed.), *The Praeger handbook of victimology* (pp. 75–76). Santa Barbara, CA: Praeger.

Goldsmith, J., & Goldsmith, S. (1976). *Crime and the elderly: Challenge and response*. Lexington, MA: D.C. Heath.

Goldstein, E. (1993). *Confabulations: Creating false memories, destroying families*. Boca Raton, FL: SIRS Books.

Goldstein, J. (1960, March). Police discretion not to invoke the criminal process. *Yale Law Journal, 69*, 543–594.

Goldstein, J., & Baker, A. (2011, July 21). City room: Young and missing. *New York Times*, p. B4.

Goldstein, K., & Martin, S. (2004, August). Intimate partner physical assault before and during pregnancy. *Violence and Victims, 19*(4), 387–398.

Goldstein, M. (2011, April 20). Special report: From Hannibal Lecter to Bernie Madoff: FBI behavioral analysts apply serial killer profiling to white collar crime. Retrieved July 23, 2011, from www.reuters.com.

Goldstein, S. (2014, January 31). 'Young Guns' special looks at the dangerous intersection of children and firearms. *New York Daily News*. Retrieved January 10, 2015, from http://www.nydailynews.com/entertainment/tv-movies/

young-guns-special-dangerous-intersection-children-fire arms-article-1.1598431.

Goleman, D. (1993, June 11). Studies reveal suggestibility of very young as witnesses. *New York Times*, pp. A1, A23.

———. (1994, October 31). Proof lacking for ritual abuse by Satanists. *New York Times*, p. A13.

Goldstein, K., & Martin, S. (2004, August). Intimate partner physical assault before and during pregnancy. *Violence and Victims, 19*(4), 387–394.

Gondolf, E. (1988). The state of the debate: A review essay on woman battering. *Response, 11*(3), 3–8.

Gonzalez, D. (1992, November 25). Sliwa admits faking crimes for publicity. *New York Times*, pp. B1, B2.

Gonzalez, T. (2013, July 22). Human trafficking survivors in Tennessee need more help, report finds. *The Tennessean*. Retrieved September 27, 2014, from http://www.tennes sean.com/article/20130722/NEWS03/307220021/Human-trafficking-survivors-TN-need-more-help-report-finds.

Goode, E. (2011, September 28). Rape definition too narrow in federal statistics, critics say. *New York Times*, p. A14.

Goodell, J. (2001, May 13). Letting go of McVeigh. *New York Times Magazine*, pp. 40–44.

Goodman, A. (2012, January 9). As Arizona remembers Tucson shooting, Virginia Tech massacre survivor calls for new gun control. Retrieved January 23, 2012, from www. democracynow.org.

———. (2013, February 20). Throwaways: Recruited by police & thrown into danger, young informants are drug war's latest victims. Retrieved September 30, 2014, from www.democracynow.org.

Goodman, D. (2013, June 24). Police unit taking closer look at deadly crashes. *New York Times,* pp. A16, A19.

———. (2014, April 8). For car thieves, the older and heavier the ride, the better. *New York Times,* pp. A10.

Goodman, R., Mercy, J., Loya, F., Rosenberg, M., Smith, J., Allen, N., et al. (1986). Alcohol use and interpersonal violence: Alcohol detected in homicide victims. *American Journal of Public Health, 76*(2), 144–148.

Goodnough, A. (2003, June 12). City to remove four teachers from classrooms. *New York Times*, p. B2.

———. (2005, April 27). Florida expands right to use deadly force in self-defense. *New York Times*, p. A18.

———. (2011, April 13). 13 former campers echo senator's claim of abuse. *New York Times*, p. A19.

Goodnough, A. (2013, October 26). For victim of ghastly crime, a new face, a new beginning. *New York Times,* pp. A1, A14.

Goodstein, L. (2011, May 19). Church abuse report authors defend findings as critics weigh in. *New York Times*, p. A19.

Goodstein, L., & Callender, D. (2010, March 27). For half century, deaf boys raised alarm on priest's abuse. *New York Times*, pp. A1, A10.

Gootman, E. (2007, September 20). Undercount of violence in schools. *New York Times*, p. B2.

Gose, B. (1997, April 18). Efforts to end fraternity hazing said to have largely failed. *Chronicle of Higher Education*. Retrieved December 28, 2011, from http://chronicle.com.

Gottesman, R., & Mountz, L. (1979). *Restitution: Legal analysis*. Reno, NV: National Council of Juvenile and Family Court Judges.

Gottfredson, M., & Gottfredson, D. (1988). *Decision making in criminal justice: Toward the rational exercise of discretion* (2nd ed.). New York: Plenum Press.

Graham, E. (1993, October 25). Education: Fortress academia sells security. *Wall Street Journal*, p. B1.

Grant, M. (2013, March). Unpacking the sex trafficking panic. *Contemporary Sexuality, 47*(2), 1–6.

Gray, E. (1986). *Child abuse: Prelude to delinquency?* Washington, DC: U.S. Department of Justice.

Gray, J. (1993, July 29). New Jersey court says victims of car chases cannot sue police. *New York Times*, pp. B1, B6.

Gray, M. (2013, March 8). Georgia town mulls mandatory gun ownership.*CNN*. Retrieved January 10, 2015, from http://www.cnn.com/2013/03/07/us/georgia-gun-requirement/index.html.

Grayson, B., & Stein, M. (1981). Attracting assault: Victims' nonverbal cues. *Journal of Communications, 31*, 65–70.

Green, A. (2008, February 15). Attacks on homeless rise, with youths mostly to blame. *New York Times*, p. A12.

Green, E. (1964, September). Inter- and intra-racial crime relative to sentencing. *Journal of Criminal Law, Criminology, and Police Science, 55*, 348–358.

Green, G. (1987, February). Citizen gun ownership and crime deterrence: Theory, research, and policy. *Criminology, 25*(1), 63–82.

Greenberg, M., & Ruback, R. (1984). Elements of crime victim decision making. *Victimology, 10*(1), 600–616.

Greenblatt, M., & Razio, D. (2010, Winter). Uncovering hidden homicides. *The IRE Journal,*30–31.

Greenfeld, L., Rand, M., & Craven, D. (1998). *Violence by intimates: Analysis of data on crimes by current or former spouses, boyfriends, and girlfriends. BJS Report.* Washington, DC: U.S. Department of Justice.

Greenhouse, L. (1989, June 22). Supreme Court roundup: First Amendment protects paper that named rape victim, justices rule. *New York Times*, p. B9.

———. (1990, June 28). Child abuse trials can shield witness. *New York Times*, pp. A1, B8.

———. (1991, December 11). High court upsets seizing of profits of convict's books. *New York Times*, pp. A1, B8.

———. (2006, June 20). 911 call is held as evidence if victim cannot testify. *New York Times,* p. A14.

———. (2008, June 27). Justices, ruling 5–4, endorse personal right to own gun. *New York Times*, p. A10.

Greenwald, G. (2008, August 1). Vital unsolved anthrax questions and ABC news. Retrieved December 28, 2011, from www.salon.com.

Greenwood, A. (2008, February). For mail-order brides, happily ever after. *ABA Journal, 94*(2), 14.

Gregory, L. (2011, Fall). President's message. *COPS* (newsletter of Concerns of Police Survivors), *25*(3), 1. Retrieved December 29, 2010, from www.nationalcops.org.

Griffin, S. (1979). *Rape: The power of consciousness*. New York: Harper & Row.

Grissom, B. (2013, January 4). Clearing Texas rape kit backlog brings hefty price tag. *The Texas Tribune*. Retrieved January 10, 2015, from http://www.texastribune.org/2013/01/04/clearing-texas-rape-kit-backlog-brings-hefty-price/.

Groeninger, S. (2014, December 30). Firearms–related fatalities spiked 56 percent while ambush attacks remained the leading cause of felonious deaths. *National Law Enforcement Officers Memorial Fund*. Retrieved January 15, 2014, from http://www.nleomf.org/newsroom/news-releases/eoy-report-2014.html.

Gross, J. (1990, September 20). 203 rape cases reopened in Oakland as the police chief admits mistakes. *New York Times*, p. A13.

———. (1992, September 15). Abused women who kill now seek way out of cells. *New York Times*, p. A16.

———. (1993, December 6). California town mourns abducted girl. *New York Times*, p. A12.

Gross, T. (2013, October 8). Elizabeth Smart says kidnapper was a 'master at manipulation.' *NPR Radio show Fresh Air*. Retrieved November 17, 2014, from http://www.npr.org/2013/10/08/230204193/elizabeth-smart-says-kidnapper-was-a-master-at-manipulation.

Grow, B. (2011, May 19). Strauss-Kahn case raises issue of abuse by diplomats in U.S. Retrieved July 3, 2011, from www.reuters.com.

Gutis, P. (1988, April 10). New head of police speaks out. *New York Times*, p. A12.

———. (1989, June 8). Attacks on U.S. homosexuals held alarmingly widespread. *New York Times*, p. A24.

Gutman, M. (2014, January 14). Wife of slain movie theater patron says her life is "shattered." *ABC News*. Retrieved September 17, 2014, from http://abcnews.go.com/US/wife-slain-movie-theater-patron-life-shattered/story?id=21629039.

Haake, G. (2014, August 2). Marcas McGowan case affidavit keeps Cady Harris' shooter a secret. *KHSB 41 TV News*. Retrieved September 5, 2014, from http://www.kshb.com/news/crime/marcas-mcgowan-case-affidavit-keeps-cady-harris-shooter-a-secret.

Hackett, G., & Cerio, G. (1988, January 18). When the victim goes on trial. *Newsweek*, p. 31.

Hafemeister, T. (1996, Spring). Protecting child witnesses: Judicial efforts to minimize trauma and reduce evidentiary barriers. *Violence and Victims, 11*(1), 71–92.

Halber, D. (2014). *The skeleton crew:How amateur sleuths are solving America's coldest cases*. New York: Simon and Schuster.

Halbfinger, D. (2002, February 20). Finding hope as an enemy ties a noose. *New York Times*, p. B1.

Hall, D. (1975). The role of the victim in the prosecution and conviction of a criminal case. *Vanderbilt Law Review, 28*(5), 932–985.

———. (1991). Victims' voices in criminal court: The need for restraint. *American Criminal Law Review, 28*, 233–243.

Hall, T. (1990, October 7). Fatal accidents are down as U.S. becomes vigilant. *New York Times*, pp. A1, A32.

Halleck, S. (1980). Vengeance and victimization. *Victimology, 5*(2), 99–109.

Hamburger, T., Wallsten, P., & Horwitz, S. (2013, January 31). NRA-backed federal limits on gun lawsuits frustrate victims, their attorneys. *Washington Post*. Retrieved December 3, 2014, from http://www.washingtonpost.com/politics/nra-backed-federal-limits-on-gun-lawsuits-frustrate-victims-their-attorneys/2013/01/31/a4f101da-69b3-11e2-95b3-272d604a10a3_story.html.

Hampton, R., Oliver, R., & Magarian, L. (2003, May). Domestic violence in the African American community: An analysis of social and structural factors. *Violence Against Women, 9*(5), 533–558.

Hanley, R. (1994, September 28). Crime victims call for hard labor. *New York Times*, p. B6.

Hansen, M. (1997, September). Repairing the damage: Citizen boards tailor sentences to fit the crimes in Vermont. *ABA Journal, 83*, 20.

Hardison, J., Walters, M., Moore, A., Stat, M., Berzofsky, M., & Langton, L. (2013, June). *Household burglary, 1994–2011.BJS Special Report*. Washington, DC: U.S. Department of Justice.

Harland, A. (1979). Restitution statutes and cases: Some substantive and procedural restraints. In B. Galaway & J. Hudson (Eds.), *Victims, offenders, and restitutive sanctions* (pp. 151–171). Lexington, MA: Lexington Books.

———. (1981a). *Restitution to victims of personal and household crimes*. Washington, DC: U.S. Department of Justice.

————. (1983). One hundred years of restitution: An international review and prospectus for research. *Victimology*, *8*(1), 190–202.

Harlow, C. (1985). *Reporting crimes to the police. BJS Special Report*. Washington, DC: U.S. Department of Justice.

————. (1987). *Robbery victims. BJS Special Report*. Washington, DC: U.S. Department of Justice.

————. (1988). *Motor vehicle theft. BJS Special Report*. Washington, DC: U.S. Department of Justice.

————. (1991). *Female victims of violent crime. BJS Special Report*. Washington, DC: U.S. Department of Justice.

————. (1999). *Prior abuse reported by inmates and probationers. BJS Selected Findings*. Washington, DC: U.S. Department of Justice.

————. (2001). *Firearm use by offenders. BJS Special Report*. Washington, DC: U.S. Department of Justice.

————. (2005). *Hate crimes reported by victims and police. BJS Special Report*. Washington, DC: U.S. Department of Justice.

Harrell, E. (2005). *Violence by gang members, 1993–2003. BJS Crime Data Brief*. Washington, DC: U.S. Department of Justice.

————. (2007). *Black victims of violent crimes. BJS Special Report*. Washington, DC: U.S. Department of Justice.

————. (2011, November). *Crime against persons with disabilities, 2008–2010 - statistical tables. BJS Special Report*. Washington, DC: U.S. Department of Justice.

————. (2014, February). *Crime against persons with disabilities, 2009–2012 - statistical tables. BJS Special Report*. Washington, DC: U.S. Department of Justice.

————., & Langton, L. (2013, December 13). *Victims of identity theft, 2012. BJS Special Report*. Washington, DC: U.S. Department of Justice.

Harrington, C. (1985). *Shadow justice: The ideology and institutionalization of alternatives to court*. Westport, CT: Greenwood Press.

Harris, A., Thomas, S., Fisher, G., & Hirsch, D. (2002, May). Murder and medicine: The lethality of criminal assault, 1960–1999. *Homicide Studies*, *6*(2), 128–166.

Harris, M. (1979). *Sentencing to community service*. Washington, DC: American Bar Association.

Harrop, F. (2003, June 1). Editorial: Boys as victims? Oh, please! *Providence* (RI) *Journal-Bulletin*, p. D9.

Harry, J. (2002, July). Focus on victims' rights in Minnesota. *Corrections Today*, *64*(4), 12–13.

Harshbarger, S. (1987, March). Prosecution is an appropriate response in child sexual abuse cases. *Journal of Interpersonal Violence*, *2*(1), 108–112.

Hart, T., & Miethe, T. (2008). Exploring bystander presence and intervention in non-fatal violent victimization. *Violence and Victims*, *23*(5), 637–653.

Hart, T., & Reaves, B. (1999). *Felony defendants in large urban counties, 1996. BJS Bulletin*. Washington, DC: U.S. Department of Justice.

Hart, T., & Rennison, C. (2003). *Reporting crime to the police, 1992–2000. BJS Special Report*. Washington, DC: U.S. Department of Justice.

Hartman, S. (2013, October 4). Okla. teen acts to right his father's wrong. *CBS News*. Retrieved from http://www.cbsnews.com/news/okla-teen-acts-to-right-his-fathers-wrong/.

Haugrud, L., Gratch, L., & Magruder, B. (1997, Summer). Victimization and perpetration rates of violence in gay and lesbian relationships: Gender issues explored. *Violence and Victims*, *12*(2), 173–185.

Hauser, C., & O'Connor, M. (2007, April 16). Virginia Tech shooting leaves 33 dead. *New York Times*, p. A1.

Hazelbaker, K. (2011, August 25). News Release: Cadillac Escalade, large pickup trucks top list of thieves' favorite vehicles, claims data show. *Insurance Institute for Highway Safety, Highway Loss Data Institute*. Retrieved October 15, 2011, from www.iihs.org/news.

Healy, K. (1995). *NIJ Research in Action. Victim and witness intimidation: New developments and emerging responses*. Washington, DC: U.S. Department of Justice.

Healy, K., & Smith, C. (1998). *NIJ Research in Action. Batterer programs: What criminal justice agencies need to know*. Washington, DC: U.S. Department of Justice.

Heinz, J. (1982, July 7). On justice to victims. *New York Times*, p. A19.

Heisler, C. (2004, November). Court orders protect victims of stalking and domestic violence. *The Crime Victims Report*, 67–69.

Hellerstein, D. (1989). The victim impact statement: Reform or reprisal? *American Criminal Law Review*, *27*, 390–434.

Hellman, P. (1993, March 8). Crying rape: The politics of date rape on campus. *New York*, pp. 32–37.

Hemenway, D., Vriniotis, M., & Miller, M. (2006). Is an armed society a polite society? Guns and road rage. *Accident Analysis and Prevention*, *38*, 687–695.

Henderson, L. (1985). Victims' rights and wrongs. *Stanford Law Review*, *37*, 937–1021.

Hendricks, J. (1992). Domestic violence legislation in the United States: A survey of the states. In E. Viano (Ed.), *Intimate violence: Interdisciplinary perspectives* (pp. 213–228). New York: Hemisphere Publishers.

Hennessy, D. A., & Wiesenthal, D. L. (2002). The relationship between driver aggression, vengeance, and violence. *Violence and Victims*, *17*, 707–718.

Henriques, D. (2010, February 3). In court, impassioned challenges of Madoff trustee's plans. *New York Times*, pp. B1, B8.

Herberman, E., & Bonczar, T. (2014, October). Probation and parole in the United States, 2013. *Probation and parole population series.* Washington, DC: U.S. Department of Justice.

Herbert, B. (2002, April 15). Take the DNA kits off the shelves. *New York Times,* p. A23.

———. (2009, March 21). The great shame. *New York Times,* p. A21.

Herdt, T. (2013, December 15). Record numbers of life-term inmates granted parole in California. *Huffington Post.* Retrieved November 15, 2014, from http://www.huffingtonpost.com/2013/12/15/california-parole_n_4447448.html.

Herman, J. (1981). *Father–daughter incest.* Cambridge, MA: Harvard University Press.

———. (1992). *Trauma and recovery.* New York: Basic Books.

Herman, S. (1998). *Viewing restorative justice through victims' eyes.* Arlington, VA: National Center for Victims of Crime.

———. (1999, November 30). Interview: The director of the National Center for Victims of Crime. *Law Enforcement News,* pp. 8–11.

———. (2000). Seeking parallel justice: A new agenda for the victims movement. Retrieved October 3, 2008, from www.ncvc.org.

———. (2010). *Parallel justice for victims of crime.* Washington, DC: NCVC.

——— & Waul, M. (2004). *Repairing the harm: A new vision for crime victims compensation in America.* Washington, DC: National Center for Victims of Crime.

Hernandez, R. (2007, April 18). Students panicked and then held off gunman. *New York Times,* p. A21.

Herrington, L. (1982). Statement of the chairman. In *President's Task Force on Victims of Crime, final report* (pp. vi–vii). Washington, DC: U.S. Government Printing Office.

———. (1986, August). Dollars and sense: The value of victim restitution. *Corrections Today,* pp. 156–160.

Herszenhorn, D. (1999, July 27). Alarm helps to fight domestic violence. *New York Times,* p. B6.

Hewitt, S. (1998). *Assessing allegations of sexual abuse in preschool children.* Thousand Oaks, CA: Sage.

Hickey, E. (1991). *Serial murderers and their victims.* Pacific Grove, CA: Brooks/Cole.

Higgins, A. (2013). Maine bill would allow electronic tracking of domestic violence suspects. Maine Public Radio. Retrieved November 22, 2014, from www.mpbn.net/home/tabid/36.

Higgins, J. (2005). *Don't let identity thieves steal your future!* Retrieved September 23, 2005, from www.ed.gov/about/offices/list/oig/misused/idtheft.html.

Hightower, K. (2014, October 31). Ex-band member guilty of manslaughter in hazing case. *Huffington Post.* Retrieved December 22, 2014, from http://www.huffingtonpost.com/news/famu-hazing-death/.

Hill, C. (2014, February 21). Do cruise lines have a crime problem? *Market Watch.* Retrieved November 17, 2014, from http://www.marketwatch.com/story/do-cruise-lines-have-a-crime-problem-2014-02-21.

Hillenbrand, S. (1990). Restitution and victim rights in the 1980s. In A. Lurigio, W. Skogan, & R. Davis (Eds.), *Victims of crime: Problems, politics, and programs* (pp. 188–204). Thousand Oaks, CA: Sage.

Hills, S. (1981). *Demystifying deviance.* Englewood Cliffs, NJ: Prentice Hall.

Hilton, N. (1993). *Legal responses to wife assault: Current trends and evaluation.* Newbury Park, CA: Sage.

Hilts, P. (1994, March 3). Six percent of women admit beatings while pregnant. *New York Times,* pp. A1, A23.

Hinchcliffe, K. (2014, April 16). 'A gift from heaven': NC pays millions to help crime victims. *WRAL TV.* Retrieved December 17, 2014, from http://www.wral.com/-a-gift-from-heaven-nc-pays-millions-to-help-crime-victims/13547297/#HUsM26G2IpM8rPvK.99.

Hindelang, M., Gottfredson, M., & Garofalo, J. (1978). *Victims of personal crime: An empirical foundation for a theory of personal victimization.* Cambridge, MA: Ballinger Publishing.

Hines, D., Malley-Morrison, K., & Dutton, L. (2013). *Family violence in the United States: Defining, understanding, and combating abuse* (2nd ed.). Thousand Oaks, CA: Sage.

Hinman, K. (2011, November 2). Lost boys. *Village Voice,* pp. 1, 11, 12.

——— (2002, November–December). Cyberstalking and law enforcement: Keeping up with the web. *The Crime Victims Report,* 6(5), 65–66, 73.

Ho, T., Zhao, J., & Brown, M. (2009, February). Examining hotel crimes from police reports. *Crime Prevention and Community Safety,* 11(1), 21–33.

Hochstedler, E. (1981). *Crime against the elderly in twenty-six cities.* Washington, DC: U.S. Department of Justice.

Hoffman, B. (2003, September 9). Syracuse sex slaves tell rapist's secrets. *New York Post,* p. 25.

Hoffman, J. (1994, April 22). May it please the public: Lawyers exploit media attention as a defense tactic. *New York Times,* pp. B1, B7.

———. (2009, September 13). Why can't she walk to school? *New York Times,* pp. F1, F14.

Hoffmaster, D., Murphy, G., McFadden, S., & Griswold, M. (2010). Police and immigration: How chiefs are leading their communities through the challenges. *Police Executive Research Foundation (PERF).* Retrieved July 23, 2010, from http://www.ncjrs.gov/App/Publications/abstract. aspx?ID=256099.

Hofmann, R. (2007, June 28). Help rape survivors quickly. *Newsday*, p. A43.

Hofstadter, R., & Wallace, M. (1970). *American violence: A documentary history*. New York: Knopf.

Holder, E. (2011, December 28). *Statement of Attorney General Holder on increase in law enforcement fatalities*. Washington, DC: U.S. Department of Justice, Office of Public Affairs.

Holmes, R. (1994). *Murder in America*. Newbury Park, CA: Sage.

Holmes, R., & DeBurger, J. (1988). *Serial murder*. Newbury Park, CA: Sage.

Holmes, R., & Holmes, S. (2009). *Profiling violent crimes: An investigative too* (4th ed.). Newbury Park, CA: Sage.

Hook, S. (1972, April). The rights of the victims: Thoughts on crime and compassion. *Encounter*, 29–35.

Hoover, J. (1994). *Technical background on the redesigned National Crime Victimization Survey*. Washington, DC: U.S. Department of Justice.

Hoover, J. E. (1966, September 22). The car theft problem: How you can help beat it. *Congressional Record: Senate*, 23621.

Hope, J. (2007, February 16). Drug rape myth exposed as study reveals binge drinking is to blame. Retrieved September 24, 2008, from www.dailymail.co.uk.

Horn, M. (1993, November 29). Memories lost and found. *U.S. News & World Report*, pp. 52–63.

Hotaling, G., Finkelhor, D., Kirkpatrick, J., & Straus, M. (1988). *Coping with family violence: Research on policy perspectives*. Newbury Park, CA: Sage.

Houppert, K. (2005, July–August). Base crimes: The military has a domestic violence problem. *Mother Jones*, pp. 8–11.

House Subcommittee on Health and Long-Term Care, Select Committee on Aging. (1992). *Hearings on elder abuse*. Washington, DC: U.S. Department of Justice.

Houston Police Department. (2014). *Robbery prevention*. Retrieved November 8, 2014, from http://www.houstontx.gov/police/pdfs/brochures/english/Robbery_Personal.pdf.

Howell, J. (1989). *Selected state legislation: A guide for effective state laws to protect children* (2nd ed.). Washington, DC: National Center for Missing and Exploited Children.

Hu, W., & Goodman, D. (2013, July 13). Wake-up call for New Yorkers as police seek abducted boy. *New York Times*, p. 12.

Hubbard, A. (2006, May/June). Flip-flopping victims. *The Crime Victims Report, 19*, 31.

Hubbard, A. (2012, March 20). Menendez brothers convicted in parents' murder 16 years ago. *Los Angeles Times*. Retrieved September 9, 2014, from http://latimesblogs.latimes.com/lanow/2012/03/menendez-brothers.html.

Hudson, D. (2012, March). 'Son of Sam' laws. *Vanderbilt University First Amendment Center*. Retrieved December 14, 2014, from http://www.firstamendmentcenter.org/son-of-sam-laws.

Hudson, J., & Chesney, S. (1978). Research on restitution: A review and assessment. In B. Galaway & J. Hudson (Eds.), *Offender restitution in theory and action* (pp. 131–148). Lexington, MA: Lexington Books.

Hudson, J., & Galaway, B. (1975). *Considering the victim: Readings in restitution and victim compensation*. Springfield, IL: Charles C. Thomas.

Hui, J. (2009). Marital rape. In J. Wilson (Ed.), *The Praeger handbook of victimology* (pp. 202–204, 305–306). Santa Barbara, CA: Praeger.

Hulse, C. (2014, July 7). Immigrant surge rooted in law to curb child trafficking. *New York Times*, p. A10.

Human Rights Watch. (2010, August 30). Defending Illinois' rape victims. *HRW.org*. Retrieved December 11, 2014, from http://www.hrw.org/news/2010/08/30/defending-illinois-rape-victims.

Humane Society of the United States. (2014). Directory of safe havens for animals programs. *Human Society*. Retrieved November 23, 2014, from http://www.humanesociety.org/issues/abuse_neglect/tips/safe_havens_directory.html#nj.

Hunzeker, D. (1992). Stalking laws. *National Conference of State Legislatures' State Legislative Report, 17*(19), 1–6.

Hurley, J. (1995, June). Home invasion robbery. *FBI Law Enforcement Bulletin, 64*(6), 9–16.

IACP. See International Association of Chiefs of Police.

IBR (Incident Based Reporting) Resource Center. (2011). Crime reporting. Retrieved December 11, 2011, from www.jrsa.org.

Identity Theft Assistance Center (ITAC). (2011, October 24). Seventy percent of identity theft victims helped by ITAC report they do not know the source of the crime. Retrieved October 30, 2011, from www.identitytheftassistance.org.

Identity Theft Resource Center (ITRC). (2014a, July 17). Your car: A four-wheeled identity. *ITRC*. Retrieved October 30, 2014, from http://www.idtheftcenter.org/Identity-Theft/your-car-a-four-wheeled-identity.html.

———. (2014b). IRCR Breach Report 2014. *ID Theft Center*. Retrieved October 21, 2014, from http://www.idtheftcenter.org/id-theft/data-breaches.html.

Inciardi, J. (1976). The pickpocket and his victim. *Victimology, 1*(3), 446–453.

Ingrassia, M., & Beck, M. (1994, July 4). Patterns of abuse. *Newsweek*, pp. 26–33.

Insurance Information Institute (III). (2011). Auto theft. Retrieved October 25, 2011, from www.iii.org/media/hottopics/insurance.

International Association Of Chiefs of Police (IACP). (2009). Enhancing law enforcement responses to victims: A 21st century strategy. *IACP*. Retrieved November 14, 2014, from http://www.iacp.org/Portals/0/pdfs/responsetovictims/pdf/pdf/IACP_Strategy_REV_09_Layout_1.pdf.

Irwin, T. (1980). *To combat and prevent child abuse and neglect*. New York: Public Affairs Committee.

Island, D., & Letellier, P. (1991). *Men who beat the men who love them*. New York: Harrington Park Press.

Italiano, L. (2010, February 24). Three years in prison for framing innocent man. *New York Post*, pp. 4–5.

Italiano, L., & Mangan, D. (2011, March 26). Family of murdered student Imette St. Guillen drops fed case for $130G. *New York Post*, p. 14.

ITRC. *See* Identity Theft Resource Center.

Jackson, L., Socolar, R., Hunter, W., Runyan, D., & Colindres, R. (2000). Directly questioning children and adolescents about maltreatment: A review of survey measures used. *Journal of Interpersonal Violence*, *15*(7), 725–760.

Jackson, N. (1998). Lesbian battering: The other closet. In N. Jackson & G. Oates (Eds.), *Violence in intimate relation-ships: Examining sociological and psychological issues* (pp. 181–194). Woburn, MA: Butterworth Heinemann.

Jackson, N. (2007). *Encyclopedia of domestic violence*. New York: Routledge.

Jacob, B. (1977). The concept of restitution: An historical overview. In J. Hudson & B. Galaway (Eds.), *Restitution in criminal justice* (pp. 45–62). Lexington, MA: Lexington Books.

Jacobs, A. (2003, April 19). Town loner charged in chilling case of sexual captivity. *New York Times*, pp. D1, D5.

Jacobs, J., & Potter, K. (1998). *Hate crimes: Criminal law and identity politics*. New York: Oxford University Press.

Jacobs, S., & Moore, D. (1994). Successful restitution as a predictor of juvenile recidivism. *Juvenile and Family Court Journal*, *45*(1), 3–14.

Jahic, G., & Finckenauer, J. (2005). Representations and misrepresentations of human trafficking. *Trends in Organized Crime, 8*(3), 24–40.

Janofsky, M. (1994, December 5). The "why" of youth's fatal beating in Philadelphia is elusive. *New York Times*, p. A16.

Jasinski, J., & Williams, L. (1998). *Partner violence*. Thousand Oaks, CA: Sage.

Jauregui, A. (2014, September 13). George Zimmerman told motorist, "Do you know who I am?" *Huffington Post*. Retrieved September 15, 2014, from http://www.huffingtonpost.com/2014/09/13/george-zimmerman-road-rage_n_5815120.html.

Javelin. (2011, February 8). Identity fraud fell 28 percent in 2010 according to new Javelin Strategy and Research Report. Retrieved October 29, 2011, from www.javelinstrategy.com.

———. (2014, February 4). A new identity fraud victim every two seconds in 2013 according to latest Javelin Strategy & Research study. *Javelin*. Retrieved November 6, 2014, from https://www.javelinstrategy.com/news/1467/92/A-New-Identity-Fraud-Victim-Every-Two-Seconds-in-2013-According-to-Latest-Javelin-Strategy-Research-Study/d,pressRoomDetail.

Jay, M. (2011, June 30). Drivers who can no longer afford their cars turn to auto theft fraud. Retrieved October 27, 2011, from www.insureme.com.

Jeffrey, C. (1971). *Crime prevention through environmental design*. Beverly Hills, CA: Sage.

Jenkins, P. (1998). *Moral panic: Changing concepts of the child molester in modern America*. New Haven, CT: Yale University Press.

Jensen, G., & Brownfield, D. (1986). Gender, lifestyles, and victimization: Beyond routine activity. *Violence and Victims*, *1*(2), 85–99.

Johann, S., & Osanka, F. (1989). *Representing battered women who kill*. Springfield, IL: Charles C. Thomas.

John Jay College Research Team. (2004). *The nature and scope of sexual abuse of minors by Catholic priests and deacons in the United States, 1950–2002*. Retrieved January 12, 2005, from www.jjay.cuny.edu.

Johnson, G. (1941). The Negro and crime. *Annals of the American Academy of Political and Social Science*, *217*, 93–104.

Johnson, J. (1989). Horror stories and the construction of child abuse. In J. Best (Ed.), *Images of issues: Typifying contemporary social problems* (pp. 5–19). New York: Aldine de Gruyter.

Johnson, K. (2005, March 3). Settlement is reached in Bryant case. *New York Times*, p. A14.

———. (2008, July 10). New DNA technology clears the family of JonBenet Ramsey. *New York Times*, p. A18.

———. (2012, September 26). Boy scouts assert 'Good faith effort' to protect youths. *New York Times,* p. A17.

Johnston, J. (2005). Profile: Jennifer Wilbanks: Runaway bride. Retrieved October 1, 2005, from http://marriage.about.com/od/proposingbeingengaged/p/wilbanks.htm.

Johnstone, G. (2001). *Restorative justice: Ideas, values, debates*. Devon, UK: Willan Publishing.

Jones, A. (1980). *Women who kill*. New York: Fawcett Columbine Books.

Jones, J. (2004). Judge revisits day he overruled jury verdict. *San Diego Union Tribune*. Retrieved January 20, 2012, from www.signonsandiego.com.

Jones, M. (2003, May–June). Amber alert system saves children's lives. *The Crime Victims Report*, *7*(2), 20, 28.

Jones, R. (2007, February 28). In secret '96 tape, doomed woman tried to bargain with kidnapper. *New York Times*, pp. B1, B5.

Jones, R., & Goodnough, A. (2008, April 18). Abuse victims warily consider Pope's words. *New York Times*, p. A18.

Jordan, B. (2014, March 6). Gillibrand's military sexual assault bill fails. Military.com. Retrieved September 17, 2014, from http://www.military.com/daily-news/2014/03/06/gillibrands-military-sexual-assault-bill-fails.html.

Jordan, C., Logan, T., Walker, R., & Nigoff, A. (2003, February). Stalking: An examination of the criminal justice response. *Journal of Interpersonal Violence*, *18*(2), 148–165.

Jordan, I. (2005, September 9). Double-shot of fear. *Spokane Spokesman-Review*, p. 12.

Jordan, J. (2004, February). Beyond belief? Police, rape, and women's credibility. *Criminal Justice*, *4*(1), 29–59.

Joyce, E. (2004, Winter). Teen dating violence: Facing the epidemic. *Networks* (newsletter of the National Center for Victims of Crime, Washington, DC), 1–8.

Kalish, C. (1988). *International crime rates*. *BJS Special Report*. Washington, DC: U.S. Department of Justice.

Kahn, J. (2007, April). The story of a snitch. *Atlantic*, pp. 20–31.

Kaiser, D., & Stannow, L. (2011, March 24). Prison rape and the government. *New York Review of Books*, pp. 26–29.

Kallestad, B. (2011, July 9). States weigh "Caylee's law" in verdict aftermath. *Associated Press*. Retrieved December 1, 2011, from www.ap.org.

Kalven, H., & Zeisel, H. (1966). *The American jury*. Boston: Little, Brown.

Kampshroer, C. (2011, March 1). New leads in the Jacob Wetterling case. *KSTP channel 5 news*. Retrieved December 1, 2011, from http://kstp.com/news/stories.

Kanin, E. (1984). Date rape: Unofficial criminals and victims. *Victimology*, *9*(1), 95–108.

———. (1994). False rape allegations. *Archives of Sexual Behavior*, *23*(1), 81–90.

Kantrowitz, B., Starr, M., & Friday, C. (1991, April 29). Naming names. *Newsweek*, pp. 27–32.

Kappeler, V., Blumberg, M., & Potter, G. (1993). *The mythology of crime and criminal justice*. Prospect Heights, IL: Waveland.

Karjane, H., Fisher, B., & Cullen, F. (2005, December). *Sexual assault on campus: What colleges and universities are doing about it*. Washington, DC: Office of Justice Programs.

Karlen, N., Greenberg, N., Gonzalez, D., & Williams, E. (1985, October 7). How many missing kids? *Newsweek*, pp. 32–33.

Karmen, A. (1979). Victim facilitation: The case of auto theft. *Victimology*, *4*(4), 361–370.

———. (1980). Auto theft: Beyond victim blaming. *Victimology*, *5*(2), 161–174.

———. (1981a). Auto theft and corporate irresponsibility. *Contemporary Crises*, *5*, 63–81.

———. (1981b, February 15). *Crime victims and Congress*. Paper presented at the meeting of the Academy of Criminal Justice Sciences, Philadelphia, PA.

———. (1989). Crime victims and the news media: Questions of fairness and ethics. In J. Sullivan & J. Victor (Eds.), *Annual editions: Criminal justice 1988–1989* (pp. 51–57). Guilford, CT: Dushkin Publishing Group.

———. (1990). The implementation of victims' rights: A challenge for criminal justice professionals. In R. Muraskin (Ed.), *Issues in justice: Exploring policy issues in the criminal justice system* (pp. 46–57). Bristol, IN: Wyndham Hall Press.

———. (1992, Fall). Who's against victims' rights? The nature of the opposition to pro-victim initiatives in criminal justice. *St. John's Journal of Legal Commentary*, *8*(1), 157–176.

———. (1995). Towards the institutionalization of a new kind of justice professional: The victim advocate. *The Justice Professional*, *9*(1), 1–16.

———. (2006). *New York murder mystery: The true story behind the crime crash of the 1990s*. Paperback edition. New York: New York University Press.

Karp, D., & Warshaw, J. (2009, February). Their day in court: The role of murder victims' families in capital juror decision making. *Criminal Law Bulletin*, *45*(1), 99–120.

Katel, P. (2005, June). Identity theft: Can Congress give Americans better protection? *Congressional Quarterly Researcher*, *15*(22), 517–540.

Kates, D. (1986). *Firearms and violence: Issues of public policy*. New York: Ballinger.

Katz, L. (1980). *The justice imperative: An introduction to criminal justice*. Cincinnati, OH: Anderson Publishing.

Katz, L., Fletcher, G., & Altman, S. (1993). Blackmail symposium. *University of Pennsylvania Law Review*, *141*(5), 1565–1989.

Kaufman, E. (2012, November 20). Elizabeth Smart memoir of her captivity is acquired by St. Martin's. *New York Times*, p. B6.

Kaukinen, C. (2014). Dating violence among college students: The risk and protective factors. *Trauma, Violence, and Abuse*, *15*(4), 283–296.

Keepgunsoffcampus. (2014). Resources. *The Campaign To Keep Guns Off Campus*. Retrieved December 1, 2014, from http://keepgunsoffcampus.org/blog/category/resources/.

Keilitz, S., Davis, C., Efkeman, H., Flango, C., & Hannaford, P. (1997, September). Civil protection orders: Victims' views on effectiveness. *NIJ Journal*, *233*, 23–24.

Kelleher, J. (2006, January 3). An identity crisis. *Newsday*, p. A8.

Kelley, T. (2008, November 15). Bad health and a thief put a woman in crisis. *New York Times*, p. A19.

Kelley, T. (2009). Child witness. In J. Wilson (Ed.), *The Praeger handbook of victimology* (pp. 43–44). Santa Barbara, CA: Praeger.

Kelly, D. (2011). *The official identity theft prevention handbook.* New York: Sterling and Ross.

Kelly, R. (1983). Addicts and alcoholics as victims. In D. MacNamara & A. Karmen (Eds.), *Deviants: Victims or victimizers?* (pp. 49–76). Newbury Park, CA: Sage.

Kenber, B. (2013, August 28). Nidal Hasan sentenced to death for Fort Hood shooting rampage. *Washington Post.* Retrieved January 7, 2014, from http://www.washingtonpost.com/world/national-security/nidal-hasan-sentenced-to-death-for-fort-hood-shooting-rampage/2013/08/28/aad28de2-0ffa-11e3-bdf6-e4fc677d94a1_story.html.

Kendall-Tackett, K., Williams, L., & Finkelhor, D. (1993, January). Impact of sexual abuse on children: A review and synthesis of recent empirical studies. *Psychological Bulletin, 113*(1), 164–181.

Kennedy, D. (2004, Spring–Summer). Rethinking law enforcement strategies to prevent domestic violence. *Networks* (newsletter of the National Center for Victims of Crime), 9–15.

Kerner, O. (1968). *Report of the National Advisory Commission on Civil Disorders.* New York: Bantam Books.

Kesler, J. (1992). *How to keep your car from being stolen.* Houston, TX: Shell Oil Company.

Kethineni, S. (2009). Battered child syndrome. In J. Wilson (Ed.), *The Praeger handbook of victimology* (pp. 21–22). Santa Barbara, CA: Praeger.

Keve, P. (1978). Therapeutic uses of restitution. In B. Galaway & J. Hudson (Eds.), *Offender restitution in theory and action* (pp. 59–64). Lexington, MA: Lexington Books.

Kidnapping summons city to action. (1993, October 15). *New York Times*, p. A24.

Kilpatrick, D. (1985, February). Survey analyzes responses of female sex assault victims. *Crime Victims Digest*, p. 9.

Kincaid, J. (1993, June 1). Purity, pederasty and a fallen heroine. *New York Times*, p. A17.

———. (1998). *Erotic innocence: The culture of child molesting.* Durham, NC: Duke University Press.

Kindermann, C., Lynch, J., & Cantor, D. (1997). *Effects of the redesign on victimization estimates. BJS National Crime Victimization Survey.* Washington, DC: U.S. Department of Justice.

King, D., & Drost, M. (2005). Recantation and false allegations of child abuse: Selected bibliography. National Children's Advocacy Center. Retrieved November 19, 2014, from http://www.nationalcac.org/professionals/images/stories/pdfs/recantations%20and%20false%20allegations%20bibliography%20updated2.pdf.

King, P. (1993, October 4). Not so different, after all. *Newsweek*, p. 75.

King, W. (1989, January 1). Violent racism attracts new breed: Skinheads. *New York Times*, p. A35.

Kingkade, T. (2014, January 25). Dozen reported shootings at college campuses in 2013. *Huffington Post.* Retrieved January 2, 2015, from http://www.huffingtonpost.com/2014/01/13/shootings-college-campuses-2013_n_4577404.html.

Kirkwood, C. (1993). *Leaving abusive partners.* Newbury Park, CA: Sage.

Klaus, P. (1999a). *Carjackings in the United States, 1992–1996. BJS Special Report.* Washington, DC: U.S. Department of Justice.

———. (1999b). *Crimes against persons age 65 and older. BJS Report.* Washington, DC: U.S. Department of Justice.

———. (2004). *Carjackings, 1993–2002. BJS Crime Data Brief.* Washington, DC: U.S. Department of Justice.

Klaus, P., DeBerry, M., & Timrots, A. (1985). *The crime of rape. BJS Bulletin.* Washington, DC: U.S. Department of Justice.

Kleck, G. (1991). *Point blank: Guns and violence in America.* New York: Aldine de Gruyter.

———. (1997). *Targeting guns: Firearms and their control.* Hawthorne, NY: Aldine de Gruyter.

——— & DeLone, M. (1993). Victim resistance and offender weapon effects in robbery. *Journal of Quantitative Criminology, 9*(1), 55–81.

——— & Gertz, M. (1995, Fall). Armed resistance to crime: The prevalence and nature of self-defense with a gun. *Journal of Criminal Law and Criminology, 86*(1), 150–187.

Klein, A. (1997). *Alternative sentencing, intermediate sanctions and probation* (2nd ed.). Cincinnati, OH: Anderson.

Klein, E., Campbell, J., Soler, E., & Ghez, M. (1997). *Ending domestic violence.* Thousand Oaks, CA: Sage.

Klinger, D. (2001, August). Suicidal intent in victim-precipitated homicide. *Homicide Studies, 5*(3), 206–226.

Klurfeld, J. (1988, June 24). Editorial: Crimes of bigotry deserve harsher punishment. *New York Newsday*, p. 92.

Kocieniewski, D. (2010, November 13). U.S. sits on data pointing to missing children. *New York Times*, pp. A1, A11.

———, & Flynn, K. (1998, November 1). New York police lag in fighting domestic violence by officers. *New York Times*, p. B1, B4.

Koehler, M. (2011, October 20). PD: Victim killed in targeted shooting. *The Long Islander, 172*(11), 1.

Kohn, A. (2005, May). Straight shooting on gun control. *Reason, 37*(1), 20–25.

Kolarik, G. (1992, November). Stalking laws proliferate. *ABA Journal, 78*, 35–36.

Koppel, H. (1987). *Lifetime likelihood of victimization: BJS Technical Report*. Washington, DC: U.S. Department of Justice.

Kosloski, A. (2009). Adult protective services. In J. Wilson (Ed.), *The Praeger handbook of victimology* (pp. 8–9). Santa Barbara, CA: Praeger.

Koss, M. (1992). The underdetection of rape: Methodological choices influence incidence estimates. *Journal of Social Issues, 48*(1), 61–75.

———. (2005, January). Empirically enhanced reflections on 20 years of rape research. *Journal of Interpersonal Violence, 20*(1), 100–107.

———. (2008). Letter to the editor of the *Los Angeles Times*. Retrieved September 24, 2008, from www.calcasa.org.

Koss, M., & Cook, S. (1998). Facing the facts: Date and acquaintance rape are significant problems for women. In R. Bergen (Ed.), *Issues in intimate violence* (pp. 147–156). Thousand Oaks, CA: Sage.

Koss, M., Gidyez, C., & Wisniewski, N. (1987). The scope of rape: Incidence and prevalence of sexual aggression and victimization in a national sample of higher education students. *Journal of Consulting and Clinical Psychology, 55*, 162–170.

Koss, M., & Harvey, M. (1991). *The rape victim: Clinical and community interventions*. Newbury Park, CA: Sage.

Kotecha, K., & Walker, J. (1976). Vigilantism and the American police. In J. Rosenbaum & P. Sederberg (Eds.), *Vigilante politics* (pp. 158–174). Philadelphia: University of Pennsylvania Press.

Kratcoski, P., Edelbacher, M., & Das, D. (2001). Terrorist victimization: Prevention, control, and recovery. *International Review of Victimology, 8*, 257–268.

Krauss, C. (1994, January 23). New York car theft draws police priority. *New York Times*, pp. 21, 26.

Krebs, C., Lindquist, C., Warner, T., Fisher, B., & Martin, S. (2009, May/June). *Journal of American College Health, 57*(6), 639–649.

Krienert, J., & Walsh, J. (2010, February). Elderly homicide in the United States, 2000–2005. *Homicide Studies, 14*(1), 52–71.

———. (2011, July). My brother's keeper. *Journal of Family Violence, 26*(5), 331–342.

Kristal, A. (1991). You've come a long way baby: The battered woman's syndrome revisited. *New York Law School Journal of Human Rights, 9*, 111–116.

Kristof, N. (2009, April 30). Is rape serious? *New York Times*, p. A24.

———. (2011, April 23). What about American girls sold on the streets? *New York Times*, p. A26.

———. (2014a, March 8). To end the abuse, she grabbed a knife. *New York Times*, p. A24.

———. (2014b, December 14). A shooter, his victim, and race. *New York Times*, pp. E1, E5.

Krueger, F. (1985, May). Violated. *Boston*, 138–141.

Kuhl, A. (1986). Implications of justifiable homicide verdicts for battered women. *Response, 9*(2), 6–10.

Kuhner, J. (2011, September 2). Martin Luther King Jr.'s mixed legacy; Embrace of victimology tainted his call for a color blind society. *Washington Times*, p. 3.

Kyckelhahn, T., & Cohen, T. (2008, April). *Felony defendants in large urban counties, 2004. Bureau of Justice Statistics*. Washington, DC: U.S. Department of Justice.

La Fave, W. (1965). *Arrest: The decision to take a suspect into custody*. Boston: Little, Brown.

Labrecque, R., Smith, P., & Wooldredge, J.(2014, July–September). Creation and validation of an inmate risk assessment for violent, nonsexual victimization. *Victims & Offenders, 9*(3), 317–333.

Labriola, M., Bradley, S., O'Sullivan, C., Rempel, M., & Moore, S. (2010). A national portrait of domestic violence courts. Center For Court Innovation. Retrieved November 21, 2014, from https://www.ncjrs.gov/pdffiles1/nij/grants/229659.pdf.

LaFontaine, D. (1997). *Speak of the devil: Allegations of satanic abuse in Britain*. New York: Cambridge University Press.

LaFree, G. (1989). *Rape and criminal justice*. Santa Fe, NM: University of New Mexico Press.

Lambert, A., & Raichle, K. (2000). The role of political ideology in mediating judgments of blame in rape victims and their assailants. *Personality and Social Psychology Bulletin, 26*(7), 853–863.

Lamborn, L. (1968). Toward a victim orientation in criminal theory. *Rutgers Law Review, 22*, 733–768.

———. (1985). The impact of victimology on the criminal law in the United States. *Canadian Community Law Journal, 8*, 23–43.

Lamm, R. (2004). Speech: I have a plan to destroy America. Retrieved September 17, 2008, from www.snopes.com.

Land, K., McCall, P., & Cohen, L. (1990, January). Structural covariates of homicidal rates: Are there any invariances across time and social space? *American Journal of Sociology, 95*(4), 922–963.

Lander, E. (1988, May 11). Rough sex defense assailed. *New York Newsday*, p. 26.

Landesman, P. (2004, January 25). The girls next door. *New York Times Magazine*, pp. 28–39.

Laner, M., & Thompson, J. (1982). Abuse and aggression in courting couples. *Deviant Behavior, 3*, 229–244.

Langan, P. (1985). *The risk of violent crime. BJS Special Report*. Washington, DC: U.S. Department of Justice.

——— & Graziadei, H. (1995). *Felony sentences in state courts, 1992. BJS Bulletin*. Washington, DC: U.S. Department of Justice.

———— & Innes, C. (1986). *Preventing domestic violence against women. BJS Special Report.* Washington, DC: U.S. Department of Justice.

————, Perkins, C., & Chaiken, J. (1994). *Felony sentences in the United States, 1990. BJS Bulletin.* Washington, DC: U.S. Department of Justice.

Langhinrichsen-Rohling, J. (2005, January). Important findings and future directions for intimate partner violence research. *Journal of Interpersonal Violence, 20,* 108–118.

Langstaff, J., & Sleeper, T. (2001). *The national center on child fatality review. OJJDP fact sheet.* Washington, DC: U.S. Department of Justice.

Langton, L. (2011, November). *Identity theft reported by households, 2005–2010. BJS Crime Data Brief.* Washington, DC: U.S. Department of Justice.

Langton, L., & Planty, M. (2010, December). *Victims of identity theft, 2008. BJS Special Report.* Washington, DC: U.S. Department of Justice.

————. (2011, June). *Hate crime, 2003–2009. BJS Special Report.* Washington, DC: U.S. Department of Justice.

Langton, L., & Truman, J. (2014, September). *Socio-emotional impact of violent crime. BJS Special Report.* Washington, DC: U.S. Department of Justice.

Lanning, K. (1992). *Child sex rings: A behavioral analysis.* Arlington, VA: National Center for Missing and Exploited Children.

Lanza, J. (2008). *Protecting your identity: Advice from FBI agent Jeff Lanza.* Retrieved July 18, 2008, from www.fbi.gov/page2/aug06/idtheft082106.htm.

LaPierre, W. (2008). Standing guard. Retrieved September 18, 2008, from www.nra.org.

Largen, M. (1981, Autumn). Grassroots centers and national task forces: A herstory of the anti-rape movement. *Aegis, 32,* 46–52.

————. (1987). A decade of change in the rape reform movement. *Response, 10*(2), 4–9.

Larson, E. (2014, January 13). Cantor wins approval of 9/11 American Airlines accord. *Bloomberg News.* Retrieved December 10, 2014, from http://www.bloomberg.com/news/2014-01-13/cantor-wins-approval-of-9-11-ameri can-airlines-accord.html.

Larzelere, R., & Baumrind, D. (2010, Spring). Are spanking injunctions scientifically supported? *Law and Contemporary Problems, 73*(2), 57–67.

Lasch, C. (1982, May 17). Why the "survival mentality" is rife in America. *U.S. News & World Report,* pp. 59–60.

Laster, R. (1970). Criminal restitution: A survey of its past history and analysis of its present usefulness. *University of Richmond Law Review, 5,* 71–98.

Lateano, T., Ituarte, S., & Davies, G. (2008, September). Does the law encourage or hinder bystander intervention? *Criminal Law Bulletin, 44*(5), 708–723.

Latson, J. (2014, July 2). Book review: The skeleton crew. *Boston Globe.* Retrieved September 24, 2014, from http://www.bostonglobe.com/arts/2014/07/02/book-review-the-skeleton-crew-how-amateur-sleuths-are-solv ing-america-coldest-cases-deborah-halber/RQaXEDCyI6-CATtjwhom8pK/story.html.

Law Center. (2012, November 12). Statistics on gun deaths and injuries. *Law Center To Prevent Gun Violence.* Retrieved December 12, 2014, from http://smartgunlaws.org/gun-deaths-and-injuries-statistics/.

Lawry, M. (1997, March). Court-appointed special advocates: A voice for abused and neglected children in court. *OJJDP Juvenile Justice Bulletin,* 1.

Leander, L., Granhag, P., & Christianson, S. (2005, August). Children exposed to obscene phone calls: What they remember and tell. *Child Abuse & Neglect, 29*(8), 871–888.

Lear, J. (2013, August 14). A cup and straw that can detect date-rape drugs? *CNN.com.* Retrieved December 1, 2014, from http://www.cnn.com/2013/08/14/us/date-rape-drug-detection/index.html.

Leary, W. (1993, October 7). Gun in home? Study finds it a deadly mix. *New York Times,* p. A18.

Lederer, L. (1980). *Take back the night.* New York: Morrow.

Lederman, D. (1994, February 2). Crime on the campuses. *Chronicle of Higher Education,* pp. A31–A42.

LeDuff, C. (2005, March 17). "Baretta" star acquitted of murder in wife's death. *New York Times,* p. A18.

Lee, J. (2005, February 26). Some tourists learn the hard way: Hawaii is not crime free. Retrieved December 9, 2008, from www.ap.org.

Lee, J. (2003a, January 23). Identity theft complaints double in '02, continuing rise. *New York Times,* p. A18.

————. (2003b, May 17). 130 arrested since Jan. 1 in Internet frauds that snared 89,000 victims, Ashcroft says. *New York Times,* p. A18.

Lee, M. (2015, January 5). Bratton's claim that more than 100 police officers annually are killed from 'anger' and 'hatred.' *Washington Post.* Retrieved January 10, 2015, from http://www.washingtonpost.com/blogs/fact-checker/wp/2015/01/05/how-often-are-police-officers-murdered-on-the-job/.

Leepson, M. (1982). Helping victims of crime. *Editorial Research Reports, 1*(17), 331–344.

LeGrande, C. (1973). Rape and rape laws: Sexism in society and law. *California Law Review, 61,* 919–941.

Lehnen, R., & Skogan, W. (1981). *The national crime survey: Working papers: Vol. 1. Current and historical perspectives.* Washington, DC: U.S. Department of Justice.

Leo, J. (1994, February 14). Watching "As the jury turns." *U.S. News & World Report*, p. 17.

———. (2002, December 23). People who blame people . . . *U.S. News & World Report*, p. 8.

Leonard, E. (2001). Convicted survivors: Comparing and describing California's battered women's inmates. *Prison Journal, 81*(1), 73–86.

Leone, B., & de Koster, K. (1995). *At issue: Rape on campus*. San Diego, CA: Greenhaven Press.

Lerner, D. (2014, September 30). Why drivers get away with murder. *New York Times*, p. A23.

Lerner, M. (1965). Evaluation of performance as a function of performer's reward and attractiveness. *Journal of Personality and Social Psychology, 1*, 355–360.

Lessmiller, K. (2013, December 24). Class claims Memphis spoiled 15,000 rape kits. *Courthouse News Service*. Retrieved December 14, 2014, from http://www.courthousenews.com/2013/12/24/64019.htm.

Letkemann, P. (1973). *Crime as work*. Englewood Cliffs, NJ: Prentice Hall.

Levin, J., & McDevitt, J. (2003). *Hate crimes revisited: America's war on those who are different*. Boulder, CO: Westview Press.

Levine, J. (1976). The potential for crime overreporting in criminal victimization surveys. *Criminology, 14*(2), 307–331.

Levitt, L. (2004, March 26). Big headache over a box of aspirins. *New York Newsday*, p. 18.

Levy, A. (2013, August 5). Trial by twitter. *The New Yorker*. Retrieved November 18, 2014, from http://www.newyorker.com/magazine/2013/08/05/trial-by-twitter.

Lewin, T. (1992, April 20). Battered men sounding equal-rights battle cry. *New York Times*, p. A12.

———. (2001, March 7). Legal action after killings at schools often fails. *New York Times*, p. A17.

———. (2002, July 28). Above expectation: A child as witness. *New York Times*, p. E3.

Li, D. (2014, May 19). Pamela's shocker: Abused from age 6, she tells Cannes. *New York Post*, p. A15.

Libai, D. (1969). The protection of the child victim of a sexual offense in the criminal justice system. *Wayne Law Review, 15*, 977–1032.

Libbey, P., & Bybee, R. (1979). The physical abuse of adolescents. *Journal of Social Issues, 35*(2), 101–126.

Lightfoot, E., & Umbreit, M. (2004, December). An analysis of state statutory provisions for victim–offender mediation. *Criminal Justice Policy Review, 15*(4), 418–436.

Limbaugh, R. (2014, September 29). Borderline millennial on victimology and redemption. *Rush Limbaugh Show Transcript*. Retrieved September 30, 2014, from http://www.rushlimbaugh.com/daily/2014/09/29/borderline_millennial_on_victimology_and_redemption.

Lindner, C., & Koehler, R. (1992). Probation officer victimization: An emerging concern. *Journal of Criminal Justice, 20*(1), 53–62.

Lindzon, J. (2011, June 3). Stolen laptop snaps key shots of alleged thief; Software allows owner to give evidence to police. Retrieved October 4, 2011, from www.nationalpost.com.

Lipkins, S. (2008). Bullying. In J. Wilson (Ed.), *The Praeger handbook of victimology* (pp. 29–30). Santa Barbara, CA: Praeger.

Lippincott, E. (2006, March/April). New kits for sexual assault protective orders. *The Crime Victims Report, 10*(1), 3.

Liptak, A. (2011, March 1). Jury can hear dying man's words, justices say. *New York Times*, p. A14.

Lipton, A. (1999). Recovered memories in the courts. In S. Taub (Ed.), *Recovered Memories of Child Sexual Abuse: Psychological, social and legal perspectives on a contemporary mental health controversy* (pp. 109–125). Springfield, IL.: Charles C. Thomas.

Lisak, D., Gardner, L., Niksa, S., & Coate, A. (2010, December). False allegations of sexual assault: An analysis of ten years of reported cases. *Violence Against Women, 16*(12), 1318–1334.

Lisefski, E., & Manson, D. (1988). *Tracking offenders, 1984. BJS Bulletin*. Washington, DC: U.S. Department of Justice.

Little, B., & Terrance, C. (2010, March). Perceptions of domestic violence in lesbian relationships. *Journal of Homosexuality, 57*, 429–440.

Little, K. (2001). *Sexual assault nurse examiner (SANE) programs: Improving the community response to sexual assault victims*. Washington, DC: Office for Victims of Crime.

Livingston, I., & Fagen, C. (2007, September 17). B'klyn mom dead for caring. *New York Post*, p. 11.

Lobasz, J. (2009). Beyond border security: Feminist approaches to human trafficking. *Security Studies, 18*, 319–344.

Lobdell, W. (2002, March 21). Priests' victims feel vindicated. *Los Angeles Times*, p. A8.

Lockwood, D. (1980). *Prison sexual violence*. New York: Elsevier.

Loftin, C. (1986). The validity of robbery murder classifications in Baltimore. *Violence and Victims, 1*(3), 191–202.

Loftus, E., & Ketcham, K. (1994). *The myth of repressed memory: False memories and allegations of sexual abuse*. New York: St. Martin's Press.

Loftus, L. (2011, October 24). Data on rape in E.U. difficult to compare. *New York Times*, p. A18.

Logan, T. (2010). *Research on partner stalking: Putting the pieces together*. Lexington, KY: University of Kentucky. Retrieved January 4, 2015, from http://www.victimsofcrime.org/docs/Common%20Documents/Research%20on%20Partner%20Stalking%20Report.pdf?sfvrsn=0.

LoJack. (2014, May 14). LoJack releases fifth annual vehicle theft recovery report. *LoJack Corporation*. Retrieved

November 16, 2014, from http://www.lojack.com/
About-LoJack/News-and-Media/Press-Releases/2014/
LoJack-Releases-Fifth-Annual-Vehicle-Theft-Recover.

Long, C. (2008, July 13). Police officer impersonation is a
common crime. *USA Today*, p. 9.

———., & Peltz, J. (2013, October 10). Wojciech Braszczok,
NYPD officer, charged in motorcycle-SUV attack, looks
to video to exonerate him. *Associated Press*. Retrieved
September 9, 2014, from http://www.huffingtonpost.
com/2013/10/10/wojciech-braszczok-motorcycle-suv-
attack-nypd-cop-_n_4076809.html.

Lonsway, K., & Fitzgerald, L. (1994). Rape myths: In review.
Psychology of Women Quarterly, *18*, 133–164.

Loseke, D. (1989). Violence is 'violence' … or is it? The social
construction of "wife abuse" and public policy. In J. Best
(Ed.), *Images of issues: Typifying contemporary social problems*
(pp. 191–206). New York: Aldine de Gruyter.

Loseke, D., Gelles, R., & Cavanaugh, M. (2005). *Current controversies on family violence* (2nd ed.). Thousand Oaks, CA:
Sage.

Lott, J. (1998). *More guns, less crime: Understanding crime and gun
control laws*. Chicago: University of Chicago Press.

Louden, R. (1998). The development of hostage negotiation
by the NYPD. In A. Karmen (Ed.), *Crime and justice in
New York City* (pp. 148–158). New York: McGraw Hill
Custom Publishing.

Louisiana State Police, Insurance Fraud Unit. (2011). Auto theft
unit: Red flags of insurance fraud. Retrieved October 26,
2011, from www.lsp.org/ifu/html.

Lourie, I. (1977). The phenomenon of the abused adolescent:
A clinical study. *Victimology*, *2*(2), 268–276.

Lovett, D. (2011, November 21). Youth pleads guilty to killing
gay classmate. *New York Times*, p. A19.

Lovett, K. (2003, June 12). Peep victim hails deal on vid-perv
law. *New York Post*, p. 12.

———. (2006, April 3). Stop in the name of the law: Queens
pol. *New York Post*, p. 12.

———. (2013, February 11). 'Rape is rape.' *New York Daily
News*. Retrieved November 25, 2014, from http://www.
nydailynews.com/new-york/survivor-expand-ny-rape-
statutes-article-1.1260437.

Lozano, J. (2014, August 27). Dad acquitted in slaying of driver
who killed sons. *Associated Press*. Retrieved January 7,
2015, from http://news.yahoo.com/texas-road-rage-
murder-case-coming-close-132319303.html.

Lubenow, G. (1983, June 27). When kids kill their parents.
Newsweek, pp. 35–36.

Lucas, L., & Melago, C. (2009, September 2). Hairy scheme vs.
Bernanke's wife. *New York Daily News*, p. 40.

Luckenbill, D. (1977). Criminal homicide as a situated transaction. *Social Problems*, *25*, 176–186.

Lukewarm reception for new crime-data plan. (1988, May 31).
Law Enforcement News, pp. 1, 7.

Lundman, R. (1980). *Police and policing: An introduction*. New
York: Holt, Rinehart & Winston.

Lundsgaarde, H. (1977). *Murder in space city: A cultural analysis of
Houston homicide patterns*. New York: Oxford University
Press.

Luo, M. (2011a, January 26). Sway of N.R.A. blocks studies,
scientists say. *New York Times*, pp. A1, A3.

———. (2011b, December 26). Guns in public, and out of
sight. *New York Times*, p. A14.

———. (2013, March 17). In some states, gun rights trump
orders of protection. *New York Times*, p. A16.

———. (2013, March 18). Ruled a threat to family, but
allowed to keep guns. *New York Times*, pp. A1, A112.

———., & McIntire, M. (2013, September 29). Children
and guns: The hidden toll. *New York Times*, pp. A1,
A24.

Lurigio, A. (1990). *Victims of crime: Problems, policies and programs*.
Newbury Park, CA: Sage.

Lyman, R. (2005, July 7). Missing woman's case spurs discussion of news coverage. *New York Times*, p. A16.

Lynch, C. (2003, October 10). Fighting crime, but diplomati-
cally, at the UN. *Washington Post*, p. A25.

Lynch, R. (1976). Improving the treatment of victims: Some
guides for action. In W. MacDonald (Ed.), *Criminal justice
and the victim* (pp. 165–176). Beverly Hills, CA: Sage.

Lynch, R., & Addington, L. (Ed.). (2007). *Understanding crime
statistics*. New York: Cambridge University Press.

Lynn, W. (1981, March 30). What scientists really mean by
"acceptable risk." *U.S. News & World Report*, p. 60.

MacDonald, H. (2007, February 9). Harvard's Faustian bargain.
America's oldest university selects a dreadful president.
City Journal. Retrieved October 13, 2008, from www.
city-journal.org.

———. (2008a, Winter). The campus rape myth: Bogus statistics, feminist victimology, and university approved sex
toys. *City Journal*, *18*(1), 15–27.

———. (2008b, March 2). A thought experiment on campus
rape. *City Journal*. Retrieved September 25, 2008, from
www.city-journal.org.

———. (2008c, September 27). Anti-elitism goes too far: Sarah
Palin's defenders shouldn't mock the value of learning.
City Journal. Retrieved October 11, 2008, from www.
city-journal.org.

———. (2013, July 22). Obama strikes out. *City Journal*.
Retrieved September 12, 2014, from http://www.city-
journal.org/2013/eon0722hm.html.

MacDonald, J. (1971). *Rape: Offenders and victims*. Springfield,
IL: Charles C. Thomas.

MacDonald, J., & Michaud, D. (1995). *Rape: Controversial issues—Criminal profiles, date rape, false reports and false memories.* Chicago: Charles C. Thomas.

MacGowan, C. (2007, October 12). Drug-chase killer gets maximum. *Long Island Newsday,* p. A16.

MacNamara, D. (1983). Prisoners as victimizers and victims. In D. MacNamara & A. Karmen (Eds.), *Deviants: Victims or victimizers?* (pp. 219–238). Beverly Hills, CA: Sage.

MacNamara, D., & Sullivan, J. (1974). Making the victim whole: Composition, restitution, and compensation. In T. Thornberry & E. Sagarin (Eds.), *Images of crime: Offenders and victims* (pp. 79–90). New York: Praeger.

MADD. *See* Mothers Against Drunk Driving.

Maddalenna, D. (2005, September 23). Syracuse officials say new date rape drug test not the answer. *Syracuse Daily Orange,* p. 3.

Madden, B. (2010, October 12). Mick was haunted by sexual abuse as a child. *New York Daily News,* p. 3.

Madison, A. (1973). *Vigilantism in America.* New York: Seabury Press.

Maghan, J., & Sagarin, E. (1983). Homosexuals as victimizers and victims. In D. MacNamara & A. Karmen (Eds.), *Deviants: Victims or victimizers?* (pp. 147–162). Newbury Park, CA: Sage.

Makepeace, J. (1981). Courtship violence among college students. *Family Relations, 30,* 97–102.

Malefyt, M., Littel, K., Walker, A., Tucker, D., & Buel, S. (1998). *Promising practices: Improving the criminal justice system's response to violence against women. Office of Justice Programs report.* Washington, DC: U.S. Department of Justice.

Malkin, C. (2013, March 1). Why do people stay in abusive relationships? *Huffington Post.* Retrieved November 20, 2014, from http://www.huffingtonpost.com/dr-craig-malkin/domestic-violence_b_2786921.html.

Maltz, W., & Holman, B. (1986). *Incest and sexuality: A guide to understanding and healing.* New York: Free Press.

Mannheim, H. (1965). *Comparative criminology.* Boston: Houghton Mifflin.

Manshel, L. (1990). *Nap time.* New York: Kensington.

Mansnerus, L. (1989, February 19). The rape laws change faster than perceptions. *New York Times,* Sec. 5, p. 20.

Maple, J. (1999). *The crime fighter: Putting the bad guys out of business.* New York: Doubleday.

Marciniak, L. (1999, Fall). Adolescent attitudes toward victim precipitation of rape. *Violence and Victims, 13*(3), 287–300.

Margolick, D. (1994, January 16). Does Mrs. Bobbitt count as another battered wife? *New York Times,* p. E5.

Markel, H. (2009, December 15). The child who put a face on abuse. *New York Times,* pp. D5, D6.

Mariner, J. (2001). *No escape: Male rape in U.S. prisons.* New York: Human Rights Watch.

Marquis, J. (2005, June). Prosecutors and victims' rights. *The Crime Victims Report, 9*(2), 17–18.

Martin, D. (1976). *Battered wives.* San Francisco: Glide.

Martin, D. E. (1989, June 7). The line of duty: Special officers help their own. *New York Times,* p. B1.

Martin, P., & Hummer, R. (1998). Fraternities and rape on campus. In R. Bergen (Ed.), *Issues in intimate violence* (pp. 157–167). Thousand Oaks, CA: Sage.

Martinez, M. (2010, October 22). O. J. Simpson loses appeal in Las Vegas armed robbery trial. *CNN Justice News.* Retrieved January 4, 2012, from www.cnn.com.

Martinson, R. (1974, Spring). What works—questions and answers about prison reform. *Public Interest, 35,* 22–54.

Martz, L., Miller, M., Hutchinson, S., Emerson, T., & Washington, F. (1989, January 16). A tide of drug killing. *Newsweek,* pp. 44–45.

Marx, B. (2005, February). Lessons learned from the last twenty years of sexual violence research. *Journal of Interpersonal Violence, 20*(2), 225–230.

Marx, G., & Archer, D. (1976). Community police patrols and vigilantism. In J. Rosenbaum & P. Sederberg (Eds.), *Vigilante politics* (pp. 129–157). Philadelphia: University of Pennsylvania Press.

Mash, E., & Wolfe, D. (1991, March). Methodological issues in research on physical child abuse. *Criminal Justice and Behavior, 18*(1), 8–29.

Maslin, J. (2011, July 17). A captivity no novelist could invent. *New York Times Book Review,* p. 3.

Mash, K. (2013, Fall). Guns on campus: A chilling effect. *Thought and Action,* pp. 57–60.

Mason, M. (2002, October 10). Drug coasters that can detect "date rape drugs" may backfire. *Associated Press Worldstream.*

Mathews, A. (1993, March 7). The campus crime wave. *New York Times Magazine,* pp. 38–47.

Mathias, A. (2008, April 16). Fear and learning on campus. *New York Times,* p. A25.

Matson, Z., & Turk, M. (2013). Delving into crime data and finding flaws. *Investigative Reporters and Editors Conference blog.* Retrieved November 13, 2014, from http://ire.org/blog/ire-conference-blog/2013/06/20/delving-crime-data-and-finding-flaws/.

Mauer, M. (1999). *Race to incarcerate.* New York: New Press.

Mawby, R. (1985). Bystander responses to the victims of crime—Is the Good Samaritan alive and well? *Victimology, 10*(4), 461–475.

Mawby, R., & Walklate, S. (1993). *Critical victimology: International perspectives.* Newbury Park, CA: Sage.

Max, W., Rice, D., Finkelstein, E., Bardwell, R., & Leadbetter, S. (2004, June). The economic toll of intimate partner violence against women in the United States. *Violence and Victims, 19*(3), 259–271.

Maxfield, M. (1987). Household composition, routine activity, and victimization: A comparative analysis. *Journal of Quantitative Criminology, 3,* 301–320.

Maxwell, C., Garner, J., & Fagan, J. (2001). *The effects of arrest on intimate partner violence.NIJ Research in Brief.* Washington, DC: U.S. Department of Justice.

May, G. (2002, Spring). Stop thief! *Journal of Texas Consumer Law, 5*(3), 72–80.

May, J. (2001). *The guide to identity theft prevention.* Bloomington, IL: First Book Library.

Mayhew, P., & Hough, M. (1988). The British crime survey: Origins and impact. In M. Maguire & J. Pointing (Eds.), *Victims of crime: A new deal?* (pp. 156–163). Philadelphia: Open University Press.

Mayor's Management Report, New York City. (2014, September). Agency performance measures FY 2014. *Office of the Mayor.* Retrieved November 13, 2014, from http://www.nyc.gov/html/ops/downloads/pdf/mmr2014/nypd.pdf.

McArdle, M. (2014, September 19). How many rape reports are false? *Bloomberg View.* Retrieved December 11, 2014, from http://www.bloombergview.com/articles/2014-09-19/how-many-rape-reports-are-false.

McCaghy, C. (1980). *Crime in American society.* New York: Macmillan.

McCaghy, C., Giordano, P., & Henson, T. (1977, November). Auto theft: Offenders and offense characteristics. *Criminology, 15,* 367–385.

McCahill, T., Williams, L., & Fischman, A. (1979). *The aftermath of rape.* Lexington, MA: Lexington Books.

McCarthy, J. (2014, October 20). More than six in 10 Americans say guns make homes safer. *Gallup Polling.* Retrieved December 13, 2014, from http://www.gallup.com/poll/179213/six-americans-say-guns-homes-safer.aspx.

McClennen, J. (2005, February). Domestic violence between same-gender partners. *Journal of Interpersonal Violence, 20,* 149–154.

McCold, P. (2003). An experiment in police-based restorative justice: The Bethlehem (Pennsylvania) Project. *Police Practice and Research, 4*(4), 379–390.

McCollister, K., French, M., & Fang, H. (2010, April 1). The cost of crime to society: New crime-specific estimates for policy and program evaluation. *Drug and Alcohol Dependence, 108*(1/2), 98–109.

McCormack, R. (1991). Compensating victims of violent crime. *Justice Quarterly, 8*(3), 329–346.

McDermott, J. (1979). *Rape victimization in 26 American cities.* Washington, DC: U.S. Government Printing Office.

McDonald, D. (1988). *NIJ crime file study guide: Restitution and community service.* Washington, DC: U.S. Department of Justice.

McDonald, R. (2011, May 27). Defense attorneys seek alleged victim's Facebook postings. *Fulton County Daily Report.* Retrieved November 21, 2011, from www.law.com/lawtechnologynews.

McDonald, W. (1976). Criminal justice and the victim. In W. McDonald (Ed.), *Criminal justice and the victim* (pp. 17–56). Beverly Hills, CA: Sage.

———. (1977). The role of the victim in America. In R. Barnett & J. Hagel, III (Eds.), *Assessing the criminal: Resti-tution, retribution, and the legal process* (pp. 295–307). Cambridge, MA: Ballinger.

———. (1978). Expanding the victim's role in the disposition decision: Reform in search of rationale. In B. Galaway & J. Hudson (Eds.), *Offender restitution in theory and action* (pp. 101–110). Lexington, MA: Lexington Books.

———. (1979). The prosecutor's domain. In W. McDonald (Ed.), *The prosecutor* (pp. 15–52). Beverly Hills, CA: Sage.

McFadden, C. (2010, September 6). Many campus assault victims stay quiet, or fail to get help. *ABC Nightline.* Retrieved December 27, 2011, from www.abcnews.go.com.

McFarland, S., Ellis, C., & Chunn, G. (2008, December 29). *Report on rape in jails in the U.S.* Retrieved December 17, 2011, from www.sheriffs.org.

McFarlane, J., Campbell, J. C., Wilt, S., Sachs, C. J., & Ulrich, Y., Xu, X. (1999, November). Stalking and intimate partner femicide. *Homicide Studies, 3*(4), 300–316.

McGillis, D. (1982). Minor dispute processing: A review of recent developments. In R. Tomasic & M. Feeley (Eds.), *Neighborhood justice: Assessment of an emerging idea* (pp. 60–76). New York: Longman.

———. (1986). *NIJ issues and practices: Crime victim restitution: An analysis of approaches.* Washington, DC: U.S. Department of Justice.

McGillis, D., & Smith, P. (1983). *Compensating victims of crime: An analysis of American programs.* Washington, DC: U.S. Department of Justice.

McGrath, K., & Osborne, M. (1989). Redressing violence against elders. *NOVA Newsletter, 13*(2), 1, 4, 5.

McIntyre, D. (1968, December). A study of judicial dominance of the charging decision. *Journal of Criminal Law, Criminology, and Police Science, 59,* 463–490.

McKinley, J. (2006, June 3). The distinction Modesto didn't need: National car-theft capital. *New York Times,* p. A8.

———. (2011, June 3). Couple sentenced to prison in 18-year kidnapping case. *New York Times,* p. A12.

———. (2013, July 26). Life term given in triple murder near Columbia University. *New York Times,* p. A16.

McKnight, D. (1981). The victim–offender reconciliation project. In B. Galaway & J. Hudson (Eds.), *Perspectives on crime victims* (pp. 292–298). St. Louis, MO: C.V. Mosby.

McPhee, M. (1999, December 20). Agonizing wait for mom. *New York Daily News*, p. 4

———. (2014, October 14). Family matters: Dzhokhar Tsarnaev and the women in his life. *Newsweek*. Retrieved December 28, 2014, from http://www.newsweek.com/2014/10/24/women-behind-boston-marathon-bombing-suspects-277760.html.

McQueary, K. (2011, September 29). Ten years of hope, trying to save abandoned newborns. *New York Times*, p. A21.

McRobbie. (2014, January) The real victims of satanic ritual abuse. *Slate Magazine*. Retrieved December 10, 2014, from http://www.slate.com/articles/health_and_science/medical_examiner/2014/01/fran_and_dan_keller_freed_two_of_the_last_victims_of_satanic_ritual_abuse.2.html.

McShane, L. (2011a, February 26). Father says don't parole cop son's killer. *New York Daily News*. Retrieved August 10, 2011, from www.nydailynews.com.

———. (2011b, April 1). Convicted cop-killer loses third bid for parole. *New York Daily News*. Retrieved August 10, 2011, from www.nydailynews.com.

McShane, M., & Emeka, T. (2011). *American victimology*. El Paso, TX: LFB Scholarly Publishing.

Mead, J. (2006, May 28). A slow war on human trafficking. *New York Times*, p. B1.

Mears, D., & Visher, C. (2005, February). Trends in understanding and addressing domestic violence. *Journal of Interpersonal Violence, 20*(2), 204–211.

Mechanic, M., & Uhlmansiek, M. (2000). The impact of severe stalking experienced by acutely battered women. *Violence and Victims, 15*(4), 443–458.

Meiners, R. (1978). *Victim compensation: Economic, political and legal aspects*. Lexington, MA: D. C. Heath.

Meloy, J. (1998). *The psychology of stalking: Clinical and forensic perspectives*. San Diego, CA: Academic Press.

Meloy, M., & Miller, S. (2010). *The victimization of women*. New York: Oxford University Press.

Memmott, M. (2005, July 16). Spotlight skips cases of missing minorities. *USA Today*, p. 6A.

Mendelsohn, B. (1940). *Rape in criminology*. Translated and cited in S. Schafer (1968), *The victim and his criminal*. New York: Random House.

———. (1956, July). The victimology. *Etudes Internationales de Psycho-Sociologie Criminelle*, 23–26.

Menninger, K. (1968). *The crime of punishment*. New York: Viking Press.

Merrill, L. (1994, April 7). A defense that won't go away. *New York Daily News*, p. 6.

Messner, S., & Golden, R. (1992). Racial inequality and racially disaggregated homicide rates: An assessment of alternative theoretical explanations. *Criminology, 30*(3), 421–447.

Messner, S., & Tardiff, K. (1985). The social ecology of urban homicide: An application of the "routine activities" approach. *Criminology, 23*, 241–267.

Miers, D. (1989). Positivist victimology: A critique. *International Review of Victimology, 1*, 3–22.

Miethe, T., Stafford, M., & Sloane, D. (1990). Lifestyle changes and risks of criminal victimization. *Journal of Quantitative Criminology, 6*(4), 357–375.

Mignon, S. (1998). Husband battering: A review of the debate over a controversial social phenomenon. In N. Jackson & G. Oates (Eds.), *Violence in intimate relationships: Examining sociological and psychological issues* (pp. 137–160). Woburn, MA: Butterworth- Heinemann.

Miller, D. (2011, September 21). James Byrd's sister: I had to forgive. *WFAA-TV 11 Dallas*. Retrieved October 12, 2011, from www.wfaa.com.

Miller, F. (1970). *Prosecution: The decision to charge a suspect with a crime*. Boston: Little, Brown.

Miller, J. (2005, September 23). Ex-pharmaceutical executive sentenced to 8 years in the beating death of his wife. *New York Times*, p. B4.

Miller, M., & Hemenway, D. (2008, September 4). Guns and suicide in the United States. *New England Journal of Medicine, 359*, 989–991.

Miller, S. (2005). *Victims as offenders: The paradox of women's violence in relationships*. New Brunswick, NJ: Rutgers University Press.

Miller, T., Cohen, M., & Wiersema, B. (1996). *Victim costs and consequences: A new look*. Washington, DC: U.S. Department of Justice.

Miller, W. (1973). Ideology and criminal justice policy: Some current issues. *Journal of Criminal Law and Criminology, 64*(2), 34–59.

Millet, K. (1970). *Sexual politics*. New York: Doubleday.

Mills, C. (1959). *The sociological imagination*. Oxford, UK: Oxford University Press.

Milner, J. (1991, March). Introduction: Current perspectives on physical child abuse. *Criminal Justice and Behavior, 18*(1), 4–7.

MIPT. (2008). *Terrorism knowledge base*. Retrieved September 16, 2008, from www.terrorisminfo.mipt.org.

Mitchell, J. (2008, March 16). Victims fund assists felons. Retrieved September 10, 2008, from www.baltimoresun.com/news/local.

Mithers, C. (1990, October 21). Incest and the law. *New York Times Magazine*, pp. 44–63.

Mixed verdict for six youths in fatal beating. (1996, February 6). *New York Times*, p. A9.

Mizell, L. (1997). Aggressive driving: Three studies. *AAA Foundation for Traffic Safety*. Retrieved January 29, 2012, from www.aaafoundation.org.

Mugulescu, K. (2014, January 31). The Superbowl and sex trafficking. *New York Times*, p. A24.

Molotsky, I. (1997, February 26). Two years later, Congress gets report on crime at colleges. *New York Times*, p. A23.

Mones, P. (1991). *When a child kills: Abused children who kill their parents*. New York: Simon & Schuster.

Montague, R., Zohra, I., Love, S., McGee, D., & Tsamis, V. (2008, April). Hazing typologies: Those who criminally haze and those who receive criminal hazing. *Victims & Offenders*, *3*(2), 258–274.

Moore, E., & Mills, M. (1990). The neglected victims and unexamined costs of white-collar crime. *Crime and Delinquency*, *36*(3), 408–418.

Moore, L. (1985, March). Your home: Make it safe. *Security Management*, pp. 115–116.

Morash, M., Hoan, B., Yan, Z., & Holtfreter, K. (2007, July). Risk factors for abusive relationships. *Violence Against Women*, *13*(7), 653–675.

Morgan, R. (2014, November). *Crimes against the elderly, 2003–2013.BJS Special Report*. Washington, DC: U.S. Department of Justice.

Morganthau, R. (2013, July 2). Suing, or taxing, the gun makers. *New York Times*, p. A25.

Morganthau, T., & Shenitz, B. (1994, August 15). Too many guns? Or too few? *Newsweek*, pp. 44–45.

Morgenstern, P., & Fisher, E. (2005, July 20). Outside counsel: New clout for victims in criminal proceedings. *New York Law Journal*, *234*, 4.

Morrison, P. (2010, February 20). Steve Cooley: L.A.'s D.A. *Los Angeles Times*. Retrieved January 4, 2012, from www.latimes.com.

Mothers Against Drunk Driving (MADD). (1988, Spring). Victim rights: How far have we come? *Maddvocate*, p. 13.

Moye, D. (2013, June 24). John Wayne Bobbitt says penis severing improved love life. *Huffington Post*. Retrieved September 7, 2014, from http://www.huffingtonpost.com/2013/06/24/john-wayne-bobbitt_n_3492202.html.

Moynihan, M., Banyard, V., Arnold, J., Eckstein, R., & Stapleton, J. (2011, June). Sisterhood may be powerful for reducing sexual and intimate partner violence. *Violence Against Women*, *17*(6), 703–716.

Muehlenhard, C., Powch, I., Phelps, J., & Giusti, L. (1992). Definitions of rape: Scientific and political implications. *Journal of Social Issues*, *48*(1), 23–44.

Mueller, B. (2014, August 5). Two decades after pair of killings on Long Island, authorities make an arrest. *New York Times*, p. A14.

Muftic, L., & Foster, R. (2010). Victim-precipitated rape. In S. Fisher & S. Lab (Eds.), *Encyclopedia of victimology and crime prevention* (pp. 881–883). Thousand Oaks, CA: Sage.

Munson, D. (1989). *The child victim as a witness: OJJDP update on research*. Washington, DC: U.S. Department of Justice.

Murphy, B. (2014, April 2). DA: Officer Nikolas Budimlic won't face charges in fatal shooting of Hofstra student Andrea Rebello. *Newsday*, p. A2.

Murphy, C. (2006, July 22). Little Rock tourism growing, but so is the rate of violent crime. *Arkansas Democrat-Gazette*, p. 1.

Murphy, K., & Barkworth, J. (2014, April–June). Victim willingness to report crime to police: Does procedural justice or outcome matter most? *Violence and Victims*, *9*(2), 178–204.

Murphy, W. (1999, September). Massachusetts initiates victim "Miranda" law. *The Crime Victims Report*, *3*(4), 49, 50, 55.

Mustaine, E., & Tewksbury, R. (1998a, November). Predicting risks of larceny theft victimization: A routine activity analysis using refined lifestyle measures. *Criminology*, *36*(4), 829–857.

Mustaine, E., & Tewksbury, R. (1998b, Fall). Victimization risks at leisure: A gender-specific analysis. *Violence and Victims*, *13*(3), 232–249.

Mydans, S. (1994, January 29). The other Menendez trial, too, ends with the jury deadlocked. *New York Times*, pp. A1, A8.

Myers, J. (1998). *Legal issues in child abuse and neglect*. Thousand Oaks, CA: Sage.

Myers, M. (1977). *The effects of victim characteristics on the prosecution, conviction, and sentencing of criminal defendants*. Unpublished doctoral dissertation, University Microfilms, Ann Arbor, MI.

Myers, M., & Hagan, J. (1979). Private and public trouble: Prosecutors and the allocation of court resources. *Social Problems*, *26*(4), 439–451.

Myers, R. (2009, February). Failure of justice results in rape victim's suicide. *The Crime Victims Report*, *12*(1), 83–84.

Myers, R., & Jacobo, J. (2006). Criminal transmission of HIV, Part IV. *The Crime Victims Report*, *9*(6), 83–84.

Myers, S. (2009, December 28). Another peril in war zones: Sexual abuse by fellow G.I.'s. *New York Times*, pp. A1, A10.

Myrdal, G. (1944). *An American dilemma: The Negro problem and modern democracy*. New York: Harper Row.

NACVCB. *See* National Association of Crime Victims Compensation Boards.

Naim, M. (2005). *Illicit: How smugglers, traffickers, and copycats are hijacking the global economy.* New York: Doubleday.

Nathan, D., & Snedeker, M. (1995). *Satan's silence: Ritual abuse and the making of a modern American witch hunt.* New York: Basic Books.

National Advisory Commission on Criminal Justice Standards and Goals. (1973). *The courts.* Washington, DC: U.S. Government Printing Office.

National Association of Crime Victims Compensation Boards. (2011). Crime victim compensation: An overview. Retrieved November 29, 2011, from www.nacvcb.org.

National Center for Child Abuse and Neglect (NCCAN). (1978). *Child sexual abuse: Incest, assault and sexual exploitation.* Washington, DC: U.S. Department of Health, Education, and Welfare.

National Center for Educational Statistics. See NCES.

(NCES). (2008). *Indicators of school crime and safety, 2007.* Washington, DC: U.S. Department of Justice. Retrieved December 20, 2011, from http://nces.ed.gov/programs/crimeindicators.

———. (2011a). Campus crime statistics online, 2007–2009. Retrieved December 22, 2011, from http://www2.ed.gov/admins/lead/safety/criminal2007-09.pdf.

———. (2013). *Indicators of school crime and safety, 2013. Table 2.1.* Washington, DC: U.S. Department of Justice. Retrieved December 2, 2014, from http://nces.ed.gov/programs/crimeindicators.

National Center for Missing Adults (NCMA). (2008). About our organization. Retrieved September 25, 2008, from www.theyaremissed.org.

National Center for Missing and Exploited Children (NCMEC). (1986). *State legislation to protect children: An update on the nation's progress to implement effective laws preventing child victimization.* Washington, DC: Author.

———. (1987). *Accomplishing great things.* Washington, DC: Author.

———. (2011). Amber Alert Annual Reports, 2005–2011. Retrieved December 12, 2014, from www.ambertalert.gov.

National Center for Victims of Crime (NCVC). (1999). *The NCVC does not support the current language of the proposed crime victims' rights constitutional amendment.* Arlington, VA: NCVC.

———. (2002). *Restitution: Making it work. Legal Series Bulletin 5.* Washington, DC: U.S. Department of Justice.

———. (2002c). *Ordering restitution to the crime victim. Legal Series Bulletin 6.* Washington, DC: U.S. Department of Justice.

———. (2002d). *Victim input into plea agreements. Legal Series Bulletin 7.* Washington, DC: U.S. Department of Justice.

———. (2003, March 9). *Vote of no confidence major factor in low crime reporting rates.* Press release. Washington, DC: Author.

———. (2004). Restitution. *NCVC.* Retrieved December 10, 2014, from http://www.victimsofcrime.org/help-for-crime-victims/get-help-bulletins-for-crime-victims/restitution.

———. (2007). *The model stalking code revisited.* Washington, DC: Author.

———. (2008). Parallel justice guiding principles. Retrieved October 3, 2008, from www.ncvc.org.

———. (2011a). Dating violence: Is it abuse? *NCVC.* Retrieved October 30, 2011, from www.ncvc.org.

———. (2011b). Issues: Constitutional Amendments. Retrieved October 30, 2011, from www.ncvc.org.

———. (2011c). VictimLaw: Son of Sam laws. Retrieved October 30, 2011, from www.ncvc.org.

National Center on Elder Abuse, U.S. Administration on Aging. (2005). Elder abuse prevalence. Retrieved October 13, 2011, from www.ncea.aoa.gov.

———. (2011). *Mission statement: What we do.* Retrieved October 13, 2011, from www.ncea.aoa.gov.

National Clearinghouse on Child Abuse and Neglect Information (NCCANI). (1997). *What is child maltreatment?* Washington, DC: Author.

National Coalition of Anti-Violence Programs (NCAVP). (2014). Lesbian, gay, bisexual, transgender, queer, and HIV-affected intimate partner violence in 2013. *avp.org.* Retrieved December 1, 2014, from www.avp.org/storage/documents/2013.

National Coalition of Victims in Action. (2008). Board of Directors. Retrieved October 4, 2008, from www.rorpf.org/NCVIABoard of Directors.htm.

National Commission on the Causes and Prevention of Violence (NCCPV). (1969a). *Crimes of violence.* Washington, DC: U.S. Government Printing Office.

———. (1969b). *The offender and his victim.* (Staff report by D. Mulvihill, L. Curtis, & M. Tumin). Washington, DC: U.S. Government Printing Office.

National Conference of State Legislatures (NCSL). (2013, April 24). Pretrial release: Victims' rights and protections. NCSL. Retrieved January 10, 2015, from www.ncsl.org/.../pretrial-release-victims-rights-and-protections.aspx.

National Consortium for the Study of Terrorism and Responses to Terrorism (START). (2012). Global Terrorism Database. Retrieved January 3, 2012, from www.start.umd.edu/gtb.

National Crime Prevention Institute (NCPI). (1978). *Understanding crime prevention.* Louisville, KY: Author.

National Crime Victim Law Institute (NCVLI). (2011). History of NCVLI and victims' rights. Retrieved January 25, 2012, from http://law.lclark.edu/centers.

———. (2014, April 23). Mixed message to crime victims from U.S. Supreme Court; victims to return to Congress.

NCVLI.org. Retrieved November 14, 2014, from http://law. lclark.edu/live/files/16898-ncvli-paroline-press-releasepdf.

National Crime Victims Bar Association. (2007). Civil justice for victims of crime: A handbook. Retrieved September 30, 2008, from www.victimbar.org/vb.

National Criminal Justice Reference Center (NCJRS). (2005). In the spotlight: Identity theft. Retrieved September 21, 2005, from www.ncjrs.org/spotlight/identitytheft.html.

National Highway Transportation Safety Administration (NHTSA). (2014). *Theft Rates 2011.* Retrieved October 23, 2014, from http://www.nhtsa.gov/cars/rules/theft/theftyears.cfm.

National Insurance Crime Bureau (NICB). (1993, Winter). The public speaks out on fraud and theft. *Spotlight on Insurance Crime, 2*(3), 1–2.

———. (2014). Hot spots report, 2013. Retrieved October 16, 2014, from www.nicb.org.

National Institute of Justice (NIJ). (1984). *Vehicle theft prevention strategies.* Washington, DC: U.S. Government Printing Office.

———. (1998). *New directions from the field: Victims' rights and services for the twenty-first century.* Washington, DC: U.S. Department of Justice.

National Organization for Victim Assistance (NOVA). (1988). *Victim rights and services: A legislative directory—1987.* Washington, DC: Author.

———. (1989). Bipartisan victim rights bill introduced in U.S. Congress. *NOVA Newsletter, 13*(3), 1, 5.

———. (1995). Basic rights revisited. *NOVA Newsletter, 17*(4), 1–2.

National Network To End Domestic Violence (NNEDV). (2014). Domestic violence counts: Census 2013 report. *NNEDV.* Retrieved November 21, 2014, from http://nnedv.org/projects/census/4225-domestic-violence-counts-census-2013-report.html.

National Prison Rape Elimination Commission (NPREC). (2008). Sexual victimization in state and federal prisons reported by inmates, 2007. Retrieved October 23, 2008, from www.nprec.us/resources.htm.

National Public Radio (NPR). (2008, March 28). StoryCorps NPR series: A victim treats his mugger right. Retrieved October 23, 2008, from www.npr.org.

National Registry of Exonerations. (2014). Exoneration news. *University of Michigan Law School.* Retrieved December 11, 2014, from http://www.law.umich.edu/special/exoneration/Pages/about.aspx.

National Rifle Association (NRA). (2008). Institute for Legislative Action: Criticism of "Castle Doctrine" bill way off target. Retrieved October 3, 2008, from www.nraila.org/news.

NRA-ILA (National Rifle Association Institute for Legislative Action). (2011). Gun ownership rises to an all-time high, violent crime falls to a 36-year low. Retrieved January 22, 2012, from www.nraila.org.

———. (2012, January 9). Firearms fact card 2012. Retrieved March 3, 2012, from www.nraila.org/news-issues.

———. (2014, October). Bloomberg ad inadvertently portrays limits on gun control agenda. *American Rifleman,* p. 91.

National Safe Haven Alliance. (2014). Abandoned infant protection laws. *Nationalsafehaven.org.* Retrieved November 19, 2014, from http://www.nationalsafehavenalliance.org/law.php.

National Sheriffs' Association. (1999). *First response to victims of crime.* Washington, DC: Office for Victims of Crime, U.S. Department of Justice.

National Victim Center (NVC). (1990). *Crime victims and corrections.* Fort Worth, TX: NVC.

———. (1991a). *America speaks out: Citizens' attitudes about victims' rights and violence.* Fort Worth, TX: NVC.

———. (1991b). *National victim services survey of adult and juvenile corrections and parole agencies. Final report.* Fort Worth, TX: NVC.

———. (1993). *Civil justice for crime victims.* Fort Worth, TX: NVC.

National Victim Constitutional Amendment Passage (NVCAP). (2008). Marsy's Law, California's new VRA, passes. Retrieved December 4, 2008, from www.nvcap.org.

———. (2011). State victims rights amendments. Retrieved December 14, 2011, from www.nvcap.org.

NCCAN. *See* National Center for Child Abuse and Neglect.

NCCANI. *See* National Clearinghouse on Child Abuse and Neglect Information.

NCAVP. *See* National Coalition of Anti-Violence Programs.

NCCPV. *See* National Commission on the Causes and Prevention of Violence.

NCEA. *See* National Center on Elder Abuse.

NCES. *See* National Center for Educational Statistics.

NCHS. *See* National Center for Health Statistics.

NCJRS. *See* National Criminal Justice Reference Center.

NCMEC. *See* National Center for Missing and Exploited Children.

NCPCA. *See* National Committee for Prevention of Child Abuse.

NCSL see National Conference of State Legislatures.

NCVC. *See* National Center for Victims of Crime.

Negrusz, A., Juhascik, M., & Gaenssler, R. (2005). Estimate of the incidence of drug-facilitated sexual assaults in the U.S. *Final report to the U.S. Department of Justice.* Retrieved December 22, 2011, from www.ncjrs.gov.

Neidig, P. (1984). Women's shelters, men's collectives and other issues in the field of spouse abuse. *Victimology, 9*(3–4), 464–476.

Nelson, D. (2014, July 3). Payback: Idaho's victims compensation fund. *KIVI Fox 9 TV.* Retrieved December11, 2014, from http://www.jrn.com/kivitv/news/Payback-Idahos-victims-compensation-fund-265771931.html.

Nemy, E. (2009, August 27). Dominick Dunne, writer who chronicled high-profile crime, is dead at 83. *New York Times*, p. B12.

Nesbo, J. (2014, May 4). Revenge, my lovely. *New York Times,* pp. E1, E6.

Neubauer, D. (1974). *Criminal justice in middle America.* Morristown, NJ: General Learning Press.

Neuilly, M., & Zgoba, K. (2006, August). Assessing the possibility of a pedophilia panic and contagion effect between France and the United States. *Victims and Offenders, 1*(3), 225–254.

New Jersey: Crime victims request only 10% of funding. (2002, September 16). *Juvenile Justice Digest, 30*(1), 7.

New Jersey Victims of Crime Compensation Agency. (2008). Benefits in a nutshell. Retrieved September 30, 2008, from www.state.nj.us/victims.

New study details dangers of holding youth in adult jails. (2008, March). *Juvenile Justice Update, 14*(1), 11.

New York Police Department (NYPD). (1992). *Auto theft: A growing business.* NYPD Auto Crime Division. New York City.

———. (2014). Crime prevention: Safeguard your house. Retrieved November 6, 2014, from http://www.nyc.gov/html/nypd/html/crime_prevention/safeguardhouse.shtml.

New York State Law Enforcement Council. (1994). *Legislative proposals, 1994.* New York: Author.

Newall, M. (2011, August 4). Her home shot up, witness' mother offered relocation aid. *Philadelphia Inquirer.* Retrieved November 20, 2011, from www.philly.com.

Newberger, E. (1987, March). Prosecution: A problematic approach to child abuse. *Journal of Interpersonal Violence, 2*(1), 112–117.

Newman, D. (1966). *Conviction: The determination of guilt or innocence without trial.* Boston: Little, Brown.

Newman, G. (2004). Identity theft. *Problem-Oriented Policing Guide, No 18.* Office of Community Oriented Policing Services (COPS). Washington, DC: U.S. Department of Justice.

Newman, O. (1972). *Defensible space: People and design in the violent city.* London: Architectural Press.

NHTSA. *See* National Highway Transportation Safety Administration.

NICB. *See* National Insurance Crime Bureau.

NICB study shows vehicle theft trends. (1993, August 3). *Corporate Security Digest*, pp. 1–2.

Nichols, A. (2014, January 2). No-drop prosecution in domestic violence cases. *Journal of Interpersonal Violence, 29*(11), 2114–2142.

Niemeyer, M., & Shichor, D. (1996, September). A preliminary study of a large victim/offender reconciliation program. *Federal Probation, 60*(3), 30–34.

Nieves, E. (1994, December 3). Prosecutors drop charges in abuse case from mid-80s. *New York Times*, pp. A25, A29.

NIJ. *See* National Institute of Justice.

Nipps, E., & Lang, M. (2011, August 9). Armed diner shoots robbery suspect outside St. Petersburg Applebee's. *Tampa Bay Times.* Retrieved January 20, 2012, from www.tampabay.com.

Nizza, M. (2007, October 6). Students sue prosecutor and city in Duke case. *New York Times*, p. A24.

———. (2008, February 15). Gunman was once "revered" on campus. *New York Times*, p. A20.

NNEDV. See National Network To End Domestic Violence.

Nobles, M., Reyns, B., Fox, K., & Fisher, B. (2014). Protection against pursuit: A conceptual and empirical comparison of cyberstalking and stalking victimization among a national sample. *Justice Quarterly, 31*(6), 986–1001.

Noe, D. (2005). The killing of Polly Klaas. *Crime Library.* Retrieved October 13, 2005, from www.courttv.com.

Noh, M., Lee, M., & Feltey, K. (2010, December). Mad, bad, or reasonable? Newspaper portrayals of the battered woman who kills. *Gender Issues, 27*(3/4), 110–130.

Nolan, J., McDevitt, J., & Cronin, S. (2004). Learning to see hate crime: A framework for understanding and clarifying ambiguities in bias crime classification. *Criminal Justice Studies, 17*(1), 91–105.

Noonan, M., & Ginder, S. (2014, October). *Mortality in local jails and state prisons, 2000–2012 - statistical tables.* BJS. Washington, DC: U.S. Department of Justice.

Normandeau, A. (1968, November). Patterns in robbery. *Acta Criminologica, 3*, 2–15.

Notalone. (2014). Schools. *Notalone.gov.* Retrieved December 6, 2014, from https://www.notalone.gov/schools/.

NOVA. *See* National Organization for Victim Assistance.

NPREC. *See* National Prison Rape Elimination Commission.

NRA. *See* National Rifle Association.

NVC. *See* National Victim Center.

NYPD Detectives. (2008). Victimology. Retrieved April 20, 2008, from www.homicidesquad.com.

Oatman, M., & Gordon, I. (2012, December 23). All we want for Christmas is...guns. *Mother Jones.* Retrieved January 10,

2015, from http://www.motherjones.com/mojo/2012/12/christmas-guns-black-friday-obama.

Obama, B. (2010, December 11). *A proclamation: National stalking awareness month, 2011.* Washington, DC: Office of the White House Press Secretary.

———. (2011, April 8). *A proclamation: National crime victims week, 2011.* Washington, DC: Office of the White House Press Secretary.

———. (2012, April 2). *Presidential proclamation -- National Sexual Assault Awareness and Prevention Month, 2012.* Washington, DC: Office of the White House Press Secretary.

———. (2013, March 7). *President Obama signs the Violence Against Women Act reauthorization.* Washington, DC: Office of the White House Press Secretary.

———. (2014, September 30). *Presidential proclamation --- National domestic violence awareness month, 2014.* Washington, DC: Office of the White House Press Secretary.

O'Brien, R. (1985). *Crime and victimization data.* Beverly Hills, CA: Sage.

Occupational Safety and Health Administration. See OSHA.

Ochberg, F. (1978). The victim of terrorism: Psychiatric considerations. *Terrorism: An International Journal, 1*(2), 147–167.

O'Connell, P., & Straub, F. (1999, Spring). Why the jails didn't explode. *City Journal, 9*(2), 28–37.

O'Connor, A., (2013, June 17). When the bully is a sibling. *New York Times,* pp. E1, 5.

———., & Pacifici, S. (2007, April 28). A fatal wound from a colleague's weapon is rare, but always a risk. *New York Times,* p. B3.

O'Donnell, N. (2013, May 5). Branded by tattoos: A lesser known form of domestic violence. *CBS TV News.* Retrieved November 20, 2014, from http://www.cbsnews.com/news/branded-by-tattoos-a-lesser-known-form-of-domestic-violence/.

Office of the Inspector General, Department of Defense. (2003). *United States Air Force Academy: Initial sexual assault survey findings.* Washington, DC: U.S. Department of Defense.

Office of Inspector General, Department of Education. (2005). Don't let identity thieves steal your future! Retrieved September 23, 2005, from www.ed.gov/about/offices/list/oig/misused/idtheft.html.

Office of Intelligence and Analysis Assessment. (2009, April). *Rightwing extremism: Current economic and political climate fueling resurgence in radicalization and recruitment.* Washington, DC: U.S. Department of Homeland Security.

Office of Justice Programs (OJP). (1997). *National Victim Assistance Academy (NVAA) handbook.* Washington, DC: U.S. Department of Justice.

———. (1998). *Stalking and domestic violence: The third annual report to Congress under the Violence Against Women Act.* Washington, DC: U.S. Department of Justice.

———. (2008b). Information on stalking victims. Retrieved August 29, 2008, from www.ojp.usdoj.gov/nij/topics/crime/stalking/victims.htm.

Office of Juvenile Justice and Delinquency Prevention. (1998a). *Guide for implementing the balanced and restorative justice model.* Washington, DC: U.S. Department of Justice.

———. (1998b). *National directory of restitution and community service programs.* Washington, DC: U.S. Department of Justice.

———. (2008, Winter). The Front Line Newsletter. Retrieved December 9, 2008, from www.missingkids.org.

Office of National Drug Control Policy. (2003). Rohypnol. Drug policy information clearinghouse fact sheet. Retrieved December 20, 2005, from www.whitehouse-drugpolicy.gov.

Office For Victims of Crime (OVC). (1997). *Restorative justice fact sheet.* Washington, DC: U.S. Department of Justice.

———. (2001). *Handbook for coping after terrorism: A guide to healing and recovery.* Washington, DC: U.S. Department of Justice.

———. (2002). *Terrorism and international victims unit. OVC fact sheet.* Washington, DC: U.S. Department of Justice.

———. (2003). *First response to victims of crime who have a disability.* Washington, DC: U.S. Department of Justice.

———. (2014). *National Crime Victims Rights Week resource guide, commemorative calendar.* Washington, DC: U.S. Department of Justice.

———. (2014b). Eight benefits of NIBRS for victim service providers. Retrieved December 13, from http://www.ovc.gov/pubs/NIBRS/index.html.

Office on Women's Health, U.S. Department of Health and Human Services. (2011). What is dating violence? Retrieved January 3, 2012, from www.womenshealth.gov.

Officer Down Memorial Page. (2015). Honoring officers killed in 2014. *ODMP.org.* Retrieved January 10, 2015, from http://www.odmp.org/search/year?year=2014.

Ofshe, R., & Watters, E. (1993). *Making monsters: False memories, psychotherapy, and sexual hysteria.* New York: Scribners.

Ogawa, B. (1999). *Color of justice: Culturally sensitive treatment of minority crime victims*(2nd ed.). Boston: Allyn & Bacon.

Ohio Insurance Board. (2011). Red flags associated with fraudulent property & casualty claims. *Ohio Department of Insurance.* Retrieved December 1, 2014, from http://www.insurance.ohio.gov/Company/Documents/RedFlagIndicators.pdf.

Ohlin, L., & Tonry, M. (1989). Family violence in perspective. In L. Ohlin & M. Tonry (Eds.), *Crime and justice: A review* of research, Volume 11: Family violence (pp. 1–18). Chicago: University of Chicago Press.

OJJDP. *See* Office of Juvenile Justice and Delinquency Prevention.

OJP. *See* Office of Justice Programs.

O'Keefe, M., & Trester, L. (1998). Victims of dating violence among high school students. *Violence Against Women, 4*(2), 195–223.

O'Neill, T. (1984). The good, the bad, and the Burger court: Victims' rights and a new model of criminal review. *Journal of Criminal Law and Criminology, 75*(2), 363–387.

Oppel, R. (2013, March 16). Accuser testifies in Ohio rape case; Verdict expected. *New York Times,*p. A12.

Orel, N. (2010). Elder abuse, neglect, and maltreatment: Institutional. In S. Fisher & S. Lab (Eds.), *Encyclopedia of Victimology and Crime Prevention* (pp. 351–353). Thousand Oaks, CA: Sage.

Orth, U., & Maercker, A. (2004). Do trials of perpetrators retraumatize crime victims? *Journal of Interpersonal Violence, 19*(2), 212–227.

OSHA. (2014). Workplace violence: Fact sheet. Retrieved December 22, 2014, from https://www.osha.gov/OshDoc/data_General_Facts/factsheet-workplace-violence.pdf.

O'Shaughnessy, P. (2008, February 25). Ex-cop terrorized her. *New York Daily News,* p. 16.

Ostling, R. (2003, June 21). Clergy abuse victims group opens meeting. *Associated Press Newswire.* Retrieved August 10, 2005, from www.ap.org.

O'Sullivan, C., Davis, R., Farole, D., & Rempel, M. (2007, September). *A comparison of two prosecution policies in cases of intimate partner violence: Executive summary by Safe Horizon.* New York: National Institute of Justice.

Ottens, A., & Hotelling, K. (Eds.). (2001). *Sexual violence on campus: Policies, programs, and perspectives.* New York: Springer.

Otterman, S., & Rivera, R. (2012, May 10). Ultra-orthodox shun their own for reporting child sexual abuse. *New York Times,* pp. A1, A24.

Outlaw, M., & Ruback, B. (1999). Predictors and outcomes of victim restitution orders. *Justice Quarterly, 16*(4), 847–869.

Oudekerk, B., Farr, R., & Reppuci, N. (2013). Is it love or sexual abuse: Young adults perceptions of statutory rape. *Journal of Child Sexual Abuse, 22*(7), 28–44.

OVC. *See* Office of Victims of Crime.

Overland, A. (2011, June 28). Peace takes practice. Retrieved January 22, 2012, from www1.umn.edu.

Owsley, S. (2005, June 25). Don't become a victim this vacation season. *Eureka-Times Standard,* p. 4.

Pacepa, I. (2005, June 16). Bolton's bravery. *National Review Online.* Retrieved September 20, 2005, from www.nationalreview.com.

Paddock, B., Schapiro, R., & Siemaszko, C. (2011, March 23). 1 funeral, 1 arrest. *New York Daily News,* p. 5.

Pagelow, M. (1984a). *Family violence.* New York: Praeger.

———. (1984b). *Women battering: Victims and their experiences.* Beverly Hills, CA: Sage.

———. (1989). The incidence and prevalence of criminal abuse of other family members. In L. Ohlin & M. Tonry (Eds.), *Crime and justice: A review of research, Volume 11: Family violence* (pp. 263–313). Chicago: University of Chicago Press.

Paglia, C. (1993, August 1). Interview on CBS's *60 Minutes.*

———. (1994). *Vamps and tramps.* New York: Vintage.

Pakhomou, S. (2004, Winter). Serial killers: Offender's relationship to the victim and selected demographics. *International Journal of Police Science & Management, 6*(4), 219–233.

Parascandola, R., (2012, January 21). Police Commissioner Raymond Kelly tells cops not to shrug off crime victims. *New York Daily News,* p. 14.

———., Feeney, M., Lauinger, J., & Hutchinson, B. (2010, April 2). Brooklyn man confesses as three are arrested in fatal subway stabbings. Retrieved January 22, 2012, from www.nydailynews.com.

Parent, D., Auerbach, B., & Carlson, K. (1992). *Compensating crime victims: A summary of policies and practices.* Washington, DC: U.S. Department of Justice.

Parker, B. (2014, July 23). Prosecutors detail second attack involving teen charged in Danvers teacher murder. *CBS Television News, Boston.* Retrieved September 24, 2014, from http://boston.cbslocal.com/2014/07/23/teen-charged-in-danvers-teacher-murder-in-court-on-assault-charge/.

Parilla, R., & Allen, E. (2010). 2010 annual report, National Center For Missing and Exploited Children. Retrieved November 30, 2011, from www.missingkids.com.

Parker, A. (2011, February 15). Lawsuit says military is rife with sexual abuse. *New York Times,* p. A11.

Parker, K. (1999, November 22). Moral pendulum swings back. *Denver Post,* p. B10.

Parker, M. (2009). Parole boards. In J. Wilson (Ed.), *The Praeger handbook of victimology* (pp. 193–194). Santa Barbara, CA: Praeger.

Parker, R. (1995). Bringing "booze" back in: The relationship between alcohol and homicide. *Journal of Research in Crime and Delinquency, 32*(1), 3–38.

Parker, R., & Rebhun, L. (1995). *Alcohol and homicide: A deadly combination of two American traditions.* Albany: SUNY Press.

Parsell, T. (2005). Personal accounts from survivors of prison sexual assaults. Retrieved August 19, 2008, from www.nprec.us/docs/sf_tjparsell_statement.pdf.

Parsonage, W. (Ed.). (1979). *Perspectives on victimology*. Beverly Hills, CA: Sage.

Parsonage, W., Bernat, F., & Helfgott, J. (1994). Victim impact testimony and Pennsylvania's parole decision-making process: A pilot study. *Criminal Justice Policy Review, 6*, 187–206.

Paternoster, R. (1984). Prosecutorial discretion in requesting the death penalty: A case of victim-based racial discrimination. *Law and Society Review, 18*, 437–478.

Patterson, L. (2009). Guardian ad litem. In J. Wilson (Ed.), *The Praeger handbook of victimology* (pp. 102–103). Santa Barbara, CA: Praeger.

Patton, C. (2005). *Anti-lesbian, gay, bisexual and transgender violence in 2004: A report of the National Coalition of Anti-Violence Programs*. New York: NCAVP.

Payne, B., & Gainey, R. (2005). *Family violence and criminal justice: A life-course approach* (2nd ed.). Florence, KY: Anderson.

Payne, L. (1989, April 27). Her boyfriend says: Tawana made it up. *New York Newsday*, pp. 1, 3.

Peacock, P. (1998). Marital rape. In R. Bergen (Ed.), *Issues in intimate violence* (pp. 223–235). Thousand Oaks, CA: Sage.

Peak, K. (1986, September). Crime victim reparation: Legislative revival of the offended ones. *Federal Probation, 50*, 36–41.

Pear, R. (2002, March 3). Unreported abuse found at nursing homes. *New York Times*, p. A8.

Pearson-Nelson, B. (2009). Subculture of violence. In J. Wilson (Ed.), *The Praeger handbook of victimology* (pp. 267–268). Santa Barbara, CA: Praeger.

Pease, K., & Laycock, G. (1996). *Revictimization: Reducing the heat on hot victims. NIJ Research in Action*. Washington, DC: U.S. Department of Justice, National Institute of Justice.

Pendergrast, M. (1994). *Victims of memory: Incest accusations and shattered lives*. San Francisco: Upper Access.

Pennington, B. (2011, November 30). New suit says coach abused boy for four years. *New York Times*, p. A16.

Pepinsky, H. (1991). Peacemaking in criminology and criminal justice. In H. Pepinsky & R. Quinney (Eds.), *Criminology as peacemaking* (pp. 299–327). Bloomington, IN: Indiana University Press.

Perez-Pena, R. (2014a, February 24). Christian school faulted for halting abuse study. *New York Times*, p. A14.

———. (2014b, December 12). Bob Jones University blamed victims of sexual assault, not abusers, report says. *New York Times*, p. A10.

PERF, see Police Executive Research Foundation.

Perillo, A., Mercado, C., & Terry, K. (2008). Repeat offending, victim gender, and extent of victim relationship in Catholic Church sexual abusers. *Criminal Justice and Behavior, 35*(5), 600–614.

Perrusquia, M. (2008, December 1). Standing their ground: More citizens enforcing the law themselves. *Memphis Commercial Appeal*, p. 4.

Perry, B. (2011). Recognition of the problem: Public health epidemic. Quoted on the website of the Texas Association for the Protection of Children. Retrieved November 30, 2011, from www.texprotects.org.

Perry, S. (2006). *Prosecutors in state courts, 2005. BJS Bulletin*. Washington, DC: U.S. Department of Justice.

Peters, D., Wyatt, G., & Finkelhor, D. (1986). Prevalence. In D. Finkelhor (Ed.), *A sourcebook on child sexual abuse* (pp. 50–60). Beverly Hills, CA: Sage.

Petherick, W., & Turvey, B. (2008). *Forensic victimology*. New York: Academic Press.

Petit, M. (2011, October 17). America's child death shame. *BBC*. Retrieved December 8, 2011, from www.bbc.co.uk/news.

Pew Research Center. (2014, December 3–7). *What do you think is more important—to protect the right of Americans to own guns, or to control gun ownership?* Retrieved December 12, 2014, from http://www.pewresearch.org/.

Peyser, S. (2012, October 10). The creep show: Sandusky adds insult to injury at sentencing. *New York Post*, p. 21.

Pfeiffer, L. (2007). To enhance or not to enhance: Civil penalty enhancements for parents of juvenile hate crime offenders. *Valparaiso University Law Review, 41*(4), 1685–1738.

Pfeiffer, S. (2002, November 9). Sex-abuse monitor favors police tipoffs. *Boston Globe*, p. 8.

Pfohl, S. (1984). The discovery of child abuse. In D. Kelly (Ed.), *Deviant behavior* (pp. 45–65). New York: St. Martin's Press.

Phillips, N., & McCoy, C. (2010, February 24). Specter introduces bill on witness intimidation. *Philadelphia Inquirer*. Retrieved November 20, 2011, from www.philly.com.

Piquero, N. L., Cohen, M., & Piquero, A. (2011, June). How much is the public willing to pay to be protected from identity theft? *Justice Quarterly, 28*(3), 437–454.

Planty, M. (2002, July). *Third-party involvement in violent crime, 1993–99. BJS Special Report*. Washington, DC: U.S. Department of Justice.

———., & Langton, L. (2013, March). *Female victims of sexual violence, 1994–2010. BJS Special Report*. Washington, DC: U.S. Department of Justice.

Plate, T. (1975). *Crime pays*. New York: Simon & Schuster.

Platell, A. (2005, August). The Date Rape "Myth." *London Daily Mail*, Sec. 2, p. 12.

Platt, A. (1968). *The child savers.* Chicago: University of Chicago Press.

Pleck, E. (1989). Criminal approaches to family violence, 1640–1980. In L. Ohlin & M. Tonry (Eds.), *Crime and justice: An annual review of research, Vol. 11: Family violence* (pp. 19–57). Chicago: University of Chicago Press.

Pleck, E., Pleck, J., Grossman, M., & Bart, P. (1978). The battered data syndrome: A comment on Steinmetz' article. *Victimology*, 2(4), 680–684.

Podhoretz, N. (1991, October). Rape in feminist eyes. *Commentary*, 30–36.

Polaris Project. (2012). Human trafficking cheat sheet. *National Human Trafficking Resource Center.* Retrieved September 26, 2014, from http://www.polarisproject.org/resources/resources-by-topic/human-trafficking.

———. (2013). Human trafficking trends in the United States, 2007–2012. *National Human Trafficking Resource Center.* Retrieved September 25, 2014, from https://na4.salesforce.com/sfc/p/#300000006E4S/a/600000004TLG/f7PldVCtt4Irtx_iljKxiGsERUTm6PUfmNxj9ijA6Sg=.

———. (2014a). Resources Overview. *National Human Trafficking Resource Center.* Retrieved September 25, 2014, from http://www.polarisproject.org/resources/overview.

———. (2014b). State ratings reveal progress in human trafficking laws, more needed to assist victims. *National Human Trafficking Resource Center.*Retrieved September 29, 2014, from http://www.polarisproject.org/media-center/news-and-press/press-releases/1044-state-ratings-reveal-progress-in-human-trafficking-laws-more-needed-to-assist-victims.

Police chief and others do not fit victim stereotypes. (1993, September). *Crime Victims Digest*, pp. 6–7.

Police Executive Research Foundation (PERF). (2011, April). Improving the police response to sexual assault. *PERF.* Retrieved December 11, 2014, from www.policeforum.org/assets/docs/Critical_Issues_Series/improving.

Pollitt, K. (1989, June 18). Violence in a man's world. *New York Times Magazine*, pp. 16, 20.

———. (1991, June 24). Naming and blaming: The media goes wild in Palm Beach. *The Nation*, 833, 847–852.

Pope, E., & Shouldice, M. (2001, January). Drugs and sexual assault: A review. *Trauma, Violence, and Abuse*, 2(1), 51–55.

Porter, E. (1986). *Treating the young male victim of sexual assault: Issues and intervention strategies.* Syracuse, NY: Safer Society Press.

Poston, B. (2012, May 22). City's violent crime rate lowered based on faulty data.*Milwaukee Journal Sentinel.* Retrieved November 13, 2014, from http://www.jsonline.com/watchdog/watchdogreports/hundreds-of-assault-cases-misreported-by-milwaukee-police-department-v44ce4p-152862135.html?ipad=y.

Povoledo, E. (2014, May 27). Pontiff to meet victims of sexual abuse. *New York Times*, p. A18.

Prah, P. M. (2006, January 6). Domestic violence. *CQ Researcher*, 16, 1–24. Retrieved June 23, 2012, from http://library.cqpress.com/cqresearcher.

Pranis, K. (1999, September). Victims in the peacemaking circle process. *The Crime Victims Report*, 3(4), 51.

President's Task Force on Identity Theft. (2007). *Combating identity theft: A strategic plan.* Washington, DC: U.S. Government Printing Office.

President's Task Force on Victims of Crime. (1982). *Final report.* Washington, DC: U.S. Government Printing Office.

Press, A., Copeland, J., Contreras, J., Camper, D., Agrest, S., Newhall, E., et al. (1981, March 23). The plague of violent crime. *Newsweek*, pp. 46–54.

Prestia, K. (1993). *Chocolates for the pillows—Nightmares for the guests.* Silver Spring, MD: Bartleby Press.

Preston, J. (2005, September 27). Judge sets Gotti's bail at $7 million. *New York Times*, pp. B1, B6.

———. (2011, March 4). Police chiefs wary of immigration role. *New York Times*, p. A15.

Price, B., & Sokoloff, N. (2003). *The criminal justice system and women* (3rd ed.). Englewood Cliffs, NJ: Prentice Hall.

Price, M. (2002). The benefits of victim-offender mediation. Retrieved November 28, 2005, from www.vorp.com.

Prison Research and Action Project. (1976). *Instead of prisons.* Genesee, NY: Author.

ProCon. (2012). Concealed guns: Should adults have the right to carry a concealed handgun? Retrieved January 20, 2012, from www.procon.org.

Prosecutorial discretion in the initiation of criminal complaints. (1969, Spring). *Southern California Law Review*, 42, 519–545.

Puckett, J., & Lundman, R. (2003, May). Factors affecting homicide clearances: Multivariate analysis of a complete conceptual framework. *Journal of Research in Crime and Delinquency*, 40(2), 171–193.

Purdum, T. (1988, April 10). The reality of crime on campus. *New York Times Education Supplement*, Sec. 12, pp. 47–51.

Purdy, M. (1994, February 14). Workplace murders provoke lawsuits and better security. *New York Times*, pp. A1, B5.

Quinn, M., & Tomita, S. (1986). *Elder abuse and neglect: Causes, diagnosis, and intervention strategies.* New York: Springer.

Radford, B. (2013, December 5). Why do some falsely claim to be victims?*Discovery Channel.* Retrieved November 14, 2014, from http://news.discovery.com/human/psychology/why-do-some-falsely-claim-to-be-victims-13120.htm.

Raeder, M., (2010). Why stereotypes don't die and ways to facilitate child testimony. *Widener Law Review*, 16(2), 239–278.

Rainville, G., & Reeves, B. (2003). *State court processing statistics: Felony defendants in large urban counties, 2000. BJS.* Washington, DC: U.S. Department of Justice.

RAINN:See Rape Abuse Incest National Network.

Ramsey, J., & Ramsey, P. (2000). *The death of innocence: The untold story of JonBenet's murder and how its exploitation compromised the pursuit of truth.* Waterville, ME: Thorndike Press.

Rand, M., & Rennison, C. (2002). True crime stories? Accounting for differences in our national crime indicators. *Chance Magazine, 15*(1), 8–12.

Rape Abuse Incest National Network (RAINN). (2014). U.S. Supreme Court affirms DNA can be collected from arrestees. *RAINN.org.* Retrieved November 16, 2014, from https://www.rainn.org/public-policy/sexual-assault-in-the-state-and-federal-courts.

———. (2014b, September 18). Rape kit backlog legislation passes Congress. Retrieved December 12, 2014, from https://www.rainn.org/news-room/congress-passes-rapekit-backlog-legislation.

Rashbaum, W. (2005, September 23). Arrest in killings of two who dared to rob the mob. *New York Times,* pp. A1, B6.

Rathbone, G., & Huckabee, J. (1999). *Controlling road rage: A literature review and pilot study.* Washington, DC: AAA Foundation for Traffic Safety.

Rauber, M. (1991, May 21). Rape victims get a legal break. *New York Post,* p. 22.

Ray, L. (1984, May). Dispute resolution: "A muffled explosion." *NIJ Reports, 185,* 9.

Rayman, G. (2012, March 7). The NYPD tapes confirmed. *Village Voice.* Retrieved March 10, 2012, from www.villagevoice.com.

Ready, J., Weisburd, D., & Farrell, G. (2002). The role of crime victims in American policing. *International Review of Victimology, 9,* 175–195.

Reaves, B. (1993). *Using NIBRS (National Incident-Based Reporting System) data to analyze violent crime.* Washington, DC: U.S. Department of Justice.

———. (1998). *Felony defendants in large urban counties, 1994. BJS State Court Processing Statistics.* Washington, DC: U.S. Department of Justice.

———. (2008, February). *Campus law enforcement, 2004–05. BJS Special Report.* Washington, DC: U.S. Department of Justice.

———. (2013, December). *Felony defendants in large urban counties, 2009. BJS Bulletin.* Washington, DC: U.S. Department of Justice.

——— & Hart, T. (2001). *Federal law enforcement officers, 2000. BJS Bulletin.* Washington, DC: U.S. Department of Justice.

——— & Hickman, M. (2002). *Police departments in large cities, 1990–2000. BJS Special Report.* Washington, DC: U.S. Department of Justice.

Reckless, W. (1967). *The crime problem.* New York: Appleton-Century-Crofts.

Redden, M. (2013, December 20). The nine worst things that were said about women, abortion, and rape in 2013. *Mother Jones Magazine.* Retrieved September 18, 2014, from http://www.motherjones.com/politics/2013/12/9-worst-things-said-womens-bodies-2013.

Reeves, H. (2006, June 18). What's that word for taking stuff? *New York Times,* Sec. 11, p. 12.

Reeves, C., & O'Leary-Kelly, A. (2007, March). The effects and costs of intimate partner violence for work organizations. *Journal of Interpersonal Violence, 22*(3), 327–344.

Regehr, C., & Bober, T. (2005). *In the line of fire: Trauma in the emergency services.* New York: Oxford University Press.

Reiff, R. (1979). *The invisible victim.* New York: Basic Books.

Reilly, J. (1981, October). Victim/witness services in prosecutors' offices. *The Prosecutor, 15,* 8–11.

Reiman, J. (1990). *The rich get richer and the poor get prison: Ideology, class, and criminal justice* (3rd ed.). New York: Wiley.

———. (2005). *The rich get richer and the poor get prison: Ideology, class, and criminal justice* (7th ed.). Boston: Allyn & Bacon.

Reiss, A. (1971). *The police and the public.* New Haven, CT: Yale University Press.

———. (1981). Toward a revitalization of theory and research on victimization by crime. *Journal of Criminal Law and Criminology, 72*(2), 704–713.

———. (1986). Official and survey statistics. In E. Fattah (Ed.), *From crime policy to victim policy* (pp. 53–79). New York: St. Martin's Press.

Rennison, C. (1999). *Criminal victimization 1998: Changes 1997–1998 with trends 1993–1998. BJS National Crime Victimization Survey.* Washington, DC: U.S. Department of Justice.

———. (2002b). *Rape and sexual assault: Reporting to police and medical attention, 1992–2000. BJS Selected Findings.* Washington, DC: U.S. Department of Justice.

———. (2003). *Intimate partner violence, 1993–2001. BJS Crime Data Brief.* Washington, DC: U.S. Department of Justice.

Rennison, C., & Addington, L. (2014). Violence against college women: A review to identify limitations in defining the problem and inform future research. *Trauma, Violence, and Abuse, 15*(3), 159–169.

Reno, J. (1999). *Cyberstalking: A new challenge for law enforcement and industry. A report from the attorney general to the vice president.* Washington, DC: U.S. Department of Justice.

Renshaw, D. (2008, October). Coping with obscene phone calls. *Psychiatric Times, 25*(11), 14–15.

Renzetti, C. (1992). *Violent betrayal: Partner abuse in lesbian relationships.* Newbury Park, CA: Sage.

Report exposes lie detector tests that await some Ohio rape victims. (2003, April 15). *Law Enforcement News,* pp. 1, 10.

Resick, P., & Nishith, P. (1997). Sexual assault. In R. Davis, A. Lurigio, & W. Skogan (Eds.), *Victims of crime* (2nd ed., pp. 27–52). Thousand Oaks, CA: Sage.

Reynald, D. (2010, August). Guardians on guardianship. *Journal of Research in Crime & Delinquency, 47*(3), 358–390.

Reynolds, G. (2007, January 16). A rifle in every pot. *New York Times,* p. A21.

Reyns, B., Henson, B., & Fisher, B. (2011, November). Being pursued online: Applying C\cyberlifestyle-routine activities theory to cyberstalking victimization. Retrieved January 2, 2015, from *Criminal Justice and Behavior, 38*(11), 1149–1163.

Rhatigan, D., Moore, T., & Street, A. (2005). Reflections on partner violence: Twenty years of research and beyond. *Journal of Interpersonal Violence, 20*(1), 82–88.

Rhode, D. (1989). *Justice and gender: Sex discrimination and the law.* Cambridge, MA: Harvard University Press.

Rhodes, N. (1992). The assessment of spousal abuse: An alternative to the conflict tactics scale. In E. Viano (Ed.), *Intimate violence: Interdisciplinary perspectives* (pp. 27–36). Washington, DC: Hemisphere Publishing.

Rhodes, W. (1978). Plea bargaining: Who gains? Who loses? *PROMIS Research Project No. 14.* Washington, DC: Institute for Law and Social Research.

Rich, F. (2010, February 2). The axis of the obsessed and deranged. *New York Times,* p. A24.

Richardson, J., Best, J., & Bromley, D. (Eds.). (1991). *The Satanism scare.* New York: Aldine de Gruyter.

Richie, B. (1996). *Compelled to crime: The gender entrapment of battered black women.* New York: Routledge.

Riczo, S. (2001). America, guns and the twenty-first century. *USA Today Magazine, 129*(2670), 16–19.

Riedel, M. (1987). Stranger violence: Perspectives, issues, and problems. *Journal of Criminal Law, 78*(2), 223–259.

Riedel, M., & Mock, L. (1985). *NIJ report: The nature and patterns of American homicide.* Washington, DC: U.S. Government Printing Office.

Rieger, A. (2007). Missing the mark. *Harvard Journal of Law and Gender, 30*(1), 231–256.

Rittenmeyer, S. (1981). Of battered wives, self-defense and double standards of justice. *Journal of Criminal Justice, 9*(5), 389–396.

Riveira, D. (2002, November–December). Internet crimes against women. *The Crime Victims Report, 6*(5), 67–68, 75.

Rivera, R. (2010a, September 24). Agency admits fault in death of child. *New York Times,* pp. A1, A16.

———. (2011b, November 18). Audit says police fall short in providing interpreters. *New York Times,* pp. A18.

Robbins, J. (2011a, March 11). Burglars in Brooklyn Heights find the doors (and windows) are open. *New York Times,* p. A20.

———. (2013, March 1). Ex-college quarterback is acquitted of rape in Montana. *New York Times,* p. A16.

Roberts, A. (1990). *Helping crime victims.* Newbury Park, CA: Sage.

———. (Ed.). (1998). *Juvenile justice: Policies, programs, and services* (2nd ed.). Thousand Oaks, CA: Sage.

———. (2002). *Handbook of domestic violence intervention strategies.* New York: Oxford University Press.

Roberts, A., & Roberts, B. (2005). *Ending intimate abuse.* New York: Oxford University Press.

Roberts, L., & Indermaur, D. (2008). Social issues as media constructions: The case of "road rage." *Crime, Media, Culture, 1*(3), 301–318.

———. (2008). The "homogamy" of road rage revisited. *Violence and Victims, 23*(6), 758–770.

Roberts, S. (1987, March 22). Criminals, authors, and criminal authors. *New York Times Book Review,* pp. 1, 34–35.

———. (1989, March 7). When crimes become symbols. *New York Times,* Sec. 4, pp. 1, 28.

Robertson, C. (2014, November 12). New Orleans police routinely ignored sex crimes, report finds. *New York Times,* p. A12.

Robin, G. (1977, April). Forcible rape: Institutionalized sexism in the criminal justice system. *Crime and Delinquency, 23*(2), 136–152.

Robin, M. (1991). The social construction of child abuse and "false allegations." *Child and Youth Services, 75,* 1–34.

Robinson, N., Davies, G., & Nettleingham, A. (2009, February). Vicarious traumatization as a consequence of jury service. *The Howard Journal, 48*(1), 1–12. Retrieved January 7, 2012, from www.onlinelibrary.wiley.com.

Robinson, P., Cahill, M., & Bartels, D. (2010, December). Competing theories of blackmail: An empirical research critique of criminal law theory. *Texas Law Review, 89*(2), 291–352.

Rochman, B. (2011, July 26). Talking to strangers? Rewriting the rules of childhood. *Time.* Retrieved November 30, 2011, from www.healthland.time.com.

RMIIA. See Rocky Mountain Insurance Information Association.

Rocky Mountain Insurance Information Association (RMIIA). (2011). U.S. auto theft statistics. *RMIIA.com.* Retrieved December 2, 2014, from http://www.rmiia.org/auto/auto_theft/statistics.asp.

Rodriguez, C. (2011, April 4). Woman who falsely accused Duke lacrosse players of rape charged with stabbing boyfriend. Retrieved December 20, 2011, from www.abcnews.go.com.

Roehl, J., & Ray, L. (1986, July). Toward the multi-door courthouse: Dispute resolution intake and referral. *NIJ Reports, 198,* 2–7.

Roger Williams University. (2011). Sexual assault: Rape myths and facts. Retrieved December 20, 2011, from www.rwu.edu.

Rohter, L. (1993, September 16). Fearful of tourism decline, Florida offers assurances on safety. *New York Times*, p. A14.

Roiphe, K. (1993). *The morning after: Sex, fear, and feminism on campus*. Boston: Little, Brown.

Roman, J. (2013, July). Race, justifiable homicides, and stand your ground laws. *Urban Institute*. Retrieved January 10, 2015, from http://www.urban.org/UploadedPDF/412873-stand-your-ground.pdf.

Rondeau, G., & Rondeau, E. (2006, February). National coalition of victims in action. *The Crime Victims Report, 87*, 90–91.

Rootsaert, D. (1987). *A prosecutor's guide to victim/witness assistance*. Alexandria, VA: National District Attorneys Association.

Roper Center for Public Opinion Research. (2004). Respondents reporting a firearm in their home. *Sourcebook of Criminal Justice Statistics, 2003*, 150. Albany, NY: State University of New York.

Rose, M., Nadler, J., & Clark, J. (2006, May). Appropriately upset? Emotion norms and perceptions of crime victims. *Law and Human Behavior, 30*, 203–219.

Rose, V. (1977, October). Rape as a social problem: A by-product of the feminist movement. *Social Problems, 25*, 75–89.

Rosenmerkel, S., Durose, M., & Farole, D. (2010, November). *Felony sentences in state courts, 2006, (revised). BJS National Judicial Reporting Program*. Washington, DC: U.S. Department of Justice.

Rosenthal, E. (1990, June 27). U.S. is by far the homicide capital of the industrialized nations. *New York Times*, p. A10.

Ross, R., & Staines, G. (1972, Summer). The politics of analyzing social problems. *Social Problems, 20*, 18–40.

Rothfeld, M. (2008, October 22). Proposition 9 would give crime victims a stronger voice, but critics say it could violate inmates rights. *Los Angeles Times*, p. A8.

Rothman, E., & Xuan, Z. (2014, September). Trends in physical dating violence victimization among U.S. high school students, 1999–2011. *Journal of School Violence, 13*(3), 277–290.

Rothstein, E. (2008, July 5). Good guys, bad guys, and spies, all wrapped in "edutainment." *New York Times*, pp. B1, B12.

Rottenberg, D. (1980, March 16). Crime victims fight back. *Parade*, 21–23.

Rubenfeld, J. (2014, November 14). Mishandling rape. *New York Times*, p. E4.

Rubin, J. (2008, March 18). Report urges LAPD to change SWAT unit. *Los Angeles Times*, p. 1.

———., & Poston, B. (2014, August 11). Inaccurate LAPD crime statistics prompt larger investigation. *Los Angeles Times*. Retrieved November 13, 2014, from http://www.latimes.com/local/lanow/la-me-ln-lapd-crime-stats-20140811-story.html.

Ruderman, W., & Goodman, D. (2012, October 25). A conscientious driver, a gunman, and a fatal encounter on L.I. *New York Times*, p. A24.

Rueda, M. (2013, February 8). The ten most violent cities in the world. *ABC News*. Retrieved October 5, 2014, from http://abcnews.go.com/ABC_Univision/10-violent-cities-world/story?id=18442706#.

Rugala, E. (2004). *Workplace violence: Issues and responses*. Quantico, VA: Federal Bureau of Investigation Academy.

Russell, D. (1975). *The politics of rape: The victim's perspective*. New York: Stein & Day.

———. (1982). *Rape in marriage*. New York: Macmillan.

———. (1984). *Sexual exploitation: Rape, child molestation, and workplace harassment*. Newbury Park, CA: Sage.

———. (1986). *The secret trauma: Incest in the lives of girls and women*. New York: Basic Books.

———. (1990). *Sexual exploitation*. Beverly Hills, CA: Sage.

Russell-Brown, K. (2008). *The color of crime* (2nd ed.). New York: NYU Press.

Ryan, W. (1971). *Blaming the victim*. New York: Vintage.

Sabo, D. (1992). Understanding men in prison: The relevance of gender studies. *Men's Studies Review, 9*(1), 4–9.

Sachs, A. (1994, January 31). Now for the movie. *Time*, p. 99.

Sagarin, E. (1975, May–June). Forcible rape and the problem of the rights of the accused. *Intellect, 103*, 515–520.

Sakheim, D., & Devine, S. (Eds.). (1992). *Out of darkness: Exploring Satanism and ritual abuse*. New York: Macmillan.

Salfati, C., James, A., & Ferguson, L. (2008). Prostitute homicides: A descriptive study. *Journal of Interpersonal Violence, 23*(4), 505–543.

Salmivalli, C., & Nieminen, E. (2002). Proactive and reactive aggression among school bullies and victims. *Aggressive Behavior, 28*, 30–44.

Salzinger, S., Feldman, R., & Hammer, M. (1991, March). Risk for physical child abuse and the personal consequences for its victims. *Criminal Justice and Behavior, 18*(1), 64–81.

Sampson, R. (2004). *Acquaintance rape of college students*. Washington, DC: Office of Community Oriented Policing Services, U.S. Department of Justice.

———. (2007a, January). Domestic violence. *Problem-Oriented Policing Guide, No. 45*. Retrieved October 2, 2011, from popcenter.org.

———. (2007b, March). *False burglar alarms* (2nd ed.). *Problem-Oriented Policing Guide, No. 5*. Retrieved October 26, 2011, from popcenter.org.

Sanday, P. (2007). Fraternity gang rape: *Sex, brotherhood and privilege on campus* (2nd ed.). New York: NYU Press.

Sander, L. (2011, December 9). Latest shootings at Virginia Tech offer a test like no other of new alert system. *Chronicle of Higher Education*. Retrieved December 28, 2011, from http://chronicle.com.

Sanderson, B. (1994, November 30). Victim fund slashes its payouts. *Bergen (NJ) Record*, pp. A1, A12.

Sandoval, E. (2011, October 17). Woman beat with pipe by McDonald's cashier faces permanent brain damage, mother claims. *New York Daily News*, p. 8.

Sargeant, G. (1991, April). Battered woman syndrome gaining legal recognition. *Trial, 27*(4), 17–20.

Sarnoff, S. (1996). *Paying for crime: The policies and possibilities of crime victim reimbursement*. Westport, CT: Praeger.

Saunders, D. (1986). When battered women use violence: Husband-abuse or self-defense? *Victims and Violence, 1*(1), 47–59.

Saunders, P. (2005). Traffic violations: Determining the meaning of violence in sexual trafficking versus sex work. *Journal of Interpersonal Violence, 20*(3), 343–360.

Savage, D. (2003, January). Getting back your name. *ABA Journal, 88*, 24–25.

Save Abandoned Babies Foundation. (2014). April is save abandoned babies month. *Saveabandonedbabiesfoundation.org*. Retrieved November 20, 2014, from http://www.saveabandonedbabies.org/breaking_news/press_releases/SAB_PressRelease_20140421.pdf.

Savitz, L. (1982). Official statistics. In L. Savitz & N. Johnston (Eds.), *Contemporary criminology* (pp. 3–15). New York: Wiley.

———. (1986). Obscene phone calls. In T. Hartnagel & R. Silverman (Eds.), *Critique and explanation: Essays in honor of Gwynne Nettles* (pp. 149–158). New Brunswick, NJ: Transaction Books.

Sawyer, S. (1987, November). Law enforcement officers and their families face special difficulties when victimized. *NOVA Newsletter, 11*(11), 1–2.

Scafidi, F. (2006, July 24). California tops nation in motorcycle thefts. Press release. *National Insurance Crime Bureau*. Retrieved July 5, 2008, from www.nicb.org.

———. (2013, November 25). NICB reports small decline in motorcycle thefts in 2012. Press release. *National Insurance Crime Bureau*.Retrieved October 15, 2014, from https://www.nicb.org/newsroom/news-releases/2012-motorcycle-theft-and-recovery-report.

———. (2014a, June 26). NICB celebrates 30th anniversary of hot spots. Press release. *National Insurance Crime Bureau*.

Retrieved October 25, 2014, from https://www.nicb.org/newsroom/news-releases/nicb-celebrates-30th-anniversary-of-hot-spots.

———. (2014b, August 18). NICB's Hot Wheels: America's ten most stolen vehicles. Press release. *National Insurance Crime Bureau*. Retrieved October 15, 2014, from https://www.nicb.org/newsroom/news-releases/hot-wheels-report.

Schafer, S. (1968). *The victim and his criminal*. New York: Random House.

———. (1970). *Compensation and restitution to victims of crime* (2nd ed.). Montclair, NJ: Patterson Smith.

———. (1977). *Victimology: The victim and his criminal*. Reston, VA: Reston Publishers.

Schanberg, S. (1984, March 27). The rape trial. *New York Times*, p. A31.

———. (1989, April 28). We should be outraged at all rapes. *New York Newsday*, pp. 94–95.

Schaye, K. (1998, July 27). Judgment called the end of the Tawana Brawley story. *New York Daily News*, p. 8.

Schechter, S. (1982). *Women and male violence*. Boston: South End Press.

Scheck, J. (2010, August 5). Stalkers exploit cell phone GPS. *Wall Street Journal*, pp. A1, A14.

Schemo, D. (2002, December 18). Harvard advertises for people abducted by aliens, but the truth is out there a little farther. *New York Times*, p. B13.

Scherer, J. (1982). An overview of victimology. In J. Scherer & G. Shepherd (Eds.), *Victimization of the weak: Contemporary social reactions* (pp. 8–30). Springfield, IL: Charles C. Thomas.

Schmidt, J. (2006, October). Victim impact statements in El Paso. *Crime Victims Report, 10*(4), 49–50.

Schmitt, E. (1994, May 23). Military struggling to stem an increase in family violence. *New York Times*, pp. A1, A12.

Schneider, A. (1981). Methodological problems in victim surveys and their implications for research in victimology. *Journal of Criminal Law and Criminology, 72*(2), 818–830.

Schneider, A., & Schneider, P. (1978). *Private and public-minded citizen responses to a neighborhood crime prevention strategy*. Eugene, OR: Institute of Policy Analysis.

———. (1981). Victim assistance programs. In B. Galaway & J. Hudson (Eds.), *Perspectives on crime victims* (pp. 364–373). St. Louis, MO: C.V. Mosby.

Schneider, E. (1980). Equal rights to trial for women: Sex bias in the law on self-defense. *Harvard Civil Rights and Civil Liberties Review, 15*, 623–647.

———. (2000). *Battered women and feminist lawmaking*. New Haven, CT: Yale University Press.

Schneider, H. (Ed.). (1982). *The victim in international perspective*. New York: Walter De Gruyter.

———. (1996). Violence in the institution. *International Journal of Offender Therapy and Comparative Criminology, 40,* 5–18.

Schneider, P. (1987, February). Lost innocents: The myth of missing children. *Harper's Magazine,* pp. 47–53.

Schneider, S. (2014). *Crime prevention: Theory and practice* (2nd ed.). Boca Raton, FL: CRC Press.

Schreiber, L. (1990, September). Campus rape. *Glamour,* pp. 23–26.

Schultz, D., Hudak, E., & Alpert, G. (2010, March). Evidence based decisions on police pursuits: The officer's perspective. *FBI Law Enforcement Bulletin, 79*(3), 4–10.

Schultz, J. (2010, October 16). Being discreet on Facebook. *New York Times,* p. B4.

Schultz, L. (1965). The violated: A proposal to compensate victims of violent crime. *St. Louis University Law Journal, 10,* 238–250.

———. (1968). The victim–offender relationship. *Crime and Delinquency, 14,* 135–141.

Schur, E. (1984). *Labeling women deviant: Gender, stigma, and social control.* New York: Random House.

Schwab, N. (2008, August 21). Self-defense techniques help you to survive on campus. Retrieved September 25, 2008, from www.usnews.com/articles/education/best-colleges/2008/08/21/self-defense-techniques-help-you-survive-on-campus.html.

Schwartz, E. (2007, December 13). Giving crime victims more of their say. *U.S. News & World Report,* p. 32.

Schwartz, M. (2005). The past and the future of violence against women. *Journal of Interpersonal Violence, 20*(1), 7–11.

Schwartz, M., & DeKeseredy, W. (1997). *Sexual assault on the college campus: The role of male peer support.* Thousand Oaks, CA: Sage.

Schwendinger, H., & Schwendinger, J. (1967). Delinquent stereotypes of probable victims. In M. Klein (Ed.), *Juvenile gangs in context* (pp. 92–105). Englewood Cliffs, NJ: Prentice Hall.

———. (1974). Rape myths in legal, theoretical, and everyday practice. *Crime and Social Justice, 1,* 18–26.

Schwirtz, M. (2013, August 16). Teenager's errant gunfire at project in Bronx leads to his fatal beating. *New York Times,* p. 18.

———. (2014, March 19). Rikers Island struggles with a rise in violence. *New York Times,* pp. A1, A8.

Sclafani, T. (2005, April 11). Fighting fire with wire. *New York Daily News,* pp. 4–5.

Scott, E., & Williams, A. (1985). *Racial and religious violence: A model law enforcement response.* Landover, MD: National Organization of Black Law Enforcement Executives (NOBLE).

Screening. (2006, May 30). Women often hide domestic abuse from doctors. *New York Times,* p. C4.

Scroggins, J. (2009). Bystander effect. In J. Wilson (Ed.), *The Praeger handbook of victimology* (pp. 33–34). Santa Barbara, CA: Praeger.

Seager, S. (2014, November 11). Where hell is other patients. *New York Times,* p. A25.

Secret, M. (2012, December 28). Suit settled over claims of sex abuse at Poly Prep. *New York Times,* p. A22.

Sedlak, A., Finkelhor, D., Hammer, H., & Schultz, D. (2002). *NISMART National estimates of missing children: An overview.* Washington, DC: U.S. Department of Justice, Office of Juvenile Justice and Delinquency Prevention.

Seebach, L. (1999, March 28). How to give the campus left a taste of its own medicine. *Denver Rocky Mountain News,* p. 2B.

Seelye, K. (2014, April 14). A year after the Boston Marathon bombings, injured brothers endure. *New York Times,* pp. A1, A10.

Seligmann, J., & Maor, Y. (1980, August 4). Punishments that fit the crime. *Newsweek,* p.60.

Senate Committee considers proposed victims' rights amendments to Constitution. (2003, April 16). *Criminal Law Reporter, 73*(3), 74–76.

Senate Committee on the Judiciary. (2003). *Report: The Violence Against Women Act of 1993.* Washington, DC: U.S. Senate.

Senate Judiciary Committee (Majority Staff). (1993). *The response to rape: Detours on the road to equal justice.* Washington, DC: U.S. Senate.

Serbin, R. (2002, May). When clergy fail their flocks. *Trial, 38*(5), 34–41.

Seward, Z. (2006, October 23). FBI stats show many colleges understate campus crime. *Wall Street Journal,* pp. B1, B12.

Sexton, J. (1994, December 3). Brooklyn drivers fear reckless young guns. *New York Times,* pp. A1, A26.

Shanahan, E. (2006, June). ID thieves' new tricks. *Readers Digest,* pp. 82–87.

Shane, S. (2010, April 2). Words as weapons: Dropping the "terrorism" bomb. *New York Times,* p. E6.

Shane, S., & Lichtblau, E. (2008a, June 28). Scientist is paid millions by U.S. in anthrax suit. *New York Times,* p. A10.

———. (2008b, September 17). Senator, target of anthrax letter, challenges FBI finding. *New York Times,* p. A14.

Shelden, R. (1982). *Criminal justice in America: A sociological approach.* Boston: Little, Brown.

Sheley, J. (1979). *Understanding crime: Concepts, issues, decisions.* Belmont, CA: Wadsworth.

Shepeard, C. (2014, August 2). Marissa Alexander faces 60 years in prison for self-defense. Retrieved September 5, 2014, from http://www.care2.com/causes/domestic-abuse-victim-marissa-alexander-faces-60-years-in-prison-for-self-defense.html.

Sheridan, R. (1994). The false child molestation outbreak of the 1980s: An explanation of the cases arising in the divorce context. In K. de Koster & K. Swisher (Eds.), *Child abuse: Opposing viewpoints* (pp. 48–55). San Diego, CA: Greenhaven Press.

Sherman, L. (1986). *NIJ crime file: Domestic violence*. Washington, DC: U.S. Department of Justice.

Sherman, L., & Berk, R. (1984, April). The specific deterrent effects of arrest for domestic assault. *American Sociological Review, 49*, 261–272.

Sherman, L., Berk, R., & Smith, D. (1992, October). Crime, punishment, and stake in conformity: Legal and informal control of domestic violence. *American Sociological Review, 57*, 680–690. Washington, DC: Police Foundation.

Sherman, L., Gartin, P., & Buerger, M. (1989, February). Hot spots of predatory crime: Routine activities and the criminology of place. *Criminology, 27*(1), 27–40.

Sherman, L., Steele, L., Laufersweiler, D., Hoffer, N., & Julian, S. (1989). Stray bullets and "mushrooms": Random shootings of bystanders in four cities, 1977–1988. *Journal of Quantitative Criminology, 5*, 297–316.

Sherman, W. (2005, May 15). How they'll steal your I.D. *New York Daily News*, p. 8.

Shichor, D., Sechrest, D., & Doocy, J. (2000). Victims of investment fraud. In H. Pontell & D. Shichor (Eds.), *Contemporary issues in crime and criminal justice* (pp. 81–96). Upper Saddle River, NJ: Prentice Hall.

Shifrel, S. (2007a, July 19). Rape victim hummed to soothe drug-crazed beast, she testifies. *New York Daily News*, p. 26.

Shipp, E. (1987, April 21). Defense lawyers' tactics: Unfair or just aggressive? *New York Times*, pp. B1, B4.

Shotland, L. (1976). Spontaneous vigilantism: A bystander response to criminal behavior. In J. Rosenbaum & P. Sederberg (Eds.), *Vigilante politics* (pp. 30–44). Philadelphia: University of Pennsylvania Press.

Shotland, L., & Goodstein, L. (1984). The role of bystanders in crime control. *Journal of Social Issues, 40*(1), 9–26.

Shulevitz, J. (2015, February 5). The best way to address campus rape. *New York Times*, p. A22.

Siedsma, A. (2012, February15). What to expect from your insurance company after a burglary. *Insure.com*. Retrieved December 7, 2014, from http://www.insure.com/home-insurance/after-a-burglary.html.

Siegel, J., Sorenson, S., Golding, J., Burnham, M., & Stein, J. (1987). The prevalence of childhood sexual assault. *American Journal of Epidemiology, 126*, 1141–1153.

Siegel, L. (1998). *Criminology* (6th ed.). Belmont, CA: West/Wadsworth.

Sieh, E. (1990). Diplomatic immunity: A reconsideration of an ancient concept. *International Journal of Comparative and Applied Criminal Justice, 14*(1/2), 269–280.

Silberman, C. (1978). *Criminal violence, criminal justice*. New York: Random House.

Silberman, M. (1995). *A world of violence: Corrections in America*. Belmont, CA: Wadsworth.

Silver, J. (2012, November 6). Can the law make us be decent? *New York Times*, p. A26. Retrieved December 8, 2014, from http://www.nytimes.com/2012/11/07/opinion/can-the-law-make-bad-samaritans-be-decent.html.

Silverman, R. (1974). Victim precipitation: An examination of the concept. In I. Drapkin & E. Viano (Eds.), *Victimology: A new focus* (pp. 99–110). Lexington, MA: DC Heath.

Silving, H. (1959). Compensation for victims of criminal violence—A roundtable. *Journal of Public Law, 8*, 236–253.

Simmons, M. (2007, April 8). Home where family died is now safe haven. *New York Times*, p. A16.

Simon, D. (1991). *Homicide: A year on the killing streets*. New York: Fawcett Columbine.

Simonelli, C., Mullis, T., Elliott, A., & Pierce, T. (2002). Abuse by siblings and subsequent experiences of violence within the dating relationship. *Journal of Interpersonal Violence, 11*(2), 103–122.

Simonson, L. (1994). The victims' rights movement: A critical view from a practicing sociologist. *Sociological Imagination, 31*, 181–196.

Sinason, V. (1994). *Treating survivors of Satanist abuse*. New York: Routledge.

Singer, S. (1981). Homogeneous victim–offender populations: A review and some research implications. *Journal of Criminal Law and Criminology, 12*(2), 779–788.

———. (1986). Victims of serious violence and their criminal behavior: Subcultural theory and beyond. *Violence and Victims, 1*(1), 61–70.

Sinozich, S., & Langton, L. (2014, December 11). *Rape and sexual assault among college-age females, 1995–2013.BJS Special Report*. Washington, DC: U.S. Department of Justice.

Sivers, H., Schooler, J., & Freyd, J. (2002). *Recovered memories*. New York: Elsevier Science.

Skogan, W. (1978). *Victimization surveys and criminal justice planning*. Washington, DC: U.S. Government Printing Office.

———. (1981a). Assessing the behavioral context of victimization. *Journal of Criminal Law and Criminology, 12*(2), 727–742.

———. (1981b). *Issues in the measurement of victimization*. Washington, DC: U.S. Department of Justice.

———. (1986). Methodological issues in the study of victimization. In E. Fattah (Ed.), *From crime policy to victim policy* (pp. 80–116). New York: St. Martin's Press.

Skogan, W., & Maxfield, M. (1981). *Coping with crime: Individual and neighborhood reactions.* Beverly Hills, CA: Sage.

Skuse, D., et al. (2003, February). Development of sexually abusive behavior in sexually victimized males: A longitudinal study. *The Lancet, 361,* 471–476.

Slosarik, K. (2002). Identify theft: An overview of the problem. *The Justice Professional, 15*(4), 329–343.

Smalley, S., & Mnookin, S. (2003, May 5). A house of horrors. *Newsweek,* p. 49.

Smart, R., & Mann, R. (2002, July). Is road rage a serious traffic problem? *Traffic Injury Prevention, 3*(3), 183–189.

Smilowitz, A. (2014, July 30). A sustainable approach to ending human trafficking. *Huffington Post.* Retrieved September 30, 2014, from http://www.huffingtonpost.com/ariel-smilowitz/a-sustainable-approach-to_b_5633604.html.

Smith, B. (1985). Trends in the victims' rights movement and implications for future research. *Victimology, 10*(1–4), 34–43.

Smith, B., Sloan, J., & Ward, R. (1990). Public support for the victims' rights movement: Results of a statewide survey. *Crime and Delinquency, 36*(4), 488–502.

Smith, E., & Farole, D. (2009, October). *Profile of intimate partner violence cases in large urban counties. BJS Special Report.* Washington, DC: U.S. Department of Justice.

Smith, J. (2014, November 20). These laws let accused rapists off the hook. *Mother Jones Magazine.* Retrieved January 2, 2015, from http://www.motherjones.com/politics/2014/11/rape-sexual-assault-statutes-limitations-laws.

Smith, K. (1994, September 19). Outrage over new attack by freed N.J. kid molester. *New York Post,* p. 6.

Smith, M. (1988). *Coping with crime on campus.* New York: American Council on Education (ACE).

Smith, N., & Harrell, S. (2013, March). Sexual abuse of children with disabilities: A national snapshot. *Vera Institute of Justice, Center on Victimization and Safety.* Retrieved September 30, 2014, from http://www.vera.org/sites/default/files/resources/downloads/sexual-abuse-of-children-with-disabilities-national-snapshot-v3.pdf.

Smith, P., & Welchans, S. (2000). Peer education: Does focusing on male responsibility change sexual assault attitudes? *Violence Against Women, 6*(11), 1255–1268.

Smith, S. (1994, July). Have screwdriver, will steal. *Car and Driver,* pp. 157–167.

Smith, S., & Freinkel, S. (1988). *Adjusting the balance: Federal policy and victim services.* New York: Greenwood Press.

Smith, S., Steadman, G., Todd, M., & Townsend, M. (1999). *Criminal victimization and perceptions of community safety in 12 cities, 1998. BJS Report.* Washington, DC: U.S. Department of Justice.

Smothers, R. (2003, September 27). New Jersey creates independent child advocate office. *New York Times,* p. B6.

Snell, J., Rosenwald, R., & Robey, A. (1964, August). The wifebeater's wife: A study of family interaction. *Archives of General Psychiatry, 11,* 107–112.

Snyder, J. (1993, Fall). A nation of cowards. *The Public Interest, 113,* 40–56.

Snyder, H., & Sickmund, M. (1995). *Juvenile offenders and victims: A focus on violence. OJJDP Statistical Summary.* Washington, DC: U.S. Department of Justice.

Sokoloff, N., & Pratt, C. (2005). *Domestic violence at the margins: Readings on race, class, gender and culture.* New Brunswick, NJ: Rutgers University Press.

Sontag, S. (2002, November 17). Fierce entanglement. *New York Times Magazine,* pp. 52–62.

Sottile, L. (2014, February 15). When adults go missing, only questions remain. *Aljazeera.com.* Retrieved November 16, 2014, from http://america.aljazeera.com/features/2014/2/when-an-adult-goesmissingonlyquestionsremain.html.

Southern Poverty Law Center (SPLC). (2001, Winter). Discounting hate. *Intelligence Report.* Atlanta: SPLC.

Southern Regional Council. (1969). *Race makes the difference: An analysis of sentence disparity among black and white offenders in southern prisons.* Atlanta, GA: Author.

Sparkman, E. (2003). SUVs, pickups, minivans favorites on thieves' shopping lists. Retrieved September 10, 2005, from www.nicb.com.

Spears, J., & Spohn, C. (1997). The effects of evidence factors and victim characteristics on prosecutors' charging decisions in sexual assault cases. *American Journal of Criminal Justice, 20,* 183–205.

Spector, M., & Kitsuse, J. (1987). *Constructing social problems.* New York: Aldine de Gruyter.

Spelman, W., & Brown, D. (1984). *NIJ report: Calling the police: Citizen reporting of serious crime.* Washington, DC: U.S. Department of Justice.

Spence-Diehl, E. (1999). *Stalking: A handbook for victims.* Holmes Beach, FL: Learning Publications.

Spitzer, N. (1986, June). The children's crusade. *Atlantic,* pp. 18–22.

Spohn, C., & Horney, J. (1992). *Rape law reform: A grassroots revolution and its impact.* New York: Plenum Press.

Spunt, B., Goldstein, P., Brownstein, H., Fendrich, M., & Langley, S. (1994). Alcohol and homicide: Interviews with prison inmates. *Journal of Drug Issues, 24*(1), 143–163.

Spunt, B., Tarshish, C., Fendich, M., Goldstein, P., & Brownstein, H. (1993, Spring). Research note: The utility of correctional data for understanding the drugs-homicide connection. *Criminal Justice Review, 18*(1), 46–60.

Stajano, F., & Wilson, P. (2011, March). Understanding scam victims: Seven principles for systems security. *Communications of the ACM (Association of Computing Machinery), 54*(3), 70–75.

Stalking Resource Center. (2009). Stalking fact sheet. Retrieved September 13, 2011, from www.ncvc.org.

Stammer, L. (2003, February 23). National advocacy group helps victims break their silence. *Los Angeles Times*, p. A8.

Stanford, T. (2011). *Annual report, fiscal year 2009–2010.* Albany, NY: New York State Crime Victims Board.

Stark, J., & Goldstein, H. (1985). *The rights of crime victims: An American Civil Liberties Union handbook.* New York: Bantam Books.

START. (2014). Data and tools. *National Consortium For The Study of Terrorism and Responses to Terrorism.* Retrieved December 6, 2014, from http://www.start.umd.edu/data-and-tools/start-datasets.

Steinhauer, J. (2013, November 7). Reports of military sexual assault rise sharply. *New York Times*, p. A8.

Steinman, M. (1991). The public policy process and woman battering: Problems and pitfalls. In M. Steinman (Ed.), *Woman battering: Policy responses* (pp. 1–18). Cincinnati, OH: Anderson.

Steinmetz, S. (1978a). The battered husband syndrome. *Victimology, 2*(4), 499–509.

———. (1978b). Battered parents. *Society, 15*(5), 54–55.

———. (1988). *Duty bound: Elder abuse and family care.* Newbury Park, CA: Sage.

Stelloh, T., & Barron, J. (2011, August 19). Husband admits he set up killing of wife in street, police say. *New York Times*, p. A12.

Stennett, D. (2014, July 16). Armed Good Samaritan holds stabbing suspect at gunpoint deputies say. *Orlando Sentinel.* Retrieved January 6, 2015, from http://articles.orlandosentinel.com/2014-07-16/news/os-armed-good-samaritan-stabbing-suspect-20140716_1_deputies-orange-county-jail-good-samaritan.

Stephens, M. (1988). *A history of the news.* New York: Penguin.

Stepp, L. (2007, September). A new kind of date rape. *Cosmopolitan*, pp. 199–203.

———. (2008). *Unhooked: How young women pursue sex, delay love, and lose at both.* New York: Penguin, Riverhead Trade.

Stets, J., & Pirog-Good, M. (1987). Violence in dating relationships. *Social Psychology Quarterly, 50*, 237–246.

Stevens, D. (1999). Interviews with women convicted of murder: Battered women's syndrome revisited. *International Review of Victimology, 6*(2), 117–135.

Stephens, D., & Matarese, L. (2013, October). The necessary truths about police safety. *Law and Order, 61*(10), 82–87.

Stewart, E., Schreck, C., & Brunson, R. (2008). Lessons of the street code. *Journal of Contemporary Criminal Justice, 24*(2), 137–147.

Stewart, M. (2014, August 21). Nissan Altima, Honda Accord top most stolen car list. *Motortrend Magazine.* Retrieved October 25, 2014, from http://wot.motortrend.com/1408_nissan_altima_honda_accord_top_most_stolen_car_list.

Stillman, F. (1987). *NIJ Research in brief. Line-of-duty deaths: Survivor and departmental responses.* Washington, DC: U.S. Department of Justice.

Stockton, D. (2014, Fall). An update on the commonsense approach to officer safety. *Rap Sheet*, p. 4.

Stolberg, S. (2005, October 21). Congress passes new legal shield for gun industry. *New York Times*, pp. A1, A21.

Stone, L. (1984). Shelters for battered women: A temporary escape from danger or the first step toward divorce? *Victimology, 9*(1), 284–289.

Stop it now! (2011). Briefing sheet: What do U.S. adults think about child sexual abuse? *Child Sex Abuse Prevention and Protection Center.* Retrieved December 10, 2011, from www.stopitnow.org.

Stowe, S. (2007, June 16). Man is guilty of manslaughter in '06 stabbing of neighbor. *New York Times*, p. A14.

Straus, M. (1978). Wife beating: How common and why? *Victimology, 2*(4), 443–458.

———. (1991). Conceptualization and measurement of battering: Implications for public policy. In M. Steinman (Ed.), *Woman battering: Policy responses* (pp. 19–42). Cincinnati, OH: Anderson.

———. (1999). The controversy over domestic violence by women. In X. Arriaga & S. Oskamp (Eds.), *Violence in intimate relationships* (pp. 109–119). Thousand Oaks, CA: Sage.

Straus, M., & Gelles, R. (1986). Societal change and change in family violence from 1975 to 1985. *Journal of Marriage and the Family, 48*, 20–30.

———. (1990). *Physical violence in American families.* New Brunswick, NJ: Transaction.

Straus, M., Gelles, R., & Steinmetz, S. (1980). *Behind closed doors: Violence in the American family.* New York: Doubleday.

Stromwall, L., Alfredsson, H., & Landstrom, S. (2013, September). Blame attributions and rape: Effects of belief in a just world and relationship level. *Legal and Criminological Psychology, 18*(2), 254–261.

Study puts facts behind some child kidnapping assumptions. (1997, August 15). *Law Enforcement News*, p. 9.

Suarez, E., & Gadalla, T. M. (2010, November). Stop blaming the victim: A meta-analysis on rape myths. *Journal of Interpersonal Violence, 25*(11), 2010–2035.

Sugarman, D., & McCoy, S. (1997, Summer). Impact of expert testimony on the believability of repressed memories. *Violence and Victims, 12*(2), 115–126.

Sullivan, A. (1993, February 9). Gay values, truly conservative. *New York Times*, p. A21.

Sullivan, D., & Tifft, L. (2001). *Restorative justice: Healing the foundations of our everyday lives.* Monsey, NY: Willow Tree Press.

Sulzberger, A., & Meehan, M. (2010, April 26). Questions surround a delay in help for a dying man. *New York Times*, p. A20.

Swartz, M. (2013, July 3). Gone girls. *New York Times*, p. F4. Retrieved January 4, 2015, from http://www.nytimes.com/2013/07/07/books/review/lost-girls-by-robert-kolker.html?_r=0.

Sweet, M. (2011, June 22). If you leave the keys in the ignition, are you liable for a thief's damages? *Law Information.* Retrieved October 26, 2011, from www.lawinfo.com.

Swift, A. (2014, October 30). Less than half of Americans support stricter gun laws. *Gallup Polling Organization.* Retrieved December 22, 2014, from http://www.gallup.com/poll/179045/less-half-americans-support-stricter-gun-laws.aspx.

Sygnatur, E., & Toscano, G. (2000, Spring). Work-related homicides: The facts. *Compensation and Working Conditions,5*(1), 1–8.

Sykes, C. (1992). *A nation of victims: The decay of the American character.* New York: St. Martin's Press.

Sykes, G., & Matza, D. (1957). Techniques of neutralization: A theory of delinquency. *American Sociological Review, 22,* 664–670.

Symonds, M. (1975). Victims of violence: Psychological effects and after-effects. *American Journal of Psychoanalysis, 35*(1), 19–26.

———. (1980a). Acute responses of victims to terror. *Evaluation and Change* (special issue), 39–42.

———. (1980b). The "second injury" to victims. *Evaluation and Change,* 7(1), 36–38.

Tabachnick, S. (2013, April 29). Shamed into silence. *The Crime Report.* Retrieved September 30, 2014, from http://www.thecrimereport.org/news/inside-criminal-justice/2013-04-shamed-into-silence.

Taibbi, M., & Sims-Phillips, A. (1989). *Unholy alliances.* San Diego, CA: Harcourt Brace.

Takooshian, H. (2014, March 24). Not just a bystander. *Psychology Today.* Retrieved September 10, 2014, from http://www.psychologytoday.com/blog/not-just-bystander/201403/the-1964-kitty-genovese-tragedy-what-have-we-learned.

Tardiff, K., Gross, E., & Messner, S. (1986). A study of homicides in Manhattan, 1981. *American Journal of Public Health,* 16(2), 139–145.

Targeted News Service. (2009, July 12). Governor Riley issues proclamation for road rage awareness week. Retrieved September 1, 2011, from www.lexisnexis.com.

Task Force on Assessment. (1967). The victims of crime. *In the President's Commission on Law Enforcement and Administration of Justice, Task force report: Crime and its impact—an assessment* (pp. 80–84). Washington, DC: U.S. Government Printing Office.

Tatara, T. (1993). Understanding the nature and scope of elder abuse with the use of state aggregate data. *Journal of Elder Abuse and Neglect, 5*(4), 35–57.

Tavernise, S. (2011, February 12). Chandra Levy's killer sentenced to 60 years. *New York Times*, p. A12.

———., & Gebeloff, R. (2013, March 9). Share of homes with guns shows 4-decade decline. *New York Times*, p. A14.

Tavris, C. (1993, January 3). Beware the incest survivor machine. *New York Times Book Review*, pp. 1, 16–17.

Taylor, A. (2011, December 18). Commentary: Sometimes it's necessary to blame the victim. *Chronicle of Higher Education.* Retrieved December 27, 2011, from http//:chronicle.com.

Taylor, B. (1989). *Redesign of the national crime survey.* Washington, DC: U.S. Department of Justice.

Teaching children how to escape from abduction. (1999, February 14). *New York Times*, p. 32.

Teevan, J. (1979). Crime victimization as a neglected social problem. *Sociological Symposium, 25,* 6–22.

Terr, L. (1994). *Unchained memories: True stories of traumatic memories, lost and found.* New York: Basic.

Terrance, C., Plumm, K., & Rhyner, K. (2012, December). Expert testimony in cases involving battered women who kill.*North Dakota Law Review, 88,* 920–945.

Tesch, B., Bekerian, D., English, P., & Harrington, E. (2010, Winter). Same-sex domestic violence: Why victims are more at risk. *International Journal of Police Science & Management* [serial online], *12*(4), 526–535.

Tewksbury, R. (2009). Male rape. In J. Wilson (Ed.), *The Praeger handbook of victimology* (pp. 161–163). Santa Barbara, CA: Praeger.

Texas Advocacy Project. (2011). Teen dating violence. Retrieved January 2, 2012, from www.texasadvocacyproject.org.

Texprotects (Texas Association For The Protection Of Children). (2011). What is child abuse? *Texprotects.org.* Retrieved December 11, 2014, from http://www.texprotects.org/facts/.

The Ticker. (2011, December 21). Settlement reached in Brown University lawsuit over student said to be falsely accused of rape. *Chronicle of Higher Education.* Retrieved December 27, 2011, from http://chronicle.com.

Thomason, T., & Babbilli, A. (1987). *Crime victims and the news media.* Fort Worth, TX: Texas Christian University Department of Journalism.

Thompson, D. (2010, July 2). California to pay $20M to kidnap victim. *Newsday*, p. 33.

Thompson, K. (2011, June). When the first responder is you. *Popular Mechanics*, *188*(6), 86–92.

Thompson, M. (1984). MADD curbs drunk drivers. *Victimology*, *9*(1), 191–192.

Thompson, S. (2008, March 16). Prosecutors fear castle law's presumption will allow real murderers to go free. *Dallas Morning News*. Retrieved September 15, 2008, from www.dallasnews.com.

Thompson-Cannino, J., & Cotton, R. (2009). *Picking Cotton: Our memoir of injustice and redemption*. New York: St. Martins Press.

Thornburgh, N. (2008, July 3). Looking kindly on vigilante justice. *Time*. Retrieved January 20, 2012, from www.time.com.

Thyfault, R. (1984). Self-defense: Battered woman syndrome on trial. *California Western Law Review*, *20*, 485–510.

Time, V., Payne, B., & Gainey, R. (2010, July). Don't help victims of crime if you don't have the time: Assessing support for Good Samaritan laws. *Journal of Criminal Justice*, *38*(4), 790–795.

Timrots, A., & Rand, M. (1987). *Violent crime by strangers and non-strangers. BJS Special Report*. Washington, DC: U.S. Department of Justice.

Timrots, A., & Snyder, E. (1994). *Drugs and crime facts, 1993. BJS Drugs and Crime Data Center and Clearinghouse*. Washington, DC: U.S. Department of Justice.

Tittle, C. (1978). Restitution and deterrence: An evaluation of compatibility. In B. Galaway & J. Hudson (Eds.), *Offender restitution in theory and action* (pp. 33–158). Lexington, MA: Lexington Books.

Titus, R., Heinzelmann, F., & Boyle, J. (1995). Victimization of persons by fraud. *Crime and Delinquency*, *41*(1), 54–72.

Tjaden, P., & Thoennes, N. (1998). *Stalking in America: Findings from the National Violence Against Women Survey*. Washington, DC: National Institute of Justice.

———. (2000). *Extent, nature, and consequences of intimate partner violence: Findings from the National Violence Against Women Survey*. Washington, DC: National Institute of Justice.

———. (2006, January). *Extent, nature, and consequences of rape victimization: Findings from the National Violence Against Women Survey*. Washington, DC: National Institute of Justice.

Tobias, B. (2009, November). Death empowers victims. *The Crime Victims Report*, 73.

Toobin, J. (2003, September 1). The consent defense, Kobe Bryant, and the changing law of rape. *New Yorker*, pp. 40–47.

Toups, D. (2014, June 27). 380 cities ranked for car thefts. *Insurance.com*. Retrieved November 14, 2014, from http://www.insurance.com/auto-insurance/claims/380-cities-ranked-for-2013-car-thefts.html.

Traister, R. (2011, July 24). Ladies, we have a problem. *New York Times Magazine*, pp. 8–9.

Treanor, W. (1986, August 25). The Missing Children's Act has been misused, abused. *Juvenile Justice Digest*, p. 7–10.

Triebwasser, J. (1986, June 28). Court says you can't run from restitution. *Law Enforcement News*, pp. 6, 8.

———. (1987a, June 9). Court leaves death penalty alive and well. *Law Enforcement News*, p. 5.

———. (1987b, September 29). Victims' non-impact on sentence. *Law Enforcement News*, p. 5.

Troup-Leasure, K., & Snyder, H. (2005, August). *Statutory rape known to law enforcement. Juvenile Justice Bulletin*. Washington, DC: Office of Juvenile Justice and Delinquency Prevention.

Truman, J. (2011, September). *Criminal victimization, 2010. BJS Report*. Washington, DC: U.S. Department of Justice.

———., & Langton, L. (2014, September). *Criminal victimization, 2013. BJS Report*. Washington, DC: U.S. Department of Justice.

———., & Morgan, (2014, April). *Non-fatal domestic violence, 2003–2012. BJS Special Report*. Washington, DC: U.S. Department of Justice.

Turman, K. (1999). *Breaking the cycle of violence: Recommendations to improve the criminal justice response to child victims and witnesses*. Washington, DC: Office for Victims of Crime, U.S. Department of Justice.

Turner, J. (1990). Preparing individuals at risk for victimization as hostages. In E. Viano (Ed.), *The victimology handbook: Research findings, treatment, and public policy* (pp. 217–226). New York: Garland.

Turner, N. (2002). *Responding to hate crimes: A police officer's guide to investigation and prevention*. Alexandria, VA: International Association of Chiefs of Police (IACP).

Tyler, K., Whitbeck, L., Hoyt, D., & Cauce, A. (2005, May). Risk factors for sexual victimization among male and female homeless and runaway youth. *Journal of Interpersonal Violence*, *19*(5), 503–520.

Tyre, P. (2001, June 18). Betrayed by a badge. *Newsweek*, pp. 38–39.

Ullman, S. (2007). Comparing gang and individual rapes in a community sample of urban women. *Violence and Victims*, *22*(1), 43–51.

Umbreit, M. (1987, March). Mediation may not be as bad as you think; some victims do benefit. *NOVA Newsletter*, pp. 1–2, 6.

———. (1989). Violent offenders and their victims. In M. Wright & B. Galaway (Eds.), *Mediation and criminal justice: Victims, offenders and community* (pp. 99–112). Newbury Park, CA: Sage.

————. (1990). Victim-offender mediation with violent offenders: Implications for modifications of the VORP model. In E. Viano (Ed.), *The victimology handbook: Research findings, treatment, and public policy* (pp. 337–352). New York: Garland.

————. (1994, Summer). Victim empowerment through mediation: The impact of victim offender mediation in four cities. *Perspectives* (special issue), 25–28. American Probation and Parole Association.

Umbreit, M., & Greenwood, D. (1998). *National survey of victim–offender mediation programs in the United States.* Washington, DC: Office of Victims of Crime, U.S. Department of Justice.

Umbreit, M., Vos, B., Coates, R., & Brown, K. (2004, April). Victim–offender dialogue in violent cases: The Texas and Ohio experience. *The Crime Victims Report, 8,* 1–2.

Underwood, T. (2009). Victim vs. survivor. In J. Wilson (Ed.), *The Praeger handbook of victimology* (pp. 305–306). Santa Barbara, CA: Praeger.

United Nations (U.N.). Office on Drugs and Crime. (2014). Global study on homicide, 2013. Retrieved October 1, 2014, from http://www.unodc.org/documents/gsh/pdfs/2014_GLOBAL_HOMICIDE_BOOK_web.pdf.

Unnever, J., & Cornell, D. (2003, February). Bullying, self-control, and ADHD. *Journal of Interpersonal Violence, 18*(2), 129–147.

U.S. Conference of Catholic Bishops (USCCB). (2002, September 19). Sex abuse committee releases preliminary survey results. *Communications.* Retrieved August 10, 2005, from www.usccb.org.

U.S. Department of Health and Human Services. (2005). National survey of family growth, 2002. Retrieved December 10, 2011, from www.childtrends.org.

U.S. Department of Justice, Fraud Division. (2008). Identity theft. Retrieved July 18, 2008, from www.usdoj.gov/criminal/fraud/websites/idtheft.html.

U.S. Department of Labor, Bureau of Labor Statistics (BLS). (2013). Census of Fatal Occupational Injuries, 2013. Chart 6: Four most frequent work-related fatal injury events, 1992–2013. Retrieved December 21, 2014, from www.bls.gov.

U.S. Department of State. (2007). What is modern slavery? Office to Monitor and Combat Trafficking in Persons. Retrieved December 8, 2011, from www.state.gov.

————. (2011). Trafficking in persons report, 2010. Country narratives: United States, prosecution. Retrieved December 10, 2011, from www.state.gov.

U.S. General Accounting Office (GAO). (2002). *Identity theft: Prevalence and cost appear to be growing.* Washington, DC: U.S. Government Printing Office.

————. (2011, July). Child maltreatment: Strengthening national data on child fatalities could aid in prevention.

GAO Highlights. Retrieved December 9, 2011, from www.gao.gov.

U.S. House Committee on the Judiciary. (1980, February 13). *Victims of Crime Act of 1979: Report together with dissenting and separate views.* 96th Cong., 2nd session. Washington, DC: U.S. Government Printing Office.

U.S. Marshals Service. (2011). Witness security program. Retrieved December 12, 2011, from www.usmarshals.gov.

U.S. Supreme Court holds: No constitutional duty to protect. (1989). *NOVA Newsletter, 13*(2), 6.

Uy, R. (2011, Winter). Blinded by red lights. *Berkeley Journal of Gender, Law, and Justice, 26*(1), 204–229.

Vacca, J. (2002). *Identity theft.* Upper Saddle River, NJ: Prentice Hall.

Vachss, A. (1993). *Sex crimes.* New York: Random House.

Valencia, N. (2010, December 15). Juarez counts 3,000th homicide of 2010. *CNN World.* Retrieved December 1, 2011, from www.cnn.com/2010.

Van Dijk, J., Van Kesteren, J., & Smit, P. (2007). Criminal victimization in international perspective: Key findings from the 2004–2005 ICVS and EU ICS. *The Hague, Ministry of Justice, WODC.*

Van Emmerik, A., Kamphuis, J., Holsbosch, A., & Emmelkamp, P. (2002). Single session debriefing after psychological trauma. *The Lancet, 360,* 766–771.

Van Ness, D. (1990). Restorative justice. In B. Galaway & J. Hudson (Eds.), *Criminal justice, restitution and reconciliation* (pp. 7–14). Monsey, NY: Willow Tree Press.

Van Ness, D., & Strong, K. (1997). *Restoring justice.* Cincinnati: Anderson.

Van Netta, D. (2011, May 29). In Florida, criminals pose as police more frequently, and for more violent ends. *New York Times,* p. A18.

Vazquez, S., Stohr, M., & Purkiss, M. (2005, March). Intimate partner violence incidence and characteristics: Idaho *NIBRS* 1995 to 2001 data. *Criminal Justice Policy Review, 16*(1), 99–114.

Velasquez, E. (2013, November 26). Why traditional crime measurements don't tell the whole story. *ITL.com.* Retrieved November 2, 2014, from http://insurancethoughtleadership.com/why-traditional-crime-measurements-dont-tell-the-whole-story/#ixzz2mjfqnuRK.

————. (2014, August 18). Is ID theft worse if you're in the military? *Credit.com.* Retrieved October 29, 2014, from http://blog.credit.com/2014/08/why-military-servers-may-face-scarier-identity-theft-consequences-93185/.

Velliquette, B. (2011, December 13). Carson asked Lovette to pray with her. *Herald Sun.* Retrieved December 14, 2011, from www.heraldsun.com.

Verhovek, S. (2001, November 7). "Code Adam" soon finds lost children in big stores. *New York Times*, p. A33.

Veraa, A. (2009, Winter). Child sexual abuse: The sources of anxiety making and the negative effects. *Issues in Child Abuse Accusations*, *18*(1), 4–8.

Viano, E. (1976). *Victims and society*. Washington, DC: Visage.

———. (1983). Victimology: The development of a new perspective. *Victimology*, *8*(1/2), 17–30.

———. (1987). Victims' rights and the constitution: Reflections on a bicentennial. *Crime and Delinquency*, *33*, 438–451.

———. (1989). Victimology today: Major issues in research and public policy. In E. Viano (Ed.), *Crime and its victims: International research and public policy issues* (pp. 3–16). New York: Hemisphere Publishing.

———. (1990a). Introduction: Victimology: A new focus of research and practice. In E. Viano (Ed.), *The victimology handbook: Research findings, treatment, and public policy* (pp. xi–xii). New York: Garland.

———. (1990b). The recognition and implementation of victims' rights in the United States: Developments and achievements. In E. Viano (Ed.), *The victimology handbook: Research findings, treatment, and public policy* (pp. 319–336). New York: Garland.

———. (1992). Violence among intimates: Major issues and approaches. In E. Viano (Ed.), *Intimate violence: Interdisciplinary perspectives* (pp. 3–12). New York: Hemisphere.

Victims Rights Caucus (VRC). (2014). Legislation. *VRC.org*. Retrieved November 17, 2014, from http://vrc.poe. house.gov/index.cfm/legislation.

Villmoare, E., & Neto, V. (1987). *NIJ research in brief: Victim appearances at sentencing under California's victims' bill of rights*. Washington, DC: U.S. Department of Justice.

Vinciguerra, T. (2011, June 5). The "murderabilia" market. *New York Times*, p. E2.

Vines, V. (2004, November 28). Press release: Data on firearms and violence too weak to settle policy debates; comprehensive research effort needed. *The National Academies*. Retrieved August 20, 2005, from www.nationalacademies.org.

Violence Policy Center. (2011). A shrinking minority: The continuing decline of gun ownership in America. *VPC*. Retrieved December 10, 2014, from http://www.vpc. org/studies/ownership.pdf.

———. (2013, April). Guns are rarely used to kill criminals or stop crimes, new VPC analysis reveals. *VPC*. Retrieved December 10, 2014, from http://www.vpc.org/press/ 1304self.htm.

———. (2014a, April). Concealed carry killers. *VPC*. Retrieved December 10, 2014, from https://www.vpc. org/ccwkillers.htm.

———. (2014b, September). When men murder women: An analysis of 2012 homicide data. *VPC*. Retrieved November 29, 2014, from http://www.vpc.org/studies/ wmmw2014.pdf.

Virella, K. (2011, June). Behind bars: Corrective measures. *City Limits*, *35*(2), 51–54.

Vitello, P. (2008, November 13). Sexual abuse complaints subpoenaed. *New York Times*, p. A33.

Voboril, M. (2005, September 6). 9/11 groups: Dedicated to the memory. *Newsday*, p. 8.

Vollmer, A., & Parker, A. (1936). *The police and modern society*. San Francisco: University of California Press.

Volpe, M. (2000). ADR in the criminal justice system: Promises and challenges. *Dispute Resolution Magazine*, *7*(1), 4–7.

Von Hentig, H. (1941, March–April). Remarks on the interaction of perpetrator and victim. *Journal of Criminal Law, Criminology, and Police Science*, *31*, 303–309.

———. (1948). *The criminal and his victim: Studies in the sociobiology of crime*. New Haven, CT: Yale University Press.

Voss, H., & Hepburn, J. (1968). Patterns in criminal homicide in Chicago. *Journal of Criminal Law, Criminology, and Police Science*, *59*, 499–508.

VPC see Violence Policy Center.

VRC see Victims Rights Caucus.

Wagner, N. (2011, June 16). Bart Johnson sentenced to death. *Shelby County Reporter*. Retrieved December 4, 2015. from http://www.shelbycountyreporter.com/2011/06/ 16/bart-johnson-sentenced-to-death/#sthash.aQcaAvkm. dpuf.

Wakin, D. (2003, April 15). Two sexual abuse lawsuits filed against L.I. diocese. *New York Times*, p. B8.

Walker, J. (2009). Child lures. In J. Wilson (Ed.), *The Praeger handbook of victimology* (pp. 42–43). Santa Barbara, CA: Praeger.

Walker, L. (2009). *The battered woman syndrome* (3rd ed.). New York: Springer.

Walker, S. (1982, October). What have civil liberties ever done for crime victims? Plenty! *ACJS Today*, pp. 4–5.

Walker, S. D. (2003). History and development of academic programs in victimology/victim services. In *Proceedings of the first American symposium on victimology* (pp. 18–25). Retrieved July 12, 2011, from www.american-society victimology.us/documents.

Walker-Rodriguez, A., & Hill, R. (2011, March). Human sex trafficking. *FBI Law Enforcement Bulletin*, 3–8.

Walklate, S. (1991). Researching victims of crime: Critical victimology. *Social Justice*, *17*(3), 25–42.

Waller, I. (2011). *Rights for victims of crime: Rebalancing justice*. Lanham, MD: Rowman & Littlefield Publishers.

Waller, I., & Okihiro, N. (1978). *Burglary: The victim and the public.* Toronto: University of Toronto Press.

Wallace, H. (2007). *Victimology: Legal, psychological, and social perspectives* (2nd ed.). Boston: Pearson.

Walsh, A. (1992). Placebo justice: Victim recommendations and offender sentences in sexual assault cases. In E. Fattah (Ed.), *Towards a critical victimology* (pp. 295–311). New York: St. Martin's Press.

Walsh, M. (2014, November 11). Boston Marathon bombing survivor bids farewell to leg before amputation. *Yahoo News.* Retrieved January 2, from http://news.yahoo.com/boston-marathon-bombing-victim-leg-amputate-205118670.html;_ylt=A0LEVz9cDINUWvkABQtXNyoA;_ylu=X3oDMTExNjdtbnJtBHNlYwNzcgRwb3MDMgRjb2xvA2JmMQR2dGlkA1VJQzFfMQ.

Walsh, M., & Schram, D. (1980). The victim of white-collar crime: Accuser or accused. In G. Geis & E. Stotland (Eds.), *White-collar crime* (pp. 32–51). Beverly Hills, CA: Sage.

Walsh, P. (2014, July 28). Son 'did what had to be done,' kills man attacking mom in N. Minn. *Minneapolis Star Tribune.* Retrieved January 7, 2015, from http://www.startribune.com/local/268888541.html.

Walsh, S. (2011, June 8). Sex assaults underreported, inquiry into V.A. concludes. *New York Times,* p. A14.

Walshe, S. (2014, April 30). Gabby Giffords tells activists she is getting better. *ABC News.* Retrieved December 23, 2014, from http://abcnews.go.com/blogs/politics/2014/04/gabby-giffords-tells-activists-she-is-getting-better-and-doing-yoga-too/.

Walters, J., Moore, A., Berzofsky, M., & Langton, L. (2013, June). *Household burglary, 1994–2011. BJS Special Report.* Washington, DC: U.S. Department of Justice.

Warchol, G. (1998). *Workplace violence, 1992–1996. BJS Special Report.* Washington, DC: U.S. Department of Justice.

Warkentin, G. (2006, June). Special victims unit. *Crime Victims Report, 10*(2), 17, 28.

Warner, J., & Burke, V. (1987). *National directory of juvenile restitution programs.* Washington, DC: U.S. Department of Justice.

Warner, P. (1988, Winter). Aural assault: Obscene telephone calls. *Qualitative Sociology, 11*(4), 300–310.

Warrick, J., & Horwitz, S. (2013, April 19). How string of events involving Tsarnaev brothers unfolded. *Washington Post.* Retrieved December 19, 2014, from http://www.washingtonpost.com/world/national-security/how-string-of-events-involving-tsarnaev-brothers-unfolded/2013/04/19/629d19c6-a929-11e2-8302-3c7e0ea97057_story.html.

Warrior, B. (1977, February). Transition house shelters battered women. *Sister Courage,* p. 12.

Warshaw, R. (1988). *I never called it rape.* New York: Harper & Row.

Washington Crime News Service. (2003, June 27). $200 million in grants to prevent child abuse. *Crime Control Digest, 37*(25), 2.

Wasserman, S. (2008, October 7). The emergent second amendment. *New York Law Journal,* pp. 8–10.

Weathers, H. (2005, August 8). Drug rape: The disturbing facts. *London Daily Mail,* p. 26.

Websdale, N., & Johnson, B. (1997). Structural approaches to reducing women-battering. *Social Justice, 24,* 54–81.

———. (2003, November). Reviewing domestic violence deaths. *NIJ Journal, 250,* 26–31.

Webster, R. (2011, July 15). Childhood maltreatment deaths being undercounted? Retrieved December 8, 2011, from www.examiner.com.

Weed, F. (1995). *Certainty of justice: Reform in the crime victim movement.* Hawthorne, NY: Aldine de Gruyter.

———. (2005). The position of the victim-activist in crime victim service organizations. *Social Science Digest, 42*(1), 97–105.

Weigend, T. (1983). Problems of victim/witness assistance programs. *Victimology, 8*(3), 91–101.

Weis, K., & Borges, S. (1973). Victimology and rape: The case of the legitimate victim. *Issues in Criminology, 8*(2), 71–115.

Weisberg, L. (2008, July 13). Home burglary: Even with insurance and good police work, odds are against a full recovery. *San Diego Union-Tribune,* p. H1.

Weisel, D. (2002). Burglary of single-family houses. *Problem-Oriented Policing Guide, No 18.* Office of Community Oriented Policing Services (COPS). Washington, DC: U.S. Department of Justice.

———. (2005). Analyzing repeat victimization. *Problem-Oriented Policing Guide, No 4.* Office of Community Oriented Policing Services (COPS). Washington, DC: U.S. Department of Justice.

Weiser, B. (2011, September 19). Family and United Airlines settle last 9/11 wrongful-death lawsuit. *New York Times,* p. A22.

———. (2011, September 23). Port Authority not liable in '93 bombing. *New York Times,* p. A26.

Wellford, C., & Cronin, J. (2000, April). Cleaning up homicide clearance rates. *NIJ Journal,* 2–8.

Wells, M. (2011, August 15). Recantation and false allegations of child abuse: Updated 2011. National Children's Advocacy Center. Retrieved November 19, 2014, from http://www.nationalcac.org/images/pdfs/CALiO/Bibliographies/recantation-false-allegations-bib6.pdf.

Wemmers, J. (2002). A victim-oriented approach to restorative justice. *International Review of Victimology, 9,* 43–59.

Wertham, F. (1949). *The show of violence*. New York: Doubleday.

Wessler, S., & Moss, M. (2001). *Hate crimes on campus: The problem and efforts to confront it*. Washington, DC: Office of Justice Programs, U.S. Department of Justice.

West, J. (2014, August 13). Georgia agency helps compensate crime victims. *Albany Herald*. Retrieved December 10, 2014, from http://www.albanyherald.com/news/2014/apr/05/georgia-agency-helps-compensate-crime-victims/.

Wetenhall, J. (2010, July 2). Investigators dig for new evidence in Wetterling case. *ABC 20/20*. Retrieved December 3, 2011, from www.abcnews.go.com.

Wexler, C., & Marx, G. (1986, April). When law and order works: Boston's innovative approach to the problem of racial violence. *Crime and Delinquency, 32*(2), 205–223.

Wexler, R. (1990). *Wounded innocents: The real victims of the war against child abuse*. Buffalo, NY: Prometheus Books.

"What a way to dye." (2008, May 6). Retrieved August 8, 2008, from www.snopes.com.

What sheriffs need to know about the Prison Rape Reduction Act of 2003. (2004, March–April). *Sheriff, 56*(2), 58–59.

When judges make the punishment fit the crime. (1978, December 11). *U.S. News & World Report*, pp. 44–46.

When technology gets diabolical: Florida trains its sights on digital stalkers. (2005, May 15). *Law Enforcement News*, p. 11.

Whitaker, C. (1989). *The redesigned National Crime Survey: Selected new data. BJS Special Report*. Washington, DC: U.S. Department of Justice.

Whitaker, L., & Pollard, J. (Eds.). (1993). *Campus violence: Kinds, causes, and cures*. Binghamton, NY: Haworth Press.

Whitcomb, D. (1986). *NIJ Research in Action: Prosecuting child sexual abuse: New approaches*. Washington, DC: U.S. Department of Justice.

———. (1988). *Evaluation of programs for the effective prosecution of child physical and sexual abuse*. Washington, DC: Institute for Social Analysis.

———. (1992). *When the victim is a child* (2nd ed.). Washington, DC: Office of Justice Programs.

White House Council on Women and Girls. (2014, January). Rape and sexual assault: A call to action. Retrieved January 5, 2015, from http://www.whitehouse.gov/sites/default/files/docs/sexual_assault_report_1-21-14.pdf.

White, J., & Wesley, J. (1987, April). Male rape survivors: Guidelines for crisis counselors. *Crime Victims Digest*, pp. 3–6.

White, N. (2009, June 16). Drink spike claims rejected. *The Australian*. Retrieved December 20, 2011, from www.theaustralian.com.au.

Whitman, H. (1951). *Terror in the streets*. New York: Dial Press.

Wicker, T. (1970, October 4). Jackson State and Orangeburg. *New York Times*, p. A10.

Widom, C. (1989). Child abuse, neglect, and violent criminal behavior. *Criminology, 21*(2), 251–270.

———. (1995). *Victims of childhood sexual abuse—later criminal consequences. NIJ Research in Brief*. Washington, DC: U.S. Department of Justice.

——— & Maxfield, M. (2001, February). An update on the "cycle of violence." *NIJ Research in Brief*. Washington, DC: U.S. Department of Justice.

——— & Shepard, R. (1996). Accuracy of adult recollections of childhood victimization. *Psychological Assessment, 8*, 412–421.

Wiehe, V. (1997). *Sibling abuse: Hidden physical, emotional, and sexual trauma* (2nd ed.). Thousand Oaks, CA: Sage.

———., & Richards, A. (1995). *Intimate betrayal: Understanding and responding to the trauma of acquaintance rape*. Thousand Oaks, CA: Sage.

Wilgoren, J. (2005, June 28). Kansas suspect pleads guilty in 10 murders. *New York Times*, pp. A1, A20.

Will, G. (1993, November 15). Are we a nation of cowards? *Newsweek*, pp. 93–94.

———. (1998, July 31). President feeds the culture of victimology. *Houston Chronicle*, p. A42.

Williams, B. (2002). *Reparation and victim-focused social work*. Philadelphia: Kingsley Publishers.

Williams, C. (2009, January 2). Rise in young killers worries DC; City recorded 186 homicides in '08, an increase of 5; Area slayings up slightly. *Washington Post*, p. B1.

Williams, K. (1976). The effects of victim characteristics on the disposition of violent crimes. In W. McDonald (Ed.), *Criminal justice and the victim* (pp. 172–214). Beverly Hills, CA: Sage.

———. (1978). *The effects of victim characteristics on judicial decisions: PROMIS Research Project Report*. Washington, DC: Institute for Law and Social Research.

———. (2005, February 14). Policing video voyeurs. *Newsweek*, p. 44.

Williams, T. (1987, February). Post-traumatic stress disorder: Recognizing it, treating it. *NOVA Newsletter*, pp. 1–2, 7.

Williams, T. (2012a, February 20). Higher crime, fewer charges on Indian land. *New York Times*, p. A10.

———. (2012b, May 22). For Native American women, scourge of rape, rare justice. *New York Times*, p. A12.

———. (2013, July 10). Freed captives in Cleveland issue messages of resolve. *New York Times*, p. A11.

Williams, T. (2013, June 19). Bill would give judges more discretion when sentencing domestic violence survivors. *Legislative Gazette*, p. A12.

Wills, K., Doyle, J., & Parascandola, R. (2011, August 19). Off-duty NYPD cop arrested mid-crime, charged with raping school teacher at gunpoint. *New York Daily News*, p. 10.

Wilson, D. (2007, June 16). Facing sanction, Duke prosecutor plans to resign. *New York Times*, pp. A1, A11.

Wilson, D. G., Walsh, W., & Kleuber, S. (2006). Trafficking in human beings: Training and services among U.S. law enforcement agencies. *Police Practice & Research: An International Journal*, 7(2), 149–160.

Wilson, J. (2005, October). Victim-centered restorative justice: An essential distinction. *The Crime Victims Report*, 9(4), 49–50.

———. (2008, June). Victim-centered victim–offender dialogue in father–daughter incest cases. *Crime Victims Report*, 12(2), 17–18.

Wilson, M. (2014, February). *Hate crime victimization, 2004–2012 - statistical tables*.*BJS Report*. Washington, DC: U.S. Department of Justice.

Winerip, M. (2014, February 7). Stepping up to stop sexual assault. *New York Times Education Supplement*, pp. 1, 6.

Winfrey, O. (2006, May 5). Ultimate betrayals. Retrieved January 22, 2012, from www.oprah.com.

Winter, R. (2010). Intimate partner violence, theories of. In S. Fisher & S. Lab (Eds.), *Encyclopedia of Victimology and Crime Prevention* (pp. 552–563). Thousand Oaks, CA: Sage.

Witkin, G. (1994, August 15). The great debate: Should you own a gun? *U.S. News & World Report*, pp. 24–31.

Wolf, R., & Pillemer, K. (1989). *Helping elderly victims: The reality of elder abuse*. New York: Columbia University Press.

Wolfgang, M. (1958). *Patterns in criminal homicide*. Philadelphia: University of Pennsylvania Press.

———. (1959). Suicide by means of victim-precipitated homicide. *Journal of Clinical and Experimental Psychopathology and Quarterly Review of Psychiatry and Neurology, 20*, 335–349.

———. (1965). Victim compensation in crimes of personal violence. *Minnesota Law Review, 50*, 229–241.

Wolfgang, M., & Ferracuti, F. (1967). *The subculture of violence: Towards an integrated theory in criminology*. London: Tavistock.

Wolfgang, M., & Riedel, M. (1973, May). Race, judicial discretion, and the death penalty. *Annals of the Academy of Political and Social Science, 407*, 119–133.

Wood, J. (2008). The Crime Victims Rights Act of 2004 and the Federal Courts: Federal Judicial Center. Retrieved December 5, 2008, from www.uscourts.gov/rules/cvra0806.pdf.

Wood, J. A. (2008). Press release: United States Attorney's Office, Western Missouri. Retrieved September 20, 2008, from http://kansascity.fbi.gov/dojpressrel/pressrel08/cyberstalking050908.htm.

Wood, N. (1990). Black homicide—a public health crisis: Introduction and overview. *Journal of Interpersonal Violence, 5*, 147–150.

Wooden, K. (1984). *Child lures: A guide to prevent abduction*. St. Louis, MO: Ralston Purina.

Wright, E. (1973). *The politics of punishment*. New York: Harper & Row.

Wright, J., Burgess, A., Burgess, B., & Laszio, A. (1996). A typology of interpersonal stalking. *Journal of Interpersonal Violence, 11*(4), 487–502.

Wright, J., Rossi, P., & Daly, K. (1983). *Under the gun: Weapons, crime, and violence in America*. New York: Aldine de Gruyter.

Wright, L. (1994). *Remembering Satan*. New York: Knopf.

Wright, M. (1985). The impact of victim–offender mediation on the victim. *Victimology, 10*(1), 630–646.

———. (1989). Introduction. In M. Wright & B. Galaway (Eds.), *Mediation and criminal justice: Victims, offenders and community* (pp. 1–13). Newbury Park, CA: Sage.

———. (1991). *Justice for victims and offenders*. Philadelphia: Open University Press.

———. (2014, July 31). Book review: Just emotions:Rituals of restorative justice. *Restorative Justice Online*. Retrieved December 23, 2014, from http://www.restorativejustice.org/RJOB/book-review-just-emotions-rituals-of-restorative-justice.

www.drivers.com Staff. (1997, Summer). The road rage epidemic: Hype or reality? *Driver Education, 7*(3), 15–18.

Wyatt, E. (2005, February 24). A Mormon daughter's book stirs a storm. *New York Times*, pp. E1, E7.

Wyatt, G. (1985). The sexual abuse of Afro-American and white American women in childhood. *Child Abuse and Neglect, 9*, 507–519.

Wyatt, G., & Powell, G. (1988). *Lasting effects of child sexual abuse*. Newbury Park, CA: Sage.

Xu, J., Kochanek, K., Murphy, S., & Arias, E. (2014, October). Mortality in the United States, 2012. *NCHS Data Brief, 168*, 150–170. Retrieved December 1, 2014, from http://www.cdc.gov/nchs/data/databriefs/db168.htm.

Yan, E. (2014, February 15). Caught on cameras. *Newsday*, pp. A2, A3.

Yanich, D. (2004). Crime creep: Urban and suburban crime in local TV news. *Journal of Urban Affairs, 26*(5), 535–563.

Yardley, W., & Raftery, I. (2012, January 3). Man believed to have killed park ranger is found dead. *New York Times*, p. A10.

Yapko, M. (1994). *Suggestions of abuse: True and false memories of childhood sexual trauma*. New York: Simon & Schuster.

Yapko, M., & Powell, G. (1988). *Lasting effects of child sexual abuse*. Newbury Park, CA: Sage.

Yardley, J. (1999, December 26). A flurry of baby abandonment leaves Houston wondering why. *New York Times*, p. A14.

———. (2014). Pope asks forgiveness from victims of sex abuse. *New York Times*, p. A8.

Yee, V. (2013, May 25). Horace Mann apologizes for abuse but won't start new inquiry. *New York Times*, pp. A17.

Yllo, K., & Bograd, M. (1988). *Feminist perspectives on wife abuse*. Newbury Park, CA: Sage.

Yoffe, E. (2013, October 15). College women: Stop getting drunk. *Slate*. Retrieved January 10, 2015, from http://www.slate.com/articles/double_x/doublex/2013/10/sexual_assault_and_drinking_teach_women_the_connection.html.

———. (2014, December 7). The college rape overcorrection. *Slate*. Retrieved January 10, 2015, from http://www.slate.com/articles/double_x/doublex/2014/12/college_rape_campus_sexual_assault_is_a_serious_problem_but_the_efforts.html.

Young, C. (1999, November 26). Feminists play the victim game. *New York Times*, p. A43.

Young, J. (2011). *The criminological imagination*. New York: John Wiley and Sons.

Young, M. (1991). NOVA protests NBC's "Naming Names." *NOVA Newsletter, 15*(4), 1.

Young, M. (2008, April 11). North Carolina deputy paralyzed by shooting sets new life in motion. *The Charlotte Observer*. Retrieved September 28, 2008, from charlotteobserver.com.

Young-Spillers, M. (2009). Child protective services. In J. Wilson (Ed.), *The Praeger handbook of victimology* (pp. 42–43). Santa Barbara, CA: Praeger.

Yu, J., Kochanek, K., Murphy, S., & Arias, E. (2014, October). Mortality in the United States, 2012. *NCHS Data Brief*, No. 168. Retrieved October 15, 2014, from http://www.cdc.gov/nchs/data/databriefs/db168.pdf.

Zagier, A. (2008, August 26). Campus training program. Retrieved September 8, 2008, from www.ap.org.

Zawitz, M. (1994). *Domestic violence: Violence between intimates. BJS Selected Findings*. Washington, DC: U.S. Department of Justice.

Zehr, H. (1998). Justice as restoration, justice as respect. *The Justice Professional, 11*(1), 71–87.

Zeoli, A., & Webster, D. (2010). Effects of domestic violence policies, alcohol taxes and police staffing levels on intimate partner homicide in large U.S. cities. *Injury Prevention, 16*, 90–95.

Zernike, K. (2003, August 3). What privacy? Everything else but the name. *New York Times*, p. D4.

———. (2014, October 4). Abuse cases at 2 schools: Technology was at root. *New York Times*, pp. A15, 16.

———., & Schweber, N. (2014, October 11). Sayreville High School arrests divide a town that lived for football. *New York Times*, pp. A16, 19.

Zgoba, K. (2004). Spin doctors and moral crusaders: The moral panic behind child safety legislation. *Criminal Justice Studies, 11*(4), 385–404.

Ziegenhagen, E. (1977). *Victims, crime, and social control*. New York: Praeger.

Zimring, F., & Hawkins, G. (1997). *Crime is not the problem: Lethal violence in America*. New York: Oxford University Press.

——— & Zuehl, J. (1986, January). Victim injury and death in urban robbery: A Chicago study. *Journal of Legal Studies, 15*(1), 1–40.

Zinzow, H., Resnick, H., Barr, S., Danielson, C., & Kilpatrick, D. (2012). Receipt of post-rape medical care in a national sample of female victims. *American Journal of Preventive Medicine, 43*(2), 183–187.

Name Index

Subject Index